July 1–3, 2019
Amsterdam, Netherlands

Association for Computing Machinery

Advancing Computing as a Science & Profession

PODS '19

Proceedings of the 38th ACM SIGMOD-SIGACT-SIGAI Symposium on Principles of Database Systems

General Chair:
Dan Suciu (University of Washington, USA)

Program Chair:
Christoph Koch (EPFL, Switzerland)

Proceedings Chair:
Sebastian Skritek (TU Wien, Austria)

Association for
Computing Machinery

Advancing Computing as a Science & Profession

The Association for Computing Machinery
1601 Broadway, 10th Floor
New York, NY 10019-7434

ISBN: 978-1-4503-6227-6 (Digital)

ISBN: 978-1-4503-7066-0 (Print)

Additional copies may be ordered prepaid from:

ACM Order Department
PO Box 30777
New York, NY 10087-0777, USA

Phone: 1-800-342-6626 (USA and Canada)
+1-212-626-0500 (Global)
Fax: +1-212-944-1318
E-mail: acmhelp@acm.org
Hours of Operation: 8:30 am – 4:30 pm ET

PODS 2019 Welcome Message

It is our great pleasure to welcome you to the 38th ACM SIGMOD-SIGACT-SIGAI Symposium on Principles of Database Systems (PODS 2019), held in Amsterdam, The Netherlands, on July 1-3, 2019, in conjunction with the 2019 ACM SIGMOD International Conference on Management of Data.

Since the first edition of the symposium in 1982, the PODS papers are distinguished by a rigorous approach to widely diverse problems in data management, often bringing to bear techniques from a variety of different areas, including computational logic, finite model theory, computational complexity, algorithm design and analysis, programming languages, and artificial intelligence.

The PODS Symposia study data management challenges in a variety of application contexts, including more recently parallel computation, streaming and realtime data, and graph data processing algorithms. PODS has a tradition of being the premier international conference on the theoretical and foundational aspects of data management, and the interested reader is referred to the web page https://databasetheory.org/pods for information on the history of this conference series.

This year's symposium continues this tradition and invited for submission papers providing original, substantial contributions in one or more of the following categories:

a) deep theoretical exploration of topical areas central to data management;

b) new formal frameworks that aim at providing a basis for deeper theoretical investigation of important emerging issues in data management; and

c) validation of theoretical approaches from the lens of practical applicability in data management. Papers in this track should provide an experimental evaluation that gives new insight in established theories. Besides, they should provide a clear message to the database theory community as to which aspects need further (theoretical) investigation, based on the experimental findings.

As in previous years, PODS operated with two submission cycles. The first cycle allowed for the possibility for papers to be revised and resubmitted. For the first cycle, 36 papers were submitted, 4 of which were directly selected for inclusion in the proceedings, and 8 were invited for a resubmission after a revision. The quality of the revised papers increased substantially with respect to the first submission, and all of the revised papers were selected for the proceedings. For the second cycle, 51 papers were submitted, 17 of which were selected, resulting in 29 papers selected overall from a total number of 87 submissions.

The program committee invited two tutorials, by Alan Fekete (University of Sydney) and by Suresh Venkatasubrahmanian (University of Utah). In addition, it selected two "Gems of PODS" speakers, Christos Papadimitriou (Columbia University) and Leopoldo Bertossi (Carleton University). "Gems of PODS" is an event, started in 2016, whose goal is to promote understanding of past seminal PODS results to the general audience. The Gems of PODS papers were selected by the Gems of PODS committee consisting of Mahmoud Abo Khamis, Christoph Koch (chair), Pierre Senellart, and Yufei Tao.

This volume contains the proceedings of PODS 2019, which include papers on the keynote addressed by Cynthia Dwork of Harvard University, the two invited tutorials, one of the two Gems talks, and 29 contributions that were selected by the Program Committee for presentation at the symposium.

The ACM PODS Alberto O. Mendelzon Test-of-Time Award is awarded every year to a paper or a small number of papers published in the PODS proceedings ten years prior that had the most impact in terms of research, methodology, or transfer to practice over the past decade. The 2019 Award Committee consisted of Jianwen Su, Dirk Van Gucht, and Victor Vianu. After careful consideration, and having solicited external nominations and advice, they selected the following paper as the award winner for the 2019 ACM PODS Alberto. O. Mendelzon Test-of-Time Award: "A General Datalog-Based Framework for Tractable Query Answering over Ontologies", by Andrea Cali, Georg Gottlob and Thomas Lukasiewicz.

The paper "Efficient Logspace Classes for Enumeration, Counting, and Uniform Generation" by Marcelo Arenas, Luis Alberto Croquevielle, Rajesh Jayaram and Cristian Riveros was selected for the PODS 2019 Best Paper Award. The paper "On the Enumeration Complexity of Unions of Conjunctive Queries" by Nofar Carmeli and Markus Kröll was selected for the Best Student Paper Award. These two papers were selected by a committee consisting of Pierre Senellart (chair), Frank Neven, and Dirk Van Gucht, with the advice of the Program Committee.

Our warmest congratulations to the authors!

We thank all authors who submitted papers to the symposium, and we look forward to welcoming you in Amsterdam!

Christoph Koch
PODS 2019 Program Chair

Dan Suciu
PODS 2019 General Chair

Sebastian Skritek
PODS 2019 Proceedings Chair

Table of Contents

PODS 2019 Symposium Organization viii

PODS 2019 Sponsors & Supporters x

Keynote

- **Differential Privacy and the US Census** 1
  Cynthia Dwork *(Harvard University)*

Session 1: Incomplete Information

- **Regularizing Conjunctive Features for Classification** 2
  Pablo Barceló *(University of Chile & IMFD Chile)*,
  Alexander Baumgartner *(University of Chile & RISC, Johannes Kepler University)*,
  Victor Dalmau *(Universitat Pompeu Fabra)*, Benny Kimelfeld *(Technion - Israel Institute of Technology)*

- **Probabilistic Databases with an Infinite Open-World Assumption** 17
  Martin Grohe, Peter Lindner *(RWTH Aachen University)*

- **Query Evaluation in Election Databases** 32
  Benny Kimelfeld *(Technion)*, Phokion G. Kolaitis *(University of California, Santa Cruz & IBM Research-Almaden)*,
  Muhammad Tibi *(Technion)*

Session: Gems of PODS and Test-of-Time Award Session

- **2019 ACM PODS Alberto O. Mendelzon Test-of-Time Award** 47
  Jianwen Su *(University of California, Santa Barbara)*, Dirk Van Gucht *(Indiana University)*,
  Victor Vianu *(University of California, San Diego)*

- **Database Repairs and Consistent Query Answering: Origins and Further Developments** 48
  Leopoldo Bertossi *(RelationalAI Inc. & Carleton University)*

Session 2: Best Paper Award, Enumeration and Counting

- **Efficient Logspace Classes for Enumeration, Counting, and Uniform Generation** 59
  Marcelo Arenas, Luis Alberto Croquevielle *(PUC & IMFD Chile)*,
  Rajesh Jayaram *(Carnegie Mellon University)*, Cristian Riveros *(PUC & IMFD Chile)*

- **Ranked Enumeration of Minimal Triangulations** 74
  Noam Ravid, Dori Medini, Benny Kimelfeld *(Technion - Israel Institute of Technology)*

- **Enumeration on Trees with Tractable Combined Complexity and Efficient Updates** 89
  Antoine Amarilli *(LTCI, CNRS, Télécom ParisTech, Université Paris-Saclay)*,
  Pierre Bourhis *(CRIStAL, CNRS UMR 9189, Inria Lille)*, Stefan Mengel *(CNRS, CRIL UMR 8188)*,
  Matthias Niewerth *(University of Bayreuth)*

- **Counting Database Repairs under Primary Keys Revisited** 104
  Marco Calautti, Marco Console, Andreas Pieris *(University of Edinburgh)*

- **The Complexity of Counting Cycles in the Adjacency List Streaming Model** 119
  John Kallaugher *(University of Texas at Austin)*, Andrew McGregor *(University of Massachusetts, Amherst)*,
  Eric Price *(University of Texas at Austin)*, Sofya Vorotnikova *(University of Massachusetts, Amherst)*

- **On the Enumeration Complexity of Unions of Conjunctive Queries** 134
  Nofar Carmeli *(Technion)*, Markus Kröll *(TU Wien)*

Session 3: Information Extraction, Hashing, and Privacy

- **Split-Correctness in Information Extraction** 149
  Johannes Doleschal *(University of Bayreuth & Hasselt University)*,
  Benny Kimelfeld *(Technion - Israel Institute of Technology)*, Wim Martens *(University of Bayreuth)*,
  Yoav Nahshon *(Technion - Israel Institute of Technology)*,
  Frank Neven *(Hasselt University & Transnational University of Limburg)*

- **Robust Set Reconciliation via Locality Sensitive Hashing** 164
  Michael Mitzenmacher *(Harvard University)*, Tom Morgan *(Harvard University & Google)*

- **What Storage Access Privacy is Achievable with Small Overhead?** 182
  Sarvar Patel *(Google LLC)*, Giuseppe Persiano *(University of Salerno & Google LLC)*, Kevin Yeo *(Google LLC)*

Session 4: Streams

- **Tight Trade-offs for the Maximum *k*-Coverage Problem in the General Streaming Model** 200
  Piotr Indyk, Ali Vakilian *(Massachusetts Institute of Technology)*

- **Weighted Reservoir Sampling from Distributed Streams** 218
  Rajesh Jayaram *(Carnegie Mellon University)*, Gokarna Sharma *(Kent State University)*,
  Srikanta Tirthapura *(Iowa State University)*, David P. Woodruff *(Carnegie Mellon University)*

- **Distributed and Streaming Linear Programming in Low Dimensions** 236
  Sepehr Assadi *(Princeton University)*, Nikolai Karpov, Qin Zhang *(Indiana University Bloomington)*

- **Better Sliding Window Algorithms to Maximize Subadditive and Diversity Objectives** 254
  Michele Borassi, Alessandro Epasto, Silvio Lattanzi,
  Sergei Vassilvitskii, Morteza Zadimoghaddam *(Google Research)*

Invited Tutorial 1

- **Making Consistency Protocols Serializable** 269
  Alan Fekete *(University of Sydney)*

Session 5: Semistructured Data and Knowledge Graphs, Logic, and Verification

- **The Space-Efficient Core of Vadalog** 270
  Gerald Berger *(TU Wien)*, Georg Gottlob *(University of Oxford & TU Wien)*,
  Andreas Pieris *(University of Edinburgh)*, Emanuel Sallinger *(University of Oxford & TU Wien)*

- **Decidable XPath Fragments in the Real World** 285
  David Baelde, Anthony Lick, Sylvain Schmitz *(ENS Paris-Saclay & CNRS, Université Paris-Saclay)*

- **Containment of Shape Expression Schemas for RDF** 303
  Sławek Staworko *(CNRS & University of Lille)*, Piotr Wieczorek *(University of Wroclaw)*

- **Complexity Bounds for Relational Algebra over Document Spanners** 320
  Liat Peterfreund *(Technion)*, Dominik D. Freydenberger *(Loughborough University)*,
  Benny Kimelfeld *(Technion)*, Markus Kröll *(Vienna University of Technology)*

- **Reachability in Database-driven Systems with Numerical Attributes under Recency Bounding** 335
  Parosh Aziz Abdulla *(Uppsala University)*, C. Aiswarya *(Chennai Mathematical Institute)*,
  Mohamed Faouzi Atig *(Uppsala University)*, Marco Montali *(Free University of Bozen-Bolzano)*

- **Compiling Existential Positive Queries to Bounded-Variable Fragments** 353
  Christoph Berkholz *(Humboldt-Universität zu Berlin)*, Hubie Chen *(Birkbeck, University of London)*

Session 6: Containment and Homomorphisms

- **Testability of Homomorphism Inadmissibility: Property Testing Meets Database Theory** 365
  Hubie Chen *(Birkbeck, University of London)*, Yuichi Yoshida *(National Institute of Informatics)*

- **The Selfish Models Property: Bounding the Complexity of Query Containment and Entailment Problems** 383
  Hubie Chen *(Birkbeck, University of London)*

- **Attacking Diophantus: Solving a Special Case of Bag Containment** 399
  George Konstantinidis *(University of Southampton)*,
  Fabio Mogavero *(Università degli Studi di Napoli Federico II)*

Session 7: Joins, Hypergraphs, and Aggregate Queries

- **On Functional Aggregate Queries with Additive Inequalities** 414
  Mahmoud Abo Khamis, Ryan R. Curtin *(relationalAI Inc.)*, Benjamin Moseley *(Carnegie Mellon University)*,
  Hung Q. Ngo *(relationalAI Inc.)*, XuanLong Nguyen *(University of Michigan)*,
  Dan Olteanu, Maximilian Schleich *(University of Oxford)*

- **Topology Dependent Bounds For FAQs** 432
  Michael Langberg, Shi Li, Sai Vikneshwar Mani Jayaraman, Atri Rudra *(University at Buffalo)*

- **Instance and Output Optimal Parallel Algorithms for Acyclic Joins** 450
  Xiao Hu, Ke Yi *(Hong Kong University of Science and Technology)*

- **HyperBench: A Benchmark and Tool for Hypergraphs and Empirical Findings** 464
  Wolfgang Fischl *(Vienna University of Technology)*,
  Georg Gottlob *(Vienna University of Technology & University of Oxford)*,
  Davide Mario Longo, Reinhard Pichler *(Vienna University of Technology)*

Invited Tutorial 2

- **Algorithmic Fairness: Measures, Methods and Representations** 481
  Suresh Venkatasubramanian *(University of Utah)*

Author Index 482

PODS 2019 Symposium Organization

General Chair: Dan Suciu *(University of Washington, USA)*

Program Chair: Christoph Koch *(EPFL, Switzerland)*

Proceedings Chair: Sebastian Skritek *(TU Wien, Austria)*

Publicity Chair: Milos Nikolic *(University of Edinburgh, UK)*

Program Committee:
Mahmoud Abo Khamis *(RelationalAI, USA)*
Pablo Barcelo *(University of Chile, Chile)*
Michael Bender *(Stony Brook University, USA)*
Angela Bonifati *(University of Lyon & CNRS, France)*
Pierre Bourhis *(CNRS CRIStAL Lille, France)*
Diego Calvanese *(Free University of Bozen-Bolzano, Italy)*
Rada Chirkova *(North Carolina State University, USA)*
Alin Deutsch *(University of California, San Diego, USA)*
Alexandre V. Evfimievski *(IBM Almaden, USA)*
Minos Garofalakis *(ATHENA Research Center and Technical University of Crete, Greece)*
Daniel Kifer *(Pennsylvania State University, USA)*
Ashwin Machanavajjhala *(Duke University, USA)*
Michael Kapralov *(EPFL, Switzerland)*
Frank Neven *(Hasselt University, Belgium)*
Hung Q. Ngo *(RelationalAI, USA)*
Dan Olteanu *(University of Oxford, UK)*
Emanuel Sallinger *(University of Oxford, UK)*
Francesco Scarcello *(University of Calabria, Italy)*
Pierre Senellart *(ENS, PSL University, France)*
Jianwen Su *(University of California, Santa Barbara, USA)*
Yufei Tao *(Chinese University of Hong Kong, Hong Kong/China)*
Jan Van den Bussche *(Hasselt University, Belgium)*
Dirk Van Gucht *(Indiana University, USA)*
Christoph Koch *(EPFL, Switzerland)*

PODS Best Paper Award Committee:
Pierre Senellart (chair) *(ENS, PSL University, France)*
Frank Neven *(Hasselt University, Belgium)*
Dirk Van Gucht *(Indiana University, USA)*

Alberto O. Mendelzon Test-of-Time Award Committee:
Jianwen Su *(University of California, Santa Barbara, USA)*
Dirk Van Gucht *(Indiana University, USA)*
Victor Vianu *(University of California, San Diego, USA)*

PODS 2019 Sponsors & Supporters

Sponsors:

Diamond Supporter:

Platinum Supporters:

Gold Supporters:

Silver Supporters:

Startup Supporter:

Platinum Publisher:

Gold Publisher:

Silver Publisher:

Differential Privacy and the US Census

Cynthia Dwork
dwork@seas.harvard.edu
Harvard University

ABSTRACT

Differential privacy is a mathematically rigorous definition of privacy tailored to statistical analysis of large datasets. Differentially private systems simultaneously provide useful statistics to the well-intentioned data analyst and strong protection against arbitrarily powerful adversarial system users – without needing to distinguish between the two. Differentially private systems "don't care" what the adversary knows, now or in the future. Finally, differentially private systems can rigorously bound and control the cumulative privacy loss that accrues over many interactions with the confidential data. These unique properties, together with the abundance of auxiliary data sources and the ease with which they can be deployed by a privacy adversary, led the US Census Bureau to adopt differential privacy as the disclosure avoidance methodology of the 2020 decennial census.

This talk will motivate the definition of differential privacy, reflect on the theory-meets-practice experiences of the decennial census, and highlight a few pressing challenges in the field.

KEYWORDS

private-preserving data analysis

ACM Reference Format:
Cynthia Dwork. 2019. Differential Privacy and the US Census. In *38th ACM SIGMOD-SIGACT-SIGAI Symposium on Principles of Database Systems (PODS'19), June 30-July 5, 2019, Amsterdam, Netherlands.* ACM, New York, NY, USA, 1 page. https://doi.org/10.1145/3294052.3322188

PODS'19, June 30-July 5, 2019, Amsterdam, Netherlands

ACM ISBN 978-1-4503-6227-6/19/06.
https://doi.org/10.1145/3294052.3322188

Regularizing Conjunctive Features for Classification

Pablo Barceló
DCC, Univ. of Chile & IMFD Chile

Alexander Baumgartner
DCC, Univ. of Chile & RISC, Johannes Kepler Univ.

Victor Dalmau
Universitat Pompeu Fabra

Benny Kimelfeld
Technion – Israel Institute of Technology

ABSTRACT

We consider the feature-generation task wherein we are given a database with entities labeled as positive and negative examples, and the goal is to find feature queries that allow for a linear separation between the two sets of examples. We focus on conjunctive feature queries, and explore two fundamental problems: (a) deciding whether separating feature queries exist (separability), and (b) generating such queries when they exist. In the approximate versions of these problems, we allow a predefined fraction of the examples to be misclassified. To restrict the complexity of the generated classifiers, we explore various ways of regularizing (i.e., imposing simplicity constraints on) them by limiting their dimension, the number of joins in feature queries, and their generalized hypertree width (ghw). Among other results, we show that the separability problem is tractable in the case of bounded ghw; yet, the generation problem is intractable, simply because the feature queries might be too large. So, we explore a third problem: classifying new entities without necessarily generating the feature queries. Interestingly, in the case of bounded ghw we can efficiently classify without ever explicitly generating the feature queries.

KEYWORDS

Classification; Feature generation; Separability; Conjunctive queries; Generalized hypertree width

PODS '19, June 30–July 5, 2019, Amsterdam, Netherlands

ACM ISBN 978-1-4503-6227-6/19/06...$15.00
https://doi.org/10.1145/3294052.3319680

ACM Reference Format:
Pablo Barceló, Alexander Baumgartner, Victor Dalmau, and Benny Kimelfeld. 2019. Regularizing Conjunctive Features for Classification. In *38th ACM SIGMOD-SIGACT-SIGAI Symposium on Principles of Database Systems (PODS '19), June 30–July 5, 2019, Amsterdam, Netherlands.* ACM, New York, NY, USA, 15 pages. https://doi.org/10.1145/3294052.3319680

1 INTRODUCTION

Feature engineering is a critical and resource-consuming task in the development of machine-learning solutions in general, and classifiers in particular [16, 18, 34]. In the framework proposed by Kimelfeld and Ré [22], the general goal is to utilize the database's knowledge of the raw data structure to provide automated assistance in feature engineering. One of the fundamental tasks discussed in that framework is that of *separability*—given a database with labeled examples, determine whether a class of queries (e.g., conjunctive queries) is rich enough to provide the features needed for classification; that is, is there a sequence of feature queries and a classifier that separate the examples according to their labels?

We first summarize the framework of Kimelfeld and Ré [22]. The database schema has a special unary relation of *entities* to be classified, known as the *entity schema.* A *feature query* is a query that selects entities, and a *statistic* is a vector of feature queries. Every entity in the database is then assigned a vector, where the ith entry is $+1$ if the entity is selected by the ith feature query in the statistic, and -1 otherwise. A *training database* consists of a database over the entity schema along with a *labeling function* that partitions of the entities into *positive examples* and *negative examples.* A *classifier* maps every vector representing an entity into $+1$, denoting the positive class, or -1, denoting the negative class. When evaluating a classifier over a database, the entities are classified into positive and negative cases by transforming each entity into a vector, via the statistic, and then applying the classifier to this vector.

As in [22], we focus on features that are *Conjunctive Queries* (CQs) without constants, and on the class of *linear* classifiers. We consider the task of feature generation that aims at automatically proposing feature queries for the statistic. In the separability problem, we are given a training database, and the goal is to determine if there exist a statistic and a classifier that separate the entities according to their labeling. When separability is tractable, we also study the ability to actually produce the statistic, i.e., *feature generation*. As we shall see, determining the existence of a separating statistic does not necessarily mean that we can produce the statistic.

The separability problem is the database variant of the classic separability from Machine Learning (cf., e.g., [2, 25]), except that, here, we are given a database and not numeric vectors, and we need to generate the features. The motivation is the practice of automatically generating features as queries, and particularly via joins, which is quite common [1, 24, 27, 29]. While such features often involve *aggregate* queries over the joins, we aim to take a step forward in understanding the theoretical ground for this practice, and we begin with seeking restricted queries that are useful as features in the sense that they provide (approximate) separation.

The plain definition of the separability problem allows for feature queries that are arbitrarily complex. This is indeed the case in the proof of coNP-completeness of separability for linear classifiers over CQs shown in [22]. Yet, allowing complex feature queries entails several problems. The first problem is the classic risk of *overfitting*—feature queries seek information that is too specific to the examples, and hence, the learned classifier fails to generalize beyond the training database. The second problem is high *computational complexity*—feature queries might be hard to evaluate (under combined complexity). In machine learning, complexity restriction and reduction for learned models is known as *regularization* [30, 31]. Finally, complex queries are complicated to interpret and manipulate by human engineers.

In this work, we explore regularization at the level of the statistic and feature queries. We consider simplicity constraints on feature CQs and study their implication on the complexity of separability and feature generation. These restrictions are twofold: bounding the *number of atoms* (join operators), and more generally bounding the *generalized hypertree width* (ghw). When these bounds are constant, the feature queries can be evaluated efficiently [9]. Restricting the number of atoms is an inherent artifact of common algorithms for feature generation from relational databases, which build joins incrementally up to a limited (small) depth [1, 24, 27, 29]. While we are not aware of ghw playing a role in features for machine learning, it has been shown that a very small width is common in "natural" queries [7]. In addition, we explore the more traditional form of regularization—bounding the *dimension* of (i.e., the number of feature CQs in) the statistic, which motivates classic notions of regularization (viewed as the number of nonzero coefficients) [11, 26]. We also study the complexity of combining the bound on the dimension with the bounds on the CQ features.

As said, in the absence of any restriction, the separability problem is coNP-complete even for a fixed schema [22]. If we fix the schema *and* pose a constant bound on the number of atoms, then there is only a polynomial number of possible feature queries up to equivalence; in that case, the statistic that consists of all feature CQs (up to equivalence) is itself a separating statistic, if any such statistic exists. In particular, both separability and feature generation become tractable. We show that this tractability continues to hold when the schema is not necessarily fixed, but rather, we keep fixed just the maximal arity of the relations. It remains open whether just bounding the number of atoms in each feature query (and not fixing the schema or its maximal arity) suffices to solve separability in polynomial time. Still, even in this case the problem is feasible by a *fixed-parameter tractable* algorithm [10] (the parameter being the arity of the schema).

When we consider the class of CQs of bounded ghw (for some bound k), we observe an interesting phenomenon: separability is solvable in polynomial time. And yet, we cannot necessarily generate the separating statistic (when it exists), simply because the feature queries may be too large. Interestingly, it turns out that, while we cannot generate the feature CQs of a separating statistic, we can still classify according to it! To make this formal, we define the *classification* problem: given a training database and an evaluation database (which is simply a database over the entity schema), classify the entities of the evaluation database in a way that is explainable by a learned statistic; i.e., there exists a statistic that agrees with both the training labels (over the training database) and the produced new labels (over the evaluation database). We prove that in the case of bound ghw, the classification problem is solvable in polynomial time. This result is obtained by applying techniques based on the *existential cover game* [9].

Next, we turn to investigating the complexity implications of bounding the dimension of the statistic. We first show a general polynomial-time reduction from a variant of the problem of *Query By Example* (QBE) [3, 32, 33]: given a database and two tables, is there a query such that the result contains all of the tuples of the first table, and none of the tuples of the second table? The reduction applies to any query language $\mathcal{L}$ that is used for both problems. Using this general reduction, we obtain complexity results about the separability problem for several classes of CQs due to known results about QBE. For other classes of CQs, we first prove their complexity in QBE and then apply our reduction to establish the complexity of separability. In particular, we prove that for every combination of positive constant bounds on the dimension of the classifier and the number of atoms per CQ, separability is NP-complete. For general CQs, the complexity rises to coNEXPTIME-completeness, and EXPTIME-completeness for bounded ghw.

Table 1: Selected complexity results for the separability problem. We assume that the schema is fixed.

Problem	$\mathcal{L}$ = CQ	$\mathcal{L}$ = CQ[m]	$\mathcal{L}$ = GHW(k)
$\mathcal{L}$-SEP	coNP-c. [22]	PTIME	PTIME
$\mathcal{L}$-SEP[ℓ]	coNEXPTIME-c.	PTIME	EXPTIME-c.

Table 1 shows selected complexity results that we obtain for separability. The classes of feature queries are the one of all CQs (denoted **CQ**), the one of all CQs with at most m atoms (denoted **CQ**[m]), and the one of all CQs of ghw bounded by k (denoted **GHW**(k)). The computational problems for each class $\mathcal{L}$ of feature queries is that of general separability ($\mathcal{L}$-SEP) and the separability by a statistic with at most ℓ features ($\mathcal{L}$-SEP[ℓ]). We assume that the schema is fixed, and throughout the paper, we explain the importance of this assumption, and moreover, when it is necessary. However, no such assumption is needed for the tractability of separability for bounded ghw (i.e., **GHW**(k)-SEP).

Our analysis so far is applied to *perfect classification*, which means that we seek a statistic and a classifier that classify the examples precisely, no errors allowed. One might wonder if our (positive and negative) complexity results are based on the perfection of the classification. This is *not* the case: most of our complexity results apply to *approximate* classification, where we are given a number $\epsilon \in [0, 1)$ and we allow an ϵ fraction of the examples to be misclassified. In particular, for the hardness results, we prove a general reduction from approximate separability to precise separability which holds for every *fixed* ϵ. We also obtain feasibility results for CQs of bounded ghw and CQs with a fixed number of atoms by revisiting the techniques we use for perfect separability.

We also study the separability problem for more expressive feature queries, in particular FO queries. We observe that FO has the *dimension-collapse property*, which means that every training database that is FO-separable is also separable by a statistics with a single FO feature. This allows us to show that FO-separability has the same complexity as the QBE problem for FO, which is known to be GI-complete [4]. We also provide a characterization based on a definability condition of when a query language has the dimension collapse property. From this we obtain that several relevant fragments of FO also have this property: most notably, the k-variable fragment of FO, for any $k \geq 1$, and the class of existential FO formulas. On the other hand, the class of CQs, the class of CQs of bounded generalized hypertreewidth, and even the existential positive FO formulas do not have such a property. In fact, we prove something stronger: All these languages have the *unbounded-dimension property*, implying that there is no bound on the number of features from the language that are needed to separate training databases.

Note that our work is restricted to the *linear* case of classification, which is commonly viewed as a classic notion for separability, at least as a baseline to compare to more expressive classifier classes (cf., e.g., [2, 25]). Moreover, in some cases, such as Lemma 5.8 of Kimelfeld and Ré [23], or Lemma 5.4 of the current paper, a linear separation exists if and only if the class of CQs can distinguish between the positive and the negative examples, regardless of the classifier class; in such cases, the complexity results immediately extend to every superclass of the linear classifiers.

The rest of the paper is organized as follows. We give basic notation and definitions in Section 2, and define the separability problem in Section 3. In the next three sections, we study the complexity implications of bounding the maximum number of atoms per CQ (Section 4), the generalized hypertree width (Section 5), and the dimension of the statistic (Section 6). In Section 7, we provide results for approximate separability. We discuss feature queries beyond CQs in Section 8 and conclude in Section 9. Due to space constraints some proofs are in the appendix.

2 PRELIMINARIES

Databases and homomorphisms. A *schema* σ is a finite set of relation symbols, each of which has an associated arity $k > 0$. A *fact* over σ is an expression of the form $R(\bar{a})$, where R is a k-ary relation symbol in σ and $\bar{a}$ is a k-tuple of elements taken from a predefined universe. A *database* D over a σ is a finite set of facts over σ. The *domain* of D, denoted dom(D), is the set of universe elements that occur in the facts of D.

Let D and D' be databases over σ. A *homomorphism* from D to D' is a mapping $h : \text{dom}(D) \longrightarrow \text{dom}(D')$ such that for each fact $R(\bar{a}) \in D$ we have that $R(h(\bar{a})) \in D'$. Here, we use the conventional notation $h(\bar{a}) := (h(a_1), \dots, h(a_k))$.

We write $D \longrightarrow D'$ if there is a homomorphism from D to D'. We also write $(D, \bar{a}) \longrightarrow (D', \bar{a}')$, where $\bar{a}$ and $\bar{a}'$ are tuples over dom(D) and dom(D'), respectively, to denote that there is a homomorphism h from D to D' such that $h(\bar{a}) = \bar{a}'$.

Conjunctive queries. We consider here conjunctive queries without constants. Formally, a *Conjunctive Query* (CQ) q over a schema σ is a First-Order (FO) formula of the form

$$\exists \bar{y} \left(R_1(\bar{x}_1) \wedge \dots \wedge R_n(\bar{x}_n) \right), \tag{1}$$

such that the following hold: (1) For each $i \in \{1, \dots, n\}$ we have that R_i is a k-ary relation symbol in σ and $\bar{x}_i$ is a k-tuple of variables, and (2) $\bar{y}$ is a tuple of variables from $\bar{x}_1, \dots, \bar{x}_n$. The expressions $R_i(\bar{x}_i)$ are the *atoms* of q. We write $q(\bar{x})$ to denote that $\bar{x}$ is a sequence that consists of all *free variables* of q, i.e., the ones that do not occur in $\bar{y}$. In this work, we mainly deal with *unary* CQs, namely CQs $q(x)$ with a single free variable x.

As conventional, we define the evaluation of a CQ in terms of homomorphisms. To do so, we associate with each CQ $q(\bar{x})$ a database D_q, known as its *canonical database*. In particular, if q is of the form (1), then $D_q = \{R_1(\bar{x}_1), \ldots, R_n(\bar{x}_n)\}$ is the database that consists precisely of the atoms in q, where variables are treated as elements from the universe. A homomorphism from $q(\bar{x})$ to a database D is then a homomorphism from D_q to D. The *evaluation* of $q(\bar{x})$ over D, denoted $q(D)$, is the set of all tuples $\bar{a}$ over dom(D) such that $(D_q, \bar{x}) \longrightarrow (D, \bar{a})$. If q is unary, then we abuse notation and view $q(D)$ as a set of *elements* rather than unary *tuples*.

When there is no risk of ambiguity, we identify q with D_q; e.g., we write $(q, \bar{x}) \longrightarrow (D, \bar{a})$ instead of $(D_q, \bar{x}) \longrightarrow (D, \bar{a})$.

Linear classifiers. A *classifier* is a function $\mathcal{H} : \{1, -1\}^n \longrightarrow \{1, -1\}$, where $n > 0$ is the *arity*. In this paper, we restrict the discussion to the class of *linear* classifiers. Recall that a tuple $\bar{w} = (w_0, w_1, \ldots, w_n)$ of real numbers defines a linear classifier $\Lambda_{\bar{w}}$ in the following way. For $(b_1, \ldots, b_n) \in \{1, -1\}^n$ we have

$$\Lambda_{\bar{w}}(b_1, \ldots, b_n) := \begin{cases} 1 & \text{if } \sum_{1 \le i \le n} w_i b_i \ge w_0, \\ -1 & \text{otherwise.} \end{cases}$$

We view a sequence $\langle(\bar{b}_1, y_1), \ldots, (\bar{b}_m, y_m)\rangle$ of vectors in $\{1, -1\}^{n+1}$ as a collection of *examples*, consisting of *positive examples* (where $y_i = 1$) and *negative examples* (where $y_i = -1$). As a shorthand notation, we write such a sequence as $(\bar{b}_i, y_i)_{i=1}^m$ and refer to it as a *training collection*. The training collection $(\bar{b}_i, y_i)_{i=1}^m$ is *linearly separable* if there is a linear classifier $\Lambda_{\bar{w}}$ such that $\Lambda_{\bar{w}}(\bar{b}_i) = y_i$ for all $i \in \{1, \ldots, m\}$; in this case, we say that $\Lambda_{\bar{w}}$ *linearly separates* $(\bar{b}_i, y_i)_{i=1}^m$.

3 THE SEPARABILITY PROBLEM

Our investigation is in the context of the classification framework introduced by Kimelfeld and Ré [22], which recall next.

An *entity schema* is a schema that includes a distinguished unary relation symbol η used to represent *entities*. To improve readability, we refer to an entity schema simply by σ and denote the corresponding entity symbol by η_σ (but if σ is clear from the context, we simply write η). Let D be a database over an entity schema σ. An *entity* of D is a constant a such that $\eta(a) \in D$. We denote by $\eta(D)$ the set of entities of D.

In this work, a *feature query* is a unary CQ $q(x)$ over an entity schema σ. We are interested in the set of entities selected by $q(x)$ over a database D of schema σ. Hence, without loss of generality, we assume that the atom $\eta(x)$ is always present in feature queries $q(x)$, and therefore it holds that $q(D) \subseteq \eta(D)$. We denote by $\mathbb{1}_{q(D)} : \eta(D) \longrightarrow \{1, -1\}$ the *indicator function* defined by $q(D)$ over $\eta(D)$; that is, for each $e \in \eta(D)$ we have that $\mathbb{1}_{q(D)}(e) = 1$ if $e \in q(D)$, and $\mathbb{1}_{q(D)}(e) = -1$ otherwise.

A *statistic* over an entity schema σ is a sequence $\Pi = (q_1, \ldots, q_n)$ of feature queries over σ. If D is a database, then we define the mapping $\Pi^D : \eta(D) \longrightarrow \{1, -1\}^n$ as follows for all entities $e \in \eta(D)$:

$$\Pi^D(e) := \big(\mathbb{1}_{q_1(D)}(e), \ldots, \mathbb{1}_{q_n(D)}(e)\big).$$

A *labeling* λ of a database D over entity schema σ is a function $\lambda : \eta(D) \longrightarrow \{1, -1\}$ that partitions the set of entities into the set $\{e \in \eta(D) \mid \lambda(e) = 1\}$ of *positive examples* and the set $\{e \in \eta(D) \mid \lambda(e) = -1\}$ of *negative examples*. A *training database* over σ is a pair (D, λ), where D is a database over σ and λ is a labeling of D.

Definition 3.1 ($\mathcal{L}$-separability). Let $\mathcal{L}$ be a class of queries and (D, λ) a training database. Then (D, λ) is *$\mathcal{L}$-separable* if there is a statistic $\Pi = (q_1, \ldots, q_n)$ such that each q_i is in $\mathcal{L}$ and $(\Pi^D(e), \lambda(e))_{e \in \eta(D)}$ is linearly separable. □

In other words, (D, λ) is $\mathcal{L}$-separable if there is a statistic Π such that each feature query $q \in \Pi$ is in $\mathcal{L}$ and a linear classifier $\Lambda_{\bar{w}}$ that satisfies $\Lambda_{\bar{w}}(\Pi^D(e)) = \lambda(e)$ for every $e \in \eta(D)$. In this case, we say that $(\Pi, \Lambda_{\bar{w}})$ *$\mathcal{L}$-separates* (D, λ); or simply that Π $\mathcal{L}$-separates (D, λ) if $\Lambda_{\bar{w}}$ is irrelevant.

This paper focuses on the *$\mathcal{L}$-separability problem*, or $\mathcal{L}$-Sep for short, for a class $\mathcal{L}$ of queries (usually CQs). Originally proposed in [22], in the problem $\mathcal{L}$-Sep the goal is to determine the existence of a separating statistic Π in $\mathcal{L}$.

Problem:	$\mathcal{L}$-Sep
Input:	A training database (D, λ)
Question:	Is (D, λ) $\mathcal{L}$-separable?

The following is known about the complexity of the $\mathcal{L}$-Sep problem, when $\mathcal{L}$ is the class CQ of all CQs.

Theorem 3.2. [22] *The problem* CQ-Sep *is* coNP*-complete. The lower bound holds even if the schema consists of a single binary relation R and the distinguished symbol η.*

We study the complexity of $\mathcal{L}$-Sep for subfamilies $\mathcal{L}$ enforcing various natural restrictions on the feature CQs. In addition, we consider two regularization variants of the separability problem:

- The *dimension* of (i.e., the number of features in) Π is bounded by a constant ℓ. We denote this variant by $\mathcal{L}$-Sep$[\ell]$.
- The dimension is not bounded, but rather is given as input. We denote this variant by $\mathcal{L}$-Sep$[*]$.

Hence, we have three variants of the separability problem, namely $\mathcal{L}$-Sep, $\mathcal{L}$-Sep$[\ell]$, and $\mathcal{L}$-Sep$[*]$.

4 BOUNDED NUMBER OF FEATURE ATOMS

As we will see next, one can overcome the high complexity of separability (and related problems), at least under the yardstick of *parameterized complexity* [10], by fixing the number of atoms allowed in feature CQs.

For every fixed $m \geq 1$, we denote by $\mathbf{CQ}[m]$ the class of CQs with at most m atoms (not counting atom $\eta(x)$ which we assume appears in every feature query $q(x)$). The following simple observation allows us to obtain a better understanding of the complexity of the separability problem when restricted to feature queries in $\mathbf{CQ}[m]$.

Proposition 4.1. *There is an algorithm that determines if a given training database (D, λ) is $\mathbf{CQ}[m]$-separable, and if so, constructs a pair $(\Pi, \Lambda_{\bar{w}})$ that $\mathbf{CQ}[m]$-separates (D, λ). The running time of is bounded by $|D|^c \cdot 2^{q(k)}$ for a constant $c \geq 1$ and polynomial $q : \mathbb{N} \to \mathbb{N}$, where $k \geq 1$ is the maximal arity of a relation in D.*

Proof. Observe that (D, λ) is $\mathbf{CQ}[m]$-classifiable iff it is classifiable by the statistic Π that contains all feature queries $q(x)$ in $\mathbf{CQ}[m]$ that mention only relation symbols that appear in D. Since m is fixed, the statistic Π can be computed in time $r^m \cdot 2^{p(k)}$, for p a polynomial, where r is the number of relation symbols mentioned in D. (Thus, $r^m \cdot 2^{p(k)}$ is also a bound for the number of different feature CQs in Π). Since $r \leq |D|$, the latter is also $|D|^m \cdot 2^{p(k)}$. Now, for each CQ $q(x)$ in Π, we can compute $q(D)$ in time $O(|D|^m)$, and thus the indicator function $\mathbb{1}_{q(D)} : \eta(D) \to \{1, -1\}$ can be computed in time $O(|D|^{m+1})$. Hence, the set of tuples of the form $\Pi^D(e)$, for $e \in \eta(D)$, can be computed in time $O(|D|^{2m+1} \cdot 2^{p(k)})$, which is $|D|^{2m+1} \cdot 2^{p'(k)}$, for some polynomial p'.

Finally, we need to determine whether $(\Pi^D(e), \lambda(e))_{e\in\eta(D)}$ is indeed linearly classifiable. Recall that linear separability can be solved in polynomial time, by a reduction to the problem of finding a solution to a linear program (which is known to be tractable by a landmark result in combinatorial optimization [19, 21]). This procedure also finds a linear classifier $\Lambda_{\bar{w}}$ that separates the training collection $(\Pi^D(e), \lambda(e))_{e\in\eta(D)}$ in case it exists. Thus, checking if (D, λ) is $\mathbf{CQ}[m]$-separable, and, if so, computing a pair $(\Pi, \Lambda_{\bar{w}})$ that $\mathbf{CQ}[m]$-separates (D, λ), can be done in time $|D|^c \cdot 2^{q(k)}$ for a constant $c \geq 1$ and polynomial q. This concludes the proof. □

From Proposition 4.1, the problem $\mathbf{CQ}[m]$-Sep can be solved in time $|D|^{O(1)} \cdot f(k)$, for a computable function $f : \mathbb{N} \to \mathbb{N}$, where k is the maximal arity of a relation symbol mentioned in D. In the terminology of parameterized complexity, this means that the problem is *Fixed-Parameter Tractable* (FPT), with the parameter being the maximum arity k of a relation symbol in the schema (or simply the *arity of the schema* from now on). Summing up:

Corollary 4.2. *For all fixed $m \geq 1$, the problem $\mathbf{CQ}[m]$-Sep is FPT with the parameter being the arity of the schema.*

The restriction on the number of atoms allowed in statistics is necessary for obtaining the positive result stated in Corollary 4.2. In fact, Theorem 3.2 states that CQ-Sep is coNP-hard even if the schema is of a fixed arity; hence, the problem cannot be FPT if the parameter is the arity of the schema (assuming PTIME ≠ NP).

It remains an open problem whether $\mathbf{CQ}[m]$-Sep is NP-hard for some fixed $m \geq 1$. Nevertheless, there is a way to restrict the problem in order to ensure tractability: bounding the arity of the schema by a fixed constant. As explained in the proof of Proposition 4.1, the implication of this restriction is that the number of different feature CQs that one can form in this case (up to equivalence) is polynomial in the size of the input. Still, we can do better than fixing the arity, since the argument remains valid if we assume only that the maximal *number of occurrences per variable* in the feature CQs is bounded by a constant. Formally, for fixed $m, p \geq 1$ let $\mathbf{CQ}[m, p]$ be the class of CQs with at most m atoms and in which each variable occurs at most p times. Then:

Proposition 4.3. *$\mathbf{CQ}[m, p]$-Sep can be solved in polynomial time, for every fixed m and p.*

Importantly, the results stated in Corollary 4.2 and Proposition 4.3 are obtained via a constructive proof that allows to perform the following tasks with the same tractability guarantees, if the input (D, λ) is indeed $\mathbf{CQ}[m]$-separable.

- *Feature generation:* Construct a pair $(\Pi, \Lambda_{\bar{w}})$ that $\mathbf{CQ}[m]$-separates the training database (D, λ).
- *Classification:* Apply $(\Pi, \Lambda_{\bar{w}})$ to a given evaluation database for performing the actual classification.

As shown next, things become more complicated if, instead of the number of atoms, we bound the *generalized hypertree-width* of feature queries.

5 BOUNDED GEN. HYPERTREE-WIDTH

In this section, we investigate the complexity implications of regularizing statistics by bounding the generalized hypertree-width of the feature CQs. We start with some background.

We introduce the classes of CQs of bounded *generalized hypertree-width* [13] (also known as *coverwidth* [9]). We adopt the definition of Chen and Dalmau [9], which better suits non-Boolean queries. A *tree decomposition* of a CQ $q = \exists \bar{y} \bigwedge_{1\leq i\leq n} R_i(\bar{x}_i)$ is a pair (T, χ), where T is a tree and χ is a mapping that assigns a subset of the existentially quantified variables in $\bar{y}$ to each node $t \in T$, such that:

(1) For all $1 \leq i \leq m$, the variables in $\bar{x}_i \cap \bar{y}$ are contained in $\chi(t)$, for some $t \in T$.
(2) For all variables y in $\bar{y}$, the node set $\{t \in T \mid y \in \chi(t)\}$ induces a connected subtree of T.

The *width* of node t in (T, χ) is the minimal size of an $I \subseteq \{1, \ldots, m\}$ such that $\bigcup_{i\in I} \bar{x}_i$ covers $\chi(t)$. The width of (T, χ) is the maximal width of the nodes of T. The *generalized hypertree-width* (*ghw* for short) of q is the minimum width of its tree decompositions.

For a fixed k, we denote by $\mathbf{GHW}(k)$ the class of CQs of ghw at most k. In contrast to the case of general CQs, the evaluation problem for CQs in $\mathbf{GHW}(k)$ can be solved in polynomial time [12]. Notice that each CQ in $\mathbf{CQ}[k]$ is also in $\mathbf{GHW}(k)$, but not viceversa.

The existential cover game. There is a link between the evaluation of CQs in $\mathbf{GHW}(k)$ and a version of the pebble game, known as *existential cover game* [9], that we recall below. The existential k-cover game (for k a natural number) is played by *Spoiler* and *Duplicator* on pairs $(D, \bar{a})$ and $(D', \bar{b})$, where D and D' are databases and $\bar{a}$ and $\bar{b}$ are n-ary ($n \geq 0$) tuples over $\text{dom}(D)$ and $\text{dom}(D')$, respectively. In each round of the game, Spoiler places (resp., removes) a pebble on (resp., from) an element of $\text{dom}(D)$, and Duplicator responds by placing (resp., removing) its corresponding pebble on an element of (resp., from) $\text{dom}(D')$. The number of pebbles is not bounded, but Spoiler is constrained as follows: At any round p of the game, if $c_1, \ldots, c_\ell$ ($\ell \leq p$) are the elements marked by Spoiler's pebbles in D, there must be a set of at most k facts in D that contain all such elements (this is why the game is called k-cover, as pebbled elements are *covered* by no more than k facts).

Duplicator wins if she has a *winning strategy*, that is, she can indefinitely continue playing the game in such a way that after each round, if $c_1, \ldots, c_\ell$ are the elements that are marked by Spoiler's pebbles in D and $d_1, \ldots, d_\ell$ are the elements marked by the corresponding pebbles of Duplicator in D', then

$$\big((c_1, \ldots, c_\ell, \bar{a}), (d_1, \ldots, d_\ell, \bar{b})\big)$$

is a *partial homomorphism* from D to D'. That is, for every atom $R(\bar{c}) \in D$, where each element c of $\bar{c}$ appears in $(c_1, \ldots, c_\ell, \bar{a})$, it is the case that $R(\bar{d}) \in D'$, where $\bar{d}$ is the tuple obtained from $\bar{c}$ by replacing each element c of $\bar{c}$ by its corresponding element d in $(d_1, \ldots, d_\ell, \bar{b})$. We write $(D, \bar{a}) \rightarrow_k (D', \bar{b})$ if Duplicator wins.

Notice that $\rightarrow_k$ "approximates" $\rightarrow$ as follows:

$$\rightarrow \subset \cdots \subset \rightarrow_{k+1} \subset \rightarrow_k \subset \cdots \subset \rightarrow_1 \qquad (k \geq 1).$$

These approximations are convenient complexity-wise: Checking whether $(D, \bar{a}) \rightarrow (D', \bar{b})$ is NP-complete, but $(D, \bar{a}) \rightarrow_k (D', \bar{b})$ can be solved efficiently (as long as k is fixed).

Proposition 5.1. [9] *For all fixed $k \geq 1$, whether $(D, \bar{a}) \rightarrow_k (D', \bar{b})$ can be determined in polynomial time.*

Moreover, there is a close connection between $\rightarrow_k$ and the evaluation of CQs in $\mathbf{GHW}(k)$.

Proposition 5.2. [9] *$(D, \bar{a}) \rightarrow_k (D', \bar{b})$ if and only if for every CQ $q(\bar{x})$ in $\mathbf{GHW}(k)$ we have that*

$$(q, \bar{x}) \rightarrow (D, \bar{a}) \quad \Longrightarrow \quad (q, \bar{x}) \rightarrow (D', \bar{b}).$$

In particular, for all CQs $q(\bar{x})$ in $\mathbf{GHW}(k)$, databases D and tuples $\bar{a}$, it holds that $\bar{a} \in q(D)$ if and only if $(q, \bar{x}) \rightarrow_k (D, \bar{a})$.

5.1 Separability

In contrast to the case of arbitrary CQs, the separability problem for the classes of CQs of bounded ghw is tractable. We prove this result by applying techniques based on the existential cover game.

Theorem 5.3. *For all fixed $k \geq 1$, the problem $\mathbf{GHW}(k)$-SEP is solvable in polynomial time.*

The proof is based on the following lemma.

Lemma 5.4. *The following statements are equivalent for all training databases (D, λ).*

(1) (D, λ) is $\mathbf{GHW}(k)$-separable.
(2) There are no entities $e, e' \in \eta(D)$ such that $\lambda(e) \neq \lambda(e')$, and yet $e \in q(D) \Leftrightarrow e' \in q(D)$ for all $q(x) \in \mathbf{GHW}(k)$.

PROOF. The fact that $1 \rightarrow 2$ is straighforward. We now prove that $2 \rightarrow 1$. For each $e \in \eta(D)$, we define a query

$$q_e(x) := \bigwedge_{e' \in \eta(D)} q_e^{e'}(x),$$

where $q_e^{e'}(x) = q(x)$ is an arbitrary CQ in $\mathbf{GHW}(k)$ such that $e \in q(D)$ and $e' \notin q(D)$—if such $q(x)$ exists at all—and it is $\eta(x)$ otherwise. Then $q_e(x)$ can be reformulated as an equivalent CQ in $\mathbf{GHW}(k)$. This is because each conjunct in $q_e(x)$ is in $\mathbf{GHW}(k)$, and $\mathbf{GHW}(k)$ is closed under taking conjunctions (see, e.g., [6]).

We denote by $\preceq$ the binary relation over $\eta(D)$ such that $e \preceq e'$ iff $e' \in q_e(D)$. It is easy to see that $\preceq$ is reflexive and transitive, that is, it is a preorder. Recall that an *equivalence class* of $\preceq$ over $\eta(D)$ is an equivalence class of the equivalence relation "$e \preceq e'$ and $e' \preceq e$". We overload notation and write $E \preceq F$, for equivalence classes E, F over $\eta(D)$ defined by $\preceq$, iff there are elements $e \in E$ and $f \in F$ such that $e \preceq f$. Since $\preceq$ is a partial order, there is a topological sort of such equivalence classes with respect to $\preceq$. Let $E_1, E_2, \ldots, E_m$ be one such a topological sort.

For each E_i, we select an arbitrary entity $e_i \in E_i$. It is not hard to see then that the following hold for each $i \in \{1, \ldots, m\}$ and entity $e \in E_i$: *(a) $e \in q_{e_i}(D)$, and (b) $e \notin q_{e_j}(D)$* for each $j \in \{1, \ldots, m\}$ with $i < j$. It follows from Kimelfeld and Ré [22] that these properties imply that the statistics $\Pi = (q_{e_1}, \ldots, q_{e_m})$ separates (D, λ). Since each q_{e_i} can be reformulated as an equivalent CQ in $\mathbf{GHW}(k)$, we conclude that (D, λ) is $\mathbf{GHW}(k)$-separable. □

Proposition 5.2 establishes that the condition of Lemma 5.4, stating that for all $q(x) \in \mathbf{GHW}(k)$ it is the case that $e \in q(D) \Leftrightarrow e' \in q(D)$, is equivalent to saying that

$$(D, e) \rightarrow_k (D, e') \text{ and } (D, e') \rightarrow_k (D, e).$$

Hence, the following test checks for $\mathbf{GHW}(k)$-separability:

> $\mathbf{GHW}(k)$*-separability test:*
> Given a training database (D, λ), accept if $(D, e) \not\rightarrow_k (D, e')$ or $(D, e') \not\rightarrow_k (D, e)$ for all $e, e' \in \eta(D)$ with $\lambda(e) \neq \lambda(e')$.

Proposition 5.5. *A training database (D, λ) is $\mathbf{GHW}(k)$-separable iff the $\mathbf{GHW}(k)$-separability test accepts (D, λ).*

From Proposition 5.1, the $\mathbf{GHW}(k)$-separability test can be performed in polynomial time, which yields Theorem 5.3.

While Theorem 5.3 establishes the tractability of $\mathbf{GHW}(k)$-Sep, the proof is *not* constructive, that is, it does not show how to efficiently construct a statistic that realizes $\mathbf{GHW}(k)$-separability. As shown next, this is not coincidental: separability and feature generation behave differently for $\mathbf{GHW}(k)$.

5.2 Feature Generation

We now look at the problem of generating a statistics that $\mathbf{GHW}(k)$-separates a training database (D, λ). It follows from Chen and Dalmau [9] that there is an exponential time algorithm that takes as input an entity $e \in \eta(D)$ and constructs a CQ $q'_e(x)$ in $\mathbf{GHW}(k)$ that is equivalent to $q_e(x)$, where $q_e(x)$ is as defined in the proof of Lemma 5.4. On the other hand, Lemma 5.4 states that if (D, λ) is $\mathbf{GHW}(k)$-separable, then it is separable by a statistic that contains only queries of the form $q'_e(x)$ for $e \in \eta(D)$. Therefore, if (D, λ) is $\mathbf{GHW}(k)$-separable, then there exists a statistic Π with polynomially many features, each of which is of at most exponential size, such that Π $\mathbf{GHW}(k)$-separates (D, λ). This statistic Π can be constructed in exponential time from (D, λ). Summing up:

Proposition 5.6. *For all fixed k, there is an exponential-time algorithm that determines whether a given training database (D, λ) is $\mathbf{GHW}(k)$-separable, and if so, generates a statistic Π that:*

- *$\mathbf{GHW}(k)$-separates (D, λ);*
- *has a dimension linear in the number of entities in $\eta(D)$;*
- *consists of CQs of size at most exponential in that of D.*

As it turns out, the size of statistic Π in Proposition 5.6 is essentially optimal.

Theorem 5.7. *For all $n, m \geq 1$ there is a training database (D, λ) with $|D| = O(n)$ and $|\eta(D)| = O(m)$ such that:*

- *(D, λ) is $\mathbf{GHW}(k)$-separable.*
- *For all statistics $\Pi = (q_1, \ldots, q_p)$ that linearly separate (D, λ), it is the case that (a) $p \geq m$, and (b) at least one of the q_is, for $i \in \{1, \ldots, p\}$, has $\Omega(2^n)$ atoms.*

We are thus faced with an apparently contradictory situation: while we can efficiently check for the existence of a statistic that $\mathbf{GHW}(k)$-separates the input (D, λ), materializing such a statistic might be infeasible. Interestingly, for *classifying* unseen entities, this statistic does not need to be materialized—we can perform this task efficiently by applying techniques based on the existential cover game. Next, we formalize this statement and prove it.

5.3 Classification

In this section, we discuss the problem of classifying an evaluation database based on a training database, without necessarily materializing a statistic. Formally, in this problem we are given a training database (D, λ) and an evaluation database D', which is a database over the same schema as D. The goal is to classify the entities of D' according to *some* statistic and linear classifier that separate D.

Problem:	$\mathcal{L}$-Cls
Input:	An $\mathcal{L}$-separable training database (D, λ) and an evaluation database D'
Output:	A labeling λ' of D' such that there is $(\Pi, \Lambda_{\bar{w}})$ that $\mathcal{L}$-separates both (D, λ) and (D', λ')

We prove the following:

Theorem 5.8. $\mathbf{GHW}(k)$-Cls *can be solved in polynomial time for all fixed $k \geq 1$.*

Proof. Consider an input for $\mathbf{GHW}(k)$-Cls that consists of a $\mathbf{GHW}(k)$-separable training database (D, λ) over an entity schema σ and an evaluation database D' over σ. We need to construct a labeling λ' of $\eta(D')$ such that there exists $(\Pi, \Lambda_{\bar{w}})$ that $\mathbf{GHW}(k)$-separates both (D, λ) and (D', λ').

Let us consider again the CQs $q_e(x)$, for $e \in \eta(D)$, defined in the proof of Lemma 5.4. From the definition of $q_e(x)$ it follows that for all $e' \in \eta(D)$ we have that $e' \in q_e(D)$ iff for all CQs $q(x) \in \mathbf{GHW}(k)$ it is the case that $e \in q(D)$ implies $e' \in q(D)$. In turn, from Proposition 5.2 we get that the latter holds iff $(D, e) \rightarrow_k (D, e')$. Therefore, the problem of testing whether $e' \in q_e(D)$, given $e, e' \in \eta(D)$, can be solved in polynomial time due to Proposition 5.1.

Let $E_1, \ldots, E_m$ be an arbitrary topological sort of the equivalence classes defined by $\preceq$ over $\eta(D)$. From the proof of Lemma 5.4 it follows that the training database (D, λ) is $\mathbf{GHW}(k)$-separable by any statistic $\Pi = (q_{e_1}(x), \ldots, q_{e_m}(x))$ such that $e_i \in E_i$.

The topological sort $E_1, \ldots, E_m$ and, therefore, also the elements $e_1, \ldots, e_m$, can be constructed in polynomial time from (D, λ). This is due to the fact that the relation $\preceq$ over $\eta(D)$ can be constructed efficiently (as we have already mentioned that $e \preceq e'$ iff $e' \in q_e(D)$ iff $(D, e) \rightarrow_k (D, e')$, which is decidable in polynomial time). In addition, it follows from [22] that one can construct in polynomial time a linear classifier $\Lambda_{\bar{w}}$ such that $(\Pi, \Lambda_{\bar{w}})$ separates (D, λ), without actually constructing Π, but rather just using $\preceq$.

We define a labeling λ' of $\eta(D')$ such that for each $f \in \eta'(D)$ it holds that $\lambda'(f) = \Lambda_{\bar{w}}(\Pi^{D'}(f))$. Clearly, $(\Pi, \Lambda_{\bar{w}})$ **GHW**(k)-separates (D, λ) and (D', λ'). We need to show that λ' can be constructed in polynomial time, or equivalently, that given $f \in \eta(D')$ we can compute $\lambda'(f) = \Lambda_{\bar{w}}(\Pi^{D'}(f))$ in polynomial time. By definition,

$$\Lambda_{\bar{w}}(\Pi^{D'}(f)) = 1 \iff \sum_{1 \le i \le m} w_i \cdot \mathbb{1}_{q_{e_i}(D')}(f) \ge w_0,$$

assuming that $\bar{w} = (w_0, \ldots, w_m)$. The latter can be checked in polynomial time, since computing $\mathbb{1}_{q_{e_i}(D')}(f)$ boils down to checking $(D, e_i) \rightarrow_k (D', f)$. The pseudo-code of the procedure is shown in Algorithm 1. □

Algorithm 1 Classification algorithm **GHW**(k)-Cls.

Require: An **GHW**(k)-separable training database (D, λ) and an evaluation database D'

$([e_1], \ldots, [e_m])$:= topological sort of the equivalence classes defined by $\rightarrow_k$ over $\eta(D)$
$\Lambda_{\bar{w}} = (w_0, \ldots, w_m)$:= linear classifier such that $(\Pi, \Lambda_{\bar{w}})$ separates (D, λ), where $\Pi = (q_{e_1}(x), \ldots, q_{e_m}(x))$ ▷ It can be computed efficiently without computing Π
for each $f \in \eta(D')$ and $i \in \{1, \ldots, m\}$ **do**
  if $(D, e_i) \rightarrow_k (D', f)$ **then**
    $\mathbb{1}_{q_{e_i}(D')}(f) = 1$
  else
    $\mathbb{1}_{q_{e_i}(D')}(f) = -1$
  end if
end for
for each $f \in \eta(D')$ **do**
  if $\sum_{1 \le i \le m} w_i \cdot \mathbb{1}_{q_{e_i}(D')}(f) \ge w_0$ **then**
    $\lambda'(f) = 1$
  else
    $\lambda'(f) = -1$
  end if
end for
return $\lambda' : \eta(D') \rightarrow \{1, -1\}$

In summary, in this section we have established that it takes polynomial time to decide whether a given training database (D, λ) is **GHW**(k)-separable (Theorem 5.3). A the same time, it may be infeasible to actually materialize the separating statistic, since it might be too large (Theorem 5.7). Then again, to classify entities of a given evaluation database D', we do not need to materialize such a statistic, and in fact, this classification can be carried out in polynomial time (Theorem 5.8).

6 BOUNDING THE DIMENSION

While the separability and classification problems become tractable if we restrict to statistics formed by CQs in **GHW**(k), for each fixed $k \ge 1$, there is one aspect of such statistics that complicates its applicability: as stated in Theorem 5.7, the number of feature queries required to separate a training database (D, λ) might depend on the number of entities in $\eta(D)$. This problem is not exclusive to the class **GHW**(k); in fact, a similar negative result can be proved for statistics based on the general class of CQs.

To address this issue, we study the separability problem for the restricted class of statistics that allow a bounded number of features only. Recall that this problem is denoted $\mathcal{L}$-Sep[$*$], for $\mathcal{L}$ a class of CQs. The input consists of a training database (D, λ) and an integer $\ell \ge 1$, and the task is to decide if there is a statistic formed by at most ℓ feature queries in $\mathcal{L}$ that separates (D, λ). If, in addition, the number ℓ of features is fixed, we denote the problem by $\mathcal{L}$-Sep[ℓ].

As we show next, the study of $\mathcal{L}$-Sep[$*$] and $\mathcal{L}$-Sep[ℓ] is directly related to *query-by-example* problem (QBE). This allow us to apply the wide arsenal of results and tools for QBE [6, 32, 33] in order to understand the complexity of $\mathcal{L}$-Sep[$*$]. We first introduce QBE.

6.1 The Query-by-Example Problem

Let D be a database, and assume that S^+ and S^- are relations over D of *positive* and *negative* examples, respectively. An $\mathcal{L}$-*explanation* for (D, S^+, S^-) is a query $q(\bar{x})$ in $\mathcal{L}$ such that $S^+ \subseteq q(D)$ and $q(D) \cap S^- = \emptyset$. Then QBE for the class $\mathcal{L}$ is defined as follows.

Problem:	$\mathcal{L}$-QBE
Input:	A database D and relations S^+ and S^- over D
Question:	Is there an $\mathcal{L}$-explanation for (D, S^+, S^-)?

The following is known regarding the complexity of QBE:

Theorem 6.1. [6, 32, 33] *The following statements hold:*

- **CQ**-QBE *is* coNEXPTIME-*complete.*
- **GHW**(k)-QBE *is* EXPTIME-*complete, for each* $k \ge 1$.

The lower bounds continue to hold even if the schema is fixed and S^+, S^- *are nonempty unary relations such that* $S^- = \mathrm{dom}(D) \setminus S^+$.

6.2 Separability for Bounded Dimension

One of the crucial properties used in the study of separability is that a training database (D, λ) is **CQ**-separable iff there are no entities $e, e' \in \eta(D)$ such that $\lambda(e) \neq \lambda(e')$, yet e and

e' are "indistinguishable" by CQs [22]. As the next example shows, this does not hold under the current restriction on the dimension of the statistic.

Example 6.2. Let σ be an entity schema with two unary symbols R and S and the entity symbol η. Consider the database $D = \{R(a), S(a), S(c), \eta(a), \eta(b), \eta(c)\}$ over σ. We define a labeling $\lambda : \eta(D) \to \{1, -1\}$ such that $\lambda(a) = \lambda(b) = 1$ and $\lambda(c) = -1$. It is not hard to see that (D, λ) is not **CQ**-separable by a statistic with one feature. This is in spite of the fact that a can be distinguished from c by the CQ $R(x)$, and b can be distinguished from c by the CQ $S(x)$. On the other hand, (D, λ) is **CQ**-separable by a statistic with two features; namely, $\Pi = (R(x), S(x))$. □

On the other hand, we can design a simple "guess-and-check" algorithm that solves $\mathcal{L}$-SEP[$*$], for an arbitrary class $\mathcal{L}$ of CQs, if we know how to solve $\mathcal{L}$-QBE.

$(\mathcal{L}, \ell)$-separability test:

Given a training database (D, λ),

- Guess a vector $\bar{\kappa}_e \in \{1, -1\}^\ell$, for each $e \in \eta(D)$;
- Check $(\bar{\kappa}_e, \lambda(e))_{e \in \eta(D)}$ for linear separability;
- For all $j \in \{1, \ldots, \ell\}$, test whether an $\mathcal{L}$-explanation for (D, S_j^+, S_j^-) exists, where $S_j^+ = \{e \mid \bar{\kappa}_e[j] = 1\}$ and $S_j^- = \{e \mid \bar{\kappa}_e[j] = -1\}$.

Here, $\bar{\kappa}_e[j]$ is the j-th component of $\bar{\kappa}_e[j]$. It is easy to see that the following holds for every class $\mathcal{L}$ of CQs.

Lemma 6.3. *A training database is $\mathcal{L}$-separable by a statistic with at most ℓ features if and only if the $(\mathcal{L}, \ell)$-separability test accepts (D, λ).*

It is not hard to see, by applying Theorem 6.1, that for every $\ell \geq 1$ the $(\mathbf{CQ}, \ell)$-separability test can be carried out in coNEXPTIME, while for every fixed $k \geq 1$, the $(\mathbf{GHW}(k), \ell)$-separability test can be carried out in EXPTIME. Then, from Lemma 6.3 we obtain an upper bound for the complexity of **CQ**-SEP[$*$] and **GHW**(k)-SEP[$*$], for every $k \geq 1$.

Proposition 6.4. **CQ**-SEP[$*$] *is in* coNEXPTIME, *while the problem* **GHW**(k)-SEP[$*$] *is in* EXPTIME *for every* $k \geq 1$.

It can be shown that these bounds are optimal by using a general reduction from QBE for any class $\mathcal{L}$ of CQs (under a mild assumption on $\mathcal{L}$). This reduction actually states something stronger: The lower bound for our problems continue to hold even if the number of features $\ell \geq 1$ is fixed.

Lemma 6.5. *Let $\mathcal{L}$ be a class of CQs such that $\mathcal{L}$ contains all CQs with only one atom (over every schema). Fix $\ell \geq 1$. Then $\mathcal{L}$-QBE, when restricted to inputs of the form (D, S^+, S^-) where S^+, S^- are nonempty unary relations such that $S^- = \text{dom}(D) \setminus S^+$, reduces in polynomial time to $\mathcal{L}$-SEP[ℓ].*

PROOF. Let D be a database over some schema σ and assume that S^+, S^- are nonempty unary relations over D such that $S^- = \text{dom}(D) \setminus S^+$. Define an entity schema σ' that extends σ with the entity symbol η and $\ell - 1$ fresh unary symbols $\kappa_1, \ldots, \kappa_{\ell-1}$. We construct a database D' over σ' that extends D with fresh constants $c^-, c_1, \ldots, c_{\ell-1}$ and facts $\kappa_1(c_1), \ldots, \kappa_{\ell-1}(c_{\ell-1})$. We define

$$\eta(D') = S^+ \cup S^- \cup \{c^-, c_1, \ldots, c_{\ell-1}\} = \text{dom}(D'),$$

and a labeling $\lambda : \eta(D') \to \{1, -1\}$ in such a way that $\lambda(e) = 1$ if $e \in S^+ \cup \{c_1, \ldots, c_{\ell-1}\}$ and $\lambda(e) = -1$ if $e \in S^- \cup \{c^-\}$.

By construction of D', for any CQ $q(x)$ over σ':

(1) If $c^- \in q(D')$ then $q(D') = \eta(D') = \text{dom}(D')$.
(2) For each $i \in \{1, \ldots, \ell - 1\}$, if $c_i \in q(D')$ then either $q(D') = \{c_i\}$ or $q(D') = \eta(D') = \text{dom}(D')$.

We claim that there is an $\mathcal{L}$-explanation for (D, S^+, S^-) iff (D', λ) is $\mathcal{L}$-separable by a statistics with ℓ features. Assume first that $q(x)$ is an $\mathcal{L}$-explanation for (D, S^+, S^-). Let $q_i(x) := \kappa_i(x)$, for each $1 \leq i \leq \ell - 1$. Then the statistic $\Pi = (q_1, \ldots, q_{\ell-1}, q)$ belongs to $\mathcal{L}$ by hypothesis. Moreover, $(\Pi, \Lambda_{\bar{w}})$ separates (D', λ), where $\bar{w} = (1 - l, 1, \ldots, 1)$. In fact, notice that for each $e \in \eta(D') = \text{dom}(D')$ it is the case that $\Lambda_{\bar{w}}(\Pi^{D'}(e)) = 1$ iff e belongs to the evaluation of at least some CQ in Π over D'. Let us first consider the elements e with $\lambda(e) = 1$. If $e = c_i$, for $i \in \{1, \ldots, \ell - 1\}$, then $e \in q_i(D')$. If $e \in S^+$ then $e \in q(D')$. Consider now an arbitrary element e in S^-. Then $e \notin q_i(D)$, for each $i \in \{1, \ldots, \ell - 1\}$, since $q_i(x) = \kappa_i(x)$. Also, $e \notin q(D')$. This is because the restriction of D' to the symbols in σ homomorphically maps to D, and, thus, if $e \in q(D')$ we would have that $e \in q(D)$. This contradicts the fact that $q(D) \cap S^- = \emptyset$. Finally, since $S^- \neq \emptyset$, it follows by property (1) above that $c^- \notin q(D')$. Otherwise, we would have that $b \in q(D')$, for some $b \in S^-$, and thus $b \in q(D)$, contradicting the fact that $q(D) \cap S^- = \emptyset$. In addition, $c^- \notin q_i(D)$, for each $i \in \{1, \ldots, \ell - 1\}$, by definition.

Assume, on the other hand, that Π separates (D', λ), where Π is a statistic with ℓ features from $\mathcal{L}$. For each $i \in \{1, \ldots, \ell - 1\}$ it is the case that $\lambda(c_i) \neq \lambda(c^-)$, and, therefore,

$$\Lambda_{\bar{w}}(\Pi^{D'}(c_i)) \neq \Lambda_{\bar{w}}(\Pi^{D'}(c^-)).$$

Hence, for each $i \in \{1, \ldots, \ell - 1\}$ there is at least some $q(x)$ in Π such that $q(D') \cap \{c^-, c_i\}$ is either $\{c^-\}$ or $\{c_i\}$. But $q(D') \cap \{c^-, c_i\} = \{c^-\}$ is ruled out by property (1), and hence for each $i \in \{1, \ldots, \ell - 1\}$ there exists a $q(x)$ in Π such that $q(D') \cap \{c^-, c_i\} = \{c_i\}$. By property (2) now, it follows that $q(D') = \{c_i\}$.

Let $c_i, c_i' \in \{c_1, \ldots, c_{\ell-1}\}$ with $c_i \neq c_i'$. Then there are queries $q(x)$ and $q'(x)$ in Π such that $q(D') = \{c_i\}$ and $q'(D') = \{c_i'\}$. It must be the case then that $q \neq q'$. Thus, there are at least $\ell - 1$ distinct feature queries $q_1, \ldots q_{\ell-1}$ in Π, such that for each $1 \leq j \leq \ell - 1$ and $e \in S^+ \cup S^- \cup \{c^-\}$ it holds that $e \notin q_j(D)$.

Aside from $\{q_1, \ldots q_{\ell-1}\}$, there is only one more feature query $q(x)$ in Π. By our previous observation, it must be the case that $e \in q(D') \Leftrightarrow e' \notin q(D')$ for each $e \in S^+$ and $e' \in S^- \cup \{c^-\}$ (as otherwise there would be entities $e \in S^+$ and $e' \in S^- \cup \{c^-\}$ such that $\Pi^{D'}(e) = \Pi^{D'}(e')$, contradicting the fact that Π separates (D', λ)). By property (1) then, it must be the case that $e \in q(D')$ for each $e \in S^+$, and $e' \notin q(D')$ for each $e' \in S^- \cup \{c^-\}$. This means that $S^+ \subseteq q(D')$ and $(S^- \cup \{c^-\}) \cap q(D') = \emptyset$.

It remains to show that we can restrict q so that it only contains symbols from σ, i.e., if q' is the query obtained from q by removing atoms of the form $\eta(x)$ and $\kappa_i(x)$, then $q'(D') = q(D')$. Since $\eta(D') = \text{dom}(D')$, an atom $\eta(x)$ is equal to the trivial condition $x \in \text{dom}(D')$ and can be removed. Let us assume then that

$$q(x) := \exists \bar{y} \left(\kappa_{i_1}(z_1) \wedge \cdots \wedge \kappa_{i_m}(z_m) \wedge R_1(\bar{x}_1) \wedge \cdots \wedge R_n(\bar{x}_n)\right),$$

where $1 \leq i_1, \ldots, i_m \leq \ell - 1$ and the R_is come from σ. Since S^+ is a nonempty unary relation, there is some $a \in q(D')$; hence $x \neq z_j$, for each $j \in \{1, \ldots, m\}$. Thus, $q(x) := \exists \bar{y}_0 \exists z_1, \ldots, z_m \left(\kappa_{i_1}(z_1) \wedge \cdots \wedge \kappa_{i_m}(z_m) \wedge R_1(\bar{x}_1) \wedge \cdots \wedge R_n(\bar{x}_n)\right)$, where z is taken from $\bar{y}$ and $\bar{y}_0$ is $\bar{y}$ without $z_1, \ldots, z_m$. By definition, for each $j \in \{1, \ldots, m\}$, the element c_{i_j} only appears twice in D', namely in the facts $\kappa_{i_j}(c_{i_j})$ and $\eta(c_{i_j})$. Therefore, z_{i_j} cannot appear in any of the atoms $R_i(\bar{x}_i)$, for $1 \leq i \leq n$. This means that we can safely remove each atom of the form $\kappa_{i_j}(z_{i_j})$ from q, as it is expressing a trivial condition; i.e., that there is an element in the interpretation of κ_{i_j} over D'. The resulting query $q'(x)$ satisfies that $q'(D') = q(D')$, and, therefore, $q'(x)$ is an $\mathcal{L}$-explanation for (D, S^+, S^-). □

In view of Theorem 6.1 and Lemma 6.5, we obtain the following:

Theorem 6.6. *It is the case that:*

- **CQ**-Sep[$*$] *is* coNEXPTIME-*complete.*
- **GHW**(k)-Sep[$*$] *is* EXPTIME-*complete, for each* $k \geq 1$.

The lower bounds continue to hold even for the $\mathcal{L}$-Sep[ℓ] *problem, for any fixed* $\ell \geq 1$, *where* $\mathcal{L}$ *is either* **CQ** *or* **GHW**(k).

The lower bounds for **CQ**-Sep[ℓ] and **GHW**(k)-Sep[ℓ] established in the previous theorem hold even for a fixed schema. This is based on the fact that the lower bounds in Theorem 6.1 hold over a fixed schema, and the reduction from QBE to $\mathcal{L}$-Sep[ℓ] provided in the proof of Lemma 6.5 enlarges the schema of the input database for QBE with only ℓ extra unary symbols (for fixed $\ell \geq 1$).

Generating a statistic. Next we establish lower bounds on the number of atoms required by feature queries under the assumption that statistics are of a bounded dimension.

Theorem 6.7. *Fix* $\ell \geq 1$. *For every* $n \geq 1$ *there is a training database* (D, λ) *such that:*

(1) $|D|$ *is polynomial in* n,
(2) (D, λ) *is* **CQ**-*separable,*
(3) for every statistics $\Pi = (q_1, \ldots, q_\ell)$ *that* **CQ**-*separates* (D, λ), *at least one* q_i *has* $\Omega(2^n)$ *atoms.*

This holds true if we restrict to the class of statistics formed by CQs in **GHW**(k), *but then, at least one* q_i *has* $\Omega(2^{2^n})$ *atoms.*

In summary, while bounding the dimension of statistics for general CQs and CQs of bounded ghw is positive from a generalization point of view, it also creates new problems that affect the practicality of the approach: (1) The complexity of separability becomes prohibitively high, and (2) feature queries can grow exponentially large (or even double exponentially if we bound their ghw).

6.3 Bounded Dimension and Number of Feature Atoms

Let us go back to the restriction on statistics introduced in Section 4: fixing the number of atoms allowed in feature CQs. Recall that this restriction is well-behaved in terms of separability; in fact, the problem becomes FPT, with the parameter being the arity of the schema (see Corollary 4.2). In addition, this restriction prevents statistics from growing too large in terms of the size of the data. In fact, the number of different CQs in **CQ**[m]—the class of CQs with at most m atoms—depends exclusively on m and the underlying schema σ (in particular, in the number $r \geq 1$ of relation symbols in σ and the maximum arity $k \geq 1$ of any such a relation symbol).

Yet, the number of different CQs in **CQ**[m] is exponential in the combined size of m and k, and thus could still be quite large for practical purposes. It might be reasonable then in this case to also bound the number of feature queries allowed in statistics. This calls for the study of **CQ**[m]-Sep[$*$] and **CQ**[m]-Sep[ℓ], that is, the separability problem for statistics based on the class of CQs with at most m atoms wherein the number of features is bounded or corresponds to the fixed $\ell \geq 1$, respectively.

It is not hard to see that **CQ**[m]-Sep[$*$] is FPT, with the parameter being the size of the schema. The proof of this fact is constructive in the sense that it yields a pair $(\Pi, \Lambda_{\bar{w}})$ that **CQ**[m]-separates the input training database (D, λ) where Π has at most ℓ features. Therefore, the classification problem **CQ**[m]-Cls[$*$] is also FPT.

Proposition 6.8. *For each* $m \geq 1$ *both* **CQ**[m]-Sep[$*$] *and* **CQ**[m]-Cls[$*$] *are* FPT, *with the parameter being the size of the schema.*

Notice the difference with Corollary 4.2, which establishes that **CQ**[m]-Sep is FPT with the parameter being the *arity* of the schema only. As we show next, the extra requirement on the parameter is necessary (under conventional complexity assumptions).

Proposition 6.9. *For each $m \geq 1$ the problem* CQ$[m]$-Sep$[*]$ *is* NP*-complete even for fixed arity schemas.*

Therefore, if for any $m \geq 1$ the problem CQ$[m]$-Sep$[*]$ is FPT with the parameter being the arity of the schema, then P = NP. The reason why CQ$[m]$-Sep$[*]$ is NP-hard is because it involves *choosing* a set of at most ℓ feature CQs in **CQ**$[m]$, for a given $\ell \geq 1$, that separates the input (D, λ). An easy reduction from Vertex Cover shows this problem to be NP-hard even for fixed arity schemas. Notice that this establishes an interesting difference with the problem CQ$[m]$-Sep, which we do not know whether it is NP-hard.

Interestingly, the intractability holds even if the number of features is fixed (but the arity of the schema is not).

Theorem 6.10. *The problem* CQ$[m]$-Sep$[\ell]$ *is* NP*-complete, for each fixed $\ell \geq 1$.*

We now explain the proof of the NP-hardness in Theorem 6.10. Recall that Lemma 6.5 provides a general way of obtaining lower bounds for separability with a fixed number of features via a reduction from a restricted version of QBE. However, unlike the case of **CQ** and **GHW**(k), for $k \geq 1$, for which the complexity of QBE is well understood, the complexity of QBE for **CQ**$[m]$, for $m \geq 1$, has not been studied in the literature. We show it to be NP-complete below, even in the restricted setting required by Lemma 6.5, which is a surprisingly negative result. In fact, the problem is NP-complete even for the class **CQ**$[1]$ of single-atom CQs.

Proposition 6.11. CQ$[m]$-QBE *is* NP*-complete for each fixed $m \geq 1$. The lower bound holds even if the input is of the form (D, S^+, S^-) and S^+, S^- are nonempty unary relations such that $S^- = \mathrm{dom}(D) \setminus S^+$.*

The lower bound in Theorem 6.10 follows directly then from Lemma 6.5 and Proposition 6.11.

Fixed number of variable occurrences. Recall from Proposition 4.3 that we can ensure tractability of separability, for statistics with an unbounded number of features, by fixing *both* the number of atoms and the number of occurrences of variables in feature queries; that is, CQ$[m,p]$-Sep is in PTIME, for fixed $m, p \geq 1$.

In the current scenario this continues to hold only if we fix the number $\ell \geq 1$ of features allowed in statistics. In turn, if the number ℓ is given as part of the input the problem becomes NP-hard.

Proposition 6.12. *Fix $m, p \geq 1$. The following holds:*

(1) *The problems* CQ$[m,p]$-Sep$[\ell]$ *and* CQ$[m,p]$-Cls$[\ell]$ *are in* PTIME*, for each fixed $\ell \geq 1$.*
(2) *The problem* CQ$[m,p]$-Sep$[*]$ *is* NP*-complete even for fixed arity schemas.*

7 APPROXIMATE SEPARABILITY

We now discuss a generalization of the separability problem, allowing some examples to be misclassified. Hence, we handle the case where a training database is inseparable due to a small amount of noise in the data. This notion of approximation captures the common goal of minimizing the number of misclassified examples [8, 20, 28], and corresponds to one of the studied notions of separation errors [5, 35]. We revise the previously obtained complexity results for the case that a relative error ϵ, for $0 \leq \epsilon < 1$, is allowed in the classification of the training examples.

Formally, a training database (D, λ) is $\mathcal{L}$-separable *with error* ϵ if there is a statistic Π, with feature queries from $\mathcal{L}$, and a linear classifier $\Lambda_{\bar{w}}$, such that

$$\{e \in \eta(D) \mid \Lambda_{\bar{w}}(\Pi^D(e)) \neq \lambda(e)\} \;\leq\; \epsilon \cdot |\eta(D)|\,.$$

We then say that $(\Pi, \Lambda_{\bar{w}})$ $\mathcal{L}$*-separates* (D, λ) with error ϵ. We study the following problem.

Problem:	$\mathcal{L}$-ApxSep
Input:	A training database (D, λ), an $\epsilon \in [0, 1)$
Question:	Is (D, λ) $\mathcal{L}$-separable with error ϵ?

As before, we study two variants of this problem in which the dimension is given as input or bounded by a constant $\ell \geq 1$. These are denoted by $\mathcal{L}$-ApxSep$[*]$ and $\mathcal{L}$-ApxSep$[\ell]$, respectively.

7.1 Intractable Cases

$\mathcal{L}$-ApxSep is at least as difficult as $\mathcal{L}$-Sep, since $\mathcal{L}$-Sep is precisely $\mathcal{L}$-ApxSep when $\epsilon = 0$. Thus all lower bounds obtained for the latter along the paper continue to hold for the former. The same holds for $\mathcal{L}$-ApxSep$[*]$ and $\mathcal{L}$-ApxSep$[\ell]$ w.r.t. $\mathcal{L}$-Sep$[*]$ and $\mathcal{L}$-Sep$[\ell]$, respectively. More interestingly, such lower bounds continue to hold even if ϵ is an arbitrary *fixed* value with $\epsilon \in [0, 1/2)$.[1] This is proved via a polynomial-time reduction from $\mathcal{L}$-Sep (resp., $\mathcal{L}$-Sep$[*]$ and $\mathcal{L}$-Sep$[\ell]$) to $(\mathcal{L}, \epsilon)$-ApxSep (resp., $(\mathcal{L}, \epsilon)$-ApxSep$[*]$ and $(\mathcal{L}, \epsilon)$-ApxSep$[\ell]$), the restriction of $\mathcal{L}$-ApxSep (resp., $\mathcal{L}$-ApxSep$[*]$ and $\mathcal{L}$-ApxSep$[\ell]$) in which ϵ is an arbitrary fixed value in the interval $[0, 1/2)$. These reductions hold for any class $\mathcal{L}$ of CQs.

Proposition 7.1. *Fix an arbitrary $\epsilon \in [0, 1/2)$. There are polynomial-time reductions:*

- *from $\mathcal{L}$-Sep to $(\mathcal{L}, \epsilon)$-ApxSep;*
- *from $\mathcal{L}$-Sep$[*]$ to $(\mathcal{L}, \epsilon)$-ApxSep$[*]$; and*
- *from $\mathcal{L}$-Sep$[\ell]$ to $(\mathcal{L}, \epsilon)$-ApxSep$[\ell]$ for all fixed $\ell \geq 1$.*

Now, as all lower bounds for $\mathcal{L}$-Sep, $\mathcal{L}$-Sep$[*]$ and $\mathcal{L}$-Sep$[\ell]$ presented in the paper are for complexity classes that

[1] For $\epsilon \geq 1/2$ the problem is trivial, since then we can always find a classifier that separates with error ϵ.

are closed under polynomial-time reductions, Proposition 7.1 implies that they continue to hold for their approximate versions, even if ϵ is an arbitrary *fixed* value with $0 \leq \epsilon < 1/2$. Therefore, our hardness results do not arise from the aim of finding a "strict" classifier, but are due to the inherent complexity of the problem.

7.2 Feasible Cases

In view of the previous discussion, we can only hope to obtain a feasible complexity for approximate separability in the cases where (perfect) separability is also feasible. As we have seen, there are two such cases: statistics formed by CQs with a bounded number of atoms, where separability is FPT (Corollary 4.2 and Proposition 6.8), and statistics of unbounded dimension formed by CQs of bounded ghw, where separability is solvable in PTIME (Theorem 5.3). We study both cases below.

Approximate **CQ**$[m]$*-separability.* We first study the approximate separability problem **CQ**$[m]$-ApxSep for statistics formed by CQs with a fixed number of atoms. It is not hard to see that this problem is FPT, if we assume the parameter to be the size of the schema. Notice again the difference with Corollary 4.2, which establishes that the exact separability problem **CQ**$[m]$-Sep is FPT with the parameter being the *arity* of the schema only. As in Proposition 6.9, the extra requirement on the parameter is necessary (under conventional complexity assumptions).

Proposition 7.2. *The following holds for each $m \geq 1$:*

1. *The problem* **CQ**$[m]$-ApxSep *is* FPT *with the parameter being the size of the schema.*
2. *The problem* **CQ**$[m]$-ApxSep *is* NP*-complete even for fixed arity schemas.*

From (2), if for any $m \geq 1$ the problem **CQ**$[m]$-ApxSep is FPT with the parameter being the arity of the schema, then P = NP. The difference in complexity between **CQ**$[m]$-Sep and **CQ**$[m]$-ApxSep stems from the nature of their underlying classification task: **CQ**$[m]$-Sep calls for *exact* linear separability, which is in PTIME [19, 21], while **CQ**$[m]$-ApxSep calls for *approximate* linear separability, which is NP-complete [17]. This yields item (2) in Proposition 7.2.

A similar situation holds for **CQ**$[m]$-ApxSep$[*]$, the restriction of **CQ**$[m]$-ApxSep to statistics with at most ℓ features, where ℓ is given as part of the input. On the other hand, if ℓ is fixed, then we can again ensure fixed-parameter tractability by using only the arity of the schema as the parameter.

Proposition 7.3. *For all fixed $m \geq 1$, the following hold:*

1. *The problem* **CQ**$[m]$-ApxSep$[*]$ *is* FPT *with the parameter being the schema.*
2. *The problem* **CQ**$[m]$-ApxSep$[*]$ *is* NP*-complete even for fixed arity schemas.*
3. *For every fixed $\ell \geq 1$, the problem* **CQ**$[m]$-ApxSep$[\ell]$ *is* FPT *with the parameter being the arity of the schema.*

We conclude this part by observing that all our feasibility results are via constructive proofs that result in the proper statistic; hence, in the cases of tractable separability (and variants), both approximate feature generation and approximate classification, namely **CQ**$[m]$-ApxCls, **CQ**$[m]$-ApxCls$[\ell]$, and **CQ**$[m]$-ApxCls$[*]$, are FPT. The problem $\mathcal{L}$-ApxCls takes as input a number $\epsilon \in [0, 1)$, a training database (D, λ) that is $\mathcal{L}$-separable with error ϵ, and an evaluation database D'. The goal is to construct a labeling λ' of D' such that there exists $(\Pi, \Lambda_{\bar{w}})$ that $\mathcal{L}$-separates (D', λ'), and at the same time, $\mathcal{L}$-separates (D, λ) with error ϵ. The problems $\mathcal{L}$-ApxCls$[\ell]$ and $\mathcal{L}$-ApxCls$[*]$ are defined analogously.

Approximate **GHW**(k)*-separability.* Now we look at approximate separability for statistics formed by CQs of bounded generalized hypertreewidth. Our main result is as follows.

Theorem 7.4. *Fix $k \geq 1$. There is a polynomial time algorithm that takes as input a training database (D, λ) and computes a labeling $\lambda' : \eta(D) \to \{1, -1\}$ such that:*

1. *(D, λ') is* **GHW**(k)*-separable; and*
2. *for every $\lambda'' : \eta(D) \to \{1, -1\}$ such that (D, λ'') is* **GHW**(k)*-separable, we have that $|\{e \in \eta(D) \mid \lambda(e) \neq \lambda'(e)\}| \leq |\{e \in \eta(D) \mid \lambda(e) \neq \lambda''(e)\}|$.*

Proof. Let (D, λ) be a given training database. For each $e \in \eta(D)$, we define $[e]$ to be the set of elements $e' \in \eta(D)$ such that $(D, e') \to_k (D, e)$ and $(D, e) \to_k (D, e')$. It is easy to see that the classes of the form $[e]$, for $e \in \eta(D)$, define a partition of $\eta(D)$. Define a new labeling $\lambda' : \eta(D) \to \{1, -1\}$ as follows:

$$\lambda'(e) := \begin{cases} 1 & \text{if } \sum_{e' \in [e]} \lambda(e') \geq 0, \\ -1 & \text{otherwise.} \end{cases}$$

Due to Theorem 5.3, there is a polynomial-time algorithm that computes every $[e]$; therefore, λ' can be constructed in polynomial time. By its definition, each equivalence class $[e]$ is consistent with λ', that is, λ' maps all elements of $[e]$ to the same value. Hence, due to Lemma 5.4, it is the case that(D, λ') is **GHW**(k)-separable.

We will show that λ' is a best approximation of λ, in terms of the cardinality of the "disagreement," among the labelings λ'' of $\eta(D)$ such that (D, λ'') is **GHW**(k)-separable. Formally, this means that for every $\lambda'' : \eta(D) \to \{1, -1\}$ such that (D, λ'') is **GHW**(k)-separable, we have that $|\{e \in \eta(D) \mid \lambda(e) \neq \lambda'(e)\}| \leq |\{e \in \eta(D) \mid \lambda(e) \neq \lambda''(e)\}|$, or, equivalently, that $\sum_{e \in \eta(D)} |\lambda'(e) - \lambda(e)| \leq \sum_{e \in \eta(D)} |\lambda''(e) - \lambda(e)|$. We will show that this inequality holds, for all such λ'', already in each equivalence class $[e]$; that is, $\sum_{e' \in [e]} |\lambda'(e') - \lambda(e')| \leq \sum_{e' \in [e]} |\lambda''(e') - \lambda(e')|$.

So, let $\lambda'' : \eta(D) \rightarrow \{1, -1\}$ be such that (D, λ'') is $\mathbf{GHW}(k)$-separable, and let $e \in \eta(D)$. Since λ' is consistent on $[e]$, either all $\lambda'(e')$ are $+1$ or all $\lambda'(e')$ are -1. Hence, either all $\lambda'(e') - \lambda(e')$ are nonnegative or all $\lambda'(e') - \lambda(e')$ are nonpositive. It follows that

$$\sum_{e' \in [e]} |\lambda'(e') - \lambda(e')| = \Big| \sum_{e' \in [e]} (\lambda'(e') - \lambda(e')) \Big| .$$

Analogously,

$$\sum_{e' \in [e]} |\lambda''(e') - \lambda(e')| = \Big| \sum_{e' \in [e]} (\lambda''(e') - \lambda(e')) \Big| .$$

So, we need to prove that

$$\Big| \sum_{e' \in [e]} (\lambda'(e') - \lambda(e')) \Big| \leq \Big| \sum_{e' \in [e]} (\lambda''(e') - \lambda(e')) \Big|$$

or, equivalently, that

$$\Big| \sum_{e' \in [e]} \lambda'(e') - \sum_{e' \in [e]} \lambda(e') \Big| \leq \Big| \sum_{e' \in [e]} \lambda''(e') - \sum_{e' \in [e]} \lambda(e') \Big| .$$

Let us define $x' = \sum_{e' \in [e]} \lambda'(e')$, define $x'' = \sum_{e' \in [e]} \lambda''(e')$, and define $y = \sum_{e' \in [e]} \lambda(e')$. We need to prove that $|x' - y| \leq |x'' - y|$. Since both λ' and λ'' are constant (either always 1 or always -1) on $[e]$, we have that $x' = x''$ or $x' = -x''$. In the first case, we are done. In the second one, we need to show that $|x' - y| \leq |-x' - y|$, i.e., $|x' - y| \leq |x' + y|$. But this is true for λ', as either both x' and y are nonnegative, or both x' and y are nonpositive. The pseudo-code of the procedure is given in Algorithm 2. □

Theorem 7.4 implies that $\mathbf{GHW}(k)$-ApxSep and $\mathbf{GHW}(k)$-ApxCls are tractable.

Corollary 7.5. *For all fixed $k \geq 1$, the problems* $\mathbf{GHW}(k)$-ApxSep *and* $\mathbf{GHW}(k)$-ApxCls *can be solved in polynomial time.*

Proof. Given a training database (D, λ), we apply Theorem 7.4 to compute in polynomial time a labeling $\lambda' : \eta(D) \rightarrow \{1, -1\}$ such that (D, λ') is $\mathbf{GHW}(k)$-separable and λ' minimizes the disagreement with respect to λ, among those labelings λ'' such that (D, λ'') is $\mathbf{GHW}(k)$-separable. Thus, the minimal error δ, for $0 \leq \delta \leq 1$, with which a statistic $\mathbf{GHW}(k)$-separates (D, λ) is $(\{e \in \eta(D) \mid \lambda'(e) \neq \lambda(e)\})/|\eta(D)|$. Then in order to determine whether (D, λ) is separable with error ϵ, we simply check whether $\delta \geq \epsilon$.

To solve $\mathbf{GHW}(k)$-ApxCls on an evaluation database D', we solve in polynomial time the problem $\mathbf{GHW}(k)$-Cls on input given by training database (D, λ') and evaluation database D'. This generates a labeling λ^* of $\eta(D')$ such that there is a pair $(\Pi, \Lambda_{\bar{w}})$ that $\mathbf{GHW}(k)$-separates both (D, λ') and (D', λ^*). Therefore, the pair $(\Pi, \Lambda_{\bar{w}})$ also $\mathbf{GHW}(k)$-separates (D, λ) with error δ, and thus with error ϵ, and $\mathbf{GHW}(k)$-separates (D', λ^*) with no error. □

Algorithm 2 Approx-separability algorithm $\mathbf{GHW}(k)$-ApxSep.

Require: A training database (D, λ)

```
([e_1], ..., [e_m]) := equivalence classes with respect to
    →_k over η(D)
for each e ∈ η(D) do
    if Σ_{e'∈[e]} λ(e') ≥ 0 then
        λ'(e) = 1
    else
        λ'(e) = −1
    end if
end for
return λ' : η(D) → {1, −1}
```

8 MORE EXPRESSIVE FEATURE QUERIES

In this section, we embark on a preliminary exploration of the separability problem for more expressive feature languages, in particular First-Order Logic (FO) and some fragments thereof. While the problems have been discussed over CQs, they naturally extend to any query language $\mathcal{L}$, and we can talk about $\mathcal{L}$-separability and about $\mathcal{L}$-Sep for arbitrary fragments $\mathcal{L}$ of FO. We write **FO** when $\mathcal{L}$ is the class of all FO formulas. We start by observing that **FO**-separability collapses to *single-feature* **FO**-separability.

Proposition 8.1. *A training database is* **FO***-separable iff it is* **FO***-separable by a statistics Π with a single* FO *formula.*

Hence, the complexity of separability for FO is the same regardless of whether the dimension of the statistic is bounded or not. That is, the complexity of the problems **FO**-Sep, **FO**-Sep$[*]$, and **FO**-Sep$[\ell]$, for any $\ell \geq 1$, is the same. It can be proved, on the other hand, that the complexity of **FO**-Sep$[1]$ coincides with that of QBE for FO (**FO**-QBE), as one can reduce in polynomial time from **FO**-Sep$[1]$ to **FO**-QBE and, on the other hand, use **FO**-QBE as a subroutine to solve **FO**-Sep$[1]$ in polynomial time. Arenas and Díaz [4] have shown that **FO**-QBE is GI-complete, where GI is the class of problems with a polynomial-time reduction to the graph-isomorphism problem. Therefore:

Corollary 8.2. *The problems* **FO**-Sep, **FO**-Sep$[*]$, *and* **FO**-Sep$[\ell]$, *for any $\ell \geq 1$, are* GI*-complete.*

What about separability for fragments of FO? As we state next, **FO**-separability collapses to separability for statistics based on a simple class of formulas, namely, *existential* FO formulas, denoted **∃FO**. Recall that these are the FO formulas of the form $\exists \bar{x} \psi$, where ψ is quantifier-free (but allows negation). On the other hand, for the restriction on **∃FO** that disallows negation on ψ (the so-called class of *existential positive* FO formulas, written $\mathbf{\exists FO}^+$), we have that separability collapses to **CQ**-separability. In summary:

Proposition 8.3. *The following statement hold for all training databases (D, λ):*

(1) (D, λ) is **FO***-separable iff it is* $\exists$**FO***-separable.*
(2) (D, λ) is **CQ***-separable iff it is* $\exists\mathbf{FO}^+$*-separable.*

Therefore, from Proposition 8.3 and Corollary 8.2 we obtain that $\mathcal{L}$-Sep is GI-complete for any fragment $\mathcal{L}$ of FO that contains $\exists$FO, and from Theorem 3.2 that $\exists\mathbf{FO}^+$-Sep is coNP-complete.

As we have seen, there is an important difference between **FO**-separability and **CQ**-separability: While the former collapses to single-feature **FO**-separability from Proposition 8.3, for the latter there is no bound on the number of features which are required for separating training databases (recall that the same holds for **GHW**(k), for $k \geq 1$, from Theorem 5.7). This motivates the two questions we study next about feature languages $\mathcal{L}$:

(1) When does $\mathcal{L}$ have the *dimension-collapse property*, i.e., every training database (D, λ) that is $\mathcal{L}$-separable is also separable by a single-feature statistic in $\mathcal{L}$?
(2) In turn, when does $\mathcal{L}$ have the *unbounded-dimension property*, that is, for all $n \geq 1$ there is a training database (D, λ) that is $\mathcal{L}$-separable only by statistics with at least n features?

The dimension-collapse property. We have seen in Proposition 8.1 that **FO** has the dimension-collapse property. In contrast, we can show that none of **CQ**, **GHW**(k) and $\exists\mathbf{FO}^+$ have this property. Next, we present a general explanation of this fact by providing a characterization of when a query language $\mathcal{L}$ has the dimension-collapse property in terms of a certain definability condition.

Theorem 8.4. *$\mathcal{L}$ has the dimension-collapse property if and only if for every database D, the set $\bigcup_{q\in\mathcal{L}}\{q(D), \eta(D)\setminus q(D)\}$ of entity sets is closed under intersection.*

Applying this characterization, one can readily see that not only **FO**, but also $\mathbf{FO}_k$, the fragment of formulas with at most k variables, has the dimension-collapse property. It is possible to prove, on the other hand, that the dimension-collapse property also holds for every class Σ_k, for $k \geq 1$, that consists of all FO queries of the form $\exists\bar{x}_1\forall\bar{x}_2\dots Qx_n\psi$, where ψ is quantifier-free and $Q = \exists$ if n is odd and $Q = \forall$ otherwise. Notice that Σ_1 is precisely $\exists$FO.

Corollary 8.5. *The languages* **FO**, $\mathbf{FO}_k$*, and Σ_k, for any $k \geq 1$, have the dimension-collapse property.*

In contrast, neither **CQ** nor **GHW**(k), for any $k \geq 1$, satisfy the condition of Theorem 8.4. This is also the case for Σ_k^+, the restriction of Σ_k where no negation is allowed in the quantifier-free formula ψ. We actually prove a stronger statement below: All of these languages have the unbounded-dimension property.

The unbounded-dimension property. We provide a simple condition that ensures the unbounded-dimension property for a language $\mathcal{L}$. A family $\mathcal{S}$ of sets is *linear* if $A \subseteq B$ or $B \subseteq A$, for every $A, B \in \mathcal{S}$.

Proposition 8.6. *Assume that for each $n \geq 1$ there is a database D such that $\{q(D) \mid q \in \mathcal{L}\}$ is linear and has cardinality at least n. Then $\mathcal{L}$ has the unbounded-dimension property.*

We can show that all of the above languages satisfy the condition expressed in Proposition 8.6. Correspondingly, they all have the unbounded-dimension property.

Theorem 8.7. *The languages* **CQ**, **GHW**(k) *and Σ_k^+, for any $k \geq 1$, have the unbounded-dimension property.*

9 FINAL REMARKS

We studied the separability problem for CQ features under various regularizations by posing upper bounds on the number of atoms per CQ, the ghw of CQs, and the dimension of (i.e., number of features in) the statistic. When the tractability proofs are *constructive*, tractability extends to the problems of feature generation and classification of an evaluation database. This is not the case for the class of CQs of a bounded ghw where the feature CQs might be overly large to materialize; yet, we showed that classification is then tractable even without materializing the feature CQs. We also proved that our complexity results extend to approximate separability, though some of our proofs require nontrivial adjustments. Finally, we gave preliminary results on separability with more expressive languages of feature queries, such as FO, and particularly, about when separability collapses to restricted fragments and a bounded number of feature queries (and even a single one).

An immediate open problem is the complexity of separability for a bounded number of CQ atoms, that is, **CQ**$[m]$-Sep for any fixed $m \geq 1$, when the schema is given as part of the input with no restrictions. Finally, an important direction is the treatment of feature generation over databases through the lens of PAC learning, for instance, by adopting the concepts of Grohe et al. [14, 15].

Acknowledgements. We are grateful to M. Romero for useful comments. Barceló is funded by Millennium Institute for Foundational Research on Data and FONDECYT Grant 1170109. Baumgartner is funded by the Austrian Science Fund (FWF) under the project J 3909-N31. Dalmau is funded by MICCIN grant TIN2016-76573-C2-1P and Maria de Maeztu Units of Excellence Programme MDM-2015-0502. The work of Benny Kimelfeld was supported in part by the Israel Science Foundation (ISF), Grant 1295/15.

REFERENCES

[1] Farrukh Ahmed, Michele Samorani, Colin Bellinger, and Osmar R. Zaïane. 2016. Advantage of integration in big data: Feature generation in multi-relational databases for imbalanced learning. In *BigData*. IEEE, 532–539.
[2] Ethem Alpaydin. 2009. *Introduction to machine learning*. MIT press.

[3] Timos Antonopoulos, Frank Neven, and Frédéric Servais. 2013. Definability problems for graph query languages. In *ICDT 2013*. 141–152.

[4] Marcelo Arenas and Gonzalo I. Diaz. 2016. The Exact Complexity of the First-Order Logic Definability Problem. *ACM TODS* 41, 2 (2016), 13:1–13:14.

[5] Boris Aronov, Delia Garijo, Yurai Núñez-Rodríguez, David Rappaport, Carlos Seara, and Jorge Urrutia. 2012. Minimizing the error of linear separators on linearly inseparable data. *Discrete Applied Math.* 160, 10-11 (2012), 1441–1452.

[6] Pablo Barceló and Miguel Romero. 2017. The Complexity of Reverse Engineering Problems for Conjunctive Queries. In *ICDT 2017*. 7:1–7:17.

[7] Angela Bonifati, Wim Martens, and Thomas Timm. 2017. An Analytical Study of Large SPARQL Query Logs. *PVLDB* 11, 2 (2017), 149–161.

[8] Olivier Chapelle, Patrick Haffner, and Vladimir Vapnik. 1999. Support vector machines for histogram-based image classification. *IEEE Trans. Neural Networks* 10, 5 (1999), 1055–1064.

[9] Hubie Chen and Víctor Dalmau. 2005. Beyond Hypertree Width: Decomposition Methods Without Decompositions. In *CP 2005*. 167–181.

[10] Jörg Flum and Martin Grohe. 2006. *Parameterized Complexity Theory*. Springer.

[11] Jerome Friedman, Trevor Hastie, and Robert Tibshirani. 2008. Sparse inverse covariance estimation with the graphical lasso. *Biostatistics* 9, 3 (2008), 432–441.

[12] Georg Gottlob, Gianluigi Greco, Nicola Leone, and Francesco Scarcello. 2016. Hypertree Decompositions: Questions and Answers. In *PODS 2016*. 57–74.

[13] Georg Gottlob, Nicola Leone, and Francesco Scarcello. 2002. Hypertree Decompositions and Tractable Queries. *J. Comput. Syst. Sci.* 64, 3 (2002), 579–627.

[14] Martin Grohe, Christof Löding, and Martin Ritzert. 2017. Learning MSO-definable hypotheses on strings. In *ALT (Proceedings of Machine Learning Research)*, Vol. 76. PMLR, 434–451.

[15] Martin Grohe and Martin Ritzert. 2017. Learning first-order definable concepts over structures of small degree. In *LICS*. IEEE Computer Society, 1–12.

[16] Isabelle Guyon, Steve Gunn, Masoud Nikravesh, and Lotfi A. Zadeh. 2006. *Feature Extraction: Foundations and Applications (Studies in Fuzziness and Soft Computing)*. Springer-Verlag New York, Inc., Secaucus, NJ, USA.

[17] Klaus-Uwe Höffgen, Hans Ulrich Simon, and Kevin S. Van Horn. 1995. Robust Trainability of Single Neurons. *J. Comput. Syst. Sci.* 50, 1 (1995), 114–125.

[18] Sean Kandel, Andreas Paepcke, Joseph M. Hellerstein, and Jeffrey Heer. 2012. Enterprise Data Analysis and Visualization: An Interview Study. *IEEE Trans. Vis. Comput. Graph.* 18, 12 (2012), 2917–2926.

[19] Narendra Karmarkar. 1984. A new polynomial-time algorithm for linear programming. *Combinatorica* 4, 4 (1984), 373–396.

[20] James M. Keller, Michael R. Gray, and James A. Givens. 1985. A fuzzy K-nearest neighbor algorithm. *IEEE Trans. Systems, Man, and Cybernetics* 15, 4 (1985), 580–585.

[21] Leonid Khachiyan. 1979. A Polynomial Algorithm in Linear Programming. *Soviet Mathematics Dodlaky* 20 (1979), 191–194.

[22] Benny Kimelfeld and Christopher Ré. 2017. A Relational Framework for Classifier Engineering. In *PODS 2017*. 5–20.

[23] Benny Kimelfeld and Christopher Ré. 2017. A Relational Framework for Classifier Engineering. In *PODS*. ACM, 5–20.

[24] Arno J. Knobbe, Marc de Haas, and Arno Siebes. 2001. Propositionalisation and Aggregates. In *Principles of Data Mining and Knowledge Discovery, 5th European Conference, PKDD 2001, Freiburg, Germany, September 3-5, 2001, Proceedings*. 277–288.

[25] Mehryar Mohri, Afshin Rostamizadeh, and Ameet Talwalkar. 2012. *Foundations of machine learning*. MIT press.

[26] C. A. Murthy. 2017. Bridging Feature Selection and Extraction: Compound Feature Generation. *IEEE Trans. Knowl. Data Eng.* 29, 4 (2017), 757–770.

[27] Claudia Perlich and Foster J. Provost. 2006. Distribution-based aggregation for relational learning with identifier attributes. *Machine Learning* 62, 1-2 (2006), 65–105. https://doi.org/10.1007/s10994-006-6064-1

[28] Massimiliano Pontil and Alessandro Verri. 1998. Support Vector Machines for 3D Object Recognition. *IEEE Trans. Pattern Anal. Mach. Intell.* 20, 6 (1998), 637–646. https://doi.org/10.1109/34.683777

[29] Michele Samorani, Manuel Laguna, Robert Kirk DeLisle, and Daniel C. Weaver. 2011. A Randomized Exhaustive Propositionalization Approach for Molecule Classification. *INFORMS Journal on Computing* 23, 3 (2011), 331–345.

[30] Bernhard Schölkopf and Alexander Johannes Smola. 2002. *Learning with Kernels: support vector machines, regularization, optimization, and beyond*. MIT Press.

[31] Shai Shalev-Shwartz and Shai Ben-David. 2014. *Understanding Machine Learning: From Theory to Algorithms*. Cambridge University Press, New York, NY, USA.

[32] Balder ten Cate and Víctor Dalmau. 2015. The Product Homomorphism Problem and Applications. In *ICDT 2015*. 161–176.

[33] Ross Willard. 2010. Testing Expressibility Is Hard. In *CP 2010*. 9–23.

[34] Ce Zhang, Arun Kumar, and Christopher Ré. 2014. Materialization optimizations for feature selection workloads.. In *SIGMOD Conference*. 265–276.

[35] Wojciech Ziarko. 1993. Variable precision rough set model. *Journal of computer and system sciences* 46, 1 (1993), 39–59.

Probabilistic Databases with an Infinite Open-World Assumption

Martin Grohe
RWTH Aachen University
Aachen, Germany
grohe@informatik.rwth-aachen.de

Peter Lindner
RWTH Aachen University
Aachen, Germany
lindner@informatik.rwth-aachen.de

ABSTRACT

Probabilistic databases (PDBs) introduce uncertainty into relational databases by specifying probabilities for several possible instances. Traditionally, they are *finite* probability spaces over database instances. Such finite PDBs inherently make a closed-world assumption: non-occurring facts are assumed to be impossible, rather than just unlikely. As convincingly argued by Ceylan et al. (KR '16), this results in implausibilities and clashes with intuition. An open-world assumption, where facts not explicitly listed may have a small positive probability can yield more reasonable results. The corresponding open-world model of Ceylan et al., however, assumes that all entities in the PDB come from a fixed finite universe.

In this work, we take one further step and propose a model of "truly" open-world PDBs with an infinite universe. This is natural when we consider entities from typical domains such as integers, real numbers, or strings. While the probability space might become infinitely large, all instances of a PDB remain finite. We provide a sound mathematical framework for infinite PDBs generalizing the existing theory of finite PDBs. Our main results are concerned with countable, tuple-independent PDBs; we present a generic construction showing that such PDBs exist in the infinite and provide a characterization of their existence. This construction can be used to give an open-world semantics to finite PDBs. The construction can also be extended to so-called block-independent-disjoint probabilistic databases.

Algorithmic questions are not the focus of this paper, but we show how query evaluation algorithms can be lifted from finite PDBs to perform approximate evaluation (with an arbitrarily small additive approximation error) in countably infinite tuple-independent PDBs.

PODS'19, June 30-July 5, 2019, Amsterdam, Netherlands

ACM ISBN 978-1-4503-6227-6/19/06...$15.00
https://doi.org/10.1145/3294052.3319681

CCS CONCEPTS

• **Theory of computation → Incomplete, inconsistent, and uncertain databases.**

KEYWORDS

Probabilistic Databases; Open-World Assumption; Tuple-Independence; Block-Independent-Disjoint Probabilistic Databases; Infinite Probabilistic Databases

ACM Reference Format:
Martin Grohe and Peter Lindner. 2019. Probabilistic Databases with an Infinite Open-World Assumption. In *38th ACM SIGMOD-SIGACT-SIGAI Symposium on Principles of Database Systems (PODS'19), June 30-July 5, 2019, Amsterdam, Netherlands.* ACM, New York, NY, USA, 15 pages. https://doi.org/10.1145/3294052.3319681

1 INTRODUCTION

Probabilistic databases (PDBs) are uncertain databases where uncertainty is quantified in terms of probabilities. The current standard model of probabilistic databases [4, 18, 37, 38] is an extension of the relational model that associates probabilities to the facts appearing in a relational database. Formally, it is convenient to view such a probabilistic database, which we shall call a *finite PDB* here, as a probability distribution over a finite set of database instances of the same schema. A very important basic class of finite PDBs is the class of *tuple-independent* finite PDBs, in which all facts, that is, events of the form "tuple t appears in relation R", are assumed to be stochastically independent. This independence assumption implies that the whole probability distribution of the PDB is fully determined by the marginal distributions of the individual facts and that the probability of all instances can easily be calculated from these marginal probabilities. Thus, a tuple-independent PDB can be represented as a table (resp. as tables) of all possible facts annotated with their respective marginal probabilities. According to [27], well-known systems that operate under the assumption of tuple-independence are, among others, Google's Knowledge Vault

[16], the NELL project [29] and DeepDive [30]. The focus on tuple-independent finite PDBs can be further justified by the fact that all finite PDBs can be represented by first-order (or relational calculus) views over tuple-independent finite PDBs (see [37]).

Modeling uncertainty by finite PDBs entails an implicit *closed-world assumption* (CWA) [31]:

- entities not appearing in the finitely many instances with positive probability do not exist and
- facts not appearing in these instances are strictly impossible, rather than just unlikely.

In tuple-independent finite PDBs, this means that facts that are not explicitly listed with a positive probability are impossible. As has already been argued by Ceylan, Darwiche, and Van den Broeck [14], operating under the CWA can be problematic. For example, consider a database that collects temperature measurements in the author's offices. Due to unreliable sensors, these measurements are inherently imprecise and the database may be regarded as uncertain and modeled as a PDB. Now suppose that the database never records a temperature between 20.2 °C and 20.5 °C. *Is it reasonable to derive that such a temperature is impossible?* Or suppose that the data show that the temperature in the first author's office is always at least 0.1 °C below the temperature of the second author's office. *Should we conclude that it is impossible that the temperature in the first author's office is higher than the temperature in the second author's office?* Given the uncertainty of the data, we would rather say it is unlikely (has low probability, where of course the exact probability depends on the distribution modeling the uncertainty in the data). Moreover, we would expect that the event "the temperature in the first author's office is 0.05 °C below that in the second author's office" has a higher probability than the event "the temperature in the first author's office is 10 °C above that in the second author's office". In a closed-world model however, both events have the exact same probability 0.

Considerations like these led Ceylan et al. [14] to proposing a model of open-world probabilistic databases. Their model is tuple-independent, but instead of probability 0, facts not appearing in the database are assumed to have a small positive probability (below some threshold λ). However, Ceylan et al. still assume that all entities in the database come from a fixed finite universe. Hence their model is "open-world" with respect to facts, but not with respect to entities or values.

In this work, we take one step further and propose a model of "truly" open-world probabilistic databases modeled by an infinite supply of entities. Formally, we define a *probabilistic database (PDB)* to be a probability space over a sample space consisting of database instances of the same schema and with entities from the same infinite universe. Note that every instance in such a PDB is still finite; it is only the probability space and the universe of potential entities that may be infinite.

There are various ways in which such probabilistic databases may arise in practice: collecting data from unreliable sources, completing incomplete databases by using statistical or machine learning models, or even having datasets entirely represented by machine learning models. This is not very different from finite PDBs, except that often it is more natural to allow infinite domains, for example for numerical values or for strings. One may argue that in practice the domains are always finite (such as 64-bit integers, 64-bit floating point numbers, or strings with fixed maximum length), but conceptually it is still much more natural to use models with an idealized infinite domain, as it is common in most other areas of computer science and numerical mathematics.

In this paper, we explore the mathematical foundations of infinite (relational) probabilistic databases. The general definition of PDBs is given and discussed in Section 3. In Section 4 we consider tuple-independent infinite PDBs and show how to construct a countable, tuple-independent PDB from specified fact probabilities. Unfortunately, the nice result, that every finite PDB can be represented by a finite tuple-independent PDB does *not* carry over to infinite PDBs (Proposition 4.9). In addition to our investigation of tuple-independence, we provide an extension of their existence results results to the practically important block-independent-disjoint PDBs (Theorem 4.15). Next, in section 5, we study the "open-world" aspect of PDBs. We start from a given discrete PDB and construct a countable "completion" that specifies probabilities for *every* imaginable instance. The key requirement for such a completion to be reasonable is that the probability measure is faithfully extended: the new probability measure should coincide with the old one, when conditioned over old instances. We extend the construction of countable tuple-independent PDBs to a construction of tuple-independent completions (Theorem 5.5). Albeit query evaluation is not the focus of this paper, in Section 6 we hint that it is algorithmically not completely out of reach even in the infinite setting. Using a naïve truncation procedure, we show how to lift query evaluation for finite PDBs to obtain approximate query answer probabilities in the case of countably infinite tuple-independent PDBs. Note, that this is only the very first step towards the algorithmic investigation of our infinite PDBs.

Related Work

We rely foundationally on the extensive work on finite PDBs (see, for example [4, 37, 38]). Although some system-oriented approaches are capable of dealing with continuous PDBs (like MCDB [22], PIP [23], ORION [34] and the extended Trio system [6]), these systems typically model probabilistic databases with an a priori bounded number of facts. In the case of probabilistic XML [3, 24] (that is, probabilistic tree databases) a continuous extension with solid theoretical foundations has been proposed [1], which however also only allows a bounded number of facts (resp. *leaf nodes*) in its instances. On the other hand, a proposed extension of probabilistic XML that allows for unbounded tree structures does not account for continuous distributions [9].

Work on *incomplete databases* [2, 18, 21, 39], which is also an important source of motivation for our work, has always naturally assumed potentially infinite domains, but not treated them probabilistically.

In the context of probabilistic databases we want to emphasize again the impact of the OpenPDB model [14] to our investigations. More recently, it has been proposed to extend OpenPDBs using domain knowledge in the form of ontologies [11, 12], yielding more intuitive query results with respect to the open-world assumption in OpenPDBs.

In the AI community and in probabilistic programming, open-universe models have been considered before. Inference in probabilistic models is closely related to query answering in probabilistic databases [38]. In this area, some related work has been conducted, although with different backgrounds and aims. Languages respectively models like BLOG [28], Infinite Domain Markov Logic [35], probabilistic logic programming [15], and Probabilistic Programming Datalog [7] are capable of describing infinite probability spaces of structures. It is also worth mentioning, that weighted first order model counting has been previously considered in an open-universe setting with given, relation-level probabilities [8].

Finally, let us point out a fundamental difference between our notion of *countable* tuple-independent PDBs and notions of limit probabilities in asymptotic combinatorics (for example, [10, 36]). For example, the classical Erdős-Rényi model $\mathscr{G}(n, p)$ of random graphs is also what we would call a tuple-independent model: the edges of an n-vertex graph are drawn independently with probability p. However, the sample space is finite, it consists of all n-vertex graphs. Then the behavior of these spaces as n goes to infinity is studied. This means that the properties of very large graphs dominate the behavior observed here. This contrasts our model of infinite tuple-independent PDBs, which is dominated by the behavior of PDBs whose size is close to the expected value (which for tuple-independent PDBs is always finite). Both views have their merits, but we believe that for studying probabilistic databases our model is better suited.

2 PRELIMINARIES

By $\mathbb{N}$ we denote the set of positive integers, and by $\mathbb{R}$ the set of real numbers. We denote open, closed and half-open intervals of reals by (r, s), $[r, s]$, $[r, s)$, $(r, s]$. If M is a set, then 2^M denotes the power set of M, that is, the set of all subsets of M.

2.1 Relational Databases and Logic

We start out by introducing basic notions of relational databases and logic (see [2]), leading us towards the definition of the standard model of probabilistic databases of [37] as it will be introduced in section 3.

We fix an arbitrary (possibly uncountable) set $\mathbb{U}$ to be the *universe* (or *domain*). A *database schema* $\tau = \{R_1, \dots, R_m\}$ consists of relation symbols where each relation symbol $R \in \tau$ has an associated *arity* $\operatorname{ar}(R) \in \mathbb{N}$. A *database instance* D of schema τ over $\mathbb{U}$ (for short: $(\tau, \mathbb{U})$*-instance*) consists of *finite* relations $R^D \subseteq \mathbb{U}^{\operatorname{ar}(R)}$ for all $R \in \tau$. We denote the set of all $(\tau, \mathbb{U})$-instances by $\mathbf{D}[\tau, \mathbb{U}]$.

In terms of logic, a $(\tau, \mathbb{U})$-instance is hence a relational structure of vocabulary τ with universe $\mathbb{U}$ in which all relations are finite.

It will often be convenient for us (and is quite common in database theory) to identify database instances as collections of *facts* of the form $R(a_1, \dots, a_k)$ where $R \in \tau$ is k-ary and $(a_1, \dots, a_k) \in \mathbb{U}^k$. By $F[\tau, \mathbb{U}]$ we denote the set of all facts of schema τ with universe $\mathbb{U}$. Then $\mathbf{D}[\tau, \mathbb{U}]$ is the set of all finite subsets of $F[\tau, \mathbb{U}]$. The size $\|D\|$ of an instance $D \in \mathbf{D}[\tau, \mathbb{U}]$ is the number of facts it contains, that is, $\|D\| = \sum_{R \in \tau} |R^D|$. The *active domain* $\operatorname{adom}(D)$ of a $(\tau, \mathbb{U})$-instance is the set of all elements of $\mathbb{U}$ occurring in the relations of D.

We use standard first-order logic FO over our relational vocabulary τ, which we may expand by constants from $\mathbb{U}$. By $\mathsf{FO}[\tau, \mathbb{U}]$ we denote the set of all first-order formulas of vocabulary $\tau \cup \mathbb{U}$. Note that in our notation we do not distinguish between an element $a \in \mathbb{U}$ and the corresponding constant and hence between a fact $R(a_1, \dots, a_k)$ and the corresponding atomic first-order formula. For an FO-formula $\varphi(x_1, \dots, x_k) \in \mathsf{FO}[\tau, \mathbb{U}]$ with free variables $x_1, \dots, x_k$ and an instance $D \in \mathbf{D}[\tau, \mathbb{U}]$, by $\varphi(D)$ we denote the set of all tuples $(a_1, \dots, a_k) \in \mathbb{U}^k$ such that D satisfies $\varphi(a_1, \dots, a_k)$ (written as $D \models \varphi(a_1, \dots, a_k)$).

FACT 2.1. *Suppose that $\mathbb{U}$ is infinite. Let φ be an FO-formula with k free variables, i. e. $\varphi(x_1, \dots, x_k) \in \mathsf{FO}[\tau, \mathbb{U}]$ and let $D \in \mathbf{D}[\tau, \mathbb{U}]$ such that $\varphi(D)$ is finite. Then $\varphi(D) \subseteq (\operatorname{adom}(D) \cup \operatorname{adom}(\varphi))^k$, where $\operatorname{adom}(\varphi)$ denotes the set of all constants from $\mathbb{U}$ occurring in φ.*

A *view* of source schema τ and target schema τ' is a mapping $V \colon \mathbf{D}[\tau, \mathbb{U}] \to \mathbf{D}[\tau', \mathbb{U}]$. A ($k$-ary) query is a view Q whose target schema consists of a single (k-ary) relation symbol R_Q. Slightly abusing notation, we usually denote the relation $R_Q^{Q(D)}$ of the image of an instance D under Q by $Q(D)$. For 0-ary (*Boolean*) queries, we identify the answer $\emptyset$ with FALSE and the answer $\{()\}$ with TRUE. We defined queries in terms of views, but of course views can also be regarded as finite sets of queries.

A view $V\colon \mathbf{D}[\tau, \mathbb{U}] \to \mathbf{D}[\tau', \mathbb{U}]$ is an FO-*view* if for every k-ary relation symbol $R \in \tau'$ there exists a first order formula $\varphi_R(x_1, \dots, x_k) \in \mathsf{FO}[\tau, \mathbb{U}]$ such that for all $D \in \mathbf{D}[\tau, \mathbb{U}]$ it holds that $R^{V(D)} = \varphi_R(D)$.

2.2 Series and Infinite Products

In the analysis of independence in infinite probabilistic databases, infinite products naturally occur. Therefore, we summarize a few important classical results from the theory of infinite products in the following. For details we refer the reader to chapter 7 of [25].

Let $(x_i)_{i\geq 1}$ be a sequence of real numbers. Consider the series $\sum_{i\geq 1} x_i$. If the range of the summation is clear, we might simply write $\sum_i x_i$. The *value* of $\sum_i x_i$ is the limit $\lim_{n\to\infty} \sum_{i=1}^{n} x_i$ of its partial sums, given that this limit exists. $\sum_i x_i$ *converges*, if its value is existent and finite (and *diverges* otherwise). The series is called *absolutely convergent*, if $\sum_i |x_i|$ converges. Being absolutely convergent is equivalent to the condition that the value of the series is invariant to reorderings of its summands.

An infinite product $\prod_i x_i$ *converges* if there exists i_0 such that

$$\lim_{n\to\infty} \prod_{i=i_0}^{n} x_i \tag{1}$$

exists, is finite and non-zero (and *diverges* otherwise). Note, how this definition differs from the definition of convergence of a series; see [25] for the technical rationale. The *value* of $\prod_i x_i$ is given by (1) for $i_0 = 0$, if it exists. Note that in particular, diverging products may have value 0 (which is the case if all the limits (1) are 0) but also converging products may have value 0 (which happens whenever the product contains a finite number of 0s and the rest of the product converges).

A necessary condition for infinite products to converge is that its factors approach 1. In analogy to series, where the corresponding criterion is that the summands approach 0, infinite products are commonly written in the form $\prod_i(1 + a_i)$. An infinite product $\prod_i(1 + a_i)$ *converges absolutely*, if $\prod_i(1 + |a_i|)$ converges.

FACT 2.2 ([25], PP. 229 AND 234).
(1) *An infinite product $\prod_i(1 + a_i)$ converges (absolutely) if and only if $\sum_i a_i$ converges (absolutely).*
(2) *An infinite product $\prod_i(1 + a_i)$ converges to the same value under arbitrary reorderings of its factors if and only if it is absolutely convergent.*

Later on, we use arbitrary countably infinite index sets I in the consideration of infinite products and series. In that case, we fix an arbitrary order on I for the summation. Since in all of these cases, the corresponding series will be absolutely convergent, this won't cause any problems.

We will at some point use the following relationship between infinite products and series. Its proof can be found in the full version of the paper [19].

LEMMA 2.3 ([33]). *Let $(a_i)_{i\in I}$ be a countably infinite sequence of real numbers such that $\sum_i a_i$ is absolutely convergent. Then*

$$\prod_{i\in I}\left(1 + a_i\right) = \sum_{\substack{J\subseteq I\\ \text{finite}}} \prod_{i\in J} a_i \tag{2}$$

and both sides of (2) *are absolutely convergent.*

2.3 Probability Theory

We review a few basic definitions from probability theory. Recall that a σ-*algebra* over a set Ω is a set $\mathfrak{A} \subseteq 2^{\Omega}$ such that $\Omega \in \mathfrak{A}$ and $\mathfrak{A}$ is closed under complementation and countable unions. A *probability space* is a triple $\mathcal{S} = (\Omega, \mathfrak{A}, P)$ consisting of

- a non-empty set Ω (the *sample space*);
- a σ-algebra $\mathfrak{A}$ on Ω (the *event space*); and
- a function $P\colon \mathfrak{A} \to [0, 1]$ (the *probability measure*) satisfying
  (1) $P(\Omega) = 1$ and
  (2) for every sequence $A_1, A_2, \dots$ of mutually disjoint events $A_i \in \mathfrak{A}$ $(i \geq 1)$

$$P\left(\bigcup_{i\geq 1} A_i\right) = \sum_{i\geq 1} P(A_i).$$

  (condition (2) is called σ-*additivity*).

A probability space is called *discrete* or *countable*, if its sample space Ω is at most countably infinite, and *uncountable* otherwise. It is called *finite*, if Ω is finite. In discrete probability spaces, $\mathfrak{A}$ is usually the power set 2^{Ω}. Then, defining $P(\{\omega\})$ for all $\omega \in \Omega$ already completely determines the whole probability distribution due to the σ-additivity of P.

If the components of a probability space $\mathcal{S}$ are anonymous, $\Pr_{S\sim\mathcal{S}}$ is the probability distribution of the random variable associated with drawing a sample from $\mathcal{S}$ (and we may omit the subscript, if it is clear from the context). We let $\mathrm{E}(X)$ denote the expectation of a random variable (RV) X.

Example 2.4. Suppose we take a universe $\mathbb{U} = \Sigma^* \cup \mathbb{R}$, where Σ is a finite alphabet, as our sample space. To define a σ-algebra $\mathfrak{A}$ on $\mathbb{U}$, we let $\mathfrak{A}_1 := 2^{\Sigma^*}$ and let $\mathfrak{A}_2$ be a standard σ-algebra over the reals $\mathbb{R}$, say, the Borel sets. Then we let $\mathfrak{A}$ be the set of all sets $A \subseteq \mathbb{U}$ such that $A \cap \mathbb{R} \in \mathfrak{A}_2$ (note that we automatically have $A \cap \Sigma^* \in \mathfrak{A}_1$). To define a probability distribution P, we take a distribution P_1 on $\mathfrak{A}_1$, for example the distribution defined by

$$P_1\big(\{w\}\big) := \frac{6}{\pi^2(n+1)^2|\Sigma|^n}$$

for all words $w \in \Sigma^*$ of length $|w| = n$ and a distribution P_2 on $\mathfrak{A}_2$, say, the normal distribution $N(0,1)$ with mean 0 and variance 1, and let $P(A) := \frac{1}{2}P_1(A \cap \Sigma^*) + \frac{1}{2}P_2(A \cap \mathbb{R})$ for all $A \in \mathfrak{A}$.

Note that in the definition of P_1 we use that $\sum_{n\geq 1} \frac{1}{n^2} = \frac{\pi^2}{6}$.

A collection $(A_i)_{i\in I}$ (with arbitrary index set I) of events of a probability space $(\Omega, \mathfrak{A}, P)$ is called *independent*, if

$$P\left(\bigcap_{i\in M} A_i\right) = \prod_{i\in M} P(A_i) \qquad \text{for every finite } M \subseteq I.$$

If $(A_i)_{i\in I}$ is independent, so is the sequence $(\overline{A_i})_{i\in I}$ of the complements of the A_i. If $(A_1, A_2, \dots)$ is a *countably infinite* sequence of independent events, then

$$P\left(\bigcap_{i\geq 1} A_i\right) = \prod_{i\geq 1} P(A_i).$$

We use a variant of an important classical result, known as the *(Second) Borel-Cantelli Lemma* (see, for example, [17]).

Lemma 2.5. *If $(\Omega, \mathfrak{A}, P)$ is a probability space and $A_1, A_2, \dots$ a sequence of pairwise independent events. If $\sum_{i\geq 1} P(A_i) = \infty$, then*

$$P\left(\bigcap_{i\geq 1}\bigcup_{j\geq i} A_i\right) = 1,$$

that is, the probability that infinitely many events A_i occur is 1.

3 PROBABILISTIC DATABASES

In the current literature (e. g. [37]), probabilistic relational databases are defined to be probability spaces whose sample space is a finite set of database instances over the same schema and the same universe. We extend this notion in a straightforward way to infinite spaces.

Let $\mathbb{U}$ be some set and τ be a database schema. *We always assume that the universe $\mathbb{U}$ implicitly comes with a σ-algebra $\mathfrak{U}$.* Moreover, we assume that $\{u\} \in \mathfrak{U}$ for all $u \in \mathbb{U}$. If $\mathbb{U}$ is countable, this implies $\mathfrak{U} = 2^{\mathbb{U}}$. A typical uncountable universe is $\Sigma^* \cup \mathbb{R}$ for some finite alphabet Σ; we described a natural construction of a σ-algebra for this universe in Example 2.4. We lift the σ-algebra $\mathfrak{U}$ to a σ-algebra $\mathfrak{F}$ on the set $F[\tau, \mathbb{U}]$ of all facts by a generic product construction. That is, we let $\mathfrak{F}$ be the σ-algebra generated by all sets of the form

$$\Big\{R(u_1, \dots, u_k) : u_1 \in U_1, \dots, u_k \in U_k\Big\}$$

for k-ary $R \in \tau$ and $U_1, \dots, U_k \in \mathfrak{U}$. Note that the assumption $\{u\} \in \mathbb{U}$ for all $u \in \mathbb{U}$ implies $\{f\} \in \mathfrak{F}$ for all $f \in F[\tau, \mathbb{U}]$ and thus $\mathfrak{F} = 2^{F[\tau,\mathbb{U}]}$ if $\mathbb{U}$ is countable.

In the following, we refer to the sets $F \in \mathfrak{F}$ as *measurable* sets of facts.

Definition 3.1. A *probabilistic database (PDB)* of schema τ and universe $\mathbb{U}$ is a probability space $\mathfrak{D} = (\Omega, \mathfrak{A}, P)$ such that Ω is a set of $(\tau, \mathbb{U})$-instances and for all measurable sets $F \subseteq F[\tau, \mathbb{U}]$ the event $\mathcal{E}_F := \{D \in \Omega : F \cap D \neq \emptyset\}$ belongs to $\mathfrak{A}$.

Note, that if the universe $\mathbb{U}$ is countable, then the containment of events $\mathcal{E}_F$ in $\mathfrak{A}$ is equivalent to the containment of the events $\mathcal{E}_f := \mathcal{E}_{\{f\}}$ for every fact f.

A set of database instances of the same schema over the same universe is often called an *incomplete database* and its elements are referred to *possible worlds* [2, ch. 19]. This terminology is also used in the context of probabilistic databases. However, we prefer to call the elements of the sample space Ω of a probabilistic database $\mathfrak{D}$ the *instances* of $\mathfrak{D}$. One reason is that we may have instances $D \in \Omega$ with probability 0 in $\mathfrak{D}$. Calling such instances "possible worlds" may be misleading. In fact, if the sample space Ω is uncountable, we typically have probability 0 for every single database instance.

Typically, the σ-algebra $\mathfrak{A}$ of a PDB $\mathfrak{D}$ will be constructed by lifting the σ-algebra on the facts (denoted by $\mathfrak{F}$ above) to a generic[1] σ-algebra $\mathfrak{A}$ on the set $\mathbf{D}[\tau, \mathbb{U}]$ of all finite subsets of $F[\tau, \mathbb{U}]$. In probability theory, probability spaces on finite or countable subsets of a probability space are known as *point processes*. There are standard, "product type" constructions for lifting σ-algebras from a set to its finite (or countable) subsets. Yet, some issues are particular to the database setting and require extra care. For example, we may want all first-order views to be measurable mappings between the corresponding spaces (cf. 3.1). However, we are not going to delve into these issues in this paper and refer to future work for details.

Example 3.2. Incomplete databases are often specified by relations with null values. In our framework, we can conveniently describe a probability distribution on the "completions" of an incomplete database.

Suppose that our universe is $\Sigma^* \cup \mathbb{R}$, where Σ is a standard alphabet like ASCII or UTF-8. Further suppose that we have a schema τ that contains a 5-ary relation symbol R with attributes *FirstName, LastName, Gender, Nationality* and *Height* (in this order).

[1] By "generic" we mean that $\mathfrak{A}$ will just be constructed in a standard way from the σ-algebra $\mathfrak{F}$. By providing such a generic construction, we can avoid worrying too much about the σ-algebras when specifying PDBs.

Assume first that in this relation R we have a single null value $\perp$ in a tuple (Peter, Lindner, male, German, $\perp$). We may assume that the missing height is distributed according to a known distribution of heights of German males, maybe a normal distribution with a mean around 180 (cm). This gives us a probability distribution on the possible completions of our incomplete database and hence a probabilistic database. Note that this is an uncountable probabilistic database with a distribution derived from a normal distribution on the reals.

Now assume that we have a null value in the first component of a tuple, for example ($\perp$, Grohe, male, German, 183). Again, we may complete it according to some distribution on Σ^*. To find this distribution, we may take a list of German names together with their frequencies. However, there may be a small probability that the missing name does not occur in the list. We can model this by giving a small positive probability to all strings not occurring in the list, decaying with increasing length. Again, this would give us a probabilistic database, this time a countable one.

If we have several null values, we can assume them to be independent and complete each of them with its own distribution. This independence assumption can be problematic, especially, if we have two null values in the same tuple. For example if the above tuples would additionally list the birth year and the year of graduation, we would want the birth year to refer to an earlier point in time than the year of graduation. If we do not want to make an independence assumption, we can directly define the joint distribution on the completions of all missing values.

Note that this example is related to recent work of Libkin [26], in which probabilistic completions of incomplete databases are studied in terms of limit probabilities as the size of the universe goes to infinity.

We call a PDB *finite / discrete / uncountable*, if its underlying probability space is *finite / discrete / uncountable*. Note especially, that these notions refer to the cardinality of the sample space rather than to the size of individual instances (which is in our framework always finite). Sometimes (in particular in Section 4), we will use the term "countable" in a looser sense for PDBs that may have an uncountable universe, but where the probability distribution is completely determined by the probabilities of countably many facts (and hence a countable "sub-PDB").

3.1 Queries and Views

In this section, we define the semantics of queries and views applied to probabilistic databases. Let $\mathcal{D} = (\Omega, \mathfrak{A}, P)$ be a PDB of schema τ with universe $\mathbb{U}$ and let V be a view of source schema τ and target schema τ'. For simplicity, let us first assume that $\mathcal{D}$ is countable. Then we let $\mathcal{D}' := V(\mathcal{D}) = (\Omega', \mathfrak{A}', P')$ be the PDB of schema τ' defined via

$$P'\big(\{D'\}\big) := P\big(V^{-1}(D')\big) \tag{3}$$

for every $D' \in \Omega'$ where Ω' is the image of V on Ω.

In the general case, let $\mathfrak{A}'$ be a σ-algebra on $\mathbf{D}[\tau', \mathbb{U}]$. Assume that the mapping V is *measurable* with respect to $\mathfrak{A}$ and $\mathfrak{A}'$, that is, $V^{-1}(A') \in \mathfrak{A}$ for all $A' \in \mathfrak{A}'$. Then, $\mathcal{D}' := V(\mathcal{D}) = (\Omega', \mathfrak{A}', P')$ is the PDB of schema τ' defined by

$$P'\big(A'\big) := P\big(V^{-1}(A')\big) \tag{4}$$

for every $A' \in \mathfrak{A}'$. Since we are mostly interested in countable PDBs in this paper, we do not want to delve into a discussion of the measurability condition.

The semantics of views defined in (3) and (4) yields a semantics of queries on probabilistic databases as a special case. However, for queries Q one is often interested in the marginal probabilities of individual tuples in the query answer,

$$\Pr_{D\sim\mathcal{D}}\big(\vec{a} \in Q(D)\big).$$

Usually, this marginal probability is only of interest in countable PDBs.

3.2 Size Distribution

Let $\mathcal{D}$ be a probabilistic database of schema τ with universe $\mathbb{U}$. Let $S_{\mathcal{D}}$ be the random variable that associates with each instance $D \in \mathbf{D}[\tau, \mathbb{U}]$ its size $\|D\|$, that is, the number of facts that D contains. Observe that if $\mathcal{D}$ is countable then the expected size of an instance of $\mathcal{D}$ is[2]

$$\mathrm{E}\big(S_{\mathcal{D}}\big) = \sum_{f \in F[\tau, \mathbb{U}]} \Pr_{D\sim\mathcal{D}}\big(D \in \mathcal{E}_f\big). \tag{5}$$

For uncountable PDBs, the sum in (5) is replaced by an integral. It is easy to construct examples of (countable) PDBs where $\mathrm{E}(S_{\mathcal{D}}) = \infty$.

Example 3.3. Let $\tau = \{R\}$ with a unary relation symbol R and $\mathbb{U} = \mathbb{N}$. For every $n \geq 1$, let $p_n := \frac{6}{\pi^2 n^2}$ (so $\sum_n p_n = 1$) and let D_n be a $(\tau, \mathbb{U})$-instance with $R^{D_n} := \{1, \dots, 2^n\}$. Then $\|D_n\| = 2^n$. Define $\mathcal{D}$ by letting $\Pr_{D\sim\mathcal{D}}(\{D_n\}) := p_n$ and $\Pr_{D\sim\mathcal{D}}(\{D\}) = 0$ for all $D \in \mathbf{D}[\tau, \mathbb{U}] - \{D_n : n \in \mathbb{N}\}$.

Then $\mathrm{E}(S_{\mathcal{D}}) = \sum_n p_n \|D_n\| = \sum_n \frac{6 \cdot 2^n}{\pi^2 n^2} = \infty$.

Probabilistic databases with infinite expected instance size may not be the most relevant in practice. We will see later that tuple-independent PDBs always have a finite expected size. While the expected instance size of a PDB can be infinite, the probability that it is large goes to zero:

$$\lim_{n\to\infty} \Pr(S_{\mathcal{D}} \geq n) = 0. \tag{6}$$

[2] $S_{\mathcal{D}}$ is the sum of the indicator RV associated with the events $\mathcal{E}_f$. The expectation of 0-1-valued RV is equal to their probability to take the value 1. Finally note, that linearity of expectation holds for countably infinite sums of $[0, \infty)$-valued RV [17, p. 50].

To see this, just consider the decreasing sequence of events

$$A_n := \{D\colon \|D\| \geq n\}$$

and let $A := \bigcap_n A_n$. Then $A = \emptyset$, because a PDB only contains finite instances. Thus $\lim_{n\to\infty} \Pr(A_n) = \Pr(A) = 0$. A consequence of this observation is the following useful proposition.

PROPOSITION 3.4. *Let $\mathfrak{D}$ be a (possibly uncountable) PDB. Then the set F_ω of all facts f with probability $p_f := \Pr_{D\sim\mathfrak{D}}(D \in \mathcal{E}_f) > 0$ is countable.*

PROOF. For every $k \in \mathbb{N}$ we let F_k be the set of all facts f with $p_f > 1/k$. Then $F_\omega = \bigcup_k F_k$. We claim that for all k the set F_k is finite; this will imply that F is countable.

To prove the claim, let $k \in \mathbb{N}$. Suppose for contradiction that F_k is infinite and let $f_1, f_2, \dots \in F_k$. By (6), there is an n such that $\Pr(S_{\mathfrak{D}} > n) < (2k)^{-1}$. Choose such an n. For every $i \in \mathbb{N}$ let X_i be the indicator random variable of the event "$S_{\mathfrak{D}}(D) \leq n$ and $f_i \in D$" and let $Y_i := \sum_{1\leq j\leq i} X_j$. Then

$$\begin{aligned}\Pr\big(X_i = 1\big) &= 1 - \Pr\big(S_{\mathfrak{D}}(D) > n \cup f_i \notin D\big)\\ &> 1 - \tfrac{1}{2k} - \big(1 - \tfrac{1}{k}\big) = \tfrac{1}{2k},\end{aligned}$$

and thus $\mathrm{E}(Y_i) > i \cdot (2k)^{-1}$. In particular, $\mathrm{E}(Y_{2kn}) > n$, which implies that $\Pr(Y_{2kn} > n) > 0$. However, every instance D with positive $Y_{2kn}(D)$ satisfies $S_{\mathfrak{D}}(D) \leq n$ and therefore $\|D\| \leq n$, but contains (since $Y_{2kn} > n$) at least n of the facts $f_1, f_2, \dots, f_{2kn}$. This is a contradiction. □

4 TUPLE-INDEPENDENCE IN THE INFINITE

With the above framework in mind, we turn our attention to an infinite extension of the idea of tuple-independence. This is motivated by the major importance of tuple-independence in the traditional finite setting. As we will see, the notions will be more involved and more fundamental questions have to be addressed. For the following discussion let $\mathfrak{D} = (\Omega, \mathfrak{A}, P)$ be a probabilistic database and let $\mathfrak{F}$ be a suitable σ-algebra on the set of all facts, whose elements we call *measurable* sets of facts. Recall from section 3 that $\mathcal{E}_f$ denotes the event "the fact f occurs in a randomly drawn instance". Finite probabilistic databases are referred to as "tuple-independent" if all these events are independent. In consideration of *infinite* probabilistic databases, we want to broaden that notion, using the events $\mathcal{E}_F = \bigcup_{f\in F} \mathcal{E}_f$. Recall that the definition of PDBs requires that $\mathcal{E}_F \in \mathfrak{A}$ for all measurable sets F of facts.

Definition 4.1. $\mathfrak{D}$ is called *tuple-independent (t. i.)* if for all collections $\mathcal{F}$ of pairwise disjoint measurable sets of facts the events $\mathcal{E}_F$ are independent, that is, if

$$P\Big(\bigcap_{F\in\mathcal{F}'} \mathcal{E}_F\Big) = \prod_{F\in\mathcal{F}'} P(\mathcal{E}_F) \tag{7}$$

for all finite $\mathcal{F}' \subseteq \mathcal{F}$.

Observe that this definition matches the definitions from the literature when applied to a countable setting.

LEMMA 4.2. *A countable PDB $(\Omega, \mathfrak{A}, P)$ is tuple-independent if and only if all events $\mathcal{E}_f$ are independent.*

PROOF. Let $\mathcal{F}$ be a collection of disjoint measurable fact sets. It has to be shown that the events $(\mathcal{E}_F)_{F\in\mathcal{F}}$ are independent (i. e., (7) holds). To see this, we show the independence of $(\overline{\mathcal{E}_F})_{F\in\mathcal{F}'}$ where $\overline{\mathcal{E}_F} = \Omega - \mathcal{E}_f$. Using the independence of the events $\mathcal{E}_f$ (respectively $\overline{\mathcal{E}_f}$) and the fact that $\overline{\mathcal{E}_F} = \bigcap_{f\in F} \overline{\mathcal{E}_f}$, we have

$$P\Big(\bigcap_{F\in\mathcal{F}'} \overline{\mathcal{E}_F}\Big) = P\Big(\bigcap_{F\in\mathcal{F}'} \bigcap_{f\in F} \overline{\mathcal{E}_f}\Big) = \prod_{F\in\mathcal{F}'} \underbrace{\prod_{f\in F} P(\overline{\mathcal{E}_f})}_{=P(\bigcap_{f\in F} \overline{\mathcal{E}_f})} = \prod_{F\in\mathcal{F}'} P(\overline{\mathcal{E}_F}).$$

□

Nevertheless, the definition can in this form be applied to uncountable PDBs, although raising multiple issues that keep this extension from being straightforward. In particular, the above lemma does not carry over to a general uncountable setting as the events $\mathcal{E}_F$ are not necessarily expressible in terms of the events $\mathcal{E}_f$ anymore using only countable union and complementation.

4.1 Construction

Tuple-independence is a convenient setting for finite PDBs as it suffices to specify probabilities for all possible facts to obtain a tuple-independent PDB. In this subsection, we investigate whether the same approach works for infinite tuple-independent PDBs. From that investigation, we will obtain a sufficient criterion for the existence of *countable* tuple-independent PDBs. We revisit the uncountable setting towards the end of the subsection.

Let us consider a schema τ and a universe $\mathbb{U}$. We let $\Omega := \mathbf{D}[\tau, \mathbb{U}]$, and we let $\mathfrak{A} \subseteq 2^\Omega$ be an arbitrary σ-algebra that contains all events $\mathcal{E}_F$ for measurable $F \subseteq F[\tau, \mathbb{U}]$. In fact, for the construction here we can simply let $\mathfrak{A} := 2^\Omega$. Moreover, we assume that we are given a family $(p_f)_{f\in F[\tau,\mathbb{U}]}$ of numbers $p_f \in [0, 1]$. The question we ask is: can we construct a tuple-independent PDB $\mathfrak{D} = (\Omega, \mathfrak{A}, P)$ such that $P(\mathcal{E}_f) = p_f$ for all f? We will see, that the question can be positively answered whenever every countable sum of numbers p_f is finite, that is,

$$\sum_{f\in F} p_f < \infty \qquad \text{for every countable } F \subseteq F[\tau, \mathbb{U}]. \tag{8}$$

In the following, we say that $\sum_f p_f$ is *convergent* if (8) is satisfied. This is justified by the following argument showing that if (8) holds then the set of all facts f with $p_f > 0$ is countable. Thus in this case, up to 0-values, the sum $\sum_f p_f$ is countable. Indeed, if (8) holds then for every $k \in \mathbb{N}$ the set F_k of all f such that $p_f > 1/k$ is finite. Thus the set $F_\omega = \bigcup_k F_k$ of all f such that $p_f > 0$ is countable. A consequence of this observation is that the convergence assumption (8) implies that the resulting PDB will be countable.

In the following, we assume that $\sum_f p_f$ is convergent and let F_ω be the (countable) set of all $f \in F[\tau, \mathbb{U}]$ with $p_f > 0$. We define a probability measure P on $(\Omega, \mathfrak{A})$ as follows. For $D \in \mathbf{D}[\tau, \mathbb{U}]$, we let

$$P(\{D\}) = \prod_{f \in D} p_f \prod_{f \in F_\omega - D} \left(1 - p_f\right).$$

It follows from Fact 2.2 that this product is well-defined, because the sum $\sum_{f \in F_\omega} p_f$ is convergent an hence the product $\prod_{f \in F_\omega} (1 - p_f)$ is convergent as well.

Note that there are only countably many $D \in \mathbf{D}[\tau, \mathbb{U}]$ such that $P(\{D\}) > 0$, because $P(\{D\}) > 0$ implies that $D \subseteq F_\omega$, and the countable set F_ω has only countably many finite subsets. Let $\mathbf{D}_\omega$ be the set of all finite subsets of F_ω. We complete the definition of the probability measure P by letting $P(A) = \sum_{D \in A \cap \mathbf{D}_\omega} P(\{D\})$ for all $A \in \mathfrak{A}$.

The following lemma (which is a variation of a statement proven in [32] by Rényi) ensures that P is a probability measure:

Lemma 4.3 (cf. [32], p. 167 et seq.). $P(\Omega) = \sum_{D \in \mathbf{D}_\omega} P(\{D\}) = 1$.

Proof. Denote $F_\omega - D$ by $\overline{D}$ for any instance D. By reordering and using Lemma 2.3, we obtain:

$$\begin{aligned}\sum_{D \in \mathbf{D}_\omega} P(\{D\}) &= \sum_{D \in \mathbf{D}_\omega} \prod_{f \in D} p_f \prod_{f \in \overline{D}} (1 - p_f) \\ &= \sum_{D \in \mathbf{D}_\omega} \prod_{f \in D} p_f \sum_{\substack{D' \subseteq \overline{D} \\ \text{finite}}} \prod_{f \in D'} (-p_f) \\ &= \sum_{D \in \mathbf{D}_\omega} \prod_{f \in D} p_f \sum_{\substack{D' \in \mathbf{D}_\omega \\ D' \supseteq D}} \prod_{f \in D' - D} (-p_f) \\ &= \sum_{D \in \mathbf{D}_\omega} \sum_{\substack{D' \in \mathbf{D}_\omega \\ D' \supseteq D}} \prod_{f \in D} p_f \prod_{f \in D' - D} (-p_f) \\ &= \sum_{D' \in \mathbf{D}_\omega} \sum_{D \subseteq D'} \prod_{f \in D} p_f \prod_{f \in D' - D} (-p_f). \qquad (9)\end{aligned}$$

Within (9), the summand for $D' = \emptyset$ collapses to a single empty product and hence equals 1. If on the other hand $D' \neq \emptyset$, fix some $f_0 \in D'$. It is easy to see that the subsums containing the factor p_{f_0} and those containing $-p_{f_0}$ exactly cancel each other out. Thus $P(\Omega) = 1$. □

The previous lemma means that we have indeed constructed a PDB. It remains to show that $\mathcal{D} = (\Omega, \mathfrak{A}, P)$ is tuple-independent and has the right marginal probabilities for the events $\mathcal{E}_f$.

Lemma 4.4. *$\mathcal{D}$ is t. i., and $P(\mathcal{E}_f) = p_f$ for all facts $f \in F[\tau, \mathbb{U}]$.*

Proof. By an argument similar to the proof of Lemma 4.2, it suffices to check the independence of the events $\mathcal{E}_f$ for facts $f \in F_\omega$.

Let $F \subseteq F_\omega$ be finite. We prove that $P\left(\bigcap_{f \in F} \mathcal{E}_F\right) = \prod_{f \in F} p_f$. Note that this implies both $P(\mathcal{E}_f) = p_f$ *and* the independence of the events $\mathcal{E}_f$ for all f. Let Ω_F denote the set of instances $D \in \mathbf{D}_\omega$ with $F \subseteq D$. We have

$$\begin{aligned}P\left(\bigcap_{f \in F} \mathcal{E}_f\right) &= \sum_{D \in \Omega_F} P(\{D\}) \\ &= \sum_{D \in \Omega_F} \prod_{f \in D} p_f \prod_{f \in F_\omega - D} \left(1 - p_f\right) \\ &= \prod_{f \in F} p_f \left(\sum_{D \in \Omega_F} \prod_{f \in D - F} p_f \prod_{f \in F_\omega - D} \left(1 - p_f\right)\right).\end{aligned}$$

We conclude the proof by showing that the parenthesized term in the last row equals 1. Note that its products range exactly over all facts in $F_\omega - F$. Recall that $\overline{\mathcal{E}_F}$ is the set of instances that are disjoint from F.

$$\begin{aligned}&\sum_{D \in \Omega_F} \prod_{f \in D - F} p_f \prod_{f \in F_\omega - D} \left(1 - p_f\right) \\ &= \sum_{D' \in \overline{\mathcal{E}_F}} \prod_{f \in D'} p_f \prod_{\substack{f \in F_\omega \\ f \notin F \cup D'}} \left(1 - p_f\right) \overbrace{\left(\sum_{F' \subseteq F} \prod_{f \in F'} p_f \prod_{f \in F - F'} \left(1 - p_f\right)\right)}^{=1} \\ &= \sum_{D' \in \overline{\mathcal{E}_F}} \sum_{F' \subseteq F} \prod_{f \in F' \cup D'} p_f \prod_{\substack{f \in F_\omega \\ f \notin F' \cup D'}} \left(1 - p_f\right) \\ &= \sum_{D \in \Omega} \prod_{f \in D} p_f \prod_{f \in F_\omega - D} \left(1 - p_f\right) = P(\Omega) = 1.\end{aligned}$$

□

The above construction, starting from a convergent series of fact probabilities thus yields a tuple-independent PDB that realizes these given probabilities. Note also that the given sequence of fact probabilities already determines the whole probability space. We summarize the result in the following proposition.

Proposition 4.5. *Given a family $(p_f)_{f \in F[\tau, \mathbb{U}]}$ of real numbers $p_f \in [0, 1]$ such that $\sum_f p_f$ is convergent, we can construct a tuple-independent PDB with $P(\mathcal{E}_f) = p_f$ for all $f \in F[\tau, \mathbb{U}]$.*

Finally, let us briefly discuss the difficulties of obtaining a similar result for "truly" uncountable PDBs, although we refer to future work for a thorough investigation of that problem. In the countable case discussed above, we expressed the probabilities of all events $\mathcal{E}_F$ using the probabilities $\mathcal{E}_f$ alone.

In general, we cannot do this, because all $\mathcal{E}_f$ may have probability 0. This raises the question even which probabilities should actually be specified beforehand for constructing the PDB. We leave it as an open problem whether uncountable tuple-independent PDBs exist that do not collapse to discrete probability spaces.

4.2 A Necessary Existence Criterion

In the previous subsection, we have seen that the convergence of $\sum_f p_f$ is a sufficient criterion for given fact probabilities to fulfill in order to ensure the existence of a tuple-independent PDB that is compatible with these probabilities. Now, we will prove that this condition is also necessary, i. e. that there is no tuple-independent PDB realizing a divergent series of fact probabilities. This result is not limited to the countable case:

Lemma 4.6. *Let $\mathcal{D} = (\Omega, \mathfrak{A}, P)$ be a tuple-independent PDB. Then*

$$\sum_{F \in \mathcal{F}} P(\mathcal{E}_F) < \infty$$

for all countably infinite collections $\mathcal{F}$ of pairwise disjoint, measurable sets of facts.

Proof. Since $\mathcal{D}$ is tuple-independent, the events $\mathcal{E}_F$ are independent. Suppose $\mathcal{F} = \{F_1, F_2, \dots\}$ and for $F = F_i$, let $\mathcal{E}_i := \mathcal{E}_F$. Then

$$\mathcal{E} := \limsup_{i \to \infty} \mathcal{E}_i = \bigcap_{i \geq 1} \bigcup_{j \geq i} \mathcal{E}_j$$

is the set of instances having a nonempty intersection with infinitely many sets $F \in \mathcal{F}$. Since the sets from $\mathcal{F}$ are disjoint and each database of Ω has only finitely many facts, $\mathcal{E} = \emptyset$ and $P(\mathcal{E}) = 0$. By Lemma 2.5 (the Borel-Cantelli Lemma), this means $\sum_{F \in \mathcal{F}} P(\mathcal{E}_F)$ converges. □

Note that in particular, if $\mathcal{D}$ is a countable tuple-independent PDB (over database schema τ and universe $\mathbb{U}$), then we have $\sum_{f \in F[\tau, \mathbb{U}]} P(\mathcal{E}_f) < \infty$. As this sum is exactly the definition of the expected instance size (5), we immediately obtain the following.

Corollary 4.7. *If $\mathcal{D}$ is a countable tuple-independent PDB, then its expected instance size is finite.*

Finally, we can combine Lemma 4.6 and Proposition 4.5 into the following characterization of countable tuple-independent PDBs.

Theorem 4.8. *Let $(p_f)_{f \in F[\tau, \mathbb{U}]}$ with $p_f \in [0, 1]$. There exists a tuple-independent PDB with fact probabilities $\Pr(\mathcal{E}_f) = p_f$ for all $f \in F[\tau, \mathbb{U}]$ if and only if $\sum_f p_f$ is convergent.*

4.3 Definability in Tuple-Independent Probabilistic Databases

The viability of t. i. PDBs in the finite is often justified by the well-known result that tuple-independent PDBs are sufficient to describe arbitrary finite PDBs by the means of "FO-views".

We call a PDB $\mathcal{D}$ FO-*definable* over a PDB $\mathcal{C}$ if there is an FO-view V such that $\mathcal{D} = V(\mathcal{C})$ (see Section 3.1). Although not every finite PDB is itself tuple-independent, every finite PDB is FO-definable over a tuple-independent PDB [37]. Unfortunately, this result does not extend to infinite PDBs.

Proposition 4.9. *There is a countably infinite PDB $\mathcal{D}$ that is not* FO-*definable over any tuple-independent PDB.*

Proof. Let $\mathbb{U} := \mathbb{N}$ and $\tau' := \{R\}$ for some unary relation symbol R. Let $\mathcal{D}$ be the database of schema τ' over $\mathbb{U}$ defined in Example 3.3. Then $\mathrm{E}(S_{\mathcal{D}}) = \infty$, where $S_{\mathcal{D}}$ was the random variable associating instances with their size.

Suppose for contradiction that $\mathcal{D} = V(\mathcal{C})$ for some t. i. PDB $\mathcal{C}$ of some schema τ. For every $f \in F[\tau, \mathbb{U}]$ let $p_f := \Pr_{C \sim \mathcal{C}}(C \in \mathcal{E}_f)$. Then, by Corollary 4.7, $\mathrm{E}(S_{\mathcal{C}}) = \sum_f p_f < \infty$. Let $X_{\mathcal{C}}$ be the random variable that maps $C \sim \mathcal{C}$ to $|\mathrm{adom}(C)|$. Let k be the maximum arity of a relation in τ and note that for every $(\tau, \mathbb{U})$-instance $|\mathrm{adom}(C)| \leq k \|C\|$. That is, $X_{\mathcal{C}} \leq k S_{\mathcal{C}}$.

Since τ' consists of a single unary relation symbol, the view V consists of a single formula $\varphi(x) \in \mathsf{FO}[\tau, \mathbb{U}]$. Let c be the number of constants from $\mathbb{U}$ appearing in φ. By Fact 2.1, for every $(\tau, \mathbb{U})$-instance we have $\|V(C)\| = |\varphi(C)| \leq |\mathrm{adom}(C)| + c$. But this implies $S_{\mathcal{D}} \leq k S_{\mathcal{C}} + c$ and therefore $\mathrm{E}(S_{\mathcal{D}}) \leq k\,\mathrm{E}(S_{\mathcal{C}}) + c < \infty$, a contradiction. □

Remark 4.10. The PDB $\mathcal{D}$ that we used in the proof of Proposition 4.9 has the property that the expected instance size is infinite. However, it is not hard to construct an analogous counterexample with finite expected input size: we simply construct a PDB $\mathcal{D}$ where $\mathrm{E}(S_{\mathcal{D}}) < \infty$ but $\mathrm{E}(S_{\mathcal{D}}^2) = \infty$. Instead of the second moment, we can use the kth moment for any k.

We do not know an example of a PDB $\mathcal{D}$ with $\mathrm{E}(S_{\mathcal{D}}^k) < \infty$ such that $\mathcal{D}$ is not FO-definable over a tuple-independent PDB. We conjecture, though, that such an example exists.

4.4 A Word on Block-Independent-Disjoint Probabilistic Databases

After studying tuple-independence, we want to turn our attention to a practically relevant generalization of tuple-independence: the notion of *block-independent-disjoint* (*b. i. d.*) PDBs [37]. As [27] notes for example, the systems Trio [5], MayBMS [20] and MystiQ [13] realize (finite) PDBs of this category. In such PDBs, the set of all facts is partitioned into *blocks* of facts with two central properties: first of all, facts within the same blocks form mutually exclusive events and; second of all, facts across different blocks are independent. Obviously, the traditional notion of tuple-independence is the special case of b. i. d. PDBs with singleton blocks.

The usual application of b. i. d. PDBs is to incorporate key constraints in PDBs. Here, we want to provide a more general definition that extends to infinite settings. In the following, let $\mathbb{U}$ be some universe and τ be a database schema. As usual, we assume that we have suitable σ algebra on $F[\tau, \mathbb{U}]$ and speak of measurable sets of facts.

Definition 4.11. Let $\mathcal{B}$ be a partition of $F[\tau, \mathbb{U}]$ into measurable sets. A PDB $\mathcal{D} = (\Omega, \mathfrak{A}, P)$ is *block-independent-disjoint (b. i. d.) with respect to* $\mathcal{B}$ or *with blocks* $\mathcal{B}$, if

(1) for all $B \in \mathcal{B}$ and all disjoint, measurable $B_1, B_2 \subseteq B$:
$$P\big(\mathcal{E}_{B_1} \cap \mathcal{E}_{B_2}\big) = 0,$$

(2) and for all mutually distinct $B_1, \dots, B_k \in \mathcal{B}$ ($k \in \mathbb{N}$) and all measurable $B_i' \subseteq B_i$ ($1 \leq i \leq k$), it holds that
$$P\Big(\bigcap_{1 \leq i \leq k} \mathcal{E}_{B_i'}\Big) = \prod_{1 \leq i \leq k} P\big(\mathcal{E}_{B_i'}\big).$$

A PDB $\mathcal{D}$ is *block-independent-disjoint (b. i. d.)*, if there exists a suitable partition $\mathcal{B}$ such that $\mathcal{D}$ is b. i. d. with respect to $\mathcal{B}$.

We want to discuss whether and if so, how the previous results generalize from t. i. to b. i. d. PDBs.

First, we note that an analogue of Lemma 4.2 holds, which means that our notion of b. i. d. PDBs in a countable setting matches the traditional definition that only mentions facts:

Lemma 4.12. *For countable PDBs with blocks $\mathcal{B}$, satisfying condition* (1) *from Definition 4.11, condition* (2) *is equivalent to*

(2') *The sequences $(\mathcal{E}_f)_{f \in F}$ are independent for every collection F of facts such that F contains at most one fact from each block.*

The easy proof can be found in the full version of the paper [19].

Next, we can construct *countable* b. i. d. PDBs similarly to the tuple-independent case.

Proposition 4.13. *Let $\mathcal{B}$ be a partition of $F[\tau, \mathbb{U}]$ into blocks and for every block B let $(p_f^B)_{f \in B}$ such that $p_f^B \in [0, 1]$ and $\sum_{f \in B} p_f^B \leq 1$. Then we can construct a PDB $\mathcal{D} = (\Omega, \mathfrak{A}, P)$ that is b. i. d. with respect to $\mathcal{B}$, realizing the given fact probabilities (i. e., $P(\mathcal{E}_f) = p_f^{B(f)}$, where $B(f)$ is the block containing f) whenever*
$$\sum_{f \in F} p_f^{B(f)} < \infty \tag{10}$$
for all countable $F \subseteq F[\tau, \mathbb{U}]$.

Proof sketch. Let $\Omega := \mathbf{D}[\tau, \mathbb{U}]$ and $\mathfrak{A} := 2^{\Omega}$. If (10) holds for all countable $F \subseteq F[\tau, \mathbb{U}]$, we say $\sum_{B \in \mathcal{B}} \sum_{f \in B} p_f^B$ converges. This notation is justified like in the case of tuple-independence. Similarly to before, it entails that the set F_ω of facts with $p_f^{B(f)} > 0$ is countable. We may thus suppose that $\mathcal{B}$ consists of countably many countable blocks $\mathcal{B}_\omega$ exactly covering the facts F_ω and that all the remaining facts are gathered in a single dummy block (this can be found in the the extended version [19] in the proof of Lemma 4.12). *Good* instances contain at most one fact from each $B \in \mathcal{B}$ and *bad* instances violate this condition. We set $p_\perp^B := 1 - \sum_{f \in F_\omega \cap B} p_f^B$ ($p_\perp^B = 1$ for B being the dummy block) and for every block B and good $D \in \mathbf{D}[\tau, \mathbb{U}]$, define
$$\beta(B, D) := \begin{cases} f & \text{if } D \cap B = \{f\}, \\ \perp & \text{if } D \cap B = \emptyset. \end{cases}$$
We set
$$P\big(\{D\}\big) := \begin{cases} \prod_{B \in \mathcal{B}} p_{\beta(B,D)}^B & \text{if } D \text{ is good,} \\ 0 & \text{if } D \text{ is bad;} \end{cases}$$
and for all other $A \in \mathfrak{A}$, $P(A) = \sum_{D \in A \cap \mathbf{D}_\omega} P(\{D\})$ where $\mathbf{D}_\omega$ is the set of finite subsets of F_ω. Analogously to section 4.1, the required convergence property (10) ensures, that this yields indeed a probability measure. Generalizing the proof of Lemma 4.4, one can show that $\mathcal{D}$ is indeed a b. i. d. PDB. These two claims are demonstrated in detail in the extended version of the paper [19]. □

Finally, the necessary condition from section 4.2 easily translates to b. i. d. PDBs:

Lemma 4.14. *Let $\mathcal{D} = (\Omega, \mathfrak{A}, P)$ be a b. i. d. PDB with blocks $\mathcal{B}$. Then, for every countable collection $(B_i)_{i \geq 1}$ of $\mathcal{B}$-blocks and all measurable subsets $B_i' \subseteq B_i$ ($i \geq 1$) it holds that $\sum_{i \geq 1} P(\mathcal{E}_{B_i'}) < \infty$.*

Proof. This is proven exactly like in the proof of Lemma 4.6 with B_i' in the role of F_i. □

Proposition 4.13 and Lemma 4.14 can be combined, yielding the following characterization of existence for countable b. i. d. PDBs:

Theorem 4.15. *Let $\mathcal{B}$ be a partition of facts and for every $B \in \mathcal{B}$ let $(p_f^B)_{f \in B}$ be a sequence with $p_f^B \in [0, 1]$ such that $\sum_{f \in B} p_f^B \leq 1$. There exists a block-independent-disjoint PDB with fact probabilities $(p_f^B)_{f \in B, B \in \mathcal{B}}$ if and only if $\sum_{B \in \mathcal{B}} \sum_{f \in B} p_f^B$ converges.*

5 COMPLETIONS OF PROBABILISTIC DATABASES

Now that we have established a model of infinite independence assumptions, we want to revisit the open-world assumption in probabilistic databases. We want to use our construction of countable tuple-independent PDBs to deploy a "completed" version of a given PDB. Let $\mathcal{D}$ be a PDB with sample space $\Omega \subsetneq \mathbf{D}[\tau, \mathbb{U}]$ where τ is a database schema and $\mathbb{U}$ a universe. Typically (but not necessarily), we think of Ω being finite. Our construction shall expand the sample space Ω to all of $\mathbf{D}[\tau, \mathbb{U}]$. In order to obtain results that are consistent with the original data from $\mathcal{D}$, this expansion should preserve the basic structure of the probability space $\mathcal{D}$, that is, its internal correlations and the proportions of already known fact probabilities.

Definition 5.1. Let $\mathcal{D} = (\Omega, \mathfrak{A}, P)$ be a PDB with $\Omega \subsetneq \mathbf{D}[\tau, \mathbb{U}]$. A *completion* of $\mathcal{D}$ is a PDB $\mathcal{D}' = (\Omega', \mathfrak{A}', P')$ with $\Omega' = \mathbf{D}[\tau, \mathbb{U}]$ and $\mathfrak{A}' \supseteq \mathfrak{A}$ such that $P'(\Omega) > 0$ and for all $A \in \mathfrak{A}$, the following *completion condition* holds:

$$P'\big(A \,\big|\, \Omega\big) = P(A). \tag{CC}$$

When considering a completion $\mathcal{D}'$ of $\mathcal{D}$, we refer to $\mathcal{D}$ (and its components) as *original.*

Remark 5.2. Applying the closed-world-assumption to a PDB corresponds to considering the completion that sets all probabilities of new instances to 0.

Remark 5.3. Although we use similar notions, the completions of Definition 5.1 are not directly related to the concept of completion of measure spaces in measure theory.

5.1 Completions by Independent Facts

As we motivated above, we want to use our construction of tuple-independent PDBs to obtain a completion of a given probabilistic database.

We let $\mathcal{D} = (\Omega, \mathfrak{A}, P)$ be a PDB of schema τ and universe $\mathbb{U}$; this is the PDB we shall complete. We assume that the occurrences of new facts are independent in the completion of $\mathcal{D}$. For the moment, we leave more sophisticated completions open as future work (see section 7). Since our constructions of tuple-independent PDBs always yield countable PDBs anyway, for convenience we assume that the universe $\mathbb{U}$ is countable. Then $\mathfrak{A} = 2^{\Omega}$. Let $F(\mathcal{D})$ be the set of facts that appear in the instances of Ω.

Definition 5.4. A completion $\mathcal{D}'$ of $\mathcal{D}$ is called *completion by independent facts* (*independent-fact completion*) if in $\mathcal{D}'$, all sequences $(\mathcal{E}_F)_{F \in \mathcal{F}}$ are independent for collections $\mathcal{F}$ of disjoint sets of facts from $F[\tau, \mathbb{U}] - F(\mathcal{D})$.

Note that the above definition itself can be easily formulated for arbitrary (even uncountable) original PDBs. As in Lemma 4.2, in the countable case, the independence condition is equivalent to the independence of $(\mathcal{E}_f)_{f \in F[\tau,\mathbb{U}]-F(\mathcal{D})}$ in $\mathcal{D}'$.

We remark that especially, we do not allow any facts from $F[\tau, \mathbb{U}] - F(\mathcal{D})$ to have probability 1 (otherwise $P'(\Omega) = 0$).

For the following, we assume that Ω (the sample space of $\mathcal{D}$) is closed under subsets and union. This restriction will be revisited later.

Theorem 5.5. *Let $(p_f)_{f \in F[\tau,\mathbb{U}]-F(\mathcal{D})}$ be a sequence of numbers $p_f \in [0, 1)$ such that $\sum_f p_f < \infty$. Then we can construct an independent-fact completion $\mathcal{D}'$ of $\mathcal{D}$ with the property that $P'(\mathcal{E}_f) = p_f$ for all $f \in F[\tau, \mathbb{U}] - F(\mathcal{D})$ where P' is the probability measure of $\mathcal{D}'$.*

Proof of Theorem 5.5. Let $\mathcal{C}$ be the t.i. PDB with sample space $\{D \subseteq F[\tau, \mathbb{U}] - F(\mathcal{D}) : D \text{ finite}\}$ that is constructed as described in section 4.1. Let P_1 denote the probability measure of $\mathcal{C}$. We now define a PDB $\mathcal{D}'$ with sample space $\Omega' = \mathbf{D}[\tau, \mathbb{U}]$: every instance of $\mathcal{D}'$ is a unique disjoint union $D' = D \uplus C$ with $D \in \Omega$ and an instance C of $\mathcal{C}$. We set

$$P'(\{D'\}) = P(\{D\}) \cdot P_1(\{C\}).$$

This yields a probability distribution (in fact, a product distribution). For original instances $D \in \Omega$, we have

$$P'(\{D\}) = P(\{D\}) \cdot P_1(\{\emptyset\}) \tag{11}$$

and $P_1(\{\emptyset\}) > 0$ since $\mathcal{C}$ contains no facts of probability 1. By distributivity, an analogous version of (11) holds for *sets* of original instances. Hence, for every $D \in \Omega$,

$$P'\big(\{D\} \,\big|\, \Omega\big) = \frac{P'(\{D\} \cap \Omega)}{P'(\Omega)} = \frac{P(\{D\}) \cdot P_1(\{\emptyset\})}{P_1(\{\emptyset\})} = P\big(\{D\}\big).$$

□

Let us now, as previously announced, review the assumption that $\mathcal{D}$ be closed under (countable) union and subsets of instances (this was used for the easy decomposed representation of new instances). Suppose, we want to complete $\mathcal{D}_0 = (\Omega_0, 2^{\Omega_0}, P_0)$ where Ω_0 is a proper subset of $\big\{D \subseteq F(\mathcal{D}_0) : D \text{ finite}\big\}$. We can add the "missing" instances in the following way: fix some $c \in [0, 1]$ and define a PDB $\mathcal{D} = (\Omega, 2^{\Omega}, P)$ with Ω being the set of (finite) subsets of $F(\mathcal{D}_0)$ such that $P(\{D\}) = cP_0(\{D\})$ whenever $D \in \Omega_0$ and $P(\Omega - \Omega_0) = 1 - c$ (by specifying probabilities for the instances of $\Omega - \Omega_0$ with a total mass of $1 - c$).

Remark 5.6. Note that this extension of $\mathcal{D}_0$ to $\mathcal{D}$ is reasonable, if $\mathcal{D}_0$ is finite but harder to motivate (although technically possible) if $\mathcal{D}_0$ is itself countably infinite and infinitely many facts are "missing". On the other hand note that countable PDBs already fulfill the required closure properties if they are tuple-independent, in which case no such extension is required.

Now execute the construction from the proof above for the resulting PDB and observe that the completion condition is satisfied.

$$P'\big(\{D\} \mid \Omega_0\big) = \frac{P'(\{D\})}{P'(\{\Omega_0\})} = \frac{c \cdot P_0(\{D\})) \cdot P_1(\{\emptyset\})}{c \cdot P_1(\{\emptyset\})} = P_0\big(\{D\}\big)$$

for every $D \in \Omega_0$.

Analogously, $\mathcal{D}$ might be, for example, augmented by finitely many, arbitrarily correlated instances of arbitrary probability mass before carrying out the completion.

Theorem 5.5 assures the existence of an infinite open-world approach for countable PDBs and establishes in some sense a generalization of the model of Ceylan et al. [14]. If the given universe $\mathbb{U}$ is finite, we can directly obtain their framework. In this case we only need to specify probabilities for finitely many new facts. In [14], the authors construct a collection of finite PDBs that contains all the completions of the original PDB by probabilities up to some (reasonably small) upper bound λ. The generalization of this idea is also achievable in our setting: instead of a fixed upper bound λ, fact probabilities could be bounded by the summands of a fixed convergent series.

Example 5.7. We want to close this section with a small, abstract example. Supposed $\mathbb{U} = \{\mathsf{A}, \mathsf{B}, \mathsf{C}, \mathsf{D}\} \cup \mathbb{N}$ and let $\tau = \{R\}$ consist of a single, binary relation symbol. Consider the following finite t.i. PDB $\mathcal{D} = (\Omega, 2^{\Omega}, P)$ where the last column displays the probabilities $P(\mathcal{E}_f)$.

R		P
A	1	0.8
B	1	0.4
B	2	0.5
C	3	0.9

Additionally, assume R is supposed to be a relation between $\{\mathsf{A}, \mathsf{B}, \mathsf{C}, \mathsf{D}\}$ and $\mathbb{N}$ (this is for instance achievable by excluding facts of the wrong shape from $F[\tau, \mathbb{U}]$). The usual closed-world interpretation of the tabular representation above would be a PDB over the universe $\mathbb{U}' = \{\mathsf{A}, \mathsf{B}, \mathsf{C}, 1, 2, 3\}$ and, for example, the probability that two facts of the shape $R(\mathsf{A}, i)$ are occurring would be 0. Also, the object D would not occur whatsoever.

Instead, we want to apply the open-world assumption to $\mathcal{D}$ by assuming that the probability of any unspecified tuple (x, i) to belong to R is given by 2^{-1} (i. e. there are up to 4 facts f with probability 2^{-i} for every i). Obviously, the sum of all fact probabilities converges. Hence, these probabilities induce an independent-fact completion $\mathcal{D}'$ of $\mathcal{D}$. In particular, in $\mathcal{D}'$, all finite Boolean combinations of (occurrences of) distinct facts have probability > 0.

6 A NAÏVE APPROXIMATION OF QUERY EVALUATION

In this section, we investigate the problem of query evaluation. Its purpose is to demonstrate, that query evaluation for infinite PDBs is not out of reach from an algorithmic perspective. This may serve as a stepping stone in further more thorough examination of the subject.

We consider the following setting. Let $\mathbb{U}$ be some countable universe and τ be a database schema. We also assume that $\mathbb{U}$ is computable, for example $\mathbb{U} = \Sigma^*$ for some finite alphabet Σ, so that an algorithm can generate all facts $f \in F[\tau, \mathbb{U}]$. Given is an infinite t.i. PDB $\mathcal{D} = (\Omega, 2^{\Omega}, P)$ over τ and $\mathbb{U}$ and a *first order* query $Q(\vec{x})$ with free variables $\vec{x}$, and we want to compute $P(Q) = P(\{D \in \Omega : D \models Q\})$. As we have to deal with an infinite PDB, we will not exactly evaluate queries but instead discuss, how query results can be approximated up to an arbitrarily small error. Our focus remains on Boolean queries Q for the moment. We will hint on how to process non-Boolean queries later.

Let $F(\mathcal{D})$ be the set of facts appearing among the instances of our PDB $\mathcal{D}$ and let $p_f := P(\mathcal{E}_f)$. We make two assumptions concerning our access to the probability measure of $\mathcal{D}$:

(i) the expected size $\mathrm{E}(S_{\mathcal{D}}) = \sum_{f \in F(\mathcal{D})} p_f$ of $\mathcal{D}$ is known and
(ii) given f, we have oracle access to p_f.

Note that these two assumptions are, for example, easily achievable if we obtained $\mathcal{D}$ by completing a finite t.i. PDB as described in section 5.

Proposition 6.1. *Let $0 < \varepsilon < \frac{1}{2}$. Then there exists an algorithm that, given a Boolean query $Q \in \mathsf{FO}[\tau, \mathbb{U}]$ and access to a tuple-independent PDB $\mathcal{D} \in \mathbf{D}[\tau, \mathbb{U}]$ (via (i),(ii)), computes an* additive *approximation p of $P(Q)$ with error guarantee ε, that is,*

$$P(Q) - \varepsilon \underset{(a)}{\leq} p \underset{(b)}{\leq} P(Q) + \varepsilon.$$

Proof sketch. We will omit some technical details of the proof in this presentation. They can be found in detail in the extended version of the paper [19].

Let $F(\mathcal{D}) = \{f_1, f_2, \dots\}$ and let $p_i := p_{f_i}$. Choose n large enough such that for all $i > n$ we have $p_i \leq \frac{1}{2}$ and $e^{\alpha_n} \leq 1+\varepsilon$ and $e^{-\alpha_n} \geq 1 - \varepsilon$. This is possible because $\alpha_n \to 0$ as n approaches ∞ and the function e^x is continuous at 0. Also, an appropriate n can be found algorithmically by *systematically* listing facts until the remaining probability mass is small enough.

Let r be the quantifier rank of the input query Q (that is, the maximum nesting depth of quantifiers), and let s be the number of constants from $\mathbb{U}$ appearing in Q. Let $\Omega_n = 2^{\{f_1, \dots, f_n\}}$. As always, we denote the complement of an event $\mathcal{E}$ by $\overline{\mathcal{E}}$. Note that every instance D of Ω_n is r-equivalent (that is, equivalent for Boolean queries up to quantifier rank r) to some finite structure of size $O(n+r+s)$. Hence, $P(Q \mid \Omega_n)$ can be computed by a traditional closed-world query evaluation algorithm for finite tuple-independent PDBs. We let p be the output of this evaluation and return p as our approximate answer.

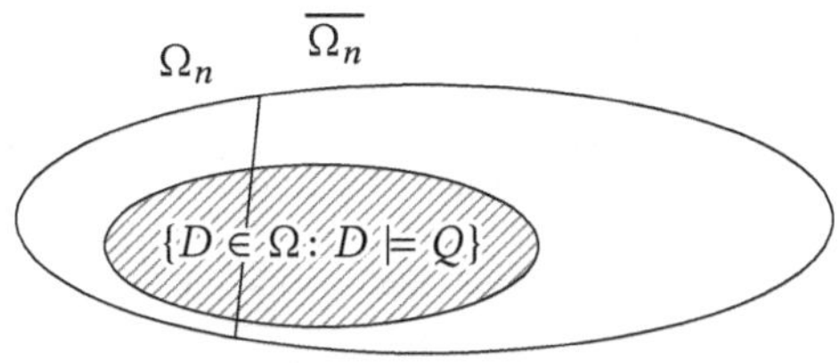

Figure 1: Our approximate answer is the probability of D satisfying Q conditioned on Ω_n (in the image, the fraction of the left side that is shaded). We use rough bounds for the remaining probability mass to derive our approximation guarantee.

We will now establish the bounds on the error of this approximation. For an illustration of the situation, see Figure 1 above.

First, we can show that

$$P(\Omega_n) = \prod_{f \notin \{f_1,\dots,f_n\}} (1 - p_f) \geq e^{-\alpha_n} \qquad (*)$$

(proven in [19]). From this inequality we infer

$$P(Q) = \underbrace{P(\Omega_n)}_{\leq 1} \cdot p + \underbrace{P(\overline{\Omega_n})}_{\leq 1 - e^{-\alpha_n} \leq \varepsilon} \cdot \underbrace{P(Q \mid \overline{\Omega_n})}_{\leq 1}$$

and therefore immediately $p \geq P(Q) - \varepsilon$, showing (a).

Towards (b), we have

$$P(Q) = \underbrace{P(\Omega_n)}_{\geq e^{-\alpha_n}} \cdot p + \underbrace{P(\overline{\Omega_n}) \cdot P(Q \mid \overline{\Omega_n})}_{\geq 0}$$

and hence $p \leq e^{\alpha_n} P(Q) \leq (1 + \varepsilon) P(Q) \leq P(Q) + \varepsilon$. □

As we noted before, the additive approximation of Proposition 6.1 can be extended to allow the evaluation of FO-queries with free variables. Here we use the relaxed version of query semantics that was introduced in Section 3.1 where we are only interested in marginal probabilities of different tuples belonging to the result. These probabilities can be approximated in the following way: suppose $Q = Q(\vec{x})$ where $\vec{x} = (x_1, \dots, x_k)$ are the free variables of the FO-formula Q. From Q we can obtain $|\mathrm{adom}(\Omega_n)|^k$ many sentences $Q(\vec{a})$ by plugging in all the possible valuations $\vec{a}$ of $\vec{x}$ from $\mathrm{adom}(\Omega_n)^k$ as constants. The probability of $\vec{a}$ to belong to the output of the query Q is equal to the probability of the sentence $Q(\vec{a})$ being satisfied in our PDB. With the procedure above, this probability can be approximated up to an additive error of ε. Note that this approximation only contains facts from Ω_n.

The following proposition shows that there is no hope to replace the additive approximation guarantee of Proposition 6.1 by a multiplicative one (which is more common in approximation algorithms). We cannot even do this for a very simple fixed conjunctive query. Let Σ be a finite alphabet and let τ be a database schema. We say that a Turing machine M *represents* a t.i. PDB over Σ, τ of *weight* w if it computes a function $p_M \colon F[\tau, \Sigma^*] \to \mathbb{Q}$ such that $\sum_{f \in F[\tau,\Sigma^*]} p_M(f) = w$. The PDB $\mathcal{D}_M$ represented by M is the tuple-independent PDB with universe $\mathbb{U} = \Sigma^*$, schema τ and fact probabilities $p_M(f)$. Note that if we have a Turing machine M representing a PDB $\mathcal{D}_M$ in this sense then the two assumptions (i), (ii) of Proposition 6.1 are again satisfied with $p_f := p_M(f)$.

Proposition 6.2. *Let $\Sigma = \{0, 1\}$ and $\tau = \{R, S\}$ for a unary relation symbols R, S. Let Q be the Boolean query $\exists x \colon R(x)$ in* FO$[\tau, \mathbb{U}]$. *Furthermore, let $c \geq 1$. There is no algorithm A that, given a Turing machine M representing a tuple-independent PDB over Σ, τ of weight 1, computes a number p such that*

$$\tfrac{1}{c} \cdot \Pr_{D \sim \mathcal{D}_M}(D \models Q) \leq p \leq c \cdot \Pr_{D \sim \mathcal{D}_M}(D \models Q).$$

The detailed proof can be found in [19].

Let us close this section with some remarks regarding complexity issues of the previously described approximation procedure. Basically, its run-time is given by the run-time of the finite evaluation algorithm when applied to a PDB with a universe of size n. In the proof of Proposition 6.1, $n = n(\varepsilon)$ was the number of facts that needed to be taken into consideration in order to obtain the error guarantee ε and is basically determined by the rate of convergence of the series of fact probabilities. The way we produced n systematically ensures its existence. In the best case, the facts $f_1, f_2, \dots$ are enumerated by decreasing probability. For a geometric series of fact probabilities for example, $n = \Omega\big(\log\big(\frac{1}{1-\varepsilon}\big)\big)$. It is worth noting, though, that series in general may converge arbitrarily slowly [25, pp. 310-311]. For the moment, we leave it at that and refer to future work for a more thorough examination of the complexity of query evaluation in infinite PDBs.

7 CONCLUSIONS

In this work, we proposed a framework for probabilistic databases that extends the standard finite notion, which dominated theoretical research on probabilistic databases so far. Our model provides a theoretical foundation for several practical systems allowing for values from infinite domains (albeit still in a restricted way) and opens avenues to new, even more flexible systems.

We discussed independence assumptions in infinite PDBs, most notably the simple model of tuple-independence. We showed how to construct countable tuple-independent PDBs realizing any given sequence of fact probabilities, provided the sum of these fact probabilities converges, and we also proved that the convergence condition is necessary. An important application of this result is that it allows us to complete PDBs to cover all potential instances (with respect to the underlying domain). We also gave a construction of countable block-independent disjoint probabilistic databases with given fact probabilities. Although we did not focus on algorithmic questions, the aforementioned completions provide the mathematical background for applying open-world semantics to (classically closed-world) finite PDBs.

In general, we expect query evaluation (even approximate) to be difficult in infinite PDBs. The way to approach it may be to combine classical database techniques with probabilistic inference techniques from AI, as they are used for relational languages like BLOG [28], ProbLog [15], and Markov logic [35]. However, the underlying inference problems have a high computational complexity, and algorithms are mostly heuristic, so we see little hope for obtaining algorithms tractable in the worst case. As we showed, the class of tuple-independent PDBs with respect to some countable universe and schema is not powerful enough to capture all possible probability spaces, even when extended with FO-views. A more detailed investigation of the exact boundaries of expressivity, as well as the corresponding considerations for b.i.d. PDBs are still pending. We think that concise and powerful representation systems for infinite PDBs are of general interest, even if they might turn out to be only possible as approximations (in some sense) of arbitrary PDBs. For whatever models or systems come forth, the consecutive goal is to have efficient (approximation) algorithms that perform query evaluation, perhaps among other database specific operations on our probability spaces.

Our technical results are, at least implicitly, mostly about countable PDBs. It would be nice to extend these results, for example the construction of tuple-independent PDBs to uncountable PDBs in meaningful way. But in fact, even more basic questions regarding the construction of suitable σ-algebras and probability spaces and the measurability of queries and views need a thorough investigation for uncountable PDBs. Of course, algorithmic tractability becomes even more challenging in the uncountable.

ACKNOWLEDGMENTS

We are very grateful to Dan Suciu, for the time he spent reading a manuscript version of this paper and his valuable comments. In particular, he proposed the condition $\mathcal{E}_F \in \mathfrak{A}$ for measurable F in Definition 3.1 as a strengthening of our original condition $\mathcal{E}_f \in \mathfrak{A}$ and made various other proposals improving our treatment of uncountable PDBs. We also highly appreciate the work of the reviewers for their suggestions and their criticism and for guiding our attention to some relevant related works and towards reconsidering some technical issues. Additionally, we would like to thank Steffen van Bergerem for helpful remarks.

This work is supported by the German Research Council (DFG) Research Training Group 2236 UnRAVeL (http://gepris.dfg.de/gepris/projekt/282652900).

REFERENCES

[1] Serge Abiteboul, Tsz-Hong Hubert Chan, Evgeny Kharlamov, Werner Nutt, and Pierre Senellart. 2011. Capturing Continuous Data and Answering Aggregate Queries in Probabilistic XML. *ACM Transactions on Database Systems (TODS)* 36, 4, Article 25 (2011), 45 pages.

[2] Serge Abiteboul, Richard Hull, and Victor Vianu. 1995. *Foundations of Databases* (1st ed.). Addison-Wesley, Boston, MA, USA.

[3] Serge Abiteboul, Benny Kimelfeld, Yehoshua Sagiv, and Pierre Senellart. 2009. On the Expressiveness of Probabilistic XML Models. *The VLDB Journal - The International Journal on Very Large Data Bases* 18, 5 (2009), 1041–1064.

[4] Charu C. Aggarwal and Philip S. Yu. 2009. A Survey of Uncertain Data Algorithms and Applications. *IEEE Transactions on Knowledge and Data Engineering (TKDE)* 21, 5 (2009), 609–623.

[5] Parag Agrawal, Omar Benjelloun, Anish Das Sarma, Chris Hayworth, Shubha Nabar, Tomoe Sugihara, and Jennifer Widom. 2006. Trio: A System for Data, Uncertainty, and Lineage. In *Proceedings of the 32nd International Conference on Very Large Data Bases (VLDB '06)*. VLDB Endowment / ACM, New York, NY, USA, 1151–1154.

[6] Parag Agrawal and Jennifer Widom. 2009. Continuous Uncertainty in Trio. In *Proceedings of the Third International Workshop on Management of Uncertain Data (MUD '09)*. Centre for Telematics and Information Technology (CTIT), Enschede, The Netherlands, 17–32.

[7] Vince Bárány, Balder Ten Cate, Benny Kimelfeld, Dan Olteanu, and Zografoula Vagena. 2017. Declarative Probabilistic Programming with Datalog. *ACM Transactions on Database Systems (TODS)* 42, 4, Article 22 (2017), 35 pages.

[8] Vaishak Belle. 2017. Open-Universe Weighted Model Counting. In *Proceedings of the Thirty-First AAAI Conference on Artificial Intelligence (AAAI '17)*. AAAI Press, Palo Alto, CA, USA, 3701–3708.

[9] Michael Benedikt, Evgeny Kharlamov, Dan Olteanu, and Pierre Senellart. 2010. Probabilistic XML via Markov Chains. In *Proceedings of the 36th International Conference On Very Large Data Bases (VLDB '10)*. VLDB Endowment / ACM, New York, NY, USA, 770–781.

[10] Béla Bollobás. 2001. *Random Graphs* (2nd ed.). Cambridge University Press, Cambridge, United Kingdom.

[11] Stefan Borgwardt, İsmail İlkan Ceylan, and Thomas Lukasiewicz. 2017. Ontology-Mediated Queries for Probabilistic Databases. In *Proceedings of the 31st AAAI Conference on Artificial Intelligence (AAAI '17)*. AAAI Press, Palo Alto, CA, USA, 1063–1069.

[12] Stefan Borgwardt, İsmail İlkan Ceylan, and Thomas Lukasiewicz. 2018. Recent Advances in Querying Probabilistic Knowledge Bases. In *Proceedings of the 27th International Joint Conference on Artificial Intelligence (IJCAI'18)*. AAAI Press, Palo Alto, CA, USA, 5420–5426.

[13] Jihad Boulos, Nilesh Dalvi, Bhushan Mandhani, Shobhit Mathur, Chris Re, and Dan Suciu. 2005. MYSTIQ: A System for Finding More Answers by Using Probabilities. In *Proceedings of the 2005 ACM SIGMOD International Conference on Management of Data (SIGMOD '05)*. ACM, New York, NY, USA, 891–893.

[14] İsmail İlkan Ceylan, Adnan Darwiche, and Guy Van den Broeck. 2016. Open-World Probabilistic Databases. In *Proceedings of the Fifteenth International Conference on Principles of Knowledge Representation and Reasoning (KR '16)*. AAAI Press, Palo Alto, CA, USA, 339–348.

[15] Luc De Raedt, Kristian Kersting, Sriraam Natarajan, and David Poole. 2016. *Statistical Relational Artificial Intelligence: Logic, Probability, and Computation*. Morgan & Claypool, San Rafael, CA, USA.

[16] Xin Dong, Evgeniy Gabrilovich, Geremy Heitz, Wilko Horn, Ni Lao, Kevin Murphy, Thomas Strohmann, Shaohua Sun, and Wei Zhang. 2014. Knowledge Vault: A Web-scale Approach to Probabilistic Knowledge Fusion. In *Proceedings of the 20th ACM SIGKDD International*

Conference on Knowledge Discovery and Data Mining (KDD '14). ACM, New York, NY, USA, 601–610.

[17] Bert E. Fristedt and Lawrence F. Gray. 1997. *A Modern Approach to Probabilitiy Theory*. Birkhäuser, Boston (MA, USA), Basel (Switzerland), Berlin (Germany).

[18] Todd J. Green and Val Tannen. 2006. Models for Incomplete and Probabilistic Information. In *Current Trends in Database Technology (EDBT '06)*. Springer-Verlag, Berlin, Heidelberg (Germany), 278–296.

[19] Martin Grohe and Peter Lindner. 2018. Probabilistic Databases with an Infinite Open-World Assumption. arXiv e-prints, arXiv:1807.00607v2 [cs.DB].

[20] Jiewen Huang, Lyublena Antova, Christoph Koch, and Dan Olteanu. 2009. MayBMS: A Probabilistic Database Management System. In *Proceedings of the 2009 ACM SIGMOD International Conference on Management of Data (SIGMOD '09)*. ACM, New York, NY, USA, 1071–1074.

[21] Tomasz Imieliński and Witold Lipski, Jr. 1984. Incomplete Information in Relational Databases. *Journal of the ACM (JACM)* 31, 4 (1984), 761–791.

[22] Ravi Jampani, Fei Xu, Mingxi Wu, Luis Leopoldo Perez, Christopher Jermaine, and Peter J. Haas. 2008. MCDB: A Monte Carlo Approach to Managing Uncertain Data. In *Proceedings of the 2008 ACM SIGMOD International Conference on Management of Data (SIGMOD '08)*. ACM, New York, NY, USA, 687–700.

[23] Oliver Kennedy and Christoph Koch. 2010. PIP: A Database System for Great and Small Expectations. In *Proceedings of the 2010 IEEE 26th International Conference on Data Engineering (ICDE '10)*. IEEE, Washington DC, USA, 157–168.

[24] Benny Kimelfeld and Pierre Senellart. 2013. Probabilistic XML: Models and Complexity. In *Advances in Probabilistic Databases for Uncertain Information Management*. Vol. 304. Springer Verlag, Berlin, Heidelberg (Germany), 39–66.

[25] Konrad Knopp. 1996. *Theorie und Anwendung der unendlichen Reihen* (6th ed.). Springer-Verlag, Berlin, Göttingen, Heidelberg (Germany); New York (NY, USA). An english translation of a previous edition is available under the title *Theory and Application of Infinite Series*, 1990, published by Dover Publications, Mineola, NY, USA.

[26] Leonid Libkin. 2018. Certain Answers Meet Zero-One Laws. In *Proceedings of the 37th ACM SIGMOD-SIGACT-SIGAI Symposium on Principles of Database Systems (PODS '18)*. ACM, New York, NY, USA, 195–207.

[27] Thomas Lukasiewicz and Dan Olteanu. 2016. Probabilistic Databases and Reasoning. https://www.cs.ox.ac.uk/dan.olteanu/tutorials/olteanu-pdb-kr16.pdf. Tutorial at the Fifteenth International Conference on Principles of Knowledge Representation and Reasoning (KR '16).

[28] Brian Milch, Bhaskara Marthi, Stuart Russell, David Sontag, Daniel L. Ong, and Andrey Kolobov. 2005. BLOG: Probabilistic Models with Unknown Objects. In *Proceedings of the 19th International Joint Conference on Artificial Intelligence (IJCAI '05)*. Morgan Kaufmann Publishers Inc., San Francisco, CA, USA, 1352–1359.

[29] Tom Mitchell, William Cohen, Estevam Hruschka, Partha Talukdar, Justin Betteridge, Andrew Carlson, Bhavana Dalvi Mishra, Matthew Gardner, Bryan Kisiel, Jayant Krishnamurthy, Ni Lao, Kathryn Mazaitis, Thahir Mohamed, Ndapa Nakashole, Emmanouil Platanios, Alan Ritter, Mehdi Samadi, Burr Settles, Richard Wang, Derry Wijaya, Abhinav Gupta, Xinlei Chen, Abulhair Saparov, Malcolm Greaves, and Joel Welling. 2015. Never-Ending Learning. In *Proceedings of the Twenty-Ninth AAAI Conference on Artificial Intelligence (AAAI '15)*. AAAI Press, Palo Alto, CA, USA, 2302–2310.

[30] Feng Niu, Ce Zhang, Christopher Ré, and Jude W. Shavlik. 2012. DeepDive: Web-scale Knowledge-Base Construction using Statistical Learning and Inference. In *Very Large Data Search: Proceedings of the Second International Workshop on Searching and Integrating New Web Data Sources) (VLDS '12)*, Vol. 884. CEUR Workshop Proceedings, Aachen, Germany, 25–28. http://ceur-ws.org/Vol-884/VLDS2012_p25_Niu.pdf

[31] Raymond Reiter. 1978. On Closed World Data Bases. In *Logic and Data Bases* (1st ed.), Herve Gallaire and Jack Minker (Eds.). Plenum Press, New York, NY, USA, 55–76.

[32] Alfred Rényi. 2007. *Foundations of Probability* (reprint ed.). Dover Publications, Mineola, NY, USA.

[33] David Simmons. 2013. Infinite Distributive Law. Mathematics Stack Exchange. https://math.stackexchange.com/q/509318

[34] Sarvjeet Singh, Chris Mayfield, Rahul Shah, Sunil Prabhakar, Susanne Hambrusch, Jennifer Neville, and Reynold Cheng. 2008. Database Support for Probabilistic Attributes and Tuples. In *Proceedings of the 2008 IEEE 24th International Conference on Data Engineering (ICDE '08)*. IEEE, Washington, DC, USA, 1053–1061.

[35] Parag Singla and Pedro Domingos. 2007. Markov Logic in Infinite Domains. In *Proceedings of the Twenty-Third Conference on Uncertainty in Artificial Intelligence (UAI '07)*. AUAI Press, Arlington, VA, USA, 368–375.

[36] Joel Spencer. 2001. *The Strange Logic of Random Graphs*. Algorithms and Combinatorics, Vol. 22. Springer-Verlag, Berlin, Heidelberg (Germany).

[37] Dan Suciu, Dan Olteanu, Christopher Ré, and Christoph Koch. 2011. *Probabilistic Databases* (1st ed.). Synthesis Lectures on Data Management, Vol. 16. Morgan & Claypool Publishers, San Rafael, CA, USA.

[38] Guy Van den Broeck and Dan Suciu. 2017. Query Processing on Probabilistic Data: A Survey. *Foundations and Trends® in Databases* 7, 3-4 (2017), 197–341.

[39] Ron van der Meyden. 1998. Logics for Databases and Information Systems. In *Logics for Databases and Information Systems*, Jan Chomicki and Gunter Saake (Eds.). Kluwer Academic Publishers, Norwell, MA, USA, Chapter Logical Approaches to Incomplete Information: A Survey, 307–356.

Query Evaluation in Election Databases

Benny Kimelfeld
Technion
Haifa, Israel
bennyk@cs.technion.ac.il

Phokion G. Kolaitis
UC Santa Cruz
and IBM Research-Almaden
California, USA
kolaitis@soe.ucsc.edu

Muhammad Tibi
Technion
Haifa, Israel
m7mdtb@cs.technion.ac.il

ABSTRACT

Election databases are the main elements of a recently introduced framework that aims to create bridges between the computational social choice and the data management communities. An election database consists of incomplete information about the preferences of voters, in the form of partial orders, alongside with standard database relations that provide contextual information. Earlier work in computational social choice focused on the computation of possible winners and necessary winners that are determined by the available incomplete information and the voting rule at hand. The presence of the relational context, however, permits the formulation of sophisticated queries about voting rules, candidates, potential winners, issues, and positions on issues. Such queries can be given possible answer semantics and necessary answer semantics on an election database, where the former means that the query is true on some completion of the given partial orders and the latter means that the query is true on every such completion.

We carry out a systematic investigation of query evaluation on election databases by analyzing how the interaction between the partial preferences, the voting rules and the relational context impacts on the complexity of query evaluation. To this effect, we focus on positional scoring rules and unions of conjunctive queries. We establish a number of results that delineate the complexity of the possible answers and of the necessary answers for different positional scoring rules and for various classes of unions of conjunctive queries. Furthermore, we show that query evaluation is fixed-parameter tractable, where the parameter is the number of candidates in the election.

PODS'19, June 30-July 5, 2019, Amsterdam, Netherlands

ACM ISBN 978-1-4503-6227-6/19/06...$15.00

CCS CONCEPTS

• **Theory of computation → Incomplete, inconsistent, and uncertain databases; Database query languages (principles);** • **Applied computing → Voting / election technologies;**

KEYWORDS

Necessary and Possible Answers; Computational Social Choice; Positional Scoring Rules.

1 INTRODUCTION

During the past two decades, computational social choice has emerged as an interdisciplinary area between social choice theory, economics, mathematics, logic, and computer science. Social choice theory studies how votes or, more broadly, preferences of individual members of a society can be aggregated in such a way that the society arrives at a collective decision. Social choice theory has a long history that spans several centuries, from the analysis of voting manipulation by Pliny the Younger in Ancient Rome to the study of particular voting rules by Jean-Charles de Borda and Marquis de Condorcet in the 18th Century (now known as the Borda rule and the Condorcet method, respectively), to, more recently, the ground-breaking work on dictatorial aggregation by Kenneth Arrow in the 1950s. (See [8] for a brief history of social choice theory.)

Computational social choice infuses an algorithmic perspective into social choice theory. In particular, the computational aspects of preference aggregation in an election have been a focal point of research in this area. It is often the case, however, that preferences are only partial, since, for example, a voter may be undecided between two candidates, or our knowledge of the voter's preference is incomplete. For this reason, Konczak and Lang [21] introduced the notions of *necessary winners* and *possible winners* as those candidates who win in *every* completion, and *at least one* completion, respectively, of the given partial preferences. This work eventually led to a classification of the computational complexity of the necessary and possible winners for a variety of voting rules [3, 4, 27].

Arguably, the *positional scoring rules* form the most extensively studied class of voting rules. Under such a rule, every candidate receives from every voter a score that is determined only by the position of the candidate in the voter's ranking. Hence, a positional scoring rule is defined by a sequence of *scoring vectors* that specify the score for each position (there is a scoring vector of length m, for each $m \geq 1$, where m stands for the number of candidates). A *winner* in an election is a candidate who achieves the highest total score from the voters. Thus, in general, there may be several winners in an election, in which case they are also referred to as *co-winners*. It is conceivable, however, that only one candidate achieves the highest total score from the voters, in which case that candidate is a *unique* winner. The *plurality* rule and the *veto* rule are two well known examples of positional scoring rules. The scoring vectors of the plurality rule are of the form $(1, 0, \ldots, 0)$, while the scoring vectors of the veto rule are of the form $(1, 1, \ldots, 1, 0)$. Thus, under the plurality rule, the winners are the candidates who are at top of the ranking of as many voters as possible, while, under the veto rule, the winners are the candidates who are the bottom of the ranking of as few voters as possible.

We focus on positional scoring rules whose scoring vectors are computable in polynomial time in the number of candidates. Under such rules, the necessary winners can be computed in polynomial time [21, 27]. The possible answers can be computed in polynomial time under the plurality and veto rules, but their computation is NP-complete for any other *pure* rule, as established in a sequence of studies [3, 4, 21, 27]. A positional scoring rule is *pure* if, for all $m > 1$, the scoring vector for m candidates is obtained from the scoring vector for $m - 1$ candidates by inserting a new score into the vector.

Elections or polls do not take place in a vacuum; instead, they take place in a context in which an abundance of additional information may be available, including information about the candidates (gender, age, education, wealth), information about issues and positions of candidates on issues, and information about campaign contributions (donors, amounts, recipients). Thus, one may be interested in formulating and answering queries that take into account both the given partial preferences and the contextual information available.

The preceding considerations motivated Kimelfeld, Kolaitis, and Stoyanovich [20] to introduce a new framework that aims to create, for the first time, bridges between the computational social choice and the database management communities.

The main conceptual contribution of [20] is the development of rigorous semantics of queries that involve both partial preferences and contextual information about candidates, issues, positions, and so on. To this effect, the notions of *necessary answers* and *possible answers* to queries were introduced as an extension of the notions of necessary winners and possible winners. To appreciate the difference between, say, necessary winners and necessary answers, consider the Boolean query q that asks whether or not there is a winner who is Republican. Given a set **P** of partial orders representing the (partial) preferences of voters, it is conceivable that no single candidate is a winner in every completion **T** of **P**, which implies that the set of necessary winners is the empty set. Yet, it is also conceivable that in every completion **T** of **P** one of the winners is a Republican, hence the necessary answers of the query q is "yes." In particular, this example shows that the necessary answers to queries cannot always be obtained from the necessary winners.

As regards technical contributions, a study of the necessary answers of conjunctive queries was initiated in [20] and some preliminary complexity results were obtained. In particular, it was shown that there are natural conjunctive queries involving winners and database relations such that computing the necessary answers of these queries under the plurality rule is coNP-complete. This contrasts sharply with earlier results in computational social choice to the effect that, as previously mentioned, there is a polynomial-time algorithm for computing the necessary winners under every positional scoring rule, including the plurality rule [21, 27].

Summary of results. We carry out a systematic investigation of the algorithmic aspects of query evaluation on *election* databases, that is, databases that consist of standard database relations and a set of partial orders representing the preferences of voters. We analyze how the interaction between the partial preferences, the voting rules and the relational context impacts on the computational complexity of query evaluation. We establish a number of results that delineate the complexity of the possible answers and of the necessary answers for various classes of unions of conjunctive queries and under different positional scoring rules.

The scope of our investigation is broader than that in [20] along several different dimensions. First, while only the necessary answers to queries were investigated in [20], here we investigate both the necessary answers and the possible answers to queries. Second, most of our results cover arbitrary pure positional scoring rules, thus they go well beyond the plurality rule and a few other voting rules studied in [20]. Third, we consider queries that involve not only winners, but also unique winners, while only queries involving winners (but not unique winners) were considered in [20].

To give a taste of our findings, we state here a few of the results obtained in this paper. For the possible answers, we show that if q is an arbitrary union of Boolean conjunctive queries that may involve winners and unique winners, then there are polynomial-time algorithms for computing the possible answers to q under the plurality rule or under the veto rule. This gives a fairly complete picture for the class of pure positional scoring rules, because the aforementioned NP-hardness results for the possible winners [3, 4, 27] imply the NP-hardness of the possible answers of unions of conjunctive queries under pure positional scoring rules other than plurality and veto.

As for the necessary answers, we consider the Boolean conjunctive query $q^k_{\mathrm{wr}}()$ for every $k \geq 1$, where

$$q^k_{\mathrm{wr}}() \text{ :- } \textsc{Winner}(x_1), \ldots, \textsc{Winner}(x_k), R(x_1, \ldots, x_k)\,.$$

We show that there are polynomial-time algorithms for computing the necessary answers of q^1_{wr} under the plurality rule or the veto rule, but computing the necessary answers of q^1_{wr} is coNP-complete under every other pure positional scoring rule. We further show how the tractable cases generalize from q^1_{wr} to a wide class of unions of conjunctive queries where, in each disjunct, the WINNER atoms are disconnected. In contrast, we prove that for every $k > 1$, computing the necessary answers of q^k_{wr} is coNP-complete under every pure positional scoring rule (including plurality and veto). For $k > 2$, this hardness applies to *every* positional scoring rule, pure or not.

Finally, we examine query evaluation using the lens of parameterized complexity and we show that evaluation of unions of conjunctive queries is fixed-parameter tractable, where the parameter is the number of candidates in the election.

Organization. The rest of the paper is structured as follows. In Section 2, we give the basic definition and terminology, and in particular, describe briefly the framework of election databases in [20]. In Sections 4 and 5, we study the possibility and necessity problems, respectively, for queries that involve winners but not *unique* winners. In Section 6, we extend our study to queries that involve unique winners. In Section 7, we study the parameterized complexity of the possibility and necessity problems, and then conclude in Section 8.

2 PRELIMINARIES

This section contains the definitions of the main concepts and background material.

2.1 Databases and Queries

A (relational) *schema* $\mathcal{S}$ is a collection of *relation symbols* with each relation symbol R in $\mathcal{S}$ having an associated arity that we denote by $ar(R)$. We assume a countably infinite set of *constants* that are used as database values. A *relation* is a set of tuples of constants, each having the same arity (length) that we denote by $ar(T)$. A *database* D (over the schema $\mathcal{S}$) is a collection of relations such that for each relation symbol R, the database D contains a relation R^D with $ar(R) = ar(R^D)$. The active domain of D, denoted by $adom(D)$, is the set of all constants occurring in relations in D.

A *query* is a function that maps databases to relations. Formally, a query q of arity $ar(q)$ is a function that maps every database over $\mathcal{S}$ to a finite relation $q(D)$ of arity $ar(q)$ on the active domain $adom(D)$. We say that each tuple in $q(D)$ is an *answer* to q on D. If the arity of q is zero, then we say that q is a *Boolean* query; in this case, $D \models q$ denotes that $q(D)$ consists of the empty tuple (), while $D \not\models q$ denotes that $q(D)$ is empty.

A *conjunctive query* (CQ) q over the schema $\mathcal{S}$ is a query definable by a first-order formula of the form

$$\exists \mathbf{y}_1 \cdots \exists \mathbf{y}_m \theta(\mathbf{x}, \mathbf{y}_1, \ldots, \mathbf{y}_m),$$

where θ is a conjunction of atomic formulas with variables among those in $\mathbf{x}, \mathbf{y}_1, \ldots, \mathbf{y}_m$. In the sequel, conjunctive queries will be written as logic rules, i.e., as expressions of the form

$$q(\mathbf{x}) \text{ :- } R_1(\mathbf{t}_1), \ldots, R_n(\mathbf{t}_m)$$

where each R_i is a relation symbol of $\mathcal{S}$, each $\mathbf{t}_i$ is a tuple of variables and constants with the same arity as R_i, and $\mathbf{x}$ is a tuple of k variables from $\mathbf{t}_1, \ldots, \mathbf{t}_m$. We call $q(\mathbf{x})$ the *head* of q, and $R_1(\mathbf{t}_1), \ldots, R_n(\mathbf{t}_m)$ the *body* of q; each $R_i(\mathbf{t}_i)$ is an *atom* of q. The variables occurring in the body but not in the head are existentially quantified. The answers to q on a database D are the projections to $\mathbf{x}$ of all homomorphisms from q to D.

A *union of conjunctive queries* (UCQ) is an expression q of the form $q_1 \cup \cdots \cup q_\ell$, where each q_i is a conjunctive query and all q_is have the same arity (i.e., the arity $ar(q)$ of q). If D is a database, then $q(D) = q_1(D) \cup \cdots \cup q_\ell(D)$.

2.2 Voting Profiles and Voting Rules

We now recall the basic terminology of voting theory in computational social choice. For additional background material, we refer the reader to the handbook of computational social choice [7] and, in particular, to the chapter on incomplete information in voting [6]. Let $C = \{c_1, \ldots, c_m\}$ be a set of *candidates*, and let $V = \{v_1, \ldots, v_n\}$ be a set of voters. A *complete voting profile* is a tuple $\mathbf{T} = (T_1, \ldots, T_n)$, where each T_i is a total order over C, representing the ranking (preference) of voter v_j of the candidates in C. A *voting rule* r is a function that maps every complete profile $\mathbf{T}$ into a set $\mathbf{W}(r, \mathbf{T}) \subseteq C$ of *winners*. We say that a candidate c is a *winner* if $c \in \mathbf{W}(r, \mathbf{T})$; we also say that c is a *unique winner* if $\mathbf{W}(r, \mathbf{T}) = \{c\}$. We write $\mathbf{U}(r, \mathbf{T})$ to denote the set of unique winners; note that $\mathbf{U}(r, \mathbf{T})$ is either a singleton or the empty set. On occasion, we will use the term "co-winner" to emphasize that we refer to a winner who is not necessarily unique.

In this paper, we focus on the class of *positional scoring rules*, which is arguably the most extensively studied class of voting rules in computational social choice.

$\mathbf{T}^1$				
T_1	D	T	H	B
T_2	H	T	B	D
T_3	D	H	B	T
T_4	D	B	H	T
T_5	B	H	T	D
$r(m,\cdot)$	1	1	0	0

WINNER
Hillary
Donald

UWINNER

$\mathbf{T}^2$				
T_1	D	T	B	H
T_2	H	D	T	B
T_3	D	H	T	B
T_4	D	B	T	H
T_5	B	H	T	D
$r(m,\cdot)$	1	1	0	0

WINNER
Donald

UWINNER
Donald

(a) Complete voting profiles $\mathbf{T}^1 = (T^1_1, \dots, T^1_5)$, $\mathbf{T}^2 = (T^2_1, \dots, T^2_5)$ over the candidates Bernie, Donald, Hillary and Ted, together with corresponding sets of winners and unique winners. Candidates are denoted by the first letter of their name (e.g., D for Donald); the order is from left to right, the leftmost being the most preferred.

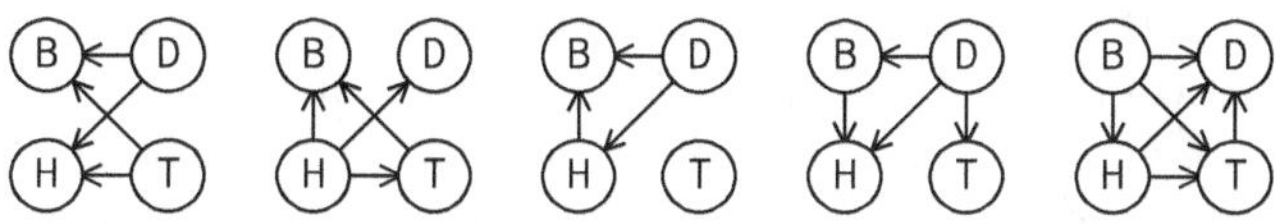

P_1 P_2 P_3 P_4 P_5

(b) A partial voting profile $\mathbf{P} = (P_1, \dots, P_5)$; an edge $c \to d$ denotes that c is preferred to d.

Cand		
name	party	birth
Bernie	D	1941
Donald	D	1947
Hillary	R	1946
Ted	R	1970

Donate		
donor	type	cand
Soros	indv	Hillary
Trump	indv	Donald
UAPE	PAC	Hillary
UAPE	PAC	Ted
Wilks	indv	Ted

Position		
cand	issue	pos
Hillary	TPP	yes
Donald	TPP	no
Bernie	TPP	no
Ted	TPP	no
Hillary	PPACA	yes
Donald	PPACA	no
Bernie	PPACA	yes
Ted	PPACA	no

(c) A database D over a schema $\mathcal{S}$

Figure 1: Examples of profiles, a partial profile, and a database. Viewed bottom up, this an example of an election database $(D, \mathbf{P})$ and two expansions $D \sqcup \mathbf{T}^1$ and $D \sqcup \mathbf{T}^2$.

A *positional scoring rule* r is a function that maps every number m to a *scoring vector* $(r(m,1), \dots, r(m,m))$ of natural numbers, called the *score values*, such that $r(m,1) \geq r(m,2) \ldots \geq r(m,m)$. Here, m is the number of candidates and $r(m,j)$ is the score that a candidate is awarded whenever she is at the jth position of a voter. We denote by $r(\cdot,m)$ the vector $(r(1,m), \dots, r(m,m))$. Suppose that $\mathbf{T} = (T_1, \dots, T_n)$ is a complete voting profile. The score $s(T_i, c)$ of a candidate c on T_i is the value $r(m,j)$ where j is the position of candidate c in T_i. When the positional scoring rule r is applied to $\mathbf{T} = (T_1, \dots, T_n)$, it assigns to each candidate c the sum $\sum_{i=1}^{n} s(T_i, c)$ as the *score* of c. A candidate is a *winner* if her score is greater or equal to the score of all candidates. Consequently, a candidate is a *unique winner* if her score is strictly greater than that of all other candidates. We now give several examples of well known positional scoring rules.

- The *plurality* rule $(1, 0, \dots, 0)$, where the winners are the candidates that voters most frequently rank first.
- The k-*approval* rule $(1, \dots, 1, 0, \dots, 0)$ that starts with k ones and then 0's, where the winners are the candidates that voters most frequently rank among the top k.
- The *veto* rule $(1, \dots, 1, 0)$, where the winners are the candidates that voters least frequently rank last.
- The k-*veto* rule that starts with 1's and ends with k zeros, where the winners are the candidates that voters least frequently rank among the bottom k.
- The *Borda* rule $(m-1, m-2, \dots, 0)$, where the score of a candidate is the position itself minus 1 in reverse order.

We assume that the scoring rule r is such that the score values $r(m,i)$ are computable in polynomial time in m. Hence, $\mathbf{W}(r,\mathbf{T})$ and $\mathbf{U}(r,\mathbf{T})$ are also computable in polynomial time in the size of T. To avoid trivialities, we assume that every $r(\cdot,m)$ contains at least two different score values, that is, $r(m,1) > r(m,m)$ holds for all $m > 1$. It follows that $\mathbf{W}(r,\mathbf{T})$ is always nonempty, while $\mathbf{U}(r,\mathbf{T})$ is either a singleton or the empty set (the latter is the case when $|\mathbf{W}(r,\mathbf{T})| > 1$). We also assume that for all $m > 1$, the score values in $r(\cdot,m)$ are co-prime numbers (i.e., their biggest common divisor is 1), since multiplying all score values by the same number has no impact on the outcome of the rule.

The rule r is *pure* if for every $m \geq 2$, the scoring vector $r(\cdot,m)$ is obtained from $r(\cdot,m-1)$ by inserting a score value at some position. All aforementioned positional scoring rules (plurality, k-approval, veto, k-veto, and Borda) are pure.

Example 2.1. Our running example is taken from the 2016 US presidential elections. There are four candidates, *Bernie*, *Donald*, *Hillary*, and *Ted*, and five voters. Figure 1a shows two voting profiles $\mathbf{T}^1$ and $\mathbf{T}^2$, each consisting of five linear orders (presented as sequences) over the candidates. (The other parts of Figure 1 will be discussed later on.) The positional scoring rule is 2-approval (which, in this case, is also 2-veto), and it is shown below each profile. The scores of the candidates *Bernie, Donald, Hillary,* and *Ted* in $\mathbf{T}^1$ are, respectively, 2, 3, 3 and 2. Hence, $\mathbf{W}(r, \mathbf{T}^1)$ consists of Donald and Hillary, while $\mathbf{U}(r, \mathbf{T}^1)$ is empty since there is no unique winner. In $\mathbf{T}^2$, the scores of these candidates are, respectively, 2, 4, 3 and 1; thus, $\mathbf{W}(r, \mathbf{T}^2)$ consists of just Donald. Since Donald is the unique winner, we have that $\mathbf{U}(t, \mathbf{T}^2)$ also consists of Donald. □

2.3 Partial Profiles

Often, our knowledge about the voter preference is only partial. Missing information in preferences is commonly modeled using a *partial order*, that is, a relation $\succeq$ that is reflexive, ($a \succeq a$), transitive, ($a \succeq b$ and $b \succeq c$ imply $a \succeq c$), and antisymmetric, ($a \succeq b$ and $b \succeq a$ imply $a = b$), but not necessarily total (it may be the case that neither $a \succeq b$ nor $b \succeq a$ holds). A *completion* of a partial order is a total order that extends that partial order. A partial order may have exponentially many completions.

A *partial voting profile* is a tuple $\mathbf{P} = (P_1, \dots, P_n)$, where each P_i is a partial order of the set C of candidates, representing the partial ranking (partial preference) of voter v_j on the candidates. A *completion* of a partial voting profile $\mathbf{P} = (P_1, \dots, P_n)$ is a complete voting profile $\mathbf{T} = (T_1, \dots, T_n)$ such that each T_i is a completion of the partial order P_i. The notions of *possible* and *necessary* winners were introduced by Konczak and Lang [21].

Let r be a voting rule and $\mathbf{P}$ a partial voting profile.

- The set $\mathrm{PW}(r, \mathbf{P})$ of the *possible winners* with respect to (w.r.t.) r and $\mathbf{P}$ is the union of the sets $\mathbf{W}(r, \mathbf{T})$, where $\mathbf{T}$ varies over all completions of $\mathbf{P}$.
- The set $\mathrm{NW}(r, \mathbf{P})$ of the *necessary winners* w.r.t. r and $\mathbf{P}$ is the intersection of the sets $\mathbf{W}(r, \mathbf{T})$, where $\mathbf{T}$ varies over all completions of $\mathbf{P}$.
- The set $\mathrm{PU}(r, \mathbf{P})$ of the *possible unique winners* w.r.t. r and $\mathbf{P}$ is the union of the sets $\mathbf{U}(r, \mathbf{T})$, where $\mathbf{T}$ varies over all completions of $\mathbf{P}$.
- The set $\mathrm{NU}(r, \mathbf{P})$ of the *necessary unique winners* w.r.t. r and $\mathbf{P}$ is the intersection of the sets $\mathbf{U}(r, \mathbf{T})$, where $\mathbf{T}$ varies over all completions of $\mathbf{P}$.

In other words, a candidate c is a possible winner (respectively, a possible unique winner) with respect to r and $\mathbf{P}$ if c is a winner (respectively, a unique winner) in at least one completion $\mathbf{T}$ of $\mathbf{P}$. Also, c is a necessary winner (respectively, a necessary unique winner) with respect to r and $\mathbf{P}$ if c is a winner (respectively, a unique winner) in every completion $\mathbf{T}$ of $\mathbf{P}$. Observe that $\mathrm{NW}(r, \mathbf{P})$, $\mathrm{PU}(r, \mathbf{P})$ and $\mathrm{NU}(r, \mathbf{P})$ can be empty, but $\mathrm{PW}(r, \mathbf{P})$ is never empty (since every completion has at least one winner). Moreover, there can be any number of *possible* unique winners, but there can be at most one *necessary* unique winner.

Example 2.2. Continuing our running example, Figure 1b depicts a partial voting profile $\mathbf{P}$ that consists of five partial orders of the five voters (represented as directed acyclic graphs) over the four candidates. It is easy to verify that both $\mathbf{T}^1$ and $\mathbf{T}^2$ in Figure 1a are completions of $\mathbf{P}$.

From the discussion in Example 2.1, we conclude that Donald and Hillary are both possible winners. Note that there is a completion in which Ted is a winner (e.g., Ted gets a unit score value from the first four voters), and, in fact, the unique winner. Bernie, however, cannot win in any completion. To see this, observe that he must be ranked no higher than third by the first three voters (so, gets a zero score from these voters), thus the maximum score he can get is 2. Among the ten units granted by the five voters, at least one candidate must get a score of 3, and therefore, will surpass Bernie. Via a similar reasoning, we conclude that the maximum score that Hillary can get is 3, and hence, it is impossible for her to be the single winner (since there is always another candidate with 3 or more units). Thus, Hillary is a possible winner, but not a possible *unique* winner.

Finally, we observe that for every one of the four candidates, there is a completion where the candidate does not win. (In particular, $\mathbf{T}^2$ provides such an example for every candidate other than Donald, so it remains to find one just for Donald.) Therefore, no candidate is a necessary winner.

In conclusion, it holds that

- $\mathrm{NW}(r, \mathbf{P}) = \mathrm{NU}(r, \mathbf{P}) = \emptyset$;
- $\mathrm{PW}(r, \mathbf{P}) = \{\text{Donald, Hillary, Ted}\}$;
- $\mathrm{PU}(r, \mathbf{P}) = \{\text{Donald, Ted}\}$. □

On the face of the definitions, computing possible and necessary (unique or not) winners requires exponential time since a partial order may have exponentially many completions. There is a substantial body of research on the computational complexity of the necessary and the possible winners for a variety of voting rules. The following *complete* classification of the complexity for *all* pure positional scoring rules was obtained through the work of Konczak and Lang [21], Xia and Conitzer [27], Betzler and Dorn [4], and Baumeister and Rothe [3].

Theorem 2.3. [Classification Theorem] *Let r be a pure positional scoring rule.*

(1) *If r is the plurality rule or the veto rule, then there is a polynomial-time algorithm for computing* $\mathrm{PW}(r, \mathbf{P})$ *and* $\mathrm{PU}(r, \mathbf{P})$, *given a partial voting profile* $\mathbf{P}$. *Otherwise, the following two problems are NP-complete: given a partial voting profile* $\mathbf{P}$ *and a candidate c, determine whether* $c \in \mathrm{PW}(r, \mathbf{P})$, *and determine whether* $c \in \mathrm{PU}(r, \mathbf{P})$.
(2) *There is a polynomial-time algorithm for computing both* $\mathrm{NW}(r, \mathbf{P})$ *and* $\mathrm{NU}(r, \mathbf{P})$, *given a partial voting profile* $\mathbf{P}$.

Put Theorem 2.3 differently, it is NP-hard to compute the possible winners for all pure positional scoring rules, with the exception of plurality and veto where the possible winners can be found in polynomial time. In contrast, the necessary winners can be computed in polynomial time for every pure positional scoring rule; in fact, this tractability result holds for *every* positional scoring rule (pure or not) [27].

3 ELECTION DATABASES

Here, we review the framework of Kimelfeld, Kolaitis, and Stoyanovich [20] that brings together computational social choice and relational databases. The aim is to have a unifying setting for analyzing partial voting profiles in the context of a database that holds information about candidates, voters, and issues.

Informally, an *election database* consists of a partial profile **P** and a database D that provides contextual information about the candidates (and beyond), as illustrated in Figure 1.[1] If r is a voting rule, then each completion **T** of **P** gives rise to an *expansion* of D obtained by augmenting D with the unary relations $\mathbf{W}(r, \mathbf{T})$ and $\mathbf{U}(r, \mathbf{T})$ of the winners and unique winners.

We now give the precise definition of an election database.

Let $\mathcal{S}$ be a schema and let WINNER and UWINNER be two new unary relation symbols that will be interpreted by the set of the winners and the set of unique winners, respectively. Let $\mathcal{S}^e$ be the schema obtained by augmenting $\mathcal{S}$ with these two unary relation symbols, that is, $\mathcal{S}^e = \mathcal{S} \cup \{\text{WINNER}, \text{UWINNER}\}$.

Definition 3.1 (Election Database). An *election database* over a schema $\mathcal{S}$ is a pair $(D, \mathbf{P})$, where D is a database over $\mathcal{S}$ and **P** is a partial voting profile. Let r be a voting rule. Each completion **T** of **P** gives rise to an *expansion* $D \sqcup \mathbf{T}$ of $(D, \mathbf{P})$ under r such that:

- $D \sqcup \mathbf{T}$ is a database over the relational schema $\mathcal{S}^e = \mathcal{S} \cup \{\text{WINNER}, \text{UWINNER}\}$;
- $R^{D \sqcup \mathbf{T}} = R^D$, for every relation symbol R of $\mathcal{S}$;
- $\text{WINNER}^{D \sqcup \mathbf{T}} = \mathbf{W}(r, \mathbf{T})$;
- $\text{UWINNER}^{D \sqcup \mathbf{T}} = \mathbf{U}(r, \mathbf{T})$.

Example 3.2. The schema $\mathcal{S}$ of our running example consists of the relation symbols *Cand, Position* and *Donate* that are instantiated in the database D of Figure 1c. The *Cand* relation includes information about the candidates (e.g., Bernie was born in 1941 and is currently with the Democratic Party), the *Position* relation contains the positions of the candidates on issues (e.g., Hillary supports the *Trans-Pacific Partnership* (TPP), and Donald opposes the *Patient Protection and Affordable Care Act* (PPACA), known as *Obamacare*), and the *Donate* relation contains information about donations to candidate (e.g., the individual Soros donated to Hillary, while the political action committee (PAC) UAPE donated to Ted). Combined with the partial profile **P** described in the figure (and discussed in Example 2.2), we get the election database $(D, \mathbf{P})$.

Recall the completions $\mathbf{T}^1$ and $\mathbf{T}^2$ of Figure 1a. Shown to the right of each completion are the WINNER and UWINNER relations of the corresponding expansion. In $\mathbf{T}^1$, the UWINNER relation is empty, since the winners are Donald and Hillary. Yet, in $\mathbf{T}^2$, the WINNER and UWINNER relations are the same, since there is a unique winner (namely, Donald). □

3.1 Necessary and Possible Answers

Next, we recall the definitions of the necessary and possible query answers from [20]. Let $\mathcal{S}$ be an schema, $(D, \mathbf{P})$ an election database, q a query over $\mathcal{S}^e$, and r a voting rule. Let **a** be a tuple of constants of arity $ar(q)$.

- We say that a tuple **a** is a *possible answer* if $\mathbf{a} \in q(D \sqcup \mathbf{T})$ for some expansion $D \sqcup \mathbf{T}$.
- We say that a tuple **a** is a *necessary answer* if $\mathbf{a} \in q(D \sqcup \mathbf{T})$ for every expansion $D \sqcup \mathbf{T}$.

In terms of data complexity, the problem of computing the possible and necessary answers of CQs and UCQs amounts to the evaluation of Boolean queries.

Definition 3.3 (Possibility/Necessity Problem). Let $\mathcal{S}$ be a schema, q a Boolean query over $\mathcal{S}^e$ and r a voting rule.

- Possibility(q, r) is the following decision problem: given $(D, \mathbf{P})$, is q possibly true (i.e., does $D \sqcup \mathbf{T} \models q$ for some expansion $D \sqcup \mathbf{T}$ of $(D, \mathbf{P})$)?
- Necessity(q, r) is the following decision problem: given $(D, \mathbf{P})$, is q necessarily true (i.e., does $D \sqcup \mathbf{T} \models q$ for every expansion $D \sqcup \mathbf{T}$ of $(D, \mathbf{P})$)?

Example 3.4. We now illustrate queries. For a candidate c, the following query asks whether c is a winner.

$$q_c() \text{ :- } \text{WINNER}(c) \qquad (1)$$

In particular, q_c is possible if and only if c is a possible winner, and q_c is necessary if and only if c is a necessary winner.

The following queries apply to our running example (Figure 1). The next one asks whether there is a Republican winner. (We use the convention of an underscore instead of a variable with a single occurrence.)

$$q_1() \text{ :- } \text{WINNER}(x)\,,\ Cand(x, \mathsf{R}, \_)$$

Hence, Possibility(q_1, r) asks whether it is possible to have a Republican winner, and Necessity(q_1, r) asks whether we necessarily have a Republican winner. As explained in Example 2.2, in every completion it is the case that either

[1] The information in the figure is taken from Diffen (https://www.diffen.com) and The New York Times (https://www.nytimes.com/interactive/2016/us/elections/top-presidential-donors-campaign-money.html).

Donald or Ted are winners. Hence, in the running example, both Possibility(q_1, r) and Necessity(q_1, r) are true. The next query asks whether there is a unique winner who is also a Republican.

$$q_1'() \text{ :- } \text{UWINNER}(x)\,,\ \mathit{Cand}(x, \mathsf{R}, \_)$$

As shown in Figure 1a, it Donald is a possible unique winner, and hence, Possibility(q, r) is true. However, Necessity(q, r) is false, simply because there is an expansion in which the UWINNER relation is empty (i.e., there are no unique winners).

The following query asks whether there are two winners who disagree on Obamacare.

$$q_2() \text{ :- } \mathit{Position}(x, \mathsf{PPACA}, \mathsf{yes})\,,\ \mathit{Position}(y, \mathsf{PPACA}, \mathsf{no})\,,\ \text{WINNER}(x)\,,\ \text{WINNER}(y)$$

Possibility(q_2, r) is true as witnessed by the completion T^1 in Figure 1a, while Necessity(q_2, r) is false due to T^2.

Finally, the following query asks whether there are two winners, one Democratic and one Republican, who get donations from the same source.

$$q_3() \text{ :- } \mathit{Cand}(x, \mathsf{R}, \_)\,,\ \mathit{Cand}(y, \mathsf{D}, \_),\ \text{WINNER}(x)\,,\ \text{WINNER}(y)\,,\ \mathit{Donate}(z, \_, x)\,,\ \mathit{Donate}(z, \_, y)$$

It is possible to build a completion where both Hillary and Ted (who both receive donations from UAPE) are winners, hence, Possibility(q_3, r) is true; moreover, both completions of Figure 1a witness that Necessity(q_3, r) is false. □

Example 3.5. For every positive integer k, let q^k_{wr} be the following Boolean conjunctive query:

$$q^k_{\mathrm{wr}}() \text{ :- } \text{WINNER}(x_1), \ldots, \text{WINNER}(x_k), R(x_1, \ldots, x_k) \quad (2)$$

This query asks whether there is a sequence of k winners that constitutes a tuple of R.

In the remainder of the paper, we will make repeated use of the family of the queries q^k_{wr}, $k \geq 1$. □

Note that a query q over $\mathcal{S}^{\mathrm{e}}$ may involve both the WINNER and UWINNER relation symbols. When q is a UCQ, we use the terms WINNER *atoms* and UWINNER *atoms* to refer to atoms that involve, respectively, the WINNER and the UWINNER relation symbol. In the sections that follow, we investigate the complexity of the decision problems Possibility(q, r) and Necessity(q, r), where q is a Boolean UCQ.

We note that other notions of databases and queries over partial orders have been studied [1, 14, 18], but none of them involves elections or social choice.

4 QUERIES WITH WINNER ATOMS: POSSIBLE ANSWERS

Next, we investigate the complexity of computing the possible answers for UCQs that involve WINNER atoms only (but no UWINNER atoms). Thus, in what follows in this section, we make the blanket assumption that the term UCQ refers to a union of conjunctive queries whose atoms are WINNER atoms or atoms with relation symbols from the schema $\mathcal{S}$.

4.1 Tractability

According to Theorem 2.3, the possible winners can be computed in polynomial time when the positional scoring rule is plurality or veto. In the remainder of this section, we show that this tractability result extends to the possible answers of every UCQ (and beyond).

To establish tractability for plurality and veto, we use the tractability of a polygamous version of the perfect-matching problem. This problem is a special case of generalizations of perfect matching that are known to be in polynomial time [12, 25]. This special case has a simple proof, which we now give to make the subsequent results as self-contained as possible.

Definition 4.1 (Polygamous Matching). Polygamous Matching is the following decision problem: Given a bipartite graph $G = (V \cup U, E)$ and natural numbers $\alpha_u \leq \beta_u$ for all $u \in U$, is there a subset of E where each $v \in V$ is incident to exactly one edge and every $u \in U$ is incident to at least α_u edges and at most β_u edges?

PROPOSITION 4.2. *Polygamous Matching is solvable in polynomial time.*

PROOF. We reduce Polygamous Matching to the problem of determining whether a *perfect* matching exists (which is solvable in polynomial time, e.g., via the Hungarian algorithm or maximum network flows). Given an input G, α, β to Polygamous Matching, we construct a bipartite graph $G' = (V' \cup U', E')$ as follows. We obtain U' from U by replacing every node u with β_u distinct *copies* of u. The set V' is the union of V and a set of $|U'| - |V|$ of new *dummy* nodes. (If $|U'| < |V|$, then no polygamous matching exists.) Next, we construct E' by considering every node $u \in U$ and connecting all its copies in U' to the all the neighbors $v \in V$ that u has in g; in addition, we connect $\beta_u - \alpha_u$ of the copies of u to all the dummy nodes in V'. The reader can verify that G is a "yes" instance of Polygamous Matching if and only if G' has a perfect matching. In particular, to obtain a polygamous matching from a perfect matching M of G', we take all edges (v, u) such that $v \in V$ and M connects v to a copy of u. □

We will also use the following lemma, which we prove using Proposition 4.2. Hereafter, we will denote by $\min(v)$ the set of candidates c that the voter v does not prefer to any other candidate (hence, such a c can be last in a completion), and by $\max(v)$ the set of candidates c that are not preceded by any other voter (hence, such a c can be first in a completion).

Lemma 4.3. *Let r be the plurality rule or the veto rule. Then the following problem is solvable in polynomial time: Given a set C of candidates, a partial profile* $\mathbf{P}$ *over C, and a subset $S \subseteq C$, is there a completion* $\mathbf{T}$ *such that $S \subseteq \mathbf{W}(r, \mathbf{T})$?*

Proof. We begin with the plurality rule. We solve the problem by considering every possible score $s = 1, \dots, n$ (where n is the number of voters), and test whether there is a completion $\mathbf{T}$ such that every candidate in S gains *precisely* s votes, and every candidate outside of S gains *at most* s votes. If the answer is true for at least one s, we return true; otherwise, we return false.

So, the question at hand is whether we can assign to each voter one of her top candidates so that every candidate in S is assigned to precisely s voters, and every candidate outside of S is assigned to at most s voters. This problem is a special case of Polygamous Matching (Definition 4.1), where

- V is the set of voters,
- U is the set of candidates,
- E connects c and v, whenever $c \in \max(v)$,
- $\alpha_u = \beta_u = s$, for every $u \in S$,
- $\alpha_u = 0$ and $\beta_u = s$, for every $u \in C \setminus S$.

We then conclude the proof via Proposition 4.2.

For the veto rule, the proof is analogous. Here, the question is whether we can assign to each voter one of her *bottom* candidates so that every candidate in S is assigned to precisely $n - s$ voters, and every candidate outside of S is assigned to *at least* $n - s$ voters. In particular, V and U are the same as in the case of plurality; furthermore,

- E connects c and v whenever $c \in \min(v)$,
- $\alpha_u = \beta_u = n - s$, for every $u \in S$,
- $\alpha_u = n - s$ and $\beta_u = n$, for every $u \in C \setminus S$.

This concludes the proof. □

We can now prove the main result for this section.

Theorem 4.4. *Let r be the plurality rule or the veto rule. If q is a Boolean UCQ, then* Possibility(q, r) *is solvable in polynomial time.*

Proof. Consider an input $(D, \mathbf{P})$ of Possibility(q, r). Then q is possible for $(D, \mathbf{P})$ if and only if one of its CQs is possible for $(D, \mathbf{P})$; thus, we can solve the problem separately for each CQ of q. So, we will assume that q is a CQ (i.e., it has one disjunct) to begin with.

Let $adom(D)$ be the active domain of D (i.e., the set of constants that occur in relations in D, let C be the set of candidates, and let $\tau(q)$ be the set of variables and constants that occur in q. By a *potential homomorphism*, we refer to a mapping $\mu : \tau(q) \rightarrow adom(D) \cup C$ that satisfies the following conditions:

(1) $\mu(t) = t$, whenever t is a constant;
(2) μ maps every non-Winner fact to a fact of D;
(3) $\mu(t) \in C$, whenever t occurs in a Winner atom (i.e., the atom Winner(t)) of q.

Then q is possible for $(D, \mathbf{P})$ if and only if there is a potential homomorphism μ and a completion $\mathbf{T}$ of $\mathbf{P}$ such that $\mu(t)$ is a winner for every term t of the third condition. More formally, for a potential homomorphism μ, let us denote by $W(\mu)$ the set of all candidates $\mu(t)$ such that t occurs in a Winner atom. Then, for a completion $\mathbf{T}$ of $\mathbf{P}$, we have that μ is a homomorphism from q to $D \sqcup \mathbf{T}$ (hence, $D \sqcup \mathbf{T} \models q$) if and only if $W(\mu) \subseteq \mathbf{W}(r, \mathbf{T})$.

In view of the above, the algorithm simply constructs all possible μ (in polynomial time) and, for each μ, tests whether there exists a completion $\mathbf{T}$ such that $W(\mu) \subseteq \mathbf{W}(r, \mathbf{T})$. By Lemma 4.3, this test can be carried out in polynomial time. □

We remark that the proof of Theorem 4.4 can be extended to the generalization of UCQs in which negated atoms are allowed. For example, if r is the plurality rule or the veto rule, then Possibility(q, r) is solvable in polynomial time, where q is the query that tests whether there are a winner and a loser both of whom are funded by the same PAC, i.e.,

$$q_4() \text{ :- } \mathit{Donate}(z, \mathsf{PAC}, x)\,,\ \mathit{Donate}(z, \mathsf{PAC}, y)$$
$$\textsc{Winner}(x)\,,\ \neg\textsc{Winner}(y)$$

4.2 Hardness

Let r be a voting rule and let q be a UCQ. To determine whether Possibility(q, r) is true, we need to, at least, be able to determine whether a candidate is a possible winner. Indeed, the possible-winner problem (i.e., determine whether a given candidate c is a possible winner in a given partial profile) is simply Possibility(q_c, r), where q_c is the query defined in (1). Theorem 2.3 implies that Possibility(q_c, r) is NP-hard, for every pure positional scoring rule other than plurality and veto (and regardless of the relational schema $\mathcal{S}$). Clearly, Possibility(q_c, r) reduces to the problem Possibility(q, r) for the query $q() \text{ :- } \textsc{Winner}(x), R(x)$, which we refer to as q^1_{wr} in Equation (2). In fact, it is an easy observation that Possibility(q_c, r) reduces to Possibility(q^k_{wr}, r) for every $k > 0$. Thus, Possibility(q^k_{wr}, r) is NP-hard, for every $k > 0$.

5 QUERIES WITH WINNER ATOMS: NECESSARY ANSWERS

In this section, we analyze the complexity of the necessity problem for CQs and UCQs that involve Winner atoms (but no UWinner atoms). Thus, we continue to make the blanket assumption that the term UCQ refers to a union of conjunctive queries whose atoms are Winner atoms or atoms with relation symbols from the schema $\mathcal{S}$.

Table 1: The complexity of Necessity(q^k_{wr}, r)**, where** q^k_{wr} **is defined in Equation** (2) **(Example 3.5).**

k	*Complexity*	*Reference*
1	P for veto, plurality; coNP-c. for all other pure pos. rules	Theorem 5.3, Proposition 5.4
>1	coNP-c. for all pure pos. rules	Theorem 5.6
>2	coNP-c. for all pos. rules	Theorem 5.7

Let c be a candidate and let q_c be the CQ

$$q_c() \text{ :- } \textsc{Winner}(c).$$

Theorem 2.3 implies that Necessity(q_c, r) is solvable in polynomial time for every pure positional scoring rule r, Indeed, Necessity(q_c, r) asks whether c is a necessary winner. In this section, we explore the boundaries of the combinations of r and q that have a tractable necessity testing. For that, we will refer to the CQs q^k_{wr} defined in Equation (2). Our results for these queries are summarized in Table 1.

5.1 Tractability

We begin with tractability results. Towards the main result of this part, we first consider the conjunctive query q^1_{wr} in Equation (2). Kimelfeld, Kolaitis, and Stoyanovich [20] showed that if r is the plurality rule, then Necessity(q^1_{wr}, r) is solvable in polynomial time. The next lemma shows that this tractability result also holds true when r is the veto rule.

Lemma 5.1. *If r is the veto rule, then* Necessity(q^1_{wr}, r) *is solvable in polynomial time.*

Proof. Consider an input $(D, \mathbf{P})$ to Necessity(q^1_{wr}, r). We solve Necessity(q^1_{wr}, r) by searching for a counterexample, that is, a completion where a candidate outside R^D beats every candidate inside R^D. Recall that, in the veto rule, the score that a candidate c gains is $n - k$, where n is the number of voters and k is the number of voters who position c last. So, we consider every $c \in C \setminus R^D$ and $k \in \{0, \dots, n-1\}$, and search for a completion of $\mathbf{P}$ in which c gains a score of at least $n-k$ and each $c' \in R^D$ gains a score of at most $n-k-1$; in other words, at most k voters position c last, and at least $k+1$ voters position c' last, for every $c' \in R^D$.

So, we fix c and k. Recall that, for a voter v, we denote by $\min(v)$ the set of candidates c that v can position last (i.e., v does not prefer c to any other candidate). We reduce the problem to Polygamous Matching (Definition 4.1), which is solvable in polynomial time (Proposition 4.2). In our construction, V is the set of voters, U is the set of candidates, and $E = \{(v, d) \mid d \in min(v)\}$. We set the bounds as follows.

- $\alpha_c = 0$ and $\beta_c = k$;
- $\alpha_{c'} = k+1$ and $\beta_{c'} = n$, for all $c' \in R^D$;

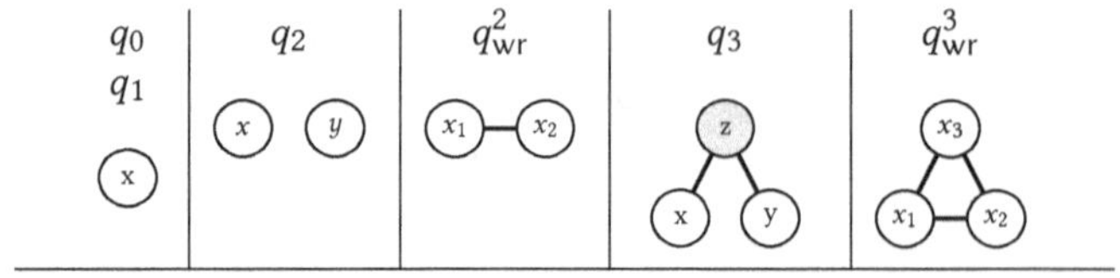

Figure 2: The Gaifman graphs of the queries from Examples 3.4 and 3.5. All the variables are Winner variables, except for the shaded z**.**

- $\alpha_{c''} = 0$ and $\beta_{c''} = n$, for all other candidates c''.

In the construction, selecting an edge (v, d) means that v positions d last. Hence, we get a "yes" instance if and only if there is a completion $\mathbf{T}$ of $\mathbf{P}$ in which the score of c is at least $n-k$ and the score of every $c' \in R^D$ is at most $n-k-1$. □

The main tractability result of this section is Theorem 5.3 below, which generalizes both Lemma 5.1 and the tractability results in [20] for the plurality rule and for UCQs in which every CQ has *pairwise disconnected* Winner atoms in its *Gaifman graph.* As is well known, the notion of the Gaifman graph plays an important role in finite model theory (see [22]). In this graph, the nodes are the variables of the CQ and the edges consist of pairs of variables occurring in the same atom. As an example, Figure 2 depicts the Gaifman graphs of the specific CQs that we mentioned so far (Examples 3.4 and 3.5). A variable x that occurs in a Winner atom Winner(x) is called a Winner *variable.* We say that the Winner atoms are *pairwise disconnected* if every two distinct Winner variables belong to different connected components of the Gaifman graph.

Example 5.2. As can be seen in Figure 2, the Winner atoms of the queries q_0, q_1 and q_2 from Example 3.4 are (pairwise) disconnected, but those of q_3 are not. In particular, this property is shared by every CQ with a single Winner atom, such as q^1_{wr} of Equation 2. In contrast, the property does not hold for the queries q^2_{wr} and q^3_{wr} in the figure. □

Theorem 5.3 concerns the class of UCQs such that each of their CQs has pairwise disconnected Winner atoms. An example of such a UCQ is the following query that asks whether there exist two winners who belong to different major parties and who disagree on the Trans-Pacific Partnership issue.

$$\big(\textsc{Winner}(x)\,,\ \mathit{Cand}(x, \mathsf{R}, \_)\,,\ \mathit{Position}(x, \mathsf{TPP}, \mathsf{yes})$$
$$\textsc{Winner}(y)\,,\ \mathit{Cand}(y, \mathsf{D}, \_)\,,\ \mathit{Position}(y, \mathsf{TPP}, \mathsf{no})\big) \bigcup$$
$$\big(\textsc{Winner}(x)\,,\ \mathit{Cand}(x, \mathsf{R}, \_)\,,\ \mathit{Position}(x, \mathsf{TPP}, \mathsf{no})$$
$$\textsc{Winner}(y)\,,\ \mathit{Cand}(y, \mathsf{D}, \_)\,,\ \mathit{Position}(y, \mathsf{TPP}, \mathsf{yes})\big)$$

Theorem 5.3. *Let q be a UCQ such that the* Winner *atoms of each of its CQs are pairwise disconnected. If r is plurality or veto, then* Necessity(q, r) *is solvable in polynomial time.*

Proof. Let q be $q_1 \cup \cdots \cup q_\ell$, and consider an input $(D, \mathbf{P})$ to Necessity(q, r). We first make and justify some structural assumptions about q. For $i = 1, \ldots, \ell$, if q_i does not involve *any* Winner atom, then either $D \models q_i$ and then q is necessarily true on $(D, \mathbf{P})$, or $D \not\models q_i$ and then we can remove q_i from q without affecting the truth of q over the expansions. Therefore, we will assume that each q_i includes at least one Winner atom. We also assume that no q_i contains two identical Winner atoms (with the same Winner variable or constant), since we can clearly remove copies of atoms from a CQ while preserving equivalence.

With the above assumptions, we will assume that each q_i has the form

$$q_i() \text{ :- } \varphi_i^1 \wedge \cdots \wedge \varphi_i^{k_i},$$

where each φ_i^j is a conjunction of atoms that includes precisely one Winner atom, and no variable is shared among two φ_i^j. We can make this assumption since the Winner atoms of q_i are pairwise disconnected. Hence, an expansion $D \sqcup \mathbf{T}$ satisfies q_i if and only if $D \sqcup \mathbf{T}$ satisfies each φ_i^j independently.

It thus follows that a counterexample to Necessity(q, r) is a completion $\mathbf{T}$ of $\mathbf{P}$ such that the expansion $D \sqcup \mathbf{T}$ violates at least one $\varphi_i^{j_i}$, for every $i = 1, \ldots, \ell$. So, we iterate through every combination $\varphi_1^{j_1}, \ldots, \varphi_\ell^{j_\ell}$ and test whether there exists a corresponding counterexample, that is, a completion $\mathbf{T}$ such that $D \sqcup \mathbf{T}$ violates *every* $\varphi_i^{j_i}$. If no such $\mathbf{T}$ is found, then q is necessarily true. So, fix $\varphi_1^{j_1}, \ldots, \varphi_\ell^{j_\ell}$. Recall that every $\varphi_i^{j_i}$ contains precisely one Winner atom. For $i = 1, \ldots, \ell$, let W_i be the set of candidates that satisfy $\varphi_i^{j_i}$, that is,

$$W_i \stackrel{\text{def}}{=} \{c \in C \mid D \cup \{\text{Winner}(c)\} \models \varphi_i^{j_i}\}.$$

Let $W = W_1 \cup \cdots \cup W_\ell$. The question at hand is whether there exists a completion $\mathbf{T}$ such that $\mathbf{W}(r, \mathbf{T})$ is *disjoint* from W. This is exactly the complement of the problem Necessity(q^1_{wr}, r) when the R relation is equal to W. Hence, the theorem follows from the tractability of Necessity(q^1_{wr}, r) when r is the plurality rule [20] and when r is the veto rule (Lemma 5.1). □

In the next section, we discuss hardness and, in particular, show that Theorem 5.3 covers *all* tractable cases of pure positional scoring rules.

5.2 Hardness

The next result asserts that if r is a pure positional scoring rule other than plurality and veto, the necessity problem is already hard for the query q^1_{wr}.

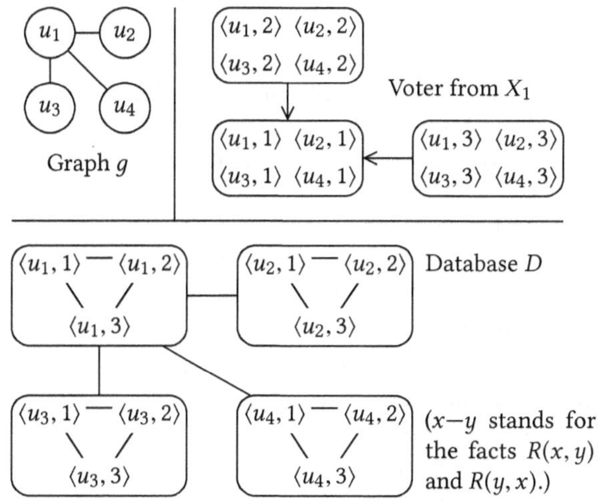

Figure 3: An illustration of the reduction in the proof of Lemma 5.5 for $k = 2$.

Proposition 5.4. Necessity(q^1_{wr}, r) *is coNP-complete for every pure positional scoring rule r other than plurality and veto.*

Proof. We exhibit a reduction from the complement of the *possible unique winner* problem: given a partial profile $\mathbf{P}$ and a candidate c, determine whether c is a possible unique winner. By Theorem 2.3, this problem is NP-complete for every pure positional scoring rule r other than plurality and veto. Given $\mathbf{P}$ and c, we construct the election database $(D, \mathbf{P})$, where D consists of a single unary relation $R^D = C \setminus \{c\}$. For a completion $\mathbf{T}$ of $\mathbf{P}$, we have that $D \sqcup \mathbf{T} \models q^1_{\text{wr}}$ if and only if $\mathbf{W}(r, \mathbf{T})$ includes a candidate other than c. Consequently, q^1_{wr} is necessary for $(D, \mathbf{P})$ if and only if c is *not* a possible unique winner in $\mathbf{P}$. □

By combining Theorem 5.3 and Proposition 5.4, we conclude that Necessity(q^1_{wr}, r) is tractable when r is plurality or veto, and intractable for every other pure positional scoring rule. Next, we show that the query q^2_{wr} is *harder* than q^1_{wr}, in the sense that q^2_{wr} is hard for *every* pure positional scoring rule, including plurality and veto. Hardness for plurality has been shown by Kimelfeld, Kolaitis, and Stoyanovich [20]. The next lemma completes the picture with the veto rule.

Lemma 5.5. *If r is the veto rule, then* Necessity(q^2_{wr}, r) *is coNP-complete.*

Proof. We exhibit a reduction from the complement of the *maximum independent set* problem. We are given as input a graph $G = (V, E)$ and a natural number k, and the goal is to determine whether G has an independent set of size k. We construct an instance $(D, \mathbf{P})$ of Necessity(q^2_{wr}, r), as illustrated in Figure 3. The partial voting profile $\mathbf{P}$ is defined as follows.

- The candidate set C consists of all pairs $\langle u, i\rangle$, where u is a node of G and $1 \leq i \leq k$. We partition C into *parties* $C_1, \dots, C_k$ such that $C_i = \{\langle u, i\rangle \mid u \in V\}$.
- There are $k \times (|V| - 1)$ voters. Let $X_1, \dots, X_k$ be a partitioning of the voters such that every X_i is of size $|V| - 1$.
- For $1 \leq i \leq k$, the voters in X_i have the same partial preference: they prefer every candidate in $C \setminus C_i$ to every candidate in C_i; there are no preferences within X_i and no preferences within $C \setminus X_i$.

The database D consists of one binary relation R^D that contains all candidate pairs $(\langle u, i\rangle, \langle u', i'\rangle)$ such that one of the following holds:

- $u = u'$ and $i \neq i'$;
- $u \neq u'$, but u is a neighbor of u' in g.

This concludes the construction. We complete the proof by proving correctness, that is, Necessity(q^2_{wr}, r) is false for $(D, \mathbf{P})$ if and only if G has an independent set of size k.

We observe that, in every completion $\mathbf{T}$ of $\mathbf{P}$, there are at least k winners. Indeed, only voters from C_i can veto (i.e., position as last) a candidate from X_i, and $|X_i| = |C_i| - 1$, and hence at least one candidate from C_i has no vetoes at all in $\mathbf{T}$. In particular, that candidate gets the highest possible score (namely, $k \times (|V| - 1)$) and must be a winner. We conclude that at least one candidates in C_i is a winner in $\mathbf{T}$, which proves the observation.

If G has an independent set $U = \{u'_1, \dots, u'_k\}$ of size k, then we construct a completion $\mathbf{T}$ of $\mathbf{P}$ as follows. For $1 \leq i \leq k$, every voter in X_i vetoes a unique candidate from $C_i \setminus \{\langle u'_i, i\rangle\}$. Then we have that, in $\mathbf{T}$, every candidate $\langle u'_i, i\rangle$ gains the maximum score $k \times (|V| - 1)$, since no candidate vetoes $\langle u'_i, i\rangle$. Every other candidate c gains the score of $k \times (|V| - 1) - 1$, since precisely one voter vetoed c. The winners in $\mathbf{T}$ are the $\langle u'_i, i\rangle$. Since no tuple in R^D contains two nodes among the $\langle u'_i, i\rangle$, we get that $D \sqcup \mathbf{T} \not\models q^2_{\text{wr}}$.

Next, suppose that $\mathbf{T}$ is a completion of $\mathbf{P}$ where $D \sqcup \mathbf{T} \not\models q^2_{\text{wr}}$. By the way we constructed R^D, the winners must correspond to different nodes in g, and no two nodes are neighbours. From the above observation, it follows that g has an independent set of size at least k. □

We then establish the following result.

Theorem 5.6. *If $k > 1$, then* Necessity(q^k_{wr}, r) *is coNP-complete, for every pure positional scoring rule r.*

Proof. We prove the theorem for $k = 2$. For $k > 2$, coNP-hardness is proved by reducing Necessity(q^2_{wr}, r) to the problem Necessity(q^k_{wr}, r). Kimelfeld, Kolaitis, and Stoyanovich [20] showed that Necessity(q^2_{wr}, r) is coNP-complete when r is the plurality rule. Lemma 5.5 shows that this is also the case when r is the veto rule. For the remaining positional rules, we reduce Necessity(q^1_{wr}, r) to Necessity(q^2_{wr}, r) and use Proposition 5.4. The reduction is simple: given an instance $(D, \mathbf{P})$ of Necessity(q^1_{wr}, r), construct an instance $(D', \mathbf{P})$ of Necessity(q^2_{wr}, r) by setting the relation $R^{D'}$ to be $\{(c, c) \mid c \in R^D\}$. □

If $k > 2$, then we can drop the assumption that the rule r is pure and establish a hardness result that is much stronger than that of Theorem 5.6. To the best of our knowledge, this is the first general hardness result that applies to *every* positional scoring rule, whether pure or not. The proof of this result will appear in the full version of this paper.

Theorem 5.7. *If $k > 2$, then* Necessity(q^k_{wr}, r) *is coNP-complete for every positional scoring rule.*

It remains an open problem to determine whether or not Theorem 5.7 holds true for $k = 2$, that is, whether Necessity(q^2_{wr}, r) is coNP-complete for every positional scoring rule, thus extending Theorem 5.6 to arbitrary positional scoring rules.

6 QUERIES WITH WINNER AND UNIQUE-WINNER ATOMS

In this section, we discuss the possibility and necessity problems for UCQs that involve UWinner atoms. Thus, in this section, the term UCQ refers to a union of conjunctive queries whose atoms are Winner atoms or UWinner atoms or atoms with relation symbols from the schema $\mathcal{S}$.

We begin with a simple observation. Consider a CQ q that contains one or more UWinner atom. For an expansion $D \sqcup \mathbf{T}$ to satisfy q, the relation UWinner$^{D\sqcup\mathbf{T}}$ should be nonempty. By the semantics of UWinner it must hold that UWinner$^{D\sqcup\mathbf{T}}$ = Winner$^{D\sqcup\mathbf{T}}$ = $\{c\}$ for some candidate c. Moreover, a homomorphism from q to $D \sqcup \mathbf{T}$ must assign all the terms (variables and constants) that occur in UWinner and Winner atoms the same value (the unique winner). Consequently, we can unify these terms in q. More formally, let Θ_q be the set of all the terms in the UWinner and Winner atoms of q.

- If Θ_q contains no constants, we select a variable $x \in \Theta_q$ and replace in q every $y \in \Theta_q$ with x.
- If Θ_q contains a single constant c, we replace in q every variable $y \in \Theta_q$ with c.
- If Θ_q contains two or more constants, q is not satisfiable (hence, if q is one of the CQs of a UCQ, then it can be removed by the UCQ while preserving equivalence.

Therefore, in the remainder of this section, we will assume that if a CQ q contains at least one UWinner atom, then it contains a single UWinner atom and no Winner atoms. We will use this assumption for analyzing the complexity of both the possibility and the necessity problems.

6.1 Possible Answers

The following theorem generalizes Theorem 4.4 to allowing UWinner atoms.

Theorem 6.1. *Let q be a Boolean UCQ (that may contain* Winner *and* UWinner *atoms). If r is the plurality rule or the veto rule, then* Possibility(q, r) *is solvable in polynomial time.*

Proof. Consider an input $(D, \mathbf{P})$ for Possibility(q, r). As in the proof of Theorem 4.4, we may assume that q is a CQ. In that proof, we have covered the case where q does not contain UWinner atom, so we assume that q contains UWinner atoms. In view of the discussion in the beginning of this section, we may assume that q contains a single UWinner atom and no Winner atoms.

For a candidate c, we denote by D_c the database over $\mathcal{S}^e$ where $R^{D_c} = R^D$ for every relation $R \in \mathcal{S}$ and $\text{UWinner}^{D_c} = \text{Winner}^{D_c} = \{c\}$. We have that a candidate c is a *possible unique winner* if and only if there is a completion $\mathbf{T}$ of $\mathbf{P}$ such that $D \sqcup \mathbf{T} = D_c$. Then, Possibility$(q, r)$ is true on $(D, \mathbf{P})$ if and only if q evaluates to true on D_c for some possible unique winner c. From Theorem 2.3, it follows that computing the set of possible unique winners, PU, can be done in polynomial time if r is the plurality rule or the veto rule. □

For the remaining pure positional scoring rules, the hardness of Possibility(q_c, r) and Possibility(q^k_{wr}, r) that we discussed in Section 4.2 continues to hold if we replace the Winner relation symbol with UWinner; this is because determining whether a candidate is a possible *unique* winner is also NP-hard (Theorem 2.3). On the other hand, consider the following query, which asks whether a winner exists.

$$q_{\exists\text{w}}() \;\text{:-}\; \text{Winner}(x)$$

The possibility (as well as necessity) of this query is trivial, as it is always true. Yet, as we show next, it becomes NP-hard for some voting rules if Winner is replaced with UWinner:

$$q_{\exists\text{uw}}() \;\text{:-}\; \text{UWinner}(x)$$

The problem Possibility$(q_{\exists\text{uw}}, r)$ asks whether there is a completion with a unique winner, which is now nontrivial. We can show NP-hardness for the case where r is the k-approval rule, for $k > 1$, by adapting the proof of Xia and Conitzer [27, Theorem 2] for the NP-hardness of the possible unique-winner problem.

Theorem 6.2. *For every $k > 1$, if r is the k-approval rule, then* Possibility$(q_{\exists\text{uw}}, r)$ *is NP-complete.*

Proof. Xia and Conitzer [27] prove that the problem of determining whether a candidate is a possible unique winner is NP-complete for k-approval, for every $k > 1$. They do so by building a reduction from 3-satisfiability. In more detail, given a propositional formula φ, they construct an instance $(\mathbf{P}, c)$ where φ is satisfiable if and only if c is a possible unique winner. In this construction, c is a necessary winner in $\mathbf{P}$. Hence, if there is *any* unique winner in a completion $\mathbf{T}$, then this unique winner must be c. Therefore, their reduction is also a reduction to the problem of whether a possible unique winner exists, that is, Possibility$(q_{\exists\text{uw}}, r)$. □

Recall that, by Theorem 6.1, we have a polynomial-time algorithm for Possibility$(q_{\exists\text{uw}}, r)$ when r is the plurality rule, i.e., when r is k-approval with $k = 1$; thus, the case of k-approval is settled for every $k \geq 1$. Nevertheless, the complexity of Possibility$(q_{\exists\text{uw}}, r)$ remains an open problem for every positional scoring rule other than k-approval and veto.

6.2 Necessary Answers

We now consider the necessity problem for UCQs that involve the UWinner relation symbol. Our result here is the tractability for the plurality and veto rules, where we generalize Theorem 5.3 to allow for arbitrary disjuncts (CQs) with UWinner atoms.

So, suppose that r is the plurality rule or the veto rule. Let us start with a conjunctive query q that contains a UWinner atom. As mentioned in the beginning of the section, we may assume that q contains a single UWinner atom and no Winner atoms. Given an input $(D, \mathbf{P})$, let U be the set of all candidates c such that $D \sqcup \mathbf{T} \models q$, whenever c is a unique winner. Then Necessity(q, r) is true if and only if Possibility(q', r) is false for $(D', \mathbf{P})$ where q' is defined by

$$q'() \;\text{:-}\; \big(\text{Winner}(x)\,,\ \text{Winner}(y)\,,\ R_{\neq}(x, y)\big) \cup \big(\text{Winner}(z)\,,\ R_{\bar{U}}(z)\big)$$

and D' consists of the fact $R_{\neq}(c_1, c_2)$ for all candidates c_1 and c_2 such that $c_1 \neq c_2$, and the fact $R_{\bar{U}}(c)$ for all candidates c that are *not* in U. Note that q' states that either there are two distinct winners (hence, UWinner is empty) or there is a winner that violates q. Theorem 6.1 implies that Possibility(q', r) is solvable in polynomial time, thus Necessity(q, r) is solvable in polynomial time. In fact, the following generalization of Theorem 5.3 shows a stronger result, the proof will appear in the full version of this paper.

Theorem 6.3. *Let q be a UCQ where in each CQ q', either q' contains a* UWinner *atom or the* Winner *atoms are pairwise disconnected. If r is the plurality or the veto rule, then* Necessity(q, r) *is solvable in polynomial time.*

For other positional scoring rules, the complexity remains unresolved, even for the query $q_{\exists\text{uw}}$, where the goal is to determine whether there is *always* a single winner (whose identity may differ from one completion to another).

7 FIXED PARAMETER TRACTABLE

Here, we investigate the possibility and necessity problems through the lens of parameterized complexity. We show that,

Table 2: Complexity of UCQs for positional scoring rules. Each row applies to *every* rule in the list. A lower bound for answers refers to the existence of a UCQ with the corresponding complexity. "U" stands for "Unique" and refers to UCQs with UWINNER atoms and no WINNER atoms, "D/U" stands for "Disconnected/Unique" and refers to the condition of Theorem 6.3, and "?" means that no complete classification is known.

Rule	*Possible Winners*	*Possible Answers*	*Necessary Winners*	*Necessary Answers*	*U Necessary Answers*	*D/U Necessary Answers*
plurality, veto	P	P (Thm 4.4, 6.1)	P	coNP-c. (Thm 5.6)	P (6.3)	P (Thm 5.3, 6.3)
pure \ {plurality, veto}	NP-c.	NP-c.	P	coNP-c. (Prop 5.4)	?	coNP-c. (Prop 5.4)
non-pure	?	?	P	coNP-c. (Thm. 5.7)	?	?

taking the number of candidates as a parameter, it is *Fixed Parameter Tractable* (FPT) to compute the possible and necessary answers to every fixed UCQ. Thus, we generalize the result by Betzler et al. [5] asserting that the possible-winner problem is FPT, where the parameter is the number of candidates. Towards this goal, we first prove the following generalization, which implies that, under fixed parameter tractability, we can actually produce all possible *winner sets.*

THEOREM 7.1. *Let r be a positional scoring rule. The following decision problem is FPT with parameter the number $|C|$ of candidates : given a partial profile $\mathbf{P}$ over the set C of candidates, and a subset $S \subseteq C$, is there a completion $\mathbf{T}$ such that $\mathbf{W}(r, \mathbf{T}) = S$?*

PROOF. We adopt the approach that has been used for designing FPT algorithms for computational social choice [5, 28], namely, an FPT reduction to the feasibility of an Integer Linear Program (ILP), where the parameter is the number of variables. This problem is known to be FPT via an algorithm designed by Lenstra [15] (and later improved by Kannan [16]).

We need some notation. We denote the partial profile $\mathbf{P}$ by $(P_1, \ldots, P_n)$. For a partial order P over C, let V_P be the set $\{i \mid P_i = P\}$ (thus, V_P represents the set of voters that have the partial preference P) and let L_P be the set of all linear extensions of P (thus, L_P consists of total orders over C). Note that the V_P's form a partition of the set of voters. Recall that for a total order T over C and for a candidate c, we denote by $s(T, c)$ the score value that T assigns to c according to r; in other words, if c is the jth element of T, then $s(T, c) = r(m, j)$. We assume that C is nonempty (otherwise, the answer is trivially false), and we fix a candidate $c_0 \in C$.

Our ILP uses a variable $X_{P,T}$ for each partial order P and linear extension $T \in L_P$. An assignment to $X_{P,T}$ represents a (feasible) number of voters i in V_P that have their partial order (i.e., P_i, which is equal to P) completed into T. Our ILP specifies constraints that assert the feasibility of the $X_{P,T}$.

$$\text{For every } P \text{ and } T: \quad X_{P,T} \in \mathbb{N}$$

$$\text{For every } P: \quad \sum_{T \in L_P} X_{P,T} = |V_P|.$$

To simplify the presentation, we also use a variable Y_c, for every candidate c, that holds the total score gained by c. Hence, the Y_c are realized via the following set of constraints.

$$\text{For every } c \in C: \quad Y_c = \sum_P \sum_{T \in L_P} s(T, c) \cdot X_{P,T}.$$

In addition, the ILP contains constraints that assert that the score of c_0 is the same as that of every $c \in S$.

$$\text{For every } c \in S: \quad Y_{c_0} = Y_c.$$

Moreover, the ILP contains constraints that assert that the score of c_0 is strictly larger than that of every candidate who is not in S.

$$\text{For every } c \in C \setminus S: \quad Y_{c_0} > Y_c.$$

This completes the description of the ILP. To complete the proof, observe that the ILP has a solution if and only if there is a completion $\mathbf{T}$ of $\mathbf{P}$ such that $\mathbf{W}(r, \mathbf{T}) = S$. Also, observe that the number of variables $X_{P,T}$ and Y_c depends (in a single-exponential manner) only on the number of candidates. In fact, the same holds for the number of constraints. The only components of the program that depend on the number of voters are the constants $|V_P|$. □

From Theorem 7.1, we derive the following fixed parameter tractability result.

COROLLARY 7.2. *Let $\mathcal{S}$ be a schema and let q be a UCQ over $\mathcal{S}^e$. There is an FPT algorithm for computing the possible and necessary answers to q, where the parameter is the number of candidates.*

PROOF. From Theorem 7.1 it follows that we can materialize all expansions $D \sqcup \mathbf{T}$ for the input $(D, \mathbf{P})$, by constructing every feasible relation WINNER$^{D \sqcup \mathbf{T}}$ and its corresponding UWINNER$^{D \sqcup \mathbf{T}}$. Then, by definition, the possible answers are the union of the $q(D \sqcup \mathrm{T})$, and the necessary answers are the intersection of the $q(D \sqcup \mathrm{T})$. □

A perusal of the proof of Theorem 7.1 reveals that Corollary 7.2 holds even for queries richer than UCQs. In fact, the corollary is true for every query q with a polynomial-time data complexity over ordinary databases (e.g., every safe query in relational calculus).

8 CONCLUDING REMARKS

We investigated the complexity of evaluating queries over election databases. We focused on the possibility and necessity problems for Boolean UCQs and positional scoring rules. The state of affairs is summarized in Table 2. While our study unveiled that these problems are often intractable, we have also established several different tractability results. In particular, the tractability side of the classification for the possible-winner problem [3, 4, 21, 27] generalizes to the possibility problem for UCQs under the plurality rule and the veto rule. In contrast, the tractability of the necessary-winner problem under every positional scoring rule [27] does not generalize to the necessity problem for Boolean UCQs; this reveals a fundamental difference between computational social choice and election databases. Finally, we showed that the possibility and necessity problems are fixed-parameter tractable when the parameter is the number of candidates; this is an appropriate parameter in such situations as political elections, where there are many voters but only a handful of candidates.

We have already listed several different open problems. We conclude the paper with additional open problems and directions for future investigation. First, as we mentioned in the body of the paper, some of our results go beyond the class of UCQs; nonetheless, very little is known at present about more expressive classes of queries. Furthermore, we have not considered voting rules that fall outside the class of positional scoring rules, such as Copeland's method, Simpson's rule, and Bucklin voting[2]. Future research also includes queries that involve multiple elections and multiple voting rules [20].

Another direction for future research is that of probabilistic voters, adopting statistical models of preferences, such as the uniform distribution over the linear extensions, Mallows [24] and the Repeated Insertion Model (RIM) [11]. The analog of computing necessary/possible winners is to compute the probability that a candidate wins [2, 13, 17, 23]. In the framework of election databases, the analog is *probabilistic query answering*, where the goal is to compute the marginal probability of query answers [10, 26]. The evaluation of CQs over databases with RIM preferences has been studied in past research [9, 19], but without the angle of elections and social choice.

[2]See, e.g., [27] for a description of these and other voting rules.

ACKNOWLEDGMENTS

This work was supported by NSF Grant 1814152 and BSF Grant 2017753. The work of Kimelfeld and Tibi was also supported by ISF Grant 1295/15.

REFERENCES

[1] Antoine Amarilli, Mouhamadou Lamine Ba, Daniel Deutch, and Pierre Senellart. 2017. Possible and Certain Answers for Queries over Order-Incomplete Data. In *TIME (LIPIcs)*, Vol. 90. Schloss Dagstuhl - Leibniz-Zentrum fuer Informatik, 4:1–4:19.

[2] Yoram Bachrach, Nadja Betzler, and Piotr Faliszewski. 2010. Probabilistic Possible Winner Determination. In *AAAI*. AAAI Press.

[3] Dorothea Baumeister and Jörg Rothe. 2012. Taking the final step to a full dichotomy of the possible winner problem in pure scoring rules. *Inf. Process. Lett.* 112, 5 (2012), 186–190.

[4] Nadja Betzler and Britta Dorn. 2010. Towards a dichotomy for the Possible Winner problem in elections based on scoring rules. *J. Comput. Syst. Sci.* 76, 8 (2010), 812–836.

[5] Nadja Betzler, Susanne Hemmann, and Rolf Niedermeier. 2009. A Multivariate Complexity Analysis of Determining Possible Winners Given Incomplete Votes. In *IJCAI*. 53–58.

[6] Craig Boutilier and Jeffrey S. Rosenschein. 2016. Incomplete Information and Communication in Voting. In *Handbook of Computational Social Choice*. 223–258.

[7] Felix Brandt, Vincent Conitzer, Ulle Endriss, Jérôme Lang, and Ariel D. Procaccia (Eds.). 2016. *Handbook of Computational Social Choice*. Cambridge University Press. https://doi.org/10.1017/CBO9781107446984

[8] Felix Brandt, Vincent Conitzer, Ulle Endriss, Jérôme Lang, and Ariel D. Procaccia. 2016. Introduction to Computational Social Choice. In *Handbook of Computational Social Choice*. 1–20.

[9] Uzi Cohen, Batya Kenig, Haoyue Ping, Benny Kimelfeld, and Julia Stoyanovich. 2018. A Query Engine for Probabilistic Preferences. In *SIGMOD Conference*. ACM, 1509–1524.

[10] Nilesh N. Dalvi and Dan Suciu. 2004. Efficient Query Evaluation on Probabilistic Databases. In *VLDB*. Morgan Kaufmann, 864–875.

[11] Jean-Paul Doignon, Aleksandar Pekec, and Michel Regenwetter. 2004. The repeated insertion model for rankings: Missing link between two subset choice models. *Psychometrika* 69, 1 (2004), 33–54.

[12] Jack Edmonds and Ellis L. Johnson. 2001. Matching: A Well-Solved Class of Integer Linear Programs. In *Combinatorial Optimization - Eureka, You Shrink!, Papers Dedicated to Jack Edmonds (Lecture Notes in Computer Science)*, Vol. 2570. Springer, 27–30.

[13] Noam Hazon, Yonatan Aumann, Sarit Kraus, and Michael Wooldridge. 2012. On the evaluation of election outcomes under uncertainty. *Artificial Intelligence* 189 (2012), 1 – 18.

[14] Marie Jacob, Benny Kimelfeld, and Julia Stoyanovich. 2014. A System for Management and Analysis of Preference Data. *PVLDB* 7, 12 (2014), 1255–1258.

[15] Hendrik W. Lenstra Jr. 1983. Integer Programming with a Fixed Number of Variables. *Math. Oper. Res.* 8, 4 (1983), 538–548.

[16] Ravi Kannan. 1987. Minkowski's Convex Body Theorem and Integer Programming. *Math. Oper. Res.* 12, 3 (1987), 415–440.

[17] Batya Kenig and Benny Kimelfeld. 2019. Approximate Inference of Outcomes in Probabilistic Elections. To appear in AAAI.

[18] Batya Kenig, Benny Kimelfeld, Haoyue Ping, and Julia Stoyanovich. 2017. Querying Probabilistic Preferences in Databases. In *PODS (PODS '17)*. ACM, New York, NY, USA, 21–36.

[19] Batya Kenig, Benny Kimelfeld, Haoyue Ping, and Julia Stoyanovich. 2017. Querying Probabilistic Preferences in Databases. In *PODS*. 21–36.
[20] Benny Kimelfeld, Phokion G. Kolaitis, and Julia Stoyanovich. 2018. Computational Social Choice Meets Databases. In *IJCAI*. ijcai.org, 317–323.
[21] Kathrin Konczak and Jérôme Lang. 2005. Voting procedures with incomplete preferences. In *Proc. IJCAI-05 Multidisciplinary Workshop on Advances in Preference Handling*, Vol. 20.
[22] Leonid Libkin. 2004. *Elements of Finite Model Theory*. Springer.
[23] Tyler Lu and Craig Boutilier. 2011. Vote Elicitation with Probabilistic Preference Models: Empirical Estimation and Cost Tradeoffs. In *ADT (Lecture Notes in Computer Science)*, Vol. 6992. Springer, 135–149.
[24] C. L. Mallows. 1957. Non-Null Ranking Models. I. *Biometrika* 44, 1-2 (1 June 1957), 114–130.
[25] Yossi Shiloach. 1981. Another Look at the Degree Constrained Subgraph Problem. *Inf. Process. Lett.* 12, 2 (1981), 89–92.
[26] Dan Suciu, Dan Olteanu, Christopher Ré, and Christoph Koch. 2011. *Probabilistic Databases*. Morgan & Claypool Publishers.
[27] Lirong Xia and Vincent Conitzer. 2011. Determining Possible and Necessary Winners Given Partial Orders. *J. Artif. Intell. Res.* 41 (2011), 25–67.
[28] Yongjie Yang. 2014. Election Attacks with Few Candidates. In *ECAI (Frontiers in Artificial Intelligence and Applications)*, Vol. 263. IOS Press, 1131–1132.

2019 ACM PODS Alberto O. Mendelzon Test-of-Time Award

The ACM PODS Alberto O. Mendelzon Test-of-Time Award is awarded every year to a paper or a small number of papers published in the PODS proceedings ten years prior that had the most impact in terms of research, methodology, or transfer to practice over the intervening decade.

The PODS Executive Committee has appointed us to serve as the Award Committee for 2019. After careful consideration and having solicited external nominations and advice, we have selected the following paper as the award winner for 2019:

A General Datalog-Based Framework for Tractable Query Answering over Ontologies

by Andrea Calì, Georg Gottlob, and Thomas Lukasiewicz

Citation. This paper introduces and studies the Datalog$^{\pm}$ framework for query answering over ontologies, which subsequently became highly influential in both the database and knowledge representation communities. Its main contribution is an in-depth study of the data complexity of Datalog$^{\pm}$, and several extensions and restrictions tailored to ontologics. The paper identifies a tractable family of Datalog$^{\pm}$ formalisms, based on linear tuple-generating dependencies, that generalizes description logics of the DL-Lite family. Extensions with keys and stratified negation are also studied. Other technical results of the paper concerning the chase have been fundamental to further developments in the field. The paper received over 450 citations, evidencing its significant impact.

The Alberto O. Mendelzon Test-of-Time Award Committee for 2019:

Jianwen Su
UC Santa Barbara

Dirk Van Gucht
Indiana University

Victor Vianu
UC San Diego

Database Repairs and Consistent Query Answering: Origins and Further Developments

Leopoldo Bertossi*
leopoldo.bertossi@relational.ai
RelationalAI Inc.
Toronto, Canada

ABSTRACT

In this article we review the main concepts around database repairs and consistent query answering, with emphasis on tracing back the origin, motivation, and early developments. We also describe some research directions that has spun from those main concepts and the original line of research. We emphasize, in particular, fruitful and recent connections between repairs and causality in databases.

CCS CONCEPTS

• **Data management systems → databases**; • **Integrity constraints**;

KEYWORDS

databases, database repairs, consistent query answering, integrity constraints, data integration, answer-set programs, causality

ACM Reference Format:
Leopoldo Bertossi. 2019. Database Repairs and Consistent Query Answering: Origins and Further Developments. In *38th ACM SIGMOD-SIGACT-SIGAI Symposium on Principles of Database Systems (PODS'19), June 30-July 5, 2019, Amsterdam, Netherlands.* ACM, New York, NY, USA, 11 pages. https://doi.org/10.1145/3294052.3322190

1 INTRODUCTION

The notions of database repair and consistent query answering (CQA) explicitly appeared in a PODS paper in 1999 [3], on databases that may not satisfy (i.e. may be inconsistent with) a given set of integrity constraints (ICs). That paper, co-authored with Marcelo Arenas and Jan Chomicki, has received many citations and has been the basis for a large body of research, until these days, and even beyond the data management community. In particular, the notion of "repair" has become ubiquitous in several areas of computer science. Most of the lines of research on repairs and CQA are well-known in the community of theoretical data management, but possible less known in more applied communities. The same applies, more generally, to some newer "conceptual" applications to other areas of data management and knowledge representation. Without attempting to provide a comprehensive review, the goal of this article is to revisit the early days, and briefly and partially fill the gap in relation to lesser known directions the original ideas have taken. There are several early reviews of the area [12, 18, 49]. The more recent monograph [14] is a rather comprehensive survey of the "core" of this area up to a certain time point. A recent survey of the vast area of CQA for conjunctive queries (CQs) under key constraints can be found in [109].

Since it not possible to introduce, in a such a limited space, formal definitions that can be found in the original papers, the presentation will be based on representative examples.

2 THE BEGINNINGS

Right after finishing my PhD in Mathematics, in mathematical logic, and working at the Catholic University of Chile (PUC), I decided to do research on applications of logic to computer science, more specifically, to knowledge representation and data management. Crucial influences in those days of the late 80s and early 90s were Ray Reiter and Alberto Mendelzon. The latter gave in 1988 an inspiring tutorial in Chile on "Logic in Databases". I was lucky to start collaboration with Ray Reiter in 1990, when I was visiting the University of Toronto. Not long after that, he started doing research on the situation calculus [97], in particular on applications to the specification of database updates and the dynamics of a database [96].[1] So, I joined in, and started working in the area.

Around that time I joined the Department of Computer Science of the School of Engineering of the PUC. Soon I noticed that there was very little research going on there. On the other side, the department was full of students, and most of them of excellent quality. Given this situation, I developed a tree-tier plan: (a) I started teaching an undergraduate course on logic for computer science, which included apart from classical logic, models of computation, elements of complexity, logic programming, and elements of knowledge representation. (This was the only course that did expose students to some computer science.) The course had a sort of a hands-on workshop associated to it, where students learned about automated theorem proving with Otter, Prolog, and at some point also answer-set programming with DLV.[2] (b) I started inviting the best students in that course to do research with me, to motivate them to pursue graduate studies (in the hope they would come back; Chileans do come back). (c) I started inviting researchers from abroad to give tutorials and engage with the local students, to create a research

*Also affiliated to Carleton University, Ottawa, Canada, and member of the "Millenium Institute for Foundational Research on Data (IMFD, Chile)

[1] It is interesting to observe that mathematical logic has been broadly applied to static aspects of databases, but very little to their dynamic aspects, which involve updates, transactions, dynamic constraints, active rules, hypothetical queries, etc.

[2] Several brilliant students helped me create that applied appendix to the course, most prominently, Cristian Ferretti and Marcelo Arenas.

PODS'19, June 30-July 5, 2019, Amsterdam, Netherlands

ACM ISBN 978-1-4503-6227-6/19/06...$15.00
https://doi.org/10.1145/3294052.3322190

atmosphere around them. Materializing this plan was not without toil; it was a colonizing and also political undertaking in may ways, but it certainly paid off. A seed of relevant research activity was sown; and several of the now established computer science researchers in Chile were exposed to this experience. I want to believe it did provide some inspiration to them.

In this context, and since I was working on dynamic aspects of databases, I invited Jan Chomicki to visit the PUC. He was a prominent researcher in temporal databases. At the same time, Marcelo Arenas was starting his masters in computer science under my supervision (we had started doing research together before that, while he was still an undergraduate student, as I described in the previous paragraph); and I invited him to join the conversations. In this way, the three of us ended up staring at a blank board, asking ourselves about how to take off. As usual in this kind of meetings, we started wandering in different directions, and at some point we became interested in comparing databases in relation to consistency, asking when can one say a database is more consistent than another database (both for the same schema). As usual again, we did not attack that question, but we became intrigued by the question about what an inconsistent database can tell us. Which led to the more precise question, but still not quite, about what is consistent in an inconsistent database. This question was further refined into "what are the consistent answers to a query posed to an inconsistent database, and how can we obtain them?" Although this question was still unprecise, it was the real start. We did not ask ourselves if this was a fashionable line of research, a well-known open problem, or if someone else was doing something along similar lines. And we started playing with examples as the one that follows.

Example 2.1. Consider the database instance D below, and the inclusion dependency

$$ID\colon\ \forall x \forall y \forall z(\mathit{Supply}(x, y, z) \longrightarrow \mathit{Articles}(z)), \quad (1)$$

requiring that the items shipped according to table *Supply* are all among the official list of items displayed in table *Articles*.

Supply	Company	Receiver	Item
	C_1	R_1	I_1
	C_2	R_2	I_2
	C_2	R_1	I_3

Articles	Item
	I_1
	I_2

This instance is inconsistent with respect to (wrt.) ID, i.e. it does not satisfy ID, usually denoted with $D \not\models ID$. Clearly there is a problem with the last tuple of table *Supply*, but the information in the other tuples of the database seems to be fine. Now, if we pose the query about the items that are supplied, i.e. the conjunctive query

$$Q(z)\colon\ \exists x \exists y \mathit{Supply}(x, y, z), \quad (2)$$

i.e. a projection on the third attribute, we intuitively expected to obtain as consistent answers only I_1 and I_2, but how? □

Not long before these conversations, I had invited Jack Minker to visit the PUC. He gave a tutorial on semantic query optimization, which is about optimizing query answering by taking advantage of integrity constraints that are satisfied by the database. This can be done via query rewriting, by appending to the query at hand "residues" from the ICs. They impose additional conditions on the query, narrowing down the search space [46]. We though we could try out locally enforcing, possibly unsatisfied, ICs on the query results (rather than on the whole database) through similar rewritings.

Example 2.2. (example 2.1 cont.) ID in (1) is logically equivalent to the (implicitly universally quantified) clause

$$\neg \mathit{Supply}(x, y, z) \vee \mathit{Articles}(z), \quad (3)$$

whose first, negative disjunct can be canceled (resolved [86]) with the (positive) query atom $\mathit{Supply}(x, y, z)$ in (2), leaving the residue $\mathit{Articles}(z)$ of ID. This residue is appended to the original query, obtaining a rewritten query:

$$Q'(z)\colon\ \exists x \exists y(\mathit{Supply}(x, y, z) \wedge \mathit{Articles}(z)). \quad (4)$$

The new query posed to the original, inconsistent database does return the intuitively expected answers. □

3 FIRST NOTIONS AND DEVELOPMENTS

The next natural research steps were about clarifying two questions: (a) The rewriting mechanism was just that, a computational approach to the original question, but what was the *semantics* of consistent answers to a query posed to an inconsistent database. (b) Assuming that the rewriting-based approach was in agreement with that semantics, what was its the scope of applicability.

3.1 Repairs and consistent query answering

In relation to question (a) above, the intuition that we were developing was that the consistent data inside the inconsistent database are those that are invariant under the process of restoring the consistency of the database. Those consistent data persisted under update actions on the database that made the database consistent. Of course, those update actions have to be restricted somehow. After all, making the database in Example 2.1 empty produces a consistent instance, but this is an unintended kind of repair process. Accordingly, the consistency-restoring updates had to be "minimal" in some way. At the same time we decided to accept only deletions and insertions of tuples as admissible updates (the rewriting approach we were considering worked at the tuple, i.e. atomic, level). This led to the notion of *database repair*.

Example 3.1. (example 2.1 cont.) A repair of the original instance D is any instance D' for the same schema that satisfies ID, is obtained from D by inserting or deleting tuples, and minimally differs from D, in the sense that the symmetric difference, $D \Delta D' := (D \smallsetminus D') \cup (D' \smallsetminus D)$, is minimal under set-inclusion. This is a reason why these repairs are also known as *S-repairs*, referring to set-minimality.

For example, $D_1 = \{\mathit{Supply}(C_1, R_1, I_1), \mathit{Supply}(C_2, R_2, I_2), \mathit{Articles}(I_1), \mathit{Articles}(I_2)\}$, obtained deleting $\mathit{Supply}(C_2, R_1, I_3)$ from D is a repair, with $D \Delta D_1 = \{\mathit{Supply}(C_2, R_1, I_3)\}$. Another repair is $D_2 = \{\mathit{Supply}(C_1, R_1, I_1), \mathit{Supply}(C_2, R_2, I_2), \mathit{Supply}(C_2, R_1, I_3), \mathit{Articles}(I_1), \mathit{Articles}(I_2), \mathit{Articles}(I_3)\}$, obtained inserting $\mathit{Articles}(I_3)$ into D, with $D \Delta D_2 = \{\mathit{Articles}(I_3)\}$.

Since $D \Delta D_1$ and $D \Delta D_2$ are incomparable under set-inclusion, both are S-repairs. However, $D_3 = \{\mathit{Supply}(C_1, R_1, I_1), \mathit{Articles}(I_1), \mathit{Articles}(I_2)\}$, obtained deleting $\mathit{Supply}(C_2, R_1, I_3)$ and $\mathit{Supply}(C_2, R_2, I_2)$ from D, is consistent, but not an S-repair: $D \Delta D_1 \subsetneqq D \Delta D_3 = \{\mathit{Supply}(C_2, R_1, I_3), \mathit{Supply}(C_2, R_2, I_2)\}$.

Looking at the two obtained repairs, we can see that the data in D that persist across repairs are the first two tuples in table *Supply* and the two tuples in table *Articles*. □

Next, given a database D, a set of ICs Σ, and a query $Q(\bar{x})$, one can define the set of *consistent answers to* Q wrt. D and Σ, denoted $Cons(Q, D, \Sigma)$, as the set of those answers that are *obtained from every repair* when the query is posed to them. So, more formally: $\bar{a} \in Cons(Q, D, \Sigma)$ iff $\bar{a} \in Q(D')$ for every repair D' of D wrt. Σ. (As usual, $Q(D)$ denotes the sets of answer to query Q from D.)

Example 3.2. (example 3.1 cont.) For the query $Q(z)$ in (2), $Q(D_1) = \{I_1, I_2\}$, $Q(D_2) = \{I_1, I_2, I_3\}$. Then, $Cons(Q, D, \{ID\}) = \{I_1, I_2\}$. □

Example 3.3. The following instance D violates the key constraint KC: *Name* $\longrightarrow$ *Salary* that requires the employee salary to functionally depend upon the employee name, i.e. every employee should have at most one salary.

Employee	Name	Salary
	page	5K
	page	8K
	smith	3K
	stowe	7K

There are two repairs, D_1 and D_2 obtained by tuple deletions:

Employee	Name	Salary
	page	5K
	smith	3K
	stowe	7K

Employee	Name	Salary
	page	8K
	smith	3K
	stowe	7K

They are consistent with KC and minimally depart from D. Now, if we want the consistent answers to the query about all tuples in the database, i.e. to $Q_1(x, y)$: *Employee*(x, y)?, we obtain: $Cons(Q_1, D, \{KC\}) = \{\langle smith, 3K\rangle, \langle stowe, 7K\rangle\}$. Now, if the query is only about employee names, i.e. $Q_2(x)$: $\exists y Employee(x, y)$?, we obtain: $Cons(Q_2, D, \{KC\}) = \{\langle smith\rangle, \langle stowe\rangle, \langle page\rangle\}$ since we find *page* as employee in each repair. □

We can see that obtaining consistent answers amounts to posing a query to a class of *possible worlds*, in this case, the class of repairs of the original instance. In this sense, the consistent answers correspond to a form of *certain answers* [74]. This notion, defined in model-theoretic terms (through the class of repairs) captures the initial intuition, but may be impractical for the computation of consistent answers: We may want to avoid computing all repairs, materialize them, and posing the same query to each of them, to finally collect the answers in common. Actually, it is easy to produce examples of databases that have exponentially many repairs in the size of the database. To start, we might try out the rewriting-based approach.

Example 3.4. (example 3.3 cont.) The key constraint KC can be rewritten into a sentence of first-order (FO) predicate logic as

$$\forall x \forall y \forall z (Employee(x, y) \land Employee(x, z) \longrightarrow y = z),$$

and in clausal form as

$$\neg Employee(x, y) \lor \neg Employee(x, z) \lor y = z. \quad (5)$$

Now, if query Q_1 is resolved with (5), we obtain a residue to be appended to the query, obtaining the rewritten query:

$$Q_1'(x, y)\colon\ Employee(x, y) \land \neg \exists z (Employee(x, z) \land z \neq y), \quad (6)$$

which asks about employees with their salaries for which there is no other employee with the same name, but a different salary. This is a query written in a FO language, and then easy to express and answer from a database. If it is posed to the original instance, the ordinary, classical answers to this query from D turn out to be the expected consistent answers to the original query, i.e. those in $Cons(Q_1, D, \{KC\})$. Notice that this rewriting amounts to rewriting the original SQL query:

```
SELECT Name, Salary
FROM   Employee;
```

into the new SQL query:

```
SELECT Name, Salary FROM Employee
WHERE NOT EXISTS (  SELECT *  FROM Employee E
    WHERE E.Name = Name AND E.Salary <> Salary);
```

which is posed to- and answered from the original instance as usual. □

3.2 Complexity of CQA and approximation

The correctness and termination of the rewriting approach was investigated in the Pods'99 paper [3], and positive cases were identified. (Termination because there could be interacting ICs which could give rise to a cycle of rewritings.) However, there was no claim of universal applicability of the FO rewriting approach when attempted on FO queries and FO ICs. Actually, no long after the appearance of [3], it became clear that the data complexity of consistent query answering (CQA) was bound to be higher than polynomial time. For example, there are Boolean conjunctive queries (BCQs) and functional dependencies (FDs), for which deciding if the query is consistently true, i.e. true in all S-repairs, is *coNP*-complete (in data complexity) [48]. For some BCQs and combinations of FDs and inclusion dependencies, CQA becomes Π^P_2-complete (again, in data complexity, as all the complexity results mentioned in this article) for repairs allowing only tuple deletions [48], and general S-repairs [25].

These complexity results made it clear that the FO rewriting approach had limitations, but its scope remained open. Actually, not long after the emergence of those first complexity results [48, 64], a thorough investigation of the FO rewriting approach and the data complexity of CQA for CQs under key constraints and FDs was started by Jef Wijsen and collaborators. This research program has provided a clear picture of the syntactic cases where FO rewritings are possible, when queries can be consistently answered in polynomial time (but may not be FO rewritable), and when CQA for them becomes intractable (cf. [77, 78, 109] for details and references).

Algorithmic and complexity research on repairs and CQA took many interesting directions. Among others, the following problems have been investigated: Complexity of CQA for aggregate queries under FDs [5], repair checking [1, 48], counting repairs [90], enumerating repairs [84], computing a particular repair [85], etc. Combined complexity results on repair checking and CQA are reported in [9].

Given the high worst-case complexity of CQA, research has also been conducted on tractable approximations to CQA [65, 69–71]. This is a promising line of research that will lead to interesting applications.

3.3 Answer-set programming approaches

In 1999 I invited Michael Kifer to the PUC in Chile. He had written a paper on a very nice multi-valued FO logic with annotations for truth-values structured as a lattice [75]. Since it could be used to do non-trivial reasoning in the presence of inconsistency, and again with the participation of Marcelo Arenas, we attempted to represent in logical terms both repairs and consistent query answers. This effort gave rise to an elegant representation [4], but it was not exploited in algorithmic terms. Short after that, when Pablo Barcelo, student of Engineering at the PUC then, asked me for a research topic for his masters thesis, I proposed to him to develop logic programs with annotations that could be used to both model repairs and do actual computations.[3] All this was inspired by the just-mentioned annotated logic approach and previous results on the use of logic programming for database repairs [6]. This was a successful undertaking that took the form of *answer-set programs* [33] (or logic programs with stable model semantics [67]) with annotations [10, 11]. The resulting *repair programs* are quite simple and general in terms of the ICs that can be handled. The stable models of a program turn out to be the repairs of the given instance, and CQA becomes certain query answering from the program, for which reasoning can be applied. It is worth mentioning that repairs programs and the problems related to repairs and CQA have the same complexity. That is, repair programs have exactly the required expressive power for the task.

Example 3.5. The following is a *denial constraint*, i.e. it prohibits combinations or joins of database atoms:

$$\kappa\colon\ \neg\exists x\exists y(S(x) \wedge R(x,y) \wedge S(y)).$$

The following database instance D violates κ.

	R	A	B
ι_1		a_4	a_3
ι_2		a_2	a_1
ι_3		a_3	a_3

	S	A
ι_4		a_4
ι_5		a_2
ι_6		a_3

Here, we are introducing, in an unessential manner, global tuple identifiers (tids), which will be useful later on to refer to individual tuples. Those tids will appear in predicates as well, in the first argument and separated from the rest by a semicolon.

Instance D has three S-repairs: $D_1 = \{R(\iota_1; a_4, a_3), R(\iota_2; a_2, a_1), R(\iota_3; a_3, a_3), S(\iota_4; a_4), S(\iota_5; a_2)\}$, $D_2 = \{R(\iota_2; a_2, a_1), S(\iota_4; a_4), S(\iota_5; a_2), S(\iota_6; a_3)\}$, and $D_3 = \{R(\iota_1; a_4, a_3), R(\iota_2; a_2, a_1), S(\iota_5; a_2), S(\iota_6; a_3)\}$.

The repair program contains the atoms in D (with tids) as facts, and the rules:

$$S'(t_1; x, \mathrm{d}) \vee R'(t_2; x, y, \mathrm{d}) \vee S'(t_3; y, \mathrm{d}) \leftarrow S(t_1; x), R(t_2; x, y), S(t_3; y).$$

$$S'(t; x, \mathrm{s}) \leftarrow S(t; x),\ \mathit{not}\ S'(t; x, \mathrm{d}).$$

$$R'(t; x, y, \mathrm{s}) \leftarrow R(t; x, y),\ \mathit{not}\ R'(t; x, y, \mathrm{d}).$$

Here, $t_1, \ldots, t$ are variables. The annotation d is constant denoting that the tuple is deleted from the original database, and annotation constant s denotes that the tuple stays in the repair. Here, the first rule captures in its body (i.e. antecedent) a violation of κ, and the head (i.e. the consequent) offers all the alternative tuples deletions that can solve that violation. The last two rules basically represent inertia: the repairs keep the original tuples that have not been deleted. Predicates R' and S' are nicknames for R and S, and have an extra argument to accommodate the annotation.

This repair-program has three stable models, with repair D_1 corresponding to the model $M_1 = \{R'(\iota_1; a_4, a_3, \mathrm{s}), R'(\iota_2; a_2, a_1, \mathrm{s}), R'(\iota_3; a_3, a_3, \mathrm{s}), S'(\iota_4; a_4, \mathrm{s}), S'(\iota_5; a_2, \mathrm{s}), S'(\iota_6; a_3, \mathrm{d})\} \cup D$, in the sense that D_1 is read off from M_1 by keeping only the tuples annotated with s. □

This is a simple example, but hopefully conveys the gist. If there are interacting ICs, i.e. that repair actions for one of them may affect satisfaction of another one, it is necessary to use a couple of extra annotations to capture a transition process (cf. the cited papers and [14] for more examples). The important points to keep in mind are: (a) there is a one-to-one correspondence between S-repairs and stable models; (b) the minimality of repairs is captured by the minimality of stable models; and (c) doing CQA becomes reasoning with the repair program. In [43] it is reported on *ConsEx*, a system for CQA based on repair programs that run on top of the answer-set programming system *DLV* [82]. *ConsEx*, for "consistency extractor", uses magic-sets for query optimization.

Repair programs have been used beyond the strict domain of CQA, as we will see in Section 7. Other independent approaches to repairs and CQA using answer-set programs are found in [6, 55, 68]. As a final remark, it is worth mentioning that repair programs as those in Example 3.5 for DCs can be transformed into non-disjunctive, unstratified programs [43]; and repair programs in general can be transformed into theories written in second-order (SO) predicate logic, and in some cases, via elimination of SO quantifiers, into FO theories [13]. This is achieved by taking advantage of a compilation of logic programs with stable model semantics into circumscriptive theories [61].

4 OTHER KINDS OF REPAIRS

As we saw in Example 2.1, inconsistencies wrt. inclusion dependencies can be solved by inserting or deleting tuples. However, we might want to accept just deletions, as done in [48]. Even more, we may not want to restrict ourselves to repairs based on minimal sets of insertions and/or deletions of tuples. In fact, other kinds of repairs have been proposed and investigated. In this direction, different *repair semantics* differ at least in two aspects: (a) the admissible repair actions; and (b) the minimality criterion, i.e. what are the consistent instances that are the "closest" to the original one. Several abstract repair semantics based on optimality criteria have been introduced and investigated in [103], with complexity results reported in [57].

Repairs based on changes of attribute values, a.k.a. "attribute-based repairs", have also been investigated and applied. For this, values for these updates can be taken from the data domain [63, 108]. Special mention deserve attribute-based repairs of databases with numerical values, numerical queries, and subject to numerical constraints [12, 20, 62]. That scenario opens completely new research challenges. In the rest of this section we give some more details on a few specific repairs semantics.

[3] Pablo has different, spicer memories of this first encounter.

4.1 Cardinality-repairs

Cardinality-repairs, a.k.a. *C-repairs*, were first considered in [6]. They are S-repairs, as in Section 3.1, that also minimize the *number* of tuples deleted or inserted, i.e. $|D \Delta D'|$. In Example 3.1, D_1 and
j

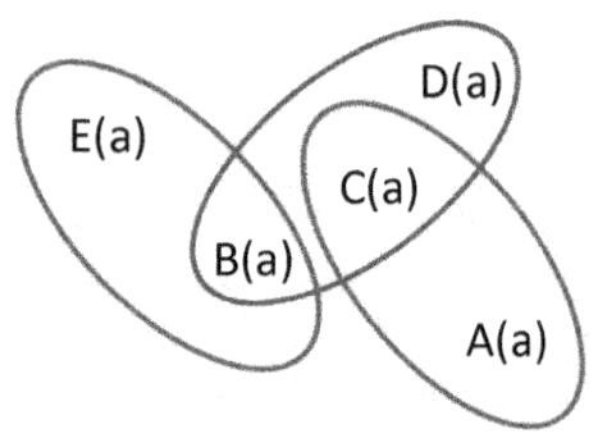

Figure 1: Conflict hyper-graph

Example 4.1. Consider $D = \{A(a), B(a), C(a), D(a), E(a)\}$, and the set of DCs

$$\Sigma = \{\neg\exists x(B(x) \land E(x)),\ \neg\exists x(B(x) \land C(x) \land D(x)),\ \neg\exists x(A(x) \land C(x))\}.$$

One can build the so-called *conflict hyper-graph* [5, 48], whose nodes are the database tuples, and hyper-edges connect tuples that simultaneously violate a DC, as shown in Figure 1. Among the S-repairs, which are maximal independent sets in the hyper-graph, we find $D_1 = \{B(a), C(a)\}$, $D_2 = \{C(a), D(a), E(a)\}$, $D_3 = \{A(a), B(a), D(a)\}$, $D_4 = \{E(a), D(a), A(a)\}$. They are all subset-maximal consistent subinstances of D. However, only D_2, D_3 and D_4 are also C-repairs, but not D_1. □

C-repairs and CQA under them were investigated in detail in [87, 88], where complexity results were obtained. This is interesting in its own right, but the complexity bound turned out to be useful to investigate the complexity of causality in databases (cf. Section 7). The complexity of computational problems related to C-repairs tends to be higher than for S-repairs. However, C-repairs seem to behave better than S-repairs under updates of the original database [87]. (By the way, the investigation of repairs and CQA under updates has received little attention; [87] just started to scratch the surface in this direction.) C-repairs were further investigated in [1]. As shown in [6, 15], repair-programs can be produced for the specification of C-repairs and CQA under them. Those programs use *weak program-constraints* [82] to capture the numerical minimization.

Example 4.2. (example 3.5 cont.) The models of the repair program corresponding to C-repairs can be obtained by adding to the program the following weak program constraints (WCs):

$$\Leftarrow\ R(t, \bar{x}), R'(t, \bar{x}, \mathrm{d}),$$
$$\Leftarrow\ S(t, \bar{x}), S'(t, \bar{x}, \mathrm{d}).$$

They can be violated by the models (meaning that the rule body becomes true), but the number of violations (value combinations in the rule body) has to be kept to a minimum. The non-minimally violating models are discarded.[4] With these WCs we are minimizing the number of deleted tuples. □

[4] In contrast, a *hard program constraint*, i.e. of the form $\leftarrow Body(\bar{x})$, would eliminate all the models where the body becomes true.

4.2 Null-based repairs: tuple level

Example 4.3. (example 2.1 cont.) Let us modify the table *Articles* in Example 2.1 as follows:

Articles	Item	Cost
	I_1	50
	I_2	30

and the inclusion dependency as follows:

$$ID':\ \forall x \forall y \forall z(Supply(x, y, z) \rightarrow \exists v\ Articles(z, v)), \qquad (7)$$

This is a more general case of inclusion dependency that the one in (1). Both are usually called tuple-generating dependencies (*tgds*). In this case, $D \not\models ID'$ due to the absence of value I_3 in the table *Articles*.

In this case, we may consider two repairs, one just deletes the third tuple from table *Supply*, and another repair inserts the tuple $\langle I_3, \mathrm{NULL}\rangle$ into *Articles*. □

The constant NULL may not have a preassign semantics, and different ones could be considered. However, a natural one is that for the single null in SQL databases. For example, it cannot be used to satisfy joins, to make true comparison atoms, or as values for key attributes, etc. To keep everything in a predicate logic-based setting, the semantics of SQL nulls can be "logically reconstructed", as done in [24] and [25, sec. 4]. (A deeper investigation of the logical foundations of SQL nulls can be found in [71] and references therein.) Other forms of nulls, e.g. multiple, labeled nulls, can be used for the same problem [92].

This repair semantics shown in Example 4.3 was applied in [25] to peer data-exchange systems, where there may be inter-peer mappings of the form (7). Peers exchange data at query-answering time using those mappings, but need to keep their local data consistent. Hence the need for local, peer-level repairs. Those repairs can be specified using repair programs when the local *tgds* are acyclic. (There have been other applications of repairs in peer-data-exchange systems, e.g. [42].)

4.3 Null-based repairs: attribute level

A particularly interesting and natural class of attribute-based repairs relies on changes of attribute values, but only by a null value that behaves as in SQL databases. This kind of repairs is particularly appropriate for DCs.

Example 4.4. (example 3.5 cont.) With the same database D and DC κ: $\neg\exists x \exists y(S(x) \land R(x, y) \land S(y))$, repairs can be obtained by "minimally" changing attribute values by a special constant NULL. Since it behaves as in SQL, it cannot be used to satisfy a join. Here we have two attribute-based repairs via NULL replacement; in each of them NULL is preventing the satisfaction of a join in κ:

R	A	B
ι_1	a_4	a_3
ι_2	a_2	a_1
ι_3	a_3	a_3

S	A
ι_4	a_4
ι_5	a_2
ι_6	NULL

R	A	B
ι_1	a_4	NULL
ι_2	a_2	a_1
ι_3	a_3	NULL

S	A
ι_4	a_4
ι_5	a_2
ι_6	a_3

The one on the left-hand side is characterized by the set of changes $\{\iota_6[1]\}$, meaning that the value in the first attribute (or position) of the tuple with tuple ID ι_6 is changed into NULL (the tids use position 0). Similarly, the repair on the right-hand side is characterized by the set of changes $\{\iota_1[2], \iota_3[2]\}$. Both sets of changes are minimal under set inclusion. □

This kind of repairs were used in [24] to hide a sensitive view contents in a database. This is achieved by virtually repairing the database wrt. an IC that specifies that the view has to be empty. Those repairs were also used to define causality for query answers at the attribute level [15] (cf. Section 7). Corresponding repair-programs can be found in [15].

5 VIRTUAL DATA INTEGRATION

In a virtual data integration system, there are independent data sources that are brought together through a *mediator*, which, without materializing data imported from the sources and without being a database, offers a database-like interface, with its own global schema. The mediated schema may be different from those for the sources, which may not even share the same schema. The mediator receives queries from a user and answers them by sending queries back to
query ai

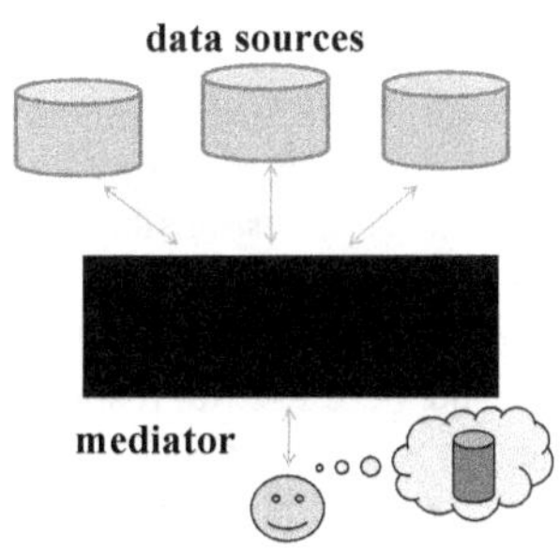

Crucial components of this architecture are the *mappings* that establish the correspondences between the global schema and the local schemata. This is usually done through view definitions, according to two main paradigms: (a) Global-as-view (GAV), under which predicates at the global level are defined as views over the source relations; and (b) Local-as-view (LAV), under which the local relations (predicates) are defined as views over the global schema. For example, the picture below shows a case of GAV, where the global predicate S is defined as a view over local predicates P and Q. It also shows a case of LAV, where the local predicate R is defined as a for
only ate
both.

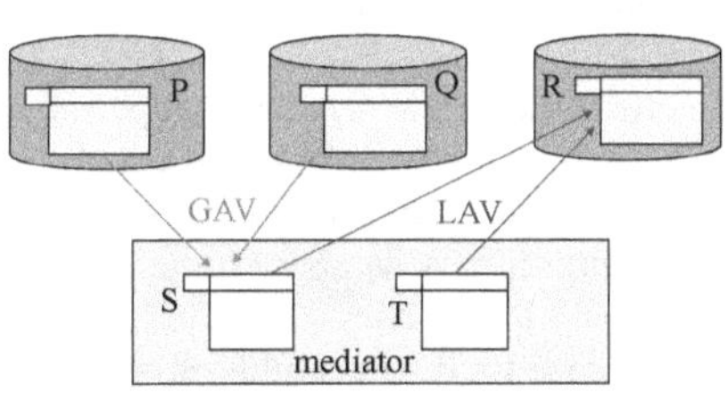

The semantics of a virtual integration system is given through a collection of admissible global instances [81], i.e. a possible-world semantics. Of course, being a virtual approach, we avoid materializing those global instances.

Example 5.1. The two universities in Ottawa want to virtually integrate their databases, the sources, that are as follows:

Sources: Carleton U.

CUstds	Number	Name
	101	john
	102	mary

SpecCU	Number	Field
	101	alg
	102	ai

Ottawa U.

OUstds	Number	Name
	103	claire
	104	peter

SpecOU	Number	Field
	103	db

We are assuming the tables at the top have the student number as a key, and this constraint is satisfied, but this is not relevant for the moment. The mediator has a single, global relation schema:

$$Stds(Number, Name, Univ, Field).$$

Under GAV, this predicate is defined as a view in terms of source predicates. We use two Datalog rules that define the view:

$$Stds(x, y, \text{'cu'}, z) \leftarrow CUstds(x, y), SpecCU(x, z). \quad (8)$$
$$Stds(x, y, \text{'ou'}, z) \leftarrow OUstds(x, y), SpecOU(x, z). \quad (9)$$

A query posed to the mediator, in a language associated to its global schema, could be about "names of students who study the same field at both universities":

$$Ans(x) \leftarrow Stds(z, x, \text{'cu'}, u), Stds(w, x, \text{'ou'}, u),$$

which can be answered from the sources via unfolding of (8) and (9).

Under LAV, we could define, for example, the first table of Carleton U. as a view over the global *Stds*:

$$CUstds(x, y) \leftarrow Stds(x, y, \text{'cu'}, z).$$ □

Now, what do we do if we want to impose ICs on the global schema? There is no material instance on which to check or enforce those global ICs, and still we would like to see them satisfied, but when and where? The only sensible answer seems to be at the level of global query answering. This is a perfect, if not unavoidable, scenario for CQA.

Example 5.2. (example 5.1 cont.) Let us assume that we have now the following table for Ottawa U.

OUstds	Number	Name
	103	claire
	104	peter
	101	**sue**

It satisfies its local key constraint. However, if we want to impose the global FD: *Stds*: *Number* $\rightarrow$ *Name*, there will be problems with the student number 101, that is shared by the two universities, but for different students. The mediator, who may be aware of the global IC, could only check the sources through queries (often of a limited kind), but it cannot update the sources. So, something along the lines of CQA has to be done. For example, the global query about students numbers and names, i.e. $Q(x, y)\colon\ \exists u \exists z Stds(x, y, u, z)$, could be consistently answered via the rewriting into $Q'(x, y)$:
$\exists u \exists z Stds(x, y, u, z) \wedge \neg\exists y'u'z'(Stds(x, y', u', z') \wedge y \neq y' \wedge u \neq u')$, where we are using the fact that the local key constraints are satisfied (and the mediator knows). □

Repairs and CQA under virtual data integration were investigated in several papers [19, 32, 37–39]. The example above is simple and can be handled via a FO rewriting. In other cases, more expressive rewriting languages are needed, such as that of answer-set programs that specify the virtual repairs of the already virtual global admissible instances [19].

6 DATA CLEANING

The notion of repair naturally appears in data cleaning and data quality assessment. After all, consistency is one of the dimensions of data quality, together with completeness, accuracy, freshness, etc. Instead of ICs, one can use formalized contexts to express data quality concerns; and in this way the context acts as semantic information on the database at hand. If the quality restrictions are not satisfied, then one can, possibly virtually, repair the database. The quality data is, as before, persistent under the repairs, and can be extracted as *quality answers* to queries (the natural generalization of the notion of consistent answer). This is exactly the approach developed in [22, 23].

Conditional functional dependencies (CFDs) were introduced in [58] as extensions of FDs, in order to capture common data quality concerns for which FDs alone are not expressive enough. Consider, for example, a database D containing the following table (taken from [58]):

CC	AC	Phone	Name	Street	City	Zip
44	131	1234567	mike	mayfield	NYC	EH4 8LE
44	131	3456789	rick	crichton	NYC	EH4 8LE
01	908	3456789	joe	mtn ave	NYC	07974

The two following FDs

$$[CC, AC, Phone] \rightarrow [Street, City, Zip]$$
$$[CC, AC] \rightarrow [City]$$

are satisfied by D. They are "global" ICs that may not capture natural data quality requirements, e.g. as related to specific data values. Instead, the CFD

$$[CC = 44, Zip] \rightarrow [Street],$$

expressing a FD of *Street* upon *Zip when* the country code is 44, is not satisfied anymore, and data cleaning may be necessary. CQA and database repairs for CFDs have been investigated in [76, 111]. Cf. [60, 98] for more connections between data quality and database repairs.

The original paper on repairs and CQA was not meant to be a contribution to data cleaning, but rather a scientific undertaking that would lead to model and compute what are the consistent data in an inconsistent database. Nevertheless, repairs still found a way into data cleaning, and have been used in many classical data cleaning problems [28, 31, 111], in particular, in entity resolution (deduplication, record-matching) with entity-linking dependencies [28, 34, 35], and the combination of entity resolution and repairs wrt. classical ICs [59, 66].

In general terms, the notion of repair has been relevant to data cleaning in that it enabled the characterization of what is a good and legal solution to a data cleaning problem, as represented by a new, clean instance or a class thereof. Maybe working with all admissible repairs is too complex, but one can think of choosing one or some of them, and also of weakening the notion of certain answer behind CQA, by considering what is true in most repairs, or introducing probability distributions, etc. Recent application of repairs to data cleaning with probabilistic elements can be found in [52, 98].

7 A CAUSALITY CONNECTION

In data management, we need to understand and compute why certain results are obtained or not, e.g. query answers or violations of semantic conditions. A database system could provide some *explanations*. The notion of *causality* can be used in this direction.

A notion of causality-based explanation for a query result was introduced in [91], as follows. Given a relational instance D and a Boolean conjunctive query (BCQ) Q, a tuple $\tau \in D$ is a *counterfactual cause* for Q if $D \models Q$ and $D \smallsetminus \{\tau\} \not\models Q$. Next, a tuple $\tau \in D$ is an *actual cause* for Q if there is a *contingency set* $\Gamma \subseteq D$, such that τ is a counterfactual cause for Q in $D \smallsetminus \Gamma$. This notion is based on [72]. The strength of an actual cause is commonly captured by the notion of *responsibility*: The responsibility of an actual cause τ for Q is defined by $\rho_D^Q(\tau) := \frac{1}{|\Gamma|+1}$, where $|\Gamma|$ is the smallest size of a contingency set for τ (and 0, otherwise). High responsibility tuples provide more interesting explanations [47].

Example 7.1. (example 3.5 cont.) Consider the same database D. Let us ignore the tids in this example. The query

$$Q\colon \exists x \exists y (S(x) \land R(x, y) \land S(y))$$

is satisfied by D: $D \models Q$. Tuple $S(a_3)$ is one of the causes for Q to be true in D, actually a counterfactual cause: If $S(a_3)$ is removed from D, Q is no longer true. Its responsibility is $\frac{1}{1+|\emptyset|} = 1$.

Tuple $R(a_4, a_3)$ is an actual cause for Q with contingency set $\{R(a_3, a_3)\}$: If $R(a_3, a_3)$ is removed from D, Q is still true, but further removing $R(a_4, a_3)$ makes Q false. Its responsibility is $\frac{1}{1+1} = \frac{1}{2}$ (its smallest contingency sets have size 1). Similarly, $R(a_3, a_3)$ and $S(a_4)$ are actual causes, with responsibility $\frac{1}{2}$. □

There are several computational problems related to causality in databases, among them: (a) Computing causes, and deciding if a tuple is a cause; (b) computing responsibilities; (c) computing most responsible actual causes (MRAC); (d) deciding if a tuple has responsibility above a threshold. By now there is a relatively clear picture of the complexity of these problems for CQs and unions thereof (UCQs). Some of these complexity and algorithmic results were obtained in [26] through connections of causality to database repairs and to *consistency-based diagnosis* [95].

Consider a BCQ: $Q\colon \exists \bar{x}(P_1(\bar{x}_1) \land \cdots \land P_m(\bar{x}_m))$, and assume that Q is true in D. It turns out that the causes for Q to be true in D and their contingency sets can be obtained from database repairs. In fact, the negation of the query, $\neg Q$, is logically equivalent to a DC $\kappa(Q)\colon \neg\exists \bar{x}(P_1(\bar{x}_1) \land \cdots \land P_m(\bar{x}_m))$; and Q holds in D iff D is inconsistent wrt. $\kappa(Q)$. The S-repairs of D wrt. $\kappa(Q)$ are associated to causes and their minimal contingency sets; and C-repairs are associated to causes, minimum contingency sets, and maximum responsibilities: A database tuple τ is an actual cause with subset-minimal contingency set Γ iff $D \smallsetminus (\Gamma \cup \{\tau\})$ is an S-repair, in which case its responsibility is $\frac{1}{1+|\Gamma|}$. Furthermore, τ is an actual cause with minimum-cardinality contingency set Γ iff $D \smallsetminus (\Gamma \cup \{\tau\})$ is a C-repair, in which case, τ is an MRAC. (Conversely, repairs can be obtained from causes and their contingency sets.) [26].

Computing/deciding actual causes can be done in polynomial time in data for CQs and UCQs [26, 91]. The definition of causality we just gave can be applied to any monotone query, e.g. to Datalog queries. It turns out that for them, cause computation can be *NP*-complete, a result that can be obtained via a connection between causality and Datalog abduction [27].

Returning to causes for CQs and their responsibilities, we can take advantage of the connection to C-repairs. It turns out that most computational problems related to repairs, in particular, C-repairs, are provably hard (in data complexity) [87], and the bounds can be applied to causality problems. For example, we can obtain that: (a) deciding if a tuple has responsibility above a certain threshold is *NP*-complete for UCQs (responsibility decision problem); (b) computing $\rho_D(\tau)$ is $FP^{NP(log(n))}$-complete for BCQs (this is the *functional*, non-decision, version of (a)); (c) deciding if a tuple is a most responsible cause is $P^{NP(log(n))}$-complete for BCQs [26].

Since ASPs can be used to specify, compute and query S- and C-repairs, another interesting consequence of the causality/repair connection is the possibility of using repair programs as a basis for causality-related specifications and computations [15].

Example 7.2. (examples 3.5 and 7.1 cont.) Consider the same database D and the DC:

$$\kappa(Q):\ \neg\exists x\exists y(S(x)\wedge R(x,y)\wedge S(y)),$$

associated to the BCQ Q for which we are finding causes. The repair program is an in Example 3.5, and its three stable models (or answer sets) are in correspondence with the S-repairs. Now, cause and responsibility computation becomes query answering on extended repair-programs, as we will show next.

First, causes (and tuples in general) will be represented by their tids. So, if we want to compute causes, we add the query rules to the repair program:

$$Ans(t) \leftarrow R'(t,x,y,\mathrm{d})$$
$$Ans(t) \leftarrow S'(t,x,\mathrm{d})$$

The causes become those tuples (with tid) ι that make the auxiliary answer predicate *Ans* true wrt. the repair program plus the query rules, i.e. $\Pi \models_{brave} Ans(\iota)$, where $\models_{brave}$ indicates a "brave" consequence of the program, in the sense that $Ans(\iota)$ becomes true in *some* model of Π.

In order to compute responsibilities, we need to specify and compute contingency sets associated to causes. We introduce a new predicate, $CauCon(t,t')$, standing for "t is actual cause, and t' is a member of the former's contingency set", which is specified as follows: For each pair of predicates P_i, P_j in $\kappa(Q)$, add the rule:

$$CauCon(t,t') \leftarrow P_i'(t,\bar{x}_i,\mathrm{d}),\ P_j'(t',\bar{x}_j,\mathrm{d}),\ t\neq t',$$

which is indicating that t' is deleted together with t. More specifically, in this example:

$$\begin{aligned}CauCon(t,t') &\leftarrow S'(t,x,\mathrm{d}),R'(t',u,v,\mathrm{d}),\\ CauCon(t,t') &\leftarrow S'(t,x,\mathrm{d}),S'(t',u,\mathrm{d}),t\neq t',\\ CauCon(t,t') &\leftarrow R'(t,x,y,\mathrm{d}),S'(t',u,\mathrm{d}),\\ CauCon(t,t') &\leftarrow R'(t,x,y,\mathrm{d}),R'(t',u,v,\mathrm{d}),t\neq t'.\end{aligned}$$

For example, from model M_2, corresponding to repair D_2, we obtain: $CauCon(\iota_1,\iota_3)$ and $CauCon(\iota_3,\iota_1)$, corresponding to the difference $D\smallsetminus D_2=\{R(a_4,a_3),R(a_3,a_3)\}$

Full contingency sets and responsibilities can be specified and computed with extensions of ASP with numerical and set-aggregation, e.g. with DLV-Complex [40, 41, 56], collecting all individual contingency elements for each cause and nothing more:

$$\begin{aligned}preCon(t,\{t'\}) &\leftarrow CauCon(t,t'),\\ preCon(t,\#union(C,\{t''\})) &\leftarrow CauCon(t,t''),preCon(t,C),\\ &\qquad not\ \#member(t'',C),\\ Con(t,C) &\leftarrow preCon(t,C),not\ aux(t,C),\\ aux(t,C) &\leftarrow CauCon(t,t'),\#member(t',C).\end{aligned}$$

In order to compute a cause's responsibilities, all we need is the rule: $preresp(t,n) \leftarrow \#count\{t' : CauCon(t,t')\} = n$. To obtain the responsibility for a cause ι, we pose the following query to the extended program, say Π^e: $\Pi^e \models_{brave} preresp(\iota,x)?$, and we keep the minimum value m returned for x (we may get different answers from different models), then $\rho_D^Q(\iota)=\frac{1}{1+m}$.

If we want maximum responsibility causes, we can concentrate on C-repairs, which, as we saw in Example 4.2, can be obtained by adding weak programs constraint to the extended program we have so far. □

It is worth mention that the expressive power and data complexity of ASPs with WCs [51, 82] is exactly what is required for maximum-responsibility computation [26].

7.1 Attribute-Level causes

One can naturally define causes at the attribute level, rather than tuple level, by appealing to attribute-based repairs of the kind introduced in Section 4.3. We illustrate the idea with an example (a detailed treatment can be found in [15]).

Example 7.3. (example 4.4 cont.) Consider the same instance with its attribute-based repairs wrt. the DC κ, whose associated conjunctive query is: Q: $\exists x\exists y(S(x)\wedge R(x,y)\wedge S(y))$. It holds $D\models Q$. The sets of changes $\{\iota_6[1]\}$ and $\{\iota_1[2],\iota_3[2]\}$ associated to the two minimal repairs allow us to define $\iota_6[1]$, the first attribute value of the sixth tuple as a counterfactual cause for Q. Similarly, $\iota_1[2]$ becomes an actual cause with contingency set $\Gamma=\{\iota_3[2]\}$, and the other way around. □

Repair programs for attribute-based repairs can be used as a basis to specify and compute attribute-level causes and their associated responsibilities [15].

7.2 Causality under integrity constraints

The problem of defining and investigating causes for database queries under ICs was addressed in [27]. In this scenario it is assumed that a given set Σ of ICs has to be satisfied. So, we start assuming that $D\models\Sigma$. Next, for τ to be actual cause for an answer $\bar{a}$ to a monotone query $Q(\bar{a})$, the associated contingency set Γ has to satisfy: (a) $D\smallsetminus\Gamma\models\Sigma$; (b) $D\smallsetminus\Gamma\models Q(\bar{a})$; (c) $D\smallsetminus(\Gamma\cup\{\tau\})\models\Sigma$; and (d) $D\smallsetminus(\Gamma\cup\{\tau\})\not\models Q(\bar{a})$. The responsibility of a cause τ under Σ, denoted $\rho_D^{Q,\Sigma}$, is defined as before.

Example 7.4. Consider the database instance D below

Dep	DName	TStaff
ι_1	Computing	John
ι_2	Philosophy	Patrick
ι_3	Math	Kevin

Course	CName	TStaff	DName
ι_4	COM08	John	Computing
ι_5	Math01	Kevin	Math
ι_6	HIST02	Patrick	Philosophy
ι_7	Math08	Eli	Math
ι_8	COM01	John	Computing

Let us first consider the query:

(A) $Q(x)\colon\ \exists y \exists z(Dep(y,x) \wedge Course(z,x,y))$.

John is an answer, denoted $\langle \text{John} \rangle \in Q(D)$; and the causes are: (a) ι_1, counterfactual; (b) ι_4, with single minimal contingency set $\Gamma_1 = \{\iota_8\}$; (c) ι_8, with single minimal contingency set $\Gamma_2 = \{\iota_4\}$. Then, $\rho_D^{Q(\text{John})}(\iota_1) = 1$, and $\rho_D^{Q(\text{John})}(\iota_4) = \rho_D^{Q(\text{John})}(\iota_8) = \frac{1}{2}$.

Now, let us consider an inclusion dependency:[5]

$$\psi\colon\quad \forall x \forall y\, (Dep(x,y) \longrightarrow \exists u\ Course(u,y,x)),$$

which is satisfied by D.

Under ψ, ι_4 and ι_8 are not actual causes anymore, and ι_1 is still a counterfactual cause, i.e. $\rho_D^{Q(\text{John}),\psi}(\iota_1) = 1$, and $\rho_D^{Q(\text{John}),\psi}(\iota_4) = \rho_D^{Q(\text{John}),\psi}(\iota_8) = 0$.

Consider now the query about the first conjunct in (A):

(B) $Q_1(x)\colon\ \exists y\ Dep(y,x)$.

John is still an answer, i.e. $\langle \text{John} \rangle \in Q_1(D)$. Under ψ, we obtain for Q_1 the same causes with the same minimal contingency sets as for Q, which is logically equivalent to Q_1 under ψ: $Q \equiv_\psi Q_1$.

And now the query about the second conjunct in (A):

(C) $Q_2(x)\colon\ \exists y \exists z Course(z,x,y)$.

It holds $\langle \text{John} \rangle \in Q_2(D)$. Without considering ψ, ι_4 and ι_8 are the only actual causes, with contingency sets $\Gamma_1 = \{\iota_8\}$ and $\Gamma_2 = \{\iota_4\}$, resp., that is: $\rho_D^{Q(\text{John})}(\iota_1) = 0$, and $\rho_D^{Q(\text{John})}(\iota_4) = \rho_D^{Q(\text{John})}(\iota_8) = \frac{1}{2}$.

Now under ψ, ι_4 and ι_8 are still actual causes, but we lose their previous contingency sets. Now, the smallest contingency sets are: $\Gamma_3 = \{\iota_8, \iota_1\}$ for ι_4; and $\Gamma_4 = \{\iota_4, \iota_1\}$ for ι_8. With them, the responsibilities decrease: $\rho_D^{Q_2(\text{John}),\psi}(\iota_4) = \rho_D^{Q_2(\text{John}),\psi}(\iota_8) = \frac{1}{3}$. We can see that ι_1 is still not an actual cause, but affects the responsibility of the actual causes. □

We can see that causes and responsibilities are affected by ICs. However, both are preserved under logical equivalence of queries under ICs. More interestingly, without ICs, deciding causality for CQs is tractable, but their presence may make the complexity grow: There are a CQ Q and an inclusion dependency ψ, for which deciding causality is *NP*-complete [27]. Finally, ASPs for computation of causes and responsibilities under ICs can be produced [15].

There is still much to investigate around the connection between database repairs and causality in databases. In a different direction, an alternative notion to that of responsibility was introduced and investigated in [102].

8 OTHER DIRECTIONS

Far from pretending to give a full account of the many other directions in which repairs and CQA have been investigated, we mention just a few of them.

Repairs have been defined and investigated for data warehouses and multidimensional databases [8, 21, 44, 45, 110]; also in spatial databases [93, 99], and temporal databases [50, 93]. In data exchange, the data sent to a target instance may collide with the local target constraints, and repairs may be considered [106]. Notions found in data exchange, such as universal solutions, now applied to repairs, can be found in [105], together with a deep investigation of data complexity of CQA, and some undecidability results (for the latter, see also [7]). Repairs of databases using probabilistic elements and repairs of probabilistic databases [104] have been investigated in [2, 69, 83].

An active area of research is that of formal ontologies, and, in particular, ontology-based data access (OBDA) [94]. In OBDA it is not unlikely that the combination of data, rules and constraints produces inconsistencies. In that case, repairs of- and consistent query answering (CQA) on the inconsistent ontology have to be considered. There are different ways of doing this, in terms of the ontological language (e.g. some Description Logic or a Datalog$^\pm$ program class), the kind of repairs considered, and the way CQA is done [29, 30, 53, 54, 79, 80, 89, 100, 107].

As a final note, let me say that it has been fascinating to see how the area has evolved since its inception in 1999. We can see that research on repairs and CQA is still going strong after twenty years. As to the problem we first started thinking about in those early days, that of measuring the degree of inconsistency of a database, it turns out that database repairs can be used as a basis for such a task. We have taken the first steps in that direction [16, 17], but that is a different story.

[5]Tuple deletions do not affect the satisfaction of monotone ICs, such as DCs. Causes and inclusion dependencies were considered without a formalization in [101].

ACKNOWLEDGMENTS

My deep gratitude goes to my coauthors of the Pods'99 paper, Marcelo Arenas and Jan Chomicki. Working with them gave me the best moments in my days at the PUC in Chile. We had a good time and stimulating exchanges of ideas. I am grateful to the several coauthors and former students who have worked with me in this area. Special gratitude goes to all those who have done research in the area of repairs and CQA. This is a community effort after all. I appreciate the support from RelationalAI while writing this paper, and the great human and research environment it provides.

REFERENCES

[1] Afrati, F. and Kolaitis, P. Repair Checking in Inconsistent Databases: Algorithms and Complexity. Proc. ICDT 2009.

[2] Andritsos, P., Fuxman, A. and Miller, R.J. Clean Answers over Dirty Databases: A Probabilistic Approach. Proc. ICDE 2006.

[3] Arenas, M., Bertossi, L. and Chomicki, J. Consistent Query Answers in Inconsistent Databases. Proc. PODS, 1999.

[4] Arenas, M., Bertossi, L. and Kifer, M. Applications of Annotated Predicate Calculus to Querying Inconsistent Databases. Proc. Computational Logic 2000, Springer LNCS 1861, pp. 926-941.

[5] Arenas, M., Bertossi, L., Chomicki, J., He, X., Raghavan, V. and Spinrad, J. Scalar Aggregation in Inconsistent Databases. *Theoretical Computer Science*, 2003, 296(3):405-434.

[6] Arenas, M., Bertossi, L. and Chomicki, J. Answer Sets for Consistent Query Answers. *Theory and Practice of Logic Programming*, 2003, 3(4&5):393-424.

[7] Arenas, M and Bertossi, L. On the Decidability of Consistent Query Answering. Proc. AMW 2010, CEUR-WS, Vol-619.

[8] Ariyan, S. and Bertossi, L. 2013. A multidimensional data model with subcategories for flexibly capturing summarizability. Proc. SSDBM 2013.

[9] Arming, S., Pichler, R. and Sallinger, E. Complexity of Repair Checking and Consistent Query Answering. Proc. ICDT 2016.

[10] Barcelo, P. and Bertossi, L. Logic Programs for Querying Inconsistent Databases. Proc. PADL 2003, Springer LNCS 2562.

[11] Barcelo, P., Bertossi, L. and Bravo, L. Characterizing and Computing Semantically Correct Answers from Databases with Annotated Logic and Answer Sets. In *Semantics in Databases*, Springer LNCS 2582, 2003, pp. 7-33.

[12] Bertossi, L. Consistent Query Answering in Databases. *ACM Sigmod Record*, 2006, 35(2):68-76.

[13] Bertossi, L. From Database Repair Programs to Consistent Query Answering in Classical Logic. Proc. AMW 2009, CEUR-WS, Vol-450.

[14] Bertossi, L. *Database Repairing and Consistent Query Answering*. Morgan & Claypool, Synthesis Lectures on Data Management, 2011.

[15] Bertossi, L. Characterizing Causes for Query Answers in Databases via Database Repairs and their Computation through Repair Programs. Corr Arxiv Paper cs.DB/1712.01001. Revised and extended version of paper in Proc. FoIKs, 2018, Springer LNCS 10833, pp. 55-76.
[16] Bertossi, L. Measuring and Computing Database Inconsistency via Repairs. Proc. SUM 2018, Springer LNAI 11142, pp. 368-372.
[17] Bertossi, L. Repair-Based Degrees of Database Inconsistency. To appear in Proc. LPNMR 2019. Extended version as Corr Arxiv Paper cs.DB/1809.10286, 2018.
[18] Bertossi, L and Chomicki, J. Query Answering in Inconsistent Databases. In *Logics for Emerging Applications of Databases*, Springer, 2003, pp. 43-83.
[19] Bertossi, L. and Bravo, L. Consistent Query Answers in Virtual Data Integration Systems. In *Inconsistency Tolerance*, Springer LNCS 3300, 2005, pp. 42-83.
[20] Bertossi, L., Bravo, L., Franconi, E. and Lopatenko, A. The Complexity and Approximation of Fixing Numerical Attributes in Databases Under Integrity Constraints. *Information Systems*, 2008, 33(4):407-434.
[21] Bertossi, L., Bravo, L. and Caniupan-Marileo, M. Consistent Query Answering in Data Warehouses. Proc. AMW 2009, CEUR-WS, Vol-450.
[22] Bertossi, L., Rizzolo, F. and Lei, J. Data Quality is Context Dependent. Proc. WS on Enabling Real-Time Business Intelligence (BIRTE 2010). Collocated with VLDB 2010. Springer LNBIP 84, 2011, pp. 52-67.
[23] Bertossi, L. and Rizzolo, F. Contexts and Data Quality Assessment. Corr Arxiv Paper cs.DB/1608.04142. Extended version of [22].
[24] Bertossi, L. and Li, L. Achieving Data Privacy through Secrecy Views and Null-Based Virtual Updates. *IEEE Trans. Knowledge and Data Engineering*, 2013, 25(5):987-1000.
[25] Bertossi, L. and Bravo, L. Consistency and Trust in Peer Data Exchange Systems. *Theory and Practice of Logic Programming*, 2017, 17(2):148-204. Extended version as Corr Arxiv Paper cs.DB/1606.01930.
[26] Bertossi, L. and Salimi, B. From Causes for Database Queries to Repairs and Model-Based Diagnosis and Back. *Theory of Computing Systems*, 2017, 61(1):191-232.
[27] Bertossi, L. and Salimi, B. Causes for Query Answers from Databases: Datalog Abduction, View-Updates, and Integrity Constraints. *International Journal of Approximate Reasoning*, 2017, 90:226-252.
[28] Beskales, G., Soliman, M., Ilyas, I. and Ben-David, S. Modeling and Querying Possible Repairs in Duplicate Detection. Proc. VLDB 2009.
[29] Bienvenu, M. On The Complexity of Consistent Query Answering in the Presence of Simple Ontologies. Proc. AAAI 2012.
[30] Bienvenu, M., Bourgaux, C. and Goasdoue, F. Computing and Explaining Query Answers over Inconsistent DL-Lite Knowledge Bases. *J. Artificial Intelligence Research*, 2019, 64:563-644.
[31] Bohannon, P, Flaster, M., Fan, F. and Rastogi, R. A Cost-Based Model and Effective Heuristic for Repairing Constraints by Value Modification. Proc. SIGMOD 2005.
[32] Bravo, L. and Bertossi, L. Logic Programs for Consistently Querying Data Integration Systems. Proc. IJCAI 2003.
[33] Brewka, G., Eiter, T. and Truszczynski, M. Answer Set Programming at a Glance. *Comm. of the ACM*, 2011, 54(12):93-103.
[34] Burdick, D., Fagin, R., Kolaitis, P., Popa, L. and Tan, W-C. A Declarative Framework for Linking Entities. *ACM Trans. Database Syst.*, 2016, 41(3):17:1-17:38.
[35] Burdick, D., Fagin, R., Kolaitis, P., Popa, L. and Tan, W-C. Expressive Power of Entity-Linking Frameworks. *J. Comput. Syst. Sci.*, 2019, 100:44-69.
[36] Calautti, M., Libkin, L. and Pieris, A. An Operational Approach to Consistent Query Answering. Proc. PODS 2018.
[37] Calì, A., Lembo, D. and Rosati, R. On The Decidability and Complexity of Query Answering over Inconsistent and Incomplete Databases. Proc. PODS 2003.
[38] Calì, A., Lembo, D. and Rosati, R. Query rewriting and Answering under Constraints in Data Integration Systems. Proc. IJCAI 2003.
[39] Calì, A., Calvanese, D., De Giacomo, G. and Lenzerini, M. Data Integration under Integrity Constraints. *Inf. Syst.*, 2004, 29(2):147-163.
[40] Calimeri, F. Cozza, S. Ianni, G. and Leone, N. Computable Functions in ASP: Theory and Implementation. Proc. ICLP 2008.
[41] Calimeri, F. Cozza, S. Ianni, G. and Leone, N. An ASP System with Functions, Lists, and Sets. Proc. LPNMR 2009.
[42] Calvanese, D., De Giacomo, G., Lembo, D., Lenzerini, M. and Rosati, R. Inconsistency Tolerance in P2P Data Integration: An Epistemic Logic Approach. *Information Systems*, 2008, 33:360Ů384.
[43] Caniupan-Marileo, M. and Bertossi, L. The Consistency Extractor System: Answer Set Programs for Consistent Query Answering in Databases. *Data & Know. Eng.*, 2010, 69(6):545-572.
[44] Caniupan-Marileo, M., Bravo, L. and Hurtado, C. Repairing inconsistent dimensions in data warehouses. *Data & Know. Eng.*, 2012, 79-80:17-39.
[45] Caniupan-Marileo, M., Vaisman, A. and Arredondo, R. Efficient repair of dimension hierarchies under inconsistent reclassification. *Data & Know. Eng.*, 2015, 95:1-22.
[46] Chakravarthy, U. S., Grant, J. and Minker, J. Logic-Based Approach to Semantic Query Optimization. *ACM Trans. Database Syst.*, 1990, 15(2):162-207.
[47] Chockler, H. and Halpern, J. Y. Responsibility and Blame: A Structural-Model Approach. *J. Artif. Intell. Res.*, 2004, 22:93-115.
[48] Chomicki, J. and Marcinkowski, J. Minimal-Change Integrity Maintenance using Tuple Deletions. *Inf. and Comput.*, 2005, 197(1-2):90-121.
[49] Chomicki, J. Consistent Query Answering: Five Easy Pieces. Proc. ICDT 2007.
[50] Chomicki, J. and Wijsen, J. Consistent Query Answering for Atemporal Constraints over Temporal Databases. Proc. TIME 2016.
[51] Dantsin, E., Eiter, T., Gottlob, G. and Voronkov, A. Complexity and Expressive Power of Logic Programming. *ACM Computing Surveys*, 2001, 33(3):374-425.
[52] De Sa, C., Ilyas, I., Kimelfeld, B., Re, C. and Rekatsinas, T. A Formal Framework For Probabilistic Unclean Databases. Proc. ICDT 2019.
[53] Du, J., Qi, G. and Shen, Y.-D. Weight-Based Consistent Query Answering over Inconsistent $\mathcal{SHIQ}$ Knowledge Bases. *KAIS*, 2012 34:335-371.
[54] Eiter, T., Fink, M. and Stepanova, D. Computing Repairs of Inconsistent DL-Programs over EL Ontologies. *J. Artif. Intell. Res.*, 2016, 56:463-515.
[55] Eiter, T., Fink, M., Greco, G. and Lembo, D. Repair Localization for Query Answering from Inconsistent Databases. *ACM Trans. Database Syst.*, 2008, 33(2):10:1-10:51.
[56] Faber, W., Pfeifer, G., Leone, N., Dell'Armi, T. and Ielpa, G. Design and Implementation of Aggregate Functions in the DLV System. *Theory and Practice of Logic Programming*, 2008, 8(5-6):545-580.
[57] Fagin, R., Kimelfeld, B. and Kolaitis, P. Dichotomies in the Complexity of Preferred Repairs. Proc. PODS 2015.
[58] Fan, W., Geerts, F., Jia, X. and Kementsietsidis, A. Conditional Functional Dependencies for Capturing Data Inconsistencies. *ACM Trans. Database Syst.*, 2008, 33(2):6:1-6:48.
[59] Fan, W., Ma, S., Tang, N. and Yu, W. Interaction between Record Matching and Data Repairing. *J. Data and Information Quality*, 2014, 4(4):16:1-16:38.
[60] Fan, W. and Geerts, F. *Foundations of Data Quality Management*. Synthesis Lectures on Data Management, Morgan & Claypool Publishers, 2012.
[61] Ferraris, P., Lee, J. and Lifschitz, V. Stable Models and Circumscription. *Artif. Intell.*, 2011, 175(1):236-263.
[62] Flesca, S., Furfaro, F. and Parisi, F. Querying and Repairing Inconsistent Numerical Databases. *ACM Trans. Database Syst.*, 2010, 35(2):14:1-14:50.
[63] Franconi, E., Laureti Palma, A., Leone, N., Perri, S. and Scarcello, F. Census Data Repair: a Challenging Application of Disjunctive Logic Programming. Proc. LPAR 2001.
[64] Fuxman, A. and Miller, R. J. First-Order Query Rewriting for Inconsistent Databases. *J. Comput. Syst. Sci.*, 2007, 73(4):610-635.
[65] Geerts, F., Pijcke, F. and Wijsen, J. First-Order under-Approximations of Consistent Query Answers. *Int. J. Approx. Reasoning*, 2017, 83:337-355.
[66] Geerts, F., Mecca, G., Papotti, P. and Santoro, D. The LLUNATIC Data-Cleaning Framework. *PVLDB*, 2013, 6(9):625-636.
[67] Gelfond, M and Vladimir Lifschitz, M. Classical Negation in Logic Programs and Disjunctive Databases. *New Generation Comput.*, 1991, 9(3/4):365-386.
[68] Greco, G., Greco, S. and Zumpano, E. A Logical Framework for Querying and Repairing Inconsistent Databases. *IEEE Trans. Knowl. Data Eng.*, 2003, 15(6):1389-1408.
[69] Greco, S. and Molinaro, C. Approximate Probabilistic Query Answering over Inconsistent Databases. Proc. ER 2008.
[70] Greco, S., Molinaro, C. and Trubitsyna, I. Computing Approximate Query Answers over Inconsistent Knowledge Bases. Proc. IJCAI 2018.
[71] Guagliardo, P. and Libkin, L. Correctness of SQL Queries on Databases with Nulls. *SIGMOD Record*, 2017, 46(3):5-16.
[72] Halpern, J. and Pearl, J. Causes and Explanations: A Structural-Model Approach: Part 1. *British J. Philosophy of Science*, 2005, 56:843-887.
[73] Ilyas, I. and Chu, X. *Trends in Cleaning Relational Data: Consistency and Deduplication*. Foundations and Trends in Databases, 2015, 5(4):281-393.
[74] Imielinski, T. and Lipski Jr., W. Incomplete Information in Relational Databases. *J. ACM*, 1984, 31(4):761-791.
[75] Kifer, M. and Lozinskii, E. A Logic for Reasoning with Inconsistency. *J. Autom. Reasoning*, 1992, 9(2):179-215.
[76] Kolahi, S. and Lakshmanan, L. On Approximating Optimum Repairs for Functional Dependency Violations. Proc. ICDT 2009.
[77] Koutris, P. and Wijsen, J. Consistent Query Answering for Self-Join-Free Conjunctive Queries Under Primary Key Constraints. *ACM Trans. Database Syst.*, 2017, 42(2):9:1-9:45.
[78] Koutris, P. and Wijsen, J. Consistent Query Answering for Primary Keys in Logspace. Proc. ICDT 2019.
[79] Lembo, D., Lenzerini, M., Rosati, R., Ruzzi, M. and Savo, D. F. Inconsistency-Tolerant Semantics for Description Logics. Proc. RR 2010.
[80] Lembo, D., Lenzerini, M., Rosati, R., Santarelli, V., Domenico, F. and Thorstensen, V. Mapping Repair in Ontology-based Data Access Evolving Systems. Proc. IJCAI, 2017.
[81] Lenzerini, M. Data Integration: A Theoretical Perspective. Proc. PODS 2002.
[82] Leone, N., Pfeifer, G., Faber,W., Eiter, T., Gottlob, G., Perri, S. and Scarcello, F. The DLV System for Knowledge Representation and Reasoning. *ACM Trans. Comput. Logic.*, 2006, 7(3):499-562.

[83] Lian, X., Chen, L. and Song, S. Consistent Query Answers in Inconsistent Probabilistic Databases. Proc. SIGMOD 2010.

[84] Livshits, E. and Kimelfeld, B. Counting and Enumerating (Preferred) Database Repairs. Proc. PODS 2017.

[85] Livshits, E., Kimelfeld, B. and Roy, S. Computing Optimal Repairs for Functional Dependencies. Proc. PODS 2018.

[86] Lloyd, J. *Foundations of Logic Programming*, Springer, 1987.

[87] Lopatenko, A. and Bertossi, L. Complexity of Consistent Query Answering in Databases under Cardinality-Based and Incremental Repair Semantics. Proc. ICDT 2007.

[88] Lopatenko, A. and Bertossi, L. Complexity of Consistent Query Answering in Databases under Cardinality-Based and Incremental Repair Semantics. Corr Arxiv Paper cs.DB/1605.07159. Extended version of [87].

[89] Lukasiewicz, T., Martinez, M. V., Pieris, A. and Simari, G. I. From Classical to Consistent Query Answering under Existential Rules. Proc. AAAI 2015.

[90] Maslowski, D. and Wijsen, J. A Dichotomy in the Complexity of Counting Database Repairs. *J. Comput. Syst. Sci.*, 2013, 79(6):958-983.

[91] Meliou, A., Gatterbauer, W., Moore, K. F. and Suciu, D. The Complexity of Causality and Responsibility for Query Answers and Non-Answers. Proc. VLDB 2010.

[92] Molinaro, C. and Greco, S. Polynomial Time Queries over Inconsistent Databases with Functional Dependencies and Foreign Keys. *Data Knowl. Eng.*, 2010, 69(7):709-722.

[93] Parisi, F. and Grant, J. Repairs and Consistent Answers for Inconsistent Probabilistic Spatio-Temporal Databases. Proc. SUM 2014.

[94] Poggi, A., Lembo, D., Calvanese, D., De Giacomo, G., Lenzerini, M. and Rosati, R. Linking Data to Ontologies. *J. Data Semantics*, 2008, 10:133-173.

[95] Reiter, R. A Theory of Diagnosis from First Principles. *Artif. Intell.*, 1987, 32(1):57-95.

[96] Reiter, R. On Specifying Database Updates. *J. Log. Program.*, 1995, 25(1):53-91.

[97] Reiter, R. *Knowledge in Action.* The MIT Press, 2001.

[98] Rekatsinas, T., Chu, X., Ilyas, I. and Re, C. HoloClean: Holistic Data Repairs with Probabilistic Inference. *PVLDB*, 2017, 10(11):1190-1201.

[99] Rodriguez, M. A., Bertossi, L. and Caniupan-Marileo, M. Consistent Query Answering under Spatial Semantic Constraints. *Inf. Syst.*, 2013, 38(2):244-263.

[100] Rosati, R. On the Complexity of Dealing with Inconsistency in Description Logic Ontologies. Proc. IJCAI 2011.

[101] Roy, S. and Suciu, D. A Formal Approach to Finding Explanations for Database Queries. Proc. SIGMOD 2014.

[102] Salimi, B., Bertossi, L., Suciu, D. and Van den Broeck, G. Quantifying Causal Effects on Query Answering in Databases. Proc. TaPP 2016.

[103] Staworko, S., Chomicki, J. and Marcinkowski, J. Prioritized Repairing and Consistent Query Answering in Relational Databases. *Ann. Math. Artif. Intell.*, 2012, 64(2-3):209-246.

[104] Suciu, D., Olteanu, D., Re, C. and Koch, C. *Probabilistic Databases.* Synthesis Lectures on Data Management, Morgan & Claypool Publishers, 2011.

[105] ten Cate, B., Fontaine, G. and Kolaitis, P. On the Data Complexity of Consistent Query Answering. *Theory Comput. Syst.*, 2015, 57(4):843-891.

[106] ten Cate, B., Halpert, R. and Kolaitis, P. Exchange-Repairs - Managing Inconsistency in Data Exchange. *J. Data Semantics*, 2016, 5(2):77-97.

[107] Troquard, N., Confalonieri, R., Galliani, P., Peñaloza, R., Porello, D. and Kutz, O. Repairing Ontologies via Axiom Weakening. Proc. AAAI 2018.

[108] Wijsen, J. Database Repairing using Updates. *ACM Trans. Database Syst.*, 2005, 30(3):722-768.

[109] Wijsen, J. A Survey of the Data Complexity of Consistent Query Answering under Key Constraints. Proc. FoIKS 2014.

[110] Yaghmaie, M., Bertossi, L. and Ariyan, S. Repair-Oriented Relational Schemas for Multidimensional Databases. Proc. EDBT 2012.

[111] Yakout, M., Elmagarmid, A., Neville, J., Ouzzani, M. and Ilyas, I. Guided Data Repair. PVLDB, 2011, 4(5):279-289.

Efficient Logspace Classes for Enumeration, Counting, and Uniform Generation

Marcelo Arenas
PUC & IMFD Chile
marenas@ing.puc.cl

Luis Alberto Croquevielle
PUC & IMFD Chile
lacroquevielle@uc.cl

Rajesh Jayaram
Carnegie Mellon University
rkjayara@cs.cmu.edu

Cristian Riveros
PUC & IMFD Chile
cristian.riveros@uc.cl

ABSTRACT

In this work, we study two simple yet general complexity classes, based on logspace Turing machines, which provide a unifying framework for efficient query evaluation in areas like information extraction and graph databases, among others. We investigate the complexity of three fundamental algorithmic problems for these classes: enumeration, counting and uniform generation of solutions, and show that they have several desirable properties in this respect.

Both complexity classes are defined in terms of nondeterministic logspace transducers (NL transducers). For the first class, we consider the case of unambiguous NL transducers, and we prove constant delay enumeration, and both counting and uniform generation of solutions in polynomial time. For the second class, we consider unrestricted NL transducers, and we obtain polynomial delay enumeration, approximate counting in polynomial time, and polynomial-time randomized algorithms for uniform generation. More specifically, we show that each problem in this second class admits a fully polynomial-time randomized approximation scheme (FPRAS) and a polynomial-time Las Vegas algorithm for uniform generation. Interestingly, the key idea to prove these results is to show that the fundamental problem #NFA admits an FPRAS, where #NFA is the problem of counting the number of strings of length n accepted by a nondeterministic finite automaton (NFA). While this problem is known to be #P-complete and, more precisely, SpanL-complete, it was open whether this problem admits an FPRAS. In this work, we solve this open problem, and obtain as a welcome corollary that every function in SpanL admits an FPRAS.

PODS'19, June 30-July 5, 2019, Amsterdam, Netherlands

ACM ISBN 978-1-4503-6227-6/19/06...$15.00
https://doi.org/10.1145/3294052.3319704

CCS CONCEPTS

• **Information systems → Query optimization**; *Information extraction*; Semi-structured data; • **Theory of computation → Turing machines**; **Complexity classes**; **Regular languages**; *Probabilistic computation*.

KEYWORDS

Enumeration, counting, uniform generation.

ACM Reference Format:
Marcelo Arenas, Luis Alberto Croquevielle, Rajesh Jayaram, and Cristian Riveros. 2019. Efficient Logspace Classes for Enumeration, Counting, and Uniform Generation. In *38th ACM SIGMOD-SIGACT-SIGAI Symposium on Principles of Database Systems (PODS'19), June 30-July 5, 2019, Amsterdam, Netherlands.* ACM, New York, NY, USA, 15 pages. https://doi.org/10.1145/3294052.3319704

1 INTRODUCTION

Arguably, query answering is the most fundamental problem in databases. In this respect, developing efficient query answering algorithms, as well as understanding when this cannot be done, is of paramount importance in the area. In the most classical view of this problem, one is interested in computing all the answers, or solutions, to a query. However, as the quantity of data becomes enormously large, the number of solutions to a query could also be enormous, so computing the complete set of solutions can be prohibitively expensive. In order to overcome this limitation, the idea of enumerating the answers to a query with a *small delay* has been recently studied in the database area [31]. More specifically, the idea is to divide the computation of the answers to a query into two phases. In a *preprocessing* phase, some data structures are constructed to accelerate the process of computing answers. Then in an *enumeration* phase, the answers are enumerated with a small delay between them. In particular, in the case of constant delay enumeration algorithms, the preprocessing phase should take polynomial time, while the time between consecutive answers should be constant.

Constant delay enumeration algorithms allow users to retrieve a fixed number of answers very efficiently, which can give them a lot of information about the solutions to a query. In fact, the same holds if users need a linear or a polynomial number of answers. However, because of the data structures used in the preprocessing phase, these algorithms usually return answers that are very similar to each other [11, 16, 31]; for example, tuples with n elements where only the first few coordinates are changed in the first answers that are returned. In this respect, other approaches can be used to return some solutions efficiently but improving the variety. Most notably, generating an answer uniformly, at random, is a desirable condition if it can be done efficiently. Notice that returning varied solutions has been identified as an important property not only in databases, but also for algorithms that retrieve information in a broader sense [1].

Efficient algorithms for either enumerating or uniformly generating the answers to a query are powerful tools to help in the process of understanding the answers to a query. But how can we know how long these algorithms should run, and how complete the set of computed answers is? A third tool that is needed then is an efficient algorithm for computing, or estimating, the number of solutions to a query. Then, taken together, enumeration, counting and uniform generation techniques form a powerful attacking trident when confronting to the problem of answering a query.

In this paper, we follow a more principled approach to study the problems of enumerating, counting and uniformly generating the answers to a query. More specifically, we begin by following the guidance of [22], which urges the use of relations to formalize the notion of solution to a given input of a problem (for instance, to formalize the notion of answer to an input query over an input database). While there are many other ways of formalizing this notion, most such formalizations only make sense for a specific kind of queries, e.g. a subset of the integers is well-suited as the solution set for counting problems, but not for sampling problems. Thus, if Σ denotes a finite alphabet, then by following [22] we represent a problem as a relation $R \subseteq \Sigma^* \times \Sigma^*$, and we say that y is a solution for an input x if $(x, y) \in R$. Note that the problem of enumerating the solutions to a given input x corresponds to the problem of enumerating the elements of the set $\{y \in \Sigma^* \mid (x, y) \in R\}$, while the counting and uniform generation problems correspond to the problems of computing the cardinality of $\{y \in \Sigma^* \mid (x, y) \in R\}$ and uniformly generating, at random, a string in this set, respectively.

Second, we study two simple yet general complexity classes for relations, based on non-deterministic logspace transducers (NL transducers), which provide a unifying framework for studying enumeration, counting and uniform generation. More specifically, given a finite alphabet Σ, an NL-transducer M is a nondeterministic Turing Machine with input and output alphabet Σ, a read-only input tape, a write-only output tape and a work-tape of which, on input $x \in \Sigma^*$, only the first $O(\log(|x|))$ cells can be used. Moreover, a string $y \in \Sigma^*$ is said to be an output of M on input x, if there exists a run of M on input x that halts in an accepting state with y as the string in the output tape. Finally, assuming that all outputs of M on input x are denoted by $M(x)$, a relation of $R \subseteq \Sigma^* \times \Sigma^*$ is said to be accepted by M if for every input x, it holds that $M(x) = \{y \in \Sigma^* \mid (x, y) \in R\}$.

The first complexity class of relations studied in this paper consists of the relations accepted by unambiguous NL-transducers. More precisely, an NL-transducer M is said to be unambiguous if for every input x and $y \in M(x)$, there exists exactly one run of M on input x that halts in an accepting state with y as the string in the output tape. For this class, we are able to achieve constant delay enumeration, and both counting and uniform generation of solutions in polynomial time. For the second class, we consider (unrestricted) NL-transducers, and we obtain polynomial delay enumeration, approximate counting in polynomial time, and polynomial-time randomized algorithms for uniform generation. More specifically, we show that each problem in this second class admits a fully polynomial-time randomized approximation scheme (FPRAS) [22] and a polynomial-time Las Vegas algorithm for uniform generation. It is important to mention that the key idea to prove these results is to show that the fundamental problem #NFA admits an FPRAS, where #NFA is the problem of counting the number of strings of length n (given in unary) accepted by a non-deterministic finite automaton (NFA). While this problem is known to be #P-complete and, more precisely, SpanL-complete [3], it was open whether it admits an FPRAS, and only quasi-polynomial time randomized approximation schemata were known for it [19, 24]. In this work, we solve this open problem, and obtain as a welcome corollary that every function in SpanL admits an FPRAS. Thus, to the best of our knowledge, we obtain the first complexity class with a simple definition based on Turing Machines, and where each problem admits an FPRAS.

Proviso. The main results of the paper are given in Section 3, while the sketches of the proofs of these results are presented in Sections 5 and 6. Due to the lack of space, the full proofs will be given in the journal version of this article.

2 PRELIMINARIES

Relations and problems. Let Σ be a finite alphabet with at least two symbols. As usual, we represent inputs as words $x \in \Sigma^*$ and the length of x is denoted by $|x|$. A problem is represented as a relation $R \subseteq \Sigma^* \times \Sigma^*$. For every pair $(x, y) \in R$, we interpret x as being the encoding of an input to some problem, and y as being the encoding of a solution or witness to that input. For each $x \in \Sigma^*$, we define the set $W_R(x) = \{y \in \Sigma^* \mid (x, y) \in R\}$, and call it the witness set for x. Also, if $y \in W_R(x)$, we call y a witness or a solution to x.

This is a very general framework, so mostly we work with relations that meet two additional properties. First, we only work with relations where both the input and the witnesses have a finite encoding. Second, we work with p-relations [22], namely, each R satisfies that (1) there exists a polynomial q such that $(x, y) \in R$ implies that $|y| \leq q(|x|)$ and (2) there exists a deterministic Turing Machine that receives as input $(x, y) \in \Sigma^* \times \Sigma^*$, runs in polynomial time and accepts if, and only if, $(x, y) \in R$. Without loss of generality, from now on we assume that for a p-relation R, there exists a polynomial q such that $|y| = q(|x|)$ for every $(x, y) \in R$. This is not a strong requirement, since all witnesses can be made to have the same length through padding.

Enumeration, counting and uniform generation. Given a p-relation R, we are interested in the following problems:

Problem:	ENUM(R)
Input:	A word $x \in \Sigma^*$
Output:	Enumerate all $y \in W_R(x)$ without repetitions

Problem:	COUNT(R)
Input:	A word $x \in \Sigma^*$
Output:	The size $|W_R(x)|$

Problem:	GEN(R)
Input:	A word $x \in \Sigma^*$
Output:	Generate uniformly, at random, a word in $W_R(x)$

Given that $|y| = q(|x|)$ for every $(x, y) \in R$, we have that $W_R(x)$ is finite and these three problems are well defined. Notice that in the case of ENUM(R), we do not assume a specific order on words, so that the elementos of $W_R(x)$ can be enumerated in any order (but without repetitions). Moreover, in the case of COUNT(R), we assume that $|W_R(x)|$ is encoded in binary and, therefore, the size of the output is logarithmic in the size of $W_R(x)$. Finally, in the case of GEN(R), we generate a word $y \in W_R(x)$ with probability $\frac{1}{|W_R(x)|}$ if the set $W_R(x)$ is not empty; otherwise, we return a special symbol $\perp$ to indicate that $W_R(x) = \varnothing$.

Enumeration with polynomial and constant delay. An enumeration algorithm for ENUM(R) is a procedure that receives an input $x \in \Sigma^*$ and, during the computation, it outputs each word in $W_R(x)$, one by one and without repetitions. The time between two consecutive outputs is called the delay of the enumeration. In this paper, we consider two restrictions on the delay: polynomial-delay and constant-delay. *Polynomial-delay enumeration* is the standard notion of polynomial time efficiency in enumeration algorithms [23] and is defined as follows. An enumeration algorithm is of polynomial delay if there exists a polynomial p such that for every input $x \in \Sigma^*$, the time between the beginning of the algorithm and the initial output, between any two consecutive outputs, and between the last output and the end of the algorithm, is bounded by $p(|x|)$.

Constant-delay enumeration is another notion of efficiency for enumeration algorithms that has attracted a lot attention in the last years [10, 13, 31]. This notion has stronger guarantees compared to polynomial delay: the enumeration is done in a second phase after the processing of the input and taking constant-time between two consecutive outputs in a very precise sense. Several notions of constant-delay enumeration have been given, most of them in database theory where it is important to divide the analysis between query and data. In this paper, we want a definition of constant-delay that is agnostic of the distinction between query and data (i.e. combined complexity) and, for this reason, we use a more general notion of constant-delay enumeration than the one in [10, 13, 31].

As it is standard in the literature [31], for the notion of constant-delay enumeration we consider enumeration algorithms on Random Access Machines (RAM) with addition and uniform cost measure [2]. Given a relation $R \subseteq \Sigma^* \times \Sigma^*$, an enumeration algorithm E for R has constant-delay if E runs in two phases over the input x.

(1) The first phase (precomputation), which does not produce output.
(2) The second phase (enumeration), which occurs immediately after the precomputation phase, where all words in $W_R(x)$ are enumerated without repetitions and satisfying the following conditions, for a fixed constant c:
  (a) the time it takes to generate the first output y is bounded by $c \cdot |y|$;
  (b) the time between two consecutive outputs y and y' is bounded by $c \cdot |y'|$ and does not depend on y; and
  (c) the time between the final element y that is returned and the end of the enumeration phase is bounded by $c \cdot |y|$,

We say that E is a constant delay algorithm for R with precomputation phase f, if E has constant delay and the precomputation phase takes time $O(f(|x|))$. Moreover, we say that ENUM(R) can be solved with constant delay if there exists a constant delay algorithm for R with precomputation phase p for some polynomial p.

Our notion of constant-delay algorithm differ from the definitions in [31] in two aspects. First, as it was previously mentioned we relax the distinction between query and data in the preprocessing phase, allowing our algorithm to take polynomial time in the input (i.e. combined complexity). Second, our definition of constant-delay is what in [10, 13] is called *linear delay in the size of the output*, namely, writing the next output is linear in its size and not depending on the size of the input. This is a natural assumption, since each output must at least be written down to return it to the user. Notice that, given an input x and an output y, the notion of polynomial-delay above means polynomial in $|x|$ and, instead, the notion of linear delay from [10, 13] means linear in $|y|$. Thus, we have decided to call the two-phase enumeration from above "constant-delay", as it does not depend on the size of the input x, and the delay is just what is needed to write the output (which is the minimum requirement for such an enumeration algorithm).

Approximate counting. Given a relation $R \subseteq \Sigma^* \times \Sigma^*$, the problem COUNT$(R)$ can be solved efficiently if there exists a polynomial-time algorithm that, given $x \in \Sigma^*$, computes $|W_R(x)|$. In other words, if we think of COUNT(R) as a function that maps x to the value $|W_R(x)|$, then COUNT(R) can be computed efficiently if COUNT$(R) \in$ FP, the class of functions that can be computed in polynomial time. As such a condition does not hold for many fundamental problems, we also consider the possibility of efficiently approximating the value of the function COUNT(R). More precisely, COUNT(R) is said to admit a fully polynomial-time randomized approximation scheme (FPRAS) [22] if there exists a randomized algorithm $\mathcal{A} : \Sigma^* \times (0,1) \to \mathbb{N}$ and a polynomial $q(u, v)$ such that for every $x \in \Sigma^*$ and $\delta \in (0,1)$:

$$\mathbf{Pr}(|\mathcal{A}(x,\delta) - |W_R(x)|| \leq \delta \cdot |W_R(x)|) \quad \geq \quad \frac{3}{4}$$

and the number of steps needed to compute $\mathcal{A}(x,\delta)$ is at most $q(|x|, \frac{1}{\delta})$. Thus, $\mathcal{A}(x,\delta)$ approximates the value $|W_R(x)|$ with a relative error of δ, and it can be computed in polynomial time in the size of x and the value $\frac{1}{\delta}$.

Las Vegas uniform generation. The problem GEN(R) can be solved efficiently if there exists a polynomial-time randomized algorithm that, given $x \in \Sigma^*$, generates an element of $W_R(x)$ with uniform probability distribution (if $W_R(x) = \varnothing$, then it returns $\perp$). However, as in the case of COUNT(R), the existence of such a generator is not guaranteed for many fundamental problems, so we also consider a relaxed notion of generation that has a probability of failing in returning a solution. More precisely, GEN(R) is said to admit a polynomial-time Las Vegas uniform generator (PLVUG) if there exists a randomized algorithm $\mathcal{G} : \Sigma^* \to \Sigma^* \cup \{\perp, \mathbf{fail}\}$, a polynomial $q(u)$ and a function $\varphi : \Sigma^* \to (0,1)$ such that for every $x \in \Sigma^*$:

(1) $\mathbf{Pr}(\mathcal{G}(x) \neq \mathbf{fail}) \geq \frac{1}{2}$;
(2) if $W_R(x) \neq \varnothing$, then $\mathbf{Pr}(\mathcal{G}(x) = \perp) = 0$;
(3) for every $(x, y) \in \Sigma^* \times \Sigma^*$:
  (a) if $(x, y) \notin R$, then $\mathbf{Pr}(\mathcal{G}(x) = y) = 0$;
  (b) if $(x, y) \in R$, then $\mathbf{Pr}(\mathcal{G}(x) = y) = \varphi(x)$;
(4) the number of steps needed to compute $\mathcal{G}(x)$ is at most $q(|x|)$.

The invocation $\mathcal{G}(x)$ can fail in generating an element of $W_R(x)$, in which case it returns **fail**. By condition (1), we know that this probability of failing is smaller than $\frac{1}{2}$, so that by invoking $\mathcal{G}(x)$ several times we can make this probability arbitrarily small (for example, the probability that $\mathcal{G}(x)$ returns **fail** in 100 consecutive independent invocations is at most $(\frac{1}{2})^{100}$). Assume that the invocation $\mathcal{G}(x)$ does not fail. If $W_R(x) = \varnothing$, then we have by condition 3 (a) that $\mathcal{G}(x) = \perp$, so the randomized algorithm indicates that there is no witness for x in this case. If $W_R(x) \neq \varnothing$, then we have by conditions (2) and (3) that $\mathcal{G}(x)$ returns an element $y \in W_R(x)$. Moreover, we know by condition 3 (b) that the probability of returning such an element y is $\varphi(x)$. Thus, we have a uniform generator in this case, as the probability of returning each $y \in W_R(x)$ is the same. Finally, we have that $\mathcal{G}(x)$ can be computed in polynomial time in the $|x|$.

It is important to notice that the notion of polynomial-time Las Vegas uniform generator corresponds to the notion of uniform generator used in [22]. However, we have decided to use the term "Las Vegas" to emphasize the fact that there is a probability of failing in returning a solution. Moreover, the notion of polynomial-time Las Vegas uniform generator imposes stronger requirements than the notion of fully polynomial-time almost uniform generator introduced in [22]. In particular, the latter not only has a probability of failing, but also considers the possibility of generating a solution with a probability distribution that is *almost* uniform, that is, an algorithm that generates a string $y \in W_R(x)$ with a probability in an interval $[\varphi(x) - \delta, \varphi(x) + \delta]$ for a given error $\delta \in (0,1)$, where φ is defined as in the notion of PLVUG.

3 NL TRANSDUCERS: DEFINITIONS AND OUR MAIN RESULTS

The goal of this section is to provide simple yet general definitions of classes of relations with good properties in terms of enumeration, counting and uniform generation. More precisely, we are first aiming at providing a class $\mathcal{C}$ of relations that has a simple definition in terms of Turing Machines and such that for every relation $R \in \mathcal{C}$, it holds that ENUM(R) can be solved with constant delay, and both COUNT(R) and GEN(R) can be solved in polynomial time. Moreover, as it is well known that such good conditions cannot always be achieved, we are then aiming at extending the definition of $\mathcal{C}$ to obtain a simple class, also defined in terms of Turing Machines and with good approximation properties. It is important to mention that we are not looking for an exact characterization in terms of Turing Machines of the class of relations that admit constant delay enumeration algorithms, as this may result in an overly complicated model. Instead, we are looking for simple yet general classes of relations with good properties in terms of enumeration, counting and uniform generation, and which can serve as a starting point for the systematic study of these three fundamental properties.

A key notion that is used in our definitions of classes of relations is that of transducer. Given a finite alphabet Σ, an NL-transducer M is a nondeterministic Turing Machine with input and output alphabet Σ, a read-only input tape, a write-only output tape where the head is always moved to the right once a symbol is written in it (so that the output cannot be read by M), and a work-tape of which, on input x, only the first $f(|x|)$ cells can be used, where $f(n) \in O(\log(n))$. A string $y \in \Sigma^*$ is said to be an output of M on input x, if there exists a run of M on input x that halts in an accepting state with y as the string in the output tape. The set of all outputs of M on input x is denoted by $M(x)$ (notice that $M(x)$ can be empty). Finally, the relation accepted by M, denoted by $\mathcal{R}(M)$, is defined as $\{(x,y) \in \Sigma^* \times \Sigma^* \mid y \in M(x)\}$.

Definition 3.1. A relation R is in RelationNL if, and only if, there exists an NL-transducer M such that $\mathcal{R}(M) = R$.

The class RelationNL should be general enough to contain some natural and well-studied problems. A first such problem is the satisfiability of a propositional formula in DNF. As a relation, this problem can be represented as follows:

$$\text{SAT-DNF} = \{(\varphi,\sigma) \mid \varphi \text{ is a proposional formula in DNF}, \sigma \text{ is a truth assignment and } \sigma(\varphi) = 1\}.$$

Thus, we have that ENUM(SAT-DNF) corresponds to the problem of enumerating the truth assignments satisfying a propositional formula φ in DNF, while COUNT(SAT-DNF) and GEN(SAT-DNF) correspond to counting and uniformly generating such truth assignments, respectively. It is not difficult to see that SAT-DNF $\in$ RelationNL. Hence, given that COUNT(SAT-DNF) is a #P-complete problem, we cannot expect COUNT(R) to be solvable in polynomial time for every $R \in$ RelationNL. However, COUNT(SAT-DNF) admits an FPRAS [25], so we can still hope for COUNT(R) to admit an FPRAS for every $R \in$ RelationNL. It turns out that proving such a result involves providing an FPRAS for another natural and fundamental problem: #NFA. More specifically, #NFA is the problem of counting the number of words of length k accepted by a non-deterministic finite automaton without epsilon transitions (NFA), where k is given in unary (that is, k is given as a string 0^k). It is known that #NFA is #P-complete [3], but it is open whether it admits an FPRAS; in fact, the best randomized approximation scheme known for #NFA runs in time $n^{O(\log(n))}$ [24]. In our notation, this problem is represented by the following relation:

$$\text{MEM-NFA} = \{((N,0^k),w) \mid N \text{ is an NFA with alphabet } \Sigma, w \in \Sigma^*, |w| = k \text{ and } w \text{ is accepted by } N\},$$

that is, we have that #NFA = COUNT(MEM-NFA). It is easy to see that MEM-NFA $\in$ RelationNL. Hence, we give a positive answer to the open question of whether #NFA admits an FPRAS by proving the following general result about RelationNL.

Theorem 3.2. *If* $R \in$ RelationNL, *then* ENUM(R) *can be solved with polynomial delay,* COUNT(R) *admits an FPRAS, and* GEN(R) *admits a PLVUG.*

It is worth mentioning a fundamental consequence of this result in computational complexity. The class of function SpanL was introduced in [3] to provide a characterization of some functions that are hard to compute. More specifically, given a finite alphabet Σ, a function $f : \Sigma^* \to \mathbb{N}$ is in SpanL if there exists an NL-transducer M with input alphabet Σ such that $f(x) = |M(x)|$ for every $x \in \Sigma^*$. The class SpanL is contained in #P, and it has been instrumental in proving that some functions are difficult to compute [3, 8, 20, 26], as if a function f is complete for SpanL and $f \in$ FP, then P = NP [3]. Given that #NFA is SpanL-complete under parsimonious reductions [3], and parsimonious reductions preserve the existence of an FPRAS, we obtain the following corollary from Theorem 3.2.

Corollary 3.3. *Every function in* SpanL *admits an FPRAS.*

Although some classes of functions C for which every $f \in C$ admits an FPRAS have been identified before [9, 29], to the best of our knowledge this is the first such a class with a simple and robust definition based on Turing Machines.

A tight relationship between the existence of an FPRAS and the existence of a schema for almost uniform generation was proved in [22], for the class of relations that are *self-reducible.* Thus, one might wonder whether the existence of a PLVUG for GEN(R) in Theorem 3.2 is a corollary of the result in [22], as in this theorem we prove the existence of an FPRAS for COUNT(R). Interestingly, the answer to this question is no, as the notion of PLVUG ask for a uniform generator without an error δ, whose existence cannot be inferred from the results in [22]. Thus, we prove in Section 6 that COUNT(R) admits an FPRAS and GEN(R) admits a PLVUG, for a relation $R \in$ RelationNL, without relaying in the aforementioned result from [22].

A natural question at this point is whether a simple syntactic restriction on the definition of RelationNL gives rise to a class of relations with better properties in terms of enumeration, counting and uniform generation. Fortunately, the answer to this question comes by imposing a natural and well-studied restriction on Turing Machines, which allows us to define a class that contains many natural problems. More precisely, we consider the notion of UL-transducer, where the letter "U" stands for "unambiguous". Formally, M is an UL-transducer if M is an NL-transducer such that for every input x and $y \in M(x)$, there exists exactly one run of M on input x that halts in an accepting state with y as the string in the output tape. Notice that this notion of transducer is based on well-known classes of decision problems (e.g. UP [32] and UL [28]) and adapted for our case, namely, problems defined as relations.

Definition 3.4. A relation R is in RelationUL if, and only if, there exists an UL-transducer M such that $\mathcal{R}(M) = R$.

For RelationUL, we obtain the following result.

Theorem 3.5. *If $R \in$ RelationUL, then ENUM(R) can be solved with constant delay, there exists a polynomial-time algorithm for COUNT(R), and there exists a polynomial-time randomized algorithm for GEN(R).*

In particular, it should be noticed that given R in the class RelationUL and an input x, the solutions for x can be enumerated, counted and uniformly generated efficiently.

Classes of problems definable by machine models and that can be enumerated with constant delay have been proposed before. In [4], it is shown that if a problem is definable by a d-DNNF circuit, then the solutions of an instance can be listed with linear preprocessing and constant delay enumeration. Still, to the best of our knowledge, this is the first class with a simple and robust definition based on Turing Machines.

4 APPLICATIONS OF THE MAIN RESULTS

Before providing proof sketches of Theorems 3.2 and 3.5, we give some implications of these results. In particular, we show how NL and UL transducers can be used to obtain positive results on query evaluation in areas like information extraction, graph databases, and binary decision diagrams.

4.1 Information extraction

In [15], the framework of document spanners was proposed as a formalization of ruled-based information extraction. In this framework, the main data objects are documents and spans. Formally, given a finite alphabet Σ, a document is a string $d = a_1 \dots a_n$ and a span is pair $s = [i, j\rangle$ with $1 \leq i \leq j \leq n+1$. A span represents a continuous region of the document d, whose content is the substring of d from positions i to $j-1$. Given a finite set of variables $\mathbf{X}$, a mapping μ is a function from $\mathbf{X}$ to the spans of d.

Variable set automata (VA) are one of the main formalisms to specify sets of mappings over a document. Here, we use the notion of extended VA (eVA) from [16] to state our main results. Given the lack of space, we only recall the main definitions (see [15, 16] for more intuition and further details). An eVA is a tuple $\mathcal{A} = (Q, q_0, F, \delta)$ such that Q is a finite set of states, q_0 is the initial state, and F is the final set of states. Further, δ is the transition relation consisting of letter transitions (q, a, q'), or variable-set transitions (q, S, q'), where $S \subseteq \{x\vdash, \dashv x \mid x \in \mathbf{X}\}$ and $S \neq \emptyset$. The symbols $x\vdash$ and $\dashv x$ are called markers, and they are used to denote that variable x is open or close by $\mathcal{A}$, respectively. A run ρ over a document $d = a_1 \cdots a_n$ is a sequence of the form: $q_0 \xrightarrow{X_1} p_0 \xrightarrow{a_1} q_1 \xrightarrow{X_2} p_1 \xrightarrow{a_2} \dots \xrightarrow{a_n} q_n \xrightarrow{X_{n+1}} p_n$ where each X_i is a (possible empty) set of markers, $(p_i, a_{i+1}, q_{i+1}) \in \delta$, and $(q_i, X_{i+1}, p_i) \in \delta$ whenever $X_{i+1} \neq \emptyset$, and $q_i = p_i$ otherwise (that is, when $X_{i+1} = \emptyset$). We say that a run ρ is valid if for every $x \in \mathbf{X}$ there exists exactly one pair $[i, j\rangle$ such that $x\vdash \in X_i$ and $\dashv x \in X_j$. A valid run ρ naturally defines a mapping μ^ρ that maps x to the only span $[i, j\rangle$ such that $x\vdash \in X_i$ and $\dashv x \in X_j$. We say that ρ is accepting if $p_n \in F$. Finally, the semantics $[\![\mathcal{A}]\!](d)$ of $\mathcal{A}$ over d is defined as the set of all mappings μ^ρ where ρ is a valid and accepting run of $\mathcal{A}$ over d.

In [17, 27], it was shown that the decision problem related to query evaluation, namely, given an eVA $\mathcal{A}$ and a document d deciding whether $[\![\mathcal{A}]\!](d) \neq \emptyset$, is NP-hard. For this reason, in [16] a subclass of eVA is considered in order to recover polynomial-time evaluation. A eVA $\mathcal{A}$ is called functional if every accepting run is valid. Intuitively, a functional eVA does not need to check validity of the run given that it knows that every run that reaches a final state will be valid.

For the query evaluation problem of functional eVA (i.e. to compute $[\![\mathcal{A}]\!](d)$), one can naturally associate the relation:

$$\text{EVAL-eVA} = \{((\mathcal{A}, d), \mu) \mid \mathcal{A} \text{ is a functional eVA}, \; d \text{ is a document, and } \mu \in [\![\mathcal{A}]\!](d)\}.$$

It is not difficult to show that EVAL-eVA is in RelationNL. Hence, by Theorem 3.2 we get the following results.

Corollary 4.1. *ENUM(EVAL-eVA) can be enumerated with polynomial delay, COUNT(EVAL-eVA) admits an FPRAS, and GEN(EVAL-eVA) admits a PLVUG.*

In [5, 16], it was shown that every functional RGX or functional VA (not necessarily extended) can be converted in polynomial time into a functional eVA. Therefore, Corollary 4.1 also holds for these more general classes. Notice that in [18], it was given a polynomial-delay enumeration algorithm for $[\![\mathcal{A}]\!](d)$. Thus, only the results about COUNT(EVAL-eVA) and GEN(EVAL-eVA) are new.

Regarding efficient enumeration and exact counting, a constant-delay algorithm with polynomial preprocessing was given in [16] for the class of deterministic functional eVA. Here, we can easily extend these results for a more general class, that we called unambiguous functional eVA. Formally, we say that an eVA is unambiguous if for every two valid and accepting runs ρ_1 and ρ_2, it holds that $\mu^{\rho_1} \neq \mu^{\rho_2}$. In other words, each output of an unambiguous eVA is witnessed by exactly one run. As in the case of EVAL-eVA, we can define the relation EVAL-UeVA, by restricting the input to unambiguous functional eVA. By using UL-transducers and Theorem 3.5, we can then extend the results in [16] for the unambiguous case.

Corollary 4.2. ENUM(EVAL-UeVA) *can be solved with constant delay, there exists a polynomial-time algorithm for* COUNT(EVAL-UeVA), *and there exists a polynomial-time randomized algorithm for* GEN(EVAL-UeVA).

Notice that this result give a constant-delay algorithm with polynomial preprocessing for the class of unambiguous functional eVA. Instead, the algorithm in [16] has linear preprocessing over documents, restricted to the case of deterministic eVA. This leaves open whether there exists a constant-delay algorithm with linear preprocessing over documents for the unambiguous case.

4.2 Query evaluation in graph databases

Enumerating, counting, and generating paths are relevant tasks for query evaluation in graph databases [7]. Given a finite set Σ of labels, a graph database G is a pair (V, E) where V is a finite set of vertices and $E \subseteq V \times \Sigma \times V$ is a finite set of labeled edges. Here, nodes represent pieces of data and edges specify relations between them [7]. One of the core query languages for posing queries on graph databases are regular path queries (RPQ). An RPQ is a triple (x, R, y) where x, y are variables and R is a regular expression over Σ. As usual, we denote by $\mathcal{L}(R)$ all the strings over Σ that conform to R. Given an RPQ $Q = (x, R, y)$, a graph database $G = (V, E)$, and nodes $u, v \in V$, one would like to retrieve, count, or uniformly generate all paths[1] in G going from u to v that satisfies Q. Formally, a path from u to v in G is a sequence of vertices and labels of the form $\pi = v_0, p_1, v_1, p_2, \ldots, p_n, v_n$, such that $(v_i, p_{i+1}, v_{i+1}) \in E$, $u = v_0$, and $v = v_n$. A path π is said to satisfy $Q = (x, R, y)$ if the string $p_1 p_2 \cdots p_n \in \mathcal{L}(R)$. The length of π is defined as $|\pi| = n$. Clearly, between u and v there can be an infinite number of paths that satisfies Q. For this reason, one usually wants to retrieve all paths between u and v of at most certain length n, namely, one usually considers the set $[\![Q]\!]_n(G, u, v)$ of all paths π from u to v in G such that π satisfies Q and $|\pi| \leq n$. This naturally defines the following relation representing the problem of evaluating an RQP over a graph database:

$$\text{EVAL-RPQ} = \{((Q, 0^n, G, u, v), \pi) \mid \pi \in [\![Q]\!]_n(G, u, v)\}.$$

Using this relation, fundamental problems for RPQs such as enumerating, counting, or uniform generating paths can be naturally represented. It is not difficult to show that EVAL-RPQ is in RelationNL, from which the following corollary can be obtained by using Theorem 3.2. Notice that giving a polynomial-delay enumeration algorithm for EVAL-RPQ is straightforward, but the existence of an FPRAS and a PLVUG for EVAL-RPQ was not known before when queries are part of the input (i.e. in combined complexity).

Corollary 4.3. COUNT(EVAL-RPQ) *admits an FPRAS, and* GEN(EVAL-RPQ) *admits a PLVUG.*

4.3 Binary decision diagrams

Binary decision diagrams (OBDDs) are an abstract representation of boolean functions which are widely used in computer science and have found many applications in areas like formal verification [12]. A binary decision diagram (BDD) is a directed acyclic graph $D = (V, E)$ where each node v is labeled with a variable $\text{var}(v)$ and has at most two edges going to children $\text{lo}(v)$ and $\text{hi}(v)$. Intuitively, $\text{lo}(v)$ and $\text{hi}(v)$ represent the next nodes when $\text{var}(v)$ takes values 0 and 1, respectively. D contains only two terminal, or sink nodes, labeled by 0 or 1, and one initial node called v_0. We assume that every path from v_0 to a terminal node does not repeat variables. Then given an assignment σ from the variables in D to $\{0, 1\}$, we have that σ naturally defines a path from v_0 to a terminal node 0 or 1. In this way, D defines a boolean function that gives a value in $\{0, 1\}$ to each assignment σ; in particular, $D(\sigma) \in \{0, 1\}$ corresponds to the sink node reached by starting from v_0 and following the values in σ. For Ordered BDDs, we also have a linear order $<$ over the variables in D such that, for every $v_1, v_2 \in V$ with v_2 a child of v_1, it holds that $\text{var}(v_1) < \text{var}(v_2)$. Notice that not necessarily all variables appear in a path from the initial node v_0 to a terminal node 0 or 1. Nevertheless, the promise in an OBDD is that variables will appear following the order $<$.

An OBDD D defines the set of assignments σ such that $D(\sigma) = 1$. Then D can be considered as a succinct representation of the set $\{\sigma \mid D(\sigma) = 1\}$, and one would like to enumerate, count and uniformly generate assignments given D. This motivates the relation:

$$\text{EVAL-OBDD} = \{(D, \sigma) \mid D(\sigma) = 1\}.$$

Given (D, σ) in EVAL-OBDD, there is exactly one path in D that witnesses $D(\sigma) = 1$. Therefore, one can easily show that EVAL-OBDD is in RelationUL, from which we obtain:

Corollary 4.4. ENUM(EVAL-OBDD) *can be enumerated with constant delay, there exists a polynomial-time algorithm*

[1] Notice that the standard semantics for RPQs is to retrieve pair of nodes. Here we consider a less standard semantics based on paths which is also relevant for graph databases [7, 8, 26].

for COUNT(EVAL-OBDD), *and there exists a polynomial-time randomized algorithm for* GEN(EVAL-OBDD).

The above results are well known. Nevertheless, they show how easy and direct is to use UL transducers to realize the good algorithmic properties that a data structure has.

Some non-deterministic variants of BDDs have been studied in the literature [6]. In particular, an nOBDD extends an OBDD with vertices u without variables (i.e. $\text{var}(u) = \bot$) and without labels on its children. Thus, an nOBDD is non-deterministic in the sense that given an assignment σ, there can be several paths that bring σ from the initial node v_0 to a terminal node with labeled 0 or 1. Without loss of generality, nOBDDs are assumed to be consistent in the sense that, for each σ, all paths of σ in D can reach 0 or 1, but not both.

As in the case of OBDDs, we can define a relation called EVAL-nOBDD that pairs an nOBDD D with an assignment σ that evaluate D to 1 (i.e. $D(\sigma) = 1$). Contrary to OBDDs, an nOBDD looses the single witness property, and now an assignment σ can have several paths from the initial node to the 1 terminal node. Thus, it is not clear whether EVAL-nOBDD is in RelationUL. Still one can easily show that EVAL-nOBDD $\in$ RelationNL, from which the following results follow.

Corollary 4.5. ENUM(EVAL-nOBDD) *can be solved with polynomial delay,* COUNT(EVAL-nOBDD) *admits an FPRAS, and* GEN(EVAL-nOBDD) *admits a PLVUG.*

It is important to stress that the existence of an FPRAS and a PLVUG for EVAL-nOBDD was not known before.

5 A SIMPLE NOTION OF COMPLETENESS, AND ITS APPLICATION TO RelationUL

The goal of this section is to define a simple notion of reduction for the classes RelationNL and RelationUL, and then to show how it can be used to prove Theorem 3.5. In Section 6, we use this notion again when proving Theorem 3.2.

A natural question to ask is which notions of "completeness" and "reduction" are appropriate for our framework. Notions of reductions for relations have been proposed before, in particular in the context of search problems [14]. However, we do not intent to discuss them here; instead, we use an idea of completeness that is very restricted, but that turns out to be useful for the classes we defined. Let $\mathcal{C}$ be a complexity class of relations, and let $R, S \in \mathcal{C}$. We say R is reducible to S if there exists a function $f : \Sigma^* \to \Sigma^*$, computable in polynomial time, such that for every $x \in \Sigma^*$: $W_R(x) = W_S(f(x))$. Also, if T is reducible to S for every $T \in \mathcal{C}$, we say S is complete for $\mathcal{C}$. Notice that this definition is very strict, since the notion of reduction requires the witness set to be exactly the same for both relations (is not sufficient that they have the same size, for example). The benefit behind this kind of reduction is that it preserves all the properties of efficient enumeration, counting and uniform generation that we introduced in Sections 2 and 3, as stated in the following result.

Proposition 5.1. *If a relation R can be reduced to a relation S, then the following properties holds:*

- *If* ENUM(S) *can be solved with constant (resp. polynomial) delay, then* ENUM(R) *can be solved with constant (resp. polynomial) delay.*
- *If there exists a polynomial time algorithm (resp. an FPRAS) for* COUNT(S)*, then there exists a polynomial time algorithm (resp. an FPRAS) for* COUNT(R).
- *If there exists a polynomial time randomized algorithm (resp. a PLVUG) for* GEN(S)*, then there exists a polynomial time randomized algorithm (resp. a PLVUG) for* GEN(R).

Therefore, by finding a complete relation S for a class $\mathcal{C}$, we can just study the aforementioned problems for S, and we know that the obtained results will extend to every relation in the class $\mathcal{C}$.

5.1 Complete problems for RelationNL and RelationUL

The notion of reduction just defined above is useful for us as RelationNL and RelationUL admit complete problems under this notion. These complete relations are defined in terms of NFAs, and the idea behind them is the following. Take a relation R in RelationNL (the case for RelationUL is very similar). We know there is an NL-transducer M that characterizes it. Consider now some input x. Since M is a non-deterministic logspace Turing Machine, there is only a polynomial number of different configurations that M can be in (polynomial on $|x|$). So we can consider the set of possible configurations as the states of an NFA N_x, which has polynomial size, and whose transitions are determined by the transitions between the configurations of M. Moreover, whenever a symbol is output by the transducer M, that symbol is read by the automaton N_x. In this way, N_x accepts exactly the language $W_R(x)$. We formalize this idea in the following result, where

$$\text{MEM-UFA} = \{((N, 0^k), w) \mid N \text{ is an unambiguous NFA with alphabet } \Sigma, w \in \Sigma^*, |w| = k \text{ and } w \text{ is accepted by } N\},$$

and an NFA is said to be unambiguous if there exists exactly one accepting run for every string accepted by it.

Proposition 5.2. MEM-NFA *is complete for* RelationNL *and* MEM-UFA *is complete for* RelationUL.

5.2 Algorithmic properties of RelationUL

Theorem 3.5 is a consequence of Propositions 5.1 and 5.2, and the following result.

Proposition 5.3. ENUM(MEM-UFA) *can be solved with constant delay, there exists a polynomial time algorithm for* COUNT(MEM-UFA), *and there exists a polynomial time randomized algorithm for* GEN(MEM-UFA).

The results for COUNT(MEM-UFA) is a corollary of the fact that there exists a polynomial time algorithm that, given an input string x, returns the number of accepting runs of a non-deterministic logspace Turing Machine with input x [3]. Moreover, the result for GEN(MEM-UFA) can be obtained by considering that COUNT(MEM-UFA) can be solved in polynomial time and MEM-UFA is a self-reducible relation [22], and then using a strategy similar to the one described in [22]. On the other hand, the result for ENUM(MEM-UFA) does require a more elaborated proof that we we outline here.

Let $(N, 0^k)$ be an input of ENUM(MEM-UFA). In the preprocessing phase of the constant-delay enumeration algorithm for this problem, the NFA N is unrolled to get rid of any cycles it might have, and keep only the accepted words of length exactly k, which are the ones we want to enumerate. For the unrolling, we create $k+1$ layers of nodes, being each layer a copy of the set of states of N. And for each transition in N, we connect each layer with the next one, by joining the corresponding nodes with a directed edge, and labeling the edge according to the symbol in the transition. Given that N is an unambiguous NFA, this gives us a directed acyclic graph G, where each word w of length k accepted by N has a unique corresponding path between a fixed start node and a fixed end node in G, such that the labels read along the way form the string w. From that, it is not difficult to see how to enumerate with constant delay. We just have to go through G, beginning in the "start node", and traversing it in a depth-first search manner. During this process, we store the symbols read, and output them any time we reach the end node of G.

6 APPROXIMATE COUNTING AND UNIFORM GENERATION OF RelationNL

The goal of this section is to provide a proof of Theorem 3.2, which considers the class RelationNL defined in terms of NL-transducers. Given that we show in Proposition 5.2 that MEM-NFA is complete for RelationNL, we have by Propositions 5.1 that Theorem 3.2 is a consequence of the following result.

Theorem 6.1. ENUM(MEM-NFA) *can be solved with polynomial delay,* COUNT(MEM-NFA) *admits an FPRAS, and* GEN(MEM-NFA) *admits a PLVUG*

As mentioned in Section 5.2, we have that MEM-NFA is a self-reducible relation [22]. Besides, the existence problem for MEM-NFA (that is, for a given input $(N, 0^k)$, decide whether there are any witnesses) can be solved in polynomial time. With all that, we can derive the existence of a polynomial delay algorithm for ENUM(MEM-NFA) as a direct application of Theorem 4.9 from [30]. In this section, we focus on the remaining part of the proof of Theorem 6.1. More specifically, we provide an algorithm that approximately counts the number of words of a given length accepted by an NFA, where this length is given in unary. This constitutes an FPRAS for COUNT(MEM-NFA), as formally stated in Theorem 6.6. As this algorithm works by simultaneously counting and doing uniform generation of witnesses, its existence not only gives us an FPRAS for COUNT(MEM-NFA), but also a PLVUG for GEN(MEM-NFA), as formally stated in Corollary 6.7.

6.1 The Algorithm Template

As mentioned in Section 3, we consider the following approximation problem. The input of the problem is an NFA N on the alphabet $\{0, 1\}$ with m states (and no epsilon transitions), a string 0^n that represents an integer $n \geq 1$ given in unary, and an error $\delta \in (0, 1)$. The problem then is to return R such that R is a $(1 \pm \delta)$-approximation of $|\mathcal{L}_n(N)|$, that is, $(1-\delta)|\mathcal{L}_n(N)| \leq R \leq (1+\delta)|\mathcal{L}_n(N)|$, where $\mathcal{L}(N)$ is the set of strings accepted by N and $\mathcal{L}_n(N) = \{w \in \{0,1\}^* \mid w \in \mathcal{L}(N) \text{ and } |w| = n\}$. Besides, such an approximation should be returned in time polynomial in m, n and $\frac{1}{\delta}$ (notice that the size of NFA N is $O(m^2)$, so being polynomial in m means being polynomial in the size of N).

Our algorithm for approximating $\mathcal{L}_n(N)$ will involve the construction of a directed acyclic graph from the NFA N. We call this directed acyclic graph N_{unroll}, as it is obtained by unrolling n times the NFA N . Formally, assume that $N = \{s_1, \ldots, s_m\}$ and s_1 is the initial state of N. Then for every state $s_i \in N$ create n states $s_i^1, \ldots, s_i^n$ in N_{unroll}, and for every transition $s_i \xrightarrow{b} s_j$ in N and $b \in \{0, 1\}$, create the transition $s_i^t \xrightarrow{b} s_j^{t+1}$ for all $t = 1, 2, \ldots, n-1$ in N_{unroll}. Moreover, include a vertex s_{start} in N_{unroll} with transitions $s_{start} \xrightarrow{b} s_i^1$ if there is a transition $s_1 \xrightarrow{b} s_i$ in N (recall that s_1 is the initial state of N). Finally, create a unique final state s_{final} for N_{unroll}, and for every accepting state s_j of N, add to N_{unroll} the transition $s_j^n \xrightarrow{1} s_{final}$. We will use the terms *vertex* and *state* interchangeably to refer to the vertices of N_{unroll}. We refer to the set $\{s_1^t, s_2^t, \ldots, s_m^t\}$ as the t-th layer of N_{unroll}. The vertex set of N_{unroll} is precisely $\{s_{start}, s_{final}\} \cup (\bigcup_{t=1}^n \{s_1^t, s_2^t, \ldots, s_m^t\})$.

Remark 1. *Notice that* s_{final} *is included in* N_{unroll} *to have a unique final state. Besides, notice that for each final state* s_j *of*

N, the last occurrence of such a state when processing a string of length n is connected with s_{final} via the same symbol 1, that is, the transition $s_j^n \xrightarrow{1} s_{final}$ is included in N_{unroll}. Hence, the size of the accepted language is not changed, as the number of distinct strings which give a path from s_{start} to s_{final} in N_{unroll} is precisely $|\mathcal{L}_n(N)|$.

We say that a string w is a *member of* a vertex $s \in N_{unroll}$ if there is a path from s_{start} to s in N_{unroll} where the string of ordered labels of the edges is precisely w. We write $U(s)$ to denote the set of strings which are members of a state s. Note that $|U(s_{final})| = |\mathcal{L}_n(N)|$, and $U(s_{start}) = \{\varepsilon\}$. Thus, our goal is to produce a good estimate of the value $|U(s_{final})|$. For a string w, let $w[t]$ denote the t-th bit in w. Thus if $w = 100101$, we have $w[1] = 1, w[2] = 0, w[3] = 0$, and so on. For strings w, v, let $w \circ v$ denote their concatenation.

Algorithm 1: Algorithmic Template for our FPRAS

(1) Construct the directed acyclic graph N_{unroll} from the NFA N.
(2) For layers $i = 1, 2, \ldots, n$ and $j = 1, 2, \ldots, m$:
  (a) Compute $R(s_j^i)$ given $\bigcup_{t=1}^{i-1} \bigcup_{j=1}^{m} \{R(s_j^t), X(s_j^t)\}$. For $i = 1$, we have that $R(s_j^i)$ is computed without any additional information.
  (b) Call a subroutine to sample k uniform elements of $U(s_j^i)$ using the value $R(s_j^i)$ and $\bigcup_{t=1}^{i-1} \bigcup_{j=1}^{m} \{R(s_j^t), X(s_j^t)\}$.
  (c) Let $X(s_j^i) \subseteq U(s_j^i)$ be the multi-set of the k uniform samples obtained.
(3) Return $R(s_{final})$.

The components of the main algorithm are as follows. We set $k = (\frac{nm}{\delta})^c$ for some sufficiently large constant c (to be defined later). Then for each vertex $s \in N_{unroll}$ (where $s = s_j^t$ for some $j \in \{1, \ldots, m\}$ and $t \in \{1, \ldots, n\}$), we store k strings $x_1, \ldots, x_k$, such that each $x_i \in U(s)$. Specifically, the x_i's are uniform samples of the set $U(s)$. We denote this set of k samples for the vertex s by $X(s) \subseteq U(s)$ (if $|U(s)| \leq k$, we set $X(s) = U(s)$). Since the samples will be uniform and independent, it is possible that we will obtain duplicates samples of a given $x \in U(s)$. Therefore, we allow $X(s)$ to be a multi-set (meaning that $X(s) = \{x_1, \ldots, x_k\}$, and the strings x_i are not necessarily distinct). Second, we store a value $R(s)$ which is a $(1 \pm \delta)$-approximation of $|U(s)|$. The algorithm proceeds like a dynamic programming algorithm, computing $R(s)$ and $X(s)$ for every state s in N_{unroll} in a breadth-first search ordering. We first compute $R(s), X(s)$ for all states s in layer 1, meaning $\{s_1^1, s_2^1, \ldots, s_m^1\}$. Then for any layer i, given the values $\bigcup_{t=1}^{i-1} \bigcup_{j=1}^{m} \{R(s_j^t), X(s_j^t)\}$, we compute the corresponding values $R(s_j^i), X(s_j^i)$ for each vertex s_j^i in layer i. So the values $R(s), X(s)$ are computed layer by layer. The final estimate for $|\mathcal{L}_n(N)|$ is $R(s_{final})$. We summarize this algorithmic template in Algorithm 1.

6.2 The Sampling Template

To carry out our main approximation algorithm, we must implement the algorithmic template given in Algorithm 1. In particular, we must implement the sampling subroutine in step 2 (b). We begin by describing a generic sampling template for this step, which will be used by our main algorithm as a subroutine. The procedure is essentially that of [22], but modified to suit our setting. The procedure to sample a uniform element of a set $U(s_j^\alpha)$ is as follows. We initialize a string w^α to be the empty string, we construct a sequence of strings $w^\alpha, w^{\alpha-1}, \ldots, w^1, w^0$, where each string w^t is of the form $b_t \circ w^{t+1}$ with $b_t \in \{0, 1\}$, and we define the result of the sample procedure to be w^0. To ensure that w^0 is an element of $U(s_j^\alpha)$ chosen with uniform distribution, we also consider a sequence of sets of strings $W^\alpha, W^{\alpha-1}, \ldots, W^1, W^0$ constructed as follows. We have that $W^\alpha = U(s_j^\alpha)$. Then we partition W^α into two sets of strings: those with last bit equal to 0 and with last bit equal to 1, which are called W_0^α and W_1^α, respectively. We estimate the size of each partition, and choose one of them with probability proportional to its size, say W_b^α. We then append the bit b the prefix of w^α to obtain $w^{\alpha-1} = b \circ w^\alpha$, we define $W^{\alpha-1}$ as $\{x \mid x \circ b \in W^\alpha \text{ and } |x| \geq 1\}$, and we recurse on $w^{\alpha-1}$ and $W^{\alpha-1}$. Thus, in general, we have that W^t is the set of strings x such that $x \circ w^t \in U(s_j^\alpha)$, and we also have that $W^0 = \varnothing$.

Since there could be an error in estimating the sizes of the partitions, it may be the case that some items were chosen with slightly larger probability than others. To remedy this and obtain a perfectly uniform sampler, at every step of the algorithm we store the probability with which we chose a partition. Thus at the end, we have computed exactly the probability φ with which we sampled the string w. We can then reject this sample with probability proportional to $1 - \varphi$, which gives a perfect sampler. As long as no string is too much more likely than another to be sampled, the probability of rejection will be a constant, and we can simply run our sampler $O(\log(\frac{1}{\mu}))$-times to get a sample with probability $1 - \mu$ for every $\mu > 0$. For the sake of simplicity, we first assume that we have perfect estimates of the sizes of the partitions in question. This procedure is given below in Algorithm 2. We call it with the initial parameters **SampleTemplate**$(W^\alpha, \varepsilon, \varphi_0)$, where ε is the empty string, corresponding to the goal of sampling a uniform element of $W^\alpha = U(s_j^\alpha)$. Here, φ_0 is a value that we will later choose. Specifically, φ_0 will be a constant times a $(1 \pm \delta)$-approximation of $|U(s_j^\alpha)|$.

At every step j of Algorithm 2, we have that $|W^j|$ is precisely the number of strings in W^α which have the suffix

w^j, as W^j is the set of strings x such that $x \circ w^j \in W^\alpha$. Note then that the set W^j *depends* on the random string w^j, so in fact we should write $W^j_{w^j}$ instead of W^j, but for notational simplicity we omit the subscript, and it is then understood that W^j is a function of w^j.

Now the probability of choosing a given element $x \in W^\alpha$ can be computed as follows. Ignoring for a moment the possibility of returning **fail**, we have that w^0 is the string returned by **SampleTemplate**$(W^\alpha, \varepsilon, \varphi_0)$ since $W^0 = \emptyset$. Thus, we probability we chose x is:

$$\mathbf{Pr}(w^0 = x) = \frac{|W^{\alpha-1}|}{|W^\alpha|} \cdot \frac{|W^{\alpha-2}|}{|W^{\alpha-1}|} \cdot \cdots \cdot \frac{|W^1|}{|W^2|} \cdot \frac{1}{|W^1|} = \frac{1}{|W^\alpha|}$$

Now at the point of return, we also have that $\varphi = \varphi_0/\mathbf{Pr}(w^0 = x)$. Thus, if $\varphi_0/\mathbf{Pr}(w^0 = x) \leq 1$, then the probability that x is output is simply φ_0. The following is then easily seen:

Fact 1. *If* $0 < \varphi_0 \leq \frac{1}{|W^\alpha|}$ *and* $w^0 \neq$ **fail** *is the output of Algorithm 2, then* $\mathbf{Pr}(w^0 = x) = \varphi_0$ *for every* $x \in W^\alpha$*. Moreover, the algorithm outputs* $w^0 =$ **fail** *with probability* $1 - |W^\alpha|\varphi_0$.

This shows that, conditioned on not failing, the above is a uniform sampler. Repeating the procedure $\ell \cdot (|W^\alpha|\varphi_0)^{-1}$ times, we get a sample with probability $1 - e^{-\ell}$ since:

$$\begin{aligned}(1 - |W^\alpha|\varphi_0)^{\ell \cdot (|W^\alpha|\varphi_0)^{-1}} &\leq (e^{-|W^\alpha|\varphi_0})^{\ell \cdot (|W^\alpha|\varphi_0)^{-1}} \\ &= e^{-|W^\alpha|\varphi_0 \cdot \ell \cdot (|W^\alpha|\varphi_0)^{-1}} = e^{-\ell}.\end{aligned}$$

Algorithm 2: SampleTemplate(W^j, w^j, φ)

(1) If $W^j = \emptyset$, then with probability φ return w^j, otherwise return **fail**.
(2) Else, partition W^j into two sets, those with last bit equal to 0, call this W^j_0, and those with last bit equal to 1, call this W^j_1.
(3) Then choose partition $b \in \{0,1\}$ with probability $p_b = \frac{|W^j_b|}{|W^j|}$, and set $W^{j-1} = \{x \mid x \circ b \in W^j \text{ and } |x| \geq 1\}$, and $w^{j-1} = b \circ w^j$.
(4) Return **SampleTemplate**$(W^{j-1}, w^{j-1}, \frac{\varphi}{p_b})$.

6.3 The Main Algorithm

We now describe our main algorithm formally. As previously mentioned, the algorithm computes the values of $R(s), X(s)$ in a breadth-first search order on the graph N_{unroll}. Thus we first compute $R(s), X(s)$ for all s in layer i, and then move on to layer $i+1$. Our algorithm for computing the samples needed in $X(s^\alpha_i)$ for a fixed state s^α_i is given in Algorithm 3, and our full FPRAS is given in Algorithm 4.

Base Case: For every state s^α_i such that $|U(s^\alpha_i)| \leq k$, compute and store $R(s) = |U(s)|$ exactly, and store the entire set $U(s) = X(s)$. We call these states *exactly handled*. To do this, we perform a breadth-first search from s_{start}. At every new state s we see, we check if all the states in the prior layer with edges into s are exactly handled (if not, then s is not exactly handled). If so, then we compute $|U(s)|$ by computing the union Y_0 of all $X(s')$, where s' ranges over all states with edges into s labeled with a 0, and then computing the union Y_1 of all $X(s'')$, where s'' ranges over all states with edges into s labeled with a 1. If $|Y_0| + |Y_1|$ is at most k, then we set $X(s)$ to be $\{x \circ 0 \mid x \in Y_0\} \cup \{x \circ 1 \mid x \in Y_1\}$, and we set $R(s) = |X(s)|$. Otherwise, we conclude that $|U(s)| > k$, and thus s is not exactly handled.

Inductive Case: Suppose we have a state s^α_i that is not exactly handled, and for which we have not computed $X(s^\alpha_i)$, $R(s^\alpha_i)$, but such that we have computed $X(s^t_j)$, $R(s^t_j)$ for $j = 1, 2, \ldots, m$ and $t = 1, 2, \ldots, \alpha - 1$. To build the set of samples $X(s^\alpha_i)$, we call the procedure **Sample**(T, w, φ) a total of k times, where T is some subset of states (all in the same layer), w is a string suffix, and $\varphi > 0$ is some small value (T, w and φ will be specified later). Notice that **Sample** is the instantiation of the procedure **SampleTemplate** described in the previous section to the specific requirements of our main algorithm. Given any fixed arbitrary linear ordering $\prec$ on the states of N_{unroll}, the procedure **Sample** is defined as shown in Algorithm 3.

Algorithm 3: Sample(T, w, φ)

(1) If $\varphi \notin (0,1)$ return **fail**.
(2) If $T = \{s_{start}\}$, then with probability φ return w. Else, with probability $1 - \varphi$, return **fail**.
(3) Else, define:

$$T_0 = \{s^{r-1}_j \in N_{unroll} \mid s^{r-1}_j \xrightarrow{0} s^r_i \text{ for some } s^r_i \in T\}$$

$$T_1 = \{s^{r-1}_j \in N_{unroll} \mid s^{r-1}_j \xrightarrow{1} s^r_i \text{ for some } s^r_i \in T\}$$

Note $T_0 \cap T_1$ may be non-empty. Then:
(a) For $q \in \{0,1\}$, compute

$$\widetilde{W}_q = \sum_{s \in T_q} R(s) \cdot \frac{|X(s) \setminus (\bigcup_{s' \in T_q : s' \prec s} U(s'))|}{|X(s)|}$$

(b) For $q \in \{0,1\}$, set $p_q = (\widetilde{W}_q)/(\widetilde{W}_0 + \widetilde{W}_1)$, and then choose $b \in \{0,1\}$ with probability p_b.
(4) Return **Sample**$(T_b, b \circ w, \frac{\varphi}{p_b})$

It is important to note that $X(s) \setminus (\bigcup_{s' \in T_q, s' \prec s} U(s'))$ in step 3 (a) can be computed in polynomial time by simply iterating through each $x \in X(s)$, and checking whether there is a path from s_{start} to some $s' \in T_q$, with $s' \prec s$, where the string of ordered labels of the edges is precisely x, which can be done by a breadth-first search.

Algorithm 4: FPRAS to estimate $|\mathcal{L}_n(N)|$ for a NFA N with $m \geq 1$ states, $n \geq 1$ given in unary and error $\delta \in (0,1)$

(1) If $n \leq 12$, then return $|\{x \in \{0,1\}^n \mid x \in \mathcal{L}(N)\}|$ (this can be done in polynomial time by an exhaustive search)
(2) Construct the directed acyclic graph N_{unroll} from N, and set $k = \lceil (\frac{nm}{\delta})^{64} \rceil$.
(3) For each vertex $s \in N_{unroll}$, if there is not a path from the starting vertex s_{start} to s, remove s from N_{unroll}.
(4) For layers $\alpha = 1, 2, \ldots, n$ and for $i = 1, 2, \ldots, m$:
  (a) For $b \in \{0,1\}$, let $T_b(s_i^\alpha) = \{s \in N_{unroll} \mid \text{there is an edge } s \xrightarrow{b} s_i^\alpha \text{ in } N_{unroll}\}$. Let $T(s_i^\alpha) = T_0(s_i^\alpha) \cup T_1(s_i^\alpha)$, and for $b \in \{0,1\}$, assume that $T_b(s_i^\alpha) = \{v_1^b, \ldots, v_{r_b}^b\}$ where $r_b = |T_b(s_i^\alpha)|$.
  (b) If $T(s_i^\alpha) = \{s_{start}\}$ (meaning if $\alpha = 1$), set $X(s_i^\alpha) = \{b \in \{0,1\} \mid s_{start} \xrightarrow{b} s_i^\alpha \text{ is an edge in } N_{unroll}\}$. Moreover, set $R(s_i^\alpha) = |X(s_i^\alpha)|$, and declare the state s_i^α to be exactly handled.
  (c) Else, if s is exactly-handled for all $s \in T(s_i^\alpha)$, set

$$R(s_i^\alpha) = \left(\sum_{j=1}^{r_0} \left|X(v_j^0) \setminus \bigcup_{t=1}^{j-1} X(v_t^0)\right|\right) + \left(\sum_{j=1}^{r_1} \left|X(v_j^1) \setminus \bigcup_{t=1}^{j-1} X(v_t^1)\right|\right),$$

  and then if $R(s_i^\alpha) \leq k$, declare s_i^α to be exactly handled, and set

$$X(s_i^\alpha) = \left(\bigcup_{t=1}^{r_0} \{x \circ 0 \mid x \in X(v_t^0)\}\right) \bigcup \left(\bigcup_{t=1}^{r_1} \{x \circ 1 \mid x \in X(v_t^1)\}\right).$$

  Otherwise, (that is, if $R(s_i^\alpha) > k$), do nothing.
  (d) Else (that is, if s is not exactly handled for at least one state $s \in T(s_i^\alpha)$) do nothing.
(5) For layers $\alpha = 1, 2, \ldots, n$ and for $i = 1, 2, \ldots, m$:
  (a) If s_i^α is exactly handled, then $R(s_i^\alpha)$ and $X(s_i^\alpha)$ are already computed. Otherwise, for $b \in \{0,1\}$ set

$$\widetilde{W}_b(s_i^\alpha) = \sum_{s \in T_b(s_i^\alpha)} R(s) \cdot \frac{\left|X(s) \setminus \left(\bigcup_{s' \in T_b(s_i^\alpha) : s' \prec s} U(s')\right)\right|}{|X(s)|}$$

  and $R(s_i^\alpha) = \widetilde{W}_0(s_i^\alpha) + \widetilde{W}_1(s_i^\alpha)$.
  (b) If $R(s_i^\alpha) = 0$, terminate the algorithm and output 0 as the estimate (failure event).
  (c) Else, set $X(s_i^\alpha) = \emptyset$. Then while $|X(s_i^\alpha)| < k$
    (i) Set $w =$ **fail**
    (ii) Run **Sample**$(\{s_i^\alpha\}, \varepsilon, \frac{e^{-4}}{R(s_i^\alpha)})$ until it returns a string $w \neq$ **fail**, and at most $\lceil (\frac{nm}{\delta})^4 \rceil$ times
    (iii) If $w =$ **fail** (that is, none of the $\lceil (\frac{nm}{\delta})^4 \rceil$ calls returned a string $w \neq$ **fail**), then terminate the algorithm and output 0 as the estimate (failure event).
    (iv) Otherwise, a sample $w \in \{0,1\}^*$ was returned, and set $X(s_i^\alpha)$ as $X(s_i^\alpha) \cup \{w\}$ (recall we allow $X(s_i^\alpha)$ to contain duplicates).
(6) Return $R(s_{final})$ as an estimate for $|\mathcal{L}_n(N)|$.

By calling the procedure **Sample** on $(\{s_i^\alpha\}, \varepsilon, \varphi_0)$ until it returns k samples (where ε the empty string, and φ_0 is a value we will later choose) we obtain the samples for $X(s_i^\alpha)$. Note that it is possible that duplicate samples will be returned by the **Sample** procedure. This will not be an issue for us, and we can instead assume that $X(s_i^\alpha)$ is a multi-set (thus, $X(s_i^\alpha)$ can have more than one copy of the same element in $U(s_i^\alpha)$). The value of φ_0 that we choose will depend on our estimate $R(s_i^\alpha)$, so before invoking the above recursive procedure to obtain $X(s_i^\alpha)$, we first show how to compute $R(s_i^\alpha)$. To do so, set $T_0(s_i^\alpha) = \{s_q^{\alpha-1} \in N_{unroll} \mid s_q^{\alpha-1} \xrightarrow{0} s_i^\alpha\}$, and $T_1(s_i^\alpha) = \{s_q^{\alpha-1} \in N_{unroll} \mid s_q^{\alpha-1} \xrightarrow{1} s_i^\alpha\}$, and define the linear ordering $\prec$ as above. Then for $b \in \{0,1\}$, compute

$$\widetilde{W}_b = \sum_{s \in T_b(s_i^\alpha)} R(s) \cdot \frac{\left|X(s) \setminus \left(\bigcup_{s' \in T_b(s_i^\alpha) : s' \prec s} U(s')\right)\right|}{|X(s)|},$$

and define $R(s_i^\alpha) = \widetilde{W}_0 + \widetilde{W}_1$. We then set the parameter $\varphi_0 = \frac{e^{-4}}{R(s_i^\alpha)}$, which we use in our calls to **Sample**. This completes the procedure to obtain the desired $X(s_i^\alpha), R(s_i^\alpha)$ pair. After computing $X(s_i^\alpha), R(s_i^\alpha)$ for all states, the final output of the algorithm is $R(s_{final})$ as the approximation to $|\mathcal{L}_n(N)|$.

Summary: We compute the sample set and estimate pair $X(s_j^t)$, $R(s_j^t)$ for all states s_j in layers $t = 1, 2, \dots, \alpha - 1$. For each state s_i^α such that $|U(s_i^\alpha)| \le k$, we declare s_i^α to be *exactly handled.* For such exactly handled states, we store $X(s_i^\alpha) = U(s_i^\alpha)$ and $R(s_i^\alpha) = |U(s_i^\alpha)|$ exactly. Otherwise, we compute $R(s_i^\alpha)$ from the samples and estimates in the prior layers $t < \alpha$. Finally, using $R(s_i^\alpha)$ and $X(s_i^t)$, $R(s_i^t)$ for all $t < \alpha$, we invoke $\mathbf{Sample}(\{s_i^\alpha\}, \varepsilon, \frac{e^{-4}}{R(s_i^\alpha)})$ repeatedly to obtain all k samples needed for $X(s_i^\alpha)$. Once this has been completed for all states in N_{unroll}, we output $R(s_{final})$ as our final estimate. Our full algorithm is given in Algorithm 4.

6.4 The Analysis of the Algorithm

We start by showing that our sampling algorithm **Sample** of Algorithm 3 performs nearly the same procedure as the one described in the template Algorithm 2. Consider the notation used in these algorithms, and fix a state s_i^α in layer α. Let T^t, T_0^t and T_1^t be the set T, T_0 and T_1, respectively, in the $(\alpha - t)$-th recursive call to **Sample**, where the original call to $\mathbf{Sample}(\{s_i^\alpha\}, \varepsilon, \frac{e^{-4}}{R(s_i^\alpha)})$ is counted as the first, that is, $t = 0$. Moreover, let w^t be the (possibly empty) string in this call, and let $\widetilde{W}_q^t$ for $q \in \{0, 1\}$ be the value of $\widetilde{W}_q$ in this call. Thus, we have that $w^\alpha = \varepsilon$, and $T^\alpha = \{s_i^\alpha\}$. We define the index t in this way so that T^t is a subset of states in the t-th layer (i.e. T^t is a set of states of the form s_j^t for some $j \in \{1, \dots, m\}$). Notice that the sets T_0^t and T_1^t will be in layers $t-1$ by definition, and $R(s_i^\alpha) = \widetilde{W}_0^\alpha + \widetilde{W}_1^\alpha$. By construction, for $t < \alpha$, we have the property that T^t is the set of states s in layer t such that there is an edge labeled with the bit $w^{\alpha-t}[1]$ to some state $s' \in T^{t+1}$. Given this, the only difference between our sampling algorithm of Algorithm 3 and the template Algorithm 2 is that the sizes of the sets $|W^t|$ are replaced with approximations $\widetilde{W}^t$, since we no longer know $|W^t|$ exactly. We now demonstrate that the procedure of Algorithm 3 does in fact follow the template of Algorithm 2, up to the fact that it uses approximations $\widetilde{W}^t$ of $|W^t|$.

Proposition 6.2. *For every t, it holds that $(\bigcup_{s \in T^t} U(s)) = W^t$, where W^t is defined as in Algorithm 2 as the set of strings x such that $x \circ w^t \in U(s_j^\alpha)$.*

Recall that for $q \in \{0, 1\}$, we defined W_q^t as the set of strings in W^t with last bit equal to q, and that W^t is the set of strings x such that $x \circ w^t \in U(s_i^\alpha)$. Also recall that we initialized $w^\alpha = \varepsilon$, so in general $w^{\alpha-i}$ is a string of length i for every $i = 0, 1, 2, \dots, \alpha$. As noted, the only difference between our algorithm **Sample** and the template **SampleTemplate** is that at any layer t, instead of choosing w^{t-1} to be $q \circ w^t$ and recursing into the set W_q^t with probability $\frac{|W_q^t|}{|W^t|}$ exactly, we choose q with the approximation probability $\frac{\widetilde{W}_q^t}{\widetilde{W}_0^t + \widetilde{W}_1^t}$ (since we do not know the exact value of $\frac{|W_q^t|}{|W^t|} = \frac{|W_q^t|}{|W_0^t + W_1^t|}$). Recall that the approximation $\widetilde{W}_q^t$ of $|W_q^t|$ is the value of $\widetilde{W}_q$ in the t-th call to **Sample** as in Algorithm 3. The following result can be found in [22], however we provide a proof here to consider the specificities of our setting. The result says that at the point where we attempt to compute uniform samples of the set $U(s_i^\alpha)$, in order to build the sample set $X(s_i^\alpha)$, assuming that we have a good estimate $R(s_i^\alpha)$ of $|U(s_i^\alpha)|$ and good estimates $\widetilde{W}_q^t$ of the sizes of the partitions $|W_q^t|$, our sampling procedure will in fact output a uniformly random sample of $U(s_i^\alpha)$ (and only output **fail** with at most $1 - O(1)$ probability).

Proposition 6.3. *Set $k = \lceil (\frac{mn}{\delta})^{64} \rceil$, where $n \ge 2$, and suppose that we have estimates $\widetilde{W}_q^t = (1 \pm k^{-1/4})^t |W_q^t|$ for all $t = 1, 2, \dots, \alpha$ and $q \in \{0, 1\}$, and an estimate $R(s_i^\alpha) = (1 \pm k^{-1/4})^\alpha |U(s_i^\alpha)|$. If $w \neq$ **fail** is the output of the procedure $\mathbf{Sample}(\{s_i^\alpha\}, \varepsilon, \frac{e^{-4}}{R(s_i^\alpha)})$, then for every $x \in U(s_i^\alpha)$:*

$$\mathbf{Pr}(w = x) \quad = \quad \frac{e^{-4}}{R(s_i^\alpha)}.$$

Moreover, it outputs **fail** *with probability at most $1 - e^{-5}$. Thus, conditioned on not failing, $\mathbf{Sample}(\{s_i^\alpha\}, \varepsilon, \frac{e^{-4}}{R(s_i^\alpha)})$ returns a uniform element $x \in U(s_i^\alpha)$.*

Proposition 6.3 demonstrates that our sampler is indeed uniform, provided our estimates $R(s_i^\alpha)$ and $\widetilde{W}_q^t$ satisfy the stated assumptions. Our next goal is to show that, when tasked with computing samples for the set $X(s_i^\alpha)$, the conditions of Proposition 6.3 will indeed hold. Note that while our sampler only returns a sample with probability e^{-5}, by repeating the procedure some τ times, at least one sample will be returned with probability $1 - e^{-c \cdot \tau}$, where $c > 0$ is a fixed constant. Since our algorithm needs only nmk samples, we can bound the probability of error by the union of getting at least one sample out of every τ attempts. This blows up the complexity of our algorithm by a τ factor only, preserving the polynomial time if τ is polynomial in $\frac{nm}{\delta}$.

To facilitate our analysis, we introduce two properties. On termination of our algorithm, we define the following properties for each state s_i^α:

Property 1: $R(s_i^\alpha) = (1 \pm k^{-1/4})^\alpha |U(s_i^\alpha)|$,

Property 2: for every subset $L \subseteq \{1, \dots, m\}$, it holds:

$$\left| \frac{|X(s_i^\alpha) \setminus (\bigcup_{j \in L} U(s_j^\alpha))|}{|X(s_i^\alpha)|} - \frac{|U(s_i^\alpha) \setminus (\bigcup_{j \in L} U(s_j^\alpha))|}{|U(s_i^\alpha)|} \right| < k^{-1/3}$$

In other words, Property 1 means that our estimate $R(s_i^\alpha)$ for the size of the set $U(s_i^\alpha)$ is within our desired error bounds. Property 2 asserts that the sampled subset $X(s_i^\alpha) \subseteq$

$U(s_i^\alpha)$ is a *good* approximation of the set $U(s_i^\alpha)$ in the following sense: for every set of the form $U(s_i^\alpha) \setminus (\bigcup_{j\in L} U(s_j^\alpha))$ such that our algorithm may at some point attempt to estimate the ratio $|U(s_i^\alpha) \setminus (\bigcup_{j\in L} U(s_j^\alpha))|/|U(s_i^\alpha)|$ as in step 3(a) of Algorithm 3, we will get a good approximation of this ratio by using $|X(s_i^\alpha) \setminus (\bigcup_{j\in L} U(s_j^\alpha))|/|X(s_i^\alpha)|$ instead. We now consider a fixed point in the execution of the algorithm, and show that if Properties 1 and 2 hold for all nodes in N_{unroll} at depth $t = 1, 2, \ldots, \alpha - 1$, then on a call to sample a string from $U(s_i^\alpha)$ for a fixed s_i^α, the assumptions of Proposition 6.3 will be satisfied.

Proposition 6.4. *Fix a state s_i^α for $i \in \{1, \ldots, m\}$ and $\alpha \in \{1, \ldots, n\}$, and set $k = \lceil (\frac{mn}{\delta})^{64} \rceil$. Suppose that for every $t \in \{1, \ldots, \alpha - 1\}$ and $j \in \{1, \ldots, , m\}$, the states s_j^t satisfy both Properties 1 and 2. Then on query to* **Sample**$(\{s_i^\alpha\}, \varepsilon, \frac{e^{-4}}{R(s_i^\alpha)})$ *for each $i \in \{1, \ldots, m\}$, the conditions of Proposition 6.3 hold: namely that $\widetilde{W}_q^t = (1 \pm k^{-1/4})^t |W_q^t|$ for every $t \in \{1, \ldots, \alpha\}$ and $q \in \{0, 1\}$, and $R(s_i^\alpha) = (1 \pm k^{-1/4})^\alpha |U(s_i^\alpha)|$. In particular, this implies that s_i^α satisfies Property 1 for all $i \in \{1, \ldots, m\}$.*

Let $\mathcal{E}^r$ be the event that Properties 1 and 2 hold for s_j^r for all $j \in \{1, \ldots, m\}$. Note for every layer r where s_j^r is exactly handled for all $j \in \{1, \ldots, m\}$, the event $\mathcal{E}^r$ holds with probability 1. Call a layer exactly handled if all the states in it are exactly handled.

The following Lemma, which is a consequence of Hoeffding inequality [21], demonstrates that if Properties 1 and 2 hold for all states s_j^t in layers $t = 1, 2, \ldots, \alpha - 1$, then after completion of the sampling procedure which constructs $X(s_i^\alpha)$ and the estimate $R(s_i^\alpha)$ for a fixed state s_i^α, we will have that s_i^α satisfies both Properties 1 and 2. This result will allow us to inductively show that all vertices in the graph N_{unroll} satisfy Properties 1 and 2. In particular, this means that Property 1 will hold for the final state s_{final}, which implies that $R(s_{final}) = (1 \pm k^{-1/4})^n |U(s_{final})| = (1 \pm \delta)\mathcal{L}_n(N)$, which is our desired approximation.

Lemma 6.5. *Conditioned on $\mathcal{E}^1 \wedge \cdots \wedge \mathcal{E}^{\alpha-1}$, for every $i \in \{1, \ldots, m\}$, state s_i^α will satisfy Properties 1 and 2 with probability at least $1 - 2e^{-k^{1/3}}$. In other words,*

$$\mathbf{Pr}(\mathcal{E}^\alpha \mid \mathcal{E}^1 \wedge \cdots \wedge \mathcal{E}^{\alpha-1}) \geq 1 - 2e^{-k^{1/3}}$$

Putting together all the previous results, we obtain the main result of this section.

Theorem 6.6. *Given an NFA N with $m \geq 1$ states over the alphabet $\{0, 1\}$, an integer $n \geq 1$ given in unary and $\delta \in (0, 1)$, there exists a randomized algorithm that receives as input N, n and δ, and returns a value R such that:*

$$\mathbf{Pr}\big(\big|R - |\mathcal{L}_n(N)|\big| \leq \delta |\mathcal{L}_n(N)|\big) \quad \geq \quad 1 - e^{-\tau n m},$$

where $\tau > 0$ is a fixed constant. Moreover, the algorithm runs in time $O((\frac{nm}{\delta})^c)$, where c is a fixed constant. Thus, we have that #NFA admits an FPRAS.

From the existence of Algorithm 4 and the form it is defined, and from the proof of Theorem 6.6, it is possible to conclude that GEN(MEM-NFA) admits a PLVUG. More precisely, we have the following result.

Corollary 6.7. *Given an NFA N with $m \geq 1$ states over the alphabet $\{0, 1\}$ and an integer $n \geq 1$ given in unary, there exists a polynomial $q(u, v)$ and a randomized algorithm $\mathcal{G}$ that receives as input N and n, and satisfies the following conditions.*

(1) If $W_{\text{MEM-NFA}}((N, 0^n)) = \varnothing$, then $\mathcal{G}(N, n)$ returns $\perp$.
(2) If $W_{\text{MEM-NFA}}((N, 0^n)) \neq \varnothing$, then
  - *(a) $\mathcal{G}(N, n)$ returns* **fail** *with a probability $p_{N,n} < \frac{1}{2}$.*
  - *(b) $\mathcal{G}(N, n)$ returns $w \in W_{\text{MEM-NFA}}((N, 0^n))$ with a probability $(1 - p_{N,n})/|W_{\text{MEM-NFA}}((N, 0^n))|$.*

(3) The number of steps needed to compute $\mathcal{G}(N, n)$ is at most $q(m, n)$.

7 CONCLUDING REMARKS

We consider this work as a first step towards the definition of classes of problems with good properties in terms of enumeration, counting and uniform generation of solutions. In this sense, there is plenty of room for extensions and improvements. In particular, the different components of the FPRAS for #NFA were designed to facilitate its proof of correctness. As such, we already know of some optimizations that significantly reduce its runtime, and we also plan on developing more such optimizations so to make this FPRAS usable in practice.

ACKNOWLEDGMENTS

M. Arenas and C. Riveros was partially funded by the Fondecyt grant 1161473 and the Fondecyt grant 11150653, respectively. M. Arenas, L. A. Croquevielle and C. Riveros were partially funded by the Millennium Institute for Foundational Research on Data.

REFERENCES

[1] Serge Abiteboul, Gerome Miklau, Julia Stoyanovich, and Gerhard Weikum. 2016. Data, Responsibly (Dagstuhl Seminar 16291). *Dagstuhl Reports* 6, 7 (2016), 42–71.
[2] Alfred V Aho and John E Hopcroft. 1974. *The design and analysis of computer algorithms.* Pearson Education India.
[3] Carme Álvarez and Birgit Jenner. 1993. A very hard log-space counting class. *Theoretical Computer Science* 107, 1 (1993), 3–30.
[4] Antoine Amarilli, Pierre Bourhis, Louis Jachiet, and Stefan Mengel. 2017. A Circuit-Based Approach to Efficient Enumeration. In *Proceedings of ICALP.* 111:1–111:15.

[5] Antoine Amarilli, Pierre Bourhis, Stefan Mengel, and Matthias Niewerth. 2019. Constant-Delay Enumeration for Nondeterministic Document Spanners. In *Proceedings of ICDT.*

[6] Antoine Amarilli, Florent Capelli, Mikaël Monet, and Pierre Senellart. 2018. Connecting Knowledge Compilation Classes and Width Parameters. *CoRR* abs/1811.02944 (2018).

[7] Renzo Angles, Marcelo Arenas, Pablo Barceló, Aidan Hogan, Juan Reutter, and Domagoj Vrgoč. 2017. Foundations of modern query languages for graph databases. *ACM Computing Surveys (CSUR)* 50, 5 (2017), 68.

[8] Marcelo Arenas, Sebastián Conca, and Jorge Pérez. 2012. Counting beyond a Yottabyte, or how SPARQL 1.1 property paths will prevent adoption of the standard. In *Proceedings of WWW.* 629–638.

[9] Marcelo Arenas, Martin Muñoz, and Cristian Riveros. 2017. Descriptive Complexity for counting complexity classes. In *32nd Annual ACM/IEEE Symposium on Logic in Computer Science, LICS 2017, Reykjavik, Iceland, June 20-23, 2017.* 1–12.

[10] Guillaume Bagan. 2006. MSO queries on tree decomposable structures are computable with linear delay. In *Proceedings of CSL.* 167–181.

[11] Guillaume Bagan, Arnaud Durand, and Etienne Grandjean. 2007. On acyclic conjunctive queries and constant delay enumeration. In *Proceedings of CSL.* 208–222.

[12] Randal E Bryant. 1992. Symbolic Boolean manipulation with ordered binary-decision diagrams. *ACM Computing Surveys (CSUR)* 24, 3 (1992), 293–318.

[13] Bruno Courcelle. 2009. Linear delay enumeration and monadic second-order logic. *Discrete Applied Mathematics* 157, 12 (2009), 2675–2700.

[14] Constantinos Daskalakis, Paul W. Goldberg, and Christos H. Papadimitriou. 2009. The Complexity of Computing a Nash Equilibrium. *SIAM J. Comput.* 39, 1 (2009), 195–259.

[15] Ronald Fagin, Benny Kimelfeld, Frederick Reiss, and Stijn Vansummeren. 2015. Document spanners: A formal approach to information extraction. *J. ACM* 62, 2 (2015), 12.

[16] Fernando Florenzano, Cristian Riveros, Martin Ugarte, Stijn Vansummeren, and Domagoj Vrgoc. 2018. Constant delay algorithms for regular document spanners. *arXiv preprint arXiv:1803.05277* (2018).

[17] Dominik D. Freydenberger. 2017. A Logic for Document Spanners. In *Proceedings of ICDT.* 13:1–13:18.

[18] Dominik D Freydenberger, Benny Kimelfeld, and Liat Peterfreund. 2018. Joining extractions of regular expressions. In *Proceedings of PODS.* 137–149.

[19] Vivek Gore, Mark Jerrum, Sampath Kannan, Z. Sweedyk, and Stephen R. Mahaney. 1997. A Quasi-Polynomial-Time Algorithm for Sampling Words from a Context-Free Language. *Inf. Comput.* 134, 1 (1997), 59–74.

[20] Lane A. Hemaspaandra and Heribert Vollmer. 1995. The satanic notations: counting classes beyond #P and other definitional adventures. *SIGACT News* 26, 1 (1995), 2–13.

[21] Wassily Hoeffding. 1963. Probability inequalities for sums of bounded random variables. *J. Amer. Statist. Assoc.* 58, 301 (1963), 13–30.

[22] Mark R Jerrum, Leslie G Valiant, and Vijay V Vazirani. 1986. Random generation of combinatorial structures from a uniform distribution. *Theor. Comput. Sci.* 43 (1986), 169–188.

[23] David S Johnson, Mihalis Yannakakis, and Christos H Papadimitriou. 1988. On generating all maximal independent sets. *Inform. Process. Lett.* 27, 3 (1988), 119–123.

[24] Sampath Kannan, Z. Sweedyk, and Stephen R. Mahaney. 1995. Counting and Random Generation of Strings in Regular Languages. In *Proceedings of SODA.* 551–557.

[25] Richard M. Karp and Michael Luby. 1983. Monte-Carlo Algorithms for Enumeration and Reliability Problems. In *Proceedings of FOCS.* 56–64.

[26] Katja Losemann and Wim Martens. 2013. The complexity of regular expressions and property paths in SPARQL. *ACM Trans. Database Syst.* 38, 4 (2013), 24:1–24:39.

[27] Francisco Maturana, Cristian Riveros, and Domagoj Vrgoc. 2018. Document Spanners for Extracting Incomplete Information: Expressiveness and Complexity. In *Proceedings of PODS.* ACM, 125–136.

[28] Klaus Reinhardt and Eric Allender. 2000. Making Nondeterminism Unambiguous. *SIAM J. Comput.* 29, 4 (2000), 1118–1131.

[29] Sanjeev Saluja, KV Subrahmanyam, and Madhukar N Thakur. 1995. Descriptive complexity of #P functions. *J. Comput. System Sci.* 50, 3 (1995), 493–505.

[30] Johannes Schmidt. 2009. Enumeration: Algorithms and complexity. *Preprint, available at https://www.thi.uni-hannover.de/fileadmin/forschung/arbeiten/schmidt-da.pdf* (2009).

[31] Luc Segoufin. 2013. Enumerating with constant delay the answers to a query. In *Proceedings of ICDT.* 10–20.

[32] Leslie G. Valiant. 1976. Relative Complexity of Checking and Evaluating. *Inf. Process. Lett.* 5, 1 (1976), 20–23.

Ranked Enumeration of Minimal Triangulations

Noam Ravid
Technion
Haifa, Israel
noamrvd@cs.technion.ac.il

Dori Medini
Technion
Haifa, Israel
dorimedi@campus.technion.ac.il

Benny Kimelfeld
Technion
Haifa, Israel
bennyk@cs.technion.ac.il

ABSTRACT

A tree decomposition of a graph facilitates computations by grouping vertices into bags that are interconnected in an acyclic structure; hence their importance in a plethora of problems such as query evaluation over databases and inference over probabilistic graphical models. The relative benefit from different tree decompositions is measured by diverse (sometime complex) cost functions that vary from one application to another. For generic cost functions like width and fill-in, an optimal tree decomposition can be efficiently computed in some cases, notably when the number of minimal separators is bounded by a polynomial (due to Bouchitte and Todinca); we refer to this assumption as "poly-MS." To cover the variety of cost functions in need, it has recently been proposed to devise algorithms for enumerating many decomposition candidates for applications to choose from using specialized, or even machine-learned, cost functions.

We explore the ability to produce a large collection of "high quality" tree decompositions. We present the first algorithm for ranked enumeration of the proper (non-redundant) tree decompositions, or equivalently minimal triangulations, under a wide class of cost functions that substantially generalizes the generic ones above. On the theoretical side, we establish the guarantee of polynomial delay if poly-MS is assumed, or if we are interested in tree decompositions of a width bounded by a constant. We describe an experimental evaluation on graphs of various domains (including join queries, Bayesian networks, treewidth benchmarks and random), and explore both the applicability of the poly-MS assumption and the performance of our algorithm relative to the state of the art.

PODS'19, June 30-July 5, 2019, Amsterdam, Netherlands

ACM ISBN 978-1-4503-6227-6/19/06...$15.00
https://doi.org/10.1145/3294052.3319678

CCS CONCEPTS

• **Mathematics of computing** → **Enumeration**; **Graph enumeration**; *Graph algorithms*; Bayesian computation; • **Information systems** → Query optimization; Join algorithms.

KEYWORDS

Tree decomposition; Minimal triangulation; Minimal separator; Ranked enumeration

ACM Reference Format:
Noam Ravid, Dori Medini, and Benny Kimelfeld. 2019. Ranked Enumeration of Minimal Triangulations. In *38th ACM SIGMOD-SIGACT-SIGAI Symposium on Principles of Database Systems (PODS'19), June 30-July 5, 2019, Amsterdam, Netherlands.* ACM, New York, NY, USA, 15 pages. https://doi.org/10.1145/3294052.3319678

1 INTRODUCTION

A *tree decomposition* of a graph G is a tree $\mathcal{T}$ such that each vertex of $\mathcal{T}$ is associated with a *bag* of vertices of G, every edge of G is contained in at least one bag, and every vertex of G occurs in a connected subtree of $\mathcal{T}$. Tree decompositions are useful in common scenarios where problems are intractable on general structures, yet tractable on acyclic ones. A *beneficial* tree decomposition allows for efficient computation. This benefit is typically estimated by a cost function, most popular being the *width*—the cardinality of the largest bag (minus one), and the *fill in*–the number of missing edges among bag neighbors. The generalization to hypergraphs, *generalized hypertree decomposition*, is a tree decomposition of the *primal* graph (consisting of an edge between hyperedge neighbors) along with a cover of each bag by hyperedges, giving rise to specialized costs [18] such as (*generalized*) *hypertree width* [19, 20], and *fractional hypertree width* [30]. The applications of (ordinary and generalized) tree decompositions include optimization of join queries in databases [17, 39], solvers for constraint satisfaction problems [26], RNA analysis in bioinformatics [40], computation of Nash equilibria in game theory [17], inference in probabilistic graphical models [27], and weighted model counting [24].

Computing an optimal tree decomposition is NP-hard for the classic cost measures as the aforementioned ones. Therefore, heuristic algorithms are often used [2, 4]. But even regardless of the computational hardness, applications often require specialized costs that are not covered by the classics. For instance, for weighted model counting there are costs associated with the "CNF-tree" of the formula [18, 24]. In the work of Kalinsky et al. [23] on database join optimization, the execution cost is dominated by the effectiveness of the *adhesions* (intersection of neighboring bags) for caching, particularly the associated *skew*. They show real-life scenarios where isomorphic tree decompositions (of minimum width) feature orders-of-magnitude difference in performance. Mediero [31] aims at minimizing the size of AND/OR trees by seeking decompositions of a low *height*. Abseher et al. [1] designed a machine-learning framework to learn the cost function of a tree decomposition in various problems, using various features of the tree decomposition.

Motivated by the above need, Carmeli et al. [10] embarked on the challenge of *enumerating* tree decompositions; that is, generating tree decompositions one by one so that an application can stop the enumeration at any time and select the decomposition that best suits its needs. As they point out, it is essential to avoid *redundancy*. For example, if a graph is already a tree, then there is no need to further group its vertices. Hence, following Carmeli et al. [10], we consider the task of enumerating the *proper* tree decompositions, which are intuitively the ones that cannot be improved by splitting a bag or removing it altogether. They showed that these tree decompositions are precisely the *clique trees* of the *minimal triangulations*. A *triangulation* of a graph G is a chordal graph H obtained from G by adding edges, called *fill edges*. A triangulation H is *minimal* if no triangulation H' has a strict subset of the fill edges. Carmeli et al. [10] proved that for enumerating tree decompositions, it suffices to enumerate the minimal triangulations. See Mediero [31] for an application of Carmeli et al. [10].

While algorithms for generating pools of tree decompositions have been proposed in the past for small graphs (representing database queries) [39], Carmeli et al. [10] have presented the first algorithm that has both completeness and efficiency guarantees; that is, it can generate *all* minimal triangulations (and by implication all proper tree decompositions), and it does so in *incremental polynomial time*, which means that the time taken for producing the Nth result is polynomial in N and in the size of the input [22]. Nevertheless, there can be exponentially many minimal triangulations, and an effective enumeration needs to produce earlier the triangulations that are likely to be low cost. In other words, we would like the algorithm to enumerate the minimal triangulations by increasing relevant cost such as width (of some version) or fill-in. In turn, the application will evaluate the complex cost function on each generated triangulation, and at a point of choice it will stop the enumeration and pick the best result found. Carmeli et al. [10] use heuristics to affect the enumeration order, but provide no guarantees. Without making assumptions it is impossible to guarantee efficient ranked enumeration for costs, as it is already NP-hard to compute the first (best) triangulation.

Yet, for some classes of graphs, there is a polynomial-time algorithm for computing a tree decomposition of a minimum width/fill-in. These include the (weakly) chordal graphs, interval graphs, circular-arc graphs, and cographs. These examples have the property we refer to as *poly-MS*: having a polynomial number of *minimal separators* [14]. A minimal separator of a graph is a vertex set S such that some vertices u and v are separated by S, but no proper subset of S separates u from v. Various problems have been studied in the context of the poly-MS assumption [14], including graph isomorphism [34]. Assuming poly-MS, a tree decomposition of a minimum width or fill-in can be computed in polynomial time [8, 9].

The decomposition algorithm of Bouchitté and Todinca [8, 9] consists of two main steps. First, they construct the set of minimal separators of the input graph, for example using the algorithm of Berry et al. [3], and from these compute the set of all *potential maximal cliques* (which are essentially the bags of the proper tree decompositions) [9]. Second, they use the potential maximal cliques in order to find an optimal triangulation. In fact, their algorithm has two variants—one for minimal width (*tree-width*) and one for minimal fill-in. The second step has been later generalized to allow for positive weights on bags (in the case of width) and edges (in the case of fill) by Furuse and Yamazaki [15], again presenting two corresponding variants of their algorithm.

Our first contribution is a generalization of the concepts of width and fill-in to general cost functions over tree decompositions. These cost functions satisfy two properties. First, they assign the same cost to tree decompositions with the same bags; hence, these are essentially costs over the set of bags. Second, and more importantly, they are *monotonic* in the following (informal) sense. Suppose that we cut a tree decomposition $\mathcal{T}$ along an edge, and replace one of the sides with an alternative subtree (which is a tree decomposition of a subgraph of the original graph), resulting in a tree decomposition $\mathcal{T}'$; if the altenative subtree does not cost more than the one it replaced, then the cost of $\mathcal{T}'$ is no greater than that of $\mathcal{T}$. We call such a cost function *split monotone*, and refer the reader to Section 3 for the precise definition. Split-monotone cost functions generalize existing costs such as fill-in, width and generalized/fractional hypertree width, as well as the weighted width and fill-in of Furuse and Yamazaki [15]. Moreover, we can come up with various motivated split-monotone costs that are not among the classic ones, such as the sum over the (exponents of the) bag cardinalities and linear combinations of width and fill-in. We present a generalization of the algorithm of Bouchitté and Todinca [8] to general split-monotone cost functions. As we explain later, the importance of supporting general cost functions is not just for the sake of richer costs; even if we are interested just in width or fill-in, we need the flexibility of the cost function in order to incorporate *constraints* that we later use to devise our algorithm for ranked enumeration.

Our main theoretical contributions are algorithms that enumerate minimal triangulations by increasing cost, for any split-monotone cost function that is polynomial-time computable (e.g., the aforementioned ones). The first algorithm enumerates *all* minimal triangulations, and does so with polynomial delay if the input is from a poly-MS class of graphs. The second enumerates all minimal triangulations of a *bounded width*, and it does so with polynomial delay if the bound on the width is a fixed constant. *Polynomial delay* [22] means that the time between every two consecutive answers is polynomial in the size of the input (graph), a guarantee that is stronger than incremental polynomial time. Due to the previously discussed connection between proper tree decompositions and minimal triangulations, we get algorithms with the same guarantees for the enumeration of proper tree decompositions. Observe that these algorithms imply polynomial-time procedures for computing top-k minimal triangulations and/or proper tree decompositions. To the best of our knowledge, these are the first enumeration algorithms for minimal triangulations (and proper tree decompositions) with completeness, efficiency, *and order* guarantees.

Our ranked enumeration algorithm adapts the generic procedure of Lawler-Murty [28, 33]. For this deployment, we use a result by Parra and Scheffler [35] who show that a minimal triangulation is fully identified by its set of minimal separators. To adopt Lawler-Murty, we rephrase the task as that of enumerating the relevant sets of minimal separators. In turn, using the technique of Lawler-Murty we reduce this enumeration to the task of finding an optimal minimal triangulation, under the cost function, constrained on *including* a given set of minimal separators and *excluding* a given set of other minimal separators. Towards that, we show that these constraints can be compiled into any split-monotone cost function so that the resulting cost remains split monotone. Furthermore, if the original cost function can be computed in polynomial time, then so can the new cost function with the constraints compiled in.

Finally, we describe an implementation of our algorithm and an experimental study. We conduct experiments over the datasets of Carmeli et al. [10] that consist of three types of graphs: probabilistic graphical models (from the 2011 *Probabilistic Inference Challenge*), database queries (TPC-H), and random (Erdős-Rényi) graphs. We also conduct experiments on graphs from the PACE 2016 competition on tree-width computation. We compare our algorithm to the enumeration of Carmeli et al. [10] on both the execution time and the quality (width/fill) of the generated triangulations. In addition, we explore the validity of the poly-MS assumption on our datasets; that is, we provide statistics on the number of minimal separators, and explore the portion of the instances where this number is "manageable."

The remainder of the paper is organized as follows. We first present preliminary definitions and terminology in Section 2. In Section 3, we describe the notion of split monotonicity. We give our main theoretical results in Section 4, and present the algorithms that realize the results in Sections 5–6. Specifically, Section 5 presents our algorithm for computing a minimum-cost minimal triangulation, and Section 6 discusses the adaptation of Lawler-Murty to our enumeration. Finally, we describe our implementation and experimental study in Section 7, and conclude in Section 8. Due to space limitation, some proofs are omitted and can be found in the archive version of this paper [36].

2 PRELIMINARIES

We begin by introducing the basic notation, terminology and formal concepts that we use throughout the paper. For convenience, Table 1 contains important notation that we present here and later.

Graphs and Cliques. All the graphs in this paper are undirected. We denote by $\mathsf{V}(G)$ and $\mathsf{E}(G)$ the set of vertices and edges, respectively, of a graph G. An edge in $\mathsf{E}(G)$ is a pair $\{u, v\}$ of distinct vertices in $\mathsf{V}(G)$. The *union* of two graphs G_1 ad G_2, denoted $G_1 \cup G_2$, is the graph G with $\mathsf{V}(G) = \mathsf{V}(G_1) \cup \mathsf{V}(G_2)$ and $\mathsf{E}(G) = \mathsf{E}(G_1) \cup \mathsf{E}(G_2)$.

A set C of vertices of a graph G is a *clique (of G)* if every two vertices in C are connected by an edge of G. The set C is a *maximal clique (of G)* if C is not strictly contained in any other clique of G. We note by *MaxClq*(G) the set of all maximal cliques of G.

Let G be a graph, and U a set of vertices of G. We denote by $\mathcal{K}_U$ the *complete* graph over a vertex set U; that is, $\mathcal{K}_U$ is the graph with $\mathsf{V}(K_U) = U$ and $\mathsf{E}(\mathcal{K}_U) = \{\{u, v\} \subseteq U \mid u \neq v\}$ (hence, U itself is a clique of $\mathcal{K}_U$). By *saturating U (in G)* we refer to the operation connecting every non-adjacent vertices in U by a new edge, thereby making U a clique of G. In other words, saturating U refers to the operation of replacing G with $G \cup \mathcal{K}_U$.

A *subgraph* of a graph G is a graph G' with $\mathsf{V}(G') \subseteq \mathsf{V}(G)$ and $\mathsf{E}(G') \subseteq \mathsf{E}(G)$. Let $U \subseteq \mathsf{V}(G)$ be a set of vertices of G. We denote by $G[U]$ the subgraph of G that is *induced* by U; that is, $G[U]$ is the graph G' with $\mathsf{V}(G') = U$ and $\mathsf{E}(G') = \{e \in \mathsf{E}(G) \mid e \subseteq U\}$. Let G be a graph, and U a set of vertices of G. We denote by $G \setminus U$ the graph obtained from G by removing all vertices in U (along with their incident edges); that is, $G \setminus U$ is the graph $G[\mathsf{V}(G) \setminus U]$.

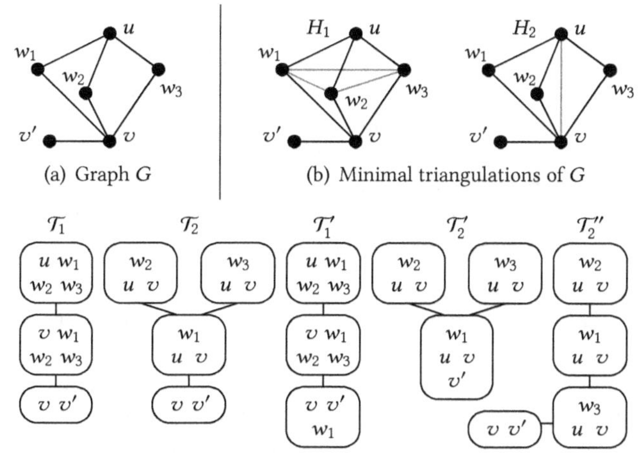

(a) Graph G (b) Minimal triangulations of G

(c) Tree decompositions of G

Figure 1: A graph G, tree decompositions of G and minimal triangulations of G.

Tree decompositions. A *tree decomposition* $\mathcal{T}$ of a graph G is a pair (T, β), where T is a tree and $\beta : \mathsf{V}(T) \to 2^{\mathsf{V}(G)}$ is a function that maps every node of T to a set of vertices of G, so that all of the following hold.

- Vertices are covered: for every vertex u of G there is a vertex v of T such that $u \in \beta(v)$.
- Edges are covered: for every edge e of G there is a vertex v of T such that $e \subseteq \beta(v)$.
- The *junction-tree* property: for all vertices u and v of T, the intersection $\beta(u) \cap \beta(v)$ is contained in every vertex along the path between u and v.

Let G be a graph, and let $\mathcal{T} = (T, \beta)$ be a tree decomposition of G. A set $\beta(v)$, for $v \in \mathsf{V}(T)$, is called a *bag* of $\mathcal{T}$. We denote by bags($\mathcal{T}$) the set $\{\beta(v) \mid v \in \mathsf{V}(\mathcal{T})\}$.

Let $\mathcal{T}_1 = (T_1, \beta_1)$ and $\mathcal{T}_2 = (T_2, \beta_2)$ be two tree decompositions of a graph G. We say that $\mathcal{T}_2$ *bag-contains* $\mathcal{T}_1$ if there is an injection $\varphi : \mathsf{V}(T_1) \to \mathsf{V}(T_2)$ such that $\beta_1(v) = \beta_2(\varphi(v))$ for all $v \in \mathsf{V}(T_1)$. We say that $\mathcal{T}_1$ and $\mathcal{T}_2$ are *bag equivalent* if $\mathcal{T}_2$ bag-contains $\mathcal{T}_1$ and vice versa. We say that $\mathcal{T}_1$ *strictly subsumes* $\mathcal{T}_2$ if $\mathcal{T}_1$ is obtained from $\mathcal{T}_2$ by splitting a bag or removing it altogether. More formally, $\mathcal{T}_1$ strictly subsumes $\mathcal{T}_2$ if there is a mapping $\varphi : \mathsf{V}(T_1) \to \mathsf{V}(T_2)$ such that $\beta_1(x) \subseteq \beta_2(\varphi(x))$ for all $x \in \mathsf{V}(T_1)$, and for at least one $y \in \mathsf{V}(T_2)$ it is the case that $\beta_1(x) \subsetneq \beta_2(y)$ whenever $\varphi(x) = y$ (hence, either no vertex is mapped to y or a vertex that is mapped to y is a strict subset of y). A tree decomposition is *proper* if it is not strictly subsumed by any other tree decomposition [10].[1]

Example 2.1. Figure 1(c) depicts five tree decompositions of the graph G of Figure 1(a). Each rectangle corresponds to a vertex x of the tree, and the bag $\beta(x)$ is depicted inside the rectangle. For example, if we denote $\mathcal{T}_1 = (T_1, \beta_1)$, then T_1 is a path of three vertices (corresponding to the three rectangles), and for the top vertex x we have $\beta_1(x) = \{u, w_1, w_2, w_3\}$. Note that $\mathcal{T}_2$ and $\mathcal{T}_2''$ are bag equivalent, since they have the exact same bags (though connected differently). The tree decomposition $\mathcal{T}_1$ strictly subsumes $\mathcal{T}_1'$, as the latter is obtained from the former by adding w_1 to the bottom bag. Moreover, $\mathcal{T}_2$ strictly subsumes $\mathcal{T}_2'$, as the former is obtained from the latter by splitting the bottom bag into two—the middle and bottom vertices of $\mathcal{T}_2$. Thus, $\mathcal{T}_1'$ and $\mathcal{T}_2'$ are not proper. We will later show that $\mathcal{T}_1$ and $\mathcal{T}_2$ (and, hence, $\mathcal{T}_2''$) are proper. □

[1] This is a simplified, yet equivalent definition to that of Carmeli et al. [10].

Table 1: Symbol table

Notation	Meaning
$\mathsf{V}(G)$ / $\mathsf{E}(G)$	Vertex/edge set of G
$MaxClq(G)$	Maximal cliques of G
$\mathcal{K}_U$	Full graph (clique) over node set U
$MinSep(G)$	Minimal separators of G
(S, C)	Block of G
$\mathcal{R}(S, C)$	Realization of (S, C), that is, $G[S \cup C] \cup \mathcal{K}_S$
$PMC(G)$	Potential maximal cliques of G
$MinSep_G(\Omega)$	Minimal separators associated to Ω of G
$Blck_G(\Omega)$	Blocks associated to Ω in G

Minimal triangulations. Let G be a graph. A *cycle* in G is a path that starts and ends with the same vertex. A *chord* of a cycle C is an edge $e \in \mathsf{E}(G)$ that connects two vertices that are non-adjacent in C. We say that G is *chordal* if every cycle of length greater than three has a chord. Whether a given graph is chordal can be decided in linear time [38].

A *triangulation* of a graph G is a chordal graph H that is obtained from G by adding edges. The *fill set* of a triangulation H of G is the set of edges added to H, that is, $\mathsf{E}(H) \setminus \mathsf{E}(G)$. A *minimal triangulation* of G is a triangulation H of G such that the fill set of H is not strictly contained in the fill set of any other triangulation; that is, there is no chordal graph G' with $\mathsf{V}(G) = \mathsf{V}(G')$ and $\mathsf{E}(G) \subseteq \mathsf{E}(G') \subsetneq \mathsf{E}(H)$. In particular, if G is already chordal then G is the only minimal triangulation of itself.

Clique trees. Let G be a graph. A *clique tree* of G is a tree decomposition $\mathcal{T} = (T, \beta)$ of G such that β is a bijection between $\mathsf{V}(T)$ and $MaxClq(G)$. In other words, $\mathcal{T}$ is a clique tree of G if bags($\mathcal{T}$) $= MaxClq(G)$ and no two bags are the same. The following is known, and recorded for later use.

Theorem 2.2. ([5, 10, 37]) *Let G be a graph.*

(1) G is chordal if and only if G has a clique tree [5].
(2) If G is chordal, then $|MaxClq(G)| < |\mathsf{V}(G)|$ [37].

(3) *A tree decomposition $\mathcal{T}$ of G is proper if and only if it is a clique tree of a minimal triangulation of G* [10].

Example 2.3. Continuing Example 2.1, observe that the graph G of Figure 1(a) is not chordal. As one evidence, it has the chordless cycle u—w_1—v—w_2—u. Figure 1(b) depicts two minimal triangulations, H_1 and H_2, of the graph G of Figure 1(a). The reader can verify that $\mathcal{T}_1$ and $\mathcal{T}_2$ of Figure 1(c) are clique trees of H_1 and H_2, respectively. In particular, we conclude that $\mathcal{T}_1$ and $\mathcal{T}_2$ are proper tree decompositions. □

Minimal separators. Let u and v be vertices of a graph G. A *(u, v)-separator (w.r.t. G)* is a set $S \subseteq \mathsf{V}(G)$ such that u and v belong to different connected components in $G \setminus S$; that is, $G \setminus S$ does not contain any path between u and v (or equivalently, every path between u and v visits one or more vertices of S). We say that S is a *minimal (u, v)-separator* if no proper subset of S is a (u, v)-separator. We say that S is a *minimal separator* of G if there are vertices u and v such that S is a minimal (u, v)-separator. We denote by *MinSep*(G) the set of all minimal separators of G. A graph may have exponentially many minimal separators.

Let G be a graph, and let S and T be two minimal separators of G. We say that S *crosses* T if there are vertices u and v in T such that S is a (u, v)-separator. Crossing is known to be a symmetric relation: if S crosses T then T crosses S [25, 35]. Hence, if S crosses T then we may also say that S and T are *crossing*. When S and T are non-crossing, then we also say that S and T are *parallel*.

Example 2.4. We continue with our running example. The top-left graph of Figure 2 depicts three minimal separators S_1, S_2 and S_3 of the graph G of Figure 1(a). For instance $S_1 = \{w_1, w_2, w_3\}$ is a minimal (u, v)-separator, $S_2 = \{u, v\}$ is a minimal (w_1, w_2)-separator, and $S_3 = \{v\}$ is a minimal (u, v')-separator. Note that S_2 is a (w_1, v')-separator but not a minimal (w_1, v')-separator, since a strict subset of S_2, namely S_3, is a (w_1, v')-separator. Also note that S_1 and S_2 are crossing, since S_1 is a (u, v)-separator (and also S_2 is a (w_1, w_2)-separator). It can be verified that S_1, S_2 and S_3 are the only minimal separators of G. Hence *MinSep*$(G) = \{S_1, S_2, S_3\}$. This example illustrates that, albeit being "minimal," a minimal separator can be a strict subset of another; for instance $S_3 \subsetneq S_2$. □

A set of *pairwise-parallel* minimal separators is a set M of minimal separators such that every two distinct members of M are parallel. Moreover, such M is said to be *maximal* if every minimal separator not in M is crossing at least one member of M. Parra and Scheffler [35] established the following connection between minimal triangulations and maximal sets of pairwise-parallel minimal separators.

Theorem 2.5. (Parra and Scheffler [35]) *Let G be a graph.*

(1) *Let M be a maximal set of pairwise-parallel minimal separators of G, and let H be obtained from G by saturating each member of M. Then H is a minimal triangulation of G having MinSep$(H) = M$.*
(2) *Conversely, if H is a minimal triangulation of G, then M = MinSep(H) is a maximal set of pairwise-parallel minimal separators in G, and H is obtained from G by saturating each member of M.*

Ranked enumeration. An *enumeration problem* P is a collection of pairs (x, Y) where x is an *input* and Y is a finite set of *answers* for x, denoted by $\mathsf{P}(x)$. A *solver* for an enumeration problem P is an algorithm that, when given an input x, produces (or *prints*) a sequence of answers such that every answer in $\mathsf{P}(x)$ is printed precisely once. A solver for an enumeration problem is also called an *enumeration algorithm*. We recall several standard yardsticks of efficiency for enumeration algorithms [22]. Let P be an enumeration problem, and let A be solver for P. We say that A runs in *(a) polynomial total time* if the total execution time of A is polynomial in $(|x| + |\mathsf{P}(x)|)$; *(b) polynomial delay* if the time between printing every two consecutive answers is polynomial in $|x|$; *and (c) incremental polynomial time* if, after printing a sequence Y of answers, the time to print the next answer is polynomial in $(|x| + |Y|)$ where Y is the size of the representation of Y. Observe that a solver that enumerates with polynomial delay also enumerates with incremental polynomial time, which, in turn, implies polynomial total time.

Let P be an enumeration problem. A *cost function* for P is a function c that associates a numerical cost $c(x, y)$ to each input x and answer y for x. A solver A for P is said to *enumerate by increasing* c, where c is cost function for P, if for every two answers a_1 and a_2 produced by A, if a_1 is produced before a_2 then $c(a_1) \leq c(a_2)$.

3 MONOTONE COST FUNCTIONS

By a *cost function over tree decompositions* we refer to a function κ that maps a graph G and a tree decomposition $\mathcal{T}$ for G to a numerical (positive, negative or zero) value $\kappa(G, \mathcal{T})$. In this section we define a class of such cost functions that includes many of the common costs such as width and fill-in. This class is defined by means of monotonicity, as we formally defined next.

Let G be a graph, and let $\mathcal{T} = (T, \beta)$ be a tree decomposition of G. Every edge $e = \{v_1, v_2\}$ of T connects two unique subtrees of T—one connected to v_1 and one connected to v_2. Let e be an edge of T, let T_1 and T_2 be the two subtrees connected by e, and let β_1 and β_2 be the restrictions of β to $\mathsf{V}(T_1)$ and $\mathsf{V}(T_2)$, respectively. Let $\mathcal{T}_1 = (T_1, \beta_1)$ and $\mathcal{T}_2 = (T_2, \beta_2)$, and let G_1 and G_2 be the subgraphs of G induced by the nodes in the bags of $\mathcal{T}_1$ and $\mathcal{T}_2$, respectively. Then we say that $\mathcal{T}$

splits (*by* e) as $\langle G_1, \mathcal{T}_1, G_2, \mathcal{T}_2 \rangle$. The following proposition is straightforward.

Proposition 3.1. *Let* G *be a graph and* $\mathcal{T} = (T, \beta)$ *a tree decomposition of* G. *If* $\mathcal{T}$ *splits as* $\langle G_1, \mathcal{T}_1, G_2, \mathcal{T}_2 \rangle$, *then* $\mathcal{T}_1$ *and* $\mathcal{T}_2$ *are tree decompositions of* G_1 *and* G_2, *respectively.*

Proposition 3.1 implies that if κ is a cost function and $\mathcal{T}$ splits as $\langle G_1, \mathcal{T}_1, G_2, \mathcal{T}_2 \rangle$, then both $\kappa(G_1, \mathcal{T}_1)$ and $\kappa(G_2, \mathcal{T}_2)$ are defined. We can now define properties of cost functions.

Definition 3.2. Let κ be a cost function over tree decompositions. We say that κ is:

(1) *invariant under bag equivalence*, if for all graphs G and tree decompositions $\mathcal{T}_1$ and $\mathcal{T}_2$ of G, if $\mathcal{T}_1$ and $\mathcal{T}_2$ are bag equivalent then $\kappa(\mathcal{T}_1) = \kappa(\mathcal{T}_2)$.
(2) *split monotone* if for all graphs G and tree decompositions $\mathcal{T}$ and $\mathcal{T}'$ of G, if $\mathcal{T}$ and $\mathcal{T}'$ split as $\langle G_1, \mathcal{T}_1, G_2, \mathcal{T}_2 \rangle$ and $\langle G_1, \mathcal{T}_1', G_2, \mathcal{T}_2' \rangle$, respectively and for $i = 1, 2$ we have $\kappa(G_i, \mathcal{T}_i) \leq \kappa(G_i, \mathcal{T}_i')$, then $\kappa(G, \mathcal{T}) \leq \kappa(G, \mathcal{T}')$.

If κ is invariant under bag equivalence, then it is essentially a scoring function over the collection of bags, and in that case we say that κ is a *bag cost.*

For illustration, the following most popular cost functions $\kappa(G, \mathcal{T})$ are both split-monotone bag costs.

- width$(G, \mathcal{T})$: the maximal bag cardinality minus one.
- fill-in$(G, \mathcal{T})$: the number of edges required to be added for saturating all bags.

Other such cost functions are the generalizations of width and fill-in introduced by Furuse and Yamazaki [15], where it is assumed that each bag b has a cost $c(b)$, and each edge e has a cost $c(e)$. Then, they define width$_c(G, \mathcal{T})$ to be the maximal score of a bag, and fill-in$_c(G, \mathcal{T})$ to be the sum of costs of the edges required to saturate all bags. As a special case, if the graph G is the primal graph of a hypergraph, then $c(b)$ can be the minimal number of hyperedges needed to cover b, or the minimal weight of a *fractional* edge cover of b, thereby establishing the popular cost functions of *hypertree width* [19] and *fractional* hypertree width [21].

Finally, another intuitive split-monotone bag costs is

$$\kappa(G, \mathcal{T}) = |\mathsf{E}(G)|^{\mathrm{width}(G, \mathcal{T})} + \text{fill-in}(G, \mathcal{T})$$

that effectively establishes the lexicographic ordering of the width followed by the fill-in of G.

We can then use a bag cost κ as a cost function over triangulations H, by defining the cost as $\kappa(\mathcal{T})$ where $\mathcal{T}$ is *any* clique tree of H. Since κ is invariant under bag equivalence (being a bag cost), then the choice of $\mathcal{T}$ does not matter. By a slight abuse of notation, we use $\kappa(G, H)$ to denote the resulting cost over triangulations H of G.

4 MAIN THEORETICAL RESULTS

In this section we present our main theoretical results. These results are upper bounds (existence of algorithms) on problems of ranked enumeration of tree decompositions and minimal triangulations. In the next two sections we will describe the algorithms.

The poly-MS assumption. Recall that a graph may have an exponential number of minimal separators. Our main result holds for the case where this number is reasonable, a case that was deeply investigated in past research [9, 15, 29, 32]. Formally, we consider classes $\mathbf{G}$ of graph such that for some polynomial p it is the case that $|\mathit{MinSep}(G)| \leq p(|\mathsf{V}(G)|)$ for all $G \in \mathbf{G}$. We then say shortly that $\mathbf{G}$ is a *poly-MS* class of graphs (where "MS" stands for *Minimal Separators*). Later in this paper we empirically study the applicability of this assumption on real and synthetic datasets.

State of the art. Before presenting our results, we recall some relevant results from the literature. Carmeli et al. [10] showed that, without making any assumption, one can enumerate in incremental polynomial time the set of all proper tree decompositions and the set of all minimal triangulations. Note, however, that no guarantee is made on the order of enumeration.

Theorem 4.1. ([10]) *Given a graph* G, *one can enumerate in incremental polynomial time all proper tree decompositions, and all minimal triangulations.*

Parra and Scheffler [35] showed that minimal triangulations are in one-to-one correspondence with the maximal independent sets of the graph that has the minimal separators as vertices, and an edge between every two crossing separators. Combining that with results on the enumeration of maximal independent sets [11, 22], we get that that for poly-MS classes of graphs, the minimal triangulations can be enumerated with polynomial delay (again with no guarantees on the order). Moreover, Carmeli et al. [10] show that such enumeration automatically translates into an algorithm for enumerating the proper tree decompositions with polynomial delay. Hence, we get the following.

Theorem 4.2. (see [10]) *If* $\mathbf{G}$ *is a poly-MS class of graphs, then one can enumerate with polynomial delay all proper tree decompositions, and all minimal triangulations.*

Bouchitté and Todinca showed that on poly-MS classes of graphs, a tree decomposition (or triangulation) of a minimal width or fill-in can be found in polynomial time.

Theorem 4.3. ([9]) *Let* $\mathbf{G}$ *be a poly-MS class of graphs. One can find in polynomial time a minimal-cost tree decomposition (or triangulation) when the cost is either the width or the fill-in.*

Furuse and Yamazaki [15] generalized the above result to the cost functions width$_c$ and fill-in$_c$ as defined in Section 3.

Main Results. We now turn to our results. The main result generalizes Theorems 4.2 and 4.3 in two directions. First, the enumeration is ranked. Second, the cost function is not just width of fill-in, but in fact every bag cost that is split monotone and computable in polynomial time.

Theorem 4.4. *Let* **G** *be a poly-MS class of graphs, and let* κ *be a bag cost that is split monotone and computable in polynomial time. On the graphs of* **G***, one can enumerate with polynomial delay all:*

(1) proper tree decompositions $\mathcal{T}$ *by increasing* $\kappa(G, \mathcal{T})$*;*
(2) minimal triangulations H *by increasing* $\kappa(G, H)$*.*

Finally, the next result applies to general graphs, and assumes that we are interested only in tree decompositions of a bounded width. In this case, we get a ranked enumeration with polynomial delay *without* assuming an upper bound on the number of minimal separators.

Theorem 4.5. *Let* b *be a fixed natural number, and let* κ *be a bag cost that is split monotone and computable in polynomial time. Given a graph, one can enumerate with polynomial delay all:*

(1) proper tree decompositions $\mathcal{T}$ *of width at most* b *by increasing* $\kappa(G, \mathcal{T})$*;*
(2) minimal triangulations H *of width at most* b *by increasing* $\kappa(G, H)$*.*

As said previously, in the next sections we prove Theorems 4.4 and 4.5 by presenting the corresponding algorithms and proving their correctness.

5 COMPUTING AN OPTIMAL MINIMAL TRIANGULATION

We now present an algorithm for computing a minimum-cost minimal triangulation, assuming that the cost function is a split-monotone bag cost. Our algorithm terminates in polynomial time if the cost function can be evaluated in polynomial time, and moreover, the input graphs belong to a poly-MS class of graphs. Our algorithm generalizes an algorithm by Bouchitté and Todinca [8] for computing the minimal width (*tree-width*) and minimum fill-in over a poly-MS class of graphs. Furthermore, we will consider restriction to triangulations of a bounded width.

5.1 Definitions and Notation

We first recall some concepts from the literature that our triangulation algorithm builds upon. For convenience, some of the notation is shown in Table 1.

Components and Blocks. Let G be a graph, and U a set of vertices of G. A U*-component* (*of* G) is a connected component of the graph $G \setminus U$. Recall that a *connected component* is a subset W of V(G) such that G contains a path from each vertex of W to every other vertex of W, and to none of the vertices outside W.

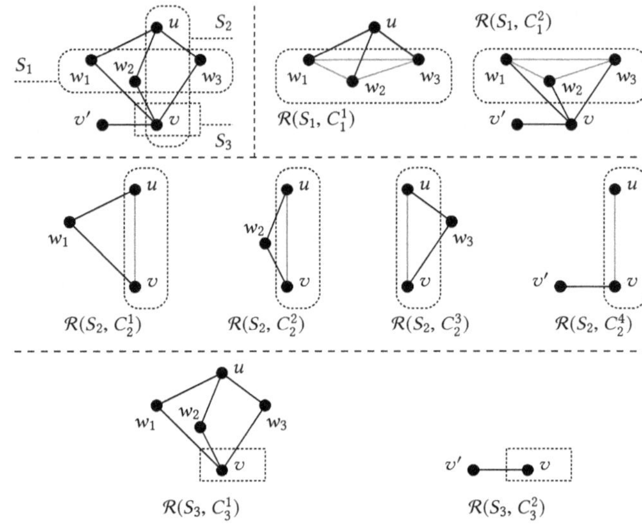

Figure 2: Minimal separators and realizations of blocks of the graph G **of Figure 1(a).**

Let S be a minimal separator of G. An S-component C is *full* if every vertex in S is connected to one or more vertices in C. A *block* (*of* G) is a pair (S, C) where S is a minimal separator and C is an S-component. By a slight abuse of notation, we often identify the block (S, C) with the vertex set $S \cup C$. A block (S, C) is *full* if C is a full component. The *realization* of the block (S, C), denoted $\mathcal{R}_G(S, C)$, is the induced graph of (S, C) after saturating S; that is:

$$\mathcal{R}_G(S, C) \stackrel{\text{def}}{=} G[S \cup C] \cup \mathcal{K}_S$$

When G is clear from the context, we may remove it from the subscripts and write simply $\mathcal{R}(S, C)$.

Example 5.1. Recall from Example 2.4 that for the graph G of our running example (Figure 1(a)) we have $MinSep(G) = \{S_1, S_2, S_3\}$, where the S_i are depicted in Figure 2 on the top left. The rest of Figure 2 shows the different realizations $\mathcal{R}(S_i, C_i^j)$ of the blocks of G. A rectangle marks the vertices of the minimal separator of the block, and the edges that have been added in the saturation are colored red. Note that all of the blocks are full, except for (S_2, C_2^4) where no vertex of C_2^4 is connected to u. □

Potential Maximal Cliques. Let G be a graph. A vertex set $\Omega \subseteq$ V(G) is a *Potential Maximal Clique* (*PMC* for short) if there is a minimal triangulation H of G such that Ω is a maximal clique of H. Due to Theorem 2.2 we conclude that a vertex set Ω is a PMC if and only if it is a bag of some proper tree decomposition of G. We denote by *PMC*(G) the set of PMCs of G.

For $\Omega \in PMC(G)$, let C be any Ω-component. Let S be the set of all vertices in Ω that are neighbors of vertices in C. It is known that S is a minimal separator of G and (S, C) is a full block of G [8], and they are said to be *associated to* Ω *(in* G*)*. Besides the minimal separators in the blocks associated to Ω, no other minimal separator of G is contained in Ω. We denote by $MinSep_G(\Omega)$ and $Blck_G(\Omega)$ the sets of minimal separators and blocks, respectively, associated to Ω. When G is clear from the context, we may omit it and write simply $MinSep(\Omega)$ and $Blck(\Omega)$.

Example 5.2. The PMCs of the graph G of Figure 1(a) are the vertex sets in all of the bags of the proper tree decompositions in Figure 1(c). For example, *PMC*(G) contains the sets $\{u_1, w_1, w_2, w_3\}$ and $\{w_1, u, v\}$. Let Ω be $\{w_1, u, v\}$. The minimal separators in $MinSep(\Omega)$ are S_2 and S_3 of Figure 2, and the blocks in $Blck(\Omega)$ are (S_2, C_2^2), (S_2, C_2^3), (S_3, C_3^2), all depicted in Figure 2. □

5.2 Algorithm Description

To describe the algorithm, we first give some background. The Bouchitté-Todinca algorithm [8] is based on the observation that a minimal triangulation of a graph is composed of minimal triangulations over realizations of its blocks. This is formalized in the following theorem:

Theorem 5.3. (Bouchitté and Todinca [8]) *The following hold for a graph G.*

(1) If H is a minimal triangulation, $\Omega \in MaxClq(H)$, and $(S_i, C_i) \in Blck_G(\Omega)$, then $H_i = H[S_i \cup C_i]$ is a minimal triangulation of the realization $\mathcal{R}_G(S_i, C_i)$.

(2) Conversely, let $\Omega \in PMC(G)$ and $k = |Blck_G(\Omega)|$. For $(S_i, C_i) \in Blck_G(\Omega)$ let H_i be a minimal triangulation of $\mathcal{R}_G(S_i, C_i)$. Then $H = \bigcup_{i=1}^{k} H_i \cup \mathcal{K}_\Omega$ is a minimal triangulation of G.

Observe that $\Omega \in MaxClq(H)$ implies that Ω is a PMC. Theorem 5.3 provides a characterization of the minimal triangulations in terms of the minimal triangulations of the block realizations. Then, how do we proceed to computing the minimal triangulations of the block realizations? This is shown in the following result.

Theorem 5.4. (Bouchitté and Todinca [8]) *Let G be a graph, $S \in MinSep(G)$, and (S, C) a full block of G. Let $G' = \mathcal{R}_G(S, C)$. Let H be a graph with $\mathsf{V}(H) = \mathsf{V}(G')$ and $\mathsf{E}(H) \supseteq \mathsf{E}(G')$. The following are equivalent.*

(1) H is a minimal triangulation of G'.

(2) There exists $\Omega \in PMC(G)$ such that $S \subset \Omega \subseteq \mathsf{V}(G')$ and $H = \bigcup_{i=1}^{k} H_i \cup \mathcal{K}_\Omega$, where $|Blck_{G'}(\Omega)| = k$ and H_i is a minimal triangulation of $\mathcal{R}_{G'}(S_i, C_i)$ for all $(S_i, C_i) \in Blck_{G'}(\Omega)$.

Algorithm MinTriang$\langle\kappa\rangle(G)$

1: Compute $MinSep(G)$ and $PMC(G)$
2: $\mathcal{B}$:= the set of full blocks of G
3: **for** $(S, C) \in \mathcal{B}$ by increasing cardinality **do**
4: $\quad \Omega(S, C) := \underset{\Omega \in PMC(S,C)}{\text{argmin}}\ \kappa(G[(S, C)], H_{\mathcal{R}(S,C)}(\Omega))$
5: $\quad \mathcal{H}(S, C) := H_{\mathcal{R}(S,C)}(\Omega(S, C))$
6: $\Omega(G) := \text{argmin}_{\Omega \in PMC(G)} \kappa(G, H_G(\Omega))$
7: **return**$(H_G(\Omega(G)))$

Figure 3: Computing an optimal minimal triangulation for a split-monotone bag cost.

For Part 2 of Theorem 5.4, it is important to note that the blocks of Ω in G' are also full blocks of G [8].

Now, consider an input G for our algorithm and $\Omega \in PMC(G)$. We will assume that for each $(S_i, C_i) \in Blck_G(\Omega)$ our algorithm has computed a minimal triangulation H_i for the realization $\mathcal{R}_G(S_i, C_i)$. We then define the following.

$$H_G(\Omega) \stackrel{\text{def}}{=} \bigcup_{(S_i, C_i) \in Blck_G(\Omega)} H_i \cup \mathcal{K}_\Omega \qquad (1)$$

Our algorithm, MinTriang, is depicted in Figure 3. It applies dynamic programming based on Equation (1). The algorithm is parameterized by a split-monotone bag cost κ, takes as input a graph G, and computes a minimum-κ minimal triangulation of G.

The first step is to compute *MinSep*(G) and *PMC*(G). Assuming G belongs to a poly-MS class of graphs, this step can be done efficiently by combining results from Berry et al. [3] and Bouchitté and Todinca [9]. Then, the set $\mathcal{B}$ of full blocks of G is computed and traversed in order of ascending cardinality (beginning with (S, C) such that $|S \cup C|$ is minimal) in the loop of line 3. In the iteration of (S, C), the optimal triangulation of $\mathcal{R}(S, C)$ is computed.

When processing a block (S, C), the algorithm selects a PMC $\Omega \in PMC(G)$ where $S \subset \Omega \subseteq S \cup C$, to be saturated according to Equation (1), such that the cost of the resulting triangulation of $\mathcal{R}(S, C)$ is minimized. The saturated vertex set is stored as $\Omega(S, C)$ (line 4). By a slight abuse of notation, we denote by $PMC(S, C)$ the set $\{\Omega \in PMC(G) \mid S \subset \Omega \subseteq (S, C)\}$. The chosen optimal triangulation of $\mathcal{R}(S, C)$ is then stored as $\mathcal{H}(S, C)$ for later use (line 5). The processing order of the blocks allows larger blocks to evaluate each member of $PMC(S, C)$ based on previously computed optimal triangulations for each of the realizations of its smaller blocks. That is, for each block $(S_i, C_i) \in Blck_{\mathcal{R}(S,C)}(\Omega)$, the term H_i in

Equation (1) (used in lines 4 and 5) will refer to previously computed $\mathcal{H}(S_i, C_i)$.

Finally, the optimal result is selected by saturating the minimal-cost PMC in the whole graph (lines 6–7). The following theorem states the correctness and efficiency of the algorithm.

Theorem 5.5. *Let κ be a split-monotone bag cost computable in polynomial time.* MinTriang$\langle\kappa\rangle(G)$ *returns a minimal triangulation of minimal cost κ in time polynomial in the number of minimal separators of the graph. Hence, if G belongs to a poly-MS class of graphs then* MinTriang *terminates in polynomial time.*

5.3 Bounded Width

Another application of the algorithm is when we are interested only in tree decompositions of a bounded (constant) width b, without making the poly-MS assumption. Bounding the width can be accomplished by attaching a high cost (∞) to triangulations with maximal cliques of a larger size than b (lines 4 and 6). Furthermore, any minimal separator larger than b cannot be saturated in our output, implying that full blocks of these separators can be completely disregarded in the main loop (line 3). The limit on the width bounds the number of minimal separators and PMCs that our algorithm should consider. Hence, if this limit is considered constant then we get a polynomial bound on the execution time of our algorithm, without assuming poly-MS, if we revise line 1 to compute only the minimal separators and PMCs of size at most b. We can generate those minimal separators in polynomial time by naively testing, for every set of b or fewer nodes, whether the set is a minimal separator; we can then similarly generate those PMCs, since we can test whether a node set is a PMC when given the minimal separators contained in the set [7]. We refer to the revised algorithm as MinTriangB$\langle b,\kappa\rangle(G)$. We have the following.

Theorem 5.6. *Let b be a fixed natural number, and κ a split monotone bag cost computable in polynomial time. The algorithm* MinTriangB$\langle b,\kappa\rangle(G)$ *returns, in polynomial time, a minimal triangulation H of width at most b (if one exists) with a minimal $\kappa(G,H)$.*

6 ENUMERATION ALGORITHM

We now present our algorithm for ranked enumeration of minimal triangulations. A strong connection between minimal triangulations and proper tree decompositions is stated in Theorem 2.2. Carmeli et al. [10] show how enumeration of proper tree decompositions reduces to that of minimal triangulations. Formally, we have the following.

Proposition 6.1. *Let* **G** *be class of graphs, and κ a bag cost. If, on graphs of* **G**, *the minimal triangulations can be enumerated with polynomial delay by increasing κ, then so can the proper tree decompositions.*

So, in the remainder of this section we consider only minimal triangulations. Our algorithm is an application of Lawler-Murty's procedure [28, 33], which reduces ranked enumeration to optimization under *inclusion* and *exclusion constraints*. The goal of this procedure is to enumerate sets A of items a by an increasing cost function $c(A)$. Here, an item a is a minimal separator of G and each set A is a maximal set of pairwise-parallel minimal separators. Recall from Theorem 2.5 that each such set A identifies a minimal triangulation H. In particular, the score $c(A)$ is $\kappa(G,H)$. A constraint of both types is represented as a minimal separator S. A minimal triangulation H satisfies sets I and X of inclusion and exclusion constraints, respectively, if $I \subseteq$ *MinSep*(H) and $X \cap$ *MinSep*$(H) = \emptyset$. We denote such a pair as $[I,X]$, and say that H satisfies $[I,X]$ if it satisfies both I and X.

In the rest of this section we will show how MinTriang can be adapted to return a minimal triangulation satisfying input constraints, and present our algorithm for ranked enumeration. Later, we adapt the algorithm to enumerate the minimal triangulations of a bounded width.

6.1 Incorporating Constraints

We would like to restrict MinTriang (Figure 3) to return a minimal triangulation that satisfies a set $[I,X]$ of inclusion and exclusion constraints. Our approach is to alter our cost function κ to assign an infinite cost to triangulations that violate the constraints. Yet, while doing so we need to verify that all needed assumptions hold.

To check constraints during the MinTriang algorithm we need to take into consideration two problems that may occur while triangulating a realization $\mathcal{R}(S,C)$ of G. First, I may include vertices that are not in $\mathcal{R}(S,C)$, so I will be violated for the wrong reasons. Second, it might be the case that a minimal separator S of G is not a minimal separator of a triangulation of $\mathcal{R}(S,C)$, but it will be a minimal separator in a triangulation that contains this triangulation. Therefore, we use the following equivalent definition (see Theorem 2.5). We say that H *satisfies* $[I,X]$, in notation $H \models [I,X]$, if for all $S \in I \cup X$ with $S \subseteq \mathrm{V}(H)$ it holds that S is a clique of H if $S \in I$ and S is *not* a clique of H if $S \in X$.

Given a constraint $[I,X]$ and a split-monotone bag cost κ (over tree decompositions), we define the cost function $\kappa[I,X]$ as follows.

$$\kappa[I,X](G,\mathcal{T}) \stackrel{\text{def}}{=} \begin{cases} \kappa(G,\mathcal{T}) & \text{if } H_{\mathcal{T}} \models [I,X]; \\ \infty & \text{otherwise.} \end{cases} \tag{2}$$

where, $H_{\mathcal{T}}$ is the graph obtained from G by saturating every bag of $\mathcal{T}$. A crucial lemma is the following, stating that if κ is a split-monotone bag cost, then so is $\kappa[I,X]$.

Lemma 6.2. *Let κ be a cost function, G a graph, and $[I, X]$ a set of constraints on minimal triangulations of G.*

(1) If κ is a split-monotone bag cost, then so is $\kappa[I, X]$.

(2) If κ can be computed in polynomial time in the size of G, then $\kappa[I, X]$ can be computed in polynomial time in the size of G, I and X.

Combining Lemma 6.2 with Theorem 5.5, we conclude the following theorem that we will use in the next section.

Theorem 6.3. *Let $\mathbf{G}$ be a poly-MS class of graphs and κ a split-monotone bag cost computable in polynomial time over $\mathbf{G}$. For all $G \in \mathbf{G}$ and constraints $[I, X]$ over G, $\mathsf{MinTriang}\langle\kappa[I, X]\rangle(G)$ returns a minimum $\kappa[I, X]$ minimal triangulation in polynomial time.*

6.2 The Enumeration Algorithm

Our enumeration algorithm, RankedTriang, is depicted in Figure 4. It is parameterized by a cost function κ, takes as input a graph G, and enumerates (via the **print** command of line 6) the minimal triangulations of G by increasing cost.

The algorithm maintains a priority queue Q. Each element in Q represents a partition of the space of minimal triangulations. Here, a *partition* is associated with an inclusion-exclusion constraint $[I, X]$, and it consists of all minimal triangulations that satisfy $[I, X]$. In Q, the partition $[I, X]$ is represented as a triple $\langle H, I, X\rangle$, where H is a minimum-cost member (minimal triangulation) in the partition. Whenever we reach the loop of line 4, Q forms a partition of the entire space of minimal triangulations that have not been printed yet. In particular, the first element inserted into Q (in line 3) is the triple $\langle H, \emptyset, \emptyset\rangle$, representing the entire space of minimal triangulations, where H is a minimal triangulation of a minimum κ.

Priority in Q is determined by the cost of the minimal triangulation. In particular, the element removed in line 5 is triple $\langle H, I, X\rangle$ such that $\kappa(H) \leq \kappa(H')$ for any triple $\langle H', I', X'\rangle$ in Q. In each iteration of the while loop, such $\langle H, I, X\rangle$ is removed and printed. Then, in the rest of the iteration (lines 7–13), the remainder of the partition $[I, X]$ (that is, every minimal triangulation there except for H) is split into new partitions, all inserted to Q (line 13). The new partitions are constructed as follows. Recall that H contains all of the minimal separators in I. Let $S_1, \dots, S_k$ be the set of minimal separators of H that are *not* in I. The first partition, $[I_1, X_1]$, is obtained from $[I, X]$ by copying I and inserting S_1 into X_1. In the second partition we add S_1 to I, but now X_2 is $X \cup \{S_2\}$. We likewise continue for $i = 2, \dots k$, where each I_i consists of I and $S_1, \dots, S_{i-1}$, and each X_i is $X \cup \{S_i\}$. It is an easy observation that the $[I_i, X_i]$ form a proper partition. In particular, observe that no other minimal triangulation can contain all of the minimal separators of H, since no two triangulations H and H' satisfy $\mathit{MinSep}(H) \subsetneq \mathit{MinSep}(H')$, as implied by Theorem 2.5. For each partition $[I_i, X_i]$ a minimum-cost minimal triangulation H_i w.r.t. $\kappa[I_i, X_i]$ is constructed (line 11). Observe that H_i satisfies $[I_i, X_i]$ if and only if this partition is nonempty; hence, the test of line 12 tests whether the partition is nonempty, and if so inserts $\langle H_i, I_i, X_i\rangle$ to Q.

The correctness and efficiency of the algorithm are stated in the following theorem.

Theorem 6.4. *$\mathsf{RankedTriang}\langle\kappa\rangle(G)$ enumerates the minimal triangulations H of G by increasing $\kappa(G, H)$. Moreover, the algorithm enumerates with polynomial delay if:*

(1) κ can be computed in polynomial time, and

(2) each $\mathsf{MinTriang}\langle\kappa[I_i, X_i]\rangle(G)$ takes polynomial time.

Combined with Theorem 6.3, we conclude the following.

Corollary 6.5. *Let $\mathbf{G}$ be a poly-MS class of graphs, and let κ be a bag cost that is split monotone and computable in polynomial time. On graphs G of $\mathbf{G}$, $\mathsf{RankedTriang}\langle\kappa\rangle(G)$ can enumerate the minimal triangulations of G by increasing κ, with polynomial delay.*

Note that Theorem 4.4 (from Section 4) is a direct consequence of Corollary 6.5.

Bounded width. We now consider the enumeration of the minimal triangulations of a width bounded by a fixed bound b without masking the assumption of poly-MS. To adjust $\mathsf{RankedTriang}\langle\kappa\rangle(G)$, it suffices to replace $\mathsf{MinTriang}\langle\kappa\rangle(G)$ and $\mathsf{MinTriang}\langle\kappa[I_i, X_i]\rangle(G)$ in lines 2 and 11 with the calls to $\mathsf{MinTriangB}\langle b, \kappa\rangle(G)$ and $\mathsf{MinTriangB}\langle b, \kappa[I_i, X_i]\rangle(G)$, respectively, building on Theorem 5.6 instead of Theorem 5.5.

Algorithm $\mathsf{RankedTriang}\langle\kappa\rangle(G)$

```
1:  Q := empty priority queue by κ (lowest first)
2:  H := MinTriang⟨κ⟩(G)
3:  Q.push(⟨H, ∅, ∅⟩)
4:  while Q ≠ ∅ do
5:      ⟨H, I, X⟩ := Q.pop()
6:      print(H)
7:      let MinSep(H) \ I be {S_1, ..., S_k}
8:      for i = 1, ..., k do
9:          I_i := I ∪ {S_1, ..., S_{i-1}}
10:         X_i := X ∪ {S_i}
11:         H_i := MinTriang⟨κ[I_i, X_i]⟩(G)
12:         if H_i satisfies [I_i, X_i] then
13:             Q.push(⟨H_i, I_i, X_i⟩)
```

Figure 4: Ranked enumeration of the minimal triangulations by a split-monotone bag cost κ.

(The algorithm MinTriangB is described right before Theorem 5.6.) We can show that all guarantees of the enumeration algorithm (as stated in Theorem 6.4) remain valid. Combined with Lemma 6.2 and Proposition 6.1, we then establish Theorem 4.5 (from Section 4).

7 EXPERIMENTAL EVALUATION

In this section, we describe our experimental study, where the goal is twofold. First and foremost, we explore the performance of our enumeration algorithm (Figures 3 and 4), namely RankedTriang. The second goal is to explore the applicability of the poly-MS assumption in reality, and particularly to get an insight on how often realistic graphs have a manageable number of minimal separators.

7.1 Experimental Setup

We first describe the general setup for the experiments.

Implementation. The algorithms have been implemented in C++, with STL data structures. We used some of the code of Carmeli et al. [10].[2] Particularly, we used their implementation of the algorithm for enumerating the minimal separators by Berry et al. [3]. To compute the PMCs of a graph, we implemented the algorithm by Bouchitté and Todinca [9]. It is important to note that the implementation of these two algorithms is direct, with no special optimization. While these algorithms might take a significant portion of the time, improving their implementation is beyond the scope of this paper, and remains an important future direction. We consider the computation of the minimal separators, PMCs and blocks of each graph (lines 1-2 of MinTriang) the *initialization* step, as they are computed once at the beginning of RankedTriang, instead of rerunning for each invocation of MinTriang as our algorithms state.

Hardware. We ran all experiments on a 2.5Ghz 48-core server with 512 GB of RAM running Ubuntu 14.04.5 LTS. The experiments ran single threaded.[3]

Compared algorithms. We compared our algorithm to that of Carmeli, Kenig and Kimelfeld [10], referred to as CKK, which enumerates with incremental polynomial time and has no guarantees on the order. To the best of our knowledge, no other published algorithms for enumerating minimal triangulations or tree decompositions with completeness guarantees exist, with the exception of DunceCap [39] that is designed for small query graphs; for more details about its performance we refer the reader to Carmeli et al. [10].

[2]https://github.com/NofarCarmeli/MinTriangulationsEnumeration

[3]In future work we will explore how RankedTriang can be parallelized for delay reduction by parallelizing the main loop or using more advanced ideas such as those of Golenberg et al. [16].

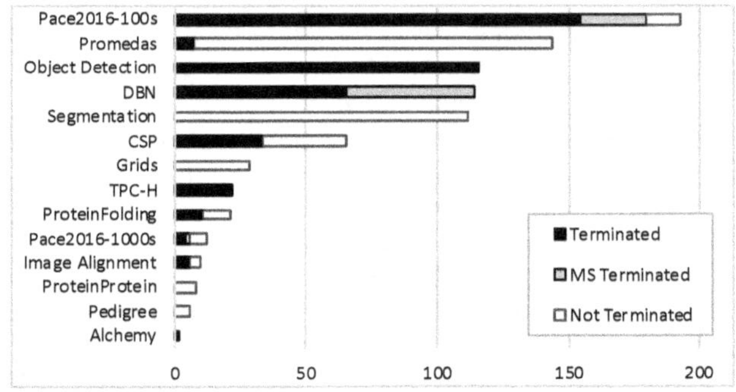

Figure 5: Tractability of computing the minimal separators and the PMCs over PIC2011 and PACE2016 graphs.

CKK requires a black-box minimal triangulator. In our experiments, we used the algorithm LB_TRIANG [4] for this matter, as it was found to allow for enumeration of triangulations of smaller width and fill [10]. In principle, we could also have used our MinTriang, but we chose not to do so since MinTriang requires a long initialization step, and CKK applies its triangulator to many graphs that change between execution calls (hence, the initialization cannot be shared across invocations).

Datasets. Our datasets contain those of Carmeli et al. [10]. These include graphs of three types: probabilistic graphical models from the PIC2011 challenge,[4] Gaifman graphs of conjunctive queries translated from the TPC-H benchmark (see [10]), and random graphs. Random graphs were generated by the $G(n, p)$ Erdös-Rényi model, where the number of vertices is n and every pair of vertices is (independently) connected by an edge with probability p.

Additionally, we used the dataset from the PACE2016 competition [12], where participants competed on the computation of tree decompositions (equivalently, minimal triangulations) of minimal width. These graphs[5] are samples from *named graphs*,[6] *control-flow graphs*,[7] and the *DIMACS graph-coloring problems*.[8] We used graphs from the tracks where time was limited to 100 and 1000 seconds.

7.2 The Poly-MS Assumption

We begin with our investigation of the poly-MS assumption, since this study is needed as context for the later evaluation of our enumeration algorithms. In this study, we attempted to generate all minimal separators, and then all PMCs, on our

[4]http://www.cs.huji.ac.il/project/PASCAL/showNet.php

[5]The PACE2016 competition graphs can be found at http://github.com/holgerdell/PACE-treewidth-testbed/tree/master/instances/pace16

[6]https://github.com/freetdi/named-graphs

[7]https://github.com/freetdi/CFGs.git

[8]URL:http://mat.gsia.cmu.edu/COLOR/instances.html

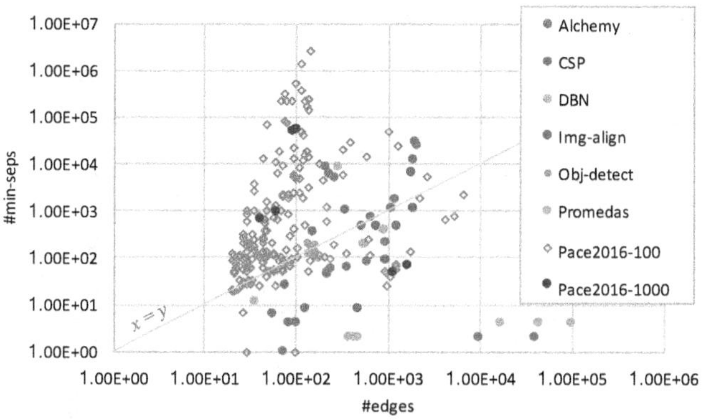

Figure 6: Distribution of the number of minimal separators on the MS tractable PIC2011 and PACE2016 graphs.

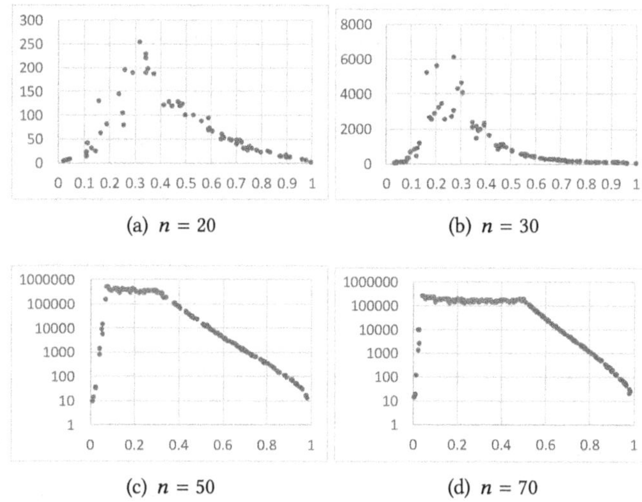

Figure 7: Number of minimal separators on random graph $G(n, p)$. The bottom charts use logarithmic scale. Red marks stand for cases where the computation took over 10 minutes and then stopped.

datasets. We describe the success rate, and for each successful case the corresponding number of results.

Real-life graphs. In Figure 5 we report, for each dataset, the number of graphs where the computation terminated in predefined time periods. The columns are as follows.

- *Terminated*: Graphs G where the time required to compute *MinSep*(G) is under a minute, and the time required to compute *PMC*(G) is under 30 minutes. These graphs will be used to test our algorithm.
- *MS terminated*: Graphs G where the time required to compute *MinSep*(G) is under a minute, but the time to compute *PMC*(G) is over 30 minutes.
- *Not terminated*: Graphs where the time to compute *MinSep*(G) is over a minute, effectively taking over ten minutes in nearly all cases, and the time to compute *PMC*(G) is over 30 minutes.

As expected, graphs often violate the poly-MS assumption (otherwise the NP-hard problem of computing the tree-width and fill-in would actually be tractable in all of these graphs). In some of the datasets, all graphs were found infeasible. Nevertheless, the positive finding is that the portion of graphs with a manageable number of minimal separators is quite substantial (around 50%). The reader can also observe that in most cases, when we were able to compute the minimal separators, we were also able to compute the PMCs (which is consistent with known theory about the relationship between the two [9]). Figure 6 shows the distribution of the number of minimal separators (in log scale) over the *terminated* and *MS terminated* cases of the PIC2011 and PACE2016. One can observe that these numbers are quite often comparable to the number of edges, and sometimes even smaller.

Random graphs. We ran a similar experiment on random graphs. As said earlier, our random graphs are $G(n, p)$ from assorted n and p. We drew graphs with $n \in \{20, 30, 50, 70\}$ vertices, drawing three graphs for each $p \in \{1/n, \dots, n/n\}$. This allowed us to observe the correlation between the fraction of edges in the graph and the number of minimal separators. Figure 7 reports the result of these tests. When the computation time exceeded ten minutes, we stopped the execution and, as observed, it happened in the case of $n = 50$ and $n = 70$ (shown by the red marks). The reader can observe an interesting phenomenon—the number of minimal separators is small for either sparse or dense graphs. In between (around $p = 0.25$) this number blows up.

7.3 Enumeration Evaluation

We now describe our evaluation of the algorithm RankedTriang, and compare it to CKK.

Real-life graphs. Table 2 compares the enumerations of the algorithms on datasets of PIC2011 and PACE2016, where we were able to compute all PMCs (i.e., "Terminated" graphs from the previous section). Each algorithm was executed twice on each graph for 30 minutes, once for minimization of width and again for fill-in. In the case of TPC-H graphs, computing all minimal triangulations is a matter of a few seconds, so we did not include those in the table. Moreover, as we look only at the set of results following a fixed execution time, RankedTriang has no apparent advantage if CKK actually terminates (computing all minimal triangulations); hence, executions where CKK terminates are excluded from the table. The table columns are as follows.

- **#trng**: Number of returned minimal triangulations.

Table 2: Results on 30-minute executions, optimizing width and fill. For each dataset, the top row relates to RankedTriang **and the bottom to** CKK. **Numbers larger than** 1000 **are rounded.**

dataset (#graphs)	#trng	init	delay	delay no init	min-w	#min-w	#≤1.1min-w	min-f	#min-f	#≤1.1min-f
CSP (12)	36493	274.8	2.4	1.7	16.5	34143	34143	146.3	1909	6747
	18625	-	0.23	-	18.5	2117(12.2%)	2151(14%)	208.2	1(0.35%)	336.8(8.2%)
Image Align. (4)	29674	36.3	0.36	0.34	20	37067	38951	135	305.5	2640
	4191	-	0.57	-	22.3	1034(1.3%)	1169(1.4%)	213.8	1(25%)	10.8(10.4%)
Object Detect. (79)	538927	0.2	0.004	0.004	5.8	579156	579156	24.9	287589	486465
	67639	-	0.03	-	7.3	15946(4.7%)	15946(4.7%)	39.3	11.9(0.15%)	3918(1.3%)
PACE2016-100s (87)	137537	108.3	13.4	7.4	5.8	113516	114250	54.4	95139	100612
	164069	-	0.15	-	9.9	87002(30.3%)	87214(30.3%)	413.4	54781(767%)	56994(904%)
PACE2016-1000s (3)	63029	3.3	0.03	0.03	15.7	36232	39418	56.7	5989	27404
	79591	-	0.13	-	16	440.7(0.4%)	1363(8.3%)	60	13(3.6%)	1405(3.6%)
Promedas (2)	1095	387.6	44.6	28.9	3.5	89.5	89.5	34.5	43	91
	10296	-	0.45	-	3.5	9166(48242%)	9166(48242%)	41.5	0.5(0.78%)	0.5(0.31%)

- **init**: For RankedTriang, the initialization time. Importantly, this time is counted into the 30 minutes of the other columns (unless stated otherwise).
- **delay**: The average delay between returned results.
- **delay no init**: The average delay between returned results, after initialization.
- **min-w**: The average minimal width among the minimal triangulations returned by the algorithm.
- **#min-w**: When the cost is width, number of triangulations returned with a minimal width.
- **#≤1.1·min-w**: Number of near-optimal (within 10%) triangulations returned by the algorithm, optimizing width.
- **min-f**: The average minimal fill-in among the minimal triangulations returned by the algorithm.
- **#min-f**: When optimizing fill-in, the number of triangulations returned with minimal fill-in.
- **#≤1.1·min-f**: Number of near optimal triangulations returned by the algorithm, optimizing fill-in.

Next to the number of optimal (or near optimal) results returned by CKK for each cost, we also report the average percent of optimal results returned, relative to the algorithm RankedTriang.

We can see that, with the exception of Promedas, the execution cost of RankedTriang is comparable to, and even lower than, CKK. Moreover, the cost of its answers are consistently lower than CKK, which returns only a fraction of the optimal triangulations. On Promedas, RankedTriang is too slow due to a high number of PMCs. For the CSP graphs, it appears as if our algorithm returns more results with a larger average delay. This is caused by two graphs where RankedTriang returns a higher number of results than CKK by an order of magnitude. This is not the case for the rest of the dataset, where the delays are longer and the number of results is smaller in RankedTriang than in CKK.

For PACE2016 100s graphs, the table shows the average percentage of optimal triangulations returned by CKK is much larger than that of RankedTriang. This is caused by only three graphs where the number of results returned by CKK is larger by several orders of magnitude than those returned by RankedTriang, due to a high initialization time and delay. The results returned by the heuristic LB_TRIANG are all optimal in fill-in for these three graphs. This is *not* the usual case for the graphs in this dataset, and for many of them CKK did not generate *any* result of a minimum fill-in. The reader can observe that under the *width* cost, the advantage of RankedTriang over CKK is substantial.

Random graphs. We evaluated both algorithms on random graphs $G(n, p)$, in the same experimental setup as for the real graphs. We drew graphs with $n \in \{20, 50\}$ vertices, drawing three graphs for each $p \in \{0.05, 0.1, 0.15, \dots, 0.75, 0.8\}$. Figure 8 reports the results. Figures 8(a) and 8(b) show the average delay between returned results, where the delay of RankedTriang is measured with and without the initialization time. Figures 8(c) and 8(d) show the relative percent of optimal cost results returned by CKK, relative to RankedTriang. We can see that for graphs where the minimal separators and PMCs can be computed, the delay of RankedTriang is smaller than that of CKK. This occurs in all graphs with 20 vertices, and some of the graphs with 50 vertices. In the case of graphs with 50 vertices, RankedTriang does not terminate initialization for probabilities 0.1 through 0.5, implying for these graphs the number of minimal separators and PMCs is high. For graphs from probabilities closer to this range, RankedTriang has a higher delay, which is caused by a larger

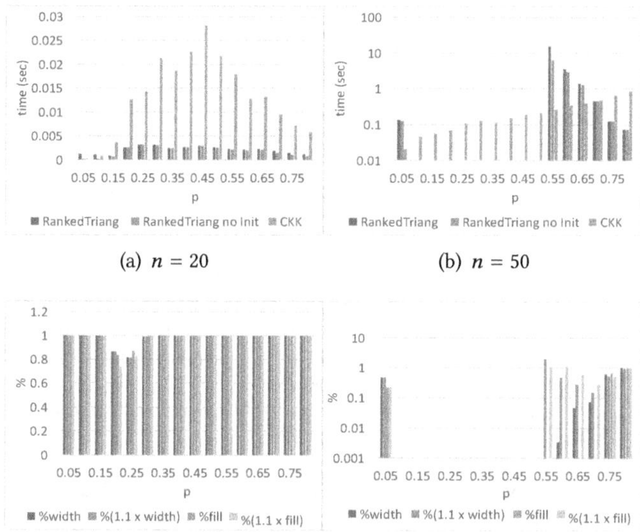

(a) $n = 20$ (b) $n = 50$

(c) $n = 20$ (d) $n = 50$

Figure 8: Delay over random graphs $G(n, p)$, and ratio of results of CKK compared to RankedTriang.

number of minimal separators. These results are consistent with the hardness results observed in Section 7.2.

8 CONCLUDING REMARKS

We presented an algorithm for enumerating minimal triangulations, and by implication proper tree decompositions, by increasing cost with polynomial delay, for arbitrary split-monotone (efficiently computable) bag costs. One variant of the algorithm enumerates *all* minimal triangulations, but requires pre-computing all minimal separators, and hence, makes the poly-MS assumption. The other variant computes all minimal triangulations of a bounded width, and does not require the poly-MS assumption. Our implementation and experimental study shows that the algorithm can lend itself to practical realization, and that the poly-MS assumption is quite often valid.

Various directions are left open for future research, beyond the ones mentioned throughout the paper. For one, it is known that computing a tree decomposition of width w is *Fixed-Parameter Tractable* (FPT) [6] when taking w as the parameter; this means that w affects only the constant (and not the degree) of the polynomial [13]. Can we extend this result to the enumeration of all tree decompositions of width at most w with FPT delay? Also, can we strengthen our algorithms with further *diversity* of results to maximize the potential value to the application? How should diversification be defined? In addition to investigating the open questions, we plan to incorporate our algorithm in the framework of Abseher et al. [1] for supervised learning of effective tree decompositions.

ACKNOWLEDGMENTS

We are very grateful to Batya Kenig for insightful discussions about the content of this paper. This work was supported by ISF Grant 1295/15.

REFERENCES

[1] Michael Abseher, Nysret Musliu, and Stefan Woltran. 2017. Improving the Efficiency of Dynamic Programming on Tree Decompositions via Machine Learning. *J. Artif. Intell. Res.* 58 (2017), 829–858.

[2] Anne Berry, Jean R. S. Blair, and Pinar Heggernes. 2002. Maximum Cardinality Search for Computing Minimal Triangulations. In *WG (WG '02)*. Springer-Verlag, London, UK, UK, 1–12.

[3] Anne Berry, Jean Paul Bordat, and Olivier Cogis. 1999. Generating All the Minimal Separators of a Graph. In *WG (LNCS)*, Vol. 1665. Springer, 167–172.

[4] Anne Berry, Jean-Paul Bordat, Pinar Heggernes, Geneviève Simonet, and Yngve Villanger. 2006. A wide-range algorithm for minimal triangulation from an arbitrary ordering. *Journal of Algorithms* 58, 1 (2006), 33–66.

[5] Jean RS Blair and Barry Peyton. 1993. An introduction to chordal graphs and clique trees. In *Graph theory and sparse matrix computation*. Springer, 1–29.

[6] Hans L. Bodlaender. 1996. A Linear-Time Algorithm for Finding Tree-Decompositions of Small Treewidth. *SIAM J. Comput.* 25, 6 (1996), 1305–1317.

[7] Vincent Bouchitté and Ioan Todinca. 1999. Treewidth and Minimum Fill-in of Weakly Triangulated Graphs. In *STACS (Lecture Notes in Computer Science)*, Vol. 1563. Springer, 197–206.

[8] Vincent Bouchitté and Ioan Todinca. 2001. Treewidth and minimum fill-in: Grouping the minimal separators. *SIAM J. Comput.* 31, 1 (2001), 212–232.

[9] Vincent Bouchitté and Ioan Todinca. 2002. Listing all potential maximal cliques of a graph. *Theor. Comput. Sci.* 276, 1-2 (2002), 17–32.

[10] Nofar Carmeli, Batya Kenig, and Benny Kimelfeld. 2017. Efficiently Enumerating Minimal Triangulations. In *PODS*. ACM, 273–287.

[11] Sara Cohen, Benny Kimelfeld, and Yehoshua Sagiv. 2008. Generating all maximal induced subgraphs for hereditary and connected-hereditary graph properties. *J. Comput. Syst. Sci.* 74, 7 (2008), 1147–1159.

[12] Holger Dell, Thore Husfeldt, Bart M. P. Jansen, Petteri Kaski, Christian Komusiewicz, and Frances A. Rosamond. 2017. The First Parameterized Algorithms and Computational Experiments Challenge. In *IPEC (Leibniz International Proceedings in Informatics (LIPIcs))*, Vol. 63. 30:1–30:9.

[13] Rodney G. Downey and Michael R. Fellows. 1999. *Parameterized Complexity*. Springer.

[14] Fedor V. Fomin, Ioan Todinca, and Yngve Villanger. 2015. Large Induced Subgraphs via Triangulations and CMSO. *SIAM J. Comput.* 44, 1 (2015), 54–87.

[15] Masanobu Furuse and Koichi Yamazaki. 2014. A revisit of the scheme for computing treewidth and minimum fill-in. *Theor. Comput. Sci.* 531 (2014), 66–76.

[16] Konstantin Golenberg, Benny Kimelfeld, and Yehoshua Sagiv. 2011. Optimizing and Parallelizing Ranked Enumeration. *PVLDB* 4, 11 (2011), 1028–1039.

[17] Georg Gottlob, Gianluigi Greco, and Francesco Scarcello. 2005. Pure Nash Equilibria: Hard and Easy Games. *J. Artif. Intell. Res. (JAIR)* 24 (2005), 357–406.

[18] Georg Gottlob, Martin Grohe, Nysret Musliu, Marko Samer, and Francesco Scarcello. 2005. Hypertree Decompositions: Structure, Algorithms, and Applications. In *WG (LNCS)*, Vol. 3787. Springer, 1–15.

[19] Georg Gottlob, Nicola Leone, and Francesco Scarcello. 2002. Hypertree Decompositions and Tractable Queries. *J. Comput. Syst. Sci.* 64, 3 (2002), 579–627.

[20] Georg Gottlob, Zoltán Miklós, and Thomas Schwentick. 2009. Generalized hypertree decompositions: NP-hardness and tractable variants. *J. ACM* 56, 6 (2009).

[21] Martin Grohe and Dániel Marx. 2014. Constraint Solving via Fractional Edge Covers. *ACM Trans. Algorithms* 11, 1 (2014), 4:1–4:20.

[22] David S. Johnson, Christos H. Papadimitriou, and Mihalis Yannakakis. 1988. On Generating All Maximal Independent Sets. *Inf. Process. Lett.* 27, 3 (1988), 119–123.

[23] Oren Kalinsky, Yoav Etsion, and Benny Kimelfeld. 2017. Flexible Caching in Trie Joins. In *EDBT*. OpenProceedings.org, 282–293.

[24] Batya Kenig and Avigdor Gal. 2015. On the Impact of Junction-Tree Topology on Weighted Model Counting. In *SUM (LNCS)*, Vol. 9310. Springer, 83–98.

[25] Ton Kloks, Dieter Kratsch, and Jeremy P. Spinrad. 1997. On Treewidth and Minimum Fill-In of Asteroidal Triple-Free Graphs. *Theor. Comput. Sci.* 175, 2 (1997), 309–335.

[26] Phokion G. Kolaitis and Moshe Y. Vardi. 2000. Conjunctive-Query Containment and Constraint Satisfaction. *J. Comput. Syst. Sci.* 61, 2 (2000), 302–332.

[27] S. Lauritzen and D. J. Spiegelhalter. 1988. Local Computations with Probabilities on Graphical Structures and Their Application to Expert Systems. *Journal of the Royal Statistical Society* B, 50, 2 (1988), 157–224.

[28] E. L. Lawler. 1972. A procedure for computing the K best solutions to discrete optimization problems and its application to the shortest path problem. *Management Science* 18, 7 (1972), 401–405.

[29] Mathieu Liedloff, Pedro Montealegre, and Ioan Todinca. 2015. Beyond Classes of Graphs with "Few" Minimal Separators: FPT Results Through Potential Maximal Cliques. In *WG (LNCS)*, Vol. 9224. Springer, 499–512.

[30] Dániel Marx. 2010. Approximating fractional hypertree width. *ACM Trans. Algorithms* 6, 2 (2010).

[31] Héctor Otero Mediero. 2017. *Search Algorithms for Solving Queries on Graphical Models and the Importance of Pseudo-trees in their Complexity.* Technical Report. University of California Irvine. UCI ICS Technical Report.

[32] Pedro Montealegre and Ioan Todinca. 2016. On Distance-d Independent Set and Other Problems in Graphs with "few" Minimal Separators. In *WG (LNCS)*, Vol. 9941. 183–194.

[33] K. G. Murty. 1968. An algorithm for ranking all the assignments in order of increasing cost. *Operations Research* 16, 3 (1968), 682–687.

[34] Yota Otachi and Pascal Schweitzer. 2014. Reduction Techniques for Graph Isomorphism in the Context of Width Parameters. In *SWAT (LNCS)*, Vol. 8503. Springer, 368–379.

[35] Andreas Parra and Petra Scheffler. 1997. Characterizations and Algorithmic Applications of Chordal Graph Embeddings. *Discrete Applied Mathematics* 79, 1-3 (1997), 171–188.

[36] Noam Ravid, Dori Medini, and Benny Kimelfeld. 2017. Ranked Enumeration of Minimal Triangulations. *CoRR* abs/1709.10254 (2017).

[37] Donald J Rose. 1970. Triangulated graphs and the elimination process. *J. Math. Anal. Appl.* 32, 3 (1970), 597–609.

[38] Robert E. Tarjan and Mihalis Yannakakis. 1984. Simple Linear-time Algorithms to Test Chordality of Graphs, Test Acyclicity of Hypergraphs, and Selectively Reduce Acyclic Hypergraphs. *SIAM J. Comput.* 13, 3 (July 1984), 566–579.

[39] Susan Tu and Christopher Ré. 2015. DunceCap: Query Plans Using Generalized Hypertree Decompositions. In *SIGMOD*. ACM, 2077–2078.

[40] Jizhen Zhao, Russell L. Malmberg, and Liming Cai. 2006. Rapid *ab initio* RNA Folding Including Pseudoknots Via Graph Tree Decomposition. In *WABI*. 262–273.

Enumeration on Trees with Tractable Combined Complexity and Efficient Updates

Antoine Amarilli
LTCI, Télécom ParisTech, Université Paris-Saclay

Pierre Bourhis
CRIStAL, CNRS UMR 9189 & Inria Lille

Stefan Mengel
CNRS, CRIL UMR 8188

Matthias Niewerth
University of Bayreuth

ABSTRACT

We give an algorithm to enumerate the results on trees of monadic second-order (MSO) queries represented by *non-deterministic* tree automata. After linear time preprocessing (in the input tree), we can enumerate answers with linear delay (in each answer). We allow updates on the tree to take place at any time, and we can then restart the enumeration after logarithmic time in the tree. Further, all our combined complexities are polynomial in the automaton.

Our result follows our previous circuit-based enumeration algorithms based on deterministic tree automata, and is also inspired by our earlier result on words and nondeterministic sequential extended variable-set automata in the context of document spanners. We extend these results and combine them with a recent tree balancing scheme by Niewerth, so that our enumeration structure supports updates to the underlying tree in logarithmic time (with leaf insertions, leaf deletions, and node relabelings). Our result implies that, for MSO queries with free first-order variables, we can enumerate the results with linear preprocessing and constant-delay and update the underlying tree in logarithmic time, which improves on several known results for words and trees.

Building on lower bounds from data structure research, we also show unconditionally that up to a doubly logarithmic factor the update time of our algorithm is optimal. Thus, unlike other settings, there can be no algorithm with constant update time.

PODS '19, June 30–July 5, 2019, Amsterdam, Netherlands

ACM ISBN 978-1-4503-6227-6/19/06...$15.00
https://doi.org/10.1145/3294052.3319702

ACM Reference Format:
Antoine Amarilli, Pierre Bourhis, Stefan Mengel, and Matthias Niewerth. 2019. Enumeration on Trees with Tractable Combined Complexity and Efficient Updates. In *38th ACM SIGMOD-SIGACT-SIGAI Symposium on Principles of Database Systems (PODS '19), June 30–July 5, 2019, Amsterdam, Netherlands.* ACM, New York, NY, USA, 16 pages. https://doi.org/10.1145/3294052.3319702

1 INTRODUCTION

Query evaluation is one of the central tasks in databases. A prominent framework for this task in theoretical work are so-called *enumeration algorithms*. Such algorithms print out query answers one after the other, without duplicates, and bound the time between each two answers, called the *delay* of the algorithm. Enumeration algorithms were introduced in database theory by the pioneering work of Durand and Grandjean [21], in which the goal was to achieve a constant bound on the delay, called *constant-delay enumeration*. In such algorithms, the delay between different solutions only depends on the query to be evaluated, in particular it is independent of the database. To ensure such a bound, the algorithm is allowed to first perform a *preprocessing phase* on the database, which in most cases is required to run in linear time. While these time bounds sound very restrictive, a surprising range of query evaluation problems allow enumeration in this regime, as surveyed, e.g., in [36]. Most notably, constant-delay enumeration with linear-time preprocessing can be achieved for acyclic free-connex queries on arbitrary databases [9] (with extensions for the case of functional dependencies [19] and for unions of conjunctive queries [13]), for first-order queries on bounded degree databases [11] and nowhere dense databases [35] (with pseudo-linear time preprocessing), for regular path queries [28], and for monadic second-order queries on trees and bounded-treewidth structures [8, 25] which is the setting that we study.

Enumerations algorithms have more recently been extended to handle the fact that practical databases are rarely static but change frequently. Specifically, it is important for enumeration algorithms to efficiently handle updates to the underlying database, and maintain their precomputed index structures without recomputing them from scratch at

Work	Data	Delay	Updates
Bagan [8], Kazana and Segoufin [25]	trees	$O(1)$	N/A
Losemann and Martens [26]	words	$O(\log n)$	$O(\log n)$
Losemann and Martens [26]	trees	$O(\log^2 n)$	$O(\log^2 n)$
Niewerth and Segoufin [31]	words	$O(1)$	$O(\log n)$
Niewerth [30]	trees	$O(\log n)$	$O(\log n)$
Amarilli, Bourhis, Mengel [4]	trees	$O(1)$	$O(\log n)$[1]
this paper	**trees**	$\mathbf{O(1)}$	$\mathbf{O(\log n)}$

[1]: Only supports *relabeling updates*

Table 1: State of the art for enumeration of MSO query results (for free FO variables) on trees under updates. All these algorithms have linear time preprocessing.

each update. This approach was inspired by the work of Balmin et al. [10] that showed how to maintain queries on trees efficiently under updates, but only for Boolean queries, i.e., without the ability to enumerate results. Losemann and Martens [26] were the first to extend this to an update-aware enumeration algorithm, which handled efficient enumeration of monadic second order logic (MSO) queries on words and trees. Note that the efficiency in such update-aware enumeration algorithms is measured by three parameters: the enumeration delay, the time for an initial preprocessing, and the time necessary for each update. Since [26], several such algorithms have been designed in several settings, namely, CQs [12] and UCQs [13], FO+MOD queries on bounded degree databases [11], and MSO queries over words and trees (see Table 1).

In this paper, we focus on the setting where we evaluate MSO queries on trees [8]. This task is motivated by, e.g., querying tree-shaped data such as XML or JSON documents, and the important special case of evaluating queries on words, e.g., for information extraction using *document spanners* [22, 23]. It is already known that for any MSO query the answers on a given tree can be enumerated in linear time [8, 25], and this was extended to updates by Losemann and Martens [26] but at the cost of increasing the enumeration delay to a polylogarithmic term (in particular making it depend on the database). This delay and update time were recently made logarithmic in [30], and two incomparable algorithms can achieve constant delay in special cases: when restricting the structure to be a word [31], or when restricting updates to *relabelings*, i.e., disallowing structural changes on the input tree. See Table 1 for an overview.

Our first contribution in this paper is to show an update-aware enumeration algorithm for MSO query evaluation on trees that achieves linear-time preprocessing, constant-delay enumeration, and supports updates in logarithmic time including node insertions and deletions. This strictly outperforms all previously known algorithms and shows that updates can be handled in this setting without worsening the delay. Further, our algorithm also handles the case of monadic second-order queries with free second-order variables, for which query answers no longer have constant size: in this case the delay is linear in the size of each produced answer, as in the static case [8].

Our result is shown using the *circuit-based approach* to enumeration developed in [2, 3] and also used in [4] to show the result for relabelings. In this approach, the input is first translated into a circuit representation, and we impose on the circuit some properties inspired by similar concepts in knowledge compilation, namely, that it is a complete structured DNNF whose width only depends on the query. Then the actual enumeration is performed on this circuit by relying on these properties. This approach of translating MSO queries on trees into circuits was first proposed for probabilistic query evaluation and provenance computation [7], and has the advantage of being applicable to different enumeration problems with very few adaptations, and of being modular (i.e., in the enumeration we no longer need to refer to the database or query). Our circuit based approach is also related to factorized [32] representations where query results are first encoded into a compact representation before performing other tasks on it, e.g., aggregation.

The circuit-based approach to enumeration lends itself well to relabeling updates, as we already presented in [4]: we can toggle the value of gates when labels change, and then propagate information upwards in the circuit. The update time then depends on the *depth* of the circuit, which in our construction is linear in the height of the input tree. In [4] we side-stepped this problem by computing a balanced tree decomposition on the input during the preprocessing phase using [14], so that we applied our construction to a tree of logarithmic height to achieve logarithmic update time when relabeling nodes of the tree. However, we did not know how to maintain such a balanced tree decomposition under other updates like leaf additions and deletions.

Our first contribution is shown by observing that we can combine the techniques of [4] with those developed in the recent independent work [30]. There, it was shown that one can represent trees as balanced *forest algebra* terms [15, 16] and efficiently maintain them under updates. We show that this technique can also be used in the circuit-based approach, formalizing the forest algebra updates via *tree hollowings* (in Section 7) and giving an entirely bottom-up presentation of circuit construction and enumeration (in Sections 3–6). This allows us to show our main result that generalizes the incomparable results of [8, 25], [31], [30], and [4].

The second contribution of this paper is an enumeration algorithm which is tractable *in combined complexity*. Indeed, the complexities given in Table 1 only apply to data complexity, i.e., complexity in the database when assuming that the query is fixed. However, if we want our enumeration algorithms to be applicable, it is important that the complexity remains tractable, e.g., polynomial, when the query is given as part of the input. This is an unreasonable hope when the query is written in MSO, as the combined complexity of Boolean MSO query evaluation (even without enumeration) is generally nonelementary [29]. However, if the query is given as a *tree automaton*, then Boolean evaluation has tractable combined complexity. But achieving combined tractability for enumeration is challenging: all results in Table 1 are either intractable in the query or are only tractable when assuming that the input query is represented as a *deterministic* tree automaton. This assumption is problematic already in the case of words, as we cannot, e.g., convert an input regular expression query on words to a deterministic automaton in polynomial time. In our recent work [5], we showed that enumeration *on words* (and without updates) could be performed with linear-preprocessing and constant delay while being polynomial in an input *nondeterministic* automaton (presented in the context of information extraction and *document spanners* [22]). We extend these techniques in the present paper to make our enumeration algorithm polynomial in an input nondeterministic tree automaton representation of the query; in other words we perform enumeration on circuits without requiring *determinism* [20]. This is done in Sections 5–6 by extending the techniques of [5] to trees. Our results also imply efficient enumeration algorithms to evaluate the matches of automata on words and efficiently maintain these results under updates, generalizing some results of [5] to the case of dynamic words.

Our third contribution is to show that our algorithm is close to optimal. We leverage known lower bounds from data structure research [1] to show unconditionally that the update time for an enumeration algorithm for MSO queries has to be $\Omega(\log n/\log\log n)$ when the delay is constant, or even when it is allowed to be in $o(\log n/\log\log n)$. This shows that our result is optimal up to a doubly logarithmic factor.

Paper Structure. We give preliminaries in Section 2. We present in Section 3 how to construct from the input tree and nondeterministic automaton a circuit representation of the results. We present our enumeration algorithm on such circuits in Sections 4–6, starting with a simple scheme in Section 4 which enumerates the results with duplicates and large delays, refining it in Section 5 to avoid duplicates, and showing how to achieve the right delay bound in Section 6. In Section 7, we show how the algorithm can support updates using [30], leading to our main results in Section 8. We present our lower bounds in Section 9, before concluding in Section 10. Full proofs are deferred to the full version [6].

2 PRELIMINARIES

We define words, trees, and valuations, present our automata and a homogenization lemma, and state our problem.

Trees and Valuations. In this paper, we work with trees that are all *rooted* and *ordered*, i.e., there is an order on the children of each node. Given a set Λ of tree labels, a Λ-*tree* T (or *tree* when Λ is clear from context) is a pair of a rooted tree (also written T) and of a *labeling function* λ that maps each node n of T to a *label* $\lambda(n) \in \Lambda$. We write $\mathrm{Leaf}(T)$ for the set of leaves of T. We abuse notation and identify T with its set of nodes, i.e., we can write that $\mathrm{Leaf}(T) \subseteq T$. An *internal node* is a node of $T \setminus \mathrm{Leaf}(T)$. Until Section 7, all trees in this paper will be *binary*, i.e., every internal node has exactly two children, which we refer to as *left* and *right* child.

When evaluating a query with *variables* $\mathcal{X}$ on a Λ-tree T, we will see its possible results as *valuations*: an $\mathcal{X}$-*valuation* of T is a function $\nu : \mathrm{Leaf}(T) \to 2^{\mathcal{X}}$ that assigns to every leaf n of T a set of variables $\nu(n) \subseteq \mathcal{X}$ called the *annotation* of n. Note that our variables are second-order, i.e., each variable can be interpreted as a set of nodes of T. We represent valuations concisely as *assignments*: an $\mathcal{X}$-*assignment* is a set S of *singletons* which are pairs of the form $\langle Z : n\rangle$, where $Z \in \mathcal{X}$ and $n \in \mathrm{Leaf}(T)$. The *size* $|S|$ of S is simply the number of singletons that it contains. There is a clear bijection between $\mathcal{X}$-valuations and $\mathcal{X}$-assignments, so we write $\alpha(\nu)$ for an $\mathcal{X}$-valuation ν to mean the assignment $\{\langle Z : n\rangle \mid Z \in \nu(n)\}$, and write $|\nu| := |\alpha(\nu)|$. We often write $\langle \mathcal{Y} : n\rangle$ for some $n \in T$ and some *non-empty* set $\mathcal{Y} \subseteq \mathcal{X}$, to mean the non-empty set of singletons $\{\langle Z : n\rangle \mid Z \in \mathcal{Y}\}$.

Tree Variable Automata. We will write our query on trees using *tree automata* that can express, e.g., queries in *monadic second-order logic* (MSO): see [37] and [3, Appendix E.1]. Formally, a *tree variable automaton* TVA on binary Λ-trees for variable set $\mathcal{X}$ (or $\Lambda, \mathcal{X}$-TVA) is a tuple $A = (Q, \iota, \delta, F)$, where Q is a finite set of *states*, $\iota \subseteq \Lambda \times 2^{\mathcal{X}} \times Q$ is the *initial relation*, $\delta \subseteq \Lambda \times Q \times Q \times Q$ is the *transition relation*, and $F \subseteq Q$ is the set of *final states*. The *size* $|A|$ of A is $|Q|+|\iota|+|\delta|$. This definition only applies to *binary* Λ-trees; the analogous automata for unranked trees will be introduced in Section 7.

To simplify notation we often see δ as a tuple of functions, i.e., for each $l \in \Lambda$ we have a function $\delta_l : Q \times Q \to 2^Q$ defined by $\delta_l(q_1, q_2) = \{q \in Q \mid (l, q_1, q_2, q) \in \delta\}$: this intuitively tells us to which states the automaton can transition on an internal node with label l when the states of the two children are respectively q_1 and q_2. Note that, following our definition of a valuation and of ι, the automaton is only reading annotations on leaf nodes.

Having fixed Λ and $\mathcal{X}$, given a Λ-tree T and an $\mathcal{X}$-valuation ν of T, given a $\Lambda, \mathcal{X}$-TVA $A = (Q, \iota, \delta, F)$, a *run* of A on T under ν is a function $\rho : T \to Q$ satisfying the following:

- For every $n \in \text{Leaf}(T)$, we have $(\lambda(n), \nu(n), \rho(n)) \in \iota$;
- For every internal node n with label l and children n_1, n_2, we have $\rho(n) \in \delta_l(\rho(n_1), \rho(n_2))$.

The run is *accepting* if it maps the root of T to a state in F, and we say that A *accepts* T under ν if there is an accepting run of A on T under ν. The *satisfying valuations* of A on T is the set of the $\mathcal{X}$-valuations ν of T such that A accepts T under ν, and the *satisfying assignments* are the corresponding assignments $\alpha(\nu)$. Thus, the automaton A defines a query on Λ-trees with second-order variables $\mathcal{X}$, and its results on a Λ-tree T are the satisfying assignments of A on T.

Homogenization. It will be useful to assume a *homogenization* property on automata. Given a $\Lambda, \mathcal{X}$-TVA $A = (Q, \iota, \delta, F)$, we call $q \in Q$ a *0-state* if there is some Λ-tree T and run ρ of A on T that maps the root of T to q under the *empty $\mathcal{X}$-valuation* $\nu_\emptyset$ of T defined as $\nu_\emptyset(n) := \emptyset$ for each $n \in \text{Leaf}(T)$. We call q a *1-state* if there is some Λ-tree T and run ρ of A on T mapping the root of T to q under some *non-empty $\mathcal{X}$*-valuation, i.e., a valuation ν different from the empty valuation. Intuitively, a 0-state is a state that A can reach by reading a tree annotated by the empty valuation, and a 1-state can be reached by reading a tree with at least one non-empty annotation. In general a state can be both a 0-state and a 1-state, or it can be neither if there is no way to reach it. We say that A is *homogenized* if every state is either a 0-state or a 1-state and no state is both a 0-state and a 1-state. We can easily make automata homogenized, by duplicating the states to remember if we have already seen a non-empty annotation:

LEMMA 2.1. *Given a $\Lambda, \mathcal{X}$-TVA A, we can compute in linear time a $\Lambda, \mathcal{X}$-TVA A' which is homogenized and equivalent to A.*

Problem statement. Our goal in this paper is to efficiently enumerate the results of queries on trees. The inputs to the problem are the Λ-tree T and the query given as a $\Lambda, \mathcal{X}$-TVA A, with Λ the tree alphabet and $\mathcal{X}$ the variables. The output is the set of the satisfying assignments of A and T. We present an *enumeration algorithm* to produce them, which first runs a *preprocessing phase* on A and T: we compute a concise representation of the output as an *assignment circuit* (Section 3), and compute an *index structure* on it (Section 6). Second, the *enumeration phase* produces each result to the query, with no duplicates, while bounding the maximal *delay* between two successive answers (Sections 4–6). Third, our algorithm must handle *updates* to T, i.e., given an edit operation on T, efficiently update the assignment circuit and index and restart the enumeration on the updated tree (Section 7).

Our main result shows how to solve this problem with preprocessing linear in T and polynomial in A; with delay independent from T, polynomial in A, and linear in each produced assignment; and with update time logarithmic in T and polynomial in A. This result is formally stated in Section 8.

3 BUILDING ASSIGNMENT CIRCUITS

In this section, we start describing the preprocessing phase of our enumeration algorithm. Given the input TVA and binary tree, we will build an *assignment circuit* that concisely represents the set of satisfying assignments: we do this by adapting the circuit constructions in our earlier work [2, 4] to give them better support for updates and handle non-deterministic automata.

We first define the circuit formalism that we will use, namely *set circuits*, and their semantics. Second, we define when a set circuit can serve as an *assignment circuit* for a TVA on a binary tree. Third, we present properties that our circuits will satisfy, namely, they are *complete structured DNNFs*, and we can bound a *width* parameter for them. Last, we state our main circuit construction result at the end of the section (Lemma 3.7): it shows that, given a homogenized TVA A and binary tree T, we can construct an assignment circuit of A on T in time $O(|A| \times |T|)$ while respecting our properties and controlling the width parameter.

The circuit produced by Lemma 3.7 will then be fed to the enumeration algorithms presented in Sections 4–6. To extend enumeration to updates in Section 7, we will leverage the fact that all our constructions work by processing T bottom-up.

Set Circuits. A *set circuit* (or just *circuit*) $C = (G, W, \mu)$ consists of a directed acyclic graph (G, W) where G are the *gates* and $W \subseteq G \times G$ are the *wires*, and of a function μ mapping each gate to a type among $\top$, $\bot$, var, $\times$, $\cup$: we will accordingly call g a $\top$-gate, $\bot$-gate, var-gate, $\times$-gate, or $\cup$-gate depending on $\mu(g)$. There is also an injective function S_{var} mapping each var-gate g to some set $\mathsf{S}_{\text{var}}(g)$ of *variables*. We write C_{var} to refer to the variables occurring in C, i.e., $C_{\text{var}} := \bigcup_{g \in G \mid \mu(g) = \text{var}} \mathsf{S}_{\text{var}}(g)$. The set of *inputs* of a gate $g \in G$ is $\{g' \in G \mid (g', g) \in W\}$. We require that:

- $\top$-, $\bot$-, and var-gates have no inputs;
- $\times$-gates have exactly 2 inputs;
- $\cup$-gates have at least 1 input;
- $\top$-gates and $\bot$-gates are never used as inputs.

The *maximal fan-in* of C is the maximum number of inputs of a gate and its *depth* is the maximum length of a directed path of wires.

The goal of set circuits is to concisely represent sets. Formally, each gate *captures* a *set*, in the following sense:

Definition 3.1. Given a set circuit $C = (G, W, \mu)$, we define for each gate $g \in G$ a *captured set* $\mathsf{S}(g)$ which is a set of subsets of C_{var} defined inductively as follows:

- If g is a var-gate then $\mathsf{S}(g) := \mathsf{S}_{\text{var}}(g)$.
- If g is a $\bot$-gate then $\mathsf{S}(g) := \emptyset$.
- If g is a $\top$-gate then $\mathsf{S}(g) := \{\emptyset\}$.
- If g is a $\times$-gate with inputs g_1 and g_2 then $S(g) := \{S_1 \cup S_2 \mid S_1 \in \mathsf{S}(g_1), S_2 \in \mathsf{S}(g_2)\}$.

- If g is a $\cup$-gate then, letting $g_1, \ldots, g_m$ be the inputs of g, we define $S(g) := \bigcup_{1 \leq i \leq m} S(g_i)$.

Example 3.2. Consider the circuit C featuring a $\times$-gate g with one input g'_1 being a var-gate with $S_{var}(g'_1) = \{x\}$, and one input g_2 being a $\cup$-gate with two input var-gates g'_2 and g''_2 with $S_{var}(g'_2) = \{y\}$ and $S_{var}(g''_2) = \{y, z\}$. We have $C_{var} = \{x, y, z\}$ and $S(g) = \{\{x, y\}, \{x, y, z\}\}$.

Assignment Circuits. An *assignment circuit* for a TVA on a tree is a set circuit where, for each automaton state q and tree node n, there is a gate $\gamma(q, n)$ capturing the assignments for which we reach state q on node n. Formally:

Definition 3.3. Given a binary Λ-tree T and a $\Lambda, \mathcal{X}$-TVA $A = (Q, \iota, \delta, F)$, an *assignment circuit* of T on A consists of a circuit C where C_{var} is the set of singletons $\{\langle Z : n \rangle \mid Z \in \mathcal{X}, n \in \text{Leaf}(T)\}$, and a mapping $\gamma : T \times Q \to C$ such that for any $n \in T$ and $q \in Q$, the gate $\gamma(n, q)$ is a $\cup$-gate, $\top$-gate, or $\bot$-gate, and for any $\mathcal{X}$-valuation ν of the subtree T_n of T rooted at n, we have $\alpha(\nu) \in S(\gamma(n, q))$ iff there is a run of A on T_n under ν that maps the root node n to state q.

Note that an assignment circuit concisely represents the satisfying assignments of A on T: they are $\bigcup_{q \in F} S(\gamma(n, q))$ where n is the root of T. Thus, our goal is to use assignment circuits to efficiently enumerate satisfying assignments. To be able to do this, we will impose certain properties on assignment circuits, which we now define.

Complete Structured DNNFs. The circuits that we build will be *complete structured DNNFs*, and we will control their *width*. The notion of structured DNNF is inspired by knowledge compilation [34], with DNNF meaning *decomposable negation normal form*, and completeness is also inspired by that field [17]; we adapt it here to set circuits rather than Boolean circuits (as we also did in [2, 4]), with no negations, and with *decomposability* intuitively implying that no variable can occur in assignments in both the left and the right input gate of some $\times$-gate. Formally:

Definition 3.4. A *v-tree* $\mathcal{T}$ for a set circuit C is a binary tree whose leaves are labeled by sets of variables that form a partition of C_{var}. A *structuring function* σ from C to T maps each gate g of C to a node $\sigma(g)$ of $\mathcal{T}$ such that:

- For every var-gate g, the node $\sigma(g)$ is a leaf of $\mathcal{T}$, and the variables that label g in C are a subset of the variables of $\sigma(g)$ in $\mathcal{T}$; formally, letting $\mathcal{Y}$ be the set of variables that labels $\sigma(g)$ in $\mathcal{T}$, we have $S_{var}(g) \subseteq \mathcal{Y}$.
- Whenever a gate g' is an input gate to a gate g, then either g and g' are mapped to the same v-tree node, or the input g' must be a $\cup$-gate that is mapped to the child of the node of g. Formally, for every wire $(g', g) \in W$ of C, either $\sigma(g) = \sigma(g')$, or g' is a $\cup$-gate and $\sigma(g')$ is a child of $\sigma(g)$ in $\mathcal{T}$.
- Each $\times$-gate g has one input gate g_1 such that $\sigma(g_1)$ is the left child of $\sigma(g)$ and one input gate g_2 such that $\sigma(g_2)$ is the right child of $\sigma(g)$; we call g_1 and g_2 the *left* and *right* inputs. Note that, by the previous point, g_1 and g_2 must be $\cup$-gates.

Note that these points ensure that C is *decomposable*, namely, for any $\times$-gate g with inputs g_1 and g_2, no variable gate in C has a path both to g_1 and to g_2. In particular, when defining $S(g)$ according to Definition 3.1, there can never be any duplicate in the union that defines the relational product.

A *complete DNNF structured by* $\mathcal{T}$ is a set circuit C together with a v-tree $\mathcal{T}$ and a structuring function σ from C to $\mathcal{T}$.

Example 3.5. The circuit C in Example 3.2 is not a complete structured DNNF. However, consider C' built from C where the first input of the $\times$-gate g is now a $\cup$-gate g_1 having the var-gate g'_1 as its only input. Then C' is a complete structured DNNF for the v-tree $\mathcal{T}'$ whose root has a left child n_1 labeled $\{x\}$ and a right child n_2 labeled $\{y, z\}$; the structuring function σ maps g to the root of $\mathcal{T}$, maps g_1 and g'_1 to n_1, and g_2, g'_2, and g''_2 to n_2.

When we have a complete structured DNNF C with a structuring function σ to a v-tree $\mathcal{T}$, we see the gates of C as partitioned into *boxes*, with each box being the preimage of some node of $\mathcal{T}$ by σ. We use $\textsc{box}(g)$ to denote the box of some gate g (formally, $\textsc{box}(g) := \sigma^{-1}(\sigma(g))$), We talk about the *tree of boxes* to mean the structure on boxes that follows $\mathcal{T}$. In particular, given a box B, letting n be the node of $\mathcal{T}$ such that $B = \sigma^{-1}(n)$, if n is an internal node then we call B a *non-leaf box* and denote by $\textsc{left}(B)$ and $\textsc{right}(B)$ its *left child box* and *right child box* in the tree of boxes, i.e., $\sigma^{-1}(n_1)$ and $\sigma^{-1}(n_2)$ respectively, where n_1 and n_2 are the children of n in $\mathcal{T}$. We will use boxes to define a structural parameter of complete structured DNNFs, called *width*, and similar to width in [17].

Definition 3.6. The *width* of a structured complete DNNF is the maximal number of $\cup$-gates in a box, i.e.,

$$\max_B |\{g \in B \mid \mu(g) = \cup\}| \ .$$

While this notion of width only bounds the number of $\cup$-gates in each box, we can always rewrite a structured complete DNNF of width w in linear time to ensure that the number of $\times$-gates in each box is also bounded by w^2 [17, Observation 3]. Intuitively, each $\times$-gate in a box B has two $\cup$-gates as input, one in $\textsc{left}(B)$ and one in $\textsc{right}(B)$, so there are at most w^2 non-equivalent combinations. Hence, we will assume that this bound holds on all circuits that we manipulate (and in fact our circuit construction obeys it directly, with no rewriting needed).

Building Assignment Circuits. We have defined the assignment circuits that we want to compute, defined the notion of a structured complete DNNF and a width parameter for them. We can now state our main result for this section, namely, that we can efficiently construct assignment circuits. Observe that, while the depth of the circuit depends on the input tree, the width only depends on $|Q|$, which will be crucial for our delay bounds.

Lemma 3.7. *Given any binary Λ-tree T and homogenized $\Lambda, \mathcal{X}$-TVA $A = (Q, \iota, \delta, F)$, we can construct in time $O(|T| \times |A|)$ a structured complete DNNF C which is an assignment circuit of A and T, a v-tree $\mathcal{T}$, and a structuring function from C to $\mathcal{T}$, such that C has width $|Q|$ and depth $O(\text{height}(T))$.*

Proof sketch. We construct $\mathcal{T}$ by taking T, removing all node labels, and labeling each leaf node n by the set of singletons $\langle \mathcal{X} : n \rangle$: thus, $\mathcal{T}$ is a v-tree for the set of variables $C_{\text{var}} = \{\langle Z : n \rangle \mid Z \in \mathcal{X}, n \in T\}$ of C given by the definition of assignment circuits.

We now build C bottom up. For a leaf node n of T with label $l \in \Lambda$, we build the box B_n for n by setting $\gamma(n, q)$ for all $q \in Q$ as:

- a $\bot$-gate, if there are no tuples of the form $(l, \mathcal{Y}, q) \in \iota$,
- a $\top$-gate, if $(l, \emptyset, q) \in \iota$, and
- a $\cup$-gate having as inputs one variable gate labeled by $\langle \mathcal{Y} : n \rangle$ for each non-empty $\mathcal{Y} \subseteq \mathcal{X}$ such that $(l, \mathcal{Y}, q) \in \iota$, otherwise.

As A is homogenized, the first and last case are disjoint, i.e., we cannot have both $(l, \emptyset, q) \in \iota$ and $(l, \mathcal{Y}, q) \in \iota$ with $\mathcal{Y} \neq \emptyset$.

For an inner node n of T with label l and child nodes n_1 and n_2, we construct the box B_n as follows. For every triple $(q_1, q_2, q) \in \delta_l$, we define a $\times$-gate g^{q_1, q_2} with inputs $\gamma(n_1, q_1)$ and $\gamma(n_2, q_2)$. If there is no such triple, we let $\gamma(n, q)$ be a $\bot$-gate. Otherwise, we let $\gamma(n, q)$ be a $\cup$-gate that has all such $\times$-gates g^{q_1, q_2} as input.

In terms of accounting, it is clear that there are at most $|Q|$ $\cup$-gates in each B_n, that the depth of the circuit is as stated, and the construction of the whole circuit is in time $O(|A| \times |T|)$ as promised. Now, a straightforward bottom-up induction on T shows that the gates $\gamma(n, q)$ capture the correct set for any n, i.e., that for any leaf node n and any $q \in Q$ we have: $\mathrm{S}(\gamma(n, q)) = \{\langle \mathcal{Y} : n \rangle \mid (\lambda(n), \mathcal{Y}, q) \in \iota\}$ and for any internal node n with label l and children n_1 and n_2 and any $q \in Q$ we clearly have:

$$\mathrm{S}(\gamma(n, q)) = \bigcup_{(q_1, q_2, q) \in \delta_l} \mathrm{S}(\gamma(n_1, q_1)) \times \mathrm{S}(\gamma(n_2, q_2))$$

It is easy to check that all rules of assignment circuits are respected with the exception of the rule that $\top$- and $\bot$-gates are never allowed as inputs to other gates. In particular, all $\cup$-gates and $\times$-gates have the right fan-in. To ensure that $\top$- and $\bot$-gates are never used as inputs, one can use a slightly modified construction (see appendix) that avoids adding outgoing wires to $\top$- and $\bot$-gates by treating these cases in a special way. This uses the fact that, as A is homogenized, there is no gate $\gamma(n, q)$ that captures both the empty assignment and some non-empty assignment. □

Algorithm 1 Simple enumeration algorithm

```
1: procedure ENUM_S^DUPES(g)
2:   for g' ∈ ENUM_↓^DUPES(g) do
3:     if g' is a var-gate then output {S_var(g')}
4:     else                                  ▷ g' is a ×-gate
5:       for S_L ∈ ENUM_S^DUPES(left input of g') do
6:         for S_R ∈ ENUM_S^DUPES(right input of g') do
7:           output S_L ∪ S_R
```

4 SIMPLE ENUMERATION ALGORITHM

In the three following sections, we will present how to enumerate the set of assignments captured by gates of assignment circuits. We start in this section by presenting an algorithm which is simple but has two important drawbacks. First, the worst-case delay is $O(\text{depth}(C))$, i.e., linear in the depth of the circuit C. Second, assignments are output multiple times. We will refine this algorithm in Section 5 to ensure that every assignment is enumerated exactly once. Last in Section 6, we show how to bound the delay by the width of the circuit (instead of the depth).

To define our enumeration algorithms in this and the following sections, we introduce some useful notation. For any $\cup$-gate g of C, for any gate g' of C, we write $g' \overset{\cup}{\leadsto} g$ if there is a path $g' = g_1, \ldots, g_n = g$ from g' to g in C where each (g_i, g_{i+1}) is a wire in W and where all intermediate gates $g_2, \ldots, g_n$ are $\cup$-gates. We then write $\Downarrow(g)$ to mean the set of var-gates and $\times$-gates g' such that $g' \overset{\cup}{\leadsto} g$. The following observation shows why $\Downarrow(g)$ is useful for enumeration: it is proven by an immediate induction on $\cup$-gates:

Observation 4.1. *For any $\cup$-gate $g \in C$, we have that $\mathrm{S}(g) = \bigcup_{g' \in \Downarrow(g)} \mathrm{S}(g')$.*

We observe that we can enumerate $\Downarrow(g)$ for every gate g by doing a simple preorder traversal of the circuit: however, doing this naively only ensures a delay of $O(\text{depth}(C))$, and it enumerates each gate g' as many times as there are paths that witness $g' \overset{\cup}{\leadsto} g$ in C. We denote by $\text{ENUM}_{\downarrow}^{\text{DUPES}}(g)$ this naive procedure.

Using this procedure, we present our enumeration algorithm for $\mathrm{S}(g)$ as Algorithm 1. The algorithm applies to any decomposable set circuit and does not use the v-tree or the structuring function.

Algorithm 1 is presented using "output" statements to produce new results (like, e.g., Python's "yield"). When we recursively use the enumeration algorithm on a subcircuit (as in lines 5 and 6), we assume that this enumeration is started in another thread, which will run until the first output is produced. Afterwards the new thread pauses until the calling thread requests the next value. Whenever the calling thread requests a new value, the called thread runs until it produces the next output. The following result is now not hard to see.

Proposition 4.2. *Given a structured complete DNNF C and $\cup$-gate g, Algorithm 1 enumerates* $\mathrm{S}(g)$ *(with duplicates) with delay* $O(\mathrm{depth}(C) \times |S|)$, *where S is the produced assignment.*

Proof. It is clear that Algorithm 1 is correct, because it directly follows Observation 4.1, and the inputs to $\times$-gates are always $\cup$-gates so we always call the algorithm on a $\cup$-gate. In terms of delay, each assignment of size k produced by the algorithm required at most $2k-1$ recursive calls, each of which correspond to a var-gate or $\times$-gate used when producing the assignment: note that this uses the decomposability of C, and uses the fact that $\top$-gates are never used as inputs to another gate. Now, each recursive call has delay $O(\mathrm{depth}(C))$ for the call to $\textsc{enum}_{\Downarrow,\textsc{dupes}}(g)$, hence the delay of the algorithm is as claimed, which completes the proof. □

As a side remark, note that the number of times that Algorithm 1 enumerates each assignment is related to the number of runs of the TVA for this assignment. Specifically, up to redefining Definition 3.1 with multisets, and up to small changes in Lemma 3.7, we could ensure that each assignment in $\mathrm{S}(\gamma(n,q))$ is enumerated exactly as many times as there are runs on the subtree rooted at n under the corresponding valuation such that the root node is mapped to q.

5 ELIMINATING DUPLICATES

In this section, we adapt Algorithm 1 to enumerate satisfying assignments without duplicates. A simple idea would be to change Algorithm 1 to enumerate the gates of $\Downarrow(g)$ without duplicates. Sadly, this would not suffice: imagine that we enumerate $\mathrm{S}(g)$ for some $\cup$-gate g having two inputs g_1 and g_2 for which $\mathrm{S}(g_1) \cap \mathrm{S}(g_2) \neq \emptyset$, then if we consider g_1 and g_2 separately we will enumerate their common assignments twice. However, the crucial point is that $\mathrm{S}(g_1) \cap \mathrm{S}(g_2) \neq \emptyset$ implies that g_1 and g_2 are in the same box, thanks to the following property of structured complete DNNFs:

Lemma 5.1. *For any structured complete DNNF C, for any* var*-gate or $\times$-gate g of C and assignment S, if we have $S \in \mathrm{S}(g)$, then the box of g is the (unique) least common ancestor of the boxes that contain the* var*-gates whose variables occur in S.*

Proof sketch. This is because $\top$-gates are not allowed as input to any gate and $\times$-gates always use inputs from both subtrees. □

This observation leads to the idea of *boxwise enumeration*, i.e., simultaneously considering a set of gates that are all in the same box, and enumerate *simultaneously* the assignments that they capture, without duplicates. This idea is reminiscent of evaluating a nondeterministic automaton on a word by determinizing the automaton on-the-fly, and it was already used in [4] in the case of words; we will extend it to trees. We will accordingly call *boxed set* a set Γ of gates that are all $\cup$-gates and that all belong in the same box. We write $B_\cup$ for a box B to mean the $\cup$-gates of B.

Given a boxed set Γ in some box B, let us denote by $\mathrm{S}(\Gamma)$ the set of assignments $\bigcup_{g\in\Gamma}\mathrm{S}(g)$, which we want to enumerate without duplicates, and let us write $\Downarrow(\Gamma) := \bigcup_{g\in\Gamma}\Downarrow(g)$. Our enumeration will rely on a procedure $\textsc{box-enum}(\Gamma)$ that enumerates the boxes B' such that $\Downarrow(\Gamma)\cap B' \neq \emptyset$ and produces for each such box B' the *$\cup$-reachability relation* between B' and Γ, i.e., the binary relation $R(B',\Gamma)$ describing which gates of $B'_\cup$ have a path of $\cup$-gates to Γ. Formally, we define the $\cup$-reachability relation between any sets of gates G' and G as $R(G',G) := \{(g',g) \in G'_\cup \times G_\cup \mid g' \overset{\cup}{\rightsquigarrow} g\}$. Pay attention to the fact that each call to $\textsc{box-enum}$ returns the complete relation $R(B',B)$ for one of the boxes B' (i.e., we do not enumerate the pairs of $R(B',B)$), and the relation for each box B' is returned only once (i.e., there should not be duplicate boxes).

It is straightforward to show that $\textsc{box-enum}(\Gamma)$ can be naively implemented with delay $O(\mathrm{depth}(C)\times\mathrm{poly}(w))$, where w is the width of the circuit, by exploring the boxes from B (traversing only $\cup$-gates and at most one other gate per level) and maintaining the information $R(B',\Gamma)$ for the boxes B' that we visit. In the next section, we show how we can implement $\textsc{box-enum}$ more efficiently.

The point of $\textsc{box-enum}$ is the following easy consequence of Observation 4.1:

Observation 5.2. *For any boxed set Γ in any box, we have:*

$$\mathrm{S}(\Gamma) \;=\; \biguplus_{R(B',\Gamma)\in\textsc{box-enum}(\Gamma)} \;\; \bigcup_{\substack{g'\in W\circ R(B',\Gamma)\\ \text{with } \mu(g')\in\{\mathrm{var},\times\}}} \mathrm{S}(g')$$

where W is the set of wires of C, where $W \circ R(B',\Gamma)$ denotes the composition of the two binary relations, and where the outermost union is without duplicates.

Proof. To see why the equality holds, first observe that for each $R(B',\Gamma)$, the inner union goes over all gates of $\Downarrow(\Gamma)\cap B'$. Indeed, the definition of the $\cup$-reachability relation ensures that $R(B',\Gamma)$ denotes the $\cup$-gates g' of B' such that $g' \overset{\cup}{\rightsquigarrow} g$ for some $g \in \Gamma$, so the inner union goes over all their inputs that are $\times$-gates and var-gates (and which must also be in box B'). Now, by definition of $\textsc{box-enum}$, the outermost union goes over all gates of $\Downarrow(\Gamma)$. Thus, we can conclude thanks to Observation 4.1. The fact that the outermost union is disjoint follows immediately from Lemma 5.1. □

Observation 5.2 suggests that we can perform enumeration without duplicates recursively by re-applying the scheme on the inputs of the gates of $\Downarrow(\Gamma)\cap B'$ to perform enumeration without duplicates. The details are subtle, however, and this

Algorithm 2 Enumeration algorithm without duplicates

1: **procedure** ENUMS(Γ)
2: $B \leftarrow$ BOX(Γ)
3: **for** $R(B', \Gamma) \in$ BOX-ENUM(Γ) **do**
4: $G' \leftarrow \pi_1(W \circ R(B', \Gamma))$ ▷ project to first component
5: $G_{\text{var}} \leftarrow \{h \in G' \mid \mu(h) = \text{var}\}$
6: **for** $g'' \in G_{\text{var}}$ **do**
7: **output** $(\mathrm{S}_{\text{var}}(g''), \{g''\} \circ W \circ R(B', \Gamma))$
8: $G_{\times} \leftarrow \{h \in G' \mid \mu(h) = \times\}$
9: $\Gamma_L \leftarrow$ set of left inputs of $G_{\times}$
10: **for** $(S_L, \Gamma_L') \in$ ENUMS(Γ_L) **do**
11: $G_{\times}' \leftarrow$ set of gates of $G_{\times}$ with left input in Γ_L'
12: $\Gamma_R \leftarrow$ set of right inputs of $G_{\times}'$
13: **for** $(S_R, \Gamma_R') \in$ ENUMS(Γ_R) **do**
14: $G_{\times}'' \leftarrow$ set of gates of $G_{\times}'$ with right input in Γ_R'
15: $\Gamma' \leftarrow G_{\times}'' \circ W \circ R(B', \Gamma)$
16: **output** $(S_L \cup S_R, \Gamma')$

is why we designed BOX-ENUM to return more than just the set $\pi_1(R(B', \Gamma))$ of the $\cup$-gates of B' having a path of $\cup$-gates to Γ (with π_1 denoting projection to the first component): we will really need the complete relation $R(B', \Gamma)$ for the recursive calls, in order to avoid duplicate assignments across multiple $\times$-gates in $\Downarrow(\Gamma) \cap B'$.

Our algorithm to enumerate $\mathrm{S}(\Gamma)$ is presented as Algorithm 2. The semantics are changed a bit relative to Algorithm 1. Algorithm 2 takes as input a boxed set Γ, and the output is the enumeration of $\mathrm{S}(\Gamma)$ without duplicates. Moreover, for each assignment S in this set, the algorithm also returns its *provenance relative to* Γ, i.e., the subset $\mathrm{Prov}(S, \Gamma) := \{g \in \Gamma \mid S \in \mathrm{S}(g)\}$, which again is used for the recursive calls.

THEOREM 5.3. *Given a structured complete DNNF C and given a boxed set Γ, we can enumerate $\mathrm{S}(\Gamma)$ (without duplicates) with delay $O(|S| \times (\Delta + w^3))$, where S is the produced assignment, Δ is the delay of* BOX-ENUM, *and w is the width of C. Further, we correctly produce for each assignment S its provenance* $\mathrm{Prov}(S, \Gamma)$ *relative to* Γ.

PROOF SKETCH. We have to show three things to establish correctness: (1) For every output (S, Γ') of the algorithm, we have $\Gamma' \subseteq \Gamma$ and $S \in \mathrm{S}(g)$ for every $g \in \Gamma'$. (2) For every assignment $S \in \mathrm{S}(g)$ with $g \in \Gamma$, we have some output (S, Γ') with $g \in \Gamma'$. (3) No assignment S is outputted twice.

Statements (1) and (2) can be shown by induction on the number of variable gates that contribute to the assignment. For the induction base case one can verify that assignments that only use one variable gate are correctly handled in Line 7. For the induction step, one can verify that the topmost $\times$-gate $g_{\times}$ that is involved in computing an assignment is handled correctly in the lines 8 to 16.

Statement (3) follows from Lemma 5.1 and the fact that for each box BOX-ENUM(Γ) returns at most one relation.

The proof for the runtime delay is similar to Proposition 4.2, with the difference that the local computations are more expensive as we need to compute relational compositions, e.g., $W \circ R(B', \Gamma)$. □

6 ENUMERATING BOXES EFFICIENTLY

We have shown in the previous section how to enumerate the assignments captured by an assignment circuit without duplicates. However the delay depends on the delay of BOX-ENUM, which for the naive implementation we discussed before was linear in the depth of the circuit. This leads to a delay for the assignment enumeration that is also linear in the depth of the circuit. In this section, we show how to speed up BOX-ENUM and make its delay independent from the depth of the circuit, using a similar idea to *jump pointers* from [5]. As the delay added by Algorithm 2 only depends on the circuit width, this will establish our overall delay bound, which we state at the end of the section.

Interesting and Bidirectional Boxes. To speed up BOX-ENUM, we will need to perform some linear-time preprocessing on the input circuit, following the tree of boxes. Let us first give the required definitions. For each boxed set Γ, the set of *interesting boxes* for Γ is defined as $\{B' \mid B' \cap \Downarrow(\Gamma) \neq \emptyset\}$: these are the boxes that BOX-ENUM(Γ) must consider. We also define the set of *bidirectional boxes* for Γ as

$$\{B' \mid \Downarrow(\Gamma) \text{ intersects boxes in both subtrees of } B'\}$$

These boxes are necessarily non-leaf boxes and have interesting boxes as descendants of their left and right child. Note that a bidirectional box may also be interesting.

One key idea to optimize BOX-ENUM is to "jump" from a box B to a bidirectional descendant box B', skipping boxes on the path from B to B' that are neither interesting nor bidirectional. To do so, we need to precompute to which box we can jump from the boxed set Γ; specifically, we need to know the *first interesting box* and the *first bidirectional box*. We thus define FIB(g) (resp., FBB(g)) for a gate g as the first interesting box (resp., bidirectional box) seen in the *preorder traversal* of T where we first visit the box of g, then recursively traverse its left subtree, and last traverse its right subtree. We then extend these definitions to Γ by:

$$\mathrm{FIB}(\Gamma) = \min_{g \in \Gamma} \mathrm{FIB}(g) \quad (1)$$

$$\mathrm{FBB}(\Gamma) = \mathrm{LCA}(\{\mathrm{FBB}(g) \mid g \in \Gamma\}) \quad (2)$$

where the min operator is according to the preorder traversal and LCA denotes the least common ancestor of a set of boxes in the tree of boxes.

Intuitively, the first bidirectional box will tell us where to jump, and the first interesting box will compensate the time spent visiting bidirectional boxes in the enumeration (as these boxes do not otherwise allow us to make progress). In addition to FIB and FBB, when jumping from a box B to a descendant box B', we will also need to know the $\cup$-reachability relation $R(B', B)$ from the $\cup$-gates of B' to the $\cup$-gates of B, i.e., a special case of what we have defined in Section 5, where all $\cup$-gates of B appear. Hence, our preprocessing will consider each box B and compute the $\cup$-reachability relation $R(B', B)$ for every box B' to which we may jump from B.

Index Structure. We summarize all information that needs to be computed by formally defining the index structure:

Definition 6.1. The *index structure* $I(C)$ of a structured complete DNNF C consists of the following, for each box B:

- For each $\cup$-gate $g \in B$, the first interesting box $\text{FIB}(g)$ of Γ and the reachability relation $R(\text{FIB}(g), \text{BOX}(g))$
- For each boxed set $\Gamma \subseteq B$ with $1 \leq |\Gamma| \leq 2$, the first bidirectional box $\text{FBB}(\Gamma)$ of Γ, and the reachability relation $R(\text{FBB}(\Gamma), \text{BOX}(\Gamma))$
- Letting $\mathcal{B}$ be the set of boxes of the form $\text{FIB}(g)$ or $\text{FBB}(g)$ for g a $\cup$-gate of B, letting $\mathcal{B}' = \{\text{LCA}(B_1, B_2) \mid B_1, B_2 \in \mathcal{B}\}$ (hence $\mathcal{B}' \supseteq \mathcal{B}$), we precompute $\mathcal{B}'$ and the linear order implied by preorder traversal over $\mathcal{B}'$.

At first glance, the index seems weaker than what we need, because we will want to determine $\text{FIB}(\Gamma)$ and $\text{FBB}(\Gamma)$ for boxed sets Γ of arbitrary size. However, Equation (1) implies that $\text{FIB}(\Gamma)$ can be evaluated from $\text{FIB}(g)$ for individual gates $g \in \Gamma$, using the fact that we have precomputed min. The same is true for FBB and boxed sets Γ of size at most two, thanks to Equation (2) and the following elementary fact about least common ancestors:

OBSERVATION 6.2. *For any set $\mathcal{B}$ of boxes, the least common ancestor of $\mathcal{B}$ is the minimal box B in the preorder traversal that is a least common ancestor of two (possibly equal) boxes B_1 and B_2 of $\mathcal{B}$. Formally: $\text{LCA}(\mathcal{B}) = \min\{\text{LCA}(B_1, B_2) \mid B_i \in \mathcal{B}\}$*

We now show how to compute the index structure:

LEMMA 6.3. *Given a structured complete DNNF circuit C with v-tree $\mathcal{T}$, we can compute $I(C)$ in time $O(|\mathcal{T}| \times w^4)$, where w is the width of C.*

PROOF SKETCH. We compute the first interesting boxes $\text{FIB}(g)$ for all $\cup$-gates g by an easy bottom-up processing of C, and we do the same for all $\text{FBB}(\Gamma)$: here we rely on Observation 6.2 to know that, when we recursively compute $\text{FBB}(\Gamma')$ for a boxed set in a child box, we can do so from the $\text{FBB}(\Gamma'')$ for $\Gamma'' \subseteq \Gamma'$ with $|\Gamma''| \leq 2$.

We compute the reachability relations by considering all boxes B bottom-up and computing $R(B', B)$ for all descendant boxes B' where this is required: we show that we can always do so from the relation $R(B'', B)$ for B'' the child of B in the direction of B', which is easy to compute from the wires, and from the relation $R(B', B'')$ which we argue must have been computed when considering B''. The complexity is $O(w^3)$, which is bounded by the complexity of computing $R(B', B'') \circ R(B'', B)$ with the naïve join algorithm. □

Algorithm 3 Box enumeration

```
 1: procedure BOX-ENUM(Γ)
 2:     B-ENUM(BOX(Γ), {(g, g) | g ∈ Γ})
 3: procedure B-ENUM(B, R)
 4:     B1 ← FIB(π1(R))                      ▷ first interesting box
 5:     R1 ← R(B1, B) ∘ R                    ▷ R(B1, B) is in the index
 6:     output R1                            ▷ relation to B1
 7:     BL ← LEFT(B1); RL ← R(BL, B1) ∘ R1
 8:     if RL ≠ ∅ then B-ENUM(BL, RL)        ▷ left subtree of B1
 9:     BR ← RIGHT(B1); RR ← R(BR, B1) ∘ R1
10:     if RR ≠ ∅ then B-ENUM(BR, RR)        ▷ right subtree of B1
11:     B' ← B; B ← FBB(π1(R))               ▷ jump to the 1st bidir. box
12:     while B is defined and is a strict ancestor of B1 do
13:         R ← R(B, B') ∘ R                 ▷ R(B, B') is in the index
14:         BR ← RIGHT(B); RR ← R(BR, B) ∘ R
15:         B-ENUM(BR, RR)                   ▷ right subtree of B
16:         B' ← LEFT(B); R ← R(B', B) ∘ R   ▷ left child
17:         B ← FBB(π1(R))                   ▷ 1st bidir. box
```

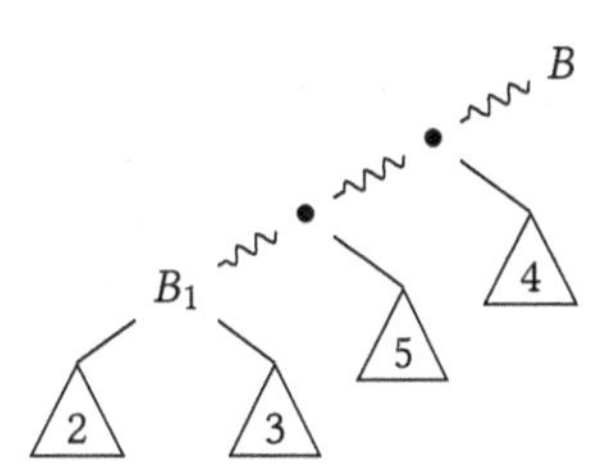

B_1 is the first interesting box and • indicates bidirectional boxes. All interesting boxes of the subtrees indicated by triangles are visited in the indicated order.

Figure 1: Sketch of the box tree of assignment circuits

Efficient Implementation of BOX-ENUM. We can now present the algorithm for efficient enumeration of $\text{BOX-ENUM}(\Gamma)$:

LEMMA 6.4. *Given a structured complete DNNF C and the index structure $I(C)$, we can implement BOX-ENUM with delay $O(w^3)$, where w is the width of C.*

PROOF SKETCH. The algorithm $\text{BOX-ENUM}(\Gamma)$ to perform the enumeration for an arbitrary boxed set Γ is in Algorithm 3. Each call of the recursive algorithm in Line 3 receives the relation $R(B, \Gamma)$ for some box B called the *current box*, and it is expected to output the relations $R(B', \Gamma)$ for interesting boxes B' in the subtree of B.

In Figure 1, we sketched the order in which boxes are enumerated, starting with the first interesting box B_1 (output in Line 6), then all descendants of B_1 (recursive calls in lines 8 and 10), and then right children of bidirectional boxes on the path to B_1 (recursive call in the loop). By the definition of bidirectional boxes, this enumerates all interesting boxes.

It is easy to show that the delay is $O(w^3)$, which stems from the computation of relational composition using naïve joins; the main subtlety is that we need to modify Algorithm 3 slightly to ensure that each last recursive call is tail-recursive, to avoid delays when unwinding the recursion stack. □

Putting it Together. We now state our main result about the complexity of enumerating the set of assignments captured by a boxed set in a complete structured DNNF circuit. Before we do so, however, we point out a small optimization trick that allows us to bring the complexity in the width w of the circuit from $O(w^3)$ down to $O(w^\omega)$, where $2 \leq \omega \leq 3$ is an exponent for Boolean matrix multiplication, i.e., a constant such that the product of two r-by-r Boolean matrices can be computed in time $O(r^\omega)$. The best possible value for ω is an open question, with the best known bound being $\omega < 2.3728639$, see [24]. Observe that, in Theorem 5.3, Lemma 6.3 and Lemma 6.4, the complexity bottleneck is to compute expressions of the form $R \circ R'$ for relations R and R' over sets of size $\leq w$, with all other operations having complexity $O(w^2)$ at most. We have used the naïve join algorithm to bound this by $O(w^3)$, but we can instead represent these relations as Boolean matrices and use any matrix multiplication algorithm to compute the product in $O(w^\omega)$.

This leads to our final enumeration result on set circuits:

Theorem 6.5. *Let ω be an exponent for Boolean matrix multiplication. Given any complete structured DNNF C of width w with its v-tree $\mathcal{T}$ and structuring function, we can preprocess C in $O(|\mathcal{T}| \times w^{\omega+1})$ to be able, given any boxed set Γ, to enumerate the assignments of $\mathrm{S}(\Gamma)$ with delay $O(|S| \times w^\omega)$ for each produced assignment S.*

Proof. We preprocess C using Lemma 6.3, and we then perform the enumeration using Theorem 5.3 with the efficient implementation of box-enum given in Lemma 6.4; modifying the algorithms to perform matrix multiplication in time $O(w^\omega)$ instead of using the naïve join algorithm. □

7 UPDATES AND BALANCING

We have presented our circuit construction result (Lemma 3.7) and enumeration result (Theorem 6.5). We will put them together to show our enumeration results for automata and queries over trees. However, before this we need to explain how we can handle updates efficiently, i.e., how we can recompute the circuit (Lemma 3.7) and the index of the enumeration structure (Lemma 6.3) whenever the underlying tree is modified.

The crucial insight is that the circuit in Lemma 3.7 is computed *bottom-up* on the input tree T, and the precomputation in Lemma 6.3 is also performed bottom-up on the tree of boxes whose structure is isomorphic to T. Hence, whenever T is updated at some node n, we can modify the circuit and the index accordingly by recomputing everything bottom-up starting at node n. The complexity of this process will be linear in the *height* of T. This is why, in this section, we will want to work on trees that are *balanced*, i.e., whose height is logarithmic in their size: this is what will guarantee that updates can be handled in logarithmic time.

As trees are in general not balanced, our technique will be to code the input tree as binary balanced trees. We will also use this as a way to allow arbitrary unranked trees as input (not just binary trees), which is more convenient because binary trees do not behave well under edit operations (e.g., adding or deleting a single leaf). Specifically, given the input unranked Λ-tree T and $\Lambda, \mathcal{X}$-TVA A running on unranked trees, we will encode T to a balanced binary tree T' over a different alphabet Λ', and we will translate the automaton A in polynomial time to a $\Lambda', \mathcal{X}$-TVA A', while ensuring that A and A' have the same satisfying assignments. Our balanced binary tree formalism will further ensure that, whenever an update is performed on T, we can update T' (and keep it balanced) to reflect the change, and we can efficiently update the circuit C and the index for this update.

In this section, we first present our model for the input unranked tree T and the edit operations that we allow on it. We then present our formalism for the automaton A, which runs on unranked trees, and the notion of *tree hollowings* to describe which kinds of updates can happen on the balanced binary tree T': intuitively, whenever we apply an edit operation on T, then we will be able to update T' in logarithmic time with a tree hollowing; and we will show that we can update the circuit and index in the same time bound. Then, we formalize the notion of encoding unranked trees to binary trees and of faithfully translating automata, and we state the result from [30] which explains how this can be efficiently performed. This allows us state our main enumeration results for automata and queries in the next section.

Edit Operations on Unranked Trees. We first present the language of edit operations that we allow on the *unranked* tree which is the input to our enumeration scheme. Fixing a set $\mathcal{X}$ of variables, we will define an $\mathcal{X}$-valuation of an unranked Λ tree T as a function ν mapping each node n of T to a set $\nu(n) \subseteq \mathcal{X}$. Note that a valuation of an unranked tree annotates all its nodes, not just the leaf nodes.

The update operations that we allow on unranked trees are leaf insertions, leaf deletions, and relabelings. More precisely:

Definition 7.1. Given an unranked Λ-tree T, a node n of T and a label $l \in \Lambda$, we allow the following edit operations:

- delete(n): remove n from T (only if n is a leaf)
- insert(n, l): insert an l-node as first child of n

- INSERT$_R(n, l)$: insert an l-node as right sibling of n
- RELABEL(n, l): change the label of n to l

For any edit operation τ, we call $\tau(T)$ the resulting tree.

Automata on Unranked Trees. Following our use of unranked binary trees, we must also extend the definition of TVAs to work on unranked trees. Our automaton model for unranked trees are stepwise tree automata extended with variables. Stepwise tree automata where first introduced in [18]. We use the formalism from [27], as it is closer to our tree model. A $\Lambda, \mathcal{X}$-*TVA on unranked* Λ-*trees* for the variable set $\mathcal{X}$ is a tuple $A = (Q, \iota, \delta, F)$, where Q are the states, $\iota \subseteq \Lambda \times 2^{\mathcal{X}} \times Q$ is the *initial relation*, $\delta \subseteq Q \times Q \times Q$ is the *transition relation*, and $F \subseteq Q$ are the *final states*. Given a Λ-tree T and an $\mathcal{X}$-valuation ν of T, we again define a *run* of A on T as a function $\rho\colon T \to Q$ satisfying some conditions. However, compared to binary trees, the use of ι and δ is different: ι assigns a set of possible initial states to every state (not only to leaves). For inner nodes, δ then consumes the states of children state by state , just as a word automaton reads its input symbol by symbol. The assigned state of a node is the state after having read the states of all children.

To formalize this, let us see δ as a function $\delta\colon 2^Q \times Q \to 2^Q$ by setting $\delta(Q', q') = \cup_{q \in Q'} \{q'' \mid (q, q', q'') \in \delta\}$, and let us inductively define the function $\delta^*\colon 2^Q \times Q^* \to 2^Q$ by $\delta^*(Q', \epsilon) := Q'$ and $\delta^*(Q', q_1 \dots q_n) := \delta^*(\delta(Q', q_1), q_2 \dots q_n)$. A *run* $\rho\colon T \to Q$ of A on T must then satisfy the following: For every node n with children $n_1, \dots, n_m$, we have $\rho(n) \in \delta^*(\iota(\lambda(n), \nu(n)), \rho(n_1)\rho(n_2) \dots \rho(n))$. Note that TVAs on unranked trees now read annotations at all nodes (and not only at leaves), as per the definition of valuations.

The definitions of accepting runs, satisfying valuations and assignments on a $\Lambda, \mathcal{X}$-TVA on unranked trees is the same as for binary trees: note that assignments now consist of singletons of the form $\langle Z : n \rangle$ where n can be any node of T, not just a leaf. Incidentally, observe that any $\Lambda, \mathcal{X}$-TVA on binary trees can clearly be converted to a $\Lambda, \mathcal{X}$-TVA on unranked trees which accepts exactly the same trees.

Tree Hollowings. We now formalize our language of updates on *binary trees*, called tree hollowings. Intuitively, when performing an update on the input unranked tree T, we want to reflect it on its balanced binary representation T'. Our encoding scheme will ensure that the edit operations of Definition 7.1 can be performed as *tree hollowings* whose *trunks* have logarithmic size. Here are the relevant definitions:

Definition 7.2. Let T' be a binary Λ'-tree. Two nodes of T' are *incomparable* if neither is a descendant of the other (in particular, they must be different). An *antichain* in T' is a set of nodes in T' that are pairwise incomparable.

A *tree hollowing* $H = (T'', \eta)$ of T' consists of a $(\Lambda' \cup \{\square\})$-tree T'' called the *trunk*, in which all internal nodes must have a label in Λ', and an injective function η from the leaves of T'' with label $\square$ to T', such that the image of η is a antichain of T'. The *result* H^{res} of the tree hollowing H is the Λ'-tree obtained by taking T'' and replacing each $\square$-labeled leaf n of T'' by the subtree of T' rooted at $\eta(n)$.

Intuitively, a tree hollowing describes how to build a new tree while reusing disjoint subtrees of the original tree. We will require that each update to the original tree T should be translatable in logarithmic time to a tree hollowing of the binary balanced representation T'—so in particular the trunk will have logarithmic size, even though the result of the hollowing will not.

The reason why hollowings are a good update language is because our constructions are strictly bottom up. Thus, given a binary Λ'-tree T' for which we have computed an assignment circuit C for some $\Lambda', \mathcal{X}$-TVA A, and given the index $I(C)$, we can follow a tree hollowing $H = (T'', \eta)$ of T' to update the circuit to an assignment circuit C^{res} of A on H^{res} and to update the index to $I(C^{\text{res}})$. Formally:

Lemma 7.3. *Given any Λ'-tree T' and $\Lambda', \mathcal{X}$-TVA A' with state space Q', given an assignment circuit C of A' on T' which is a structured complete DNNF of width $|Q'|$ and given the index structure $I(C)$, given any tree hollowing $H' = (T'', \eta)$ of T', we can compute in time $O(|T''| \times |Q'|^{\omega+1})$ a circuit C^{res} and the index structure $I(C^{res})$ such that C^{res} is a structured complete DNNF of width $|Q'|$ which is an assignment circuit of A' on T'^{res}, and $I(C^{res})$ is the index structure for C^{res}.*

Proof. We use the circuit construction from Lemma 3.7 to compute a box B_n for each node n in T'' that is not labeled $\square$ (total time $O(|T''| \times |A'|)$) and we thus compute C^{res}, which has size $O(|T''| \times |A'|)$. Afterwards we use the computation from the proof of Lemma 6.3 (using efficient matrix multiplication as explained in the proof of Theorem 6.5) to compute the index structure for the new boxes in total time $O(|T'| \times w^{\omega+1})$. $\square$

Encoding Unranked Trees in Balanced Binary Trees. We will now explain how we can encode an unranked tree T into a balanced binary tree T' on which update operations can be reflected, i.e., every update on T in the language of Definition 7.1 translates to an update of T' that can be represented by a tree hollowing whose trunk has logarithmic size. It will be more convenient to formalize the encoding by describing the *decoding function* which decodes a binary tree to an unranked tree. Specifically, a *tree encoding scheme* for the tree alphabet Λ consists of a tree alphabet Λ' and of a function ω defined on some subset of the binary Λ'-trees (called the *well-formed trees*) and which decodes any such binary Λ'-tree T' to an unranked Λ-tree T and to a bijection $\varphi_{T'}$ from the leaves of T' to the nodes of T. We require ω to be surjective, i.e., every unranked Λ-tree has some preimage in ω. Now, given a set $\mathcal{X}$ of variables, a $\Lambda, \mathcal{X}$-TVA A and a binary $\Lambda, \mathcal{X}'$-TVA A', we say that ω is A, A'-*faithful* if for any Λ-tree T, for any preimage T' of T in ω, letting $\varphi_{T'}$ be the bijection from the leaves of T' to the nodes of T, for any $\mathcal{X}$-valuation ν of T, we have that A accepts T under ν iff A' accepts T' under the valuation $\nu \circ \varphi_{T'}$.

Our tree encoding method can then be formalized as the following result, which easily follows from [30]:

LEMMA 7.4. *For any tree alphabet Λ and set $\mathcal{X}$ of variables, there is an encoding scheme ω for Λ such that:*

- *The encoding is linear-time computable, i.e., given any unranked Λ-tree T, we can compute in linear time some Λ'-tree T' with $\omega(T') = T$, as well as the bijection $\varphi_{T'}$.*
- *The encoded trees have logarithmic height, i.e., each well-formed Λ'-tree T' has height in $O(\log |T'|)$.*
- *We can efficiently perform updates, i.e., given any binary Λ-tree T, preimage T' of T, and update τ on T in the language of Definition 7.1, we can compute in time $O(\log |T|)$ a tree hollowing $H = (T'', \eta)$ of T' such that $\omega(H^{res}) = \tau(\omega(T'))$.*
- *We can efficiently translate automata, i.e., given any unranked $\Lambda, \mathcal{X}$-TVA A with state space Q, we can build in time $O(|Q|^6)$ a binary $\Lambda', \mathcal{X}$-TVA A' with $O(|Q|^4)$ states and $O(|Q|^6)$ transitions such that ω is A, A'-faithful. Furthermore, A' has a single accepting state.*

PROOF SKETCH. The proof idea is to convert unranked trees to binary trees that represent terms in the free forest algebra. Intuitively, a forest algebra term T' is a binary Λ'-tree that describes an unranked Λ-tree: the leaves of T' correspond to the nodes of T, and each internal node corresponds to a forest computed from its children by one of two operations: forest concatenation or context application. In [30, Section 3], it is described how we can convert an unranked tree T in linear time to a balanced term T' that represents T, and how updates on T can be reflected on T'. Although this is not stated explicitly in [30], the resulting updates on T' can be described as tree hollowings of logarithmic size. We can also easily show that an automaton A on unranked Λ-trees can be converted in PTIME to an automaton A' on binary Λ'-trees. □

8 MAIN RESULTS

We can now present our main results by combining our results about tree balancing and hollowing updates (Lemma 7.4 and Lemma 7.3) with our circuit construction and enumeration results (Lemma 3.7 and Theorem 6.5). The first phrasing of our main result deals with the enumeration of the satisfying assignments to TVAs under updates, while ensuring the right complexity bounds, and in particular guaranteeing tractable combined complexity:

THEOREM 8.1. *Let ω be an exponent for Boolean matrix multiplication. Given an unranked $\Lambda, \mathcal{X}$-TVA A with state space Q and an unranked Λ-tree T, we can enumerate the satisfying assignments of A on T with preprocessing time $O(|T| \times |Q|^{4(\omega+1)})$, update time $O(\log(|T|) \times |Q|^{4(\omega+1)})$, and delay $O(|Q|^{4\omega} \times |S|)$, where S is the produced assignment.*

Thanks to Theorem 8.1, we can now obtain as a corollary our main result on enumeration for monadic second-order logic (MSO). Recall that MSO is a logic that extends first-order logic on Λ-trees defined on a signature featuring the edge relation of the tree, the order relation among siblings, and unary predicates for the node labels. MSO extends first-order logic by adding the ability to quantify over sets. Given a Λ-MSO formula $\Phi(X_1, \ldots, X_n)$ and a Λ-tree T where all free variables are second-order, letting $\mathcal{X} = \{X_1, \ldots, X_n\}$, the *satisfying valuations* of Φ on T are the $\mathcal{X}$-valuations ν of T such that T satisfies the Boolean Λ-MSO formula Φ where the predicates $X_1, \ldots, X_n$ are interpreted according to ν. Similarly to what we did for TVAs, we represent any $\mathcal{X}$-valuation ν as an *assignment* $\alpha(\nu) := \{\langle Z : n\rangle \mid Z \in \nu(n)\}$, and the *satisfying assignments* of Φ on T are the images by α of the satisfying valuations.

Our main result for MSO enumeration is then the following; it improves on the earlier results for MSO enumeration on trees under updates [4, 26, 30]. Note that unlike Theorem 8.1, this result only considers *data complexity*, i.e., complexity in the input tree (and in the produced assignments), assuming that the MSO query is fixed.

COROLLARY 8.2. *For any fixed tree alphabet Λ, for any fixed Λ-MSO query Φ with free second-order variables, given an unranked Λ-tree T, after preprocessing T in linear time, we can enumerate the satisfying assignments of Φ with delay linear in each produced assignment, and we can handle updates to T in logarithmic time in T.*

PROOF. Let $\mathcal{X}$ be the variables of Φ. We see Φ as a Boolean query on the tree signature $\Lambda \cup 2^{\mathcal{X}}$, and rewrite Φ to a tree automaton on $\Lambda \cup 2^{\mathcal{X}}$ using the well-known result by Thatcher and Wright [37]: see also [3, Appendix E.1]. The automaton can equivalently be seen as an unranked $\Lambda, \mathcal{X}$-TVA, so we can enumerate its assignments on T using Theorem 8.1. □

In the common case of an MSO formula $\Phi(x_1, \ldots, x_n)$ with free *first-order* variables, Corollary 8.2 implies that we can enumerate the satisfying assignments on a tree T, with the delay being constant, i.e., independent from T.

COROLLARY 8.3. *For any fixed tree alphabet Λ, for any fixed Λ-MSO query Φ with free first-order variables, given an unranked Λ-tree T, after preprocessing T in linear time, we can enumerate the satisfying assignments of Φ with constant delay, and we can handle updates to T in logarithmic time in T.*

Note that enumerating satisfying assignments also allows us to enumerate the *answer tuples* $(a_1, \dots, a_n) \in T^n$ such that T satisfies $\Phi(a_1, \dots, a_n)$, as we can simply translate each satisfying assignment in linear time to an answer tuple.

Results on Words. We conclude the section by presenting consequences of our results for *words*. As words are a special case of trees, our results on trees imply results for the enumeration on words of the satisfying assignments of word automata, with the ability to efficiently handle updates to the underlying word. This can be used in the context of *document spanners* [22] for information extraction, allowing us to efficiently enumerate the matches of a document spanner represented as a sequential extended VA [23], and to update the enumeration structure when the word changes.

Given a set Λ of labels, we call a Λ-*word* a finite sequence w of letters from Λ. Given a variable set $\mathcal{X}$, an $\mathcal{X}$-*valuation* of w is a function $\nu : \{1, \dots, |w|\} \to 2^{\mathcal{X}}$, and the corresponding $\mathcal{X}$-*assignment* $\alpha(\nu)$ is the set $\{\langle Z : n \rangle \mid Z \in \nu(n)\}$. On words we allow the usual local edits: (1) inserting a character, (2) deleting a character, and (3) replacing a character.

We next present the formalism that we use to write queries on words, which is analogous to *extended sequential variable automata* [23]. A *word variable automaton* WVA on Λ-words for variable set $\mathcal{X}$ (or $\Lambda, \mathcal{X}$-WVA) is a tuple $A = (Q, \delta, I, F)$, where Q is a set of *states*, I is the set of initial states, $\delta \subseteq Q \times \Lambda \times 2^{\mathcal{X}} \times Q$ is the *transition relation*, and $F \subseteq Q$ is the set of *final states*. Note that, like an unranked TVA, a WVA can read variables at any position.

When working with WVAs rather than TVAs, the translation to balanced binary trees can be done with a better complexity. Specifically, the following is obvious from the details of the construction of A' in Lemma 7.4.

Corollary 8.4. *Lemma 7.4 holds for words instead of trees and a WVA A instead of an unranked TVA as input, with the difference that the binary tree automaton A' can be constructed in time $O(|Q|^3)$, has $O(|Q|^2)$ states and $O(|Q|^3)$ transitions, where Q is the state space of A.*

We can conclude the following theorem.

Theorem 8.5. *Given a $\Lambda, \mathcal{X}$-WVA A with state space Q and Λ-word w, we can enumerate the satisfying assignments with preprocessing time $O(|w| \times |Q|^{2(\omega+1)})$, update time $O(\log(|w|) \times |Q|^{2(\omega+1)})$, and delay $O(|Q|^{2\omega} \times |\nu|)$, for ν the current valuation.*

In terms of document spanners, this theorem is the analogue of the result of [5] which showed that we can efficiently enumerate the results of an extended sequential nondeterministic VA on an input word, and it extends this result to handle updates to the word in logarithmic time. However, in exchange for the support for updates, the complexity in the automaton is less favorable, with a higher polynomial degree (due to the need to balance the word); and the memory usage of Theorem 8.5 is not constant like it was in [5]. We also note that our results in this paper do *not* recapture the results for *non-extended VAs* from [5]: we believe that our techniques here would extend to such automata, but that it would require some changes to the tree automaton model.

9 LOWER BOUND

In this section, we will show that the logarithmic update time of Section 8 is optimal up to a doubly logarithmic factor. In fact, we will show that either the update time or the enumeration delay of any MSO enumeration algorithm on trees must be $\Omega\left(\frac{\log(n)}{\log\log(n)}\right)$. In particular, in contrast to the settings in [11, 12], there is no algorithm with constant update time for MSO queries on trees even if we allow the enumeration delay to be slightly superconstant.

To show our lower bound, we rely heavily on a result from [1], so let us introduce some notation from there: consider a tree T on n nodes in which some of the nodes are *marked* while the others are *unmarked*. For every node v of T, let $\pi(v)$ denote the path from v to the root of T. The *existential marked ancestor query* is, given a node v, to decide if v has a marked ancestor, i.e., there is a marked node on $\pi(v)$. An *update* in the marked ancestor problem is an operation that marks or unmarks a node of T. An algorithm for the marked ancestor problem is an algorithm that maintains a data structure that allows updates and marked ancestor queries. A main result of [1] is then the following:

Theorem 9.1. *Consider an algorithm that solves the marked ancestor problem and let t_u be a bound on the time to handle an update and t_q be a bound on the time to answer a query. Then we have $t_q = \Omega\left(\frac{\log(n)}{\log(t_u \log(n))}\right)$.*

We remark that Theorem 9.1 is unconditional and holds for the standard model of unit cost RAMs with logarithmic word size; for different word sizes the result is slightly different. We also remark that Theorem 9.1 even stays true if all runtimes are assumed to be amortized, so in a non-worst case setting. Finally, Theorem 9.1 makes no assumption whatsoever about the runtime of a potential preprocessing phase. So even with generous runtime in the preprocessing, the result holds.

We now show that we get a lower bound for MSO query enumeration easily from Theorem 9.1.

Theorem 9.2. *There is an MSO query Φ on trees such that any enumeration algorithm for Φ under relabelings with update time $\hat{t}_u$ and enumeration delay $\hat{t}_e$ has*

$$\max(\hat{t}_u, \hat{t}_e) \;\geq\; \Omega\left(\frac{\log(n)}{\log\log(n)}\right).$$

Proof sketch. We reduce from the existential marked ancestor problem. To this end, we consider trees in which nodes can have three labels: marked, unmarked, or special. Fix the query $\Phi(x)$ that selects all special nodes that have a marked ancestor: we can easily write it in MSO.

We give an algorithm for the marked ancestor problem: We start with the input tree T, i.e., a tree without any node marked special. To answer the marked ancestor query for a node v, we label v as a special node, enumerate the answer to Φ, and make v non-special again. Finally we return 'yes' if and only if we enumerated any answer to Φ.

To see that this algorithm is correct, observe that v is the only special node in T when evaluating Φ. So either we enumerate v or nothing depending on if v has a marked ancestor, and the answer we give is correct. Now, Theorem 9.1 applies to the marked ancestor queries, i.e., to $2\hat{t}_u + \hat{t}_e$, from which we can mathematically derive our claimed bound. □

From Theorem 9.2 we get easily that the update time in Theorem 8.1 is optimal up to a doubly logarithmic factor even if we allow the enumeration delay to be close to logarithmic.

Corollary 9.3. *There is an MSO query Φ on trees such that any enumeration algorithm for Φ under relabelings with enumeration delay $o\left(\frac{\log(n)}{\log\log(n)}\right)$ has update time $\Omega\left(\frac{\log(n)}{\log\log(n)}\right)$.*

As Theorem 9.1 from [1], our Theorem 9.2 also works for amortized time and with arbitrary preprocessing. Note also that the query Φ in the proof does not use the full power of MSO but can in fact be expressed in first-order logic with transitive closure, so our lower bound already holds for that fragment. Note that it is not clear if we can show an analogous result for FO without transitive closure: in particular, we cannot apply the results of [11] about enumeration for FO on bounded-degree structures, because the lower bound in [1] uses trees of unbounded degree.

10 CONCLUSION

We have shown an efficient algorithm to enumerate the assignments of MSO formulae on trees under updates (relabeling, leaf insertions, leaf deletions), with linear preprocessing in the input tree, linear delay in each produced assignment (so constant if all free variables are first-order), and with logarithmic update time (in the tree). Our work is the first to match the bounds of the original results on MSO enumeration on trees without updates, while allowing general updates on trees (refer back to Table 1 for a comparison). Our algorithm is also the first to be tractable in combined complexity when the query is given as a (generally nondeterministic) tree variable automaton, with the preprocessing phase, enumeration delay, and update time being polynomial in the automaton; this extends our previous results on words [5] to trees and to efficient updates.

Our results leave several directions open for future work. One question is to improve the complexity in terms of the automaton, i.e., lowering the polynomial degree, as we have shown to be possible in the case of queries on words. A related question would be to perform enumeration for a more concise automaton model, in particular allowing the automaton to represent possible sets of captured variables more concisely, like non-extended VAs [5, 23]: we believe that this should be possible. We could also aim for more expressive automata models, e.g., alternating automata or two-way automata; or other query languages on trees, e.g., tree pattern queries. Another open question is the support for more expressive update operations. In the case of words, it would be natural to support bulk updates, i.e., moving a part of the text to a different place (see the conclusion of [5]). We believe that our techniques could adapt for such updates on words. As for trees, we currently do not know how to handle updates that split a subtree or attach a subtree.

One issue that we have not explored in the current paper is memory usage. Constant memory usage was achieved in [5] (for nondeterministic sequential VAs) and in [5, 8, 25] (for MSO queries with free first-order variables), but it does not hold for our results (the memory usage may be linear in the circuit). We do not know if we can achieve constant memory.

Finally, there is a gap of $\log\log(n)$ between our upper bound and the lower bound, which it would be interesting to close. Note that the marked ancestor problem in fact has an algorithm with update complexity $O(\log(n)/\log\log(n))$, so we cannot hope to close the gap by improving the lower bound in Theorem 9.1. It may be the case that better lower bounds can be shown for our enumeration problem, but, going beyond $\Omega(\log(n)/\log\log(n))$ is generally considered very challenging. Indeed, the only paper that we are aware of that achieves a lower bound of $\Omega(\log(n))$ for any dynamic problem is [33], but it does not imply a lower bound in our setting because they allow more powerful updates than we do. Alternatively, it may be possible to improve our update complexity to $O(\log(n)/\log\log(n))$, e.g., by adapting the techniques of [1], but we have not been able to do so.

It would also be interesting to see what happens if we allow more generous enumeration delay, say $O(\log(n))$. Can we get an algorithm with updates faster than the lower bound of Corollary 9.3 in that case, maybe even constant? This might be an interesting trade-off in applications where updates are much more frequent than enumeration queries.

ACKNOWLEDGMENTS

Bourhis was partially founded by the DeLTA French ANR project (ANR-16-CE40-0007). Niewerth was supported by the Deutsche Forschungsgemeinschaft (MA 4938/4-1).

REFERENCES

[1] Stephen Alstrup, Thore Husfeldt, and Theis Rauhe. 1998. Marked ancestor problems. In *FOCS*.

[2] Antoine Amarilli, Pierre Bourhis, Louis Jachiet, and Stefan Mengel. 2017. A Circuit-based approach to efficient enumeration. In *ICALP*.

[3] Antoine Amarilli, Pierre Bourhis, Louis Jachiet, and Stefan Mengel. 2019. A Circuit-based approach to efficient enumeration. Extended version with proofs. https://arxiv.org/abs/1702.05589.

[4] Antoine Amarilli, Pierre Bourhis, and Stefan Mengel. 2018. Enumeration on trees under relabelings. In *ICDT*.

[5] Antoine Amarilli, Pierre Bourhis, Stefan Mengel, and Matthias Niewerth. 2019. Constant-delay enumeration for nondeterministic document spanners. In *ICDT*.

[6] Antoine Amarilli, Pierre Bourhis, Stefan Mengel, and Matthias Niewerth. 2019. Enumeration on trees with tractable combined complexity and efficient updates. Extended version with proofs. https://arxiv.org/abs/1812.09519.

[7] Antoine Amarilli, Pierre Bourhis, and Pierre Senellart. 2015. Provenance circuits for trees and treelike instances. In *ICALP*.

[8] Guillaume Bagan. 2006. MSO queries on tree decomposable structures are computable with linear delay. In *CSL*.

[9] Guillaume Bagan, Arnaud Durand, and Etienne Grandjean. 2007. On Acyclic conjunctive queries and constant delay enumeration. In *CSL*.

[10] Andrey Balmin, Yannis Papakonstantinou, and Victor Vianu. 2004. Incremental validation of XML documents. *TODS* 29, 4 (2004).

[11] Christoph Berkholz, Jens Keppeler, and Nicole Schweikardt. 2017. Answering FO+MOD queries under updates on bounded degree databases. In *ICDT*.

[12] Christoph Berkholz, Jens Keppeler, and Nicole Schweikardt. 2017. Answering conjunctive queries under updates. In *PODS*.

[13] Christoph Berkholz, Jens Keppeler, and Nicole Schweikardt. 2018. Answering UCQs under updates and in the presence of integrity constraints. In *ICDT*.

[14] Hans L. Bodlaender and Torben Hagerup. 1998. Parallel algorithms with optimal speedup for bounded treewidth. *SIAM J. Comput.* 27, 6 (1998).

[15] M. Bojańczyk. 2010. Algebra for trees. In *Handbook of Automata Theory*. European Mathematical Society Publishing.

[16] M. Bojańczyk and I. Walukiewicz. 2007. Forest algebras. In *Automata and Logic: History and Perspectives*. Amsterdam University Press.

[17] Florent Capelli and Stefan Mengel. 2019. Tractable QBF by knowledge compilation. In *STACS*.

[18] J. Carme, J. Niehren, and M. Tommasi. 2004. Querying unranked trees with stepwise tree automata. In *RTA*.

[19] Nofar Carmeli and Markus Kröll. 2018. Enumeration complexity of conjunctive queries with functional dependencies. In *ICDT*.

[20] Adnan Darwiche. 2001. On the tractable counting of theory models and its application to truth maintenance and belief revision. *J. Applied Non-Classical Logics* 11, 1-2 (2001).

[21] Arnaud Durand and Etienne Grandjean. 2007. First-order queries on structures of bounded degree are computable with constant delay. *TOCL* 8, 4 (2007).

[22] Ronald Fagin, Benny Kimelfeld, Frederick Reiss, and Stijn Vansummeren. 2015. Document spanners: A formal approach to information extraction. *JACM* 62, 2 (2015).

[23] Fernando Florenzano, Cristian Riveros, Martin Ugarte, Stijn Vansummeren, and Domagoj Vrgoc. 2018. Constant delay algorithms for regular document spanners. In *PODS*.

[24] François Le Gall. 2014. Powers of tensors and fast matrix multiplication. In *ISSAC*.

[25] Wojciech Kazana and Luc Segoufin. 2013. Enumeration of monadic second-order queries on trees. *TOCL* 14, 4 (2013).

[26] Katja Losemann and Wim Martens. 2014. MSO queries on trees: enumerating answers under updates. In *CSL-LICS*.

[27] W. Martens and J. Niehren. 2007. On the Minimization of XML Schemas and tree automata for unranked trees. *JCSS* 73, 4 (2007).

[28] Wim Martens and Tina Trautner. 2018. Evaluation and enumeration problems for regular path queries. In *ICDT*.

[29] Albert R Meyer. 1975. Weak monadic second order theory of succesor is not elementary-recursive. In *Logic Colloquium*.

[30] Matthias Niewerth. 2018. MSO queries on trees: Enumerating answers under updates using forest algebras. In *LICS*.

[31] Matthias Niewerth and Luc Segoufin. 2018. Enumeration of MSO queries on strings with constant delay and logarithmic updates. In *PODS*.

[32] Dan Olteanu and Maximilian Schleich. 2016. Factorized databases. *SIGMOD Record* 45, 2 (2016).

[33] Mihai Patrascu and Erik D. Demaine. 2006. Logarithmic lower bounds in the cell-probe model. *SIAM J. Comput.* 35, 4 (2006).

[34] Knot Pipatsrisawat and Adnan Darwiche. 2008. New compilation languages based on structured decomposability. In *AAAI*.

[35] Nicole Schweikardt, Luc Segoufin, and Alexandre Vigny. 2018. Enumeration for FO queries over nowhere dense graphs. In *PODS*.

[36] Luc Segoufin. 2014. A glimpse on constant delay enumeration (Invited talk). In *STACS*.

[37] James W. Thatcher and Jesse B. Wright. 1968. Generalized finite automata theory with an application to a decision problem of second-order logic. *Math. Systems Theory* 2, 1 (1968).

Counting Database Repairs under Primary Keys Revisited

Marco Calautti
School of Informatics
University of Edinburgh
mcalautt@inf.ed.ac.uk

Marco Console
School of Informatics
University of Edinburgh
mconsole@inf.ed.ac.uk

Andreas Pieris
School of Informatics
University of Edinburgh
apieris@inf.ed.ac.uk

ABSTRACT

Consistent query answering (CQA) aims to deliver meaningful answers when queries are evaluated over inconsistent databases. Such answers must be certainly true in all repairs, which are consistent databases whose difference from the inconsistent one is somehow minimal. An interesting task in this context is to count the number of repairs that entail the query. This problem has been already studied for conjunctive queries and primary keys; we know that it is #P-complete in data complexity under polynomial-time Turing reductions (a.k.a. Cook reductions). However, as it has been already observed in the literature of counting complexity, there are problems that are "hard-to-count-easy-to-decide", which cannot be complete (under reasonable assumptions) for #P under weaker reductions, and, in particular, under standard many-one logspace reductions (a.k.a. parsimonious reductions). For such "hard-to-count-easy-to-decide" problems, a crucial question is whether we can determine their exact complexity by looking for subclasses of #P to which they belong. Ideally, we would like to show that such a problem is complete for a subclass of #P under many-one logspace reductions. The main goal of this work is to perform such a refined analysis for the problem of counting the number of repairs under primary keys that entail the query.

CCS CONCEPTS

• **Information systems → Inconsistent data**; • **Theory of computation → Complexity classes; Numeric approximation algorithms**;

PODS'19, June 30-July 5, 2019, Amsterdam, Netherlands

ACM ISBN 978-1-4503-6227-6/19/06...$15.00
https://doi.org/10.1145/3294052.3319703

KEYWORDS

inconsistency, repairs, primary keys, first-order queries, counting, complexity, approximation schemes

ACM Reference Format:
Marco Calautti, Marco Console, and Andreas Pieris. 2019. Counting Database Repairs under Primary Keys Revisited. In *38th ACM SIGMOD-SIGACT-SIGAI Symposium on Principles of Database Systems (PODS'19), June 30-July 5, 2019, Amsterdam, Netherlands.* ACM, New York, NY, USA, 15 pages. https://doi.org/10.1145/3294052.3319703

1 INTRODUCTION

Inconsistent databases, that is, databases that do not conform to their specifications in the form of integrity constraints, are a real-life phenomenon that arises due to many reasons such as integration of conflicting sources. With the aim of obtaining conceptually meaningful answers to queries posed over inconsistent databases, Arenas, Bertossi, and Chomicki introduced in the late 1990s the notion of Consistent Query Answering (CQA) [2]. The key elements of the CQA approach can be summarized as follows: (1) the notion of *repair* of an inconsistent database D, i.e., a consistent database whose difference with D is minimal, and (2) the notion of query answering based on *certain answers*, i.e., answers that are entailed by every repair. Here is a simple example.

Example 1.1. Consider the schema $\mathbf{S}$ consisting of a single relation Employee(id, name, dept) that comes with the key constraint key(Employee) $= \{1\}$, which states that the first attribute, i.e., the id, is the key of the relation Employee. Consider now the database D over $\mathbf{S}$ consisting of the atoms:

$$\text{Employee}(1, \text{Bob}, \text{HR}) \qquad \text{Employee}(1, \text{Bob}, \text{IT})$$
$$\text{Employee}(2, \text{Alice}, \text{IT}) \qquad \text{Employee}(2, \text{Tim}, \text{IT}).$$

Observe that the above database is inconsistent w.r.t. the key constraint since we are uncertain about Bob's department, and the name of the employee with id 2. In this case, to devise a repair, we only need to keep one of the two atoms that are in a conflict. In this way, we obtain a $\subseteq$-maximal subset of D that is consistent. Now, consider the Boolean query Q

$$\exists x \exists y \exists z (\text{Employee}(1, x, y) \wedge \text{Employee}(2, z, y)),$$

which asks whether employees 1 and 2 work in the same department. This query is true only in two repairs, and thus, according to the certain answer semantics, is not entailed. ∎

The constraint used in the above example is a primary key. Primary keys, which means that each relation of the schema has at most one key, form a central class of constraints that is heavily used in real-life applications. As we have seen above, in the presence of primary keys, a repair of a database D is a maximal consistent subset of D. The rest of this work deals only with primary keys.

1.1 Counting Database Repairs

Example 1.1, despite its simplicity, illustrates one of the limitations of the standard CQA approach. The notion of certain answers only says that a tuple is entailed by all repairs, or is not entailed by some repair. But, as discussed in [4], the former is too strict, while the latter is not very useful in a more practical context. Instead, we would like to know how often a tuple is a consistent answer, i.e., its relative frequency. For instance, in Example 1.1, the relative frequency of the query (in fact, of the empty tuple) is $\frac{1}{2}$ since, out of four repairs in total, two of those entail the query. Of course, to compute the relative frequency of a tuple, we need a way to compute (i) the number of repairs that entail a tuple (the numerator), and (ii) the total number of repairs (the denominator).

It is easy to show that, assuming a fixed query and set of primary keys (i.e., focussing on the data complexity), computing the total number of repairs is an easy task, i.e., feasible in polynomial time; see, e.g., [8]. However, computing the number of repairs that entail a given tuple is #P-complete in data complexity, under polynomial-time Turing reductions, when we focus on conjunctive queries [8, 9]. Recall that #P is a hard counting complexity class, which, roughly speaking, collects the function problems that ask for the number of solutions to an NP problem. Maslowski and Wijsen analyzed further this counting problem. They proved in [8] that, for every self-join-free conjunctive query and set of primary keys, it is either tractable, i.e., in FP, or #P-hard under polynomial-time Turing reductions, and they lifted this result to conjunctive queries with self-joins in [9].

1.2 Our Main Goal

From the above brief discussion, it is fair to conclude that, at least for conjunctive queries, the data complexity of the problem of counting the number of repairs that entail a given tuple is rather well-understood. Recall, however, that all the aforementioned completeness results rely on polynomial-time Turing reductions, a.k.a. Cook reductions. As it has been already observed in the literature (see, e.g., [6, 10]), there are problems that are "hard-to-count-easy-to-decide", which cannot be complete (under reasonable assumptions) for #P under standard many-one logspace (or even polynomial-time) reductions; these reductions are also called parsimonious. Note that the decision version of a counting problem asks whether the number of solutions is greater than zero. In our case, it asks whether there is a repair that entails a given tuple.

As stated in [10], Cook reductions blur structural differences between counting problems and complexity classes. The reason is that #P is not closed under Cook reductions (under reasonable assumptions). Therefore, for such "hard-to-count-easy-to-decide" problems, a crucial question is whether we can determine their exact complexity by looking for subclasses of #P to which they belong. Ideally, we would like to show that such a problem is complete for a subclass C of #P under many-one logspace reductions, where C is closed under many-one logspace reductions.

The main goal of this work is to perform such a refined complexity analysis for the problem of counting the number of repairs that entail a given tuple, always focussing on its data complexity. The query can be an arbitrary first-order query, or a query from important fragments such as positive existential queries, while the constraints are primary keys.

1.3 Research Challenges

After a preliminary complexity analysis, we have concluded that in the case of arbitrary first-order queries, our problem is not only "hard-to-count", but also "hard-to-decide". We can show that the decision problem is NP-complete, while the counting problem is #P-complete, both under many-one logspace reductions. This tells us that #P is the right complexity for our problem when we focus on first-order queries.

On the other hand, the situation for positive existential queries is more interesting. We can show that in this case we are dealing with a typical "hard-to-count-easy-to-decide" problem, and therefore, further investigation is needed. We know several counting complexity classes inside #P. One of those, which is central for our work, is SpanL, which, roughly speaking, collects all the functions that compute the number of distinct accepted outputs of a nondeterministic logspace transducer [1]. Although we can place our problem inside SpanL, it is unlikely to be complete for SpanL under many-one logspace reductions since this implies that L = NL. In view of the fact that we do not know much about subclasses of SpanL for which our problem can be complete under logspace reductions, this brings us to our first question:

Question 1: *Can we isolate a complexity class $C \subsetneq$ SpanL, which is closed under many-one logspace reductions, for which our problem is complete under many-one logspace reductions?*

At this point, let us stress one more time that we focus on the data complexity of our problem. This means, by convention, that we deal, not with a single problem, but with a family of problems; as usual, each query and set of primary keys gives rise to a new problem. Furthermore, establishing a completeness result for a certain complexity class C boils down to showing that (i) every problem in this family belongs to C, and (ii) there exists one problem that is C-complete. But there is no guarantee that there exists a problem in this family such that all the other problems of the family are logspace reducible to it. This means that there is no guarantee that the answer to the above question is affirmative. This brings us to our second research question, which concerns the case where Question 1 is answered negatively:

Question 2: *Can we characterize the data complexity of a parameterized version of our problem, i.e., when the query and the set of primary keys enjoy additional properties?*

Such a property can be, for example, a constant bound on the keywidth of the query w.r.t. the set of primary keys, i.e, the number of atoms occurring in the query with a relation that has a key. Indeed, as we shall see, the notion of keywidth plays a critical role in our analysis.

1.4 Summary of Contributions

Our main results can be summarized as follows; let us clarify that all the complexity results refer to the data complexity:

▶ In Section 3, we perform a preliminary complexity analysis under many-one logspace reductions. We show that our problem is "hard-to-count-hard-to-decide" for arbitrary first-order queries, but "hard-to-count-easy-to-decide" for positive existential queries. For the latter case, we further show that our problem is in SpanL, which is essentially the starting point of our subsequent investigation.

▶ In Section 4, we isolate a hierarchy of complexity classes inside SpanL, dubbed the Λ-hierarchy. The main technical challenge here is to understand how to limit the power of logspace nondeterministic transducers in such a way that will lead to the desired complexity classes. Note that the Λ-hierarchy, apart from the 0th and 1st levels, consists of hard complexity classes. In particular, if the second level is inside polynomial-time, then P = NP.

▶ We then proceed, in Section 5, to show that our problem, assuming that the keywidth of the query w.r.t. the set of primary keys is bounded by $k \geq 0$, is $\Lambda[k]$-complete under many-one logspace reductions, where $\Lambda[k]$ denotes the kth level of the Λ-hierarchy. This provides a firm answer to our second question above.

▶ By exploiting the above result, we can partially answer our first question. In Section 5, we show that: either our problem is $\Lambda[k]$-complete, for some $k \geq 0$, or there is no class $C \subseteq$ SpanL, which is closed under logspace reductions, for which our problem is complete; both statements are under many-one logspace reductions. As the reader may have already suspected, the existence of an integer $k \geq 0$ such that $\Lambda[k]$ is the right complexity class for our problem is equivalent to the fact that the Λ-hierarchy collapses. The latter is a difficult question that remains open.

▶ Since our problem is hard, it is natural to try to approximate it. In Section 6, we target fully polynomial-time randomized approximation schemes, FPRAS for short. Although for arbitrary first-order queries our problem does not admit an FPRAS (under reasonable assumptions), in the case of positive existential queries an FPRAS can be devised. Actually, this is not a new result since we can inherit the FPRAS for query answering over disjoint-independent probabilistic databases [5]. The novelty lies in the fact that our FPRAS is conceptually simpler than the one from [5]. Note that this result is obtained by showing a more general result, i.e., every function in $\Lambda[k]$, for $k > 1$, admits an FPRAS.

▶ Finally, in Section 7, we provide more completeness results for the Λ-hierarchy, which justifies even further its meaningfulness. In particular, we show that counting the satisfying assignments of disjoint positive kDNF formulas, as well as counting the number of forbidden colorings of k-uniform hypergraphs, are $\Lambda[k]$-complete.

2 PRELIMINARIES

In this section, we recall the basics on relational databases, key constraints, and queries. We also recall some fundamental notions from complexity theory.

2.1 Databases, Constraints and Queries

Relational Databases. We assume a countably infinite set $\mathbf{C}$ of *constants* from which database elements are drawn. A *(relational) schema* $\mathbf{S}$ is a finite set of relation symbols (or predicates) with associated arity. We write R/n to denote that R has arity n. A *fact* over $\mathbf{S}$ is an expression of the form $R(c_1, \ldots, c_n)$, where $R/n \in \mathbf{S}$ with $n > 0$, and $c_i \in \mathbf{C}$ for each $i \in \{1, \ldots, n\}$. A *database* over $\mathbf{S}$ is a finite set of facts over $\mathbf{S}$. The *active domain* of a database D, denoted $\mathrm{dom}(D)$, is the set of constants occurring in D.

Primary Key Constraints. A *key constraint* (or simply *key*) κ over a schema $\mathbf{S}$ is an expression of the form $\mathrm{key}(R) = A$, where $R/n \in \mathbf{S}$ and $A \subseteq \{1, \ldots, n\}$. Such an expression is called an R-key. A database D satisfies κ if, for every two facts $R(\bar{t}), R(\bar{s}) \in D$, $\bar{t}[A] = \bar{s}[A]$ implies $\bar{t} = \bar{s}$. We say that D is *consistent* w.r.t. a set Σ of keys, written $D \models \Sigma$, if D satisfies each key in Σ; otherwise, is *inconsistent* w.r.t. Σ. In this work, we focus on sets of *primary keys*, i.e., sets of keys that, for each predicate R of the underlying schema, have at most one R-key. For technical clarity, we assume, w.l.o.g., that each key constraint is of the form $\mathrm{key}(R) = \{1, \ldots, m\}$, i.e., always the first m attributes of R/n, for some $m \leq n$, form the key.

Queries. Let $\mathbf{V}$ be a countably infinite set of *variables* disjoint from $\mathbf{C}$. An atom over a schema $\mathbf{S}$ is an expression of the form $R(t_1, \ldots, t_n)$, where $R/n \in \mathbf{S}$, and $t_i \in \mathbf{C} \cup \mathbf{V}$ for each $i \in \{1, \ldots, n\}$. Notice that a fact is an atom without variables. A *first-order query* $Q(\bar{x})$ over a schema $\mathbf{S}$ is an expression $\{\bar{x} \mid \varphi\}$, where φ is a first-order formula with free variables $\bar{x}$ that mentions only atoms over $\mathbf{S}$. The class of first-order queries is denoted $\mathbb{FO}$. We are also going to consider key fragments of $\mathbb{FO}$, in particular, *existential positive queries* ($\exists\mathbb{FO}^+$), *conjunctive queries* ($\mathbb{CQ}$), and *unions of conjunctive queries* ($\mathbb{UCQ}$). The answer to $Q(\bar{x})$ over a database D, denoted $Q(D)$, is the set of tuples $\{\bar{c} \in \mathsf{dom}(D)^{|\bar{x}|} \mid D \models \varphi(\bar{c})\}$.

Database Repairs and Blocks. For an inconsistent database D w.r.t. a set Σ of primary keys, a *repair* of D w.r.t. Σ is a maximal subset of D that is consistent w.r.t. Σ; i.e., if $D' \subseteq D$ is a repair, then there is no $D'' \subseteq D$ that is consistent w.r.t. Σ and $D' \subsetneq D''$. Let $\mathsf{rep}(D, \Sigma)$ be the set of repairs of D w.r.t Σ.

When we focus on primary keys, there is a convenient way to construct repairs. We first collect all the facts of the database that are in a conflict, i.e., they have the same predicate R and agree on $\mathsf{key}(R)$, into disjoint sets called blocks. A repair can then be constructed by keeping exactly one fact from each block. Formally, for a fact $\alpha = R(c_1, \ldots, c_n)$, the *key value* of α w.r.t. Σ is defined as

$$\mathsf{key}_\Sigma(\alpha) = \begin{cases} \langle R, \langle c_1, \ldots, c_m \rangle \rangle & \text{if } \mathsf{key}(R) = \{1, \ldots, m\} \in \Sigma, \\ \langle R, \langle c_1, \ldots, c_n \rangle \rangle & \text{otherwise.} \end{cases}$$

Then, given a database D, we define

$$\mathsf{block}_\Sigma(\alpha, D) = \{\beta \in D \mid \mathsf{key}_\Sigma(\beta) = \mathsf{key}_\Sigma(\alpha)\}.$$

For $\alpha, \beta \in D$, if $\mathsf{key}_\Sigma(\alpha) = \mathsf{key}_\Sigma(\beta)$, then $\mathsf{block}_\Sigma(\alpha, D)$ and $\mathsf{block}_\Sigma(\beta, D)$ coincide. Moreover, $\mathsf{block}_\Sigma(\alpha, D) = \{\alpha\}$ means that α is not in a conflict. A repair can be constructed by keeping one fact from each block. Formally, with $\mathsf{block}_\Sigma(D) = \{\mathsf{block}_\Sigma(\alpha, D) \mid \alpha \in D\}$ and $\Pi_{D,\Sigma} = \times_{B \in \mathsf{block}_\Sigma(D)} B$, it holds that $\mathsf{rep}(D, \Sigma) = \{\{\alpha_1, \ldots, \alpha_n\} \mid \langle \alpha_1, \ldots, \alpha_n \rangle \in \Pi_{D,\Sigma}\}$.

For a database D and set Σ of primary keys, we write $\prec_{D,\Sigma}$ for the lexicographic ordering over the set of key values $\{\mathsf{key}_\Sigma(\alpha) \mid \alpha \in D\}$. Observe that $\prec_{D,\Sigma}$ induces a sequence $B_1, \ldots, B_n$ of the sets of $\mathsf{block}_\Sigma(D)$: assuming that $\kappa_1 \prec_{D,\Sigma} \cdots \prec_{D,\Sigma} \kappa_n$, the key value of the facts of B_i is κ_i. Note that in case D is empty, the above sequence is empty, i.e., $n = 0$.

Counting Database Repairs. An interesting problem, which has been already studied in [8, 9], and is the main concern of this work, is the following; $\mathbb{Q}$ is a class of queries:

PROBLEM :	$\#\mathsf{CQA}(\mathbb{Q})$
INPUT :	A database D, a set Σ of primary keys, $Q(\bar{x}) \in \mathbb{Q}$, and a tuple $\bar{t} \in \mathsf{dom}(D)^{|\bar{x}|}$.
OUTPUT :	$\lvert\{D' \in \mathsf{rep}(D, \Sigma) \mid \bar{t} \in Q(D')\}\rvert$.

The goal of this work is to revisit the above problem with the aim of providing more insights about its computational complexity. As usual, we are interested in its *data complexity*, where the set of constraints and the query are fixed, and only the database and the tuple are considered input. Let us make this more precise as it is very crucial for our work. For every pair of a query $Q(\bar{x}) \in \mathbb{Q}$ and a set Σ of primary keys, we can define the following problem:

PROBLEM :	$\#\mathsf{CQA}(Q(\bar{x}), \Sigma)$
INPUT :	A database D, and a tuple $\bar{t} \in \mathsf{dom}(D)^{|\bar{x}|}$.
OUTPUT :	$\lvert\{D' \in \mathsf{rep}(D, \Sigma) \mid \bar{t} \in Q(D')\}\rvert$.

Let C be a complexity class, and $\mathcal{R}$ a class of reductions; details about complexity classes and reductions are given below. We say that $\#\mathsf{CQA}(\mathbb{Q})$ is $\mathcal{R}$-complete for C in data complexity if: (i) for each $Q \in \mathbb{Q}$ and set Σ of primary keys, $\#\mathsf{CQA}(Q, \Sigma)$ is in C, and (ii) there is $Q' \in \mathbb{Q}$ and a set Σ' of primary keys such that $\#\mathsf{CQA}(Q', \Sigma')$ is $\mathcal{R}$-complete for C.

The above counting problems have a natural decision version, denoted $\#\mathsf{CQA}_{>0}(\mathbb{Q})$ and $\#\mathsf{CQA}_{>0}(Q, \Sigma)$, respectively, that simply asks whether $\lvert\{D' \in \mathsf{rep}(D, \Sigma) \mid \bar{t} \in Q(D')\}\rvert > 0$. The data complexity of $\#\mathsf{CQA}_{>0}(\mathbb{Q})$ is defined in the same way as for $\#\mathsf{CQA}(\mathbb{Q})$. Henceforth, we focus on Boolean queries, but all the results extend to non-Boolean queries.

2.2 Complexity Toolbox

Counting Complexity Classes. We recall well-known counting complexity classes, i.e., classes of counting functions of the form $\{0, 1\}^* \to \mathbb{N}$, that are crucial for our analysis. We first recall the counting analog of polynomial-time:

$$\mathrm{FP} = \{f \mid f \text{ is computable in polynomial-time}\}.$$

Given a nondeterministic Turing machine (NTM) M, let accept_M be the function $\{0, 1\}^* \to \mathbb{N}$ such that $\mathsf{accept}_M(x)$ is the number of accepting computations of M on input x. We can then define:

$$\begin{aligned} \#\mathrm{P} &= \{\mathsf{accept}_M \mid M \text{ is a polynomial-time NTM}\} \\ \#\mathrm{L} &= \{\mathsf{accept}_M \mid M \text{ is a logarithmic-space NTM}\}. \end{aligned}$$

Given an NTM M with output tape, i.e., a nondeterministic transducer (NTT), let span_M be the function $\{0, 1\}^* \to \mathbb{N}$ such that $\mathsf{span}_M(x)$ is the number of *distinct valid* outputs of M on input x; the output of a computation is considered to be valid if the machine halts in an accepting state. Then:

$$\mathrm{SpanL} = \{\mathsf{span}_M \mid M \text{ is a logarithmic-space NTT}\}.$$

For the above classes we know that $\#\mathrm{L} \subseteq \mathrm{FP}$, $\mathrm{SpanL} \subseteq \#\mathrm{P}$. It is also believed that the above inclusions are strict (under reasonable complexity-theoretic assumptions) [1].

Let us recall that every counting problem f has a natural decision version, denoted by $f_{>0}$, defined as expected: given $x \in \{0, 1\}^*$, is it the case that $f(x) > 0$? Actually, we have already seen this for #CQA($\mathbb{Q}$) and #CQA(Q, Σ) in the previous section. Of course, for pinpointing the complexity of $f_{>0}$ we rely on standard complexity classes.

Reductions. Consider two functions $f, g : \{0,1\}^* \to \mathbb{N}$. We say that f is *Cook reducible* to g, denoted $f \leq_{\mathrm{T}}^{\mathrm{P}} g$, if there exists a polynomial-time deterministic transducer M, with access to an oracle for g, such that, for every $x \in \{0,1\}^*$, $f(x) = M(x)$. In other words, a (functional) Cook reduction is a polynomial-time (functional) Turing reduction. Moreover, we say that f is *many-one logspace reducible* to g, denoted $f \leq_{\mathrm{m}}^{\log} g$, if there is a function $h : \{0,1\}^* \to \{0,1\}^*$ that is computable in logarithmic-space such that, for every $x \in \{0,1\}^*$, $f(x) = g(h(x))$. Let us say that when referring to counting functions, many-one reductions are also called *parsimonious* reductions. A class C is *closed* under Cook (resp., many-one logspace) reductions if, for every two functions f, g, $f \leq_{\mathrm{T}}^{\mathrm{P}} g$ (resp., $f \leq_{\mathrm{m}}^{\log} g$) and $g \in C$ implies $f \in C$.

3 COMPLEXITY OF #CQA: A GLIMPSE

The complexity of #CQA has been already studied by Maslowski and Wijsen in [8, 9]. Notice that all the complexity results for #CQA and #CQA$_{>0}$ that will be given in the rest of the paper concern their data complexity. Thus, for brevity, we will sometimes avoid to explicitly mention the term data complexity. We know that:

Theorem 3.1 ([8, 9]). *#CQA($\mathbb{CQ}$) is $\leq_{\mathrm{T}}^{\mathrm{P}}$-complete for* #P.

The above result relies on Cook reductions. However, as it has been already discussed in Section 1, there are problems that are "hard-to-count-easy-to-decide", which cannot be complete (under reasonable assumptions) for #P under many-one logspace (or even polynomial-time) reductions. For such problems, a crucial question is whether we can determine their exact complexity by looking for subclasses of #P to which they belong. Our main goal here is to perform such an analysis for #CQA($\mathbb{Q}$), where $\mathbb{Q}$ is one of the standard query languages mentioned in Section 2.

3.1 Arbitrary First-Order Queries

Is #CQA($\mathbb{FO}$) an "easy-to-decide" problem? Unfortunately, the answer to this question is negative. We can show that:

Theorem 3.2. *#CQA$_{>0}$($\mathbb{FO}$) is $\leq_{\mathrm{m}}^{\log}$-complete for* NP.

For the upper bound (assume a fixed query $Q \in \mathbb{FO}$ and a set Σ of primary keys), given a database D, we simply need to guess a database $D' \subseteq D$, and then verify that $D' \in \mathrm{rep}(D, \Sigma)$ and $D' \models Q$. It is clear that this nondeterministic procedure runs in polynomial time. For the lower bound, we show that there is a query $Q \in \mathbb{FO}$ and a set Σ of primary keys such that 3SAT $\leq_{\mathrm{m}}^{\log}$ #CQA$_{>0}(Q, \Sigma)$.

With Theorem 3.2 in place, it is not surprising that #CQA($\mathbb{FO}$) is also "hard-to-count". It is easy to show that:

Theorem 3.3. *#CQA($\mathbb{FO}$) is $\leq_{\mathrm{m}}^{\log}$-complete for* #P.

Proof. For the lower bound, since #3SAT, i.e., the counting version of 3SAT, is $\leq_{\mathrm{m}}^{\log}$-complete for #P [11], we can exploit the construction given in the proof of Theorem 3.2. For the upper bound, fix a query $Q \in \mathbb{FO}$ and a set Σ of primary keys. We need to show that #CQA(Q, Σ) is a function of the form accept_M, where M is a polynomial-time NTM. Consider a database D, and let $B_1, \ldots, B_n$ be the sequence of blocks induced by $\prec_{D,\Sigma}$. The machine M, on input D, performs two simple steps: (1) for $i = 1$ to n: guess a fact $\alpha_i \in B_i$, and (2) if $\{\alpha_1, \ldots, \alpha_n\} \models Q$, then accept; otherwise, reject. It is clear that $D' = \{\alpha_1, \ldots, \alpha_n\} \in \mathrm{rep}(D, \Sigma)$. Moreover, since D' is constructed according to a fixed ordering, each computation of M on input D builds a distinct repair of $\mathrm{rep}(D, \Sigma)$. Thus, the number of accepting computations of M on D is the number of repairs of $\mathrm{rep}(D, \Sigma)$ that entail Q. Since the machine M runs in polynomial time, the claim follows. □

Since #P is closed under many-one logspace reductions, Theorem 3.3 implies that #P is the right complexity for #CQA($\mathbb{FO}$), and thus, there is no room for further analysis.

3.2 Existential Positive First-Order Queries

The situation for existential positive queries is more interesting. According to the following result, we are dealing with a typical "hard-to-count-easy-to-decide" problem.

Theorem 3.4. *#CQA$_{>0}$($\exists\mathbb{FO}^+$) is in* L.

Proof. Fix a query $Q \in \exists\mathbb{FO}^+$ and a set Σ of primary keys. We need to show that #CQA$_{>0}(Q, \Sigma)$ is in L. We first recall that Q can be equivalently rewritten in constant time (since the query is not part of the input) as a query $Q' \in \mathbb{UCQ}$ of the form $\bigvee_{i=1}^{n} Q_i$, where each Q_i is a Boolean conjunctive query. Thus, it suffices to show that #CQA$(Q', \Sigma)_{>0}$ is in L. The crucial observation, which is easy to verify, is the following; we write $\mathrm{var}(Q_i)$ for the variables in Q_i:

Lemma 3.5. *Given a database D, there exists $D' \in \mathrm{rep}(D, \Sigma)$ such that $D' \models Q'$ iff there exists $i \in \{1, \ldots, n\}$ and a mapping h from $\mathrm{var}(Q_i)$ to $\mathrm{dom}(D)$ such that $h(Q_i) \subseteq D$ and $h(Q_i) \models \Sigma$.*

We then get the following logspace procedure: if there is $i \in \{1, \ldots, n\}$ and mapping $h : \mathrm{var}(Q_i) \to \mathrm{dom}(D)$ such that $h(Q_i) \subseteq D$ and $h(Q_i) \models \Sigma$, then accept; otherwise, reject. □

The following is an easy consequence of Theorem 3.4:

Proposition 3.6. *If #CQA($\exists\mathbb{FO}^+$) is $\leq_{\mathrm{m}}^{\log}$-complete for #P, then* P = NP. *This holds even for polynomial-time reductions.*

```
Input: a database D
Output: a member of rep(D, Σ)

guess i ∈ {1, ..., m} and mapping
h : var(Q_i) → dom(D);
if h(Q_i) ⊈ D or h(Q_i) ⊭ Σ then
    reject;
j := 1;
while j ≤ n do
    if B_j ∩ h(Q_i) = {R(t̄)} and Σ has an R-key then
        output R(t̄);
    else
        guess α ∈ B_j;
        output α;
    j := j + 1;
accept.
```

Algorithm 1: The nondeterministic transducer $M_{Q,\Sigma}$.

Towards pinpointing the complexity of #CQA($\exists\mathbb{FO}^+$), Proposition 3.6 tells us that first we should look for a subclass of #P, closed under many-one logspace reductions, in which we can place our problem. The obvious candidate is SpanL:

THEOREM 3.7. *#CQA($\exists\mathbb{FO}^+$) is in* SpanL.

PROOF. It suffices to show that #CQA($\mathbb{UCQ}$) is in SpanL. Fix a query $Q \in \mathbb{UCQ}$ of the form $\bigvee_{i=1}^{m} Q_i$, and a set Σ of primary keys. We need to show that #CQA(Q, Σ) is a function of the form span_M, where M is a logarithmic-space NTT. Consider the transducer $M_{Q,\Sigma}$, depicted in Algorithm 1, that accepts as input a database D, and outputs a member of rep(D, Σ). Let $B_1, \ldots, B_n$ be the sequence of blocks from $\text{block}_\Sigma(D)$ induced by $\prec_{D,\Sigma}$. It can be shown that $M_{Q,\Sigma}$ uses only logarithmic-space. It is also not difficult to see that (1) for each $D' \in \text{rep}(D,\Sigma)$, $D' \models Q$ iff there exists an accepting computation of $M_{Q,\Sigma}$ on D that outputs D', and (2) for each output $\alpha_1, \ldots, \alpha_n$ of an accepting computation of $M_{Q,\Sigma}$ on D, $\alpha_i \in B_i$, i.e., facts from a certain block always appear at the same position of the output. The latter statement ensures that it is not possible for two different accepting computations to produce the same repair, while their output strings are syntactically different by producing the same facts in different order. Hence, from (1) and (2), we get that the number of distinct valid outputs of $M_{Q,\Sigma}$ on input D is exactly the number of repairs of rep(D, Σ) that entail Q. □

At this point, one may be tempted to think that SpanL is the right complexity for #CQA($\exists\mathbb{FO}^+$). Unfortunately, the situation is more complex. The following consequence of Theorem 3.4 states that it is unlikely to be the case:

PROPOSITION 3.8. *If #CQA($\exists\mathbb{FO}^+$) is $\leq_{\text{m}}^{\log}$-complete for* SpanL, *then* L = NL.

What about subclasses of SpanL? From Section 2.2, we know that #L ⊆ SpanL. However, since this class is tractable, while our problem is hard (i.e., $\leq_{\text{T}}^{\text{P}}$-complete for #P), it is again unlikely that this is the class that we are looking for.

PROPOSITION 3.9. *If #CQA($\exists\mathbb{FO}^+$) is in #L, then* P = NP.

Note that the above holds even if we replace #L with FP.

Our Main Research Questions

The above discussion brings us to our main questions, already discussed in Section 1. We proceed to expand a bit more on those questions in order to make them more precise.

Question 1: *Is there a class $C \subseteq$* SpanL, *closed under logspace reductions, such that #CQA($\exists\mathbb{FO}^+$) is $\leq_{\text{m}}^{\log}$-complete for C?*

One may think that the above question is trivial since, for every function $f \in$ SpanL, there is a class $C \subseteq$ SpanL, closed under logspace reductions, such that f is $\leq_{\text{m}}^{\log}$-complete for C: define C as $\{g \in \text{SpanL} \mid g \leq_{\text{m}}^{\log} f\}$. However, it should not be forgotten that we concentrate on the data complexity of #CQA($\exists\mathbb{FO}^+$), which means that we deal with a family F of functions and not a single function, and, by convention, F is $\leq_{\text{m}}^{\log}$-complete for C if (i) F ⊆ C, and (ii) there is a function of F that is $\leq_{\text{m}}^{\log}$-complete for C. But there is no guarantee that there is $f \in$ F such that, for every $g \in$ F, $g \leq_{\text{m}}^{\log} f$. This means that it might be the case that a class $C \subseteq$ SpanL, closed under logspace reductions, for which #CQA($\exists\mathbb{FO}^+$) is $\leq_{\text{m}}^{\log}$-complete does not exist. This brings us to our second question, which is a refined version of the first one:

Question 2: *Can we characterize the data complexity of a parameterized version of #CQA($\exists\mathbb{FO}^+$)?*

Let us make this more precise. A *covering function for* #CQA($\exists\mathbb{FO}^+$) is a function that maps pairs of the form (Q, Σ), where Q is a query from $\exists\mathbb{FO}^+$ and Σ is a set of primary keys, to the natural numbers. Such a function *cov* is called covering for #CQA($\exists\mathbb{FO}^+$) since it induces a cover for F = {#CQA(Q, Σ) | $Q \in \exists\mathbb{FO}^+$ and Σ is a set of primary keys}, i.e., the family of problems that we have to deal with in order to pinpoint the data complexity of #CQA($\exists\mathbb{FO}^+$). More precisely, *cov* induces a sequence $\mathsf{F}_0, \mathsf{F}_1, \ldots$ of subsets of F, where F_k = {#CQA(Q, Σ) | $cov(Q,\Sigma) = k$}, that covers F in the sense that F = $\bigcup_{i \geq 0} \mathsf{F}_i$. We can now consider a parameterized version of #CQA($\exists\mathbb{FO}^+$) defined as follows:

PROBLEM :	#CQA$_k^{cov}$($\exists\mathbb{FO}^+$)
INPUT :	A database D, a set Σ of primary keys, and $Q \in \exists\mathbb{FO}^+$ such that $cov(Q,\Sigma) = k$.
OUTPUT :	$\lvert\{D' \in \text{rep}(D,\Sigma) \mid D' \models Q\}\rvert$.

The data complexity of the above problem is defined as expected. In case Question 1 is answered negatively, the best that we can hope for is to isolate a covering function *cov* that allows us to pinpoint the data complexity of $\#\text{CQA}_k^{cov}(\exists\mathbb{FO}^+)$. Question 2 asks whether such a covering function exists.

Plan of Attack. We will first focus on our second question and provide a definite answer, which will then allow us to partially answer the first question. Despite our efforts, we have not managed to provide a firm answer to the first question. As we shall see, it is equivalent to a problem concerning the collapsing of a hierarchy of complexity classes inside SpanL. Our plan is as follows:

▶ We show that the *keywidth function* (*kw*), which computes the number of atoms in Q that use a predicate with a key (w.r.t. to Σ), is a covering function that allows us to pinpoint the complexity of $\#\text{CQA}_k^{kw}(\exists\mathbb{FO}^+)$. To this end, we first isolate (in Section 4) a hierarchy of classes inside SpanL, which are closed under logspace reductions, dubbed the Λ-*hierarchy*. We then show (in Section 5) that, for each $k \geq 0$, $\#\text{CQA}_k^{kw}(\exists\mathbb{FO}^+)$ is $\leq_m^{\log}$-complete for $\Lambda[k]$, i.e., the kth level of the Λ-hierarchy.

▶ Then, we proceed (in Section 5) to partially answer our first question. By exploiting the above result, we show the following: either $\#\text{CQA}(\exists\mathbb{FO}^+)$ is $\leq_m^{\log}$-complete for $\Lambda[k]$, for some $k \geq 0$, or there is no $C \subseteq$ SpanL, closed under logspace reductions, such that $\#\text{CQA}(\exists\mathbb{FO}^+)$ is $\leq_m^{\log}$-complete for C. The existence of an integer $k \geq 0$ such that $\Lambda[k]$ is the right complexity class for $\#\text{CQA}(\exists\mathbb{FO}^+)$ is equivalent to the fact that the Λ-hierarchy collapses. Whether the latter holds seems to be a difficult question that remains open.

4 THE Λ-HIERARCHY

We now proceed to introduce our hierarchy of complexity classes. The main technical challenge is to understand how to limit the computational power of logarithmic-space NTTs, which in turn will lead to our new complexity classes inside SpanL that serve the purpose described in our plan of attack. To this end, we first give a semi-formal discussion on a couple of structural properties that our problem enjoys, which will provide important insights on how to overcome our main technical challenge. Interestingly, these properties are shared by several natural problems inside SpanL.

4.1 The Guess-Check-Expand Paradigm

It turned out that there exists a generic paradigm, which we call *guess-check-expand*, that a logspace NTT can follow in order to place problems inside SpanL, assuming that the following structural properties are fulfilled:

Small Certificates. A solution (in our case, a repair that entails the query) is witnessed via a *small certificate*, i.e., of logarithmic size, that is verifiable in logspace.

For the next property, we first need to give some auxiliary terminology. Given a sequence of sets $S_1, \ldots, S_n$, an ℓ-*selector* of it, for $\ell \geq 0$, is a sequence of pairs $\sigma = (i_1, e_1), \ldots, (i_\ell, e_\ell)$, where $1 \leq i_1 < \cdots < i_\ell \leq n$, and $e_j \in S_{i_j}$ for each $j \in \{1, \ldots, \ell\}$. Intuitively, a pair (i, e) in σ tells us to "keep the element e from the set S_i". We can then define the *cartesian product of* $S_1, \ldots, S_n$ *w.r.t.* σ, denoted $[S_1, \ldots, S_n]^\sigma$, as $S_1^\sigma \times \cdots \times S_n^\sigma$, where $S_i^\sigma = \{e\}$ if σ contains a pair (i, e), otherwise, $S_i^\sigma = S_i$. In simple words, $[S_1, \ldots, S_n]^\sigma$ is the cartesian product of $S_1, \ldots, S_n$ with the difference that ℓ sets are first replaced by a singleton set as dictated by the ℓ-selector σ.

We can now discuss the second property. For brevity, for an input instance x, let $\mathsf{sol}(x)$ be the set of solutions, and $\mathsf{cert}(x)$ the set of certificates that witness a solution of $\mathsf{sol}(x)$.

Solutions via Certificate Expansion. There is $k \geq 0$ such that, for every input instance x, there is a sequence of logspace computable sets $S_1, \ldots, S_n$, called *solution domains*, such that

$$|\mathsf{sol}(x)| = \left| \bigcup_{c \in \mathsf{cert}(x)} [S_1, \ldots, S_n]^{\sigma_c} \right|,$$

where σ_c is an ℓ-selector, with $\ell \leq k$, for $S_1, \ldots, S_n$ determined by the small certificate c. In fact, there is a bijection $enc : \mathsf{sol}(x) \to \bigcup_{c \in \mathsf{cert}(x)} [S_1, \ldots, S_n]^{\sigma_c}$, and $enc(s)$ should be seen as an encoding of the solution s.

A function that enjoys the above properties can be placed in SpanL via a simple guess-check-expand algorithm:

(1) **(Guess)** Guess a candidate small certificate c.
(2) **(Check)** If c is not a valid certificate, then reject.
(3) **(Expand)** Expand c into an encoding of a solution witnessed by c using the solution domains $S_1, \ldots, S_n$ as follows: for $i = 1$ to n, if the ℓ-selector σ_c determined by c mentions (i, e), then output e; otherwise, guess $e \in S_i$ and output e.

It is clear that, on an input x, the above NTT uses logarithmic space in the size of x since the small certificates are logspace verifiable, and the solution domains are logspace computable. It is also clear that the number of distinct valid outputs of the NTT coincides with $\left|\bigcup_{c \in \mathsf{cert}(x)} [S_1, \ldots, S_n]^{\sigma_c}\right|$, and thus, with $|\mathsf{sol}(x)|$, as needed.

$\#\text{CQA}(Q, \Sigma)$ via a Guess-Check-Expand Algorithm. It is interesting to observe that the problem $\#\text{CQA}(Q, \Sigma)$, for some UCQ Q and set Σ of primary keys, enjoys the two structural properties discussed above; recall that an existential positive query can be rewritten as a UCQ. In fact, on input D:

- A small certificate for a repair of $\mathsf{rep}(D, \Sigma)$ that entails Q, is a pair (Q', h), where Q' is a disjunct of Q, and $h : \mathsf{var}(Q') \to \mathsf{dom}(D)$ with $h(Q') \subseteq D$ and $h(Q') \models \Sigma$.

- The sequence of solution domains corresponds to the sequence $B_1, \ldots, B_n$ of the sets of $\mathsf{block}_\Sigma(D)$ induced by $\prec_{D,\Sigma}$. The ℓ-selector $\sigma_{(Q',h)}$ for $B_1, \ldots, B_n$ determined by a certificate (Q', h) mentions the pair $(i, R(\bar{t}))$, i.e., it keeps the fact $R(\bar{t})$ from B_i, iff $h(Q') \cap B_i = \{R(\bar{t})\}$ and Σ has an R-key. The latter implies that ℓ is bounded by the maximum number of atoms with a predicate that has a key over all disjuncts of Q, which does not depend on the input database D. Clearly, the number of repairs of $\mathsf{rep}(D, \Sigma)$ that entail Q is the number

$$\left| \bigcup_{(Q',h) \in \mathsf{cert}(D)} [B_1, \ldots, B_n]^{\sigma(Q',h)} \right|.$$

Therefore, the fact that $\#\mathsf{CQA}(Q, \Sigma)$ is in SpanL can be shown via a guess-check-expand algorithm. Actually, the logspace NTT presented in Algorithm 1 is such an algorithm:

(1) **(Guess)** It first guesses a candidate certificate (Q', h).
(2) **(Check)** If $h(Q') \nsubseteq D$ or $h(Q') \not\models \Sigma$, then it rejects.
(3) **(Expand)** It expands (Q', h) into an encoding of a solution witnessed by (Q', h) as follows: for $i = 1$ to n, if $h(Q') \cap B_i = \{R(\bar{t})\}$ and Σ has an R-key, then outputs $R(\bar{t})$; otherwise, it guesses a fact $\alpha \in B_i$ and outputs α.

Ubiquity of the Guess-Check-Expand Paradigm. It turned out that there are several natural problems that enjoy the above structural properties, and thus, can be placed in SpanL via the guess-check-expand paradigm. Here we give a partial list of such problems, which ask for the number of:

- Satisfying assignments of a positive kDNF formula.
- Non-independent sets of an undirected graph.
- Non-3-colorings of an undirected graph.
- Non-vertex-covers of an undirected graph.

Let us stress that the above list is by no means exhaustive, which is a strong indication that the guess-check-expand paradigm is a fundamental algorithm design paradigm that deserves our attention.

Problems Beyond Guess-Check-Expand. At this point, one may think that the structural properties discussed above are trivial, i.e., they are fulfilled by every problem inside SpanL. In such a case, all the functions inside SpanL admit a guess-check-expand algorithm, and thus, it would be of little use towards understanding how to limit the computational power of logarithmic-space NTTs, which in turn will lead to our new complexity classes. The small certificate property implies that the decision version of a counting problem is in L. Actually, this is how Theorem 3.4, which states that $\#\mathsf{CQA}_{>0}(\exists\mathbb{FO}^+)$ is in L, is shown. Thus, if a $\leq_{\mathrm{m}}^{\log}$-complete problem for SpanL enjoys the small certificate property, then L = NL. Hence, it is unlikely that $\leq_{\mathrm{m}}^{\log}$-complete problems for SpanL can be solved via guess-check-expand algorithms (this is shown in Theorem 4.3).

4.2 Guess-Check-Expand via Compactors

The previous discussion suggests that our new complexity classes inside SpanL, which will form the Λ-hierarchy, should be defined by relying on logarithmic-space NTTs whose computational power does not go beyond guess-check-expand algorithms. In other words, we should limit the nondeterminism of logspace NTTs in such a way that they can only implement algorithms that follow the guess-check-expand paradigm. However, it is not clear at all how this can be achieved, while keeping the definition of the obtained class of NTTs compact and elegant.

Towards such an elegant definition, we observe that the "solutions via certificate expansion" property essentially tells us the following. On an input x, assuming that $S_1, \ldots, S_n$ are the solution domains, for a valid certificate $c \in \mathsf{cert}(x)$, we can deterministically compute in logspace a compact representation of $[S_1, \ldots, S_n]^{\sigma_c}$. This is simply the sequence of sets $S_1^{\sigma_c}, \ldots, S_n^{\sigma_c}$, while its unfolding

$$\mathsf{unfolding}\left(S_1^{\sigma_c}, \ldots, S_n^{\sigma_c}\right) = S_1^{\sigma_c} \times \cdots \times S_n^{\sigma_c}$$

gives us back the set $[S_1, \ldots, S_n]^{\sigma_c}$. Having this simple observation in place, we can implement guess-check-expand algorithms via deterministic logspace transducers, called *compactors*, which are responsible for computing compact representations as the one above. Somehow, a logspace compactor implements the deterministic part of a guess-check-expand algorithm, while the nondeterministic part is taken care by the unfolding of the compact representations. As we shall see, logspace compactors, together with the notion of unfolding, will allow us to provide an elegant definition for our hierarchy. Before giving the formal definitions, let us give some more details how compactors work.

Logspace Compactors and Unfolding. Consider a function f that enjoys the two main properties. Let x be an input instance, and $S_1, \ldots, S_n$ the solution domains. A logspace compactor M_f accepts as input x and a candidate certificate c, and performs two steps:

(1) **(Check)** If c is not valid, then output ϵ and halt.
(2) **(Compact)** For $i = 1$ to n, if the selector σ_c determined by c mentions (i, e), then output $\{e\}$; else, output S_i.

Let $\mathsf{unfolding}(\epsilon) = \emptyset$, and assume that $\mathsf{ccert}(x)$ collects all the candidate small certificates. It is not difficult to see that

$$f(x) = \left| \bigcup_{c \in \mathsf{ccert}(x)} \mathsf{unfolding}\left(M_f(x, c)\right) \right|.$$

Note that $\mathsf{unfolding}(\epsilon) = \emptyset$ reflects the fact that invalid candidate certificates should not be taken into count.

4.3 The Λ-hierarchy: Definition and Results

The previous, rather extensive, semi-formal discussion provides important insights on how to limit the power of logspace NTTs, which in turn will lead to our new complexity classes that form the Λ-hierarchy. This will be done via logspace compactors and unfolding as sketched above. We proceed with the formal definitions.

Shape of Compact Representations. We first need to fix the syntactic shape of compact representations, and formalize the notion of unfolding. Let $S_1, \dots, S_n \subseteq \{0,1\}^*$ be non-empty sets of strings, where $n \geq 0$; assume that, for $i \in \{1, \dots, n\}$, $S_i = \{s_i^1, \dots, s_i^{\ell_i}\}$. We write $[\![S_1, \dots, S_n]\!]^k$, where $k \geq 0$, for the set of strings

$$\{\epsilon\} \cup \{s_1\$s_2\$\cdots\$s_n \mid \text{either } s_i \in S_i \text{ or } s_i = \#s_i^1\$\cdots\$s_i^{\ell_i}\# \text{ and } |\{i \in \{1, \dots, n\} \mid s_i \in S_i\}| \leq k\}.$$

Given a string $s_1\$\cdots\$s_n \in [\![S_1, \dots, S_n]\!]^k \setminus \{\epsilon\}$, we define

$$\mathsf{unf}(s_i) = \begin{cases} \{s_i\} & \text{if } s_i \in S_i \\ S_i & \text{otherwise,} \end{cases}$$

for each $i \in \{1, \dots, n\}$. The *unfolding* of $s \in [\![S_1, \dots, S_n]\!]^k$, denoted $\mathsf{unfolding}(s)$, is defined as

$$\begin{cases} \mathsf{unf}(s_1) \times \cdots \times \mathsf{unf}(s_n) & \text{if } s = s_1\$\cdots\$s_n \\ \emptyset & \text{if } s = \epsilon. \end{cases}$$

Logspace Compactors. We are now ready to introduce logspace compactors. A *logspace 2-2-transducer* has two read-only two-way input tapes. Our logspace compactors are essentially logspace 2-2-transducers that output strings of the shape introduced above. We use the notion of *certificate function*, which is a logspace computable function $g : \{0,1\}^* \to \mathbb{N}$ such that $g(x) \in O(\log |x|)$.

Definition 4.1 (**Logspace Compactor**). A *logspace k-compactor*, where $k \geq 0$, is a logspace 2-2-transducer M such that, for some certificate function g, the following holds: for each $x \in \{0,1\}^*$, there are non-empty sets $S_1, \dots, S_n \subseteq \{0,1\}^*$, for $n \geq 0$, such that, for each $c \in \{0,1\}^*$ with $|c| \leq g(x)$, $M(x,c) \in [\![S_1, \dots, S_n]\!]^k$. ■

In simple words, a logspace k-compactor accepts as input an instance $x \in \{0,1\}^*$, and a candidate certificate $c \in \{0,1\}^*$ of logarithmic size, and outputs ϵ, or a compact representation of $[S_1, \dots, S_n]^{\sigma_c}$, where σ_c is the ℓ-selector for $S_1, \dots, S_n$ determined by c.

The Λ-hierarchy. Given a logspace k-compactor M, let unfold_M be the function $\{0,1\}^* \to \mathbb{N}$ such that $\mathsf{unfold}_M(x)$ is the number

$$\left| \bigcup_{c \in \{0,1\}^*, |c| \leq g(x)} \mathsf{unfolding}(M(x,c)) \right|.$$

For each $k \geq 0$, we can then define the complexity class

$$\Lambda[k] \;=\; \{\mathsf{unfold}_M \mid M \text{ is a logspace } k\text{-compactor}\}.$$

The Λ-hierarchy is defined as the infinite union

$$\Lambda \;=\; \bigcup_{k \geq 0} \Lambda[k].$$

We proceed to establish some fundamental results concerning the Λ-hierarchy. The first one is crucial for our analysis:

Proposition 4.2. *For each $k \geq 0$, $\Lambda[k]$ is closed under many-one logspace reductions.*

The above proposition, shown by exploiting the fact that many-one logspace reductions can be composed, simply says that, if $f \leq_{\mathrm{m}}^{\log} g$ and $g \in \Lambda[k]$, then $f \in \Lambda[k]$. The next result confirms that Λ is a hierarchy of classes inside SpanL:

Theorem 4.3. $\Lambda[0] \subseteq \Lambda[1] \subseteq \cdots \subseteq \Lambda \subseteq \mathrm{SpanL}$*; furthermore, unless* $\mathrm{L} = \mathrm{NL}$, $\Lambda \subsetneq \mathrm{SpanL}$.

The fact that $\Lambda[i] \subseteq \Lambda[i+1]$, for $i \geq 0$, follows by definition. For showing that $\Lambda \subseteq \mathrm{SpanL}$, we essentially show that a logspace k-compactor, for $k \geq 0$, can be converted into a logspace NTT that follows the guess-check-expand paradigm. This should be already clear from the previous semi-formal discussion on guess-check-expand algorithms and logspace compactors. Finally, for showing that $\Lambda \subsetneq \mathrm{SpanL}$ (unless $\mathrm{L} = \mathrm{NL}$), we first establish that, for every $f \in \Lambda$, its decision version $f_{>0}$ is in L; the latter uses the fact that the existence of a solution is witnessed by a small, logspace verifiable, certificate. Since every problem in NL is the decision version of some problem in SpanL, $\mathrm{SpanL} \subseteq \Lambda$ implies $\mathrm{L} = \mathrm{NL}$.

The next result establishes that, apart from $\Lambda[0]$ and $\Lambda[1]$, the rest of the hierarchy consists of "hard" classes:

Theorem 4.4. *The following statements hold:*
(1) $\Lambda[1] \subseteq \#\mathrm{L}$*; furthermore, unless* $\mathrm{L} = \mathrm{NL}$, $\Lambda[1] \subsetneq \#\mathrm{L}$.
(2) $\mathrm{FP}^{\Lambda[2]} = \mathrm{FP}^{\#\mathrm{P}}$.

For showing that $\Lambda[1] \subseteq \#\mathrm{L}$, for every function $f \in \Lambda[1]$, we provide a logspace NTM M_f such that, for each $x \in \{0,1\}^*$, $f(x) = \mathsf{accept}_{M_f}(x)$. The fact that the inclusion is strict (unless $\mathrm{L} = \mathrm{NL}$) is a consequence of (i) for each $f \in \Lambda[1]$, $f_{>0} \in \mathrm{L}$ (actually, as discussed above, this holds for the whole hierarchy), and (ii) every problem in NL is the decision version of a problem in #L. For showing the second claim, i.e., $\mathrm{FP}^{\Lambda[2]} = \mathrm{FP}^{\#\mathrm{P}}$, it suffices to show $\mathrm{FP}^{\#\mathrm{P}} \subseteq \mathrm{FP}^{\Lambda[2]}$ (the other direction is trivial), which is equivalent to $\#\mathrm{P} \subseteq \mathrm{FP}^{\Lambda[2]}$. The latter boils down to showing that there exists $f \in \Lambda[2]$ that is $\leq_{\mathrm{T}}^{\mathrm{P}}$-complete for #P. Such a function is #Pos2DNF, which computes the number of satisfying assignments of a positive 2DNF formula. Indeed, we can easily show that #Pos2DNF $\in \Lambda[2]$, while the #P-hardness is implicit in [12]; for a formal proof see [8].

The second statement of Theorem 4.4 has a couple of interesting implications, which confirm that beyond $\Lambda[1]$ we deal with "hard" complexity classes. More precisely, the fact that $\mathrm{FP}^{\Lambda[2]} = \mathrm{FP}^{\#\mathrm{P}}$, combined with the fact that the polynomial-hierarchy (PH) is included in $\mathrm{P}^{\#\mathrm{P}}$ (this is a consequence of Toda's powerful theorem [13]), we get that:

Corollary 4.5. *(1) If* $\Lambda[2] \subseteq \mathrm{FP}$*, then* $\mathrm{P} = \mathrm{NP}$.
(2) $\mathrm{PH} \subseteq \mathrm{P}^{\Lambda[2]} = \mathrm{P}^{\#\mathrm{P}}$.

Notice that claim (1) of Theorem 4.4, together with claim (1) of the above corollary, imply that the 1st level of the Λ-hierarchy is strictly contained in the 2nd level, unless $\mathrm{P} = \mathrm{NP}$. We can also show, assuming that there are infinitely many Mersenne primes, i.e., prime numbers of the form $2^n - 1$, for some integer n, that the 0th level is strictly contained in the 1st level. The above assumption is known as the Lenstra-Pomerance-Wagstaff conjecture. Therefore:

Proposition 4.6. *(1) Unless* $\mathrm{P} = \mathrm{NP}$, $\Lambda[1] \subsetneq \Lambda[2]$.
(2) Unless the Lenstra-Pomerance-Wagstaff conjecture does not hold, $\Lambda[0] \subsetneq \Lambda[1]$.

This brings us to the crucial question whether the same can be established (possibly under reasonable assumptions) for the other levels of the hierarchy. Unfortunately, we do not known whether the inclusions beyond $\Lambda[2]$ are strict. This essentially asks whether the Λ-hierarchy collapses to its kth level for some $k \geq 2$, i.e., whether $\Lambda = \Lambda[k]$. This is a difficult question that, despite our efforts, has remained open. We strongly believe that:

Conjecture 4.7. *The Λ-hierarchy does not collapse.*

An interesting issue is whether our new classes ensure the existence of efficient approximation schemes; this is studied in Section 6. But now the question is whether the Λ-hierarchy serves its purpose. This is the subject of the next section.

5 COMPLEXITY OF #CQA($\exists\mathbb{FO}^+$)

We are now ready to analyze the complexity of #CQA($\exists\mathbb{FO}^+$) under the lenses of many-one logspace reductions. We first study, in Section 5.1, the question whether a covering function for #CQA($\exists\mathbb{FO}^+$) that allows to pinpoint the data complexity of the parameterized version of the problem exists. Then, in Section 5.2, we partially answer the question whether we can characterize the data complexity of #CQA($\exists\mathbb{FO}^+$) via a class $C \subseteq$ SpanL.

Input: a database D, and a pair (Q', h)
Output: a string from $[\![B_1, \ldots, B_n]\!]^k$

```
if h(Q') ⊈ D or h(Q') ⊭ Σ then
    halt;
i := 1;
while i ≤ n do
    if B_i ∩ h(Q') = {R(t̄)} and Σ has an R-key then
        output R(t̄);
    else
        output #α_i^1$ ··· $α_i^{ℓ_i}#;
    if i < n then
        output $;
    i := i + 1;
```

Algorithm 2: The k-compactor $M_{Q,\Sigma}$.

5.1 #CQA($\exists\mathbb{FO}^+$) and the Keywidth Function

Recall that the keywidth function (kw) maps pairs (Q, Σ), where $Q \in \exists\mathbb{FO}^+$ and Σ is a set of primary keys, to $\mathbb{N}$, while

$$kw(Q, \Sigma) = |\{R(\bar{t}) \mid R(\bar{t}) \text{ occurs in } Q, \text{ and } \Sigma \text{ has an } R\text{-key}\}|.$$

It is clear that kw is a covering function for #CQA($\exists\mathbb{FO}^+$). We focus on the parameterized version of #CQA($\exists\mathbb{FO}^+$), denoted $\#\mathrm{CQA}_k^{kw}(\exists\mathbb{FO}^+)$, which is defined in the same way as #CQA($\exists\mathbb{FO}^+$) with the key difference that the input query Q and set Σ of primary keys are such that $kw(Q, \Sigma) = k$.

Theorem 5.1. $\#\mathrm{CQA}_k^{kw}(\exists\mathbb{FO}^+)$ *is* $\leq_{\mathrm{m}}^{\log}$*-complete for* $\Lambda[k]$.

For brevity, let $\mathsf{F}_k^{kw} = \{\#\mathrm{CQA}(Q, \Sigma) \mid kw(Q, \Sigma) = k\}$. The above result boils down to showing that, for each $k \geq 0$:

(1) **(Membership)** For each $f \in \mathsf{F}_k^{kw}$, $f \in \Lambda[k]$.
(2) **(Hardness)** There exists $f \in \mathsf{F}_k^{kw}$ that is $\leq_{\mathrm{m}}^{\log}$-complete for $\Lambda[k]$.

The rest of this subsection is devoted to showing the above statements. In the sequel, fix an arbitrary $k \geq 0$.

Proof of Membership

Since an existential positive query can be converted into a UCQ, we can assume that the function $f \in \mathsf{F}_k^{kw}$ is of the form #CQA(Q, Σ), where $Q \in \mathbb{UCQ}$, and Σ is a set of primary keys. We need to show that #CQA(Q, Σ) is a function of the form unfold_M, where M is a logspace k-compactor. Actually, we simply need to convert the guess-check-expand NTT, depicted in Algorithm 1, into a check-compact transducer. It should be clear from our semi-formal discussion how this can be done, but, for the sake of completeness, we provide here the details and the formal definition.

Consider the 2-2-transducer $M_{Q,\Sigma}$, depicted in Algorithm 2 (notice the similarity with Algorithm 1), that accepts as input a database D, and a candidate certificate (Q', h), where Q' is a disjunct of Q and $h : \mathsf{var}(Q') \to \mathsf{dom}(D)$. The database D is stored on the first tape, while the pair (Q', h) on the second tape. As usual, $B_1, \dots, B_n$ is the sequence of the sets of $\mathsf{block}_\Sigma(D)$ induced by $\prec_{D,\Sigma}$. For brevity, let $B_i = \{\alpha_i^1, \dots, \alpha_i^{\ell_i}\}$, for each $i \in \{1, \dots, n\}$. Let us clarify that if the transducer halts without writing anything on the output tape, this means that the output tape contains the empty string ϵ. It can be shown that $M_{Q,\Sigma}$ uses only logarithmic-space; in fact, the argument is the same as for the logspace NTT depicted in Algorithm 1. It is also clear that $M_{Q,\Sigma}$ is a k-compactor. Notice that the latter is a consequence of the fact that the number of atoms $R(\bar{t})$ occurring in Q' such that Σ has an R-key is at most k, which in turn implies that indeed $M_{Q,\Sigma}(D, (Q', h)) \in [\![B_1, \dots, B_n]\!]^k$. Finally, with C being the set of all candidate certificates, i.e., pairs of the form (Q', h), where Q' is a disjunct of Q, and $h : \mathsf{var}(Q') \to \mathsf{dom}(D)$, it is easy to see that the number of repairs that entail Q is

$$\left| \bigcup_{(Q',h) \in C} \mathsf{unfolding}\left(M_{Q,\Sigma}(D, (Q', h))\right) \right|,$$

and the claim follows.

Proof of Hardness

We proceed to show that there exists a query $Q \in \exists\mathbb{FO}^+$ (actually, a conjunctive query), and a set Σ of primary keys, with $kw(Q, \Sigma) = k$, such that, for every function $\lambda \in \Lambda[k]$, λ is many-one logspace reducible to $\#\mathsf{CQA}(Q, \Sigma)$. The conjunctive query Q is defined as

$$\exists x_1 \exists y_1 \cdots \exists x_k \exists y_k \exists z \Big(\mathrm{Selector}(z, x_1, y_1, \dots, x_k, y_k) \wedge \bigwedge_{i=1}^{k} \mathrm{Element}(x_i, y_i) \Big),$$

while the set Σ consists of the single key

$$\mathsf{key}(\mathrm{Element}) = \{1\}.$$

Roughly, the predicate Selector stores ℓ-selectors, with $\ell \leq k$, for the solution domains, while the predicate Element stores elements of the solution domains (e.g., Element(i, s) refers to the element s from the ith solution domain). It is clear that $kw(Q, \Sigma) = k$. We proceed to show that, for each function $\lambda \in \Lambda[k]$, $\lambda \leq_{\mathrm{m}}^{\log} \#\mathsf{CQA}(Q, \Sigma)$.

Fix $\lambda \in \Lambda[k]$. By definition, λ is a function of the form unfold_M, where M is a logspace k-compactor. Therefore, for some certificate function g, the following holds: for each $x \in \{0, 1\}^*$, there are non-empty sets $S_1, \dots, S_n \subseteq \{0, 1\}^*$ such that, for each $c \in \{0, 1\}^*$ with $|c| \leq g(x)$, $M(x, c) \in [\![S_1, \dots, S_n]\!]^k$. Consider an arbitrary instance $x \in \{0, 1\}^*$. We define the database D_x as the union of two databases: $D_{element}$ and $D_{selector}$. The first one collects all the elements of the solution domains that the compactor outputs:

$$\begin{aligned}&\{\mathrm{Element}(\star, \star)\} \cup \\ &\{\mathrm{Element}(i, s) \mid i \in \{1, \dots, n\}, s \in S_i, \text{ and there exists} \\ &\qquad c \in \{0, 1\}^* \text{ with } |c| \leq g(x) \text{ such that} \\ &\qquad M(x, c) = s_1\$ \cdots \$s_n \text{ with } s_i = s \text{ or } s_i = \# \cdots s \cdots \#\}.\end{aligned}$$

Let us clarify that Element$(\star, \star)$ is an auxiliary fact, which is needed for dealing with selectors that select less than k elements. The other database collects all the ℓ-selectors for the solution domains. For brevity, given a string $s_1\$ \cdots \$s_n \in [\![S_1, \dots, S_n]\!]^k$, let $\mathsf{single}(s_1\$ \cdots \$s_n) = \{(i, s_i) \mid i \in \{1, \dots, n\} \text{ and } s_i \in S_i\}$. Let also $C = \{c \in \{0, 1\}^* \mid |c| \leq g(x), M(x, c) \neq \epsilon\}$. $D_{selector}$ follows:

$$\bigcup_{c \in C} \Big\{ \mathrm{Selector}(c, i_1, s_1, \dots, i_\ell, s_\ell, \underbrace{\star, \dots, \star}_{2(k-\ell)}) \mid \mathsf{single}(M(x, c)) = \big\{(i_j, s_j)\big\}_{j \in \{1, \dots, \ell\}} \Big\}.$$

This completes the definition of D_x. We can show that

$$\lambda(x) = |\{D \in \mathsf{rep}(D_x, \Sigma) \mid D \models Q\}|.$$

This is done by exhibiting a bijection

$$h : \{D \in \mathsf{rep}(D_x, \Sigma) \mid D \models Q\} \to \bigcup_{\substack{c \in \{0,1\}^* \\ |c| \leq g(x)}} \mathsf{unfolding}(M(x, c));$$

$h(D') = s_1, \dots, s_n$, where, for $i \in \{1, \dots, n\}$, Element$(i, s_i) \in D' \setminus$ Element$(\star, \star)$. We can also show, via simulation of the compactor M, that D_x can be constructed in logarithmic space. Thus, the above is a many-one logspace reduction.

5.2 Non-parameterized #CQA($\exists\mathbb{FO}^+$)

We now focus our attention on #CQA($\exists\mathbb{FO}^+$). By exploiting Theorem 5.1, we can partially answer the question whether there is a class $C \subsetneq$ SpanL, closed under many-one logspace reductions, such that #CQA($\exists\mathbb{FO}^+$) is $\leq_{\mathrm{m}}^{\log}$-complete for C.

THEOREM 5.2. *The following are equivalent:*

1. *There exists a complexity class $C \subsetneq$ SpanL, closed under many-one logspace reductions, such that #CQA($\exists\mathbb{FO}^+$) is $\leq_{\mathrm{m}}^{\log}$-complete for C in data complexity.*
2. *There exists an integer $k \geq 0$ such that #CQA($\exists\mathbb{FO}^+$) is $\leq_{\mathrm{m}}^{\log}$-complete for $\Lambda[k]$ in data complexity.*
3. *The Λ-hierarchy collapses.*

Theorem 5.2 essentially tells that either #CQA($\exists\mathbb{FO}^+$) is $\leq_{\mathrm{m}}^{\log}$-complete for $\Lambda[k]$, for some $k \geq 0$, or there is no complexity class $C \subsetneq$ SpanL, closed under logspace reductions, such that #CQA($\exists\mathbb{FO}^+$) is $\leq_{\mathrm{m}}^{\log}$-complete for C. Thus, the right complexity class that characterizes the data complexity of our problem, if it exists, is one of the levels of the Λ-hierarchy. Moreover, whether such a class exists boils down to the question whether the Λ-hierarchy collapses. Thus, the latter question begs for an answer, which will complete the picture concerning the data complexity of #CQA($\exists\mathbb{FO}^+$).

6 EFFICIENT APPROXIMATION SCHEMES

When a counting problem is computationally hard, it is natural to approximate it. In general, approximations to such problems can be computed via randomized algorithms with some probabilistic guarantees. Here we target fully polynomial-time randomized approximations schemes, FPRAS for short. As we shall see, for arbitrary first-order queries, our problem does not admit an FPRAS (under a reasonable assumption). On the other hand, for positive existential queries, we already know that our problem admits an FPRAS; this is implicit in [5]. However, by exploiting the fact that, for every $Q \in \exists\mathbb{FO}^+$ and set Σ of primary keys, #CQA(Q, Σ) is in $\Lambda[kw(Q, \Sigma)]$, we can provide a conceptually simpler FPRAS. But let us first recall some basic notions.

Probability Spaces and Random Variables. A *probability space* is a pair PS $= (\Omega, \pi)$, where Ω is a finite set, called *sample space*, and $\pi : \Omega \rightarrow [0, 1]$ is a function such that $\sum_{\omega \in \Omega} \pi(\omega) = 1$. A subset $E \subseteq \Omega$ is called an *event*. The probability of an event E, denoted $\Pr(E)$, is defined as $\sum_{\omega \in E} \pi(\omega)$. A *random variable* over PS is a function $X : \Omega \rightarrow \mathbb{Q}$. The *probability distribution* of X is a function π_X from the image of X to $[0, 1]$ such that $\pi_X(x) = \Pr(X = x)$, where $X = x$ denotes the event $\{\omega \in \Omega \mid X(\omega) = x\}$.

FPRAS. Consider a function $f : \{0, 1\}^* \rightarrow \mathbb{N}$. A *fully polynomial-time randomized approximation scheme* (FPRAS) for f is a randomized algorithm A that accepts as input $x \in \{0, 1\}^*$, and numbers $\epsilon > 0$ and $0 < \delta < 1$, runs in polynomial time in $|x|$, $1/\epsilon$ and $\log(1/\delta)$, and produces a random variable $\mathsf{A}(x, \epsilon, \delta)$ such that

$$\Pr(|\mathsf{A}(x, \epsilon, \delta) - f(x)| \leq \epsilon \cdot f(x)) \geq 1 - \delta.$$

Let us clarify that, assuming the random variable $\mathsf{A}(x, \epsilon, \delta)$ is over the sample space (Ω, π), $|\mathsf{A}(x, \epsilon, \delta) - f(x)| \leq \epsilon \cdot f(x)$ denotes the event $\{\omega \in \Omega \mid |\mathsf{A}(x, \epsilon, \delta)(\omega) - f(x)| \leq \epsilon \cdot f(x)\}$.

6.1 Approximation via FPRAS

As said above, for arbitrary first-order queries, our problem does not admit an FPRAS, under the assumption that RP $\neq$ NP. This is a consequence of the fact that #CQA($\mathbb{FO}$) is $\leq_{\mathrm{m}}^{\log}$-complete for #P (Theorem 3.3). Recall that RP is the class of problems that are efficiently solvable by a randomized algorithm with a bounded one-sided error (i.e., the answer may mistakenly be "no") [3].

```
Input: a string x ∈ {0,1}*
Output: 0 or 1

for i = 1 to n do
  | choose s_i ∈ S_i with probability 1/|S_i|;
if there exists c ∈ {0,1}* with |c| ≤ g(x) such that
(s_1, ..., s_n) ∈ unfolding(M(x, c)) then
  | return 1;
else
  | return 0;
```

Algorithm 3: The randomized algorithm Sample.

THEOREM 6.1. *Unless* RP = NP, *there exists a query* $Q \in \mathbb{FO}$ *and a set* Σ *of primary keys such that* #CQA(Q, Σ) *does not admit an FPRAS.*

We now proceed to provide an FPRAS for the case of positive existential queries which, as mentioned above, is conceptually simpler than the one inherited from [5]. Actually, we are going to establish a more general result, which will immediately imply the desired FPRAS. Interestingly, we can show that every problem that falls in the Λ-hierarchy admits such a conceptually simple FPRAS:

THEOREM 6.2. *For* $k \geq 0$, *every function in* $\Lambda[k]$ *admits an FPRAS.*

PROOF. Fix $k \geq 0$, and consider a function $f \in \Lambda[k]$. By definition, f is a function of the form unfold_M, where M is a logspace k-compactor. Let g be the certificate function associated with M. Consider an arbitrary $x \in \{0, 1\}^*$, and let $S_1, \ldots, S_n \subseteq \{0, 1\}^*$ be the solution domains of M on input x. The FPRAS for f relies on a randomized algorithm, called Sample, which is depicted in Algorithm 3. We define U as the cartesian product $S_1 \times \cdots \times S_n$. We can show that:

LEMMA 6.3. *The following statements hold:*

(1) Sample(x) *terminates after polynomially many steps.*

(2) $\Pr(\mathsf{Sample}(x) = 1) = \frac{f(x)}{|U|}$.

Sample is a polynomial-time randomized algorithm that, on input x, outputs a random variable X_x over (U, π), with π being the uniform distribution, that maps U to $\{0, 1\}$, and $\Pr(X_x = 1) = \frac{f(x)}{|U|}$. Consider now the random variable

$$X_x^{(t)} = \frac{|U|}{t} \cdot \sum_{i=1}^{t} X_x^i,$$

where $t > 0$, and $X_x^1, \ldots, X_x^t$ are independent random variables, which are essentially copies of X_x. Having $X_x^{(t)}$ in place, we define the randomized algorithm Apx_f, which accepts as input x, and numbers $\epsilon > 0$ and $0 < \delta < 1$, and performs the following steps:

(1) $m := \max_{1 \leq i \leq n} \{|S_i|\}$;
(2) $t := \frac{(2+\epsilon)m^k}{\epsilon^2} \cdot \ln\left(\frac{2}{\delta}\right)$;
(3) return $X_x^{(t)}$.

It is easy to see that Apx_f runs in polynomial time in $|x|$, $1/\epsilon$ and $\ln(1/\delta)$. It remains to show that Apx_f is indeed an FPRAS for f. To this end, we exploit Chernoff's inequality. Since $X_x^{(t)}$ is the product of $|U|$ and the random mean of t Bernoulli random variables,

$$\Pr\left(\left|X_x^{(t)} - f(x)\right| \leq \epsilon \cdot f(x)\right) \geq 1 - 2e^{-\frac{t\epsilon^2}{2+\epsilon} \cdot \frac{f(x)}{|U|}}.$$

By replacing t with $\frac{(2+\epsilon)m^k}{\epsilon^2} \cdot \ln\left(\frac{2}{\delta}\right)$, we obtain that

$$\Pr\left(\left|X_x^{(t)} - f(x)\right| \leq \epsilon \cdot f(x)\right) \geq 1 - 2e^{-m^k \cdot \ln\left(\frac{2}{\delta}\right) \cdot \frac{f(x)}{|U|}}.$$

Observe that, if we could replace $\frac{f(x)}{|U|}$ with $\frac{1}{m^k}$, then

$$\Pr\left(\left|X_x^{(t)} - f(x)\right| \leq \epsilon \cdot f(x)\right) \geq 1 - \delta,$$

which proves the claim. Thus, it remains to show that $\frac{f(x)}{|U|} \geq \frac{1}{m^k}$. Consider a small certificate $c \in \{0,1\}^*$ with $|c| \leq g(x)$, and let $s = s_1\$ \cdots \$s_n = M(x,c)$. Since M is a k-compactor, $|\mathsf{single}(s)| = \ell \leq k$; recall that $\mathsf{single}(s) = \{(i, s_i) \mid s_i \in S_i\}$. We can assume, w.l.o.g., that $\mathsf{single}(s) = \{(i, s_i)\}_{1 \leq i \leq \ell}$. Hence,

$$|\mathsf{unfolding}(M(x,c))| = \prod_{i=\ell+1}^{n} |S_i|.$$

By definition of $\Lambda[k]$, $f(x) \geq |\mathsf{unfolding}(M(x,c))|$. Thus,

$$\frac{f(x)}{|U|} \geq \frac{\prod_{i=\ell+1}^{n} |S_i|}{\prod_{i=1}^{n} |S_i|} = \frac{1}{\prod_{i=1}^{\ell} |S_i|} \geq \frac{1}{\prod_{i=1}^{k} |S_i|}.$$

Recall that $m = \max_{1 \leq i \leq n} \{|S_i|\}$. Consequently,

$$\frac{f(x)}{|U|} \geq \frac{1}{\prod_{i=1}^{k} m} = \frac{1}{m^k},$$

and the claim follows. □

An immediate corollary of Theorem 6.2 is that:

Corollary 6.4. *For every query $Q \in \exists\mathbb{FO}^+$ and set Σ of primary keys, #CQA(Q, Σ) admits an FPRAS.*

As already said, it is known that the above statement holds. In particular, in [5] it is shown that, for every positive existential Boolean query Q, the problem of computing the probability of Q over a disjoint-independent probabilistic database, denoted $\mathsf{DisjPDB}(Q)$, admits an FPRAS.[1] But, it is an easy task, given a query $Q \in \exists\mathbb{FO}^+$ and a set Σ of primary keys, to reduce #CQA(Q, Σ) to $\mathsf{DisjPDB}(Q)$ via an approximation-preserving polynomial-time Turing reduction, which in turn implies that #CQA(Q, Σ) admits an FPRAS. Therefore, the novelty here is not the statement itself, but the actual FPRAS, which is conceptually simpler than the one inherited from [5].

[1]In fact, the result is given for conjunctive queries, but it can be easily generalized to positive existential queries.

The simplicity of our FPRAS lies in the fact that we can sample from the natural sample space, i.e., the solution domains of the problem (see Algorithm 3). This is not the case for $\mathsf{DisjPDB}(Q)$, where the natural sample space consists of all the possible worlds of the probabilistic database. However, by using this sample space, in general, we need exponentially many samples in order to achieve the desired error and confidence guarantees. Thus, the sampling should be performed over a more complex sample space consisting of pairs of the form (W, h), where W is a possible world, and h is a homomorphism from the query to the database.

7 MORE ON THE Λ-HIERARCHY

In this last section, we provide more completeness results for the Λ-hierarchy, which justifies even further its meaningfulness. This analysis led to the definition of another natural complexity class that goes beyond the Λ-hierarchy, but is still inside SpanL.

7.1 More Complete Problems

We present two families of problems that have a problem that is complete for every level of the Λ-hierarchy. The first one is about counting satisfying assignments of Boolean formulas, while the second one is about counting forbidden colorings for hypergraphs.

Counting Satisfying Assignments. Let $X = \{x_1, \ldots, x_n\}$ be a (possibly empty) set of Boolean variables, and let $P = \{X_1, \ldots, X_n\}$ be a partition of X. A *P-assignment* for X is a function $\mu : X \to \{0,1\}$ such that, for each $i \in \{1, \ldots, n\}$, exactly one $x \in X_i$ is such that $\mu(x) = 1$. A positive kDNF formula over X is a Boolean formula of the form $\varphi = C_1 \vee \cdots \vee C_n$, where each C_i is a conjunction of $\ell \leq k$ variables from X occurring positively in C_i, i.e., the variables occurring in φ form a subset of X. A P-assignment μ for X *satisfies* φ if $\mu(\varphi)$, i.e., the formula obtained after replacing each variable x with $\mu(x)$, evaluates to 1. Then:

PROBLEM :	#DisjPos$k$DNF
INPUT :	A set of variables X, a partition P of X, and a positive kDNF formula φ over X.
OUTPUT :	Number of P-assignments for X that satisfy φ.

The above problem is a generalization of the problem of counting the number of satisfying assignments of a positive kDNF formula, and is the counting variant of a probabilistic extension of kDNF presented in [5]. It is possible to show that, for each $k \geq 0$:

THEOREM 7.1. *#DisjPos$k$DNF is $\leq_{\mathrm{m}}^{\log}$-complete for $\Lambda[k]$.*

Counting Forbidden Colorings. Consider a hypergraph $H = (V, E)$; H is called *k-uniform*, for $k \geq 0$, if, for each $e \in E$, $|e| = k$. Let $C = \{C_v\}_{v \in V}$ be sets of colors for each node $v \in V$. A *C-assignment* for a set $S \subseteq V$ is a function $\mu : S \rightarrow \bigcup_{v \in V} C_v$ such that $\mu(v) \in C_v$. Given a set $F = \{F_e\}_{e \in E}$, where F_e is a set of C-assignments for e, a *forbidden C-coloring for H w.r.t. F* is a C-assignment μ for V such that, for some $e \in E$ and $\nu \in F_e$, $\mu(v) = \nu(v)$, for each $v \in e$. Then:

PROBLEM :	#kForbColoring
INPUT :	A k-uniform hypergraph $H = (V, E)$, sets of colors $C = \{C_v\}_{v \in V}$, and sets of C-assignments $F = \{F_e\}_{e \in E}$.
OUTPUT :	Number of forbidden C-colorings for H w.r.t. F.

The above problem generalizes the problem of counting the number of non-list-colorings of a hypergraph; see, e.g., [7]. It is possible to show that, for each $k \geq 0$:

THEOREM 7.2. *#kForbColoring is $\leq_{\mathrm{m}}^{\log}$-complete for $\Lambda[k]$.*

7.2 Beyond the Λ-hierarchy

The above results consider the "bounded" version of the problems in question; #DisjPos$k$DNF bounds the number of variables in a clause, while #kForbColoring the number of nodes in a hyperedge. But, what about the complexity of their "unbounded" version, i.e., #DisjPosDNF and #ForbColoring? This question led to a new complexity class, dubbed SpanLL, which is of independent interest, that goes beyond the Λ-hierarchy, but is strictly contained in SpanL (unless L = NL).

The Complexity Class SpanLL. As the reader may have already suspected, this class is defined in the same way as $\Lambda[k]$, for some $k \geq 0$, with the key difference that an arbitrary logspace compactor, instead of a k-compactor, is used, which is able to choose an element from an unbounded number of solution domains. Formally, with $[\![S_1, \ldots, S_n]\!]$ (as usual, $S_1, \ldots, S_n \subseteq \{0,1\}^*$ are non-empty sets of strings) defined as the set of strings

$$\{\epsilon\} \cup \{s_1\$s_2\$\cdots\$s_n \mid \text{ either } s_i \in S_i \text{ or } s_i = \#s_i^1\$\cdots\$s_i^{\ell_i}\#\},$$

i.e., is the same as $[\![S_1, \ldots, S_n]\!]^k$ but without the condition that $|\{i \in \{1, \ldots, n\} \mid s_i \in S_i\}| \leq k$, a *logspace compactor* is defined in exactly the same way as a logspace k-compactor (see Definition 4.1) with the crucial difference that $M(x, c) \in [\![S_1, \ldots, S_n]\!]$. Then:

$$\mathrm{SpanLL} \quad = \quad \{\mathsf{unfold}_M \mid M \text{ is a logspace compactor}\}.$$

We can indeed show that SpanLL goes beyond the Λ-hierarchy, buy stays inside SpanL. In particular:

THEOREM 7.3. $\Lambda \subseteq$ SpanLL $\subseteq$ SpanL; *furthermore, unless* L = NL, SpanLL $\subsetneq$ SpanL.

We can also show that:

THEOREM 7.4. *Every function in* SpanLL *admits an FPRAS.*

Notice, however, that for devising an FPRAS for functions from SpanLL, we are forced to sample from a more complex sample space, similar in spirit to that for DisjPDB(Q); see the discussion at the end of Section 6. Sampling from the natural sample space, i.e., the solution domains of the problem, will lead to an exponential time algorithm. Observe that the FPRAS given in the previous section for functions from $\Lambda[k]$ becomes exponential if we do not bound k.

Back to our Problems. Coming back to the problems in question, we can show the following:

THEOREM 7.5. *#DisjPosDNF and #ForbColoring are $\leq_{\mathrm{m}}^{\log}$-complete for* SpanLL.

An immediate consequence of Theorem 7.4 and Theorem 7.5 is that #DisjPosDNF and #ForbColoring admit an FPRAS. Notice, however, that for the "bounded" version of the problems, one can use the simpler FPRAS where the sampling is performed over the natural sample space.

8 THE NEXT STEPS

Although we have provided a definite answer to our second question (Theorem 5.1), our first question is only partially answered (Theorem 5.2). Providing a firm answer to this question boils down to answering the question whether the Λ-hierarchy collapses. Our conjecture is that it does not collapse. Proving or disproving this conjecture is one of our main priorities, which will complete the picture concerning the data complexity of #CQA($\exists\mathbb{FO}^+$).

We have stressed a couple of times that the new FPRAS provided for each level of the Λ-hierarchy is conceptually simpler than the one inherited from the literature. The question is how this will perform in practice. The right way to answer this question is to implement this approximation scheme, and design a proper set of experiments, which we intend to do in the followup work.

Acknowledgements. We thank the anonymous referees for their useful feedback. This work was supported by the EPSRC grant EP/S003800/1 EQUID, and the EPSRC Programme Grant EP/M025268/ VADA.

REFERENCES

[1] Carme Àlvarez and Birgit Jenner. 1993. A Very Hard log-Space Counting Class. *Theor. Comput. Sci.* 107, 1 (1993), 3–30.

[2] Marcelo Arenas, Leopoldo E. Bertossi, and Jan Chomicki. 1999. Consistent Query Answers in Inconsistent Databases. In *PODS*. 68–79.

[3] Sanjeev Arora and Boaz Barak. 2009. *Computational Complexity - A Modern Approach*. Cambridge University Press.

[4] Marco Calautti, Leonid Libkin, and Andreas Pieris. 2018. An Operational Approach to Consistent Query Answering. In *PODS*. 239–251.

[5] Nilesh N. Dalvi and Dan Suciu. 2007. Management of probabilistic data: foundations and challenges. In *PODS*. 1–12.

[6] Arnaud Durand, Miki Hermann, and Phokion G. Kolaitis. 2005. Subtractive reductions and complete problems for counting complexity classes. *Theor. Comput. Sci.* 340, 3 (2005), 496–513.

[7] Penny E. Haxell and Jacques Verstraëte. 2010. List Coloring Hypergraphs. *Electr. J. Comb.* 17, 1 (2010).

[8] Dany Maslowski and Jef Wijsen. 2013. A dichotomy in the complexity of counting database repairs. *J. Comput. Syst. Sci.* 79, 6 (2013), 958–983.

[9] Dany Maslowski and Jef Wijsen. 2014. Counting Database Repairs that Satisfy Conjunctive Queries with Self-Joins. In *ICDT*. 155–164.

[10] Aris Pagourtzis and Stathis Zachos. 2006. The Complexity of Counting Functions with Easy Decision Version. In *MFCS*. 741–752.

[11] Christos H. Papadimitriou. 1994. *Computational complexity*. Addison-Wesley.

[12] J Scott Provan and Michael O. Ball. 1983. The Complexity of Counting Cuts and of Computing the Probability that a Graph is Connected. *SIAM J. Comput.* 12 (1983), 777–788.

[13] Seinosuke Toda. 1991. PP is as Hard as the Polynomial-Time Hierarchy. *SIAM J. Comput.* 20, 5 (1991), 865–877.

The Complexity of Counting Cycles in the Adjacency List Streaming Model

John Kallaugher
UT Austin
jmgk@cs.utexas.edu

Andrew McGregor
UMass Amherst
mcgregor@cs.umass.edu

Eric Price
UT Austin
ecprice@cs.utexas.edu

Sofya Vorotnikova
UMass Amherst
svorotni@cs.umass.edu

ABSTRACT

We study the problem of counting cycles in the adjacency list streaming model, fully resolving in which settings there exist sublinear space algorithms. Our main upper bound is a two-pass algorithm for estimating triangles that uses $\widetilde{O}(m/T^{2/3})$ space, where m is the edge count and T is the triangle count of the graph. On the other hand, we show that no sublinear space multipass algorithm exists for counting ℓ-cycles for $\ell \geq 5$. Finally, we show that counting 4-cycles is intermediate: sublinear space algorithms exist in multipass but not single-pass settings.

CCS CONCEPTS

• **Theory of computation → Streaming, sublinear and near linear time algorithms**;

KEYWORDS

Data streams, triangles, cycles.

ACM Reference Format:
John Kallaugher, Andrew McGregor, Eric Price, and Sofya Vorotnikova. 2019. The Complexity of Counting Cycles in the Adjacency List Streaming Model. In *38th ACM SIGMOD-SIGACT-SIGAI Symposium on Principles of Database Systems (PODS'19), June 30-July 5, 2019, Amsterdam, Netherlands.* ACM, New York, NY, USA, 15 pages. https://doi.org/10.1145/3294052.3319706

ACM ISBN 978-1-4503-6227-6/19/06...$15.00
https://doi.org/10.1145/3294052.3319706

1 INTRODUCTION

Subgraph counting is a fundamental graph problem and an important primitive in massive graph analysis. It has many applications in data mining and analyzing the structure of large networks. In particular, triangle counting and the related problems of estimating the transitivity and clustering coefficients arise in spam detection [4], community detection in social networks [7], identification of web pages with a common topic [14], and evaluation of large graph models [24]; see Tsourakakis et al. [33] for an overview of applications.

Triangle counting has been studied in various models of computation for large inputs, such as MapReduce [32], other parallel models [2, 6], and external memory models [1]. In the data stream model, triangle counting was first introduced by Bar-Yossef, Kumar, and Sivakumar [3]. Subsequent work has studied algorithms in a number of streaming models [5, 9, 12, 13, 16–18, 21, 23, 26–28]. Other subgraphs have received less attention in the streaming community, with most work focused on cycles and cliques [5, 25, 28] and a few papers considering arbitrary subgraphs of constant size [5, 18, 20].

1.1 Prior Work

Triangle Counting. Two adversarial *insertion-only* streaming models have been studied in the literature: *arbitrary order*, where the edges can arrive in any order, and *adjacency list order*, where edges incident to the same vertex arrive together (and therefore every edge is required to appear twice). In discussing related work, we use T to denote the number of triangles in the graph and $\widetilde{O}(\cdot)$ to hide factors polynomial in $\log n$ and ε^{-1}. In the single-pass arbitrary order model, $\Omega(m)$ space is required to even distinguish between graphs with 0 and T triangles [9] for any $T < n$, and thus work has largely concentrated on providing space bounds parameterized by properties of the graph, such as the maximum degree [17, 28], tangle coefficient [28], number of paths of length two [16], or the maximum number of triangles sharing an edge or a vertex [18, 27]; see [5] for a summary of these results. The best known results without such additional

Cycle	Passes	Space	Comments	Source
Triangle	1	$\widetilde{O}(P_2/T)$	P_2 = number of paths of length two	[12]
	1	$\widetilde{O}(m/\sqrt{T})$	-	[26]
	3	$\widetilde{O}(\sqrt{m} + m^{3/2}/T)$	-	[21]
	3	$\widetilde{O}(m^{3/2}/T)$	-	[26]
	2	$\widetilde{O}(m/T^{2/3})$	Distinguishing between 0 and T triangles	[26]
	2	$\widetilde{O}(m/T^{2/3})$	-	Theorem 3.7
	1	$\Omega(f_{pj}(m/\sqrt{T}))$	$\Omega(f_{pj}(r))$ = communication complexity of 3-PJ$_r$; $T = O(m)$	Theorem 5.1
	const	$\Omega(f_d(m/T^{2/3}))$	$\Omega(f_d(r))$ = communication complexity of 3-DISJ$_r$; $T = O(m^{3/2})$	Theorem 5.2
$\ell = 4$	2	$\widetilde{O}(m/T^{3/8})$	$O(1)$-factor approximation	Theorem 4.6
	1	$\Omega(m)$	$T = O(n^{1/3})$	Theorem 5.3
	const	$\Omega(m/T^{2/3})$	$T = O(n^{3/4})$	Theorem 5.4
$\ell \geq 5$	const	$\Omega(m)$	$T = O(n)$	Theorem 5.5

Table 1: Cycle counting in adjacency list insertion-only streams. Unless specified otherwise, upper bounds are for $(1+\varepsilon)$-estimating the number of cycles and lower bounds for distinguishing between graphs with 0 and T cycles.

parameters are either the trivial $O(m)$ or—for graphs with many triangles—$\widetilde{O}(mn/T)$ [12].

More recently, it has been shown that algorithms using a constant number of passes over the stream can achieve sublinear space for any $T = \omega(1)$. The optimal lower bound depending on m and T only was given by Bera and Chakrabarti in [5]. They proved an $\Omega(\min\{m^{3/2}/T, m/\sqrt{T}\})$ bound and gave an $\widetilde{O}(m^{3/2}/T)$ space algorithm matching one of the terms. Independently, McGregor, Vorotnikova, and Vu [26] gave two algorithms matching both terms of the lower bound, and Cormode and Jowhari [13] gave a different algorithm with $\widetilde{O}(m/\sqrt{T})$ space[1].

In the adjacency list model, on the other hand, it is possible to achieve sublinear space without additional parameters. Prior to this work, the two state-of-the-art algorithms for $(1+\varepsilon)$-approximating the number of triangles were a single-pass algorithm using $\widetilde{O}(m/\sqrt{T})$ space and a two-pass algorithm using $\widetilde{O}(m^{3/2}/T)$ space by McGregor et al. [26]. They also gave a two-pass algorithm for distinguishing triangle-free graphs from those with at least T triangles that uses only $\widetilde{O}(m/T^{2/3})$ space.

Counting Other Subgraphs. Prior to this work, counting constant size subgraphs other than triangles had only been considered in the arbitrary order setting.

Bera and Chakrabarti [5] describe an algorithm $(1+\varepsilon)$-approximating the number of occurrences of a particular subgraph H of size h using $\widetilde{O}(m^{\beta(H)}/T)$ space and two passes over the stream, where $\beta(H)$ denotes the size of an edge cover of H. They improve on this algorithm for cliques and cycles, achieving $\widetilde{O}(m^{h/2}/T)$ space, and provide a matching lower bound. For single-pass algorithms they show lower bounds of $\Omega(m^h/T^2)$ for cliques and odd-length cycles and $\Omega(m^{h/2}/T)$ for even-length cycles. Kallaugher and Price [18] presented an algorithm for counting copies of an arbitrary subgraph H which depends on how much the subgraphs overlap with each other; it is sublinear as long as no constant-size set of vertices contains a constant fraction of the copies of H.

1.2 Our Setting

Streaming model. We consider the *adjacency list* streaming model. In this model, we assume that the stream consists of a sequence of ordered pairs xy. For each edge $\{x, y\}$, both xy and yx will be present in the stream. The promise on the ordering is that all pairs with the same first vertex (the adjacency list of that vertex) appear consecutively in the stream. Within the adjacency lists the stream is ordered arbitrarily. For example, for the graph consisting of a cycle on three vertices $V = \{v_1, v_2, v_3\}$, a possible ordering of the stream could be $\langle v_3v_1, v_3v_2, v_1v_2, v_1v_3, v_2v_3, v_2v_1\rangle$. In this example, we say that the adjacency list for v_3 came first, then the adjacency list for v_1, and finally the adjacency list for v_2.

[1]Note that in the original version of the paper, Cormode and Jowhari initially claimed that their algorithm returned a $(1+\varepsilon)$-approximation but this claim was incorrect. Instead, their proposed algorithm returned a $(3+\varepsilon)$-estimate. Subsequently, they designed a new $(1+\varepsilon)$- approximation algorithm which appeared in the revised version of the paper.

Cycle Counting. For $\ell \geq 3$, we will consider algorithms for counting the number of ℓ-cycles in a graph G presented as an adjacency list stream. G has T cycles, with T unknown to the algorithm, and the problem is to compute a multiplicative approximation to T with probability $1-\delta$. The approximation factor may be $(1 \pm \varepsilon)$, with ε an arbitrary parameter, or it may be a fixed constant.

Our algorithms are parametrized in terms of T, which is a convention widely adopted in the literature on subgraph counting. While T cannot be assumed to be known in advance, it suffices to know a lower bound on $T' \leq T$, and then set our space usage based on T', as our bounds will only be tighter if $T > T'$. Furthermore, if T is in fact smaller than T', then we will not be able to accurately estimate T, but we will be able to determine that it is smaller than T'. This is because our bounds are variance-based, with variance that is increasing in T.

We will be primarily concerned with the *space* complexity of the algorithms, expressed in terms of the edge count m, T, ε, and δ. When ε and δ are omitted, this denotes the complexity when ε and δ are constant.

1.3 Our Results

We present new upper and lower bounds for cycle counting in adjacency list streams. See Table 1 for a summary of known results and our contributions. For triangle counting we give a two-pass $(1 + \varepsilon)$-estimation algorithm using $\widetilde{O}(m/T^{2/3})$ space, improving on the previous best known multipass algorithm. We also present the first adjacency list algorithm for approximately counting 4-cycles, using $\widetilde{O}(m/T^{3/8})$ space and two passes over the stream to return a constant-factor approximation to T. We complement our upper bounds with lower bound results for all cycle lengths. These are the first lower bounds for subgraph counting in the adjacency list model and they fully resolve in which settings there exist sublinear space cycle counting/distinguishing algorithms.

Both of our algorithms are based on sampling. Sampling-based approaches to this problem are very sensitive to "heavy" edges, i.e., edges which are involved in a large number of cycles. Heavy edges often introduce unacceptably large variance to the estimator. In our triangle counting algorithm, we deal with this by defining, for each triangle, a "lightest" edge, and ensuring that the triangle is only counted if it is initially sampled at that edge. See Sections 2.1 and 3 for more in-depth discussion.

In our 4-cycle counting algorithm, we deal with this problem by showing that a sufficient fraction of the 4-cycles have at least one wedge that is sufficiently "light". The difference from triangle counting is that the algorithm cannot *identify* the "light" wedge during the stream; this leads to a constant factor approximation to the cycle count, rather than $1 + \varepsilon$. See Sections 2.2 and 4 for details.

We present lower bounds for counting cycles of all length, both in one pass and constant number of passes. We use reductions from four known communication complexity problems: Index (INDEX_r), three-player Number on Forehead Pointer-jumping (3-PJ_r), two-player Disjointness (DISJ_r) and three-player NOF Disjointness (3-DISJ_r), where r indicates the size of the input. The communication complexity of the two multi-player Number on Forehead (NOF) problems have not yet been fully resolved [10, 31] and thus we present our lower bounds for triangle counting as conditional on the best communication complexity lower bounds for these problems. It is generally believed that both of these problems have communication complexity $\widetilde{\Omega}(r)$, which would imply lower bounds of $\widetilde{\Omega}(m/\sqrt{T})$ and $\widetilde{\Omega}(m/T^{2/3})$ for one pass and multipass triangle counting respectively, matching the corresponding algorithms (from [26] and here) up to polylog factors; certainly any result to the contrary would be a breakthrough. For 4-cycle counting we show that solving the problem in one pass requires $\Omega(m)$ space, but in two passes it can be done using sublinear amount of space. We then show that counting larger cycles requires $\Omega(m)$ space for any constant number of passes. The details can be found in Sections 2.3 and 5.

2 TECHNIQUES

2.1 Triangle Counting Algorithm

Our main upper bound is a two-pass adjacency list streaming algorithm that counts the number of triangles in a graph using $O\left(m/T^{2/3} \cdot \log n\right)$ space, where T is the number of triangles in the graph and m is the number of edges. To motivate our methods, consider first the following algorithm for distinguishing graphs with T triangles from graphs with no triangles described in [26]:

First Pass Sample m' edges from the graph.

Second Pass Check if any of these edges are in a triangle.

Note that the second pass can be accomplished with only $2m'$ extra bits of storage by, for each adjacency list presented in the second pass, flagging any endpoint of a sampled vertex if it appears in the adjacency list. If both endpoints of an edge are flagged in the adjacency list of some vertex v, that edge forms a triangle with v.

It can be shown (see, e.g., [15]) that any graph with T triangles must have at least $T^{2/3}$ edges involved in those triangles, so provided $m' \geq m/T^{2/3}$, at least one such edge will be sampled in the first pass with good probability, and so the algorithm will detect that the graph has at least one triangle.

This algorithm gives an unbiased estimator for T, as the number of triangles found by the algorithm is $3m'T/m$ in expectation (if triangles with multiple sampled edges are counted with multiplicity). However, this estimator has high variance, due to "heavy" edges—edges involved in many triangles. We can reduce the variance by discarding excessively heavy edges (for instance, if we discard every edge involved in at least $100T^{1/3}$ triangles we can reduce the variance to $O(T^2)$), but at the cost of biasing the estimator. This approach will allow us a constant-factor approximation to T, but not the $(1 \pm \varepsilon)$-multiplicative approximation we want.

Instead, consider the following three-pass algorithm, which only counts a triangle as being sampled if its "lightest" edge was sampled:

First Pass Sample a size-m' set S of edges from the graph.
Second Pass Collect the set Q of triangles that include at least one edge in S.
Third Pass For every triangle $uvw \in Q$, calculate T_{uv}, T_{vw}, T_{wu}, the number of triangles in G that use uv, vw, and wu, respectively.
Post-Processing For each edge $e \in S$, and each triangle τ using e, count τ iff $e = \arg\min_{e' \in \tau} T_{e'}$, breaking ties arbitrarily.

This algorithm discards most "heavy edges" (it is possible for a heavy edge to be the lightest edge of *some* triangle, but not of *most* triangles), while providing an unbiased estimator, as each triangle has an exactly m'/m chance of being counted. One can show that this leads to an unbiased estimator with good variance.

However, there are two problems with this algorithm. Firstly, it takes an extra pass, and secondly, we need to store Q, which is size $m'T/m$ in expectation. Therefore, its space complexity is, in the worst case,

$$O\left(\max\left(m/T^{2/3}, T^{1/3}\right)\log n\right)$$

To deal with the second problem, we sample a size-m' subset of the triangles we would collect in the second pass, or all of them if we see fewer than m'. This gives us a true $O\left(m/T^{2/3} \cdot \log n\right)$-space algorithm.

Now we consider the first problem. Our algorithm depends on, for each triangle sampled, determining whether it was sampled at its "lightest" edge. It is impossible to determine this exactly in only two passes, as for each edge e' in a triangle τ, we will only be able to count triangles that involve e' in the postfix of the stream that appears *after* τ is first detected.

To solve this, we first note that, if we sample the edge uv in our first pass, we will be able to add it to S when the first of the adjacency lists of u, v arrive (assuming we use a hash-based sampling method). Suppose this is u. Then, if uv is completed by a vertex w to form τ, either w appears after u, in which case τ can be found during the first pass, or it appears before u, in which case τ can be found in the second pass as soon as w arrives. In either case, we can find τ by the time its first vertex arrives in the second pass.

We can therefore replace $\arg\min_{e' \in \tau} T_{e'}$ from the three-pass algorithm with $\arg\min_{e' \in \tau} H_{e',\tau}$, where

$$H_{e',\tau} = |\{\tau' : e' \in \tau',\ (\tau' \setminus e') \text{ arrives after } (\tau \setminus e')\ \}|,$$

because we can compute $H_{e',\tau}$ in the second pass for every $\tau \in Q$ and edge $e' \in \tau$.

For any given edge e' and triangle, this can be arbitrarily small, but on average across all triangles that use an edge e', $H_{e',\tau}$ will be approximately $T_{e'}/2$, which will suffice to bound the variance of our algorithm (for further details, see the full discussion in Section 3). This gives us the following algorithm:

First Pass Sample a size-m' set S of edges from the graph.
First and Second Pass Collect the set Q of triangles that include at least one edge in S.
Second Pass For each $\tau \in Q$ and each $e' \in \tau$, calculate $H_{e',\tau}$.
Post-Processing For each edge $e \in S$, and each triangle τ using e, count τ iff $e = \arg\min_{e' \in \tau} H_{e',\tau}$, breaking ties arbitrarily.

Combining with the aforementioned fix—only storing a sample of Q—gives our final algorithm.

2.2 4-Cycle Counting Algorithm

Our second result is a two-pass adjacency list streaming algorithm that returns an $O(1)$ multiplicative approximation to the 4-cycle count of a graph using $\widetilde{O}\left(m/T^{3/8}\right)$ space, where T is the number of 4-cycles in the graph and m is the number of edges. In the first pass, we collect a set of edges S and in the second, count how many 4-cycles G has that contain a wedge in S. To sample even one cycle reliably, we need S to be size at least $m/T^{3/8}$, as any wedge will be sampled with probability about $(|S|/m)^2$, and there can be as few as $T^{3/4}$ wedges in a graph with T 4-cycles. We show that this also gives a $O(1)$-factor multiplicative approximation to T by showing that at least a constant fraction of the cycles in G have at least one wedge that is "good", i.e. that is not used by too many 4-cycles and has neither of its edges used by too many 4-cycles.

2.3 Lower Bounds

Our last set of results consists of five lower bounds on the space complexity of cycle counting in the adjacency list streaming model. All of them involve the standard method of using reductions from known communication complexity problems. We let C_r be a two or three-player communication complexity problem with input of size $\Theta(r)$ and a

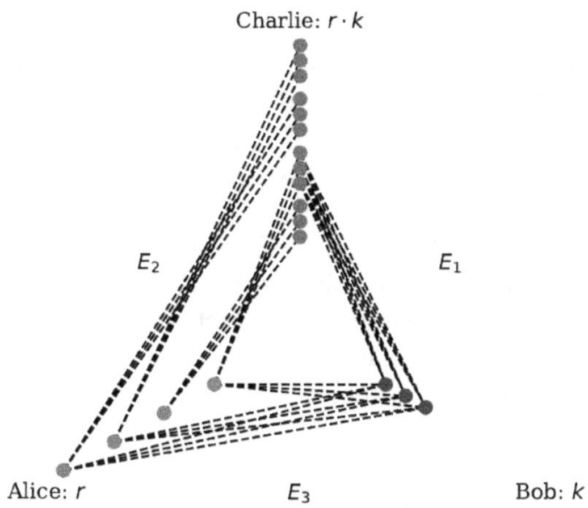

(a) One-pass Triangle Counting
$\widetilde{\Omega}(m/\sqrt{T})$ **from** 3-PJ
(conditional)

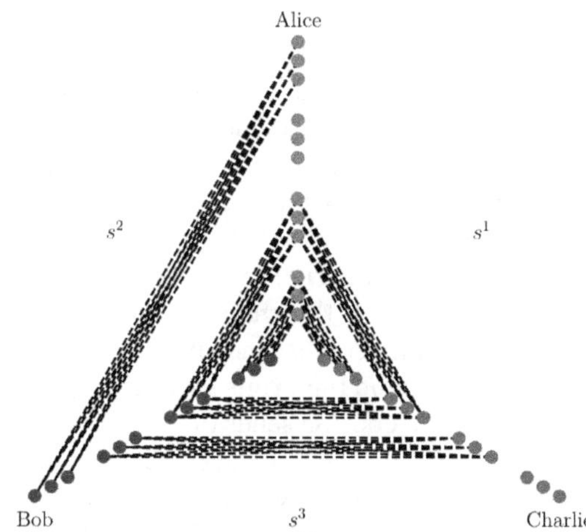

(b) Multi-pass Triangle Counting
$\widetilde{\Omega}(m/T^{2/3})$ **from** 3-DISJ
(conditional)

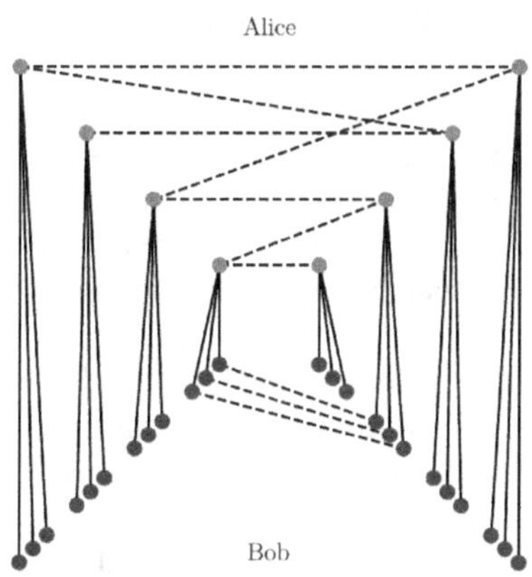

(c) One-pass 4-cycle Counting
$\Omega(m)$ **from** INDEX

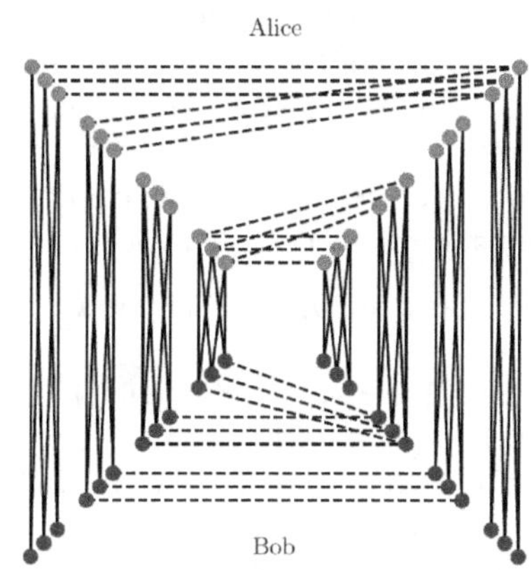

(d) Multi-pass 4-cycle Counting
$\Omega(m/T^{2/3})$ **from** DISJ

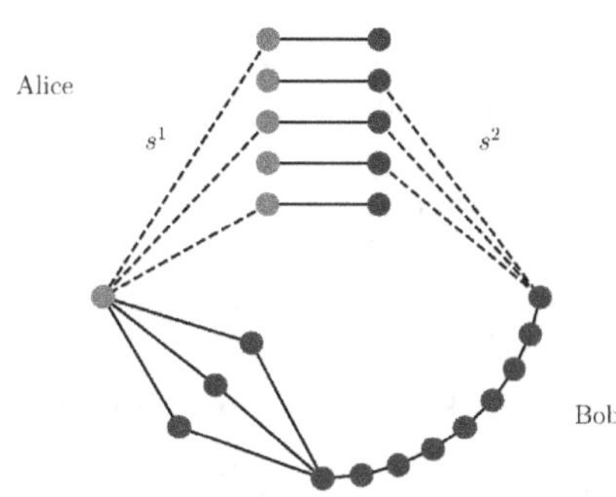

(e) Multi-pass ℓ-cycle Counting, $\ell \geq 5$
$\Omega(m)$ **from** DISJ

Figure 1: Lower bound constructions.

single bit as output. Suppose $\mathcal{A}$ is an algorithm that can distinguish between graphs with T ℓ-cycles and ℓ-cycle-free graphs with probability 2/3 in the one-pass adjacency list streaming model. We then construct a protocol for C_r which sends messages whose size is the internal space of $\mathcal{A}$. Based on an instance of C_r we construct a graph G, such that G is ℓ-cycle-free if the output is 0 and has T ℓ-cycles if the output is 1. Alice, Bob (and possibly Charlie) each encode their input as adjacency lists of vertices in the graph G. The protocol is then for Alice to run $\mathcal{A}$ on her adjacency lists, and send the algorithm's state to Bob, who then runs it on his adjacency lists. If there are three players, Bob sends the state to Charlie, who then runs $\mathcal{A}$ on his lists. The last player can tell whether G has 0 or T ℓ-cycles and therefore whether the output of C_r is 0 or 1. This implies that if C_r requires $\Omega(f(r))$ one-way communication, $\mathcal{A}$ must use $\Omega(f(r))$ space.

To obtain a bound on the space used by multi-pass algorithms, we allow players to communicate for an arbitrary number of rounds and consider total communication. If total communication complexity of C_r is $\Omega(f(r))$, then any algorithm $\mathcal{A}$ with c passes must use $\Omega(f(r)/c)$ space, which is $\Omega(f(r))$ for constant c.

For our reductions, we use the following communication complexity problems (formally defined in Section 5):

- INDEX: Alice has $s \in \{0,1\}^r$, Bob has $x \in [r]$, and must output s_x.
- DISJ: Alice and Bob have $s^1, s^2 \in \{0,1\}^r$ and must determine if any $s^1_x = s^2_x = 1$.
- 3-PJ: Three-player Number on Forehead (NOF) Pointer-jumping. This problem can be viewed as an extension of Index to the multi-party NOF setting.
- 3-DISJ: Three-player NOF Disjointness.

Using reductions from Index and Disjointness is standard for proving lower bounds on the space of one-pass and multi-pass arbitrary order streaming algorithms. In adjacency list streams, they are only applicable for obtaining bounds on counting subgraphs with two disjoint edges, and thus cannot be used for triangles. Since the input of a given communication complexity problem is encoded in the edges of the graph and each player sees every edge on certain vertices, assigning two vertices of a triangle to Alice and the third one to Bob (or vice versa) would lead to the player with two vertices having information about the other player's input. On the other hand, in a 4-cycle (or a larger cycle) we can assign two adjacent vertices to Alice and two other adjacent vertices to Bob, which would insure that both of them have private input. To circumvent this problem for triangles, we employ three-player communication complexity problems, where each player knows two thirds of the input. This is a special case of the k-player Number on Forehead (NOF) model, where the input consists of k parts I_1 through I_k and i-th player knows all I_j *except* I_i. Showing bounds on communication complexity in this model has proven harder than in the more standard Number in Hand model. For multiparty NOF Pointer Jumping and Disjointness there is currently a gap between best known upper and lower bounds on the communication complexity. The best known lower bound for three players is currently $\Omega(\sqrt{r})$ for both problems, where r is the size of input [30, 34]. Thus, we reference $f_{pj}(r)$ and $f_d(r)$ as (currently unknown) complexities of NOF Pointer Jumping and Disjointness respectively in our triangle counting lower bounds. It is conjectured, that the communication complexity of both problems is $\widetilde{\Omega}(r)$, where $\widetilde{\Omega}(\cdot)$ notation hides inverse polylog factors. If that is the case, our triangle counting bounds become tight.

For $\ell \geq 4$, we encode classic one-way (for one-pass) or two-way (for multi-pass) communication complexity problems as subgraph counting problems. This requires us to encode the players' inputs in *disjoint* edges, as if we use incident edges the players will share information, and so it is not available for $\ell = 3$.

In two of our reductions concerning counting 4-cycles we aim to construct a graph with a large number of 4-cycles for instances with output 1 and a similar 4-cycle-free graph for 0-instances. To achieve that, we employ bipartite 4-cycle-free graphs on $2r$ vertices with $\Theta(r^{3/2})$ edges. An example of such a graph is an incidence graph of a special kind of projective plane called a field plane. If the order of the plane is q, it has $q^2 + q + 1$ points, the same number of lines, and each line passes through exactly $q + 1$ points. Thus, the incidence graph has $2(q^2 + q + 1)$ vertices, each with degree $q + 1$. The graph is 4-cycle-free since by definition of a projective plane, for any two distinct points, there is exactly one line passing through both of them, and for any two distinct lines, there is exactly one point both of them pass through. We also note that there are no 4-cycle-free graphs on r vertices with $\omega(r^{3/2})$ edges [8].

When $\ell \geq 5$ our lower bounds become $\Omega(m)$ for any constant number of passes regardless of the number of cycles in the graph. This is because we can encode Disjointness (which is known to require linear communication even in two-way complexity) as an ℓ-cycle-counting problem. This encoding will depend on the fact that a pair of disjoint edges can be shared by many different ℓ-cycles, which does not hold for $\ell = 4$.

For illustrations of the lower bound constructions see Figure 1. Solid edges are fixed and dashed edges correspond to players' input. For detailed definitions of communication complexity problems and descriptions of the reductions see Section 5.

3 TWO PASS TRIANGLE COUNTING ALGORITHM

3.1 Notation

For any edge or subset of edges x in G, write $L(x)$ for the set of triangles involving x, and write $T(x)$ for $|L(x)|$. Let $T = T(G)$. For each triangle $\tau \in L(G)$, and each edge $e \in \tau$, let τ^{-e} denote the unique vertex in τ that is not an endpoint of e.

3.2 Algorithm

Our algorithm will take two passes over the stream. Call these passes P_1, P_2. We will require that P_2 have the same ordering as P_1. For each $i \in [2]$, $u \in V(G)$ and $v \in \Gamma(u)$, let $P_i^{<uv}$ denote the prefix of P_i that appears before v appears in the adjacency list of u, and $P_i^{>uv}$ denote the postfix of P_i that appears afterwards. Similarly, let $P_i^{<u}$,$P_i^{>v}$ denote the prefix and postfix of P_i that occur before and after the adjacency list of v, respectively. For each $e \in G$, define an order on the triangles of the graph as follows: $\tau_1 <_e \tau_2$ if τ_2^{-e} arrives after τ_1^{-e} in the stream.

Now, let τ be a triangle and e an edge. Define:

$$H_{e,\tau} = |\{\tau' \in L(e) : \tau <_e \tau'\}|$$

Then, for each triangle τ, let $\rho(\tau)$ be the unique edge $e \in \tau$ that minimizes $H_{e,\tau}$, breaking ties arbitrarily. Let

$$\widetilde{T}_e = |\{\tau \in L(e) : \rho(\tau) = e\}|$$

Note that $\sum_{e \in E} \widetilde{T}_e = T$. Our algorithm is then as follows:

(1) Choose a sample size m'.
(2) While passing through P_1, keep a uniformly chosen size-m' subset S of $E(G)$, adding an edge to S the first time of the two times it appears in P_1. If $m' > m$, instead keep all of $E(G)$.
(3) While passing through P_1 and P_2, perform the following steps in parallel:
  (a) Calculate $m = |E(G)|$. Define $k = \max(m/m', 1)$.
  (b) Calculate $T' = \sum_{e \in S} T_e$.
  (c) Sample a size-m' subset Q uniformly from $\{(e, \tau) : e \in S, \tau \in L(e)\}$, or let Q be the entire set if it is smaller than m'.
  (d) For each $(e', \tau) \in Q$ and for each $e \in \tau$, calculate $H_{e,\tau}$.
(4) Return $\widetilde{T}' = \frac{k^2 T'}{m} |\{(e, \tau) \in Q : \rho(\tau) = e\}|$.

3.3 Analysis

3.3.1 Space Complexity. To see that this can be implemented, first note that, if we are storing an edge $e = uv$, whenever the adjacency list of a vertex w appears in the stream we can check whether uvw forms a triangle in G with the use of only two extra bits per such edge e. This is because, while scanning the adjacency list of w, we can flag u if uw appears, and v if vw appears, concluding at the end of the adjacency list that uvw exists iff v and w are flagged.

Therefore, we can perform step 3b with $O(|S| \log n)$ space, and step 3c with $O(|Q| \log n)$ space. We can perform step 3a in $O(\log n)$ space just by maintaining a counter.

Then, for step 3d, consider any $(e, \tau) \in Q$. The first time this can be added to Q is the first time the vertex $w = \tau^{-e}$ is seen after adding e to S. Suppose e appears in P_1 for the first time as the vertex v in the adjacency list of u. Then, as P_1, P_2 have the same order, the adjacency list of w appears either in $P_1^{>uv}$ or $P_2^{<uv}$. So in particular, all of $P_2^{>uv} \cup P_2^{>w}$ is seen *after* (e, τ) is added to Q. Since u arrives before v, this means that $P_2^{>u} \cup P_2^{>v} \cup P_2^{>w}$ is seen after (e, τ) is added to Q.

Then, for any $f \in \tau$ and $\sigma \in L(e')$ such that $\tau <_f \sigma$, σ^{-f} appears after τ^{-f} in P_2, by the definition of $<_f$. Since τ^{-f} must be one of u, v, w, σ^{-f} is in $P_2^{>u} \cup P_2^{>v} \cup P_2^{>w}$, and it appears after (e, τ) is added to Q. Therefore,

$$H_{e,\tau} = |\{\tau' \in L(e) : \tau <_e \tau'\}|$$

can be counted with only $O(|Q| \log n)$ space.

Therefore, the space complexity of this algorithm is:

$$O\left((|Q| + |S|) \log n\right) = O(m' \log n)$$

3.3.2 Correctness.

Lemma 3.1.

$$\mathbb{E}\left[\widetilde{T}'\right] = T$$

Proof. Fix any ordering of the stream. Condition on the set S of edges sampled from P_1. Then, for each triangle $\tau \in G$ such that $e \in S$ and $\rho(\tau) = e$, $(e, \tau) \in Q$ with probability $\frac{m'}{T'} = \frac{m}{kT'}$. Therefore,

$$\mathbb{E}\left[\widetilde{T}'|S\right] = k \sum_{e \in S} \widetilde{T}_e$$

and as each $e \in G$ is included in S with probability $\frac{m'}{m} = 1/k$,

$$\mathbb{E}\left[\widetilde{T}'\right] = \sum_{e \in G} \widetilde{T}_e$$

and since for each τ there is exactly one $e \in \tau$ such that $\rho(\tau) = e$:

$$\mathbb{E}\left[\widetilde{T}'\right] = T$$

□

To bound the accuracy of this estimator, we will need the following combinatorial lemma concerning the values $\widetilde{T}_e$.

Lemma 3.2.

$$\sum_{e \in G} \widetilde{T}_e^2 = O\left(T^{4/3}\right)$$

Proof. For all $i \in \{0, \ldots, \lfloor \log T \rfloor\}$, let $E_i = \{e \in G : \widetilde{T}_e \in [2^i, 2^{i+1}]\}$, and let $A_i = \{\tau \in G : \rho(\tau) \in E_i\}$.

Then, let $B_i = \{\tau \in A_i : H_{\rho(\tau),\tau} \geq \widetilde{T}_{\rho(\tau)}/2\}$, and let $F_i = \bigcup B_i$, so F_i contains all of the edges of triangles in B_i. Then, for any $e \in E_i$, at least half of the triangles τ such that $\rho(\tau) = e$ have $H_{\rho(\tau),\tau} \geq \widetilde{T}_{\rho(\tau)}/2$, so $|B_i| \geq |A_i|/2$. Furthermore, by [15], any graph with m edges has at most $m^{3/2}$ triangles, and so $|F_i|^{3/2} \geq |A_i|/2$. Then,

$$\sum_{e\in G} \widetilde{T}_e^2 \leq \sum_{i=0}^{\lfloor \log T \rfloor} 2^{i+1} \sum_{e \in E_i} \widetilde{T}_e$$

While

$$\sum_{e\in E_i} \widetilde{T}_e = |A_i| \leq 2|F_i|^{3/2}$$

Then, for any $e \in F_i$, $\exists \tau \in B_i$ such that $e \in \tau$, and therefore $H_{e,\tau} \geq H_{\rho(\tau),\tau} \geq \widetilde{T}_{\rho(\tau)}/2$. Therefore:

$$T_e \geq H_{e,\tau} \geq \widetilde{T}_{\rho(\tau)}/2 \geq 2^{i-1}$$

Thus, $|F_i|2^{i-1} \leq 3T$, and so $|F_i|^{3/2} \leq T^{3/2}2^{-3(i-1)/2}/3^{3/2}$. At the same time, $\sum_{e\in E_i} \widetilde{T}_e$ is clearly at most T, and so by breaking our sum at $i = \lfloor \log T/3 \rfloor$:

$$\sum_{e\in G} \widetilde{T}_e^2 \leq \sum_{i=0}^{\lfloor \log(T)/3 \rfloor} 2^i T + \sum_{i=\lfloor \log(T)/3 \rfloor}^{\lfloor \log T \rfloor} 2^{-i/2+5/2} T^{3/2}/3^{3/2} = O\left(T^{4/3}\right) + O\left(T^{4/3}\right) = O\left(T^{4/3}\right)$$

□

We are now ready to analyze the accuracy of the algorithm. First, we will show that $k\sum_{e\in S} \widetilde{T}$ is a good estimator for T.

Lemma 3.3.

$$\forall \varepsilon > 0, \mathbb{P}\left[k\sum_{e\in S} \widetilde{T}_e \in ((1-\varepsilon)T, (1+\varepsilon)T)\right] \geq 1 - O\left(\frac{k}{\varepsilon^2 T^{2/3}}\right)$$

Proof. As each $e \in G$ is included in S with probability $m'/m = 1/k$,

$$\mathbb{E}\left[k\sum_{e\in S} \widetilde{T}_e\right] = T$$

We will now proceed to bound the variance. Let I_e be the indicator variable that is 1 if $e \in S$ and 0 otherwise. Then, since a fixed number of edges are included in S, the family $\{I_e\}_{e\in G}$ is negatively associated, and so

$$\mathrm{Var}\left(k\sum_{e\in S} \widetilde{T}_e\right) = k^2 \sum_{e\in G} \widetilde{T}_e^2 \,\mathrm{Var}\left(I_e\right) \leq k^2 \sum_{e\in G} \widetilde{T}_e^2 (1/k - 1/k^2) \leq k\sum_{e\in G} \widetilde{T}_e^2 \leq kT^{4/3}$$

by applying Lemma 3.2. The result then follows by Chebyshev's inequality. □

We will now bound, for any sample set S, the accuracy with which the algorithm estimates $k\sum_{e\in S} \widetilde{T}_e$.

Lemma 3.4.

$$\forall \varepsilon > 0, \mathbb{P}\left[\widetilde{T}' \in \left(k\sum_{e\in S} \widetilde{T}_e - \varepsilon T, k\sum_{e\in S} \widetilde{T}_e + \varepsilon T\right) \middle| S\right] \geq 1 - \frac{k^3 T'}{\varepsilon^2 T^2 m} \sum_{e\in S} \widetilde{T}_e$$

Proof. We may assume $|Q| = m'$, since otherwise $Q = \bigcup_{e\in S}(e, L(e))$ and so $\widetilde{T}' = k\sum_{e\in S} \widetilde{T}_e$ exactly. Conditioned on S, for any τ such that $\rho(\tau) \in S$, let J_τ be 1 if $(\rho(\tau), \tau) \in Q$, and 0 otherwise. As Q is fixed size, the family $\{J_\tau\}_{\tau\in G}$ is negatively associated, and so

$$\mathrm{Var}\left(\widetilde{T}' \middle| S\right) \leq \left(\frac{kT'}{m'}\right)^2 \sum_{e\in S} \sum_{\tau:\rho(\tau)=e} \mathrm{Var}(J_\tau) = \left(\frac{kT'}{m'}\right)^2 \sum_{e\in S} \sum_{\tau:\rho(\tau)=e} \left(\frac{m'}{T'} - \left(\frac{m'}{T'}\right)^2\right) \leq \frac{k^2 T'}{m'} \sum_{e\in S} \widetilde{T}_e \leq \frac{k^3 T'}{m} \sum_{e\in S} \widetilde{T}_e$$

The result then follows from Chebyshev's inequality. □

To make use of the bound above, we will need to bound the probability that T' is too large.

Lemma 3.5.

$$\mathbb{P}\left[kT' \leq 30T\right] \geq 9/10$$

Proof. Each edge in G is included in S with probability $1/k$, so

$$\mathbb{E}\left[T'\right] = \sum_{e\in G} T_e/k = 3T/k$$

The result then follows from Markov's inequality. □

Putting these results together will allow us to bound the accuracy of the estimator.

Lemma 3.6. *There exists a constant $D > 0$ such that, $\forall \varepsilon \in (0, 1)$, if*

$$k \leq \varepsilon^2 D T^{2/3}$$

then

$$\mathbb{P}\left[\widetilde{T}' \in ((1-\varepsilon)T, (1+\varepsilon)T)\right] \geq 2/3$$

Proof. Using Lemmas 3.3 and 3.4, choose $D \leq 1$ such that

$$\mathbb{P}\left[k \sum_{e \in S} \widetilde{T}_e \in ((1-\varepsilon/2)T, (1+\varepsilon/2)T)\right] \geq 99/100$$

$$\mathbb{P}\left[\widetilde{T}' \in \left(k \sum_{e \in S} \widetilde{T}_e - \varepsilon T/2, k \sum_{e \in S} \widetilde{T}_e + \varepsilon T/2\right) \middle| S\right]$$
$$\geq 1 - \frac{kT'}{3000 T^{4/3} m} k \sum_{e \in S} \widetilde{T}_e$$

Then, if $\mathcal{E}$ is the event that $k \sum_{e \in S} \widetilde{T}_e = (1 \pm \varepsilon/2)T$ and $kT' \leq 30T$, by Lemma 3.5 and the union bound

$$\mathbb{P}[\mathcal{E}] \geq 89/100$$

Thus,

$$\mathbb{P}\left[\widetilde{T}' \in \left(k \sum_{e \in S} \widetilde{T}_e - \varepsilon T/2, k \sum_{e \in S} \widetilde{T}_e + \varepsilon T/2\right) \middle| S, \mathcal{E}\right]$$
$$\geq 1 - \frac{kT'}{2670 T^{4/3} m} k \sum_{e \in S} \widetilde{T}_e$$
$$\geq 1 - \frac{1}{89 T^{1/3} m} k \sum_{e \in S} \widetilde{T}_e$$
$$\geq 1 - \frac{1+\varepsilon}{89m} T^{2/3}$$
$$\geq \frac{87}{89}$$

as $T \leq m^{3/2}$. Therefore, with probability at least $89/100 \times 87/89 - 1/100 > 2/3$

$$\widetilde{T}' \in \left(k \sum_{e \in S} \widetilde{T}_e - \varepsilon T/2, k \sum_{e \in S} \widetilde{T}_e + \varepsilon T/2\right)$$

and

$$k \sum_{e \in S} \widetilde{T}_e \in ((1-\varepsilon/2)T, (1+\varepsilon/2)T)$$

Therefore,

$$\widetilde{T}' = ((1-\varepsilon)T, (1+\varepsilon)T)$$

□

Theorem 3.7. *For all $\varepsilon, \delta \in (0, 1)$, there is a 2-pass triangle counting algorithm that uses*

$$O\left(\frac{m \log n}{\varepsilon^2 T^{2/3}} \log 1/\delta\right)$$

space and returns a $(1 \pm \varepsilon)$ multiplicative approximation to T with probability $1 - \delta$.

Proof. Let $m' = \Theta\left(m/(\varepsilon^2 T^{2/3})\right)$, with constants chosen so that $k = \Theta(\varepsilon^2 T^{2/3})$ meets the requirements of Lemma 3.6. This gives an algorithm that runs in

$$O\left(\frac{m \log n}{\varepsilon^2 T^{2/3}}\right)$$

space and returns a $(1 \pm \varepsilon)$ multiplicative approximation to T with probability $2/3$. Then, for an appropriately chosen constant $D' \in \mathbb{N}$, run $D' \log 1/\delta$ copies of the algorithm in parallel, and take the median of their outputs. If D' is chosen to be a sufficiently large constant, at least half the algorithms will return a result within εT of T with probability $1 - \delta$, and so the median will give a $(1 \pm \varepsilon)$ multiplicative approximation. □

4 TWO PASS 4-CYCLE COUNTING ALGORITHM

4.1 Notation

For any edge or wedge x, let T_x denote the number of 4-cycles that contain x, let T denote the number of 4-cycles in our graph G, and let m denote the number of edges in G.

4.2 Algorithm

Our algorithm will take two passes over the stream. Call these passes P_1, P_2. We will *not* require P_2 to have the same ordering as P_1. Our algorithm is then as follows:

(1) Choose a sample size m'.
(2) While passing through P_1, keep a uniformly chosen size-m' subset S of $E(G)$. If $m' > m$, instead keep all of $E(G)$. Record m.
(3) Let Q be the set of wedges consisting of edges in S.
(4) While passing through P_2, for each $w \in Q$, calculate T_w.
(5) Let $k = m/m'$.
(6) Return $T' = k^2 \cdot \sum_{w \in Q} T_w$.

4.3 Analysis

4.3.1 Space Complexity. For any wedge uvw in Q, and any vertex $z \in V(G)$, we may check whether $uvwz$ forms a 4-cycle in G while passing over the adjacency list of z with only extra $2|S|$ bits of storage, by flagging whether u and w are in the adjacency list of z. Therefore, the algorithm can be implemented with the use of

$$O(|S| \log n) = O(m' \log n)$$

space.

4.3.2 Correctness. To show that the algorithm obtains an $O(1)$ factor approximation to T, we will need to show that at least a constant fraction of cycles in our graph G are easy to find.

Definition 4.1. *We call an edge $e \in E(G)$ "heavy" if it is contained in at least $40\sqrt{T}$ 4-cycles, and "light" otherwise. We call a wedge w "overused" if it is contained in at least $40T^{1/4}$ 4-cycles, "heavy" if it contains a heavy edge, "bad" if it is either overused or heavy, and "good" otherwise. We call a cycle "good" if it contains at least one good wedge. We will denote the set of good cycles as F_G.*

Lemma 4.2. $|F_G| = \Omega(T)$

Proof. See appendix. □

For each cycle τ that has at least one good wedge, let $\rho(\tau)$ denote an arbitrarily chosen good wedge in τ. Let f_G denote the number of 4-cycles τ such that $\rho(\tau)$ is in the sampled wedge set Q. Let f_B denote the number of 4-cycles τ such that $\rho(\tau) \notin Q$, but some other wedge in τ is in Q. The estimate returned by the algorithm is then $k^2(f_G + f_B)$.

Lemma 4.3. *There exists a constant $D > 0$ such that, if*

$$k \le DT^{3/8}$$

then $\mathbb{P}\left[k^2 f_G \in [|F_G|/4, 2|F_G|]\right] \ge 9/10$.

Proof. For each $\tau \in F_G$, there is a

$$\frac{m'(m'-1)}{m(m-1)} \in [1/(2k^2), 1/k^2]$$

probability that both edges in $\rho(\tau)$ will be included in S, so

$$\mathbb{E}\left[k^2 f_G\right] \in [|F_G|/2, |F_G|]$$

Next we bound the variance. For any two 4-cycles τ_1, τ_2, the probability that both $\rho(\tau_1)$ and $\rho(\tau_2)$ are in Q is $\prod_{i=0}^{r-1} \frac{m'-i}{m-i} \le k^{-r}$, where r is the total number of distinct edges between $\rho(\tau_1)$ and $\rho(\tau_2)$ (varying from 4 if they are disjoint to 2 if they are the same wedge).

$$\begin{aligned}
\mathrm{Var}(k^2 f_G) &= k^4\,\mathbb{E}\left[f_G^2\right] - k^4\,\mathbb{E}[f_G]^2 \\
&\le k^4 \sum_{\tau_1,\tau_2 \in F_G} \mathbb{P}[\rho(\tau_1), \rho(\tau_2) \in Q] - k^4\,\mathbb{E}[f_G]^2 \\
&\le k^4 \sum_{\substack{\tau_1,\tau_2 \in F_G: \\ \rho(\tau_1)\cap\rho(\tau_2)\neq\emptyset}} \mathbb{P}[\rho(\tau_1), \rho(\tau_2) \in Q] \\
&\le k^4 \left(\sum_{\tau \in F_G} \left(k^{-2} T_{\rho(\tau)} + k^{-3} \sum_{e \in \rho(\tau)} T_e \right) \right) \\
&\le \sum_{\tau \in F_G} \left(40k^2 T^{1/4} + 80k T^{1/2} \right) \\
&\le 120DT^2
\end{aligned}$$

where the penultimate step uses the fact that $\rho(\tau)$ is good and the last step uses the fact that $k \le DT^{3/8}$. The result then follows for sufficiently small $D > 0$ by Lemma 4.2 and Chebyshev's inequality. □

Lemma 4.4.

$$\mathbb{P}\left[k^2 f_B \le 40T\right] \ge 9/10$$

Proof. Each cycle has 4 wedges, and each one has at most a $1/k^2$ probability of contributing to f_B, so $\mathbb{E}\left[k^2 f_B\right] \le 4T$. The result then follows by Markov's inequality. □

Lemma 4.5. *There exists a constant $D > 0$ such that, if*

$$k \le DT^{3/8}$$

then with probability $4/5$, the algorithm outputs an $O(1)$ multiplicative approximation to T.

Proof. Apply the union bound to the above two lemmas. □

Theorem 4.6. *For every $\delta \in (0,1)$, there exists a two-pass 4-cycle counting algorithm that uses*

$$O\left(\frac{m \log n}{T^{3/8}} \log 1/\delta\right)$$

space and returns a $O(1)$ multiplicative approximation to T with probability $1 - \delta$.

Proof. Let $m' = \Theta(m/T^{3/8})$, with constants chosen so that $k = \Theta(T^{3/8})$ meets the requirement of Lemma 4.5. This gives an algorithm that runs in $O((m \log n)/T^{3/8})$ space and returns an $O(1)$ multiplicative approximation to T with probability 2/3. Running $\Theta(\log 1/\delta)$ copies of the algorithm in parallel and taking the median of their outputs then gives the desired result. □

5 LOWER BOUNDS

We will make use of reductions from the following communication complexity problems. In each case, the players are allowed to use (shared) randomness, and the lower bounds mentioned will be for solving the problem with probability 2/3.

> Index (INDEX$_r$)
> Alice holds a binary string s of length r and Bob holds an index $x \in [r]$. Alice sends a message to Bob, who must compute s_x. This requires $\Omega(r)$ communication[22].

THREE PARTY NOF POINTER-JUMPING (3-PJ$_r$)
Alice, Bob, and Charlie share edges from a graph with four layers of vertices: $V_1 = \{v^*\}$, $V_2 = \{v_{2i}\}_{i=1}^r$, $V_3 = \{v_{3i}\}_{i=1}^r$, $V_4 = \{v_{40}, v_{41}\}$ and three layers of edges E_1, E_2, E_3, where E_i contains edges from V_i to V_{i+1}. Edges of the graph are directed, and every vertex in layers 1 through 3 has out-degree exactly one. Vertices in V_4 have out-degree 0. Alice has the edges in E_2 and E_3, Bob has E_1 and E_3, and Charlie has E_1 and E_2. Using one way communication — Alice sends a message to Bob, who then sends a message to Charlie — the players must compute whether v^* is connected by a directed path to v_{40} or v_{41}, answering 0 in the first case and 1 in the second. The best known lower bound on the communication complexity of this problem is $\Omega(\sqrt{r})$ [34], while the best known upper bound is $\widetilde{O}(r \log\log r / \log r)$ [11], and it is conjectured that the true complexity of the problem is close to linear.

TWO PARTY DISJOINTNESS (DISJ$_r$)
Alice holds a binary string s^1 of length r and Bob holds a string s^2 of the same length. Using multi-way communication, they must determine whether there exists an index x such that $s^1_x = s^2_x = 1$, answering 1 if there is and 0 otherwise. The communication complexity of this problem is $\Omega(r)$ [19, 29].

THREE PARTY NOF DISJOINTNESS (3-DISJ$_r$)
Alice, Bob, and Charlie share three binary strings of length r: s^1, s^2, and s^3. Each of the three players holds two of the strings: Alice has s^1 and s^2, Bob s^2 and s^3, Charlie s^3 and s^1. Using multi-way communication, they must determine whether there exists an index x such that $s^1_x = s^2_x = s^3_x = 1$, answering 1 if there is and 0 otherwise. The best known lower bound on the communication complexity of this problem is $\Omega(\sqrt{r})$ [30]. No sublinear protocol is known, and it is conjectured that the true complexity is $\widetilde{\Omega}(r)$.

5.1 Reduction Structure

Each of the lower bounds will take the following form: an encoding of an instance of the problem into a graph where the vertices are "assigned" to players. Each player must be able to insert the adjacency list corresponding to their "assigned" vertices, and thus any edges between the assigned vertices of two different players must be determined by state shared by both players.

In each case, we will embed an instance of the problem in a graph which has no ℓ-cycles (for ℓ the length we are considering) if the correct output of the game is 0, and T cycles if it is 1. Therefore, any algorithm that can distinguish between 0 and T ℓ-cycles (in particular, any algorithm for counting ℓ-cycles) would provide a protocol for the communication problem, with communication complexity equal to the space cost of the algorithm. For one-pass lower bounds, we will reduce from one-way communication problems, and for multi-pass lower bounds we will reduce from multi-way communication problems, so that each pass over the input corresponds to one round of communication.

5.2 Girth-6 Graphs

In two of our reductions concerning counting 4-cycles we will need to construct a graph with a large number of 4-cycles for instances with output 1 and a similar 4-cycle-free graph for 0-instances. To achieve this, we employ bipartite 4-cycle-free graphs on $2r$ vertices with $\Theta(r^{3/2})$ edges. An example of such a graph is an incidence graph of a special kind of projective plane called field plane. If the order of the plane is q, it has $q^2 + q + 1$ points, the same number of lines, and each line passes through exactly $q + 1$ points. Thus, the incidence graph has $2(q^2 + q + 1)$ vertices, each with degree $q + 1$. The graph is 4-cycle-free since by the definition of a projective plane, for any two distinct points, there is exactly one line passing through both of them, and for any two distinct lines, there is exactly one point both of them pass through. We also note that there are no 4-cycle-free graphs on r vertices with $\omega(r^{3/2})$ edges [8].

5.3 One-Pass Triangle Counting

THEOREM 5.1. *If 3-PJ$_r$ requires $\Omega(f_{pj}(r))$ communication, then for any m and $T \le m$, there exist $m' = \Theta(m)$ and $T' = \Theta(T)$ such that any adjacency list streaming algorithm that distinguishes between m'-edge graphs with 0 and T' triangles with at least 2/3 probability in one pass requires $\Omega(f_{pj}(m/\sqrt{T}))$ space.*

PROOF. We will describe an encoding of an instance of 3-PJ$_r$ as a graph G, illustrated in Figure 1a. Let $r, k \in \mathbb{N}$ be variables to be fixed later, and consider an instance of 3-PJ$_r$ with edge sets E_1, E_2, E_3. $V(G)$ will be the union of the following sets:

- $A = \{a_i\}_{i=1}^r$ of size r, assigned to Alice.
- B of size k, assigned to Bob.
- $C_1, C_2, \ldots, C_r$, each of size k, assigned to Charlie.

The edges of the graph will be:

- For the edge $(v^*, v_{2i}) \in E_1$, k^2 edges connecting every vertex in B to every vertex in C_i.
- For each edge $(v_i, v_{3j}) \in E_2$, k edges connecting every vertex in C_i to a_j.
- For each edge $(v_i, v_{41}) \in E_3$, k edges connecting a_i to every vertex in B. Edges $(v_i, v_{40}) \in E_3$ will be ignored.

G will have $O(rk + k^2)$ edges. If v^* has a path to v_{41} it will have k^2 triangles. Otherwise it will have 0 triangles. We can therefore set $k = \Theta(\sqrt{T})$ and $r = \Theta(m/\sqrt{T})$ to complete the proof. □

5.4 $O(1)$-Pass Triangle Counting

THEOREM 5.2. *If 3-DISJ$_r$ requires $\Omega(f_d(r))$ communication, then for any m and $T \leq m^{3/2}$, there exist $m' = \Theta(m)$ and $T' = \Theta(T)$ such that any adjacency list streaming algorithm that distinguishes between m'-edge graphs with 0 and T' triangles with at least 2/3 probability in a constant number of passes requires $\Omega(f_d(m/T^{2/3}))$ space.*

PROOF. We will describe an encoding of an instance of 3-DISJ$_r$ as a graph G, illustrated in Figure 1b. $V(G)$ will be the union of the following sets:

- $A_1, A_2, \ldots, A_r$, each of size k, assigned to Alice.
- $B_1, B_2, \ldots, B_r$, each of size k, assigned to Bob.
- $C_1, C_2, \ldots, C_r$, each of size k, assigned to Charlie.

The edges of the graph will be:

- For each $i \in [r]$, k^2 edges between A_i and C_i iff $s_i^1 = 1$.
- For each $i \in [r]$, k^2 edges between A_i and B_i iff $s_i^2 = 1$.
- For each $i \in [r]$, k^2 edges between B_i and C_i iff $s_i^3 = 1$.

G will have $\Theta(rk)$ vertices and $O(rk^2)$ edges. If there exists an index x such that $s_x^1 = s_x^2 = s_x^3 = 1$, A_x, then B_x, and C_x will form k^3 triangles. Otherwise, the graph will be triangle-free. Therefore, for any m and $T \leq m^{3/2}$, we may set $k = \Theta(T^{1/3})$ and $r = m/T^{2/3}$, and the result follows. □

5.5 One Pass 4-Cycle Counting

THEOREM 5.3. *For any m and $T \leq m^{1/3}$, there exists $m' = m$ such that any adjacency list streaming algorithm that distinguishes between m'-edge graphs with 0 and T 4-cycles with at least 2/3 probability in one pass requires $\Omega(m)$ space.*

PROOF. We will describe an encoding of an instance of INDEX$_{\Theta(r^{3/2})}$ as a graph G, illustrated in Figure 1c. $V(G)$ will be the union of the following sets:

- $A = \{a_i\}_{i=1}^r$ and $B = \{b_i\}_{i=1}^r$, each of size r, assigned to Alice.
- $C_1, C_2, \ldots, C_r, D_1, D_2, \ldots, D_r$, each of size k, assigned to Bob.

Using the construction in Section 5.2, fix a bipartite 4-cycle-free graph H with both partitions of size r and $\Theta(r^{3/2})$ edges. Let the size of Alice's string (and therefore the size of the instance) be $|E(H)|$, and associate each edge of H with a different index of Alice's string. The edges of our graph are then the following:

- A copy of H between A and B, with the edges corresponding to bits of Alice's string that are 0 removed.
- A matching of size k between C_i and D_j, where ij is the edge of H corresponding to Bob's index.
- For each $i \in [r]$, k edges between a_i and C_i.
- For each $i \in [r]$, k edges between b_i and D_i.

The resulting graph has $\Theta(rk)$ vertices and $O(r^{3/2}+rk)$ edges. If $s_x = 1$, the graph has k 4-cycles, otherwise it is 4-cycle-free. Therefore, by setting $k = T$ and $r = \Theta(m^{2/3})$, the result follows. □

5.6 $O(1)$-Pass 4-Cycle Counting

THEOREM 5.4. *For any m and $T \leq m^{3/5}$, there exists $m' = \Theta(m)$ such that any any adjacency list streaming algorithm that distinguishes between m'-edge graphs with 0 and T 4-cycles with at least 2/3 probability in a constant number of passes requires $\Omega(m/T^{2/3})$ space.*

PROOF. We will describe an encoding of an instance of DISJ$_{\Theta(r^{3/2})}$ as a graph G, illustrated in Figure 1d.

Using the construction in Section 5.2, fix a bipartite 4-cycle-free graph H_1 with both partitions of size r and $\Theta(r^{3/2})$ edges and another bipartite 4-cycle-free graph H_2 with both partitions of size k and $\Theta(k^{3/2})$ edges. Let the size of Alice and Bob's strings (and therefore the size of the instance) be $|E(H_1)|$, and associate each edge of H_1 with an index i from 1 to $|E(H_1)|$, so each edge in H_1 corresponds to bits s_i^1 and s_i^2 in Alice and Bob's strings.

$V(G)$ will be the union of the following sets:

- Sets $A_1, A_2, \ldots A_r$ and $B_1, B_2, \ldots B_r$, each of size k, assigned to Alice.
- Sets $C_1, C_2, \ldots C_r$ and $D_1, D_2, \ldots D_r$, each of size k, assigned to Bob.

The edges of the graph will be:

- A copy of H_2 between A_i and C_i for all $i \in [r]$
- A copy of H_2 between B_i and D_i for all $i \in [r]$.
- For each edge (v_i, u_j) in H_1, a matching of size k between A_i and B_j iff corresponding Alice's bit is 1.
- For each edge (v_i, u_j) in H_1, a matching of size k between C_i and D_j iff corresponding Bob's bit is 1.

G will have $\Theta(rk)$ vertices and $\Theta(rk^{3/2} + kr^{3/2})$ edges. If there exists an index x such that $s_x^1 = s_x^2 = 1$, G will have $k^{3/2}$ 4-cycles, and otherwise it will be 4-cycle-free. Therefore, the result follows by setting $k = T^{2/3}$ and $r^{3/2} = \Theta(m/T^{2/3})$, so that as $T \leq m^{3/5}$, $rk^{3/2} + kr^{3/2} = \Theta(m^{2/3}T^{5/9} + m) = \Theta(m)$. □

5.7 $O(1)$-Pass ℓ-cycle Counting for $\ell \geq 5$

THEOREM 5.5. *For any constant $\ell \geq 5$, and for any m and $T \leq m$, there exists $m' = \Theta(m)$ such that any adjacency list streaming algorithm that distinguishes between m'-edge graphs with 0 and T ℓ-cycles with at least 2/3 probability in a constant number of passes requires $\Omega(m)$ space.*

PROOF. We will describe an encoding of an instance of DISJ$_k$ as a graph G, illustrated in Figure 1e. $V(G)$ will be the union of the following sets:

- $A = \{a_i\}_{i=1}^{r+1}$ of size $r + 1$, assigned to Alice.
- $B = \{b_i\}_{i=1}^{r}$ of size r, assigned to Bob.
- $C = \{c_i\}_{i=1}^{k}$ of size k, assigned to Bob.
- $D = \{d_i\}_{i=1}^{\ell-4}$ of size $\ell - 4$, assigned to Bob.

The edges of the graph will be:

- (a_i, b_i) for all $i \in [r]$.
- (a_{r+1}, c_i) for all $i \in [k]$.
- $(d_{\ell-4}, c_i)$ for all $i \in [k]$.
- A path $d_1 - d_2 - \cdots - d_{\ell-4}$. Note that for $\ell = 5$, this path has 1 vertex and 0 edges.
- (a_i, a_{r+1}) for every i such that the i-th bit of Alice's string is 1.
- (b_i, d_1) for every i such that the i-th bit of Bob's string is 1.

G will have $O(r + k)$ edges, as ℓ is a constant. If there exists an index x such that $s_x^1 = s_x^2 = 1$, then the graph will have k ℓ-cycles, otherwise it will be ℓ-cycle-free. Therefore, if $T \leq m$, the result follows by setting $r = m, k = T$. □

ACKNOWLEDGMENTS

This work was done in part while John Kallaugher, Eric Price, and Sofya Vorotnikova were visiting the Simons Institute for the Theory of Computing. Sofya Vorotnikova was supported by a Simons-Berkeley Research Fellowship. This material is based upon work supported by the National Science Foundation under Grant No. 1637536 and Grant No. 1751040.

REFERENCES

[1] Lars Arge, Michael T. Goodrich, and Nodari Sitchinava. 2010. Parallel external memory graph algorithms. In *24th IEEE International Symposium on Parallel and Distributed Processing, IPDPS 2010, Atlanta, Georgia, USA, 19-23 April 2010 - Conference Proceedings*. 1–11. https://doi.org/10.1109/IPDPS.2010.5470440

[2] Shaikh Arifuzzaman, Maleq Khan, and Madhav V. Marathe. 2013. PATRIC: a parallel algorithm for counting triangles in massive networks. In *22nd ACM International Conference on Information and Knowledge Management, CIKM'13, San Francisco, CA, USA, October 27 - November 1, 2013*. 529–538. https://doi.org/10.1145/2505515.2505545

[3] Ziv Bar-Yossef, Ravi Kumar, and D. Sivakumar. 2002. Reductions in streaming algorithms, with an application to counting triangles in graphs. In *Proceedings of the Thirteenth Annual ACM-SIAM Symposium on Discrete Algorithms, January 6-8, 2002, San Francisco, CA, USA*. 623–632. http://dl.acm.org/citation.cfm?id=545381.545464

[4] Luca Becchetti, Paolo Boldi, Carlos Castillo, and Aristides Gionis. 2008. Efficient Semi-streaming Algorithms for Local Triangle Counting in Massive Graphs. In *Proceedings of the 14th ACM SIGKDD International Conference on Knowledge Discovery and Data Mining (KDD '08)*. ACM, New York, NY, USA, 16–24. https://doi.org/10.1145/1401890.1401898

[5] Suman K. Bera and Amit Chakrabarti. 2017. Towards Tighter Space Bounds for Counting Triangles and Other Substructures in Graph Streams. In *34th Symposium on Theoretical Aspects of Computer Science (STACS 2017) (Leibniz International Proceedings in Informatics (LIPIcs))*, Heribert Vollmer and Brigitte Vallée (Eds.), Vol. 66. Schloss Dagstuhl–Leibniz-Zentrum fuer Informatik, Dagstuhl, Germany, 11:1–11:14. https://doi.org/10.4230/LIPIcs.STACS.2017.11

[6] Jonathan W. Berry, Bruce Hendrickson, Simon Kahan, and Petr Konecny. 2007. Software and Algorithms for Graph Queries on Multithreaded Architectures. In *21th International Parallel and Distributed Processing Symposium (IPDPS 2007), Proceedings, 26-30 March 2007, Long Beach, California, USA*. 1–14. https://doi.org/10.1109/IPDPS.2007.370685

[7] Jonathan W. Berry, Bruce Hendrickson, Randall A. LaViolette, and Cynthia A. Phillips. 2011. Tolerating the community detection resolution limit with edge weighting. *Phys. Rev. E* 83 (May 2011), 056119. Issue 5. https://doi.org/10.1103/PhysRevE.83.056119

[8] J. Bondy and M. Simonovits. 1974. Cycles of even length in graphs. *Journal of Combinatorial Theory, Series B* (1974), 97–105.

[9] Vladimir Braverman, Rafail Ostrovsky, and Dan Vilenchik. 2013. How Hard Is Counting Triangles in the Streaming Model?. In *Automata, Languages, and Programming - 40th International Colloquium, ICALP 2013, Riga, Latvia, July 8-12, 2013, Proceedings, Part I*. 244–254. https://doi.org/10.1007/978-3-642-39206-1_21

[10] Joshua Brody and Amit Chakrabarti. 2008. Sublinear communication protocols for multi-party pointer jumping and a related lower bound. *arXiv preprint arXiv:0802.2843* (2008).

[11] Joshua Brody and Mario Sanchez. 2015. Dependent Random Graphs and Multiparty Pointer Jumping. *CoRR* abs/1506.01083 (2015). arXiv:1506.01083

[12] Luciana S. Buriol, Gereon Frahling, Stefano Leonardi, Alberto Marchetti-Spaccamela, and Christian Sohler. 2006. Counting triangles in data streams. In *Proceedings of the Twenty-Fifth ACM SIGACT-SIGMOD-SIGART Symposium on Principles of Database Systems, June 26-28, 2006, Chicago, Illinois, USA*. 253–262. https://doi.org/10.1145/1142351.1142388

[13] Graham Cormode and Hossein Jowhari. 2014. A second look at counting triangles in graph streams. *Theor. Comput. Sci.* 552 (2014), 44–51. https://doi.org/10.1016/j.tcs.2014.07.025

[14] Jean-Pierre Eckmann and Elisha Moses. 2002. Curvature of co-links uncovers hidden thematic layers in the World Wide Web. *Proceedings of the National Academy of Sciences* 99, 9 (2002), 5825–5829. https://doi.org/10.1073/pnas.032093399

[15] emab (http://math.stackexchange.com/users/74964/emab). 2014. Number of triangles in a graph based on number of edges. Mathematics Stack Exchange. URL:http://math.stackexchange.com/q/823650 (version: 2014-06-07).

[16] David GarcÃŋa-Soriano and Konstantin Kutzkov. [n. d.]. Triangle counting in streamed graphs via small vertex covers. In *Proceedings of the 2014 SIAM International Conference on Data Mining*. 352–360. https://doi.org/10.1137/1.9781611973440.40

[17] Hossein Jowhari and Mohammad Ghodsi. 2005. New Streaming Algorithms for Counting Triangles in Graphs. In *Computing and Combinatorics, 11th Annual International Conference, COCOON 2005, Kunming, China, August 16-29, 2005, Proceedings*. 710–716. https://doi.org/10.1007/11533719_72

[18] John Kallaugher and Eric Price. 2017. A Hybrid Sampling Scheme for Triangle Counting. In *Proceedings of the Twenty-Eighth Annual ACM-SIAM Symposium on Discrete Algorithms (SODA '17)*. Society for Industrial and Applied Mathematics, Philadelphia, PA, USA, 1778–1797. http://dl.acm.org/citation.cfm?id=3039686.3039802

[19] B. Kalyanasundaram and G. Schintger. 1992. The Probabilistic Communication Complexity of Set Intersection. *SIAM Journal on Discrete Mathematics* 5, 4 (1992), 545–557. https://doi.org/10.1137/0405044

[20] Daniel M. Kane, Kurt Mehlhorn, Thomas Sauerwald, and He Sun. 2012. Counting Arbitrary Subgraphs in Data Streams. In *Proceedings of the 39th International Colloquium Conference on Automata, Languages, and Programming - Volume Part II (ICALP'12)*. Springer-Verlag, Berlin, Heidelberg, 598–609. https://doi.org/10.1007/978-3-642-31585-5_53

[21] Mihail N. Kolountzakis, Gary L. Miller, Richard Peng, and Charalampos E. Tsourakakis. 2012. Efficient Triangle Counting in Large Graphs via Degree-Based Vertex Partitioning. *Internet Mathematics* 8, 1-2 (2012), 161–185. https://doi.org/10.1080/15427951.2012.625260
[22] Ilan Kremer, Noam Nisan, and Dana Ron. 1995. On Randomized One-round Communication Complexity. In *Proceedings of the Twenty-seventh Annual ACM Symposium on Theory of Computing (STOC '95)*. ACM, New York, NY, USA, 596–605. https://doi.org/10.1145/225058.225277
[23] Konstantin Kutzkov and Rasmus Pagh. 2014. Triangle Counting in Dynamic Graph Streams. In *Algorithm Theory - SWAT 2014 - 14th Scandinavian Symposium and Workshops, Copenhagen, Denmark, July 2-4, 2014. Proceedings*. 306–318. https://doi.org/10.1007/978-3-319-08404-6_27
[24] Jure Leskovec, Lars Backstrom, Ravi Kumar, and Andrew Tomkins. 2008. Microscopic evolution of social networks. In *Proceedings of the 14th ACM SIGKDD International Conference on Knowledge Discovery and Data Mining, Las Vegas, Nevada, USA, August 24-27, 2008*. 462–470. https://doi.org/10.1145/1401890.1401948
[25] Madhusudan Manjunath, Kurt Mehlhorn, Konstantinos Panagiotou, and He Sun. 2011. Approximate Counting of Cycles in Streams. In *Algorithms - ESA 2011 - 19th Annual European Symposium, Saarbrücken, Germany, September 5-9, 2011. Proceedings*. 677–688. https://doi.org/10.1007/978-3-642-23719-5_57
[26] Andrew McGregor, Sofya Vorotnikova, and Hoa T. Vu. 2016. Better Algorithms for Counting Triangles in Data Streams. In *Proceedings of the 35th ACM SIGMOD-SIGACT-SIGAI Symposium on Principles of Database Systems, PODS 2016, San Francisco, CA, USA, June 26 - July 01, 2016*. 401–411. https://doi.org/10.1145/2902251.2902283
[27] Rasmus Pagh and Charalampos E. Tsourakakis. 2012. Colorful triangle counting and a MapReduce implementation. *Inf. Process. Lett.* 112, 7 (2012), 277–281. https://doi.org/10.1016/j.ipl.2011.12.007
[28] A. Pavan, Kanat Tangwongsan, Srikanta Tirthapura, and Kun-Lung Wu. 2013. Counting and Sampling Triangles from a Graph Stream. *PVLDB* 6, 14 (2013), 1870–1881. http://www.vldb.org/pvldb/vol6/p1870-aduri.pdf
[29] A. A. Razborov. 1992. On the Distributional Complexity of Disjointness. *Theor. Comput. Sci.* 106, 2 (Dec. 1992), 385–390. https://doi.org/10.1016/0304-3975(92)90260-M
[30] Alexander A. Sherstov. 2014. Communication Lower Bounds Using Directional Derivatives. *J. ACM* 61, 6, Article 34 (Dec. 2014), 71 pages. https://doi.org/10.1145/2629334
[31] Alexander A Sherstov. 2016. The multiparty communication complexity of set disjointness. *SIAM J. Comput.* 45, 4 (2016), 1450–1489.
[32] Siddharth Suri and Sergei Vassilvitskii. 2011. Counting triangles and the curse of the last reducer. In *Proceedings of the 20th International Conference on World Wide Web, WWW 2011, Hyderabad, India, March 28 - April 1, 2011*. 607–614. https://doi.org/10.1145/1963405.1963491
[33] Charalampos E. Tsourakakis, Mihail N. Kolountzakis, and Gary L. Miller. 2011. Triangle Sparsifiers. *J. Graph Algorithms Appl.* 15, 6 (2011), 703–726. https://doi.org/10.7155/jgaa.00245
[34] Emanuele Viola and Avi Wigderson. 2009. One-way multiparty communication lower bound for pointer jumping with applications. *Combinatorica* 29, 6 (01 Nov 2009), 719–743. https://doi.org/10.1007/s00493-009-2667-z

A PROOFS OMITTED FROM 4-CYCLE COUNTING

Definition 4.1. *We call an edge $e \in E(G)$ "heavy" if it is contained in at least $40\sqrt{T}$ 4-cycles, and "light" otherwise. We call a wedge w "overused" if it is contained in at least $40T^{1/4}$ 4-cycles, "heavy" if it contains a heavy edge, "bad" if it is either overused or heavy, and "good" otherwise. We call a cycle "good" if it contains at least one good wedge. We will denote the set of good cycles as F_G.*

Lemma 4.2. $|F_G| = \Omega(T)$

We split the proof of this into three subsidiary lemmas.

Lemma A.1. *There are at least $\frac{13}{50}T$ cycles containing no more than one heavy edge.*

Proof. Call a wedge "very heavy" if it contains two heavy edges. We note that there are at most $\sqrt{T}/10$ heavy edges, as each cycle contains 4 edges. Therefore, there are at most $T/100$ distinct pairs of disjoint heavy edges, and so there are at most $T/50$ cycles containing a pair of disjoint heavy edges, as each such pair may participate in at most two distinct cycles.

Therefore, the remaining $\frac{49}{50}T$ cycles all either contain no more than one heavy edge, or consist of one light wedge joined with one very heavy wedge. Let the number of cycles of the second type be B.

For each pair of vertices uv, let g_{uv} be the number of light wedges of the form uwv for some vertex w, and b_{uv} be the number of very heavy wedges of that form. Then we have:

$$B = \sum_{uv \in V(G)^2} g_{uv} b_{uv}$$

Furthermore,

$$\sum_{\substack{uv \in V(G)^2: \\ g_{uv} \leq 2}} g_{uv} b_{uv} \leq 2 \sum_{uv \in V(G)^2} b_{uv} \leq T/50$$

and so we have:

$$B \leq \sum_{\substack{uv \in V(G)^2: \\ g_{uv} > 2}} g_{uv} b_{uv} + T/50$$

Furthermore, between any pair of vertices there are at least $\binom{b_{uv}}{2}$ cycles consisting of two very heavy wedges with endpoints at those vertices, and at least $\binom{g_{uv}}{2}$ cycles consisting of two light wedges with endpoints at those vertices. Furthermore, each of those cycles will appear between at most two pairs of vertices in this fashion. Therefore:

$$
\begin{aligned}
T &\geq B + \frac{1}{2} \sum_{uv \in V(G)^2} \left(\binom{g_{uv}}{2} + \binom{b_{uv}}{2} \right) \\
&\geq B + \frac{1}{2} \sum_{\substack{uv \in V(G)^2: \\ g_{uv} > 2}} \left(\binom{g_{uv}}{2} + \binom{b_{uv}}{2} \right) \\
&= B + \frac{1}{4} \sum_{\substack{uv \in V(G)^2: \\ g_{uv} > 2}} \left(g_{uv}^2 - g_{uv} + b_{uv}^2 - b_{uv} \right) \\
&\geq B + \frac{1}{4} \sum_{\substack{uv \in V(G)^2: \\ g_{uv} > 2}} \left(\frac{2}{3} g_{uv}^2 + b_{uv}^2 \right) - T/400 \\
&\geq B + \frac{1}{\sqrt{6}} \sum_{\substack{uv \in V(G)^2: \\ g_{uv} > 2}} g_{uv} b_{uv} - T/400 \\
&\geq B + \frac{1}{\sqrt{6}} (B - T/50) - T/400
\end{aligned}
$$

where the last step plugs in the previous expression. Hence:

$$B \leq T(1 + \frac{1}{50\sqrt{6}} + \frac{1}{400})/(1 + \frac{1}{\sqrt{6}}) < 0.72T$$

So the number of cycles that contain no more than one heavy edge is at least $\frac{49}{50}T - 0.72T = \frac{13}{50}T$. □

For the next two lemmas, note that there are at most $4T/40T^{1/4} = T^{3/4}/10$ overused wedges, as each cycle contains 4 distinct wedges. We will distinguish between two kinds of vertices. Let a vertex $v \in V(G)$ be "primary" if it is an endpoint of at least $\sqrt{T}$ overused wedges, and "secondary" otherwise. There are at most $2 \cdot T^{3/4}/10 \cdot 1/\sqrt{T} = T^{1/4}/5$ primary vertices.

Lemma A.2. *There are at most $\frac{3}{25}T$ 4-cycles containing all overused wedges.*

Proof. Any 4-cycle that contains all overused wedges *and* at least one primary vertex can be uniquely specified by one primary vertex and an overused wedge that is disjoint from it. There are therefore at most

$$T^{1/4}/5 \cdot T^{3/4}/10 \leq T/50$$

such cycles. Now, for any pair of secondary vertices $u, v \in V(G)$, let X_{uv} be the number of 4-cycles that contain u and v as opposite vertices (that is, not connected by any edge in the cycle), and have only overused wedges. As both u and v are secondary, $X_{uv} \leq \sqrt{T}$. Note also that there are at least $\sqrt{X_{uv}}$ overused wedges with u and v as their endpoints. Then, the number of 4-cycles containing only secondary vertices and all overused wedges is at most:

$$
\begin{aligned}
\sum_{\substack{uv \in V(G)^2: \\ u,v \text{ secondary}}} X_{uv} &\leq T^{1/4} \sum_{\substack{uv \in V(G)^2: \\ u,v \text{ secondary}}} \sqrt{X_{uv}} \\
&\leq T^{1/4} \# \text{ of overused wedges} \\
&\leq T/10
\end{aligned}
$$

So the total number of cycles that contain all overused wedges is at most $\frac{1}{50}T + \frac{1}{10}T = \frac{3}{25}T$. □

Lemma A.3. *There are at most $\frac{3}{25}T$ 4-cycles containing one heavy edge e and with the two wedges not containing e being overused.*

Proof. First we bound the number of such 4-cycles where e has at least one primary endpoint, v. For any such cycle, v has an overused wedge that is disjoint from it, and v together with this wedge uniquely determine the cycle, so the number of such cycles is at most:

$$T^{1/4}/5 \cdot T^{3/4}/10 = T/50$$

Second, we bound the number of such 4-cycles where e has at least one secondary endpoint v. Each such cycle can be characterised by the choices of e and the choice of overused wedge that connects to e at v. As v is secondary, there are at most $\sqrt{T}$ choices of this overused wedge, so the total number of such cycles is at most:

$$\sqrt{T}/10 \cdot \sqrt{T} = T/10$$

So the total number of cycles that contain one bad edge e and with the two wedges not containing e being overused is at most $\frac{1}{50}T + \frac{1}{10}T = \frac{3}{25}T$. □

By combining the previous three lemmas, there are at least $\frac{13}{50}$ cycles that contain no more than one heavy edge, no more than $\frac{3}{25}T$ of which have all overused cycles, and no more than $\frac{3}{25}T$ of which have one heavy edge e and both wedges that do not contain e overused. So the number of cycles which contain at least one good wedge is at least:

$$\frac{13}{50}T - \frac{3}{25}T - \frac{3}{25}T = \frac{1}{50}T = \Omega(T)\ .$$

On the Enumeration Complexity of Unions of Conjunctive Queries

Nofar Carmeli
Technion
Haifa, Israel
snofca@cs.technion.ac.il

Markus Kröll
TU Wien
Vienna, Austria
kroell@dbai.tuwien.ac.at

ABSTRACT

We study the enumeration complexity of Unions of Conjunctive Queries (UCQs). We aim to identify the UCQs that are tractable in the sense that the answer tuples can be enumerated with a linear preprocessing phase and a constant delay between every successive tuples. It has been established that, in the absence of self joins and under conventional complexity assumptions, the CQs that admit such an evaluation are precisely the free-connex ones. A union of tractable CQs is always tractable. We generalize the notion of free-connexity from CQs to UCQs, thus showing that some unions containing intractable CQs are, in fact, tractable. Interestingly, some unions consisting of only intractable CQs are tractable too. The question of a finding a full characterization of the tractability of UCQs remains open. Nevertheless, we prove that for several classes of queries, free-connexity fully captures the tractable UCQs.

CCS CONCEPTS

• **Theory of computation** → **Database theory**; *Complexity classes*; *Database query languages (principles)*; *Database query processing and optimization (theory)*.

KEYWORDS

unions of conjunctive queries, enumeration, complexity, constant delay

ACM Reference Format:
Nofar Carmeli and Markus Kröll. 2019. On the Enumeration Complexity of Unions of Conjunctive Queries. In *38th ACM SIGMOD-SIGACT-SIGAI Symposium on Principles of Database Systems (PODS'19), June 30-July 5, 2019, Amsterdam, Netherlands.* ACM, New York, NY, USA, 15 pages. https://doi.org/10.1145/3294052.3319700

PODS'19, June 30-July 5, 2019, Amsterdam, Netherlands

ACM ISBN 978-1-4503-6227-6/19/06...$15.00
https://doi.org/10.1145/3294052.3319700

1 INTRODUCTION

Evaluating a query Q over a database instance D is a fundamental and well-studied problem in database management systems. Most of the complexity results dealing with query evaluation so far aim to solve a decision or counting variant of it. Starting with Durand and Grandjean in 2007 [7], there has been a renewed interest in examining the enumeration problem of all answers to a query, focusing on fine-grained complexity [6, 8, 15, 16]. When evaluating a non-Boolean query over a database, the number of results may be larger than the size of the database itself. Enumeration complexity offers specific measures for the hardness of such problems. In terms of data complexity, the best time guarantee we can hope for is to output all answers with a constant delay between consecutive answers. In the case of query evaluation, this enumeration phase comes after a linear preprocessing phase required to read the database and decide the existence of a first answer. The enumeration class achieving these time bounds is denoted by $\mathsf{DelayC_{lin}}$. Hereafter, we refer to queries in $\mathsf{DelayC_{lin}}$ as tractable, and queries outside of this class as intractable.

Results by Bagan et al. [2] and Brault-Baron [5] form a dichotomy that fully classifies which self-join free Conjunctive Queries (CQs) are in the class $\mathsf{DelayC_{lin}}$ based on the structure of the query: the class of *free-connex* queries is exactly the class that admits tractable enumeration. In the years following this dichotomy, much work has been conducted to achieve similar results for other classes of queries [17]. Unions of CQs (UCQs) are a natural extension of CQs, as they describe the union of the answers to several CQs. UCQs form an important class of queries, as it captures the positive fragment of relational algebra. Previous work which implies results on the enumeration complexity of UCQs imposes strong restrictions on the underlying database [18]. We aim to understand the enumeration complexity of UCQs without such restrictions and based solely on their structure.

Using known methods [19], it can be shown that a union of tractable problems is again tractable. However, what happens if some CQs of a union are tractable while others are not? Intuitively, one might be tempted to expect a union of enumeration problems to be harder than a single problem within the union, making such a UCQ intractable as well. As we will show, this is not necessarily the case.

Example 1. Let $Q = Q_1 \cup Q_2$ with

$$Q_1(x, y) \leftarrow R_1(x, y), R_2(y, z), R_3(z, x) \text{ and}$$
$$Q_2(x, y) \leftarrow R_1(x, y), R_2(y, z).$$

Even though Q_1 is hard while Q_2 is easy, a closer look shows that Q_2 contains Q_1. This means that Q_1 is redundant, and the entire union is equivalent to the easy Q_2.

To avoid cases like these, where the UCQ can be translated to a simpler one, it makes sense to consider non-redundant unions. It was claimed that in all cases of a non-redundant union containing an intractable CQ, the UCQ is intractable too [4]. The following is a counter example which refutes this claim.

Example 2. Let $Q = Q_1 \cup Q_2$ with

$$Q_1(x, y, w) \leftarrow R_1(x, z), R_2(z, y), R_3(y, w) \text{ and}$$
$$Q_2(x, y, w) \leftarrow R_1(x, y), R_2(y, w).$$

According to the dichotomy of Bagan et al. [2], the enumeration problem for Q_2 is in $\mathsf{DelayC_{lin}}$, while Q_1 is intractable. Yet, it turns out that Q is in fact in $\mathsf{DelayC_{lin}}$. The reason is that, since Q_1 and Q_2 are evaluated over the same database, we can use $Q_2(I)$ to find $Q_1(I)$. We can compute $Q_2(I)$ efficiently, and try to extend every such solution to solutions of Q_1 with a constant delay: for every new combination a, c of an output $(a, b, c) \in Q_2(I)$, we find all d values with $(b, d) \in R_3^I$ and then output the solution $(a, c, d) \in Q_1(I)$. Intuitively, the source of intractability for Q_1 is the join of R_1 with R_2 as we need to avoid duplicates that originate in different z values. The union is tractable since Q_2 returns exactly this join. □

As the example illustrates, to compute the answers to a UCQ in an efficient way, it is not enough to view it as a union of isolated instances of CQ enumeration. In fact, this task requires an understanding of the interaction between several queries. Example 2 shows that the presence of an easy query within the union may give us enough time to compute auxiliary data structures, which we can then add to the hard queries in order to enumerate their answers as well. In Example 2, we can assume we have a ternary relation holding the result of Q_2. Then, adding the auxiliary atom $R_{Q_2}(x, z, y)$ to Q_1 results in a tractable structure. We generalize this observation and introduce the concept of *union-extended* queries. We then use union extensions as a central tool for evaluating the enumeration complexity of UCQs, as the structure of such queries has implications on the tractability of the UCQ.

Interestingly, this approach can be taken a step further: We show that the concept of extending the union by auxiliary atoms can even be used to efficiently enumerate the answers of UCQs that *only* contain hard queries. By lifting the concept of free-connex queries from CQs to UCQs via union-extended queries, we show that free-connex UCQs are always tractable. This gives us a sufficient global condition for membership in $\mathsf{DelayC_{lin}}$ beyond any classification of individual CQs.

Finding a full characterization of the tractability of UCQs with respect to $\mathsf{DelayC_{lin}}$ remains an open problem. Nevertheless, we prove that for several classes of queries, free-connexity fully captures the tractable UCQs. A non-free-connex union of two CQs is intractable in the following cases: both CQs are intractable, or they both represent the same CQ up to a different projection. The hardness results presented here use problems with well-established assumptions on the lower bounds, such as Boolean matrix-multiplication [13] or finding a clique or a hyperclique in a graph [14].

Why is establishing lower bounds on UCQ evaluation, even when it contains only two CQs, a fundamentally more challenging problem than the one for CQs? In the case of CQs, hardness results are often shown by reducing a computationally hard problem to the task of answering a query. The reduction encodes the hard problem to the relations of a self-join free CQ, such that the answers of the CQ correspond to an answer of this problem [2, 3, 5, 6]. However, using such an encoding for CQs within a union does not always work. Similarly to the case of CQs with self-joins, relational symbols that appear multiple times within a query can interfere with the reduction. Indeed, when encoding a hard problem to an intractable CQ within a union, a different CQ in the union evaluates over the same relations, and may also produce answers. A large number of such supplementary answers, with constant delay per answer, accumulates to a long delay until we obtain the answers that correspond to the computationally hard problem. If this delay is larger than the lower bound we assume for the hard problem, we cannot conclude that the UCQ is intractable.

The lower bounds presented in this paper are obtained either by identifying classes of UCQs for which we can use similar reductions to the ones used for CQs, or by introducing alternative reductions. As some cases remain unclassified, we spend the last section of this paper inspecting such UCQs, and describing the challenges that will need to be resolved in order to achieve a full classification.

Our main contributions are as follows:

- We show that some non-redundant UCQs containing intractable CQs are tractable, and even that unions containing only intractable CQs may be tractable.
- We extend the notion of free-connexity to UCQs, and show that free-connex UCQs can be evaluated with linear time preprocessing and constant delay.

- We establish lower bounds on UCQs w.r.t. $\mathsf{DelayC_{lin}}$, and prove that free-connexity captures exactly the tractable cases in some classes of UCQs.
- We provide a discussion accompanied by examples, describing the challenges that need to be resolved to achieve a full characterization of the tractable UCQs.

This work is organized as follows: In Section 2 we provide definitions and state results that we use. Section 3 formalizes how CQs within a union can make each other easier, defines free-connex UCQs, and proves that free-connex UCQs are in $\mathsf{DelayC_{lin}}$. In Section 4 we prove conditional lower bounds and conclude a dichotomy for some classes of UCQs. Section 5 discusses the future steps required for a full classification, and demonstrates examples of queries of unknown complexity. Concluding remarks are given in Section 6.

2 PRELIMINARIES

In this section we provide preliminary definitions as well as state results that we will use throughout this paper.

Unions of Conjunctive Queries. A *schema* $\mathcal{S}$ is a set of *relational symbols* $\{R_1,\dots,R_n\}$. We denote the *arity* of a relational symbol R_i as arity(R_i). Let *dom* be a finite set of constants. A database I over schema $\mathcal{S}$ is called an *instance* of $\mathcal{S}$, and it consists of a finite relation $R_i^I \subseteq dom^{\text{arity}(R_i)}$ for every relational symbol $R_i \in \mathcal{R}$.

Let *var* be a set of variables disjoint from *dom*. A *Conjunctive Query* (CQ) over schema $\mathcal{S}$ is an expression of the form $Q(\vec{p}) \leftarrow R_1(\vec{v}_1),\dots,R_m(\vec{v}_m)$, where $R_1,\dots,R_m$ are relational symbols of $\mathcal{S}$, the tuples $\vec{p},\vec{v}_1,\dots,\vec{v}_m$ hold variables, and every variable in $\vec{p}$ appears in at least one of $\vec{v}_1,\dots,\vec{v}_m$. We often denote this query as Q. Define the variables of Q as $var(Q) = \bigcup_{i=1}^{m}\vec{v}_i$, and define the *free variables* of Q as free$(Q) = \vec{p}$. We call $Q(\vec{p})$ the head of Q, and the atomic formulas $R_i(\vec{v}_i)$ are called *atoms*. We further use atoms(Q) to denote the set of atoms of Q. A CQ is said to be *self-join free* if no relational symbol appears in more than one atom.

The *evaluation* $Q(I)$ of a CQ Q over a database I is the set of all *mappings* $\mu|_{\text{free}(Q)}$ such that μ is a homomorphism from $R_1(\vec{v}_1),\dots,R_m(\vec{v}_m)$ into I, and $\mu|_{\text{free}(Q)}$ is the restriction (or projection) of μ to the variables free(Q). A CQ Q_1 is *contained* in a CQ Q_2, denoted $Q_1 \subseteq Q_2$, if for every instance I, $Q_1(I) \subseteq Q_2(I)$. A *homomorphism* from Q_2 to Q_1 is a mapping $h: var(Q_2) \to var(Q_1)$ such that: (1) for every atom $R(\vec{v})$ of Q_2, $R(h(\vec{v}))$ is an atom in Q_1; (2) $h(\text{free}(Q_2)) = \text{free}(Q_1)$.

A *Union of Conjunctive Queries (UCQ)* Q is a set of CQs, denoted $Q = \bigcup_{i=1}^{\ell} Q_i$, where free$(Q_{i_1})$ = free(Q_{i_2}) for all $1 \le i_1, i_2 \le \ell$. Semantically, $Q(I) = \bigcup_{i=1}^{\ell} Q_i(I)$. Given a UCQ Q and a database instance I, we denote by $\textsc{Decide}\langle Q\rangle$ the problem of deciding whether $Q(I) \neq \emptyset$.

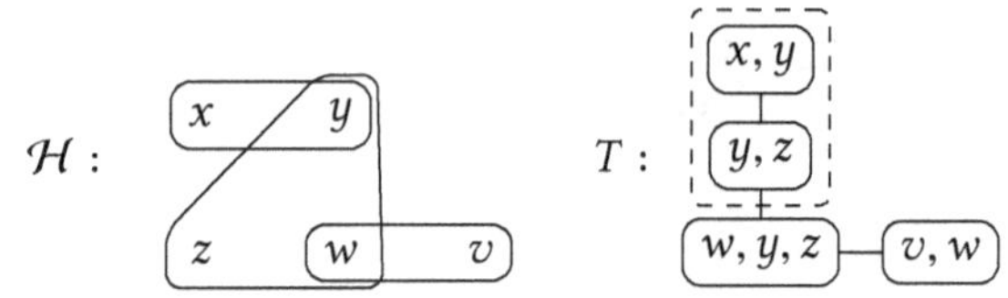

Figure 1: T is an ext-$\{x,y,z\}$-connex tree for hypergraph $\mathcal{H}$.

Hypergraphs. A *hypergraph* $\mathcal{H} = (V,E)$ is a set V of *vertices* and a set E of non-empty subsets of V called *hyperedges* (sometimes *edges*). A *join tree* of a hypergraph $\mathcal{H} = (V,E)$ is a tree T where the nodes are the hyperedges of $\mathcal{H}$, and the *running intersection* property holds, namely: for all $u \in V$ the set $\{e \in E \mid u \in e\}$ forms a connected subtree in T. A hypergraph $\mathcal{H}$ is *acyclic* if there exists a join tree for $\mathcal{H}$.

Two vertices in a hypergraph are *neighbors* if they appear in the same edge. A *clique* of a hypergraph is a set of vertices, which are pairwise neighbors in $\mathcal{H}$. If every edge in $\mathcal{H}$ has k many vertices, we call $\mathcal{H}$ k-*uniform*. An l-*hyperclique* in a k-uniform hypergraph $\mathcal{H}$ is a set V' of $l > k$ vertices, such that every subset of V' of size k forms a hyperedge.

A hypergraph $\mathcal{H}'$ is an *inclusive extension* of $\mathcal{H}$ if every edge of $\mathcal{H}$ appears in $\mathcal{H}'$, and every edge of $\mathcal{H}'$ is a subset of some edge in $\mathcal{H}$. A tree T is an *ext-S-connex tree* for a hypergraph $\mathcal{H}$ if: (1) T is a join-tree of an inclusive extension of $\mathcal{H}$, and (2) there is a subtree T' of T that contains exactly the variables S [2] (see Figure 1).

Classes of CQs. We associate a hypergraph $\mathcal{H}(Q) = (V,E)$ to a CQ Q where the vertices are the variables of Q, and every hyperedge is a set of variables occurring in a single atom of Q. That is, $E = \{\{v_1,\dots,v_n\} \mid R_i(v_1,\dots,v_n) \in \text{atoms}(Q)\}$. With a slight abuse of notation, we identify atoms of Q with edges of $\mathcal{H}(Q)$. A CQ Q is said to be *acyclic* if $\mathcal{H}(Q)$ is acyclic

A CQ Q is *S-connex* if $\mathcal{H}(Q)$ has an ext-S-connex tree, and it is *free-connex* if it has an ext-free(Q)-connex tree [2]. Equivalently, Q is free-connex if both Q and $(V, E \cup \{\text{free}(Q)\})$ are acyclic [5]. A *free-path* in a CQ Q is a sequence of variables $(x, z_1,\dots,z_k, y)$ with $k \ge 1$, such that: (1) $\{x,y\} \subseteq \text{free}(Q)$ (2) $\{z_1,\dots,z_k\} \subseteq V \setminus \text{free}(Q)$ (3) It is a *chordless path* in $\mathcal{H}(Q)$: that is, every two succeeding variables are neighbors in $\mathcal{H}(Q)$, but no two non-succeeding variables are neighbors. An acyclic CQ has a free-path iff it is not free-connex [2].

Computational Model. The size of the input to most of our problems is measured only by the size of the database instance I. We denote by $||o||$ the size of an object o (i.e., the number of integers required to store it), whereas $|o|$ is its cardinality. Let I be a database over a schema $\mathcal{S} = (\mathcal{R},\Delta)$. Flum et al. describe a reasonable encoding $||I||$ of the database as a word over integers bound by $\max\{|dom|, max_{R\in\mathcal{R}}|R^I|\}$ [9].

In this paper we adopt the *Random Access Machine* (RAM) model with uniform cost measure. For an input of size n, every register is of length $O(\log(n))$. Operations such as addition of the values of two registers or concatenation can be performed in constant time. In contrast to the Turing model of computation, the RAM model with uniform cost measure can retrieve the content of any register via its unique address in constant time. This enables the construction of large lookup tables that can be queried within constant time.

We use a variant of the RAM model named DRAM [10], where the values stored in registers are at most n^c for some fixed integer c. As a consequence, the amount of available memory is polynomial in n.

Enumeration Complexity. Given a finite alphabet Σ and binary relation $R \subseteq \Sigma^* \times \Sigma^*$, the *enumeration problem* $\text{ENUM}\langle R\rangle$ is: given an instance $x \in \Sigma^*$, output all $y \in \Sigma^*$ such that $(x, y) \in R$. Such y values are often called *solutions* or *answers* to $\text{ENUM}\langle R\rangle$. An *enumeration algorithm* $\mathcal{A}$ for $\text{ENUM}\langle R\rangle$ is a RAM that solves $\text{ENUM}\langle R\rangle$ without repetitions. We say that $\mathcal{A}$ enumerates $\text{ENUM}\langle R\rangle$ with *delay* $d(|x|)$ if the time before the first output, the time between any two consecutive outputs, and the time between the last output and termination are each bound by $d(|x|)$. Sometimes we wish to relax the requirements of the delay before the first answer, and specify a *preprocessing* time $p(|x|)$. In this case, the time before the first output is only required to be bound by $p(|x|)$. The enumeration class $\text{DelayC}_{\text{lin}}$ is defined as the class of all enumeration problems $\text{ENUM}\langle R\rangle$ which have an enumeration algorithm $\mathcal{A}$ with preprocessing $p(|x|) \in O(|x|)$ and delay $d(|x|) \in O(1)$. Note that we do not impose a restriction on the memory used. In particular, such an algorithm may use additional constant memory for writing between two consecutive answers.

Let $\text{ENUM}\langle R_1\rangle$ and $\text{ENUM}\langle R_2\rangle$ be enumeration problems. There is an *exact reduction* from $\text{ENUM}\langle R_1\rangle$ to $\text{ENUM}\langle R_2\rangle$, denoted as $\text{ENUM}\langle R_1\rangle \leq_e \text{ENUM}\langle R_2\rangle$, if there exist mappings σ and τ such that: (1) for every $x \in \Sigma^*$, $\sigma(x)$ is computable in $O(|x|)$ time; (2) for every y such that $(\sigma(x), y) \in R_2$, $\tau(y)$ is computable in $O(1)$ time; and (3) in multiset notation, $\{\tau(y) \mid (\sigma(x), y) \in R_2\} = \{y' \mid (x, y') \in R_1\}$. Intuitively, σ maps instances of $\text{ENUM}\langle R_1\rangle$ to instances of $\text{ENUM}\langle R_2\rangle$, and τ maps solutions of $\text{ENUM}\langle R_2\rangle$ to solutions of $\text{ENUM}\langle R_1\rangle$. If $\text{ENUM}\langle R_1\rangle \leq_e \text{ENUM}\langle R_2\rangle$ and $\text{ENUM}\langle R_2\rangle \in \text{DelayC}_{\text{lin}}$, then $\text{ENUM}\langle R_1\rangle \in \text{DelayC}_{\text{lin}}$ as well [2].

Computational Hypotheses. In the following, we will use the following well-established hypotheses for lower bounds on certain computational problems:

MAT-MUL: two Boolean $n \times n$ matrices cannot be multiplied in time $O(n^2)$. This problem is equivalent to the evaluation of the query $\Pi(x, y) \leftarrow A(x, z), B(z, y)$ over the schema $\{A, B\}$ where $A, B \subseteq \{1, \ldots, n\}^2$. It is strongly conjectured that this problem cannot be solved in $O(n^2)$ time, and the best algorithms today require $O(n^\omega)$ time for some $2.37 < \omega < 2.38$ [1, 13].

HYPERCLIQUE: for all $k \geq 3$, finding a k-hyperclique in a $(k-1)$-uniform graph is not possible in time $O(n^{k-1})$. This is a special case of the (ℓ, k)– Hyperclique Hypothesis [14], which states that, in a k-uniform hypergraph of n vertices, $n^{k-o(1)}$ time is required to find a set of ℓ vertices such that each of it subsets of size k forms a hyperedge. The HYPERCLIQUE hypothesis is sometimes called Tetra$\langle k\rangle$ [5].

4-CLIQUE: it is not possible to determine the existence of a 4-clique in a graph with n nodes in time $O(n^3)$.
This is a special case of the k-Clique Hypothesis [14], which states that detecting a clique in a graph with n nodes requires $n^{\frac{\omega k}{3} - o(1)}$ time, where $\omega < 2.373$ is the matrix multiplication exponent.

Enumerating Answers to UCQs. Given a UCQ Q over some schema $\mathcal{S}$, we denote by $\text{ENUM}\langle Q\rangle$ the enumeration problem $\text{ENUM}\langle R\rangle$, where R is the binary relation between instances I over $\mathcal{S}$ and sets of mappings $Q(I)$. We consider the size of the query as well as the size of the schema to be fixed. In the case of CQs, Bagan et al. [2] showed that a self-join free acyclic CQ is in $\text{DelayC}_{\text{lin}}$ iff it is free-connex. In addition, Brault-Baron [5] showed that self-join free cyclic queries are not in $\text{DelayC}_{\text{lin}}$. In fact, the existence of a single answer to a cyclic CQ cannot be determined in linear time.

Theorem 3 ([2, 5]). *Let Q be a self-join free CQ.*

(1) If Q is free-connex, then $\text{ENUM}\langle Q\rangle \in \text{DelayC}_{\text{lin}}$.
(2) If Q is acyclic and not free-connex, then $\text{ENUM}\langle Q\rangle$ is not in $\text{DelayC}_{\text{lin}}$, assuming MAT-MUL.
(3) If Q is cyclic, then $\text{ENUM}\langle Q\rangle \notin \text{DelayC}_{\text{lin}}$, as $\text{DECIDE}\langle Q\rangle$ cannot be solved in linear time, assuming HYPERCLIQUE.

The positive case of this dichotomy can be shown using the *Constant Delay Yannakakis* (CDY) algorithm [11]. It uses an ext-free(Q)-connex tree T for Q. First, it performs the classical Yannakakis preprocessing [20] over T to obtain a relation for each node in T, where all tuples can be used for some answer in $Q(I)$. Then, it considers only the subtree of T containing free(Q), and joins the relations corresponding to this subtree with constant delay.

3 UPPER BOUNDS VIA UNION EXTENSIONS

In this section we generalize the notion of free-connexity to UCQs and show that such queries are in $\text{DelayC}_{\text{lin}}$. We do so by introducing the concepts of *union extensions* and variable sets that a single CQ can *provide* to another CQ in the union in order to help evaluation. First, note that using known techniques [19, Proposition 2.38] a union of tractable CQs is also tractable.

Theorem 4. *Let Q be a UCQ. If all CQs in Q are free-connex, then* $\textsc{Enum}\langle Q\rangle \in \mathsf{DelayC}_{\mathsf{lin}}$.

Proof. The following is an algorithm to evaluate a union of two CQs. In case of a union $Q = \bigcup_{i=1}^{\ell} Q_i$ of more CQs, we can use this recursively by treating the second query as $Q_2 \cup \ldots \cup Q_\ell$.

Algorithm 1 Answering a union of two tractable CQs

```
1: while a ← Q1(I).next() do
2:     if a ∉ Q2(I) then
3:         print a
4:     else
5:         print Q2(I).next()
6: while a ← Q2(I).next() do
7:     print a
```

By the end of the run, the algorithm prints $Q_1(I) \setminus Q_2(I)$ over all iterations of line 3, and it prints $Q_2(I)$ in lines 5 and 7. Line 5 is called $Q_1(I) \cap Q_2(I)$ times, so the command $Q_2(I).next()$ always succeeds there. Since free-connex CQs can be enumerated in constant delay and tested in constant time after a linear time preprocessing phase, this algorithm runs within the required time bounds. □

The technique presented in the proof of 4 has the advantage that it does not require more than constant memory available for writing in the enumeration phase. Alternatively, this theorem is a consequence of the following lemma, which gives us a general approach to compile several enumeration algorithms into one. This lemma is useful to show upper bounds for UCQs even in cases not covered by Theorem 4.

Lemma 5. *Let $R \subseteq \Sigma^* \times \Sigma^*$, and let $\mathcal{A}$ be an algorithm that outputs the solutions to* $\textsc{Enum}\langle R\rangle$ *such that:*

- *the delay of $\mathcal{A}$ is bound by $p(x)$ at most n times and bound by $d(x)$ otherwise;*
- *every result is produced at most m times.*

Then, there exists an enumeration algorithm $\mathcal{A}'$ for $\textsc{Enum}\langle R\rangle$, *with $np(x) + md(x)$ preprocessing time and $md(x)$ delay.*

Proof. $\mathcal{A}'$ simulates $\mathcal{A}$ and maintains a lookup table and a queue that are initialized as empty. When $\mathcal{A}$ returns a result, $\mathcal{A}'$ checks the lookup table to determine whether it was found before. If it was not, the result is added to both the lookup table and the queue. $\mathcal{A}'$ first performs $np(x)$ computation steps, and then after every $md(x)$ computation steps, it outputs a result from the queue. $\mathcal{A}'$ returns its ith result after $np(x) + imd(x)$ computation steps. At this time, $\mathcal{A}$ produced at least mi results, which form at least i unique results, so the queue is never empty when accessed. When it is done simulating $\mathcal{A}'$, $\mathcal{A}$ outputs all remaining results in the queue. $\mathcal{A}'$ outputs all results of $\mathcal{A}$ with no duplicates since every result enters the queue exactly once. □

A direct consequence of Lemma 5 is that to show that a problem is in $\mathsf{DelayC}_{\mathsf{lin}}$, it suffices to find an algorithm for this problem where the delay is usually constant, but it may be linear a constant number of times, and the number of times every result is produced is bound by a constant.

As Example 2 shows, Theorem 4 does not cover all tractable UCQs. We now address the other cases and start with some definitions. We define *body-homomorphisms* between CQs to have the standard meaning of homomorphism, but without the restriction on the heads of the queries.

Definition 6. Let Q_1, Q_2 be CQs.

- A *body-homomorphism* from Q_2 to Q_1 is a mapping $h : var(Q_2) \rightarrow var(Q_1)$ such that for every atom $R(\vec{v})$ of Q_2, $R(h(\vec{v})) \in Q_1$.
- If Q_1, Q_2 are self-join free and there exists a body-homomorphism h from Q_2 to Q_1 and vice versa, we say that Q_2 and Q_1 are *body-isomorphic*, and h is called a *body-isomorphism.*

We now formalize the way that one CQ can help another CQ in the union during evaluation by providing variables.

Definition 7. Let Q_1, Q_2 be CQs. We say that Q_2 *provides* a set of variables $V_1 \subseteq var(Q_1)$ to Q_1 if:

(1) There is a body-homomorphism h from Q_2 to Q_1.
(2) There is $V_2 \subseteq \text{free}(Q_2)$ such that $h(V_2) = V_1$.
(3) There is $V_2 \subseteq S \subseteq \text{free}(Q_2)$ such that Q_2 is S-connex.

Intuitively, the first condition requires that Q_2 provides complete information regarding the possible assignments to some variables of Q_1, the second condition ensures that these include the provided variables, and the third condition guarantees that these assignments can easily be computed as part of Q_2. The following lemma shows why provided variables play an important role for UCQ enumeration: If Q_2 provides a set of variables to Q_1, then we can produce an auxiliary relation for Q_1 containing all possible value combinations of these variables. This can be done efficiently while producing some answers to Q_2.

Lemma 8. *Let Q_1, Q_2 be CQs such that Q_2 provides V_1 to Q_1. Given an instance I, one can compute with linear time preprocessing and constant delay a set of mappings $M \subseteq Q_2(I)$, which can be translated to $Q_1(I)|_{V_1}$ in time $O(|M|)$.*

Proof. Let h, V_2 and S be a body-homomorphism and two sets of variables meeting the conditions of Definition 7. Take an ext-S-connex tree T for Q_2, and perform the CDY algorithm on Q_2 while treating S as the free-variables. This results in a set N of mappings from the variables of S to the domain such that $N = Q_2(I)|_S$.

For every mapping $\mu \in N$, extend it once to obtain a mapping from all variables of Q_2 as follows. Go over all vertices of T starting from the connected part containing S and treating a neighbor of an already treated vertex at every step. Consider a step where in its beginning μ is a homomorphism from a set S_1, and we are treating an atom $R_i(\vec{v}_i, \vec{u}_i)$ where $\vec{v}_i \subseteq S_1$ and $\vec{u}_i \cap S_1 = \emptyset$. We take some tuple in R_i of the form $(\mu(\vec{v}_i), t_i)$ and extend μ to also map $\mu(\vec{u}_i) = t_i$. Such a tuple exists since the CDY algorithm has a preprocessing step that removes dangling tuples. This extension takes constant time, and in its end we have that $\mu|_{free(Q)} \in Q_2(I)$. These extensions form $M \subseteq Q_2(I)$. When computing M, the delay for the first element may be linear due to the preprocessing phase of the CDY algorithm, but the delay after that is constant.

We now describe how M can be translated to $Q_1(I)|_{V_1}$. As $M|_{V_2} = Q_2(I)|_{V_2}$, we need to use the body-homomorphism in the opposite direction. For every variable $v_1 \in V_1$, define $h^{-1}(v_1) = \{v_2 \in V_2 \mid h(v_2) = v_1\}$. Given a mapping μ in $Q_2(I)$, if $\mu(v_2)$ is the same for all $v_2 \in h^{-1}(v_1)$, denote it by $\mu(h^{-1}(v_1))$. Otherwise, $\mu(h^{-1}(v_1))$ is undefined, and in the following μ is skipped. As h is a body-homomorphism, we have that $M|_{V_2} \circ h^{-1} = Q(I)|_{V_1}$. Given $\mu \in M$, we can compute $\mu|_{V_2} \circ h^{-1}$ (or determine it is undefined) in constant time. Doing this for every $\mu \in M$ computes $Q_1(I)|_{V_1}$ in time $O(|M|)$. □

Note that without the first condition of Definition 7, the lemma above does not hold in general. Here is an example.

Example 9. Consider $Q = Q_1 \cup Q_2$, which is a slight modification of the UCQ in from Example 2, with

$$Q_1(x, y, w) \leftarrow R_1(x, z), R_2(z, y), R_3(y, w) \text{ and}$$
$$Q_2(x, y, w) \leftarrow R_1(x, y), R_2(y, w), R_4(y).$$

Since R_4 is not a relational symbol in Q_1, there is no body-homomorphism from Q_2 to Q_1. If, $R_4^I = dom$, then we can take the same approach as in Example 2, as the answers of Q_2 form $Q_1(I)|_{\{x,z,y\}}$. However, if R_4^I is smaller, this extra atom may filter the answers to Q_2, and we do not obtain all of $Q_1(I)|_{\{x,z,y\}}$ in general. □

During evaluation, a set of variables provided to a CQ can form an auxiliary relation accessible by an auxiliary atom. The CQ with its auxiliary atoms is called a *union extension.*

Definition 10. Let $Q = Q_1 \cup \ldots \cup Q_n$ be a UCQ.

- A *union extension* Q_1^+ of $Q_1(\vec{v}) \leftarrow R_1(\vec{v}_1), \ldots, R_s(\vec{v}_s)$ is

$$Q_1^+(\vec{v}) \leftarrow R_1(\vec{v}_1), \ldots, R_s(\vec{v}_s), P_1(\vec{u}_1), \ldots, P_k(\vec{u}_k)$$

  where $k \geq 0$, each $\vec{u}_i$ is provided by some $Q_j \in Q$, and $P_1, \ldots, P_k$ are fresh relational symbols. By way of recursion, the variables $\vec{u}_i$ may alternatively be provided by a union extension of some $Q_j \in Q$.
- *Virtual atoms* are atoms appearing in Q_1^+ but not in Q_1.

Union extension can transform an intractable query to a free-connex one.

Definition 11. Let $Q = Q_1 \cup \ldots \cup Q_n$ be a UCQ.

- Q_1 is said to be *union-free-connex* with respect to Q if it has a free-connex union extension.
- Q is *free-connex* if all CQs in Q are union-free-connex.

Note that the term free-connex for UCQs is a generalization of that for CQs: If a UCQ Q contains only one CQ, then Q is free-connex iff the CQ it contains is free-connex. We next show that tractability of free-connex queries also carries over to UCQs.

Theorem 12. *Let Q be a UCQ. If Q is free-connex, then* $\textsc{Enum}\langle Q\rangle \in \mathsf{DelayC_{lin}}$.

Proof. For each query Q_1 in the union (in an order imposed by the recursive definition of union extensions), we first instantiate its free-connex union extension Q_1^+, and then evaluate the resulting free-connex CQ using the CDY algorithm: For every virtual atom containing some variables V_1, use Lemma 8 to generate a subset of $Q_2(I)$ while obtaining a relation $Q_1(I)|_{V_1}$ assigned to this atom. After instantiating all virtual relations, we have an instance I^+ for Q_1^+, and we can evaluate it as usual using the CDY algorithm. We have that $Q_1(I) = Q_1^+(I^+)$ since all virtual atoms in Q_1^+ are assigned relations that contain merely a projection of the results.

Overall, there is a constant number of times where the delay is linear: once per query and once per virtual atom. Similarly, every result is produced at most a constant number of times: once per query and once per virtual atom. According to Lemma 5 this means that $\textsc{Enum}\langle Q\rangle \in \mathsf{DelayC_{lin}}$. □

We can now revisit Example 2 and explain its tractability using the terminology and results introduced in this section. There is a body-homomorphism $h : Q_2 \to Q_1$ with $h((x, y, w)) = (x, z, y)$. The query Q_2 provides $\{x, z, y\}$ to Q_1, as $\{x, y, w\} \subseteq \text{free}(Q_2)$, and Q_2 is $\{x, y, w\}$-connex. Adding $R'(x, z, y)$ to Q_1 results in a free-connex union extension $Q_1^+(x, y, w) \leftarrow R_1(x, z), R_2(z, y), R_3(y, w), R'(x, z, y)$, as illustrated in Figure 2. Since every query in Q is union-free-connex, we have that $\textsc{Enum}\langle Q\rangle \in \mathsf{DelayC_{lin}}$ by Theorem 12.

Remark 1. Example 2 is a counter example to a past made claim [4, Theorem 4.2b]. The claim is that if a UCQ contains an intractable CQ and does not contain redundant CQs (a CQ contained in another CQ in the union), then the union is intractable. In contrast, none of the CQs in Example 2 is redundant, Q_1 is intractable, and yet the UCQ is tractable.

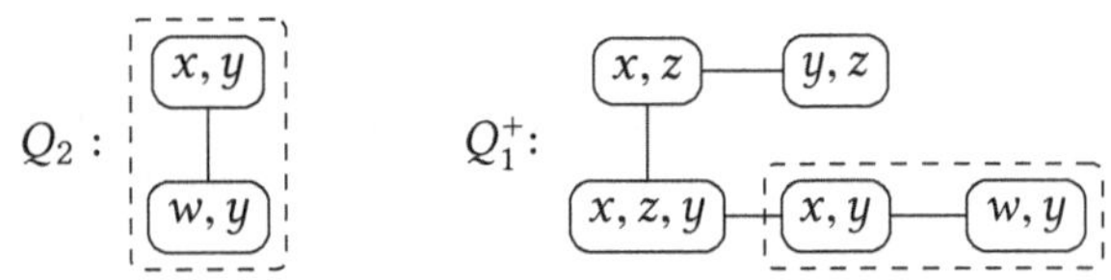

Figure 2: A $\{x, y, w\}$-connex tree for query Q_2 and a $\{x, y, w\}$-connex tree for query Q_1^+.

The intuition behind the proof of the past claim is reducing the hard CQ Q_1 to Q. This can be done by assigning each variable of Q_1 with a different and disjoint domain (e.g., by concatenating the variable names to the values in the relations corresponding to the atoms), and leaving the relations that do not appear in the atoms of Q_1 empty. It is well known that $Q_1 \subseteq Q_2$ iff there exists a homomorphism from Q_2 to Q_1. The claim is that since there is no homomorphism from another CQ in the union to Q_1, then there are no answers to the other CQs with this reduction. However, it is possible that there is a body-homomorphism from another CQ to Q_1 even if it is not a full homomorphism (the free variables do not map to each other). Therefore, in cases of a body-homomorphism, the reduction from the Q_1 to Q does not work. In such cases, the union may be tractable, as we show in Theorem 12. In Lemma 14, we use the same proof described here, but restrict it to UCQs where there is no body-homomorphism from other CQs to Q_1. □

The tractability result in Theorem 12 is based on the structure of the union-extended queries. This means that the intractability of any query within a UCQ can be resolved as long as another query can provide the right variables. The following example shows that this can even be the case for a UCQ only consisting of non-free-connex CQs. Moreover, the example illustrates why we need the definition of union extensions to be recursive.

Example 13. Let $Q = Q_1 \cup Q_2 \cup Q_3$ with

$$\begin{aligned} Q_1(x, y, v, u) \leftarrow & R_1(x, z_1), R_2(z_1, z_2), R_3(z_2, z_3), \\ & R_4(z_3, y), R_5(y, v, u), \\ Q_2(x, y, v, u) \leftarrow & R_1(x, y), R_2(y, v), R_3(v, z_1), \\ & R_4(z_1, u), R_5(u, t_1, t_2), \\ Q_3(x, y, v, u) \leftarrow & R_1(x, z_1), R_2(z_1, y), R_3(y, v), \\ & R_4(v, u), R_5(u, t_1, t_2). \end{aligned}$$

Each of three CQs is intractable on its own: Q_1 has the free-path (x, z_1, z_2, z_3, y), while Q_2 has the free-path (v, z_1, u), and Q_3 has the free-path (x, z_1, y). The CQ Q_2 provides the variables $\{x, z_1, y\}$ to Q_3, as Q_2 is $\{x, y, v\}$-connex, $\{x, y, v\}$ are free in Q_2, and there is a body-homomorphism h from Q_2 to Q_3 with $h((x, y, v)) = (x, z_1, y)$. Extending the body of Q_3 by the virtual atom $R'(x, z_1, y)$ yields the free-connex union extension Q_3^+. Similarly, we have that Q_3 provides $\{v, z_1, u\}$ to Q_2, and extending Q_2 by $R''(v, z_1, u)$ yields the free-connex union extension Q_2^+. Since Q_2^+ and Q_3^+ provide $\{x, z_1, z_2, y\}$ and respectively $\{x, z_2, z_3, y\}$ to Q_1, we obtain a free-connex union extension Q_1^+ by adding virtual atoms with the variables (x, z_1, z_2, y) and (x, z_2, z_3, y) to Q_1. Thus, Q is free-connex and $\text{Enum}\langle Q \rangle \in \mathsf{DelayC_{lin}}$ by Theorem 12. □

Remark 2. The approach presented here can also be used when there are functional dependencies in the schema. By taking functional dependencies into account, we can find even more tractable cases. If there are functional dependencies, some intractable CQs have a tractable FD-extension that can be computed efficiently [6]. Given a UCQ over a schema with functional dependencies, we can first take the FD-extensions of all CQs in the union, and then take the union extensions of those and evaluate the union. □

4 LOWER BOUNDS

In this section, we prove lower bounds for evaluating UCQs within the time bounds of $\mathsf{DelayC_{lin}}$. We begin with some general observations regarding cases where a single CQ is not harder than a union containing it, and then continue to handle other cases. In Section 4.1 we discuss unions containing only intractable CQs, and in Section 4.2 we discuss unions containing two body-isomorphic CQs. In both cases such UCQs may be tractable, and in case of such a union of size two, we show that our results from Section 3 capture all tractable unions.

In order to provide some intuition for the choices we make throughout this section, we first explain where the approach used for proving the hardness of single CQs fails. Consider Example 2. The original proof that shows that Q_1 is hard describes a reduction from Boolean matrix multiplication [2, Lemma 26]. Let A and B be binary representations of Boolean $n \times n$ matrices, i.e. $(a, b) \in A$ corresponds to a 1 in the first matrix at index (a, b). Define a database instance I as $R_1^I = A$, $R_2^I = B$, and $R_3^I = \{1, \dots, n\} \times \{\bot\}$. One can show that $Q_1(I)$ corresponds to the answers of AB. If $\text{Enum}\langle Q_1 \rangle \in \mathsf{DelayC_{lin}}$, we can solve matrix multiplication in time $O(n^2)$, in contradiction to MAT-MUL. Since Q_2 evaluates over the same relations, Q_2 also produces answers over this construction. Since the number of results for Q_2 might reach up to n^3, evaluating Q in constant delay does not necessarily compute the answers to Q_1 in $O(n^2)$ time, and does not contradict the complexity assumption.

So in general, whenever we show a lower bound to a UCQ by computing a hard problem through answering one CQ in the union, we need to ensure that the other CQs cannot have too many answers over this construction. As a first step to resolve this issue, we describe cases where there is a way to encode any arbitrary instance of Q_1 to an instance of Q, such that no other CQ in the union returns results.

Lemma 14. *Let Q be a UCQ of self-join free CQs, and let $Q_1 \in Q$ such that for all $Q_i \in Q \setminus \{Q_1\}$ there is no body homomorphism from Q_i to Q_1. Then* $\textsc{Enum}\langle Q_1 \rangle \leq_e \textsc{Enum}\langle Q \rangle$.

Proof sketch. Given an instance of $\textsc{Enum}\langle Q_1 \rangle$, we assign each variable of Q_1 with a different and disjoint domain by concatenating the variable names to the values in their corresponding relations. We leave the relations that do not appear in the atoms of Q_1 empty. Since there is no body-homomorphism from Q_i to Q_1, then there are now no answers to Q_i over this construction, and the answers to Q are exactly those of Q_1. □

The lemma above implies that if there is an intractable CQ in a union where no other CQ maps to it via a body-homomorphism, then the entire union is intractable. This also captures cases such as a union of CQs where one of them is hard, and the others contain a relation that does not appear in the first.

Using the same reduction, a similar statement with relaxed requirements can be made in case it is sufficient to consider the decision problem.

Lemma 15. *Let Q be a UCQ of self-join free CQs, and let $Q_1 \in Q$ such that for all $Q_i \in Q$, either there exists no body-homomorphism from Q_i to Q_1, or Q_1 and Q_i are body-isomorphic. Then* $\textsc{Decide}\langle Q_1 \rangle \leq \textsc{Decide}\langle Q \rangle$ *via a linear-time many-one reduction.*

Proof sketch. We use the same encoding as in Lemma 14. A CQ with no body-homomorphism to Q_1 has no answers. A CQ which is body-isomorphic to Q_1 has an answer iff Q_1 has an answer. Therefore $Q(I) \neq \emptyset$ iff $Q_1(I) \neq \emptyset$. □

Theorem 3 states that deciding whether a cyclic CQ has any answers cannot be done in linear time (assuming hyperclique). Following Lemma 15, if a UCQ Q containing a cyclic Q_1 where the conditions of Lemma 15 are satisfied, the entire union cannot be decided in linear time, and thus $\textsc{Enum}\langle Q \rangle \notin \mathsf{DelayC_{lin}}$.

4.1 Unions of Intractable CQs

We now discuss unions containing only CQs classified as hard according to Theorem 3. In the following, *intractable CQs* refers to self-join-free CQs that are not free-connex. The following lemma can be used to identify a CQ on which we can apply Lemma 14 or Lemma 15.

Lemma 16. *Let Q be a UCQ. There exists a query $Q_1 \in Q$ such that for all $Q_i \in Q$ either there is no body-homomorphism from Q_i to Q_1 or Q_1 and Q_i are body-isomorphic.*

Proof sketch. Consider a longest sequence $(Q^1, \dots, Q^m)$ such that for every $2 \leq j \leq m$ there is a body-homomorphism from Q^j to Q^{j-1}, but no body-homomorphism in the opposite direction. The CQ Q^m satisfies the conditions of the lemma: For every Q_i not on the sequence, if there is a body homomorphism from Q_i to Q^m, then there is also one in the opposite direction due to the maximality of the sequence; For every Q_i on the sequence, there is a body-homomorphism from Q^m to Q_i, so either there is no body-homomorphism in the opposite direction, or the CQs are body-isomorphic. □

Using the results obtained so far, we deduce a characterization of all cases of a union of intractable CQs, except those that contain a pair of body-isomorphic acyclic CQs.

Theorem 17. *Let Q be a UCQ of intractable CQs that does not contain two body-isomorphic acyclic CQs. Then, $Q \notin \mathsf{DelayC_{lin}}$, assuming mat-mul and hyperclique.*

Proof. Let Q_1 be a CQ in Q given by Lemma 16. We treat the two possible cases of the structure of Q_1. In case Q_1 is acyclic, since we know that Q does not contain body-isomorphic acyclic CQs, then for all $Q_i \in Q \setminus \{Q_1\}$ there is no body-homomorphism from Q_i to Q_1. According to Lemma 14, $\textsc{Enum}\langle Q_1 \rangle \leq_e \textsc{Enum}\langle Q \rangle$. Since Q_1 is self-join free acyclic non-free-connex, we have that $\textsc{Enum}\langle Q_1 \rangle \notin \mathsf{DelayC_{lin}}$ assuming mat-mul. Therefore $\textsc{Enum}\langle Q \rangle$ is not in $\mathsf{DelayC_{lin}}$ either. In case Q_1 is cyclic, we use Lemma 15 to conclude that $\textsc{Decide}\langle Q_1 \rangle \leq \textsc{Decide}\langle Q \rangle$. According to Theorem 3, since Q_1 is self-join free cyclic, $\textsc{Decide}\langle Q_1 \rangle$ cannot be solved in linear time assuming hyperclique. Therefore $\textsc{Decide}\langle Q \rangle$ cannot be solved in linear time, thus $\textsc{Enum}\langle Q \rangle \notin \mathsf{DelayC_{lin}}$. □

In the next example, we demonstrate how the reductions from Lemma 15 and Theorem 3 combine in Theorem 17.

Example 18. Consider the UCQ $Q = Q_1 \cup Q_2 \cup Q_3$ with

$$Q_1(x, y) \leftarrow R_1(x, y), R_2(y, u), R_3(x, u),$$
$$Q_2(x, y) \leftarrow R_1(y, v), R_2(v, x), R_3(y, x),$$
$$Q_3(x, y) \leftarrow R_1(x, z), R_2(y, z).$$

The queries Q_1 and Q_2 are cyclic, and Q_3 is acyclic but not free-connex. This union is intractable according to Theorem 17. Note that Q_1 and Q_2 are body-isomorphic, but there is no body-homomorphism from Q_3 to Q_1. The proof of Theorem 3 states the following: If $\textsc{Enum}\langle Q_1 \rangle \in \mathsf{DelayC_{lin}}$, then given an input graph G, we can use Q_1 to decide the existence of triangles in G in time $O(n^2)$, in contradiction to hyperclique. The same holds true for the $\textsc{Enum}\langle Q \rangle$. For every edge (u, v) in G with $u < v$ we add $((u, x), (v, y))$ to R_1^I, $((u, y), (v, z))$ to R_2^I and $((u, x), (v, z))$ to R_3^I. The query detects triangles: for every triangle a, b, c in G with $a < b < c$, the query Q_1 returns $((a, x), (b, y))$. The union only returns answers corresponding to triangles:

- For every answer $((d,x),(e,y))$ to Q_1, there exists some f such that d,e,f is a triangle in G with $d<e<f$.
- For every answer $((g,z),(h,x))$ to Q_2, there exists some i such that g,h,i is a triangle in G with $h<i<g$.
- The query Q_3 returns no answers over I. □

Theorem 17 does not cover the case of a UCQ containing acyclic non-free-connex queries with isomorphic bodies. Since this requires a more intricate analysis, we first restrict ourselves to such unions of size two. In the next section we discuss unions of two body-isomorphic CQs in general, and show in Theorem 28 that such a UCQ is tractable iff the UCQ is free-connex. By combining this with Theorem 17, we have the following dichotomy for the case of unions containing exactly two intractable CQs.

Theorem 19. *Let $Q=Q_1\cup Q_2$ be a union of intractable CQs.*

- *If Q is free-connex, then* $\text{ENUM}\langle Q\rangle \in \text{DelayC}_{\text{lin}}$.
- *If Q is not free-connex, then* $\text{ENUM}\langle Q\rangle \notin \text{DelayC}_{\text{lin}}$, *assuming MAT-MUL, HYPERCLIQUE and 4-CLIQUE.*

4.2 Unions of Two Body-Isomorphic CQs

Consider a set of body-isomorphic CQs. As all of them have the same structure, either every CQ in this set is cyclic, or every CQ is acyclic. In the case of a union of two cyclic CQs, the UCQ is intractable according to Theorem 17. So in this section, we discuss the union of body-isomorphic acyclic CQs. Note that, unlike the previous section, we allow a CQ in the union to be free-connex. We first introduce a new notation for body-isomorphic UCQs that we use hereafter.

Consider a UCQ of the form $Q_1\cup Q_2$, where there exists a body-isomorphism h from Q_2 to Q_1. That is, the CQs have the structure:

$$Q_1(\vec{v}_1) \leftarrow R_1(h(\vec{w}_1)),\dots,R_n(h(\vec{w}_n)),$$
$$Q_2(\vec{v}_2) \leftarrow R_1(\vec{w}_1),\dots,R_n(\vec{w}_n).$$

Applying h^{-1} to the variables of Q_1 does not affect evaluation, so we can rewrite Q_1 as $Q_1(h^{-1}(\vec{v}_1)) \leftarrow R_1(\vec{w}_1),\dots,R_n(\vec{w}_n)$. Since now the two CQs have exactly the same body, we can treat the UCQ as a query with one body and two heads:

$$Q_1(h^{-1}(\vec{v}_1)), Q_2(\vec{v}_2) \leftarrow R_1(\vec{w}_1),\dots,R_n(\vec{w}_n)$$

We use this notation from now on for UCQs containing only body-isomorphic CQs. Note that when treating a UCQ as one CQ with several heads, we can use the notation atoms(Q), as the atoms are the same for all CQs in the union, and the notation free(Q_i), as the free variables may differ between different queries Q_i in the union. With this notation at hand, we now inspect some examples of two body-isomorphic acyclic CQs.

Example 20. Consider $Q=Q_1\cup Q_2$ with

$$Q_1(x,y,v) \leftarrow R_1(x,z),R_2(z,y),R_3(y,v),R_4(v,w) \text{ and}$$
$$Q_2(x,y,v) \leftarrow R_1(w,v),R_2(v,y),R_3(y,z),R_4(z,x).$$

Since Q_1 and Q_2 are body-isomorphic, Q can be rewritten as

$$Q_1(w,y,z),Q_2(x,y,v) \leftarrow R_1(w,v),R_2(v,y),R_3(y,z),R_4(z,x).$$

In this case we can use the same approach used for single CQs in Theorem 3, and show that this UCQ is not in $\text{DelayC}_{\text{lin}}$ assuming MAT-MUL. Let A and B be binary representations of Boolean $n\times n$ matrices as explained in the beginning of this section. Define a database instance I with $R_1^I=A$, $R_2^I=B$, $R_3^I=\{1,\dots,n\}\times\{\bot\}$ and $R_4^I=\{(\bot,\bot)\}$. Since $Q_1(I)$ corresponds to the answers of AB, and $|Q_2(I)|=O(n^2)$, we cannot enumerate Q within the time bounds of $\text{DelayC}_{\text{lin}}$ unless we can solve matrix multiplication in time $O(n^2)$. □

A union of two intractable body-isomorphic acyclic CQs may also be tractable. In fact, by adding a single variable to the heads in Example 20, we obtain a tractable UCQ.

Example 21. Let Q be the UCQ

$$Q_1(w,y,x,z),Q_2(x,y,w,v) \leftarrow R_1(w,v),R_2(v,y),R_3(y,z),R_4(z,x).$$

Both CQs are acyclic non-free-connex. As Q_2 provides the variables $\{v,w,y\}$ and Q_1 provides $\{x,y,z\}$, both CQs have free-connex union extension:

$$Q_1^+(w,y,x,z) \leftarrow R_1(w,v),R_2(v,y),R_3(y,z),R_4(z,x),P_1(v,w,y),$$
$$Q_2^+(x,y,w,v) \leftarrow R_1(w,v),R_2(v,y),R_3(y,z),R_4(z,x),P_2(x,y,z).$$

By Theorem 12 it follows that $\text{ENUM}\langle Q\rangle \in \text{DelayC}_{\text{lin}}$. □

Intuitively, the reason why the reduction of Example 20 fails in Example 21 is the fact that all the variables of the free-paths in one CQ, which are used to encode matrix multiplication, are free in the other CQ. Indeed, if we encode matrices A and B to the relations of the free path w,v,y in Q_1, there can be n^3 answers to Q_3. The answer set in this case is too large to contradict the assumed lower bound for matrix multiplication. As it turns out, there are cases where we cannot reduce matrix multiplication to a union in this manner, and yet we can show that it is intractable using an alternative problem.

Example 22. Let Q be the UCQ

$$Q_1(x,y,t),Q_2(x,y,w) \leftarrow R_1(x,w,t),R_2(y,w,t).$$

This union is intractable under the 4-CLIQUE assumption. For a given graph $G=(V,E)$ with $|V|=n$, we compute

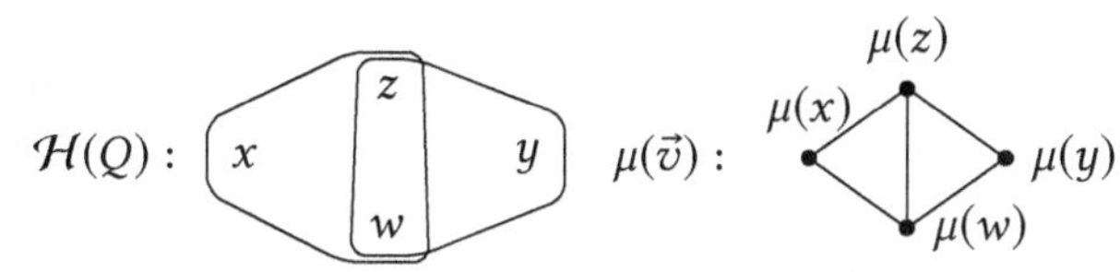

Figure 3: If $\mu|_{free(Q_i)} \in Q(I)$, the induced subgraph of $\mu(w, x, y, z)$ forms a clique where one edge might be missing.

the set T of all triangles in G in time n^3. Define a database instance I as $R_1^I = R_2^I = T$. For every output $\mu|_{free(Q_i)}$ in $Q(I)$ with $i \in \{1, 2\}$, we know that $(\mu(x), \mu(z), \mu(w))$ and $(\mu(y), \mu(w), \mu(z))$ are triangles. If $\mu(x) \neq \mu(y)$, this means that $\mu((x, y)) \in E$ if and only if $(\mu(x), \mu(y), \mu(w), \mu(z))$ forms a 4-clique (see Figure 3). Since there are $O(n^3)$ answers to Q, if $\text{ENUM}\langle Q\rangle \in \text{DelayC}_{\text{lin}}$, we can check whether $\mu((x, y)) \in E$ for every answer in $Q(I)$, and determine whether a 4-clique appears in G in time $O(n^3)$. □

Note that we can use the 4-CLIQUE assumption in Example 22, since, in addition to the free-path variables, there is another variable in both free-path relations. We now generalize the observations from the examples.

Definition 23. Let $Q = Q_1 \cup Q_2$ be a UCQ where Q_1 and Q_2 are body-isomorphic.

- Q_1 is said to be *free-path guarded* if for every free-path P in Q_1, we have that $var(P) \subseteq \text{free}(Q_2)$.
- Consider a path $P = (u_1, \dots u_k)$ in Q_1. Two atoms $R_1(\vec{v}_1)$ and $R_2(\vec{v}_2)$ of Q_1 are called *subsequent P-atoms* if $\{u_{i-1}, u_i\} \subseteq \vec{v}_1$ and $\{u_i, u_{i+1}\} \subseteq \vec{v}_2$ for some $1 < i < k$.
- Q_1 is said to be *bypass guarded* if for every free-path P in Q_1 and variable u that appears in two subsequent P-atom, we have that $u \in \text{free}(Q_2)$.

Note that every free-connex CQ is trivially free-path guarded and bypass guarded. In the following two lemmas, we show that if some CQ in a union is either not free-path guarded or bypass-guarded, then the UCQ is intractable.

In Example 20, Q_1 is not free-path guarded, so we can use the reduction from matrix multiplication.

Lemma 24. *Let $Q = Q_1 \cup Q_2$ be a UCQ of self-join free body-isomorphic acyclic CQs. If Q_1 is not free-path guarded, then* $\text{ENUM}\langle Q\rangle$ *is not in* $\text{DelayC}_{\text{lin}}$*, assuming MAT-MUL.*

PROOF SKETCH. Let A and B be Boolean matrices and let $P = (z_0, \dots, z_{k+1})$ be a free-path in Q_1. In the proof of part (2) in Theorem 3, the matrix multiplication AB is reduced to $\text{ENUM}\langle Q_1\rangle$ by encoding the matrices to the relations of Q_1 [2, Lemma 26]. They define $V_x = \{z_0\}$, $V_z = \{z_1, \dots, z_k\}$ and $V_y = \{z_{k+1}\}$. Since P is chordless, no atom contains both a variables of V_x and a variable of V_y. For every atom $R_i(\vec{v}_i)$ that has no variables in V_y and for every 1 in the matrix A in indices (a, b), we add a tuple to R_i where every variable in V_x corresponds to the value a, every variable in V_z corresponds to the value b, and all other variables are assigned the constant $\perp$. Similarly, we encode the matrix B to the other atoms. Since $V_x \cup V_y$ are free, we get the answers to matrix multiplication in $Q_1(I)$, and as no variable in V_z is free, we do not have duplicates. We extend this encoding as follows. If z_0 or z_{k+1} are not free in Q_2, we use the exact same reduction. In this case, $V_x \cap \text{free}(Q_2) = \emptyset$ or $V_y \cap \text{free}(Q_2) = \emptyset$. Otherwise, let z_i be the first variable in P that is not free in Q_2. We define $V_x = \{z_0, \dots, z_{i-1}\}$, $V_z = \{z_i\}$ and $V_y = \{z_{i+1} \dots, z_{k+1}\}$, and we have that $V_z \cap \text{free}(Q_2) = \emptyset$. With this encoding Q_1 still computes matrix multiplication, and as the CQs both have the same body, we have that Q_2 has at most n^2 answers. To distinguish the answers of Q_1 from those of Q_2, we can concatenate the variable names to the values, as we did in Lemma 14. Thus, enumerating $\text{ENUM}\langle Q\rangle$ in $\text{DelayC}_{\text{lin}}$ solves matrix multiplication in $O(n^2)$, which contradicts MAT-MUL. □

In Example 22, we encounter a UCQ where both CQs are free-path guarded, but Q_1 is not bypass guarded. In every UCQ with this property we can encode 4-CLIQUE.

Lemma 25. *Let $Q = Q_1 \cup Q_2$ be a UCQ of self-join free body-isomorphic acyclic CQs. If Q_1 and Q_2 are free-path guarded and Q_1 is not bypass guarded, then* $\text{ENUM}\langle Q\rangle \notin \text{DelayC}_{\text{lin}}$*, assuming 4-CLIQUE.*

PROOF. Let $G = (V, E)$ be a graph with $|V| = n$. We show how to solve the 4-CLIQUE problem on G in time $O(n^3)$ if $\text{ENUM}\langle Q\rangle$ is in $\text{DelayC}_{\text{lin}}$. Let P be a free-path in Q_1 and let $u \notin \text{free}(Q_2)$ such that u appears in two subsequent P-atoms. It can be shown that, under the conditions of this lemma, P is of the form (z_0, z_1, z_2). Let R_1 and R_2 be atoms with $\{z_0, z_1, u\} \subseteq var(R_1)$ and $\{z_1, z_2, u\} \subseteq var(R_1)$. Further let (a, b, c) be a triangle in G. We define a mapping $\tau_{(a,b,c)}$ on variables of Q in order to encode this triangle to tuples $r \in R^I$ of a database over Q, such that $var(R)$ either contains $\{z_0, z_1, u\}$ or $\{z_1, z_2, u\}$. That is, given $v \in var(Q)$, we define

$$\tau_{a,b,c}(v) = \begin{cases} a & \text{if } v = z_0 \text{ or } v = z_2, \\ b & \text{if } v = z_1, \\ c & \text{if } v = u, \\ \perp & \text{otherwise.} \end{cases}$$

For every atom $R(v_1, \dots, v_s) \in \text{atoms}(Q)$, we define

$$R^I = \{(\tau_{a,b,c}(v_1), \dots, \tau_{a,b,c}(v_s)) \mid (a, b, c) \text{ a triangle in } G\}.$$

Note that $|R^I| \in O(n^3)$, as there are at most n^3 triangles in G, and that we can construct I within $O(n^3)$ steps. Now consider a homomorphism $\mu : var(Q) \to V$ mapping Q into the database. Since $(\mu(z_0), \mu(z_1), \mu(u))$ and $(\mu(z_1), \mu(z_2), \mu(u))$ form triangles in G, we have that G contains a 4-clique iff $(\mu(z_0), \mu(z_2)) \in E(Q)$. As $z_0, z_1 \in$ free(Q_1) it suffices to check every $\mu|_{free(Q_1)} \in Q(I)$ for this property. We have that $\{z_0, z_1, z_2, u\}$ is neither contained in free(Q_1) nor in free(Q_2). Thus, $|Q(I)| \in O(n^3)$. If ENUM$\langle Q\rangle$ is in DelayC$_{\text{lin}}$, we can construct I, output $Q(I)$ and check every output for an edge of the form $(\mu(z_0), \mu(z_2))$ in time $O(n^3)$, which contradicts 4-CLIQUE. □

We show that any UCQ that is not covered by Lemma 24 and Lemma 25 is in fact union-free-connex. To prove this, we need a structural property given as follows.

Lemma 26. *Let $Q = Q_1 \cup Q_2$ be a UCQ of body-isomorphic acyclic CQs, where Q_1 and Q_2 are free-path guarded, and Q_1 is bypass guarded, and let P be a free-path in Q_1. There exists a join-tree T for Q with a subtree T_P such that $var(P) \subseteq var(T_P)$, and every variable that appears in two different atoms of T_P is in* free(Q_2).

Proof. Consider a path $A_1, \ldots, A_s$ between two atoms on a join tree. We define a *contraction step* for a path of length 2 or more: if there is A_j such that $A_j \cap A_{j+1} \subseteq A_1 \cap A_s$, then remove the edge (A_j, A_{j+1}) and add the edge (A_1, A_s). The new graph is still a join-tree since all of the atoms on the path between A_1 and A_s contain $A_1 \cap A_s$, and in particular they contain $A_j \cap A_{j+1}$. The unique path on the join-tree between the atoms A_1 and A_s is now of length one. A path on a join-tree is said to be *fully-contracted* if none of its subpaths can be contracted.

Now let T be a join-tree of Q, and let $P = (z_0, \ldots, z_{k+1})$. We consider some path in T between an atom containing $\{z_0, z_1\}$ and an atom containing $\{z_k, z_{k+1}\}$. Take the unique subpath T_P of it containing only one atom with $\{z_0, z_1\}$ and one atom with $\{z_k, z_{k+1}\}$, and fully contract it. Note that T_P contains $var(P)$ due to the running intersection property.

First, we claim that every variable u that appears in two or more atoms of T_P is part of a chordless path from z_0 to z_{k+1}. We first show a chordless path from u to z_{k+1}. Denote the last atom on T_P containing u by A_i. If A_i contains z_{k+1}, we are done. Otherwise, consider the subpath A_{i-1}, A_i, A_{i+1}. Since it is fully contracted, $A_i \cap A_{i+1} \not\subseteq A_{i-1} \cap A_{i+1}$. This means that there is a variable v in A_i and in A_{i+1} that does not appear in A_{i-1}. Now consider the last atom containing v, and continue with the same process iteratively until reaching z_{k+1}. Do the same symmetrically to find a chordless path from u to z_0. Note that the concatenation of the two paths is chordless by construction and since z_0 and z_{k+1} are not neighbors.

Assume by contradiction that some variable $u \notin$ free(Q_2) appears in two distinct atoms of T_P. There is a chordless path from z_0 to z_{k+1} that contains u. Take a subpath of it starting with the first variable before u which is in free(Q_2), and ending with the first variable after u which is in free(Q_2). This is a free-path in Q_2, and since Q_2 is free-path guarded, $u \in$ free(Q_1). Next consider two neighboring atoms on T_P that contain u. There exists some z_i that appears in both atoms. Note that $i > 0$ and $i < k + 1$ since the path only contains one atom with z_0 and one atom with z_{k+1}. Since Q_1 is bypass guarded, u is not a neighbor of both z_{i-1} and z_{i+1}. Without loss of generality, assume it is not a neighbor of z_{i+1}. Then there is a chordless path $(u, z_i, z_{i+1}, \ldots, z_{k+1})$. Since $u \in$ free(Q_1), it is a free-path. This contradicts the fact that Q_1 is free-path guarded since $u \notin$ free(Q_2). □

We are now ready to show that the properties free-path guardedness and bypass guardedness imply free-connexity.

Lemma 27. *Let $Q = Q_1 \cup Q_2$ be a UCQ of body-isomorphic acyclic CQs. If Q_1 and Q_2 are both free-path guarded and bypass guarded, then Q is free-connex.*

Proof. We describe how to iteratively build a union extension for each CQ. In every step we take one free-path among the queries in Q and add a virtual atom in order to eliminate this free-path. We show that this eventually leads to free-connex union extensions.

Let $P = (z_0, \ldots, z_{k+1})$ be a free-path in Q_1. Take T_P according to Lemma 26, and denote by V_P the variables $var(P)$ and all variables that appear in more than one atom of T_P. First we claim that Q_2 provides V_P. It is guaranteed that $V_P \subseteq$ free(Q_2), so we only need to show that Q_2 is acyclic V_P-connex. Take the join-tree T from Lemma 26. For every vertex A_i in T_P, add another vertex with $A'_i = var(A_i) \cap V_P$ and an edge (A_i, A'_i). Then, for every edge (A_i, A_j) in T_P, add the edge (A'_i, A'_j) and remove (A_i, A_j). The running intersection property is maintained since for every edge (A_i, A_j) removed, $var(A_i) \cap var(A_j) \subseteq V_P$, meaning that all vertices on the path A_i, A'_i, A'_j, A_j contain $var(A_i) \cap var(A_j)$. The subtree containing the new vertices contains exactly V_P.

We add the atom $R(V_P)$ to both Q_1 and Q_2 and obtain Q_1^+ and Q_2^+ respectively. After this extension there are no free-paths that start in z_0 and end in z_{k+1} since they are now neighbors. If both of the CQs are now free-connex, then we are done. Otherwise, we use the extension iteratively, as one can show that for the UCQ $Q_1^+ \cup Q_2^+$, both Q_1^+ and Q_2^+ are free-path guarded and bypass guarded. Note that after a free-path from z_0 to z_{k+1} is treated, and even after future extension, there will never be a free-path from z_0 to z_{k+1} since they are now neighbors. Since there is a finite number of variable pairs, at some point all pairs that have a free-path between them are resolved, this process stops, and there are no free-paths. □

Since Lemma 24, Lemma 25 and Lemma 27 cover all cases of a union of two self-join-free body-isomorphic acyclic CQs, we have a dichotomy that characterizes the UCQs discussed in this section.

Theorem 28. *Let $Q = Q_1 \cup Q_2$ be a UCQ of self-join free body-isomorphic CQs.*

- *If Q_1 and Q_2 are free-path guarded and bypass guarded, then Q is free-connex and* ENUM$\langle Q\rangle \in$ DelayC$_{\text{lin}}$.
- *Otherwise, Q is not free-connex and* ENUM$\langle Q\rangle$ *is not in* DelayC$_{\text{lin}}$, *under the assumptions* HYPERCLIQUE, MAT-MUL *and* 4-CLIQUE.

PROOF. By Theorem 17, if the CQs are cyclic, ENUM$\langle Q\rangle$ is not in DelayC$_{\text{lin}}$ assuming HYPERCLIQUE. Now assume that the CQs are acyclic. By Lemma 27, if Q_1 and Q_2 are both free-path guarded and bypass guarded, then Q is free-connex, and ENUM$\langle Q\rangle \in$ DelayC$_{\text{lin}}$ by Theorem 12. By Lemma 24 and Lemma 25, if one of Q_1 and Q_2 are not free-path guarded or not bypass guarded, then ENUM$\langle Q\rangle$ is not in DelayC$_{\text{lin}}$ (assuming MAT-MUL and 4-CLIQUE), and then Q is not free-connex by Theorem 12. □

5 TOWARDS A DICHOTOMY

In this section we examine the next steps that are required to fully characterize which UCQs are in DelayC$_{\text{lin}}$. We pinpoint some of the difficulties that must be tackled when formulating such a dichotomy, accompanied by examples. In Section 5.1 we discuss unions containing only acyclic CQs, and in Section 5.2 we discuss those that contain at least one cyclic CQ.

5.1 Unions of Acyclic CQs

We inspect two ways of extending the results of Section 4.2. The first such extension is to a union of two CQs that are not body-isomorphic. If there is an intractable CQ Q_1 in the union where for every other CQ Q_i in the union there is no body-homomorphism from Q_i to Q_1, we can reduce Q_1 to the union as described in Lemma 14. Since Q_1 is intractable, the union is intractable too. In case there is a body-homomorphism to the hard queries, one might think that it is sufficient for intractability to have unguarded intractable structures similarly to the previous section. This is incorrect.

Example 29. Let $Q = Q_1 \cup Q_2$ with

$$Q_1(x, y, w) \leftarrow R_1(x, z), R_2(z, y), R_3(y, w) \text{ and}$$
$$Q_2(x, y, w) \leftarrow R_1(x, t_1), R_2(t_2, y), R_3(w, t_3).$$

The query Q_1 is acyclic non-free-connex, while Q_2 is free-connex. Further Q_1 is not contained in Q_2 but there is a body-homomorphism from Q_2 to Q_1. The variable z is part of the free-path (x, z, y) in Q_1, but the variables t_1 and t_2 that map to it via the body-homomorphism are not free in Q_2. If we extend the notion of guarding to non-body-isomorphic CQs in the natural way, the free-path (x, z, y) is not guarded. Nevertheless, we cannot compute matrix multiplication in $O(n^2)$ time by encoding it to the free-path (x, z, y) like before. Over such a construction, there can be n^3 many results to Q_2 as w and y are not connected in Q_2, and they can have distinct values. This is not an issue when discussing body-isomorphic CQs. We do not know whether this example is in DelayC$_{\text{lin}}$. □

A future characterization of the union of CQs that are not body-isomorphic would need an even more careful approach than the one used in Section 4.2 in order to handle the case that variables mapping to the free-path are not connected via other variables mapping to the free-path.

A second way of extending Section 4.2 is to consider more than two body-isomorphic acyclic CQs. This case may be tractable or intractable, and for some queries of this form, we do not have a classification yet. Example 13 shows a tractable union of such form, while the following example shows that free-paths that share edges can be especially problematic within a union.

Example 30. Let $k \geq 4$ and consider the UCQ Q containing k body-isomorphic CQs, with an atom $R_i(x_i, z)$ for every $1 \leq i \leq k-1$. The heads are all possible combinations of $k-1$ out of the k variables of the query, $\{z, x_1, \ldots, x_{k-1}\}$. In the case of $k = 4$ we have the following UCQ:

$$Q_1(x_1, x_2, x_3), Q_2(x_1, x_2, z), Q_3(x_1, x_3, z), Q_4(x_2, x_3, z)$$
$$\leftarrow R_1(x_1, z), R_2(x_2, z), R_3(x_3, z).$$

The query Q_1 has free-paths (x_i, z, x_j) between all possible pairs of i and j. In this case, enumerating the solutions to the UCQ is not in DelayC$_{\text{lin}}$, assuming 4-CLIQUE: Encode each relation with all edges in the input graph, and concatenate the variable names. That is, for every edge (u, v) in the graph, add $((u, x_1), (v, z))$ to R_1. By concatenating variable names, we can identify which solutions come from which CQ, and ignore the answers to all CQs other than Q_1. The answers to Q_1 gives us 3 vertices that have a common neighbor. We can check in constant time if every pair of the 3 vertices are neighbors, and if so, we found a 4-clique. As there can be $O(n^3)$ solutions the the UCQ, we solve 4-clique in $O(n^3)$ time. This proves that the UCQ is intractable assuming 4-CLIQUE.

With the same strategy, we can solve k-clique in time $O(n^{k-1})$, but this does not result in a lower bound for large k values: It is assumed that one can not find a k-clique in time $n^{\frac{\omega k}{3}-o(1)}$, which does not contradict an $O(n^{k-1})$ algorithm. However, this reduction does not seem to fully capture the hardness of this query, as it encodes all relations with the same set of edges. We do not know if queries of the structure given here are hard in general, or if they become easy for larger k values, as any current approach that we know of for constant delay enumeration fails for them. □

We briefly describe some classification we can achieve when we exclude cases like Example 30. First note that when generalizing the notion of guarding free-paths to unions of several CQs, a free-path does not have to be guarded by a single CQ.

Definition 31. Let $Q = Q_1 \cup \ldots \cup Q_n$ be a union of body-isomorphic CQs, and let $P = (z_0, \ldots, z_{k+1})$ be a free-path in Q_1. We say that a set $\mathcal{U} \subseteq 2^{var(P)}$ is a *union guard* for P if:

- $\{z_0, z_{k+1}\} \in \mathcal{U}$.
- For every $\{z_a, z_c\} \subseteq u \in \mathcal{U}$ with $a + 1 < c$, we have that $\{z_a, z_b, z_c\} \in \mathcal{U}$ for some $a < b < c$.
- For every $u \in \mathcal{U}$, we have $u \subseteq \text{free}(Q_i)$ for some $1 \leq i \leq n$.

We now show that if a UCQ contains a free-path with no union guard, then the entire union is intractable.

Theorem 32. *Let $Q = Q_1 \cup \ldots \cup Q_n$ be a UCQ of body-isomorphic acyclic CQs. If there exists a free-path in Q_1 that is not union guarded, then* ENUM$\langle Q \rangle \notin$ DelayC$_{\text{lin}}$*, assuming* MAT-MUL.

PROOF SKETCH. If some path $P = (z_0, \ldots, z_{k+1})$ is not union guarded, then there exist some a and b such that $0 \leq a + 1 < b \leq k + 1$, and $\{z_a, z_b\} \subseteq \text{free}(Q_r)$ for some $Q_r \in Q$, but for all $Q_s \in Q$ and for all $a < b < c$ we have $\{z_a, z_b, z_c\} \notin \text{free}(Q_s)$. Then, $P' = (z_a, z_{a+1}, \ldots, z_c)$ is a free-path of Q_r. We can use a construction similar to Lemma 24 on the path P' to compute matrix multiplication in $O(n^2)$ by evaluating the union in linear time preprocessing and constant delay. □

As we do not know of a classification for Example 30, we restrict the UCQs we consider to cases where the free-paths within each CQ do not share variables. Then, we manage to obtain a similar characterization to that of Section 4.2.

Definition 33. Let $Q = Q_1 \cup \ldots \cup Q_n$ be a union of body-isomorphic CQs, and let P be a free-path of Q_1. We say that P is *isolated* if the following two conditions hold:

- Q is $var(P)$-connex and
- $var(P') \cap var(P) = \emptyset$ for all free-paths $P' \neq P$ in Q_1.

Note that isolated is a stronger property than bypass-guarded. Given a free-path P, A bypass-guarded query can have a variable in two subsequent P-atoms as long as this variable is free in another CQ. An isolated free-path cannot have such a variable at all. If all free-paths in a union of body-isomorphic acyclic CQs are union guarded and isolated, we can show that the union is tractable.

Theorem 34. *Let $Q = Q_1 \cup \ldots \cup Q_n$ be a union of body-isomorphic acyclic CQs. If every free-path in Q is union guarded and isolated, then* ENUM$\langle Q \rangle \in$ DelayC$_{\text{lin}}$.

PROOF SKETCH. If every free-path in Q is union guarded and isolated, then we can apply an iterative process that eliminates free-paths without introducing new ones. Imagine a union guard as the nodes of a tree, where the first condition of Definition 31 defines the root and the second condition defines the children of each node. The leaves of such a tree are of the form $\{z_i, z_{i+1}, z_{i+2}\}$. Using the third condition of Definition 31 and the first condition of Definition 33, it is possible to show via a bottom-up induction on this tree that every vertex is provided by some union extension of a CQ in the union. Adding these variables sets as virtual atoms results in a union extension without the treated free-path. Due to the second condition of Definition 33, this extension does not introduce new free-paths. As we can apply this process to all free-paths, we obtain a free-connex union extension for every CQ in the union, and conclude that Q is free-connex. According to Theorem 12, ENUM$\langle Q \rangle \in$ DelayC$_{\text{lin}}$. □

Following Theorem 32 and Theorem 34, it is left to handle cases like Example 30, of unions containing body-isomorphic acyclic CQs where some free-path is union guarded but not isolated. After solving this case, and regarding unions of intractable CQs, we should also explore unions containing body-isomorphic acyclic CQs but also other intractable CQs.

5.2 Unions Containing Cyclic CQs

We now discuss UCQs containing at least one cyclic query. We first mention that many of the observations we have regarding acyclic CQs also apply here. In the following examples, Q_1 is cyclic while Q_2 is free-connex. Example 35 shows that unions containing cyclic CQs may be tractable and covered by Theorem 12. Example 36 demonstrates that it is not enough to resolve the cyclic structures in CQs, but that we should also handle free-paths. Finally, Example 37 shows that, much like Example 29 in the acyclic case, even if all intractable structures are unguarded, the original reductions showing the intractability of single CQs may not work.

Example 35. Let $Q = Q_1 \cup Q_2$ with

$$Q_1(x, y, z, w) \leftarrow R_1(y, z, w, x), R_2(t, y, w), R_3(t, z, w), R_4(t, y, z),$$
$$Q_2(x, y, z, w) \leftarrow R_1(x, z, w, v), R_2(y, x, w).$$

The query Q_2 provides $\{t, y, z, w\}$ to Q_1. Adding the virtual atom $R'(t, y, z, w)$ to Q_1 results in a free-connex union-extension, so the union $Q_1 \cup Q_2$ is tractable. □

Example 36. Let $Q = Q_1 \cup Q_2$ with

$$Q_1(x, y, v) \leftarrow R_1(v, z, x), R_2(y, v), R_3(z, y) \text{ and}$$
$$Q_2(x, y, v) \leftarrow R_1(y, v, z), R_2(x, y).$$

The union $Q_1 \cup Q_2$ is intractable despite the fact that Q_2 guards and provides the cycle variables $\{v, y, z\}$. This is due to the unguarded free-path (x, z, y) in Q_1. Similarly to Example 20, we can encode matrix multiplication to x, z, y. □

Example 37. Let $Q = Q_1 \cup Q_2$ with

$$Q_1(x,z,y,v) \leftarrow R_1(x,z,v), R_2(z,y,v), R_3(y,x,v) \text{ and}$$
$$Q_2(x,z,y,v) \leftarrow R_1(x,z,v), R_2(y,t_1,v), R_3(t_2,x,v).$$

We do not know the complexity of this example. As Q_2 does not have a free variable that maps to y via a homomorphism, Q_1 is not union-free-connex, so we cannot conclude using Theorem 12 that $Q_1 \cup Q_2$ is tractable. The only intractable structure in Q_1 is the cycle x, y, z, but encoding the triangle finding problem to this cycle in Q_1, like we did in Example 18, could result in n^3 answers to Q_2. This means that if the input graph has triangles, we are not guaranteed to find one in $O(n^2)$ time by evaluating the union efficiently. □

In addition to these issues, in the cyclic case, even if the original intractable structures are resolved, the extension may introduce new ones. Resolving the following example in general is left for future work.

Example 38. We start with a single case of a general example. Let $Q = Q_1 \cup Q_2$ with

$$Q_1(x_2,x_3,x_4) \leftarrow R_1(x_2,x_3,x_4), R_2(x_1,x_3,x_4), R_3(x_1,x_2,x_4),$$
$$Q_2(x_2,x_3,x_4) \leftarrow R_1(x_2,x_3,x_1), R_2(x_4,x_3,v).$$

There is a body-homomorphism from Q_2 to Q_1, but Q_1 is not contained in Q_2. Q_1 is cyclic, as it has the cycle (x_1, x_2, x_3). This is the only intractable structure in Q_1, i.e. $\mathcal{H}(Q_1)$ does not contain a hyperclique or a free-path. The query Q_2 is both free-connex and $\{x_2, x_3, x_4\}$-connex, and it provides $\{x_1, x_2, x_3\}$ to Q_1. Nevertheless, extending Q_1 with a virtual atoms $R(x_1, x_2, x_3)$ does not result in a free-connex CQ. Even though the extension "removes" all intractable structures from Q_1, it is intractable as it introduces a new intractable structure, namely the hyperclique $\{w, x, y, z\}$.

In this case, we have $\textsc{Enum}\langle Q_1 \cup Q_2\rangle \notin \mathsf{DelayC_{lin}}$ assuming 4-CLIQUE, with a reduction similar to that of Example 22: Given an input graph, compute all triangles and encode them to the three relations. For every triangle $\{a, b, c\}$, add the tuple $((a, x_2), (b, x_3), (c, x_4))$ to R_1, $((a, x_1), (b, x_3), (c, x_4))$ to R_2 and $((a, x_1), (b, x_2), (c, x_4))$ to R_3. By concatenating variable names, we can identify which solutions correspond to which CQ, and thus are able to ignore the answers to Q_2. The answers to Q_1 represent 3 vertices that appear in a 4-clique: For every answer $((b, x_2), (c, x_3), (d, x_4))$ to Q_1, we know that $((b, x_2), (c, x_3), (d, x_4)) \in R_1$, and there exists some a with $((a, x_1), (c, x_3), (d, x_4)) \in R_2$ and $((a, x_1), (b, x_2), (d, x_4)) \in R_3$. This means that $\{a, b, c, d\}$ is a 4-clique. In the opposite direction, for every 4-clique $\{a, b, c, d\}$ we have that $\{b, c, d\}$, $\{a, c, d\}$ and $\{a, b, d\}$ are triangles. By construction, the tuple $((b, x_2), (c, x_3), (d, x_4))$ is an answer to Q_1. As there are $O(n^3)$ triangles and there can be at most $O(n^3)$ solutions to Q_2, we solve 4-clique in $O(n^3)$ time. This proves that the UCQ is intractable assuming 4-CLIQUE.

This example can be generalized to higher orders. There, we do not have a similar lower bound. Consider the union of the following:

$$Q_1(x_2,\ldots,x_k) \leftarrow \{R_i(\{1,\ldots,k\} \setminus \{i\}) \mid 1 \le i \le k-1\}$$
$$Q_2(x_2,\ldots,x_k) \leftarrow R_1(x_2,\ldots,x_{k-1},x_1), R_2(x_k,x_3,\ldots,x_{k-1},v).$$

Again, the query Q_1 is cyclic and Q_2 is free-connex. Even though Q_2 provides $\{x_1, \ldots, x_{k-1}\}$, adding a virtual atom with these variables does not result in a free-connex extension, as this extension is again cyclic. Just like in Example 30, we can encode k-clique to this example in general, but this does not imply a lower bound for large k values. □

6 CONCLUSIONS

In this paper we study the enumeration complexity of UCQs with respect to $\mathsf{DelayC_{lin}}$. We formalized how CQs within a union can make each other easier by providing variables, and we introduced union extensions. Then, we defined free-connex UCQs, and showed that these are tractable. In particular, we demonstrated that UCQs containing only intractable CQs may be tractable.

We showed that in case of a union of two intractable CQs or two acyclic body-isomorphic CQs, free-connexity fully captures the tractable cases. Nevertheless, achieving a full classification of UCQs remains an open problem. In Section 5 we described the next steps we plan to tackle in this vein, and provided examples with unknown complexity. Resolving these examples is a necessary step on the way to a future dichotomy.

In this paper, we only considered time bounds. The class CD∘Lin describes the problems that can be solved with the same time bounds, but with the additional restriction that the available space for writing during the enumeration phase is constant. Evaluating free-connex CQs is in this class, and Kazana offers a comparison between $\mathsf{DelayC_{lin}}$ and CD∘Lin [12, Section 8.1.2]. The lower bounds we showed naturally hold for CD∘Lin. The tractability of unions containing only free-connex CQs also holds for this class. However, the memory we used in our techniques for the tractable UCQs that do not contain only tractable CQs may increase in size by a constant with every new answer. An interesting question is whether we can achieve the same time bounds when restricting the memory according to CD∘Lin.

ACKNOWLEDGMENTS

The work of Nofar Carmeli was supported by the Irwin and Joan Jacobs Fellowship. The work of Markus Kröll was supported by the Austrian Science Fund (FWF): P30930-N35, W1255-N23.

REFERENCES

[1] Amir Abboud and Virginia Vassilevska Williams. 2014. Popular conjectures imply strong lower bounds for dynamic problems. In *Foundations of Computer Science (FOCS), 2014 IEEE 55th Annual Symposium on*. IEEE, 434–443.

[2] Guillaume Bagan, Arnaud Durand, and Etienne Grandjean. 2007. On acyclic conjunctive queries and constant delay enumeration. In *International Workshop on Computer Science Logic*. Springer, 208–222.

[3] Christoph Berkholz, Jens Keppeler, and Nicole Schweikardt. 2017. Answering Conjunctive Queries under Updates. In *Proceedings of the 36th ACM SIGMOD-SIGACT-SIGAI Symposium on Principles of Database Systems, PODS 2017, Chicago, IL, USA, May 14-19, 2017*. 303–318.

[4] Christoph Berkholz, Jens Keppeler, and Nicole Schweikardt. 2018. Answering UCQs under Updates and in the Presence of Integrity Constraints. In *21st International Conference on Database Theory, ICDT 2018, March 26-29, 2018, Vienna, Austria*. 8:1–8:19.

[5] Johann Brault-Baron. 2013. *De la pertinence de lâĂŹénumération: complexité en logiques propositionnelle et du premier ordre*. Ph.D. Dissertation. Université de Caen.

[6] Nofar Carmeli and Markus Kröll. 2018. Enumeration Complexity of Conjunctive Queries with Functional Dependencies. In *ICDT 2018, March 26-29, 2018, Vienna, Austria (LIPIcs)*, Benny Kimelfeld and Yael Amsterdamer (Eds.), Vol. 98. Schloss Dagstuhl - Leibniz-Zentrum fuer Informatik, 11:1–11:17.

[7] Arnaud Durand and Etienne Grandjean. 2007. First-order Queries on Structures of Bounded Degree Are Computable with Constant Delay. *ACM Trans. Comput. Logic* 8, 4, Article 21 (Aug. 2007). https://doi.org/10.1145/1276920.1276923

[8] Fernando Florenzano, Cristian Riveros, Martín Ugarte, Stijn Vansummeren, and Domagoj Vrgoc. 2018. Constant Delay Algorithms for Regular Document Spanners. In *PODS*. ACM, 165–177.

[9] Jörg Flum, Markus Frick, and Martin Grohe. 2002. Query evaluation via tree-decompositions. *J. ACM* 49, 6 (2002), 716–752.

[10] Etienne Grandjean. 1996. Sorting, Linear Time and the Satisfiability Problem. *Ann. Math. Artif. Intell.* 16 (1996), 183–236. https://doi.org/10.1007/BF02127798

[11] Muhammad Idris, Martin Ugarte, and Stijn Vansummeren. 2017. The Dynamic Yannakakis Algorithm: Compact and Efficient Query Processing Under Updates. In *Proceedings of the 2017 ACM International Conference on Management of Data (SIGMOD '17)*. ACM, New York, NY, USA, 1259–1274. https://doi.org/10.1145/3035918.3064027

[12] Wojciech Kazana. 2013. *Query evaluation with constant delay*. Theses. École normale supérieure de Cachan - ENS Cachan. https://tel.archives-ouvertes.fr/tel-00919786

[13] François Le Gall. 2014. Powers of Tensors and Fast Matrix Multiplication. In *Proceedings of the 39th International Symposium on Symbolic and Algebraic Computation (ISSAC '14)*. ACM, New York, NY, USA, 296–303. https://doi.org/10.1145/2608628.2608664

[14] Andrea Lincoln, Virginia Vassilevska Williams, and R. Ryan Williams. 2018. Tight Hardness for Shortest Cycles and Paths in Sparse Graphs. In *Proceedings of the Twenty-Ninth Annual ACM-SIAM Symposium on Discrete Algorithms, SODA 2018, New Orleans, LA, USA, January 7-10, 2018*. 1236–1252.

[15] Matthias Niewerth and Luc Segoufin. 2018. Enumeration of MSO Queries on Strings with Constant Delay and Logarithmic Updates. In *Proceedings of the 37th ACM SIGMOD-SIGACT-SIGAI Symposium on Principles of Database Systems, Houston, TX, USA, June 10-15, 2018*, Jan Van den Bussche and Marcelo Arenas (Eds.). ACM, 179–191. https://doi.org/10.1145/3196959.3196961

[16] Nicole Schweikardt, Luc Segoufin, and Alexandre Vigny. 2018. Enumeration for FO Queries over Nowhere Dense Graphs. In *Proceedings of the 37th ACM SIGMOD-SIGACT-SIGAI Symposium on Principles of Database Systems, Houston, TX, USA, June 10-15, 2018*, Jan Van den Bussche and Marcelo Arenas (Eds.). ACM, 151–163. https://doi.org/10.1145/3196959.3196971

[17] Luc Segoufin. 2015. Constant Delay Enumeration for Conjunctive Queries. *SIGMOD Rec.* 44, 1 (May 2015), 10–17. https://doi.org/10.1145/2783888.2783894

[18] Luc Segoufin and Alexandre Vigny. 2017. Constant Delay Enumeration for FO Queries over Databases with Local Bounded Expansion. In *ICDT 2017 (Leibniz International Proceedings in Informatics (LIPIcs))*, Michael Benedikt and Giorgio Orsi (Eds.), Vol. 68. Schloss Dagstuhl–Leibniz-Zentrum fuer Informatik, Dagstuhl, Germany, 20:1–20:16.

[19] Y. Strozecki. 2010. *Enumeration complexity and matroid decomposition*. Ph.D. Dissertation. Université Paris Diderot - Paris 7.

[20] Mihalis Yannakakis. 1981. Algorithms for Acyclic Database Schemes. In *Proceedings of the Seventh International Conference on Very Large Data Bases - Volume 7 (VLDB '81)*. VLDB Endowment, 82–94. http://dl.acm.org/citation.cfm?id=1286831.1286840

Split-Correctness in Information Extraction

Johannes Doleschal
University of Bayreuth & Hasselt University
johannes.doleschal@uni-bayreuth.de

Benny Kimelfeld
Technion, Israel
bennyk@cs.technion.ac.il

Wim Martens
University of Bayreuth
wim.martens@uni-bayreuth.de

Yoav Nahshon
Technion, Israel
yoavn@cs.technion.ac.il

Frank Neven
Hasselt University & transnational University of Limburg
frank.neven@uhasselt.be

ABSTRACT

Programs for extracting structured information from text, namely *information extractors*, often operate separately on document segments obtained from a generic splitting operation such as sentences, paragraphs, k-grams, HTTP requests, and so on. An automated detection of this behavior of extractors, which we refer to as *split-correctness*, would allow text analysis systems to devise query plans with parallel evaluation on segments for accelerating the processing of large documents. Other applications include the incremental evaluation on dynamic content, where re-evaluation of information extractors can be restricted to revised segments, and debugging, where developers of information extractors are informed about potential boundary crossing of different semantic components.

We propose a new formal framework for split-correctness within the formalism of document spanners. Our preliminary analysis studies the complexity of split-correctness over regular spanners. We also discuss different variants of split-correctness, for instance, in the presence of black-box extractors with "*split constraints*".

CCS CONCEPTS

• **Information systems → Information extraction;** • **Theory of computation →** *Formal languages and automata theory; Parallel algorithms.*

PODS '19, June 30–July 5, 2019, Amsterdam, Netherlands

ACM ISBN 978-1-4503-6227-6/19/06...$15.00
https://doi.org/10.1145/3294052.3319684

KEYWORDS

Information Extraction, Spanners, Complexity

ACM Reference Format:
Johannes Doleschal, Benny Kimelfeld, Wim Martens, Yoav Nahshon, and Frank Neven. 2019. Split-Correctness in Information Extraction. In *38th ACM SIGMOD-SIGACT-SIGAI Symposium on Principles of Database Systems (PODS '19), June 30–July 5, 2019, Amsterdam, Netherlands.* ACM, New York, NY, USA, 15 pages. https://doi.org/10.1145/3294052.3319684

1 INTRODUCTION

Information extraction (IE), the extraction of structured data from text, is a core operation when dealing with text in data analysis. Programming frameworks for IE, and especially *declarative* ones, are designed to facilitate the development of IE solutions. For example, IBM's SystemT [5] exposes an SQL-like declarative language, *AQL* (Annotation Query Language), which provides a collection of "primitive" extractors (e.g., tokenizer, dictionary lookup, Part-Of-Speech (POS) tagger, and regular-expression matcher) alongside the relational algebra for manipulating these relations. In Xlog [29], user-defined functions are used as primitive extractors, and Datalog is used for relation manipulation. In DeepDive [28, 30], rules are used for generating features that are translated into the factors of a statistical model with machine-learned parameters.

When applied to a large document, an IE function may incur a high computational cost and, consequently, an impractical execution time. However, it is frequently the case that the program, or at least most of it, can be distributed by separately processing smaller chunks in parallel. For instance, *Named Entity Recognition* (NER) is often applied separately to different sentences [17, 18], and so are instances of *Relation Extraction* [20, 36]. Algorithms for *coreference resolution* (identification of places that refer to the same entity) are typically bounded to limited windows; for instance, Stanford's well known *sieve* algorithm [27] for coreference resolution processes separately intervals of three sentences [19]. Sentiment extractors typically process individual paragraphs or even sentences [26]. It is also common for extractors to operate on windows of a bounded number N of words (tokens), also known as N*-grams* or *local contexts* [4, 13]. Finally, machine logs often have a natural split into semantic chunks: query logs into queries, error logs into exceptions, web-server logs into HTTP messages, and so on.

Tokenization, N-gram extraction, paragraph segmentation (identifying paragraph breaks, whether or not marked explicitly [15]), sentence boundary detection, and machine-log itemization are all examples of what we call *splitters.* When IE is programmed in a development framework such as the aforementioned, we aspire to deliver the premise of being declarative—the developer specifies *what* end result is desired, and not *how* it is accomplished efficiently. In particular, we would like the system to automatically detect the ability to split and distribute. This ability may be crucial for the developer (e.g., data scientist) who often lacks the expertise in software and hardware engineering. In this paper, we embark on a principled exploration of automated inference of *split-correctness* for information extractors. That is, we explore the ability of a system to detect whether an IE function can be applied separately to the individual segments of a given splitter, *without changing the semantics.*

The basic motivation comes from the scenario where a long document is pre-split by some conventional splitters (as the above), and developers provide different IE functions. If the system detects that the provided IE function is correctly splittable, then it can utilize its multi-processor or distributed hardware to parallelize the computation. Moreover, the system can detect that IE programs are frequently splittable, and recommend the system administrator to materialize splitters upfront. Even more, the split guarantee facilitates *incremental maintenance*: when a large document undergoes a minor edit, like in the Wikipedia model, only the relevant segments (e.g., sentences or paragraphs) need to reprocessed. Later in this section, we discuss additional motivations to split-correctness.

Formal framework. Our framework adopts the formalism of *document spanners* (or just *spanners* for short) [7]. In this framework, we consider *documents* (strings) over a fixed finite alphabet. A spanner is associated with a relational schema, and it extracts from every input document a relation of intervals within the document. An interval, called *span,* is represented simply by its starting and ending indices in the document. An example of a spanner is a *regex formula*—a regular expression with capture variables that correspond to the relational attributes. The most studied spanner language is that of the *regular* spanners, which is the closure of regex formulas under a subset of relational algebra: projection, natural join, union, and difference [7].[1] Other equally expressive formalisms are non-recursive Datalog over regex formulas [8] and the *variable-set automaton* or (or VSet-automaton for short), which is an NFA that can open and close variables while running [7].

Our framework is based on the following formal concepts. A *splitter* is a spanner S that outputs a *set of intervals* (e.g., sentences, paragraphs, N-grams, HTTP requests, etc.). A spanner P is *self-splittable* by a splitter S if for all documents d, evaluating P on d gives the same result as the union of the evaluations of P on each of the chunks produced by S. We also consider the more general case where we allow the spanner on the chunks produced by S to be some spanner P_S different from P. In this case, we say that P *is splittable by* S *via* P_S. If, for a given P and S, such a spanner P_S exists, then we say that P is *splittable* by S. With these definitions, we formally define several computational problems, each parameterized by a class C of spanners. In the *split-correctness* problem, we are given P, S, and P_S, and the goal is to determine whether P is splittable by S via P_S. In the *splittability* (resp. *self-splittability*) problem, we are given P and S and the goal is to determine whether P is splittable (resp. *self-splittable*) by S.

In our preliminary analysis, we consider the classes of regex formulas and VSet-automata, as well as VSet-automata in known normal forms, namely *functional* and *deterministic.* As we discuss later on, we use a slightly stronger definition of determinism than [24].

We show several complexity results about the studied classes of spanners. For one, the problems Split-correctness and Self-splittability are PSPACE-complete for regex formulas and VSet-automata. For Splittability, we require an additional condition for PSPACE-completeness, namely that the splitter is *disjoint.* This is a natural property of splitters S, meaning that for all input documents, the spans produced by S are pairwise disjoint (non-overlapping), such as in the case of tokenization, sentence boundary detection, paragraph splitting, and paragraph segmentation. Examples of *non-disjoint* splitters include N-grams and pairs of consecutive sentences. It turns out that disjointness is also a useful condition for Split-correctness and Self-splittability. For VSet-automata that are both functional and deterministic, Split-correctness and Self-splittability are solvable in polynomial time if the splitter is disjoint.

Interestingly, to establish the tractability result, we needed to revisit past notions and findings regarding determinism in VSet-automata. Specifically, our notion of determinism is *stronger* than that of Maturana et al. [24] (without loss of expressive power). We require that whenever the VSet-automata handle multiple variables on the same position of

[1] Adding selection would result in *Core-Spanners,* which are more powerful.

the document, it does so in a predefined order on the variables. This requirement is crucial, since our tractability proof uses the fact that containment of functional and deterministic VSet-automata is solvable in polynomial time (and, in fact, in NL), which we prove in Section 4. In contrast, we show that with the determinism of Maturana et al. [24], containment is PSPACE-complete. As we explain in Section 4.3, this stands in contradiction to a claim they make about membership in coNP. Our notion of deterministic VSet-automata is similar to the extended deterministic VSet-automata by Florenzano et al. [9]. Note that these results are of independent interest.

Following our analysis of split-correctness and splittability for regular spanners, we turn to discussing additional problems that arise in our framework. In Section 6, we discuss basic *reasoning* tasks about spanners. For example, if we wish to materialize two splitters, can we evaluate one of them over the result of the other, possibly given that documents adhere to some regular language? As an example, if we wish to split by sentences and documents are already split by paragraphs, then we can parallelize the task by splitting each paragraph individually. Similarly, an K-gram extractor can be applied to the chunks of an N-gram extractor whenever $K \leq N$.

In Section 7, we discuss problems that arise by natural extensions of the basic framework. One of these problems captures the case where some of the spanners in the query are treated as *black boxes* in a formalism that we do not understand well enough to analyze (as opposed to, e.g., regex formulas), and yet, are known to be splittable by the splitters at hand. For example, a coreference resolver may be implemented as a decision tree over a multitude of features [32] but still be splittable by sequences of three sentences, and a NER and a POS tagger may be implemented by a bidirectional LSTM [6] and a bidirectional dependency network [34], respectively, but still be splittable by sentences. Additional problems we discuss are split-correctness and splittability under the assumption that the document conforms to a regular language.

Our framework can be seen as an extension of the *parallel-correctness* framework as proposed by Ameloot et al. [2, 3]. That work considers the parallel evaluation of relational queries. In our terms, that work studies self-splittability where spanners are replaced by relational queries and splitters by *distribution policies*.

Further motivation. Besides the obvious, there are additional, perhaps less straightforward, motivations. For one, even if the document is *not* split at evaluation time (as opposed to pre-split), this split allows to parallelize the evaluation *following* a sequential split. When the IE function is expensive, this can be quite beneficial. For example, we have extracted N-grams from 1.53 GB Wikipedia sentences and observed that this method (first split to sentences and then distribute) gives a runtime improvement of 2.1x for $N = 2$ and 3.11x for $N = 3$, all over 5 cores. In a similar experiment on 279 MB of PubMed[2] sentences, the speedup was 1.9x.

Another motivation comes from programming over distribution frameworks such as Apache Hadoop [14] and Apache Spark [35]. In common cases, the text is already given as a collection of small documents (e.g., tweets, reviews, abstracts) that allow for a parallel evaluation to begin with. While we have not seen this scenario as a motivation for our framework, it turns out that splitting can make a considerable difference even then. For illustration, we ran a simple event extractor of financial transactions between organizations from sentences of around 9,000 Reuters articles over Spark. When we broke each article into sentences, the running time reduced by 1.99x on a 5-node cluster. We ran a similar experiment on sentences of around 570,000 reviews from the Amazon Fine Food Reviews dataset,[3] where the goal is to extract targets of a negative sentiment; we observed a 4.16x speedup. We found this remarkable, because the same amount of parallelization was used both before and after splitting. To the best of our understanding, this improvement can be explained by the fact that splitting provides Spark with parallelizable tasks that are smaller in cost and larger in number; hence, we provide Spark with considerably more (smartly exploited) control over scheduling and resource allocation.[4]

Finally, another motivation comes from *debugging*. For illustration, suppose that the developer seeks HTTP requests to a specific host on a specific date, and for that she seeks Host and Date headers that are close to each other; the system can warn the developer that the program is not splittable by HTTP requests like other frequent programs over the log (i.e., it can extract the Host of one request along with the Date of another), which is indeed a bug in this case. In the general case, the system can provide the user with the different splitters (sentences, paragraphs, requests, etc.) that the program is split-correct for, in contrast with what the developer believes should hold true.

Organization. The remainder of the paper is organized as follows. In Section 2, we give preliminary definitions and notation. We define the concepts of splitter, split-correctness and splittability in Section 3, and present our analysis for regular spanners in Sections 4 and 5. We discuss the extensions of the framework to other problems in Section 6 and 7. Finally, we conclude and discuss open problems in Section 8. Due to space constraints, we sometimes omit proofs or only provide a proof sketch.

[2]https://www.ncbi.nlm.nih.gov/pubmed/
[3]https://www.kaggle.com/snap/amazon-fine-food-reviews
[4]See [25] for more detail on the experiments.

2 BASIC DEFINITIONS

Our framework is within the formalism of *document spanners* by Fagin et al. [7]. We first revisit some definitions from this framework. Let Σ be a finite set of symbols called the *alphabet*. By Σ^* we denote the set of all finite strings over Σ and by Σ^+ the set of all finite strings over Σ that have at least one symbol. A string s in Σ^* is also called a *document*.

Let $d = \sigma_1 \cdots \sigma_n \in \Sigma^*$ be a document, where every $\sigma_i \in \Sigma$. We denote by $|d|$ the length n of d. A *span* of d is an expression of the form $[i, j\rangle$ with $1 \leq i \leq j \leq n + 1$. For a span $[i, j\rangle$ of d, we denote by $d_{[i,j\rangle}$ the string $\sigma_i \cdots \sigma_{j-1}$. For a document d, we denote by *Spans(d)* the set of all possible spans of d. Two spans $[i_1, j_1\rangle$ and $[i_2, j_2\rangle$ are *equal* if $i_1 = i_2$ and $j_1 = j_2$. In particular, $d_{[i_1,j_1\rangle} = d_{[i_2,j_2\rangle}$ does not imply that $[i_1, j_1\rangle = [i_2, j_2\rangle$. Two spans $[i, j\rangle$ and $[i', j'\rangle$ *overlap* if $i \leq i' < j$ or $i' \leq i < j'$, and are *disjoint* otherwise. Finally, $[i, j\rangle$ *contains* $[i', j'\rangle$ if $i \leq i' \leq j' \leq j$.

The framework focuses on functions that extract spans from documents and assigns them to variables. To this end, we fix an infinite set SVars of *span variables*, which range over spans, i.e., pairs of integers. The sets Σ and SVars are disjoint. For a finite set $V \subseteq$ SVars of variables and a document $d \in \Sigma^*$, a (V, d)*-tuple* is a mapping $t : V \to$ Spans(d) that assigns a span of d to each variable. If V is clear from context, or V is irrelevant, we may also just write *"d-tuple."* A set of (V, d)-tuples is called a (V, d)*-relation*, which is also called a *span-relation (over d)*.

A *document spanner* (or *spanner* for short) is a function that transforms a document into a span relation. More formally, a spanner is a function $P : \Sigma^* \to \mathcal{S}$ where Σ^* is the set of documents and $\mathcal{S}$ the set of span relations. A spanner is always associated with a finite set $V \in$ SVars and maps each document d to a (V, d)-relation $P(d)$. By SVars(P) we denote the set V. We say that a spanner P is *n-ary* if $|\text{SVars}(P)| = n$. We denote by $P = P'$ the fact that the spanners P and P' define the same function.

3 SPLITTERS AND MAIN PROBLEMS

In this work, we are particularly interested in spanners that split documents into (possibly overlapping) segments. Formally, a *document splitter* (or *splitter* for short) is a unary document spanner P, that is, $|\text{SVars}(P)| = 1$. Referring back to the Introduction, a splitter can split the document into paragraphs, sentences, N-grams, HTTP messages, error messages, and so on.

In the sequel, we denote a splitter by S and its unique variable by x_S or simply by x if S is clear from the context. Furthermore, since a splitter outputs unary span relations, its output on a document d can be identified with the set of spans $\{t(x) \mid t \in S(d)\}$. We often use this simplified view on a splitter in the paper and treat its output as a set of spans.

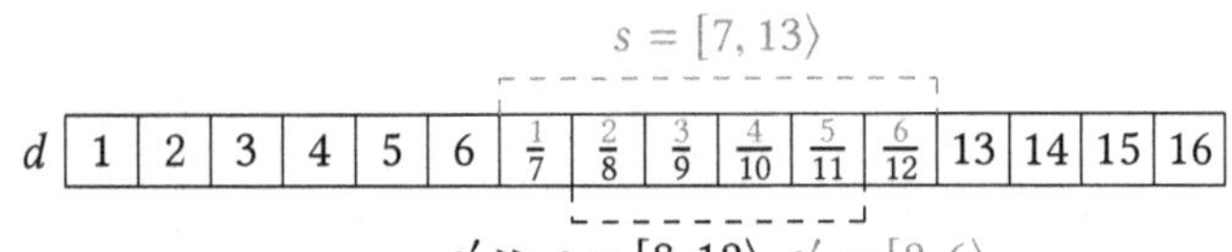

Figure 1: Visualization of the shift span operator, with $[8, 12\rangle = [2, 6\rangle \gg [7, 13\rangle$.

A splitter S is *disjoint* if the spans extracted by S are always pairwise disjoint, that is, for all $d \in \Sigma^*$ and $t, t' \in S(d)$, the spans $t(x)$ and $t'(x)$ are disjoint. For example, the paragraph and sentence splitters are disjoint, but N-gram extractors are not disjoint for $N > 1$.

Next, we want to define when a spanner is *splittable* by a splitter, that is, when documents can be decomposed such that the operation of a spanner can be distributed over the components. To this end, we first need some notation. Let d be a document, let $s = [i, j\rangle$ be a span of d, and let $s' = [i', j'\rangle$ be a span of the document $d_{[i,j\rangle}$. Then s' also marks a span of the original document d, namely the one obtained from s' by shifting it $i - 1$ characters to the right. We denote this shifted span by $s' \gg s$ (c.f., Figure 1). Hence, we have:

$$s' \gg s := [i' + (i - 1), j' + (i - 1)\rangle.$$

Let t be a (V, d)-tuple and $s = [i, j\rangle$ be a span. Slightly overloading notation, we define the (V, d)-tuple $t \gg s$ as the tuple that results from shifting each span in t by s. More formally, for all variables $x \in V$ we have:[5]

$$(t \gg s)(x) := (t(x)) \gg s.$$

As a splitter S always selects a set of unary tuples, in the following we abuse notation, and simply write s rather than $s(x_S)$ when $s \in S(d)$ for some document d.

We now define the *composition* $P \circ S$ of a spanner P and splitter S. Intuitively, $P \circ S$ is the spanner that results from evaluating P on every substring extracted by S, with a proper indentation of the indices. More formally, on every document d,

$$(P \circ S)(d) := \bigcup_{s \in S(d)} \{t \gg s \mid t \in P(d_s)\}.$$

As an example, if P extracts person names and S is a sentence splitter, then $P \circ S$ is the spanner obtained by applying P to every sentence independently and taking the union of the results. Furthermore, if P extracts close mentions of email addresses and phone numbers, and S is the 5-gram splitter, then $P \circ S$ is obtained by applying P to each 5-gram individually. An interesting question is if there is any difference between executing P and $P \circ S$. This property clearly depends

[5]Notice that when the first index of t is too large, $t \gg s$ could technically not be a (V, d)-relation anymore. However, we only use the operator in situations where this can never happen.

on the definitions of P and S. We will define it formally in Section 3.1 under the name *self-splittability*.

3.1 Splittability and Split-Correctness

A spanner P is *splittable* by a splitter S via a spanner P_S if evaluating P gives the same result as evaluating P_S on every substring extracted by S (again with proper indentation of the indices). If such a P_S exists, then we say that P is *splittable* by S; and if P_S is P itself, then we say that P is *self-splittable* by S. We define these notions more formally.

Definition 3.1. Let P be a spanner and S a splitter. We say that:

(1) P is *splittable by* S *via* a spanner P_S, if $P = P_S \circ S$;
(2) P is *splittable by* S if there exists a spanner P_S such that $P = P_S \circ S$;
(3) P is *self-splittable by* S if $P = P \circ S$.

We refer to P_S as the *split-spanner.*

As a simple example, suppose that we analyze a log of many HTTP requests separated by blank lines and assume for simplicity that the log only consists of GET requests. Furthermore, assume that S splits the document into individual requests (without the blank lines) and that P extracts the request line, which is always the first line of the request. If P identifies the request line as the one following the blank line, then P is splittable by S via P_S, which is the same as P but replaces the requirement to follow a blank line with the requirement of being the first line. If, on the other hand, P identifies the request line as being the one starting with the word GET, then P is self-splittable by S, since we can apply P itself to every HTTP message independently.

Other examples are as follows. Many spanners P that extract person names do not look beyond the sentence level. This means that, if S splits to sentences, it is the case that P is self-splittable by S. Now suppose that P extracts mentions of email addresses and phone numbers based on the formats of the tokens, and moreover, it allows at most three tokens in between; if S is the N-gram splitter, then P is self-splittable by S for $N \geq 5$ but not for $N < 5$.

3.2 Decision Problems

The previous definitions and the motivating examples from the introduction directly lead to the corresponding decision problems. We use C to denote a class of spanner representations (such as **VSA** or **RGX** that we define later on).

Split-correctness[C]	
Input:	Spanners $P, P_S \in C$ and splitter $S \in C$.
Question:	Is $P = P_S \circ S$?

Splittability[C]	
Input:	Spanner $P \in C$ and splitter $S \in C$.
Question:	Is P splittable by S?

In addition, Self-splittability[C] is the special case of the problem Splittability[C] where we ask if P is *self-splittable* by S.

4 PRELIMINARIES ON REGULAR SPANNERS

In this section, we recall the terminology and definition of *regular* spanners [7]. We use two main models for representing spanners: *regex-formulas* and *VSet-automata.* For both, we follow Freydenberger [10], defining the semantics of these models using so-called *ref-words.* We also introduce here a class of VSet-automata, **dfVSA**, that have determinism properties essential to the tractability of problems we study in the paper. In particular, we show that containment of regex formulas and VSet-automata is PSPACE-complete (Theorem 4.1), even under some determinism assumptions introduced in the past work [24] (Theorem 4.2), but is it solvable in polynomial time, and even NL, for **dfVSA** (Theorem 4.3).

Ref-words. For a finite set $V \subseteq$ SVars of variables, ref-words are defined over the extended alphabet $\Sigma \cup \Gamma_V$, where $\Gamma_V := \{x\vdash, \dashv x \mid x \in V\}$. We assume that Γ_V is disjoint with Σ and SVars. Ref-words extend strings over Σ by encoding opening ($x\vdash$) and closing ($\dashv x$) of variables.

A ref-word $\mathbf{r} \in (\Sigma \cup \Gamma_V)^*$ is *valid for* V if each variable is opened and closed exactly once. More formally, for each $x \in V$, the string $\mathbf{r}$ has exactly one occurrence of $x\vdash$ and precisely one occurrence of $\dashv x$, which is after the occurrence of $x\vdash$. If V is clear from the context, we simply say that a ref-word is *valid.*

To connect ref-words to documents and spanners, we define a morphism $\text{clr} : (\Sigma \cup \Gamma_V)^* \to \Sigma^*$ (pronounced "clear"), as $\text{clr}(\sigma) := \sigma$ for every $\sigma \in \Sigma$ and $\text{clr}(\sigma') := \varepsilon$ for every $\sigma' \in \Gamma_V$. For $d \in \Sigma^*$, let $\text{Ref}(d) := \{\mathbf{r} \in (\Sigma \cup \Gamma_V)^* \mid \text{clr}(\mathbf{r}) = d \text{ and } \mathbf{r} \text{ is valid}\}$ be the set of all valid ref-words with $\text{clr}(\mathbf{r}) = d$ and for a regular language $\mathcal{L}$ we define $\text{Ref}(\mathcal{L}) := \bigcup_{d \in \mathcal{L}} \text{Ref}(d)$ to be the language of all valid ref-words over $\mathcal{L}$.

By definition, every valid $\mathbf{r} \in \text{Ref}(d)$ over $(\Sigma \cup \Gamma_V)$ has a unique factorization $\mathbf{r} = \mathbf{r}_x^{\text{pre}} \cdot x\vdash \cdot \mathbf{r}_x \cdot \dashv x \cdot \mathbf{r}_x^{\text{post}}$ for each $x \in V$. We can therefore interpret $\mathbf{r}$ as a (V, d)-tuple $t^{\mathbf{r}}$ by defining $t^{\mathbf{r}}(x) := [i, j\rangle$, where $i := |\text{clr}(\mathbf{r}_x^{\text{pre}})| + 1$ and $j := i + |\text{clr}(\mathbf{r}_x)|$.

4.1 Regex Formulas

A *regex-formula (over* Σ*)* is a regular expression that may also include variables (called capture variables). Formally, we define the syntax with the recursive rule

$$\alpha := \emptyset \mid \varepsilon \mid \sigma \mid (\alpha \vee \alpha) \mid (\alpha \cdot \alpha) \mid \alpha^* \mid x\{\alpha\},$$

where $\sigma \in \Sigma$ and $x \in V$. We use α^+ as a shorthand for $\alpha \cdot \alpha^*$ and Σ as a shorthand for $\bigvee_{\sigma \in \Sigma} \sigma$. The set of variables that occur in α is denoted by $\text{SVars}(\alpha)$ and the size $|\alpha|$ is defined as the number of symbols in α.

Every regex-formula can be interpreted as a generator of a (regular) ref-word language $\mathcal{R}(\alpha)$ over the extended alphabet $\Sigma \cup \Gamma_{\text{SVars}(\alpha)}$. If α is of the form $x\{\beta\}$, then $\mathcal{R}(\alpha) := \{x\vdash\} \cdot \mathcal{R}(\beta) \cdot \{\dashv x\}$. Otherwise, $\mathcal{R}(\alpha)$ is defined as the language $\mathcal{L}(\alpha)$, that is $\mathcal{R}(\emptyset) := \emptyset$, $\mathcal{R}(a) := \{a\}$ for every $a \in \Sigma \cup \{\varepsilon\}$, $\mathcal{R}(\alpha \vee \beta) := \mathcal{R}(\alpha) \cup \mathcal{R}(\beta)$, $\mathcal{R}(\alpha \cdot \beta) := \mathcal{R}(\alpha) \cdot \mathcal{R}(\beta)$, $\mathcal{R}(\alpha^*) := \{\mathcal{R}(\alpha)^i \mid i \geq 0\}$.

By $\text{Ref}(\alpha)$ we denote the set of all ref-words in $\mathcal{R}(\alpha)$ which are valid for $\text{SVars}(\alpha)$;[6] and, for every string $d \in \Sigma^*$, we define $\text{Ref}(\alpha, d) := \text{Ref}(\alpha) \cap \text{Ref}(d)$. In other words, $\text{Ref}(\alpha, d)$ contains exactly those valid ref-words from $\text{Ref}(\alpha)$ that clr maps to d. Finally, the spanner $[\![\alpha]\!]$ is the one that defines the following $(\text{SVars}(\alpha), d)$-relation for every string $d \in \Sigma^*$:

$$[\![\alpha]\!](d) := \{t^{\mathbf{r}} \mid \mathbf{r} \in \text{Ref}(\alpha, d)\}$$

Slightly abusing notation, we will sometimes simply write $\alpha(d)$ rather than $[\![\alpha]\!](d)$ to denote the span-relation α defines on d. We say that a regex-formula is *functional* if $\mathcal{R}(\alpha) = \text{Ref}(\alpha)$; that is, every ref-word in $\mathcal{R}(\alpha)$ is valid. The set of all functional regex formulas is also denoted by **RGX**. Following previous work [7, 12], we assume regex formulas are functional unless explicitly stated otherwise.

4.2 Variable Set-Automata

A *variable-set automaton (VSet-automaton)* with variables from a finite set $V \subseteq \text{SVars}$ can be understood as an ε-NFA that is extended with edges that are labeled with variable operations Γ_V. Formally, a VSet-automaton is a sextuple $A := (\Sigma, V, Q, q_0, Q_F, \delta)$, where Σ is a finite set of alphabet symbols, V is a finite set of variables, Q is a finite set of states, $q_0 \in Q$ is a start state, $Q_F \subseteq Q$ is a set of final states, and $\delta : Q \times (\Sigma \cup \{\varepsilon\} \cup \Gamma_V) \rightarrow 2^Q$ is the transition function. By $\text{SVars}(A)$ we denote the set V. To define the semantics of A, we first interpret A as an ε-NFA over the terminal alphabet $\Sigma \cup \Gamma_V$, and define its *ref-word language* $\mathcal{R}(A)$ as the set of all ref-words $\mathbf{r} \in (\Sigma \cup \Gamma_V)^*$ that are accepted by the ε-NFA A. Analogously to regex formulas, we define $\text{Ref}(A)$ as the set of ref-words in $\mathcal{R}(A)$ that are valid for V, and define $\text{Ref}(A, d)$ and $[\![A]\!](d)$ accordingly for every $d \in \Sigma^*$. We say that A is *functional* if $\text{Ref}(A) = \mathcal{R}(A)$, i.e., every accepting run of A generates a valid ref-word. Furthermore, two VSet-automata A_1, A_2 are *equivalent* if and only if $[\![A_1]\!] = [\![A_2]\!]$.

[6]Notice that not all ref-words in a ref-word language have to be valid. For instance, the ref-word $\varepsilon \in \mathcal{R}((x\{a\})^*)$ is not valid for $\text{SVars}((x\{a\})^*) = \{x\}$, since it does not contain $x\vdash$ and $\dashv x$.

We refer to the set of all VSet-automata as **VSA**. Similar to regex formulas, we sometimes simply denote the relation $[\![A]\!](d)$ by $A(d)$, for a VSet automaton A.

Deterministic VSet-Automata. We use the notion of determinism for VSet-automata as introduced by [24], but refer to it as *weakly* deterministic because, as we will show, it still allows for sufficient nondeterminism to make reasoning equally hard than for general VSet-automata. Formally, a VSet-automaton $A = (\Sigma, V, Q, q_0, Q_F, \delta)$ is *weakly deterministic*, if it does not use ε-transitions and $|\delta(q, v)| \leq 1$ for every $q \in Q$ and every $v \in \Sigma \cup \Gamma_V$.

In Theorem 4.2 we show that weakly deterministic VSet-automata still have sufficient nondeterminism to make the containment problem PSPACE-hard.[7] We therefore define a stronger notion of determinism, which will lead to an NL-complete containment problem (Theorem 4.3).

We fix a total, linear order $\prec$ on the set Γ_{SVars} of variable operations, such that $v\vdash \prec \dashv v$ for every variable v. A VSet-automaton $A = (\Sigma, V, Q, q_0, Q_f, \delta)$ is *deterministic*, if

(1) $|\delta(q, v)| \leq 1$ for every $q \in Q$ and every $v \in \Sigma \cup \Gamma_V$;

(2) $v \prec v'$ for every $v, v' \in \Gamma_V$ for which there are $q_1, q_2, q_3 \in Q$ such that $\delta(q_1, v) = q_2$ and $\delta(q_2, v') = q_3$.

Condition (1) is the requirement for weakly deterministic automata, whereas condition (2) ensures that for every document $d \in \Sigma^*$ and every tuple $t \in A(d)$ there is exactly one ref-word $\mathbf{r} \in \text{Ref}(A)$ with $t^{\mathbf{r}} = t$.[8] Moreover, all adjacent variable operations in $\mathbf{r}$ are ordered according to $\prec$. We discuss expressiveness and complexity of deterministic VSet-automata in Section 4.3. In particular, none of the conditions (1–2) restrict the expressiveness of regular spanners. In the following, we denote by **dVSA** (resp., **dfVSA**) the class of deterministic (resp., deterministic and functional) VSet-automata.

4.3 Complexity and Expressiveness

Containment is the problem that asks, given VSet-automata A and A', whether $A(d) \subseteq A'(d)$ for every document d. The next theorem establishes the complexity of containment. We note that the VSet-automata are not required to be functional. The following is essentially [24, Theorem 6.4].

Theorem 4.1. *Containment of regex-formulas (***RGX***) and VSet-automata (***VSA***) is PSPACE-complete.*

Since weakly deterministic VSet-automata restrict the transition function to a singleton set, which is a standard way

[7]This result contradicts Theorem 6.6 in Maturana et al. [24] unless coNP = PSPACE. We will further discuss this in Section 4.3.

[8]Deterministic VSet-automata are very similar to the *extended deterministic VSet-automata* by Florenzano et al. [9], which allow multiple variable operations on a single transition and force each variable transition to be followed by a transition processing an alphabet symbol.

to define determinism, one may expect their containment problem to be in NL (just as for their finite automata counterparts). However, the next theorem shows that containment is hard for PSPACE, as they can use different variable orderings to introduce nondeterministic choice.

Theorem 4.2. *Containment of weakly deterministic functional VSet-automata is PSPACE-hard.*

Proof sketch. We reduce from the PSPACE complete problem of DFA union universality [16]. Given deterministic finite automata $A_1, \ldots, A_n$ over the alphabet Σ, the union universality problem asks whether

$$L(\Sigma^*) \subseteq \bigcup_{1 \leq i \leq n} L(A_i). \qquad (\dagger)$$

As usual, $L(A_i)$ denotes the language accepted by A_i. We construct VSet-automata A, A' using the variable set $V = \{x_1, \ldots, x_n\}$, such that $A(d) \subseteq A'(d)$ for all documents $d \in \Sigma^*$ if and only if $(\dagger)$ holds. To this end, let A accept the language defined by the regex-formula

$$\alpha_A = x_1\{x_2\{\cdots x_n\{\Sigma^*\}\cdots\}\},$$

selecting the whole document with every variable. Clearly, the regex-formula α_A can be represented by a weakly deterministic VSet-automaton A. We now abuse notation and describe the language accepted by A' by a hybrid regex-formula

$$\alpha_{A'} = x_1\{\alpha_1\} + \cdots + x_n\{\alpha_n\},$$

where the DFAs A_i are plugged in. In particular,

$$\alpha_i = x_1\{\cdots x_{i-1}\{x_{i+1}\{\cdots\{x_n\{L(A_i)\}\}\cdots\},$$

for $1 \leq i \leq n$. Every branch i starts by first opening variable x_i, continues to open all other variables in increasing order, and finally selects for every variable the whole document when it is accepted by A_i. Clearly, as every disjunct starts with a different symbol, this hybrid formula can be transformed into an equivalent weakly deterministic VSet-automaton. It is easy to verify that $A(d) \subseteq A'(d)$ for every document $d \in \Sigma^*$ if and only if $(\dagger)$ holds. □

The previous theorem contradicts Theorem 6.6 in Maturana et al. [24] (unless coNP = PSPACE), where it is argued that containment for sequential weakly deterministic automata is in coNP (even allowing partial mappings to variables).[9] As the VSet-automata we consider are indeed sequential, we show that the latter problem is hard for PSPACE (already without allowing partial mappings). Our definition of determinism resolves this complexity issue.

Theorem 4.3. *Containment for* **dfVSA** *is in NL.*

The following proposition shows that deterministic VSet-automata are equally expressive as VSet-automata in general.

Proposition 4.4. *For every VSet-automaton A there is a deterministic VSet-automaton A' such that $A(d) = A'(d)$ for every document $d \in \Sigma^*$. This property still holds if A' is additionally required to be functional.*

Finally, we recall that it is well known that **RGX** is less expressive than VSet-automata [7]. To reach the expressiveness of VSet-automata, **RGX** needs to be extended with projection, natural join, union, and difference.

5 SPLITTING WITH REGULAR SPANNERS

We now give preliminary results for the decision problems we introduced in Section 3 in the case of regular spanners. We consider split-correctness in Section 5.1, and discuss splittability and self-splittability in Sections 5.2 and 5.3, respectively. In particular, we show that split-correctness is PSPACE-complete for all spanners formalisms that we discuss in the paper (Theorem 5.1); nevertheless, if we make the natural assumption of *disjointness* of the splitter, then the complexity reduces to polynomial time for **dfVSA** (Theorem 5.7). For splittability, we show a PSPACE-completeness result under the assumption of splitter disjointness (Theorem 5.15), while membership in PSPACE for general splitters remains an open question. For self-splittability, we prove PSPACE-completeness (Theorem 5.16) in general, and again, that disjointness reduces the complexity to polynomial time for **dfVSA** (Theorem 5.17).

5.1 Split-Correctness

5.1.1 General cases. The following theorem states the complexity of Split-correctness for the classes defined in Section 4.

Theorem 5.1. *Split-correctness[C] is PSPACE-complete for each of the classes $C \in \{$***RGX, VSA, dVSA, dfVSA***$\}$.*

Proof sketch. For the lower bound, we need to prove hardness separately for **dfVSA** and for **RGX**, since the models are incomparable (**dfVSA** are more expressive; **RGX** have more non-determinism). For the lower bound for **dfVSA**, we reduce from the PSPACE-complete problem of DFA union universality [16]. To this end, let $A_1, \ldots, A_n$ be regular languages, given as deterministic finite automata over the alphabet Σ and let $\Sigma' = \Sigma \uplus \{a\}$. Let $P = a^n \cdot y\{\Sigma^*\}$ and

[9]The error is in the upper bound of Maturana et al. [24], as can be seen in the version that includes the proofs [23]. The specific error is in the pumping argument for proving a polynomial size witness property for non-containment. The polynomial size witness property is not necessarily true, due to the nondeterminism entailed in the ability of the automaton to open variables in different orders. At any specific position in the string, the execution can be in $\Theta(n)$ possible states, where n is the number of states, implying that a minimal witness may require a length of $2^{\Theta(n)}$.

$S = x\{a^n \cdot A_1\} + a \cdot x\{a^{n-1} \cdot A_2\} + \cdots + a^{n-1} \cdot x\{a \cdot A_n\}$. Furthermore, let $P_S = a^* \cdot z\{\Sigma^*\}$. Then $P = P_S \circ S$ if and only if $L(\Sigma^*) \subseteq \bigcup_{1 \le i \le n} L(A_i)$.

The lower bound for **RGX** is immediate by a reduction from the **RGX** containment problem, which is PSPACE-hard (c.f. Theorem 4.1). Indeed, let $P, P_S \in$ **RGX** be spanners and $S = x\{\Sigma^*\} \in$ **RGX** be a splitter. Then P is splittable by S via P_S if and only if $P \subseteq P_S$ and $P \supseteq P_S$.

For the upper bound, one can construct a spanner P' such that $P = P_S \circ S$ if and only if $P = P'$. (For readers familiar with spanner algebra, P' is the spanner $\pi_{\text{SVars}(P)}((\Sigma^* \cdot x\{P_S\} \cdot \Sigma^*) \bowtie S)$.) Furthermore, P' can be constructed in polynomial time and therefore the upper bound follows from the fact that equivalence between spanners can be tested in PSPACE (Theorem 4.1). □

5.1.2 The cover condition. In this section, we introduce a necessary condition for splittability, called the *cover condition.* We show that it is PSPACE-complete to check if the condition holds for **RGX**, **VSA**, **dVSA**, and **dfVSA**. In Section 5.1.3, we leverage the condition to obtain a tractable split-correctness result. Furthermore, we use the cover condition as a part of the splittability condition to obtain a characterization for splittability in Section 5.2.

Definition 5.2 (Cover Condition). A spanner P and splitter S satisfy the *cover condition* if, for every document d and every tuple $t \in P(d)$, there exists a span $s \in S(d)$ that contains every span in t. That is, s contains $t(v)$ for every $v \in \text{SVars}(P)$. In this case, we also say that s *covers* t.

The cover condition is indeed necessary for splittability.

Lemma 5.3. *For a spanner P and a splitter S, if P is splittable by S, then P and S satisfy the cover condition.*

The following lemma determines the complexity of testing the cover condition.

Lemma 5.4. *Let P be a spanner and S be a splitter, both coming from one of the classes* **RGX**, **VSA**, **dVSA**, *or* **dfVSA**. *Then it is PSPACE-complete to check whether P and S satisfy the cover condition.*

Proof sketch. We start with the PSPACE upper bound. Let P be a spanner and let S be a splitter both in **VSA**. Let $V = \text{SVars}(P)$. We assume $x_S \notin V$. We define a spanner P_V that selects every possible span in every variable. More formally: $P_V = (\Sigma, V, \{q_0\}, q_0, \{q_0\}, \delta)$, where $\delta = \{(q_0, c, q_0) \mid c \in \Sigma \cup \Gamma_V\}$. We argue next that the cover condition holds if and only if $P \subseteq P_V \circ S$. The PSPACE upper bound then follows from Theorem 4.1.

(if): Assume that the cover condition does not hold. Then there is a document $d \in \Sigma^*$ and a tuple $t \in P(d)$, such that there is no split $s \in S(d)$ which covers t. Therefore, $t \notin P_V \circ S$.

(only if): Assume that the cover condition holds. Let $d \in \Sigma^*$ be a document and $t \in P(d)$ be a tuple. Due to the cover condition, there is a split $s \in S(d)$ which covers t. Thus, per definition of P_V, there is a tuple $t' \in P_V$, such that $t = t' \gg s$. Therefore $P \subseteq P_V \circ S$ also holds.

For the lower bounds, we reduce from DFA union universality and regular expression union universality, which are both PSPACE-complete [16, 21]. We prove the lower bound for **dfVSA**. (The proof for **RGX** is analogous.) Let $A_1, \ldots, A_n$ be regular languages, given as deterministic finite automata over the alphabet Σ.

Let $\Sigma' = \Sigma \uplus \{a\}$. Furthermore, let $P = a^n \cdot y\{\Sigma^*\}$ be a spanner and $S = x\{a^n \cdot A_1\} + a \cdot x\{a^{n-1} \cdot A_2\} + \cdots + a^{n-1} \cdot x\{a \cdot A_n\}$ be a splitter. It is easy to see that P and S can be represented as deterministic functional VSet-automata whose size is quadratic in the input. For every document $d \in \Sigma'^*$ and every tuple $t \in P(d)$ there is a split $s \in S(d)$ that covers t if and only if $L(\Sigma^*) \subseteq \bigcup_{1 \le i \le n} L(A_i)$. □

5.1.3 Tractability for disjoint splitters. We now show that split-correctness for deterministic functional VSet-automata is decidable in polynomial time in the case where splitters are *disjoint*. The next proposition shows that deciding whether a splitter is disjoint is tractable.

Proposition 5.5. *For every splitter $S \in C$ it can be checked in NL whether S is disjoint, if C in* {**VSA**, **dVSA**, **dfVSA**}. *Furthermore, for $S \in$* **RGX**, *disjointness can be checked in PTIME.*

Recall from the Introduction that disjointness is a natural property that splitters often satisfy in real life (e.g., tokenization, sentence boundary detection, paragraph splitting and segmentation). Technically, we rely on a polynomial-time algorithm to test the cover condition for deterministic functional automata.

Lemma 5.6. *Let P be a spanner and S a disjoint splitter, both from* **dfVSA**. *Whether P and S satisfy the cover condition can be decided in polynomial time.*

Proof sketch. We reduce this problem to the containment problem of unambiguous finite automata, which can be solved in polynomial time [33]. Essentially we construct unambiguous automata A_P and A_S that accept *ref-words over an expanded alphabet.* That is, A_P accepts words $\mathbf{r}' = (\sigma_1, i_1) \cdots (\sigma_n, i_n)$ such that $\sigma_1 \cdots \sigma_n$ is a ref-word for P and $i_1 \cdots i_n \in 0^*1^+0^*$ is a bit sequence that indicates from where to where the ref-word uses its variables. The automaton A_S accepts precisely those words in the language of A_P that correspond to an output tuple that is covered by some span of S. (We need the disjointness of S for A_S to be unambiguous.) Therefore, $A_P \subseteq A_S$, if and only if for every output tuple of P, there is an output tuple of S that covers it. □

Theorem 5.7. *Let P, P_S be spanners and S be a disjoint splitter, all from* **dfVSA**. *Split-correctness for P, P_S, and S (i.e., whether $P = P_S \circ S$) is decidable in polynomial time.*

Proof Sketch. We explain how to decide the complement problem. We begin by checking the cover condition. If the cover condition is not satisfied, it follows by Lemma 5.3 that $P \neq P_S \circ S$. Using Lemma 5.6, this test can be done in polynomial time. Assuming that the cover condition holds, we look for a split s on which P and P_S behave differently. This can be done by guessing a ref-word $\mathbf{r} \in (\Sigma \cup \Gamma_{\text{SVars}(P)} \cup \Gamma_{\{x_S\}})$, symbol by symbol and simulating P, S, and P_S on the fly. □

5.2 Splittability

In this section, we address the splittability problem. In particular, we show that Splittability[**VSA**] and Splittability[**RGX**] are PSPACE-complete for disjoint splitters.

Before we begin, it is useful to note the following insight about the splittability problem. When a spanner P is splittable by a splitter S, there can be different split-spanners P_S and P'_S witnessing splittability. This is illustrated next.

Example 5.8. Consider $P = ay\{b\}b$ and $S = x\{ab\}b + ax\{bb\}$. Then, both $P = P_S \circ S$ and $P = P'_S \circ S$ for $P_S = ay\{b\}$ and $P'_S = y\{b\}b$ but $P_S \neq P'_S$. The reason this happens is that S selects two different spans $s = [1, 3\rangle$ and $s' = [2, 4\rangle$ both containing the span $[2, 3\rangle$ selected by P on abb. Since the selected spans are different, the split-spanners P_S and P'_S need to be different as well to be able to simulate P. Notice that S is not a disjoint splitter, as $[1, 3\rangle \cap [2, 4\rangle \neq \emptyset$. □

However, when S is disjoint and P is splittable by S, we show that there exists a *canonical* split-spanner P_S^{can} for which $P = P_S^{\text{can}} \circ S$. In particular, for every document d, the canonical split-spanner selects a tuple t, if there is a larger document d' on which S selects d and P selects t on d', with proper indentation of the indexes. Formally, P_S^{can} is defined such that, for every document d,

$$P_S^{\text{can}}(d) := \{t \mid \exists d' \in \Sigma^*, s \in S(d'), d'_s = d, \text{ and } (t \gg s) \in P(d')\}$$

In the following proposition, we prove that we can construct the canonical spanner in polynomial time. Essentially, P_S^{can} is a cross product between P and S, properly adjusted to use the same variables, operating on substrings of documents selected by S.

Proposition 5.9. *Let P be a spanner and S be a disjoint splitter, both coming from one of the classes* **RGX** *or* **VSA**. *Then a VSet-automaton can be constructed in time polynomial in the sizes of P and S that defines the spanner P_S^{can}.*

Proof sketch. Let $P = (\Sigma, V, Q_P, q_{0,P}, Q_{F,P}, \delta_P)$ be a VSet-automaton and let $S = (\Sigma, \{x\}, Q_S, q_{0,S}, Q_{F,S}, \delta_S)$ be a splitter, with $x \notin V$.

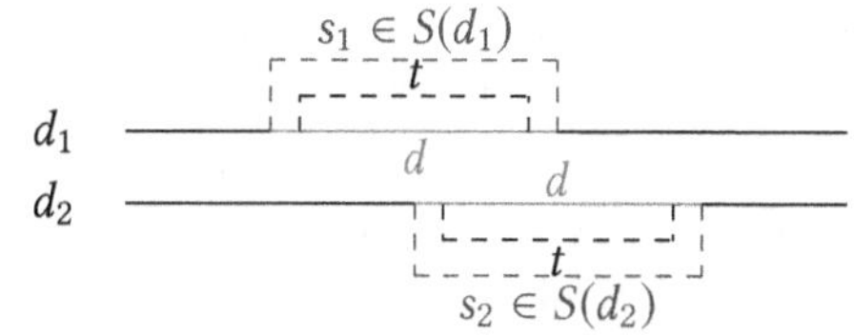

Figure 2: Visualization of the splittability condition (2).

By P^Σ we denote the VSet-automaton obtained from P by eliminating all Γ_V-transitions, that is, only keeping the Σ-transitions. For a symbol c, let $P \cdot_c P$ be the VSet-automaton consisting of two disjoint copies of P where every state of the first copy is connected to its corresponding state in the second copy by a transition labeled with c. Then define $P^x = P^\Sigma \cdot_{x\vdash} P \cdot_{\dashv x} P^\Sigma$. We denote by S^{+V} the VSet-automaton obtained from S by adding self-loops labeled with $v\vdash$ and $\dashv v$ to every state of S for $v \in V$. That is, for every state q of S, add the transitions $(q, v\vdash, q)$ and $(q, \dashv v, q)$ for every $v \in V$. Then, notice that both P^x and S^{+V} define ref-words over the same extended alphabet $\Sigma \cup \Gamma_{V \cup \{x\}}$. Moreover, for every document $d \in \Sigma^*$, the spanner $(P^x \cap S^{+V})$ defines precisely those tuples t where $t(x) \in S(d)$ and $t(v)$ is contained in $t(x)$ for every $v \in V$. Then, the spanner accepting the ref-word language $\{w_2 \mid w_1 \cdot x\vdash \cdot w_2 \cdot \dashv x \cdot w_3 \in \text{Ref}(P^x \cap S^{+V})\}$ is exactly P_S^{can}. □

Notice that, due to Lemma 5.3, whenever P is splittable by S, $P \subseteq P_S^{\text{can}} \circ S$. However, when S is not disjoint, the converse inclusion $P_S^{\text{can}} \circ S \subseteq P$ does not always hold as the next example shows.

Example 5.10. Consider again P and S from Example 5.8 and let $d = abb$. Notice that $P(d) = \{[2, 3\rangle\}$, and $P(d') = \emptyset$ for every $d' \neq d$. We now compute $(P_S^{\text{can}} \circ S)(d)$. Since $S(d) = \{[1, 3\rangle, [2, 4\rangle\}$, we need to consider the documents $d_{[1,3\rangle} = ab$ and $d_{[2,4\rangle} = bb$ for the definition of P_S^{can}. We have $P_S^{\text{can}}(ab) = \{[2, 3\rangle\}$ and $P_S^{\text{can}}(bb) = \{[1, 2\rangle\}$. Finally,

$$\begin{aligned}(P_S^{\text{can}} \circ S)(d) &= \bigcup_{s \in S(d)} \{t \gg s \mid t \in P_S^{\text{can}}(d_s)\} \\ &= \bigcup_{s \in \{[1,3\rangle, [2,4\rangle\}} \{t \gg s \mid t \in P_S^{\text{can}}(ab) \cup P_S^{\text{can}}(bb)\} \\ &= \{[1, 2\rangle, [2, 3\rangle, [3, 4\rangle\}.\end{aligned}$$

The reason is that the canonical split-spanner considers all combinations of output tuples $t' = t \gg s$ of P with splits s of S that cover t'. However, the split-spanner does not "remember" the relevant combinations of the t and s that lead to an output tuple t' and arbitrarily combines them. Therefore, if S is not disjoint and there is more than one split that covers some output tuple t', this may lead to combinations that don't correspond to outputs of P. □

We define the splittability condition that will characterize splittability for disjoint splitters.

Definition 5.11 (Splittability Condition). Let P be a spanner and S a splitter. We say that P and S satisfy the *splittability condition* if the following holds:

(1) P and S satisfy the cover condition; and,
(2) for all $d, d^1, d^2 \in \Sigma^*$, $[i_1, j_1\rangle \in S(d^1), [i_2, j_2\rangle \in S(d^2)$ such that $d = d^1_{[i_1,j_1\rangle} = d^2_{[i_2,j_2\rangle}$ and for all (SVars(P), d)-tuples t with $t_1 = t \gg [i_1, j_1\rangle$, $t_2 = t \gg [i_2, j_2\rangle$ it must hold that

$$t_1 \in P(d^1) \Leftrightarrow t_2 \in P(d^2).$$

Recall that the cover condition states that for every $d \in \Sigma^*$ and for all $t \in P(d)$ there is a span $s \in S(d)$ that covers t. The second requirement of the splittability condition is visualized in Figure 2. In essence, it says that whenever the same subdocument d is selected by S from two larger documents d_1 and d_2, and for every tuple t within d, if we consider the corresponding tuples t_1 and t_2 within the larger documents d_1 and d_2 then P should behave the same with respect to t_1 and t_2 on d_1 and d_2, respectively. That is, P selects t_1 in d_1 if and only if P selects t_2 in d_2.

Lemma 5.12. *Let P be a spanner and S be a disjoint splitter. Then the following three statements are equivalent:*

(1) P is splittable by S;
(2) P and S satisfy the splittability condition; and,
(3) $P = P^{\text{can}}_S \circ S$.

Proof. Per definition (3) implies (1). Thus we need to prove that (1) implies (2) and that (2) implies (3).

(1) $\Rightarrow$ (2) : Let spanner P be splittable by S. The first requirement of the splittability condition follows directly from Lemma 5.3. It remains to show that the second requirement holds. Towards a contradiction, assume the requirement does not hold. Thus, there are $d, d^1, d^2 \in \Sigma^*$, $[i_1, j_1\rangle \in S(d^1), [i_2, j_2\rangle \in S(d^2)$ such that $d = d^1_{[i_1,j_1\rangle} = d^2_{[i_2,j_2\rangle}$ and there is a (SVars(P), d)-tuple t with $t_1 = t \gg [i_1, j_1\rangle$, and $t_2 = t \gg [i_2, j_2\rangle$ such that $t_1 \in P(d^1)$ and $t_2 \notin P(d^2)$. Let P_S be a spanner for which P is splittable by S via P_S. Since S is disjoint, the span $[i_1, j_1\rangle \in S(d^1)$ is the only span of d^1 that covers t_1. Therefore, due to $t_1 \in P(d^1)$ and $P = P_S \circ S$ it must hold that $t \in P_S(d^1_{[i_1,j_1\rangle})$. However, using the same argument, $[i_2, j_2\rangle \in S(d^2)$ is the only span of d^2 that covers t_2. Thus, as $t_2 \notin P(d^2)$ and $P = P_S \circ S$ it must hold that $t \notin P_S(d^2_{[i_2,j_2\rangle})$. But $P_S(d^2_{[i_2,j_2\rangle}) = P_S(d^1_{[i_1,j_1\rangle})$ as $d = d^1_{[i_1,j_1\rangle} = d^2_{[i_2,j_2\rangle}$ which leads to the desired contradiction.

(2) $\Rightarrow$ (3) : Assume that the splittability condition holds. We show that P is splittable by S via the canonical split-spanner P^{can}_S.

We first argue that $P \subseteq P^{\text{can}}_S \circ S$. Indeed, by construction, P^{can}_S simulates P on every span selected by S. Moreover, by the cover condition and disjointness of S, every tuple selected by P is included in exactly one split selected by S. Formally, let $d \in \Sigma^*$ be a document and $t \in P(d)$ be a tuple, selected by P. Then, there is exactly one $s \in S(d)$ such that s covers t. Let $d = d_{\text{pre}} \cdot d_{\text{mid}} \cdot d_{\text{post}}$ such that $s = [|d_{\text{pre}}| + 1, |d_{\text{pre}} \cdot d_{\text{mid}}| + 1\rangle$. Due to s covering t, there must be a tuple t' with $t = t' \gg s$. Thus it follows, per definition of P^{can}_S, that $t' \in P^{\text{can}}_S(d_{\text{mid}})$ and, therefore, $t \in (P^{\text{can}}_S \circ S)(d)$.

We now show the other inclusion, that is, $P^{\text{can}}_S \circ S \subseteq P$. To this end, let $d^1 \in \Sigma^*$ be a document and $t \in (P^{\text{can}}_S \circ S)$ be a tuple. Thus, d^1 can be written as $d^1 = d^1_{\text{pre}} \cdot d \cdot d^1_{\text{post}}$, such that $[i_1, j_1\rangle = [|d^1_{\text{pre}}| + 1, |d^1_{\text{pre}} \cdot d| + 1\rangle \in S(d^1)$ and $t' \in P^{\text{can}}_S(d)$ is a tuple with $t = t' \gg [i_1, j_1\rangle$. Per definition of P^{can}_S and $t' \in P^{\text{can}}_S(d)$ there must be a document $d^2 = d^2_{\text{pre}} \cdot d \cdot d^2_{\text{post}} \in \Sigma^*$ such that $[i_2, j_2\rangle = [|d^2_{\text{pre}}| + 1, |d^2_{\text{pre}} d| + 1\rangle \in S(d^2)$ and $t' \gg [i_2, j_2\rangle \in P(d^2)$. By the second requirement of the splittability condition it directly follows that $t \in P(d_1)$. □

The following example shows that Lemma 5.12 does not hold in general if S is not disjoint.

Example 5.13. Let $P = aby\{b\} + cy\{b\}b$ and $S = x\{\Sigma^*\} + \Sigma^* x\{bb\}\Sigma^*$. Furthermore, let $d = bb, d_1 = abb, d_2 = cbb$, and $t = \{(y, [2, 3\rangle)\}$. With $s = [2, 4\rangle$, it is easy to see that $s \in S(d_1)$ and $s \in S(d_2)$. With $t_1 = t_2 = t \gg s$, we have that $t_1 \in P(d_1)$, but $t_2 \notin P(d_2)$. Therefore, the second requirement of the splittability condition does not hold. Nevertheless, it is easy to see that P is self-splittable. □

Lemma 5.14. *Let P, P_S be regular spanners and S be a disjoint splitter, such that $P = P_S \circ S$. Then $P^{\text{can}}_S \subseteq P_S$.*

We note that the inclusion $P^{\text{can}}_S \subseteq P_S$ does not hold if S is not disjoint, since P^{can}_S can select arbitrary tuples on documents for which S does not produce any output.

We are now ready to state the main complexity result of this section:

Theorem 5.15. *Deciding Splittability[C] for disjoint splitters and $C \in$ {RGX, VSA} is PSPACE-complete.*

Proof sketch. The upper bound directly follow from Lemma 5.12, Proposition 5.9, and Theorem 5.1. For the lower bound, we give a reduction from the inclusion problem for regular expressions that is known to be PSPACE-complete. Let r_1 and r_2 be regular expressions. It can be shown that the boolean spanner $P = r_1$ is splittable by the disjoint splitter $S = x\{r_2\}$ if and only if $L(r_1) \subseteq L(r_2)$. □

5.3 Self-Splittability

Next, we discuss self-splittability.

Theorem 5.16. *Deciding Self-splittability[C] for $C \in$ {RGX, VSA} is PSPACE-complete.*

Proof sketch. The upper bounds follow directly from Theorem 5.1. The lower bound for Self-splittability[**VSA**] follows directly from the lower bound of Self-splittability[**RGX**], since regex-formulas can be transformed into VSet-automata in polynomial time.

We give a reduction from the containment problem for **RGX** to Self-splittability[**RGX**]. To this end, let $r_1, r_2 \in$ **RGX** be regex-formulas over the alphabet Σ with $\mathrm{SVars}(r_1) = \mathrm{SVars}(r_2)$ and let $a \notin \Sigma$ be a new symbol and $\Sigma' = \Sigma \cup \{a\}$. Furthermore, let $x, y \notin \mathrm{SVars}(r_1)$ be new variables. We define the spanner $P = r_1 + (a \cdot r_2)$ and splitter $S = a? \cdot x\{\Sigma^*\}$. Then P is self-splittable by S if and only if $[\![r_1]\!] \subseteq [\![r_2]\!]$. □

The following is immediate from Theorem 5.7.

Theorem 5.17. *Let P be a spanner and S be a disjoint splitter, both from* **dfVSA**. *Self-splittability for P and S is decidable in polynomial time.*

6 REASONING ABOUT SPLITTABILITY

In a complex pipeline that involves multiple spanners and splitters, it may be beneficial to reason about the manipulation or replacement of operators for the sake of query planning (in a similar way as we reason about query plans in a database system). In this section, we consider questions of this sort. For the class of regular spanners, we prove PSPACE-completeness for deciding on splitter *commutativity* (Theorem 6.2) and *subsumption*, that is, whether a splitter can always be executed after another (Theorem 6.3). We also discuss conditions for the *transitivity* of splitters (Observation 6.4 and Lemma 6.5).

Commutativity. An obvious problem is whether two splitters commute (possibly with respect to a context, which we abstract as a regular language). For example, suppose that we are given a program that processes a text document, and suppose that the query plan first splits by pages and then by paragraphs. This is the same as splitting by paragraphs and then by pages. So, the query planner can choose between the two options.

Formally, let S_1 and S_2 be two splitters and R a regular language. We say that S_1 and S_2 *commute w.r.t.* R if and only if $(S_1 \circ S_2)(d) = (S_2 \circ S_1)(d)$ for all $d \in R$. For instance, if S_1 and S_2 commute and S_1 is more selective than S_2, then it is beneficial to apply S_1 before S_2. The next lemma shows that the composition of splitters can be explicitly constructed.

Lemma 6.1. *Let S_1 and S_2 be splitters given as VSet-automata. Then a VSet-automaton for the splitter $(S_2 \circ S_1)$ can be computed in polynomial time.*

We now establish the complexity of the decision problem.

Theorem 6.2. *Let S_1, S_2, all coming from one of the classes* **RGX** *or* **VSA** *and let R be an NFA. Then deciding if S_1 and S_2 commute w.r.t. R is PSPACE-complete. The problem is PSPACE-hard even if $L(R) = \Sigma^*$.*

Subsumption. Another form of optimization is *subsumption*. We say that S *subsumes* S' *w.r.t.* R if $S(d) = (S' \circ S)(d)$ for all $d \in R$. For example, suppose that we are told that a spanner is splittable by a splitter S (e.g., the sentence splitter); does it also imply that it is splittable by S' (e.g., the paragraph splitter)? In Section 7, we discuss an extension of the framework where such knowledge is provided on arbitrary spanners as *split constraints.*

Theorem 6.3. *Let S, S', and R, all coming from one of the classes* **RGX** *or* **VSA**. *Then deciding if S subsumes S' w.r.t. R is PSPACE-complete.*

Proof. The upper bound is immediate from Lemma 6.1 and Theorem 4.1. The lower bound follows from regular expression universality. Let E be a regular expression and let $S' = x\{E\}$. Then $S = x\{\Sigma^*\}$ subsumes S' if and only if $L(E) = \Sigma^*$. □

Transitivity. We conclude the section with a few initial observations about the *transitivity* of splittability.

Observation 6.4. Let P, P_S be spanners and S_1, S_2 be splitters, such that $P = P_S \circ S_1$ and $S_1 = S_1 \circ S_2$. Then it is not necessarily true that $P = P_S \circ S_2$.

Proof. Let $P = \Sigma^* \cdot y\{a\} \cdot \Sigma^*$, $P_S = y\{a\}$, $S_1 = \Sigma^* \cdot x\{\Sigma\} \cdot \Sigma^*$, and $S_2 = \Sigma^* \cdot x\{\Sigma \cdot \Sigma\} \cdot \Sigma^* + x\{\Sigma\}$. It's easy to see that $P = P_S \circ S_1$ and $S_1 = S_1 \circ S_2$, but $P \neq P_S \circ S_2$. □

However, self-splittability transfers from one splitter to another more general splitter:

Lemma 6.5. *Let P be a spanner and S_1, S_2 be splitters, such that $P = P \circ S_1$ and $S_1 = S_1 \circ S_2$. Then $P = P \circ S_2$.*

7 BEYOND THE BASIC FRAMEWORK

We now discuss three problems that are based on the concept of splittability, but go beyond the basic framework discussed in the previous sections. The first problem is that of deciding on the splittability in the presence of *black-box* spanners that are known to follow *split constraints* (Section 7.1). The second problem is that of deciding on the splittability under a regular precondition on the input documents (Section 7.2). Finally, the third problem is that of deciding on the splittability under splitters that can *annotate* the splits as they run (Section 7.3).

7.1 Split-Constrained Black Boxes

We begin with motivating examples. Since the examples and our definitions afterwards use the natural join of spanners, we briefly recall it from Fagin et al. [7]. The spanner $P_1 \bowtie P_2$

is defined as follows. We have $\text{SVars}(P_1 \bowtie P_2) = \text{SVars}(P_1) \cup \text{SVars}(P_2)$, and $(P_1 \bowtie P_2)(d)$ consists of all d-tuples t that agree with some $t_1 \in P(d)$, and $t_2 \in P_2(d)$; note that the existence of t implies that t_1 and t_2 agree on the common variables of P_1 and P_2, that is, $t_1(x) = t_2(x)$ for all $x \in \text{SVars}(P_1) \cap \text{SVars}(P_2)$.

Example 7.1. In this example and the next, we'll denote by $P(x, y)$ that spanner P uses the variables x and y. Consider the spanner P that seeks to extract adjectives for Galaxy phones from reports. We define this spanner by joining three spanners:

The spanner $\alpha(x, y)$ is the regex formula

$$\Sigma^* \cdot x\{\text{Galaxy [A-Z]\textbackslash d}^*\} \cdot \Sigma^* \cdot y\{\Sigma^*\}. \cdot \Sigma^*$$

that extracts mentions of Galaxy brands (e.g., Galaxy A6 and Galaxy S8) followed by substrings y that occur right before a period.

The spanner $P_1(x, x')$ is a coreference resolver (e.g., the *sieve* algorithm [27]) that finds spans x' that coreference spans x. The spanner $P_2(x', y)$ finds pairs of noun phrases x' and attached adjectives y (e.g., based on a Recursive Neural Network [31]).

For example, consider the review *"I am happy with my Galaxy A6. It is stable."* Here, in one particular match, x will match (the span of) *Galaxy A6*, x' will match *it* (which is an anaphor for *Galaxy A6*), and y will match *stable.* (Other matches are possible too.)

How should a system find an efficient query plan to this join on a long report? Natively materializing each relation might be too costly: $\alpha(x, y)$ may produce too many matches, and $P_1(x, x')$ and $P_2(x', y)$ may be computationally costly. Nevertheless, we may have the information that P_1 is splittable by paragraphs, and that P_2 is splittable by sentences (hence, by paragraphs). This information suffices to determine that the entire join $\alpha(x, y) \bowtie P_1(x, x') \bowtie P_2(x', y)$ is splittable, hence parallelizable, by paragraphs. □

Example 7.2. Now consider the spanner that joins two spanners: $\alpha'(x)$ extracts spans x followed by the phrase *"is kind"* (e.g., *"Barack Obama is kind"*). The spanner $P'(x)$ extracts all spans x that match person names. Clearly, the spanner $\alpha'(x)$ does not split by any natural splitter, since it includes, for instance, the entire prefix of the document before *"is kind"*. However, by knowing that $P'(x)$ splits by sentences, we know that the join $\alpha'(x) \bowtie P'(x)$ splits by sentences. Moreover, by knowing that $P'(x)$ splits by 3-grams, we can infer that $\alpha'(x) \bowtie P'(x)$ splits by 5-grams. Here, again, the holistic analysis of the join infers splittability in cases where intermediate spanners are not splittable. □

We now formalize the splittability question that the examples give rise to. A *spanner signature* Π is a collection $\{\pi_1, \ldots, \pi_k\}$ of *spanner symbols*, where each π_i is associated with a set $\text{SVars}(\pi_i)$ of span variables. In Example 7.1, π_1 and π_2 would correspond to the name of a coreference resolver and an adjective extractor, respectively, with $\text{SVars}(\pi_1) = \{x, x'\}$ and $\text{SVars}(\pi_2) = \{x', y\}$. We assume that Π is connected, that is, the underlying hypergraph where every π_i is interpreted as the hyperedge consisting of $\text{SVars}(\pi_i)$ is connected. An *instance* I of Π associates with each spanner symbol π_i an actual spanner P_i such that $\text{SVars}(P_i) = \text{SVars}(\pi_i)$. In Example 7.1, these would be P_1 and P_2, respectively.

Let Π be a spanner signature, I an instance of Π, and α a regular spanner. We denote by $\alpha \bowtie I$ the spanner that is given by

$$\alpha \bowtie P_1 \bowtie \cdots \bowtie P_k.$$

We note that this is well-defined due to the associativity and commutativity of the $\bowtie$-operator.

A *regular split constraint* over a spanner signature Π is an expression of the form "π_i is self-splittable by the regular splitter S," which we denote by $\pi_i \sqsubseteq S$. An instance I of Π *satisfies* a set C of regular split constraints, denoted $I \models C$, if for every constraint $\pi_i \sqsubseteq S$ in C it is the case that P_i is self-splittable by S. The problem of *split-correctness with black boxes* is the following:

Black Box Split-Correctness	
Input:	A spanner signature Π, a set C of regular split constraints, a regular spanner α, and a splitter S.
Question:	Is $\alpha \bowtie I$ splittable by S whenever I is an instance of Π such that $I \models C$?

A natural question to ask is the following. Assume that α is self-splittable by S and we have all split constraints $\pi_i \sqsubseteq S$, that is, all spanners are self-splittable by the same splitter S. Is it the case that $\alpha \bowtie I$ is splittable by S? The following Lemma shows that this is not the case in general.

Lemma 7.3. *There are spanners P_1 and P_2 and a splitter S, such that P_1 and P_2 are self-splittable by S, but $P_1 \bowtie P_2$ is not splittable (and thus also not self-splittable) by S.*

Proof. Let $P_1 = \Sigma^* \cdot x_1\{a\} \cdot x_2\{b\} \cdot \Sigma^*$ and $P_2 = \Sigma^* \cdot x_2\{b\} \cdot x_3\{a\} \cdot \Sigma^*$ be spanners. Furthermore, let $S = \Sigma^* \cdot x\{(a \cdot \Sigma) + (\Sigma \cdot a)\} \cdot \Sigma^*$ be a splitter. Then both P_1 and P_2 are self-splittable by S. However, the join $P := P_1 \bowtie P_2$ can not be splittable by S since for $d = aba$, $S(d) = \{[1, 3\rangle, [2, 4\rangle\}$ and $P(d) = \{([1, 2\rangle, [2, 3\rangle, [3, 4\rangle)\}$, and therefore the cover condition is violated. □

The next result shows that in the presence of disjoint splitters the join operator preserves self-splittability.

Theorem 7.4. *Let S be a disjoint splitter, α be a spanner that is splittable by S, Π be a spanner signature, and $C = \{\pi_1 \sqsubseteq S, \ldots, \pi_k \sqsubseteq S\}$ be a set of regular split constraints. Then Π, C, α, and S are black box split-correct.*

Proof. Let I be an instance of Π, such that $I \models \Pi$ and let P_i be the spanner interpreting π_i. We have to show, that $\alpha \bowtie I = P_S \circ S$ for some spanner P_S. Per assumption, α is splittable by S and P_i is self-splittable by S for all $1 \leq i \leq k$. Let α_S be a spanner such that $\alpha = \alpha_S \circ S$ and let $P_S = \alpha_S \bowtie P_1 \bowtie \cdots \bowtie P_k$.

We argue that $\alpha \bowtie I$ is splittable by S via P_S (i.e. $\alpha \bowtie I = P_S \circ S$). To this end, let $d \in \Sigma^*$ be a document and $t \in \alpha \bowtie I$ be a tuple. Then there are tuples $t_\alpha \in \alpha(d)$, and $t_i \in P_i(d)$ for $1 \leq i \leq k$, such that $t = t_\alpha \bowtie t_1 \bowtie \cdots \bowtie t_k$. Furthermore, as S is disjoint and Π is connected there is a unique split $s \in S(d)$ covering all tuples $t, t_\alpha, t_1, \ldots, t_k$. By $\alpha = \alpha_S \circ S$ there is a tuple $t'_\alpha \in \alpha_S(d_s)$ such that $t_\alpha = t'_\alpha \gg s$. Furthermore, by self-splittability of P_i there also is a tuple $t'_i \in P_i(d_s)$ such that $t_i = t'_i \gg s$. Thus, it must hold that $t' = t'_\alpha \bowtie t'_1 \bowtie \cdots \bowtie t'_k \in P_S(d_s)$ and $t = t' \gg s$. Hence, $t \in P_S \circ S$.

For the other direction, assume that there is a document $d \in \Sigma^*$, a split $s \in S(d)$ and a tuple $t' \in P_S(d_s)$. Then it follows by the same argument, that the tuple $t = t' \gg s \in \alpha \bowtie I$. □

7.2 Regular Precondition

Sometimes a spanner is not splittable by a given splitter, because of a reason that seems marginal. For instance, the spanner may first check that the document conforms to some standard format, such as Unicode, UTF-8, CSV, HTTP, etc. We provide two ways to deal with such kind of scenarios: *regular preconditions* (here) and *annotated splitters* (in Section 7.3).

A *splitter with filter* is a pair (S, L) where S is a splitter and L is a word language. We denote such splitters as $S[L]$. The spanner defined by $S[L]$ is the function that maps each document d to $S(d)$ if $d \in L$ and to $\emptyset$ otherwise.

It is easy to see that splitters with filter are not more powerful than ordinary splitters. However, they give rise to new problems that can be studied. For instance, it may be the case that we already have a spanner and splitter available that we do not want to change, but we can use a regular language as a filter to obtain split-correctness on all documents that satisfy the filter.

Split-correctness[C] with regular filter	
Input:	Spanners $P, P_S \in C$ and splitter $S \in C$.
Question:	Is there a regular language L such that $P = P_S \circ S[L]$?

Splittability[C] with regular filter	
Input:	Spanners $P \in C$ and splitter $S \in C$.
Question:	Is there a regular language L such that P is splittable by $S[L]$?

Furthermore, Self-splittability[C] with regular filter is the special case of Splittability[C] with regular splitter where we ask if P is self-splittable by $S[L]$.

The next lemma shows that there is a minimal filter language for each spanner. For a regular spanner P, define $L_P = \{d \mid P(d) \neq \emptyset\}$. That is, L_P is the set of strings on which P produces a non-empty result.

Lemma 7.5. *Let P and P_S be spanners, S be a splitter and L be a regular language. Then, $P = P_S \circ S[L]$ implies that:*

(1) $L_P \subseteq L$; and,
(2) $P = P_S \circ S[L_P]$.

Proof. Per definition of L_P it holds that $d \in L_P \Leftrightarrow P(d) \neq \emptyset$, for every $d \in \Sigma^*$. For the sake of contradiction, assume that $L_P \nsubseteq L$ and $d \in L_P$ such that $d \notin L$. By $d \in L_P$, it holds that $P(d) \neq \emptyset$, but due to $d \notin L$ the document d is filtered out by $S[L]$ (i.e. $S[L](d) = \emptyset$), contradicting $P = P_S \circ S[L]$. The second condition (2) follows directly from (1) and $P = P_S \circ S[L]$. □

Due to Lemma 7.5, we can decide Split-correctness with regular filter by constructing a splitter S' that is equivalent to the splitter with filter $S[L_P]$ and then testing if $P = P_S \circ S'$.

Theorem 7.6. *Deciding Split-correctness[C] with regular filter and Self-splittability[C] with regular filter are PSPACE-complete, if $C \in \{\mathbf{RGX}, \mathbf{VSA}\}$ and P is functional.*

Proof sketch. If P is functional, we can construct a splitter S' in polynomial time, which computes the same function as $S[L_P]$ (for readers familiar with spanner algebra, $S' = S \bowtie \pi_\emptyset P$). Therefore, using Lemma 7.5 there is a regular language L such that $P = P_S \circ S[L]$ if and only if $P = P_S \circ S[L_P]$. Thus, PSPACE-completeness follows directly from Theorem 5.1 (and Theorem 5.16 in the case of Self-splittability[C] with regular filters). □

Theorem 7.7. *Deciding Splittability[C] with regular filter is PSPACE-complete, if $C \in \{\mathbf{RGX}, \mathbf{VSA}\}$, P is functional, and S is disjoint.*

Proof. Immediate from Theorem 7.6 and Theorem 5.15. □

7.3 Annotated Splitters

Annotated splitters form a natural extension of splitters that can propagate annotations to the splitted strings. That is, instead of mapping documents to relations of spans, annotated splitters map documents to relations of key-span pairs (in analogy to the key-value pairs from the MapReduce framework). They extend *splitters with filters* in the following way. A splitter with filter can be seen as a function that annotates each of the splits with the Boolean value 1 or 0, depending on whether the input document satisfies the precondition or not. More precisely, given a splitter with filter (S, L), we can define a function $S[L]_{\text{ann}}$ as $S[L]_{\text{ann}}(d) := S(d) \times \{1\}$ if $d \in L$ and $S[L]_{\text{ann}}(d) := S(d) \times \{0\}$ otherwise, for every document d. An annotated splitter generalizes this idea in the sense that (1) it can choose from an arbitrary set of *keys* instead of the set of Boolean values and (2) it can annotate different splits with different keys.

As an example, assume that one wants to extract information from an HTTP log and wants to process the information extracted from GET requests differently than that extracted from POST requests. An annotated splitter can split the document and annotate each split with the type of request from which the split was extracted. This annotation can then be used to choose different split-spanners that work on the splits with different annotations.

We omit formal details, due to space constraints, but note that complexity results on *annotated* split-correctness and splittability that are in-line with those on ordinary split-correctness and splittability can be obtained.

8 CONCLUDING REMARKS

We embarked on an exploration of the task of automating the distribution of information-extraction programs across splitters. Adopting the formalism of *document spanners* [7] and the concept of *parallel-correctness* [2], our framework focuses on two computational problems, split-correctness and splittability, as well as their special case of self-splittability. We presented a preliminary analysis of these problems within the class of regular spanners. We have also discussed several natural extensions of the framework, considering the reasoning about the application about multiple splitters, black-box spanners with split constraints, preconditions, and splitters with annotation capabilities. Our principal goal is to open up new directions for research within the framework, and indeed, a plethora of open problems are left for future investigation. We discuss these problems in the remainder of this paper.

Among the basic problems, we know the least about the splittability problem. For example, we do not know even whether the problem is *decidable* without the assumption of disjointness. Moreover, what is the complexity of splittability when restricting to **dfVSA** and disjoint splitters? A fundamental problem is the existence of a *canonical split spanner* P_S such that, similarly to Proposition 5.9, if splittablity holds for P and S, then it can be realized by P_S.

We know more about split-correctness and self-splittablity, but there are some basic open problems there as well. Can we relax any of the assumptions of determinism and disjointedness and still retain tractability? What other natural assumptions lead to tractability? For instance, N-gram splitters and N-consecutive-sentence splitters are not disjoint; but do they possess any general (and easily detectable) properties that can be used for general efficient solvers of our problems? All of these open problems are within *regular* spanners; when considering more expressive languages for spanners (e.g., the class of *core* spanners [7, 11] that allow for string equalities), all problems reopen.

A variant of splittability that we have not touched upon is that of deciding, given a spanner P, whether it can be decomposed in a nontrivial way. We can show that this variant closely relates to the *language primality* problem—can a given regular language be decomposed as the concatenation of non-trivial regular languages? Interestingly, Martens et al. [22] showed that language primality is also related to the work of Abiteboul et al. [1] on typing in distributed XML, which is quite reminiscent, yet different from, our work.

For the extensions of reasoning about splitters, and deciding on splittability with black-box spanners, we barely scratched the surface. Specifically, we believe that reasoning about split constraints over black-box extractors can have a profound implication on the usability of IE systems to developers of varying degrees of expertise, while embracing the advances of the Machine Leaning and Natural Language Processing communities on learning complex functions such as artificial neural networks.

ACKNOWLEDGMENTS

We thank the anonymous reviewers for PODS 2019 for many helpful remarks. The work of Johannes Doleschal was supported by the Special Research Fund (BOF) of Hasselt University and the Deutsche Forschungsgemeinschaft (DFG), Grant MA 4938/4-1. The work of Benny Kimelfeld and Yoav Nahshon was supported in part by the Israel Science Foundation (ISF), Grant 1295/15.

REFERENCES

[1] S. Abiteboul, G. Gottlob, and M. Manna. Distributed XML design. *Journal of Computer and System Sciences*, 77(6):936–964, 2011.

[2] T. J. Ameloot, G. Geck, B. Ketsman, F. Neven, and T. Schwentick. Parallel-correctness and transferability for conjunctive queries. *Journal of the ACM*, 64(5):36:1–36:38, 2017.

[3] T. J. Ameloot, G. Geck, B. Ketsman, F. Neven, and T. Schwentick. Reasoning on data partitioning for single-round multi-join evaluation in massively parallel systems. *Communications of the ACM*, 60(3):93–100, 2017.

[4] J. Chen, D. Ji, C. L. Tan, and Z. Niu. Unsupervised feature selection for relation extraction. In *International Joint Conference on Natural Language Processing (IJCNLP), Companion Volume*, 2005.

[5] L. Chiticariu, R. Krishnamurthy, Y. Li, S. Raghavan, F. Reiss, and S. Vaithyanathan. SystemT: An algebraic approach to declarative information extraction. In *Annual Meeting on Association for Computational Linguistics (ACL)*, pages 128–137, 2010.

[6] J. P. C. Chiu and E. Nichols. Named entity recognition with bidirectional LSTM-CNNs. *Transactions of the ACL*, 4:357–370, 2016.

[7] R. Fagin, B. Kimelfeld, F. Reiss, and S. Vansummeren. Document spanners: A formal approach to information extraction. *Journal of the ACM*, 62(2):12:1–12:51, 2015.

[8] R. Fagin, B. Kimelfeld, F. Reiss, and S. Vansummeren. Declarative cleaning of inconsistencies in information extraction. *ACM Transactions on Database Systems*, 41(1):6:1–6:44, 2016.

[9] F. Florenzano, C. Riveros, M. Ugarte, S. Vansummeren, and D. Vrgoc. Constant delay algorithms for regular document spanners. In *Symposium on Principles of Database Systems (PODS)*, pages 165–177, 2018.

[10] D. D. Freydenberger. A Logic for Document Spanners. In *International Conference on Database Theory (ICDT)*, volume 68, pages 13:1–13:18, 2017.

[11] D. D. Freydenberger and M. Holldack. Document spanners: From expressive power to decision problems. *Theory of Computing Systems*, 62(4):854–898, 2018.

[12] D. D. Freydenberger, B. Kimelfeld, and L. Peterfreund. Joining extractions of regular expressions. In *Symposium on Principles of Database Systems (PODS)*, pages 137–149, 2018.

[13] C. Giuliano, A. Lavelli, and L. Romano. Exploiting shallow linguistic information for relation extraction from biomedical literature. In *Conference of the European Chapter of the Association for Computational Linguistics (EACL)*, 2006.

[14] Hadoop, apache, http://hadoop.apache.org, 2009.

[15] M. A. Hearst. Texttiling: Segmenting text into multi-paragraph subtopic passages. *Computational Linguistics*, 23(1):33–64, 1997.

[16] D. Kozen. Lower bounds for natural proof systems. In *Symposium on Foundations of Computer Science (FOCS)*, pages 254–266. IEEE, 1977.

[17] G. Lample, M. Ballesteros, S. Subramanian, K. Kawakami, and C. Dyer. Neural architectures for named entity recognition. In *Conference of the North American Chapter of the Association for Computational Linguistics (NAACL-HLT)*, pages 260–270, 2016.

[18] R. Leaman and G. Gonzalez. BANNER: an executable survey of advances in biomedical named entity recognition. In *Pacific Symposium on Biocomputing (PSB)*, volume 13, pages 652–663, 2008.

[19] H. Lee, Y. Peirsman, A. Chang, N. Chambers, M. Surdeanu, and D. Jurafsky. Stanford's multi-pass sieve coreference resolution system at the conll-2011 shared task. In *Conference on Computational Natural Language Learning (CoNLL), Shared Task*, pages 28–34, 2011.

[20] A. Madaan, A. Mittal, Mausam, G. Ramakrishnan, and S. Sarawagi. Numerical relation extraction with minimal supervision. In *AAAI Conference on Artificial Intelligence*, pages 2764–2771, 2016.

[21] W. Martens, F. Neven, and T. Schwentick. Complexity of decision problems for XML schemas and chain regular expressions. *SIAM Journal on Computing*, 39(4):1486–1530, 2009.

[22] W. Martens, M. Niewerth, and T. Schwentick. Schema design for XML repositories: complexity and tractability. In *Symposium on Principles of Database Systems (PODS)*, pages 239–250, 2010.

[23] F. Maturana, C. Riveros, and D. Vrgoč. Document spanners for extracting incomplete information: Expressiveness and complexity. *CoRR*, abs/1707.00827, 2017.

[24] F. Maturana, C. Riveros, and D. Vrgoč. Document spanners for extracting incomplete information: Expressiveness and complexity. In *Symposium on Principles of Database Systems (PODS)*, pages 125–136, 2018.

[25] Y. Nahshon. Relational framework for information extraction. Master's thesis, Technion - Computer Science Department, 2018.

[26] B. Pang and L. Lee. A sentimental education: Sentiment analysis using subjectivity summarization based on minimum cuts. In *Annual Meeting on Association for Computational Linguistics (ACL)*, pages 271–278, 2004.

[27] K. Raghunathan, H. Lee, S. Rangarajan, N. Chambers, M. Surdeanu, D. Jurafsky, and C. D. Manning. A multi-pass sieve for coreference resolution. In *Conference on Empirical Methods in Natural Language Processing (EMNLP)*, pages 492–501, 2010.

[28] C. D. Sa, A. Ratner, C. Ré, J. Shin, F. Wang, S. Wu, and C. Zhang. DeepDive: Declarative knowledge base construction. *SIGMOD Record*, 45(1):60–67, 2016.

[29] W. Shen, A. Doan, J. F. Naughton, and R. Ramakrishnan. Declarative information extraction using Datalog with embedded extraction predicates. In *Conference on Very Large Data Bases (VLDB)*, pages 1033–1044, 2007.

[30] J. Shin, S. Wu, F. Wang, C. D. Sa, C. Zhang, and C. Ré. Incremental knowledge base construction using DeepDive. *Proceedings of the VLDB Endowment (PVLDB)*, 8(11):1310–1321, 2015.

[31] R. Socher, C. C. Lin, A. Y. Ng, and C. D. Manning. Parsing natural scenes and natural language with recursive neural networks. In *International Conference on International Conference on Machine Learning (ICML)*, pages 129–136, 2011.

[32] W. M. Soon, H. T. Ng, and C. Y. Lim. A machine learning approach to coreference resolution of noun phrases. *Computational Linguistics*, 27(4):521–544, 2001.

[33] R. E. Stearns and H. B. Hunt III. On the equivalence and containment problems for unambiguous regular expressions, regular grammars and finite automata. *SIAM Journal on Computing*, 14(3):598–611, 1985.

[34] K. Toutanova, D. Klein, C. D. Manning, and Y. Singer. Feature-rich part-of-speech tagging with a cyclic dependency network. In *Conference of the North American Chapter of the Association for Computational Linguistics (NAACL-HLT)*, 2003.

[35] M. Zaharia, R. S. Xin, P. Wendell, T. Das, M. Armbrust, A. Dave, X. Meng, J. Rosen, S. Venkataraman, M. J. Franklin, A. Ghodsi, J. Gonzalez, S. Shenker, and I. Stoica. Apache spark: a unified engine for big data processing. *Communications of the ACM*, 59(11):56–65, 2016.

[36] D. Zeng, K. Liu, Y. Chen, and J. Zhao. Distant supervision for relation extraction via piecewise convolutional neural networks. In *Conference on Empirical Methods in Natural Language Processing (EMNLP)*, pages 1753–1762, 2015.

Robust Set Reconciliation via Locality Sensitive Hashing

Michael Mitzenmacher
Harvard University
michaelm@eecs.harvard.edu

Tom Morgan
Harvard University; Google, Inc.
tdmorgan@seas.harvard.edu

ABSTRACT

We consider variations of set reconciliation problems where two parties, Alice and Bob, each hold a set of points in a metric space, and the goal is for Bob to conclude with a set of points that is close to Alice's set of points in a well-defined way. This setting has been referred to as robust set reconciliation. In one variation, the goal is for Bob to end with a set of points that is close to Alice's in earth mover's distance, and in another the goal is for Bob to have a point that is close to each of Alice's. The first problem has been studied before; while previous results achieved an $O(d)$ approximation, where d is the dimension of the space, we achieve an $O(\log n)$ approximation, where n is the number of points. The second problem appears new, and here we find schemes that, under certain conditions, use sublinear communication.

Our primary novelty is utilizing Invertible Bloom Lookup Tables in combination with locality sensitive hashing. This combination allows us to cope with the geometric setting in a communication-efficient manner.

CCS CONCEPTS

• **Theory of computation → Approximation algorithms analysis; Distributed algorithms; Data exchange;**

KEYWORDS

set reconciliation; locality sensitive hashing; invertible Bloom lookup table; peeling algorithms

ACM Reference Format:
Michael Mitzenmacher and Tom Morgan. 2019. Robust Set Reconciliation via Locality Sensitive Hashing. In *38th ACM SIGMOD-SIGACT-SIGAI Symposium on Principles of Database Systems (PODS '19), June 30–July 5, 2019, Amsterdam, Netherlands.* ACM, New York, NY, USA, 18 pages. https://doi.org/10.1145/3294052.3319690

PODS '19, June 30–July 5, 2019, Amsterdam, Netherlands

ACM ISBN 978-1-4503-6227-6/19/06...$15.00
https://doi.org/10.1145/3294052.3319690

1 INTRODUCTION

Set reconciliation. Set reconciliation is a basic paradigm for data synchronization, for distributed databases and other distributed systems. In a standard set reconciliation problem, two parties, Alice and Bob, hold sets of elements from a shared universe, and the goal is for them to communicate so that one or both of them has the union of both sets. In many settings, the size of the set difference may be very small even though the sets may be large, and therefore the goal is for the communication to be proportional to the size of the set difference, rather than the size of each of the sets (which could be achieved simply by transferring the sets themselves). We provide further description and references below.

Robust set reconciliation. Robust set reconciliation, introduced in [5], generalizes set reconciliation to the scenario where the set elements lie in a metric space, and sufficiently close points should be thought of as equal. As a natural example, set elements might be geometric coordinates for objects, as determined by sensors. Each sensor corresponds to a set, and for the same object, each sensor might have slightly different, noisy measurements. Indeed, in some cases, the sensors might measure different collections of objects, or a sensor might erroneously measure the same object twice in different positions. We might wish two sensor databases to synchronize their collections of known objects, and objects within a certain measured distance are either assumed to be (or for practical purposes may be treated as) the same. Other applications would include reconciling other potentially noisy data, such as databases with floating point measurements or calculations, or databases with image data that has been subjected to varying compression schemes. In such cases, the databases would not end up with the same data; but this would suffice for numerical data sets where having points that are close enough may be all that is needed [5]. This would, for example, be useful when the databases are used for machine learning via clustering or nearest neighbor search. Here the most valuable new data to reconcile would be the outliers.

We study two different models of robust set reconciliation that achieve different types of guarantees. In both settings Alice has a point set S_A and Bob has a point set S_B, where all the points lie in a metric space (U, f), where U is a discretized metric space (as our bounds may depend on $|U|$) such as $[\Delta]^d$. They communicate over a constant number of rounds so as to *reconcile* Alice's data with Bob's; that is, Bob's final point set S'_B is close to Alice's, where the notion of closeness depends on the model. We limit ourselves to computationally efficient (polynomial time) protocols; what can be achieved without this limitation is an interesting open question.

Earth Mover's Distance model. The first model, the Earth Mover's Distance model, was originally introduced in [5]. As in [5], we restrict ourselves to metric spaces of the form $(U, f) = ([\Delta]^d, \ell_p)$. We require that $|S_A| = |S_B| = |S'_B|$. The goal here is for Bob to compute an S'_B which minimizes $\mathrm{EMD}(S_A, S'_B)$, the earth mover's distance between S_A and S'_B, with only reasonable amounts of communication.[1] The earth mover's distance is the min-cost perfect matching between the point sets, where the cost is the distance function f.

The following notation will be helpful. Let $\mathrm{EMD}_k(X, Y)$ be the minimum earth mover's distance achievable between X and Y after excluding k points from each set. In other words, if we were able to exactly identify the optimal k points to remove from S_B and the optimal k points from S_A to replace those with, we would obtain $\mathrm{EMD}(S_A, S'_B) = \mathrm{EMD}_k(S_A, S_B)$. Given a communication bound of $O(k \log |U|)$ bits (where k is an input parameter), the smallest $\mathrm{EMD}(S_A, S'_B)$ one could reasonably hope to achieve is $\mathrm{EMD}(S_A, S'_B) = \mathrm{EMD}_k(S_A, S_B)$. Indeed, [5] provided lower bounds for this model, which confirm that achieving $\mathrm{EMD}(S_A, S'_B) = \mathrm{EMD}_k(S_A, S_B)$ requires $\tilde{\Omega}(k \log |U|)$ bits of communication.

We achieve an $O(\log n)$ approximation; that is, we find S'_B so that $\mathrm{EMD}(S_A, S'_B) = O(\mathrm{EMD}_k(S_A, S_B) \cdot \log n)$, using $\tilde{O}(k)$ communication.[2] Our result improves over the $O(d)$ approximation (where d is the dimension) of [5] for high dimensional data. (One might think the results of [5], in combination with dimension-reduction via the Johnson-Lindenstrauss lemma [14], would achieve this for, for example, the ℓ_2 norm. However, "inverting" the dimensionality reduction, by somehow mapping points in the projected space back into points in the original space, would require additional rounds of communication; moreover, our result holds for metrics where such general dimensionality reduction does not exist, such as the ℓ_1 norm [1].) The setting where our improvement is most obvious is for Hamming space, where an $O(d)$ approximation is essentially useless, as the space has diameter d, while an $O(\log n)$ approximation would be useful, for example, when $n = \mathrm{poly}(d)$.

Our results for this model are presented in section 3.

Gap Guarantee model. The second model, which we believe is novel, aims for a stronger guarantee of closeness for every point. Here Bob's final point set S'_B will be of the form $S_B \cup T_A$, where $T_A \subset S_A$ includes every point in S_A which is at least some chosen distance r_2 from every point in S_B. Note that T_A is allowed to contain additional points from S_A beyond these. That is, Bob is guaranteed that every point in the union of Alice's and Bob's original sets is close to some point in his final set. In order to achieve nontrivial communication bounds for this guarantee, we introduce an additional parameter $r_1 < r_2$, with the intuition being that most of the points in S_A are already within a distance r_1 of some points in S_B. Our communication bounds are then in terms of the number of points that are not within r_1, and the gap between r_1 and r_2. We call this model the Gap Guarantee model, and study it in section 4.

We believe this model to be quite natural given our motivating sensor network example. We would expect sensors observing the same object to have similar measurements, so the objects are measured as below some distance r_1 apart, while discrete objects would yield very different measurements, above some distance r_2. (Alternatively, objects within some distance r_1 might have reason to be treated as the same by the system.) Moreover, sensors may occasionally mistakenly observe the same object as multiple objects close by in space, or may fail to observe an object at all due to interference or gaps in the coverage. As such, the earth mover's distance may not be appropriate, as we are not seeking a matching, since the number of observations of each sensor may be different. This model guarantees the recovery of all differing objects, while the Earth Mover's Distance model gives a much weaker guarantee on the recovered set. However, to achieve this distinct guarantee we may require significantly more communication.

Our main protocol uses $O((k + \rho n)\mathrm{poly}\log n + k \log |U|)$ bits of communication, where k is a bound on the number of points each party has that are more than r_1 from any of the other party's points and ρ is a parameter of the locality sensitive hash family used in the protocol, which depends on r_1 and r_2. (In many metric spaces, $\rho = r_1/r_2$; we will explain further in context.) The improvement this achieves over the naive $O(n \log |U|)$ communication is twofold: its dependence on $\log |U|$ is proportional to k and not n, which is very relevant for high dimensional data (where $\log |U|$ may be linear in the dimension d), and for a sufficiently small (sub-constant) ρ, it yields sublinear total communication.

[1] We note that Definition 2 of [5] makes the additional stipulation that $S'_B \subset S_A \cup S_B$, however neither our protocol nor the protocol of [5] meet this requirement. Both include points in S'_B that approximate, without necessarily equaling, points from S_A.

[2] The $\tilde{O}$ here hides log factors of n and log factors of parameters depending on the metric space, in particular $|U|$.

One-way reconciliation. Both of our models are defined for *one-way* reconciliation, which we define to mean that which Bob wants to conclude with something approximating Alice's data, but Alice makes no changes to her own data. For standard set reconciliation, the two-way reconciliation problem is natural, as we can have both parties conclude with the union of their original sets. For robust set reconciliation problems, the one-way variation is more natural. For example, for both models we consider, we can easily achieve a natural version of two-way reconciliation by having both Alice and Bob run the protocol once in each direction; however, they will generally not end with the same point set. Furthermore, it is unclear what the natural guarantee for a two-way version of the Earth Mover's Distance model would be, especially since we don't expect Alice and Bob to end with the same set.

1.1 Related Work

Here, we briefly describe important related work. Standard set reconciliation has been studied in the context of distributed synchronization, with many possible applications, see e.g. [8, 19, 22, 24, 28] and citations therein. As a fairly recent example, IBLTs (described below) have been proffered as a technique for scalable synchronization of transactions for Bitcoin, and have been discussed as an addition to the Bitcoin protocol [3].

Two technologies underlying our results are locality sensitive hashing and invertible Bloom lookup tables (IBLTs). Locality sensitive hashing hashes items that are close into the same bucket. Here we follow the framework established by Indyk and Motwani [12], though countless other works in locality sensitive hashing provide inspiration [2, 4, 6]. Invertible Bloom lookup tables [7, 8, 11] provide a particularly efficient approach for standard set reconciliation; they allow sets with d differences to be synchronized, after preprocessing taking time linear in the set sizes, in $O(d)$ space and time with some small probability of error. We describe IBLTs in more detail below. One of our primary technical contributions in this paper is an analysis of how errors due to noisy or otherwise inexact data propagate when using IBLTs, as we wish to limit this effect; our analysis here may prove useful for other work.

The idea of using hash-based data structures to handle close matches appears in the work of Kirsch and Mitzenmacher [16], who consider generalizing Bloom filters (for membership queries) to distance-sensitive Bloom filters by making use of locality-sensitive hash functions to return a positive result if a query is close to a set element. Chen et. al. [5] introduce the concept of robust set reconciliation, and use a randomly offset quadtree with IBLTs to develop protocols for the earth mover's distance problem variation we consider here. Chen et. al. discuss many reasons why numerical data sets may have slightly different values, including noise, lossy compression, rounding errors, and privacy-preserving transformations. Applications for the settings they describe are similarly relevant for our results.

We also make use of the recent work of Mitzenmacher and Morgan [20] on reconciling sets of sets. In this setting, Alice and Bob each hold a parent set filled with child sets, and the goal is to synchronize their sets of sets using communication proportional to the number of child set operations by which they differ. This model generalizes to reconciling various other sets of objects such as lists and unlabeled graphs.

Some of our analysis requires some technology from the theory of branching processes; here [10, 13] proved helpful.

As mentioned, Chen et. al.'s work [5] is the most closely related work. Indeed, like [5] we utilize locality-sensitive hashing in combination with IBLTs. We differ in that, as mentioned, Chen et. al. specifically use a randomly offset quadtree, while we allow for any of a large class of locality sensitive hash families. We call this class *multi-scale* locality sensitive hash families, and they have the property that the probability of collision between two points gracefully degrades as a function of the points' distance. Our main innovation comes from how we use our IBLTs. [5] simply rounds points to the center of their quadtree cell, and insert those into an IBLT, while we insert key-value pairs where the key is a point's locality sensitive hash value and the value is the point itself. Handling these pairs, which may have different values for the same key, requires a robust variant of an IBLT, along with some in depth analysis of an IBLT's peeling process. We expect these ideas (multi-scale locality sensitive hashing and robust IBLTs) to be more generally useful.

2 PRELIMINARIES / TECHNIQUES

In this section, we provide some preliminary definitions and frameworks. We note that we utilize variations on the standard notions of locality sensitive hashing and invertible Bloom lookup tables for our results. We therefore encourage the reader not to skip this section even if they are familiar with these topics.

We assume throughout that Alice and Bob's data points lie in a metric space (U, f). For technical simplicity, we often assume that $U = [\Delta]^d$ for some $\Delta, d \in \mathbb{Z}^+$. In the Earth Mover's Distanced model, Alice and Bob have have point sets $S_A, S_B \subset U$ respectively, and $|S_A| = |S_B| = n$. For the Gap Guarantee model, Alice and Bob may have sets of different size.

We work in the word RAM model, with words of size $\Omega(\log n + \log \Delta)$. All protocols are performed assuming public coins, meaning that the random bits used are shared by Alice and Bob without requiring any communication. This in particular allows us to assume that all hash functions are shared between Alice and Bob, without worrying about the cost required to communicate them. There are standard methods for converting protocols with public coins into ones with private coins using minimal additional communication [26]. In practice, one can often approximate protocols with public coins by first sharing a small random seed. We sometimes refer to the number of rounds of communication a protocol uses, which is equal to the number of messages sent. In particular, a protocol using only one round consists of a single message from Alice to Bob (or vice-versa).

2.1 Locality Sensitive Hash Functions

We start with the standard definition of locality sensitive hashing [12].

Definition 2.1 (LSH). *A family* $\mathcal{H} \subseteq \{h \mid h\colon U \to V\}$ *is a* locality sensitive hash *(LSH) family with respect to* (U, f) *with parameters* (r_1, r_2, p_1, p_2) *if* $r_1 < r_2, p_1 > p_2$ *and for any* $x, y \in U$,

- *if* $f(x,y) \leq r_1$ *then* $\Pr_{h\sim H}[h(x) = h(y)] \geq p_1$, *and*
- *if* $f(x,y) > r_2$ *then* $\Pr_{h\sim H}[h(x) = h(y)] \leq p_2$.

A commonly defined meta-parameter for locality sensitive hash functions is $\rho = \log p_1/\log p_2$, which is the key parameter of in interest in the analysis of many approximate nearest neighbor algorithms, and appears in our analysis as well. It is known for example that there exist LSH families for the ℓ_1 metric with $\rho = \Theta(r_1/r_2)$ ([6]) and for ℓ_2 with $\rho = \Theta((r_1/r_2)^2)$ ([2]).

For some of our results, we require a slightly stronger formulation. We have not found this formulation in the literature, although related ideas can be found in for example [4], which includes a condition that has the probability that two hash values collide fall with their distance in a natural way.

Definition 2.2 (MLSH). *A family* $\mathcal{H} \subseteq \{h \mid h\colon U \to V\}$ *is a* multi-scale locality sensitive hash *(MLSH) family with respect to* (U, f) *with parameters* (r, p, α) *if* $r > 0, 0 < p < 1$, $0 < \alpha < 1$, *and, for any* $x, y \in U$,

- $\Pr_{h\sim\mathcal{H}}[h(x) = h(y)] \leq p^{\alpha \cdot f(x,y)}$, *and*
- *if* $f(x,y) \leq r$ *then* $p^{f(x,y)} \leq \Pr_{h\sim\mathcal{H}}[h(x) = h(y)]$.

Many standard LSH families are also MLSH families for the right setting of their parameters. One simple example is the standard LSH family for $(\{0,1\}^d, f_H)$ where f_H is the Hamming distance. The standard LSH here simply samples a random bit from the input. The probability of collision between $x, y \in \{0,1\}^d$ is $1 - f_H(x,y)/d$ which is at most $e^{-f_H(x,y)/d}$ and at least $e^{-2f_H(x,y)/d}$ for $f_H(x,y) \leq .79d$. We can replace the d in these bounds with any $w \geq d$ by padding our points with 0s until they are w-dimensional before choosing a bit to sample.[3] This yields the following lemma.

Lemma 2.3. *For any* $w \geq d$, *there exists an MLSH family with respect to* $(\{0,1\}^d, f_H)$ *with parameters*

$$(.79w, e^{-2/w}, 1/2).$$

Many other simple MLSH families exist. For example, inspection of simple random grid hashing and p-stable distribution hashing [6] yields the following lemmas. (Proofs are in the full (arxiv) version of this paper [21].)

Lemma 2.4. *For any* $w > 0$, *there exists an MLSH family with respect to* $([\Delta]^d, \ell_1)$ *with parameters*

$$(.79w, e^{-2/w}, 1/2).$$

Lemma 2.5. *For any* $w > 0$, *there exists an MLSH family with respect to* $([\Delta]^d, \ell_2)$ *with parameters*

$$(.99w, e^{-2\sqrt{2/\pi}/w}, 1/(4\sqrt{2})).$$

2.2 Invertible Bloom Lookup Tables

We briefly review the basic properties of IBLTs; more details can be found in [7, 11]. An IBLT is a hash table using q hash functions and m cells to store key-value pairs, where the keys and values are assumed to have a fixed-size representation. (In cases where there are no associated values, IBLTs can be used to just hold keys.) A key has q associated hash values, with each hash value indexing a cell of the table. (We assume these cells are distinct; for example, one can use a partitioned hash table, with each hash function mapping to m/q cells.) Each cell maintains a count of the number of key-value pairs hashed to it, an XOR of all of the keys hashed to it, an XOR of the values hashed to it, and an XOR of checksums (e.g. fingerprints), one for each key hashed to it; adding a key-value pair simply updates the values in the q associated cells. The checksum, obtained using another hash function, is sufficiently large so as to ensure that with high probability, none of the distinct keys' checksums collide. Deleting a key from an IBLT is similar to adding it, except that now we decrement the counts instead of incrementing them.

We can find all the elements in an IBLT, or *invert* it, using a peeling process, if m is large enough compared to the number of key-value pairs stored. Whenever a cell in the table has a count of 1, the XOR of the key values in that cell equals the key hashed to that cell, and similarly for the value, so we can recover and then delete them from the table. Such deletions may yield more cells with a count of 1, allowing the process to continue until no keys remain in the table. By viewing the IBLT as a random hypergraph with the cells being m vertices

[3] Equivalently, and more efficiently, with probability d/w our hash function will sample a random bit, and with probability $1 - d/w$ it will be a constant function always equaling 0.

and the keys corresponding to hyperedges of cardinality q, we can analyze this peeling process; all key-value pairs are recovered unless the hypergraph has a nonempty 2-core, the probability of which can be directly bounded. This gives the following theorem.

Theorem 2.6 (Theorem 1 of [11]). *There exists a constant $0 < c < 1$ so that an IBLT with m cells and at most cm keys will successfully extract all key-value pairs with probability at least $1 - O(1/\text{poly}(m))$, and the process takes $O(m)$ time.*

We can apply IBLTs to standard set reconciliation when Alice and Bob have an upper bound d on the size of their set difference. Alice constructs an $O(d)$ cell IBLT by adding each of his set elements to it. (The elements can be treated as keys, no values are needed.) She then sends it to Bob who deletes each of his set elements from it. Note that after this process the only elements in the IBLT are from the set difference, as elements in both sets are added but then deleted. Now cells with a count of 1 or -1 may hold a single element, but such a cell may also hold multiple elements; a cell with a count of 1 may hold two elements from Alice and one from Bob. The checksum can be used to double-check that a cell with a count of 1 corresponds to a single key. Bob can therefore extract all the keys from the IBLT using a variation of the peeling process described above, and can reconcile the sets after finding this difference. We will sometimes refer to this process of recovering a set difference from an IBLT as "decoding" it.

For some of our results we require a variation of the IBLT that we call a Robust Invertible Bloom Lookup Table (RIBLT). This variation is important because when we have noisy values our inversion process may accumulate the discrepancy between values that are "close" but not equal as we peel elements away in the IBLT; this issue does not arise with standard set reconciliation. We discuss this fully in section 3, where we utilize results from [13] that were used to analyze a parallel version of this peeling process; our modifications allow us to bound the accumulation of noise with additional analysis. For now, we describe the ways in which an RIBLT differs from an IBLT (throughout, n will refer to an upper-bound on the number of key-value pairs inserted or deleted from the table):

(1) The peeling occurs in a specific "breadth-first," first-come first-served order. By this we mean that if a cell (vertex) u has a single key (hyperedge) remaining earlier in the process than another cell v, then u must be peeled before v.
(2) RIBLTs are sparser than IBLTs, but still require only a number of cells linear in the number of keys. In particular, we require that $c < 1/(q(q-1))$, which results in an underlying hypergraph that is all trees and unicyclic components with high probability. See [9] for a discussion of and definitions for trees and unicyclic components in the hypergraph.
(3) Rather than each cell maintaining an XOR of all its keys and key checksums, it maintains a sum for each. When we add an key-value pair to the table, we add the binary representation of the key to the key sum in each cell, and similarly for the checksum of the key. This may require more space per cell to avoid overflow. If the original universe of keys is U, and thus their binary representations take $O(\log|U|)$ bits, then we now need $O(\log(|U|n))$ bits to store each cell's key sum.
(4) Similarly, rather than each cell maintaining an XOR of all its values, it maintains a sum. We restrict ourselves to values from a universe of the form $[\Delta]^d$. Now the sum of values stored in each cell will actually store a binary representation of a point from $\{-n\Delta, \ldots, n\Delta\}^d$. To update a cell's value sum, we map the binary representation back to a point from this space, add or subtract the new value from that point, then re-encode the resulting point into binary. This requires $O(d\log(n\Delta))$ bit per cell.
(5) These changes allows us to decode an RIBLT even when there are duplicate keys in the table. Now rather than peeling a key from a cell only when a single key is mapped to that cell (and thus the count is ±1), we also peel when the multiset of keys mapped to a cell are all equal. Let C be the cell's count field, $\mathcal{K}$ be its key sum field, $\mathcal{V}$ be its value sum field, $\mathcal{S}$ its sum of checksums field, and checksum() be our checksum function. We recognize that cell's contents correspond to copies of the same key when $\mathcal{K}$ and $\mathcal{V}$ are divisible by C, and checksum$(\mathcal{K}/C) = \mathcal{S}/C$. If this occurs, then with high probability there are C copies of the same key $\mathcal{K}/C$ added to that cell.

To peel such a cell, as before we subtract (or add) its cell contents from each cell $\mathcal{K}/C$ hashes to. We then extract C key-value pairs, where each pair's key is $\mathcal{K}/C$ and each pair's value is independently determined by the following procedure. First we take $\mathcal{V}$ and interpret it as a point in $\mathbb{R}^d$. We then divide each entry by C and shift the result into $[0, \Delta]$ by changing entries less than 0 to 0 and entries greater than Δ to Δ. Each entry not falling in $[\Delta]$ (those that aren't integers) are randomly rounded up or down to the nearest integer, with the probability of rounding up equal to the fractional remainder. This guarantees that even when multiple pairs are added with the same key but differing values, the extracted pairs all have values from our desired $[\Delta]^d$ space.

3 EARTH MOVER'S DISTANCE

First, we formally define the Earth Mover's Distance model.

Definition 3.1 (EMD model). *Suppose Alice and Bob have sets of points, S_A and S_B respectively, from a metric space of the form $([\Delta]^d, \ell_q)$, and $|S_A| = |S_B| = n$. The goal of the* Earth Mover's Distance model *of robust set reconciliation is for Bob to find a point set $S'_B \subset U$, $|S'_B| = n$, such that the earth mover's distance* EMD(S_A, S'_B) *is minimized while adhering to a given upper bound on communication.*

Definition 3.2 (EMD). *Given point sets $X = \{x_1, \ldots, x_n\}$ and $Y = \{y_1, \ldots, y_n\}$ from a metric space (U, f),*

$$\text{EMD}(X, Y) = \min_{\text{bijection } \pi:[n]\to[n]} \sum_{i=1}^{n} f(x_i, y_{\pi(i)}).$$

Our protocol will ultimately relate $\text{EMD}(S_A, S'_B)$ to $\text{EMD}_k(S_A, S_B)$, which is the minimum achievable earth mover's distance between S_A and S_B after excluding k points from each.

Definition 3.3 (EMD_k). *Given point sets $X = \{x_1, \ldots, x_n\}$ and $Y = \{y_1, \ldots, y_n\}$ from a metric space (U, f),*

$$\text{EMD}_k(X, Y) = \min_{X' \subseteq X, Y' \subseteq Y, |X'|=|Y'|=n-k} \text{EMD}(X', Y').$$

The basic idea behind our protocol for the Earth Mover's Distance model is that we use an MLSH family $\mathcal{H}$ to hash Alice and Bob's points at various different resolutions. We achieve finer resolutions by concatenating more and more hash functions from $\mathcal{H}$, and thereby partition the $[\Delta]^d$ into progressively smaller regions. For each of these resolutions, Alice sends Bob an RIBLT consisting of (key, value) pairs where the key is the hash of one of her points and the value is the point itself. Bob deletes his hashed points from the RIBLTs, and then finds the highest resolution RIBLT which is decodable, and uses the decoded points extracted from it to form his S'_B. Since non-equal points can have the same key (their hash value), they won't fully "cancel" when decoding the RIBLT, and thus the decoded points will have some error. Much of our technical work is bounding this error.

In what follows we assume we have parameters D_1 and D_2 such that $D_1 \leq \text{EMD}_k(S_A, S_B) \leq D_2$ and $\max_{a \in S_A, b \in S_B} f(a, b) < M$. In the case where $q = 1$ and we have no prior knowledge about S_A and S_B, we can simply use $D_1 = 1, D_2 = n \cdot d \cdot \Delta$, and $M = d \cdot \Delta$. (Note that if $\text{EMD}_k(S_A, S_B) = 0$, this problem can be solved exactly with a standard set reconciliation protocol, so it sensible to assume that $D_1 \geq 1$.) We also require an MLSH family for $([\Delta]^d, \ell_q)$ with parameters (r, p, α) such that $r \geq \min(M, D_2)$ and $p \geq e^{-k/(24D_2)}$.[4] The full protocol appears in Algorithm 1.

[4]Note that given p and D_2 we must choose an MLSH family with p large enough to meet this condition. All of our example MLSH families allow for arbitrarily large p values, and in general it is easy to increase p by adding some set of constant functions to the MLSH family. It may be unintuitive that we would want to increase p in this way, but it is necessary to avoid over-partitioning the space while still allowing us to use enough independent functions from our MLSH family that the probability of different pairs of points colliding is sufficiently independent for our analysis.

Algorithm 1 EMD Protocol

- Alice creates $t = \log_2(D_2/D_1) + 1$ RIBLTs $T_1, \ldots, T_t$, each with $q \geq 3$ hash functions and $m = 4q^2k$ cells.
- Alice draws $s = \frac{k}{8D_1 \ln(1/p)}$ hash functions $g_1, \ldots, g_s$ from $\mathcal{H}$. She draws h from a 2-wise independent class of hash functions with range $\{0, 1\}^{\Theta(\log n)}$.
- For each $i \in \{1, \ldots, t\}$ and $a \in S_A$, Alice forms a key-value pair and inserts it into T_i. The key is $\text{key}_i(a) = h\left(g_1(a), \ldots, g_{2^{i-1}sD_1/D_2}(a)\right)$, and the value is a.
- Alice sends $T_1, \ldots, T_t$ to Bob.
- For each $i \in \{1, \ldots, t\}$ and $b \in S_B$, Bob deletes the pair $(\text{key}_i(b), b)$ from T_i. (Note that he knows $g_1, \ldots, g_s$ and h due to public coins.)
- Bob finds i^*, the largest i such that T_i successfully decodes to at most $4k$ key-value pairs ($2k$ pairs per party). Let X_B be the values that T_{i*} decodes from his side, and X_A the values it decodes from Alice's side. If no T_i successfully decodes Bob reports failure.
- Bob finds Y_B, the subset of S_B matched in the min cost matching between X_B and S_B. He then outputs $S'_B = (S_B \setminus Y_B) \cup X_A$.

Theorem 3.4. *Algorithm 1 uses $O(kd \log(\Delta n) \log(D_2/D_1))$ bits of communication and*

$$O\left(tnk/(D_1 \log(1/p)) + dn \log(D_2/D_1) + dnk + nk^2\right)$$

time. If $\text{EMD}_k(S_A, S_B) \leq D_2$, it reports failure with probability at most 1/8. If $\text{EMD}_k(S_A, S_B) \geq D_1$ and it does not report failure, then $\text{EMD}(S_A, S'_B) \leq O(\alpha^{-1} \log n) \cdot \text{EMD}_k(S_A, S_B)$ with probability at least 3/4. Here t is an upper bound on the time to evaluate functions from $\mathcal{H}$.

Before proving this theorem, let us discuss its implications for some settings. Suppose our metric space is $(\{0, 1\}^d, f_H)$, and we have no assumptions on D_1, D_2, and M. Applying the MLSH family of Lemma 2.3 to Theorem 3.4 yields the following.[5]

Corollary 3.5. *There is a protocol for the Earth Mover's Distance model on $(\{0, 1\}^d, f_H)$ using $O(kd \log n \log(dn))$ bits of communication, $O(dn^2 + nk^2)$ time that successfully computes S'_B such that $\text{EMD}(S_A, S'_B) \leq O(\log n) \cdot \text{EMD}_k(S_B, S_A)$. with probability at least 5/8.*

Now suppose we are working in $([\Delta]^d, \ell_2)$. In this case we can divide the range $[D_1, D_2]$ into $I = O(\log(D_2/D_1))$ intervals $[D_1^{(1)}, D_2^{(1)}], [D_1^{(2)}, D_2^{(2)}], \ldots, [D_1^{(I)}, D_2^{(I)}]$ such that $D_1^{(1)} =$

[5]In order to meet the restriction that $p \geq e^{-k/(24D_2)}$ we choose $w = 48nd/k$ when applying Lemma 2.3. This is already factored into the stated bounds of the corollary.

D_1, $D_2^{(I)} = D_2$, and for all j, $D_2^{(j)}/D_1^{(j)} = O(1)$ and $D_1^{(j+1)} = D_2^{(j)}$. We run Algorithm 1 in parallel for each of these intervals, and have Bob use the output of the version for the smallest index interval which did not report failure. For the jth interval, the MLSH family of Lemma 2.5 (with $w = \Theta(\min(M, D_2^{(j)}) + D_2^{(j)}/k)$) yields the following bounds.

Corollary 3.6. *There is a protocol for the Earth Mover's Distance model on $([\Delta]^d, \ell_2)$ using $O(kd\log(n\Delta)\log(D_2/D_1))$ bits of communication and $O((dnk + nk^2)\log(D_2/D_1))$ time that successfully computes S'_B such that $\mathrm{EMD}(S_A, S'_B) \leq O(\log n) \cdot \mathrm{EMD}_k(S_A, S_B)$ with probability at least 5/8.*

Note that this kind of scaling strategy could be applied in the Hamming distance case too, which would change the running time of Corollary 3.5 to $O((dnk + nk^2)\log(nd))$.

We now prove the theorem. The communication cost of this protocol is immediate. There are $O(\log(D_2/D_1))$ RIBLTs, each of which has $O(k)$ cells. Each cell takes $O(d\log(|\Delta|n))$ bits to store the value, and $O(\log n)$ bits to store the key.

The computation bound is similarly straightforward. Each of the n points is hashed $\frac{k}{8D_1\ln(1/p)}$ times, and each item is inserted/deleted from an RIBLT $O(\log(D_2/D_1))$ times. It takes $O(dnk)$ time for Bob to compute all of the distances between the points in S_B and those in X_B, and then $O(nk^2)$ time to use the Hungarian method (see, e.g., [18]) to find the min-cost matching between X_B and S_B.[6] The time to attempt decoding of the RIBLTs is dominated by the time spent constructing them.

Our proof of the approximation bound requires several steps. In order to bound $\mathrm{EMD}(S_A, S'_B)$, we find a matching between the points of S_A and S'_B, and use the cost of that matching as an upper bound. This matching consists of three pieces. For each bucket, where a bucket in this context is the set of points hashing to the same value at level i^*, we choose a maximum size matching between Alice and Bob's points within the bucket. The remaining points are those that we wish to approximately extract from T_{i^*}. The total cost of the matching is then bounded by the cost of the matching within each bucket (the *in-bucket-matching*), which we call μ, plus the minimum cost matching between our desired extracted points, plus the distance between what we wished to extract and what we actually did (X_A and X_B).

More formally, we identify $Z_A \subset S_A$ and $Z_B \subset S_B$ such that $|Z_A| = |Z_B| = |X_A| = |X_B|$. Z_A and Z_B are the points excluded from the in-bucket-matching. Using the definition of EMD, the fact that EMD obeys the triangle inequality, and the definition of Y_B (the subset of S_B matched in the min cost

[6]This assumes the distances fit into a constant number of words so they can be computed on in $O(1)$ time. If this is not the case the nk^2 term in the running time increases by a factor of the number of words it takes to represent a distance.

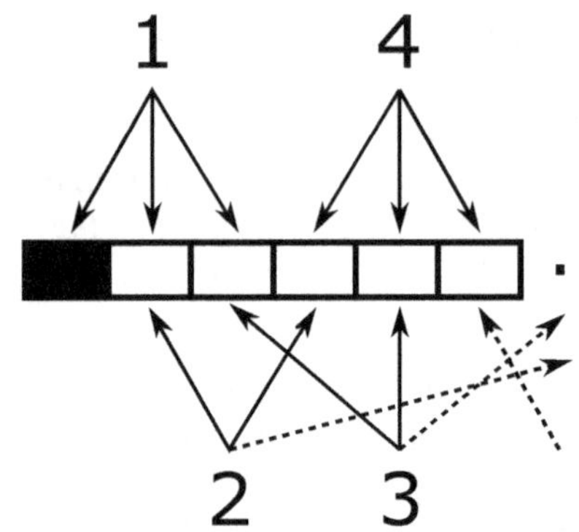

Figure 1: An example of error propagating in an (R)IBLT.

matching between X_B and S_B), we find

$$\begin{aligned}\mathrm{EMD}(S'_B, S_A) &= \mathrm{EMD}((S_B \setminus Y_B) \cup X_A, S_A)\\ &\leq \mathrm{EMD}(S_B \setminus Z_B, S_A \setminus Z_A) + 2 \cdot \mathrm{EMD}(X_B, Z_B)\\ &\quad + \mathrm{EMD}(X_A, Z_A).\end{aligned}$$

By definition, $\mathrm{EMD}(S_A \setminus Z_A, S_B \setminus Z_B) \leq \mu$. We prove later in this section that with probability at least 7/8, $\mathrm{EMD}(X_A, Z_A) + \mathrm{EMD}(X_B, Z_B) \leq O(1) \cdot \mu$. The challenge in proving this bound is that the difference between each matched pair is an error which is added to various other cell values in the RIBLT during the peeling process. In particular, the error can "propagate" when removing an element without a matching key; the error is incorporated into other cells as the element is peeled from those cells. That error can be incorporated into further cells if unmatched keys are then peeled from the cells that have incorporated the error, and so on. (See Figure 1.) We argue that in expectation, each error is only added to a constant number of other cells, thus the expected sum of the errors on all of the extracted points is at most a constant times the cost of the in-bucket matching. Putting these pieces together, we get that with probability at least 7/8, $\mathrm{EMD}(S_A, S'_B) \leq O(1) \cdot \mu$. What remains is to find an in-bucket-matching such that $\mu = O(\alpha^{-1}\log n) \cdot \mathrm{EMD}_k(S_A, S_B)$ with probability at least 7/8.

Example 3.7. *Figure 1 shows an example of error propagating in an (R)IBLT. The first black cell had a point from Bob and a point from Alice with different values but the same key hashed to it. We consider these two points to be part of Z_A and Z_B. They canceled out all of their entries in the cell except for the difference in their values, which we call the error. When item 1 is peeled, the point we extract will have its value offset by the error. The peeling of 1 will add that error to the second and third cells so when items 2 and 3 are peeled their values will also be offset by the error. The peeling of 2 and 3 will in turn propagate the error to the fourth and fifth cells so item 4 will also be extracted with the error.*

When choosing the in-bucket-matching, whenever possible we match points that are part of the $n-k$ closest pairs in the optimal matching between S_A and S_B (the one defining $\mathrm{EMD}_k(S_A, S_B)$). Matching these pairs costs at most $\mathrm{EMD}_k(S_A, S_B)$. All that remains is to find matchings among the remaining points within the buckets that has expected cost bounded by $O(\alpha^{-1}\log n)\cdot\mathrm{EMD}_k(S_A, S_B)$. Informally, we achieve this by upper bounding each points' expected matching cost by the distance from it to the furthest unmatched point in its bucket. To do this we must first reason about i^*. Going forward, we assume that the $\Theta(\log n)$-bit pairwise independent h did not produce any collisions between differing MLSH vectors. With high probability no such collision occurs, so checking equality between the hash values is equivalent to checking equality between the MLSH vectors.

We start with a simple lemma, whose proof appears in Appendix A.

Lemma 3.8. *The expected number of pairs that hash differently among the $n-k$ closest pairs in the optimal matching between S_A and S_B is at most $\frac{2^{i-4}k}{D_2}\mathrm{EMD}_k(S_A, S_B)$.*

We use this lemma to bound the level at which Bob can successfully decode the RIBLT. Once the number of pairs hashing differently is at most k, the RIBLT decodes successfully with high probability, so we choose $i' = \log_2\left(\frac{2D_2}{\mathrm{EMD}_k}\right)$ so that the expected number of differing pairs is at most $\frac{2^{i'-4}k}{D_2}\mathrm{EMD}_k(S_A, S_B) = k/8$. We can then use Markov's inequality to say that with probability at least $7/8$ we can decode $T_{i'}$, thus $i^* \geq i'$. Now that we have a bound on i^*, we can turn to bounding μ.

Lemma 3.9. *For a level $i \geq i'$, the expected value of μ, the cost of the best in-bucket-matching, is $O(\alpha^{-1}\log n)\cdot\mathrm{EMD}_k(S_A, S_B)$.*

To prove this, whenever a pair from the optimal matching (which makes up $\mathrm{EMD}_k(S_A, S_B)$) appears in the same bucket, we match them to each other, which contributes a total cost of at most $\mathrm{EMD}_k(S_A, S_B)$. For the remaining points, we upper bound their matching cost by the maximum distance from them to every point from the other party in their bucket that is not paired with its optimal match. In order to bound this last part, we exploit the fact that, because we are using sufficiently many MLSHs, conditioning on two points not falling into the same bucket has little impact on whether one of those points falls into the same bucket as some specific other point, such as its optimal match. The full proof is in Appendix A.

In the event that every matched pair in the in-bucket-matching is in fact the same point, then they would exactly cancel out and T_{i^*} would be equivalent to if we only added the points from Z_A and Z_B. If Z_A and Z_B also have no duplicate keys, then the RIBLT peeling procedure would be identical to the standard IBLT peeling procedure and we would recover Z_A and Z_B with no error. However, since in general the points will not be equal, when their keys cancel out, their values will leave behind some error, and when the RIBLT undergoes the peeling procedure, this error may be added to various other cells of the RIBLT. Additionally, RIBLTs introduce error when extracting key-value pairs that have the same keys but different values, as their values are averaged (and then randomly rounded).

Let Q_A and Q_B be what we would recover from T_i^* if the points in Z_A and Z_B all had different keys, and thus no averaging or rounding need to occur in their extraction. For now we will bound the error without this averaging and rounding, and then we later come back to it.

We argue that with constant probability, the average number of cells a given error is added to is $O(1)$. Since the sum of these errors is μ, this implies that with (a different) constant probability, $\mathrm{EMD}(Q_A, Z_A) + \mathrm{EMD}(Q_B, Z_B) \leq O(1)\cdot\mu$. Note that the RIBLT does not exactly extract the value in Z_A or Z_B plus error because it floors/ceilings the values back into $[0,\Delta]^d$, but this only decreases $\mathrm{EMD}(Q_A, Z_A)+\mathrm{EMD}(Q_B, Z_B)$ since $Z_A, Z_B \in [\Delta]^d$.

As discussed in subsection 2.2, we can view the (R)IBLT peeling procedure as the process of peeling vertices of degree one from a random hypergraph. In particular, this random hypergraph is $G^q_{m,cm}$, an m vertex hypergraph with cm q-regular hyperedges drawn uniformly at random from the $\binom{m}{q}$ possible q-regular hyperedges. We model our problem as having a single random vertex initially have an "error", and then whenever we peel a vertex v, we add its error count C_v to every adjacent vertex. We then argue that the expected final sum of the C_v values is $O(1)$, implying that the error only contributed to an expected constant number of extracted points as desired. In what follows, we assume $q = O(1)$. Since Algorithm 1 required that T_{i^*} decodes to at most $4k$ points and has $4q^2k$ cells, we have that $c < 1/(q(q-1))$. Thus, the following lemma gives us that with constant probability, $\mathrm{EMD}(Q_A, Z_A) + \mathrm{EMD}(Q_B, Z_B) \leq O(1)\cdot\mu$.

Lemma 3.10. *For $c < 1/(q(q-1))$, after performing breadth first peeling of $G^q_{m,cm}$ we have with probability at least 7/8, $\sum_{v=1}^m C_v = O(1)$.*

The structure of our proof of this lemma is similar to that of [13], in that we relate the peeling process to an idealized branching process. We argue that the lemma holds in this idealized branching process via careful analysis, and then argue that the branching process is sufficiently close to our peeling process that the lemma still holds there. The full details of our proof are presented in Appendix A.

Now with our bound on $\mathrm{EMD}(Q_A, Z_A) + \mathrm{EMD}(Q_B, Z_B)$, we complete our proof of Theorem 3.4 with the following lemma.

Lemma 3.11. *With probability at least* $3/4$,

$$\mathrm{EMD}(Z_A, X_A) + \mathrm{EMD}(Z_B, X_B) = O(\alpha^{-1}\log n)\cdot \mathrm{EMD}_k(S_A, S_B).$$

The proof of this (which appears in Appendix A) follows similarly to that of Lemma 3.9. We bound the distance between a point in Q_A and the rounded average of the other points in Q_A falling into its bucket, by the maximum distance between Q_A and those other points from Q_A in its bucket.

4 GAP GUARANTEE

In this section we discuss the Gap Guarantee model, which provides a generally stronger guarantee than the Earth Mover's distance model. Here Bob and Alice may have differing numbers of points, and Bob's final set only consists of points from his and Alice's original point sets. Furthermore, Alice is guaranteed to not have any points that are too far from Bob's final point set.

Definition 4.1 (Gap Guarantee model). *The* Gap Guarantee model *of robust set reconciliation is defined for a metric space* (U, f) *and two distance parameters* $0 < r_1 < r_2$ *as follows. Alice and Bob have sets of points* $S_A, S_B \subset U$ *respectively.* $|S_A| \leq n$ *and* $|S_B| \leq n$. *There exist subsets* $C_A \subset S_A$ *and* $C_B \subset S_B$ *such that* $|C_A| \geq n-k$, $|C_B| \geq n-k$, $\forall a \in C_A, \min_{b\in S_B} f(a,b) \leq r_1$, *and* $\forall b \in C_B, \min_{a\in S_A} f(a,b) \leq r_1$.

The goal of the model is to minimize communication while allowing Bob to compute a set $S'_B = S_B \cup T_A$ *where* $T_A \subset S_A$ *such that* $\forall a \in S_A, \exists b \in S'_B$ s.t. $f(a,b) \leq r_2$.

Going forward, we refer to $a \in S_A$ and $b \in S_B$ as *close* if $f(a,b) \leq r_1$ and *far* if $f(a,b) \geq r_2$. We also describe C_A and C_B as Alice and Bob's close points, and T_A as Alice's far points.

4.1 General Protocol

Our scheme hinges upon the application of a good locality sensitive hash function for our data. Let $\mathcal{H}$ be an LSH family for our metric space with parameters (r_1, r_2, p_1, p_2). We assume that $p_2 \geq 1/2$. (This assumption simplifies the analysis, and is readily achieved for standard LSH families.) The scheme operates as follows.

Each party constructs a *key* for each of their elements. A key is a vector of $h = \Theta(\log n)$ hashes. Each of these hashes is $O(\log n)$ bits and is the evaluation of a pairwise independent hash function on a tuple of $m = \log_{p_2}(1/2)$ LSH values. The point of the keys is that two far points have very different keys, and two close points have keys that match in all or almost all of their entries.

More concretely, we start by sampling hm functions from $\mathcal{H}$. To construct an element x's key, we evaluate all of these hm functions on it. We partition these evaluations into h batches of m. We apply a pairwise independent hash function to each batch, and then our key is the vector of these hashes. We then interpret each key as a set of (hash, vector index) pairs. Alice and Bob then engage in a multisets of sets reconciliation protocol ([20]) so that Alice recovers the multiset of Bob's keys.

Alice then compares their keys. If one of her keys differs in sufficiently many of its entries from every one of Bob's keys (the exact number depends on the parameters of the LSH and is detailed below), then she transmits every one of her elements that matches that key to Bob. This protocol yields the following bounds.

Theorem 4.2. *Given a locality sensitive hash function with* $\rho \leq 1-\varepsilon$ *for some constant* $\varepsilon > 0$, *there exists a protocol for the Gap Guarantee model using 4 rounds of*

$$O\left((k+\rho n)\log^2 n\left(\frac{\log n}{\log(k+\rho n)+\log\log n} + \log\log n\right) + k\log|U|\right)$$

bits of communication and $O(tn\log n/\log(1/p_2) + (k+\rho n)^2\log^3 n)$ *time, where* t *is the time to evaluate the LSH. This protocol succeeds with probability at least* $1 - 1/n$.

The first three rounds of the protocol come from the following protocol for reconciling (multi)sets of sets from [20], and the final round is Alice's transmission of elements. In the multisets of sets reconciliation problem, Alice and Bob each have a parent multiset of at most s child sets, each containing at most h elements from a universe of size u. The sum of the sizes of of all of the child sets is at most n'. z is the sum over each of Alice and Bob's child sets of their minimum set difference with one of the other party's child sets. $\widehat{z} = \min(z, s)$. The goal of the problem is for Bob to successfully recover Alice's multiset of sets.

Theorem 4.3 (Theorem 3.11 of [20]). *Multisets of sets reconciliation can be solved in 3 rounds using*

$$O(\lceil\log_{\widehat{z}}(1/\delta)\rceil\widehat{z}\log s + \log(\widehat{z}/\delta)\widehat{z}\log h + \lceil\log_z(1/\delta)\rceil z\log(un'))$$

bits of communication and

$$O(\log(\widehat{z}/\delta)(n' + \widehat{z}^2) + z^2 + \min(zh, n'\sqrt{z}, n'\log^2 h))$$

time with probability at least $1-\delta$.

Using this, we can prove the correctness of our protocol.

Proof of Theorem 4.2. We chose m so that the probability that two far elements match on one of their hashes is at most $1/2$. By a Chernoff bound, the probability that two far elements have keys matching in more than $h(1/2+\varepsilon/6)$ entries is at most

$$e^{-O(h)} = 1/\mathrm{poly}(n)$$

so with high probability, no pair of far keys match in more than $h(1/2+\varepsilon/6)$ entries.

Now consider a close pair of elements. The expected number of matches in their keys is at least

$$h \cdot p_1^m = h \cdot p_1^{\log_{p_2}(1/2)} = h(1/2)^\rho$$
$$\geq h(1/2)^{1-\varepsilon} \geq h(1/2)^{-\log_2(1/2+\varepsilon/3)} = h(1/2 + \varepsilon/3),$$

where the final inequality follows from a Taylor expansion of $-\log_2(1/2 + \varepsilon/3)$.

By a Chernoff bound, the probability that a close pair matches in less than $h(1/2 + \varepsilon/6)$ LSHs is at most

$$e^{-O(h)} = 1/\text{poly}(n),$$

so with high probability, no pair of close keys matches in less than $h(1/2 + \varepsilon/6)$ entries.

The total number of differences between the multisets of sets, excluding the far points, is at most

$$nh(1 - p_1^m) = nh(1 - (1/2)^\rho) = \Theta(nh\rho) = \Theta(\rho n \log n)$$

in expectation. By a Chernoff bound, the total number is no more than $(1 + c)$ times this with probability at most $e^{-O(c\rho n \log n)}$. If $\rho > 1/n$, then this is at most $1/\text{poly}(n)$ for $c = 1$. If $\rho \leq 1/n$, then this is at most $1/\text{poly}(n)$ for $c = 1/(\rho n)$. Therefore, with high probability the total number of differences between the multisets of sets, including the far points, is at most

$$O(\max(\rho n \log n, \log n) + k \log n) = O((k + \rho n) \log n).$$

We reconcile the LSH vectors via Theorem 4.3. Here $n' = n \log n$, $\widehat{z} \leq z = k \log n + \rho n \log n$, $s = n$, $\log u = \log n$, $h = \log n$, and $\delta = 1/n$. We get communication

$$O\left(\left\lceil \frac{\log n}{\log z} \right\rceil z \log n + \log(zn) z \log\log n\right) =$$

$$O\left((k + \rho n) \log^2 n \left(\frac{\log n}{\log(k+\rho n)+\log\log n} + \log\log n\right)\right)$$

and time

$$O(\log(zn)(n + z^2) + z^2$$
$$+ \min(z \log n, n \log n\sqrt{z}, n \log n \log^2 \log n))$$
$$= O(n \log n + (k + \rho n)^2 \log^3 n).$$

Now we have already argued that, with high probability, every far key is successfully identified, and no close key is misidentified as a far key. Note that we must have at most k elements corresponding to those identified far keys. The far keys may not be unique, but if a pair of elements corresponds to the same far key, then by our analysis both of the elements must not be close elements so by transmitting all of them, we only use $O(k \log |U|)$ communication.

The time to construct the keys is

$$O(thmn) = O(tn \log n / \log(1/p_2)).$$

All that remains is to determine which keys of Alice's keys differ in at least $h(1/2 + \varepsilon/6)$ entries from every one of Bob's keys. There are at most $k \log n + \rho n \log n$ keys that differ between Alice and Bob, so it takes $O((k + \rho n)^2 \log^3 n)$ to compare all of the differing keys. □

Intuitively, the locality sensitive hashing here buys us two things. First, if ρ is sufficiently small then sufficiently many of the close elements will have matching keys so that we only need $o(n)$ communication. Second, even when ρ is large, it serves as a form of dimensionality reduction, allowing us to only transmit $O(\text{poly} \log n)$ bits per close element, and only transmit the full $O(\log |U|)$ bits for the k far elements. While the latter could be accomplished by traditional dimensionality reduction techniques for ℓ_2 distance [14], there are some metrics, such as ℓ_1 distance, for which no sufficiently strong general dimensionality reduction scheme exists [1].

Suppose we are working in $(\{0, 1\}^n, f_H)$, the space of n-bit vectors under the Hamming metric. (Note that for this example we are choosing the dimension of the space to be equal to the number of points in it). Via the standard bit sampling LSH for Hamming distance used in Lemma 2.3, we see that Theorem 4.2 yields the optimal $O(kn)$ communication as long as $r_2/r_1 = \Omega(\log^2 n \log\log n)$.

Corollary 4.4. *There exists a protocol for the Gap Guarantee model on $(\{0, 1\}^n, f_H)$ for $r_2/r_1 = \Omega(\log^2 n \log\log n)$ using 4 rounds of $O(kn)$ bits of communication and $O(n^2 \log n/r_2 + k^2 \log^3 n)$ time. This protocol succeeds with probability at least $1 - 1/n$.*

If we are working in $([\Delta]^d, \ell_1)$ with only a constant gap r_2/r_1, the grid LSH of Lemma 2.4 or the p-stable LSH of Lemma 2.5 give us the following result.

Corollary 4.5. *There exists a protocol for the Gap Guarantee model on $([\Delta]^d, \ell_1)$ for $r_2/r_1 \geq 2$ using 4 rounds of $O\left(n \log^2 n \log\log n + kd \log \Delta\right)$ bits of communication and $O(dn \log n + n^2 \log^3 n)$ time. This protocol succeeds with probability at least $1 - 1/n$.*

Note that even with $r_2/r_1 = O(1)$, for large d we still improve significantly over the naive solution (direct transmission) that uses $\Theta(nd \log \Delta)$ communication.

4.2 Protocol for Low Dimensions

While the previous protocol works with any provided LSH, we can do slightly better in low dimensional ℓ_p metric spaces by using a special class of LSHs. Specifically, we can construct an LSH with the property that $p_2 = 0$, but otherwise degrades with increased dimension.

The following is an LSH scheme with this kind of one-sided error that we can use for an $([\Delta]^d, \ell_p)$ metric space. Construct a randomly shifted grid of width $r_2/d^{1/p}$. A point's hash value is the grid cell it falls into. Since the maximum distance apart two points falling in the same grid cell can be is exactly r_2, $p_2 = 0$ as desired. Now we bound p_1.

Let $x_1, \ldots, x_d$ be the absolute values of the differences between two points in each dimension. Since we are looking at p_1, we want the total distance to be r_1 so $(\sum_{i=1}^d x_i^p)^{1/p} = r_1$. In order for the two points to round to the different grid point, they must have at least one dimension that rounds to a different value. By a union bound, the probability of this is at most

$$\sum_{i=1}^{d} \frac{x_i \cdot d^{1/p}}{r_2} \le \frac{d^{1+1/p}}{r_2}\left(\sum_{i=1}^{d}\frac{x_i^p}{d}\right)^{1/p} \quad \text{(Jensen's inequality)}$$
$$= \frac{d}{r_2}\left(\sum_{i=1}^{d} x_i^p\right)^{1/p} = \frac{r_1 d}{r_2}.$$

Thus $p_1 \ge 1 - \frac{r_1 d}{r_2}$.

We use the same basic protocol as before, except now this one sided LSH allows us to use $m = 1$, since we don't need any replication to reduce the probability of far points colliding. Furthermore we now only have to choose h large enough that each close pair matches in at least one hash, which we achieve with $h = \Theta\left(\log n / \log\left(\frac{r_2}{r_1 d}\right)\right)$. This yields the following bound.

THEOREM 4.6. *There exists a protocol for the Gap Guarantee model on $([\Delta]^d, \ell_p)$ using 4 rounds of*

$$O\left(\left\lceil \frac{k+\hat{\rho}n}{\log(1/\hat{\rho})}\right\rceil \log^2 n \cdot \left(\frac{\log n}{\log\left\lceil\frac{k+\hat{\rho}n}{\log(1/\hat{\rho})}\right\rceil + \log\log n} + \log\log n\right) + k\log|U|\right)$$

bits of communication and

$$O\left(dn\left\lceil\frac{\log n}{\log(1/\hat{\rho})}\right\rceil + n\log n + \left\lceil\frac{k+\hat{\rho}n}{\log(1/\hat{\rho})}\right\rceil^2 \log^3 n\right)$$

time, where $\hat{\rho} = r_1 d / r_2$. This protocol succeeds with probability at least $1 - 1/n$.

For constant dimensional ℓ_p metrics with $p \in [1, 2)$, this improves over Theorem 4.2 by roughly a factor of $\log(r_2/r_1)$ in communication. The full proof, which follows very similarly to that of Theorem 4.2, appears in the full version of this paper [21].

4.3 Lower Bound for One Round

Our protocols for the Gap Guarantee model use four rounds of communication. One might hope to find a protocol using only a single round, as we have for the Earth Mover's Distance model. Our protocols could be reduced to two rounds with only a small weakening of the bounds by using a different protocol for reconciling sets of sets [20], but it is not obvious how to further reduce them to one round. In this section we demonstrate that we cannot hope to achieve a one round protocol with competitive bounds, at least for f_H, the Hamming metric.

THEOREM 4.7. *There exists no one round protocol for the Gap Guarantee on $(\{0,1\}^d, f_H)$, $d = \Omega(\log n + r_2)$, $r_1 = 1$, and $k = 1$, using $O(n)$ bits of communication that succeeds with probability at least 2/3.*

PROOF. We reduce from the index problem, in which Alice has an n-bit string $x \in \{0,1\}^n$, Bob has an integer $i \in [n]$, and Alice wishes to send a message to Bob so that he can recover x_i. The randomized communication complexity of the index problem is known to be $\Omega(n)$ [17]. We reduce the index problem to the relevant form of the Gap Guarantee as follows.

In advance, the two parties agree on a set of $n+1$ $(d-1)$-bit strings $c_1, \ldots, c_{n+1} \in \{0,1\}^{d-1}$ such that for all $i \ne j \in [n+1]$, $f_H(c_i, c_j) \ge r_2$. This is achievable for our setting of $d = \Omega(\log n + r_2)$ by a variety of error-correcting codes, such as Reed-Muller codes [29].

Alice constructs her set of n points as

$$S_A = \{c_1||x_1, \ldots, c_n||x_n\},$$

where $||$ is the concatenation operator. In other words, she takes the first n agreed upon codewords and appends her corresponding bit to each one. Bob's point set is

$$S_B = \{c_1||0, \ldots, c_{i-1}||0, c_{i+1}||0, \ldots, c_{n+1}||0\}.$$

He takes the set of codewords except for the ith one, and appends a 0 to each one.

Now, Alice sends Bob a message so that he recovers S'_B according to the Gap Guarantee definition. S'_B must contain $c_i||x_i$, and it can not have any other points within r_2 of that, so Bob simply finds the only new point that is at least r_2 from all of his original points, and reports its final bit as the solution to the index problem. □

We note that Theorem 4.2, which uses more than one round, would use $O(\lceil n/r_2\rceil \log^3 n/\log\log n + r_2)$ bits of communication in this regime, which beats this lower bound for one-round protocols when $r_2 = \omega(\log^3 n/\log\log n)$ and also $r_2 = o(n)$.

5 CONCLUSION

Robust set reconciliation is a natural communication problem with several distributed system applications that has received relatively little study. We have provided new results for the EMD model utilizing IBLTs, where we analyzed error propagation during decoding; this analysis may prove useful for other problems. We have also considered a new variation, based on guaranteeing a small gap for all data points. However, there remains room to improve our results, both in terms of communication and computation, and in both the lower and upper bounds.

ACKNOWLEDGMENTS

The authors Michael Goodrich for describing applications of robust set reconciliation to machine learning settings. Michael Mitzenmacher was supported in part by NSF grants CNS-1228598, CCF-1320231, CCF-1563710 and CCF-1535795. Tom Morgan was supported in part by NSF grants CNS-1228598 and CCF-1320231.

REFERENCES

[1] Alexandr Andoni, Moses S Charikar, Ofer Neiman, and Huy L Nguyen. 2011. Near linear lower bound for dimension reduction in l1. In *Proc. of the 52nd Annual Symposium on Foundations of Computer Science*. IEEE, 315–323.

[2] Alexandr Andoni and Piotr Indyk. 2006. Near-optimal hashing algorithms for approximate nearest neighbor in high dimensions. In *Proc. of the 47th Annual Symposium on Foundations of Computer Science*. 459–468.

[3] G. Andresen. [n. d.]. *$O(1)$ Block Propagation, https://gist.github.com/gavinandresen/e20c3b5a1d4b97f79ac2*. Technical Report.

[4] Moses S Charikar. 2002. Similarity estimation techniques from rounding algorithms. In *Proceedings of the 35th Annual ACM Symposium on Theory of Computing*. ACM, 380–388.

[5] Di Chen, Christian Konrad, Ke Yi, Wei Yu, and Qin Zhang. 2014. Robust set reconciliation. In *Proceedings of the 2014 ACM SIGMOD International Conference on Management of Data*. 135–146.

[6] Mayur Datar, Nicole Immorlica, Piotr Indyk, and Vahab S Mirrokni. 2004. Locality-sensitive hashing scheme based on p-stable distributions. In *Proceedings of the 20th Annual Symposium on Computational Geometry*. ACM, 253–262.

[7] David Eppstein and Michael Goodrich. 2011. Straggler identification in round-trip data streams via Newton's identities and invertible Bloom filters. *IEEE Transactions on Knowledge and Data Engineering* 23, 2 (2011), 297–306.

[8] David Eppstein, Michael Goodrich, Frank Uyeda, and George Varghese. 2011. What's the difference?: efficient set reconciliation without prior context. *ACM SIGCOMM Computer Communication Review* 41, 4 (2011), 218–229.

[9] David Eppstein, Michael T Goodrich, Michael Mitzenmacher, and Paweł Pszona. 2014. Wear minimization for cuckoo hashing: How not to throw a lot of eggs into one basket. In *International Symposium on Experimental Algorithms*. Springer, 162–173.

[10] Jochen Geiger. 1999. Elementary new proofs of classical limit theorems for Galton–Watson processes. *Journal of Applied Probability* 36, 2 (1999), 301–309.

[11] Michael Goodrich and Michael Mitzenmacher. 2011. Invertible Bloom lookup tables. In *Proceedings of the 49th Annual Allerton Conference on Communication, Control, and Computing*. 792–799.

[12] Piotr Indyk and Rajeev Motwani. 1998. Approximate nearest neighbors: towards removing the curse of dimensionality. In *Proceedings of the 30th Annual ACM Symposium on Theory of Computing*. ACM, 604–613.

[13] Jiayang Jiang, Michael Mitzenmacher, and Justin Thaler. 2014. Parallel peeling algorithms. In *Proceedings of the 26th ACM Symposium on Parallelism in Algorithms and Architectures*. ACM, 319–330.

[14] William B Johnson and Joram Lindenstrauss. 1984. Extensions of Lipschitz mappings into a Hilbert space. *Contemp. Math.* 26, 189-206 (1984), 1.

[15] Michał Karoński and Tomasz Łuczak. 2002. The phase transition in a random hypergraph. *J. Comput. Appl. Math.* 142, 1 (2002), 125–135.

[16] Adam Kirsch and Michael Mitzenmacher. 2006. Distance-sensitive bloom filters. In *Proceedings of the Eighth Workshop on Algorithm Engineering and Experiments (ALENEX)*. SIAM, 41–50.

[17] Ilan Kremer, Noam Nisan, and Dana Ron. 1999. On randomized one-round communication complexity. *Computational Complexity* 8, 1 (1999), 21–49.

[18] Harold W Kuhn. 1955. The Hungarian method for the assignment problem. *Naval Research Logistics (NRL)* 2, 1-2 (1955), 83–97.

[19] Yaron Minsky, Ari Trachtenberg, and Richard Zippel. 2003. Set reconciliation with nearly optimal communication complexity. *IEEE Transactions on Information Theory* 49, 9 (2003), 2213–2218.

[20] Michael Mitzenmacher and Tom Morgan. 2018. Reconciling graphs and sets of sets. In *Proceedings of the 35th ACM SIGMOD-SIGACT-SIGAI Symposium on Principles of Database Systems*. ACM, 33–47.

[21] Michael Mitzenmacher and Tom Morgan. 2019. Robust Set Reconciliation via Locality Sensitive Hashing. *arXiv preprint arXiv:1807.09694* (2019).

[22] Michael Mitzenmacher and Rasmus Pagh. 2013. Simple multi-party set reconciliation. *arXiv preprint arXiv:1311.2037* (2013).

[23] Michael Mitzenmacher and Eli Upfal. 2005. *Probability and computing: Randomized algorithms and probabilistic analysis*. Cambridge University Press.

[24] Michael Mitzenmacher and George Varghese. 2012. The complexity of object reconciliation, and open problems related to set difference and coding. In *Proceedings of the 50th Annual Allerton Conference on Communication, Control, and Computing*. IEEE, 1126–1132.

[25] Michael Molloy. 2004. The pure literal rule threshold and cores in random hypergraphs. In *Proceedings of the 15th Annual ACM-SIAM Symposium on Discrete Algorithms*. Society for Industrial and Applied Mathematics, 672–681.

[26] Ilan Newman. 1991. Private vs. common random bits in communication complexity. *Inform. Process. Lett.* 39, 2 (1991), 67–71.

[27] Jeanette Schmidt-Pruzan and Eli Shamir. 1985. Component structure in the evolution of random hypergraphs. *Combinatorica* 5, 1 (1985), 81–94.

[28] David Starobinski, Ari Trachtenberg, and Sachin Agarwal. 2003. Efficient PDA synchronization. *IEEE Transactions on Mobile Computing* 2, 1 (2003), 40–51.

[29] Jacobus Hendricus Van Lint. 2012. *Introduction to Coding Theory*. Vol. 86. Springer Science & Business Media.

[30] Abraham Wald. 1944. On cumulative sums of random variables. *The Annals of Mathematical Statistics* 15, 3 (1944), 283–296.

A PROOFS FROM THE EMD MODEL

Here we present the proofs for proving the correctness of our protocol for the Earth Mover's Distance model.

Lemma A.1. *The probability that a pair of points at distance x hash differently on level i is at most $\frac{2^{i-4}k}{D_2}x$.*

PROOF. The probability that they hash differently is

$$1-\Pr\left[\text{all } \frac{2^{i-4}k}{D_2\ln(1/p)} \text{ hashes match}\right]$$
$$\leq 1-p^{\frac{2^{i-4}k}{D_2\ln(1/p)}x} = 1-e^{-\frac{2^{i-4}k}{D_2}x} \leq \frac{2^{i-4}k}{D_2}x. \qquad \square$$

Lemma 3.8. *The expected number of pairs that hash differently among the $n-k$ closest pairs in the optimal matching between S_A and S_B is at most $\frac{2^{i-4}k}{D_2}\mathrm{EMD}_k(S_A,S_B)$.*

Proof. Let x_j be the distance between the two parties' ith points when they are ordered for minimum EMD and $x_j \le x_{j+1}$.

$$\begin{aligned}&\mathbb{E}[\text{num of } n-k \text{ that hash differently}]\\&= \sum_{j=1}^{n-k} \Pr\left[\text{points at distance } x_j \text{ hash differently}\right]\\&\le \sum_{j=1}^{n-k} \frac{2^{i-4}k}{D_2}x_j = \frac{2^{i-4}k}{D_2}\mathrm{EMD}_k(S_A,S_B).\end{aligned}$$

□

Lemma 3.9. *For a level $i \ge i'$, the expected value of μ, the cost of the best in-bucket-matching, is $O(\alpha^{-1}\log n)\cdot \mathrm{EMD}_k(S_A,S_B)$.*

Proof. We will often refer to $\mathrm{EMD}_k(S_A,S_B)$ by simply EMD_k. Whenever a pair from the optimal matching (which makes up EMD_k) appears in the same bucket, we match them to each other, which contributes a total cost of at most EMD_k. For the remaining points, we upper bound their matching cost by the maximum distance from them to every point from the other party in their bucket that is not paired with its optimal match. We refer to Alice and Bob's k points that don't appear in the optimal matching as their *far* points, and the remaining points as *close* points.

Our analysis is divided into three pieces: the cost of matching Bob's far points to Alice's far points, the cost of matching Bob's far points to Alice's close points (and vice versa) and the cost of matching Bob's close points to Alice's close points. We then sum these three cases to obtain an upper bound on μ.

First let's bound the cost of matching far points to far points. Consider one of Bob's k far points. Let $y_1,\dots,y_k$ be the distance from it to each of Alice's points, ordered such that $y_j \ge y_{j+1}$. Let E_j be the event that Alice's jth far point in this ordering collides with Bob's point. Let F_j be the event that Alice's far points 1 through $j-1$ do not collide with Bob's point. The expected cost of Bob's point's matching with Alice's far points is

$$\mathbb{E}[\text{far to far matching cost}] = \sum_{j=1}^{k} y_j \Pr[E_j \cap F_j].$$

Let $\phi_j = \Pr[E_j \cap F_j]$. We know that $\sum_{j=1}^{k}\phi_j \le 1$, since they are disjoint events. We also have

$$\phi_j \le \Pr[E_j] \le p^{\alpha y_j \frac{2^{i-4}k}{D_2\ln(1/p)}}$$

which implies that

$$y_j \le \frac{D_2\ln(1/\phi_j)}{\alpha 2^{i-4}k},$$

and thus

$$\begin{aligned}\mathbb{E}[\text{far to far matching cost}] &\le \sum_{j=1}^{k}\frac{D_2\ln(1/\phi_j)}{\alpha 2^{i-4}k}\phi_j\\&= \frac{D_2}{\alpha 2^{i-4}k}\sum_{j=1}^{k}\phi_j\ln(1/\phi_j)\\&\le \frac{D_2}{\alpha 2^{i'-4}k}\sum_{j=1}^{k}\phi_j\ln(1/\phi_j)\\&= \frac{8\mathrm{EMD}_k}{\alpha k}\sum_{j=1}^{k}\phi_j\ln(1/\phi_j)\\&\le \frac{8\mathrm{EMD}_k}{\alpha k}\ln k \text{ (Jensen's inequality).}\end{aligned}$$

Summing over Bob's k far points gives us $O(\alpha^{-1}\log k)\cdot \mathrm{EMD}_k$.

Now let's consider the cost of matching one of Bob's far points to Alice's unmatched close points. Here $y_1,\dots,y_{n-k}$ are the distances from Bob's point to each of Alice's close points, ordered such that $y_j \ge y_{j+1}$. We also have $x_1,\dots,x_{n-k}$ which are the distances from Alice's close points to their optimal matches. Let H_j be the event that Alice's jth close point in this ordering cannot be matched to its optimal match (they do not fall in the same bucket). Let E_j be the event that Alice's jth close point collides with Bob's point. Let F_j be the event that Alice's close points 1 through $j-1$ do not collide with Bob's point.

We will use two facts there that we didn't use in the previous case. The first is Lemma B.1, which implies that conditioning on a pair being unmatched effectively only conditions one of their MLSHs. More specifically, $\Pr[E_j \mid H_j]$ is at most the probability that Alice's jth close point matches with Bob's on the first $2^{i-4}k/(D_2\ln(1/p))-1$ hash functions. The second fact is that, due to our bound on p,

$$\frac{2^{i'-4}k}{D_2\ln(1/p)} = \frac{k}{8\ln\left(\frac{1}{p}\right)\mathrm{EMD}_k} \ge 3. \quad (1)$$

Similar to the previous case, we compute the expected cost of Bob's far point matching with one of Alice's unmatched close ones.

$$\mathbb{E}[\text{far to close matching cost}] = \sum_{j=1}^{n-k} y_j \Pr[H_j \cap E_j \cap F_j].$$

Let $\phi_j = \Pr[H_j \cap E_j \cap F_j]$. We know that $\sum_{j=1}^{k}\phi_j \le 1$, since they are disjoint events. We also have

$$\begin{aligned}\phi_j &\le \Pr[H_j]\Pr[E_j \mid H_j]\\&\le \frac{2^{i-4}kx_j}{D_2}p^{\alpha y_j\left(\frac{2^{i-4}k}{D_2\ln(1/p)}-1\right)} \text{ (Lemma B.1)}\end{aligned}$$

$$\leq \frac{2^{i-4}kx_j}{D_2} p^{\alpha y_j \frac{2^{i-5}k}{D_2 \ln(1/p)}} \text{ (Equation 1).}$$

This implies that

$$y_j \leq \frac{D_2 \ln\left(\frac{2^{i-5}kx_j}{D_2 \phi_j}\right)}{\alpha k \cdot 2^{i-2}},$$

and thus

$$\mathbb{E}[\text{far to close matching cost}] \leq \sum_{j=1}^{n-k} \frac{D_2 \ln\left(\frac{2^{i-5}kx_j}{D_2\phi_j}\right)}{\alpha k \cdot 2^{i-2}} \phi_j$$

$$= \frac{D_2}{\alpha k \cdot 2^{i-5}} \sum_{j=1}^{n-k} \phi_j \ln\left(\frac{2^{i-4}kx_j}{D_2\phi_j}\right)$$

$$\leq \frac{D_2}{\alpha k \cdot 2^{i-5}} \ln\left(\sum_{j=1}^{n-k} \frac{2^{i-4}kx_j}{D_2}\right) \text{ (Jensen's inequality)}$$

$$= \frac{D_2}{\alpha k \cdot 2^{i-5}} \ln\left(\frac{2^{i-4}k}{D_2} \mathrm{EMD}_k\right)$$

$$\leq \frac{D_2}{\alpha k \cdot 2^{i'-5}} \ln\left(\frac{2^{i'-4}k}{D_2} \mathrm{EMD}_k\right)$$

$$= \frac{16\mathrm{EMD}_k}{\alpha k} \ln\left(\frac{k}{8}\right).$$

Summing over Bob's k far points gives us $O(\alpha^{-1} \log k) \cdot \mathrm{EMD}_k$.

Finally we bound the cost of matching Bob's unmatched close points (those whose optimal match does not appear in the same bucket) to Alice's unmatched close points. We order the points by their optimal matching, so Bob's jth point's optimal match is Alice's jth point. Let x_j be the cost of that optimal matching. For $j, r \in [n-k]$, $m_{j,r}$ is the index of Alice's point which is the rth furthest from Bob's jth point, and $y_{j,r}$ is its distance. Let $H_{j,r}$ be the event that Alice's $m_{j,r}$th point cannot be matched to its optimal match (they do not fall in the same bucket). Let $E_{j,r}$ be the event that Alice's $m_{j,r}$th point collides with Bob's jth point. Let $F_{j,r}$ be the event that Alice's close points $m_{j,1}, \ldots, m_{j,r-1}$ do not collide with Bob's jth point. Let I_j be the event that Bob's jth point cannot be matched to its optimal match. The expected cost of matching all of the unmatched close points is then at most

$$\sum_{j=1}^{n-k} \Pr[I_j] \sum_{r=1}^{n-k} y_{j,r} \Pr[H_{j,r} \cap E_{j,r} \cap F_{j,r} \mid I_j]$$

$$\leq \sum_{j=1}^{n-k} \frac{2^{i-4}kx_j}{D_2} \sum_{r=1}^{n-k} y_{j,r} \Pr[H_{j,r} \cap E_{j,r} \cap F_{j,r} \mid I_j].$$

Let $\phi_{j,r} = \Pr[H_{j,r} \cap E_{j,r} \cap F_{j,r} \mid I_j]$. We know that $\sum_{j=1}^{k} \phi_{j,r} \leq 1$, since they are disjoint events. We also have

$$\phi_{j,r} \leq \Pr[H_{j,r} \mid I_j] \Pr[E_{j,r} \mid I_j \cap H_{j,r}]$$

$$\leq 1 \cdot p^{\alpha y_{j,r}\left(\frac{2^{i-4}k}{D_2 \ln(1/p)} - 2\right)} \text{ (Lemma B.2)}$$

$$\leq p^{\alpha y_{j,r} \frac{2^{i-4}k}{3D_2 \ln(1/p)}} \text{ (Equation 1).}$$

This implies that

$$y_{j,r} \leq \frac{3D_2 \ln(1/\phi_{j,r})}{\alpha k \cdot 2^{i-4}},$$

and thus the expected cost of matching all of the unmatched close points is upper bounded by

$$\sum_{j=1}^{n-k} \frac{2^{i-4}kx_j}{D_2} \sum_{r=1}^{n-k} \frac{3D_2 \ln(1/\phi_{j,r})}{\alpha k \cdot 2^{i-4}} \phi_{j,r}$$

$$= \frac{3}{\alpha} \sum_{j=1}^{n-k} x_j \sum_{r=1}^{n-k} \ln(1/\phi_{j,r}) \phi_{j,r}$$

$$\leq \frac{3}{\alpha} \sum_{j=1}^{n-k} x_j \ln(n-k) \text{ (Jensen's inequality)}$$

$$= \frac{3\ln(n-k)}{\alpha} \mathrm{EMD}_k = O(\alpha^{-1} \log n) \cdot \mathrm{EMD}_k. \quad \square$$

Now we turn to the main piece of our analysis, bounding the propagation of errors in the RIBLT. Recall that we are modeling the propagation of error during the peeling process by having a single random vertex initially have an error, and then whenever we peel a vertex v, we add its error count C_v to every adjacent vertex.

Lemma 3.10. *For $c < 1/(q(q-1))$, after performing breadth first peeling of $G^q_{m,cm}$ we have with probability at least 7/8, $\sum_{v=1}^{m} C_v = O(1)$.*

The following lemmas allow us to restrict our analysis to the case where the hypergraph consists of only trees and unicyclic components. First, we have a lemma that allows us to reason about G^q_c (a q-uniform hypergraph on m vertices where each edge appears independently at random with probability $cm/\binom{m}{q}$) instead of $G_{m,cm}$.

Lemma A.2. *Suppose that for all $c < 1/(q(q-1))$, with probability at least $9/10 - o(1)$, $\sum_{v=1}^{m} C_v = O(1)$ on G^q_c. Then for all $c < 1/(q(q-1))$, with probability at least $9/10 - o(1)$, $\sum_{v=1}^{m} C_v = O(1)$ on $G^q_{m,cm}$.*

Proof. Key here is the fact that $\sum_{v=1}^{m} C_v$ monotonically increases with the addition of random edges. Let c' be any constant such that $c < c' < 1/(q(q-1))$. With probability $1-o(1)$ $G^q_{c'}$ has more than cm edges. Therefore, if $\sum_{v=1}^{m} C_v = O(1)$ on $G^q_{c'}$ with probability at least $9/10 - o(1)$, then $\sum_{v=1}^{m} C_v = O(1)$ on $G^q_{m,cm}$ with probability $9/10 - o(1)$. $\square$

Lemma A.3 ([15, 27]). *When $c < 1/(q(q-1))$, all connected components of G^q_c are either trees or unicyclic with probability $1 - O(1/n)$.*

Given these lemmas, we now first prove the theorem in the case that the breadth first search tree around each vertex v in the graph is generated according to an idealized branching process. Each vertex in the tree has an i.i.d. number of child edges drawn according to Poisson(cq), which each in turn connect to $q-1$ child vertices. We also assume that each component is a tree, so that the breadth first search tree is exactly v's connected component, and then relax this assumption to include unicyclic components later.

Using this model we can show that the probability that a vertex's error propagates out to a given a radius shrinks doubly exponentially in that radius, while the number of vertices in that radius is only singly exponential, thus the expected number of vertices the error propagates to is constant. Later we will use the results of [13] to argue that this idealized branching process is sufficiently close to the true distribution and thus our results still hold.

Recall that we are performing the peeling in a breadth first fashion. Let L_v be the round (starting from 1) in which vertex v was peeled, and let $K_{v,j}$ be the event that vertex v has not been peeled after j rounds. Initially only one random vertex has an error, and all the rest are 0, so each vertex has an expected starting error of $1/m$. Let $V_{v,r}$ be the number of vertices within radius r of v. Because we assume v's component is a tree,

$$\begin{aligned}
&\mathbb{E}[C_v] \\
&\leq \mathbb{E}[\text{number of errors in vertices within radius } L_v \text{ of } v] \\
&= \frac{1}{m}\mathbb{E}[V_{v,L_v}] = \frac{1}{m}\sum_{j=1}^{\infty}\Pr[L_v=j]\,\mathbb{E}[V_{v,j}\mid L_v=j] \\
&\leq \frac{1}{m}\sum_{j=1}^{\infty}\Pr[K_{v,j-1}]\,\mathbb{E}[V_{v,j}\mid L_v=j] \\
&\leq \frac{1}{m}\sum_{j=1}^{\infty}\Pr[K_{v,j-1}]\,\mathbb{E}[V_{v,j}\mid K_{v,j-1}].
\end{aligned}$$

The idealized branching process allows us to bound $L[K_{v,j-1}]$ with the following procedure. Consider the neighborhood of a vertex v of distance t. For $j=1$ up to $j=t-1$, we delete all vertices at distance $t-j$ from v which have 0 child edges (those edges branching out from our process). Then, at round t, we delete v if after all of that it has degree at most 1. Let λ_t be the probability that vertex v is not deleted after this t round procedure. Although this procedure forces a certain ordering on the deletion of vertices, it is still the case that $\Pr[K_{v,t}]=\lambda_t$. This is because although in the real peeling process v might be deleted before t rounds, if it is not deleted after t rounds of this ordering, then it also will not be deleted after t rounds of the real process.

Let ρ_j be the probability that a vertex u, which is a distance $t-j$ from v, is not deleted after j rounds. Here $p_0=1$, and we find that $\rho_j=\Pr[\text{Poisson}(\rho_{j-1}^{q-1}cq)\geq 1]$. This then yields that $\lambda_j=\Pr[\text{Poisson}(\rho_{j-1}^{q-1}cq)\geq 2]$.

These equations come from the fact that each node u has Poisson(cq) child edges, each of which survives the previous round with probability ρ_{j-1}, independent of each other child edge. By the splitting property of Poisson distributions [23], the number of surviving child edges of u is thus distributed as Poisson($\rho_{j-1}^{q-1}cq$).

For sufficiently small c (in our case $c<1/(q(q-1))$ suffices), this procedure is guaranteed to delete v for sufficiently large t. In other words, $\lim_{t\to\infty}\lambda_t=0$. [13] uses this fact to argue that for some constant $I>0$ and $0<\tau<1$, $\lambda_{I+t}\leq\tau^{2(q-1)^t}$, giving us a strong bound on $\Pr[K_{v,j-1}]$. All that remains is to bound $\mathbb{E}[V_{v,j}\mid K_{v,j-1}]$. We use the same branching process to reason about the number of vertices at some distance j from v.

First lets look at the expectation $\mathbb{E}[V_{v,j}]$. without any conditioning. Each vertex has Poisson(cq) child edges, meaning $\mathbb{E}[V_{v,1}]=cq(q-1)+1$, and an iterative application of Wald's equation [30] yields

$$\mathbb{E}[V_{v,t}]=\sum_{j=0}^{t}(cq(q-1))^j.$$

Conditioning on $K_{v,j-1}$ increases the values of each of these Poisson distributions. For $j=2$, it means that v has at least two child edges. For $j=3$, it means that v has at least 2 *saturated* child edges. We say a child edge is saturated if each of its $(q-1)$ vertices has at least one child edge. For $j=4$, the conditioning means that at least 2 of v's child edges are saturated by saturated child edges (on each of v's child edge's vertices, there is at least one saturated child edge). In general, conditioning on j means that v has 2 child edges that are saturated by child edges that are saturated by child edges that are saturated by child edges, etc. $j-2$ times. We analyze this case in Lemma C.3 and show that

$$\mathbb{E}[V_{v,j}\mid K_{v,j-1}]=O((q-1)^j).$$

Finally putting this all together we have,

$$\begin{aligned}
\mathbb{E}[C_v] &\leq \frac{1}{m}\sum_{j=1}^{\infty}\Pr[K_{v,j-1}]\,\mathbb{E}[V_{v,j}\mid K_{v,j-1}] \\
&\leq \frac{1}{m}\sum_{t=1}^{\infty}\lambda_{t-1}O((q-1)^t) \\
&= \frac{1}{m}\left(\sum_{t=1}^{I}\lambda_{t-1}O((q-1)^t)+\sum_{t=1}^{\infty}\lambda_{I+t-1}O((q-1)^{I+t})\right) \\
&\leq \frac{1}{m}\left(\sum_{t=1}^{I}O((q-1)^t)+\sum_{t=1}^{\infty}\tau^{2(q-1)^t}O((q-1)^{I+t})\right) \\
&\leq \frac{O(1)}{m}.
\end{aligned}$$

In the last line, $O(1)$ is using that I, q, ϕ and τ are all constants, together with the fact that $O((q-1)^{I+t})$ grows exponentially in t while $\tau^{2(q-1)^t}$ shrinks doubly exponentially, so $\tau^{2(q-1)^t}O((q-1)^{I+t})$ converges to 0. Thus $\mathbb{E}[C_v] = \frac{O(1)}{m}$ for all v, so $\mathbb{E}[\sum_{v=1}^m C_v] = O(1)$.

Now we address the case when a component is unicyclic. We can bound $\mathbb{E}\left[\sum_{v=1}^m C_v\right]$ in this case by its value in the tree case with the addition of one additional edge, making a cycle. Peeling this extra edge can only increase $\mathbb{E}\left[\sum_{v=1}^m C_i\right]$ by a factor of at most $q = O(1)$, since it only adds a single C_v to $q-1$ other vertices, each of which ultimately contributes only $O(1)$ times its value to final sum.

Thus, if the components are all trees or unicyclic and the breadth first search tree from each vertex is generated according to the idealized branching process, then by Markov's inequality, $\sum_{v=1}^m C_v = O(1)$ with probability at least $9/10$. We argue that the actual peeling process is sufficiently close to this idealized branching process. To do this we need a few lemmas from [13].

Lemma A.4 (Theorem 1 of [13]). *Let $q \geq 3$, and let $c < c_q^*$. With probability $1-o(1)$, the breadth-first process of the 2-core in a random hypergraph G_c^q terminates after $\log\log n/\log(q-1) + O(1)$ rounds.*

Here c_q^* is the threshold density below which random hypergraphs have empty 2-cores with high probability. [25] gives the formula for c_q^* as

$$c_q^* = \min_{x>0} \frac{x}{q(1-e^{-x})^{q-1}}.$$

It is important to note that $c_q^* > 1/(q(q-1))$, so our choice of c satisfies the conditions of the theorem.

Let E_1 be the event that, for all vertices $v \in G_c^q$, there are at most $\log^{c_2} n$ vertices within a radius of $c_1 \log\log n$ around v. There exist constants $c_1, c_2 > 0$ depending on c and q such that the following lemma holds.

Lemma A.5 (Lemma 3 of [13]). *For any event E, $\Pr[E] \geq \Pr[E \mid E_1] - 1/n$.*

Lemma A.6 (Lemma 5 of [13]). *Let $X_1(v)$ denote the random variable describing the tree of depth $i = O(\log\log n)$ rooted at v in the idealized branching process. Let $X_2(v)$ denote the random variable describing the BFS tree of depth i rooted at v in G_c^q, conditioned on the event E_1 occurring. The total variation distance between $X_1(v)$ and $X_2(v)$ is at most $\operatorname{poly}\log(n)/n$.*

Proof of Lemma 3.10. By Lemma A.4, the peeling process completes in $O(\log\log n)$ rounds with probability $1-o(1)$ in G_c^q. This, together with our analysis of the idealized branching process, Lemma A.3, and Lemma A.6 implies that, conditioned on E_1, with probability at least $9/10 - o(1) - O(1/n) - \operatorname{poly}\log(n)/n$, $\sum_{v=1}^m C_v = O(1)$ on G_c^q. Putting this together with Lemma A.5 and Lemma A.2 yields that with probability at least

$$9/10 - o(1) - O(1/n) - \operatorname{poly}\log(n)/n - 1/n,$$

$\sum_{v=1}^m C_v = O(1)$ on $G_{m,cm}^q$. For sufficiently large n, we have the lemma. □

Finally we prove the final piece to bound $\mathrm{EMD}(Z_A, X_A) + \mathrm{EMD}(Z_B, X_B)$ by reasoning about the averaging and rounding that occurs in the peeling process of RIBLTs.

Lemma 3.11. *With probability at least $3/4$,*

$$\mathrm{EMD}(Z_A, X_A) + \mathrm{EMD}(Z_B, X_B) = O(\alpha^{-1}\log n)\cdot \mathrm{EMD}_k(S_A, S_B).$$

Proof. We will prove this for $\mathrm{EMD}(Z_A, X_A)$, and the argument for $\mathrm{EMD}(Z_B, X_B)$ is identical.

By an argument identical to that of Lemma 3.9, the expected sum over each point in Z_A of the distance from that point to the furthest other point in Z_A falling in the same bucket is bounded by $O(\alpha^{-1}\log n)\cdot \mathrm{EMD}_k(S_A, S_B)$. Also, by Lemma 3.10, with probability at least $7/8$, the sum of these maximum distances in Q_A grows by $O(\mu)$, so by Lemma 3.9 the sum is still $O(\alpha^{-1}\log n)\cdot \mathrm{EMD}_k(S_A, S_B)$.

We now show that the averaging and rounding the occurs when the RIBLT extracts multiple points with the same key doesn't have too large an impact. We will prove the case when $[\Delta]^d = \{0,1\}^d$, which intuitively can be though of as the "hard" case since the rounding has maximum impact here. The general case then follows. Let $x_1, \ldots, x_m \in \{0,1\}^d$ be our points that that hash to the same bucket, which we wish to extract. Let r be the randomized rounding of $\sum_{i=1}^m x_i/m$. For $j \in [d]$, let $p_j = \sum_{i=1}^m x_{i,j}/m$. $r_j = 1$ with probability p_j. Let $B = \max_{i=1}^m ||x_1 - x_i||_q$. Without loss of generality, let $x_1 = \{0\}^d$.

$$\mathbb{E}[||x_1 - r||_q] \leq \mathbb{E}[||x_1 - r||_q^q]^{1/q} \text{ (Jensen's inequality)}$$
$$= \left(\sum_{j=1}^d p_j\right)^{1/q} \leq \left(\frac{m-1}{m}B^q\right)^{1/q} < B.$$

The second to last inequality here used the fact that

$$n\sum_{j=1}^d p_j = \sum_{i=1}^m \sum_{j=1}^d x_{i,j} \leq (m-1)B^q.$$

Thus, since the expected sum of the maximum distances is $O(\alpha^{-1}\log n)\cdot \mathrm{EMD}_k(S_A, S_B)$, the expected sum of distances between points and the averages of their colliding points (and thus $\mathrm{EMD}(Q_A, X_A)$) is $O(\alpha^{-1}\log n)\cdot \mathrm{EMD}_k(S_A, S_B)$. Then by Markov's inequality and the triangle inequality, we have the lemma. □

B CONDITIONAL PROBABILITY LEMMAS

In our proofs, we sometimes have subtle conditioned events. While intuitively these do not cause problems for our proofs, conditional probability is notoriously surprising. We therefore formalize some necessary conditioning results; while these may be known, we have not found them in existing literature. The proof are somewhat complex; we acknowledge that simpler proofs would be desirable, and leave finding such proofs as open problems.

Let $X_1, \ldots, X_n$ and $Y_1, \ldots, Y_n$ be $\{0, 1\}$ random variables. We will sometimes abuse notation slightly and use X_i to refer to the event that $X_i = 1$. The pairs $(X_1, Y_1), \ldots, (X_n, Y_n)$ are i.i.d. and $\Pr[X_i = 1] = p$ and $\Pr[Y_i = 1] = q$. We assume $n \geq 2$, and $0 < p, q < 1$.

Lemma B.1. $\Pr[\cap_i X_i \mid \cup_i Y_i] \leq p^{n-1}$.

We use this in Lemma 3.9 by letting X_i be the event that a given pair of points (u and v) have equal values for their ith MLSH function. Y_i is the event that the v and v's optimal matching point do not have equal values for their ith MLSH function. Since each MLSH function is drawn i.i.d., these collision events are i.i.d. but correlations can exist between collision events for a given one of these functions, so this setting of (X_i, Y_i) fulfills our criteria. Thus $\Pr[\cap_i X_i \mid \cup_i Y_i]$ is the probability that u and v have all equal hash values (they land in the same bucket) given that v does not have all equal hash values with its optimal match (they don't land in the same bucket).

Proof of Lemma B.1. Since the (X_i, Y_i) pairs are i.i.d., the effect of conditioning on some function of the Y_is on the probability of $\cap_i X_i$ can be quantified in terms of the conditioning's effect on the distribution of $C_Y = \sum_i Y_i$. In particular, for any function $f : \{0, 1\}^n \to \{0, 1\}$,

$$\Pr[\cap_i X_i \mid f(Y_1, \ldots, Y_n)] = \sum_{j=0}^{n} \Pr[X_1 \mid Y_1]^j \Pr[X_1 \mid \bar{Y}_1]^{n-j} \Pr[C_Y = j \mid f(Y_1, \ldots, Y_n)]. \tag{2}$$

We will use this to relate $\Pr[\cap_i X_i \mid \cup_i Y_i]$ to $\Pr[\cap_i X_i]$ and $\Pr[\cap_i X_i \mid Y_1]$.

Let us divide our analysis in two cases, based on whether or not X_1 and Y_1 are positively correlated. First, consider the case that $\Pr[X_1 \mid Y_1] \leq \Pr[X_1]$. In this case we argue that

$$\Pr[\cap_i X_i \mid \cup_i Y_i] \leq \Pr[\cap_i X_i] = p^n.$$

To see this, we compare $\Pr[\cap_i X_i \mid \cup_i Y_i]$ and $\Pr[\cap_i X_i]$ via Equation 2. First note that for all $j \in [n]$, $\Pr[C_Y \geq j] \leq \Pr[C_Y \geq j \mid \cup_i Y_i]$. Therefore, $f(Y_1, \ldots, Y_n) = \cup_i Y_i$ shifts the probability mass of $\Pr[C_Y = j \mid f(Y_1, \ldots, Y_n)]$ later in the series than $f(Y_1, \ldots, Y_n) = 1$. This shift decreases the value of the sum because
$\Pr[X_1 \mid Y_1]^j \Pr[X_1 \mid \bar{Y}_1]^{n-j}$ is decreasing in j (since $\Pr[X_1 \mid Y_1] \leq \Pr[X_1 \mid \bar{Y}_1]$).

Now consider the case that $\Pr[X_1 \mid Y_1] > \Pr[X_1]$. Here we show that

$$\Pr[\cap_i X_i \mid \cup_i Y_i] \leq \Pr[\cap_i X_i \mid Y_1] \leq p^{n-1}.$$

Now $\Pr[X_1 \mid Y_1] > \Pr[X_1 \mid \bar{Y}_1]$, so in Equation 2,

$$\Pr[X_1 \mid Y_1]^j \Pr[X_1 \mid \bar{Y}_1]^{n-j}$$

is increasing in j, so it suffices to show that for all $j \in [n]$, $\Pr[C_Y \geq j \mid Y_1] \geq \Pr[C_Y \geq j \mid \cup_i Y_i]$. Let $F_Y \in [n] \cup \{\emptyset\}$ be a random variable equal to the first index i for which $Y_i = 1$. $F_Y = \emptyset$ if $Y_i = 0$ for all $i \in [n]$. We observe that

$$\begin{aligned}
&\Pr[C_Y \geq j \mid \cup_i Y_i] \\
&= \sum_{i=1}^{n} \Pr[C_Y \geq j \mid (\cup_i Y_i) \cap (F_Y = i)] \Pr[F_Y = i \mid \cup_i Y_i] \\
&= \sum_{i=1}^{n} \Pr[C_Y \geq j \mid F_Y = i] \Pr[F_Y = i \mid \cup_i Y_i].
\end{aligned}$$

Clearly $\Pr[C_Y \geq j \mid F_Y = i] \geq \Pr[C_Y \geq j \mid F_Y = i + 1]$, thus

$$\begin{aligned}
\Pr[C_Y \geq j \mid Y_1] &= \Pr[C_Y \geq j \mid F_Y = 1] \\
&\geq \sum_{i=1}^{n} \Pr[C_Y \geq j \mid F_Y = i] \Pr[F_Y = i \mid \cup_i Y_i] \\
&= \Pr[C_Y \geq j \mid \cup_i Y_i].
\end{aligned}$$

□

We prove an analogous lemma for the case when we are conditioning on two points missing their optimal matches. Let $X_1, \ldots, X_n$, $Y_1, \ldots, Y_n$ and $Z_1, \ldots, Z_n$ be $\{0, 1\}$ random variables. The triples $(X_1, Y_1, Z_1), \ldots, (X_n, Y_n, Z_n)$ are i.i.d., $\Pr[X_i = 1] = p$, $\Pr[Y_i = 1] = q$ and $\Pr[Z_i = 1] = r$. We assume $n \geq 3$, and $0 < p, q, r < 1$.

Lemma B.2. $\Pr[\cap_i X_i \mid (\cup_i Y_i) \cap (\cup_i Z_i)] \leq p^{n-2}$.

Our application of this lemma in Lemma 3.9 is very similar to that of Lemma B.1. X_i is the event that a given pair of points (u and v) have equal values for their ith MLSH function. Y_i is the event that v and v's optimal matching point do not have equal values for their ith MLSH function. Z_i is the event that u and u's optimal match have unequal values for their ith MLSH function. Since each MLSH function is drawn i.i.d., these collision events are i.i.d. but correlations can exist between collision events for a given one of these functions, so this setting of (X_i, Y_i, Z_i) fulfills our criteria. Therefore $\Pr[\cap_i X_i \mid (\cup_i Y_i) \cap (\cup_i Z_i)]$ is the probability that u and v collide across all hash values given that u and v do not collide with their optimal matches. The proof is given in the full (arxiv) version of the paper [21].

C POISSON BRANCHING PROCESSES

In this section we analyze $\mathbb{E}[V_{v,j} \mid K_{v,j-1}]$, where recall $V_{v,j}$ is the number of vertices within radius j of v, in the model of the idealized Poisson branching process. We build on the work of [10] on Galton-Watson trees; Poisson branching processes are a special case. They studied the distribution of tree sizes conditioned on the tree surviving to some depth. Our setting is similar, except that our conditioning is more complicated, relating to the fact that our process generates hypertrees.

Let $p_k = (cq)^k e^{-cq}/k!$ be the probability that a node has k child edges. Let Z_n be the number of descendant vertices (recalling that each child edge connects to $q-1$ child vertices) the root has n levels below it. Let S_n be the event that the root has n levels of saturated child edges below it. Here S_1 means that the root has at least one child edge. S_2 mean the root has at least one saturated child edge. S_3 means the root has at least one child edge saturated by by saturated child edges, etc. Let R_{n+1} be the index of the leftmost child edge of the root whose vertices all have n levels of saturated child edges below them. The following fact is immediate from the independence of the vertices.

Fact C.1. *For $n \geq 0$ and $1 \leq j \leq k < \infty$,*

$$\Pr[R_{n+1} = j, Z_1 = k \mid S_{n+1}] = \frac{p_k(1 - \Pr[S_n]^{q-1})^{j-1} \Pr[S_n]^{q-1}}{\Pr[S_{n+1}]}.$$

Let A_{n+1} be the event that the root has at least two child edges, each of whose vertices have n levels of saturation. Let R'_{n+1} be the index of the second child edge (counting from the left) whose vertices have n levels of saturation.

Fact C.2. *For $n \geq 0$ and $1 \leq j < m \leq k < \infty$,*

$$\Pr[R_{n+1} = j, R'_{n+1} = m, Z_1 = k \mid A_{n+1}] = \frac{p_k(1 - \Pr[S_n]^{q-1})^{m-2} \Pr[S_n]^{2q-2}}{\Pr[A_{n+1}]}.$$

Using these facts, we can bound our desired quantity

$$\mathbb{E}[V_{v,j} \mid K_{v,j-1}] = \mathbb{E}\left[\sum_{i=0}^{j} Z_i \mid A_j\right].$$

Lemma C.3. *For $n \geq 0$, $c < 1/(q(q-1))$, $q \geq 3$, and $q = O(1)$,*

$$\mathbb{E}\left[\sum_{i=0}^{n+1} Z_i \mid A_{n+1}\right] = O((q-1)^n).$$

Proof sketch. The full details of this proof can be found in the full version of this paper [21].

The expected number of descendants up to m levels below an unconditioned vertex is

$$\mathbb{E}\left[\sum_{i=0}^{m} Z_i\right] = \sum_{i=0}^{m} (cq(q-1))^i.$$

We can use Fact C.1 to bound this quantity conditioned on S_n.

$$\mathbb{E}\left[\sum_{i=0}^{n+1} Z_i \mid S_{n+1}\right] \leq (q-1)\mathbb{E}\left[\sum_{i=0}^{n} Z_i \mid S_n\right] + 1 + (q-1)(cq)^2 \sum_{i=0}^{n} (cq(q-1))^i.$$

Solving this recurrence gives us

$$E\left[\sum_{i=0}^{n+1} Z_i \mid S_{n+1}\right] = O((q-1)^n).$$

Combining this with Fact C.2, we can show that

$$\mathbb{E}\left[\sum_{i=0}^{n+1} Z_i \mid A_{n+1}\right] = O((q-1)^n)$$

as desired. □

What Storage Access Privacy is Achievable with Small Overhead?

Sarvar Patel
Google LLC
sarvar@google.com

Giuseppe Persiano
Università di Salerno
Google LLC
giuper@gmail.com

Kevin Yeo
Google LLC
kwlyeo@google.com

ABSTRACT

Oblivious RAM (ORAM) and private information retrieval (PIR) are classic cryptographic primitives used to hide the access pattern to data whose storage has been outsourced to an untrusted server. Unfortunately, both primitives require considerable overhead compared to plaintext access. For large-scale storage infrastructure with highly frequent access requests, the degradation in response time and the exorbitant increase in resource costs incurred by either ORAM or PIR prevent their usage. In an ideal scenario, a privacy-preserving storage protocols with small overhead would be implemented for these heavily trafficked storage systems to avoid negatively impacting either performance and/or costs. In this work, we study the problem of the best *storage access privacy* that is achievable with only *small overhead* over plaintext access.

To answer this question, we consider *differential privacy access* which is a generalization of the *oblivious access* security notion that are considered by ORAM and PIR. Quite surprisingly, we present strong evidence that constant overhead storage schemes may only be achieved with privacy budgets of $\epsilon = \Omega(\log n)$. We present asymptotically optimal constructions for differentially private variants of both ORAM and PIR with privacy budgets $\epsilon = \Theta(\log n)$ with only $O(1)$ overhead. In addition, we consider a more complex storage primitive called key-value storage in which data is indexed by keys from a large universe (as opposed to consecutive integers in ORAM and PIR). We present a differentially private key-value storage scheme with $\epsilon = \Theta(\log n)$ and $O(\log \log n)$ overhead. This construction uses a new oblivious, two-choice hashing scheme that may be of independent interest.

PODS'19, June 30-July 5, 2019, Amsterdam, Netherlands

ACM ISBN 978-1-4503-6227-6/19/06.
https://doi.org/10.1145/3294052.3319695

ACM Reference Format:
Sarvar Patel, Giuseppe Persiano, and Kevin Yeo. 2019. What Storage Access Privacy is Achievable with Small Overhead?. In *38th ACM SIGMOD-SIGACT-SIGAI Symposium on Principles of Database Systems (PODS'19), June 30-July 5, 2019, Amsterdam, Netherlands.* ACM, New York, NY, USA, 18 pages. https://doi.org/10.1145/3294052.3319695

1 INTRODUCTION

Privacy-preserving storage primitives consider the outsourcing of the storage of a database to an untrusted server with the ability for clients to retrieve database records while maintaining the privacy of the retrievals. Even though encryption can be used to hide the content of the database, patterns of how the encrypted data is accessed are revealed. The leakage of access patterns has been shown to compromise privacy in many important practical settings [14, 31]. Privacy-preserving storage primitives that guarantee retrieval privacy have been used as a critical component in many systems such as advertisement [29], discovery of identities [8] and publish-subscribe [18]. Therefore, a very important question involves the construction of privacy-preserving storage schemes guaranteeing retrieval privacy while ensuring that record retrieval can be performed efficiently.

A common way to formulate the privacy of retrievals is *obliviousness.* Obliviousness guarantees that for any two fixed sequences of record retrievals of the same length, any adversary that views all accesses to stored data cannot determine which of the two sequences induced the resulting access pattern to stored data. Obliviousness has been considered with both statistical security, providing protection from adversaries with unbounded computational resources, and computational security, where the adversary is assumed to be probabilistic polynomial time (PPT). Oblivious RAM (ORAM) and private information retrieval (PIR) are two oblivious storage primitives that have been the objective of extensive research [12, 19, 24–27, 34, 35, 43, 47]. For ORAM, it has been shown that $\Omega(\log n)$ overhead is necessary [36]. On the other hand, the best constructions for PIR require at least $\Omega(n)$ server computation over the entire outsourced database.

For integral storage infrastructure that handle many access requests per second, the increased response time and server costs caused by the usage of ORAM and PIR prevent their implementation in these important systems. In a perfect world, there would exist a storage scheme with strong privacy with only small overhead that could be implemented for these frequently accessed storage infrastructures without negatively affecting the performance and/or expenses. In our work, we address the natural question of the best privacy that may be achieved by any storage scheme with only small overhead compared to plaintext access. To our knowledge, our work is the first that considers the question of maximizing privacy for a specific efficiency goal. Previous works consider minimizing the efficiency for primitives with a specific privacy notion.

To consider this problem, we use another formulation for storage access privacy through *differential privacy* [21–23]. Typically, differential privacy is used in the context of *privacy-preserving data analysis* where global properties of the entire database are disclosed while maintaining the privacy of individual database records. In particular, differential privacy guarantees that any fixed disclosure is just as likely, usually within a multiplicative factor, regardless of whether an individual belonged to the sample population or not. Our work focuses on the notion of *differentially private access* which attempts to maintain privacy for individual record retrievals, but may reveal information about the entire sequence of retrievals. Roughly speaking, differential privacy guarantees that any sequence of accesses to stored data caused by the execution of a sequence of record retrievals will be just as likely, except for a multiplicative factor, caused by another sequence attained by replacing a single retrieval for a database record with a single retrieval for any other database record. Differentially private access is a generalization of oblivious access as oblivious access is achieved by fixing the differential privacy parameters to be $\epsilon = 0$ and $\delta = \mathtt{negl}(n)$.

With this definition, readers might now ask the following two questions. When does differentially private access make sense as a security notion? Or, might there exist a stronger security notion that is achievable with small overhead?

To answer the first question, we revisit the scenario of privacy-preserving data analysis on outsourced databases. In these scenarios, there is no sense in using storage schemes providing obliviousness to hide entire record retrieval sequences when differentially private disclosures only maintain privacy for single records. For example, suppose we wish to disclose a differentially private model trained over a sample from the database. Obliviousness would unnecessarily hide the identity of the entire retrieved sample at a high cost yet the differential privacy would guarantee the privacy about individuals in the sample. Therefore, differentially private access is the privacy notion that is complementary to differential privacy disclosures on outsourced databases. In general, differentially private access guarantees privacy for individual retrievals. For the second question, recent work by Persiano and Yeo [46] show that $\Omega(\log n)$ overhead is necessary for differentially private RAMs with parameters of $\epsilon = O(1)$ and $\delta \leq 1/3$. Therefore, the task of finding good parameters for differential privacy that provide both meaningful privacy as well as while permitting small overhead seems non-trivial.

We study differentially private variants of both PIR and ORAM. PIR enables clients to obliviously retrieve database records outsourced to a server. In PIR, both the client and the server are stateless which means that no information may be maintained between multiple record retrievals beyond the server storing the database. Since both the client and the server are stateless, PIR requires the server to perform an operation on each database record: if a record is not involved in computing the server's reply, then it cannot be the record retrieved by the client. The majority of PIR constructions use homomorphic encryption [2, 4] or other expensive encryptions with useful properties [12, 24, 35]. Some recent works consider PIR with stateful clients [45] or super-linear server storage [10, 13, 30]. All single-server PIR schemes consider computational security. PIR has also been studied in the multiple, non-colluding server setting where constructions only require servers to perform computation sublinear in the number of database records and provide statistical security [7, 19].

On the other hand, ORAM allows both the client and server to be stateful and maintain information between multiple queries and allows the client to perform both record retrievals and overwrites. Additionally, ORAM allows a setup phase where the untrusted server receives an encrypted version of the database to store and the client is given a secret key. As a result of state, the server is no longer required to perform computation on every database record. With this efficiency, the majority of ORAM schemes consider only simple upload and download operations and forego the use of expensive encryption schemes of PIR that require the server to perform untrusted computation, although some previous works consider ORAM with homomorphic encryption [20]. For a database with n records, it has been shown that ORAM requires overhead of $\Omega(\log n)$ records [26, 36] and that $O(\log n \cdot \log\log n)$ communication suffices [43]. We also examine an extension to ORAM, which we denote as *oblivious key-value storage* (previously also denoted as oblivious storage), where database records are uniquely identified by keys from a large universe and clients might also attempt to retrieve a non-existent key [28].

In our work, we study the differentially private variants of these three primitives, which we denote as *differentially private information retrieval* (DP-IR), *differentially private RAM* (DP-RAM) and *differentially private key value storage* (DP-KVS). We focus on the question the best privacy that can be achieved by each of these primitives that only require small overhead over plaintext access.

Our Contributions. We present both negative and positive results for both DP-IR and DP-RAM as well as other natural variants of these primitives.

Our lower bounds for DP-IR and DP-RAM apply for a wide range of privacy budgets when the database is stored in a natural encoding. In particular, we consider the balls and bins model of storage (previously considered in [11, 15, 26]) where each database record is considered as an opaque ball along with a key containing important metadata. While not covering all database encodings, in our opinion, the balls and bins models encompasses all natural database representations that maximize practical utility and efficiency. In particular, the contents of each record are assumed to be placed together, which is typically done to maximize data locality.

For positive results, we show that a class of simple constructions are optimal for large sets of privacy budgets. These schemes may be viewed as inserting noise into the sequence of record retrievals and/or overwrites. In particular, the real record retrievals and/or overwrites are disguised within a set that also contain fake record retrievals and/or overwrites. These schemes suffice to construct the best privacy-preserving storage protocols with very small overhead for DP-IR, DP-RAM and DP-KVS. While our constructions are simple, we draw attention to the fact that designing differentially private storage systems is delicate even with weak security notions. Some simple constructions are very appealing and, at first, seem to match our lower bounds. However, many variants of simple constructions (including our constructions) end up being completely insecure. As an example, in Section 4, we consider a simple and tempting DP-IR construction and show that it only guarantees differential privacy with $\delta \longrightarrow 1$, i.e., no privacy at all. Additionally, while our constructions are simple, the security proofs end up being quite involved (especially for DP-RAM). Furthermore, to handle the additional functionalities of DP-KVS, a more complex algorithm using a novel, oblivious adaptation of the two-choice hashing scheme [40] is required.

DP-IR Results. To our knowledge, previous works on DP-IR consider only the multiple, non-colluding server scenarios [48]. Our work is the first to consider DP-IR in the single server scenario.

We show that for any ϵ-DP-IR that must always output the right answer and any value of $\epsilon \geq 0$, then the server must operate on all stored n records. This result is very strong and somewhat surprising as there does not exist any weakening of privacy that will improve the server computational costs.

Theorem 1.1 (informal). *For any $\epsilon, \delta \geq 0$, any (ϵ, δ)-DP-IR scheme in the balls and bins model must operate on $(1 - \delta)n$ records.*

On the other hand, we show that this strong negative result may be circumvented by considering DP-IR schemes with non-zero error probabilities $0 < \alpha \leq 1$. Here, the error probability is over the internal randomness of the DP-IR scheme and does not depend on the queries and/or stored data. For this case, we present the following weaker lower bound.

Theorem 1.2 (informal). *For any $\epsilon, \delta \geq 0$, any (ϵ, δ)-DP-IR scheme in the balls and bins model with error probability $\alpha > 0$ must operate on*

$$\Omega\left(\frac{(1 - \alpha - \delta) \cdot n}{e^{\epsilon}}\right)$$

records.

As we are focusing on schemes with very small overhead, the above theorem leads credulence that there might exist a ϵ-DP-IR scheme with some small, constant error probability $\alpha > 0$ that only performs $O(1)$ operations when $\epsilon = \Theta(\log n)$. We show that there exists a simple construction with these properties.

Theorem 1.3 (informal). *There exists an ϵ-DP-IR with $\epsilon = \Theta(\log n)$ and constant error probability $\alpha > 0$ that only operates on $O(1)$ records.*

Due to our lower bounds, the above construction seems to be the best privacy that can be achieved by any DP-IR with only constant overhead compared to plaintext storage access.

We also consider natural extensions of our DP-IR with multiple, non-colluding servers. There exist several multiple-server PIR schemes [7, 19] in literature. In our full paper, we present asymptotically tight lower bounds for the constructions in [48].

DP-RAM Results. For DP-RAM, we once again start with describing our lower bound results. Unlike DP-IR, there is no separation between the best lower bound for perfectly correct DP-RAM and DP-RAM with error probability $\alpha > 0$. We now present our DP-RAM lower bound which applies for all values $0 \leq \alpha \leq 1$.

Theorem 1.4 (informal). *For any $\epsilon \geq 0$, any ϵ-DP-RAM with error probability $\alpha \geq 0$ in the balls and bins model and a client that stores at most c blocks must operate on*

$$\Omega\left(\log_c\left(\frac{(1 - \alpha) \cdot n}{e^{\epsilon}}\right)\right)$$

records.

The above theorem essentially states that there are two ways that one can achieve very efficient ϵ-DP-RAM constructions: either increase the amount of client storage (c) or increase the privacy budget (ϵ). In most scenarios, it is impractical to suppose that the client can store large portions of data. As our desire is to construct schemes that should be easily usable in complex systems, we minimize the requirements of our clients by assuming clients have very small amounts of storage. In [46], an $\Omega(\log(n/c))$ lower bound is given for constant ϵ and $\delta \leq 1/3$. However, their lower bound can be generalized to $\Omega(\log(n/c)/e^{\epsilon})$ for any $\epsilon \geq 0$. Their lower bound has an exponentially worse dependence on ϵ compared to our lower bound. For example, the lower bound in [46] does not preclude the existence of a ϵ-DP-RAM with $\epsilon = \Theta(\log\log n)$ and constant overhead. On the other hand, our lower bound improves the privacy budget lower bound showing that an ϵ-DP-RAM that operates on $O(1)$ records must have $\epsilon = \Omega(\log n)$. We show the existence of a constant overhead ϵ-DP-RAM with asymptotically optimal $\epsilon = \Theta(\log n)$ privacy.

Theorem 1.5 (informal). *There exists an ϵ-DP-RAM with $\epsilon = \Theta(\log n)$ that only operates on $O(1)$ records.*

Once again, this construction seems to be the best privacy that can be achieved by any DP-RAM scheme with only $O(1)$ overhead over the baseline, unprotected storage access due to our lower bounds. Our scheme improves on prevous DP-RAM schemes in [49] which starts from Path ORAM [47] and degrades security to improve efficiency. For their scheme to achieve even client storage of $O(\sqrt{n})$, their construction recursively stores position maps which costs both logarithmic overhead and client-to-server roundtrips. On the other hand, our DP-RAM construction uses both $O(1)$ overhead and roundtrips while achieving small client storage.

DP-KVS Results. Finally, we consider DP-KVS which is an extension of DP-RAM. As a result, all DP-RAM lower bounds also apply to DP-KVS. Therefore, the best construction that is achievable by DP-KVS with $O(1)$ overhead could be $\epsilon = \Theta(\log n)$. Due to the difficulties of handling a larger universe of queries and possibility that clients request on-existent keys, we present a construction with slightly worse than constant overhead. In addition, we can only achieve privacy in the approximate differential privacy framework.

Theorem 1.6 (informal). *There exists a ϵ-DP-KVS with $\epsilon = \Theta(\log n)$ that operates on $O(\log\log n)$ records.*

While the scheme has non-constant overhead, the $O(\log\log n)$ overhead is exponentially smaller than the best oblivious key-value storage schemes based on ORAMs.

To construct our DP-KVS scheme, we present an improved, oblivious variant of the power of two choices hashing scheme [40] that may be of separate, independent interest. Traditional power of two choices hashing guarantees that bins do not exceed $O(\log\log n)$ items except with probability negligible in n. Our desired oblivious variant must hide the sizes of bins. One way to hide bin sizes is to pad all bins with dummy items up to a maximum. This technique requires padding all n bins to $O(\log\log n)$ items meaning $O(n\log\log n)$ storage. By using a tree-like structure to allow bins to share storage, we present a new scheme using $O(n)$ storage.

Related Work. DP-RAM was considered previously in [49] which present a construction based on Path ORAM [47]. However, their scheme requires recursively stored position maps which requires $\Theta(\log n)$ client-to-server roundtrips to get client storage of even $O(\sqrt{n})$. We present DP-RAM schemes that only require $O(1)$ overhead with small client storage. A construction of DP-IR in the multiple, non-colluding server scenario was considered in [48], which we show is optimal for certain parameters. Lower bounds for DP-RAM have been considered in [46], which are stronger and weaker in different dimensions. Their lower bound has an exponentially worse dependence on the privacy budget, ϵ. On the other hand, their lower bound applies to general storage encodings whereas our work only apply to the balls and bins model. A variant of DP-RAM that only maintains privacy for database record insertions is considered in [15]. A privacy notion stronger than obliviousness is considered in [33] where accesses are protected using obliviousness while the number of accesses is protected using differential privacy. Obliviousness has been considered for other problems such as sorting [3, 6] and shuffling [42, 44, 50]. The problem of relaxing the security notion of obliviousness to differential privacy has also been studied in the context of multi-party protocols. A simple multi-party protocol for single-bit inputs is shown in [32] that maximizes the accuracy for any privacy budget. The multi-party computation problem for larger input sizes is studied in [38]. Additionally, the problem of differentially private disclosure of specific analysis such as subspace clustering [51], deep learning [1] and many others have also been studied where the database is assumed to be stored on a trusted server.

2 DEFINITIONS

We suppose the database D contains n records denoted $B_1, \ldots, B_n$. We will interchangeably use the terms records and blocks. We will refer to a query as a single operation involving either a record retrieval or overwrite and a query sequence as a list consisting of record retrievals and/or overwrites. We use $[n]$ to refer to the set $\{1, \ldots, n\}$. We refer to Q as the space of all possible queries and let $Q_1, Q_2 \in Q^l$ be two query sequences of length l. We define the Hamming distance between Q_1 and Q_2, which we denote by $d(Q_1, Q_2)$, as the number of queries where Q_1 and Q_2 differ.

2.1 Storage Primitives

The *information retrieval* (IR) primitive stores a database D of n equal sized records where only record retrievals are allowed. The initialization of IR consists of the server receiving $D = (B_1, \ldots, B_n)$ and simply processing and storing D. The server is only allowed to store the database and may not keep any other information between multiple queries. Similarly, the client is stateless and may not use any storage between multiple queries. A query to IR is described using an integer $q \in [n]$, which is interpreted as retrieving record B_q. We denote two query sequences $Q_1, Q_2 \in [n]^l$ as adjacent if their Hamming distance is exactly 1. That is, Q_1 and Q_2 retrieve a different record at exactly one query.

The *random access memory* (RAM) primitive will store a database D of n equal sized records where both record retrievals and overwrites are permitted. The initialization of RAM consists of a setup phase consisting of a protocol run between the client and the server. The client will receive a private key, process D using the private key and send the processed database to the server to store. Both the client and server may be stateful and maintain information between multiple queries. A query to RAM is a pair $q = (i, \text{op})$ where $i \in [n]$ refers to record B_i and $\text{op} \in \{\text{read}, \text{write}\}$ describes whether the query is a retrieval or overwrite. Two query sequences $Q_1, Q_2 \in ([n] \times \{\text{read}, \text{write}\})^l$ are adjacent if their Hamming distance is exactly 1. That is, at exactly one query, Q_1 and Q_2 operate on a different record and/or perform a different operation.

Finally, the *key-value storage* (KVS) primitive is an extension to RAM. Queries to KVS consist of a pair $q = (k, \text{op})$ where $k \in U$ is the key and U is universe of all keys and $\text{op} \in \{\text{read}, \text{write}\}$ refers to whether the query is a retrieval or overwrite. Unlike RAM, the universe of keys is very large and might be exponentially larger than the number of operations that will be performed. Furthermore, a retrieval operation $q = (k, \text{read})$ may request a key k that has never been previoulsy inserted into the storage protocol. In this case, the KVS protocol should output $\perp$. Identical to RAM, two query sequences $Q_1, Q_2 \in (U \times \{\text{read}, \text{write}\})^l$ are adjacent if there exists exactly one query that operates on a different key and/or performs a different operation.

We note that IR, RAM and KVS are the most studied storage primitives to provide oblivious access. There are many other extensions to these primitives that have also been studied [9, 10, 13, 16, 17, 28, 30, 37].

2.2 Differentially Private Access to Data

Our privacy notion for a storage primitive $\mathcal{S}$ storing a database $D = (B_1, \ldots, B_n)$ with a query space $\boldsymbol{Q}$ will consider the random variable of the *view* of the adversarial server for a query sequence $Q \in \boldsymbol{Q}^l$ of length l. With a slight abuse of notation, we refer to the transcript, $\mathcal{S}(Q)$, as the random variable of the adversary's view on query sequence Q. The transcript contains all movement of records performed by the server, as well as all, possibly encrypted, records that have been uploaded and downloaded and the initial database.

Definition 2.1 (Differentially Private Access). Let $\mathcal{S}$ be a storage primitive with query space $\boldsymbol{Q}$. $\mathcal{S}$ provides (ϵ, δ)-*differentially private access* if for all pairs of query sequences $Q_1, Q_2 \in \boldsymbol{Q}^l$ of length l that are adjacent, that is $d(Q_1, Q_2) = 1$, and for any subset S of the set of possible views of the adversary, then the following holds:

$$\Pr[\mathcal{S}(Q_1) \in S] \le e^{\epsilon} \cdot \Pr[\mathcal{S}(Q_2) \in S] + \delta.$$

The ϵ parameter is referred to as the *privacy budget.* When $\delta = 0$, the above definition is referred to as *pure differential privacy* and the δ is typically dropped from notation. We denote IR, RAM and KVS primitives that provide pure differentially private access with privacy budget ϵ as ϵ-DP-IR, ϵ-DP-RAM and ϵ-DP-KVS. When $\delta > 0$, the definition is referred to as *approximate differential privacy*, which is a weakening of pure differential privacy. We denote IR, RAM and KVS primitives that provide differentially private access with parameters ϵ and δ as (ϵ, δ)-DP-IR, (ϵ, δ)-DP-RAM and (ϵ, δ)-DP-KVS.

3 LOWER BOUNDS

In this section, we present negative results about DP-IR and DP-RAM in the single-server setting. As DP-KVS is an extension of DP-RAM with more functionality requirements, all DP-RAM lower bounds apply directly to DP-KVS.

3.1 Balls and Bins Model

Our lower bounds are presented in the balls and bins model of data manipulation. The n database records are treated as immutable, opaque balls. Each ball is associated with a mutable key containing metadata about the record. The formal definition involves a server_m with storage for m balls and a client_c with storage for c balls.

Definition 3.1 (Balls and Bins Model). A client_c and server_m operate in the balls and bins model if all client memory is initially empty and client-server interactions are restricted to the following:

(1) Download ball from server_m to client_c. For some $i \in [m]$ and $j \in [c]$, store the block at address i at server_m in address j at client_c.

(2) Upload ball from client_c to server_m. For some $i \in [m]$ and $j \in [c]$, store the block at address j at client_c in address i at server_m.

The above definition assumes a passive server acting only as storage. As a result, only lower bounds on communication can be proven directly. However, for algorithms with general computation by the server, lower bounds on communication in the balls and bins model may be modified to provide lower bounds on server computation. The modification simply views the transcript as the balls that must be operated on by the server.

Discussion about storage model. The balls and bins model does not include all possible encodings of databases that may be stored. In particular, we assume that database records are all stored together and the contents do not emit special properties. In general, related information should be stored in nearby memory locations so that all required data can be found with the minimal number of cache misses. Therefore, assuming database records are stored together captures real world scenarios. In addition, opaque balls rule out bothersome corner cases where non-trivial lower bounds cannot hold such as when records are dependent and record contents may be generated using superficial methods.

3.2 DP-IR

We prove our lower bounds directly for approximately differential privacy (in this case, $\delta \geq 0$). However, one can interpret the results for pure differential privacy by setting $\delta = 0$.

To prove our lower bounds, we first define the notion of *transcripts*. For a single-server information retrieval protocol IR in the balls and bins model, the transcript $\mathsf{IR}(i)$ is the random variable denoting the set of blocks requested when retrieving B_i. The query algorithm of an IR algorithm in the balls and bins model only issues download commands to the server.

The main observation to prove the above theorem is that the initialization phase of DP-IR is public which implies that the adversary has knowledge of the identity of each record. By the restriction on correctness, the queried record must always be retrieved. Using the privacy requirement, it turns out all other blocks must also be retrieved. We summarize this in the following main lemma.

Lemma 3.2. *Let* IR *be an* (ϵ, δ)-DP-IR *scheme in the balls and bins model. For any* $a, b, c \in [n]$,

(1) $\Pr[B_c \in \mathsf{IR}(a)] \leq e^{\epsilon} \Pr[B_c \in \mathsf{IR}(b)] + \delta$.
(2) $\Pr[B_c \notin \mathsf{IR}(a)] \leq e^{\epsilon} \Pr[B_c \notin \mathsf{IR}(b)] + \delta$.

Proof. Define $S \subseteq \text{Range}(\mathsf{IR})$ to be all transcripts where the block B_c is downloaded. So, for any query q,

$$\Pr[B_c \in \mathsf{IR}(q)] = \Pr[\mathsf{IR}(q) \in S].$$

By (ϵ, δ)-DP, we know

$$\Pr[\mathsf{IR}(a) \in S] \leq e^{\epsilon} \Pr[\mathsf{IR}(b) \in S] + \delta$$

completing the first point. The second point follows identically if we choose $S \subseteq \text{Range}(\mathsf{IR})$ to be all transcripts where block B_c is not downloaded. □

Using the above lemma, we present very strong negative results for DP-IR that are errorless. That is, they always return the correct record. We show the following result:

Theorem 3.3. *If* IR *is an* (ϵ, δ)-DP-IR *scheme in the balls and bins model then* IR *performs at least* $(1 - \delta)n$ *operations in expectation.*

Proof. By Lemma 3.2, we know that

$$\Pr[B_j \notin \mathsf{IR}(i)] \leq e^{\epsilon} \Pr[B_j \notin \mathsf{IR}(j)] + \delta = \delta$$

since IR is errorless and $\Pr[B_j \notin \mathsf{IR}(j)] = 0$. Therefore, we know that $\Pr[B_j \in \mathsf{IR}(i)] \geq 1 - \delta$ and

$$\mathbb{E}[|\mathsf{IR}(i)|] = \sum_{j \in [n]} \Pr[B_j \in \mathsf{IR}(i)] \geq (1 - \delta)n$$

completing the proof. □

For algorithms with general server computation, we can the interpret the above results as a lower bound on server computation. This result is extremely strong since n server operations must be executed even when increasing the privacy budget. Therefore, the relaxation to ϵ-DP-IR does not result in any gain compared to PIR. For (ϵ, δ)-DP-IR, one could increase δ to decrease costs. However, typical privacy requires $\delta = \mathtt{negl}(n)$ resulting in almost no gain.

To circumvent this result, we move to the case where DP-IR has a non-zero error rate $0 < \alpha \leq 1$. That is, DP-IR will only retrieve the desired record with probability $1 - \alpha$ depending only on the internal randomness of DP-IR. Our hope is that a very small α may significantly improve efficiency of DP-IR and bypass this negative result. We show:

Theorem 3.4. *If* IR *is an* (ϵ, δ)-DP-IR *scheme in the balls and bins model with error probability* $\alpha > 0$, *then* IR *performs*

$$\Omega\left(\frac{(1 - \alpha - \delta) \cdot n}{e^{\epsilon}}\right)$$

operations in expectation.

Proof of Theorem 3.4. Since IR has error probability at most α, $\Pr[B_j \in \mathsf{IR}(j)] \geq 1 - \alpha$, for all $j \in [n]$. By Lemma 3.2, for all $j \neq i$,

$$\Pr[B_j \in \mathsf{IR}(j)] \leq e^{\epsilon} \Pr[B_j \in \mathsf{IR}(i)] + \delta.$$

Equivalently, this means that $\Pr[B_j \in \mathsf{IR}(i)] \geq \frac{1-\alpha-\delta}{e^\epsilon}$. So,

$$\mathbb{E}[|\mathsf{IR}(i)|] \geq \sum_{j \neq i} \Pr[B_j \in \mathsf{IR}(i)] \geq (n-1)\frac{1-\alpha-\delta}{e^\epsilon}$$

that yields the theorem. □

For any constant error $\alpha > 0$ and typical privacy budgets of $\epsilon = \Theta(1)$, errorless DP-IR schemes require $\Omega(n)$ server operations. However, it seems possible to bypass the first negative result with very small error. The above lower bound does not preclude the existence of a ϵ-DP-IR with $\epsilon = \Omega(\log n)$ and small error probability $\alpha > 0$ that only requires a constant number of server operations. In Section 5, we present an ϵ-DP-IR scheme that uses $O(1)$ communication when $\epsilon = O(\log n)$. It turns out this ϵ-DP-IR scheme asymptotically matches the lower bound for all values of $\epsilon \geq 0$.

We also extend our negative results for DP-IR in Section C where we present lower bounds when outsourcing storage to multiple, non-colluding servers.

3.3 DP-RAM

We now move to our negative results for DP-RAM. Proving lower bounds for DP-RAM is more challenging than DP-IR due to the private setup phase and the client's private memory. We can no longer directly bound the probability that blocks need to be retrieved and, instead, examine the transcripts seen by the adversary. Let us fix any transcript $\mathcal{T}$ that has non-zero probability of being viewed by the adversary on any query sequence Q of length l. We show that every other query sequence of length l must also induce $\mathcal{T}$ with non-zero probability. In fact, the probabilities that any two fixed query sequences induce $\mathcal{T}$ as the view of the adversary are strong related by their Hamming distance and the privacy budget, ϵ, as described in the following:

Lemma 3.5. *Let* RAM *be a* ϵ-DP-RAM *scheme for any* $\epsilon \geq 0$. *For every distribution* $\mathcal{D}$ *on query sequences of length* l, *random variable* $D \sim \mathcal{D}$ *and for any two fixed sequences* Q_1, Q_2 *such that* $\Pr[D = Q_2] > 0$, *then*

$$\frac{\Pr[D = Q_1 \mid \mathsf{RAM}(D) = \mathcal{T}]}{\Pr[D = Q_2 \mid \mathsf{RAM}(D) = \mathcal{T}]} \geq e^{-\epsilon \cdot d(Q_1, Q_2)} \frac{\Pr[D = Q_1]}{\Pr[D = Q_2]}.$$

Proof. By Bayes' law, we have

$$\begin{aligned}\Pr[\, \mathsf{D} = Q \mid \mathsf{RAM}(\mathsf{D}) = \mathcal{T}] &= \frac{\Pr[\mathsf{RAM}(\mathsf{D}) = \mathcal{T} \mid \mathsf{D} = Q]\Pr[\mathsf{D} = Q]}{\Pr[\mathsf{RAM}(\mathsf{D}) = \mathcal{T}]} \\ &\geq e^{-\epsilon \cdot d_H(Q,Q')} \frac{\Pr[\mathsf{RAM}(\mathsf{D}) = \mathcal{T} \mid \mathsf{D} = Q']\Pr[\mathsf{D} = Q]}{\Pr[\mathsf{RAM}(\mathsf{D}) = \mathcal{T}]} \\ &= e^{-\epsilon \cdot d_H(Q,Q')} \frac{\Pr[\mathsf{D} = Q' \mid \mathsf{RAM}(\mathsf{D}) = \mathcal{T}]\Pr[\mathsf{D} = Q]}{\Pr[\mathsf{D} = Q']}\end{aligned}$$

giving us our result. □

Next, we prove that if a query sequence has positive probability, then it stays so even after seeing a transcript. This holds for all *a priori* query sequences distributions $\mathcal{D}$.

Lemma 3.6. *Let* RAM *be an* ϵ-DP-RAM *and let* $\mathcal{T}$ *be a transcript for which there exists at least one query sequence* Q *such that*

$$\Pr[\mathsf{RAM}(Q) = \mathcal{T}] > 0.$$

Then for all distributions D *on the set of query sequences and for all* Q' *such that* $\Pr[\mathsf{D} = Q'] > 0$ *it holds that*

$$\Pr[\mathsf{D} = Q' | \mathsf{RAM}(\mathsf{D}) = \mathcal{T}] > 0.$$

Proof. Let Q be any query sequence such that $\Pr[\mathsf{D} = Q] > 0$ and $\Pr[\mathsf{RAM}(\mathsf{D}) = \mathcal{T} \mid \mathsf{D} = Q] > 0$. Assume by contradiction that $\Pr[\mathsf{D} = Q'] > 0$ but $\Pr[\mathsf{D} = Q' \mid \mathsf{RAM}(\mathsf{D}) = \mathcal{T}] = 0$ for some query sequence Q'. By Bayes' Law,

$$\begin{aligned}0 &= \Pr[\mathsf{D} = Q' \mid \mathsf{RAM}(\mathsf{D}) = \mathcal{T}] \\ &= \frac{\Pr[\mathsf{RAM}(\mathsf{D}) = \mathcal{T} \mid \mathsf{D} = Q'] \cdot \Pr[\mathsf{D} = Q']}{\Pr[\mathsf{RAM}(\mathsf{D}) = \mathcal{T}]}\end{aligned}$$

which implies that $\Pr[\mathsf{RAM}(\mathsf{D}) = \mathcal{T} \mid \mathsf{D} = Q'] = 0$. On the other hand, by ϵ-differential privacy, we have that for all q such that $\Pr[\mathsf{D} = Q] > 0$,

$$\begin{aligned}&\Pr[\mathsf{RAM}(\mathsf{D}) = \mathcal{T} \mid \mathsf{D} = Q] \\ &\quad \leq e^{d_H(Q,Q')\epsilon} \cdot \Pr[\mathsf{RAM}(\mathsf{D}) = \mathcal{T} \mid \mathsf{D} = Q'] = 0\end{aligned}$$

providing our contradiction. □

We are now ready to prove our DP-RAM lower bound. For the sake of the completeness, we suppose that the DP-RAM scheme only retrieves the desired block with probability at least $1 - \alpha$ based only on internal randomness. We show that:

Theorem 3.7. *If* RAM *is an* ϵ-DP-RAM *scheme in the balls and bins model with error probability* $\alpha \geq 0$ *then* RAM *performs*

$$\Omega\left(\log_c\left(\frac{(1-\alpha) \cdot n}{e^\epsilon}\right)\right)$$

expected amortized operations per query when the client has storage for c *balls.*

Proof. Fix $Q = (q_1, \ldots, q_l)$ to be any sequence of queries of length $l > c$. Then, client$_c$ can only perform upload/download operations with server$_M$. Denote the expected amortized bandwidth by k. The server locations of all operations are given by the transcript, $\mathsf{RAM}(q)$. However, which of the c client locations used for each operation remains hidden. For each download and upload, there are c possible execution paths, one path for each of the c client memory locations. Also, after each operation, client$_c$ may use the data stored in any of the c client memory locations to answer a query. Altogether, at most kl blocks of bandwidth are used for all l queries. Therefore, there are at most c^{2kl} different sequences of blocks that may be returned. Since RAM can only fail with α probability for each query, it must satisfy at least $(1-\alpha)^l n^l$ different access patterns. So, $c^{2kl} \geq (1-\alpha)^l n^l$.

Let $\mathcal{T}$ be any transcript with positive probability and consider the uniform distribution U over the set $[n]^l$ of query sequences of length l. By Lemma 3.6, there exists $Q \in [n]^l$ such that

$$\Pr[U = Q \mid \mathsf{RAM}(U) = \mathcal{T}] \geq \frac{1}{n^l} \geq \frac{(1-\alpha)^l}{c^{2kl}}.$$

For every $Q' \neq Q$, by Lemma 3.5, we have

$$\Pr[U = Q' \mid \mathsf{RAM}(U) = \mathcal{T}] \geq e^{-l\epsilon}\frac{(1-\alpha)^l}{c^{2kl}}.$$

Finally, we know that

$$1 \geq \sum_{Q' \neq Q} \Pr[U = Q' \mid \mathsf{RAM}(U) = \mathcal{T}] \geq e^{-l\epsilon}(n^l - 1)\frac{(1-\alpha)^l}{c^{2kl}}$$

completing the proof. □

Unlike DP-IR, we do not need a non-zero error probability to get a constant overhead scheme. From the above lower bound, it seems like the best one can achieve is a perfectly correct ϵ-DP-RAM with $\epsilon = \Theta(\log n)$ that only requires $O(1)$ overhead with small client storage. In Section 6, we show that such a scheme does exist.

Discussion about lower bounds. It has been shown that previous ORAM lower bounds come with many cavaets. The first lower bound [26] in the balls and bins model was for statistical security as pointed out in [11]. The assumption of statistical security is troublesome due to the fact that all ORAM schemes require the use of encryption which only provides computational security. To abstract away this issue, it is assumed that records were opaque balls and were hidden even against computationally unbounded adversaries. However, this abstraction was still not sufficient since the majority of ORAM schemes still required the use of pseudorandom functions. Furthermore, the DP-RAM constructions of [49] and [15] require encryption and are burdened by the same cavaets. We explain why these issues do not apply to our results. In our work, we consider typical differential privacy notions (not the computational variants described in [39]) where adversaries are computationally unbounded. Our DP-RAM scheme in Section 6 when only allowing retrievals does not require encryption and provides differentially private access to public data against computationally unbounded adversaries. All ORAM schemes still require encryption even when only retrievals are permitted. In the case that we wish to store encrypted data or protect overwrites in our DP-RAM scheme, we must apply the abstraction of opaque balls to go around encryption. With this abstraction, our DP-RAM scheme is differentially private. Recent results in [36] present $\Omega(\log(n/c))$ lower bounds for ORAM against computational adversaries with passive servers and general storage schemes. Furthermore, work in [46] extends the lower bound for (ϵ, δ)-DP-RAM where $\epsilon = O(1)$ and $\delta \leq 1/3$. However, the lower bounds in [46] have an exponentially worse dependency on ϵ compared to our results.

4 AN INSECURE CONSTRUCTION

Before presenting our constructions, we consider a simple and tempting, but insecure, construction. The lower bounds presented in Section 3 show that the best privacy any constant overhead storage primitive can achieve will be $\epsilon = \Theta(\log n)$. With such weak privacy requirements, it might seem very easy to construct these primitives at first. We caution that schemes with these weak privacy requirements must be constructed carefully as slight variants of our later schemes could also end up being insecure. To our knowledge, our schemes are the simplest constructions that achieve $\epsilon = \Theta(\log n)$ differential privacy and small overhead.

The main idea of the strawman solution derives from the fact that $\epsilon = \Theta(\log n)$. As a result, the desired block should be queried with probability a multiplicative factor of $\mathsf{poly}(n)$ larger to compared to any other block. To achieve this, one could query the desired block with probability 1 and all other blocks with probability $1/n$. This scheme would have $O(1)$ bandwidth in expectation, perfect correctness and no client storage requirements. However, we show that this scheme is really an (ϵ, δ)-DP-IR with $\epsilon = \Theta(\log n)$ and $\delta = (n-1)/n$. Denote the above scheme by IR and $\mathsf{IR}(i)$ the set of blocks returned when querying for i. Pick any two queries $i \neq j$. Note, $\Pr[B_i \notin \mathsf{IR}(i)] = 0$ and $\Pr[B_i \notin \mathsf{IR}(j)] = (n-1)/n$. Then, $(n-1)/n = \Pr[B_i \notin \mathsf{IR}(j)] \leq e^{\epsilon}\Pr[B_i \notin \mathsf{IR}(i)] + \delta$ which means that $\delta \geq (n-1)/n$. Therefore, the above scheme would not provide as much privacy as possible as δ approaches 1 as n increases.

We use the above strawman to show that attentiveness and rigor are required when constructing differentially private storage schemes even with such weak privacy guarantees. The schemes that we will present for DP-IR, DP-RAM and DP-KVS are the simplest algorithms that, to our knowledge, achieve our desired privacy of $\epsilon = \Theta(\log n)$ and small overhead in efficiency.

5 DP-IR CONSTRUCTION

For errorless DP-IR, the asymptotically optimal balls and bins algorithms is required to download the entire database regardless of the privacy budget. With active servers that can perform computation, servers must perform n operations which is identical to PIR. Therefore, there is no reason to use differentially private access when oblivious access has the same efficiency.

We now move to the more interesting case of DP-IR with errors. By introducing a small amount of error $\alpha > 0$, we hope to find algorithms more efficient than PIR for larger privacy budgets where our lower bounds from Section 3 no longer hold. We show that the simplest algorithm ends up being optimal. In particular, the client will download the desired block as well as several other blocks simultaneously. The hope is that the adversary cannot determine the real retrieval from all the fake retrievals. In addition, with probability α, we only perform fake retrievals and error. The pseudocode of this scheme can be found in Appendix G. The proof of the following theorem is found in Appendix B

Theorem 5.1. *For any $\epsilon \geq 0$, there exists a ϵ-DP-IR that returns $O(n/e^{\epsilon})$ blocks for any constant error probability $\alpha > 0$.*

The above upper bound asymptotically matches the lower bound of Theorem 3.4 for all values of $\epsilon \geq 0$. Furthemore, by fixing the privacy budget to be $\epsilon = \Theta(\log n)$, we can achieve a constant overhead DP-IR scheme with the best privacy according to Theorem 3.4.

6 DP-RAM CONSTRUCTION

In this section, we give an errorless construction DP-RAM supporting both retrieval and overwrite operations. Before describing our DP-RAM scheme, we note that one could also use the DP-IR scheme from Section 5 as a DP-RAM scheme without any client storage requirements. However, this DP-IR scheme has non-zero error probabilities which is inherently unavoidable for DP-IR due to our lower bounds in Section 3. On the other hand, our DP-RAM lower bounds do not preclude the existence of a perfectly correct DP-RAM scheme with $\epsilon = \Theta(\log n)$. In this section, we work towards constructing such a DP-RAM scheme.

Our scheme will require the client to store some records in a local *stash*. Our DP-RAM scheme is parameterized by a probability p describing the independent probability that each record is stored in the stash. We assume that (Enc, Dec) is an IND-CPA symmetric-key encryption scheme. The server's storage will consist of an array, A, of n records.

The setup phase of DP-RAM will consist of populating the server-stored array A. For security parameter λ, key $K \to \{0,1\}^{\lambda}$ is randomly selected. A is initialized by setting $A[i] = \mathsf{Enc}(K, B_i)$ for $i \in [n]$. The stash is initialized by independently selecting each record to be in the stash with probability p. In addition, the client keeps the key K in local storage.

The querying (either retrieval or overwrite) for a record B_i consists of two phases: the *download* phase followed by the *overwrite* phase. In the download phase, the client looks for B_i in the stash. If B_i is found, then B_i is removed and returned. The client asks the server for $A[j]$, with j chosen uniformly at random from $[n]$. If, instead, B_i is not in the stash, the client asks the server for $A[i]$ that contains an encryption of B_i. If the client is performing a write operation, then B_i is updated with the new version. At this point, the client holds the current version of B_i.

In the overwrite phase, the current version of B_i is added to the stash with probability p. If B_i is stored in the stash, then another record is randomly selected, downloaded from the server, decrypted and then re-encrypted with fresh randomness and uploaded to the server. If B_i is not stored in the stash, then the client asks the server for $A[i]$, discards the record received and then uploads to $A[i]$ a freshly computed ciphertext carrying the current version of B_i.

The pseudocode of the algorithms are presented in Appendix H. We note that while the above algorithm is simple, the analysis of privacy is quite complicated. We show the following about this scheme when $p \leq \Phi(n)/n$ for any $\Phi(n) = \omega(\log n)$:

Theorem 6.1. *There exists an $O(\log n)$-DP-RAM that returns $O(1)$ blocks. For any function $\Phi(n) = \omega(\log n)$, the client stores $\Phi(n)$ blocks of client storage except with probability $\mathtt{negl}(n)$.*

This scheme is, essentially, the best privacy that can be achieved by an errorless DP-RAM scheme with constant overhead according to Theorem 3.7. Since we use encryption, our DP-RAM satisfies computational differentially privacy using simulators (see SIM-CDP in [39]). Our proof uses a simulator that replaces all encryptions of records with randomly generated contents.

Discussion about encryption. The above DP-RAM scheme assumes that both record retrievals and overwrites are permitted. To hide whether queries are overwrites or retrievals, any DP-RAM scheme must use encryption. In the case that we wish to only permit retrievals, we note that the above DP-RAM scheme no longer requires encryption and can provide differentially private access to public data without computational assumptions. In particular, the entire overwrite phase may be skipped. Retrieval-only DP-RAM and DP-IR only differ by their requirements on the client's state. Therefore, using client state is another way to bypass the strong lower bound shown in Theorem 3.3 for errorless DP-IR schemes.

6.1 Roadmap of the Proof

To start, we show that if we choose that $p \leq c/n$ where $c = \omega(\log n)$, then the client will store at most $O(c)$ blocks. The proof is an application of Chernoff Bounds and postponed to Appendix D.

The technical crux of the privacy analysis lies in bounding the following ratio, for every transcript $\mathcal{T}$ seen by the adversary, and for every two neighboring query sequences

Q and Q',

$$\frac{\Pr[\mathsf{RAM}(Q') = \mathcal{T}]}{\Pr[\mathsf{RAM}(Q) = \mathcal{T}]} \tag{1}$$

where $\Pr[\mathsf{RAM}(Q) = \mathcal{T}]$ denotes the probability that RAM executing on Q produces the transcript $\mathcal{T}$. In the first step, we show that the transcript of the adversary at a single query on B_q is only dependent on the most recent query that also queries for B_q. In other words, the ratio is upper bounded by

$$\prod_{i=1}^{l} \frac{\Pr[\mathsf{RAM}_i(Q') = \mathcal{T}_i \mid \mathsf{RAM}_{\mathsf{pr}(Q',i)}(Q') = \mathcal{T}_{\mathsf{pr}(Q',i)}]}{\Pr[\mathsf{RAM}_i(Q) = \mathcal{T}_i \mid \mathsf{RAM}_{\mathsf{pr}(Q,i)}(Q) = \mathcal{T}_{\mathsf{pr}(Q,i)}]}$$

where $\mathsf{pr}(Q,i)$ is the most recent query for block B_{q_i} before the i-th query. The second step consists of giving an upper bound that holds for each factor of the product in the above equation. The third step shows that the upper bound computed in the second step is too pessimistic and that, all factors, except for 3, in the product in the right hand side of the above equation are 1 when Q and Q' differ in exactly one position.

We now proceed to define notation and terminology used throughout our proof. First, we observe that the transcript of an execution only includes the ciphertexts of the blocks and not the actual content of the blocks transferred. Assuming IND-CPA of the underlying encryption scheme (Enc, Dec), it is straightforward to prove that, for a sequence $Q = (q_1, \ldots, q_l)$ of l queries, the transcript generated by Q for blocks $B_1, \ldots, B_n$ is indistinguishable from the transcript generated by the same sequence Q for n blocks that are $\mathbf{0}$. For this reason, we shall not consider the ciphertexts of the blocks as part of the transcript and consider a transcript $\mathcal{T}$ for query sequence Q as a sequence $\mathcal{T} = ((d_1, o_1), \ldots, (d_l, o_l))$ of l pairs $\mathcal{T}_j = (o_j, d_j)$ of indices of the blocks that are accessed during the download phase and the overwrite phase. We set $\mathcal{T}_{[j]} = ((d_1, o_1), \ldots, (d_j, o_j))$. We define $\mathsf{RAM}_j^D(Q)$ and $\mathsf{RAM}_j^O(Q)$ to be the random variables of the indices of the download and of the overwrite block of the j-th query for all $j \in [l]$. Also, for $S \subseteq [l]$ we define $\mathsf{RAM}_S(Q)$ to be the set of random variables $\{\mathsf{RAM}_j^D(Q), \mathsf{RAM}_j^O(Q)\}_{j \in S}$. Also, we set $\mathsf{RAM}(Q) := \mathsf{RAM}_{[n]}(Q)$. It turns out to be convenient to extend the random variable RAM for indices $\pm\infty$ by setting $\mathsf{RAM}_{\pm\infty}^D(Q)$ and $\mathsf{RAM}_{\pm\infty}^O(Q)$ to be random variables that give probability 1 to $\perp$.

We also let $\mathsf{pr}(Q,j)$ be the index of the most recent *previous* query to block B_{q_j} that happened before the j-th query of Q; that is, $\mathsf{pr}(Q,j) = \max\{i < j : q_i = q_j\}$. If query q_j is the first query of sequence Q that asks for block B_{q_j}, then $\mathsf{pr}(Q,j) = +\infty$. Similarly, we define $\mathsf{nx}(Q,j)$ to be the index of the nearest *next* query for block B_{q_j}; that is, $\mathsf{nx}(Q,j) = \min\{i > j : q_i = q_j\}$. If the j-th query of Q is the last query of Q to ask for block B_{q_j}, then $\mathsf{nx}(Q,j) = -\infty$.

6.2 Step I: Reducing dependencies

The next lemmas outline the dependencies of the random variables of the download blocks and of the overwrite blocks. We start by showing that the overwrite block of each query is independent of all previous history and only depends on the current query.

LEMMA 6.2. *For every query sequence Q of length l, for every transcript $\mathcal{T} = ((d_1, o_1), \ldots, (d_l, o_l))$ and for every $j \leq l$*

$$\Pr[\mathsf{RAM}_j^O(Q) = o_j \mid \mathsf{RAM}_{[j-1]}(Q) = \mathcal{T}_{[j-1]} \wedge \mathsf{RAM}_j^D(Q) = d_j] = \Pr[\mathsf{RAM}_j^O(Q) = o_j].$$

Moreover, if Q and Q' are two sequences with $q_j = q'_j$, then the distributions $\mathsf{RAM}_j^O(Q)$ and $\mathsf{RAM}_j^O(Q')$ coincide.

PROOF. The lemma follows by observing that the distribution of the j-th overwrite block depends only on whether B_{q_j} is added to the block stash during the j-th overwrite phase which, in turn, depends only on q_j and the random value of r in the overwrite phase of the j-th query. □

LEMMA 6.3. *For every query sequence Q of length l, for every transcript $\mathcal{T} = ((d_1, o_1), \ldots, (d_l, o_l))$ and for every $j \leq l$,*

$$\Pr[\mathsf{RAM}_j^D(Q) = d_j \mid \mathsf{RAM}_{[j-1]}(Q) = \mathcal{T}_{[j-1]}] = \Pr[\mathsf{RAM}_j^D(Q) = d_j \mid \mathsf{RAM}_{\mathsf{pr}(Q,j)}^O = o_{\mathsf{pr}(Q,j)}].$$

Moreover, if Q and Q' are two sequences with $q_j = q'_j$ and $\mathsf{pr}(Q,j) = \mathsf{pr}(Q',j)$ then for all $d \in [n]$ and for all $o \in [n] \cup \{\perp\}$ such that $\Pr[\mathsf{RAM}_{\mathsf{pr}(Q,j)}^O = o] > 0$,

$$\Pr[\mathsf{RAM}_j^D(Q) = d \mid \mathsf{RAM}_{\mathsf{pr}(Q,j)}^O = o] = \Pr[\mathsf{RAM}_j^D(Q') = d \mid \mathsf{RAM}_{\mathsf{pr}(Q',j)}^O = o].$$

PROOF. The j-th download block of sequence Q depends on whether B_{q_j} is in the block stash at the start of the j-th download phase. We distinguish two cases.

If $\mathsf{pr}(Q,j) = +\infty$, then block B_{q_j} has not been queried in the first $j-1$ queries and its probability of being found in the stash at the start of j-th download phase is equal to the probability of being placed in the stash by RAMSetup which, obviously, is independent from the previous history.

Suppose instead that $\mathsf{pr}(Q,j) \in [j-1]$. Then the probability that B_{q_j} is in the stash at the beginning of the j-th query depends only on the random variable, $\mathsf{RAM}_{\mathsf{pr}(Q,j)}^O(Q)$, of the overwrite block of query $\mathsf{pr}(Q,j)$. □

The first part of Lemma 6.2 and the first part of Lemma 6.3 imply

$$\Pr[\mathsf{RAM}_j(Q) = (d_j, o_j) \mid \mathsf{RAM}_{[j-1]}(Q) = \mathcal{T}_{[j-1]}] =$$
$$\Pr[\mathsf{RAM}^D_j(Q) = d_j \mid \mathsf{RAM}_{[j-1]}(Q) = \mathcal{T}_{[j-1]}]\cdot$$
$$\Pr[\mathsf{RAM}^O_j(Q) = o_j \mid \mathsf{RAM}_{[j-1]}(Q) = \mathcal{T}_{[j-1]} \wedge \mathsf{RAM}^D_j(Q) = d_j] =$$
$$\Pr[\mathsf{RAM}^D_j(Q) = d_j \mid \mathsf{RAM}_{\mathsf{pr}(Q,j)}(Q) = o_{\mathsf{pr}(Q,j)}] \cdot \Pr[\mathsf{RAM}^O_j(Q) = o_j].$$

Thus, we can write

$$\frac{\Pr[\mathsf{RAM}(Q') = \mathcal{T}]}{\Pr[\mathsf{RAM}(Q) = \mathcal{T}]} = \prod_{j=1}^{l} \frac{\Pr[\mathsf{RAM}^O_j(Q) = o_j]}{\Pr[\mathsf{RAM}^O_j(Q') = o_j]}$$
$$\times \prod_{j=1}^{l} \frac{\Pr[\mathsf{RAM}^D_j(Q') = d_j \mid \mathsf{RAM}_{\mathsf{pr}(Q',j)}(Q) = o_{\mathsf{pr}(Q',j)}]}{\Pr[\mathsf{RAM}^D_j(Q) = d_j \mid \mathsf{RAM}_{\mathsf{pr}(Q,j)}(Q') = o_{\mathsf{pr}(Q,j)}]}$$

6.3 Step II: Upper bounding factors

In the next two lemmata, we give an upper bound on the contribution of each $j \in [l]$ to the product in the equation above.

Lemma 6.4. *Let Q and Q' be two query sequences of length l. For every transcript $\mathcal{T} = ((d_1, o_1), \ldots, (d_l, o_l))$ and every $j \in [l]$*

$$\frac{\Pr[\mathsf{RAM}^D_j(Q') = d_j \mid \mathsf{RAM}^O_{\mathsf{pr}(Q',j)}(Q') = o_{\mathsf{pr}(Q',j)}]}{\Pr[\mathsf{RAM}^D_j(Q) = d_j \mid \mathsf{RAM}^O_{\mathsf{pr}(Q,j)}(Q) = o_{\mathsf{pr}(Q,j)}]} \leq \frac{n^2}{p}.$$

Lemma 6.5. *Let Q and Q' be two query sequences of length l. For every transcript $\mathcal{T} = ((d_1, o_1), \ldots, (d_l, o_l))$ and every $j \in [l]$*

$$\frac{\Pr[\mathsf{RAM}^O_j(Q') = o_j]}{\Pr[\mathsf{RAM}^O_j(Q) = o_j]} \leq \frac{n}{p}.$$

Both of these lemmata consider the various cases that can occur. As the proofs are case analysis that do not provide better intuition to the problem, we postpone them to Section D.

6.4 Step III: Identifying the many good cases

The bounds given by Lemma 6.4 and Lemma 6.5 would give an $n^{O(l)}$ upper bound on the ratio in Equation 1. This is a very weak bound as it depends on the length l of the sequences. In this section, we tighten the upper bound to $n^{O(1)}$ which is instrumental to prove that RAM is private with $\epsilon = O(\log n)$. Specifically, the next lemma gives sufficient conditions under which the ratio is actually 1 and then we show that, if the two sequences only differ in one position, then there are only three values of j for which the conditions are not satisfied and for those position we use the upper bound of the previous section.

The following lemma follows directly from the second parts of Lemma 6.2 and 6.3.

Lemma 6.6. *For any two sequences Q and Q' of the same length, every transcript $\mathcal{T} = ((d_1, o_1), \ldots, (d_l, o_l))$ and every $j \in [l]$ with $\mathsf{pr}(Q, j) = \mathsf{pr}(Q', j)$ and $q_j = q'_j$,*

$$\Pr[\mathsf{RAM}^O_j(Q) = o_j]$$
$$\cdot \Pr[\mathsf{RAM}^D_j(Q) = d_j \mid \mathsf{RAM}^O_{\mathsf{pr}(Q,j)}(Q) = o_{\mathsf{pr}(Q,j)}] =$$
$$\Pr[\mathsf{RAM}^O_j(Q') = o_j]$$
$$\Pr[\mathsf{RAM}^D_j(Q') = d_j \mid \mathsf{RAM}^O_{\mathsf{pr}(Q',j)}(Q') = o_{\mathsf{pr}(Q',j)}].$$

The lemma above says that the distributions of the transcripts associated with two query sequences Q and Q' may differ only at indices j for which $\mathsf{pr}(Q, j) \neq \mathsf{pr}(Q', j)$ or $q_j \neq q'_j$. The next lemma identifies the indices j for which this happens when Q and Q' differ in exactly one position.

Lemma 6.7. *Let Q and Q' be two query sequences of length l differing only at position $k \in [l]$. If $j \notin \{k, \mathsf{nx}(Q, k), \mathsf{nx}(Q', k)\}$, then $\mathsf{pr}(Q, j) = \mathsf{pr}(Q, j')$.*

Proof. For $j < k$, we have $(q_1, \ldots, q_j) = (q'_1, \ldots, q'_j)$ and thus $\mathsf{pr}(Q, j) = \mathsf{pr}(Q', j)$. For $j > k$ such that $q_j \neq q_k, q'_k$ we have $q_j = q'_j$ and $\mathsf{pr}(Q, j) = \mathsf{pr}(Q', j)$. Next consider the indices $j_1 < \ldots < j_l$ such that $q_k = q_{j_1} = \ldots = q_{j_l}$. Clearly, if $l > 0$ then $j_1 = \mathsf{nx}(Q, k)$ and, for $i = 2, \ldots, l$, we have $q_{j_i} = q'_{j_i}$ and $\mathsf{pr}(Q', j_i) = \mathsf{pr}(Q', j_i)$. A similar argument applies for the indices $j > k$ such $q'_j = q'_k$ thus completing the proof of the theorem. □

6.5 Wrapping up the proof

Proof of Theorem 6.1. Bounds on bandwidth and server storage are obvious and the one on client storage follows from Lemma D.1.

Consider sequences Q and Q' of length l that differ only in position $k \in [l]$. Let $\mathcal{T} = ((d_1, o_1), \ldots, (d_l, o_l))$ be transcript. By Lemma 6.6 and 6.7, we obtain that the ratio $\frac{\Pr[\mathsf{RAM}(Q') = \mathcal{T}]}{\Pr[\mathsf{RAM}(Q) = \mathcal{T}]}$ is

$$\prod_{j \in S} \frac{\Pr[\mathsf{RAM}_j(Q') = \mathcal{T}_j \mid \mathsf{RAM}_{[j-1]}(Q') = \mathcal{T}_{[j-1]}]}{\Pr[\mathsf{RAM}_j(Q) = \mathcal{T}_j \mid \mathsf{RAM}_{[j-1]}(Q) = \mathcal{T}_{[j-1]}]}$$

where $S = \{k, \mathsf{nx}(Q, k), \mathsf{nx}(Q', k)\}$. By Lemma 6.4 and 6.5,

$$\frac{\Pr[\mathsf{RAM}(Q') = \mathcal{T}]}{\Pr[\mathsf{RAM}(Q) = \mathcal{T}]} = \left(\frac{n}{p}\right)^{O(1)}.$$

Since, the above holds for any single transcript, we get that the ratio holds for any set of transcripts. This implies that $\epsilon = O(\log n)$. □

7 DP-KVS CONSTRUCTION

In this section, we present DP-KVS, our KVS construction with privacy budget $\epsilon = O(\log n)$ and small overhead. Recall that a KVS is an extension of RAM where each of the n blocks is identified by a unique key taken from a possibly large universe of keys U. In contrast, a block in RAM is uniquely identified by an integer in $[n]$. One could use the DP-RAM construction from Section 6, which results in server storage on the order of $|U| \gg n$. For efficiency, we would like a DP-KVS scheme that stores $O(n)$ blocks on the server.

Our approach to constructing a DP-KVS scheme consists of two steps. First, we show that we can construct a DP-KVS scheme using a DP-RAM scheme and a *mapping scheme* which associates keys in the universe U to subsets of server storage. Next, we present an efficient mapping scheme by constructing a non-trivial *oblivious* variant of two-choice hashing [40] that uses $O(n)$ server storage and which may be of independent interest. Our oblivious two-choice hashing variant hides the number of real items that are stored in each bin at any point in time. Finally, combined with our DP-RAM scheme of Section 6, we present a (ϵ, δ)-DP-KVS with $\epsilon = O(\log n)$ and $\delta = \mathtt{negl}(n)$ using only $O(\log \log n)$ overhead. While non-constant, this is exponentially better than any previous oblivious KVS scheme built from ORAMs. Furthermore, for all practical sizes of n, $O(\log \log n)$ is very small.

7.1 Composing Mapping Schemes and DP-RAM

In this section, we present a generic reduction of DP-KVS to a mapping scheme and our DP-RAM from Section 6. First, we define mapping schemes. Afterwards, we present the reduction.

A mapping scheme is defined as the tuple $(\Pi, \mathcal{S})$ where Π is the *mapping function* and $\mathcal{S}$ is the *storing algorithm*. To store n items each uniquely identified by an key from the universe U, a mapping scheme arranges the server storage into $b(n)$ buckets each consisting of at most $s(n)$ blocks. Each bucket is uniquely identified by an index from $[b(n)]$. We note that buckets are not necessarily disjoint and the total number of blocks may be much smaller than $b(n) \cdot s(n)$. In addition, the mapping scheme assumes that the client will hold a *mapping stash* which will contain at most $c(n)$ blocks except with probability $\mathtt{negl}(n)$. For each item $u \in U$, the mapping function maps u to a subset of at most $s(n)$ buckets defined by $\Pi(u) \subseteq [b(n)]$. For convenience, we denote $k(n) := \max_{u \in U} |\Pi(u)|$. When inserting a new item with identifier u, the storing algorithm $\mathcal{S}$ determines whether u is placed into a bucket of $\Pi(u)$ or the mapping stash according to the sizes of buckets in $\Pi(u)$. We now show how to use mapping schemes to construct a DP-KVS.

Our DP-KVS scheme works as follows. We construct the server storage into $b(n)$ buckets as described by the mapping scheme. We build a DP-RAM to be able to query and update the $b(n)$ buckets. In Appendix E, we show that our DP-RAM construction from Section 6 remains secure and efficient when querying possibly overlapping buckets with minor modifications. When querying our DP-KVS for a key $u \in U$, we perform $k(n)$ DP-RAM queries to retrieve the $s(n)$ blocks from each bucket in $\Pi(u)$. If $|\Pi(u)| < k(n)$, we pick random buckets to pad $\Pi(u)$ to size $k(n)$. Now, we are guaranteed that if u exists in DP-KVS, it appears in a bucket of $\Pi(u)$ or in the mapping stash and can be thus returned. To update an existing key, we can simply update either the bucket or the mapping stash that contains the block associated to key u. For insertion, we can execute the storing algorithm $\mathcal{S}$ as all the contents of buckets $\Pi(u)$ and the mapping stash are available to the client. $\mathcal{S}$ determines the insertion location for the block associated to key u. Finally, we execute $k(n)$ DP-RAM updates to all buckets in $\Pi(u)$. Only the bucket containing the block associated with key u is updated. The other buckets will perform fake updates where the contents remain unchanged. For read operations, none of the contents of buckets in $\Pi(u)$ will be changed. We prove the following theorem about our DP-KVS construction.

THEOREM 7.1. *For n blocks, the above* KVS *scheme is an ϵ-*DP-KVS *with $\epsilon = O(k(n) \cdot \log n)$ that returns at most $O(k(n) \cdot s(n))$ blocks. For any function $\Phi(n) = \omega(\log n)$, the client stores $O(s(n) \cdot \Phi(n) + c(n))$ blocks of storage except with probability* $\mathtt{negl}(n)$.

PROOF. The bounds on bandwidth and server storage follow from the mapping scheme properties. The client storage bound follows from Lemma D.1 and the mapping scheme properties. Each query results in at most $2 \cdot k(n)$ queries over the repertoire Σ of the n buckets. By the composition theorem and the discussion in Appendix E, we obtain that $\epsilon = O(k(n) \cdot \log n)$. □

7.2 Oblivious Two-Choice Hashing

Before presenting our new mapping scheme, we revisit the two-choice hashing scheme [40] (see Section A.1 for more details). This scheme considers n buckets to store up to n keys. The mapping function $\Pi : U \rightarrow [n]$ sets $\Pi(u)$ as $k(n) := 2$ independently and uniformly at random chosen buckets. Typically, Π is succintly represented using two keys, $\mathsf{key}_1, \mathsf{key}_2$, of a pseudorandom function F and by $\Pi(u) := \{F(\mathsf{key}_1, u), F(\mathsf{key}_2, u)\}$. The storing algorithm $\mathcal{S}$ for $u \in U$, checks which of the two buckets in $\Pi(u)$ is less loaded and places u into the less loaded bucket. There are several different proofs that show that the largest bucket will contain at most $s(n) := O(\log \log n)$ items except with probability $\mathtt{negl}(n)$.

Unfortunately, we are unable to use two-choice hashing directly into our DP-KVS scheme without incurring into a server storage blockup. The DP-KVS scheme from Section 7.1 requires that all buckets are the same size for privacy. The naive approach is to simply increase all buckets to the worst case size which results in $O(n \log\log n)$ server storage. Instead, we now present a variant of two-choice hashing which will only use $O(n)$ server storage by arranging buckets to share memory.

Our bucket arrangement is best described as $\Theta(n/\log n)$ identical binary trees, each with $\Theta(\log n)$ leaf nodes and $\Theta(\log\log n)$ depth. Leaf nodes are denoted as *height* 0 and the height increases going towards the root. This results in a total of $\Theta(n)$ nodes over all binary trees. Each node in the tree will be able to store up to $t = \Theta(1)$ blocks. Furthermore, we pick the binary trees such that there are exactly n leaf nodes overall. Finally, there is a single root node that has $\Theta(n/\log n)$ children corresponding to the roots of the $\Theta(n/\log n)$ binary tree roots. We denote this node as the *super root.* Unlike all other nodes, the super root is stored on the client. We shall show that the probability that the super root holds more then $\Phi(n)$ blocks for any $\Phi(n) = \omega(\log n)$ is negligible in n.

Each of the n buckets is uniquely associated with a leaf node. The memory locations of a bucket consist of all the blocks stored in the nodes on the unique path between the leaf node and the super root. Therefore, a bucket consists of $\Theta(\log\log n)$ server memory locations in addition to the memory locations in the super root. We now describe our new storing algorithm, $\mathcal{S}$, given this bucket arrangement. When inserting u, $\mathcal{S}$ places u into the node with minimal height (that is, closest to the leaf nodes) in either of the buckets in $\Pi(u)$ with empty space. Note that u might end up being stored in the super root. If all the nodes of both buckets of $\Pi(u)$ are filled then the mapping scheme fails to store u. We show that when inserting any set of at most n keys, if we limit the capacity of the super root to $\Phi(n)$, for some $\Phi(n) = \omega(\log n)$, the above mapping scheme fails with probability $\mathtt{negl}(n)$. The analysis adapts techniques from [5].

Theorem 7.2. *Let $\Phi(n) = \omega(\log n)$. The probability that, when inserting n keys, mapping scheme $\mathcal{S}$ places more than $\Phi(n)$ keys into the super root is* $\mathtt{negl}(n)$.

Proof. Our key observation is that a block is stored in a level-$(i+1)$ slot if and only if the two selected buckets are filled up to level i. If we denote by H_i the number of filled node at level i, the probability of selecting a bucket that is filled up to level i is $H_i \cdot 2^i/n$. For a block to be allocated to a slot at level $i+1$, it must be the case that both selected buckets are filled up to level i which has probability $\left(\frac{H_i \cdot 2^i}{n}\right)^2$. For convenience, we define the sequence β_i by setting $\beta_0 = \frac{n}{e \cdot 3^4}$ and $\beta_{i+1} = \frac{e}{n} \cdot \beta_i^2 \cdot 2^{2(i+1)}$, which we will use later in the proof. First, we present a useful property about the sequence and then we show that the probability that $H_i > \beta_i$ is $\mathtt{negl}(n)$. The proof of Lemma 7.3 can be found in Appendix F.

Lemma 7.3. *For all $i \geq 0$,*

$$\beta_i = \frac{n}{e} \cdot \left(\frac{2}{3}\right)^{2^{i+2}} \left(\frac{1}{2}\right)^{2(i+2)}.$$

Lemma 7.4. *If $\beta_i = \omega(\log n)$ then,* $\Pr[H_i > \beta_i] \leq i/n^{\omega(1)}$.

Proof. We proceed by induction on i. The base case $i = 0$ is established by setting $c > 3^4 \cdot e$. We next upper bound the probability that after inserting n blocks there are more than β_{i+1} filled nodes at level $i+1$, given that we start with H_i nodes filled at level i. To do so, we define X_j to be that 0/1 random variable that is 1 iff the j-th block ends up at level $i+1$. Clearly, $\Pr[X_j = 1] = \left(\frac{H_i \cdot 2^{i+1}}{n}\right)^2$ and, if $H_i \leq \beta_i$,

$$\mu_{i+1} := \mathbb{E}\left[\sum_j X_j\right] \leq \frac{\beta_i^2 \cdot 2^{2(i+1)}}{n} = \frac{\beta_{i+1}}{e}.$$

We thus have

$$\Pr[H_{i+1} > \beta_{i+1} \mid H_i \leq \beta_i] \leq \frac{\Pr[H_{i+1} > \beta_{i+1}]}{\Pr[H_i \leq \beta_i]}$$

$$= \frac{\Pr[\sum_j X_j > e \cdot \mu_{i+1}]}{\Pr[H_i \leq \beta_i]} \leq \frac{e^{-e \cdot \beta_{i+1}}}{\Pr[H_i \leq \beta_i]}$$

where the last inequality follows by Theorem A.2. By Lemma 7.3, the sequence β_i decreases with i and thus $\beta_i \geq \beta_{i+1} = \omega(\log n)$. The proof is then completed by observing that

$$\begin{aligned}\Pr[H_{i+1} > \beta_{i+1}] &\\ \leq \Pr[H_{i+1} > \beta_{i+1} \mid H_i \leq \beta_i] \cdot \Pr[H_i \leq \beta_i] + \Pr[H_i > \beta_i] &\\ \leq 1/n^{\omega(1)} + i/n^{\omega(1)} \leq (i+1)/n^{\omega(1)} &\end{aligned}$$

using our hypothesis that $\Pr[H_i > \beta_i] = i/n^{\omega(1)}$. □

We now conclude the proof of Theorem 7.2. Fix a function $\Phi(n) = \omega(\log n)$ and let $i^\star$ be the largest index such that $\beta_{i^\star} \geq \Phi(n)$. By Lemma 7.3, we obtain that $i^\star = \Theta(\log\log n)$. Following a reasoning similar to the one adopted in proof of Lemma 7.4, we can prove that the expected number of filled nodes at level $i^\star + 1$ is at most $\beta_{i^\star+1}/e$, given that no more than $\beta_{i^\star}$ nodes are filled at level $i^\star$. By Lemma 7.4, the condition holds except with negligible probability. From the definition of $\beta_{i^\star+1}$, we obtain that, for some constant α such that $c \geq \alpha \cdot \beta_{i^\star+1}$, the probability that more than c nodes are filled at level $i^\star + 1$ is inverse exponential in c by Chernoff Bounds, and thus $\mathtt{negl}(n)$. □

7.3 Wrapping up the Proof

We complete our DP-KVS construction by observing that the mapping scheme described above has $k(n) = 2$, $s(n) = \Theta(\log\log n)$ and $c(n) = \Phi(n)$ for any $\Phi(n) = \omega(\log n)$.

Theorem 7.5. *The above* KVS *scheme is a ϵ-*DP-KVS *with $\epsilon = O(\log n)$ that returns $O(\log\log n)$ blocks. The server uses $O(n)$ blocks of storage and, for any function $\Phi(n) = \omega(\log n)$,* *the probabilty that the client stores more than $O(\Phi(n) \cdot \log\log n)$ blocks is* $\mathtt{negl}(n)$.

8 CONCLUSIONS

We consider privacy-preserving storage protocols with small overhead that could be implemented with large-scale, frequently accessed storage infrastructures without negatively impacting response times or resource costs. Our main question is to find the best privacy that can be achieved by small overhead storage schemes.

We formulate our privacy notion using differentially private access, which is a generalization of the oblivious access provided by both ORAM and PIR. We present strong evidence that the best privacy achievable by any constant overhead differentially private storage schemes must have privacy budgets $\epsilon = \Omega(\log n)$. For DP-RAM and DP-IR, we present constructions with asymptotically optimal $\epsilon = \Theta(\log n)$ privacy budgets and $O(1)$ overhead. For DP-KVS, we present a scheme with asymptotically optimal $\epsilon = \Theta(\log n)$ privacy budgets and only $O(\log\log n)$ overhead which is exponentially better than previous constructions. Our DP-KVS uses a novel, oblivious variant of two-choice hashing that uses only $O(n)$ server storage that may be of independent interest.

Therefore, we answer that the best privacy achievable by privacy-preserving storage systems with small overhead is differentially private access with $\epsilon = \Theta(\log n)$. On the other hand, any storage scheme achieving stronger privacy most likely must incur non-trivial overhead compared to plaintext access.

REFERENCES

[1] M. Abadi, A. Chu, I. Goodfellow, H. B. McMahan, I. Mironov, K. Talwar, and L. Zhang. Deep learning with differential privacy. In *CCS*, pages 308–318, 2016.

[2] C. Aguilar-Melchor, J. Barrier, L. Fousse, and M.-O. Killijian. XPIR: Private information retrieval for everyone. *Proceedings on Privacy Enhancing Technologies*, 2016(2):155–174, 2016.

[3] M. Ajtai, J. Komlós, and E. Szemerédi. An $O(N \log N)$ sorting network. In *Proceedings of the Fifteenth Annual ACM Symposium on Theory of Computing*, STOC '83, pages 1–9. ACM, 1983.

[4] S. Angel, H. Chen, K. Laine, and S. Setty. PIR with compressed queries and amortized query processing.

[5] Y. Azar, A. Z. Broder, A. R. Karlin, and E. Upfal. Balanced allocations. *SICOMP*, 29(1):180–200, 1999.

[6] K. E. Batcher. Sorting networks and their applications. In *Proceedings of the April 30–May 2, 1968, Spring Joint Computer Conference*, AFIPS '68 (Spring), pages 307–314. ACM, 1968.

[7] A. Beimel, Y. Ishai, and T. Malkin. Reducing the servers computation in private information retrieval: PIR with preprocessing. In *CRYPTO*, pages 55–73, 2000.

[8] N. Borisov, G. Danezis, and I. Goldberg. DP5: A private presence service. *POPET*, 2015(2):4–24, 2015.

[9] E. Boyle, K.-M. Chung, and R. Pass. Oblivious parallel RAM and applications. In *TCC*, pages 175–204, 2016.

[10] E. Boyle, Y. Ishai, R. Pass, and M. Wootters. Can we access a database both locally and privately? In *TCC*, pages 662–693, 2017.

[11] E. Boyle and M. Naor. Is there an oblivious RAM lower bound? In *Proceedings of the 2016 ACM Conference on Innovations in Theoretical Computer Science*, pages 357–368. ACM, 2016.

[12] C. Cachin, S. Micali, and M. Stadler. Computationally private information retrieval with polylogarithmic communication. In *EUROCRYPT*, pages 402–414, 1999.

[13] R. Canetti, J. Holmgren, and S. Richelson. Towards doubly efficient private information retrieval. In *TCC*, pages 694–726, 2017.

[14] D. Cash, P. Grubbs, J. Perry, and T. Ristenpart. Leakage-abuse attacks against searchable encryption. In *CCS*, pages 668–679, 2015.

[15] T. H. Chan, K.-M. Chung, B. Maggs, and E. Shi. Foundations of differentially oblivious algorithms. Eprint 2017/1033, 2017.

[16] T.-H. H. Chan, Y. Guo, W.-K. Lin, and E. Shi. Oblivious hashing revisited, and applications to asymptotically efficient ORAM and OPRAM. In *ASIACRYPT*, pages 660–690, 2017.

[17] B. Chen, H. Lin, and S. Tessaro. Oblivious parallel RAM: improved efficiency and generic constructions. In *TCC*, pages 205–234, 2016.

[18] R. Cheng, W. Scott, B. Parno, A. Krishnamurthy, and T. Anderson. Talek: A private publish-subscribe protocol. Technical report, Technical Report. University of Washington, 2016.

[19] B. Chor, O. Goldreich, E. Kushilevitz, and M. Sudan. Private information retrieval. In *FOCS*, pages 41–50. IEEE, 1995.

[20] S. Devadas, M. van Dijk, C. W. Fletcher, L. Ren, E. Shi, and D. Wichs. Onion ORAM: A constant bandwidth blowup oblivious RAM. In *TCC*, pages 145–174, 2016.

[21] C. Dwork. A firm foundation for private data analysis. *Communications of the ACM*, 54(1):86–95, 2011.

[22] C. Dwork, F. McSherry, K. Nissim, and A. Smith. Calibrating noise to sensitivity in private data analysis. In *TCC*, pages 265–284, 2006.

[23] C. Dwork and A. Roth. The algorithmic foundations of differential privacy. *Foundations and Trends in Theoretical Computer Science*, 9(3–4):211–407, 2014.

[24] C. Gentry and Z. Ramzan. Single-database private information retrieval with constant communication rate. In *ICALP*, pages 803–815, 2005.

[25] O. Goldreich. Towards a theory of software protection and simulation by oblivious RAMs. In *STOC*, pages 182–194, 1987.

[26] O. Goldreich and R. Ostrovsky. Software protection and simulation on oblivious RAMs. *Journal of the ACM*, 43:431–473, 1996.

[27] M. T. Goodrich and M. Mitzenmacher. Privacy-preserving access of outsourced data via oblivious RAM simulation. In *ICALP*, pages 576–587, 2011.

[28] M. T. Goodrich, M. Mitzenmacher, O. Ohrimenko, and R. Tamassia. Practical oblivious storage. In *Proceedings of the second ACM conference on Data and Application Security and Privacy*, pages 13–24. ACM, 2012.

[29] M. Green, W. Ladd, and I. Miers. A protocol for privately reporting ad impressions at scale. In *CCS*, pages 1591–1601, 2016.

[30] A. Hamlin, R. Ostrovsky, M. Weiss, and D. Wichs. Private anonymous data access. ePrint Report 2018/363, 2018.

[31] M. S. Islam, M. Kuzu, and M. Kantarcioglu. Access pattern disclosure on searchable encryption: Ramification, attack and mitigation. In *NDSS*, volume 20, page 12, 2012.

[32] P. Kairouz, S. Oh, and P. Viswanath. Secure multi-party differential privacy. In *Advances in Neural Information Processing Systems 28*, pages 2008–2016. 2015.

[33] G. Kellaris, G. Kollios, K. Nissim, and A. O'Neill. Accessing data while preserving privacy. *arXiv preprint arXiv:1706.01552*, 2017.

[34] E. Kushilevitz, S. Lu, and R. Ostrovsky. On the (in) security of hash-based oblivious RAM and a new balancing scheme. In *SODA*, pages 143–156, 2012.

[35] E. Kushilevitz and R. Ostrovsky. Replication is not needed: Single database, computationally-private information retrieval. In *FOCS*, pages 364–373. IEEE, 1997.
[36] K. G. Larsen and J. B. Nielsen. Yes, there is an oblivious RAM lower bound! In *CRYPTO*, 2018.
[37] T. Mayberry, E.-O. Blass, and G. Noubir. Multi-client oblivious RAM secure against malicious servers. Cryptology ePrint Archive, Report 2015/121, 2015. https://eprint.iacr.org/2015/121.
[38] S. Mazloom and S. D. Gordon. Differentially private access patterns in secure computation. ePrint Report 2017/1016, 2017.
[39] I. Mironov, O. Pandey, O. Reingold, and S. Vadhan. Computational differential privacy. In *CRYPTO*, pages 126–142. 2009.
[40] M. Mitzenmacher. The power of two choices in randomized load balancing. *IEEE Transactions on Parallel and Distributed Systems*, 12(10):1094–1104, 2001.
[41] M. Mitzenmacher, A. W. Richa, and R. Sitaraman. The power of two random choices: A survey of techniques and results. In *Handbook of Randomized Computing*, pages 255–312, 2000.
[42] O. Ohrimenko, M. T. Goodrich, R. Tamassia, and E. Upfal. The Melbourne Shuffle: Improving oblivious storage in the cloud. In *ICALP*, pages 556–567, 2014.
[43] S. Patel, G. Persiano, M. Raykova, and K. Yeo. PanORAMa: Oblivious RAM with logarithmic overhead. In *59th IEEE Annual Symposium on Foundations of Computer Science, FOCS*, pages 871–882, 2018.
[44] S. Patel, G. Persiano, and K. Yeo. CacheShuffle: A family of oblivious shuffles. In *45th International Colloquium on Automata, Languages, and Programming (ICALP 2018)*, 2018.
[45] S. Patel, G. Persiano, and K. Yeo. Private stateful information retrieval. In *Proceedings of the 2018 ACM SIGSAC Conference on Computer and Communications Security*, CCS '18. ACM, 2018.
[46] G. Persiano and K. Yeo. Lower bounds for differentially private RAMs. Cryptology ePrint Archive, Report 2018/1051, 2018.
[47] E. Stefanov, M. Van Dijk, E. Shi, C. Fletcher, L. Ren, X. Yu, and S. Devadas. Path ORAM: an extremely simple oblivious RAM protocol. In *CCS*, pages 299–310.
[48] R. R. Toledo, G. Danezis, and I. Goldberg. Lower-cost ϵ-private information retrieval. *Proceedings on Privacy Enhancing Technologies*, 2016(4):184–201, 2016.
[49] S. Wagh, P. Cuff, and P. Mittal. Root ORAM: A tunable differentially private oblivious RAM. *arXiv:1601.03378*, 2016.
[50] A. Waksman. A permutation network. *J. ACM*, 15(1):159–163, Jan. 1968.
[51] Y. Wang, Y.-X. Wang, and A. Singh. Differentially private subspace clustering. In *Advances in Neural Information Processing Systems 28*, pages 1000–1008. 2015.

A TOOLS

In this section we briefly review some tools that we use in the design and in the analysis of our constructions.

A.1 Power of Two Choices

The *power of two choices* concept was motivated from the classical *balls and bins* problem. The balls and bins concepts considers n balls and n bins. Each of the n balls chooses a single bin independently and uniformly at random. The *load* of a bin is the number of balls that occupy the bin. It has been shown that with high probability, the load of every bin does not exceed $O(\log n/\log\log n)$ [?]. Consider the case where each of the n balls now chooses two bins independently and uniformly at random. The ball occupies the least loaded of the two chosen bins. This slight alteration ensures that with high probability, the load of each bin does not exceed $O(\log\log n)$ [40]. This result demonstrates that having two choices significantly improves bounds on the maximum load. Furthermore, it turns out that increasing the number of choices to $d \geq 3$ only improves the maximum load bounds by a constant. It is important to note that the allocation of each is chosen independently from the allocation of all other balls.

THEOREM A.1. *At any time, the load of any bin produced by the power of two choices process exceeds $O(\log\log n)$ with probability at most $1/n^{\Omega(\log\log n)}$.*

A.2 Chernoff Bound

The next theorem gives a bound on the tails of a binomial distribution that we will use to analyze our constructions. See [41] for a proof.

THEOREM A.2. *Let X_i, for $i = 1, \ldots, n$ be independent binary random variables with $\Pr[X_i = 1] = p$ and let $\mu := np$. Then for every $t \geq \mu$, it holds that*

$$\Pr\left[\sum_{i=1}^{n} X_i \geq t\right] \leq \frac{\mu^t}{t^t} \cdot e^{t-\mu}$$

and, in particular,

$$\Pr\left[\sum_{i=1}^{n} X_i \geq e \cdot \mu\right] \leq e^{-\mu}.$$

B PROOF OF THEOREM 5.1

We remind the reader that, for $i \in [N]$, $\mathsf{IR}(i)$ is the random variable of the set of blocks transferred by the server when the client wishes to access block B_i. We next compute $\Pr[\mathsf{IR}(i) = \mathcal{T}]$ for a subset $\mathcal{T}$ of K blocks.

Case 1: $B_i \in \mathcal{T}$. With probability $1-\alpha$, we know that $B_i \in \mathcal{T}$ and the remaining $K - 1$ blocks are chosen uniformly at random. On the other hand, with probability α, for $B_i \in \mathcal{T}$, we need to choose B_i as one of the K blocks that are chosen randomly. Therefore,

$$\Pr[\mathsf{IR}(i) = \mathcal{T}] = \frac{1-\alpha}{\binom{N-1}{K-1}} + \frac{\alpha}{\binom{N}{K}}.$$

Case 2: $B_i \notin \mathcal{T}$. In this case, we know with probability $(1-\alpha)$, $\mathcal{T}$ is not possible. With probability α, we need to ensure that B_i is not one of the K blocks chosen. So,

$$\Pr[\mathsf{IR}(i) = \mathcal{T}] = \frac{\alpha}{\binom{N}{K}}.$$

Let Q and Q' be any two query sequences of length L for which $d_H(Q, Q') = 1$. Since, the above algorithm is stateless, we know that its behavior depends solely on the query index. Therefore, it suffices to consider two different sequences queries of length one, $q \neq q' \in [N]$. If we choose a transcript $\mathcal{T}$ such that $B_q, B_{q'} \notin \mathcal{T}$ or $B_q, B_{q'} \in \mathcal{T}$, then we see that $\Pr[\mathsf{IR}(q) = \mathcal{T}] = \Pr[\mathsf{IR}(q') = \mathcal{T}]$. If, instead, $B_q \in \mathcal{T}$ and $B_{q'} \notin \mathcal{T}$ we have

$$\frac{\Pr[\mathsf{IR}(q) = \mathcal{T}]}{\Pr[\mathsf{IR}(q') = \mathcal{T}]} \leq \frac{(1-\alpha)\binom{N}{K}}{\alpha\binom{N-1}{K-1}} + 1 \leq \frac{(1-\alpha)N}{\alpha K} + 1 = e^{\epsilon}.$$

Since this holds for any single transcript $\mathcal{T}$, the same ratio holds for any set of transcripts completing the proof.

C LOWER BOUND FOR MULTIPLE-SERVER DP-IR

We extend the single server lower bound to the multiple server IR model with D servers and D_A adversarial servers. If $D_A = D$, then the scenario collapses to the single adversarial server case of Section 3.2. In this section, we assume that $D_A < D$ and there is always at least one honest server. For convenience, we define $t = \frac{D_A}{D}$ to be the fraction of servers corrupted by $\mathcal{A}$ where $0 < t < 1$.

The choice of adversarial servers is modeled as a challenger C with a IR protocol and an adversary $\mathcal{A}$ with the power to corrupt t fraction of servers. Using the knowledge of IR but not the internal randomness of IR, $\mathcal{A}$ picks t fraction of the D servers to corrupt. C then runs IR and $\mathcal{A}$ gets the transcript of downloads sent by IR to the t fraction of corrupted servers. We denote the adversary's transcript on query sequence Q as $\mathsf{IR}^{\mathcal{A}}(Q)$. We now proceed to present our lower bound in the multi-server model.

THEOREM C.1. *If* IR *is a (ϵ, δ)-DP D-server IR in the balls and bins model for any $\epsilon, \delta \geq 0$ and error probability $\alpha < 1 - (\delta/t)$, then* IR *performs*

$$\Omega\left(\frac{((1-\alpha)t - \delta)\cdot n}{e^{\epsilon}}\right)$$

expected operations.

PROOF. We prove our lower bound for the adversary $\mathcal{A}$ that corrupts $D_A \leq tD$ randomly and uniformly chosen servers. We know

$$\Pr[B_i \in \mathsf{IR}(i)] \geq 1 - \alpha.$$

If B_i appears in $\mathsf{IR}^{\mathcal{A}}(i)$, $\Pr[B_i \in \mathsf{IR}^{\mathcal{A}}(i)] \geq (1-\alpha)t$. The rest of the proof follows identically to the proof of Theorem 3.4. □

As a result, we show that the DP-IR scheme in [48] is optimal when t is considered constant.

D REMAINING DP-RAM PROOFS

In this section we give the proofs that were postponed from Section 6. We start by showing that the client uses $O(c)$ memory except with negligible probability for $c = \omega(\log n)$.

LEMMA D.1. *If $p \leq \frac{c}{n}$ and $c = \omega(\log n)$, then* RAM *stores at most $O(c)$ blocks in the block stash on client storage at any point in time except with negligible probability.*

PROOF. Pick any point in time. We note that each block B_i has independent probability p of being stored in the client. We let $X_i = 1$ if and only if B_i is stored on the client memory. Let X be the number of blocks stored in client memory, so $X = X_1 + \ldots + X_n$. So, we know that $\mathbb{E}[X] = \mathbb{E}[X_1 + \ldots + X_n] = pn \leq c$. By Chernoff Bounds, for any $\delta > 0$,

$$\Pr[X > (1+\delta)c] \leq \exp\left(\frac{-c\delta^2}{2+\delta}\right)$$

which is $\mathsf{negl}(n)$ when $c = \omega(\log n)$. The lemma follows, by a union bound over all points in time (that is, the length of the queries which is polynomial in n). □

PROOF OF LEMMA 6.4. The numerator is trivially upper bounded by 1 and the denominator is lower bounded by the conjunctive probability. We prove the lemma by showing that the latter is at least p/n^2. To this aim, we consider three cases depending on the values of $\mathsf{pr}(Q,j)$ and $o_{\mathsf{pr}(Q,j)}$. Note that, if $\mathsf{pr}(Q,j) \neq +\infty$, $q_{\mathsf{pr}(Q,j)} = q_j$ by definition.

Case 1: $\mathsf{pr}(Q,j) \neq +\infty$ and $o_{\mathsf{pr}(Q,j)} = q_j$.

Consider first the case $d_j = q_j$. If during the overwrite phase of query $\mathsf{pr}(Q,j)$ block B_{q_j} is stored in block stash (and this has probability p), then $\mathsf{RAM}^O_{\mathsf{pr}(Q,j)}(Q) = q_j$ with probability $1/n$. Then at the download phase of query j, B_{q_j} is found in block stash and therefore the probability that $\mathsf{RAM}^D_j(Q) = q_j$ is $1/n$. On the other hand if during the overwrite phase of query $\mathsf{pr}(Q,j)$ block B_{q_j} is not stored in block stash (this has probability $1-p$), then certainly $\mathsf{RAM}^O_{\mathsf{pr}(Q,j)}(Q) = q_j$ and, since B_{q_j} is not found in block stash at the start of the download phase of query j, $\mathsf{RAM}^D_j(Q) = q_j$ with probability 1. Altogether, we have $\Pr[\mathsf{RAM}^O_{\mathsf{pr}(Q,j)}(Q) = q_j \wedge \mathsf{RAM}^D_j(Q) = q_j] = 1-p+1/n^3 \geq 1/n^3$. If, instead, $d_j \neq q_j$ then it means that B_{q_j} must have been stored in the block stash during the overwrite phase of query $\mathsf{pr}(Q,j)$ (this has probability p) and then $\mathsf{RAM}^O_{\mathsf{pr}(Q,j)}(Q) = q_j$ with probability $1/n$. Then, since B_{q_j} is in stash at the start of the download phase of query j $\mathsf{RAM}^D_j(Q) = d_j$ with probability $1/n$. Altogether, we have $\Pr[\mathsf{RAM}^O_{\mathsf{pr}(Q,j)}(Q) = q_j \wedge \mathsf{RAM}^D_j(Q) = q_j] = p/n^2$.

Case 2. $\mathsf{pr}(Q,j) \neq +\infty$ and $o_{\mathsf{pr}(Q,j)} \neq q_j$.

If $o_{\mathsf{pr}(Q,j)} \neq q_j$ then it must be the case that, during the overwrite phase of query $\mathsf{pr}(Q,j)$, block B_{q_j} is stored in block stash (and this happens with probability p) and $o_{\mathsf{pr}(Q,j)}$ is chosen as overwrite block (and this happens with probability $1/n$). When the download phase of query j starts, block B_{q_j} is found in the stash and so the probability that d_j is selected as download blocks is $1/n$. Whence $\Pr[\mathsf{RAM}_j^D(Q) = d_j \wedge \mathsf{RAM}^O_{\mathsf{pr}(Q,j)}(Q) = o_{\mathsf{pr}(Q,j)}] = p/n^2$.

Case 3. $\mathsf{pr}(Q,j) = +\infty$. In this case, $o_{\mathsf{pr}(Q,j)} = \perp$ and B_{q_j} has not been queried before query j. Therefore, at the start of the download phase of query j, B_{q_j} is found in block stash with probability p. By using arguments similar to the ones of the previous cases, we have

$$\begin{aligned}&\Pr[\mathsf{RAM}_j^D(Q) = q_j \wedge \mathsf{RAM}^O_{\mathsf{pr}(Q,j)}(Q) = \perp]\\ &\quad = \Pr[\mathsf{RAM}_j^D(Q) = q_j] = (1-p) + p/n\end{aligned}$$

and, for $d_j \neq q_j$,

$$\begin{aligned}&\Pr[\mathsf{RAM}_j^D(Q) = d_j \wedge \mathsf{RAM}^O_{\mathsf{pr}(Q,j)}(Q) = \perp]\\ &\quad = \Pr[\mathsf{RAM}_j^D(Q) = d_j] = p/n\end{aligned}$$

which completes the proof. □

Proof of Lemma 6.5. As in the proof of the previous lemma, we upper bound the numerator by 1 and show that the denominator is at least n/p starting from the case $o_j = q_j$. If, in the overwrite phase of the j-th query, block B_{q_j} is added to the block stash (and this happens with probability $1/n$) then the same block is chosen as overwrite block with probability $1/n$. In the remaining $1-p$ probability, q_j is the overwrite block with probability 1. Therefore $\Pr[\mathsf{RAM}_j^O(Q) = q_j] = (1-p) + p/n$. If, instead, $o_j \neq q_i$, then the only case in which o_j is the overwrite block of phase j is when B_{q_j} is added to the block stash and this gives $\Pr[\mathsf{RAM}_j^O(Q) = o_j] = p/n$, for every $o_j \neq q_j$. For any $j \neq i$, $Q_j = Q'_j$ showing the first point. For any o, $\Pr[\mathsf{RAM}_i^O(Q') = o] \geq p/n$ giving the second result. □

E DP-RAM GENERALIZATION

Our proof of differential privacy of DP-RAM of Section 6 can be seen to give a more general form of differential privacy. Suppose DP-RAM stores n blocks and there exists a repertoire Σ of size $b = O(n)$. We interpret Σ as the specification of b buckets where each bucket contains exactly s blocks. Note, buckets may overlap and two different buckets may contain the same block. Our privacy proof of DP-RAM carries over to the case in which a query retrieves all blocks in a bucket. In other words, we interpret query sequences Q of length $s \cdot l$ as l subsequences each of length s taken from the Σ of size n (that is, each subsequence corresponds to a bucket). In this framework, a query sequence $Q = (q_1, \ldots, q_{s\cdot l})$ is associated with sequence $Q = (\sigma_1, \ldots, \sigma_l)$ of length l over Σ; that is,

$$Q = (\underbrace{q_1, \ldots, q_s}_{\sigma_1}, \underbrace{q_{s+1}, \ldots, q_{2\cdot s}}_{\sigma_2}, \cdots \underbrace{q_{(l-1)s+1}, \ldots, q_{l\cdot s}}_{\sigma_l}),$$

and $\sigma_1, \sigma_2, \ldots, \sigma_l \in \Sigma$ and $|\Sigma| = b = O(n)$.

The proof of Section 6 handles the case $s = 1$ in which an access sequence is a sequence of n requests taken from the repertoire $\Sigma = [n]$.

To argue the general case let us consider first the case in which the server explicitly stores the subsequences of Σ; specifically, each element of Σ is a sequence of s of the original n blocks and each is stored using storage equal to s blocks. Then an access sequence Q of length $s \cdot l$ over $[n]$ is simply an access sequence $(\sigma_1, \ldots, \sigma_l)$ of length l over Σ and, as it is easily seen, our proof still works and guarantees differential privacy with $\epsilon = \Theta(\log n)$.

This approach, unfortunately, has the drawback that the server storage grows by a factor of s. However, we observe that the blocks that constitute the subsequence of Σ need not to be explicitly stored by the server that instead can store just the n original blocks and, each time it receives a request $\sigma \in \Sigma$, the server fetches the needed blocks. Note that this transformation preserves differential privacy with $\epsilon = \Theta(\log n)$ as this property is independent of the actual layout of the parts of the individual atomic blocks (in this case the subsequences $\sigma \in \Sigma$) on which the RAM is built. The only modification required is that when retrieving or updating a bucket i, the DP-RAM must also check if the any block is stored on the client as part of another bucket $j \neq i$. If so, the block on client storage must be returned as opposed to the one from the server for retrievals. For updates, both the server copy and client copy must be updated.

F REMAINING DP-KVS PROOFS

[Proof of Lemma 7.3] We proceed by induction and we verify the base case by plugging in $i = 0$. For $i \geq 0$, we have

$$\begin{aligned}\beta_{i+1} &= \frac{e}{n} \cdot \beta_i^2 \cdot 2^{2(i+1)}\\ &= \frac{e}{n} \cdot \frac{n^2}{e^2} \cdot \left(\frac{2}{3}\right)^{2^{i+3}} \left(\frac{1}{2}\right)^{4(i+2)} \cdot 2^{2(i+1)}\\ &= \frac{n}{e} \cdot \left(\frac{2}{3}\right)^{2^{i+3}} \left(\frac{1}{2}\right)^{4(i+2)-2(i+1)}\\ &= \frac{n}{e} \cdot \left(\frac{2}{3}\right)^{2^{i+3}} \left(\frac{1}{2}\right)^{2(i+3)}.\end{aligned}$$

G DP-IR PSEUDOCODE

We present the pseudocode for our DP-IR scheme of Section 5.

Algorithm 1 DP-IR.Query: read a block

```
Input: i, ε, α
  Set 𝒯 = ∅.        {initializing the download set}
  Pick random number r ∈ [0, 1].
  if r > α then
    𝒯 ← 𝒯 ∪ {i}.
  end if
  Set K = ⌈(1 − α)N/(e^ε − 1)⌉.
  while |𝒯| < K do
    Pick j uniformly at random from [N] \ 𝒯.
    𝒯 ← 𝒯 ∪ {j}.
  end while
  Send 𝒯 to server and receive {B_j}_{j∈𝒯} from server.
  if r > α then
    return B_i.
  else
    return ⊥.
  end if
```

H DP-RAM PSEUDOCODE

We present the pseudocode for the algorithm in Section 6.

Algorithm 2 DP-RAMSetup: initialize client and server storage

```
Input: 1^λ, B_1, ..., B_N
  Randomly select K ← {0, 1}^λ.
  Initialize array A of size N on server.
  Initialize hash table bStash on client.
  for i ← 1, ..., N do
    Set A[i] ← Enc(K, B_i).
    Pick r uniformly at random from [N].
    if r ≤ C then
      Set bStash[i] ← B_i.
    end if
  end for
```

Algorithm 3 DP-RAM.Query: reading and writing a data block

```
Input: i, op, B_new
  {Download Phase}
  if i ∈ bStash then
    Pick d uniformly at random from [N].
    Download A[d] and discard.
    Set B ← bStash[i] and remove i from bStash.
  else
    Set d ← i.
    Download A[d].
    Set B ← Dec(K, A[d]).
  end if

  if op = write then
    Set B ← B_new.
  end if

  {Overwrite Phase}
  Draw r uniformly at random from [N].
  if r ≤ C then
    Set bStash[i] ← B.
    Pick o uniformly at random from [N].
    Download A[o], decrypt it and re-encrypt it obtaing ct.

    Upload ct as A[o].
  else
    Set o = i.
    Download A[o] and discard it.
    Set ct ← Enc(K, B).
    Upload ct as A[o].
  end if
```

Tight Trade-offs for the Maximum k-Coverage Problem in the General Streaming Model

Piotr Indyk
indyk@mit.edu
CSAIL, MIT

Ali Vakilian
vakilian@mit.edu
CSAIL, MIT

ABSTRACT

We study the *maximum k-coverage* problem in the general *edge-arrival* streaming model: given a collection of m sets $\mathcal{F}$, each subset of a ground set of elements $\mathcal{U}$ of size n, the task is to find k sets whose coverage is maximized. The sets are specified as a sequence of (element, set) pairs in an *arbitrary* order. Our main result is a *tight* (up to polylogarithmic factors) trade-off between the space complexity and the approximation factor $\alpha \in (1/(1-1/e), \widetilde{\Omega}(\sqrt{m})]$ of any single-pass streaming algorithm that estimates the maximum coverage size. Specifically, we show that the optimal space bound is $\widetilde{\Theta}(m/\alpha^2)$. Moreover, we design a single-pass algorithm that reports an α-approximate solution in $\widetilde{O}(m/\alpha^2 + k)$ space.[1]

Our algorithm heavily exploits data stream sketching techniques, which could lead to further connections between vector sketching methods and streaming algorithms for combinatorial optimization tasks.

CCS CONCEPTS

• **Theory of computation → Streaming models**; **Sketching and sampling**; Lower bounds and information complexity.

KEYWORDS

max k-cover, sketching/streaming, heavy hitters

ACM Reference Format:

Piotr Indyk and Ali Vakilian. 2019. Tight Trade-offs for the Maximum k-Coverage Problem in the General Streaming Model. In *38th ACM SIGMOD-SIGACT-SIGAI Symposium on Principles of Database Systems (PODS '19), June 30–July 5, 2019, Amsterdam, Netherlands.* ACM, New York, NY, USA, 19 pages. https://doi.org/10.1145/3294052.3319691

[1] $\widetilde{O}, \widetilde{\Omega}, \widetilde{\Theta}$ suppress polylog factors.

PODS '19, June 30–July 5, 2019, Amsterdam, Netherlands

ACM ISBN 978-1-4503-6227-6/19/06...$15.00
https://doi.org/10.1145/3294052.3319691

1 INTRODUCTION

Maximum k-coverage (Max k-Cover) is a classic problem in combinatorial optimization. Given a ground set $\mathcal{U}$ of n elements, a family of m sets $\mathcal{F}$ (each is a subset of $\mathcal{U}$), and a parameter k, the goal is to select k sets in $\mathcal{F}$ whose union has the largest cardinality. Max k-Cover is an important problem in submodular maximization, with applications in many areas, including operations research, machine learning, information retrieval and data mining [1, 19, 37].

The classic greedy algorithm for this problem [35] guarantees an approximation ratio of $1/(1-1/e)$, which is known to be tight under $P \neq NP$ [23]. Unfortunately, the standard greedy algorithm does not scale very well to massive data sets [19]. This has led to considerable interest in developing maximum coverage algorithms tailored to modern architectures specifically designed for massive data processing. In particular [37] gave the first algorithm for the problem in the data streaming model, where the algorithm is required to make a single pass over the input $\mathcal{F}$ while using a sub-linear amount of memory. Since then, there has been a large body of work designing space-efficient streaming algorithms for maximum coverage [6, 12, 33, 34], as well as its dual variant, *set cover* [6, 7, 12, 17, 21, 22, 26–28].

The initial algorithms were developed in the *set arrival* model, where the input sets are listed contiguously. This restriction is natural from the perspective of submodular optimization, but limits the applicability of the algorithms[2]. Avoiding this limitation can be difficult, as streaming algorithms can no longer operate on sets as "unit objects". As a result, the first maximum coverage algorithm for the general *edge arrival* model, where pairs of (set, element) can arrive in arbitrary order, have been developed recently. In particular [12] presented a one-pass algorithm with space linear in m and constant approximation factor[3]. We remark that many of

[2] For example, consider a situation where the sets correspond to neighborhoods of vertices in a directed graph. Depending on the input representation, for each vertex, either the ingoing edges or the outgoing edges might be placed non-contiguously.

[3] Note that in [12] m denotes the number of elements and n denotes the number of sets.

the prior bounds (both upper and lower bounds) on set cover and max k-cover problems in set-arrival streams also work in edge arrival streams (e.g. [6, 7, 21, 26, 27, 34]). However, the design of efficient streaming algorithms for the coverage problems on edge arrival streams was first studied explicitly in [12].

A particularly interesting line of research in set arrival streaming set cover and max k-cover is to design efficient algorithms that only use $\widetilde{O}(n)$ space [9, 17, 22, 34, 37]. Previous work have shown that we can adopt the existing greedy algorithm of max k-cover to achieve constant factor approximation in $\widetilde{O}(n)$ space [9, 37] (which later improved to $\widetilde{O}(k)$ by [34]). However, the complexity of the problem in the "low space" regime is very different in edge-arrival streams: [12] showed that as long as the approximation factor is a constant, any algorithm must use $\Omega(m)$ space. Still, our understanding of approximation/space trade-offs in the general case is far from complete. Table 1 summarizes the known results.

Other related work. Another important related question in this area is to design a "low-approximation" (i.e., better than the 2-approximation guarantee of the greedy approach) streaming algorithm for the max k-cover problem in the *set arrival* setting. Recently, Norouzi-Fard et al. [36] presented the first streaming algorithm that improves upon 2-approximation guarantee of greedy approach on *random arrival* streams. Very recently, Agrawal et al. [2] achieved an almost $1/(1-1/e)$-approximation in $\widetilde{O}(n)$ space which is essentially the optimal bound [34][4]. Still it is an important question to design such algorithms on adversarial order streams. We also remark that the algorithms of [2, 36] do not work on *edge arrival* streams.

In many scenarios, space is the most critical factor, and thus the question becomes: what approximation guarantees are possible within the given space bounds? This question has been studied before in the context of *set cover* in set arrival streams (e.g. [17, 22]), leading to poly(n, m)-factor approximation algorithms.

Our results. In this paper, we complement the work of [12] by designing space-efficient algorithms for super-constant approximation factors α. In fact, we show a tight (up to polylogarithmic factors) trade-off between the two: the optimal space bound is $\widetilde{O}(\frac{m}{\alpha^2})$ for estimating the maximum coverage value, and $\widetilde{O}(\frac{m}{\alpha^2}+k)$ for reporting an approximately optimal solution[5]. The approximation factor α can take any value in $(1/(1-1/e), \widetilde{\Omega}(\sqrt{m})]$.

Our techniques. In the edge arrival model, elements of each set can arrive irregularly and out of order. This necessitates the use of methods that aggregate the information about the input sets, or their coverage. In particular, distinct element sketches were used both in [12] (implicitly) and [34] (explicitly). In this paper we expand the use of sketching toolkit. Specifically, in addition to distinct element estimation [5, 11, 13, 30, 31], we also need algorithms for *heavy hitters* with respect to the L_2 norm [14, 15, 18, 39], as well as a frequency-based partitioning of elements, and detecting sets that "substantially contribute" to the solution [29]. Application of vector-sketching techniques (e.g. L_p-sampling/estimation and heavy hitters) in graph streaming settings have been studied extensively (e.g. [3, 4, 8, 20, 25, 32]). We believe that our algorithms can lead to further connections between vector sketching methods and streaming algorithms for the coverage problems.

Lower bound. Our algorithm was inspired by the lower bound. Specifically, it was previously shown by [12] that approximating Max k-Cover by a factor better than 2 requires $\Omega(m)$ space. Similar approach works for larger values of α, by showing a reduction from the α-player *set disjointess* problem ($\mathsf{DSJ}_{[m]}$) with *unique intersection* guarantee (i.e., either players' sets are disjoint or there is a unique item that appears in all sets) to the task of α-approximating Max k-Cover.

The specific hard instances in the aforementioned lower bound can be distinguished in the streaming model using space $O(\frac{m}{\alpha^2})$. To this end, we compute an α-approximation to the L_∞-norm of a vector v that, for each element e, counts the number of sets e belongs to. This problem can be solved in $O(\frac{m}{\alpha^2})$ space, by using L_2-norm sketches [5]. This suggests that it might be possible to solve the *general* Max k-Cover using sketching techniques as well.

Upper bound. We start our algorithm with a "coverage boosting" *universe reduction* technique which constructs a reduced size instance (i.e. with reduced ground set) whose optimal k-cover has constant fraction coverage (see Section 3.1). This step is particularly important as the space complexity of the existing methods for Max k-Cover is proportional to the reciprocal of the fraction of covered elements in an optimal solution.

Once we have a constant fraction coverage guarantee, our algorithm exploits three different approaches so that on any instance, at least one of them reports a "good" approximate solution.

[4]Both [2, 36] study the more general problem of submodular maximization and their results are stated with different notation and assuming *oracle* access. Here, we state their guarantees for max cover on set arrival streams

[5]We note that similar trade-offs were previously obtained for the set cover problem, as [7] showed a $\Theta(mn/\alpha^2)$ bound for estimation, and a $\Theta(mn/\alpha)$ bound for reporting. Interestingly, the $1/\alpha^2$ vs. $1/\alpha$ gap does not occur for our problem.

Estimation/ Reporting	Set/Edge Arrival	Approximation	Space Upper Bound	Space Lower Bound
Estimation	Set Arrival	$1/(1-\varepsilon)$	–	$\widetilde{\Omega}(\frac{m}{\varepsilon^2})$[6]
Estimation	Set Arrival	$1/(1-1/e-\varepsilon)$	–	$\Omega(\frac{m}{k^2})$[34]
Reporting	Edge Arrival	$1/(1-1/e-\varepsilon)^a$	$\widetilde{O}(\frac{m}{\varepsilon^3})$[12], $\widetilde{O}(\frac{m}{\varepsilon^2})$[34]	–
Reporting	Set Arrival	4 [37], 2 [9]^b	$\widetilde{O}(n)$	–
Reporting	Set Arrival	$2+\varepsilon$	$\widetilde{O}(\frac{k}{\varepsilon^3})$[34]	–
Estimation	Edge Arrival	α	$\widetilde{O}(\frac{m}{\alpha^2})$ **[here]**	$\Omega(\frac{m}{\alpha^2})$ **[here]**,[12]
Reporting	Edge Arrival	α	$\widetilde{O}(\frac{m}{\alpha^2}+k)$ **[here]**	–

Table 1: The summary of known results on the complexity of single-pass streaming algorithms of Max k-Cover.

^{a}Allowing exponential runtime, the approximation factor becomes $\frac{1}{1-\varepsilon}$ which matches the information theoretic lower bound of [6] up to a factor of $\frac{1}{\varepsilon}$.
^{b}Their result works for the general submodular maximization assuming access to a value oracle that given a collection of sets computes their coverage. A careful adoption of their result to Max k-Cover (without the value oracle) uses $\widetilde{O}(n)$ space.

Multi-layered set sampling. By extending the *set sampling* approach (see Section 2.1) and trying a larger range of sampling rate, $[\frac{k}{m}, \frac{\alpha k}{m}]$, we design a *smooth* variant of set sampling: a collection of sets sampled uniformly and independently[6] at rate $\widetilde{O}(\frac{\beta k}{m})$ w.h.p., covers all elements that appear in at least $\frac{m}{\beta k}$ sets. Besides expanding the application of set sampling in finding α-approximate k-cover, this smooth variant implies more structure on the number of elements in a wider range of frequency levels which is specifically crucial in our approach for detecting sets with "low contribution".

Unlike the set sampling based technique whose success in finding an α-approximate k-cover *only* depends on the structure of the set system, the performance of the next two approaches rely on the structure of optimal solutions as well: whether the majority of the coverage (in a specific optimal k-cover) is due to (few) "large" sets or, (many) "small" sets.

Heavy hitters and contributing frequencies. The high level idea in this approach is that *if in an optimal solution, a sufficiently*[7] *small number of sets cover the majority of the elements (covered by the optimal solution), it is enough to find a single large set*, which naturally hints the use of ideas related to heavy hitters. For the sake of efficiency (in space complexity), we *randomly* partition sets into *supersets* of size at most k. However, once we merge sets into a single superset, we can no longer distinguish between their coverage and their total size. Since we combine sets at random, if all elements have "low" frequency in the set system, then the gap between the total size of all sets in a superset and their coverage is just $\widetilde{O}(1)$. This observation implies that if there is no "common" element in the set system, then we can use the total size of the sets in a superset as an estimate of its coverage size. To get around the case with (many) "common" elements, we show that performing the heavy hitter based algorithm on a sampled set of elements will find a sufficiently large superset as desired (see Section B).

Detecting k-covers with many small sets. Finally, we address the case in which an optimal k-cover consists of many "small" sets. In this case, we can show that after subsampling sets uniformly with probability $1/\alpha$, a $(\frac{k}{\alpha})$-cover with coverage at least $\Theta(1/\alpha)$ times the coverage of an optimal k-cover survives. This sampling method will save us a factor of α in the memory usage of the algorithm. Further, by exploiting the structural property guaranteed due to the multi-layered set sampling[8], we can show that element sampling can save another factor of α in the space complexity once applied to find a constant factor approximate Max $(\frac{k}{\alpha})$-Cover of the subsampled sets.

2 PRELIMINARIES AND NOTATIONS

2.1 Sampling Methods for Max k-Cover

Here we describe two sampling methods that have been used widely in the design of streaming algorithms for Max k-Cover and Set Cover [6, 7, 12, 21, 26, 27, 33, 34]. For a collection of sets Q, we define $C(Q)$ to denote the set of elements that are covered by Q; $C(Q) := \bigcup_{S\in Q} S$. Moreover, we denote an optimal k-cover of $(\mathcal{U}, \mathcal{F})$ by OPT.

Set Sampling. Roughly speaking, it says that by selecting sets *uniformly at random*, with high probability, all elements that appear in large number of sets will be covered.

Definition 2.1 (λ-common element). An element $e \in \mathcal{U}$ is called *λ-common* if it appears in at least $c \cdot m \cdot \text{polylog}(m, n)/\lambda$

[6]In fact, $O(\log mn)$-wise independent is sufficient for all applications in this paper.
[7]Depending on how large our desired approximation factor α is.
[8]If the multi-layered set sampling fails to return an α-approximate estimate, we can infer strong conditions on the maximum number of elements that belong to each frequency level in $[\frac{m}{k}, \frac{m}{\alpha k}]$.

sets in $\mathcal{F}$. Furthermore, We denote the set of λ-common elements by $\mathcal{U}_{\lambda}^{\mathrm{cmn}}$.

Observation 2.2. *For any $0 \le \lambda_1 \le \lambda_2$, $\mathcal{U}_{\lambda_1}^{\mathrm{cmn}} \subseteq \mathcal{U}_{\lambda_2}^{\mathrm{cmn}}$.*

Lemma 2.3 (Set Sampling [21]). *Consider a set system $(\mathcal{U}, \mathcal{F})$ and let $\mathcal{F}^{\mathrm{rnd}} \subseteq \mathcal{F}$ be a collection of sets such that each set S is picked in $\mathcal{F}^{\mathrm{rnd}}$ with probability $\frac{\lambda}{m}$. With high probability, $\mathcal{F}^{\mathrm{rnd}}$ covers all elements that appear in $\widetilde{\Omega}(m/\lambda)$ sets (i.e. λ-common elements).*

Observation 2.4. *Let Q be a subset of $\mathcal{F}$ of size (βk). Then, in any partitioning of Q into β groups, there exists one group with coverage at least $|C(Q)|/\beta$. In particular, an optimal k-cover in Q covers at least $|C(Q)|/\beta$.*

This simple observation is in particular interesting because it relates the task of α-approximating Max k-Cover to solving instances of Max (βk)-Cover where $\beta \le \alpha$.

Element Sampling for Max k-Cover. This sampling method shows that if we sample elements of $\mathcal{U}$ uniformly with a large enough rate (i.e. proportional to $(k|\mathcal{U}|)/|C(\mathrm{OPT})|$), then a constant factor approximate k-cover over the sampled elements w.h.p., is a constant factor approximate solution of the original instance.

Lemma 2.5 (Element Sampling Lemma [21, 33]). *Consider an instance of* Max k-Cover$(\mathcal{U}, \mathcal{F})$. *Let's assume that an optimal k-cover of $(\mathcal{U}, \mathcal{F})$ covers $(1/\eta)$-fraction of $\mathcal{U}$. Let $\mathcal{L} \subset \mathcal{U}$ be a set of elements of size $\widetilde{\Theta}(\eta k)$ picked uniformly at random. Then, with high probability, a $\Theta(1)$-approximate k-cover of $(\mathcal{L}, \mathcal{F})$ is a $\Theta(1)$-approximate k-cover of $(\mathcal{U}, \mathcal{F})$.*

2.2 HeavyHitters and Contributing Classes

Suppose that a sequence of items $p_1, \cdots, p_T$ arrive in a data stream where for each $j \le T$, $p_j \in [m]$. We can think of the stream as a sequence of (insertion only) updates on an initially zero vector $\vec{a}$ such that upon arrival of p_j in the stream, $\vec{a}[j] \leftarrow \vec{a}[j] + 1$. Here, we review the notion of F_2-*heavy hitter* and *contributing coordinates* that are used in our algorithm for approximating Max k-Cover.

Definition 2.6 (F_2-HeavyHitters). Given an m-dimensional vector $\vec{a}$, an item j (corresponding to $\vec{a}[j]$) is a ϕ-HeavyHitter of $F_2(\vec{a})$, if $\vec{a}[j]^2 \ge \phi \cdot F_2(\vec{a}) = \phi \cdot \sum_{j \in [m]} \vec{a}[j]^2$. Intuitively, the set of items that appear frequently in the stream are the heavy hitters.

We conceptually partition coordinates of $\vec{a}$ into classes

$$R_i = \{j \mid 2^{i-1} < \vec{a}[j] \le 2^i\}.$$

Definition 2.7 (γ-contributing coordinates). A class of coordinates R_t is γ-**contributing** if $|R_t| \cdot 2^{2t} \ge \gamma F_2(\vec{a}) = \gamma \sum_{j \in [m]} \vec{a}[j]^2$.

Let R_{t^*} be a γ-contributing class and let n_{t^*} denote the size of R_{t^*}; $n_{t^*} = |R_{t^*}|$. Further, let's assume that $i^* = \lceil \log n_{t^*} \rceil$; $2^{i^*-1} < n_{t^*} \le 2^{i^*}$. Let $h : [m] \to [(12 m \log m)/2^{i^*}]$ be a function chosen uniformly at random from a family of $\Theta(\log(mn))$-wise independent hash functions. We define $\mathcal{S}_{i^*}$ as a *sampled substream* of the input stream with rate $1/2^{i^*}$. More precisely, $\mathcal{S}_{i^*}$ only contains the updates corresponding to the coordinates $\mathcal{F}_{i^*} = \{j \mid h(j) = 1\}$ that are mapped to one under h. Next, we show that the survived coordinates of R_{t^*} ($j \in R_{t^*}$) in $\vec{a}_{i^*}$, which is the vector $\vec{a}$ restricted to the items in $\mathcal{F}_{i^*}$, are $\widetilde{\Omega}(\gamma)$-HeavyHitters of $F_2(\vec{a}_{i^*})$; $\vec{a}[j]^2 \ge \widetilde{\Omega}(\gamma) \cdot F_2(\vec{a}_{i^*})$. Roughly speaking, if we subsample the stream so that only polylog(m) coordinates of R_{t^*} survive, then with high probability these coordinates are $\widetilde{\Omega}(\gamma)$-HeavyHitters of the sampled substream.

Claim 2.8. *With probability at least $1 - m^{-1}$, the number of survived coordinates in the sampled substream $\mathcal{S}_{i^*}$ is at least $(6m \log m)/2^{i^*}$.*

Lemma 2.9. *With probability at least $1 - 2/(9 \log^2 n \log^c m)$, a coordinate $j \in R_{t^*}$ is a $(\frac{\gamma}{162 \log^2 n \log^{c+1} m})$-HeavyHitter in the sampled substream $\mathcal{S}_{t^*}$.*

Next, we can use the exiting algorithms for F_2-HeavyHitters to complete this section.

Theorem 2.10 (F_2-heavy hitters algorithm [14, 15, 18, 39]). *Let's assume that $\vec{a}$ is a m-dimensional vector initialized to zero. Let $\mathcal{S}$ be a stream of items $p_1, \cdots, p_T$ where for each $j \in [T]$, $p_j \in [m]$. Then, there is a single pass algorithm F_2-*HeavyHitter *that uses $\widetilde{O}(1/\gamma)$ space and with high probability returns all coordinates i such that $\vec{a}[i]^2 \ge \gamma F_2(\vec{a})$. In addition, it returns $(1 \pm \frac{1}{2})$-approximate values of these coordinates.*

Finally, there exists an algorithm that with probability at least $1 - 2/(9 \log n \log^c m)$, finds at least one coordinate in each γ-contributing class of $\vec{a}$ using $\widetilde{O}(1/\gamma)$ space.

Theorem 2.11 (γ-contributing algorithm [29]). *Let's assume that $\vec{a}$ is an m-dimensional vector initialized to zero. Let $\mathcal{S}$ be a stream of items $p_1, \cdots, p_T$ where for each $j \in [T]$, $p_j \in [m]$. Moreover, let's assume no item in $\mathcal{S}$ has frequency more than n. There exists a single pass algorithm F_2-*Contributing *that uses $\widetilde{O}(1/\gamma)$ space and with probability at least $1 - 2/(9 \log n \log^c m)$ returns a coordinate i from each γ-contributing class. In addition, it returns $(1 \pm \frac{1}{2})$-approximate frequency of these coordinates.*

Proof. There are at most $\log n$ (the total number of classes) γ-contributing classes for $\vec{a}$ and for each γ-contributing class R_t, by Lemma 2.9, with probability at least $1 - 2/(9 \log^2 n \log^c m)$, a coordinate in R_t will be a $\widetilde{\Omega}(\gamma)$-HeavyHitter of $F_2(\vec{a}_{i^*})$ (where $i^* = \lceil \log(n_t) \rceil$). By trying all values of $i^* \in [\log n]$, with probability at least

$$1 - \log n(\frac{2}{9\log^2 n \log^c m}) \geq 1 - \frac{2}{9\log n \log^c m}$$

F_2-CONTRIBUTING algorithm outputs a coordinate from each γ-contributing class. □

```
F2-CONTRIBUTING(γ, r):
for each n_t ∈ {2^i | i ∈ [log r]} do in parallel
    ▷ n_t : #coordinates in a γ-contributing class
    let φ ← (γ / (432 log n log^{c+1} m))  ▷ φ-HeavyHitter
    let HH be a instance of F2-HEAVYHITTER(φ)
    let ρ ← (12 log m)/2^i  ▷ sample rate
    pick h : [m] → [m/ρ] from a family of
        Θ(log(mn))-wise independent hash functions
    for each i in the data stream
        if h(i) = 1 then feed i to HH
    ▷ heavy coordinates with their approximate freq.
    return output of HH
```

2.3 L_0-Estimation

Norm estimation is one of the fundamental problems in the area of streaming algorithms where we are given an m-dimensional vector $\vec{a}$ which is initialized to zero and a sequence of items $p_1, \cdots, p_T$ (updates for the vector $\vec{a}$) where for each $j \in [T]$, $p_j \in [m]$ arrive in a data stream. In the well-studied task L_0-estimation (also known as Count-distinct problem), the goal is to output a $(1 \pm \varepsilon)$-estimate of the number of distinct elements (i.e., $L_0(\vec{a}) := |\{i \mid \vec{a}[i] \neq 0\}|$) after reading the whole stream.

THEOREM 2.12 (L_0-ESTIMATION [5, 11, 13, 30, 31]). *Let's assume that $\vec{a}$ is an m-dimensional vector initialized to zero. Let $\mathcal{S}$ be a stream of items $p_1, \cdots, p_T$ where for each $j \in [T]$, $i_j \in [m]$. There exists a single pass algorithm that returns a $(1 \pm 1/2)$-approximation of $L_0(\vec{a})$ and uses $\widetilde{O}(1)$ space.*

3 ESTIMATING SIZE OF MAXIMUM COVERAGE

In this section, we describe the outline of our single-pass algorithm that approximates the coverage size of an optimal k-cover of $(\mathcal{U}, \mathcal{F})$ within a factor of α using $\widetilde{O}(m/\alpha^2)$ space in *arbitrary order* edge arrival streams. The input to our algorithm is $k, \alpha, n = |\mathcal{U}|$ and $m = |\mathcal{F}|$. In high level, we perform three different subroutines in parallel and show that for any given Max k-Cover instance, at least one of the subroutines estimates the optimal coverage size within the desired factor in the promised space.

THEOREM 3.1. *For any $\alpha \in [\widetilde{O}(1), \widetilde{\Omega}(\sqrt{m})]$, the single-pass algorithm* ESTIMATEMAXCOVER *uses $\widetilde{O}(m/\alpha^2)$ space and with probability at least 3/4 computes the* **size of an optimal coverage** *of* Max k-Cover$(\mathcal{U}, \mathcal{F})$ *within a factor of α in edge-arrival streams.*

Note that Theorem 3.1 together with the $O(1)$-approximation algorithms of [12, 34] that use $\widetilde{O}(m)$ space, imply that for any $\alpha \in (1/(1-1/e), \widetilde{\Omega}(\sqrt{m})]$, there exists a single-pass streaming algorithm that computes an α-approximation of the optimal coverage size of Max k-Cover$(\mathcal{U}, \mathcal{F})$ in $\widetilde{O}(\frac{m}{\alpha^2})$ space. In the longer version of the paper, we extend our approach further to achieve a single pass algorithm that computes an α-approximate k-cover in $\widetilde{O}(\frac{m}{\alpha^2} + k)$ space.

THEOREM 3.2. *For any $\alpha \in [\widetilde{O}(1), \widetilde{\Omega}(\sqrt{m})]$, there exists a single-pass algorithm that uses $\widetilde{O}(\frac{m}{\alpha^2} + k)$ space and with probability at least 3/4 returns an α-***approximate solution** *of* Max k-Cover *$(\mathcal{U}, \mathcal{F})$ in edge-arrival streams.*

Finally, we complement our upper bounds with a matching lower bound in Section 5.

THEOREM 3.3. *Any single pass (possibly randomized) algorithm on edge-arrival streams that α-approximates the optimal coverage size of* Max k-Cover *requires $\Omega(\frac{m}{\alpha^2})$ space.*

As a first step, we provide a mapping from the ground set $\mathcal{U}$ to a small size set of *pseudo-elements* such that the optimal k-cover on the pseudo-elements covers a constant fraction of the pseudo-elements. This reduction is in particular useful for bounding the number of required samples in methods such as element sampling.

3.1 Universe Reduction

In this section we show that in order to solve Max k-Cover on *edge-arrival* streams, it suffices to solve the instances whose optimal coverage size are at least a constant fraction of $|\mathcal{U}|$. This reduction is particularly important as the space complexity of the existing methods for Max k-Cover is proportional to the reciprocal of the fraction of covered elements in an optimal solution. To this end, suppose that we have an algorithm $\mathcal{A}$ for Max k-Cover in edge-arrival streams with the following properties:

Definition 3.4 ((α, δ, η)-oracle for Max k-Cover*).* An algorithm $\mathcal{A}$ is an (α, δ, η)*-oracle* for Max k-Cover if it satisfies the following properties (α denotes the approximation guarantee, δ denotes the failure probability and η is the promised coverage of an optimal k-cover):

- If the optimal coverage size of Max k-Cover$(\mathcal{U}, \mathcal{F})$ is at least $|\mathcal{U}|/\eta$, then with probability at least $1 - \delta$, $\mathcal{A}$ returns an α-approximation of the optimal coverage size.
- If $\mathcal{A}$ returns z, then an optimal solution of Max k-Cover $(\mathcal{U}, \mathcal{F})$ with high probability, has coverage at least z.

EstimateMaxCover (as in Figure 1) is an $\widetilde{O}(\alpha)$-approximation algorithm for Max k-Cover on edge arrival streams that invokes (α, δ, η)-oracles for Max k-Cover.

```
EstimateMaxCover(k, α):
if kα ≥ m then do return n/α   ▷ trivial bound
▷ different guesses of optimal coverage size
for each z ∈ {2^i | i ∈ [log n]} do in parallel
  est_z ← 0
  repeat log(1/δ) times   ▷ boosting success probability
     pick h : U → [z] from a family of 4-wise
          independent hash functions.
     for each (S, e) in the data stream
          feed (S, h(e)) to (α, δ, η)-oracle A   ▷ S_h
     est_z ← max(output of A on S_h, est_z)
return max{est_z | est_z ≥ z/(4α)}
```

Figure 1: A single-pass algorithm that computes an $\widetilde{O}(\alpha)$-approximation of the optimal coverage size of Max k-Cover.

As in EstimateMaxCover, let $h : \mathcal{U} \to [z]$ be a hash function picked uniformly at random from a family of 4-wise independent hash functions mapping the ground set $\mathcal{U}$ onto *pseudo-elements* $\mathcal{V} = \{1, \cdots, z\}$. Furthermore, for a subset of elements S, we define $h(S) := \bigcup_{e \in S} h(e)$.

Lemma 3.5. *Let $h : \mathcal{U} \to [z]$ be a hash function picked uniformly at random from a family of 4-wise independent hash functions where $z \geq 32$. Further, let S be a subset of $\mathcal{U}$ of size at least z. Then, with probability at least $3/4$, $|h(S)| \geq z/4$.*

Proof. For any pair of elements $e_i, e_j \in S$, let $X_{i,j}$ be a random variable which is *one* if $h(e_i) = h(e_j)$ (i.e. they collide) and *zero* otherwise. Let $X := \sum_{e_i, e_j \in S} X_{i,j}$ denote the the total number of collision among the elements of S under h.

First, we show that if $X \leq |S|^2/\gamma$, then $|h(S)| \geq \gamma/4$. Let's assume $h(S) = \{v_1, \cdots, v_q\}$ and let n_i denote the number of elements in S that are mapped to v_i by h. Then, the total number of collision, X, is

$$X = \sum_{i=1}^{q} \binom{n_i}{2} \geq \sum_{i=1}^{q} (\frac{n_i}{2})^2 \geq \frac{1}{4} \cdot q \cdot (\frac{|S|}{q})^2 = \frac{|S|^2}{4q}.$$

This implies that $q = |h(S)| \geq \gamma/4$. Using this observation, it only remains to show that with probability at least $3/4$, $|X| \leq |S|^2/z$. Since h is selected from a family of 4-wise independent hash functions, $\{X_{i,j}\}_{e_i, e_j \in S}$ are *pairwise independent*. Hence,

$$\mathbf{E}[X] = \sum_{e_i, e_j \in S} \mathbf{E}[X_{i,j}] = \binom{|S|}{2} \cdot (\frac{1}{z}) \leq \frac{|S|^2}{2z},$$

$$\mathbf{Var}[X] = \sum_{e_i, e_j \in S} \mathbf{Var}[X_{i,j}] = \binom{|S|}{2} \cdot (\frac{1}{z} - \frac{1}{z^2}) \geq \frac{z}{8}.$$

Applying Chebyshev's inequality,

$$\Pr(X > |S|^2/z) \leq \Pr(X > \mathbf{E}[X] + \mathbf{Var}[X]) \leq \frac{1}{\mathbf{Var}[X]} \leq \frac{8}{z} \leq \frac{1}{4}.$$

Hence, with probability at least $3/4$, $X \leq |S|^2/z$ which implies that with probability at least $3/4$, $|h(S)| \geq z/4$. □

Theorem 3.6. *Suppose that there exists a (α, δ, η)-oracle for* Max k-Cover *on edge-arrival streams that uses $f(m, \alpha)$ space with $\eta \geq 4$ where m denotes the number of sets in the input. Then, EstimateMaxCover is an $O(\alpha)$-approximation algorithm for* Max k-Cover *with failure probability at most $4\delta \log n$ that uses $\widetilde{O}(f(m, \alpha))$ space on edge-arrival streams.*

Proof. Let OPT denote an optimal solution of Max k-Cover on $(\mathcal{U}, \mathcal{F})$. First, we show that with high probability, EstimateMaxCover returns $\Omega(|C(\text{OPT})|/\alpha)$. Note that for each guess on the optimal coverage size $z \leq |C(\text{OPT})|$, by Lemma 3.5, the probability that in none of $\log(1/\delta)$ iterations $|h(C(\text{OPT}))| > |C(\text{OPT})|/4$ is at most δ (i.e., none of the iterations preserve the optimal coverage size up to a factor of 4). Moreover, by the guarantee of (α, δ, η)-oracles for Max k-Cover, each run of $\mathcal{A}$ fails with probability at most δ. Thus, by an application of union bound, with probability at least $1 - 2\delta \log n$, est_z is at least $z/(4\alpha)$ for all $z \leq |C(\text{OPT})|$. This in particular implies that the solution returned by EstimateMaxCover is at least $|C(\text{OPT})|/(8\alpha)$. Moreover, since the coverage of a k-cover never increases after applying the "universe reduction" step (i.e. for each $S \subseteq \mathcal{U}$, $|h(C(S))| \leq |S|$) and the estimate returned by the (α, δ, η)-oracle $\mathcal{A}$ is with high probability less than the optimal coverage size, the output of EstimateMaxCover is in $[|C(\text{OPT})|/(8\alpha), |C(\text{OPT})|]$ with probability at least $1 - 4\delta \log n$.

Finally, since EstimateMaxCover runs $\log n \log(\frac{1}{\delta})$ instances of $\mathcal{A}$ with parameter (α, δ, η) in parallel and each instance has m sets, the total space of EstimateMaxCover is $\widetilde{O}(f(m, \alpha))$. □

The *universe reduction* step basically enables us to only focus on the instances of Max k-Cover in which the optimal solution covers a constant fraction of the ground set, namely at least $|\mathcal{U}|/4$ elements. Next, in Section 4, we design an $\widetilde{O}(m/\alpha)$-space (α, δ, η)-oracle for Max k-Cover with $\alpha = \widetilde{\Omega}(1)$, $\eta \geq 4$ and $\delta = O(1/\log n)$, which together with Theorem 3.6 complete the proof of Theorem 3.1. Our (α, δ, η)-oracle for Max k-Cover performs three different subroutines in parallel that together guarantee the required properties of (α, δ, η)-oracles and only use $\widetilde{O}(m/\alpha^2)$ space:

Set sampling based approach. This subroutine which provides the guarantee of (α, δ, η)-oracles when the number of *common* elements is large (see Definition 2.1) is an application of a "multi-layered" variant of set sampling. This subroutine is presented in Section 4.1.

HeavyHitter based approach. We relate the problem of α-estimating/approximating of Max k-Cover to the problem of finding *contributing classes* and *heavy hitters* on properly sampled substreams (see Section 2.2) when the main contribution of an optimal solution of Max k-Cover is due to "large" sets. In particular, this subroutine finds an α-estimation of the optimal coverage size when $\alpha = \Omega(k)$. This approach is presented in Section 4.2.

Element sampling based approach. Finally, we employ element sampling together with a new sampling technique that samples a collection of sets to find a desired estimate of Max k-Cover on instances for which the main contribution to an optimal solution comes from "small" sets. Here, we also take advantage of the structure guaranteed by the multi-layered set sampling on the number of elements in different frequency levels. This subroutine is presented in Section 4.3.

4 (α, δ, η)-ORACLE OF MAX k-COVER

In this section, we design the promised (α, δ, η)-oracle for Max k-Cover. Let OPT denote an optimal solution of Max k-Cover $(\mathcal{U}, \mathcal{F})$. As described in Definition 3.4, the solution returned by a (α, δ, η)-oracle with high probability, is smaller than $|C(\mathrm{OPT})|$ and if $|C(\mathrm{OPT})| \geq |\mathcal{U}|/\eta$, with probability at least $(1 - \delta)$, it outputs a value not smaller than $|C(\mathrm{OPT})|/\alpha$. The following Theorem together with Theorem 3.6 prove Theorem 3.1.

THEOREM 4.1. *ORACLE(α, k) performs a single pass on edge arrival streams and implements a $(\widetilde{O}(\alpha), (\log n \,\mathrm{polylog}(m))^{-1}, \eta)$-oracle of* Max k-Cover$(\mathcal{U}, \mathcal{F})$ *using $\widetilde{O}(m/\alpha^2)$ space.*

PROOF. The proof follows from the guarantees of LARGECOMMON (Theorem 4.4), LARGESET (Theorem 4.8) and SMALLSET (Theorem 4.22). The total space of the algorithm is clearly $\widetilde{O}(m/\alpha^2)$ which is the space complexity of the each of subroutines invoked by ORACLE. □

To design the promised (α, δ, η)-oracle, we design different subroutines such that each guarantees the properties required by the oracle if certain conditions based on the the size/value of following notions hold.

Common elements. An important property in design of our oracle is whether there exists $\beta \leq \alpha$ such that the number of (βk)-*common* elements is relatively large (see Definition 2.1).

We also take advantage of another useful notion which is a property of a k-cover (though, here we only describe it for optimal k-covers).

Contribution to the optimal coverage. Given the input argument α and a parameter s as defined in Table 2, we define the following notion of *contribution* for the sets in an (optimal) k-cover.

Definition 4.2. For a k-cover OPT $= \{O_1, \cdots, O_k\}$, we consider an arbitrary ordering of the sets in OPT and define the *contribution* of O_i to $C(\mathrm{OPT})$ as $|O'_i|$ where $O'_i := O_i \setminus \bigcup_{1\leq j<i} O_i$. Note that O'_i are disjoint and $|\bigcup_{i\in[k]} O'_i| = |C(\mathrm{OPT})| = z$. We (conceptually) define $\mathrm{OPT}_{\mathrm{large}}$ to be the collection of all sets in OPT that contribute more than $z/(\mathrm{s}\alpha)$ to $C(\mathrm{OPT})$ according to O'_is; $\mathrm{OPT}_{\mathrm{large}} = \{O_i \in \mathrm{OPT} \mid |O'_i| \geq z/(\mathrm{s}\alpha)\}$ for $\mathrm{s} < 1$ (as in Table 2). Note that since O'_is are disjoint, $|\mathrm{OPT}_{\mathrm{large}}| \leq \mathrm{s}\alpha$.

$\mathrm{w} = \min\{k, \alpha\}$,	$\mathrm{s} = \frac{9}{5000\sqrt{2\eta}\log(\mathrm{s}\alpha)\log^2(mn)} \cdot \frac{\mathrm{w}}{\alpha}$
$\mathrm{f} = 7\log(mn)$,	$\sigma = \frac{1}{2500\log^2(mn)}$
$\mathrm{t} = \frac{5000\log^2(mn)}{\mathrm{s}}$,	$\eta = 4$

Table 2: Values of the parameters used in this section.

Design of (δ, α, η)-oracle of max k-cover. Here we sketch a high-level outline of our (δ, α, η)-oracle for Max k-Cover (refer to Figure 2 for a formal description). In the following cases, $\sigma = \Omega(\frac{1}{\log^2(mn)})$ (as in Table 2).

I. If there exists a $\beta \leq \alpha$ such that $|\mathcal{U}^{\mathrm{cmn}}_{\beta k}| \geq \frac{\sigma\beta|\mathcal{U}|}{\alpha}$. In this case, by Observation 2.4, to approximate the optimal solution size within a factor of $\widetilde{O}(\alpha)$, it suffices to find βk sets that cover $\mathcal{U}^{\mathrm{cmn}}_{\beta k}$ which can be done via set sampling (see Section 4.1).

II. $|C(\mathrm{OPT}_{\mathrm{large}})| \geq \frac{|C(\mathrm{OPT})|}{2}$ and $\forall\beta \leq \alpha, |\mathcal{U}^{\mathrm{cmn}}_{\beta k}| < \frac{\sigma\beta|\mathcal{U}|}{\alpha}$. The subroutine for this case which is presented in Section 4.2, handles the instances of the problem in which $\mathrm{s}\alpha \geq 2k$ or, $\mathrm{s}\alpha < 2k$ and there exists an optimal solution OPT such that $|C(\mathrm{OPT}_{\mathrm{large}})| \geq |C(\mathrm{OPT})|/2$.

CLAIM 4.3. *If $\mathrm{s}\alpha \geq 2k$, then $|C(OPT_{\mathrm{large}})| \geq |C(OPT)|/2$.*

PROOF. Consider the optimal solution OPT and ignore the sets in OPT whose contribution to the coverage is less than $|C(\mathrm{OPT})|/(2k)$. Note that the survived sets belong to $\mathrm{OPT}_{\mathrm{large}}$ and their total coverage is at least $|C(\mathrm{OPT})| - k \cdot \frac{|C(\mathrm{OPT})|}{2k} \geq |C(\mathrm{OPT})|/2$. □

III. $|C(\mathrm{OPT}_{\mathrm{large}})| < \frac{|C(\mathrm{OPT})|}{2}$ and $\forall\beta \leq \alpha, |\mathcal{U}^{\mathrm{cmn}}_{\beta k}| < \frac{\sigma\beta|\mathcal{U}|}{\alpha}$. In this case, the main contribution to the coverage of OPT comes from "small" sets. This enables us to show that if we sample sets with probability $1/\alpha$, then $\widetilde{\Omega}(1/\alpha)$-fraction of sets in OPT survive and with high probability, their coverage is $\widetilde{\Omega}(|C(\mathrm{OPT})|/\alpha)$. In Section 4.3, we show that element sampling method with some new ideas can take care of this case which can only happen when $\mathrm{s}\alpha < 2k$.

Oracle(k, α):
▷ For instances in which $\exists \beta \le \alpha$ s.t. $|\mathcal{U}^{\text{cmn}}_{\beta k}| \ge \frac{\sigma\beta|\mathcal{U}|}{\alpha}$
$\text{SOL}_{\text{cmn}} \leftarrow$ LargeCommon(k, α)
if $s\alpha \ge 2k$ **then do**
 ▷ If $s\alpha \ge 2k$, then $|\text{OPT}_{\text{large}}| \ge |\text{OPT}|/2$
 $\text{SOL}_{\text{HH}} \leftarrow$ LargeSet(k, α, k)
else do
 ▷ For instances with $s\alpha < 2k$ and $|\text{OPT}_{\text{large}}| \ge |\text{OPT}|/2$
 $\text{SOL}_{\text{HH}} \leftarrow$ LargeSet(k, α, α)
 ▷ For instances with $|\text{OPT}_{\text{large}}| < |\text{OPT}|/2$
 $\text{SOL}_{\text{small}} \leftarrow$ SmallSet(k, α)
return $\max(\text{SOL}_{\text{cmn}}, \text{SOL}_{\text{HH}}, \text{SOL}_{\text{small}})$

Figure 2: An (α, δ, η)-oracle of Max k-Cover.

4.1 Multi-layered Set Sampling

Here, we first guess the value of β (more precisely, a 2-approximate estimate of β) and then pick βk sets $\mathcal{F}^{\text{rnd}}_{\beta}$ at random and compute their coverage in one pass using $\widetilde{O}(1)$ space. To get the desired space complexity, we use the implementation of set sampling with $O(\log(mn))$ random bits as described in Section A.1.

Theorem 4.4. *Consider an instance $(\mathcal{U}, \mathcal{F})$ of Max k-Cover. The LargeCommon algorithm uses $\widetilde{O}(1)$ space and if there exists $\beta \le \alpha$ such that $|\mathcal{U}^{\text{cmn}}_{\beta k}| \ge \frac{\sigma\beta|\mathcal{U}|}{\alpha}$, then with high probability, the algorithm returns at least $\sigma|\mathcal{U}|/(6\alpha)$. Moreover, with high probability the output of LargeCommon is smaller than the coverage size of an optimal solution of Max k-Cover$(\mathcal{U}, \mathcal{F})$.*

LargeCommon(k, α):
for each $\beta_g \in \{2^i \mid 1 \le i \le \log \alpha\}$ **do in parallel**
 ▷ Perform set sampling in one pass using $\widetilde{O}(1)$ space.
 pick $h_g : \mathcal{F} \to [\frac{cm \log m}{\beta_g k}]$ at random from $\Theta(\log(mn))$-wise independent hash functions
 let DE_g be a $(1 \pm 1/2)$-approximation streaming algorithm of L_0-estimation
 for each (S, e) in the data stream **do**
  if $h_g(S) = 1$ **then** feed e to DE_g ▷ computes $C(\mathcal{F}^{\text{rnd}}_{\beta_g})$
 if $\text{VAL}(\text{DE}_g) \ge \sigma\beta_g|\mathcal{U}|/(4\alpha)$ **then return** $2\text{VAL}(\text{DE}_g)/(3\beta_g)$
return infeasible ▷ $\nexists \beta \in [\alpha]$ s.t. $|\mathcal{U}^{\text{cmn}}_{\beta k}| \ge \frac{\sigma\beta|\mathcal{U}|}{\alpha k}$

Figure 3: A (α, δ, η)-oracle of Max k-Cover that handles the case where the number of common elements is large.

Claim 4.5. *For each $\beta_g \in \{2^i \mid 1 \le i \le \log \alpha\}$, with high probability, $|\mathcal{F}^{\text{rnd}}_{\beta_g}| \le \beta_g k$.*

Lemma 4.6. *If there exists $\beta \le \alpha$ such that $|\mathcal{U}^{\text{cmn}}_{\beta k}| \ge \sigma\beta|\mathcal{U}|/\alpha$, then with high probability the output of LargeCommon is at least $\sigma|\mathcal{U}|/(6\alpha)$.*

Proof. Let 2^i be the smallest power of two which is larger than or equal to β; $i := \lceil \log \beta \rceil$. Consider the iteration of LargeCommon in which $\beta_g = 2^i$. Since $2\beta > \beta_g \ge \beta$ and by Observation 2.2,

$$|\mathcal{U}^{\text{cmn}}_{\beta_g k}| \ge |\mathcal{U}^{\text{cmn}}_{\beta k}| \ge \frac{\sigma\beta|\mathcal{U}|}{\alpha} \ge \frac{\sigma\beta_g|\mathcal{U}|}{2\alpha}.$$

Hence, by the guarantee of existing streaming algorithms for L_0-estimation (Theorem 2.12) and set sampling (Lemma 2.3 and A.7), w.h.p., $\text{VAL}(\text{DE}_g) \ge \frac{1}{2} \cdot \frac{\sigma\beta_g|\mathcal{U}|}{2\alpha} = \frac{\sigma\beta_g|\mathcal{U}|}{4\alpha}$. Hence, the estimate returned by the algorithm which is a lower bound on the coverage of the best k sets in $\mathcal{F}^{\text{rnd}}_{\beta_g}$ (see Observation 2.4), w.h.p., is at least $\frac{2}{3} \cdot \frac{1}{\beta_g} \cdot \frac{\sigma\beta_g|\mathcal{U}|}{4\alpha} = \frac{\sigma|\mathcal{U}|}{6\alpha}$.

Moreover, it is straightforward to check that by the guarantee of the streaming algorithm for L_0-estimation (Theorem 2.12), the value returned by LargeCommon with high probability is not more than the actual coverage of the best k-cover in the collection of sampled sets using h_g. □

Lemma 4.7. *If LargeCommon returns* **infeasible**, *then with high probability, for all $\beta \le \alpha$, $|\mathcal{U}^{\text{cmn}}_{\beta k}| \le \frac{\sigma \cdot \beta \cdot |\mathcal{U}|}{\alpha}$.*

Proof. Since the algorithm returns **infeasible**, by the guarantee of the $(1 \pm 1/2)$-approximation algorithm for L_0-estimation (Theorem 2.12) and set sampling (Lemma 2.3), for all values of $\beta_g \in \{2^i \mid i \le \log \alpha\}$, with high probability,

$$|\mathcal{U}^{\text{cmn}}_{\beta_g k}| \le |C(\mathcal{F}^{\text{rnd}}_{\beta_g})| \le 2\text{VAL}(\text{DE}_g) < \frac{\sigma \cdot \beta_g \cdot |\mathcal{U}|}{2\alpha}. \quad (1)$$

Now, for any given value $\beta \le \alpha$, consider $\beta_g := 2^{\lceil \log \beta \rceil}$ (i.e. set β_g to be the smallest power of two which is larger than or equal to β). By Observation 2.2, $|\mathcal{U}^{\text{cmn}}_{\beta k}| \le |\mathcal{U}^{\text{cmn}}_{\beta_g k}|$ which together with Eq. 1 imply that $|\mathcal{U}^{\text{cmn}}_{\beta k}| \le \frac{\sigma \cdot \beta_g \cdot |\mathcal{U}|}{2\alpha} \le \frac{\sigma \cdot \beta \cdot |\mathcal{U}|}{\alpha}$. □

Proof of Theorem 4.4. The guarantee on the quality of the output follows from Lemma 4.6. Moreover, by Theorem 2.12, the total amount of space to compute the coverage of each collection $\mathcal{F}^{\text{rnd}}_{\beta_g}$ (via existing L_0-estimation algorithms in streams) is $\widetilde{O}(1)$. Hence, the total space to compute the coverage of all $\log \alpha$ collections considered in LargeCommon is $\widetilde{O}(1)$. □

4.2 Heavy Hitters and Contributing Classes: $|C(\textbf{OPT}_{\text{large}})| \ge |C(\textbf{OPT})|/2$.

In this section, we show that if there exists an optimal solution OPT of Max k-Cover$(\mathcal{U}, \mathcal{F})$ such that the main contribution in the coverage of OPT is due to *large* sets, which are formally defined to be the sets whose contribution to $C(\text{OPT})$ is at least $|C(\text{OPT})|/(s\alpha)$, then we can approximate the optimal coverage size within a factor of $\widetilde{O}(\alpha)$ by detecting $\widetilde{\Omega}(\frac{\alpha^2}{m})$-HeavyHitters in properly sampled substreams. Following is the main result of this section.

THEOREM 4.8. *Consider an instance $(\mathcal{U}, \mathcal{F})$ of* Max k-Cover. *In a single pass,* LARGESET *uses $\widetilde{O}(m/\alpha^2)$ space and if the optimal coverage size of the instance is $\Omega(|\mathcal{U}|)$, then with probability at least $1 - (\log n \,\text{polylog}(m))^{-1}$, it returns at least $\widetilde{\Omega}(|\mathcal{U}|/\alpha)$. Moreover, with high probability, the estimate returned by* LARGESET *is smaller than the optimal coverage size.*

We defer the proof of Theorem 4.8 to Section B. In this section, we prove the same guarantees on the performance of a simplified variant of LARGESET, LARGESETSIMPLE, when $\mathcal{U}$ contains no "common" elements (wee will define them formally later in this section) which essentially presents the main technical ideas.

Partitioning sets into supersets. We partition the sets of $\mathcal{F}$ *randomly* into $\frac{cm\log m}{\mathrm{w}}$ *supersets* $Q := \{\mathcal{D}_1, \cdots, \mathcal{D}_{\frac{cm\log m}{\mathrm{w}}}\}$ via a hash function $h : \mathcal{F} \to [(cm\log m)/\mathrm{w}]$ chosen from a family of $\Theta(\log(mn))$-wise independent hash functions. More precisely, each set $S \in \mathcal{F}$ belongs to the superset $\mathcal{D}_{h(S)}$.

The parameter w denotes the desired upper bound on the maximum number of sets in a superset in Q defined by h and is set to $\min(\alpha, k)$. In fact, given w, we define h to be a function picked uniformly at random from a family of $\Theta(\log(mn))$-wise independent hash functions $\{\mathcal{F} \to [(cm\log m)/\mathrm{w}]\}$.

CLAIM 4.9. *W.h.p., no superset in Q has more than* w *sets.*

CLAIM 4.10. *With high probability, for each $e \in \mathcal{U} \setminus \mathcal{U}^{\text{cmn}}_{\mathrm{w}}$ and $\mathcal{D} \in Q$, the number of sets in $\mathcal{D}$ that contain e is at most* f *where* $\mathrm{f} = \Theta(\log(mn))$.

This implies if $\mathcal{U}^{\text{cmn}}_{\mathrm{w}} = \emptyset$, to get an $\widetilde{O}(\alpha)$-approximation of Max k-Cover$(\mathcal{U}, \mathcal{F})$, it suffices to find a superset whose total size of its sets is $\widetilde{\Omega}(1/\alpha)$ times the optimal coverage size. Now, we are ready to exploit the results on F_2-heavy hitters and F_2-contributing classes mentioned in Section 2.2 to describe our (α, δ, η)-oracle for Max k-Cover assuming $\mathcal{U}^{\text{cmn}}_{\mathrm{w}} = \emptyset$. Later in Section B, we show how to remove this assumption by performing our algorithm on a set of sampled elements in $\mathcal{U}$ instead.

Partitioning supersets by their total size. First, setting $z = |C(\text{OPT})|$, we partition the supersets in Q (conceptually) according to the total size of their sets into $O(\log\alpha)$ classes as follows:

$$Q_0 = \{\mathcal{D} \mid \sum_{S\in\mathcal{D}} |S| \geq \frac{z}{2}\}, \tag{2}$$

$$Q_i = \{\mathcal{D} \mid \frac{z}{2^{i+1}} \leq \sum_{S\in\mathcal{D}} |S| < \frac{z}{2^i}\}, \quad \forall i \in [1, \log(\alpha)) \tag{3}$$

$$Q_{\text{small}} = \{\mathcal{D} \mid \sum_{S\in\mathcal{D}} |S| < z/\alpha\}. \tag{4}$$

Further, let n_i denote the number of supersets in Q_i; $n_i = |Q_i|$. Next, we define the vector $\vec{v}$ of size $(cm\log m)/\mathrm{w}$ such that $\vec{v}[i] = \sum_{S\in\mathcal{D}_i} |S|$ denotes the total size of the sets in $\mathcal{D}_i$. In the following, we show that a subset of supersets with large total size form an $\widetilde{\Omega}(\frac{m}{\alpha^2})$-contributing class of $F_2(\vec{v})$ and any superset in this $\widetilde{\Omega}(\frac{m}{\alpha^2})$-contributing class is an α-*approximate* k-cover of $(\mathcal{U}, \mathcal{F})$.

We consider the following two cases depending on whether the coordinates corresponding to small supersets, Q_{small}, contribute to $F_2(\vec{v})$; $F_2(\vec{v}_{\text{small}}) \geq F_2(\vec{v})/2$ where $\vec{v}_{\text{small}}$ denotes the vector $\vec{v}$ restricted to the coordinates corresponding to supersets in Q_{small}.

Case 1: Supersets with total size less than z/α contribute to $F_2(\vec{v})$. This implies that

$$F_2(\vec{v}) \leq 2F_2(\vec{v}_{\text{small}}) \leq \frac{2cm\log m}{\mathrm{w}} \cdot \frac{z^2}{\alpha^2}. \tag{5}$$

CLAIM 4.11. *If $F_2(\vec{v}_{\text{small}}) \geq F_2(\vec{v})/2$, then there exists an $\widetilde{\Omega}(\frac{\alpha^2}{m})$-contributing class Q_{i^*} of $F_2(\vec{v})$ for an index $i^* < \log(s\alpha)$.*

PROOF. Since each set in $\text{OPT}_{\text{large}}$ has contribution at least $\frac{z}{s\alpha}$ to $C(\text{OPT})$, sets in $\text{OPT}_{\text{large}}$ land in one of $Q_0, \cdots, Q_{\log(s\alpha)-1}$. Moreover, since $\text{OPT}_{\text{large}}$ has coverage at least $z/2$,

$$\sum_{i=0}^{\log(s\alpha)-1} n_i \cdot \frac{z}{2^i} \geq \sum_{O_i \in \text{OPT}_{\text{large}}} |O_i| \geq |C(\text{OPT}_{\text{large}})| \geq z/2,$$

which implies that there exists an index $i^* < \log(s\alpha)$ such that $n_{i^*} \geq 2^{i^*}/(2\log(s\alpha))$. Hence, Q_{i^*} is an $\widetilde{\Omega}(\frac{\alpha^2}{m})$-contributing class of $F_2(\vec{v})$:

$$\begin{aligned} |Q_{i^*}| \cdot (\frac{z}{2^{i^*+1}})^2 &\geq \frac{2^{i^*}}{2\log(s\alpha)} \cdot \frac{z^2}{4(2^{i^*})^2} \\ &\geq \frac{\mathrm{w}}{2cm\log m} \cdot \alpha^2 \cdot \frac{1}{2^{i^*+3}\log(s\alpha)} \cdot F_2(\vec{v}) \quad \rhd \text{By (5)} \\ &\geq (\frac{\mathrm{w}}{s\alpha} \cdot \frac{1}{8c\log(s\alpha)\log m}) \cdot \frac{\alpha^2}{m} \cdot F_2(\vec{v}) \end{aligned}$$

More formally, since $\frac{\mathrm{w}}{s\alpha} = \widetilde{\Omega}(1)$ (see Table 2), Q_{i^*} is a ϕ_1-contributing class of $F_2(\vec{v})$ where

$$\phi_1 = (\frac{\mathrm{w}}{s\alpha} \cdot \frac{1}{8c\log(s\alpha)\log m}) \cdot \frac{\alpha^2}{m} = \widetilde{\Omega}(\frac{\alpha^2}{m}). \tag{6}$$

□

Hence, by Theorem 2.11, a superset of total size at least $\frac{2}{3} \cdot \frac{1}{2} \cdot \frac{z}{s\alpha}$ will be identified by the subroutine F_2-CONTRIBUTING$(\phi_1, s\alpha)$ using $\widetilde{O}(m/\alpha^2)$ space.

Remark 4.12. *Recall that in order to find a coordinate in a ϕ-contributing class R_{t^*}, F_2-CONTRIBUTING subsamples the stream proportional to $1/|R_{t^*}|$ (so that only $O(1)$ coordinates of R_{t^*} survive) and then with high probability any survived coordinate of R_{t^*} becomes a $\widetilde{\Omega}(\phi)$-HeavyHitter in the sampled substream. However, here we show that there exists a ϕ-contributing class R_{t^*} whose intersection with OPT_{large} is a ϕ-contributing class of coordinates too. Hence, it suffices to only search for a coordinate in a ϕ-contributing class of size at most $|OPT_{\text{large}}| \leq s\alpha$.*

We emphasis that bounding the size of a ϕ-contributing class is not required for the simplified case of this section (i.e., $\mathcal{U}_{\text{w}}^{\text{cmn}} = \emptyset$). However, since we estimate the coverage size of a superset by the total size of its sets, in Section B where we solve the general case (i.e., $\mathcal{U}_{\text{w}}^{\text{cmn}} \neq \emptyset$) it is crucial to only consider ϕ-contributing classes of small size. Otherwise, in the superset returned by our algorithm, the gap between its actual coverage size and total size of the sets in the superset can be very large.

Case 2. Supersets with coverage less than z/α do not contribute to $F_2(\vec{v})$.

CLAIM 4.13. *If $F_2(\vec{v}_{\text{small}}) < F_2(\vec{v})/2$, then there exists an $\widetilde{\Omega}(1)$-contributing class Q_{i^*} of $F_2(\vec{v})$ for an index $i^* < \log \alpha$.*

PROOF. In this case, since supersets in Q_{small} are not contributing, there exists an index $i^* < \log(\alpha)$ (note that we consider all classes $Q_0, \cdots, Q_{\log \alpha - 1}$ in this case) such that

$$n_{i^*} \cdot \left(\frac{z}{2^{i^*}}\right)^2 \geq \frac{F_2(\vec{v})}{2 \log \alpha};$$

in other words, Q_{i^*} is a ϕ_2-contributing class of $F_2(\vec{v})$ where $\phi_2 = (\frac{1}{2 \log \alpha})$. □

Note that, by Theorem 2.11, a superset of total size at least $\frac{2}{3} \cdot \frac{1}{2} \cdot \frac{z}{\alpha}$ will be identified by F_2-CONTRIBUTING$(\phi_2, \frac{cm \log m}{\text{w}})$ using $\widetilde{O}(1)$ space.

LEMMA 4.14. *If $|C(OPT)| \geq \frac{|\mathcal{U}|}{\eta}$, then w.p. at least $1 - 1/(3 \log n \log^c m)$, the estimate returned by LARGESETSIMPLE with parameters $(\mathcal{V} = \mathcal{U}, \text{w}, \text{thr}_1 = \frac{|\mathcal{U}|}{\eta s \alpha}, \text{thr}_2 = \frac{|\mathcal{U}|}{\eta \alpha})$ has coverage at least $|\mathcal{U}|/(3\text{f}\eta\alpha) = \widetilde{\Omega}(|\mathcal{U}|/\alpha)$.*

PROOF. By Theorem 2.11, w.p. at least $1 - 2/(9 \log n \log^c m)$, the algorithm returns a superset whose total size is at least $\frac{2}{3} \cdot \frac{|\mathcal{U}|}{2\eta\alpha} \geq \frac{|\mathcal{U}|}{3\eta\alpha}$ (in fact, if it is in Case 1, then the estimate is at least $\frac{|\mathcal{U}|}{3s\alpha\eta}$). Then, by Claim 4.10 and assumption $\mathcal{U}_{\text{w}}^{\text{cmn}} = \emptyset$, the coverage of the reported superset is at least $\frac{1}{\text{f}} \cdot \frac{|\mathcal{U}|}{3\eta\alpha}$. □

```
LARGESETSIMPLE(V, w, thr_1, thr_2):
▷ Input: w is a bound on the number of sets in a superset
▷ Parameters: φ_1 = Ω̃(α^2/m) and φ_2 = Ω̃(1)
▷ For Case 1:
Cntr_small ← instance of F_2-CONTRIBUTING(φ_1, sα)
▷ For Case 2:
Cntr_large ← instance of F_2-CONTRIBUTING(φ_2, (cm log m)/w)
pick h : F → [(cm log m)/w] from Θ(log(mn))-wise
   independent hash functions
for each (S, e) in the data stream do
   if e ∈ V then feed h(S) to both Cntr_small and Cntr_large
▷ output(Cntr) returns (1 ± 1/2)-estimate of the frequencies
▷ ∀i ∈ output(Cntr), ṽ_i denotes the estimated frequency of i
if there exists i ∈ output(Cntr_small) such that ṽ_i ≥ 1/2 · thr_1
   return 2ṽ_i/(3f)
if there exists i ∈ output(Cntr_large) such that ṽ_i ≥ 1/2 · thr_2
   return 2ṽ_i/(3f)
return infeasible
```

Figure 4: An (α, δ, η)-oracle of Max k-Cover that handles the case in which the majority of the coverage in an optimal solution is by the sets whose coverage contributions are at least $1/(s\alpha)$ fraction of the optimal coverage size.

LEMMA 4.15. *The amount of space used by LARGESETSIMPLE is $\widetilde{O}(m/\alpha^2)$.*

PROOF. By Theorem 2.11, the amount of space to perform $\text{Cntr}_{\text{small}}$ and $\text{Cntr}_{\text{large}}$ as defined in Figure 4 is respectively $\widetilde{O}(1/\phi_1) = \widetilde{O}(m/\alpha^2)$ and $\widetilde{O}(1/\phi_2) = \widetilde{O}(1)$. □

4.3 Element Sampling: $|C(\mathbf{OPT}_{\text{large}})| < \frac{|C(\mathbf{OPT})|}{2}$

We design an (α, δ, η)-oracle of Max k-Cover with the desired parameters for the case $|C(\text{OPT}_{\text{small}})| > |C(\text{OPT}_{\text{large}})|$. Intuitively speaking, in this case, after sampling each set in $\mathcal{F}$ with probability $\widetilde{\Theta}(\frac{1}{\alpha})$ still we can find $O(\frac{k}{\alpha})$ sets whose coverage size is at least $\widetilde{\Omega}(\frac{|C(\text{OPT})|}{\alpha})$. As proved in Claim 4.3, if $\alpha = \widetilde{\Omega}(k)$, then the main contribution to the coverage of OPT is due to $\text{OPT}_{\text{large}}$ and we can α-approximate the optimal coverage size by LARGESET. Hence, in this section we assume that $\alpha = \widetilde{O}(k)$. Moreover, throughout this section we assume that for all $\beta \leq \alpha$, $|\mathcal{U}_{\beta k}^{\text{cmn}}| < \frac{\sigma \cdot \beta \cdot |\mathcal{U}|}{\alpha}$ (otherwise, our multi-layered set sampling approach described in Section 4.1 returns an α-approximation of the optimal coverage size).

LEMMA 4.16. *Consider an instance of Max k-Cover $(\mathcal{U}, \mathcal{F})$. Suppose that $\mathcal{D}$ is a collection of k disjoint sets with coverage z such that no $S \in \mathcal{D}$ has size more than $z/(s\alpha)$ where $s < 1$*

and $s = \widetilde{\Omega}(1)$. *Let's assume that* $\mathcal{D}_{\text{smp}} := \mathcal{D} \cap \mathcal{M}$ *where each* $S \in \mathcal{F}$ *survives in* $\mathcal{M}$ *with probability* $c/(s\alpha)$ *where* $c > 1$ *is a fixed constant. Then, with probability at least* $(1 - 6/c)$, $\mathcal{D}_{\text{smp}}$ *has size at most* $(2ck)/(s\alpha)$ *and covers at least* $(cz)/(2s\alpha)$ *elements.*

Proof. Let $\mathcal{D} = \{S'_1, \cdots, S'_k\}$ and for each i, let X_i to be the random variable corresponding to S'_i such that $X_i = |S'_i|$ if $S'_i \in \mathcal{D}_{\text{smp}}$ and zero otherwise.

Claim 4.17. $\mathbf{E}[X_i] = \frac{c}{s\alpha} \cdot |S'_i|$ *and* $\mathbf{Var}[X_i] \le \frac{c}{s\alpha} \cdot |S'_i|^2$.

Next, we define $X := X_1 + \cdots + X_k$. Note that $\mathbf{E}[X] = (cz)/(s\alpha)$ and, by the pairwise independence of X_is and the assumption that $|S'_i| \le z/(s\alpha)$,

$$\mathbf{Var}[X] \le \frac{c}{s\alpha} \cdot \sum_{i=1}^{k} |S'_i|^2 \le \frac{c}{s\alpha} \cdot s\alpha \cdot (\frac{z}{s\alpha})^2 = c \cdot (\frac{z}{s\alpha})^2,$$

Finally, applying Chebyshev inequality,

$$\Pr[X < \frac{cz}{2s\alpha}] = \Pr[X < (\frac{cz}{s\alpha} - \frac{\sqrt{c}}{2} \cdot (\frac{\sqrt{c}}{s\alpha} \cdot z)] < 4/c.$$

Hence, with probability at least $1 - 4/c$, $\mathcal{D}_{\text{smp}}$ covers at least $(cz)/(2s\alpha)$ elements.

Next, we show that with probability at least $1 - 2/c$, $0 < |\mathcal{D}_{\text{smp}}| < (2ck)/(s\alpha)$. For each i, let Y_i denote the random variable corresponding to S_i which is equal to one if $S_i \in \mathcal{D}_{\text{smp}}$ and zero otherwise.

Claim 4.18. $\mathbf{E}[Y_i] = (c/s\alpha)$ *and* $\mathbf{Var}[Y_i] \le (c/s\alpha)$.

We define $Y = Y_1 + \cdots + Y_\ell$ which denotes the size of $\mathcal{D}_{\text{smp}}$. Then by pairwise independence of Y_is, $\mathbf{E}[Y] = (ck)/(s\alpha)$ and $\mathbf{Var}[Y] \le (ck)/(s\alpha)$. Applying Chebyshev inequality ($\Pr[|Y - \mathbf{E}[Y]| \ge t\mathbf{Var}[Y]] \le 1/(t^2\mathbf{Var}[Y])$), with probability at least $1 - (s\alpha)/(ck) \ge 1 - 2/c$ (since in this case, $\alpha \le 2k/s$), $0 < |\mathcal{D}_{\text{smp}}| < (2ck)/(s\alpha)$.

Hence, with probability at least $(1 - 6/c)$, $\mathcal{D}_{\text{smp}}$ is a subset of size at most $(2ck)/(s\alpha)$ that covers at least $(cz)/(2s\alpha)$ elements. □

Corollary 4.19. *Consider an instance* $(\mathcal{U}, \mathcal{F})$ *of* Max k-Cover *and let OPT be an optimal solution of this instance such that* $|C(OPT_{\text{small}})| \ge \frac{1}{2} \cdot |C(OPT)| \ge |\mathcal{U}|/(2\eta)$. *Moreover, let* $\mathcal{M} \subset \mathcal{F}$ *be a collection of* $\widetilde{O}(|\mathcal{F}|/\alpha)$ *pairwise independent sets picked uniformly at random such that each* $S \in \mathcal{F}$ *belongs to* $\mathcal{M}$ *with probability* $\frac{18}{s\alpha}$. *With probability at least* $2/3$, Max $(\frac{36k}{s\alpha})$-Cover$(\mathcal{U}, \mathcal{M})$ *has an optimal solution with coverage size at least* $\frac{9|\mathcal{U}|}{s\cdot\alpha\cdot\eta}$.

Proof. By definition of $\text{OPT}_{\text{small}}$, for each $O \in \text{OPT}_{\text{small}}$, the contribution of O to OPT (i.e. O') is at most $z/(s\alpha)$ (see Definition 4.2). Then, the result follows from an application of Lemma 4.16 on collection $\mathcal{D} := \{O' \mid O \in \text{OPT}_{\text{small}}\}$ by setting $c = 18$ and $z = |\text{OPT}_{\text{small}}| \ge |\mathcal{U}|/(2\eta)$. □

Next, we show that we can perform "element sampling" and find an $\widetilde{O}(1)$-approximation of Max $(\frac{36k}{s\alpha})$-Cover of the specified instance in Corollary 4.19, $(\mathcal{U}, \mathcal{M})$, in one pass and using $\widetilde{O}(m/\alpha^2)$ space. To this end, first we compute the space complexity of $(\mathcal{L}, \mathcal{F})$ where $\mathcal{L} \subseteq \mathcal{U}$ is a subset of size $\widetilde{O}(k)$ which is picked by element sampling.

Lemma 4.20. *Suppose that coverage size of an optimal solution of* Max $(\frac{k}{\alpha})$-Cover$(\mathcal{U}, \mathcal{F})$ *is* $|\mathcal{U}|/\gamma = \widetilde{\Omega}(|\mathcal{U}|/\alpha)$. *Let* $\mathcal{L} \subset \mathcal{U}$ *be a collection of elements of size* $\widetilde{O}(\frac{k\gamma}{\alpha})$ *picked uniformly at random. With high probability, the total amount of space to store the set system* $(\mathcal{L}, \mathcal{F})$ *is* $\widetilde{O}(m/\alpha)$.

Proof. Recall that $(\mathcal{U}, \mathcal{F})$ has the property that for all $\beta \le \alpha$, $|\mathcal{U}^{\text{cmn}}_{\beta k}| < \sigma\beta|\mathcal{U}|/\alpha$ (otherwise, the result of Section 4.1 can be applied). Next, we (conceptually) partition the elements in $\mathcal{U}$ into $\log\alpha + 1$ groups as follows:

$$\mathcal{W}_0 = \mathcal{U} \setminus \mathcal{U}^{\text{cmn}}_{\alpha k}, \text{ and } \mathcal{W}_i = \mathcal{U}^{\text{cmn}}_{(\frac{\alpha}{2^{i-1}})k} \setminus \mathcal{U}^{\text{cmn}}_{(\frac{\alpha}{2^i})k} \quad \forall i \in [\log\alpha].$$

Note that $|\mathcal{W}_0| \le |\mathcal{U}|$ and for each $i \in [\log\alpha]$, $|\mathcal{W}_i| \le \sigma|\mathcal{U}|/2^{i-1}$. Since each element $e \in \mathcal{U}$ survives in $\mathcal{L}$ with probability $\widetilde{O}(\frac{k\gamma}{\alpha|\mathcal{U}|})$, w.h.p., for each $i \in [\log\alpha]$, $|\mathcal{W}_i \cap \mathcal{L}| = \widetilde{O}(1 + \frac{\sigma\cdot\gamma\cdot k}{\alpha 2^{i-1}})$. Furthermore, since each element in $\mathcal{W}_i$ appears in at most $\widetilde{O}(\frac{2^i m}{\alpha k})$ sets in $\mathcal{F}$, the total amount of space required to store $(\mathcal{L}, \mathcal{F})$ is at most

$$\begin{aligned} S(\mathcal{L}, \mathcal{F}) &= \sum_{i=0}^{\log\alpha} |\mathcal{W}_i \cap \mathcal{L}| \cdot \max_{e\in\mathcal{W}_i} \text{freq}(e) \\ &= \widetilde{O}(\frac{k\gamma}{\alpha}) \cdot \widetilde{O}(\frac{m}{\alpha k}) + \sum_{i=1}^{\log\alpha} \widetilde{O}(1 + \frac{\sigma\gamma k}{\alpha 2^{i-1}}) \cdot \widetilde{O}(\frac{2^i m}{\alpha k}) \\ &= \widetilde{O}(\frac{\gamma m}{\alpha^2}) + \sum_{i=1}^{\log\alpha} \widetilde{O}(\frac{2^i m}{\alpha k} + \frac{\sigma\gamma m}{\alpha^2}) = \widetilde{O}(m/\alpha). \end{aligned}$$

□

Next, we show that after subsampling the sets by a factor of $\widetilde{\Theta}(1/\alpha)$, we can save another factor of $\widetilde{\Omega}(\alpha)$ in the space complexity; in other words, $(\mathcal{L}, \mathcal{M})$ uses $\widetilde{O}(\frac{m}{\alpha^2})$ space. Note that since $k\alpha$ may be as large as $\widetilde{\Omega}(m)$ we cannot hope to show directly that each element in $\mathcal{W}_i$ appears in at most $\widetilde{O}(\frac{m}{2^i\alpha k})$. However, we can show that the total size of the intersection of all sets in $\mathcal{M}$ with $\mathcal{L}$ is $\widetilde{O}(\frac{m}{\alpha^2})$ using the properties of the max cover instance.

Lemma 4.21. *Suppose that the coverage size of an optimal solution of* Max $(\frac{k}{\alpha})$-Cover$(\mathcal{U}, \mathcal{F})$ *is* $|\mathcal{U}|/\gamma = \widetilde{\Omega}(|\mathcal{U}|/\alpha)$. *Let* $\mathcal{L} \subset \mathcal{U}$ *be a collection of elements of size* $\widetilde{O}(\frac{k\gamma}{\alpha})$ *picked uniformly at random and let* $\mathcal{M} \subset \mathcal{F}$ *be a collection of sets of size* $\widetilde{O}(m/\alpha)$ *picked uniformly at random. With high probability, the total amount of space required to store the set system* $(\mathcal{L}, \mathcal{M})$ *is* $\widetilde{O}(m/\alpha^2)$.

Proof. First note that since an optimal $(\frac{k}{\alpha})$-cover of $(\mathcal{U}, \mathcal{F})$ has coverage $|\mathcal{U}|/\gamma$, with high probability, for each set $S \in \mathcal{M}$, $|S \cap \mathcal{L}| = \widetilde{O}(k/\alpha)$. Moreover, by Lemma 4.20, the size of the intersection of all sets in $\mathcal{F}$ with $\mathcal{L}$ is $\widetilde{O}(m/\alpha)$. Next, we (conceptually) partition the sets of $\mathcal{F}$ into $O(\log k)$ groups based on their intersection size with $\mathcal{L}$ as follows ($c = \widetilde{O}(1)$):

$$Q_i = \{S \in \mathcal{F} \mid \frac{1}{2^i} \cdot \frac{ck}{\alpha} \leq |S \cap \mathcal{L}| < \frac{1}{2^{i-1}} \cdot \frac{ck}{\alpha}\}, \ \forall 1 \leq i \leq \log k$$

Since the total size of the intersection of all sets with the sampled set $\mathcal{L}$ is w.h.p. $\widetilde{O}(m/\alpha)$, for each $i \leq \log k$, $|Q_i| \leq \frac{\widetilde{O}(m/\alpha)}{(ck)/(2^i\alpha)} = \widetilde{O}(\frac{2^i \cdot m}{k})$. Since we have the assumption that $\frac{m}{k\alpha} \geq 1$ (we took care of the case $m < k\alpha$ in the first line of EstimateMaxCover separately), w.h.p., for each Q_i, $|Q_i \cap \mathcal{M}| = \widetilde{O}(\frac{2^i m}{k\alpha})$. Hence, the total amount of space to store $(\mathcal{L}, \mathcal{M})$ is at most

$$\sum_{i=1}^{\log k} \frac{1}{2^{i-1}} \cdot \frac{ck}{\alpha} \cdot \widetilde{O}(\frac{2^i m}{k\alpha}) = \widetilde{O}(\frac{m}{\alpha^2}).$$

□

SmallSet(k, α):
▷ estimate of the optimal coverage of $\widetilde{O}(\frac{k}{\alpha})$-cover
for each $\gamma_g \in \{2^{-i} \mid i \in [\log \alpha]\}$ **do in parallel**:
  repeat $\log n$ times **in parallel**:
    $\mathcal{M} \leftarrow$ uniformly selected samples of size $\widetilde{\Theta}(m/\alpha)$ from $\mathcal{F}$
    $\mathcal{L} \leftarrow$ uniformly selected samples of size $\widetilde{\Theta}(\gamma_g \cdot (\frac{k}{\alpha}))$ from $\mathcal{U}$
    ▷ $S(\mathcal{L}, \mathcal{M})$ stores $(\mathcal{L}, \mathcal{M})$
    initialize $S(\mathcal{L}, \mathcal{M})$ to be an empty set
    for each (S, e) in the data stream **do**
      if $S \in \mathcal{M}$ and $e \in \mathcal{L}$ **then**
        add (S, e) to $S(\mathcal{L}, \mathcal{M})$
      if $S(\mathcal{L}, \mathcal{M}) > \widetilde{O}(m/\alpha^2)$ **then**
        terminate
  $\text{sol}_{\gamma_g} \leftarrow \max_{\mathcal{L},\mathcal{M}}\{O(1)$-approximation of the coverage of Max $(\frac{36k}{s\alpha})$-Cover$(S(\mathcal{L}, \mathcal{M}))\}$
return $\max_{\gamma_g}\{(\frac{|\mathcal{U}|}{\gamma_g(k/\alpha)} \cdot \text{sol}_{\gamma_g}) \mid \text{sol}_{\gamma_g} = \widetilde{\Omega}(k/\alpha)\}$

Figure 5: A single pass streaming algorithm that estimates the optimal coverage size of Max k-Cover$(\mathcal{U}, \mathcal{F})$ **within a factor of** $\widetilde{O}(\alpha)$ **in** $\widetilde{O}(\frac{m}{\alpha^2})$ **space.**

Theorem 4.22. *If* $|C(OPT_{\text{small}})| \geq |\mathcal{U}|/(2\eta)$ *and for all* $\beta \leq \alpha$, $|\mathcal{U}^{\text{cmn}}_{\beta k}| < \frac{\sigma \cdot \beta \cdot |\mathcal{U}|}{\alpha}$, *then with high probability, SmallSet outputs an* $\widetilde{O}(\alpha)$*-approximation of the size of an optimal solution of* Max k-Cover$(\mathcal{U}, \mathcal{F})$ *in* $\widetilde{O}(m/\alpha^2)$ *space.*

Proof. By Corollary 4.19, for any sampled collection of sets $\mathcal{M}$ of size $\widetilde{\Theta}(m/\alpha)$ (as in SmallSet), with probability at least $2/3$, there exists a subset of size at most $(\frac{36k}{s\alpha})$ in $\mathcal{M}$ whose coverage is $9|\mathcal{U}|/(s \cdot \alpha \cdot \eta) = |\mathcal{U}|/\gamma$. Moreover, by the guarantee of element sampling, Lemma 2.5, when $\gamma/2 < \gamma_g \leq \gamma$, an $O(1)$-approximate solution of Max k-Cover$(\mathcal{L}, \mathcal{M})$ w.h.p. is an $O(1)$-approximate solution of Max k-Cover$(\mathcal{U}, \mathcal{M})$. Hence, with probability $1 - n^{-1}$, in at least one of the $(\log n)$ instances with the desired γ_g, sol_{γ_g} has coverage $\widetilde{\Omega}(\frac{|\mathcal{U}|}{\gamma} \cdot \gamma_g \cdot \frac{(k/\alpha)}{|\mathcal{U}|}) = \widetilde{\Omega}(k/\alpha)$ over the sampled elements $\mathcal{L}$. Note that we need to scale sol_{γ_g} by a factor of $\widetilde{\Theta}(|\mathcal{U}|/(\gamma_g \cdot \frac{k}{\alpha}))$ to reflect its coverage on $\mathcal{U}$.

Further, by Lemma 4.21, the amount of space required to store each $(\mathcal{L}, \mathcal{M})$ with high probability is $\widetilde{O}(\frac{m}{\alpha^2})$ and since SmallSet stores $\widetilde{O}(1)$ different instances $(\mathcal{L}, \mathcal{F})$, the total space of the algorithm is $\widetilde{O}(\frac{m}{\alpha^2})$. □

To complete the SmallSet is indeed an (α, δ, η)-oracle with the desired parameters, we need to show that it never overestimates the optimal coverage size.

Lemma 4.23. *The output of SmallSet with high probability is not larger than the optimal coverage size of* Max k-Cover$(\mathcal{U}, \mathcal{F})$.

Proof. The proof follows from the fact that if the optimal coverage size Max $(\widetilde{O}(\frac{k}{\alpha}))$-Cover$(\mathcal{L}, \mathcal{M})$ is not $\widetilde{\Omega}(|\mathcal{U}|/(\alpha \cdot \gamma_g))$, then with high probability in none of the $\log n$ iterations $\text{sol}_{\gamma_g} = \widetilde{\Omega}(k/\alpha)$. Hence, SmallSet with high probability does not overestimate the size of an optimal $\widetilde{O}(k/\alpha)$-cover in $(\mathcal{U}, \mathcal{F})$. □

5 LOWER BOUND FOR ESTIMATING MAXIMUM k-COVERAGE IN EDGE ARRIVAL STREAMS

By the result of [12], it is known that estimating the size of an optimal coverage of Max k-Cover within a factor of two requires $\Omega(m)$ space. Their argument relies on a reduction from Set Disjointness problem and implies the mentioned bound for 1-cover instances. In the following, we generalize their approach and provide lower bounds for the all range of approximation guarantees α smaller than $\sqrt{m}$. We remark that both our lower bound result and the lower bound result of [12] are basically similar to the lower bound of L_∞ and L_k estimation first proved in [5, 10].

The lower bound result we explain in this section is based on the well-known r-player Set Disjointness problem with unique set intersection promise which has been studied extensively in communication complexity (e.g. [11, 16, 24]). The setting of the problem is as follows: There are r players and each has a set $T_i \subseteq [m]$. The promise is that the input is in one of the following forms:

- **No Case:** There is a unique element $j \in [m]$ such that for all $i \leq r, j \in T_i$.
- **Yes Case:** All sets are pair-wise disjoint.

Moreover, a round of communication consists of each player i sending a message to player $i+1$ in order from $i = 1$ to $r-1$. The goal is that at end of a single round, player r be able to correctly output whether the input belongs to the family of **Yes** instances or **No** instances. Chakrabarti et al. [16] showed the following tight lower bound on the one-way communication complexity of the r-player Set Disjointness problem with unique set intersection promise.

THEOREM 5.1 (FROM [16]). *Any randomized one-way protocol that solves r-player* Set Disjointness(m) *with success probability at least $2/3$ requires $\Omega(m/r)$ bits of communication.*

We remark that the same $\Omega(m/r)$ communication lower bound was later proved for the general model (i.e. with multiple rounds) by Gronemeier [24]. However, for our application, the lower bound on the one-way communication model suffices.

COROLLARY 5.2. *Any single-pass streaming algorithm that solves r-player* Set Disjointness(m) *with success probability at least $2/3$ consumes $\Omega(m/r^2)$ space.*

Next, we sketch a reduction from r-player Set Disjointness(m) to Max k-Cover with m sets such that an α-approximation protocol of Max k-Cover solves the corresponding instance of r-player Set Disjointness(m). To this end, consider an arbitrary instance $\mathcal{I}$ of α-player Set Disjointness(m) problem in which each player i has a set $T_i \subset [m]$. Define $\mathcal{U}_\mathcal{I} = \{e_1, \cdots, e_\alpha\}$ to be the set of elements in the Max 1-Cover instance and for each player i if $j \in T_i$ then add $(e_i, S_{j,})$ to the stream. In other words, in the constructed Max 1-Cover $(\mathcal{U}_\mathcal{I}, \mathcal{F}_\mathcal{I} := \{S_1, \cdots, S_m\})$ instance, we have an element e_i corresponding to each player i and there exists a set S_j corresponding to each item $j \in [m]$. Moreover, each set S_j in the Max 1-Cover instance $(\mathcal{U}_\mathcal{I}, \mathcal{F}_\mathcal{I})$ denotes the set of players in the Set Disjointness(m) instance $\mathcal{I}$ whose input sets contain j; $S_j := \{i \in [\alpha] \mid j \in T_i\}$.

CLAIM 5.3. *If $\mathcal{I}$ is a* **No** *instance, then the optimal coverage of the* Max 1-Cover *instance $(\mathcal{U}_\mathcal{I}, \mathcal{F}_\mathcal{I})$ is α.*

PROOF. In this case, by the unique intersection promise, there exists an item j that belongs to all T_i (for $i \in [\alpha]$). Hence, by the construction of the Max 1-Cover instance, S_j covers the whole $\mathcal{U}_\mathcal{I}$. Thus, the optimal 1-cover has size α. □

CLAIM 5.4. *If $\mathcal{I}$ is a* **Yes** *instance, then the optimal coverage of the* Max 1-Cover *instance $(\mathcal{U}_\mathcal{I}, \mathcal{F}_\mathcal{I})$ is 1.*

PROOF. Since T_is are disjoint, for each $j \in [m]$, the set S_j has cardinality one. □

Corollary 5.2 together with Claims 5.3 and 5.4 imply the stated lower bound on α-approximating the optimal coverage size of Max k-Cover in edge-arrival streams in Theorem 3.3: *Any single pass (possibly randomized) algorithm on edge-arrival streams that α-approximates the optimal coverage size of* Max k-Cover *requires $\Omega(\frac{m}{\alpha^2})$ space.*

ACKNOWLEDGMENTS

This work was supported by grants from the NSF and the Simons Investigator award.

REFERENCES

[1] Z. Abbassi, V. S. Mirrokni, and M. Thakur. 2013. Diversity maximization under matroid constraints. In *Proceedings of the 19th ACM SIGKDD international conference on Knowledge discovery and data mining*. ACM, 32–40.

[2] Shipra Agrawal, Mohammad Shadravan, and Cliff Stein. 2019. Submodular Secretary Problem with Shortlists. In *10th Innovations in Theoretical Computer Science Conference (ITCS)*. 1:1–1:19.

[3] K. J. Ahn, S. Guha, and A. McGregor. 2012. Analyzing graph structure via linear measurements. In *Proc. 23rd ACM-SIAM Sympos. Discrete Algs.* (SODA). 459–467.

[4] K. J. Ahn, S. Guha, and A. McGregor. 2012. Graph sketches: sparsification, spanners, and subgraphs. In *Proc. 31st ACM Sympos. on Principles of Database Systems* (PODS). 5–14.

[5] N. Alon, Y. Matias, and M. Szegedy. 1999. The space complexity of approximating the frequency moments. *Journal of Computer and system sciences* 58, 1 (1999), 137–147.

[6] S. Assadi. 2017. Tight Space-Approximation Tradeoff for the Multi-Pass Streaming Set Cover Problem. In *Proc. 36th ACM Sympos. on Principles of Database Systems* (PODS). 321–335.

[7] S. Assadi, S. Khanna, and Y. Li. 2016. Tight Bounds for Single-Pass Streaming Complexity of the Set Cover Problem. In *Proc. 48th Annu. ACM Sympos. Theory Comput.* (STOC). 698–711.

[8] S. Assadi, S. Khanna, Y. Li, and G. Yaroslavtsev. 2016. Maximum matchings in dynamic graph streams and the simultaneous communication model. In *Proc. 27th ACM-SIAM Sympos. Discrete Algs.* (SODA). 1345–1364.

[9] A. Badanidiyuru, B. Mirzasoleiman, A. Karbasi, and A. Krause. 2014. Streaming submodular maximization: Massive data summarization on the fly. In *Proceedings of the 20th ACM SIGKDD international conference on Knowledge discovery and data mining*. 671–680.

[10] Z. Bar-Yossef, T. S. Jayram, R. Kumar, and D. Sivakumar. 2004. An information statistics approach to data stream and communication complexity. *J. Comput. Sys. Sci.* 68, 4 (2004), 702–732.

[11] Z. Bar-Yossef, T. S. Jayram, R. Kumar, D. Sivakumar, and L. Trevisan. 2002. Counting distinct elements in a data stream. In *International Workshop on Randomization and Approximation Techniques in Computer Science*. 1–10.

[12] M. Bateni, H. Esfandiari, and V. S. Mirrokni. 2017. Almost Optimal Streaming Algorithms for Coverage Problems. In *Proc. 29th ACM Sympos. Parallel Alg. Arch.* (SPAA). 13–23.

[13] J. Blasiok. 2018. Optimal streaming and tracking distinct elements with high probability. In *Proc. 29th ACM-SIAM Sympos. Discrete Algs.* (SODA). 2432–2448.

[14] V. Braverman, S. R. Chestnut, N. Ivkin, J. Nelson, Z. Wang, and D. P. Woodruff. 2017. BPTree: An ℓ_2 Heavy Hitters Algorithm Using Constant Memory. In *Proc. 36th ACM Sympos. on Principles of Database Systems* (PODS). 361–376.

[15] V. Braverman, S. R. Chestnut, N. Ivkin, and D. P. Woodruff. 2016. Beating CountSketch for heavy hitters in insertion streams. In *Proc. 48th Annu. ACM Sympos. Theory Comput.* (STOC). 740–753.

[16] A. Chakrabarti, S. Khot, and X. Sun. 2003. Near-optimal lower bounds on the multi-party communication complexity of set disjointness. In *18th Annual IEEE Conference on Computational Complexity*. 107–117.

[17] A. Chakrabarti and A. Wirth. 2016. Incidence Geometries and the Pass Complexity of Semi-Streaming Set Cover. In *Proc. 27th ACM-SIAM Sympos. Discrete Algs.* (SODA). 1365–1373.

[18] M. Charikar, K. Chen, and M. Farach-Colton. 2002. Finding frequent items in data streams. In *Proc. 29th Int. Colloq. Automata Lang. Prog.* (ICALP). 693–703.

[19] F. Chierichetti, R. Kumar, and A. Tomkins. 2010. Max-cover in map-reduce. In *Proc. 19th Int. Conf. World Wide Web* (WWW). 231–240.

[20] R. Chitnis, G. Cormode, H. Esfandiari, M. Hajiaghayi, A. McGregor, M. Monemizadeh, and S. Vorotnikova. 2016. Kernelization via sampling with applications to finding matchings and related problems in dynamic graph streams. In *Proc. 27th ACM-SIAM Sympos. Discrete Algs.* (SODA). 1326–1344.

[21] E. D. Demaine, P. Indyk, S. Mahabadi, and A. Vakilian. 2014. On Streaming and Communication Complexity of the Set Cover Problem. In *Proc. 28th Int. Symp. Dist. Comp.* (DISC), Vol. 8784. 484–498.

[22] Y. Emek and A. Rosén. 2014. Semi-Streaming Set Cover. In *Proc. 41st Int. Colloq. Automata Lang. Prog.* (ICALP) *(Lect. Notes in Comp. Sci.)*, Vol. 8572. 453–464. https://doi.org/10.1007/978-3-662-43948-7_38

[23] U. Feige. 1998. A threshold of ln n for approximating set cover. *Journal of the ACM (JACM)* 45, 4 (1998), 634–652.

[24] A. Gronemeier. 2009. Asymptotically Optimal Lower Bounds on the NIH-Multi-Party Information Complexity of the AND-Function and Disjointness. In *26th International Symposium on Theoretical Aspects of Computer Science, STACS 2009, February 26-28, 2009, Freiburg, Germany, Proceedings*. 505–516.

[25] S. Guha, A. McGregor, and D. Tench. 2015. Vertex and hyperedge connectivity in dynamic graph streams. In *Proc. 34th ACM Sympos. on Principles of Database Systems* (PODS). 241–247.

[26] S. Har-Peled, P. Indyk, S. Mahabadi, and A. Vakilian. 2016. Towards Tight Bounds for the Streaming Set Cover Problem. In *Proc. 35th ACM Sympos. on Principles of Database Systems* (PODS). 371–383.

[27] P. Indyk, S. Mahabadi, R. Rubinfeld, J. Ullman, A. Vakilian, and A. Yodpinyanee. 2017. Fractional Set Cover in the Streaming Model. *Approximation, Randomization, and Combinatorial Optimization* (APPROX/RANDOM) (2017), 198–217.

[28] P. Indyk, S. Mahabadi, R. Rubinfeld, A. Vakilian, and A. Yodpinyanee. 2018. Set Cover in Sub-linear Time. In *Proc. 29th ACM-SIAM Sympos. Discrete Algs.* (SODA). 2467–2486.

[29] P. Indyk and D. P. Woodruff. 2005. Optimal approximations of the frequency moments of data streams. In *Proc. 37th Annu. ACM Sympos. Theory Comput.* (STOC). 202–208.

[30] D. M. Kane, J. Nelson, and D. P. Woodruff. 2008. Revisiting norm estimation in data streams. *arXiv preprint arXiv:0811.3648* (2008).

[31] D. M. Kane, J. Nelson, and D. P. Woodruff. 2010. An optimal algorithm for the distinct elements problem. In *Proc. 29th ACM Sympos. on Principles of Database Systems* (PODS). 41–52.

[32] M. Kapralov, Y. T. Lee, C. Musco, C. Musco, and A. Sidford. 2017. Single pass spectral sparsification in dynamic streams. *SIAM J. Comput.* 46, 1 (2017), 456–477.

[33] S. Lattanzi, B. Moseley, S. Suri, and S. Vassilvitskii. 2011. Filtering: a method for solving graph problems in mapreduce. In *Proc. 23rd ACM Sympos. Parallel Alg. Arch.* (SPAA). ACM, 85–94.

[34] A. McGregor and H. T. Vu. 2017. Better Streaming Algorithms for the Maximum Coverage Problem. In *20th International Conference on Database Theory (ICDT)*. 22:1–22:18.

[35] G. L. Nemhauser, L. A. Wolsey, and M. L. Fisher. 1978. An analysis of approximations for maximizing submodular set functions–I. *Mathematical Programming* 14, 1 (1978), 265–294.

[36] Ashkan Norouzi-Fard, Jakub Tarnawski, Slobodan Mitrovic, Amir Zandieh, Aidasadat Mousavifar, and Ola Svensson. 2018. Beyond 1/2-Approximation for Submodular Maximization on Massive Data Streams. In *International Conference on Machine Learning (ICML)*. 3826–3835.

[37] B. Saha and L. Getoor. 2009. On Maximum Coverage in the Streaming Model & Application to Multi-topic Blog-Watch. In *Proc. SIAM Int. Conf. Data Mining* (SDM). 697–708.

[38] J. P. Schmidt, A. Siegel, and A. Srinivasan. 1995. Chernoff–Hoeffding bounds for applications with limited independence. *SIAM Journal on Discrete Mathematics* 8, 2 (1995), 223–250.

[39] M. Thorup and Y. Zhang. 2012. Tabulation-based 5-independent hashing with applications to linear probing and second moment estimation. *SIAM J. Comput.* 41, 2 (2012), 293–331.

[40] S. Vadhan. 2012. Pseudorandomness. *Foundations and Trends® in Theoretical Computer Science* 7, 1–3 (2012), 1–336.

A CHERNOFF BOUND FOR APPLICATIONS WITH LIMITED INDEPENDENCE

In this section, we mention some of the results in [38] on applications of Chernoff bound with limited independence that are used in our analysis.

Definition A.1 (Family of d-wise Independent Hash Functions). A family of functions $\mathcal{H} = \{h : [m] \to [n]\}$ is d-wise independent, if for any set of d distinct values $x_1, \cdots, x_d$, the random variables $h(x_1), \cdots, h(x_d)$ are independent and uniformly distributed in $[n]$ when h is picked uniformly at random from $\mathcal{H}$.

Next, we exploit the results that show for small values of d, we can store a family of d-wise hash function in small space and in the same time it suffices for our application of Chernoff bound.

Lemma A.2 (Corollary 3.34 in [40]). *For every values of m, n, and d, there is a family of d-wise independent hash functions $\mathcal{H} = \{h : [m] \to [n]\}$ such that a selecting a random function from $\mathcal{H}$ only requires $d \cdot \log(mn)$.*

Lemma A.3 (Theorem 5 in [38]). *Let $X_1, \cdots X_n$ be binary d-wise independent random variables and let $X := X_1 + \cdots + X_n$. Then,*

$$\Pr(|X - \mathrm{E}[X]| \geq \delta \mathrm{E}[X]) \leq \begin{cases} e^{-\frac{\mathrm{E}[X]\delta^2}{3}} & : \textit{if } \delta < 1 \textit{ and } d = \Omega(\delta^2 \mathrm{E}[X]); \\ e^{-\frac{\mathrm{E}[X]\delta}{3}} & : \textit{if } \delta \geq 1 \textit{ and } d = \Omega(\delta \mathrm{E}[X]). \end{cases}$$

Lemma A.4 (Theorem 6 in [38]). *Let $X_1, \cdots, X_n$ and $Y_1, \cdots, Y_n$ be Bernoulli trials such that for each i, $\mathrm{E}[X_i] = \mathrm{E}[Y_i] = p_i$. Let assume that Y_is are independent, but X_is are only d-wise independent. Further, let $p(r)$ and $p_d(r)$ respectively denote $\Pr(\sum_{i=1}^n Y_i = r)$ and $\Pr(\sum_{i=1}^n X_i = r)$ and let $\mu = \sum_{i=1}^n p_i$ be the expected number of success in the trials.*

If $d \geq e\mu + \ln(1/p(0)) + r + D$, then $|p_d(r) - p(r)| \leq e^{-D} p(r)$.

A.1 An Application: Set Sampling with $\Theta(\log(mn))$-wise Independence

Consider a set system $(\mathcal{U}, \mathcal{F})$ and let $h : \mathcal{F} \to [(cm \log m)/\gamma]$ be a function selected uniformly at random from a family of $\Theta(\log(mn))$-wise independent hash functions where c is a sufficiently large constant. Then, we think of our randomly selected sets $\mathcal{F}^{\mathrm{rnd}}$ to be the collection of sets in $\mathcal{F}$ that are mapped to one by h; $\mathcal{F}^{\mathrm{rnd}} := \{S \in \mathcal{F} \mid h(S) = 1\}$.

Lemma A.5. *Assuming $\gamma \geq 6c \log^2 m$, with probability at least $1 - m^{-1}$, $|\mathcal{F}^{\mathrm{rnd}}| \leq \gamma$.*

Proof. Let X_i be a random variable which is one if $S_i \in \mathcal{F}^{\mathrm{rnd}}$ and zero otherwise. We define $X := X_1 + \cdots + X_m$. Note that X_i are $\Theta(\log(mn))$-wise independent and $\mathrm{E}[X] = \gamma/(c \log m)$. Then, by an application of Chernoff bound with limited independence (Lemma A.3),

$$\Pr(X > \gamma) \leq \Pr(X > \underbrace{(1 + \sqrt{\frac{6c}{\gamma}} \log m)\mathrm{E}[X]}_{\leq 2\gamma/c}) < m^{-1}.$$

Hence, with high probability, $\mathcal{F}^{\mathrm{rnd}}$ has size at most γ. □

Next, we show that $\mathcal{F}^{\mathrm{rnd}}$ covers the set of elements $\mathcal{U}^{\mathrm{cmn}}_{\gamma}$ (see Definition 2.1).

Lemma A.6. *With probability at least $1 - n^{-1}$, $\mathcal{F}^{\mathrm{rnd}}$ covers $\mathcal{U}^{\mathrm{cmn}}_{\gamma}$.*

Proof. Let $e \in \mathcal{U}^{\mathrm{cmn}}_{\gamma}$ and let $S_1, \cdots, S_q$ be the sets in $\mathcal{F}$ that cover e: for each $i \leq q$, $e \in S_i$. We define X_i to be a random variable which is one if $S_i \in \mathcal{F}^{\mathrm{rnd}}$ and is zero otherwise. We also define $X := X_1 + \cdots + X_q$ to denote the number of sets in $\mathcal{F}^{\mathrm{rnd}}$ that cover e. Note that X_i are $\Theta(\log(mn))$-wise independent and $\mathrm{E}[X] = (\gamma/(cm \log m)) \cdot q \geq \log n \log(mn)$. Then, applying Chernoff bound on random variables with limited independence (Lemma A.3),

$$\Pr(X < 1) < \Pr(X < \underbrace{(1 - \sqrt{(6 \log n)/\mathrm{E}[X]})}_{\leq 1/2}\mathrm{E}[X]) < n^{-2}.$$

Hence, by union bound over all elements in $\mathcal{U}^{\mathrm{cmn}}_{\gamma}$, with high probability, $\mathcal{F}^{\mathrm{rnd}}$ covers $\mathcal{U}^{\mathrm{cmn}}_{\gamma}$. □

Lemma A.7 (Set Sampling with limited independence). *$\Theta(\log(mn))$ random bits suffice to implement set sampling method.*

B GENERALIZATION OF SECTION 4.2

In this section we generalize the approach of Section 4.2 which relates the results on heavy hitters and contributing classes to approximating the optimal coverage size. In Section 4.2, to simplify the presentation, we had the assumption that $\mathcal{U}^{\mathrm{cmn}}_{\mathrm{w}}$ is empty. This is in particular important since we can then assume that the total size of k-covers are roughly the same as their coverage size (up to polylogarithmic factors).

Here, we take care of the case in which $\mathcal{U}^{\mathrm{cmn}}_{\mathrm{w}}$ is non-empty and complete the description of our (α, δ, η)-oracle of Max k-Cover for the case $|C(\mathrm{OPT}_{\mathrm{large}})| \geq |C(\mathrm{OPT})|/2$. The high-level idea is to sample enough number of elements so that the algorithm using heavy hitters and contributing classes still works but in the same time no w-common element is among the sampled elements with at least a constant probability.

Step 1. Sampling Elements. We sample a subset $\mathcal{L} \subset \mathcal{U}$ in which each element e is in $\mathcal{L}$ with probability $\rho = (\mathrm{ts} \cdot \alpha\eta)/|\mathcal{U}| = \tilde{O}(\alpha/|\mathcal{U}|)$ where $\mathrm{t} = \tilde{O}(1)$ (see Table 2 for the exact values). We implement the process of sampling $\mathcal{L}$ via a hash function from a family of $\Theta(\log(mn))$-wise independent functions $\mathcal{H} = \{h : \mathcal{U} \to [\frac{n}{\mathrm{t} \cdot \mathrm{s}\alpha \cdot \eta}]\}$ such that $\mathcal{L} = \{e \in \mathcal{U} \mid h(e) = 1\}$.

Claim B.1. *With high probability, $\frac{\rho|\mathcal{U}|}{2} \leq |\mathcal{L}| \leq \frac{3\rho|\mathcal{U}|}{2}$.*

For each collection of set $\mathcal{D}$, we define $\mathcal{D}'$ to be the intersection of $\mathcal{D}$ with $\mathcal{L}$; $\mathcal{D}' := \{S \cap \mathcal{L} \mid S \in \mathcal{D}\}$.

Claim B.2. *If $|C(\mathcal{D})| \geq |\mathcal{U}|/(54\mathrm{f}\eta\alpha)$, then with probability at least $1 - m^{-2}$, $|C(\mathcal{D}')| \geq \rho|C(\mathcal{D})|/2$. Moreover, if $|C(\mathcal{D})| < |\mathcal{U}|/(54\mathrm{f}\eta\alpha)$, then with probability at least $1 - m^{-2}$, $|C(\mathcal{D}')| < \mathrm{ts}/(36\mathrm{f})$.*

Proof. Since $\mathrm{ts} \geq 27 \cdot 24\mathrm{f} \log m$ (as in Table 2), it follows from two applications of Chernoff bound on random variables with limited independence (Lemma A.3). □

Similarly to Lemma 4.14, we have the following guarantee for LargeSetSimple using the sampled set of elements $\mathcal{L}$.

Lemma B.3. *If $|C(OPT)| \geq |\mathcal{U}|/\eta$ and $\mathcal{L} \cap \mathcal{U}^{\mathrm{cmn}} = \emptyset$, then with probability at least $1 - (2 \log n \,\mathrm{polylog}\, m)^{-1}$, the output of LargeSetSimple with parameters $(\mathcal{L}, \mathrm{w}, \mathrm{r}_1 = \mathrm{s}_{\mathcal{L}}\alpha, \mathrm{r}_2 = \frac{cm \log m}{\mathrm{w}}, \mathrm{thr}_1 = \frac{|\mathcal{L}|}{18\eta\mathrm{s}\alpha}, \mathrm{thr}_2 = \frac{|\mathcal{L}|}{6\eta\alpha})$ is a superset whose coverage is at least $|\mathcal{U}|/(54\mathrm{f}\eta\alpha)$.*

Proof. By Claim B.1, $(\rho|\mathcal{U}|)/2 \leq |\mathcal{L}| \leq (3\rho|\mathcal{U}|)/2$. Moreover, by Claim B.2 and since $|C(\mathrm{OPT})| \geq |\mathcal{U}|/\eta$, with probability at least $1 - m^{-2}$, $|C(\mathrm{OPT}_{\mathrm{large}}) \cap \mathcal{L}| \geq \rho|C(\mathrm{OPT})|/4 \geq |\mathcal{L}|/(6\eta)$. We define $\eta_{\mathcal{L}} := 6\eta$ to denote the coverage of $\mathrm{OPT}_{\mathrm{large}}$ on the sampled elements $\mathcal{L}$.

Now, consider the collection $\mathrm{OPT}_{\mathrm{large}} := \{O_1, \cdots, O_q\}$. Since for each $i \leq q$, the contribution of O_i to the coverage of OPT is at least $1/(\mathrm{s}\alpha)$ fraction (i.e. $|O_i \setminus \bigcup_{j<i} O_j| \geq |C(\mathrm{OPT})|/(\mathrm{s}\alpha) \geq |\mathcal{U}|/(\eta\mathrm{s}\alpha)$), by Claim B.2, with probability at least $1 - m^{-1}$, for all $i \leq q$,

$$|(O_i \setminus \bigcup_{j<i} O_j) \cap \mathcal{L}| \geq \rho|C(\mathrm{OPT})|/(2\mathrm{s}\alpha).$$

This implies that $\{O_i \cap \mathcal{L} \mid O_i \in \mathrm{OPT_{large}}\}$ is a collection of sets whose contribution to $C(\mathrm{OPT}) \cap \mathcal{L}$ w.h.p. is at least $(\frac{\rho|C(\mathrm{OPT})|}{2s\alpha})/(\frac{3\rho|C(\mathrm{OPT})|}{2}) = 1/(3s\alpha)$. We define $\mathsf{s}_{\mathcal{L}} := 3\mathsf{s}$ which denotes the contribution of sets in $\mathrm{OPT_{large}}$ compared to the coverage of OPT on the sampled elements $\mathcal{L}$.

By an application of Lemma 4.14 with parameters ($\mathcal{V} := \mathcal{L}, \mathrm{thr}_1 := \frac{|\mathcal{L}|}{\eta_{\mathcal{L}} \mathsf{s}_{\mathcal{L}} \alpha}, \mathrm{thr}_2 := \frac{|\mathcal{L}|}{\eta_{\mathcal{L}} \alpha}$), with probability at least $1 - 1/(3 \log n \log^c m)$, the algorithm returns a superset $\mathcal{D}_i'$ whose coverage on the sampled set $\mathcal{L}$ is at least

$$\frac{|\mathcal{L}|}{3\mathsf{f}\eta_{\mathcal{L}}\alpha} \geq \frac{\rho|\mathcal{U}|}{36\mathsf{f}\alpha\eta} = \frac{\mathsf{ts}}{36\mathsf{f}}.$$

Then, by Claim B.2, with probability at least $1 - m^{-2}$, $\mathcal{D}_i$ has coverage at least $|\mathcal{U}|/(54\mathsf{f}\eta\alpha)$. □

Step 2. Handling Common Elements. Next, we turn our attention to the case $\mathcal{L} \cap \mathcal{U}_{\mathsf{w}}^{\mathsf{cmn}} \neq \emptyset$. Although common elements may be covered $\widetilde{\Omega}(1)$ times within a single superset, the contribution of common elements to all supersets is roughly the same.

Claim B.4. *Let $\mathcal{L}_{\mathsf{w}}^{\mathsf{cmn}} := \mathcal{L} \cap \mathcal{U}_{\mathsf{w}}^{\mathsf{cmn}}$ be the set of* w*-common elements that are sampled in $\mathcal{L}$. Then, with high probability, for each superset $\mathcal{D}$, the total number of times that elements of $\mathcal{L}_{\mathsf{w}}^{\mathsf{cmn}}$ appear in $\mathcal{D}$ (counting duplicates) belongs to $[P, 2P]$ where P is a fixed number larger than $\log n$.*

Proof. Let $e \in \mathcal{U}_{\mathsf{w}}^{\mathsf{cmn}}$ be a w-common element and let $S_1, \cdots, S_q$ be the collection of sets that contain e. For a superset $\mathcal{D}_j$, define $X_{i,j}$ to be a binary random variable that denotes whether $S_i \in \mathcal{D}_j$. Moreover, let $Y_{j,e} := X_{1,j} + \cdots + X_{q,j}$. Then, $\mathbf{E}[Y_{j,e}] = \frac{\mathsf{w}q}{cm \log m}$. By an application of Chernoff bound with limited independence (Lemma A.3) and since $\mathsf{w}q \geq cm \log m \log n \log(mn)$ (see Definition 2.1),

$$\Pr(|Y_{j,e} - \mathbf{E}[Y_{j,e}]| \geq \underbrace{\sqrt{\frac{6c\log(mn)m\log m}{\mathsf{w}q}}}_{\leq 1/3} \mathbf{E}[Y_{j,e}]) \leq (mn)^{-2}. \tag{7}$$

Note that for any w-common element e and any pair of supersets $\mathcal{D}_j, \mathcal{D}_i$, $\mathbf{E}[Y_{j,e}] = \mathbf{E}[Y_{i,e}]$. In particular, we define $Y_e := \mathbf{E}[Y_{j,e}]$ whose value is independet of the supersets. Next, we define $Y_{\mathsf{cmn}} := \sum_{e \in \mathcal{U}_{\mathsf{w}}^{\mathsf{cmn}}} Y_e$ to denote the expected contribution of w-common elements to any superset. Hence, for each superset $\mathcal{D}_j$, with probability at least $1 - 1/(nm^2)$, the total number of times that w-common elements are covered by $\mathcal{D}_j$ belongs to the range $[2Y_{\mathsf{cmn}}/3, 4Y_{\mathsf{cmn}}/3]$. Hence, with probability at least $1 - (mn)^{-1}$, the contribution of sampled w-common elements to each superset belongs to $[2Y_{\mathsf{cmn}}/3, 4Y_{\mathsf{cmn}}/3]$ where $Y_{\mathsf{cmn}} \geq \log n \log(mn) |\mathcal{L}_{\mathsf{w}}^{\mathsf{cmn}}| \geq \log n$. □

Next, we show that if a w-common element is picked in $\mathcal{L}$ the algorithm still does not return a superset with small coverage (though it may missed all large supersets). To this end, we modify LargeSetSimple and design a new subroutine LargeSetComplete as in Figure 6. The high-level idea is to guarantee that if the main contribution of a superset is just from the duplicate counts of w-common elements ($\propto P$), it will not be returned. To achieve this, unlike LargeSetSimple we do not allow F_2-Contributing to consider contributing classes of any size (up to $|Q|$). Instead, we set parameters r_1 and r_2 which denotes how large the size of a contributing class that we are looking for is. To handle the case in which the size of a contributing class is large (i.e. larger than r_2), we sample supersets proportional to $1/\mathsf{r}_2$ and compute their coverage by existing L_0-estimation algorithms.

Lemma B.5. *Even if $\mathcal{L} \cap \mathcal{U}_{\mathsf{w}}^{\mathsf{cmn}} \neq \emptyset$, with probability at least $1 - m^{-1}$, none of the solutions returned by* LargeSetComplete *with parameters ($\mathcal{L}, \mathsf{w}, \mathsf{r}_1 = \mathsf{s}_{\mathcal{L}}\alpha, \mathsf{r}_2 = \widetilde{\Theta}(\frac{cm \log m}{\mathsf{w}}), \mathrm{thr}_1 = \frac{|\mathcal{L}|}{18\eta s \alpha}, \mathrm{thr}_2 = \frac{|\mathcal{L}|}{6\eta\alpha}$) is a superset with coverage less than $|\mathcal{U}|/(54\mathsf{f} \cdot \eta \cdot \alpha)$.*

Proof. Here, we need to revisit Case 1 and Case 2 of Section 4.2 and redo the calculations with respect to the sampled elements $\mathcal{L}$.

Case 1. Suppose that F_2-Contributing$(\widetilde{\Omega}(\frac{\alpha^2}{m}), \mathsf{s}_{\mathcal{L}} \cdot \alpha)$ returns a solution whose coverage is less than $|\mathcal{U}|(54\mathsf{f} \cdot \eta \cdot \alpha)$.

Let $\vec{r}$ be a vector of size at most $(cm \log m)/\mathsf{w}$ whose ith entry denotes the total size of the intersection of sets in $\mathcal{D}_i$ and $\mathcal{L}_{\mathsf{w}}^{\mathsf{rare}} := \mathcal{L} \setminus \mathcal{U}_{\mathsf{w}}^{\mathsf{cmn}}$; $\vec{r}[i] := \sum_{S \in \mathcal{D}_i} |S \cap \mathcal{L}_{\mathsf{w}}^{\mathsf{rare}}|$. By Claim B.2, if $|C(\mathcal{D}_j)| < |\mathcal{U}|/(54\mathsf{f}\eta\alpha)$, with probability at least $1 - m^{-2}$, $|C(\mathcal{D}_i) \cap \mathcal{L}_{\mathsf{w}}^{\mathsf{rare}}| < |C(\mathcal{D}_i) \cap \mathcal{L}| < \mathsf{ts}/(36\mathsf{f})$. Hence, together with Claim 4.10, with probability at least $1 - 2m^{-2}$, $\vec{r}[i] < \mathsf{ts}/36$.

Similarly, let $\vec{v}$ be a vector of size $(cm \log m)/\mathsf{w}$ whose ith entry denotes the total size of the intersection of sets in $\mathcal{D}_i$ with the sampled elements $\mathcal{L}$; $\vec{v}[i] := \sum_{S \in \mathcal{D}_i} |S \cap \mathcal{L}|$. Note that Since $P \geq 1$, for each superset $\mathcal{D}_i$ with coverage less than $|\mathcal{U}|/(54\mathsf{f} \cdot \eta \cdot \alpha)$, $\vec{v}[i] \leq 2P + \vec{r}[i] \leq (\mathsf{ts}/36)P$. On the other hand, by Claim B.4, with probability at least $1 - m^{-1}$, the value of $\vec{v}[j]$ for all j in the sampled substream is at least P.

Moreover, since the size of contributing classes in this case is at most $\mathsf{s}_{\mathcal{L}} \cdot \alpha = 3\mathsf{s}\alpha$ (more precisely, we can always find at most $3\mathsf{s}\alpha$ sets that are $\widetilde{\Omega}(\frac{\alpha^2}{m})$-contributing), by Claim 2.8, with probability at least $1 - \frac{\log m}{m}$, all sampled substreams considered by F_2-Contributing$(\phi_1, \mathsf{s}_{\mathcal{L}} \cdot \alpha)$ have size at least $cm \log m/(\mathsf{w} \cdot \mathsf{s} \cdot \alpha)$. Hence, by Claim B.4, with probability at least $1 - \frac{2 \log m}{m}$,

$$F_2(\vec{v}_{\mathsf{smp}}) \geq (\frac{cm \log m}{\mathsf{w} \cdot \mathsf{s} \cdot \alpha})P^2,$$

```
LargeSetComplete(𝒱, w, r_1, r_2, thr_1, thr_2):
▷ Input: w is an upper bound on the size of a superset
▷ Parameters: φ_1 = Ω̃(α^2/m) and φ_2 = Ω̃(1)
▷ For Case 1
let Cntr_small be an instance of F_2-Contributing(φ_1, r_1)
▷ For Case 2
let Cntr_large be an instance of F_2-Contributing(φ_2, r_2)
pick h : ℱ → [(cm log m)/w] from Θ(log(mn))-wise
        independent hash functions
for each (S, e) in the data stream do
   if e ∈ 𝒱 then feed h(S) to both Cntr_small and Cntr_large
▷ output(Cntr) returns (1 ± 1/2)-estimate of frequencies
if there exists i* ∈ output(Cntr_small) such that ṽ_i* ≥ 1/2 · thr_1
   return 2ṽ_i*/(3f)
▷ add return {S | h(S) = i*} to get a k-cover
if there exists i* ∈ output(Cntr_large) such that ṽ_i* ≥ 1/2 · thr_2
   return 2ṽ_i*/(3f)
▷ add return {S | h(S) = i*} to get a k-cover

▷ Case 2: if size of the contributing class is large; Ω̃(|Q|)
let ℳ ⊂ Q be a collection of size 12|Q| log m/r_2
        picked uniformly at random
for each i ∈ ℳ do
   ▷ DE estimates the coverage of the supersets in ℒ
   let DE_i be a (1/2)-approximation algorithm of
        L_0-estimation initialized to zero
pick h : ℱ → [(cm log m)/w] from Θ(log(mn))-wise
        independent hash functions
for each (S, e) in the data stream do
   if e ∈ 𝒱 and h(S) ∈ ℳ then feed h(S) to DE_h(S)
if there exists i* ∈ ℳ such that VAL(DE_i*) ≥ 1/2 · thr_2
   return 2VAL(DE_i*)/3
   ▷ add return {S | h(S) = i*} to get the k-cover
return infeasible
```

Figure 6: A (α, δ, η)-oracle of Max k-Cover **that handles the case in which the majority of the coverage in an optimal solution is due to the sets whose coverage contributions are at least $1/(s\alpha)$ fraction of the optimal coverage size.**

where $\vec{v}_{\mathsf{smp}}$ is a vector corresponding to a sampled substream considered in F_2-Contributing$(\phi_1, \mathsf{s}_{\mathcal{L}} \cdot \alpha)$. Since $\mathsf{s}^4\mathsf{t}^2 \leq \frac{81}{2\eta\log(s\alpha)}$ (see Table 2) and by the value of ϕ_1 as in Eq. (6), the following holds:

$$(\frac{\mathsf{ts}}{36})^2 P^2 < \phi_1 \cdot \frac{cm \log m}{\mathsf{w} \cdot \mathsf{s} \cdot \alpha} P^2,$$

which implies that with probability at least $1 - 3\log m/m$, an entry corresponding to a superset with coverage less than $|\mathcal{U}|/(54\mathsf{f} \cdot \eta \cdot \alpha)$ cannot be a ϕ_1-HeavyHitter in any of the sampled substreams considered in F_2-Contributing$(\phi_1, \mathsf{s}_{\mathcal{L}} \cdot \alpha)$.

Case 2. The high-level idea in this case is similar to the previous case. In Case 1, we heavily used the fact that there exists a class containing at most $\mathsf{s}_{\mathcal{L}} \cdot \alpha$ coordinates that is $\widetilde{\Omega}(\frac{\alpha^2}{m})$-contributing.

This observation is crucial because then we can show that all sampled substreams considered in F_2-Contributing with parameters $(\phi_1, \mathsf{s}_{\mathcal{L}}\alpha)$ have size at least $\widetilde{\Omega}(m/(\mathsf{w} \cdot \mathsf{s}_{\mathcal{L}} \cdot \alpha))$ which rules out the possibility that a coordinate corresponding to a small superset is a $\widetilde{\Omega}(\frac{\alpha^2}{m})$-HeavyHitter for sufficiently small values of s (recall that $\mathsf{s}_{\mathcal{L}} = 3\mathsf{s}$).

However, in this case, a contributing class may have size $\widetilde{\Omega}(m/\mathsf{w})$ which results in a sampled substream with only $\widetilde{O}(1)$ coordinates in the run of F_2-Contributing! To address the issue, we handle the case in which a contributing class has more than $\mathsf{r}_2 : \frac{cm \log m}{\mathsf{w}} \cdot \gamma$ coordinates separately:

1. $\widetilde{\Omega}(1)$-contributing class has size less than r_2. Since $P \geq 1$ and by Claim B.2 and 4.10, for each superset $\mathcal{D}_j$ with coverage less than $|\mathcal{U}|/(54\mathsf{f} \cdot \eta \cdot \alpha)$, with probability at least $1 - 2m^{-2}$, $\vec{v}[j] \leq (\mathsf{ts}/36)P$. On the other hand, by Claim B.4, with probability at least $1 - m^{-1}$, the value of $\vec{v}[j]$ for all j in the sampled substream is at least P. Moreover, by Claim 2.8, with probability at least $1 - \frac{\log m}{m}$, all sampled substreams considered in F_2-Contributing$(\phi_2 = \frac{1}{2\log(\alpha)}, \mathsf{r}_2)$ invoked by LargeSetComplete (which is to handle Case 2) have at least $(\frac{3cm\log m}{\mathsf{w}\cdot\mathsf{r}_2}) = \frac{3}{\gamma}$ coordinates. Hence, $F_2(\vec{v}_{\mathsf{smp}}) \geq \frac{3}{\gamma} \cdot P^2$. By setting

$$\gamma < \frac{3\phi_2}{(\mathsf{ts}/36)^2} = \frac{1944}{\log(\alpha)\mathsf{t}^2\mathsf{s}^2}, \tag{8}$$

$\vec{v}[j]^2 \leq (\mathsf{ts}/36)^2P^2 < (\frac{1}{2\log\alpha}F_2(\vec{v}_{\mathsf{smp}}))$, which implies that an entry corresponding to a superset with coverage less than $\frac{|\mathcal{U}|}{27\mathsf{f}\cdot\eta\cdot\alpha}$ cannot be a ϕ_2-HeavyHitter in any of the sampled substream considered in F_2-Contributing(ϕ_2, r_2).

2. $\widetilde{\Omega}(1)$-contributing class has size at least r_2. Here, we need to consider an extra case compared to Lemma 4.14 and B.3 because we do not allow r_2 to try all values up to $(\frac{cm\log m}{\mathsf{w}})$. To address the case in which the number of coordinates in a contributing class is larger than r_2, we sample $\ell = (12\log m)|Q|/\mathsf{r}_2$ supersets $\mathcal{M}$ uniformly at random from Q; with high probability, $\mathcal{M}$ contains a superset from the contributing class. Then, we compute the coverage of sampled supersets via an existing algorithm for L_0-estimation. By Claim 4.13, the coverage of supersets corresponding to the ϕ_2-contributing class whose size is larger than r_2 on the sampled set $\mathcal{L}$ is at least $|\mathcal{L}|/(\eta_{\mathcal{L}} \cdot \alpha) \geq \mathsf{ts}/(12\mathsf{f})$. Hence, the algorithm finds a superset with coverage at least $\mathsf{ts}/(36\mathsf{f})$ on $\mathcal{L}$ which by Claim B.2, it implies that the returned superset has coverage at least $|\mathcal{U}|/(54\mathsf{f} \cdot \eta \cdot \mathsf{s} \cdot \alpha)$. □

Theorem B.6. *If $|C(OPT)| \geq |\mathcal{U}|/\eta$, then with probability at least $1-(\log n \operatorname{polylog} m)^{-1}$, LargeSet$(k, \alpha)$ returns at least $\frac{|\mathcal{U}|}{54f\cdot\eta\cdot\alpha}$. Moreover, if LargeSet$(k, \alpha)$ returns a value other than* **infeasible**, *then with probability at least $1-4m^{-1}$, $|C(OPT)| \geq \frac{|\mathcal{U}|}{54f\cdot\eta\cdot\alpha}$.*

Proof. By Lemma B.5, with probability at least $1-3m^{-1}$, LargeSet never returns a superset with coverage less than $|\mathcal{U}|/(27f\eta\alpha)$; either it returns a large enough estimate or returns **infeasible**. Here, we show that if $|C(\text{OPT})| > |\mathcal{U}|/\eta$, then the algorithm will return an estimate at least $|\mathcal{U}|/(54f\cdot\eta\cdot\alpha)$ with probability at least $1-1/(2\log n\log^c m)-n^{-1}$. To this end, we show that with high probability, in one of the $O(\log n)$ parallel runs of LargeSet, the sampled sets of elements $\mathcal{L}$ does not contain any common element. Then, by Lemma B.3, the algorithm with probability at least $1-1/(2\log n\log^c m)$ returns $|\mathcal{U}|/(54f\cdot\eta\cdot\alpha)$ in the iteration in which the sampled set of elements that does not contain any common elements.

Now, we show that with probability at least $1-n^{-1}$, in one of $O(\log n)$ parallel runs of LargeSet, the sampled set does not contain any common elements. Let $q = |\mathcal{U}_{w}^{cmn}|$ and define $Y_1, \cdots, Y_q$ to be independent Bernoulli trials with probability of success equal to ρ. Recall that, we have the assumption that $|\mathcal{U}_{k}^{cmn}| \leq \frac{\sigma|\mathcal{U}|}{\alpha}$ and since $w \leq k$, $|\mathcal{U}_{w}^{cmn}| \leq |\mathcal{U}_{k}^{cmn}| \leq \frac{\sigma|\mathcal{U}|}{\alpha}$,

$$\mu = \mathbf{E}[\sum_{i=1}^{q} Y_i] \leq \frac{\sigma|\mathcal{U}|}{\alpha}\cdot\rho = t\cdot s\cdot\eta\cdot\sigma$$

$$\Pr(\sum_{i=1}^{q} Y_i = 0) = (1-\rho)^q \geq e^{-2\rho q} \geq e^{-2t\cdot s\cdot\eta\cdot\sigma}$$

Next, let's assume that $\mathcal{U}_{w}^{cmn} = \{e_1, \cdots, e_q\}$. Further, define $X_1, \cdots, X_q$ to be random variables such that $X_i = 1$ if $e_i \in \mathcal{L}$. Hence, $X_1, \cdots, X_q$ are $\Theta(\log(mn))$-wise independent Bernoulli trials with success probability $\mathbf{E}[X_i] = \rho$. Next, by Lemma A.4 with the following parameters:

$r = 0, \ln(1/p(0)) \leq 2t\cdot s\cdot\eta\cdot\sigma, \mu = t\cdot s\cdot\eta\cdot\sigma, D = 12\log(mn)$,

and show that

$$\Pr(\mathcal{L}\cap\mathcal{U}_{w}^{cmn} = \emptyset) = \Pr(\sum_{i=1}^{q} X_i = 0) \geq \Pr(\sum_{i=1}^{q} Y_i)(1-e^{-D}) \geq e^{-2t\cdot s\cdot\eta\cdot\sigma}/2.$$

Hence, since $t\cdot s\cdot\eta\cdot\sigma = \eta = O(1)$ (see Table 2),

$$\Pr(\text{In all runs, } \mathcal{L}\cap\mathcal{U}^{cmn} \neq \emptyset) \leq (1-e^{-2t\cdot s\cdot\eta\cdot\sigma})^{O(\log n)} \leq n^{-1}.$$

The second property follows from Lemma B.5: if the algorithm returns a value other than **infeasible**, then with probability at least $1-4m^{-1}$, $|C(\text{OPT})| \geq |\mathcal{U}|/(54f\cdot\eta\cdot\alpha)$. □

```
LargeSet(k, α, w):
▷ Run LargeSetComplete on sampled set of elements
repeat O(log n) times in parallel
  let ℒ ⊆ 𝒰 s.t. each e ∈ ℒ w.p. ρ = t·sα·η / |𝒰|
  r1 ← s_ℒ α, r2 ← (cm log m / w) · γ   ▷ γ := 1944 / (t² s² log α)
  thr1 ← |ℒ|/(18ηsα), thr2 ← |ℒ|/(6ηα)
  SOL ← LargeSetComplete(ℒ, w, r1, r2, thr1, thr2)
      if SOL ≠ infeasible then return |𝒰|/(54f · η · α)
return infeasible
```

Figure 7: A single pass streaming algorithm.

Lemma B.7. *The amount of space used by LargeSet is $\widetilde{O}(\frac{m}{\alpha^2})$.*

Proof. Note that LargeSet performs $O(\log n)$ instances of LargeSetComplete in parallel. Hence, the total amount of space use by LargeSet is $O(\log n)$ times the space complexity of LargeSetComplete.

Similarly to the space analysis of LargeSetSimple, the amount of space to perform $\mathsf{Cntr}_{\mathsf{small}}$ and $\mathsf{Cntr}_{\mathsf{large}}$ as defined in LargeSetComplete is respectively $\widetilde{O}(1/\phi_1) = \widetilde{O}(m/\alpha^2)$ and $\widetilde{O}(1/\phi_2) = \widetilde{O}(1)$. Moreover, for the last case in which the contributing class has size larger than r_2, by Theorem 2.12, in total $\widetilde{O}(\frac{m}{w\cdot r_2}) = \widetilde{O}(1)$ space is required to compute the coverage of sampled supersets in $\mathcal{M}$. Note that, in all cases, by Lemma A.2, the algorithm can store h in $\widetilde{O}(1)$ space.

Hence, the total amount of space required to implement LargeSet is $\widetilde{O}(\frac{m}{\alpha^2})$. □

Proof of Theorem 4.8. The guarantee on the quality of the returned estimate follows from Theorem B.6 with $w = \min\{\alpha, k\}$ and $s = \widetilde{O}(w/\alpha)$ (as in Table 2). Moreover, Lemma B.7 shows that the space complexity of LargeSet is $\widetilde{O}(\frac{m}{\alpha^2})$.

Moreover, since with high probability the estimate returned by the algorithm is a lower bound on the coverage size of a k-cover of $\mathcal{F}$, the output of LargeSet with high probability, is smaller than the optimal coverage size of Max k-Cover$(\mathcal{U}, \mathcal{F})$. □

Weighted Reservoir Sampling from Distributed Streams

Rajesh Jayaram
Carnegie Mellon University
rkjayara@cs.cmu.edu

Gokarna Sharma
Kent State University
gsharma2@kent.edu

Srikanta Tirthapura
Iowa State University
snt@iastate.edu

David P. Woodruff
Carnegie Mellon University
dwoodruf@cs.cmu.edu

ABSTRACT

We consider message-efficient continuous random sampling from a distributed stream, where the probability of inclusion of an item in the sample is proportional to a weight associated with the item. The unweighted version, where all weights are equal, is well studied, and admits tight upper and lower bounds on message complexity. For weighted sampling with replacement, there is a simple reduction to unweighted sampling with replacement. However, in many applications the stream may have only a few heavy items which may dominate a random sample when chosen with replacement. Weighted sampling *without replacement* (weighted SWOR) eludes this issue, since such heavy items can be sampled at most once.

In this work, we present the first message-optimal algorithm for weighted SWOR from a distributed stream. Our algorithm also has optimal space and time complexity. As an application of our algorithm for weighted SWOR, we derive the first distributed streaming algorithms for tracking *heavy hitters with residual error.* Here the goal is to identify stream items that contribute significantly to the residual stream, once the heaviest items are removed. Residual heavy hitters generalize the notion of ℓ_1 heavy hitters and are important in streams that have a skewed distribution of weights. In addition to the upper bound, we also provide a lower bound on the message complexity that is nearly tight up to a $\log(1/\epsilon)$ factor. Finally, we use our weighted sampling algorithm to improve the message complexity of distributed L_1 tracking, also known as count tracking, which is a widely studied problem in distributed streaming. We also derive a tight message lower bound, which closes the message complexity of this fundamental problem.

KEYWORDS

Random Sampling, Continuous Streams, Weighted Sampling, Heavy Hitters, L_1 Tracking

ACM Reference Format:

Rajesh Jayaram, Gokarna Sharma, Srikanta Tirthapura, and David P. Woodruff. 2019. Weighted Reservoir Sampling from Distributed Streams. In *38th ACM SIGMOD-SIGACT-SIGAI Symposium on Principles of Database Systems (PODS'19), June 30-July 5, 2019, Amsterdam, Netherlands.* ACM, New York, NY, USA, 18 pages. https://doi.org/10.1145/3294052.3319696

PODS'19, June 30-July 5, 2019, Amsterdam, Netherlands

ACM ISBN 978-1-4503-6227-6/19/06...$15.00
https://doi.org/10.1145/3294052.3319696

1 INTRODUCTION

We consider the fundamental problem of maintaining a random sample of a data stream that is partitioned into multiple physically distributed streams. In the streaming setting, it is often observed that many distributed monitoring tasks can be reduced to sampling. For instance, a search engine that uses multiple distributed servers can maintain the set of "typical" queries posed to it through continuously maintaining a random sample of all the queries seen thus far. Another application is network monitoring, one of the driving applications for data stream processing, which deploys multiple monitoring devices within a network. Each device receives extremely high rate data streams, and one of the most commonly desired aggregates is a random sample over all data received so far [15, 16]. Oftentimes, the predominant bottleneck in distributed data processing is the network bandwidth, and so it is highly desirable to have algorithms that communicate as few messages as possible. In particular, as the volume of the data and the number of distributed sites observing the streams scale, it becomes infeasible to communicate all of the data points observed to a central coordinator. Thus, it is necessary to develop algorithms which send significantly fewer messages than the total number of data points received.

The above applications have motivated the study of the *continuous, distributed, streaming model [14]*, where there are k physically distributed sites, numbered 1 through k. Each site i receives a local stream of data $\mathcal{S}_i$. The sites are connected to a central coordinator, to which they can send and recieve messages. Queries are posed to the coordinator, asking for an aggregate over $\mathcal{S} = \cup_{i=1}^k \mathcal{S}_i$, the union of all streams observed so far. The goal is to minimize the *message complexity*, i.e., number of messages sent over the network, over the entire observation.

We now define the **distributed weighted random sampling** problem. Each local stream $\mathcal{S}_i$ consists of a sequence of items of the form (e, w) where e is an item identifier and w is a positive weight. The streams $\mathcal{S}_i$ are assumed to be disjoint. Let n denote the size of $\mathcal{S} = \cup_{i=1}^k \mathcal{S}_i$. The task is for the coordinator to continuously maintain a weighted random sample of size $s = \min\{n, s\}$ from $\mathcal{S}$. Note that the same identifier e can occur multiple times, perhaps in different streams with different weights, and each such occurrence is to be sampled as if it were a different item. We consider two variations of weighted random sampling – sampling with replacement and sampling without replacement.

A single weighted random sample from $\mathcal{S}$ is defined to be an item chosen from $\mathcal{S}$ where *the probability of choosing item (e, w) is proportional to w, i.e., equal to* $\frac{w}{\sum_{(e',w')\in\mathcal{S}} w'}$.

Definition 1.1. A *weighted random sample without replacement* (weighted SWOR) from $\mathcal{S}$ is a set S generated according to the following process. Initially S is empty. For i from 1 to s, a single weighted random sample is chosen from $(\mathcal{S} \setminus S)$ and added to S.

Definition 1.2. A *weighted random sample with replacement* (weighted SWR) from $\mathcal{S}$ is a set S generated according to the following process. Initially S is empty. For i from 1 to s, a single weighted random sample is chosen from $\mathcal{S}$ and added to S.

Definition 1.3. A distributed streaming algorithm $\mathcal{P}$ is a weighted sampler without (with) replacement if for each $t > 0$, the coordinator maintains a set S of size $\min\{t, s\}$ such that S is a weighted random sample chosen without (with) replacement from all items seen so far, $\{(e_1, w_1), \ldots, (e_t, w_t)\}$.

Distributed random sampling generalizes the classic *reservoir sampling* problem [28, 33] from a centralized to a distributed setting. Random sampling serves as a building block in other aggregation tasks, such as estimation of the number of distinct elements [12, 13] and identifying heavy hitters [5, 26, 29, 36]. Distributed random sampling has also been used in approximate query processing in big data systems such as BlinkDB [1]. Unweighted distributed sampling, where all weights are equal, is well studied and admits tight upper and lower bounds on message complexity [10, 14, 31]. However, to the best of the authors' knowledge, weighted distributed sampling has not been studied so far, though there is prior work in the centralized setting [7, 18].

Designing a message-efficient distributed sampler is non-trivial. One challenge is that the system state is distributed across multiple sites. It is not possible to keep the distributed state tightly synchronized, since this requires a significant message overhead. Since the states of the sites are not synchronized with the coordinator, sites may send updates to the coordinator even though the sample at the coordinator does not change. A second challenge is that the traditional metrics for a centralized sampling algorithm, such as space complexity and time per item, do not affect the message complexity of a distributed algorithm. For instance, a centralized algorithm that uses $O(1)$ update time and optimal $O(s)$ space need not lead to a distributed algorithm with optimal messages, since the number of messages sent depends on how many times the random sample changes according to the views of the sites and the coordinator. Finally, we emphasize the fact that, in Definition 1.3, the protocol must maintain a weighted SWOR *at all times* in the stream. There is no notion of failure in the definition of a weighted sampler – the protocol can never fail to maintain the sample S. These two features make the problem substantially more challenging.

1.1 Contributions

Let k denote the number of sites, s the desired sample size, and W the total weight received across all sites.

– We present an algorithm for weighted SWOR that achieves an optimal expected message complexity of $O\left(k\frac{\log(W/s)}{\log(1+k/s)}\right)$. The algorithm uses an optimal $\Theta(1)$ space at each site, and an optimal $\Theta(s)$ space at the coordinator. The update time of our algorithm is also optimal: $\Theta(1)$ for a site to process an update, and $O\left(k\frac{\log(W/s)}{\log(1+k/s)}\right)$ total runtime at the coordinator. Our algorithm is the first message-optimal algorithm for distributed weighted SWOR. We note that a message-efficient algorithm for weighted SWR follows via a reduction to the unweighted case, and obtaining an algorithm for SWOR is significantly harder, as described below.

– As an application of our weighted SWOR, we provide the first distributed streaming algorithm with small message complexity for continuously monitoring heavy hitters with a *residual* error guarantee. This allows us to identify heavy hitters in the residual stream after extremely heavy elements are removed. A residual error guarantee is stronger than the guarantee provided by ℓ_1 heavy hitters, and is especially useful for streams where the weight of items is highly skewed [6]. The expected message complexity of our algorithm is $O(k\log(W)/\log(k)+\log(1/\epsilon)\log(W)/\epsilon)$. We prove that our algorithm is nearly optimal, by also giving a $\Omega(k\log(W)/\log(k) + \log(W)/\epsilon)$ lower bound, which is tight up to a $\log(1/\epsilon)$ factor in the second term.

– We demonstrate another application of our sampling algorithms to the well-studied problem of L_1 tracking (or count tracking) in distributed streams, which requires the coordinator to maintain a $(1 \pm \epsilon)$ relative error approximation of the total weight seen so that at any given time, with constant probability, the estimate is correct.

For the case $k \geq 1/\epsilon^2$, the best known upper bound was $O(k\log W)$ messages in expectation [23]. Our algorithm for L_1 tracking uses $O(k\log(W)/\log(k) + \log(\epsilon W)/\epsilon^2)$ messages in expectation, which improves on the best known upper bound when $k \geq 1/\epsilon^2$. In this setting, we also improve the lower bound from $\Omega(k)$ to $\Omega(k\frac{\log(W)}{\log(k)})$.

For the case $k \leq 1/\epsilon^2$, matching upper and lower bounds of $\Theta((\sqrt{k}/\epsilon)\log W)$ were known [23]. When $k \geq 1/\epsilon^2$, the lower bound of [23] becomes $\Omega(\log(W)/\epsilon^2)$. So if $k \geq 1/\epsilon^2$ and $k\frac{\log(W)}{\log(k)} < \log(W)/\epsilon^2$, our upper bound is $O(\log(W)/\epsilon^2)$, which is tight, and otherwise our upper bound is $O(k\log(W)/\log(k))$, which is also tight. Thus, combined with the upper and lower bounds of [23], our results close the complexity of the distributed L_1 tracking problem.

1.2 Our Techniques

For the problem of sampling *with* replacement, there is a relatively straightforward reduction from the weighted to the unweighted case, which we elaborate on in Section 2.2. The reduction involves duplicating a item (e, w) a total of w times into *unweighted* updates, and does not require an increase in message complexity. On the other hand, there are inherent difficulties in attempting to carry out a similar reduction for sampling *without* replacement, which we will now discuss.

On the Difficulty of a Reduction from Weighted SWOR to Unweighted SWOR: We now examine the difficulties which arise when attempting to reduce the problem of weighted SWOR to unweighted SWOR. We consider the following natural candidate reduction. Given a weighted stream of items $\mathcal{S} = \{(e_i, w_i) | i = 1 \ldots n\}$, consider an unweighted stream $\mathcal{S}'$ where for each $(e_i, w_i) \in \mathcal{S}$, there are w_i copies of e_i in $\mathcal{S}'$. Note that $\mathcal{S}'$ can be constructed in a streaming manner as items of $\mathcal{S}$ are seen.

Let S' be an unweighted SWOR of s items from $\mathcal{S}'$. We remark that *if S' consists of s distinct identifiers*, then those distinct identifiers are in fact a weighted SWOR of $\mathcal{S}$. The difficulty of using this reduction is that of ensuring s distinct items within S'. One could consider a method that maintains an unweighted SWOR of size greater than s in S', expecting to get at least s distinct identifiers among them. However, this is not straightforward either, due to the presence of heavy-hitters (items with very large weight) which may contribute to a large fraction of the total weight in $\mathcal{S}$. For instance, if there are $s/2$ items that contribute to a more than $1 - 1/(100s)$ fraction of the total weight within $\mathcal{S}$, then S' is likely to contain only identifiers corresponding to these items. This makes it very unlikely that S' has s distinct identifiers, even if the size of S' is much larger than s. If the number of distinct items in S' falls below s, then one could invoke a "recovery" procedure that samples further items from the stream to bring the sample size back to s, but this itself will be a non-trivial distributed algorithm. Moreover, re-initializing or recovering the algorithm would be costly in terms of message complexity, and introduce unintended conditional dependencies into the distribution of the output. Note that one cannot apply distinct sampling [20, 21] to maintain s distinct items from $\mathcal{S}'$, since distinct sampling completely ignores the frequency of identifiers in $\mathcal{S}'$ (which correspond to weights in $\mathcal{S}$), while we do not want this behavior – items with a greater weight should be chosen with a higher probability.

Thus, one of the primary difficulties with an algorithm for weighted SWOR is to handle heavy hitters. One could next consider a method that explicitly maintains heavy hitters within the stream (using a streaming algorithm). On the remainder of the stream excluding the heavy hitters, one could attempt to apply the reduction to unweighted SWOR as described above. However, this does not quite work either, since after removing the heavy hitters from the stream, the remaining weight of the stream may still be dominated by just a few items, and the same difficulty persists. One has only swapped one set of heavy hitters for another. Such "residual heavy hitters" may not be heavy hitters in the original stream, and may have evaded capture when the first heavy hitters were identified. This may proceed recursively, where the weight of the stream is still dominated by only a few items after removing the heavy hitters and the residual heavy hitters. Therefore, heavy hitter identification does not solve our problem and further ideas are needed.

Algorithmic Ideas for Weighted SWOR: Our main algorithm for weighted SWOR combines two key ideas. Our first key technical contribution is to divide the items into multiple "level sets" according to the magnitude of their weights. All items within a single "level set" have weights that are close to each other. Our algorithm withholds an item from being considered by the sampler until the level set that the item belongs to has a (pre-specified) minimum number of items. This property ensures that when an item is considered for sampling, there are at least a minimum number of items of the same (or similar) weight, so that the difficulty that we faced with extreme heavy hitters does not surface. When a level set reaches a certain size, all items within the level set are released for further sampling. By choosing the weights of different levels to increase geometrically, we ensure that the number of level sets remains small, and the overhead of additional messages for filling up the level sets is small. While an item is withheld, we also run a procedure so that, at every time step, it will still be output in the sample at that time with the correct probability. Thus, the notion of withholding an item applies means only that it is withheld from an internal sampling algorithm (a subroutine), and not the overall sampler. Note that, for a distributed sampler to be correct, it cannot entirely withhold an item from being sampled, even for a single time step.

The second idea is that of "precision sampling". Originally used in [2] for sampling in non-distributed data streams, and then extended by [24, 25], the idea of precision sampling is to scale each weight w_i by an i.i.d. random variable x_i, which generates a "key" $v_i = w_i x_i$ for each item (e_i, w_i). One then looks at the resulting vector $v = (v_1, v_2, \ldots, v_n)$ of keys, and returns the largest coordinates in v. In particular, [24] used the random variables $x_i = 1/t_i^{1/p}$ where t_i is *exponentially distributed*, to develop perfect L_p samplers. A similar idea is also used in "priority sampling" [17] which was developed in the context of network monitoring to estimate subset sums. We use precision sampling to generate these keys for each item, such that the items with the s largest keys form the weighted SWOR of the stream.

It is not difficult to see that if each site independently ran such a sampler on its input–storing the items with the s largest keys–and sent each new sample to the coordinator, who then stores the items with the overall s largest keys, one would have a correct protocol with $O(ks\log(W))$ expected communication. This could be carried out by generating the keys w_i/t_i with exponential variables t_i, or also by using the keys u_i^{1/w_i} with u_i uniform on $(0, 1)$, as used for non-distributed weighted sampling without replacement in [18]. Thus, a key challenge addressed by our work is to improve the naïve multiplicative bound of $\tilde{O}(ks)$ to an additive bound of $\tilde{O}(k+s)$.

We also remark that by duplicating weighted items *in combination* with our new level set technique, it may be possible to adapt the message-optimal *unweighted* sampling algorithms of [14, 31] (see also [32]) to yield a weighted SWOR. The approach would nonetheless require the use of level sets, along with a similar analysis as provided in this work, to remove extremely heavy items from the stream which would cause issues with these samplers. We believe that our approach by scaling an entire weight by a random variable, rather than manually duplicating weighted items (e, w) into w unweighted items, is more natural and simpler to understand. Moreover, it is likely that we obtain improved runtime bounds at the sites by using the algorithm presented in this paper (which are runtime optimal).

Residual Heavy Hitters: For the problem of monitoring heavy hitters, the technique of sampling *with replacement* has been frequently applied. By standard coupon collector arguments, taking $O(\log(1/\epsilon)/\epsilon)$ samples with replacement is enough to find all items which have weight within an ϵ fraction of the total. On the other hand, it is possible and frequently the case that there are very few items which contain nearly all the weight of the stream. This is precisely the domain where SWOR achieves remarkably better results, since a with replacement sampler would only ever see the heavy items. Using this same number of samples *without replacement*, we demonstrate that we can recover all items which have weight within an ϵ fraction of the total *after* the top $1/\epsilon$ largest items are removed. This is *residual error* guarantee is much stronger in the case of skewed distributions of weights, and is a important application of SWOR.

L_1 **Tracking:** Finally, we observe that the following desirable property of our weighted SWOR: namely that, once the heavy hitters are withheld, the values of the keys stored by the algorithm at any time provide good estimates of the total L_1 (the sum of all the weights seen so far). By taking enough samples, we can show that the s-th order statistic, that is the s-largest key overall, concentrates around the value W^t/s, up to a $(1 \pm \epsilon)$ factor, where W^t is the sum of all the weights up to a given time t. Unfortunately, withholding heavy items alone is not sufficient for good message complexity, as one must naively withhold an extra $\Theta(1/\epsilon)$ factor more heavy items than the size of s to obtain good concentration. To avoid a $\Theta(1/\epsilon)$ blow-up in the complexity, we must remove heavy hitters in another way. To do this, we duplicate updates instead of withholding them, a trick used in [24] for a similar sampler. This observation yields an optimal algorithm for distributed L_1 tracking for $k \geq 1/\epsilon^2$, by using our weighted SWOR as a subroutine. Previously an optimal algorithm for L_1 tracking was known only for $k < 1/\epsilon^2$.

1.3 Related Work

Random sampling from a stream is a fundamental problem and there has been substantial prior work on it. The reservoir sampling algorithm (attributed to Waterman [28]) has been known since the 1960s. There has been much follow-up work on reservoir sampling including methods for speeding up reservoir sampling [33], sampling over a sliding window [4, 8, 19, 22, 35], and sampling from distinct elements in data [20, 21].

The sequential version of weighted reservoir sampling was considered by Efraimidis and Spirakis [18], who presented a one-pass $O(s)$ algorithm for weighted SWOR. Braverman et al. [7] presented another sequential algorithm for weighted SWOR, using a reduction to sampling with replacement through a "cascade sampling" algorithm.

Unweighted random sampling from distributed streams has been considered in prior works [10, 14, 31], which have yielded matching upper and lower bounds on sampling without replacement. Continuous random sampling for distinct elements from a data stream in a distributed setting has been considered in [11].

There has been a significant body of research on algorithms and lower bounds in the continuous distributed streaming model. This includes algorithms for frequency moments, [12, 13], entropy estimation [3, 9], heavy hitters and quantiles [36], distributed counts [23], and lower bounds on various statistical and graph aggregates [34].

Roadmap: We present preliminaries and basic results in Section 2, followed by an optimal algorithm for weighted SWOR in Section 3, applications to residual heavy hitters and lower bounds in Section 4, applications to L_1 tracking and lower bounds in Section 5, and concluding remarks in Section 6. Some proofs are deferred to Appendix.

2 PRELIMINARIES AND BASIC RESULTS

2.1 Preliminaries

As in prior work in the continuous distributed streaming model, we assume a *synchronous* communication model, where the system operates in *rounds*, and in each round, each site can observe (at most) one item, and send a message to the coordinator, and receive a response from the coordinator. We assume that the messages are delivered in FIFO order (no overtaking of messages), there is no message loss, and the sites and the coordinator do not crash. We make no assumption on the sizes of the different local streams received by different sites, the order of arrival, and the interleaving of the streams at different sites. The only assumption we have is a global ordering of the stream items by their time of arrival onto one of the sites. If n is the total number of items observed in the system, then for $j = 1 \dots n$, $o^j = (e_j, w_j)$ is the jth item observed in the total order. The partitioning of the items across different processors is carried out by an adversary.

Our space bounds are in terms of machine words, which we assume are of size $\Theta(\log(nW))$ bits, and that arithmetic operations on machine words can be performed in $O(1)$ time. We also assume that an element identifier and weight fits in a constant number of words. In our algorithms, the length of a message is a constant number of words, so that the number of messages is of the same order as the number of words communicated over the network. For simplicity (but without loss of generality), in the following sections we assume each weight w_j satisfies $w_j \geq 1$. Since each weight w_j can be written in a constant number of machine words by assumption, it follows that we could always scale the weights by a polynomial factor to ensure $w_j \geq 1$, which blows up the complexity of our algorithms only by a constant, since we only have logarithmic dependency on the total weight.

2.2 Basic Results

We first present some basic results for weighted SWR and weighted SWOR. Let n denote the number of items received in the stream.

Algorithm for Weighted SWR: We first derive a message-efficient algorithm for weighted SWR using a reduction to unweighted SWR. For this reduction, we assume that the weights w_i are integers. We first note the following result, from [14].

Theorem 2.1 ([14]). *There is a distributed algorithm for unweighted SWR with message complexity $O((k + s\log s)\frac{\log n}{\log(2+k/s)})$. The coordinator needs $O(s)$ space and $O((k + s\log s)\frac{\log n}{\log(2+k/s)})$ total time; each site needs $O(1)$ space and $O(1 + \frac{s}{n}\log s\frac{\log n}{\log(2+k/s)})$ time per item amortized.*

Corollary 2.2. *There is a distributed algorithm for weighted SWR with message complexity $O((k + s\log s)\frac{\log W}{\log(2+k/s)})$ where W is the total weight received so far. The coordinator needs $O(s)$ space and $O((k + s\log s)\frac{\log W}{\log(2+k/s)})$ total time. Each site needs $O(1)$ space and the amortized processing time per item at a site is $O(1 + \frac{1}{n}(k + s\log s)\frac{\log W}{\log(2+k/s)})$.*

Proof. We reduce weighted SWR to unweighted SWR as follows. Given stream of items with weights $\mathcal{S} = (e_i, w_i)$, $i = 1 \dots n$, consider an unweighted stream $\mathcal{S}'$ where for each $(e_i, w_i) \in \mathcal{S}$, there are w_i copies of e_i in $\mathcal{S}'$. Note that $\mathcal{S}'$ can be constructed in a streaming manner as items of $\mathcal{S}$ are seen.

Note that an unweighted SWR of s items chosen from $\mathcal{S}'$ is a weighted SWR of s items chosen from $\mathcal{S}$. To prove this, let S' denote an unweighted SWR of size s from $\mathcal{S}'$. Consider an arbitrary item in S'. Since there are w_i copies of e_i in $\mathcal{S}'$, this item is likely to be e_i with probability $w_i/\sum_j w_j$, and hence obeys the distribution we desire of a single item in a weighted SWR of $\mathcal{S}$. Since the items of S' are chosen independent of each other, the entire sample S' has the same distribution as a weighted SWR of s items from $\mathcal{S}$. The number of items in $\mathcal{S}'$ is equal to W, the total weight of $\mathcal{S}$. The message complexity, as well as the space complexity at the sites and the coordinator follow from Theorem 2.1.

The processing time per item at the site needs additional work. An unweighted SWR sampler simulates the execution of s independent copies of a single element sampler. Each element (e, w) in the weighted input stream leads to w elements into each of the s samplers. Naively done, this reduction leads to a total runtime of $O(sw)$, which can be very large. To improve on this, we speed up the sampling as follows. We note that in the algorithm in Section 3.2 of [14] for a single element unweighted SWR, in round j, an element is sent to the coordinator with probability 2^{-j} [1] When w elements are inserted, as in our reduction, the probability that at least one of them is sent to the coordinator is $\alpha(w, j) = 1 - (1 - 2^{-j})^w$. The site can simply send the element (e, w) to the coordinator with probability $\alpha(w, j)$. Repeating this s times leads to a runtime of $O(s)$ per element. To further improve on this, note that across all the s single element samplers, the number of samplers that send a message to the coordinator is a binomial random variable $B(s, \alpha(w, j))$. In the improved algorithm, the site samples a number X from this distribution. If $X > 0$, it chooses a random size X subset of the s samplers, and send (e, w) to the coordinator for each chosen sampler – as also noted in [14], this leads to the same distribution as making an independent decision for each sampler. The total time taken at the sites is now of the same order as the number of messages sent to the coordinator, which is $O\left((k + s\log s)\frac{\log W}{\log(2+k/s)}\right)$. The amortized time per element at the site is thus $O\left(1 + \frac{1}{n}(k + s\log s)\frac{\log W}{\log(2+k/s)}\right)$. □

Lower Bound for Weighted SWOR: We next present a lower bound on the message complexity of weighted SWOR, which follows from prior work on the message complexity of unweighted sampling without replacement. Let s denote the desired sample size and k the number of sites.

Theorem 2.3 ([31]). *For a constant $q, 0 < q < 1$, any correct algorithm that continuously maintains an unweighted random sample without replacement from a distributed stream must send $\Omega\left(\frac{k\log(n/s)}{\log(1+(k/s))}\right)$ messages with probability at least $1 - q$ and where the probability is taken over the algorithm's internal randomness, and where n is the number of items.*

Corollary 2.4. *For a constant $q, 0 < q < 1$, any correct algorithm that continuously maintains a weighted random sample without replacement from $\mathcal{S}$ must send $\Omega\left(\frac{k\log(W/s)}{\log(1+(k/s))}\right)$ messages with probability at least $1 - q$, where the probability is taken over the algorithm's internal randomness, and W is the total weight of all items so far.*

Proof. This lower bound follows since unweighted SWOR is a special case of weighted SWOR. We consider an input stream of W items, each with a weight of 1, and apply Theorem 2.3. □

[1]The algorithm in [14] divides execution into rounds; the exact definition of a round does not impact our analysis here, and is hence not provided.

3 WEIGHTED SWOR VIA PRECISION SAMPLING

We now present an algorithm for weighted SWOR on distributed streams. Our algorithm utilizes the general algorithmic framework of *precision sampling*, introduced by Andoni, Krauthgamer, and Onak [2]. The framework of the algorithm is relatively straightforward. When an update (e_i, w_i) is received at a site, the site generates a "key" $v_i = w_i/t_i$, where t_i is a generated exponential random variable. The coordinator then keeps the stream items (e_i, w_i) with the top s largest keys v_i. We first state a result on exponential scaling that allows for the basic correctness of our sampling algorithm.

Proposition 3.1 ([30], Equation 11.7 and Remark 1). *Let $\mathcal{S} = \{(e_1, w_1), (e_2, w_2), \ldots, (e_n, w_n)\}$ be a set of items, where each item has an identifier e_i and a weight w_i. Suppose for each $i \in [n]$ we generate a key $v_i = w_i/t_i$, where the t_is are i.i.d. exponential random variables with rate 1 (i.e., with pdf $p(x) = e^{-x}$ for $x \geq 0$). For $k \in [n]$, let the anti-ranks $D(k)$ be defined as the random variable indices such that $v_{D(1)} \geq v_{D(2)} \geq \cdots \geq v_{D(n)}$. For $s \leq n$, let $S(s) \subset [n]$ be the set of items (e_i, w_i) such that $i = D(k)$ for some $k \in [s]$ (i.e. v_i is among the top s largest keys). Then,*

- *$S(s)$ is a weighted SWOR from the set of items $\mathcal{S}$.*
- *We have the distributional equality:*

$$v_{D(k)} = \left(\sum_{j=1}^{k} \frac{E_j}{\sum_{q=j}^{n} w_{D(q)}}\right)^{-1}$$

where the random variables $E_1, \ldots, E_n$ are i.i.d. exponential random variables with rate 1, and are independent of the anti-rank vector $(D(1), D(2), \ldots, D(n))$.

The above remark demonstrates that taking the items with the top s largest keys indeed gives a weighted sample without replacement. The distributional equality given in the second part of Proposition 3.1 will be used soon in our analysis. Note that while the above results require continuous random variables to be used, we show that our results are not effected by limiting ourselves to a machine word of precision when generating the exponentials (Proposition 3.11). Thus our expected message complexity and runtime take into account the complexity required to generate the exponentials to the precision needed by our algorithm.

To reduce the number of messages sent from the sites to the coordinator, each site locally filters out items whose keys it is sure will not belong to the globally s largest keys. In order to achieve this, our algorithm divides the stream into *epochs*. The coordinator continuously maintains a threshold u, equal to the value of the smallest key v of an item (e, w, v) held in its sample set S, where S always holds the items (e_i, w_i, v_i) with the s largest values of v_i. For $r = \max\{2, k/s\}$, whenever $u \in [r^j, r^{j+1})$, the coordinator declares to all sites that the algorithm is in epoch i (at the beginning, the epoch is 0 until u first becomes equal to or larger than r). Note that this announcement requires k messages to be sent from the coordinator, and must be done once per epoch.

If the algorithm is in epoch j, and a site receives an update (e_i, w_i), it generates key v_i and sends (e_i, w_i, v_i) to the coordinator if and only if $v_i > r^j$. The coordinator will add the update (e_i, w_i, v_i) to the set S, and if this causes $|S| > s$, it removes the item (e, w, v) from S which has the smallest key v of all items in S. This way, at any time step t, the coordinator holds the items with the s-largest key values $v_i = w_i/t_i$, and outputs the set S as its weighted sample.

A complication in analyzing this algorithm is that it is not possible to directly connect the total weight received so far to the number of epochs that have progressed. For instance, it is not always true that the larger the total weight, the more epochs have elapsed (in expectation). For instance, if a few (fewer than s) items with a very large weight are received, then the total weight received can be large, but the sth largest key is still 0, so that we are still in the zeroth epoch.

To handle this situation, we introduce a *level set* procedure. The idea is to *withhold* heavy items seen in the stream from being sent to the sampler until they are no longer heavy. Here, by releasing an update (e_i, w_i) to the sampler we mean generating a key v_i for the item (e_i, w_i) and deciding whether to accept (e_i, w_i, v_i) into the sample set S. Specifically, we only release a heavy item to the sampler when its weight is no more than a $1/4s$ fraction of the total weight released to the sampler so far. We now defined the *level* of an update (e, w) below (Definition 3.2).

Definition 3.2. The level of an item (e, w) is the integer $j \geq 0$ such that $w \in [r^j, r^{j+1})$. If $w \in [0, r)$, we set $j = 0$.

For $j > 0$, the *level set* D_j will consist of the first $4rs$ items in the stream that are in level j. We do this for all $j \geq 0$, but note that we can clearly stop at $j = \log(W)/\log(r)$, and we do not need to explicitly initialize a level set until at least one item is sent to the set. The coordinator stores the set D_j. As long as $|D_j| < 4rs$, if a site received an item (e, w) that is in level j, the item is sent directly to the coordinator without any filtering at the site, and then placed into D_j. We call such a message an "early" message, as the item (e, w) is withheld from the sampling procedure. We call all other messages which send an item (e, w, v) from the site to the coordinator "regular" messages. Similarly, we call an update that resulted in an early message as an "early update", and all other updates as "regular updates". Note that a regular update may not result in a regular message, if the key of the regular update is smaller than the threshold for the current epoch.

We call the level set D_j *unsaturated* if $|D_j| < 4rs$ at a given time, and *saturated* otherwise. Each site stores a binary value $\texttt{saturated}_j$, which is initialized to `false`, indicating that $|D_j| < 4rs$. Once $|D_j| = 4rs$, the level set is saturated, and the coordinator generates keys $v_i = w_i/t_i$ for all items $(e_i, w_i) \in D_j$. For each new item-key pair, it then adds (e_i, w_i, v_i) to S if v_i is in the top s largest keys in $S \cup \{(e_i, w_i, v_i)\}$. At this point, the coordinator announces to all the sites that the level set D_j has been saturated (who then set $\texttt{saturated}_j = \texttt{true}$), and thereafter no early updates will be sent for this level set.

Note that in this procedure, the set S will only be a weighted sample over the updates in level sets that are saturated. Since our algorithm must always maintain a weighted sample over *all* stream items which have been received so far, we can simply simulate generating the keys for all items in the unsaturated level sets D_j, and take the items with the top s largest keys in $S \cup (\cup_{j\geq 0} D_j)$ as the weighted sample (see the description of this in the proof of Theorem 3.12). The algorithm for weighted SWOR is described in Algorithm 1 (algorithm at the site), and Algorithms 2, 3 (algorithm at the coordinator).

We now observe the following result of this level-set procedure.

Lemma 3.3. *At any time step, let $(e_1, w_1), \ldots, (e_t, w_t)$ be all items so far that are in saturated level sets. For any $i \in [t]$, $w_i \leq \frac{1}{4s} \sum_{p \in [t]} w_p$.*

Proof. The reason is that for each item (e_i, w_i) in a saturated level set, there are at least $4rs$ items in the same level set, whose weights are within a factor of r of w_i. Thus w_i can be no more than $\frac{1}{4s}$ of the total weight of this level set, and hence no more than $\frac{1}{4s}$ of the total weight. □

3.1 Analysis

We now analyze the message complexity of the algorithm. Let $r = \max\{2, k/s\}$, and let u be the s-th largest value of the keys v_j's given to the coordinator. As described, we define an epoch i as the sequence of updates such that $u \in [r^i, r^{i+1})$. Set $W = \sum_{i=1}^{n} w_i$, where n is the total number of updates at the end of the stream.

Let $(e_1, w_1), \ldots, (e_n, w_n)$ be the set of all stream items. For the sake of analysis, we consider a new ordering of the stream items, which corresponds to the order in which the keys v_i are generated for the items e_i in our algorithm. In other words, we assume the items are ordered $(e_1, w_1), \ldots, (e_{n'}, w_{n'})$, such that the key v_i for e_i was generated before the key for e_{i+1}, and so on. This reordering is simply accomplished by adding each regular item to the ordering as they arrive, but withholding each early item, and only adding an early item to the ordering once the level set D_j that it was sent to is saturated. Note that at the end of the

Algorithm 1: Weighted SWOR: Algorithm at Site i

```
// Initialization
for each level j ≥ 0 do
    saturated_j ← false
// we will have that u_i = r^j whenever the
    algorithm is in epoch j
u_i ← 0, r ← max{2, k/s}
// End Initialization
while true do
    if receive item (e, w) then
        // e an item id and w a positive weight
        Let j be the level set of (e, w), i.e. the integer j
          such that w ∈ [r^j, r^{j+1}). If w ∈ (0, 1), we set
          j = 0
        if saturated_j = false then
            Send (early, e, w) to the coordinator
        else
            // saturated_j = true
            Let t be an exponential random variable
            v ← w/t
            if v > u_i then
                Send (regular, e, w, v) to the
                  coordinator
    if receive ("level saturated", j) from coordinator then
        Set saturated_j ← true
    if receive ("update epoch", r^j) from coordinator then
        u ← r^j
```

Algorithm 2: Weighted SWOR: Algorithm at Coordinator

```
// Initialization
for each level j ≥ 0 do
    saturated_j ← false
    D_j ← ∅ // set of early messages in level j
u ← 0 // sth max of keys of regular items
S ← ∅ // the current sample at the coordinator
r ← max{2, k/s}
// End Initialization
while true do
    if receive (early, e, w) from site i then
        Let j be the level set of (e, w), i.e. the integer j
          such that w ∈ [r^j, r^{j+1}). If w ∈ (0, 1), we set
          j = 0
        Generate exponential t with rate 1
        Generate key v = w/i
        Add (e, w, v) to D_j
        if |D_j| ≥ 4sr then
            for each (e', w', v') ∈ D_j: do
                Add-to-Sample(S, (e', w', v'))
            D_j ← ∅, saturated_j ← true
            Broadcast ("level saturated", j) to all sites
    if receive (regular, e, w, v) from site i then
        if v > u then
            Add-to-Sample(S, (e, w, v))
    if receive query for sample of s items then
        Return items with the s largest keys in
          S ∪ (∪_j D_j)
```

Algorithm 3: Weighted SWOR: Add-to-Sample($S, (e_i, w_i, v_i)$)

```
Input: S is the current sample at the coordinator, and
       (e_i, w_i, v_i) the item to be inserted
S ← S ∪ {(e_i, w_i, v_i)}
if (|S| > s) then
    Let v_{jmin} = arg min_{v_t} {v_t | (e_t, w_t, v_t) ∈ S}
    S ← S \ {(e_{jmin}, w_{jmin}, v_{jmin})}
u_old ← u
u ← min_{(e,w,v)∈S} v
if u ∈ [r^j, r^{j+1}) and u_old ∉ [r^j, r^{j+1}) for some j then
    Broadcast ("update epoch", r^j) to all sites
```

stream, some level sets may not be saturated, thus $n' \leq n$. The remaining $n - n'$ items will have already been sent to the coordinator as early messages, and since no exponentials t_i will have been generated for them when the stream ends, we can ignore them when analyzing the message complexity of the regular stream items. Note that this ordering is a deterministic function of the original ordering and weights of the stream, and has no dependency on the randomness of our algorithm.

Now let $(e_{p_1}, w_{p_1}), (e_{p_2}, w_{p_2}), \ldots, (e_{p_\tau}, w_{p_\tau})$ be the subsequence of the regular items in $(e_1, w_1), \ldots, (e_{n'}, w_{n'})$, so that $p_1 \leq p_2 \leq \cdots \leq p_\tau$. We group the regular items $e_{p_1}, e_{p_2}, \ldots, e_{p_\tau}$ into sets Ω_i^j as follows. For any $t \in [n']$, let W_t be the total weight seen in the stream up to time t under the new ordering. Thus $W_t = \sum_{i=1}^{t} w_i$. We know by construction of the level sets, at any point in time that if e_{p_i} is a regular item then $w_{p_i} \leq \epsilon_0 W_{p_i - 1}$, where $\epsilon_0 = \frac{1}{4s}$. For any $i \geq 1$, let Ω_j be the set of all regular items (e_{p_i}, w_{p_i}) such that $W_{p_i} \in (sr^{j-1}, sr^j)$. Note that by definition, $\Omega_j = \emptyset$ for all $j > z$, where $z = \lceil \log(W/s)/\log(r) \rceil$. We now further break Ω_i into blocks $\Omega_i^1, \Omega_i^2, \ldots, \Omega_i^{q_i}$, such that Ω_i^t consists of all regular items (e_{p_i}, w_{p_i}) such that $W_{p_i} \in (sr^{i-1}(1+\epsilon)^{t-1}, sr^{i-1}(1+\epsilon)^t)$, for some value $\epsilon = \Theta(1)$ which we will later fix. Note that $q_i < \epsilon^{-1}\log(r)$.

Let Y_i indicate the event that the i-th regular item caused a message to be sent, where we order the items via the new ordering as above. If $\mathfrak{p}$ is the total number of regular items, then we would like to bound $\mathbb{E}\left[\sum_{i=1}^{\mathfrak{p}} Y_i\right]$. Note that the property of an item being regular is independent of the randomness in the algorithm, and is defined deterministically as a function of the ordering and weights of the stream. Thus $\mathfrak{p}$ is a fixed value depending on the stream itself. Then $\mathbb{E}[Y_i] = \sum_{j=1}^{\infty} \mathbb{E}\left[Y_i | \mathcal{E}_{i,j}\right] \Pr\left[\mathcal{E}_{i,j}\right]$ where $\mathcal{E}_{i,j}$ is the event that we are in epoch j when the i-th update is seen. Note that since $\mathcal{E}_{i,j}$ only depends on the values $t_1, \ldots, t_{i-1}$, it follows that $\mathbb{E}\left[Y_i | \mathcal{E}_{i,j}\right] = \Pr\left[t_i < w_i/r^j\right] \leq w_i/r^j$. Thus

$$\mathbb{E}[Y_i] \leq w_i \sum_{j=1}^{\infty} r^{-j} \Pr\left[\mathcal{E}_{i,j}\right]$$

Our goal will now be to bound the above quantity. We will only concern ourselves with $\mathcal{E}_{i,j}$ when e_i is a regular message, since the early messages will be sent to the coordinator deterministically.

To bound $\Pr\left[\mathcal{E}_{i,j}\right]$, we must bound the probability that we are in an epoch j much longer than expected. To do this, we develop a tail bound on the probability that the s-th largest key $v_i = w_i/t_i$ is much smaller than expected. To do so, we will first need the following standard tail bound on sums of exponential random variables.

Proposition 3.4. *Let $E_1, \ldots, E_k$ be i.i.d. mean 1 exponential random variables, and let $E = \sum_{i=1}^{k} E_i$. Then for any $c \geq 1/2$,*

$$\Pr[E > ck] < \lambda e^{-Cc}$$

where $\lambda, C > 0$ are fixed, absolute constants.

Proof. The moment generating function of an exponential E_i with mean 1 is given by $\mathbb{E}\left[e^{tE_i}\right] = \frac{1}{1-t}$ for $t < 1$. Thus $\mathbb{E}\left[e^{tE}\right] = \mathbb{E}\left[e^{t\sum_{i=1}^{k} E_i}\right] = \prod_{i=1}^{k} \mathbb{E}\left[e^{tE_i}\right] = (\frac{1}{1-t})^k$. Setting $t = 1/2$, then by Markov's inequality, $\Pr[E > ck] < \Pr\left[e^{tE} > e^{tck}\right] \leq \frac{2^k}{e^{1/2ck}} \leq e^{-1/2ck+k} = \lambda e^{-\Omega(c)}$ for any $c \geq 1/2$ and a fixed constant $\lambda > 0$ as needed. □

We now introduce our main tail bound on the behaviour of the s-th largest key v_i.

Proposition 3.5. *Let $w_1, \ldots, w_t$ be any fixed set of weights, and let $W = \sum_{i=1}^{t} w_i$. Fix $\ell \in [t]$, and suppose that $w_i \leq \frac{1}{2\ell} W$ for all $i \in [t]$. Let $v_i = w_i/t_i$ where the t_i's are i.i.d. exponential random variables. Define the anti-ranks $D(k)$ for $k \in [t]$ as the random variables such that $v_{D(1)} \geq v_{D(2)} \geq \cdots \geq v_{D(t)}$. Then for any $c \geq 1/2$, we have*

$$\Pr\left[v_{D(\ell)} \leq \frac{W}{c\ell}\right] \leq O(e^{-Cc})$$

where $C > 0$ is a fixed constant.

Proof. We note that $1/v_i$ is distributed as an exponential with rate w_i. The exponential order statistics of independent non-identical exponential random variables were studied by Nagaraja [30], who demonstrates that the ℓ-th largest value of v_k in $\{v_1, v_2, \ldots, v_t\}$ is distributed as (see Proposition 3.1, or equation 11.7 in [30]):

$$v_{D(\ell)} = \left(\sum_{j=1}^{\ell} \frac{E_j}{W - \sum_{q=1}^{j-1} w_{D(q)}}\right)^{-1} \geq \frac{W}{2}\left(\sum_{j=1}^{\ell} E_j\right)^{-1}$$

where the E_i's are i.i.d. exponential random variables with mean 1 that are independent of the anti-ranks $D(1), \ldots, D(t)$. Here, for the inequality, we used the fact that each regular item is at most a $1/(2\ell)$ heavy hitter at every intermediary step in the stream. It follows that if $v_{D(\ell)} \leq W/(c\ell)$, then $\sum_{j=1}^{\ell} E_j \geq \ell c/2$ Which occurs with probability $O(e^{-Cc})$ for some fixed constant $C > 0$ by Proposition 3.4. □

Proposition 3.6. *Let (e_i, w_i) be any regular stream item, and let a_i, b_i be such that $e_i \in \Omega_{a_i}^{b_i}$. Then we have:*

$$\sum_{j=1}^{\infty} r^{-j} \Pr\left[\mathcal{E}_{i,j}\right] \leq O\left(r^{-a_i+2} e^{-C\frac{(1+\epsilon)^{b_i-1}}{(1+\epsilon_0)}} + r^{-a_i+1}\right)$$

where $C > 0$ is some absolute constant.

Proof. First note for $j \geq a_i - 1$, we have $\sum_{j \geq k_i}^{\infty} r^{-j} \Pr\left[\mathcal{E}_{i,j}\right] \leq 2r^{-a_i+1}$. So we now bound $\Pr\left[\mathcal{E}_{i,j}\right]$ for $j < a_i$. Let $v_q = w_q/t_q$ for $q \in [i-1]$, and let $D(p)$ be the anti-ranks of the set $\{v_1, \ldots, v_{i-1}\}$. We note then that if $\mathcal{E}_{i,j}$ holds, then $v_{D(s)} < r^{j+1}$ by definition. Thus $\Pr\left[\mathcal{E}_{i,j}\right] \leq \Pr\left[v_{D(s)} \leq r^{j+1}\right]$. Note that by definition of the level sets $\Omega_{a_i}^{b_i}$, the total weight of all items seen up to time $i-1$ is $W_{i-1} > W_i \frac{1}{(1+\epsilon_0)} > sr^{a_i-1}\frac{(1+\epsilon)^{b_i-1}}{(1+\epsilon_0)}$. Here we have used the fact that, by construction of the ordering, no item w_i has weight greater than $\epsilon_0 W_i$ where $\epsilon_0 = \frac{1}{4s}$. This fact will also be needed to apply Proposition 3.5.

It then suffices to bound $\Pr\left[v_{D(s)} < r^{j+1}\right] = \Pr\left[v_{D(s)} < \frac{1}{c} W_{i-1}/s\right]$, where $c = W_{i-1}/(r^{j+1}s) \geq \frac{(1+\epsilon)^{b_i-1}}{(1+\epsilon_0)} r^{a_i-j-2}$. Note that since $j \leq i-2, b_i \geq 1$ and $\epsilon_0 = \frac{1}{4s} < 1/2$, we have $c > 1/2$. So by Proposition 3.5, $\Pr\left[\mathcal{E}_{i,j}\right] \leq \Pr\left[v_{D(s)} < \frac{1}{c} W_{i-1}/s\right] = O(e^{-Cc}) = O(e^{-C\frac{(1+\epsilon)^{b_i-1}}{(1+\epsilon_0)} r^{a_i-j-2}})$, where $C > 0$ is some absolute constant. Thus

$$r^{-j} \Pr\left[\mathcal{E}_{i,j}\right] \leq O\left(e^{-C\frac{(1+\epsilon)^{b_i-1}}{(1+\epsilon_0)} r^{a_i-j-2}} r^{-j}\right).$$

If $j = a_i - 2$, this is $O(r^{-a_i+2}e^{-\frac{C(1+\epsilon)^{b_i-1}}{(1+\epsilon_0)}})$. In general, if $j = a_i - 2 - \ell$ for any $\ell \geq 1$, then this bound becomes:

$$O\left(r^{-a_i+2+\ell}e^{-\frac{C(1+\epsilon)^{b_i-1}}{(1+\epsilon_0)}}r^{\ell}\right) = O\left(r^{-a_i+2-\ell}e^{-\frac{C(1+\epsilon)^{b_i-1}}{(1+\epsilon_0)}}\right)$$

where here we used the fact that $(e^{-x})^y = O(e^{-y}x^{-2})$ for any $x \geq 2$ and $y \geq \tau$ where $\tau > 0$ is some constant. Thus $\sum_{\ell=0}^{a_i-1} r^{-a_i+2-\ell}\Pr\left[\mathcal{E}_{i,j}\right] = O(r^{-a_i+2}e^{-C\frac{(1+\epsilon)^{b_i-1}}{(1+\epsilon_0)}})$ since $r \geq 2$, which completes the proof. □

Lemma 3.7. *Let $\mathfrak{p}$ be the number of regular items in the stream. If $Y_1, Y_2, \ldots$ are such that Y_i indicates the event that the i-th regular stream item (in the ordering defined above) causes a message to be sent, then:*

$$\mathbb{E}\left[\sum_{i=1}^{\mathfrak{p}} Y_i\right] = O\left(sr\frac{\log(W/s)}{\log(r)}\right).$$

Proof. Let $\mathcal{W}_i^j$ be the weight in set Ω_i^j. In other words, $\mathcal{W}_i^j = \sum_{w_{p_t}\in\Omega_i^j} w_{p_t}$. Recall we set $z = \lceil\log(W/s)/\log(r)\rceil$, and note that $\Omega_i = \emptyset$ for $i > z$. Also note that by construction we have $W_i^j < sr^{i-1}(1+\epsilon)^j$. Recall q_i is the number of sets of the form Ω_i^j for some j, and that $q_i \leq O(\epsilon^{-1}\log(r))$ by construction. Using Proposition 3.6, we have:

$$\begin{aligned}
\mathbb{E}\left[\sum_i Y_i\right] &\leq \sum_{i=1}^{z}\sum_{j=1}^{q_i}\sum_{e_{p_i}\in\Omega_i^j} w_{p_i}O\left(r^{-i+2}e^{-\frac{C(1+\epsilon)^{j-1}}{(1+\epsilon_0)}} + r^{-i+1}\right)\\
&\leq \sum_{i=1}^{z}\sum_{j=1}^{q_i}\mathcal{W}_i^j O\left(r^{-i+2}e^{-\frac{C(1+\epsilon)^{j-1}}{(1+\epsilon_0)}} + r^{-i+1}\right)\\
&\leq O(s)\sum_{i=1}^{z}\sum_{j=1}^{q_i}(1+\epsilon)^j\left(re^{-\frac{C(1+\epsilon)^{j-1}}{(1+\epsilon_0)}} + 1\right)\\
&= O(rs)\sum_{i=1}^{z}\sum_{j=1}^{q_i}(1+\epsilon)^j e^{-\frac{C(1+\epsilon)^{j-1}}{(1+\epsilon_0)}}\\
&\quad + O(s)\left(\sum_{i=1}^{z}\sum_{j=1}^{q_i}(1+\epsilon)^j\right)
\end{aligned}$$

Setting $\epsilon = .5$, we have $(1+\epsilon_0) < (1+\epsilon)$, this is

$$\leq O(sr)\sum_{i=1}^{z}\sum_{j=1}^{q_i}\frac{1.5^j}{\exp\left(C(1.5)^{j-2}\right)} + s\left(\sum_{i=1}^{z}O(r)\right)$$

Now by the ratio test $\sum_{j=1}^{\infty}\frac{(1.5)^j}{\exp(C(1.5)^{j-2})}$ converges absolutely to a constant (recalling $C > 0$ is just some absolute constant), so the whole sum is:

$$\leq sr\sum_{i=1}^{z}O(1) + sr\left(\sum_{i=1}^{z}O(1)\right) = O\left(sr\frac{\log(W/s)}{\log(r)}\right)$$

where we used $z = \lceil\log(W/s)/\log(r)\rceil$. □

We now bound the number of epochs used in the algorithm. We let the random variable ζ denote the total number of epochs in the algorithm.

Proposition 3.8. *If ζ is the number of epochs in the algorithm, then if $z = \lceil\frac{\log(W/s)}{\log(r)}\rceil$, then*

$$\mathbb{E}[\zeta] \leq 3\left(\frac{\log(W/s)}{\log(r)} + 1\right).$$

Proof. After epoch $z + \ell$ for any $\ell \geq 0$, we have that $u > r^{\ell}W$, where u is the value of the s-th largest key at the coordinator. Let $Y = |\{i \in [n] \mid v_i \geq r^{\ell}W\}|$. Since the pdf of an exponential random variable is upper bounded by 1, it follows that $\Pr\left[v_i \geq r^{\ell}W/s\right] = \Pr\left[t_j \leq sr^{-\ell}\frac{w_j}{W}\right] \leq sr^{-\ell}\frac{w_j}{W}$, thus $\mathbb{E}[Y] \leq sr^{-\ell}$. Thus $\Pr[\zeta \geq z+\ell] \leq \Pr[Y \geq s] \leq r^{-\ell}$, where the last inequality follows by a Markov bound. Thus

$$\begin{aligned}
\mathbb{E}[\zeta] &\leq z + \sum_{\ell\geq 1}(z+\ell)\Pr[\zeta \geq z+\ell]\\
&\leq z + \sum_{\ell\geq 1}(z+\ell)r^{-\ell} \leq 3z.
\end{aligned}$$

□

Lemma 3.9. *The total expected number of messages sent by the algorithm is $O\left(sr\frac{\log(W/s)}{\log(r)}\right)$, where $r = \max\{2, k/s\}$. Thus this can be rewritten as*

$$O\left(k\frac{\log(W/s)}{\log(1+k/s)}\right).$$

Proof. For each level set B_t for $t < \log(W/s)/\log(r)$, at most $4rs + k$ messages are sent, corresponding to the $4rs$ messages sent by sites to saturate the set, and then k messages coming from the reply from the coordinator to all k sites announcing that the set B_t is full. This gives a total of $(4rs + k)\log(W/s)/\log(r)$ messages. Finally, there are at most s items with weight greater than W/s, and thus we pay one message for each of these when they arrive at a site. The level sets corresponding to values greater than W/s will never be saturated, so the total message complexity to handle the early messages is $O(sr\log(W/s)/\log(r))$ as needed.

Next, we pay k messages at the end of every epoch. Thus if ζ is the number of epochs in the algorithm, the expected number of messages sent due to the end of epochs is

$$\mathbb{E}\left[\sum_{i=1}^{\zeta}k\right] = k\mathbb{E}[\zeta] < k\frac{\log(W/s)}{\log(r)} = O(sr\frac{\log(W/s)}{\log(r)})$$

by Proposition 3.8. Finally, the expected number of messages sent due to regular stream items is $O(sr\log(W/s)/\log(r))$ due to Lemma 3.7, which completes the proof of the message complexity. □

Proposition 3.10. *The algorithm described in this section can be implemented, without changing its output behavior, to* *use $O(s)$ memory and $O\left(k\frac{\log(W/s)}{\log(1+k/s)}\right)$ expected total runtime at the coordinator, and $O(1)$ memory and $O(1)$ processing time per update at each site. Note that all four of these bounds are optimal.*

Proof. We first consider the sites. Note that each site only generates a random variable, checks a bit to see if a level set is saturated, and then makes a single comparison to decide whether to send an item, all in $O(1)$ time. For space, note that each site only needs to store a bit that determines whether level set D_j is full for $j \leq \log(W)/\log(r)$. For all level sets j with $j \geq \log(W)/\log(r)$, no item will ever arrive in this level since no item has weight more than W. Thus, to store the bits $\texttt{saturated}_j$, it suffices to store a bit string of length $\log(W)/\log(r)$, which is at most $O(1)$ machine words.

We now consider the coordinator. For space, we demonstrate how the level-set procedure can be carried out using less than $O(sr\log(W)/\log(r))$ space (which is the total numer of items that can be sent to level sets). For each item that arrives at a level set, we generate its key right away. Now note that the items in the level sets with keys that are not among the s largest keys in all of the level sets will never be sampled, and thus never change the set S or the behavior of the algorithm, thus there is no point of keeping them. So at any time, we only store the identities of the items in the level sets with the top s keys (and which level they were in). Call this set S_{level} To determine when a level set becomes saturated, we keep an $O(\log(rs))$-bit counter for each level set D_j, which stores $|D_j|$. Note that we only need to store this for the levels $j \leq \log(W/s)/\log(r)$, since at most s items have weight more than W/s, and such level sets will never be saturated. When a level set D_j becomes saturated, for each item $(e, w, v) \in S_{level}$ such that (e, w) is in level j, we send this item to the main sampler (i.e., we decide whether or not to include it in S based on the size of its key). The result is the same had the entire level set been stored at all times, and only $O(s)$ machine words are required to store S_{level}, and $O(\log(sr)\log(W)/\log(r)) = O(\log(s)\log(W))$-bits for the counters, which is $O(\log(s)) < O(s)$ machine words, so the total space is $O(s)$ machine words.

For the runtime of the coordinator, each early item and regular item is processed in $O(1)$ time. When a set is saturated, it takes at most $O(s)$ work to send these new items into the main sampler, and this occurs at most $O(\log(W/s)/\log(r))$ times, for a total of $O(s\log(W/s)/\log(r))$ work. Since every other message the coordinator recieves requires $O(1)$ work, the result follows from Lemma 3.9. □

We now remark that, up until this point, we have not considered the bit complexity of our messages, or the runtime required to generate the exponentials to the required precision. We address this issue now.

Proposition 3.11. *The algorithm for weighted SWOR can be implemented so that each message requires an expected $O(1)$ machine words, and moreover, for any constant $c \geq 1$ uses $O(1)$ machine words with probability at least $1 - W^{-c}$. Each exponential can be generated in time $O(1)$ in expectation, and, for any constant $c \geq 1$, time $O(1)$ with probability at least $1 - W^{-c}$.*

Proof. To see this, we note that a site only needs to generate enough bits to determine whether a given key is large enough to be sent. Recall that the quantile function for the exponential distribution is given by $F^{-1}(p) = -\ln(1-p)$ and, since $1-p$ and p are distributed the same for a uniform variable, an exponential variable t_i can be generated by first generating a uniform random variable U, and outputting $-\ln(U)$ [27]. Thus, if the algorithm is in epoch j, one can simply generate U bit by bit, until one can determine whether $w_i/t_i > r^j$ or not. So each bit of U generated cuts the remaining probability space by a factor of 2. So for any threshold τ, it requires only $O(1)$ bits to be generated in expectation to determine whether $-\ln(U) < \tau$, and since the probability space is cut by a constant factor with each bit, only $O(\log(W))$ bits (or $O(1)$ machine words) are needed with high probability in W. Thus the coordinator generates the message in expected $O(1)$ time and with high probability, and the size of the message is an expected $O(1)$ machine words with high probability. Similarly, when the coordinator decides whether to accept a sample into the set, it again needs only to check the exponential against a threshold, which requires generating at most an additional expected $O(1)$ bits and with high probability, which completes the proof. □

Theorem 3.12. *The algorithm of this section for weighted sampling without replacement uses an expected $O\left(k\frac{\log(W/s)}{\log(1+k/s)}\right)$ messages and maintains continuously at every point in the stream a uniform weighted sample size s of the items seen so far in the stream. The space required for the coordinator is $O(s)$ machine words, and the space required for each site is $O(1)$ words. Each site requires $O(1)$ processing time per update, and the total runtime of the coordinator is $O\left(k\frac{\log(W/s)}{\log(1+k/s)}\right)$.*

Proof. The message complexity follows from Lemma 3.9, and the space and time complexity follow from Proposition 3.10. The bit complexity issues which arise from dealing with exponentials are dealt with in Proposition 3.11. For correctness, note that at any point in time, the coordinator maintains two kinds of sets: the set S which consists of the top s samples, and the level sets $D = \cup_{j\geq 0} D_j$. To obtain a true weighted SWOR of the stream up to any point i, the coordinator can simply generate an exponential t_j for each $(e_j, w_j) \in D$, and set $v_j = w_j/t_j$. It then constructs $D' = \{(e_j, w_j, v_j) | (e_j, w_j) \in D\}$, and returns the identifiers e_j in

$D' \cup S$ with the s largest keys v_j. The result is that at any point in time, the coordinator can output the set S of the entries (e_j, w_j, v_j) with the top s largest values of v_j.

Let Δ_ℓ be the identifiers e_j with the top ℓ values of v_j. Since $1/v_j$ is exponentially distributed with rate w_j, for any $\ell \geq 1$, if $v_j \notin \Delta_{\ell-1}$ then it follows that the probability that $1/v_j$ is the ℓ-th smallest (or v_j is the ℓ-th largest) is $\frac{w_j}{\sum_{e_t \notin \Delta_{\ell-1}} w_t}$ (via Proposition 3.1). Thus the coordinator indeed holds a uniform weighted sample of the stream continuously at all points in time. Note that this sample may contain items in a level set D_j which has not yet been filled at the time of query. However, this does not affect the behavior of the algorithm, since an exponential can be generated for such an item early and used as the sample (see proof of Proposition 3.10). By this, we mean that when the algorithm is queried for a weighted sample S over *all* stream items seen so far, it can simply generate a key for each item that is held in an unsaturated level set D_j, and keep the items with the top s largest keys in $S \cup (\cup_{j \geq 0} D_j)$. Note, however, that the true set S will not be modified by this procedure, and the actual items will not be sent into the set S to potentially be sampled until the level set D_j is full. □

4 TRACKING HEAVY HITTERS WITH RESIDUAL ERROR

In this section we demonstrate that our sampling algorithm results in a new algorithm for continuously monitoring heavy hitters with a *residual* error guarantee. This is also known as the heavy hitters tracking problem. We show an $O\left(\left(\frac{k}{\log(k)} + \frac{\log(1/(\epsilon\delta))}{\epsilon}\right)\log(\epsilon W)\right)$ upper bound for the message complexity of the problem, along with a nearly tight lower bound $\Omega\left(\left(\frac{k}{\log(k)} + \frac{1}{\epsilon}\right)\log(\epsilon W)\right)$.

While the monitoring of heavy hitters has been studied substantially in the streaming and distributed streaming literature, to date no distributed algorithm has been designed which obtains heavy hitters with a residual error guarantee. We first formalize these variations of the heavy hitters problem. For a vector $x \in \mathbb{R}^n$, and any $t \in [n]$, let $x_{\text{tail}(t)} \in \mathbb{R}^n$ be the vector which is equal to x except that the top t largest coordinates $|x_i|$ of x are set to 0. The following is the standard notion of the heavy hitters tracking problem.

Definition 4.1. Let $\mathcal{S} = (e_1, w_1), \ldots, (e_n, e_n)$, and let $x^t \in \mathbb{R}^n$ be the vector with $x_i = w_i$ for $i \leq t$, and $x_i = 0$ otherwise. Then an algorithm $\mathcal{P}$ solves the (ϵ, δ) heavy hitters tracking problem if, for any fixed $t \in [n]$, with probability $1 - \delta$, it returns a set S with $|S| = O(1/\epsilon)$ such that for every $i \in [t]$ with $x_i \geq \epsilon \|x^t\|_1$, we have $x_i \in S$.

Now, we introduce the variant of the heavy hitters tracking problem that requires residual error.

Definition 4.2. Let $\mathcal{S} = (e_1, w_1), \ldots, (e_n, e_n)$, and let $x^t \in \mathbb{R}^n$ be the vector with $x_i = w_i$ for $i \leq t$, and $x_i = 0$ otherwise. Then an algorithm $\mathcal{P}$ solves the (ϵ, δ) heavy hitters tracking problem *with residual error* if, for any fixed $t \in [n]$, with probability $1 - \delta$ it returns a set S with $|S| = O(1/\epsilon)$ such that for every $i \in [t]$ with $x_i \geq \epsilon \|x^t_{\text{tail}(1/\epsilon)}\|_1$, we have $x_i \in S$.

Note that the residual error guarantee is strictly stronger, and captures substantially more information about the data set when there are very large heavy items.

THEOREM 4.3. *There is a distributed streaming algorithm $\mathcal{P}$ which solves the (ϵ, δ) heavy hitters problem with residual error, and sends an expected $O\left(\left(\frac{k}{\log(k)} + \frac{\log(1/(\epsilon\delta))}{\epsilon}\right)\log(\epsilon W)\right)$ messages. The algorithm uses $O(1)$ space per site, $O(1)$ update time per site, $O(\frac{\log(1/(\delta\epsilon))}{\epsilon})$ space at the coordinator, and $O\left(\left(\frac{k}{\log(k)} + \frac{\log(1/(\epsilon\delta))}{\epsilon}\right)\log(\epsilon W)\right)$ overall runtime at the coordinator.*

PROOF. To obtain the bound, we run our weighted SWOR of Theorem 3.12 with $s = 6\frac{\log(1/(\delta\epsilon))}{\epsilon}$, where $C > 0$ is a sufficently large constant. Fix a time step t, and let S^t be the sample obtained by the weighted SWOR at that time. We know that S^t is a weighted SWOR from $(e_1, w_1), \ldots, (e_t, w_t)$. Let x^t be the vector corresponding to these weights, and let $T \subset [t]$ be the set of coordinates such that $x_i \geq \epsilon \|x^t_{\text{tail}(1/\epsilon)}\|_1$. Let $T_0 \subset T$ be the subset of i such the x^t_i is one of the $1/\epsilon$ largest values in x^t. Now fix any $i \in T$, and break S into blocks $S^1, S^2, \ldots, S^{2\log(1/(\delta\epsilon))}$, each of size $3/\epsilon$. Now for each $j \in [2\log(1/(\delta\epsilon))]$, there are at least $2/\epsilon$ items which are not in T_0 (which follows since $|T_0| \leq 1/\epsilon$). Conditioned on a sample $s \in S^j$ not being in T_0, since $x_j \geq \epsilon \|x^t_{\text{tail}(1/\epsilon)}\|_1$ by assumption, the probability that $s = i$ is at least ϵ. Thus the probability that $i \notin S^j \leq (1-\epsilon)^{2/\epsilon} < 1/2$. Repeating $2\log(1/\epsilon)$ times, the probability that $i \in S$ is at least $1 - (\frac{1}{2})^{2\log(1/(\delta\epsilon))} < 1 - (\epsilon\delta)^2$. We can then union bound over all $|T| < 2/\epsilon$ items, so that $T \subset S$ with probability at least $1 - \delta$. To restrict the set S to $O(1/\epsilon)$ items, we simply order the items in S by weight and output the top $2/\epsilon$, which will contain T if S does, which completes the proof of correctness. The remainder of the Theorem then follows from the complexity bounds of Theorem 3.12. □

4.1 Lower Bound for Tracking Heavy Hitters

We now demonstrate an $\Omega(k\log(W)/\log(k) + \log(W)/\epsilon))$ lower bound on the expected message complexity of any distributed algorithm that monitors the heavy hitters in a weighted stream (Definition 4.1). Since the residual error guarantee is strictly stronger, this lower bound extends to monitoring heavy hitters with residual error. The proof can be found in Appendix A.1

THEOREM 4.4. *Fix any constant $0 < q < 1$, and let $\epsilon \in (0, 1/2)$. Then any algorithm which $(\epsilon/2, \delta) = (\epsilon, q^2/64)$ solves the heavy hitters tracking problem (Definition 4.1), must send at least $\Omega(k \log(W)/\log(k) + \epsilon^{-1}\log(W))$ messages with probability at least $1 - q$ (assuming $1/\epsilon < W^{1-\xi}$ for some constant $\xi > 0$). In particular, the expected message complexity of such an algorithm with $\delta = \Theta(1)$ is $\Omega(k \log(W)/\log(k) + \epsilon^{-1}\log(W))$.*

5 L_1 TRACKING

In this section, we demonstrate how our sampling algorithm from Section 3 can be used to design a message-optimal L_1 tracking algorithm, which will close the complexity of this problem. We first recall the definition of an L_1 tracking algorithm.

Definition 5.1. Given a distributed weighted data stream $\mathcal{S} = (e_1, w_1), (e_2, w_2), \dots, (e_n, w_n)$ and parameters $\epsilon, \delta > 0$, a distributed streaming algorithm (ϵ, δ) solves the L_1 tracking problem if the coordinator continuously maintains a value $\widetilde{W}$ such that, at any fixed time $t \in [n]$, we have $\widetilde{W} = (1 \pm \epsilon)W_t$ with probability $1 - \delta$, where $W_t = \sum_{i=1}^{t} w_i$.

In [14], an L_1 tracker was given that had $O(k \log(W) \log(1/\delta))$ expected messages. An improved bound of $O((k + \sqrt{k}\log(1/\delta)/\epsilon)\log(W))$ expected messages was then provided in [23], along with a lower bound of $\Omega(\frac{\sqrt{k}}{\epsilon}\log(W))$ for all $k \leq \frac{1}{\epsilon^2}$. We remark that while the bounds of [23] are stated as $O(\sqrt{k}/\epsilon \log(W))$ (for constant δ), the actual expected message complexity of their algorithm is $O((k + \sqrt{k}\log(1/\delta)/\epsilon)\log(W))$ (in [23] the authors assume that $k < 1/\epsilon^2$). Nevertheless, the aforementioned bound is, up to this point, the current best known distributed algorithm for L_1 tracking.

In this section, we give tight bounds for the case $k > 1/\epsilon^2$. More specifically, we prove an L_1 tracking algorithm with expected message complexity $O(\frac{k\log(\epsilon W)}{\log(k)} + \frac{\log(\epsilon W)\log(1/\delta)}{\epsilon^2})$. In the following section, we also provide an $\Omega(k\frac{\log(W)}{\log(k)})$ lower bound for the problem. We remark that the results of [23] show an $\Omega(\frac{\sqrt{k}}{\epsilon}\log(W))$ lower bound assuming that $k < \frac{1}{\epsilon^2}$, and they give a matching upper bound in this regime. When $k > \frac{1}{\epsilon^2}$, the lower bound becomes $\Omega(\frac{1}{\epsilon^2}\log(W))$, which can be seen by simply applying the same lower bound on a subset of $1/\epsilon^2$ of the sites. Then when $k > 1/\epsilon^2$, if $k\log(W)/\log(k) < \log(W)/\epsilon^2$, our upper bound is $O(\log(W)/\epsilon^2)$, which is tight. Otherwise, our upper bound is $O(k\log(W)/\log(k))$, which matches our lower bound of $\Omega(k\log(W)/\log(k))$. Thus our protocol is optimal whenever $k > 1/\epsilon^2$. Since tight upper and lower bounds were known for the case of $k < 1/\epsilon^2$ by [23], this closes the complexity of the problem.

We also note that our lower bound assumes $1/\epsilon < W^{1-\xi}$ for some fixed constant $\xi > 0$. Thus our lower bound does not contradict our upper bound of $\Omega(k\log(\epsilon W)/\log(k) + \log(\epsilon W)/\epsilon^2)$ (for $\delta = \Theta(1)$). Observe that for $1/\epsilon = \Theta(W)$, one can simply send every stream update for $O(W)$ communication, which is also clearly a lower bound since any stream update not immediately sent would cause the coordinator to no longer have a $(1 \pm \epsilon)$ approximation.

Note for an L_1 tracking such that the coordinator has a value $\widetilde{W}$ such that $(1-\epsilon)W_t \leq \widetilde{W} \leq (1+\epsilon)W_T$ for *every* step $t = 1, 2, \dots, n$ with probability $1-\delta$, our algorithm uses $O(\frac{k\log(W/\epsilon)}{\log(k)} + \frac{\log(W/\epsilon)\log(\frac{\log(W)}{\epsilon\delta})}{\epsilon^2})$ expected message complexity. This second result simply comes from union bounding over the $\frac{\log(W)}{\epsilon\delta}$ points in the stream where the L_1 increases by a factor of $(1+\epsilon)$.

Citation	Message Complexity (upper or lower bound)
[14] + folklore	$O\left(\frac{k}{\epsilon}\log(W)\right)$
[23]	$O\left(k\log(W) + \frac{\sqrt{k}\log(W)\log(1/\delta)}{\epsilon}\right)$
This work	$O\left(\frac{k\log(\epsilon W)}{\log(k)} + \frac{\log(\epsilon W)}{\epsilon^2}\right)$
[23]	$\Omega\left(\frac{\sqrt{\min\{k, 1/\epsilon^2\}}}{\epsilon}\log(W)\right)$
This work	$\Omega\left(k\frac{\log(W)}{\log(k)}\right)$

Algorithm 1: Tracking L_1

Input: Distributed stream $\mathcal{S}$
Output: a value $\tilde{W}$ such that $\tilde{W} = (1 \pm \epsilon)W_t$ at any step time t with probability $1-\delta$.
Initalization:
Instantiate weighted SWOR algorithm $\mathcal{P}$ of Theorem 3.12 with $s = \Theta(\frac{1}{\epsilon^2}\log(\frac{1}{\delta}))$
On Stream item (e, w)
(1) Duplicate (e, w), a total of $\ell = \frac{s}{2\epsilon}$ times, to yield $(e^1, w), (e^2, w), \dots, (e^\ell, w)$. Insert each into the algorithm $\mathcal{P}$.
On Query for L_1 at time t:
(1) Let u be the value stored at the coordinator of the s-th smallest key held in the sample set S.
(2) Output $\tilde{W} = \frac{su}{\ell}$.

The known upper and lower bounds for L_1 tracking on a single time step with failure probability $\delta = \Theta(1)$ are summarized below. Note again, constant L_1 tracking at all points in the stream is accomplished in all cases by setting $\delta = \log(W)/\epsilon$, and note that the $\log(1/\delta)$ does not multiply the $O(k\log(W)/\log(k))$ term in our upper bound. With the combination of the upper and lower bounds of [23], this completely closes the complexity of the problem.

The proof of Proposition 5.2 and Theorem 5.3 can be found in Appendix A.

Proposition 5.2. *Let $E_1, E_2, \dots, E_s$ be i.i.d. exponential random variables with mean 1. Then for any $\epsilon > 0$, we have:*

$$\Pr\left[|\sum_{j=1}^{s} E_j - s| > \epsilon s \right] < 2e^{-\epsilon^2 s/5}$$

Theorem 5.3. *There is a distributed algorithm (Algorithm 1), where at every time step the coordinator maintains a value $\widetilde{W}$ such that at any fixed time $\tau \in [n]$, we have*

$$(1-\epsilon)W_\tau \le \widetilde{W} \le (1+\epsilon)W_\tau$$

with probability $1-\delta$, where $W_\tau = \sum_{i=1}^{\tau} w_i$ is the total weight seen so far at step τ. The expected message complexity of the algorithm is $O\left(\left(\frac{k}{\log(k)} + \epsilon^{-2}\log(1/\delta)\right)\log\left(\frac{\epsilon W}{\log(\delta^{-1})}\right)\right)$

Corollary 5.4. *There is a distributed algorithm where at every time step the coordinator maintains a value $\widetilde{W}$ such that*

$$(1-\epsilon)W_\tau \le \widetilde{W} \le (1+\epsilon)W_\tau$$

for every $\tau \in [n]$ with probability $1-\delta$. The expected message complexity of the algorithm is

$$O\left(\left(\frac{k}{\log(k)} + \epsilon^{-2}\log(\frac{\log(W)}{\delta\epsilon})\right)\log\left(\frac{\epsilon W}{\log(\delta^{-1})}\right)\right).$$

Proof. The result follows from running Theorem 5.3 with $\delta' = \log(W)/(\delta\epsilon)$, and union bounding over the $\log(W)/\epsilon$ time steps t in the stream where W_t increases by a factor of $(1+\epsilon)$. □

5.1 Lower Bound for L_1 Tracking

We now demonstrate an $\Omega(k\log(W)/\log(k) + \log(W)/\epsilon))$ lower bound on the expected message complexity of any distributed L_1 tracker. We remark again that our lower bound does not contradict out upper bound of $O(k\log(\epsilon W)/\log(k) + \log(\epsilon W)/\epsilon^2)$, since it requires $1/\epsilon < W^{1-\xi}$ for some constant ξ.

Note that the lower bound holds for both weighted and unweighted streams, as the hard example in the proof is a stream where all weights are equal to 1. We remark that the $\Omega(\log(W)/\epsilon)$ portion of the bound is only interesting when $k < \frac{1}{\epsilon}$, and in this regime a better lower bound of $\Omega(\frac{\sqrt{k}}{\epsilon}\log(W))$ is given by [23]. We include this portion of the bound in the Theorem for completeness, but remark that the main contribution of the Theorem is the lower bound of $\Omega(k\log(W)/\log(k))$. The proof of the Theorem can be found in Appendix A.2

Theorem 5.5. *Fix any constant $0 < q < 1$. Then any algorithm which $(\epsilon, \delta) = (\epsilon, q^2/64)$ solves the L_1 tracking problem (Definition 5.1), must send at least $\Omega(k\log(W)/\log(k) + \epsilon^{-1}\log(W))$ messages with probability at least $1-q$ (assuming $1/\epsilon < W^{1-\xi}$ for some constant $\xi > 0$). In particular, the expected message complexity of such an algorithm with $\delta = \Theta(1)$ is $\Omega(k\log(W)/\log(k) + \epsilon^{-1}\log(W))$.*

6 CONCLUSIONS

We presented message-efficient algorithms for maintaining a weighted random sample from a distributed stream. Our algorithm for weighted SWOR is optimal in its message complexity, space, as well as processing time. We also presented an optimal algorithm for L_1 tracking and the first distributed algorithms for tracking heavy hitters with residual error. One open question is whether we can obtain matching upper and lower bounds for weighted (or unweighted) sampling with replacement. While we can reduce weighted sampling with replacement to unweighted, known upper bounds are still a $\log(s)$ factor larger than the lower bounds. Another problem is to extend our algorithm for weighted sampling to the sliding window model of streaming, where only the most recent data is taken into account for the sample. Finally, for the residual heavy hitters problem, can one remove the $\log(1/\epsilon)$ factor from our bounds?

Acknowledgments: Rajesh Jayaram and David P. Woodruff thank the Simons Institute for the Theory of Computing where part of this work was done. They also acknowledge support by the National Science Foundation under Grant No. CCF-1815840. Srikanta Tirthapura acknowledges support by the National Science Foundation under grants 1527541 and 1725702.

REFERENCES

[1] Sameer Agarwal, Barzan Mozafari, Aurojit Panda, Henry Milner, Samuel Madden, and Ion Stoica. 2013. BlinkDB: Queries with Bounded Errors and Bounded Response Times on Very Large Data. In *ACM EuroSys*. 29–42.

[2] Alexandr Andoni, Robert Krauthgamer, and Krzysztof Onak. 2010. Streaming algorithms from precision sampling. *arXiv preprint arXiv:1011.1263* (2010).

[3] Chrisil Arackaparambil, Joshua Brody, and Amit Chakrabarti. 2009. Functional Monitoring Without Monotonicity. In *ICALP*. 95–106.

[4] Brian Babcock, Mayur Datar, and Rajeev Motwani. 2002. Sampling from a Moving Window over Streaming Data. In *SODA*. 633–634.

[5] Brian Babcock and Chris Olston. 2003. Distributed Top-k Monitoring. In *ACM SIGMOD*. 28–39.

[6] Radu Berinde, Piotr Indyk, Graham Cormode, and Martin J. Strauss. 2009. Space-optimal heavy hitters with strong error bounds. *PODS*.

[7] Vladimir Braverman, Rafail Ostrovsky, and Gregory Vorsanger. 2015. Weighted sampling without replacement from data streams. *IPL* 115, 12 (2015), 923–926.

[8] Vladimir Braverman, Rafail Ostrovsky, and Carlo Zaniolo. 2012. Optimal sampling from sliding windows. *J. Comput. System Sci.* 78 (2012), 260 – 272.

[9] Jiecao Chen and Qin Zhang. 2017. Improved Algorithms for Distributed Entropy Monitoring. *Algorithmica* 78, 3 (2017), 1041–1066.

[10] Yung-Yu Chung, Srikanta Tirthapura, and David P. Woodruff. 2016. A Simple Message-Optimal Algorithm for Random Sampling from a Distributed Stream. *IEEE Trans. Knowl. Data Eng.* 28, 6 (2016), 1356–1368.

[11] Yung-Yu Chung and Srikanta Tirthapura. 2015. Distinct Random Sampling from a Distributed Stream. In *IPDPS*. 532–541.

[12] Graham Cormode and Minos Garofalakis. 2005. Sketching Streams Through the Net: Distributed Approximate Query Tracking. In *VLDB*. VLDB Endowment, 13–24. http://dl.acm.org/citation.cfm?id=1083592.1083598

[13] Graham Cormode, S. Muthukrishnan, and Ke Yi. 2011. Algorithms for Distributed Functional Monitoring. *ACM Trans. Algorithms* 7, 2 (2011), 21:1–21:20.

[14] Graham Cormode, S. Muthukrishnan, Ke Yi, and Qin Zhang. 2012. Continuous Sampling from Distributed Streams. *JACM* 59, 2 (2012), 10:1–10:25.

[15] Nick G. Duffield, Carsten Lund, and Mikkel Thorup. 2003. Estimating flow distributions from sampled flow statistics. In *SIGCOMM*. 325–336.

[16] Nick G. Duffield, Carsten Lund, and Mikkel Thorup. 2004. Flow sampling under hard resource constraints. In *SIGMETRICS*. 85–96.

[17] Nick G. Duffield, Carsten Lund, and Mikkel Thorup. 2007. Priority sampling for estimation of arbitrary subset sums. *J. ACM* 54, 6 (2007), 32.

[18] Pavlos S. Efraimidis and Paul G. Spirakis. 2006. Weighted random sampling with a reservoir. *IPL* 97, 5 (2006), 181 – 185.

[19] Rainer Gemulla and Wolfgang Lehner. 2008. Sampling Time-based Sliding Windows in Bounded Space. In *ACM SIGMOD*. 379–392.

[20] Phillip B. Gibbons. 2001. Distinct Sampling for Highly-Accurate Answers to Distinct Values Queries and Event Reports. In *VLDB*. 541–550.

[21] Phillip B. Gibbons and Srikanta Tirthapura. 2001. Estimating Simple Functions on the Union of Data Streams. In *ACM SPAA*. 281–291.

[22] Phillip B. Gibbons and Srikanta Tirthapura. 2002. Distributed Streams Algorithms for Sliding Windows. In *ACM SPAA*. 63–72.

[23] Zengfeng Huang, Ke Yi, and Qin Zhang. 2012. Randomized algorithms for tracking distributed count, frequencies, and ranks. In *ACM PODS*. 295–306.

[24] Rajesh Jayaram and David P Woodruff. 2018. Perfect Lp Sampling in a Data Stream. In *IEEE FOCS*. 544–555.

[25] Hossein Jowhari, Mert Sağlam, and Gábor Tardos. 2011. Tight Bounds for Lp Samplers, Finding Duplicates in Streams, and Related Problems. In *PODS*. 49–58.

[26] Ram Keralapura, Graham Cormode, and Jeyashankher Ramamirtham. 2006. Communication-efficient Distributed Monitoring of Thresholded Counts. In *ACM SIGMOD*. 289–300.

[27] D. Knuth. 1997. *The art of computer programming: sorting and searching*. Vol. 3.

[28] D. Knuth. 1997. *The Art of Computer Programming, Volume 2 (3rd Ed.): Seminumerical Algorithms.*

[29] Amit Manjhi, Vladislav Shkapenyuk, Kedar Dhamdhere, and Christopher Olston. 2005. Finding (Recently) Frequent Items in Distributed Data Streams. In *IEEE ICDE*. 767–778.

[30] HN Nagaraja. 2006. Order statistics from independent exponential random variables and the sum of the top order statistics. *Advances in Distribution Theory, Order Statistics, and Inference* (2006), 173–185.

[31] Srikanta Tirthapura and David P. Woodruff. 2011. Optimal Random Sampling from Distributed Streams Revisited. In *DISC*. Springer-Verlag, Berlin, Heidelberg, 283–297. http://dl.acm.org/citation.cfm?id=2075029.2075065

[32] Srikanta Tirthapura and David P. Woodruff. 2019. Optimal Random Sampling from Distributed Streams Revisited. *CoRR* (2019). https://arxiv.org/abs/1903.12065

[33] J. S. Vitter. 1985. Random Sampling with a Reservoir. *ACM Trans. Math. Software* 11, 1 (1985), 37–57.

[34] David P. Woodruff and Qin Zhang. 2017. When distributed computation is communication expensive. *Distributed Computing* 30, 5 (2017), 309–323.

[35] Bojian Xu, Srikanta Tirthapura, and Costas Busch. 2008. Sketching asynchronous data streams over sliding windows. *Distributed Computing* 20, 5 (2008), 359–374.

[36] Ke Yi and Qin Zhang. 2013. Optimal Tracking of Distributed Heavy Hitters and Quantiles. *Algorithmica* 65, 1 (2013), 206–223.

A MISSING PROOFS

We first include a proof of Proposition 5.2.

PROPOSITION A.1 (PROPOSITION 5.2). *Let $E_1, E_2, \ldots, E_s$ be i.i.d. exponential random variables with mean 1. Then for any $\epsilon > 0$, we have:*

$$\Pr\left[|\sum_{j=1}^{s} E_j - s| > \epsilon s \right] < 2e^{-\epsilon^2 s/5}$$

PROOF. The moment generating function of $\sum_{j=1}^{s} E_j$ is given by $(\frac{1}{1-t})^s$ for $t < 1$,

$$\Pr\left[\sum_{j=1}^{s} E_j > (1+\epsilon)s \right] < \frac{(\frac{1}{1-t})^s}{e^{t(1+\epsilon)s}}$$
$$\leq \exp\left(-t(1+\epsilon)s + s\log(\frac{1}{1-t}) \right)$$

Setting $t = \epsilon$ and taking $\epsilon < 1/2$ we obtain

$$\leq \exp\left(-\epsilon^2 s - \epsilon s - s\log(1-\epsilon)\right)$$
$$\leq \exp\left(-\epsilon^2 s - \epsilon s + s(\epsilon + \epsilon^2/2 + \epsilon^3/3 + \ldots)\right)$$
$$\leq \exp\left(-\epsilon^2 s/5\right)$$

as needed. Next, we have

$$\Pr\left[\sum_{j=1}^{s} E_j < (1-\epsilon)s \right] < \Pr\left[e^{-t\sum_{j=1}^{s} E_j} > e^{-t(1-\epsilon)s} \right]$$
$$\leq \frac{(\frac{1}{1+t})^s}{\exp(-t(1-\epsilon)s)}$$
$$\leq \exp\left(t(1-\epsilon)s - s\log(1+t)\right)$$

setting $t = \epsilon$:

$$\leq \exp\left(-\epsilon^2 s + \epsilon s - s(\epsilon + \epsilon^2/2 + \epsilon^3/3 + \ldots)\right)$$
$$\leq \exp\left(-\epsilon^2 s/5\right)$$

and union bounding over the upper and lower tail bound gives the desired result. □

Below is a restatement and the proof of Theorem 5.3, for the correctness of our L_1 tracking algorithm.

THEOREM A.2 (THEOREM 5.3). *There is a distributed algorithm (Algorithm 1), where at every time step the coordinator maintains a value $\widetilde{W}$ such that at any fixed time $\tau \in [n]$, we have*

$$(1-\epsilon)W_\tau \le \widetilde{W} \le (1+\epsilon)W_\tau$$

with probability $1-\delta$, where $W_\tau = \sum_{i=1}^{\tau} w_i$ is the total weight seen so far at step τ. The expected message complexity of the algorithm is $O\left(\left(\frac{k}{\log(k)} + \epsilon^{-2}\log(1/\delta)\right)\log\left(\frac{\epsilon W}{\log(\delta^{-1})}\right)\right)$

PROOF. If W_τ is the total weight seen so far in the stream, then after duplication the weight of the new stream $\mathcal{S}'$ that is fed into $\mathcal{P}$ is $W_\tau \frac{2s}{\epsilon}$. Call the total weight seen up to time τ of the new stream $\overline{W}_\tau$. The duplication has the effect that at any time step τ in the original stream, every item $(e_j^i, w_j) \in \mathcal{S}'$, corresponding to a duplicate of $(e_j^i, w_j) \in \mathcal{S}$, is such that $w_j \le \frac{\epsilon}{2s}\overline{W}_\tau$. Thus once an update to $\mathcal{S}$ is finished being processed, no item in $\mathcal{S}'$ is more than an $\frac{\epsilon}{2s}$ heavy hitter. Since there are $\ell > s$ duplications made to each update, the level sets used in $\mathcal{P}$ will be immediately saturated the moment the first update in $\mathcal{S}$ with a weight in that level set arrives. Thus there is never any intermediate point in the stream $\mathcal{S}$ where some of the weight of the stream is being withheld in the level sets used by $\mathcal{P}$. Thus the total weight of the stream seen so far at any given time has already been sent to the sample, so each item (e_i, w_i) seen so far in the stream has had a key v_i generated for it.

Now the coordinator holds the value u such that u is the s-th largest value in $\{v_1, v_2, \dots, v_{\ell\tau}\}$, where ℓ was the number of duplications. Here $v_i = w_i/t_i$, where t_i is an exponetial variable and w_i is a weight of one of the duplicates sent to the stream $\mathcal{S}'$. By results on the order statistics of collections of exponential variables ([30]), we have the distributional equality

$$u = \left(\sum_{j=1}^{s} \frac{E_j}{\overline{W}_\tau - \sum_{q=1}^{j-1} w_{D(q)}}\right)^{-1}$$

where $E_1, E_2, \dots, E_s$ are i.i.d. exponential random variables, and $D(q)$ are the random variable indices such that $v_{D(1)} \ge V_{D(2)} \ge \cdots \ge V_{D(\tau\ell)}$ (the $D(q)$'s are known as anti-ranks). Since $w_{D(q)} \le \frac{\epsilon}{2s}\overline{W}_\tau$, it follows that

$$\begin{aligned} u &= \left((1\pm\epsilon)\sum_{j=1}^{s}\frac{E_j}{\overline{W}_\tau}\right)^{-1} \\ &= (1\pm O(\epsilon))\overline{W}_\tau\left(\sum_{j=1}^{s}E_j\right)^{-1} \\ &= (1\pm O(\epsilon))\ell W_\tau\left(\sum_{j=1}^{s}E_j\right)^{-1} \end{aligned}$$

Now by Proposition 5.2, we have $\Pr\left[|\sum_{j=1}^{s} E_j - s| > \epsilon s\right] < 2e^{-\epsilon^2 s/5} < \delta$, where here we set $s = 10\log(\delta^{-1})/\epsilon^2$. Conditioned on this not occurring, we have $u = (1\pm O(\epsilon))\ell W_\tau \frac{1}{s}$, thus $u\frac{s}{\ell} = (1\pm O(\epsilon))W_\tau$ as required, and the expected message complexity follows by Theorem 3.12 setting $s = \Theta(\frac{1}{\epsilon^2}\log(\frac{1}{\delta}))$. □

A.1 Proof of Heavy Hitters Lower Bound

THEOREM A.3 (THEOREM 4.4). *Fix any constant $0 < q < 1$, and let $\epsilon \in (0, 1/2)$. Then any algorithm which $(\epsilon/2, \delta) = (\epsilon, q/64)$ solves the heavy hitters tracking problem (Definition 4.1), must send at least $\Omega(k\log(W)/\log(k) + \epsilon^{-1}\log(W))$ messages with probability at least $1-q$ (assuming $1/\epsilon < W^{1-\xi}$ for some constant $\xi > 0$). In particular, the expected message complexity of such an algorithm with $\delta = \Theta(1)$ is $\Omega(k\log(W)/\log(k) + \epsilon^{-1}\log(W))$.*

PROOF. Create $s = \Theta(\frac{1}{\epsilon}\log(W))$ global stream updates (e_i, w_i), such that $w_i = (1+\epsilon)^i\epsilon$ and $w_0 = 1$. Then note for each $i \ge 0$, we have that w_i is an $\epsilon/(1+\epsilon) > \epsilon/2$ heavy hitter in $w_1, w_2, \dots, w_i$. Note that the total weight of the stream is $\sum_{i=1}^{s} w_i = W$.

Now consider any algorithm $\mathcal{P}$ for $(\epsilon/2, q^2/64)$ heavy hitter tracking, and at any time step t let S denote the set of heavy hitters held by $\mathcal{P}$,). On a given time step $t \in [n]$, let S_t denote the value of S at time t. and let R denote the concatenation of all random coin flips used by the algorithm $\mathcal{P}$ for both the sites and the coordinator. We first claim the following:

CLAIM 1. *Let $0 < q < 1$ be any constant. Suppose $\mathcal{P}$ is a randomized algorithm which $(\epsilon/2, q/64)$-solves the heavy hitter tacking problem. Suppose the set of heavy hitters it maintains at all times is called S. Then there is a constant $C' = C'(q) > 0$ such that:*

- *The set S changes at least $\frac{C'}{\epsilon}\log(n)$ times with probability at least $1-q$.*

PROOF. Consider the above stream instance. Note that on each time step, the new update (e_i, w_i) becomes an $\epsilon/2$ heavy hitter, and therefore should be accepted into the set S. Note moreover that at any time step t, the total weight is

$(1+\epsilon)^t$. Suppose there is a randomized algorithm $\mathcal{P}$ which for each $t \in T$, succeeds in outputting all the ϵ heavy hitters in a set S at time t with probability $1 - q/64$. Let X_t be a random variable that indicates that $\mathcal{P}$ is correct on t. We have $\mathbb{E}[X_t] > 1-q/64$, and clearly $\mathbb{E}[X_t X_{t'}] \le 1$ for any t, t'. Thus $\text{Var}(\sum_{i=1}^{\frac{1}{\epsilon}\log(n)} X_i) \le \frac{1}{\epsilon}\log(n)(1-q/64) + \frac{1}{\epsilon^2}\log^2(n) - \frac{1}{\epsilon^2}\log^2(n)(1-q/64)^2 \le (q/30)\frac{1}{\epsilon^2}\log^2(n)$ for n larger than some constant. By Chebyshev's inequality:

$$\Pr\left[\left|\frac{1}{\epsilon}\log(n)(1-q/64) - \sum_{i\le\epsilon^{-1}\log(n)} X_i\right| > \frac{1}{q}\sqrt{q/30}\frac{\log(n)}{\epsilon}\right] < q$$

Thus with probability at least $1-q$, $\mathcal{P}$ is correct on at least a $\frac{C'}{\epsilon}\log(n)$ number of the points in T, for $C' = (1 - q/64 - \frac{1}{\sqrt{30}}-) > 1/2$. Now suppose that, conditioned on this, the algorithm changed S fewer than $\frac{C'}{\epsilon}\log(n)$ times. Note that every time a new item (e_i, w_i) arrives, if $\mathcal{P}$ is correct on time i, it must be the case that $(e_i, w_i) \in S$ once update i is done processing. Thus if S did not change, but $(e_i, w_i) \in S_t$, this means $(e_i, w_i) \in S_{t-1}$ – the coordinator contained e_i in its set before the item arrived! By having e_i's being $O(\log(W))$ bit identifiers and randomizing the identities in the stream, it follows that the probability that this could occur at any time step t is less than $(W/\epsilon)(1/\text{poly}(W)) < W^{-100}$ for e_i's with $O(\log(W))$ bits and a sufficiently large constant. So we can safely condition on this event not occurring without affecting any of the claims of the theorem. It follows that S must change on every time step t on which it is correct, which completes the first claim that S must change at least $\frac{C'}{\epsilon}\log(n)$ times with probability at least $1-q$. □

Observe that the lower bound of of $\Omega(\log(W)/\epsilon)$ messages being sent with probability at least $1-q$ follows directly from the last claim. For the $\Omega(k\log(W)/\log(k))$ lower bound, we construct a new weighted stream. Define $\eta = \Theta(\frac{\log(W)}{\log(k)})$ *epochs*, as follows. In the i-th epoch, each site j receives *one* weighted update (e_i^j, k^i). Note then at the very beginning of the i-th epoch (for any i), the total weight seen in the stream so far is at most $2k^i$. Thus the first update (e_i^j, k^i) that arrives in the i-th epoch will be a $1/2$ heavy hitter, and thus must be accepted into S for the protocol to be correct on that time step.

Now consider any epoch i, and let X_i be the number of sites which sent or received a message from the coordinator in epoch i. Note that X_i is a lower bound on the number of messages sent in epoch i. Let X_i^j indicate that site j sent or recieved a message from the coordinator in epoch i, so that $X_i = \sum_{j\in[k]} X_i^j$. We claim $\mathbb{E}[X_i] = \Omega(k)$. To demonstrate this, consider the first site j^* which recieves an update in epoch i. Since item $(e_i^{j^*}, k^i)$ is immediately a $1/2$ heavy hitter, it must be sent to be correct. Since the protocol is correct on the $ki+1$'st time step with probability at least $1-q/64$, it follows that site j^* must send a message after receiving its update in epoch i with probability $1-q/64$, so $\mathbb{E}\left[X_i^{j^*}\right] > 1-q/64$.

But note that when a site j receives its update in the i-th epoch, if it has not communicated to the coordinator since the start of the epoch, it does not know the order in which it recieved the item. In particular, it does not know whether it was the first site to receive an item. Since the randomized protocol must be correct on any advesarial fixing of the ordering, it follows that if site j does not know if it recieved the first update, it must nevertheless send it with probability at least $1-q/64$ to be a correct protocol. In other words $\mathbb{E}\left[X_i^j\right] > 1-q/64$ *for all* $j \in [k]$, from which $\mathbb{E}[X_i] > (1-q/64)k$, and therefore $\mathbb{E}\left[\sum_{i=1}^{\eta} X_i\right] > (1-q/64)k$ follows. Thus $\mathbb{E}\left[k\eta - \sum_{i=1}^{\eta} X_i\right] < k\eta q/64$, and so by a Markov bound over the last expectation, $\Pr\left[\sum_{i=1}^{\eta} X_i < (1-1/64)k\eta\right] < q$. Since X_i lower bounds the number of messages sent in the i-th epoch, this completes the proof. □

A.2 Proof of L_1 Tracking Lower Bound

We now give the proof of the lower bound stated in Theorem 5.5. We first restate the result.

Theorem A.4 (Theorem 5.5). *Fix any constant $0 < q < 1$. Then any algorithm which $(\epsilon, \delta) = (\epsilon, q/64)$ solves the L_1 tracking problem (Definition 5.1), must send at least $\Omega(k\log(W)/\log(k) + \epsilon^{-1}\log(W))$ messages with probability at least $1-q$ (assuming $1/\epsilon < W^{1-\xi}$ for some constant $\xi > 0$). In particular, the expected message complexity of such an algorithm with $\delta = \Theta(1)$ is $\Omega(k\log(W)/\log(k) + \epsilon^{-1}\log(W))$.*

Proof. We proceed much in the way of Theorem 4.4. We define $\eta = \Theta(\frac{\log(W)}{\log(k)})$ epochs as follows: at the end of the $i-th$ epoch, for $i = 0, 1, 2, \ldots, \eta - 1$, there will have been exactly k^i global stream updates processed since the start of the stream, each with weight 1. Thus each epoch i is deterministically defined, and contains $k^{i+1} - k^i$ global updates. Let the unweighted updates be $e_1, e_2, \ldots, e_n$ (we can make these weighted by simply adding a weight of 1. Here $n = W$, so the stream is both weighted and unweighted. In each epoch, we partition the updates arbitrarily over the sites k.

Now consider any algorithm $\mathcal{P}$ for L_1 tracking, and at any time step t let u denote the value held by $\mathcal{P}$ which tracks the L_1 (total weight seen so far in the stream). On a given time step $t \in [n]$, let u_t denote the value of u at time t, and let R denote the concatination of all random coin flips used by the algorithm $\mathcal{P}$ for both the sites and the coordinator. We first claim the following:

CLAIM 2. *Let $0 < q < 1$ be any constant. Suppose $\mathcal{P}$ is a randomized algorithm which $(\epsilon, q/64)$-solves the L_1 tracking problem. Suppose the value it maintains for the L_1 approximation at all times is called u. Then there is a constant $C' = C'(q) > 0$ such that the following holds:*

- *The value u changes at least $\frac{C'}{\epsilon}\log(W)$ times with probability at least $1 - q$.*

PROOF. Consider the time steps $T = \{1, \text{rnd}(1 + \epsilon), \text{rnd}((1+\epsilon)^2), \ldots, \ldots, n\}$, where the L_1 changes be a factor of $(1+\epsilon)$, where rnd rounds the vaue to the nearest integer (note we can assume n is a power of $(1+\epsilon)$ by construction). Suppose there is a randomized algorithm $\mathcal{P}$ which for each $t \in T$, succeeds in outputting a $(1 \pm \epsilon)$ approximation to t at time t with probability $1 - q^2/64$. Assuming that $1/\epsilon < W^{1-\xi}$ for some constant $\xi > 0$, we have $|T| > \frac{1}{\epsilon}\log(W)$ distinct such points. Let X_t be a random variable that indicates that $\mathcal{P}$ is correct on t. We have $\mathbb{E}[X_t] > 1 - q/64$, and clearly $\mathbb{E}[X_t X_{t'}] \le 1$ for any t, t'. Thus $\text{Var}(\sum_{i=1}^{\frac{1}{\epsilon}\log(W)} X_i) \le \frac{1}{\epsilon}\log(W)(1 - q/64) + \frac{1}{\epsilon^2}\log^2(W) - \frac{1}{\epsilon^2}\log^2(W)(1-q/64)^2 \le (q/30)\frac{1}{\epsilon^2}\log^2(n)$ for n larger than some constant. By Chebyshev's inequality:

$$\Pr\left[\left|\frac{1}{\epsilon}\log(W)(1-q/64) - \sum_{i \le \epsilon^{-1}\log(W)} X_i\right| > \frac{1}{\sqrt{q}}\sqrt{q/30}\frac{\log(W)}{\epsilon}\right] < q$$

Thus with probability at least $1 - q$, $\mathcal{P}$ is correct on at least a $\frac{C'}{\epsilon}\log(W)$ number of the points in T, for $C' = (1 - q/64 - \frac{1}{\sqrt{30}} -) > 1/2$. Now suppose that, conditioned on this, the algorithm changed u less than $\frac{C'}{\epsilon}\log(W)$ times. But each time u changes, it can be correct for at most one of the values in T, which contradicts the fact that $\mathcal{P}$ is correct on at least a $\frac{C'}{\epsilon}\log(W)$ of these points. So with probability at least $1 - q$, the value of u must change at least $\frac{C'}{\epsilon}\log(W)$ times, as needed. □

Note that the lower bound of $\Omega(\log(W)/\epsilon)$ messages being sent with probability at least $1 - q$ follows directly from the last claim. Note moreover, that our lower bound reduces to $\Omega(\log(W)/\epsilon)$ when $k < 8/\epsilon$, so we can now assume that $k > 8/\epsilon$.

Now consider any epoch i, and let X_i be the number of sites which sent or received a message from the coordinator in epoch i. Let X_i^j indicate that site j sent or recieved a message from the coordinator in epoch i, so that $X_i = \sum_{j \in [k]} X_i^j$. We claim $\mathbb{E}[X_i] = \Omega(k)$. To demonstrate this, first note that at the beginning of an epoch, the current L_1 of the stream is k^i. First condition on the event $\mathcal{E}_i$ that the estimate of the algorithm is correct at the beginning of the epoch. Note $\Pr[\mathcal{E}_i] > 1 - q/64$. By the law of total expectation: $\mathbb{E}[X_i] \ge \mathbb{E}[X_i \mid \mathcal{E}_i](1 - q/64)$.

Now consider the stream of updates σ_i^j in epoch i which send exactly $2k^i$ consecutive updates to each site j. Consider any stream σ_i constructed by composing σ_i^j's for any arbitrary permutation of the j's. Note that if site j^* recieved the first set of updates in σ_i and does not send a message after these updates, the algorithm will have an incorrect L_1 estimate at time $3k^i$. Since this does not occur with probability at least $1 - q/64$, it follows that $\mathbb{E}\left[X_i^{j^*}\right] \ge (1 - q/64)$. But note that this must hold for all sites j, and once a site j receives its set of $2k^i$ updates, since it could have been the first one to recieve the updates (unless it hears otherwise from the coordinator). In other words, since the randomized protocol must maintain the same guarantee for any ordering of the stream, it follows that every site j must also send a message to the coordinator with probability at least $1 - q/64$ after it sees its $2k^i$ updates (unless the coordinator sends a message to it first). Thus $\mathbb{E}\left[X_i^j\right] \ge (1 - q/64)$ for all j, which completes the claim that $\mathbb{E}[X_i] \ge (1 - q/64)k$, giving $\mathbb{E}\left[\sum_{i=1}^{\eta} X_i\right] > k\eta(1 - q/64)$. Thus $\mathbb{E}\left[k\eta - \sum_{i=1}^{\eta} X_i\right] < k\eta q/64$, and so by a Markov bound over the last expectation, $\Pr\left[\sum_{i=1}^{\eta} X_i < (1 - 1/64)k\eta\right] < q$. Since X_i lower bounds the number of messages sent in the i-th epoch, this completes the proof. □

Distributed and Streaming Linear Programming in Low Dimensions

Sepehr Assadi*
Princeton University
Princeton, NJ, USA
sassadi@princeton.edu

Nikolai Karpov†
Indiana University Bloomington
Bloomington, IN, USA
nkarpov@iu.edu

Qin Zhang†
Indiana University Bloomington
Bloomington, IN, USA
qzhangcs@indiana.edu

Abstract

We study linear programming and general LP-type problems in several big data (streaming and distributed) models. We mainly focus on low dimensional problems in which the number of constraints is much larger than the number of variables. Low dimensional LP-type problems appear frequently in various machine learning tasks such as robust regression, support vector machines, and core vector machines. As supporting large-scale machine learning queries in database systems has become an important direction for database research, obtaining efficient algorithms for low dimensional LP-type problems on massive datasets is of great value. In this paper we give both upper and lower bounds for LP-type problems in distributed and streaming models. Our bounds are almost tight when the dimensionality of the problem is a fixed constant.

ACM Reference Format:
Sepehr Assadi, Nikolai Karpov, and Qin Zhang. 2019. Distributed and Streaming Linear Programming in Low Dimensions. In *38th ACM SIGMOD-SIGACT-SIGAI Symposium on Principles of Database Systems (PODS '19), June 30–July 5, 2019, Amsterdam, Netherlands.* ACM, New York, NY, USA, 18 pages. https://doi.org/10.1145/3294052.3319697

*Supported in part by the Simons foundation Algorithms and Geometry collaboration. Majority of the work done while the author was a graduate student at University of Pennsylvania.
†Supported in part by NSF CCF-1525024, IIS-1633215 and CCF-1844234.

ACM ISBN 978-1-4503-6227-6/19/06...$15.00
https://doi.org/10.1145/3294052.3319697

1 Introduction

As machine learning becomes pervasive, how to effectively support machine learning tasks in database systems has become an imminent question. In a recent paper [31], Makrynioti *et al.* observed that many machine learning problems can be expressed by *linear programs* (LP). They designed a level of abstraction called *SolverBlox* on top of a declarative language *LogiQL*[1] as a framework for expressing linear program formulations. The query in the format of SolverBlox will then be translated to a format supported by an LP solver for computing the solution. In this paper we consider the algorithmic side of this research direction, that is, we focus on the design of efficient LP solvers for large-scale datasets. In particular, we propose algorithms for linear programming in three popular "big data" models, namely, the *coordinator* model [38], the *streaming* model [2, 37], and *massively parallel computation* (MPC) [5, 23, 29]. We also provide almost matching lower bounds when the dimensionality of the linear program is a fixed constant.

In the rest of the introduction we will start with the definition of the problem and the description of the computation models, and then present our results and discuss previous work.

Problem Definition. The basic linear programming problem can be described as follows: we have a set of d variables $(x_1, \ldots, x_d)$ and a set of n linear constraints each of which (indexed by j) is in the form of $\sum_{i=1}^{d} a_i^j x_i \leq b^j$, where a_i^j, b^j are coefficients and d is the *dimension* of the problem. We also have an objective function $\sum_{i=1}^{d} c_i x_i$. The goal is to find an assignment for variables that minimizes the objective function while satisfying all the constraints.

Linear programming is a special case of a more general problem called *LP-type problem* [32], which we will discuss in details in Section 2.1. Besides linear programming, LP-type problems also include several other important problems in machine learning, such as *Linear Support Vector Machines (SVM)* [7], which is widely used in classification and regression analysis [10, 19, 22]), and *Core Vector Machines* [42], which is used to speed up general SVM computation (or,

[1]An extended version of Datalog [3].

Linear SVM augmented by the kernel trick [7]). We will give the formal definitions of these problems in Section 4. The algorithms we propose in this paper work for general LP-type problems.

In this paper we are interested in the scenario when the dimension of the linear program (and LP-type problem in general) is small compared to the number of constraints. Various examples of linear programming and LP-type problems in machine learning are of this type: SVMs and regression problems (in particular, least absolute error regression that can be modeled by linear programming) are often overconstrained; in the problems of Chebyshev approximation and linear separability, the number of variables are typically small.

Computational Models. We study linear programming and LP-type problems in the following big data models.

- *The (multi-pass) streaming model.* In this model, we have a single machine which can make linear scans of the input data sequence. The task is to compute some function defined on the input data sequence. The goal is to minimize the *memory space usage* and the *number of passes* needed. This model captures data that cannot fit the memory, and on which sequential scan is much more efficient than random access.
- *The coordinator model.* In this model, we have k sites and a central coordinator. Each site is connected by a two-way communication channel with the coordinator. The input is initially partitioned among the k sites. The task is for the sites and coordinator to jointly compute some function defined on the union of the k datasets. The computation proceeds in rounds: At the beginning of each round, the coordinator sends a message to each site, and then each site replies with a message back to the coordinator. At the end of the computation, the coordinator outputs the answer. The goal is to minimize the *total bits of the communication* and the *rounds of the computation.* This model fits data that is inherently distributed or cannot fit the storage of a single machine
- *Massively parallel computation (MPC).* In this model, we have k machines interconnected in a network that allows communication between any pairs of machines. Similar to the coordinator model, the input is partitioned among the k machines, and the task is for them to compute some function defined on the union of the k datasets. The computation is again in terms of rounds. At each round, the machines communicate with each other over the network by sending and receiving messages. The message sent by a machine at each round is a function of its input data and all messages it has received in previous rounds. Our goal is to minimize the *number of rounds of the computation,* and the *maximum bits of information sent or received by a machine at any round* (often called the *load* in the literature). MPC has already become the model of choice for studying parallel computation in computer clusters.

Description of the input. Since we are dealing with low-dimensional problems, we assume that the memory on each site/machine in each model is at least proportional to d, the dimension of the problem, but is significantly smaller than n, the number of constraints. As a result, the input is presented by giving the constraints one by one to the algorithm in the streaming model, or partitioning them across different sites/machines in the coordinator and MPC models.

1.1 Our Contributions and Related Work

In the following, we present our results for linear programming in the three big data models described above, and postpone the specifics of their generalization to LP-type problems to later sections. Our main upper bound result is the following.

Result 1. We give the following *polynomial time* algorithms for d-dimensional linear programming with n constraints. For any integer $r \geq 1$ and parameter $\delta \in (0, 1)$:

- *Streaming:* An $O(d \cdot r)$-pass streaming algorithm with $O(n^{1/r}) \cdot \text{poly}(d, \log n)$ space.
- *Coordinator:* An $O(d \cdot r)$-round distributed algorithm with $O(n^{1/r} + k) \cdot \text{poly}(d, \log n)$ total communication.
- *MPC:* An $O(d/\delta^2)$-round algorithm with $O(n^{\delta}) \cdot \text{poly}(d, \log n)$ load per machine.

Our algorithms are randomized and output the correct answer with probability $1 - 1/n^c$ for any desired constant $c \geq 1$.

By Result 1 for $r = \log n$ and $\delta = 1/\sqrt{\log n}$, we obtain linear programming algorithms that use $O(d \log n)$ passes or rounds, and have space, communication, or load requirements in each model that is almost independent of the number of constraints. For low-dimensional instances, this results in a dramatic saving compared to direct implementations of standard LP algorithms in these models.

Previously, Chan and Chen [13] proposed an $O(r^{d-1})$-pass streaming algorithm for linear programming that uses $O(n^{1/r}) \cdot \text{poly}(d, \log n)$ space. Result 1 improves upon this result by achieving an exponentially smaller pass-complexity in terms of d.

In the coordinator model, Daumé et al. [26] gave an algorithm using $O(r^{d+O(1)} \cdot k \cdot n^{1/r})$ communication based on an adaptation of the algorithm of [13]. The round-complexity and communication cost of this algorithm again depends exponentially on d.

In the MPC model, very recently Tao [41] gave a $d^{O(\log(1/\delta))}$-round MPC algorithm with load $O(n^{\delta})$ when $d = \text{polylog}(n)$

(for any $\delta \in (0,1)$). This algorithm is then used as a building block for an interesting database application called *entity matching with linear classification.* The round complexity of our MPC algorithm in Result 1 improves that of [41] by an exponential factor.

To summarize, Result 1 *exponentially* improves upon the pass/round complexities of the state-of-the-art, while using the same or smaller space, communication, or load, in the considered big data models.

We complement our algorithms by giving almost *tight* lower bounds for any fixed dimension (even $d = 2$) in the streaming and coordinator model.

Result 2. We give the following lower bounds for 2-dimensional linear programming with n constraints. For any integer $r \geq 1$:

- *Streaming:* Any r-pass algorithm requires $\Omega(n^{1/2r})$ space.
- *Coordinator:* Any r-round algorithm requires $\Omega(n^{1/2r})$ communication even when number of sites is only $k = 2$.

Our lower bounds hold even for randomized algorithms that output the correct answer with probability at least 2/3.

A few remarks about Result 2: Firstly, it is easy to see that linear programming in one dimension in the models we consider is a trivial task. Result 2 thus proves the lower bound for the smallest non-trivial dimension. We note that unlike Result 1 that worked in all the three models, Result 2 does *not* prove any lower bound for MPC algorithms. Proving lower bounds for MPC algorithms is considered to be a challenging task as it has serious implications for long standing open problems in complexity theory [39]. Hence, no *unconditional* lower bounds are known so far in the literature for *any* MPC problem and Result 2 is of no exception.

Prior to our work, Chan and Chen [13] gave a lower bound for 2-dimensional linear programming for a *restricted* family of *deterministic* streaming algorithms in the *decision tree* model (the only permitted operation of these streaming algorithms is testing the sign of a function evaluated at the coefficients of a subset of stored hyperplanes). Their lower bound states that this type of algorithms require $\Omega(n^{1/r})$ space to compute the solution in r passes. Our lower bound in Result 2 is much stronger in that it proves a similar pass-space tradeoff for *all* streaming algorithms (even randomized). Finally, Guha and McGregor [24] showed that there is a fixed dimensional optimization problem for which any r-pass streaming algorithm requires $\Omega(n^{1/r})$ space. However, it is not clear how to adapt their proof to linear programming since their optimization problem involves quadratic constraints [33].

Further Related Work. Special cases of linear programming have been studied previously in the big data models. In particular, Ahn and Guha gave multi-pass streaming algorithms for $(1+\varepsilon)$-approximation of *packing* LPs [1] and Indyk *et al.* [27] gave similar algorithms for *covering* LPs (see also [4]). These results focus on high-dimensional linear programs (non-constant d) and only packing/covering LPs, and are hence quite different from our approach in this paper.

Unlike the case for big data models, low-dimensional linear programming has been studied extensively in the RAM model since the 1980s. Megiddo [34] gave an algorithm for d-dimensional linear programming with time complexity $O(2^{2^d} n)$, which is linear in terms of the number of constraints n. This bound was consequently improved by a series of papers [8, 12, 15–17, 20, 21, 28, 32].

2 Preliminaries

Notations. For integers $1 \leq a \leq b$, we define $[a]$ as the set $\{1,\ldots,a\}$, $[a:b] := \{a, a+1, \ldots, b\}$, and $(a:b] := [a:b] \setminus \{a\}$ (we define $[a:b)$ and $(a:b)$ analogously). We use capital letters for sets and random variables and calligraphic letters for set families. We use the notation $\widetilde{O}(f)$ to denote a function of the form $O(f \cdot \text{polylog}(f))$.

Throughout the paper, we say an event happens "with high probability" if its probability can be lower bounded by $1 - 1/n^c$ for any desired constant $c \geq 1$ (n is the number of constraints).

We use the following standard variant of Chernoff bound.

Proposition 2.1 (Chernoff bound). *Suppose $X_1, \ldots, X_t$ are t independent random variables taking value in $[0,1]$ and $X := \sum_{i=1}^{t} X_i$. Then, for any $\varepsilon > 0$,*

$$\mathbf{Pr}\left(|X - \mathbb{E}[X]| > \varepsilon \cdot \mathbb{E}[X] \right) \leq 2 \cdot \exp\left(\frac{-\varepsilon^2 \cdot \mathbb{E}[X]}{3} \right).$$

2.1 LP-type Problems

We consider a generalization of linear programming referred to as LP-type problems[2]. An LP-type problem consists of a pair (S, f), where S is a finite set of elements, and $f : 2^S \to R$ is a set function with a range R which is assumed to have a total order. The function f satisfies two properties:

- *Monotonicity*: for any two sets $X \subseteq Y \subseteq S$, $f(X) \leq f(Y) \leq f(S)$.
- *Locality*: for any two sets $X \subseteq Y \subseteq S$, and any elements $e \in S$, if $f(X) = f(Y) = f(X \cup \{e\})$, then $f(Y) = f(Y \cup \{e\})$.

For an LP-type problem (S, f), we call a set $B \subseteq S$ a *basis* of S if $f(B) = f(S)$, and for all $B' \subset B$ we have $f(B') < f(B)$. The goal is to compute a basis $B_S \subseteq S$ such that $f(B_S) = f(S)$. We

[2] LP-type problems is also known as *abstract linear programming* [6].

say an element $e \in S$ *violates* $X \subseteq S$ if $f(X \cup \{e\}) > f(X)$. It helps to think of an LP-type problem (S, f) as an optimization problem in which elements of S are the constraints, and $f(A)$ computes the best *feasible* solution on the set of constraints A. In the case when the optimal solution is not unique, we just break the tie arbitrarily. Computing $f(B_S) = f(S)$ hence amounts to computing the optimal solution subject to all the constraints (we will make this connection explicit in the context of linear programming and other problems in Section 4).

Combinatorial Dimension. Note that an LP-type problem may have several bases which are of different sizes. We define the *combinatorial dimension* of an LP-type problem to be the *maximum* cardinality of a basis for S, denoted by $\nu_{S,f}$ (ν for short when S and f are clear from the context).

2.2 ε-Nets and VC Dimension

We now define another important notion that we use in designing our algorithms.

VC Dimension. A set-system is a tuple $(\mathcal{H}, U)$ consists of a universe U and a set family $\mathcal{H} \subseteq 2^U$. Let $C \subseteq U$ be a set. Define the intersection between a set family and a set to be the set family

$$\mathcal{H} \cap C := \{H \cap C \mid H \in \mathcal{H}\}.$$

We say that a set C is *shattered* by $\mathcal{H}$ if $\mathcal{H} \cap C$ contains all the subsets of C, i.e., $|\mathcal{H} \cap C| = 2^{|C|}$. The *VC dimension* of set-system $(\mathcal{H}, U)$, denoted by $\lambda_{\mathcal{H}}$ (or λ for short when $\mathcal{H}$ is clear in the context), is then the cardinality of the *largest* set C that is shattered by $\mathcal{H}$.

ε-Net. Given a set-system $(\mathcal{X}, U)$, and a weight function $w : \mathcal{X} \to \mathbb{R}$, for any $\mathcal{Y} \subseteq \mathcal{X}$, let $w(\mathcal{Y}) := \sum_{Y \in \mathcal{Y}} w(Y)$. We say a set $\mathcal{N} \subseteq \mathcal{X}$ is an ε-net of $\mathcal{X}$ with respect to w for a parameter $\varepsilon \in (0, 1)$, iff for any point $u \in U$ such that $\sum_{X \in \mathcal{X}: u \notin X} w(X) \geq \varepsilon \cdot w(\mathcal{X})$, it holds that $\{X \in \mathcal{N} \mid u \notin X\} \neq \emptyset$.

The notion of ε-net is well-studied in the literature (particularly in the computational geometry community [9, 25, 36]), and has been used in the algorithm design for many problems. We use the following simple randomized construction of ε-net for designing a distributed version of Clarkson's algorithm for LP-type problems.

Lemma 2.2 ([25]). *For any set-system $(\mathcal{X}, U)$ of VC dimension λ, any weight function $w : \mathcal{X} \to \mathbb{R}$, and $\varepsilon \in (0, 1)$, a set family $\mathcal{N} \subseteq \mathcal{X}$ obtained by randomly sampling*

$$m_{\varepsilon,\lambda,\delta} = \max\left(\frac{8\lambda}{\varepsilon}\log\frac{8\lambda}{\varepsilon}, \frac{4}{\varepsilon}\log\frac{2}{\delta}\right) \quad (1)$$

sets with probability proportional to their weights is an ε-net of $\mathcal{X}$ with probability at least $1 - \delta$.

3 Algorithms

In this section we present our algorithms for Result 1. We will work with a special class of LP-type problems that contains the most natural LP-type problems that we are aware of, including linear programming, Linear SVMs, and Core SVMs mentioned earlier. In particular, we require the LP-type problem $(\mathcal{S}, f)$ to satisfy the following properties:

(P1) Each constraint $X \in \mathcal{S}$ is associated with a set of elements $S_X \subseteq R$ (R is the range of f).
(P2) For any $\mathcal{A} \subseteq \mathcal{S}$, $f(\mathcal{A})$ is the minimal element of $\bigcap_{X \in \mathcal{A}} X$.

It is useful to think of R as the set of feasible solutions. For example, in the case of linear programming, $R = \mathbb{R}^d$ with the natural ordering induced by scalar product with the vector c in the objective function. Each constraint (inequality) $X \in \mathcal{S}$ corresponds to the subset of points S_X which satisfy the constraint, and $f(\mathcal{A})$ is equal to the point which satisfies all constraints in $\mathcal{A}$ and has a minimal scalar product with c. For convenience, we use X and S_X interchangeably.

For this special class of LP-type problems, we define the VC dimension of the problem $(\mathcal{S}, f)$ as the VC dimension of the set system $(\mathcal{S}, R)$.

In the following, we first give a general meta-algorithm for solving LP-type problems with Properties (P1) and (P2), and then show how to implement this meta-algorithm efficiently in each model.

3.1 The Meta Algorithm for LP-Type Problems

Our meta-algorithm follows Clarkson's algorithm [16] for linear programming, but we use a different sampling procedure (by using ε-net) which enables us to work with general LP-type problems with bounded VC dimension; it also significantly simplifies the analysis and facilitates the implementation of our algorithm in the big data models we consider. We further use a different weight increase rate after each iteration, which is essential for reducing the number of passes in the streaming, and the number of rounds in the coordinator and MPC models.

The algorithm proceeds in iterations. We maintain a weight function $w : \mathcal{S} \to \mathbb{R}$ throughout the algorithm which is initialized by setting $w(S) = 1$ for all $S \in \mathcal{S}$. In each iteration, we first sample a set family $\mathcal{N}$ of $m := m_{\varepsilon,\lambda_{\mathcal{S}},\frac{2}{3}}$ sets from $\mathcal{S}$ with probability proportional to their weights so as to obtain an ε-net $\mathcal{N}$ of $\mathcal{S}$ (according to Lemma 2.2). We then compute a basis $\mathcal{B}$ of $\mathcal{N}$, and the set $\mathcal{V}$ of constraints which violate the basis $\mathcal{B}$. If $w(\mathcal{V}) \leq \varepsilon \cdot w(\mathcal{S})$, then we say this iteration "succeeds", and update the weights of all sets $S \in \mathcal{V}$ by setting $w(S) \leftarrow (n^{1/r}) \cdot w(S)$. Otherwise, we say this iteration

ALGORITHM 1: A Meta-Algorithm for LP-Type Problems

Input: An LP-type problem $(\mathcal{S}, f)$ satisfying Properties (P1) and (P2) and integer $r \leq \ln n$.
Output: $f(\mathcal{S})$.

```
1  Let ε := 1/(10·v_{S,f}·n^{1/r}), and λ as the VC dimension of the
     LP-type problem (S, f).
2  Set w(S) = 1 for every S ∈ S.
3  repeat
4      Sample a family N ⊆ S of size m := m_{ε,λ,2/3} by
         picking each set in S with probability
         proportional to w for the parameter m_{ε,λ,2/3} in
         Lemma 2.2.
5      Compute a basis B of N.
6      Let V = {S ∈ S | f(B ∪ {S}) > f(B)} be the
         family of sets in S that violate B.
7      if w(V) ≤ ε · w(S) then
8          Set w(S) = (n^{1/r}) · w(S) for every set S ∈ V.
9      end
10 until V = ∅;
11 return f(B).
```

"fails", and continue to the next one without modifying the weights. A pseudo-code is provided in Algorithm 1.

In the following, we first establish the correctness of the meta-algorithm and then bound the number of iterations it needs.

Lemma 3.1. *When Algorithm 1 stops, it correctly computes* $f(\mathcal{S})$.

Proof. At the end of the algorithm, we have $\mathcal{V} = \emptyset$. This means that for any $S \in \mathcal{S} \setminus \mathcal{B}$, we have $f(\mathcal{B} \cup \{S\}) = f(\mathcal{B})$ by the monotonicity property of f. By the locality property and induction we obtain that $f(\mathcal{B}) = f(\mathcal{B} \cup (\mathcal{S} \setminus \mathcal{B})) = f(\mathcal{S})$, finalizing the proof. ∎

We now bound the number of iterations. We say that an iteration of Algorithm 1 (at Lines 4 to 8) is *successful* iff $w(\mathcal{V}) \leq \varepsilon \cdot w(\mathcal{S})$ in this iteration.

Claim 3.2. *Each iteration of Algorithm 1 is successful with probability at least* $2/3$.

Proof. Since the VC dimension of $(\mathcal{S}, R)$ is λ, by Lemma 2.2, with probability at least $2/3$, the family $\mathcal{N}$ sampled in Line 4 is an ε-net for $(\mathcal{S}, R)$ with respect to the weight function w. In the following, we condition on this event.

Let $x := f(\mathcal{B})$. By Property (P2) of the LP-type problems we consider, we know that x is the minimal element in the intersection of all sets in $\mathcal{B}$ according to the ordering of R. For any set $S \in \mathcal{S}$ to violate $\mathcal{B}$, we need to have $x \notin S$; otherwise $f(\mathcal{B} \cup \{S\}) = x$ which is in contradiction with $f(\mathcal{B} \cup \{S\}) > f(\mathcal{B})$. Recall that $\mathcal{V}$ is the family of all sets in $\mathcal{S}$ that violate $\mathcal{B}$. Suppose towards a contradiction that $w(\mathcal{V}) > \varepsilon \cdot w(\mathcal{S})$. Since none of the sets in $\mathcal{V}$ contain x, and $\mathcal{N}$ is an ε-net, by definition there is a set $S' \in \mathcal{N}$ where S' does not contain x. But this is in contradiction with $\mathcal{B}$ being a basis. To see this, if $f(\mathcal{B}) = f(\mathcal{N})$, then x belongs to all sets in $\mathcal{N}$, and consequently it should also be in S'. We thus have $w(\mathcal{V}) \leq \varepsilon \cdot w(\mathcal{S})$, finalizing the proof. ∎

Lemma 3.3. *The number of iterations in Algorithm 1 is* $O(v \cdot r)$ *with probability at least* $1 - e^{-\Omega(v \cdot r)}$, *where* v *denotes the combinatorial dimension of* $(\mathcal{S}, f)$.

Proof. Recall that the weight function $w(\cdot)$ is updated only when an iteration is successful, and each iteration succeeds with probability at least $2/3$ by Claim 3.2. By Chernoff bound (Proposition 2.1), we have that if the algorithm terminates in t iterations, then with probability at least $1 - e^{-\Omega(t)}$, at least $t/2$ of these iterations are successful.

We now focus on successful iterations. Let $w_i(\cdot)$ be the weight function $w(\cdot)$ after the i-th successful iteration. Initially, for any $S \in \mathcal{S}$ we have $w_0(S) = 1$ (and thus $w_0(\mathcal{S}) = n$). We claim that for any integer $t \geq 1$, if Algorithm 1 reaches the t-th successful iteration, then

$$n^{t/vr} \leq w_t(\mathcal{S}) \leq e^{t/10v} \cdot n. \tag{2}$$

We establish Eq (2) in the following two claims.

Claim 3.4. *For any integer* $t \geq 1$, *we have* $n^{t/vr} \leq w_t(\mathcal{S})$.

Proof. Fix an arbitrary basis $\mathcal{B}^* = \{B_1, \ldots, B_k\}$ of $\mathcal{S}$ for some $k \leq v$ (recall that by definition, v is size of the largest basis). Since $\mathcal{B}^* \subseteq \mathcal{S}$, we have $w_t(\mathcal{B}^*) \leq w_t(\mathcal{S})$ for any $t > 0$. We thus only need to show $n^{t/vr} \leq w_t(\mathcal{B}^*)$.

The first observation is that in any iteration, if $\mathcal{V} \neq \emptyset$ then we must have $\mathcal{V} \cap \mathcal{B}^* \neq \emptyset$. Indeed, if $\mathcal{V} \cap \mathcal{B}^* = \emptyset$, then $f(\mathcal{B}) = f(\mathcal{B} \cup \mathcal{B}^*) = f(\mathcal{S})$, where the first equality is by the locality property of f and induction, and the second equality holds since $\mathcal{B}^*$ is a basis for $\mathcal{S}$. However, this is in contradiction with the fact that $\mathcal{V} \neq \emptyset$.

Let us now define $\mathcal{B}_i$ as the basis of the ε-net computed in the i-th successful iteration. For any $j \in [k]$, let a_j be the number of iterations i such that $B_j \in \mathcal{B}^*$ violates $\mathcal{B}_i$. That is,

$$a_j = \left|\{i \in [t] \mid f(\mathcal{B}_i) < f(\mathcal{B}_i \cup \{B_j\})\}\right|.$$

Since $\mathcal{V} \cap \mathcal{B}^* \neq \emptyset$ in each of the first t successful iterations, there must exist at least one B_j which violates $\mathcal{B}_i$ for each $j \in [t]$. We thus have $\sum_{j=1}^{k} a_j \geq t$. Moreover, by the weight update rule of the algorithm, we can write the weight of $\mathcal{B}^*$ as $w_t(\mathcal{B}^*) = \sum_{j=1}^{k} \left(n^{1/r}\right)^{a_j}$. By combining these and Jensen's inequality we have

$$w_t(\mathcal{B}^*) \geq k \left(n^{1/r}\right)^{\sum_{j=1}^{k} a_j/k} \geq \left(n^{1/r}\right)^{t/k} \geq n^{t/vr},$$

since $k \le v$. This concludes the proof of Claim 3.4. ∎

Claim 3.5. *For any integer $t \ge 1$, we have*

$$w_t(\mathcal{S}) \le e^{t/10v} \cdot n\,.$$

Proof. For any iteration $t \ge 1$, the weight update procedure at Line 8 of Algorithm 1 gives

$$w_{t+1}(\mathcal{S}) = w_t(\mathcal{S}) + (n^{1/r} - 1) \cdot w_t(\mathcal{V}) \le w_t(\mathcal{S}) + (n^{1/r}) \cdot w_t(\mathcal{V}). \quad (3)$$

Moreover, by the condition at Line 7 of the algorithm, we have,

$$w_t(\mathcal{V}) \le \varepsilon \cdot w_t(\mathcal{S}) = \frac{1}{10v \cdot n^{1/r}} \cdot w_t(\mathcal{S}), \quad (4)$$

by the choice of ε in the algorithm. Combining (3) and (4) we have

$$w_t(\mathcal{S}) \le \left(1 + \frac{1}{10v}\right)^t \cdot w_0(\mathcal{S}) \le e^{t/10v} \cdot n. \quad ∎$$

We get back to the analysis of the number of iterations. By Eq (2) we have $n^{t/vr} \le e^{t/10v} n$, hence, $\frac{t}{v} \le \frac{10r \ln n}{10 \ln n - r}$. Since $r \le \ln n$, we have $\frac{t}{v} \le \frac{10}{9} r$. Therefore the number of successful iterations cannot exceed $\frac{10}{9} vr$, and hence the total number of iterations is bounded by $\frac{20}{9} vr$ with probability $1 - e^{-\Omega(vr)}$. ∎

Remark 3.6. We can easily turn our Las-Vegas algorithm in this section (Algorithm 1) into a Monte-Carlo algorithm by the following modifications: First we pick an ε-net of size $m_{\varepsilon,\lambda_S,1/(nv)}$, and second, the algorithm return "FAIL" whenever $w(\mathcal{V}) > \varepsilon w(\mathcal{S})$, which will not happen in the first $O(vr) = O(v \log n)$ iterations with probability at least $1 - v \log n \cdot 1/(nv) \ge 1 - o(1)$.

3.2 Implementation in the Streaming Model

Starting from this section, we show how to implement Algorithm 1 in the three big data models considered in the paper. We start with the streaming algorithm. In the multi-pass streaming model the elements of $\mathcal{S}$ arrive one by one, and $f(\cdot)$ is known to the algorithm at the beginning. We allow the algorithm to make multiple linear scans of the input.

The main challenge in the streaming implementation of Algorithm 1 is that we cannot afford to store the weights of all elements in $\mathcal{S}$ which are needed in the ε-net sampling. To resolve this issue, we instead store the set of bases computed at all the *successful* iterations – these are the only iterations that we change the weight function – in a collection $\mathfrak{B}$, using which we can compute the weight of each element of $\mathcal{S}$ *on the fly*. In particular, the weight of a set $S_i \in \mathcal{S}$ in iteration j of the algorithm, namely, $w_j(S_i)$, is computed as $w_j(S_i) := (n^{1/r})^{a_i}$ where $a_i := |\{\mathcal{B} \in \mathfrak{B} \mid f(\mathcal{B} \cup \{S_i\}) > f(\mathcal{B})\}|$. It is immediate to verify that this indeed implements the same weight function in Algorithm 1. It is also easy to see that having access to these weights, we can sample each set with probability proportional to its weight using the weighted version of reservoir sampling [14], and hence implement each iteration of Algorithm 1 in one pass over the stream.

The rest of Algorithm 1 can be implemented in the streaming model in a straightforward way. Let $T_b(m)$ be the time complexity of computing a basis for a set of size m, and $T_v(t, b)$ be the time complexity of finding all elements in a set $\mathcal{T} \subseteq \mathcal{S}$ of size t which violate a set $\mathcal{B}$ of size b, i.e., all $S \in \mathcal{S}$ such that $f(\mathcal{B} \cup S) > f(\mathcal{B})$. This allows us to prove the following theorem.

Theorem 1. *Suppose $(\mathcal{S}, f)$ is an LP-type problem with combinatorial dimension v, VC dimension λ, and bit-complexity $\mathtt{bit}(\mathcal{S})$ for each element of $\mathcal{S}$. For any integer $r \le \ln n$, we can compute $f(\mathcal{S})$ with high probability in the streaming model, using $O(vr)$ passes, and $\widetilde{O}(\lambda n^{1/r} \cdot v + v^2) \cdot \mathtt{bit}(\mathcal{S})$ space. The total running time of the algorithm is also $O(vr \cdot T_v(n, v) + vr \cdot T_b(\lambda n^{1/r} \cdot v))$.*

Proof. The correctness of the algorithm follows from Lemma 3.1. As each iteration of Algorithm 1 can be implemented in one pass, the total number of passes needed by our streaming algorithm is $O(vr)$ with high probability by Lemma 3.3.

Recall that the size of each ε-net $\mathcal{N}$ sampled in Algorithm 1 is $m = m_{\varepsilon,\lambda,\frac{2}{3}} = \widetilde{O}\left(\lambda v n^{1/r}\right)$, by the choice of ε in the algorithm and $m_{\varepsilon,\lambda,\frac{2}{3}}$ in Lemma 2.2. The space needed by the algorithm to store $\mathcal{N}$ in each iteration is $O(m) \cdot \mathtt{bit}(\mathcal{S})$, which is equal to $\widetilde{O}\left(\lambda v n^{1/r}\right) \cdot \mathtt{bit}(\mathcal{S})$ bits. We also need to store all bases in successful iterations, which requires $O(v \cdot r) \cdot O(v) \cdot \mathtt{bit}(\mathcal{S}) = \widetilde{O}(v^2) \cdot \mathtt{bit}(\mathcal{S})$ (since $r = O(\log n)$) as each basis requires $O(v) \cdot \mathtt{bit}(\mathcal{S})$ bits to represent and there are total of $O(vr)$ such bases.

Each pass of the algorithm involves performing a violation test over the n elements of $\mathcal{S}$, which takes $O(T_v(n, v))$ time. And computing a basis of m elements which takes $O(T_b(m))$ times. The running time follows by multiplying these numbers by the number of passes, and by the choice of m. ∎

3.3 Implementation in the Coordinator Model

Recall that in the coordinator model the input set $\mathcal{S}$ is arbitrarily partitioned among k sites $P_1, \ldots, P_k$ such that for any $i \in [k]$, the site P_i receives the elements $\mathcal{S}_i$. The k sites and the coordinator want to jointly compute $f(\mathcal{S}) = f(\mathcal{S}_1 \cup \cdots \cup \mathcal{S}_k)$ via communication. The function f is a public knowledge, that is, all parties know how to evaluate the function $f(\mathcal{T})$ for any $\mathcal{T} \in 2^{\mathcal{S}}$ assuming $\mathcal{T}$ resides entirely on that machine.

Similar to the streaming model, the main step here is also the implementation of the ε-net sampling procedure in Algorithm 1. We show in Appendix A.1 how this step can be performed efficiently, leading to the following theorem.

Theorem 2. *Suppose $(\mathcal{S}, f)$ is an LP-type problem with combinatorial dimension ν, VC dimension λ, and bit-complexity $\mathtt{bit}(\mathcal{S})$ for each element of $\mathcal{S}$. For any integer $r \leq \ln n$, we can compute $f(\mathcal{S})$ with high probability in the coordinator model with $k \geq 2$ machines, using $O(\nu r)$ rounds, and $\widetilde{O}(\lambda n^{1/r} \cdot \nu^2 + k \cdot \nu^2) \cdot \mathtt{bit}(\mathcal{S})$ communication in total. The local computation time of the coordinator is $O(\nu r \cdot (T_b(\lambda n^{1/r} \cdot \nu) + k\nu))$ and the local computation time of the i-th site is $O(\nu r \cdot T_v(n_i, \nu))$ where $n_i := |\mathcal{S}_i|$.*

3.4 Implementation in the MPC Model

The implementation of Algorithm 1 in the MPC model can be done similarly as that in the coordinator model, by choosing one of the machines to play the role of coordinator. The only problem is that when the number of machines is large, the machines cannot simply send all the messages to the coordinator directly, as it will blow up the load in the coordinator. In Appendix A.2 we show how to get around this using standard primitives in MPC model. We have the following theorem.

Theorem 3. *Suppose $(\mathcal{S}, f)$ is an LP-type problem with combinatorial dimension ν, VC dimension λ, and bit-complexity $\mathtt{bit}(\mathcal{S})$ for each element of $\mathcal{S}$. For any $\delta \in (0, 1)$, we can compute $f(\mathcal{S})$ with high probability in the MPC model using $O(\nu/\delta^2)$ rounds with $\widetilde{O}(\lambda n^{\delta} \cdot \nu^2) \cdot \mathtt{bit}(\mathcal{S})$ load per machine.*

4 Examples and Applications

We now give examples of the application of our algorithms for general LP-type problems. We will discuss several fundamental optimization problems in machine learning, namely, linear programming, Linear SVM, and Core SVM. Recall that when implementing our meta algorithm in each model, we have left two functions $T_v(\cdot)$ (the time needed for performing the violation test) and $T_b(\cdot)$ (the time for computing the basis) unspecified. In this section we will provide concrete bounds for these functions in the context of the concrete problems we study. Throughout this section, we assume that the bit-complexity of each number in the input is $O(\log n)$ bits.

4.1 Linear Programming

A linear program is an optimization problem of the type:

$$\min_{x \in \mathbb{R}^d} \sum_{i=1}^{d} c_i x_i \quad \text{subject to} \quad \sum_{i=1}^{d} a_i^j x_i \leq b^j \quad \text{for all } j \in [n]. \tag{5}$$

A d-dimensional linear program can be modeled as an LP-type problem as follows. Let $\mathcal{S}$ be a set family of size n such that for every constraint in (5), there exists a unique element $S \in \mathcal{S}$ which is the half-space in the d-dimensional Euclidean space $\mathbb{R}^d$ containing the points that satisfy this single constraint. We define the function f over subsets of $\mathcal{S}$ such that for every $\mathcal{A} \subseteq \mathcal{S}$, $f(\mathcal{A})$ is the lexicographically smallest point that minimizes the objective value of LP while satisfying only the constraints in $\mathcal{A}$. The linear program (5) now corresponds to the LP-type problem $(\mathcal{S}, f)$ (we use $\mathcal{S}$ as opposed to our previous notation S, since each element of $\mathcal{S}$ is now itself a subset of $\mathbb{R}^d$, and hence $\mathcal{S}$ forms a set family). We refer the interested readers to [32] for more details on connection between linear programming and LP-type problems.

It is known that the combinatorial dimension ν of this particular LP-type problem $(\mathcal{S}, f)$ is at most $d + 1$ [32]. The VC dimension λ is also at most $d+1$ [43]. Finding the basis of any given set of constraints and the violating constraints can also be done easily using standard results (see Appendix B.1 for details). We can thus prove the following theorem using Theorems 1, 2, and 3.

Theorem 4. *We give the following randomized algorithms for d-dimensional linear programming with n constraints. For any $r \geq 1$ and $\delta \in (0, 1)$:*

- Streaming: *An $O(d \cdot r)$-pass algorithm with $\widetilde{O}(d^3 \cdot n^{1/r})$ space in $\widetilde{O}(n) \cdot \mathrm{poly}(d)$ time.*
- Coordinator: *An $O(d \cdot r)$-round algorithm with $\widetilde{O}(d^4 n^{1/r} + d^3 k)$ total communication in which the coordinator and each site $i \in [k]$ spend $\widetilde{O}(n^{1/r} + k) \cdot \mathrm{poly}(d)$ time and $\widetilde{O}(n_i) \cdot \mathrm{poly}(d)$ time, respectively, where n_i is the number of constraints on site i.*
- MPC: *An $O(d/\delta^2)$-round algorithm with $\widetilde{O}(d^3 n^{\delta})$ load per machine and $\widetilde{O}(n) \cdot \mathrm{poly}(d)$ time in total.*

4.2 Linear Support Vector Machine

In Linear Support Vector Machine (SVM) problem [7], we have a set of tuples $\{(x_1, y_1), \ldots, (x_n, y_n)\}$ such that for each index $j \in [n]$, $x_j \in \mathbb{R}^d$ and $y_j \in \{-1, +1\}$. The goal is to compute a hyperplane $u = (u_1, \ldots, u_d)$ which is the outcome of the following quadratic optimization problem [7]:

$$\min_{u \in \mathbb{R}^d} \|u\|_2^2 \quad \text{s.t.} \quad y_j \cdot \langle u, x_j \rangle \geq 1 \quad \text{for all } j \in [n]. \tag{6}$$

From a geometrical point of view, the problem (6) corresponds to finding a hyperplane which separates the set of point $\{x_1, \ldots, x_n\}$ according to their labels with the maximum margin value (if possible); see, e.g., [7] for more information on this fundamental problem.[3] Note that the problem (6) is *not* a linear program. However, one can show that it is an LP-type problem $(\mathcal{S}, f)$ where $\mathcal{S}$ is a set family in $\mathbb{R}^d$ in which every set contains the points that satisfy a particular constraint, and $f(\mathcal{A})$ for $\mathcal{A} \subseteq \mathcal{S}$ computes the optimal solution of (6) given only the constraints to $\mathcal{A}$ [32] (unlike linear programming, the optimal solution to (6) under any set of constraints is unique and hence we do not need the lexicographically first constraint).

The combinatorial dimension of $(\mathcal{S}, f)$ is $\nu \leq d+1$ [32], and the VC dimension of $(\mathcal{S}, \mathbb{R}^d)$ is $\lambda \leq d+1$ [43]. One can again use standard results to find a basis of any given set of constraints and all violating constraints of a given basis for this problem (see Appendix B.2). This allows us to prove the following theorem using Theorems 1, 2, and 3.

Theorem 5. *We give the following randomized algorithms for d-dimensional linear support vector machine problem with n constraints. For any $r \geq 1$ and $\delta \in (0,1)$:*

- Streaming: *An $O(d \cdot r)$-pass algorithm with $\widetilde{O}(d^3 \cdot n^{1/r})$ space in $\widetilde{O}(n) \cdot \mathrm{poly}(d)$ time.*
- Coordinator: *An $O(d \cdot r)$-round algorithm with $\widetilde{O}(d^4 n^{1/r} + d^3 k)$ total communication in which the coordinator and each site $i \in [k]$ spend $\widetilde{O}(n^{3/r} + k) \cdot \mathrm{poly}(d)$ time and $\widetilde{O}(n_i) \cdot \mathrm{poly}(d)$ time, respectively, where n_i is the number of constraints on site i.*
- MPC: *An $O(d/\delta^2)$-round algorithm with $\widetilde{O}(d^3 n^{\delta})$ load per machine and $\widetilde{O}(n + n^{3\delta}) \cdot \mathrm{poly}(d)$ time in total.*

4.3 Core Vector Machine

Tsang at el. [42] proposed *core vector machines* as a way of speeding up kernel methods in SVM training (see [7]). This is achieved by reformulating the original kernel method as an instance of the *minimum enclosing ball* (MEB) problem, defined as follows: Given a set of points $P := \{p_1, \ldots, p_n\}$ in $\mathbb{R}^d$, find a center p and a minimum radius r such that all the points in P are within a d-dimensional sphere of radius r centered at p. MEB can be formulated as the following optimization problem:

$$\min_{r \in \mathbb{R}, p \in \mathbb{R}^d} r \quad \text{subject to} \quad \left\|p - p_j\right\|_2 \leq r \quad \text{for all } j \in [n]. \quad (7)$$

This problem is also an LP-type problem $(\mathcal{S}, f)$ formulated similarly to linear programming and Linear SVM [32]. The combinatorial dimension of $(\mathcal{S}, f)$ is $\nu \leq d+1$ [32] and the VC dimension of $(\mathcal{S}, \mathbb{R}^d)$ is $\lambda \leq d+1$ [44]. We obtain the following theorem for this problem using Theorems 1, 2, and 3 (see Appendix B.3).

Theorem 6. *We give the following randomized algorithms for d-dimensional core vector machine problem with n constraints. For any integer $r \geq 1$:*

- Streaming: *An $O(d \cdot r)$-pass algorithm with $\widetilde{O}(d^3 \cdot n^{1/r})$ space in $\widetilde{O}(n + n^{3/r}) \cdot \mathrm{poly}(d)$ time.*
- Coordinator: *An $O(d \cdot r)$-round algorithm with $\widetilde{O}(d^4 n^{1/r} + d^3 k)$ total communication in which the coordinator and each site $i \in [k]$ spend $\widetilde{O}(n^{3/r} + k) \cdot \mathrm{poly}(d)$ time and $\widetilde{O}(n_i) \cdot \mathrm{poly}(d)$ time, respectively, where n_i is the number of constraints on site i.*
- MPC: *An $O(d/\delta^2)$-round algorithm with $\widetilde{O}(d^3 n^{\delta})$ load per machine and $\widetilde{O}(n + n^{3\delta}) \cdot \mathrm{poly}(d)$ time in total.*

5 Lower Bounds

In this section we prove information-theoretic lower bounds for linear programming that hold against *any* algorithm. We obtain our lower bounds by establishing the *communication complexity* for 2-dimensional linear programming, and then translating it to lower bounds in the big data models. In the following, we first give some background on communication complexity and then present an intermediate problem, called two-curve intersection problem (TCI), that we consider en route to proving our result for linear programming. We then prove a lower bound for TCI and present its implications for linear programming in the streaming and coordinator models.

5.1 Background

Communication Complexity. We focus on the standard two-party communication complexity model of Yao [45]. In this model, Alice and Bob receive an input $X \in \mathcal{X}$ and $Y \in \mathcal{Y}$, respectively. In an r-round protocol, Alice and Bob can communicate up to r messages with each other. In particular, for an even r, Bob first sends a message to Alice, followed by a message from Alice to Bob, and so on, until Bob receives the last message and outputs the answer. For an odd r, the only difference is that Alice starts first and then the players continue like before until Bob outputs the answer.

The communication complexity of a problem $P : \mathcal{X} \times \mathcal{Y} \to \mathcal{Z}$, denoted by $\mathrm{CC}(P)$, is the minimum worst-case communication cost of any protocol (possibly randomized) that can solve P with probability at least $2/3$. The r-round communication complexity of P, denoted by $\mathrm{CC}^r(P)$, is similarly defined with respect to protocols that are allowed at most r rounds of communication.

Augmented Indexing. In the Augmented Indexing Problem, denoted by $\mathsf{Aug\text{-}Index}_n$, Alice is given a binary string

[3] Our algorithm works effectively for the hard-margin Linear SVM. In the case of the soft-margin Linear SVM, the optimization problem can also be formulated in the form of LP-type problem, but the dimension of such formulation is large – proportional to the size of input.

$x \in \{0,1\}^n$, and Bob is given an index $i \in \{0,1\}$ plus the first $i-1$ bits of the string x, i.e., $x_1, \ldots, x_{i-1}$. The goal is for Bob to output the bit x_i. It is well-known that 1-round communication complexity of this problem is $\mathsf{CC}^1(\mathsf{Aug\text{-}Index}_n) = \Omega(n)$ (see, e.g. [35]).

Information Theory. Throughout this section, we use bold-face fonts, say $\boldsymbol{A}$, to denote random variables, and normal font, say A, to denote their realizations. For a random variable $\boldsymbol{A}$, $\text{supp}(\boldsymbol{A})$ denotes its support and $\text{dist}(\boldsymbol{A})$ its distribution. We sometimes abuse the notation and use $\boldsymbol{A}$ and $\text{dist}(\boldsymbol{A})$ interchangeably. Furthermore, for a t-tuple $(X_1, \ldots, X_t)$ and any integer $i \in [t]$, we define $X^{<i} := (X_1, \ldots, X_{i-1})$ and $X^{>i} := (X_{i+1}, \ldots, X_t)$.

For random variables $\boldsymbol{A}, \boldsymbol{B}$, let $\mathbb{H}(\boldsymbol{A})$ and $\mathbb{I}(\boldsymbol{A}\,;\boldsymbol{B})$ denote the Shannon entropy and mutual information, respectively. We use $\mathbb{D}(\boldsymbol{A} \mid\mid \boldsymbol{B})$ and $\|\boldsymbol{A} - \boldsymbol{B}\|_{tvd}$ to denote the KL-divergence and total variation distance between $\boldsymbol{A}$ and $\boldsymbol{B}$, respectively. Appendix C.1 provides formal definitions and basic properties of these functions.

5.2 The Two-Curve Intersection Problem (TCI)

We consider the following problem, whose lower bound implies a lower bound for linear programming in the two-dimensional Euclidean space (as we show shortly).

Alice and Bob are given sequences of n numbers $A := \langle a_1, \ldots, a_n \rangle$ and $B := \langle b_1, \ldots, b_n \rangle$ in $\mathbb{Q}^n$, respectively, such that:

(1) *Monotonicity:* A is monotonically increasing and B is monotonically decreasing.
(2) *Convexity:* For any $i \in [n]$, in A we have $a_i - a_{i-1} \leq a_{i+1} - a_i$ and conversely in B we have $b_i - b_{i-1} \geq b_{i+1} - b_i$.

The goal is to find the *smallest index* $i^* \in [n]$ such that $a_{i^*} \leq b_{i^*}$ but $a_{i^*+1} > b_{i^*+1}$, under the promise that such an index always exists. We can interpret the sequence A as a two-dimensional curve in $\mathbb{R}^2$ that goes through the points $(1, a_1), (2, a_2), \cdots (n, a_n)$ (similarly for B). We refer to this problem as the *two-curve intersection* problem and denote it by TCI_n for sequences of length n (or TCI in general). See Figure 1a for an illustration of this problem.

Connection to 2-Dimensional Linear Programming. We can reduce the two-curve intersection problem to an instance of 2-dimensional linear programming as follows (see Figure 1b). Extend each segment of the curve in Alice's and Bob's input to obtain a line that defines a constraint in which all points above this line are feasible (blue region for Alice and green region for Bob in Figure 1b). The feasible region of this linear program is the set of points in $\mathbb{R}^2$ that lie above both of Alice's and Bob's curve. By minimizing the y-axis on the feasible region, we obtain the first "fractional" point in which Alice's curve goes above Bob's curve, and by rounding down the x-axis of this point, we obtain the index i^* of TCI.

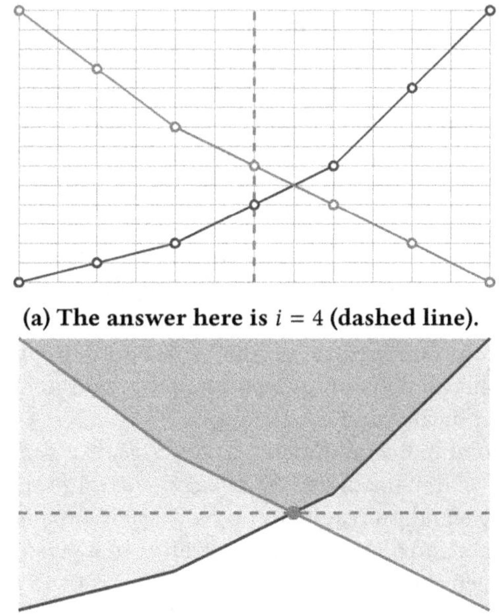

(a) The answer here is $i = 4$ (dashed line).

(b) Linear programming formulation.

Figure 1: An illustration of the two-curve intersection problem and its connection to linear programming.

Geometric Notations. We work in the two-dimensional Euclidean space $\mathbb{R}^2$. We use $p \in \mathbb{R}^2$ to denote a point, and $p.x$ and $p.y$ to denote its x and y coordinates respectively. Throughout, all the points used have rational coordinates (i.e., in $\mathbb{Q}^2$). For two points p_1, p_2 and integers $a \leq b$, we define $\mathsf{LineSegment}(p_1, p_2, a, b)$ as the sequence of $b - a + 1$ numbers $\langle z_a, z_{a+1}, \ldots, z_b \rangle$ such that for all $i \in [a:b]$, (i, z_i) belongs to the unique line in $\mathbb{R}^2$ that passes through the points p_1 and p_2. We use the following elementary geometric facts.

FACT 5.1. *Let* $\langle z_a, \ldots, z_b \rangle := \mathsf{LineSegment}(p_1, p_2, a, b)$.
(1) For every $i \in (a:b]$, $z_i - z_{i-1} := \frac{p_2.y - p_1.y}{p_2.x - p_1.x}$.
(2) For every $i \in [a:b]$, $z_i = \frac{p_2.y - p_1.y}{p_2.x - p_1.x} \cdot (i - p_1.x) + p_1.y = \frac{p_2.y - p_1.y}{p_2.x - p_1.x} \cdot (i - p_2.x) + p_2.y$.

We also define a notion called *step curve*. For a string $X = (x_1, \ldots, x_m) \in \{0,1\}^m$ and a parameter $\alpha \geq 1$, $\mathsf{StepCurve}(X, \alpha)$ is the sequence of $m+1$ numbers z_i such that $z_0 = 0$ and for all $i \in [m]$, $z_i := z_{i-1} + \alpha + i + x_i$.

5.3 Communication Complexity of TCI

Our goal is to prove the following theorem.

THEOREM 7. *For any* $r \geq 1$, $\mathsf{CC}^r(\mathsf{TCI}_n) = \Omega(\frac{1}{r^2} \cdot n^{1/r})$.

The proof of Theorem 7 is based on an inductive argument, following the general *round-elimination* approach in communication complexity (see, e.g. [35, 40]). In this approach, one proves the lower bound for r-round problems by showing that a "too good" r-round protocol will imply a too good $(r-1)$-round protocol, by reducing the r-round problem to *multiple* instances of the $(r-1)$-round problem. Following this argument inductively, we will end up with a protocol using only 1 round. We then directly prove that such a too good 1-round protocol *cannot* exist.

5.3.1 Base Case: One-Round Protocols As a warm-up, we first prove Theorem 7 for $r = 1$, i.e., 1-round protocols.

Lemma 5.2. $\mathsf{CC}^1(\mathsf{TCI}_n) = \Omega(n)$.

Proof. We prove this lemma using a reduction from the Augmented Indexing Problem on a universe of size $n-1$. Given an instance of Aug-Index$_{n-1}$ with input $x \in \{0,1\}^{n-1}$ to Alice and $i^* \in [n-1]$ plus $x_1, \ldots, x_{i^*-1}$ to Bob, the players construct the following instance of TCI_n (without any communication):

(1) Alice creates $A := \langle a_1, \ldots, a_n \rangle := \mathsf{StepCurve}(x, 0)$.
(2) Bob creates

$$B := \langle b_1, \ldots, b_n \rangle = \mathsf{LineSegment}(p_1, p_2, 1, n),$$

where $p_1 := (n, 1)$ and $p_2 := (i^*, a_{i^*} + i^* + 1)$.

The players then run the protocol for TCI_n on this instance and Bob outputs $x_{i^*} = 1$ (in answer to the Aug-Index instance) iff i^* is returned by the protocol for TCI_n as the answer on this instance.

Correctness of the reduction. We first verify that the sequences A and B constructed by Alice and Bob satisfy the promise of the TCI_n input. By Fact 5.1, B is both monotone and convex. It is also easy to see that A is monotonically increasing: for all $i \geq 2$, $a_i \geq a_{i-1} + i \geq a_{i-1}$. Finally, to verify the convexity of A, notice that $a_i - a_{i-1} = i + x_{i-1} \leq i + 1$ while $a_{i+1} - a_i = i + 1 + x_i \geq i + 1$.

We now prove the correctness of the output in the reduction. Suppose first that $x_{i^*} = 0$. In this case, $a_{i^*+1} = a_{i^*} + i^* + 1 + x_{i^*} = a_{i^*} + i^* + 1 = b_{i^*}$ by definition. On the other hand, $a_{i^*+2} > b_i$ for all $i > i^*$ as $b_i < b_{i^*}$ and $a_{i^*+2} > a_{i^*+1} = b_{i^*}$. As a result, the correct index in TCI_n is $i^* + 1$. Now suppose $x_{i^*} = 1$. In this case, $a_{i^*+1} > b_{i^*}$ while $a_{i^*} < b_{i^*}$. As such, the correct index in TCI_n is i^*, finalizing the proof of the correctness of the reduction.

Communication cost of the reduction. The instance of TCI_n can be created with no communication. As such,

$$\mathsf{CC}^1(\mathsf{TCI}_n) \geq \mathsf{CC}^1(\text{Aug-Index}_{n-1}) = \Omega(n). \quad \blacksquare$$

5.3.2 General Lower Bound: The Outline We now switch to the main part of the argument in which we prove Theorem 7 for all integers $r \geq 1$. In this section we outline our high level approach. In this section, we will oversimplify many details, and the discussions will be informal for the sake of intuition.

We design a family of distribution $\mathcal{D}_1, \mathcal{D}_2, \ldots$, where $\mathcal{D}_r$ is hard distribution for r-round protocols. Distribution $\mathcal{D}_1$ is the distribution of hard instances obtained in Lemma 5.2 (from the hard distribution of Aug-Index). Each instance I in the distribution $\mathcal{D}_r$ is then constructed roughly as follows: we sample $n^{1/r}$ instances from the distribution $\mathcal{D}_{r-1}$ each over $n^{(r-1)/r}$ points. Let us call these instances $I_1, \ldots, I_{n^{1/r}}$. We *embed* these instances inside I so that the following two properties are satisfied: (i) the answer to TCI_n on instance I is the same as the answer to $\mathsf{TCI}_{n^{(r-1)/r}}$ on instance $I_{z^\star}$ for some $z^\star \in [n^{1/r}]$ chosen uniformly at random, and (ii) the first player to speaks (namely Alice for odd r and Bob for even r) is *oblivious* to the identity of $z^\star$.

The proof of the communication lower bound then goes as follows. Using information-theoretic arguments, we can argue that if the first message of the protocol is of size $o(n^{1/r})$, then it only reveals $o(1)$ bits of information about an "average" embedded instance I_i for $i \in [n_r]$ of $\mathcal{D}_{r-1}$. In particular, since the sender of the first message is oblivious to the identity of the $z^\star$ (by property (ii)), the first message only reveals $o(1)$ bits of information about the instance $I_{z^\star}$. This effectively means that the distribution of the instance $I_{z^\star}$ is essentially the same as $\mathcal{D}_{r-1}$ even after the first round. However, by property (i), the players now need to solve the instance $I_{z^\star}$ on $n^{(r-1)/r}$ elements sampled from distribution $\mathcal{D}_{r-1}$ in $r-1$ rounds. By induction, this requires $\Omega((n^{(r-1)/r})^{1/r-1}) = \Omega(n^{1/r})$ bits, which implies the desired lower bound for r-round protocols.

The outline above is arguably the most straightforward application of round-elimination (see, e.g. the tree-pointer-jumping problem in [11]). Unfortunately however, this approach does not work directly in our application. In particular, in the discussion above, we left the specifics of how the $(r-1)$-round instances $I_1, \ldots, I_{n^{1/r}}$ are embedded together to form I. For the above information-theoretic arguments to work, these instances need to be sampled *independently* of each other. On the other hand, for us to be able to embed them together in a valid instance of TCI, we need to ensure that they collectively preserve monotonicity and convexity properties of TCI. This requires *correlating* the instances $I_1, \ldots, I_{n^{1/r}}$, impeding the use of previous information-theoretic argument.

We get around this challenge by carefully "revealing extra information" about the inputs of the players to each other (similar to the reduction from Aug-Index in Lemma 5.2), which allows to "control" the correlation between different instances $I_1, \ldots, I_{n^{1/r}}$ in terms of these revealed information. We then show that even with this extra information, the two properties above for embedded instances continue to hold, and at the same time, we have enough independence in the instances to make the information-theoretic arguments outlined above work.

We comment that this construction of hard instances of TCI and the proof of the corresponding communication lower bound is one of the main technical contributions of this paper.

5.3.3 General Lower Bound: The Hard Input Distribution

We use an integer $N \geq 1$ as a parameter in defining all other parameters of our hard distribution. In particular, for r-round instances, $n_r = N^r$ is the number of points given to Alice and Bob, and $m_r := N$ is the number of $(r-1)$-round instances "embedded" inside the r-round instance. We also define the following two *operators* on instances that are used in our lower bound construction (their roles will become more evident once we give the proper definition of the hard distribution).

- **Slope-Shift Operator:** In any instance I of our hard distribution $\mathcal{D}_r$, the input to Alice is constructed using several (potentially different) StepCurve functions. By applying slope-shift operator on instance I with parameter α, we increase the second parameter in every application of StepCurve in constructing Alice's input by an *additive* factor of α. As a result, any segment in Alice's input constructed with StepCurve$(*, \beta)$ becomes StepCurve$(*, \alpha+\beta)$. We ensure that the operator also changes the slope of Bob's input by α.
- **Origin-Shift Operator:** By applying the origin-shift operator with point $p_A \in \mathbb{R}^2$ from Alice's side in an instance I of $\mathcal{D}_r$, we shift *all* points in the instance I along the same line so that the *left-most* point of Alice's input will be on the point p_A. Similarly, by applying the origin-shift operator with $p_B \in \mathbb{R}^2$ from Bob's side, we shift *all* points along the same line so that the *right-most* point of Bob's input will be on p_B. This operator clearly does not change the slope of any line segment in players' inputs.

We are now ready to describe our hard input distribution.

Distribution $\mathcal{D}_r$: The Hard Distribution for r-round Protocols of TCI. We define the procedure Instance that given a parameter r, construct an instance of TCI.

> Instance(r).
> (1) If $r = 1$, sample (A, B) from the distribution of Lemma 5.2; otherwise, define
> $(A, B) :=$ EvenInstance(r) for even r and
> $(A, B) :=$ OddInstance(r) for odd r.
> (2) Return the points (A, B) as the r-round instance.

We now define the EvenInstance procedure inside Instance.

> EvenInstance(r).
> (1) Sample m_r instances (C_i, D_i) *independently* from Instance$(r-1)$.
> (2) For $i = m_r$ down to 1 do:
>   (a) Let p_B^{i+1} be the left-most point of Bob's input in (C_{i+1}, D_{i+1}) (define $p_B^{m_r+1} := (n_r, 0)$). Apply the origin-shift operator with point p_B^{i+1} from Bob's side on the instance (C_i, D_i).
>   (b) Let α_r^{i+1} be the largest slope of any segment in (C_{i+1}, D_{i+1}). Apply the slope-shift operator with slope α_r^{i+1} on (C_i, D_i).
> (3) Sample $z_r^\star \in [m_r]$ uniformly at random.
> (4) Define $A := (A_1, \ldots, A_{m_r})$ where $A_{z_r^\star} = C_{z_r^\star}$; the remaining A_i's for $i \neq z_r^\star$ are constructed by extending the curve in $A_{z_r^\star}$ on both its endpoints along straight lines.
> (5) Define $B := (B_1, \ldots, B_{m_r})$ where $B_i = D_i$ for all $i \in [m_r]$.

We refer to instances (C_i, D_i) as *sub-instances*. Several remarks are in order about these sub-instances. Firstly, even though they were originally sampled independently, by applying the origin-shit and slope-shift operators, we have correlated these instances. In particular, each instance (C^i, D^i) depends on instances (C^j, D^j) for $j > i$. Moreover, note that *not* all the points in these instances appear in the final instance (A, B). In particular, we only use the points in $C_{z_r^\star}$ to define $A_{z_r^\star}$; the remaining points in $A \setminus A_{z_r^\star}$ are obtained differently from $C_1, \ldots, C_{m_r}$ (the points in B are however identical to the points in $D_1, \ldots, D_{m_r}$). Nevertheless, the remaining instances still play a marginal role in the definition of the players' inputs because these points define the starting point and starting slope of each sub-instance. In the following, we refer to (A, B) as the *actual* input of Alice and Bob, and refer to the points in $(C_1, D_1), \ldots, (C_{m_r}, D_{m_r})$ that are not part of (A, B) as *fooling* inputs. Figure 2a gives an illustration of EvenInstance.

We use the term sub-instance for both (A_i, B_i) and (C_i, D_i) pairs. For any $i \in [m_r]$, we use $A_i := (a_{i,1}, \ldots, a_{i,n_{r-1}})$ and $B_i := (b_{i,1}, \ldots, b_{i,n_{r-1}})$ to denote the points in sub-instance (A_i, B_i). The following proposition ensures that instances sampled by EvenInstance do not violate the monotonicity

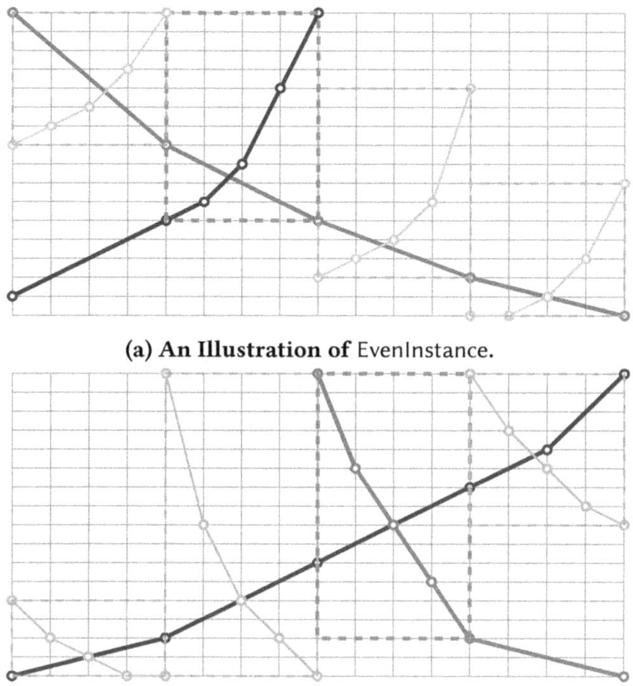

(a) An Illustration of EvenInstance.

(b) An Illustration of OddInstance.

Figure 2: An illustration of EvenInstance and OddInstance. Thick blue and green curves denote the actual inputs of Alice and Bob. Similarly, light blue and green curves denote the fooling inputs. Each red dashed rectangle denotes one sub-instance (thick ones show the special sub-instance).

and convexity properties of TCI across sub-instances (proof appears in Appendix C.2).

Proposition 5.3. *For (A, B) sampled from* EvenInstance, *assuming each sub-instance (A_i, B_i) satisfies monotonicity and convexity of* TCI, *then (A, B) also satisfies monotonicity and convexity.*

We refer to the instance $(A_{z_r^\star}, B_{z_r^\star}) = (C_{z_r^\star}, D_{z_r^\star})$ as the *special* sub-instance of (A, B). The next proposition signifies the role of the special sub-instance in EvenInstance (see Appendix C.2).

Proposition 5.4. *For instances (A, B) sampled from* EvenInstance, *the answer to* $\mathsf{TCI}(A, B)$ *is the same as the answer to* $\mathsf{TCI}(C_{z_r^\star}, D_{z_r^\star})$.

The definition of OddInstance procedure is similar to EvenInstance by switching the role of Alice and Bob. Due to space constraints, we postpone this description to Appendix C.3 (the odd-round analogues of the lemmas and claims also appear in Appendix C.3).

Actual vs Fooling Inputs. As we already observed in the proof of Lemma 5.2, providing the players with extra information about the input of the other player (i.e., giving Bob the first i^* points in Alice's input) facilitates the proof of the lower bound. This is also the case for our hard instances for $r > 1$ round protocols. In the following observations, we state several properties of this extra information which is crucial for our information-theoretic lower bound for TCI (the observations for odd rounds appear in C.3).

Observation 5.5. In EvenInstance, there is a one-to-one mapping between $(A_{z_r^\star}, B_{z_r^\star})$ and the original $(C_{z_r^\star}, D_{z_r^\star})$ (before applying any operator), assuming we are given $(C^{>z_r^\star}, D^{>z_r^\star})$.

The reason behind Observation 5.5 is simply the operators applied to each (C_i, D_i) are functions of $(C^{>i}, D^{>i})$ in EvenInstance and the special sub-instance is just a "copy" of $(C_{z_r^\star}, D_{z_r^\star})$.

Observation 5.5 implies that if players have access to $(C^{>z_r^\star}, D^{>z_r^\star})$ in EvenInstance as an extra input, then they can determine the original distribution of their special sub-instance. This is the main reason that we provide the players with this extra input in our reduction.

Observation 5.6. In EvenInstance, the index $z_r^\star \in [m_r]$ is chosen independently of B and $(C_1, D_1), \ldots, (C_{m_r}, D_{m_r})$.

This observation follows directly from the construction of the instances. Observation 5.6 implies that *even given the extra input*, the player that sends the first message is oblivious to the identity of the special sub-instance.

5.3.4 General Lower Bound: The Communication Complexity

We prove Theorem 7 by induction on the number of rounds, with Lemma 5.2 forming the base of the induction. We have the following lemma.

Lemma 5.7. *For any $r \geq 1$ and any $(1/3)$-error protocol π_r for instances of* TCI *sampled from the distribution $\mathcal{D}_r$, the communication cost of π_r is $\Omega(N/r^2)$.*

From now on we fix a *deterministic* protocol π_r for TCI on $\mathcal{D}_r$; we later use Yao's minimax principle [46] to extend the lower bound to randomized protocols. We use $\mathbf{\Pi}$ to denote the random variable for messages communicated in the protocol, and write $\mathbf{\Pi} = (\mathbf{\Pi}_1, \ldots, \mathbf{\Pi}_r)$, where $\mathbf{\Pi}_\ell$ denotes the message communicated in round ℓ. We further use $\mathbf{Z}$ to denote the index $z_r^\star$, which corresponds to the index of the special sub-instance. Let $(\mathbf{A}_1, \ldots, \mathbf{A}_{m_r})$ and $(\mathbf{B}_1, \ldots, \mathbf{B}_{m_r})$ denote the random variables for the points A and B and their partitioning into sub-instances respectively, and $(\mathbf{C}_1, \ldots, \mathbf{C}_{m_r})$ and $(\mathbf{D}_1, \ldots, \mathbf{D}_{m_r})$ for C and D.

We start with the following lemma that formalizes our intuition that players cannot reveal information about the special sub-instance in their first round. We first consider even-round protocols (see Appendix C.3 for the lemma for odd-round protocols). .

Lemma 5.8. *For any even integer r, and any r-round protocol π_r with worst-case message length ℓ on instances of $\mathcal{D}_r$,*

$$\mathbb{I}((A_Z, B_Z); \Pi_1 \mid C^{>Z}, D^{>Z}, Z) \le \ell/N.$$

Proof. We start by expanding the LHS:

$$\begin{aligned}
&\mathbb{I}((A_Z, B_Z); \Pi_1 \mid C^{>Z}, D^{>Z}, Z) \\
&\quad = \mathop{\mathbb{E}}_{z \in [m_r]} \left[\mathbb{I}((A_z, B_z); \Pi_1 \mid C^{>z}, D^{>z}, Z = z)\right] \\
&\qquad \text{(definition of conditional mutual information)} \\
&\quad = \frac{1}{m_r}\sum_{z=1}^{m_r} \mathbb{I}((A_z, B_z); \Pi_1 \mid C^{>z}, D^{>z}, Z = z) \\
&\qquad \text{(distribution of } Z \text{ is uniform over } [m_r]) \\
&\quad = \frac{1}{m_r}\sum_{z=1}^{m_r} \mathbb{I}((C_z, D_z); \Pi_1 \mid C^{>z}, D^{>z}, Z = z) \\
&\qquad \text{(by Observation 5.5)} \\
&\quad = \frac{1}{m_r}\sum_{z=1}^{m_r} \mathbb{I}((C_z, D_z); \Pi_1 \mid C^{>z}, D^{>z}),
\end{aligned}$$

where the last equality is due to the fact that the joint distribution of all random variables $(C_z, D_z), \Pi_r, C^{>z}, D^{>z}$ is independent of the event $Z = z$. Indeed, for even r, the message Π_1 sent by Bob is a function of $(B_1, \ldots, B_{m_r})$ and $(C_1, D_1), \ldots, (C_{m_r}, D_{m_r})$, and by Observation 5.6, these random variables are all independent of $z_r^\star$. As such, removing the conditioning on the event $Z = z$ does not change the distribution of variables above. Finally,

$$\begin{aligned}
&\frac{1}{m_r}\sum_{z=1}^{m_r} \mathbb{I}((C_z, D_z); \Pi_r \mid C^{>z}, D^{>z}) \\
&\quad = \frac{1}{m_r} \cdot \mathbb{I}(C_1, \ldots, C_{m_r}, D_1, \ldots, D_{m_r}; \Pi_1) \\
&\qquad \text{(chain rule of mutual information)} \\
&\quad \le \frac{1}{m_r} \cdot \mathbb{H}(\Pi_1) \le \frac{\ell}{m_r}. \qquad (\mathbb{H}(\Pi_1) \le \ell)
\end{aligned}$$

The lemma follows by noting that $m_r = N$. ∎

To continue, we need the following definition.

Distribution μ_e for even r: For an assignment $(\Pi_1, C^{>z}, D^{>z}, z)$ (denoted by E for short) to $(\Pi_1, C^{>Z}, D^{>Z}, Z)$, we define $\mu_e(E)$ as the distribution of (A_z, B_z) in $\mathcal{D}_r$ conditioned on $\Pi_r = \Pi_r, Z = z$, $C^{>z} = C^{>z}, D^{>z} = D^{>z}$.

Using Lemma 5.8, we have the following claim (see Appendix C.3 for the claim for odd-round protocols).

Claim 5.9. *For any even integer r and any r-round protocol π_r with worst-case message length $o(N/r^2)$,*

$$\mathop{\mathbb{E}}_{E=(\Pi_1, C^{>z}, D^{>z}, z)} \left[\|\mu_e(E) - \mathcal{D}_{r-1}\|_{tvd}\right] = o(1/r).$$

Proof. By the connection between mutual information and KL-divergence (Fact C.1), we have,

$$\begin{aligned}
&\mathbb{I}((A_Z, B_Z); \Pi_1 \mid C^{>Z}, D^{>Z}, Z) = \\
&\mathop{\mathbb{E}}_{E=(\Pi_1, C^{>z}, D^{>z}, z)} \left[\mathbb{D}(\text{dist}(A_Z, B_Z \mid E \setminus \Pi_1) \mid\mid \text{dist}(A_Z, B_Z \mid E))\right] \\
&= \mathop{\mathbb{E}}_{E=(\Pi_1, C^{>z}, D^{>z}, z)} \left[\mathbb{D}(\mathcal{D}_{r-1} \mid\mid \mu_e(E))\right];
\end{aligned}$$

Conditioned on $Z = z$, distribution of (A_Z, B_Z) is the same as the original distribution of (C_Z, D_Z) by Observation 5.5. Furthermore,

$$\begin{aligned}
&\mathop{\mathbb{E}}_{E=(\Pi_1, C^{>z}, D^{>z}, z)} \left[\mathbb{D}(\mathcal{D}_{r-1} \mid\mid \mu_e(E))\right] \\
&\quad \ge \mathop{\mathbb{E}}_{E=(\Pi_r, C^{>z}, D^{>z}, z)} \left[2 \cdot \|\mathcal{D}_{r-1} - \mu_e(E)\|_{tvd}^2\right] \\
&\qquad \text{(Pinsker's inequality (Fact C.3))} \\
&\quad \ge 2 \cdot \left(\mathop{\mathbb{E}}_{E=(\Pi_r, C^{>z}, D^{>z}, z)} \left[\|\mathcal{D}_{r-1} - \mu_e(E)\|_{tvd}\right]\right)^2. \\
&\qquad \text{(Jensen's inequality)}
\end{aligned}$$

By Lemma 5.8, $\mathbb{I}((A_Z, B_Z); \Pi_r \mid C^{>Z}, D^{>Z}, Z) = o(1/r^2)$, implying that,

$$\mathop{\mathbb{E}}_{E=(\Pi_r, C^{>z}, D^{>z}, z)} \left[\|\mathcal{D}_{r-1} - \mu_e(E)\|_{tvd}\right] = o(1/r).$$

This finalizes the proof. ∎

Define the recursive function $\delta(k) = \delta(k-1) - o(1/r)$ with base case $\delta(1) = 1/4$ (here r is the number of rounds).

Lemma 5.10. *Any deterministic $\delta(r)$-error protocol π_r on $\mathcal{D}_r$ requires $\Omega(N/r^2)$ communication.*

Proof. The proof is by induction on the number of rounds. The base case for $r = 1$ follows from Lemma 5.2. We now prove the induction step.

Suppose the lemma holds for all integers up to $r - 1$, we prove it for r-round protocols. Given a r-round protocol π_r for $\mathcal{D}_r$ that violates the induction hypothesis, we construct a $(r-1)$-round protocol π_{r-1} for $\mathcal{D}_{r-1}$ that also violates the induction hypothesis, a contradiction. The protocol π_{r-1} is constructed in two steps: we first construct a randomized protocol π' from π_r, and then fix the randomness of the protocol to achieve a deterministic protocol.

We now describe π'. For simplicity, we only give the protocol for even choices of r; the extension to odd values is straightforward. Given an instance $(A, B) \sim \mathcal{D}_{r-1}$, protocol π' works as follows:

(1) Using public randomness, the players sample $(\Pi_1, C^{>z}, D^{>z}, z_r^\star)$ from the distribution $\mathcal{D}_r$.
(2) Bob samples remaining coordinates (C_j, D_j) for $j < z_r^\star$ using private randomness from distribution
$$\mathcal{D}_r \mid (\Pi_1, C^{>z}, D^{>z}, z_r^\star).$$
(3) Alice sets $A_{z_r^\star} = A$ and Bob sets $B_{z_r^\star} = B$ by applying the appropriate slope-shift and origin-shift operators based on $C^{>z}, D^{>z}$ which is known to both Alice and Bob.
(4) The players then fill the rest of their input in $(A_1, \ldots, A_{m_r})$ and $(B_1, \ldots, B_{m_r})$; Bob knows all of $(C_1, D_1), \ldots, (C_{m_r}, D_{m_r})$ and can perform the needed slope-shift and origin-shift operators, and Alice simply needs to extend $A_{z_r^\star}$ across straight lines.
(5) The players run π_r on these new points from the second round onwards, assuming that the first communicated message was Π_1. They output the index returned by π_r.

Communication cost of π' is clearly at most as the communication cost of π_r. We now prove the correctness of π'.

Claim 5.11. *Assuming π_r is a $\delta(r)$-error protocol for $\mathcal{D}_r$, π' will be a $(\delta(r) + o(1/r))$-error protocol for $\mathcal{D}_{r-1}$.*

Proof. We have,

$$\Pr_{\mathcal{D}_{r-1}}(\pi' \text{ errs}) = \mathop{\mathbb{E}}_{E=(\Pi_1, C^{>z}, D^{>z}, z_r^\star)}\left[\Pr_{\mathcal{D}_{r-1}}(\pi_r \text{ errs} \mid E)\right] \quad \text{(by Proposition 5.4)}$$

$$\leq \mathop{\mathbb{E}}_{E=(\Pi_1, C^{>z}, D^{>z}, z_r^\star)}\left[\Pr_{\mu_e(E)}(\pi_r \text{ errs}) + \|\mu_e(E) - \mathcal{D}_{r-1}\|_{tvd}\right] \quad \text{(by Fact C.2)}$$

$$\leq \delta(r) + o(1/r^2), \quad (\pi_r \text{ is a } (\delta(r))\text{-error protocol, and by Claim 5.9})$$

finalizing the proof. ∎

We are now ready to complete the proof of Lemma 5.10. By Claim 5.11, π' is a $(\delta(r)+o(1/r))$-error protocol for $\mathcal{D}_{r-1}$. π' is a randomized protocol. However, by an averaging argument, we can fix the randomness of π' to obtain a deterministic $(\delta(r) + o(1/r))$-error protocol for $\mathcal{D}_{r-1}$ with the same communication cost $o(N/r^2)$. As $\delta(r) + o(1/r) = \delta(r-1)$, this contradicts the induction hypothesis. We thus have that the communication cost of π_r is $\Omega(N/r^2)$, proving the induction step. This concludes the proof. ∎

Lemma 5.7 now follows immediately from Lemma 5.10 as $\delta(r) = 1/4 + \sum_{k=1}^{r} o(1/r) = 1/4 + o(1) < 1/3$, and by the easy direction of Yao's minimax principle [46].

5.3.5 *Proof of Theorem 7*

Proof of Theorem 7. By Lemma 5.7, any $(1/3)$-error r-round protocol for TCI_n requires $\Omega(N/r^2)$ communication on instances of $\mathcal{D}_r$. In these instances, $n = N^r$ by the construction of $\mathcal{D}_r$. Plugging in $N = n^{1/r}$, we obtain $\mathsf{CC}^r(\mathsf{TCI}_n) = \Omega(\frac{1}{r^2} \cdot n^{1/r})$.

We conclude this proof by making the following remark: A r-round instance of our problem consists of at most N^{r-1} applications of StepCurve, each having a larger slope than the previous one by an additive factor of N. As a result, the largest slope using in our construction is $N^{O(r)}$. This implies that the bit-complexity of the numbers we use is bounded by $\log(N^{O(r)}) = O(\log n)$. ∎

As a corollary of Theorem 7, using the connection between two-curve intersection problem and linear programming outlined in Section 5.2, we obtain the following.

Corollary 8. *For any integer $r \geq 1$, any two-player r-round protocol for 2-dimensional linear programming with n constraints requires $\Omega(\frac{1}{r^2} \cdot n^{1/r})$ communication.*

5.4 Lower Bounds for Linear Programming in Big Data Models

We now give some straightforward applications of our communication complexity lower bound for linear programming to streaming and coordinator models, and formalize Result 2.

The Streaming Model. It is well-known that communication complexity lower bounds imply space lower bounds on the space complexity of streaming algorithms (see, e.g. [2, 24]). Using this connection in conjunction with Corollary 8, we have, to establish the following theorem.

Theorem 9. *For any integer $r \geq 1$, any streaming algorithm that makes r passes over the constraints of a 2-dimensional linear program with n constraints and finds the optimal solution with probability at least $2/3$ requires $\Omega(\frac{1}{r^3} \cdot n^{1/2r})$ space.*

The Coordinator Model. Any r-round distributed protocol implies a $2r$-round protocol in our communication model. Hence,

Theorem 10. *For any integer $r \geq 1$, any r-round algorithm that finds the optimal solution of a 2-dimensional linear program with n constraints partitioned across $k \geq 2$ sites in the coordinator model with probability at least $2/3$ requires $\Omega(\frac{1}{r^2} \cdot n^{1/2r})$ communication.*

Acknowledgments

Qin Zhang would like to thank Yufei Tao for introducing the problem (as well as the two-curve intersection problem as a way of proving a lower bound for linear programming).

References

[1] Kook Jin Ahn and Sudipto Guha. Linear programming in the semi-streaming model with application to the maximum matching problem. In *ICALP 2011*, pages 526–538, 2011.

[2] Noga Alon, Yossi Matias, and Mario Szegedy. The space complexity of approximating the frequency moments. *J. Comput. Syst. Sci.*, 58(1):137–147, 1999.

[3] Molham Aref, Balder ten Cate, Todd J. Green, Benny Kimelfeld, Dan Olteanu, Emir Pasalic, Todd L. Veldhuizen, and Geoffrey Washburn. Design and implementation of the logicblox system. In *SIGMOD*, pages 1371–1382, 2015.

[4] Sepehr Assadi, Sanjeev Khanna, and Yang Li. Tight bounds for single-pass streaming complexity of the set cover problem. In *STOC*, pages 698–711, 2016.

[5] Paul Beame, Paraschos Koutris, and Dan Suciu. Communication steps for parallel query processing. *J. ACM*, 64(6):40:1–40:58, 2017.

[6] Robert G Bland and Michel Las Vergnas. Orientability of matroids. *Journal of Combinatorial Theory, Series B*, 24(1):94–123, 1978.

[7] Bernhard E. Boser, Isabelle Guyon, and Vladimir Vapnik. A training algorithm for optimal margin classifiers. In *COLT*, pages 144–152, 1992.

[8] Hervé Brönnimann, Bernard Chazelle, and Jiří Matoušek. Product range spaces, sensitive sampling, and derandomization. *SIAM J. Comput.*, 28(5):1552–1575, 1999.

[9] Hervé Brönnimann and Michael T. Goodrich. Almost optimal set covers in finite vc-dimension. *Discrete & Computational Geometry*, 14(4):463–479, 1995.

[10] Christopher J. C. Burges. A tutorial on support vector machines for pattern recognition. *Data Min. Knowl. Discov.*, 2(2):121–167, 1998.

[11] Amit Chakrabarti, Graham Cormode, and Andrew McGregor. Robust lower bounds for communication and stream computation. In *STOC*, pages 641–650, 2008.

[12] Timothy M. Chan. Improved deterministic algorithms for linear programming in low dimensions. In *SODA*, pages 1213–1219, 2016.

[13] Timothy M. Chan and Eric Y. Chen. Multi-pass geometric algorithms. *Discrete & Computational Geometry*, 37(1):79–102, 2007.

[14] M. T. Chao. A general purpose unequal probability sampling plan. *Biometrika*, 69:653–656, 1982.

[15] Kenneth L. Clarkson. Linear programming in $o(n3^{d^2})$ time. *Inf. Process. Lett.*, 22(1):21–24, 1986.

[16] Kenneth L. Clarkson. Las vegas algorithms for linear and integer programming when the dimension is small. *J. ACM*, 42(2):488–499, 1995.

[17] Kenneth L. Clarkson and Peter W. Shor. Application of random sampling in computational geometry, II. *Discrete & Computational Geometry*, 4:387–421, 1989.

[18] Thomas M. Cover and Joy A. Thomas. *Elements of information theory (2. ed.)*. Wiley, 2006.

[19] David J. Crisp and Christopher J. C. Burges. A geometric interpretation of v-svm classifiers. In *NIPS*, pages 244–250, 1999.

[20] Martin E. Dyer. On a multidimensional search technique and its application to the euclidean one-centre problem. *SIAM J. Comput.*, 15(3):725–738, 1986.

[21] Martin E. Dyer and Alan M. Frieze. A randomized algorithm for fixed-dimensional linear programming. *Math. Program.*, 44(1-3):203–212, 1989.

[22] Bernd Gärtner and Martin Jaggi. Coresets for polytope distance. In *SOCG*, pages 33–42, 2009.

[23] Michael T. Goodrich, Nodari Sitchinava, and Qin Zhang. Sorting, searching, and simulation in the mapreduce framework. In *ISAAC*, pages 374–383, 2011.

[24] Sudipto Guha and Andrew McGregor. Tight lower bounds for multi-pass stream computation via pass elimination. In *ICALP*, pages 760–772, 2008.

[25] David Haussler and Emo Welzl. epsilon-nets and simplex range queries. *Discrete & Computational Geometry*, 2:127–151, 1987.

[26] Hal Daumé III, Jeff M. Phillips, Avishek Saha, and Suresh Venkatasubramanian. Efficient protocols for distributed classification and optimization. In *ALT*, pages 154–168, 2012.

[27] Piotr Indyk, Sepideh Mahabadi, Ronitt Rubinfeld, Jonathan Ullman, Ali Vakilian, and Anak Yodpinyanee. Fractional set cover in the streaming model. In *APPROX/RANDOM 2017*, pages 12:1–12:20, 2017.

[28] Gil Kalai. A subexponential randomized simplex algorithm (extended abstract). In *STOC*, pages 475–482, 1992.

[29] Howard J. Karloff, Siddharth Suri, and Sergei Vassilvitskii. A model of computation for mapreduce. In *SODA*, pages 938–948, 2010.

[30] Yin Tat Lee and Aaron Sidford. Path finding methods for linear programming: Solving linear programs in õ(vrank) iterations and faster algorithms for maximum flow. In *FOCS*, pages 424–433, 2014.

[31] Makrynioti, Nantia and Vasiloglou, Nikolaos and Pasalic, Emir and Vassalos, Vasilis. Data Science with Linear Programming. http://delbp.github.io/DeLBP-2017/papers/DeLBP-2017_paper_2CR.pdf, 2017.

[32] Jiří Matoušek, Micha Sharir, and Emo Welzl. A subexponential bound for linear programming. *Algorithmica*, 16(4/5):498–516, 1996.

[33] Andrew McGregor. private communication.

[34] Nimrod Megiddo. Linear programming in linear time when the dimension is fixed. *J. ACM*, 31(1):114–127, 1984.

[35] Peter Bro Miltersen, Noam Nisan, Shmuel Safra, and Avi Wigderson. On data structures and asymmetric communication complexity. *J. Comput. Syst. Sci.*, 57(1):37–49, 1998.

[36] Ketan Mulmuley. *Computational geometry - an introduction through randomized algorithms*. Prentice Hall, 1994.

[37] J. Ian Munro and Mike Paterson. Selection and sorting with limited storage. *Theor. Comput. Sci.*, 12:315–323, 1980.

[38] Jeff M. Phillips, Elad Verbin, and Qin Zhang. Lower bounds for number-in-hand multiparty communication complexity, made easy. In *SODA*, pages 486–501, 2012.

[39] Tim Roughgarden, Sergei Vassilvitskii, and Joshua R. Wang. Shuffles and circuits: (on lower bounds for modern parallel computation). In *SPAA*, pages 1–12, 2016.

[40] Pranab Sen and Srinivasan Venkatesh. Lower bounds for predecessor searching in the cell probe model. *J. Comput. Syst. Sci.*, 74(3):364–385, 2008.

[41] Yufei Tao. Massively parallel entity matching with linear classification in low dimensional space. In *ICDT*, pages 20:1–20:19, 2018.

[42] Ivor W. Tsang, James T. Kwok, and Pak-Ming Cheung. Core vector machines: Fast SVM training on very large data sets. *Journal of Machine Learning Research*, 6:363–392, 2005.

[43] Vladimir N Vapnik and A Ya Chervonenkis. On the uniform convergence of relative frequencies of events to their probabilities. In *Measures of complexity*, pages 11–30. Springer, 2015.

[44] Roberta S. Wenocur and Richard M. Dudley. Some special vapnik-chervonenkis classes. *Discrete Mathematics*, 33(3):313–318, 1981.

[45] Andrew Chi-Chih Yao. Some complexity questions related to distributive computing (preliminary report). In *STOC*, pages 209–213, 1979.

[46] Andrew Chi-Chih Yao. Lower bounds by probabilistic arguments (extended abstract). In *FOCS*, pages 420–428, 1983.

[47] Yinyu Ye and Edison Tse. An extension of karmarkar's projective algorithm for convex quadratic programming. *Math. Program.*, 44(1-3):157–179, 1989.

A Missing Details from Section 3

A.1 Implementation in the Coordinator Model

The main step is to perform the sampling of ε-net which is captured by the following lemma.

LEMMA A.1. *The coordinator can sample a subset $\mathcal{N} \subseteq \mathcal{S}$ of size m according to the weight function $w : \mathcal{S} \longrightarrow \mathbb{R}$ using 2 rounds and $O(m \cdot \texttt{bit}(\mathcal{S}) + k(\ell/r + 1)\log n)$ bits of communication, where ℓ is the number of times the weight function $w(\cdot)$ has been updated when simulating Algorithm 1 in the coordinator model.*

PROOF. The sampling algorithm is as follows. In the first round each site P_i sends $w(\mathcal{S}_i)$ to the coordinator. Note that $w(\mathcal{S}_i)$ for any $i \in [k]$ can be described in $\log(1 + n^{1/r})^{\ell} = O(\ell/r \cdot \log n)$ bits.

In the second round the coordinator generates m i.i.d. random numbers $x_1, \ldots, x_m$ from $[k]$ from the distribution $\mathbf{Pr}[i \text{ is sampled}] = \frac{w(\mathcal{S}_i)}{w(\mathcal{S})}$, and sends the i-th site the number $y_i = |\{j \mid x_j = i\}|$. After obtaining y_i, site P_i samples y_i elements from its local set $\mathcal{S}_i$ according to the distribution $\mathbf{Pr}[S \text{ is sampled}] = \frac{w(S)}{w(\mathcal{S}_i)}$, and sends the sampled elements to the coordinator. Note that $y_i \leq m \leq n$ for any $i \in [m]$, and thus the communication cost of this round is bounded by $O(k) \cdot O(\ell/r \cdot \log n) + O(m) \cdot \texttt{bit}(\mathcal{S})$ bits.

Finally, the sampling is indeed with respect to the weight function $w(\cdot)$, since $\mathbf{Pr}[S \text{ is sampled}] = \frac{w(\mathcal{S}_i)}{w(\mathcal{S})} \cdot \frac{w(S)}{w(\mathcal{S}_i)} = \frac{w(S)}{w(\mathcal{S})}$. This concludes the proof. ∎

In order to implement Algorithm 1, each site should also be able to determine the set of violating elements in its input. This can be done easily by asking the coordinator to share the basis computed in each iteration with every site. The proof of Theorem 2 follows directly from that of Theorem 1 by plugging in Lemma A.1.

A.2 Implementation in the MPC Model

Our general strategy is to simulate our implementation of the meta-algorithm for the coordinator model in the MPC model for $r = 1/\delta$ round protocols. The main challenge in implementing this is that once we require the load of roughly n^{δ} per machine, we need to start with $k = n^{1-\delta}$ machines to begin with to fit the whole input across all machines. This means that the number of sites in the simulation is k. But then, if all these machines need to send even one bit to the designated coordinator machine (or vice versa), this requires a load of $n^{1-\delta}$ on the coordinator machine which is prohibitively large for any $\delta < 1/2$.

In order to fix this, we are going to use the by now standard approach of [23]. There are only two steps that the coordinator and the machines need to communicate with each other: (1) when the machines need to send a sample of the ε-net, and (2) when the coordinator needs to send the basis to the machines. The latter can be done easily in $O(1/\delta)$ MPC rounds on machines of memory $O(n^{\delta})$: the coordinator first shares this information with n^{δ} other machines in one round; each of these machines next shares this information with another set of n^{δ} machines (unique to each original machine). In $O(1/\delta)$ rounds all the $n^{1-\delta}$ machines would receive this information (see [23] for more details).

To handle the part when the machines need to send the ε-net $\mathcal{N}$ to the coordinator, we do as follows. Recall that the size of $\mathcal{N}$ is at most $\tilde{O}(\lambda n^{\delta} \nu^2)$, and thus it will fit the memory of the coordinator. However, we first need to sample this according to the correct distribution. In order to do this, we use our approach for implementing the streaming algorithm. Since by the previous part we managed to share the basis computed in each iteration with every machine, as in the case of streaming algorithms, the machines can compute the weights of every constraint they have. The total weight of the constraints can also be computed in $O(1/\delta)$ rounds using the sort and search method of [23]. As a result, each machine can locally perform the sampling of $\mathcal{N}$ and send this information to the coordinator.

To summarize, we can implement each round of the algorithm in the coordinator model for $r = 1/\delta$ in $O(1/\delta)$ MPC rounds, hence proving Theorem 3.

B Missing Details from Section 4

B.1 Linear Programming

Let $\mathrm{T}_{LP}(m, t)$ denotes the time needed to solve a linear program with $\Theta(m)$ constraints and $\Theta(t)$ variables.

PROPOSITION B.1. *For any linear program with n constraints and dimension d:*

- *The time needed to compute a basis of $m \geq d$ given constraints is $T_b(m) = O(d \cdot \mathrm{T}_{LP}(m, d))$.*
- *The time needed to compute all constraints that violate a given basis of size $b = O(d)$ among t constraints is $T_v(t, b) = O(t \cdot d + d \cdot \mathrm{T}_{LP}(d, d))$.*

PROOF. To find a basis $\mathcal{B}$ of a set $\mathcal{N}$ of m constraints, we first solve the LP only given the constraints in $\mathcal{N}$ to obtain a point $x^* = (x_1^*, \ldots, x_d^*)$ with optimal value c^*. Recall that in our mapping of LP to an LP-type problem, we need to find a lexicographically smallest optimal solution on constraints in $\mathcal{N}$, which may not be the point x^* even though the objective value is still c^*. We thus write another linear program:

$$\min_{x \in \mathbb{R}^d} x_1$$

$$\text{s.t.} \quad \sum_{i=1}^{d} c_i x_i = c^* \quad \text{and} \quad \sum_{i=1}^{d} a_i^j x_i \leq b^j \quad \text{for all } j \in \mathcal{N}.$$

This allows us to find an optimal solution to the LP with the minimum value of x_1. Repeating this procedure for d iterations and for i-th iteration fixing $x_1, .., x_{i-1}$ computed so far, and finding the minimum value for x_i, allows us to find the lexicographically smallest optimal solution. These LPs all are d-dimensional with $\Theta(m)$ constraints, and hence can be solved in $O(d \cdot T_{LP}(m, d))$ time in total, finalizing the first part.

A basis of size b in a linear program consists of b constraints of the LP that are all tight by the assignment of the variables. Hence, given the basis, we only need to solve the linear program on a system of b linear inequalities to determine a value of x^* that is tight for all the constraints in the basis. This can be done in $O(dT_{LP}(d, d))$ time (as we do before). After this, we can simply check the d-dimensional vector x^* against all the t constraints and add each one as a violating set if x^* does not satisfy the constraint in $O(t \cdot d)$ time, finalizing the second part. ∎

Plugging in the currently best known bound for linear programming $T_{LP}(m, d) = \widetilde{O}(\sqrt{d}\,(dm + d^{2.373}))$ ([30], Proposition B.1), and the aforementioned bounds on $\nu, \lambda = O(d)$, we can prove Theorem 4 using Theorems 1, 2, and 3.

B.2 Linear Support Vector Machine

In the following, let $T_{SVM}(m, d)$ denote the time needed to solve an instance of Linear SVM problem with m constraints and d variables. We show how to implement the basis computation and violation test for Linear SVM in the following proposition.

Proposition B.2. *For any Linear SVM problem with n constraints and dimension d:*

- *The time needed to compute a basis of* $m \geq d$ *given constraints is* $T_b(m) = O(T_{SVM}(m, d))$.
- *The time needed to compute all constraints that violate a given basis of size b among t constraints is* $T_v(t, b) = O(t \cdot d + T_{SVM}(d, d))$.

Proof. To find a basis $\mathcal{B}$ of a set $\mathcal{N}$ of m constraints, we simply need to solve another instance of Linear SVM, i.e., (6), only on the given constraints. This can be done in $O(T_{SVM}(m, d))$ by definition. The second part can also be solved by solving a linear equation exactly as in the case in Proposition B.1. ∎

Plugging in the currently best known bound for Linear SVM $T_{SVM}(m, d) = O((m + d)^3)$ ([47], Proposition B.2), and the aforementioned bounds on $\nu, \lambda = O(d)$, we can prove Theorem 5 using Theorems 1, 2, and 3.

B.3 Core Vector Machine

Let $T_{MEB}(m, d)$ denote the time needed to solve an instance of MEB problem with m constraints and d variables. The following proposition show how to implement the basis computation and violation test for MEB (the proof is identical to Proposition B.2 and is hence omitted).

Proposition B.3. *For any Linear SVM problem with n constraints and dimension d:*

- *The time needed to compute a basis of* $m \geq d$ *given constraints is* $T_b(m) = O(T_{MEB}(m, d))$.
- *The time needed to compute all constraints that violate a given basis of size b among t constraints is* $T_v(t, b) = O(t \cdot d + T_{MEB}(d, d))$.

As MEB can be cast as a convex quadratic program, we have $T_{MEB}(m, d) = O((m + d)^3)$ by [47] as before. Hence, Theorems 1, 2, and 3 imply the following result.

C Missing Details from Section 5

C.1 Background on Information Theory

Our proof relies on basic concepts from information theory, which we review briefly here. For a broader introduction, we refer the interested reader to the excellent text by Cover and Thomas [18].

Entropy and Mutual Information. The Shannon entropy is defined as $\mathbb{H}(\boldsymbol{A}) := \sum_{A \in \text{supp}(\boldsymbol{A})} \Pr(\boldsymbol{A} = A) \cdot \log\left(\frac{1}{\Pr(\boldsymbol{A}=A)}\right)$. The conditional entropy of $\boldsymbol{A}$ on random variable $\boldsymbol{B}$ is defined as $\mathbb{H}(\boldsymbol{A} \mid \boldsymbol{B}) := \mathbb{E}_{B \sim \boldsymbol{B}}\left[\mathbb{H}(\boldsymbol{A} \mid \boldsymbol{B} = B)\right]$. The (conditional) mutual information between $\boldsymbol{A}$ and $\boldsymbol{B}$ is $\mathbb{I}(\boldsymbol{A} ; \boldsymbol{B} \mid \boldsymbol{C}) := \mathbb{H}(\boldsymbol{A} \mid \boldsymbol{C}) - \mathbb{H}(\boldsymbol{A} \mid \boldsymbol{B}, \boldsymbol{C})$. We shall use the following basic properties of entropy and mutual information throughout.

Measures of Distance Between Distributions. For two distributions μ and ν, the *Kullback-Leibler divergence* between μ and ν is denoted by $\mathbb{D}(\mu \mid\mid \nu)$ and defined as:

$$\mathbb{D}(\mu \mid\mid \nu) := \mathop{\mathbb{E}}_{a \sim \mu}\left[\log \frac{\Pr_\mu(a)}{\Pr_\nu(a)}\right]. \tag{8}$$

We have the following relation between mutual information and KL-divergence.

Fact C.1. *For random variables* $\boldsymbol{A}, \boldsymbol{B}, \boldsymbol{C}$,

$$\mathbb{I}(\boldsymbol{A} ; \boldsymbol{B} \mid \boldsymbol{C}) = \mathop{\mathbb{E}}_{(b,c) \sim (\boldsymbol{B}, \boldsymbol{C})}\Big[\mathbb{D}(\text{dist}(\boldsymbol{A} \mid \boldsymbol{C} = c) \mid\mid \text{dist}(\boldsymbol{A} \mid \boldsymbol{B} = b, \boldsymbol{C} = c))\Big].$$

We denote the total variation distance between two distributions μ and ν on the same support Ω by $\|\mu - \nu\|_{tvd}$, defined as:

$$\|\mu - \nu\|_{tvd} := \max_{\Omega' \subseteq \Omega} (\mu(\Omega') - \nu(\Omega')) = \frac{1}{2} \cdot \sum_{x \in \Omega} |\mu(x) - \nu(x)|. \tag{9}$$

We use the following basic properties of total variation distance.

Fact C.2. *Suppose μ and ν are two distributions for $\mathcal{E}$, then,* $\mathbf{Pr}_{\mu}(\mathcal{E}) \leq \mathbf{Pr}_{\nu}(\mathcal{E}) + \|\mu - \nu\|_{tvd}$.

The following Pinskers' inequality bounds the total variation distance between two distributions based on their KL-divergence,

Fact C.3 (Pinsker's inequality). *For any distributions μ and ν,* $\|\mu - \nu\|_{tvd} \leq \sqrt{\frac{1}{2} \cdot \mathbb{D}(\mu \mid\mid \nu)}$.

C.2 Missing Proofs of Section 5.3

Proposition (Restatement of Proposition 5.3). *For (A, B) sampled from* EvenInstance, *assuming each sub-instance (A_i, B_i) satisfies monotonicity and convexity of* TCI, *then (A, B) also satisfies monotonicity and convexity.*

Proof. For B_i's, the monotonicity and convexity follow from the origin-shift operator and slope-shift operator, respectively. For A_i's, different sub-instances are obtained by extending two line segments in $A_{z_r^\star}$, and hence A trivially satisfies the properties. ∎

Proposition (Restatement of Proposition 5.4). *For instances (A, B) sampled from* EvenInstance, *the answer to* $\mathsf{TCI}(A, B)$ *is the same as the answer to* $\mathsf{TCI}(C_{z_r^\star}, D_{z_r^\star})$.

Proof. Since $(A_{z_r^\star}, B_{z_r^\star}) = (C_{z_r^\star}, D_{z_r^\star})$, and $(C_{z_r^\star}, D_{z_r^\star})$ form a valid instance of TCI, clearly A and B also only cross each other between the points in $(A_{z_r^\star}, B_{z_r^\star})$. ∎

C.3 OddInstance and Odd-Round Protocols

We now turn to the definition of the OddInstance procedure inside Instance.

OddInstance(r).

1. Sample m_r instances (C_i, D_i) *independently* from Instance($r-1$).
2. For $i = 1$ to m_r do:
   (a) Let p_A^{i-1} be the right-most point of Alice's input in (C_{i-1}, D_{i-1}) (define $p_A^0 := (0, 0)$). Apply the origin-shift operator with point p_A^{i-1} from Alice's side on instance (C_i, D_i).
   (b) Let α_r^{i-1} be the largest slope of any segment in (C_{i-1}, D_{i-1}). Apply the slope-shift operator with slope α_r^{i-1} on (C_i, D_i).
3. Sample $z_r^\star \in [m_r]$ uniformly at random.
4. Define $A := (C_1, \ldots, C_{m_r})$.
5. Define $B := (B_1, \ldots, B_{m_r})$ where $B_{z_r^\star} := D_{z_r^\star}$; the remaining B_i's for $i \neq z_r^\star$ are constructed by extending the curve in $B_{z_r^\star}$ on both its endpoints along straight lines.

Similar to EvenInstance, instances of OddInstance also consists of m_r sub-instances among which $(C_{z_r^\star}, D_{z_r^\star})$ is called the *special* sub-instance. Figure 2b gives an illustration of instances sampled by OddInstance.

Analogues of Even-Round Results. We list the following results as odd-round analogues of the bounds in the paper for even-round protocols. Their proofs all follow immediately from the proof of their even-round counter part.

The following two properties are analogous to Propositions 5.3 and 5.4 for EvenInstance.

Proposition C.4. *For (A, B) sampled from* OddInstance, *assuming each sub-instance (A_i, B_i) satisfies monotonicity and convexity of* TCI, *then (A, B) also satisfies monotonicity and convexity.*

Proposition C.5. *For instances (A, B) sampled from* OddInstance, *the answer to* $\mathsf{TCI}(A, B)$ *is the same as the answer to* $\mathsf{TCI}(C_{z_r^\star}, D_{z_r^\star})$.

The following two observations are analogous to Observations 5.5 and 5.6 for EvenInstance.

Observation C.6. In OddInstance, there is a one-to-one mapping between $(A_{z_r^\star}, B_{z_r^\star})$ and the original sub-instance $(C_{z_r^\star}, D_{z_r^\star})$ (before applying any operator), assuming we are given $(C^{<z_r^\star}, D^{<z_r^\star})$.

Observation C.7. In OddInstance, the index $z_r^\star \in [m_r]$ is chosen independently of $A = (A_1, \ldots, A_{m_r})$ and

$$(C_1, D_1), \ldots, (C_{m_r}, D_{m_r}).$$

The following lemma for odd-round protocols is analogous to Lemma 5.8 for even-round ones (but note the change in the order of conditioning).

Lemma C.8. *For any odd integer r and any r-round protocol π_r with worst-case message length ℓ on instances of $\mathcal{D}_r$,*

$$\mathbb{I}((\mathbf{A_Z}, \mathbf{B_Z}) ; \Pi_1 \mid \mathbf{C}^{<\mathbf{Z}}, \mathbf{D}^{<\mathbf{Z}}, \mathbf{Z}) \leq \ell/N.$$

The following definition is analogous to definition of μ_e.

Distribution μ_o for odd r: For an assignment

$$(\Pi_r, C^{<z}, D^{<z}, z)$$

(denoted by O for short) to $(\mathbf{\Pi}_1, \mathbf{C}^{<\mathbf{Z}}, \mathbf{D}^{<\mathbf{Z}}, \mathbf{Z})$, we define $\mu_o(O)$ as the distribution of $(\mathbf{A}_z, \mathbf{B}_z)$ in $\mathcal{D}_r$ conditioned on $\mathbf{\Pi}_r = \Pi_r, \mathbf{Z} = z, \mathbf{C}^{<z} = C^{<z}, \mathbf{D}^{<z} = D^{<z}$.

The following claim for odd-round protocols is analogous to Claim 5.9 for even-round ones (again note the change in the order of conditioning and the distribution).

Claim C.9. *For any odd integer r and any r-round protocol π_r with worst-case message length $o(N/r^2)$,*

$$\mathop{\mathbb{E}}_{O=(\Pi_1, C^{<z}, D^{<z}, z)} \left[\|\mu_o(O) - \mathcal{D}_{r-1}\|_{tvd} \right] = o(1/r).$$

Better Sliding Window Algorithms to Maximize Subadditive and Diversity Objectives

Michele Borassi
borassi@google.com
Google Research
Zurich, Switzerland

Alessandro Epasto
aepasto@google.com
Google Research
New York, NY, USA

Silvio Lattanzi
silviol@google.com
Google Research
Zurich, Switzerland

Sergei Vassilvitskii
sergeiv@google.com
Google Research
New York, NY, USA

Morteza Zadimoghaddam
zadim@google.com
Google Research
Zurich, Switzerland

ABSTRACT

The streaming computation model is a standard model for large-scale data analysis: the input arrives one element at a time, and the goal is to maintain an approximately optimal solution using only a constant, or, at worst, polylogarithmic space.

In practice, however, recency plays a large role, and one often wishes to consider only the last w elements that have arrived, the so-called *sliding window* problem. A trivial approach is to simply store the last w elements in a buffer; our goal is to develop algorithms with space and update time sublinear in w. In this regime, there are two frameworks: *exponential histograms* and *smooth histograms*, which can be used to obtain sliding window algorithms for families of functions satisfying certain properties.

Unfortunately, these frameworks have limitations and cannot always be applied directly. A prominent example is the problem of maximizing submodular function with cardinality constraints. While some of these difficulties can be rectified on a case-by-case basis, here, we describe an alternative approach to designing efficient sliding window algorithms for maximization problems. Then we instantiate this approach on a wide range of problems, yielding better algorithms for submodular function optimization, diversity optimization and general subadditive optimization. In doing so, we *improve* state-of-the art results obtained using problem-specific algorithms.

PODS'19, June 30-July 5, 2019, Amsterdam, Netherlands

ACM ISBN 978-1-4503-6227-6/19/06.
https://doi.org/10.1145/3294052.3319701

CCS CONCEPTS

• Theory of computation → Streaming models; Approximation algorithms analysis; Streaming, sublinear and near linear time algorithms; • Mathematics of computing → Discrete optimization.

ACM Reference Format:
Michele Borassi, Alessandro Epasto, Silvio Lattanzi, Sergei Vassilvitskii, and Morteza Zadimoghaddam. 2019. Better Sliding Window Algorithms to Maximize Subadditive and Diversity Objectives. In *38th ACM SIGMOD-SIGACT-SIGAI Symposium on Principles of Database Systems (PODS'19), June 30-July 5, 2019, Amsterdam, Netherlands.* ACM, New York, NY, USA, 15 pages. https://doi.org/10.1145/3294052.3319701

1 INTRODUCTION

Since their introduction in a seminal work by Alon et al. [2], data streams have emerged as a tool for processing large volumes of data. In a standard data stream setting, the input arrives one element at a time. The goal of the algorithm designer is to compute (or approximate) some function of the entire input in space *sublinear* in the input size. Classical results include estimating frequency moments [2]; estimating the number of distinct values [7, 25]; approximating important graph properties, such as graph cuts [1]; and preserving an approximately maximum matching [33]. A survey of applications is provided in [34].

While data stream algorithms have received a lot of well-deserved attention, they treat all the elements equally: in particular, there is no difference between an element that arrived at the beginning of the stream and one that arrived at the end. In practice, however, recent data is often far more important; one way to model this assumption is to consider only the last w elements of the stream during the computation. While w is typically much smaller than the total size of the stream (since the latter can be arbitrarily large), the goal is still to design algorithms with both space and update time sublinear in w. Note that sliding window problems are a subset of dynamic stream problems [29, 34], where any element can be deleted at any time. Nonetheless, they form a challenging special case and have been studied extensively, see, for instance, [3, 4, 11, 13, 15, 16, 18, 26, 28, 31, 32, 36, 38].

Sliding Window Frameworks. To aid in designing sliding window algorithms, Datar et. al [23], and later Braverman and Ostrovsky [15] introduced techniques for special families of instances. Both of these, as well as the approach we propose in our work, rely on the existence of an efficient algorithm for the insertion-only version of the problem. The frameworks are discussed in detail in the related work section, here we introduce them briefly.

Exponential Histograms. Datar et al. [23] introduced the *exponential historgram* framework for estimating a non-negative set function f over a fixed-size sliding window. Their approach assumes that the function is weakly additive and that there exists a small space sketch that can be computed in an insertion-only stream. They show that if the sketch is composable, that is, an estimate of $f(A \cup B)$ can be obtained from the sketches of A and B, then polylogarithmically many sketches are sufficient to approximate the function over a sliding window.

Smooth Histograms. The work of Braverman and Ostrovsky [15] further generalized this approach. Instead of looking at composability, the authors consider *smooth* functions. At a high level, these are functions that do not experience sharp transitions from the addition (or deletion) of a single element, see [15] for a precise definition. Their key idea is to prove that for such smooth functions, one only needs to remember the value of the function for logarithmically many substreams over the course of any window. Such a result can be achieved by imposing that the difference between the values of the function on consecutive substreams be sufficiently large.

This approach is strictly more general than the exponential histogram of [23]; however, it also comes with some strong limitations. To the best of our knowledge, the biggest downside of smooth histograms is that to be directly applied, they require the ability to compute the function almost exactly, as a $(1-\epsilon)$-approximation of the function f leads to a $1-5\epsilon$ approximation of the value of the function over the sliding window. Thus, anything worse than a 0.8-approximation results in a trivial solution. In itself, this rules out their method for many important problems in which providing such an approximation is NP-hard. A prominent example is that of submodular function optimization subject to a cardinality constraint, where a $1-1/e$ approximation is the best possible.

This limitation can be overcome on a case-by-case basis, (see Section 2 below for examples), but doing so requires intricate reasoning in every case. In this work, we introduce a different approach to designing sliding window algorithms for maximization problems, and we apply it to diversity maximization and subadditive optimization.

Our Results. In order to solve maximization problems in the sliding window setting, we take a different perspective on the problem: instead of identifying a property of *functions* that makes them amenable to sliding window computations, we ask for an *algorithmic primitive* and prove that it is sufficient to turn any insertion-only algorithm into a sliding window algorithm. Then we show that this algorithmic primitive is easy to design for our problems.

Our proof is entirely constructive, so we obtain efficient sliding window algorithms for our problems. Briefly, our main observation is that it is possible to design an algorithm that, given two consecutive parts of the stream A and B, reduces the problem of producing an approximate solution for the substream represented by any suffix of the first summary, A concatenated with B with the additional assumption that the substream A itself does not contain a good approximation of the solution. This additional assumption significantly simplifies the design of sliding window algorithms for maximization problems. For example, under this assumption, the solution of the problem for a submodular function is trivial; in fact, it is enough to simply return the solution contained in B.

Our reduction algorithm is also simple. It is based on the observation that for every stream and every sliding window size, one can easily construct three substreams A, A^+, and B, so that a good solution to the sliding window problem is contained either in A^+, in B, or in a suffix of the first summary, A, and B.

Furthermore, we show that for many of the problems, our approach improves upon the hand-tuned implementations (Table 1 contains a summary of our results). For example, we give the first sliding window algorithms for a number of problems, such as the many variants of selection with diversity constraints problem, submodular maximization under p-matchoid constraints and, more generally, subadditive function maximization.

Roadmap. We start by reviewing related work in Section 2. Then we provide a formal formulation of our approach in Section 3, followed by specific applications. We apply the result to subadditive function optimization in Section 4.1, and in Section 4.2, we apply our maximization methods/sketches for selection with diversity constraints. Finally, we provide an even stronger version of our approach for submodular function optimization in Section 5.

Problem	Space (prev.)	Space (current)	Approx. (prev.)	Approx. (current)
Maximizing a subadditive function	-	$O(s \log w)$	-	$\alpha^2/2 - \epsilon$
Submodular maximization (card. const.)	$O(k \log^2 w)$	$O(k \log w)$	$1/3 - \epsilon$	$1/3 - \epsilon$
Submodular maximization (p-matchoid const.)	-	$O(k \log w)$	-	$O(1/p)$
Diversity maximization (linear instances)	-	$O(k \log^2 w)$	-	$\zeta/5 - \epsilon$
Diversity maximization (other instances)	-	$O(k^2 \log^2 w)$	-	$\zeta/5 - \epsilon$

Table 1: A summary of the results obtained in this paper. For simplicity, we assume that the ratio between the maximum and the minimum values is polynomial in the size w of the sliding window. We use n for the size of the stream. In subadditive maximization, we denote by α (resp., s) the approximation factor (resp., the space used) by a streaming algorithm. In diversity maximization, we denote by ζ the best approximation factor that a centralized algorithm can achieve.

2 RELATED WORK

For brevity, we restrict our literature review mostly to the sliding window streaming model of computation; we first review in detail the two main frameworks used to solve problems in the sliding window streaming model, then we list algorithms known for specific problems.

Sliding window model. The sliding window model of computation [23] is a powerful computational paradigm that allows one to naturally model data recency constraints in streaming settings. In this model, the algorithm receives a potentially unlimited stream of data points $x_1, x_2, \ldots$, and, at any point in time t, it is required to provide the result of a function f over the *active-window* W, i.e., the set of the latest w data points received (the points x_i for $i \in [\min(t-w, t)]$. This model encompasses multiple challenging data streaming problems and has received significant attention in the past [3, 4, 11, 13, 15, 16, 18, 26, 28, 31, 32, 36, 38].

We now review some of the main algorithmic techniques in this model. In their pioneering work on the sliding window problem, Datar et al. [23] and later Braverman and Ostrovsky [15] introduced two techniques that have been used successfully for providing low-space complexity algorithms for a multitude of problems in the sliding window setting.

Exponential histograms. Datar et al. [23] jump-started the study of the sliding window model in their seminal paper. They introduced *exponential histograms*, a general framework for estimating non-negative set functions f over a fixed-size sliding window. The framework assumes that the function is weakly additive and that there exists a low-space, composable sketch that can be computed in an insertion-only stream. More precisely, the authors assume that the function f is polynomially bounded by the size of the stream $f(A) \leq \text{poly}(|A|)$ and has the following weak-additivity properties: $f(A \cup B) \geq f(A) + f(B)$ and $f(A \cup B) \leq c_f(f(A) + f(B))$ for a constant $c_f \geq 1$. Finally, they assume that the function f admits low-space sketches that can be computed efficiently in insertion-only streams and can be *composed*, i.e., an estimate of $f(A \cup B)$ can be obtained from the sketches of A and B. Under these assumptions, they show that polylogarithmically many sketches are sufficient to approximate the function.

Smooth Histograms. Braverman and Ostrovsky [15] introduced the smooth histogram technique. The key idea is to preserve a subset of indices $t_1, t_2, \ldots, t_s$ of time in the stream such that one only needs to keep the value of the function f for the substream $[t_i, n]$, starting at one of these indices and ending with the last inserted item. Such an exact (or approximate) value can be computed using an (insertion-only) streaming algorithm. Braverman and Ostrovsky show that for any function f that respects certain smoothness assumptions, it is possible to keep $\text{poly}\log(w)$ many such indices and obtain a good approximation of f over the latest w items. The main idea is to look at the values of the function in the intervals mentioned above and ensure that for any pair of indices at distance 2, t_{i-1}, t_{i+1} the value of $f([t_{i+1}, t]) \leq (1-\beta)g([t_{i-1}, t])$ for some constant β, where $f([a, b])$ is the value of function f on the interval $[a, b]$ of the stream. For this method to work, the function f to be estimated needs to be polynomially bounded $f(A) \leq \text{poly}(|A|)$, monotone non-decreasing, and, crucially, (α, β)-smooth, a definition that we now recall.

Definition 2.1. *A function f is (α, β)-smooth if for all times $a < b < c < d$, we have: $(1-\beta)f([a, c]) \leq f([b, c]) \implies (1-\alpha)f([a, d]) \leq f([b, d])$.*

Braverman and Ovstrovsky then show that it is enough to maintain $O(\log_{1+\beta} M/m)$ such histogram indices, where M/m is the ratio of the max and min value of the function, to obtain a $1-\alpha$ approximation for any (α, β) smooth function f that can be computed exactly in the streaming setting. They also extend their results to functions f for which a $(1-\epsilon)$-approximation algorithm exists, in which case Theorems 2 and 3 in [15] show a $1-5\epsilon$-approximation algorithm in a sliding window. Notice that the smooth histogram provides a non-trivial result only if the function admits a good enough approximation ($\epsilon < 1/5$). Hence, it is not applicable to many problems addressed in the paper (e.g., maximizing submodular functions).

The authors use the smooth histogram technique to provide multiple improved results, including better approximations of weakly-additive functions from [23], memory-optimal algorithms for frequency moments in L^p for $p > 0$ and algorithms to find the longest increasing sequence.

Recent Developments. Very recently, and concurrently with our work, two new generalizations of the smooth histogram approach have been introduced [10, 12].

In the first of these [12] Braverman et al. introduce the composable histogram method, which is an adaptation of the smooth histogram framework that leads to near optimal results for the heavy hitters problem. Similar to the smooth histogram framework, this approach applies to function estimation and requires the underlying function to be smooth. Additionally, it needs a good approximation algorithm for obtaining estimates of all suffixes on insertion-only streams.

In the second, [10], Braverman et al. specialize the smooth histogram approach to linear algebra questions by defining a notion of smooth functions for positive semidefinite matrices. They use the framework to obtain improved results for many problems, including spectral and graph sparsification and low-rank approximation.

These developments are elegant modifications of the smooth histogram framework tailored to specific classes of problems and are in contrast to the work presented here, which gives a new algorithmic primitive that leads to sliding window results for a wide range of classic maximization problems.

Our work is orthogonal to the presented frameworks and presents a simple technique for designing sliding window algorithms for maximization problems.

2.1 Specific Sliding Window Algorithms

In addition to the frameworks presented, there have been a number of ad hoc solutions modifying these frameworks for specific problems. We give a full overview below.

Sampling from sliding windows. Several authors have addressed the problem of sampling k items from the sliding window [4, 16]. In this context, the problem is made non-trivial by the implicit nature of element deletions in the model: the algorithm is not notified when an element expires and naively storing all elements' expiration times would require $\Omega(w)$ space. Babcock et al. [4] introduced the chain-sampling algorithm, which extends the reservoir sampling method to sample k items with space $O(k \log(w))$ for a window of fixed size w. They also show results for sliding windows of varying lengths. These results were later improved by Braverman et al. [16] who showed how to do this in optimal space $O(k)$ in the fixed size window model.

Heavy hitters and statistics for the sliding window. Several authors [3, 11, 28, 38] studied the problem of finding heavy-hitters in sliding window streams under the L^p norm, where one wants to find elements that appear more than a certain constant fraction of the L^p norm of the frequency vector of the sliding window. It is known that algorithms with $\mathrm{poly}\log(w)$ space are possible only for $p \leq 2$ because of a lower bound on computing the L^p norm in streams [35]. Several authors have provided results for the L^1 norm [3, 28, 38].

Braverman et al. [11] provided the first results for the L^2 norm which do not allow the use of the smooth histogram technique. This result implies a $\mathrm{poly}\log(w)$ algorithm for all $0 < p \leq 2$, closing the gap with the impossibility results. The authors introduce a *semi-smooth* algorithm technique that borrows in part from the smooth histogram method. In a related problem, Homem et al. [27] provided a data structure for maintaining the top-k most frequent elements in a sliding window stream. Recently, Basat et al. [8] provided upper and lower bounds on the memory needed to approximate sums over binary sliding window streams.

Sliding window over graphs. Crouch et al. [22] presented the first results in the sliding window model for graphs. In particular, they study a model where edges arrive one at a time and in which one wants to preserve properties for the graph induced by the sliding window of the latest edges to arrive. They provide algorithms for graph sparsifiers and approximate spanners and estimators of the size of the maximum matching and minimum spanning tree. More precisely, they show how to preserve an approximate spanner that allows one to estimate the distance of nodes up to a multiplicative factor and a $(1 + \epsilon)$-sparsifier that almost exactly preserves edge cuts. Applications of these methods include verifying k-edge-connectivity in a graph or that the graph is bipartite. The results on matchings show a constant factor approximation that is based on a method similar to the smooth histogram technique. The authors show, in fact, that while the matching function is not smooth, it holds a smooth-like property.

Submodular maximization. Epasto et al. [24] gave a $(1/3 - \epsilon)$-approximation algorithm for arbitrary monotone submodular functions subject to cardinality constraints that requires $\tilde{O}(k \,\mathrm{poly}\log(w))$ space (for polynomially bounded functions). Submodular functions are not in general smooth, and they do not admit approximations $\geq 1 - \frac{1}{5}$, as required by the smooth histogram framework; however, the authors design an algorithm based on a variation of the smooth histogram technique for the problem. They also show a $1/2 - \epsilon$-approximation algorithm but with significantly more space. Concurrently, Chen et al. [20] showed a $(1/4 - \epsilon)$-approximation $\tilde{O}(k \text{ poly} \log(w))$ space for the same classes of functions. They also show that the same method can be extended to arbitrary hereditary constraints and provide a $(\frac{1}{4p+(1+\epsilon)16p^2})$-approximation for p-matroid of rank k using $\tilde{O}(k \text{ poly} \log(w))$ space in the sliding window.

Clustering. The problem of clustering in sliding windows has also been studied [5, 14]. Braverman [14] shows results for the fundamental k-median and k-means problem in the metric and Euclidean cases of the sliding window model. They provide the first constant factor approximation algorithm that uses polylogarithmic space for metric k-median and metric k-means problems in the sliding window. The algorithm uses $O(k^3 \log^6(w))$ space, where k is the number of centers to output. Their work improves and addresses an open problem posed by the work of Babcock et al. [5], which designed an algorithm with space poly(w). The algorithm is based on a core-set method and an extension of the smooth histogram technique.

In a related line of work, Cohen-Addad et al. [21] studied the problem of approximating the diameter and the k-center clustering in the sliding window model. They gave a $(3 + \epsilon)$-approximation for the diameter problem using space $\log(\frac{M}{m})$, where M, m are the minimum and maximum distances in the space, respectively. For the k-center problem, they show a $(6 + \epsilon)$-approximation $O(k \log(\frac{M}{n}))$ space.

Other applications. Beame et al. [9] provide multiple results in the sliding window model, including an algorithm for the distinctness problem.

Wang et al. [37] study the problem related to influence maximization. They cast the problem as a stream mining problem in which user actions are observed in real time and one wants to select a set of users with maximum influence over the most recent actions. The authors observe that the problem does not respect the requirements of the exponential and smooth histogram techniques. Then they introduce a technique based on keeping $O(\log(w))$ snapshots of the problem using an insertion-only algorithm that allows one to obtain a constant factor approximation to the problem.

3 A GENERAL APPROACH TO SOLVE MAXIMIZATION PROBLEMS

Definition 3.1 (Evaluation functions and monotonicity). *Let $\mathcal{X}$ and $\mathcal{Y}$ be the set of all inputs and solutions for an optimization problem. A solution $Y \in \mathcal{Y}$ is feasible for input $X \in \mathcal{X}$ if it satisfies the constraints of the optimization problem. Let $f : \mathcal{Y} \to \mathbb{R}^{\geq 0}$ be a function that evaluates the quality of a solution $Y \in \mathcal{Y}$. We focus on maximization problems. We say that the maximization problem represented by the function f is monotone if, for every two inputs $X \subset X'$, if Y is a feasible solution for X, it is also a feasible solution for X'.*

Notice that the monotonicity implies that for $X \subset X'$, we have $\text{OPT}^*(X) \leq \text{OPT}^*(X')$, where $\text{OPT}^*(X)$ is the value of the optimal solution in X. To simplify the notation, we allow $\mathcal{Y}$ to include non-feasible solutions and assume that $f(Y) = 0$ when Y is not a feasible solution.

In the paper, we assume that $w \geq 2$, otherwise, the problem is trivial. To summarize the data, we use a pair of functions (Z, z). The first function, Z, takes an input X and encodes it into a small summary $Z(X)$, while the second function, z, decodes $Z(X)$ and produces a feasible solution Y. This means that $f(z(Z(X))$ is the value of the solution found by the summary algorithm. We allow the summaries to be general data structures (we do not restrict their representations to be subsets of the input). We only need to assume that Z can be computed in insertion-only streams (i.e., it supports an insert operation), and z is a (polynomial-time) computable function of the summary.

To simplify the notation, we assume that $\mathcal{X}$ contains all possible summaries.

Definition 3.2 (Approximate summaries). *We say (Z, z) is a* summary *for any pair of functions $Z : \mathcal{X} \to \mathcal{X}$ and $z : \mathcal{X} \to \mathcal{Y}$. For a maximization problem f, we say the summary is α-approximate for X if:*

$$f(z(Z(X))) \geq \alpha \, \text{OPT}^*(X) \quad (1)$$

We say a summary is α-approximate (without specifying any particular X), if it is α-approximate for every $X \in \mathcal{X}$.

To allow for randomization in the summary algorithm, we say (Z, z) is a *randomized summary* if the aforementioned conditions hold on any input with high probability, where the probability is defined on the space of the random choices of the algorithm. Whenever clear from the context, we will call a randomized summary simply a summary.

Definition 3.3 (Space of a summary). *We denote the size of a summary by s_Z.*

We now present a technique that uses approximate summaries to compute approximately optimal solutions for maximization problems in the sliding window setting. The general intuition is to keep two consecutive approximate summaries for every possible guess of the optimum value, and then use the summaries to obtain a sliding window algorithm.

For simplicity, we assume that we have access to a streaming α-approximation summary, (Z, z), as well as the minimum, m, and maximum, M, value of a function f. Fix $\delta > 0$ and let $\Lambda = \{\lambda_1, \lambda_2, \ldots\}$ be a set of thresholds such that $\lambda_{i+1} = \lambda_i(1 + \delta)$; we will specify the bounds of Λ later. For each threshold $\lambda \in \Lambda$, we maintain a pair of summaries, A_λ and B_λ, computed as follows.

Initially, each $A_\lambda = B_\lambda = \emptyset$, and the corresponding summaries are $Z(\emptyset)$. When an element x arrives, we check if the value of the solution computed by the summary on $B_\lambda \cup \{x\}$ remains smaller than λ. If so, we simply extend B_λ to $B_\lambda \cup \{x\}$, and update the corresponding summary. Otherwise, we reset A_λ to the current value of B_λ, and set $B_\lambda = \{x\}$. We show the pseudocode in Algorithm 1.

Function Summaries(X, λ)
  $Z(A_\lambda) \leftarrow Z(\emptyset)$; $Z(B_\lambda) \leftarrow Z(\emptyset)$;
  foreach $x \in X$ **do**
    if $f(z(Z(B_\lambda \cup \{x\}))) \leq \lambda$ **then**
      $Z(B_\lambda) \leftarrow Z(B_\lambda \cup \{x\})$;
    else
      $Z(A_\lambda) \leftarrow Z(B_\lambda)$; $Z(B_\lambda) \leftarrow Z(\{x\})$;
    end
  end
  return $(Z(A_\lambda), Z(B_\lambda))$

Algorithm 1: The high level algorithm for maintaining approximate summaries.

Now we observe some basic properties of our summaries that will be useful to show our main result.

Lemma 3.4. *For a set A_λ, let A_λ^+ be the set A_λ together with the first element of the corresponding B_λ. The following are invariants maintained by the algorithm.*
(i) A_λ and B_λ are two disjoint consecutive substreams of X,
(ii) A_λ precedes B_λ, and
(iii) B_λ ends with the current time t and always contains the last element of the stream.
(iv) When $|A_\lambda| \geq 1$:

$$f(z(Z(A_\lambda^+))) > \lambda. \tag{2}$$

(v) When $|A_\lambda| \geq 2$:

$$f(z(Z(A_\lambda))) \leq \lambda \tag{3}$$

(vi) When $|B_\lambda| \geq 2$:

$$f(z(Z(B_\lambda))) \leq \lambda \tag{4}$$

Proof. The first three points follow from construction. Equation 2 follows from the fact that A_λ is set to a non-empty summary only when $B_\lambda \cup \{x\}$ has value $> \lambda$, and this property is maintained thereafter. Equation 3 follows from the fact that $|A_\lambda| \geq 2$ implies that A_λ has been set as a copy of a prior B_λ that was not a singleton, and this happens only if B_λ has value $\leq \lambda$. Equation 4 follows from the same property. □

So far we have described how to maintain two summaries, A_λ and B_λ, with the properties in Lemma 3.4 for every threshold λ. Now we need to show how to use these two summaries to provide a solution for an active window.

To do so, we assume to have access to an additional function h that takes two summaries and an index, and produces a good summary for the stream starting at the index. Clearly, if we require h to work in every setting, designing such h would be equivalent to solving the initial problem. Interestingly, we can show that we need to use such a function only when A_λ contains a solution of "small" value.

More formally, consider a stream $x_0, x_1, x_2, \ldots, x_a, x_{a+1}, \ldots, x_b$. Let A be the sequence $x_0, \ldots, x_a$ and let B be the sequence $x_{a+1}, \ldots, x_b$. Let A_λ, B_λ be corresponding summaries. Finally, for $t \in [0, a]$, let A^t be the sequence $x_t, x_{t+1}, \ldots, x_a$.

Definition 3.5 (Mergeable summary for maximization problems). *Let f be a monotone function. We say that an α-approximate maximization problem summary (Z, z) is (α', β)-mergeable for $\beta \leq 1$, if there exists a composer function $h : \mathcal{X} \times \mathcal{X} \times \mathbb{Z} \to \mathcal{X}$ such that for any $A, B \in \mathcal{X}$ and for any $0 \leq t \leq |A|$, $H = h(Z(A), Z(B), t)$ verifies*
(i) $z(H)$ is a valid solution for $A^t \cup B$;
(ii) if $f(z(Z(A))) \leq \beta\,\mathrm{OPT}^*(A^t \cup B)$, then: $(h(Z(A), Z(B), t), z)$ is an α'-approximate summary for $A^t \cup B$.

Note that in (ii), with a slight abuse of notation, we are denoting with $h(Z(A), Z(B), t)$ the function that computes the sketch. Similarly to the previous case to allow for randomization in the summary algorithm we define a (α', β)-mergeable *randomized summary* if the aforementioned conditions hold on any input with high probability.

We note that we are not providing a general method of designing the composer function h. For every maximization problem, one needs to design a tailored function.

To simplify exposition, we use intervals of timestamps such as $[a, b]$ for $a, b \in \mathbb{N}$ to refer to the stream of items appearing between time a and b (inclusive) in order. We refer to W as the active window of size w, (i.e., for $t \in \mathbb{N}$, $W = [\max(t - w, 1), t]$).

Remark 3.6. *For some of the maximization problems such as subadditive or submodular maximization, the composer function h defined in Definition 3.5 is very simple. If the solution of the summary for the first sequence A is small enough compared to the optimum of the active window $A^t \cup B$, we can just discard the summary of A and output only the solution for the summary of B.*

However, for the diversity maximization problem, this simple trick will not work, and we need to provide more involved mergeable summaries and an actual composer function to obtain the desired approximation algorithms for sliding window setting.

Before presenting our algorithmic result, we pause to analyze the requirements of Definition 3.5 in terms of extracting solutions for suffixes of the first stream. Notice that we never require in our algorithms to compose with an empty set

$B = \emptyset$, however, the Definition 3.5 allows that. This does not imply that a mergeable summary is able to obtain a solution for any suffix A^t of A. The key here is that if $B = \emptyset$, we need to output a good approximation solution only if $f(A, z(Z(A))) \le \beta\,\mathrm{OPT}^*(A^t)$, which makes the problem significantly simpler (sometimes trivial). For example, note that if $\beta < \alpha$, by monotonicity this condition never happens.

We now present our first algorithmic result. We show that, given a family of mergeable summaries, it is possible to obtain a sliding window algorithm that uses only logarithmically many summaries.

Let the set of thresholds be $\Lambda := \{\alpha m, (1+\delta)\alpha m, (1+\delta)^2\alpha m, \dots (1+\delta)M\}$.

We run the algorithm presented in Algorithm 2.

Input The stream X, upper and lower bounds m, M; $\delta > 0$; the size of the window w.
Output Solution for the last active window W.
Phase 1: Consume the stream X in order, maintaining, in parallel, all the summaries.
$\Lambda \leftarrow \{\alpha m, (1+\delta)\alpha m, \dots, (1+\delta)M\}$;
foreach $\lambda \in \Lambda$ **do**
  | $Z(A_\lambda), Z(B_\lambda) \leftarrow$ `Summaries`(X, λ);
end
Phase 2: Extract the solution for the window W at the end of X.
$t_0 \leftarrow \max(|X| - w, 1)$;
$\lambda^* \leftarrow \max(\{\lambda : A_\lambda \subsetneq W \text{and } |A_\lambda| \ge 1\})$;
$S_1 \leftarrow z(Z(A^+_{\lambda^*}))$
$\lambda' \leftarrow \lambda^*(1+\delta)$;
if $W \cap A_{\lambda'} \ne \emptyset$ **then**
  | $H \leftarrow h(Z(A_{\lambda'}), Z(B_{\lambda'}), t_0)$; $S_2 \leftarrow z(H)$;
else if $W = B_{\lambda'}$ **then**
  | $S_2 \leftarrow z(Z(B_{\lambda'}))$;
else
  | **return** S_1
end
return $\mathrm{argmax}_{S\in\{S_1,S_2\}} f(S)$;

Algorithm 2: The pseudocode of our main algorithm.

When asked for a solution for the current active window $W = [t_0, t]$, where $t_0 = \max(t - w, 1)$, we find the maximum $\lambda^* \in \Lambda$ such that A_{λ^*} is a proper subset of the current active window and it is non-empty (we show that such a λ^* exists in Lemma 3.7). Let, $A^+_{\lambda^*}$ be A_{λ^*} combined with the first element of B_{λ^*}, and let $S_1 = z(Z(A^+_{\lambda^*}))$, be the candidate solution computed for λ^*.

Now consider $\lambda' = (1+\delta)\lambda^*$ (we show in Lemma 3.8 that $\lambda' \in \Lambda$): by construction, either $A_{\lambda'}$ is not initialized or $A_{\lambda'} \not\subset W$ (the case $A_{\lambda'} = W$ is excluded by construction). In either case, this implies that $W \subseteq A_{\lambda'} \cup B_{\lambda'}$.

We now construct a solution S_2 as follows, depending on the particular position of W:
(i) If W intersects with $A_{\lambda'}$. Then, we have $W = A^{t_0}_{\lambda'} \cup B_{\lambda'}$. We set $S_2 = h(Z(A_{\lambda'}), Z(B_{\lambda'}), t_0)$.
(ii) $W = B_{\lambda'}$. Then we set $S_2 = z(Z(B_{\lambda'}))$.
(iii) W is a suffix of $B_{\lambda'}$. In this case we show that S_1 is a good solution, so we do not use S_2.
Finally, the algorithm outputs the solution of maximum value between S_1 and S_2.

Before proving our main result, we show that the algorithm above is well defined.

Lemma 3.7. *There exists a $\lambda^* \in \Lambda$ such that A_{λ^*} is non-empty and $A_{\lambda^*} \subsetneq W$.*

Proof. This statement is true for $\lambda = \alpha m$. Observe that the function has a value $\ge m$ on any non-empty subset of the stream by assumption (as m is the minimum value of the function); therefore, any α-approximate summary computed over any subset of the stream has value at least αm, so the value returned by the summary B_λ is at least αm every time the summary consumes one element of the stream. As a result, the algorithm resets A_λ and B_λ at every step, such that A_λ contains the second to last item observed, which is part of the sliding window by assumption of $w \ge 2$. Notice that this property continues to hold any other time the summary is reset. Finally, notice that the last element of the stream is always in B_λ, so A_λ is a proper subset of W. □

Lemma 3.8. *Let λ^* defined as in Algorithm 2, and $\lambda' = (1+\delta)\lambda^*$. Then $\lambda' \in \Lambda$.*

Proof. Clearly if $A_{\lambda^*} \subset W$ and $|A_{\lambda^*}| \ge 1$, then $A^+_{\lambda^*} \subseteq W$ as well. Moreover, by Equation 2 and monotonicity of f:

$$\lambda^* < f(z(Z(A^+_{\lambda^*}))) \tag{5}$$

Notice that this property cannot hold for $\lambda^* = M(1+\delta)$, as this would imply that $f(z(Z(A^+_{\lambda^*}))) > M(1+\delta) > \mathrm{OPT}^*(W)$. Therefore $\lambda' \in \Lambda$. □

We are now ready for the main result.

Theorem 3.9 (Sliding window algorithm for maximization problems). *Let (Z, z) be an α-approximate maximization problem summary and let it be (α', β)-mergeable for a monotone function f. Let h be its composer function. The algorithm described above computes a $\min(\alpha', \frac{\alpha\beta}{1+\delta})$-approximation to the maximization f in space $O\left(s_Z \log_{1+\delta} \frac{M}{\alpha m}\right)$.*

Proof. First we consider the quality of the solution obtained by S_1. Suppose that $\lambda^* \ge \frac{\alpha\beta}{1+\delta}\mathrm{OPT}^*(W)$. Then, Equation 5 implies that $S_1 = z(Z(A^+_{\lambda^*}))$ is an $\frac{\alpha\beta}{1+\delta}$ approximation to the optimum solution.

For the remainder of the proof, assume otherwise that $\lambda^* < \frac{\alpha\beta}{1+\delta}\mathrm{OPT}^*(W)$. This is equivalent to saying that $\lambda' <$

$\alpha\beta\,\mathrm{OPT}^*(\mathrm{W})$. We will show that in this case S_2 gives an $\min(\alpha, \alpha')$-approximate solution. We have to consider 3 cases:

(1) W intersects with $A_{\lambda'}$ and hence $\mathrm{W} \subseteq A_{\lambda'} \cup B_{\lambda'}$. Note that $|A'_\lambda| \geq 2$.[1] In this case we use the function h guaranteed by the mergeable summaries. We have: $\beta\,\mathrm{OPT}^*(\mathrm{W}) > \alpha\beta\,\mathrm{OPT}^*(\mathrm{W}) > \lambda' \geq f(z(Z(A_{\lambda'})))$ where the third inequality follows by the invariant of the algorithm. Therefore, the precondition for mergeable summaries holds, and the result is an α'-approximation.

(2) $\mathrm{W} = B_{\lambda'}$. In this case, considering $z(Z(B_{\lambda'}))$ will lead to an $\alpha \geq \frac{\alpha\beta}{1+\delta}$-approximation since Z is an α-approximate summary.

(3) $\mathrm{W} \subsetneq B_{\lambda'}$ Finally, we show that this case is not possible. Since $\lambda' < \alpha\beta\,\mathrm{OPT}^*(\mathrm{W})$, it must be that $\lambda' < \alpha\,\mathrm{OPT}^*(\mathrm{W})$. However, in this case, since Z is an α-approximate summary, we know that: $\alpha\,\mathrm{OPT}^*(\mathrm{W}) \leq f(z(Z(B_{\lambda'}))) \leq \lambda' < \alpha\,\mathrm{OPT}^*(\mathrm{W})$, which is a contradiction.

Therefore, the best of the two solutions is guaranteed to give at least a $\min(\alpha', \frac{\alpha\beta}{1+\delta})$-approximation.

To obtain the space bound, observe that there are $\log_{1+\delta}(\frac{M}{\alpha m})$ values of λ to consider, and for each of them our algorithm computes three sketches each of size less than s_Z. Hence, the total space complexity is $O(s_Z \log_{1+\delta} \frac{M}{\alpha m})$. □

4 EXAMPLES OF APPLICATIONS

We now apply our new technique to some prototypical problems.

4.1 Subadditive Function Maximization

In this subsection, we apply our new technique to subadditive optimization under downward closed constraints. Let V be a ground set: a set function $g : 2^V \longrightarrow \Re$ is subadditive if $g(Y_1 \cup Y_2) \leq g(Y_1) + g(Y_2)$, $\forall Y_1, Y_2 \subseteq V$. A set system $\mathcal{I} \subset P(V)$, where $P(V)$ is the powerset of V, is downward closed iff $I \in \mathcal{I} \implies I' \in \mathcal{I}\ \forall I' \subset I$. We seek to maximize the function g subject to a downward closed constraint (i.e., we seek to find $\max_{I \in \mathcal{I}} g(I)$). A special and widely studied case of a downward closed set system is the cardinality constraint (i.e., $\mathcal{I} = \{I \subset V \mid |I| \leq k\}$ for some $k \in \mathcal{Z}^+$). Let g be a non-negative and subadditive set function whose non-zero co-domain is in $[m, M]$. We show that if there exists a α-approximate summary using space s_Z for maximizing g subject to a downward closed constraint then there exists a sliding window algorithm for maximizing g that gets a $\frac{\alpha^2}{2(1+\delta)}$-approximation using space $O(s_Z \log_{1+\delta} \frac{M}{m\alpha})$ for every constant $\delta > 0$.

[1]Note that $|A_{\lambda'}| \neq 1$, otherwise $A_{\lambda'} \subsetneq W$ which would contradict the definition of λ.

We reformulate the problem in the following natural way. We assume that the points from V arrive one at a time, and that at time t, we are allowed to output sets in $\mathcal{I} \cap P(\{x_1, \ldots, x_t\})$. Given a solution Y to the stream $X = \{x_1, \ldots, x_t\}$, we let $f(Y) = g(Y)$, if $Y \in \mathcal{I} \cap P(X)$, and $f(Y) = 0$ otherwise. Notice that f is non-negative and bounded in $[m, M] \cup \{0\}$. Notice also that this implies that the function f satisfies our monotonicity property, $\mathrm{OPT}^*(X') \leq \mathrm{OPT}^*(X')$ whenever $X \subseteq X'$, even if g is not monotone, simply by the monotonicity of $P(\{x_1, \ldots, x_t\})$.

Note that, for general subadditive functions, it is not clear how to compute an α-approximate summary, even in the specific case of cardinality constraints; however, whenever such a summary exists, we show that it is possible to modify it to get a $(\frac{\alpha}{2}, \frac{\alpha}{2})$ mergeable summary. We actually prove a slightly stronger lemma that works for any C-"weakly" subadditive function g; that is, any function such that $g(Y_1 \cup Y_2) \leq C(g(Y_1) + g(Y_2))$, $\forall Y_1, Y_2$ (the subadditive case is the specific case of $C = 1$). We say that f is C-weakly subadditive if it models a maximization problem for a function g that is C-weakly subadditive.

Lemma 4.1. *Let f be a bounded and C-weakly subadditive function subject to downward closed constraints. If there exists an α-approximate summary using space s_Z for maximizing f, then for the same problem, there exists also a $(\frac{\alpha}{2C}, \frac{\alpha}{2C})$-mergeable summary using the same space.*

Proof. Recall that function f has an α-approximate summary so we know that there exist (z, Z) such that $f(z(Z(X))) \geq \alpha\,\mathrm{OPT}^*(X)$, $\forall X \in \mathcal{X}$.

Now, fix $\beta = \frac{\alpha}{2C}$: we need to show that if $f(z(Z(A))) \leq \frac{\alpha}{2C}\,\mathrm{OPT}^*(A^t \cup B)$, then there exist h such that $(h(Z(A), Z(B), t), z)$ is an α'-approximate summary for $A^t \cup B$. We show that it is enough to define $h(Z(A), Z(B), t) = Z(B)$. In fact, $f(z(Z(B))) \geq \alpha\,\mathrm{OPT}^*(B) \geq \frac{\alpha}{C}(\mathrm{OPT}^*(A^t \cup B) - C\,\mathrm{OPT}^*(A^t)) \geq \frac{\alpha}{C}(\mathrm{OPT}^*(A^t \cup B) - C\,\mathrm{OPT}^*(A)) \geq \frac{\alpha}{C}\left(\mathrm{OPT}^*(A^t \cup B) - \frac{Cf(z(Z(A)))}{\alpha}\right)$ which is $\geq \frac{\alpha}{C}(\mathrm{OPT}^*(A^t \cup B) - \frac{1}{2}\,\mathrm{OPT}^*(A^t \cup B)) \geq \frac{\alpha}{2C}\,\mathrm{OPT}^*(A^t \cup B)$.

Furthermore, note that $(h(Z(A), Z(B), t), z)$ is a valid solution of $A^t \cup B$ for the downward closed property of the constraints.

So by fixing $h(Z(A), Z(B), t) = Z(B)$ we get a $(\frac{\alpha}{2C}, \frac{\alpha}{2C})$-mergeable summary. □

From Lemma 4.1 and Theorem 3.9 we obtain the following result:

Corollary 4.2. *Let f be a bounded and C-weakly subadditive function, if there exists an α-good summary using space s_Z for maximizing f under downward closed constraints, then for the same problem, there exists a sliding window algorithm that computes a $\frac{\alpha^2}{2C(1+\delta)}$-approximation for f that uses space $O(s_Z \log_{(1+\delta)} \frac{M}{m})$, for any constant $\delta > 0$.*

By using the streaming algorithm of Badanidiyuru et al. [6] that gives a $(\frac{1}{2}-\epsilon)$-approximate summary using space $O(k \log \frac{M}{m})$, we get the following corollary.

Corollary 4.3. *Let f be a monotone, bounded and submodular function subject to cardinality constraints. Then there exists a sliding window algorithm that computes a $\frac{1}{8(1+\delta)}$-approximation for f that uses space $O(k(\log_{(1+\delta)} \frac{M}{m})^2)$, for any constant $\delta > 0$.*

Similarly, it is possible to show a sliding window $O(1/p)$-approximation algorithm for non-monotone submodular optimization under p-Matroid constraint as in [20]. Using the streaming algorithm of Chekuri et al. [19], it is also possible to get a sliding window $O(1/p)$-approximation algorithm for non-monotone submodular optimization under the more general class of p-Matchoid constraints.

We note that the previous bound does not improve on previously known results [20, 24]. Nevertheless, in Section 5, we show how to strengthen the approach to get tighter bounds on a few maximization problems, including submodular optimization[2].

4.2 Diversity Maximization

In diversity maximization problems, we are given a stream X of points in a metric space, and we are asked to find a subset $Y \subset X$ of k points with maximum diversity. The diversity of a set Y, $\text{div}(Y)$, depends on the distances between the points in Y. Indyk et al. [30] studied multiple variants of diversity each with its own div function, as explained in the second column of Table 2. We also list the approximation ratio and space of our new streaming and sliding window algorithms for each of these problems in Table 2 (note that all previously known streaming algorithms use space $\Omega(\sqrt{W})$ [30] or are limited to certain special cases like spaces with bounded doubling dimension [17]). In constructing the summaries, we sometimes need a centralized algorithm for solving the diversity maximization problems. Various constant approximation centralized algorithms exist for each of these problems in the literature; any of the algorithms can be used into our construction. The parameter ζ denotes the approximation factor of the centralized algorithm for the relevant diversity objective. The solution evaluation function $fY)$ is defined, as before, to be $\text{div}(Y)$ for a feasible solution Y of at most k points and 0 otherwise.

Diversity of a size k subset Y is always the sum of some number of distances, (i.e., $k(k-1)$ pairwise distances in Remote-clique, $k-1$ distances in Remote-tree, 1 distance in remote-edge, etc). To simplify the proofs, we normalize the diversity function, and instead consider the average distance.

Definition 4.4. *Let $\text{div}'(Y)$ be $\frac{1}{n_k}\text{div}(X)$, where n_k is the number of pairwise distances that are summed in div. In this section, we use $f(Y) = \text{div}'(Y)$ as our objective function for a feasible solution Y.*

Remark 4.5. *Any α-approximate solution Y for div′ is also an α-approximate solution for div, because the rescaling parameter is the same for Y and for the optimum. Hence, from now on, we only work with div′.*

We start by stating two useful properties and prove that our problems satisfy them.

(1) Given two sets of points $Y = \{y_1, \ldots, y_k\}$, and $Y' = \{y'_1, \ldots, y'_k\}$, if $d(y_i, y'_i) \le \mu$ for each i, then $|f(Y) - f(Y')| \le 2\mu$;
(2) Given $Y = \{y_1, \ldots, y_k\}$, if $d(y_i, y_j) \ge \mu$ for each $i < j$, then $f(Y) \ge \mu$;

Lemma 4.6. *All the diversity problems in Table 2 satisfy Properties 1 and 2.*

Proof. We focus on the mapping from Y to Y' that transforms each y_i to y'_i. Every point in this transformation moves by at most μ distance; therefore, by triangle inequality, the distance between any pair of points in Y is at most the distance of their projections in Y' minus 2μ. So the average distance of any subset of points in Y is also at most the average distance of the projected subset in Y' minus 2μ. Therefore, $f(Y') \ge f(Y) - 2\mu$. Similarly, one can show that $f(Y) \ge f(Y') - 2\mu$ which concludes the proof of Property 1.

The value of $f(Y)$ is the average of some subset of distances, and each distance is at least μ. Therefore, $f(Y)$ is also at least μ, which proves Property 2. □

4.2.1 *Solving remote-edge, remote-tree, remote-cycle, remote t-trees, remote t-cycles.*

Constructing approximate summary. Given lower and upper bounds m and M, we maintain a set of I_μ points with minimum pairwise distance of at least μ for each μ in $\{m, (1+\epsilon)m, \ldots, M\}$. We initialize each set I_μ to $\emptyset$ and process the stream X. For every new arriving point x and every μ, if there are fewer than k points in I_μ and the minimum distance of x to points in I_μ is at least μ, we insert x to I_μ.

This way, for each μ, either we have k points at distance μ from each other, and by Property 2 we find a solution with value at least μ, or we can move all points by at most μ so that they coincide with points of the sketch, then, by Property 1, we find a solution with value at least $\text{OPT}^*(X) - 2\mu$. By choosing the proper value of μ (as we will show in Lemma 4.7), in both cases we find a constant approximation of $\text{OPT}^*(X)$. So outputting the set I_μ with the highest diversity yields a

[2]Note that the algorithm presented in Section 5 is not problem-specific, but it is as general as the method presented in the previous section. We prefer to present the simpler method in the main body of the paper simply for clarity of exposition.

Name	Diversity Function	App. str	Space str	App. SW	Space SW
Remote-edge	$\min_{u,v \in Y} d(u,v)$	$1/5-\epsilon$	$O(k \log \Delta)$	$\zeta/5-\epsilon$	$O(k \log^2 \Delta)$
Remote-clique	$\sum_{u \neq v \in Y} d(u,v)$	$\zeta/5-\epsilon$	$O(k^2 \log \Delta)$	$\zeta/5-\epsilon$	$O(k^2 \log^2 \Delta)$
Remote-tree	weight of minimum spanning tree of Y	$1/5-\epsilon$	$O(k \log \Delta)$	$\zeta/5-\epsilon$	$O(k \log^2 \Delta)$
Remote-cycle	weight of minimum TSP tour of Y	$1/5-\epsilon$	$O(k \log \Delta)$	$\zeta/5-\epsilon$	$O(k \log^2 \Delta)$
Remote t-trees	minimum weight of t trees spanning Y	$1/5-\epsilon$	$O(k \log \Delta)$	$\zeta/5-\epsilon$	$O(k \log^2 \Delta)$
Remote t-cycles	minimum weight of t cycles spanning Y	$1/5-\epsilon$	$O(k \log \Delta)$	$\zeta/5-\epsilon$	$O(k \log^2 \Delta)$
Remote-star	$\min_{u \in Y} \sum_{v \in Y} d(u,v)$	$\zeta/5-\epsilon$	$O(k^2 \log \Delta)$	$\zeta/5-\epsilon$	$O(k^2 \log^2 \Delta)$
Remote-bipartition	$\min_{Y=Y_1 \cup Y_2, \lvert Y_1 \rvert = \lfloor \frac{k}{2} \rfloor} \sum_{u \in Y_1} \sum_{v \in Y_2} d(u,v)$	$\zeta/5-\epsilon$	$O(k^2 \log \Delta)$	$\zeta/5-\epsilon$	$O(k^2 \log^2 \Delta)$
Remote-pseudoforest	$\sum_{u \in Y} \min_{v \in Y-\{u\}} d(u,v)$	$\zeta/5-\epsilon$	$O(k^2 \log \Delta)$	$\zeta/5-\epsilon$	$O(k^2 \log^2 \Delta)$
Remote-matching	min weight of a perfect matching (for even k)	$\zeta/5-\epsilon$	$O(k^2 \log \Delta)$	$\zeta/5-\epsilon$	$O(k^2 \log^2 \Delta)$

Table 2: The summary of results for Diversity Maximization problems under different metrics for diversity. Parameter ζ denotes the approximation factor of the offline algorithm for the relevant diversity objective and δ is the ratio between the minimum and the maximum distance in the dataset.

constant factor approximation for the diversity maximization problem in the streaming setting. Therefore, we can define the summary $Z(X)$ to be the union of all I_μ sets and the solution finder function $z(Z(X))$ to be the maximizer set I_μ to be $\text{argmax}_{I_\mu} f(I_\mu)$.

Mergeable summary. We need to supplement our summary with a set of backup points to recover selected points in I_μ in case they expire (fall out of sliding window). We denote the ith point in I_μ by $P_{\mu,i}$. We aim to find a representative point $P'_{\mu,i}$ for $P_{\mu,i}$ such that the distance between them is at most μ. We also want the representative points of set I_μ to be distinct, (i.e., we need $|I_\mu|$ distinct representative points for points in I_μ). However, it is possible for a point P' to represent two points from two different sets, I_μ and $I_{\mu'}$.

We find and maintain representative points as follows. Whenever a new point x is added to set I_μ, we make x its own representative point. Otherwise, we check to see whether x is at distance of at most μ to any point in I_μ. If such a point $P_{\mu,i}$ exists, we make x the new representative point of $P_{\mu,i}$; i.e., $P'_{\mu,i}$ is set to x (if there are multiple options, we select one arbitrarily).

Now, let us define the function h used to compose two summaries $Z(A)$ and $Z(B)$ of two streams given time t (start of the active window). For each μ, the summaries of A and B each have a I_μ set. We call them $I_\mu(A)$ and $I_\mu(B)$. Let $I'_\mu(A)$ and $I'_\mu(B)$ be the set of representative points for these two sets. We define H_μ to be the union of $I_\mu(B)$ and the representative points of $I'_\mu(A)$ that arrive at or after t. Clearly, all points in H_μ are in the active window. Let ALG be some centralized ζ-approximation algorithm for our diversity problem. Function h returns $\mathsf{ALG}(H_{\mu^*})$, where $\mathsf{ALG}(X)$ is the solution of ALG on input X, and $\mu^* = \text{argmax}_\mu f(\mathsf{ALG}(H_\mu))$.

Lemma 4.7. *The summary (Z, z) defined above is $(\frac{1}{5}-\epsilon)$-approximate. Moreover, it is $(\frac{\zeta}{5}-\epsilon, \frac{1}{5}-\epsilon)$-mergeable when accompanied by the composer function h defined above. Here, ζ is the approximation factor of the centralized algorithm* ALG *used to construct the function h.*

Proof. We start by proving the $(\frac{1}{5}-\epsilon)$-approximation for an arbitrary stream X. Recall that we refer by $\text{OPT}^*(X)$ to the value of the optimum on X and by $Y(X)$ to the optimal solution. The set of μ values that we try ensures that there exists a μ' such that $\frac{1}{5}\,\text{OPT}^*(X) \le \mu' \le \frac{1}{5}(1+\epsilon)\,\text{OPT}^*(X)$, for which we maintain set $I_{\mu'}$. If there are k points in $I_{\mu'}$, this set itself has k points, and its diversity is at least μ' by Property 2. Therefore, we have a $\frac{1}{5}$ approximation by applying $\mu' \ge \frac{1}{5}\,\text{OPT}^*(X)$.

Otherwise, $I_{\mu'}$ has fewer than k points, which means that every point in the stream has distance at most μ' to some point in $I_{\mu'}$. Let OPT be the optimum solution of stream X. We map every point in OPT to its closest point in $I_{\mu'}$. Note that this is a many-to-one mapping. Let OPT$'$ be the multiset of projected points. By Property 1, $f(\text{OPT}')$ is at least $f(\text{OPT}(X)) - 2\mu'$. We want to upper bound $f(\text{OPT}')$ in terms of $f(I_{\mu'})$.

For remote-edge, if there are duplicate points in OPT$'$, $f(\text{OPT}')$ is zero, which makes the claim trivial. Otherwise, OPT$'$ should be the same as $I_{\mu'}$, as they both have k distinct points, and the former is a subset of the latter.

For the other objectives (remote-tree, remote-cycle, remote t-trees, remote t-cycles), we remove duplicate points of OPT$'$ to achieve the set OPT$''$. This operation does not decrease the diversity, so $f(\text{OPT}'')$ is also at least $f(\text{OPT}(X)) - 2\mu'$. On the other hand, OPT$''$ is a subset of $I_{\mu'}$. Therefore, $f(\text{OPT}'')$ is at most $2f(I_{\mu'})$, since any tree or tour spanning a set of points Q can be transformed to a tree or tour spanning $Q' \subseteq Q$ with total distance of, at most, twice the original one. This can be done by doubling all the edges in the tree or tour and traversing over the Eulerian tour of the doubled set of edges. We conclude that: $f(I_{\mu'}) \ge \frac{f(\text{OPT}'')}{2} \ge \frac{f(\text{OPT}')}{2}$, which is, $\ge \frac{f(\text{OPT}(X))}{2} - \mu' \ge (0.3-\epsilon)\,\text{OPT}^*(X)$, which concludes the first claim of this lemma.

For mergeability, we show that, whenever $f(z(Z(A))) \leq (\frac{1}{5} - \epsilon)\,\mathrm{OPT}^*(A^t \cup B)$, we have $f(h(Z(A), Z(B), t)) \geq (\frac{1}{5} - \epsilon)\,\mathrm{OPT}^*(A^t \cup B)$. We know that the solution produced by composer function $h(Z(A), Z(B), t)$ is $\mathrm{ALG}(H_{\mu^*})$, where $\mu^* = \mathrm{argmax}_\mu f(\mathrm{ALG}(H_\mu))$. We note that in this particular case, composer function h returns a feasible solution, and therefore we can directly evaluate it in the term $f(h(Z(A), Z(B), t))$ without applying a decoder z.

The solution $z(Z(A))$ is the solution of summary on A which is the maximizer of $\max_\mu f(I_\mu(A))$. In particular, $f(z(Z(A)))$ is at least $f(I_{\mu''}(A))$, where μ'' is chosen such that $\frac{1}{5}\,\mathrm{OPT}^*(A^t \cup B) \leq \mu'' \leq \frac{1}{5}(1+\epsilon)\,\mathrm{OPT}^*(A^t \cup B)$, and $\mathrm{OPT}^*(A^t \cup B)$ is the optimum value of the active window $A^t \cup B$.

Since $f(z(Z(A))) \leq (\frac{1}{5} - \epsilon)\,\mathrm{OPT}^*(A^t \cup B)$, we also have $f(I_{\mu''}(A)) \leq (\frac{1}{5} - \epsilon)\,\mathrm{OPT}^*(A^t \cup B)$. Therefore, $I_{\mu''}(A)$ cannot have k points, otherwise, its value will be at least μ'', contradicting the upper bound on it by definition of μ''.

We now lower bound the value of the composed solution, $f(\mathrm{ALG}(H_{\mu^*}))$. By definition of μ^* and approximation factor of ALG, we have $f(\mathrm{ALG}(H_{\mu^*})) \geq f(\mathrm{ALG}(H_{\mu''}) \geq \zeta\,\mathrm{OPT}^*(H_{\mu''})$. So, we focus on $\mathrm{OPT}^*(H_{\mu''})$.

If $I_{\mu''}(B)$ has k points, $f(I_{\mu''}(B))$ will be at least $\mu'' \geq \frac{\mathrm{OPT}^*(A^t \cup B)}{5}$. The claim is proved by noting that $I_{\mu''}(B)$ is a subset of $H_{\mu''}$, and therefore $\mathrm{OPT}^*(H_{\mu''}) \geq f(I_{\mu''}(B))$.

Now, we can focus on the case that $I_{\mu''}(A)$ and $I_{\mu''}(B)$ have strictly fewer than k points. We show that every point x in the active window has distance of at most $2\mu''$ to some point in $H_{\mu''}$ (the union of $I_{\mu''}(B)$ and points in $I'_{\mu''}(A)$ that arrive at or after t). Since $I_{\mu''}(B)$ has fewer than k points, every point in B has distance of at most μ'' to some point in $I_{\mu''}(B)$. For a point $x \in A^t$, we have two options. Either x is in $I_{\mu''}(A)$, which means its representative is present in $H_{\mu''}$. Or, if x was not added to $I_{\mu''}(A)$, it was because x had distance of at most μ'' to some point in $y \in I_{\mu''}(A)$. The representative of y is present in $H_{\mu''}$ and has distance of at most $2\mu''$ to x by triangle inequality.

Therefore, we can move the points of optimum solution of $A^t \cup B$ each by at most $2\mu''$ such that they are all present in $H_{\mu''}$. This transformation cannot decrease the value of optimum by more than $4\mu''$ (similar to the first part of the proof). We conclude that $\mathrm{OPT}^*(H_{\mu''})$ is at least $\mathrm{OPT}^*(A^t \cup B) - 4\mu'' \geq \frac{1-4-4\epsilon}{5}\,\mathrm{OPT}^*(A^t \cup B)$. Combining this with the centralized approximation factor ζ yields an overall approximation of at least $\frac{\zeta}{5} - \epsilon$, completing the proof. □

Corollary 4.8. *There is a $\frac{\zeta}{5}$-approximation algorithm in sliding window for remote-edge, remote-tree, remote-cycle, remote t-trees, remote t-cycles. The space used is $O(k \log^2 \Delta)$.*

4.2.2 Solving remote-clique, remote-star, remote-bipartition, remote-pseudoforest, remote-matching. We design a summary that is very similar to the one in Subsection 4.2.1. The main difference is in the number of representative points we keep. Instead of keeping just one representative point for selected point $P_{\mu,i}$, we keep up to k of them.

Constructing approximate summary. Like before, we maintain a set I_μ of at most k points for each μ. Whenever a new point x arrives, if its distance to points I_μ is at least μ, we add it to I_μ. Otherwise, we find the first (based on arrival time) point $y \in I_\mu$ whose distance to x is at most μ. We add x to the set of representatives of y, and if there are already k representatives for y, we delete the most outdated (with the earliest arrival time) representative and replace it with x. Like before, for a fixed μ, the representative sets are disjoint. The summary Z consists of all sets I_μ and the representatives of their points. The solution finder function z returns the maximizer of $\max_\mu f(I_\mu)$.

Mergeable summary. We define H_μ to be the union of $I_\mu(B)$ and all representative points $I'_\mu(A)$ that arrive at or after time t. Function h runs some ζ-approximation centralized algorithm ALG on each H_μ and returns the highest diversity solution (the maximizer of $max_\mu f(\mathrm{ALG}(H_\mu))$). We note that with this definition of composer function h, it returns a feasible solution, and therefore we can directly evaluate it via function f without applying any decoder z.

Lemma 4.9. *The summary (Z, z) defined above is $(\frac{\zeta}{5} - \epsilon)$-approximate for diversity maximization problems: remote-clique, remote-star, remote-bipartition, remote-pseudoforest, and remote-matching. Moreover, the summary (Z, z) is $(\frac{\zeta}{5} - \epsilon, \frac{1}{5} - \epsilon)$-mergeable for these problems when accompanied with the composer function h and centralized algorithm* ALG *defined above. Here, ζ is the approximation factor of centralized algorithm* ALG.

Proof. The proof of the first claim is identical to the first part of the proof of Lemma 4.7. Recall that the second claim is essentially proving $f(h(Z(A), Z(B), t)) \geq (\frac{1}{5} - \epsilon)\,\mathrm{OPT}^*(A^t \cup B)$ whenever we have $f(z(Z(A))) \leq (\frac{1}{5} - \epsilon)\,\mathrm{OPT}^*(A^t \cup B)$.

Let μ be such that $\frac{1}{5}\,\mathrm{OPT}^*(A^t \cup B) \leq \mu \leq \frac{1}{5}(1+\epsilon)\,\mathrm{OPT}^*(A^t \cup B)$. Identical to the proof of Lemma 4.7, we can assume that $I_\mu(A)$ and $I_\mu(B)$ both have strictly fewer than k points.

We assign points in the optimum solution of $A^t \cup B$ to selected centers in $I_\mu(A)$ and $I_\mu(B)$. Each optimum point x that is in A as well is assigned to the first (earliest arrival time) point in $I_\mu(A)$ with distance of at most μ from x. We perform a similar assignment of optimum points in B.

If L optimum points are assigned to a point y in $I_\mu(A)$ (the claim for $I_\mu(B)$ is identical), all these L points were valid candidates of being a representative for y. Therefore, y has at least L representative points in the active window. So we can map each optimum point in x to a distinct point in the summary H_μ with a distance of at most 2μ. Similar to the proof of Lemma 4.7, the rest of the claim follows by a) property 1, b) the fact that diversity of any size k subset of H_μ is a lower bound on its optimum value $\text{OPT}^*(H_\mu)$, and c) ALG is a ζ approximation algorithm. □

5 REFINED APPROACH FOR MAXIMIZATION

We now present a stronger, more complex technique for maximization problems that allows for tighter bounds. The main goal of this section is to show that it is possible to trade-off space at the cost of some additional complexity. In the refined method presented in this section, we guess the value of the optimum solution and then run a copy of the summary algorithms for each guess, λ. In this way, we can reduce the total space used by our algorithms by a $\log \Delta$ factor.

The main idea behind the refined approach is to allow the algorithm to select the optimal λ to optimize the approximation factor and to reduce the memory used by a logarithmic factor. In fact, toward the end of the section, we will show that the new approach can be used to improve the state-of-the-art algorithm for submodular maximization under cardinality constraints.

In this section, we use the same notation as before for the evaluation function f encoding the maximization problem and its constraints. We assume that the function is monotone, as defined above.

Definition 5.1 (Good summary for maximization problems). *Fix $\lambda \in \Lambda$. Let $Z_\lambda : \mathcal{X} \to \mathcal{X}$ and $z_\lambda : \mathcal{X} \to \mathcal{Y}$. A summary is $(\lambda, \alpha, \delta)$-good if:*

Whenever there exists a $X' \subseteq X$ and $Y \in \mathcal{Y}$, such that Y is a feasible solution of X', with value $\lambda \in [f(Y), (1+\delta)f(Y)]$; then we have:

$$f(z_\lambda(Z_\lambda(X))) \geq \alpha\lambda.$$

The key to our definition is that the quality of the solution only needs to be approximately optimal w.r.t. λ when there is a solution of value comparable to λ in any subset of X. Note that we do not require any guarantee on the quality of the solution returned by the summary when the value of λ is significantly different from that of any feasible solution of any subset of X.

Definition 5.2 (Good family of summaries for maximization problems). *Let $(Z, z)_\lambda$ be a family of summaries for a maximization problem f for every $\lambda \in \mathbb{R}^{\geq 0}$. We say that the family is an (α, δ) good family of summaries for the problem f if for every λ and for a stream X, (Z_λ, z_λ) is a $(\lambda, \alpha, \delta)$ good summary for X.*

We now give the adapted definition of *strong mergeable summaries.*

Definition 5.3 (Strong mergeable summary). *We say that a family of (α, δ) good summaries is $(\alpha', \delta', \beta)$-mergeable if there exists a composition function $h : \mathcal{X} \times \mathcal{X} \times \mathbb{Z} \to \mathcal{X}$ such that for any λ, A, B, t, and $H = h(A_\lambda, B_\lambda, t)$: if $f(z_\lambda(A_\lambda)) \leq \beta \cdot \lambda$, then H is a $(\lambda, \alpha', \delta')$ good summary of $A^t \cup B$.*

Also in this case, while we do not explicitly forbid the composition with $B_\lambda = \emptyset$, the definition does not require us to be able to extract arbitrary suffixes. In fact, if $\alpha > \beta$, it is easy to see that by applying the composition with an empty set, then the condition $f(z_\lambda(A_\lambda)) \leq \beta \cdot \lambda$ is not satisfied whenever λ is close to the value of a feasible solution of A^t.

We now show that, given a family of mergeable summaries, it is possible to obtain a sliding window algorithm that uses only logarithmically many summaries. Also in this algorithm, for every λ, we will keep only three summaries for intervals A_λ, A_λ^+, and B_λ.

Theorem 5.4 (Tighter sliding window algorithm for maximization problems). *Let $(Z, z)_\lambda$ be a (α, δ)-good family of summaries and let $(Z, z)_\lambda$ be $(\alpha', \delta', \beta)$-mergeable where $\beta < \alpha$. Let $\delta_0 = \min(\delta, \delta')$ and let $\alpha_0 = \min(\alpha', \beta)$. There exists a sliding window algorithm that given m, M and the stream X preserves a α_0-approximation of a maximization problem f in space $O\left(s_Z \cdot \log_{1+\delta_0} \frac{M}{m}\right)$.*

Proof. As before, let $\Lambda' := \{m, (1+\delta_0)m, (1+\delta_0)^2 m, \ldots, M(1+\delta_0)\}$. For each $\lambda \in \Lambda'$, we maintain at all time $(\lambda, \alpha, \delta)$-good summaries A_λ, A_λ^+ and B_λ almost as in Algorithm 1. At any time we maintain the following invariants: A_λ and B_λ are intervals for which we keep summaries that have processed, respectively, the items from the stream appearing in two disjoint consecutive intervals of timesteps $A_\lambda = [t_{\lambda,0}, t_{\lambda,1}]$ and $B_\lambda = [t_{\lambda,1}+1, t]$ with the second interval ending with the last item (the first interval may be empty, in which case the associated summary $Z(A_\lambda)$ is empty). Moreover, we preserve at all times that $f(z(Z(A_\lambda))) \leq \beta\lambda$ (unless A_λ has size one and it contains a single element of value $> \beta\lambda$) and either $f(z(Z(B_\lambda))) \leq \beta\lambda$ or the second interval contains a single element of value $> \beta\lambda$. Finally, unless the first interval is empty, we ensure that $f(z(Z(A_\lambda^+))$ is larger than $\beta\lambda$. Notice that it is always possible to preserve the previous invariants using Algorithm 1 by substituting $\leq \lambda$ with $\leq \beta\lambda$ in the condition of the first if statement at line 4.

Now, whenever we are asked for a solution for the current active window $W = [\max(t-w, 1), t]$, we compute a series of pairs of candidate solutions Y_λ and candidate summaries X_λ, one for each $\lambda \in \Lambda'$ that respects some properties outlined below, and later we output the one with larger value among the ones computed. For each λ, we have four cases, depending on the position of the intervals associated to λ:

- Case 1: The active window is exactly coincident with the second interval. We set $X_\lambda = Z(B_\lambda)$ and set $Y_\lambda = z_\lambda(X_\lambda)$.
- Case 2: The two intervals are both non-empty subsets of the active window. Then we use $X_\lambda = A^+_\lambda$, and $z(Z(A^+_\lambda))$ as a solution.
- Case 3: The active window intersects both intervals, and the first interval contains elements not in the active window. We use h to obtain a good solution by analyzing the summary $X_\lambda = h(Z(A_\lambda), Z(B_\lambda), t)$ and its associated solution.
- Case 4: Finally, if the active window is strictly contained in the second interval, we ignore this λ (we will show later it is not needed), and Y_λ is not set.

Let λ^* be such that $\lambda^* \in [\mathrm{OPT}^*(W), (1+\delta_0)\,\mathrm{OPT}^*(W)] \cap \Lambda'$; we know that such lambda exists by construction. The main idea of the proof is to lower-bound the value of $f(Y_{\lambda^*})$. We now show that the solution output is an α_0-approximation. We consider the four cases.

In case 1, we provide an $\alpha \geq \alpha_0$-approximation, as we are using a $(\lambda^*, \delta, \alpha)$-good summary on W, so there exists a solution of value close to λ^*, and the summary will output a solution of value at least $\alpha\lambda^* \geq \alpha_0\,\mathrm{OPT}^*(W)$.

Now consider case 2. Here, by construction we know that $f(Y_{\lambda^*}) \geq \beta\lambda^* \geq \alpha_0\,\mathrm{OPT}^*(W)$.

For case 3, it is enough to notice that we are composing a $(\lambda^*, \alpha, \delta)$-good summary with value $\leq \beta\lambda^*$ with another $(\lambda^*, \alpha, \delta)$-good summary and a start time inside the first summary interval corresponding to the beginning of the active window. Hence the output summary X^*_λ is a $(\lambda^*, \alpha', \delta')$-good summary of the active window $[\max(t-w, 1), t]$. So again we get an α_0-approximation.

For case 4, we show that this cannot happen for λ^* as $\beta < \alpha$. In fact, in this case we know that B_{λ^*} is a $(\lambda^*, \alpha, \delta)$-good summary with value $\leq \beta\lambda^*$. But B_{λ^*} needs to output a solution of value $\geq \alpha\lambda^* > \beta\lambda^*$ when computed over a superset of W, so this gives a contradiction.

Finally, note that our algorithm requires us to compute $O(\log_{1+\delta_0}(\frac{M}{m}))$ many summaries, each of size less than s_Z, so the total space is $O(s_Z \log_{1+\delta_0} \frac{M}{m})$. □

Note that the summaries constructed are independent of the size of the active window (in contrast, for example, to the smooth histogram technique). Only the post-processing uses the value w to obtain the solution. This means that the algorithm preserves an approximate solution for any window size at all time.

Now, we explore an applications of our more refined approach for *submodular maximization with cardinality constraints*. As in Section 4.1, we write $f(Y) = g(Y)$ for a submodular function g whenever Y is a valid solution (i.e., in the case of a cardinality constraint k, when $|Y| \leq k$). Recall that a function g is submodular if for each $X_1 \subseteq X_2$ and for each $x \in X \setminus X_2$, $g(X_1 \cup \{x\}) - g(X_1) \geq g(X_2 \cup \{x\}) - g(X_2)$. Since f is determined by g, as long as the solution returned is feasible, to simplify the notation, we are concerned with optimizing g.

In the following, we improve all previous results by defining a $(\frac{1}{3}-\delta, \delta, \frac{1}{3}-\delta)$-mergeable summary that uses space $O(k)$ for monotone submodular maximization under cardinality constraints. Consequently, we obtain a $(\frac{1}{3}-\delta)$-approximation in sliding window that uses space $O(k \log_{1+\delta} \frac{M}{n})$.

Our summary function Z_λ maps a stream of elements X into a feasible solution Y_λ (i.e., a subset of size $\leq k$). When we receive the next element x_t, we add it to the current solution Y_λ if Y_λ has $< k$ elements and $g(Y_\lambda \cup \{x_t\}) - g(Y_\lambda) > c\frac{\lambda}{k}$ (c will be chosen later). The function z_λ is simply the identity, and will therefore be omitted in the rest of the proof. We now show our main lemma (whose proof is similar in spirit to the proof in [24])

Lemma 5.5. *The summary Z_λ is $(\lambda, \min(c, 1-c(1+\delta)), \delta)$-good.*

Proof. Suppose there exist $X' \subseteq X$ and $Y \in \mathcal{Y}$ such that $\lambda \in [f(Y), (1+\delta)f(Y)]$ and Y is a valid solution for X', otherwise the proof is trivial. If our summary contains k elements, then $g(Y_\lambda) \geq c\lambda$. Otherwise, let $Y = \{y_1, \ldots, y_\ell\}$, where $\ell \leq k$: for each y_i, either $y_i \in Y_\lambda$ or, when we processed y_i, the old solution Y'_λ verified $g(Y'_\lambda \cup \{y_i\}) - g(Y'_\lambda) < c\frac{\lambda}{k}$. Since $Y'_\lambda \subseteq Y_\lambda$, by submodularity, this means that $g(Y_\lambda \cup \{y_1, \ldots, y_{i-1}\} \cup \{y_i\}) - g(Y_\lambda \cup \{y_1, \ldots, y_{i-1}\}) < c\frac{\lambda}{k}$.

We conclude that:

$$\begin{aligned} g(Y) &\leq g(Y_\lambda \cup Y) \\ &= g(Y_\lambda) + \sum_{i=1}^{\ell} g(Y_\lambda \cup \{y_1, \ldots, y_i\}) - g(Y_\lambda \cup \{y_1, \ldots, y_{i-1}\}) \\ &\leq g(Y_\lambda) + c\lambda \\ &\leq g(Y_\lambda) + c(1+\delta)g(Y) \end{aligned}$$

Hence, $g(Y_\lambda) \geq g(Y)(1-c(1+\delta)) \geq \lambda(1-c(1+\delta))$. □

Lemma 5.6. *The family of summaries $\{Z_\lambda\}$ is $(\min(c, 1-2c(1+\delta)), \delta, \frac{c}{1+\delta})$-mergeable.*

Proof. Let A_λ be the summary of A and B_λ be the summary of B, we define $h(A_\lambda, B_\lambda, t) = B_\lambda$. We need to prove that for any λ, A, B, t, if $g(A_\lambda) \leq \frac{c}{1+\delta}\lambda$, then B_λ is a $(\lambda, \alpha', \delta)$-good summary with $\alpha' = \min(c, 1-2c(1+\delta))$.

In other words, if there exist $X' \subseteq A^t \cup B$ and $Y \in \mathcal{Y}$ such that Y is a feasible solution of X' and $\lambda \in [f(Y), (1+\delta)f(Y)]$, we want to show that $g(B_\lambda) \geq \min(c, 1-2c(1+\delta))\lambda$. Now, suppose the condition is true, as the other case is trivial.

First, if B_λ has at least k elements, $g(B_\lambda) \geq c\lambda$, and we are done. Hence, we can assume that B_λ has $< k$ elements.

Furthermore, $g(A_\lambda) \le \frac{c}{1+\delta}\lambda < c\lambda$ by assumption, and consequently A_λ has $< k$ elements.

Let $Y := \{a_1, \ldots, a_i, b_1, \ldots, b_{l-i}\}$, $l \le k$, where $a_j \in A^t$ and $b_j \in B$. As in the previous proof, $g(\{a_1, \ldots, a_i\}) \le g(\{a_1, \ldots, a_i\} \cup A_\lambda) \le g(A_\lambda) + c\lambda\frac{i}{k} \le c\lambda(\frac{1}{1+\delta} + \frac{i}{k}) \le c\lambda(1 + \frac{i}{k}) \le c(1 + \frac{i}{k})(1+\delta)\lambda$. Similarly, $g(\{b_1, \ldots, b_{l-i}\}) \le g(B_\lambda) + c\frac{l-i}{k}(1+\delta)\lambda$.

By merging the two inequalities, we obtain $g(Y) = g(\{a_1, \ldots, a_i, b_1, \ldots, b_{l-i}\}) \le g(\{a_1, \ldots, a_i\}) + g(\{b_1, \ldots, b_{l-i}\}) \le c(1 + \frac{i}{k})(1+\delta)\lambda + g(B_\lambda) + c\frac{l-i}{k}(1+\delta)\lambda = g(B_\lambda) + 2c(1+\delta)\lambda$.

We conclude that $g(B_\lambda) \ge [1 - 2c(1+\delta)]\lambda$. □

Corollary 5.7. *There exists a sliding window $(\frac{1}{3} - \delta)$-approximation algorithm for submodular maximization that uses space $O(k \log_{1+\delta} \frac{M}{m})$.*

Proof. By Lemmas 5.5 and 5.6, there is a $(\lambda, \min(c, 1 - c(1+\delta)), \delta)$-good, $(\min(c, 1 - 2c(1+\delta)), \delta, \frac{c}{1+\delta})$-mergeable family of summaries. Plugging this into Theorem 5.4, we obtain a $\min(\frac{c}{1+\delta}, 1 - 2c(1+\delta))$-approximation in the sliding window model. By choosing $c = \frac{1}{3}$, we conclude the proof. □

6 CONCLUSION

In this work, we have presented a new approach for solving maximization problems in sliding window streams, in essence showing that augmenting standard insertion-only algorithms with an additional property of suffix composability is enough to obtain state-of-the-art approaches. We provide examples of our approach for constrained subadditive and submodular optimization problems as well as for diverse set selection. In many of the instances, we provide state-of-the art results that beat previously developed, hand-tuned algorithms. An obvious open problem is how to apply this approach to more problems (including minimization problems) and to tighten some of the approximation constants we derived. A more ambitious program should take this work as a building block towards developing a better understanding of the structure of sliding window problems, with the goal of designing new techniques to give provable upper and *lower* bounds for this important class of problems.

REFERENCES

[1] Kook Jin Ahn, Sudipto Guha, and Andrew McGregor. 2012. Graph Sketches: Sparsification, Spanners, and Subgraphs. In *Proceedings of the 31st ACM SIGMOD-SIGACT-SIGAI Symposium on Principles of Database Systems (PODS '12)*. ACM, New York, NY, USA, 5–14. https://doi.org/10.1145/2213556.2213560

[2] Noga Alon, Yossi Matias, and Mario Szegedy. 1996. The space complexity of approximating the frequency moments. In *Proceedings of the twenty-eighth annual ACM symposium on Theory of computing*. ACM, 20–29.

[3] Arvind Arasu and Gurmeet Singh Manku. 2004. Approximate counts and quantiles over sliding windows. In *Proceedings of the twenty-third ACM SIGMOD-SIGACT-SIGART symposium on Principles of database systems*. ACM, 286–296.

[4] Brian Babcock, Mayur Datar, and Rajeev Motwani. 2002. Sampling from a moving window over streaming data. In *Proceedings of the thirteenth annual ACM-SIAM symposium on Discrete algorithms*. Society for Industrial and Applied Mathematics, 633–634.

[5] Brain Babcock, Mayur Datar, Rajeev Motwani, and Liadan O'Callaghan. 2003. Maintaining Variance and K-medians over Data Stream Windows. In *Proceedings of the Twenty-second ACM SIGMOD-SIGACT-SIGART Symposium on Principles of Database Systems (PODS '03)*. ACM, New York, NY, USA, 234–243. https://doi.org/10.1145/773153.773176

[6] Ashwinkumar Badanidiyuru, Baharan Mirzasoleiman, Amin Karbasi, and Andreas Krause. 2014. Streaming submodular maximization: Massive data summarization on the fly. In *ACM SIGKDD*. ACM, 671–680.

[7] Ziv Bar-Yossef, TS Jayram, Ravi Kumar, D Sivakumar, and Luca Trevisan. 2002. Counting distinct elements in a data stream. In *International Workshop on Randomization and Approximation Techniques in Computer Science*. Springer, 1–10.

[8] Ran Ben Basat, Gil Einziger, Roy Friedman, and Yaron Kassner. 2016. Efficient summing over sliding windows. *arXiv preprint arXiv:1604.02450* (2016).

[9] Paul Beame, Raphael Clifford, and Widad Machmouchi. 2013. Element Distinctness, Frequency Moments, and Sliding Windows. In *Proceedings of the 2013 IEEE 54th Annual Symposium on Foundations of Computer Science (FOCS '13)*. IEEE Computer Society, Washington, DC, USA, 290–299. https://doi.org/10.1109/FOCS.2013.39

[10] Vladimir Braverman, Petros Drineas, Jalaj Upadhyay, and Samson Zhou. 2018. Numerical Linear Algebra in the Sliding Window Model. *arXiv preprint arXiv:1805.03765* (2018).

[11] Vladimir Braverman, Ran Gelles, and Rafail Ostrovsky. 2014. How to catch l2-heavy-hitters on sliding windows. *Theoretical Computer Science* 554 (2014), 82–94.

[12] Vladimir Braverman, Elena Grigorescu, Harry Lang, David P Woodruff, and Samson Zhou. 2018. Nearly Optimal Distinct Elements and Heavy Hitters on Sliding Windows. *arXiv preprint arXiv:1805.00212* (2018).

[13] Vladimir Braverman, Harry Lang, Keith Levin, and Morteza Monemizadeh. 2016. Clustering Problems on Sliding Windows. In *SODA*. 1374–1390. https://doi.org/10.1137/1.9781611974331.ch95

[14] Vladimir Braverman, Harry Lang, Keith Levin, and Morteza Monemizadeh. 2016. Clustering problems on sliding windows. In *Proceedings of the Twenty-Seventh Annual ACM-SIAM Symposium on Discrete Algorithms*. Society for Industrial and Applied Mathematics, 1374–1390.

[15] Vladimir Braverman and Rafail Ostrovsky. 2007. Smooth Histograms for Sliding Windows. In *FOCS*. 283–293. https://doi.org/10.1109/FOCS.2007.55

[16] Vladimir Braverman, Rafail Ostrovsky, and Carlo Zaniolo. 2009. Optimal sampling from sliding windows. In *Proceedings of the twenty-eighth ACM SIGMOD-SIGACT-SIGART symposium on Principles of database systems*. ACM, 147–156.

[17] Matteo Ceccarello, Andrea Pietracaprina, Geppino Pucci, and Eli Upfal. 2017. MapReduce and streaming algorithms for diversity maximization in metric spaces of bounded doubling dimension. *Proceedings of the VLDB Endowment* 10, 5 (2017), 469–480.

[18] Ho-Leung Chan, Tak Wah Lam, Lap-Kei Lee, and Hing-Fung Ting. 2012. Continuous Monitoring of Distributed Data Streams over a Time-Based Sliding Window. *Algorithmica* 62, 3-4 (2012), 1088–1111. https://doi.org/10.1007/s00453-011-9506-5

[19] Chandra Chekuri, Shalmoli Gupta, and Kent Quanrud. 2015. Streaming algorithms for submodular function maximization. In *International Colloquium on Automata, Languages, and Programming*. Springer, 318–330.

[20] Jiecao Chen, Huy L. Nguyen, and Qin Zhang. 2016. Submodular Maximization over Sliding Windows. *CoRR* abs/1611.00129 (2016). arXiv:1611.00129 http://arxiv.org/abs/1611.00129

[21] Vincent Cohen-Addad, Chris Schwiegelshohn, and Christian Sohler. 2016. Diameter and k-Center in Sliding Windows. In *43rd International Colloquium on Automata, Languages, and Programming (ICALP 2016) (Leibniz International Proceedings in Informatics (LIPIcs))*, Ioannis Chatzigiannakis, Michael Mitzenmacher, Yuval Rabani, and Davide Sangiorgi (Eds.), Vol. 55. Schloss Dagstuhl–Leibniz-Zentrum fuer Informatik, Dagstuhl, Germany, 19:1–19:12. https://doi.org/10.4230/LIPIcs.ICALP.2016.19

[22] Michael S Crouch, Andrew McGregor, and Daniel Stubbs. 2013. Dynamic graphs in the sliding-window model. In *European Symposium on Algorithms*. Springer, 337–348.

[23] Mayur Datar, Aristides Gionis, Piotr Indyk, and Rajeev Motwani. 2002. Maintaining stream statistics over sliding windows. *SIAM journal on computing* 31, 6 (2002), 1794–1813.

[24] Alessandro Epasto, Silvio Lattanzi, Sergei Vassilvitskii, and Morteza Zadimoghaddam. 2017. Submodular Optimization Over Sliding Windows. In *Proceedings of the 26th International Conference on World Wide Web (WWW '17)*. International World Wide Web Conferences Steering Committee, Republic and Canton of Geneva, Switzerland, 421–430. https://doi.org/10.1145/3038912.3052699

[25] Philippe Flajolet and G Nigel Martin. 1985. Probabilistic counting algorithms for data base applications. *Journal of computer and system sciences* 31, 2 (1985), 182–209.

[26] Phillip B Gibbons and Srikanta Tirthapura. 2002. Distributed streams algorithms for sliding windows. In *SPAA*. ACM, 63–72.

[27] Nuno Homem and Joao Paulo Carvalho. 2011. Finding top-k elements in a time-sliding window. *Evolving Systems* 2, 1 (2011), 51–70.

[28] Regant YS Hung and Hing-Fung Ting. 2008. Finding heavy hitters over the sliding window of a weighted data stream. *Lecture Notes in Computer Science* 4957 (2008), 699–710.

[29] Piotr Indyk. 2007. Sketching, streaming and sublinear-space algorithms. *Graduate course notes, available at* (2007).

[30] Piotr Indyk, Sepideh Mahabadi, Mohammad Mahdian, and Vahab S. Mirrokni. 2014. Composable Core-sets for Diversity and Coverage Maximization. In *Proceedings of the 33rd ACM SIGMOD-SIGACT-SIGART Symposium on Principles of Database Systems (PODS '14)*. ACM, New York, NY, USA, 100–108. https://doi.org/10.1145/2594538.2594560

[31] Lap-Kei Lee and HF Ting. 2006. Maintaining significant stream statistics over sliding windows. In *Proceedings of the seventeenth annual ACM-SIAM symposium on Discrete algorithm*. Society for Industrial and Applied Mathematics, 724–732.

[32] Lap-Kei Lee and HF Ting. 2006. A simpler and more efficient deterministic scheme for finding frequent items over sliding windows. In *Proceedings of the twenty-fifth ACM SIGMOD-SIGACT-SIGART symposium on Principles of database systems*. ACM, 290–297.

[33] Andrew McGregor. 2005. Finding graph matchings in data streams. In *APPROX-RANDOM*, Vol. 3624. Springer, 170–181.

[34] Shanmugavelayutham Muthukrishnan et al. 2005. Data streams: Algorithms and applications. *Foundations and Trends® in Theoretical Computer Science* 1, 2 (2005), 117–236.

[35] Michael Saks and Xiaodong Sun. 2002. Space Lower Bounds for Distance Approximation in the Data Stream Model. In *Proceedings of the Thiry-fourth Annual ACM Symposium on Theory of Computing (STOC '02)*. ACM, New York, NY, USA, 360–369. https://doi.org/10.1145/509907.509963

[36] Hing-Fung Ting, Lap-Kei Lee, Ho-Leung Chan, and Tak Wah Lam. 2011. Approximating Frequent Items in Asynchronous Data Stream over a Sliding Window. *Algorithms* 4, 3 (2011), 200–222. https://doi.org/10.3390/a4030200

[37] Yanhao Wang, Qi Fan, Yuchen Li, and Kian-Lee Tan. 2017. Real-time influence maximization on dynamic social streams. *Proceedings of the VLDB Endowment* 10, 7 (2017), 805–816.

[38] Linfeng Zhang and Yong Guan. 2008. Frequency estimation over sliding windows. In *Data Engineering, 2008. ICDE 2008. IEEE 24th International Conference on*. IEEE, 1385–1387.

Making Consistency Protocols Serializable

Alan Fekete
alan.fekete@sydney.edu.au
University of Sydney
Australia

ABSTRACT

A tutorial given at PODS 2019, focussed on several research agendas in the past decade or so, that examine weak isolation levels, and obtain many (or all) of the benefits for application integrity, traditionally achieved by serializable concurrency control. The tutorial presents both the mechanisms and the reasoning approaches from these research works.

CCS CONCEPTS

• **Information systems** → **Database transaction processing**; • **Theory of computation** → *Distributed computing models*; • **Software and its engineering** → *Formal methods*.

KEYWORDS

transaction, isolation, robustness, data integrity, serializability

ACM Reference Format:
Alan Fekete. 2019. Making Consistency Protocols Serializable. In *38th ACM SIGMOD-SIGACT-SIGAI Symposium on Principles of Database Systems (PODS'19), June 30-July 5, 2019, Amsterdam, Netherlands.* ACM, New York, NY, USA, ?? pages. https://doi.org/10.1145/3294052.3322191

1 TUTORIAL OVERVIEW

Concurrency control is among the central components of a database management system platform. Jim Gray produced seminal work in the 1970s, among many contributions for which he won the Turing Award in 1998. All university students in a database class will learn some classic algorithms such as two-phase locking (2PL), and they will be shown some of the classic theory that defines serializability, proves that any integrity constraint is maintained in a serializable execution of transactions that are individually consistent, and can be used to prove that a protocol such as 2PL has serializable executions. But in practice, many database applications do not use these serializable techniques, perhaps because the performance degradation is too great, or just because most platforms have weaker support as the default. Instead, many applications are running at isolation levels such as "Read Committed" with concurrency control that releases read locks earlier than allowed by 2PL, and gives executions that do not guarantee preserving arbitrary undeclared integrity constraints. In recent years, a lot of research focus shifted to studying the properties of these practically important cases of weak isolation mechanisms.

In this tutorial, we will give expositions of several different kinds of contribution from the research community. Some are system designs that allow weak isolation to be strengthened to serializability, by tracking conflicts and aborting transactions as needed; these are modern and more efficient variants of Casanova and Bernstein's Serialization Graph Testing. Others are theoretical or tool supported approaches to finding robust applications: those whose executions are serializable, even when run in a system with weaker isolation mechanisms. A third category of result, shows how to ensure preservation of certain integrity constraints, rather than arbitrary ones as happens with serializable behavior. As a framework for the presentation, we will discuss some of the reasoning techniques that are used in this research, to define isolation properties, to describe concurrency control mechanisms, and to prove properties of systems. This tutorial is intended both to show theoretical database researchers about some recent work in the systems community, and also to give systems and application researchers an introduction to the theory aspects.

PODS'19, June 30-July 5, 2019, Amsterdam, Netherlands

ACM ISBN 978-1-4503-6227-6/19/06.
https://doi.org/10.1145/3294052.3322191

The Space-Efficient Core of Vadalog

Gerald Berger
Institute of Logic and Computation
TU Wien

Georg Gottlob
Department of Computer Science
University of Oxford & TU Wien

Andreas Pieris
School of Informatics
University of Edinburgh

Emanuel Sallinger
Department of Computer Science
University of Oxford & TU Wien

ABSTRACT

Vadalog is a system for performing complex reasoning tasks such as those required in advanced knowledge graphs. The logical core of the underlying Vadalog language is the warded fragment of tuple-generating dependencies (TGDs). This formalism ensures tractable reasoning in data complexity, while a recent analysis focusing on a practical implementation led to the reasoning algorithm around which the Vadalog system is built. A fundamental question that has emerged in the context of Vadalog is the following: can we limit the recursion allowed by wardedness in order to obtain a formalism that provides a convenient syntax for expressing useful recursive statements, and at the same time achieves space-efficiency? After analyzing several real-life examples of warded sets of TGDs provided by our industrial partners, as well as recent benchmarks, we observed that recursion is often used in a restricted way: the body of a TGD contains at most one atom whose predicate is mutually recursive with a predicate in the head. We show that this type of recursion, known as piece-wise linear in the Datalog literature, is the answer to our main question. We further show that piece-wise linear recursion alone, without the wardedness condition, is not enough as it leads to the undecidability of reasoning. We finally study the relative expressiveness of the query languages based on (piece-wise linear) warded sets of TGDs.

CCS CONCEPTS

• **Information systems → Query languages;**

KEYWORDS

reasoning, query answering, Datalog, tuple-generating dependencies, complexity, expressive power

ACM Reference Format:
Gerald Berger, Georg Gottlob, Andreas Pieris, and Emanuel Sallinger. 2019. The Space-Efficient Core of Vadalog. In *38th ACM SIGMOD-SIGACT-SIGAI Symposium on Principles of Database Systems (PODS'19), June 30-July 5, 2019, Amsterdam, Netherlands.* ACM, New York, NY, USA, 15 pages. https://doi.org/10.1145/3294052.3319688

ACM ISBN 978-1-4503-6227-6/19/06...$15.00
https://doi.org/10.1145/3294052.3319688

1 INTRODUCTION

In recent times, thousands of companies world-wide wish to manage their own knowledge graphs (KGs), and are looking for adequate knowledge graph management systems (KGMS). The term knowledge graph originally only referred to Google's Knowledge Graph, i.e., "a knowledge base used by Google and its services to enhance its search engine's results with information gathered from a variety of sources.[1]" In the meantime, several other large companies have constructed their own knowledge graphs, and many more companies would like to maintain a private corporate knowledge graph incorporating large amounts of data in form of database facts, both from corporate and public sources, as well as rule-based knowledge. Such a corporate knowledge graph is expected to contain relevant business knowledge, for example, knowledge about customers, products, prices, and competitors, rather than general knowledge from Wikipedia and similar sources. It should be managed by a KGMS, that is, a knowledge base management system, which performs complex rule-based reasoning tasks over very large amounts of data and, in addition, provides methods and tools for data analytics and machine learning [6].

1.1 The Vadalog System

Vadalog is a system for performing complex reasoning tasks such as those required in advanced knowledge graphs [7]. It is Oxford's contribution to the VADA research project,[2]

[1]https://en.wikipedia.org/wiki/Knowledge_Graph
[2]http://vada.org.uk/

a joint effort of the universities of Oxford, Manchester, and Edinburgh, as well as around 20 industrial partners such as Facebook, BP, and the NHS (UK national health system). One of the most fundamental reasoning tasks performed by Vadalog is *ontological query answering*: given a database D, an ontology Σ (which is essentially a set of logical assertions that allow us to derive new intensional knowledge from D), and a query $q(\bar{x})$ (typically a conjunctive query), the goal is to compute the certain answers to q w.r.t. the knowledge base consisting of D and Σ, i.e., the tuples of constants $\bar{c}$ such that, for every relational instance $I \supseteq D$ that satisfies Σ, I satisfies the Boolean query $q(\bar{c})$ obtained after instantiating $\bar{x}$ with $\bar{c}$. Due to Vadalog's ability to perform ontological query answering, it is currently used as the core deductive database component of the overall Vadalog KGMS, as well as at various industrial partners including the finance, security, and media intelligence industries.

The logical core of the underlying Vadalog language is a rule-based formalism known as *warded Datalog*$^{\exists}$ [17], which is a member of the Datalog$^{\pm}$ family of knowledge representation languages [11]. Warded Datalog$^{\exists}$ generalizes Datalog with existential quantification in rule heads, and at the same time applies a restriction on how certain "dangerous" variables can be used; details are given in Section 3. Such a restriction is needed as basic reasoning tasks, e.g., ontological query answering, under arbitrary Datalog$^{\exists}$ rules become undecidable; see, e.g., [5, 10]. Let us clarify that Datalog$^{\exists}$ rules are essentially *tuple-generating dependencies* (TGDs) of the form $\forall\bar{x}\forall\bar{y}(\varphi(\bar{x},\bar{y}) \rightarrow \exists\bar{z}\,\psi(\bar{x},\bar{z}))$, where φ (the *body*) and ψ (the *head*) are conjunctions of atoms. Therefore, knowledge representation and reasoning should be seen as a modern application of TGDs, which have been introduced decades ago as a unifying framework for database integrity constraints.

The key properties of warded Datalog$^{\exists}$, which led to its adoption as the logical core on top of which the Vadalog language is built, can be summarized as follows:

(1) *Recursion over KGs.* It is able to express full recursion and joins, needed to express complex reasoning tasks over KGs. Moreover, navigational capabilities, empowered by recursion, are vital for graph-based structures.
(2) *Ontological Reasoning over KGs.* After adding a very mild and easy to handle negation, the language is able to express SPARQL reasoning under the OWL 2 QL entailment regime. Recall that SPARQL is the standard language for querying the Semantic Web,[3] while OWL 2 QL is a prominent profile of the OWL 2 Web Ontology Language, the standard formalism for modeling Semantic Web ontologies.[4]
(3) *Low Complexity.* Reasoning, in particular, ontological query answering, is tractable (in fact, polynomial time) in data complexity, which is a minimal requirement for allowing scalability over large volumes of data.

Warded Datalog$^{\exists}$ turned out to be powerful enough for expressing all the tasks given by our industrial partners, while a recent analysis of it focusing on a practical implementation led to the reasoning algorithm around which the Vadalog system is built [7].

1.2 Research Challenges

With the aim of isolating more refined formalisms, which will lead to yet more efficient reasoning algorithms, the following fundamental question has emerged in the context of Vadalog:

Can we limit the recursion allowed by wardedness in order to obtain a formalism that provides a convenient syntax for expressing useful statements, importantly, most of the scenarios provided by our partners, and at the same time achieves space-efficiency, in particular, NLogSpace *data complexity?*

Let us stress that NLogSpace data complexity is the best that we can hope for, since navigational capabilities are vital for graph-based structures, and already graph reachability is NLogSpace-hard. It is known that NLogSpace is contained in the class NC_2 of highly parallelizable problems. This means that reasoning in the more refined formalism that we are aiming is principally parallelizable, unlike warded Datalog$^{\exists}$, which is PTime-complete and intrinsically sequential. Our ultimate goal is to exploit this in the future for the parallel execution of reasoning tasks in both multi-core settings and in the map-reduce model. In fact, we are currently in the process of implementing a multi-core implementation for the refined formalism proposed by the present work.

Extensive benchmark results are available for the Vadalog system, based on a variety of scenarios, both synthetic and industrial scenarios, including: ChaseBench [8], a benchmark that targets data exchange and query answering problems; iBench, a data exchange benchmark developed at the University of Toronto [4]; iWarded, a benchmark specifically targeted at warded sets of TGDs; a DBpedia based benchmark; and a number of other synthetic and industrial scenarios [7]. Let us stress that all the above benchmarks contain only warded sets of TGDs. In fact, a good part of them are not *warded by chance*, i.e., they contain joins among "harmful" variables, which is one of the distinctive features of wardedness [7]. After analyzing the above benchmarks, we observed that recursion is often used in a restricted way. Approximately 70% of the TGD-sets use recursion in the following way: the body of a TGD contains at most one atom whose predicate is mutually recursive with a predicate in the head. More specifically, approximately 55% of the TGD-sets

[3] http://www.w3.org/TR/rdf-sparql-query
[4] https://www.w3.org/TR/owl2-overview/

directly use the above type of recursion, while 15% can be transformed into warded sets of TGDs that use recursion as above. This transformation relies on a standard elimination procedure of unnecessary non-linear recursion. For example,

$$\begin{aligned} \forall x \forall y (E(x,y) &\rightarrow T(x,y)) \\ \forall x \forall y \forall z (T(x,y) \wedge T(y,z) &\rightarrow T(x,z)), \end{aligned}$$

which compute the transitive closure of the binary relation E using non-linear recursion, can be rewritten as the set

$$\begin{aligned} \forall x \forall y (E(x,y) &\rightarrow T(x,y)) \\ \forall x \forall y \forall z (E(x,y) \wedge T(y,z) &\rightarrow T(x,z)) \end{aligned}$$

that uses linear recursion. Interestingly, the type of recursion discussed above has been already studied in the context of Datalog, and is known as *piece-wise linear*, see, e.g., [1]. It is a refinement of the well-known *linear* recursion [24, 25], already mentioned in the above example, which allows only one intensional predicate to appear in the body, while all the other predicates are extensional.

Based on this key observation, the following research questions have immediately emerged:

(1) Does warded Datalog$^\exists$ with piece-wise linear recursion achieve space-efficiency for query answering?[5]
(2) Is the combination of wardedness and piece-wise linearity justified? In other words, can we achieve the same with piece-wise linear Datalog$^\exists$ without the wardedness condition?
(3) What is the expressiveness of the query language based on warded Datalog$^\exists$ with piece-wise linear recursion relative to prominent languages such as Datalog?

These are top-priority questions in the context of the Vadalog system since they may provide useful insights towards more efficient reasoning algorithms, in particular, towards parallel execution of reasoning tasks. The ultimate goal of this work is to analyze piece-wise linearity, and provide definite answers to the above questions.

1.3 Summary of Contributions

Our main results can be summarized as follows:

(1) Ontological query answering under warded Datalog$^\exists$ with piece-wise linear recursion is NLogSpace-complete in data complexity, and PSpace-complete in combined complexity, which provides a definite answer to our first question. This is a rather involved result that heavily relies on a novel notion of resolution-based proof tree, which is of independent interest. In particular, we show that ontological query answering under warded Datalog$^\exists$ with piece-wise linear recursion boils down to the problem of checking whether a proof tree that enjoys certain properties exists, which in turn can be done via a space-bounded non-deterministic algorithm. Interestingly, our machinery allows us to re-establish the complexity of ontological query answering under warded Datalog$^\exists$ via an algorithm that is significantly simpler than the one employed in [17]. This algorithm is essentially the non-determinisitc algorithm for piece-wise linear warded Datalog$^\exists$ with the crucial difference that it employs alternation.
(2) To our surprise, ontological query answering under piece-wise linear Datalog$^\exists$, without the wardedness condition, is undecidable. This result, which is shown via a reduction from the unbounded tiling problem, provides a definite answer to our second question: the combination of wardedness and piece-wise linearity is indeed justified.
(3) We finally investigate the relative expressive power of the query language based on warded Datalog$^\exists$ with piece-wise linear recursion, which consists of all the queries of the form $Q = (\Sigma, q)$, where Σ is a warded set of TGDs with piece-wise linear recursion, and q is a conjunctive query, while the evaluation of Q over a database D is precisely the certain answers to q w.r.t. D and Σ. By exploiting our novel notion of proof tree, we show that it is equally expressive to piece-wise linear Datalog. The same approach allows us to elucidate the relative expressiveness of the query language based on warded Datalog$^\exists$ (with arbitrary recursion), showing that it is equally expressive to Datalog. We also adopt the more refined notion of program expressive power, introduced in [2], which aims at the decoupling of the set of TGDs and the actual conjunctive query, and show that the query language based on warded Datalog$^\exists$ (with piece-wise linear recursion) is strictly more expressive than Datalog (with piece-wise linear recursion). This exposes the advantage of value invention that is available in Datalog$^\exists$-based languages.

2 PRELIMINARIES

Basics. We consider the disjoint countably infinite sets **C**, **N**, and **V** of *constants*, *(labeled) nulls*, and *variables*, respectively. The elements of $(\mathbf{C} \cup \mathbf{N} \cup \mathbf{V})$ are called *terms*. An *atom* is an expression of the form $R(\bar{t})$, where R is an n-ary predicate, and $\bar{t}$ is an n-tuple of terms. We write $\text{var}(\alpha)$ for the set of variables in an atom α; this notation extends to sets of atoms. A *fact* is an atom that contains only constants. A *substitution* from a set of terms T to a set of terms T' is a function $h \colon T \rightarrow T'$. The restriction of h to a subset S of T, denoted $h_{|S}$, is the substitution $\{t \mapsto h(t) \mid t \in S\}$. A *homomorphism* from a set of atoms A to a set of atoms B is a substitution h from the set of terms in A to the set of terms

[5] The idea of combining wardedness with piece-wise linearity has been already mentioned in the invited paper [6], while the obtained formalism is called strongly warded.

in B such that h is the identity on $\mathbf{C}$, and $R(t_1, \ldots, t_n) \in A$ implies $h(R(t_1, \ldots, t_n)) = R(h(t_1), \ldots, h(t_n)) \in B$. We write $h(A)$ for the set of atoms $\{h(\alpha) \mid \alpha \in A\}$. For brevity, we may write $[n]$ for the set $\{1, \ldots, n\}$, where $n \geq 0$.

Relational Databases. A *schema* $\mathbf{S}$ is a finite set of relation symbols (or predicates), each having an associated *arity*. We write R/n to denote that R has arity $n \geq 0$. A *position* $R[i]$ in $\mathbf{S}$, where $R/n \in \mathbf{S}$ and $i \in [n]$, identifies the i-th argument of R. An *instance* over $\mathbf{S}$ is a (possibly infinite) set of atoms over $\mathbf{S}$ that contain constants and nulls, while a *database* over $\mathbf{S}$ is a finite set of facts over $\mathbf{S}$. The *active domain* of an instance I, denoted $\mathsf{dom}(I)$, is the set of all terms occurring in I.

Conjunctive Queries. A *conjunctive query* (CQ) over $\mathbf{S}$ is a first-order formula of the form

$$q(\bar{x}) \;:=\; \exists \bar{y}\,(R_1(\bar{z}_1) \wedge \cdots \wedge R_n(\bar{z}_n)),$$

where each $R_i(\bar{z}_i)$, for $i \in [n]$, is an atom without nulls over $\mathbf{S}$, each variable mentioned in the $\bar{z}_i$'s appears either in $\bar{x}$ or $\bar{y}$, and $\bar{x}$ are the *output variables* of q. For convenience, we adopt the rule-based syntax of CQs, i.e., a CQ as the one above will be written as the rule

$$Q(\bar{x}) \;\leftarrow\; R_1(\bar{z}_1), \ldots, R_n(\bar{z}_n),$$

where Q is a predicate used only in the head of CQs. Let $\mathsf{atoms}(q) = \{R_1(\bar{z}_1), \ldots, R_n(\bar{z}_n)\}$. The *evaluation* of $q(\bar{x})$ over an instance I, denoted $q(I)$, is the set of all tuples $h(\bar{x})$ of constants, where h is a homomorphism from $\mathsf{atoms}(q)$ to I.

Tuple-Generating Dependencies. A *tuple-generating dependency* (TGD) σ is a first-order sentence

$$\forall \bar{x} \forall \bar{y}\,(\phi(\bar{x}, \bar{y}) \rightarrow \exists \bar{z}\,\psi(\bar{x}, \bar{z})),$$

where $\bar{x}, \bar{y}, \bar{z}$ are tuples of variables of $\mathbf{V}$, and ϕ, ψ are conjunctions of atoms without constants and nulls. For brevity, we write σ as $\phi(\bar{x}, \bar{y}) \rightarrow \exists \bar{z}\,\psi(\bar{x}, \bar{z})$, and use comma instead of $\wedge$ for joining atoms. We refer to ϕ and ψ as the *body* and *head* of σ, denoted $\mathsf{body}(\sigma)$ and $\mathsf{head}(\sigma)$, respectively. The *frontier* of the TGD σ, denoted $\mathsf{front}(\sigma)$, is the set of variables that appear both in the body and the head of σ. We also write $\mathsf{var}_{\exists}(\sigma)$ for the existentially quantified variables of σ. The schema of a set Σ of TGDs, denoted $\mathsf{sch}(\Sigma)$, is the set of predicates in Σ. An instance I satisfies a TGD σ as the one above, written $I \models \sigma$, if the following holds: whenever there exists a homomorphism h such that $h(\phi(\bar{x}, \bar{y})) \subseteq I$, then there exists $h' \supseteq h_{|\bar{x}}$ such that $h'(\psi(\bar{x}, \bar{z})) \subseteq I$.[6] The instance I satisfies a set Σ of TGDs, written $I \models \Sigma$, if $I \models \sigma$ for each $\sigma \in \Sigma$.

Query Answering under TGDs. The main reasoning task under TGD-based languages is *conjunctive query answering*. Given a database D and a set Σ of TGDs, a *model* of D and Σ is an instance I such that $I \supseteq D$ and $I \models \Sigma$. Let $\mathsf{mods}(D, \Sigma)$ be the set of all models of D and Σ. The *certain answers* to a CQ q w.r.t. D and Σ is

$$\mathsf{cert}(q, D, \Sigma) \;:=\; \bigcap \{q(I) \mid I \in \mathsf{mods}(D, \Sigma)\}.$$

Our main task is to compute the certain answers to a CQ w.r.t. a database and a set of TGDs from a certain class C of TGDs; concrete classes of TGDs are discussed below. As is customary when studying the complexity of this problem, we focus on its decision version:

PROBLEM :	CQAns(C)
INPUT :	A database D, a set $\Sigma \in \mathsf{C}$ of TGDs, a CQ $q(\bar{x})$, and a tuple $\bar{c} \in \mathsf{dom}(D)^{\lvert\bar{x}\rvert}$.
QUESTION :	Is it the case that $\bar{c} \in \mathsf{cert}(q, D, \Sigma)$?

We consider the standard complexity measures: *combined complexity* and *data complexity*, where the latter measures the complexity of the problem assuming that the set of TGDs and the CQ are fixed.

A useful algorithmic tool for tackling the above problem is the well-known *chase procedure*; see, e.g., [10, 15, 19, 23]. We start by defining a single chase step. Let I be an instance and $\sigma = \phi(\bar{x}, \bar{y}) \rightarrow \exists \bar{z}\,\psi(\bar{x}, \bar{z})$ a TGD. We say that σ is *applicable* w.r.t. I if there exists a homomorphism h such that $h(\phi(\bar{x}, \bar{y})) \subseteq I$. In this case, *the result of applying σ over I with h* is the instance $J = I \cup \{h'(\psi(\bar{x}, \bar{z}))\}$, where $h'(z)$ is a fresh null not occurring in I, for every $z \in \bar{z}$. Such a single chase step is denoted $I\langle\sigma, h\rangle J$. Consider now an instance I, and a set Σ of TGDs. A *chase sequence for I under Σ* is a sequence $(I_i\langle\sigma_i, h_i\rangle I_{i+1})_{i \geq 0}$ of chase steps such that: (1) $I = I_0$; (2) for each $i \geq 0$, $\sigma_i \in \Sigma$; and (3) $\bigcup_{i \geq 0} I_i \models \Sigma$. We call $\bigcup_{i \geq 0} I_i$ the *result* of this chase sequence, which always exists. Although the result of a chase sequence is not necessarily unique (up to isomorphism), each such result is equally useful for query answering purposes, since it can be homomorphically embedded into every other result. Hence, we denote by $\mathsf{chase}(I, \Sigma)$ the result of an arbitrary chase sequence for I under Σ. The following is a classical result:

Proposition 2.1. *Given a database D, a set Σ of TGDs, and a CQ q, $\mathsf{cert}(q, D, \Sigma) = q(\mathsf{chase}(D, \Sigma))$.*

3 THE LOGICAL CORE OF VADALOG

A crucial component of the Vadalog system is its reasoning engine, which in turn is built around the Vadalog language, a general-purpose formalism for knowledge representation and reasoning. The logical core of this language is the well-behaved class of warded sets of TGDs [3, 17].

An Intuitive Description. Wardedness applies a syntactic restriction on how certain "dangerous" variables of a set of TGDs are used. These are body variables that can be unified

[6] By abuse of notation, we sometimes treat a tuple of variables as a set of variables, and a conjunction of atoms as a set of atoms.

with a null during the chase, and that are also propagated to the head. For example, given

$$P(x) \rightarrow \exists z\, R(x,z) \quad \text{and} \quad R(x,y) \rightarrow P(y)$$

the variable y in the body of the second TGD is dangerous. Indeed, once the chase applies the first TGD, an atom of the form $R(\_, \perp)$ is generated, where $\perp$ is a null value, and then the second TGD is triggered with the variable y being unified with $\perp$ that is propagated to the obtained atom $P(\perp)$. It has been observed that the liberal use of dangerous variables leads to a prohibitively high computational complexity of the main reasoning tasks, in particular of CQ answering [10]. The main goal of wardedness is to limit the use of dangerous variables with the aim of taming the way that null values are propagated during the execution of the chase procedure. This is achieved by posing the following conditions:

(1) all the dangerous variables should appear together in a single body atom α, called a ward, and
(2) α can share only harmless variables with the rest of the body, i.e., variables that unify only with constants.

We proceed to formalize the above description.

The Formal Definition. We first need some auxiliary notions. The set of positions of a schema S, denoted pos(S), is defined as $\{R[i] \mid R/n \in \mathrm{S}, \text{ with } n \geq 1, \text{ and } i \in [n]\}$. Given a set Σ of TGDs, we write pos(Σ) instead of pos(sch(Σ)). The set of *affected positions* of sch(Σ), denoted aff(Σ), is inductively defined as follows:

- if there exists $\sigma \in \Sigma$ and a variable $x \in \mathsf{var}_{\exists}(\sigma)$ at position π, then $\pi \in \mathsf{aff}(\Sigma)$, and
- if there exists $\sigma \in \Sigma$ and a variable $x \in \mathsf{front}(\sigma)$ in the body of σ only at positions of aff(Σ), and x appears in the head of σ at position π, then $\pi \in \mathsf{aff}(\Sigma)$.

Let $\mathsf{nonaff}(\Sigma) = \mathsf{pos}(\Sigma) \setminus \mathsf{aff}(\Sigma)$. We can now classify the variables in the body of a TGD into harmless, harmful, and dangerous. Fix a TGD $\sigma \in \Sigma$ and a variable x in body(σ):

- x is *harmless* if at least one occurrence of it appears in body(σ) at a position of nonaff(Σ),
- x is *harmful* if it is not harmless, and
- x is *dangerous* if it is harmful and belongs to front(σ).

We are now ready to formally introduce wardedness.

Definition 3.1 (**Wardedness**). A set Σ of TGDs is *warded* if, for each $\sigma \in \Sigma$, there are no dangerous variables in body(σ), or there is an atom $\alpha \in \mathsf{body}(\sigma)$, called a *ward*, such that: (i) all the dangerous variables in body(σ) occur in α, and (ii) each variable of $\mathsf{var}(\alpha) \cap \mathsf{var}(\mathsf{body}(\sigma) \setminus \{\alpha\})$ is harmless. Let WARD be the class of all (finite) warded sets of TGDs. ∎

The problem of CQ answering under warded sets of TGDs has been recently investigated in [3, 17]:

Proposition 3.2. CQAns(WARD) *is* ExpTime-*complete in combined complexity, and* PTime-*complete in data complexity.*

Note that [3, 17] deals only with data complexity. However, the same algorithm provides an ExpTime upper bound in combined complexity. The lower bounds are inherited from Datalog since a set of Datalog rules (seen as TGDs) is warded.

A Key Application. One of the distinctive features of wardedness, which is crucial for the purposes of the Vadalog system, is the fact that it can express every SPARQL query under the OWL 2 QL direct semantics entailment regime, which is inherited from the OWL 2 direct semantics entailment regime; for details, see [2, 17, 22]. Recall that SPARQL is the standard language for querying the Semantic Web,[7] while OWL 2 QL is a prominent profile of OWL 2.[8]

4 LIMITING RECURSION

We now focus on our main research question: can we limit the recursion allowed by wardedness in order to obtain a formalism that provides a convenient syntax for expressing useful recursive statements, and at the same time achieve space-efficiency? The above question has been extensively studied in the 1980s for Datalog programs, with *linear Datalog* being a key fragment that achieves a good balance between expressivity and complexity; see, e.g., [24, 25]. A Datalog program Σ is *linear* if, for each rule in Σ, its body contains at most one intensional predicate, i.e., a predicate that appears in the head of at least one rule of Σ. In other words, linear Datalog allows only for linear recursion, which is able to express many real-life recursive queries. However, for our purposes, linear recursion does not provide the convenient syntax that we are aiming at. After analyzing several real-life examples of warded sets of TGDs, provided by our industrial partners, we observed that the employed recursion goes beyond linear recursion. On the other hand, most of the examples coming from our industrial partners use recursion in a restrictive way: each TGD has at most one body atom whose predicate is mutually recursive with a predicate occurring in the head of the TGD. Interestingly, this more liberal version of linear recursion has been already investigated in the context of Datalog, and it is known as *piece-wise linear*, see, e.g., [1]. Does this type of recursion lead to the space-efficient fragment of warded sets of TGDs that we are looking for? The rest of this section is devoted to showing this rather involved result.

Let us start by formally defining the class of piece-wise linear sets of TGDs. To this end, we need to define when two predicates are mutually recursive, which in turn relies on the well-known notion of the predicate graph. The *predicate graph* of a set Σ of TGDs, denoted pg(Σ), is a directed graph

[7] http://www.w3.org/TR/rdf-sparql-query
[8] https://www.w3.org/TR/owl2-overview/

(V, E), where $V = \mathsf{sch}(\Sigma)$, and there exists an edge from a predicate P to a predicate R, i.e., $(P, R) \in E$, iff there exists a TGD $\sigma \in \Sigma$ such that P occurs in $\mathsf{body}(\sigma)$ and R occurs in $\mathsf{head}(\sigma)$. Two predicates $P, R \in \mathsf{sch}(\Sigma)$ are *mutually recursive* (w.r.t. Σ) if there exists a cycle in $\mathsf{pg}(\Sigma)$ that contains both P and R (i.e., R is reachable from P, and vice versa). We are now ready to define piece-wise linearity for TGDs.

Definition 4.1 (**Piece-wise Linearity**). A set Σ of TGDs is *piece-wise linear* if, for each TGD $\sigma \in \Sigma$, there exists at most one atom in $\mathsf{body}(\sigma)$ whose predicate is mutually recursive with a predicate in $\mathsf{head}(\sigma)$. We write PWL for the class of (finite) piece-wise linear sets of TGDs. ∎

The main result of this section follows:

THEOREM 4.2. $\mathsf{CQAns}(\mathsf{WARD} \cap \mathsf{PWL})$ *is* PSPACE-*complete in combined, and* NLOGSPACE-*complete in data complexity.*

The lower bounds are inherited from linear Datalog. The difficult task is to establish the upper bounds. This relies on a novel notion of proof tree, which is of independent interest. As we shall see, our notion of proof tree leads to space-bounded algorithms that allow us to show the upper bounds in Theorem 4.2, and also re-establish in a transparent way the upper bounds in Proposition 3.2. Moreover, in Section 6, we are going to use proof trees for studying the relative expressive power of (piece-wise linear) warded sets of TGDs.

4.1 Query Answering via Proof Trees

It is known that given a CQ q and a set Σ of TGDs, we can unfold q using the TGDs of Σ into an infinite union of CQs q_Σ such that, for every database D, $\mathsf{cert}(q, D, \Sigma) = q_\Sigma(D)$; see, e.g., [16, 21]. Let us clarify that in our context, an unfolding, which is essentially a resolution step, is more complex than in the context of Datalog due to the existentially quantified variables in the head of TGDs. The intention underlying our notion of proof tree is to encode in a tree the sequence of CQs, generated during the unfolding of q with Σ, that leads to a certain CQ q' of q_Σ in such a way that each intermediate CQ, as well as q', is carefully decomposed into smaller subqueries that form the nodes of the tree, while the root corresponds to q and the leaves to q'. As we shall see, if we focus on well-behaved classes of TGDs such as (piece-wise linear) warded sets of TGDs, we can establish upper bounds on the size of these subqueries, which in turn allow us to devise space-bounded algorithms for query answering. In what follows, we define the notion of proof tree (Definition 4.7), and establish its correspondence with query answering (Theorem 4.8). To this end, we need to introduce the main building blocks of a proof tree: chunk-based resolution (Definition 4.3), a query decomposition technique (Definition 4.5), and the notion of specialization for CQs (Definition 4.6).

Chunk-based Resolution. Let A and B be non-empty sets of atoms that mention only constants and variables. The sets A and B *unify* if there is a substitution γ, which is the identity on $\mathbf{C}$, called *unifier for A and B*, such that $\gamma(A) = \gamma(B)$. A *most general unifier* (MGU) for A and B is a unifier for A and B, denoted $\gamma_{A,B}$, such that, for each unifier γ for A and B, $\gamma = \gamma' \circ \gamma_{A,B}$ for some substitution γ'. Notice that if two sets of atoms unify, then there exists always a MGU, which is unique (modulo variable renaming).

Given a CQ $q(\bar{x})$ and a set of atoms $S \subseteq \mathsf{atoms}(q)$, we say that a variable $y \in \mathsf{var}(S)$ is *shared*, if $y \in \bar{x}$ or $y \in \mathsf{var}(\mathsf{atoms}(q) \setminus S)$. A *chunk unifier* of q with a TGD σ (where q and σ do not share variables) is a triple (S_1, S_2, γ), where $\emptyset \subset S_1 \subseteq \mathsf{atoms}(q)$, $\emptyset \subset S_2 \subseteq \mathsf{head}(\sigma)$, and γ is a unifier for S_1 and S_2 such that, for each $x \in \mathsf{var}(S_2) \cap \mathsf{var}_\exists(\sigma)$,

1. $\gamma(x) \notin \mathbf{C}$, i.e., $\gamma(x)$ is not constant, and
2. for every variable y different from x, $\gamma(x) = \gamma(y)$ implies y occurs in S_1 and is not shared.

The chunk unifier (S_1, S_2, γ) is *most general* (MGCU) if γ is an MGU for S_1 and S_2. Notice that the variables of $\mathsf{var}_\exists(\sigma)$ occurring in S_2 unify (via γ) only with non-shared variables of S_1. This ensures that S_1 is a "chunk" of q that can be resolved as a whole via σ using γ.[9] Without the additional conditions on the substitution γ, we may get unsound resolution steps. Consider, e.g., the CQ and TGD

$$Q(x) \leftarrow R(x, y), S(y) \quad \text{and} \quad P(x') \rightarrow \exists y'\, R(x', y').$$

Resolving the atom $R(x, y)$ in the query with the given TGD using $\gamma = \{x \mapsto x', y \mapsto y'\}$ would be an unsound step since the shared variable y is lost. This is because y' is unified with the shared variable y. On the other hand, $R(x, y), S(y)$ can be resolved with the TGD $\sigma = P(x') \rightarrow \exists y'\, R(x', y'), S(y')$ using γ; in fact, the chunk unifier is $(\mathsf{atoms}(q), \mathsf{head}(\sigma), \gamma)$.

Definition 4.3 (**Chunk-based Resolution**). Let $q(\bar{x})$ be a CQ and σ a TGD. A *σ-resolvent* of q is a CQ $q'(\gamma(\bar{x}))$ with $\mathsf{body}(q') = \gamma((\mathsf{atoms}(q) \setminus S_1) \cup \mathsf{body}(\sigma))$ for a MGCU (S_1, S_2, γ) of q with σ. ∎

Query Decomposition. As discussed above, the purpose of a proof tree is to encode a finite branch of the unfolding of a CQ q with a set Σ of TGDs, which is obtained by applying chunk-based resolution. Such a branch is a sequence $q_0, \ldots, q_n$ of CQs, where $q = q_0$, while, for each $i \in [n]$, q_i is a σ-resolvent of q_{i-1} for some $\sigma \in \Sigma$. Here is a simple example, which will serve as a running example in the rest of the section, that illustrates the notion of unfolding.

Example 4.4. Consider the set Σ of TGDs consisting of

$$R(x) \quad \rightarrow \quad \exists y\, T(y, x)$$

[9] A similar notion known as piece unifier has been defined in [21].

$$T(x,y), S(y,z) \rightarrow T(x,z)$$
$$T(x,y), P(y) \rightarrow G()$$

and the CQ that simply asks whether $G()$ is entailed, i.e., the CQ $Q \leftarrow G()$. Since the unfolding of q with Σ should give the correct answer for *every* input database, and thus for databases of the form

$$\{R(c^{n-1}), S(c^{n-1}, c^{n-2}), \ldots, S(c^2, c^1), P(c^1)\} \quad \text{for some } n > 1,$$

one of its branches should be $q = q_0, q_1, \ldots, q_n$, where

$$q_1 = Q \leftarrow T(x, y^1), P(y^1)$$

obtained by resolving q_0 using the third TGD,

$$q_i = Q \leftarrow T(x, y^i), S(y^i, y^{i-1}), \ldots, S(y^2, y^1), P(y^1),$$

for $i \in \{2, \ldots, n-1\}$, obtained by resolving q_{i-1} using the second TGD, and finally

$$q_n = Q \leftarrow R(y^{n-1}), S(y^{n-1}, y^{n-2}), \ldots, S(y^2, y^1), P(y^1)$$

obtained by resolving q_{n-1} using the first TGD. ∎

At this point, one may think that the proof tree that encodes the branch $q_0, \ldots, q_n$ of the unfolding of q with Σ is the finite labeled path $v_0, \ldots, v_n$, where each v_i is labeled by q_i. However, another crucial goal of such a proof tree, which is not achieved via the naive path encoding, is to split each resolvent q_i, for $i > 0$, into smaller subqueries $q_i^1, \ldots, q_i^{n_i}$, which are essentially the children of q_i, in such a way that they can be processed independently by resolution. The crux of this encoding is that it provides us with a mechanism for keeping the CQs that must be processed by resolution small. It should be clear from Example 4.4 that by following the naive path encoding, without splitting the resolvents into smaller subqueries, we may get CQs of unbounded size.

The key question here is how a CQ q can be decomposed into subqueries that can be processed independently. The subtlety is that, after splitting q, occurrences of the same variable may be separated into different subqueries. Thus, we need a way to ensure that a variable in q, which appears in different subqueries after the splitting, is indeed treated as the same variable, i.e., it has the same meaning. We deal with this issue by restricting the set of variables in q of which occurrences can be separated during the splitting step. In particular, we can only separate occurrences of an output variable. This relies on the convention that output variables correspond to fixed constant values of **C**, and thus their name is "frozen" and never renamed by subsequent resolution steps. Hence, we can separate occurrences of an output variable into different subqueries, i.e., different branches of the proof tree, without losing the connection between them.

Summing up, the idea underlying query decomposition is to split the CQ at hand into smaller queries that keep together all the occurrences of a non-output variable, but with the freedom of separating occurrences of an output variable.

Definition 4.5 (**Query Decomposition**). Given a CQ $q(\bar{x})$, a *decomposition* of q is a set of CQs $\{q_1(\bar{y}_1), \ldots, q_n(\bar{y}_n)\}$, where $n \geq 1$ and $\bigcup_{i \in [n]} \mathsf{atoms}(q_i) = \mathsf{atoms}(q)$, such that, for each $i \in [n]$: (1) $\bar{y}_i$ is the restriction of $\bar{x}$ on the variables in q_i, and (2) for every $\alpha, \beta \in \mathsf{atoms}(q)$, if $\alpha \in \mathsf{atoms}(q_i)$ and $\mathsf{var}(\alpha) \cap \mathsf{var}(\beta) \not\subseteq \bar{x}$, then $\beta \in \mathsf{atoms}(q_i)$. ∎

Query Specialization. From the above discussion, one expects that a proof tree of a CQ q w.r.t. a set Σ of TGDs can be constructed by starting from q, which is the root, and applying two steps: resolution and decomposition. Unfortunately, this is not enough for our purposes as we may run into the following problem: some of the subqueries will mistakenly remain large since we have no way to realize that a non-output variable corresponds to a fixed constant value, which in turn allows us to "freeze" its name and separate different occurrences of it during the decomposition step. This is illustrated by Example 4.4. Observe that the size of the CQs $\{q_i\}_{i>0}$ grows arbitrarily, while our query decomposition has no effect on them since they are Boolean queries, i.e., queries without output variables, and thus, we cannot split them into smaller subqueries. The above issue can be solved by having an intermediate step between resolution and decomposition, the so-called specialization step. A specialization of a CQ is obtained by converting some non-output variables of it into output variables, while keeping their name, or taking the name of an existing output variable.

Definition 4.6 (**Query Specialization**). Let $q(\bar{x})$ be a CQ with $\mathsf{atoms}(q) = \{\alpha_1, \ldots, \alpha_n\}$. A *specialization* of q is a CQ

$$Q(\bar{x}, \bar{y}) \leftarrow \rho_{\bar{z}}(\alpha_1, \ldots, \alpha_n)$$

where $\bar{y}, \bar{z}$ are (possibly empty) disjoint tuples of non-output variables of q, and $\rho_{\bar{z}}$ is a substitution from $\bar{z}$ to $\bar{x} \cup \bar{y}$. ∎

Consider, for example, the CQ q_1 from Example 4.4

$$Q \leftarrow T(x, y^1), P(y^1)$$

obtained by resolving $q = q_0$ using the third TGD. The query decomposition cannot split it onto smaller subqueries since the variable y^1 is a non-output variable, and thus, all its occurrences should be kept together. We can consider the following specialization of q_1

$$Q(y^1) \leftarrow T(x, y^1), P(y^1),$$

which simply converts y^1 into an output variable, and now by query decomposition we can split it into the atomic queries

$$Q(y^1) \leftarrow T(x, y^1) \qquad Q(y^1) \leftarrow P(y^1),$$

which represent the original query q_1.

Proof Trees. We are now ready to introduce our new notion of proof tree. We first explain the high-level idea by exploiting our running example. Consider the set Σ of TGDs and the CQ q from Example 4.4. The branch $q_0, \ldots, q_n$ of the

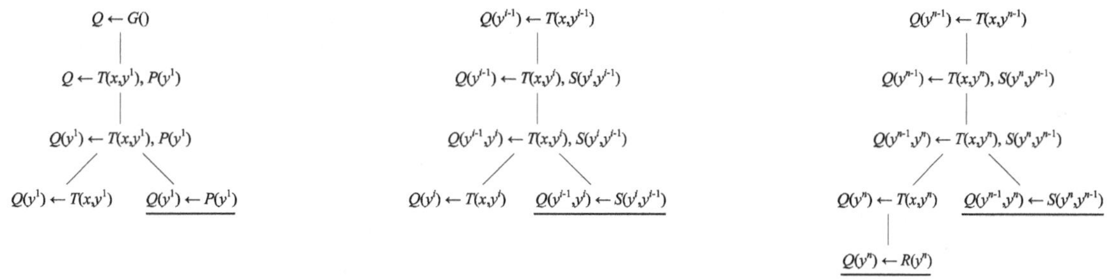

Figure 1: Partial trees of the proof tree that encodes the branch $q = q_0, \dots, q_n$ of the unfolding of q with Σ from Example 4.4.

unfolding of q with Σ given in Example 4.4 is encoded via a proof tree of the form

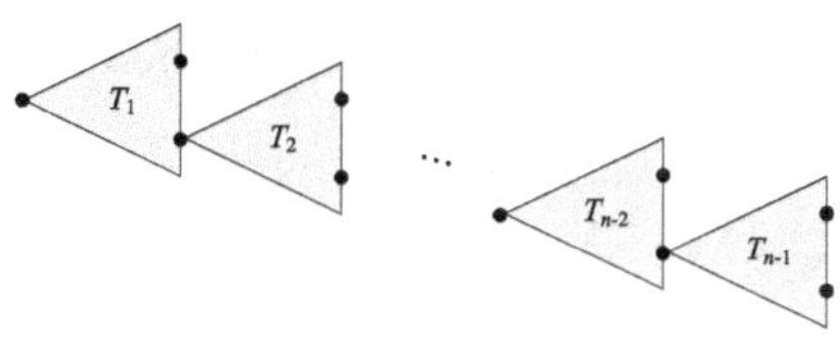

where each T_i, for $i \in [n-1]$, is a rooted tree with only two leaf nodes. The actual trees are depicted in Figure 1; the left one is T_1, the middle one is T_i for $i \in \{2, \dots, n-2\}$, while the right one is T_{n-1}. For each $i \in [n-1]$, the child of the root of T_i is obtained via resolution, then we specialize it by converting the variable y^i into an output variable, and then we decompose the specialized CQ into two subqueries. In T_{n-1}, we also apply an additional resolution step in order to obtain the leaf node $Q(y^{n-1}) \leftarrow R(y^{n-1})$. The underlined CQs are actually the subqueries that represent the CQ q_n of the unfolding. Indeed, the conjunction of the atoms occurring in the underlined CQs is precisely the CQ q_n.

We proceed to give the formal definition. Given a partition $\pi = \{S_1, \dots, S_m\}$ of a set of variables, we write eq_π for the substitution that maps the variables of S_i to the same variable x_i, where x_i is a distinguished element of S_i. We should not forget the convention that output variables cannot be renamed, and thus, a resolution step should use a MGCU that preserves the output variables. In particular, given a CQ q and a TGD σ, a σ-resolvent of q is called *IDO* if the underlying MGCU uses a substitution that is the identity on the output variables of q (hence the name IDO). Finally, given a TGD σ and some arbitrary object o (e.g., o can be the node of a tree, or an integer number), we write σ_o for the TGD obtained by renaming each variable x in σ into x_o. This is a simple mechanism for uniformly renaming the variables of a TGD in order to avoid undesirable clatter among variables during a resolution step.

Definition 4.7 (**Proof Tree**). Let $q(\bar{x})$ be a CQ with $\mathsf{atoms}(q) = \{\alpha_1, \dots, \alpha_n\}$, and Σ a set of TGDs. A *proof tree* of q w.r.t. Σ is a triple $\mathcal{P} = (T, \lambda, \pi)$, where $T = (V, E)$ is a finite rooted tree, λ a labeling function that assigns a CQ to each node of T, and π a partition of $\bar{x}$, such that, for $v \in V$:

(1) If v is the root node of T, then $\lambda(v)$ is the CQ $Q(\mathsf{eq}_\pi(\bar{x})) \leftarrow \mathsf{eq}_\pi(\alpha_1, \dots, \alpha_m)$.
(2) If v has only one child u, $\lambda(u)$ is an IDO σ_v-resolvent of $\lambda(v)$ for some $\sigma \in \Sigma$, or a specialization of $\lambda(v)$.
(3) If v has the children $u_1, \dots, u_k$ for $k > 1$, then $\{\lambda(u_1), \dots, \lambda(u_k)\}$ is a decomposition of $\lambda(v)$.

Assuming that $v_1, \dots, v_m$ are the leaf nodes of T, the *CQ induced by* $\mathcal{P}$ is defined as

$$Q(\mathsf{eq}_\pi(\bar{x})) \leftarrow \alpha_1, \dots, \alpha_\ell,$$

where $\{\alpha_1, \dots, \alpha_\ell\} = \bigcup_{i \in [m]} \mathsf{atoms}(\lambda(v_i))$. ■

The purpose of the partition π is to indicate that some output variables correspond to the same constant value – this is why variables in the same set of π are unified via the substitution eq_π. This unification step is crucial in order to safely use, in subsequent resolution steps, substitutions that are the identity on the output variables. If we omit this initial unification step, we may lose important resolution steps, and thus being incomplete for query answering purposes. The main result of this section, which exposes the connection between proof trees and CQ answering, follows. By abuse of notation, we write $\mathcal{P}$ for the CQ induced by $\mathcal{P}$.

Theorem 4.8. *Consider a database D, a set Σ of TGDs, a CQ $q(\bar{x})$, and $\bar{c} \in \mathsf{dom}(D)^{|\bar{x}|}$. The following are equivalent:*

(1) $\bar{c} \in \mathsf{cert}(q, D, \Sigma)$.
(2) There is a proof tree $\mathcal{P}$ of q w.r.t. Σ such that $\bar{c} \in \mathcal{P}(D)$.

The proof of the above result relies on the soundness and completeness of chunk-based resolution. Given a set Σ of TGDs and a CQ $q(\bar{x})$, by exhaustively applying chunk-based resolution, we can construct a (possibly infinite) union of CQs q_Σ such that, for every database D, $\mathsf{cert}(q, D, \Sigma) = q_\Sigma(D)$; implicit in [16, 21]. In other words, given a tuple $\bar{c} \in \mathsf{dom}(D)^{|\bar{x}|}$, $\bar{c} \in \mathsf{cert}(q, D, \Sigma)$ iff there exists a CQ $q'(\bar{x})$ in q_Σ such that $\bar{c} \in q'(D)$. It is now not difficult to show that the latter statement is equivalent to the existence of a proof tree $\mathcal{P}$ of q w.r.t. Σ such that $\bar{c} \in \mathcal{P}(D)$, and the claim follows.

4.2 Well-behaved Proof Trees

Theorem 4.8 states that checking whether a tuple $\bar{c}$ is a certain answer boils down to deciding whether there exists a proof tree $\mathcal{P}$ such that $\bar{c}$ is an answer to the CQ induced by $\mathcal{P}$ over the given database. Of course, the latter is an undecidable problem in general. However, if we focus on (piece-wise linear) warded sets of TGDs, it suffices to check for the existence of a well-behaved proof tree with certain syntactic properties, which in turn allows us to devise a decision procedure. We proceed to make this more precise. For technical clarity, we assume, w.l.o.g., TGDs with only one atom in the head since we can always convert a warded set of TGDs into one with single-atom heads, while certain answers are preserved; for the transformation see, e.g., [12].

Piece-wise Linear Warded Sets of TGDs. For piece-wise linear warded sets of TGDs, we can strengthen Theorem 4.8 by focussing on a certain class of proof trees that enjoy two syntactic properties: (i) they have a path-like structure, and (ii) the size of the CQs that label their nodes is bounded by a polynomial. The first property is formalized via linear proof trees. Let $\mathcal{P} = (T, \lambda, \pi)$, where $T = (V, E)$, be a proof tree of a CQ q w.r.t. a set Σ of TGDs. We call $\mathcal{P}$ *linear* if, for each node $v \in V$, there exists at most one node $u \in V$ such that $(v, u) \in E$ and u is not a leaf in T, i.e., v has at most one child that is not a leaf. For example, the proof tree given above, which consists of the partial trees depicted in Figure 1, is linear. The second property relies on the notion of node-width of a proof tree. The *node-width* of $\mathcal{P}$ is

$$\mathsf{nwd}(\mathcal{P}) \ := \ \max_{v \in V}\{|\lambda(v)|\},$$

i.e., the size of the largest CQ that labels a node of T.

Before we strengthen Theorem 4.8, let us define the polynomial that will allow us to bound the node-width of the linear proof trees that we need to consider. This polynomial relies on the notion of predicate level. Consider a set Σ of TGDs. For a predicate $P \in \mathsf{sch}(\Sigma)$, we write $\mathsf{rec}(P)$ for the set of predicates of $\mathsf{sch}(\Sigma)$ that are mutually recursive to P according to $\mathsf{pg}(\Sigma) = (V, E)$. Let $\ell_\Sigma : \mathsf{sch}(\Sigma) \longrightarrow \mathbb{N}$ be the unique function that satisfies

$$\ell_\Sigma(P) \ = \ \max\{\ell_\Sigma(R) \mid (R, P) \in E, R \notin \mathsf{rec}(P)\} + 1,$$

with $\ell_\Sigma(P)$ being the *level* (w.r.t. Σ) of P, for each $P \in \mathsf{sch}(\Sigma)$. We define the polynomial

$$f_{\mathsf{WARD} \cap \mathsf{PWL}}(q, \Sigma) := (|q| + 1) \cdot \max_{P \in \mathsf{sch}(\Sigma)}\{\ell_\Sigma(P)\} \cdot \max_{\sigma \in \Sigma}\{|\mathsf{body}(\sigma)|\}.$$

We can now strengthen Theorem 4.8. Let us first clarify that, in the case of piece-wise linear warded sets of TGDs, apart from only one atom in the head, we also assume, w.l.o.g., that the level of a predicate in the body of TGD σ is k or $k - 1$, where k is the level of the predicate in the head of σ.

Theorem 4.9. *Consider a database D, a set $\Sigma \in \mathsf{WARD} \cap \mathsf{PWL}$ of TGDs, a CQ $q(\bar{x})$, and $\bar{c} \in \mathsf{dom}(D)^{|\bar{x}|}$. The following are equivalent:*

(1) $\bar{c} \in \mathsf{cert}(q, D, \Sigma)$.
(2) There is a linear proof tree $\mathcal{P}$ of q w.r.t. Σ with $\mathsf{nwd}(\mathcal{P}) \leq f_{\mathsf{WARD} \cap \mathsf{PWL}}(q, \Sigma)$ such that $\bar{c} \in \mathcal{P}(D)$.

Warded sets of TGDs. Now, in the case of arbitrary warded sets of TGDs, we cannot focus only on linear proof trees. Nevertheless, we can still bound the node-width of the proof trees that we need to consider by the following polynomial, which, unsurprisingly, does not rely anymore on the notion of predicate level:

$$f_{\mathsf{WARD}}(q, \Sigma) := 2 \cdot \max\left\{|q|, \max_{\sigma \in \Sigma}\{|\mathsf{body}(\sigma)|\}\right\}.$$

Theorem 4.8 can be strengthened as follows:

Theorem 4.10. *Consider a database D, a set $\Sigma \in \mathsf{WARD}$ of TGDs, a CQ $q(\bar{x})$, and $\bar{c} \in \mathsf{dom}(D)^{|\bar{x}|}$. The following are equivalent:*

(1) $\bar{c} \in \mathsf{cert}(q, D, \Sigma)$.
(2) There exists a proof tree $\mathcal{P}$ of q w.r.t. Σ with $\mathsf{nwd}(\mathcal{P}) \leq f_{\mathsf{WARD}}(q, \Sigma)$ such that $\bar{c} \in \mathcal{P}(D)$.

A Proof Sketch. Let us now provide some details on how Theorems 4.9 and 4.10 are shown. For both theorems, (2) implies (1) readily follows from Theorem 4.8. We thus focus on the other direction. The main ingredients of the proof can be described as follows:

- We introduce the auxiliary notion of chase tree, which can be seen as a concrete instantiation of a proof tree. It serves as an intermediate structure between proof trees and chase derivations, which allows us to use the chase as our underlying technical tool. Note that the notions of linearity and node-width can be naturally defined for chase trees.
- We then show that, if the given tuple of constants $\bar{c}$ is a certain answer to the given CQ q w.r.t. the given database D and (piece-wise linear) warded set Σ of TGDs, then there exists a (linear) chase tree for the image of q to $\mathsf{chase}(D, \Sigma)$ such that its node-width respects the bounds given in the above theorems (Lemma 4.12).
- We finally show that the existence of a (linear) chase tree for the image of q to $\mathsf{chase}(D, \Sigma)$ with node-width at most m implies the existence of a (linear) proof tree $\mathcal{P}$ of q w.r.t. Σ with node-width at most m such that $\bar{c} \in \mathcal{P}(D)$ (Lemma 4.13).

Let us make the above description more formal. In order to introduce the notion of chase tree, we first need to recall the notion of chase graph, then introduce the notion of unraveling of the chase graph, and finally introduce the notions of unfolding and decomposition for sets of atoms in the unraveling of the chase graph.

Fix a chase sequence $\delta = (I_i\langle\sigma_i, h_i\rangle I_{i+1})_{i\geq 0}$ for a database D under a set Σ of TGDs. The *chase graph* for D and Σ (w.r.t. δ) is a directed edge-labeled graph $\mathcal{G}^{D,\Sigma} = (V, E, \lambda)$, where $V = \mathsf{chase}(D, \Sigma)$, and an edge (α, β) labeled with (σ_k, h_k) belongs to E iff $\alpha \in h_k(\mathsf{body}(\sigma_k))$ and $\beta \in I_{k+1} \setminus I_k$, for some $k \geq 0$. In other words, α has an edge to β if β is derived using α, and if β is new in the sense that it has not been derived before. Notice that $\mathcal{G}^{D,\Sigma}$ has no directed cycles. Notice also that $\mathcal{G}^{D,\Sigma}$ depends on δ – however, we can assume a fixed sequence δ since, as discussed in Section 2, every chase sequence is equally useful for our purposes.

We now discuss the notion of unraveling of the chase graph; due to space reasons, we keep this discussion informal. Given a set $\Theta \subseteq \mathsf{chase}(D, \Sigma)$, the *unraveling of* $\mathcal{G}^{D,\Sigma}$ *around* Θ is a directed node- and edge-labeled forest $\mathcal{G}^{D,\Sigma}_{\Theta}$ that has a tree for each $\alpha \in \Theta$ whose branches are backward-paths in $\mathcal{G}$ from α to a database atom. Intuitively, $\mathcal{G}^{D,\Sigma}_{\Theta}$ is a forest-like reorganization of the atoms of $\mathsf{chase}(D, \Sigma)$ that are needed to derive Θ. Due to its forest-like shape, it may contain multiple copies of atoms of $\mathsf{chase}(D, \Sigma)$. The edges between nodes are labeled by pairs (σ, h) just like in $\mathcal{G}^{D,\Sigma}$, while the nodes are labeled by atoms and, importantly, the atoms along the paths in $\mathcal{G}^{D,\Sigma}$ may be duplicated and labeled nulls are given new names. We write $U(\mathcal{G}^{D,\Sigma}, \Theta)$ for the set of all atoms that appear as labels in $\mathcal{G}^{D,\Sigma}_{\Theta}$, and $\mathsf{succ}_{\sigma,h}(v)$ for the set of children of a node v of $\mathcal{G}^{D,\Sigma}$ whose incoming edge is labeled with (σ, h). It is important to say that there exists a homomorphism h_Θ that maps Θ to $U(\mathcal{G}^{D,\Sigma}, \Theta)$.

Let us now introduce the notions of unfolding and decomposition. For sets $\Gamma, \Gamma' \subseteq U(\mathcal{G}^{D,\Sigma}, \Theta)$, Γ' *is an unfolding of* Γ, if there are $\alpha \in \Gamma$ and $\beta_1, \ldots, \beta_k \in U(\mathcal{G}^{D,\Sigma}, \Theta)$ such that

(1) $\mathsf{succ}_{\sigma,h}(v) = \{\beta_1, \ldots, \beta_k\}$, for some $\sigma \in \Sigma$ and h, and some node v of $\mathcal{G}^{D,\Sigma}_{\Theta}$ labeled with α,
(2) for every null that occurs in α, either it does not appear in $\Gamma \setminus \{\alpha\}$, or it appears in $\{\beta_1, \ldots, \beta_k\}$, and
(3) $\Gamma' = (\Gamma \setminus \{\alpha\}) \cup \{\beta_1, \ldots, \beta_k\}$.

Let $\Gamma \subseteq U(\mathcal{G}^{D,\Sigma}, \Theta)$ be a non-empty set. A *decomposition* of Γ is a set $\{\Gamma_1, \ldots, \Gamma_n\}$, where $n \geq 1$, of non-empty subsets of Γ such that (i) $\Gamma = \bigcup_{i\in[n]} \Gamma_i$, and (ii) $i \neq j$ implies that Γ_i and Γ_j do not share a labeled null. We can now define the key notion of chase tree:

Definition 4.11 (**Chase Tree**). Consider a database D, a set Σ of TGDs, and a set $\Theta \subseteq \mathsf{chase}(D, \Sigma)$. A *chase tree* for $\Gamma \subseteq U(\mathcal{G}^{D,\Sigma}, \Theta)$ (w.r.t. $\mathcal{G}^{D,\Sigma}_{\Theta}$) is a pair $C = (T, \lambda)$, where $T = (V, E)$ is a finite rooted tree, and λ a labeling function that assigns a subset of $U(\mathcal{G}^{D,\Sigma}, \Theta)$ to each node of T, such that, for each $v \in V$:

(1) If v is the root node of T, then $\lambda(v) = \Gamma$.
(2) If v has only one child u, $\lambda(u)$ is an unfolding of $\lambda(v)$.
(3) If v has children $u_1, \ldots, u_k$ for $k > 1$, then $\{\lambda(u_1), \ldots, \lambda(u_k)\}$ is a decomposition of $\lambda(v)$.
(4) If v is a leaf node, then $\lambda(v) \subseteq D$.

The *node-width* of C is $\mathsf{nwd}(C) := \max_{v\in V}\{|\lambda(v)|\}$. Moreover, we say that C is *linear* if, for each $v \in V$, there exists at most one $u \in V$ such that $(v, u) \in E$ and u is not a leaf. ■

We can now state our auxiliary technical lemmas. In what follows, fix a database D, and a set Σ of TGDs.

Lemma 4.12. *Let* $\Theta \subseteq \mathsf{chase}(D, \Sigma)$ *and* $\Gamma \subseteq U(\mathcal{G}^{D,\Sigma}, \Theta)$*:*

(1) If $\Sigma \in \mathsf{WARD} \cap \mathsf{PWL}$*, then there exists a linear chase tree* C *for* Γ *such that* $\mathsf{nwd}(C) \leq f_{\mathsf{WARD}\cap\mathsf{PWL}}(\Gamma, \Sigma)$.
(2) If $\Sigma \in \mathsf{WARD}$*, then there exists a chase tree* C *for* Γ *such that* $\mathsf{nwd}(C) \leq f_{\mathsf{WARD}}(\Gamma, \Sigma)$.

The next technical lemma exposes the connection between chase trees and proof trees:

Lemma 4.13. *Consider a set* $\Theta \subseteq \mathsf{chase}(D, \Sigma)$*, and let* $q'(\bar{x})$ *be a CQ and* $\bar{c}$ *a tuple of constants such that* $h'(\mathsf{atoms}(q')) \subseteq U(\mathcal{G}^{D,\Sigma}, \Theta)$ *and* $h'(\bar{x}) = \bar{c}$*, for some homomorphism* h'*. If there is a (linear) chase tree* C *for* $h'(\mathsf{atoms}(q'))$ *with* $\mathsf{nwd}(C) \leq m$*, then there is a (linear) proof tree* $\mathcal{P}$ *for* q' *w.r.t.* Σ *such that* $\mathsf{nwd}(\mathcal{P}) \leq m$ *and* $\bar{c} \in \mathcal{P}(D)$.

We can now show Theorem 4.9, while Theorem 4.10 can be shown analogously. Consider a CQ $q(\bar{x})$ and a tuple $\bar{c} \in \mathsf{dom}(D)^{|\bar{x}|}$ such that $\bar{c} \in \mathsf{cert}(q, D, \Sigma)$. We need to show that if $\Sigma \in \mathsf{WARD} \cap \mathsf{PWL}$, then there exists a linear proof tree $\mathcal{P}$ of q w.r.t. Σ with $\mathsf{nwd}(\mathcal{P}) \leq f_{\mathsf{WARD}\cap\mathsf{PWL}}(q, \Sigma)$ such that $\bar{c} \in \mathcal{P}(D)$. By hypothesis, there is a homomorphism h such that $h(\mathsf{atoms}(q)) \subseteq \mathsf{chase}(D, \Sigma)$ and $h(\bar{x}) = \bar{c}$. Let Θ_q be the set of atoms $h(\mathsf{atoms}(q))$. Recall that there is a homomorphism h_{Θ_q} that maps Θ_q to $U(\mathcal{G}^{D,\Sigma}, \Theta_q)$. Thus, the homomorphism $h' = h_{\Theta_q} \circ h$ is such that $h'(\mathsf{atoms}(q)) \subseteq U(\mathcal{G}^{D,\Sigma}, \Theta_q)$ and $h'(\bar{x}) = \bar{c}$. By Lemma 4.12, there exists a chase tree C for $h'(\mathsf{atoms}(q))$ with $\mathsf{nwd}(C) \leq f_{\mathsf{WARD}\cap\mathsf{PWL}}(h'(\mathsf{atoms}(q)), \Sigma)$. By Lemma 4.13, there exists a linear proof tree $\mathcal{P}$ of q w.r.t Σ with $\mathsf{nwd}(\mathcal{P}) \leq f_{\mathsf{WARD}\cap\mathsf{PWL}}(h'(\mathsf{atoms}(q)), \Sigma) \leq f_{\mathsf{WARD}\cap\mathsf{PWL}}(q, \Sigma)$ such that $\bar{c} \in \mathcal{P}(D)$, and the claim follows.

4.3 Complexity Analysis

We now have all the tools for showing that CQ answering under piece-wise linear warded sets of TGDs is in PSpace in combined complexity, and in NLogSpace in data complexity, and also for re-establishing the complexity of warded sets of TGDs (see Proposition 3.2) in a more transparent way than the approach of [3, 17].

The Case of $\mathsf{CQAns}(\mathsf{WARD} \cap \mathsf{PWL})$**.** Given a database D, a set $\Sigma \in \mathsf{WARD} \cap \mathsf{PWL}$ of TGDs, a CQ $q(\bar{x})$, and a tuple

Input: D, $\Sigma \in \mathsf{WARD} \cap \mathsf{PWL}$, $q(\bar{x})$, $\bar{c} \in \mathsf{dom}(D)^{|\bar{x}|}$
Output: Accept if $\bar{c} \in \mathsf{cert}(q, D, \Sigma)$; otherwise, Reject

$p := Q \leftarrow \alpha_1, \ldots, \alpha_n$ with $\mathsf{atoms}(q(\bar{c})) = \{\alpha_1, \ldots, \alpha_n\}$
repeat
  guess $op \in \{\mathsf{r}, \mathsf{d}, \mathsf{s}\}$
  if $op = \mathsf{r}$ **then**
    guess a TGD $\sigma \in \Sigma$
    if $\mathsf{mgcu}(p, \sigma) = \emptyset$ **then**
      Reject
    else
      guess $U \in \mathsf{mgcu}(p, \sigma)$
      if $|p[\sigma, U]| > f_{\mathsf{WARD} \cap \mathsf{PWL}}(q, \Sigma)$ **then**
        Reject
      else
        $p' := p[\sigma, U]$
  if $op = \mathsf{d}$ **then**
    $p' := p[-D]$
  if $op = \mathsf{s}$ **then**
    guess $V \subseteq \mathsf{var}(p)$ and $\gamma : V \rightarrow \mathsf{dom}(D)$
    $p' := \gamma(p)$
  $p := p'$
until $\mathsf{atoms}(p) \subseteq D$;
return Accept

$\bar{c} \in \mathsf{dom}(D)^{|\bar{x}|}$, by Theorem 4.9, our problem boils down to checking whether there exists a linear proof tree $\mathcal{P}$ of q w.r.t. Σ with $\mathsf{nwd}(\mathcal{P}) \leq f_{\mathsf{WARD} \cap \mathsf{PWL}}(q, \Sigma)$ such that $\bar{c} \in \mathcal{P}(D)$. This can be easily checked via a space-bounded algorithm that is trying to build such a proof tree in a level-by-level fashion. Essentially, the algorithm builds the i-th level from the $(i-1)$-th level of the proof tree by non-deterministically applying the operations introduced above, i.e., resolution, decomposition and specialization.

The algorithm is depicted in the box above. Here is a semi-formal description of it. The first step is to store in p the Boolean CQ obtained after instantiating the output variables of q with $\bar{c}$. The rest of the algorithm is an iterative procedure that non-deterministically constructs p' (the i-th level) from p (the $(i-1)$-th level) until it reaches a level that is a subset of the database D. Notice that p and p' always hold one CQ since at each level of a linear proof tree only one node has a child, while all the other nodes are leaves, which essentially means that their atoms appear in the database D. At each iteration, the algorithm constructs p' from p by applying resolution (r), decomposition (d), or specialization (s):

Resolution. It guesses a TGD $\sigma \in \Sigma$. If the set $\mathsf{mgcu}(p, \sigma)$, i.e., the set of all MGCUs of p with σ, is empty, then rejects; otherwise, it guesses $U \in \mathsf{mgcu}(p, \sigma)$. If the size of the σ-resolvent of p obtained via U, denoted $p[\sigma, U]$, does not exceed the bound given by Theorem 4.9, then it assigns $p[\sigma, U]$ to p'; otherwise, it rejects. Recall that during a resolution step we need to rename variables in order to avoid undesirable clutter. However, we cannot blindly use new variables at each step since this will explode the space used by the algorithm. Instead, we should reuse variables that have been lost due to their unification with an existentially quantified variable. We only need polynomially many variables, while this polynomial depends only on q and Σ.

Decomposition. It deletes from p the atoms that occur in D, and it assigns the obtained CQ $p[-D]$ to p'. Notice that $p[-D]$ may be empty in case $\mathsf{atoms}(p) \subseteq D$. Essentially, the algorithm decomposes p in such a way that the subquery of p consisting of $\mathsf{atoms}(p) \cap D$ forms a child of p that is a leaf, while the subquery consisting of $\mathsf{atoms}(p) \setminus D$ is the non-leaf child.

Specialization. It assigns to p' a specialized version of p, where some variables are instantiated by constants of $\mathsf{dom}(D)$. The convention that output variables correspond to constants is implemented by directly instantiating them with actual constants from $\mathsf{dom}(D)$.

After constructing p', the algorithm assigns it to p, and this ends one iteration. If $\mathsf{atoms}(p) \subseteq D$, then a linear proof tree $\mathcal{P}$ such that $\bar{c} \in \mathcal{P}(D)$ has been found, and the algorithm accepts; otherwise, it proceeds with the next iteration.

It is easy to see that the algorithm uses polynomial space in general. Moreover, in case the set of TGDs and the CQ are fixed, the algorithm uses logarithmic space, which is the space needed for representing constantly many elements of $\mathsf{dom}(D)$; each element of $\mathsf{dom}(D)$ can be represented using logaritmically many bits. The desired upper bounds claimed in Theorem 4.2 follow.

The Case of CQAns(WARD). The non-deterministic algorithm discussed above cannot be directly used for warded sets of TGDs since it is not enough to search for a linear proof tree as in the case of piece-wise linear warded sets of TGDs. However, by Theorem 4.10, we can search for a proof tree that has bounded node-width. This allows us to devise a space-bounded algorithm, which is similar in spirit as the one presented above, with the crucial difference that it constructs in a level-by-level fashion the branches of the proof tree in parallel universal computations using alternation. Since this alternating algorithm uses polynomial space in general, and logarithmic space when the set of TGDs and the CQ are fixed, we immediately get an ExpTime upper bound in combined, and a PTime upper bound in data complexity. This confirms Proposition 3.2 established in [3, 17]. However, our new algorithm is significantly simpler than the one employed in [3, 17], while Theorem 4.10 reveals the main property of warded sets of TGDs that leads to the desirable complexity upper bounds.

5 A JUSTIFIED COMBINATION

It is interesting to observe that the class of piece-wise linear warded sets of TGDs generalizes the class of *intensionally linear* sets of TGDs, denoted IL, where each TGD has at most one body atom whose predicate is intensional. Therefore, Theorem 4.2 immediately implies that CQAns(IL) is PSPACE-complete in combined complexity, and NLOGSPACE-complete in data complexity. Notice that IL generalizes linear Datalog, which is also PSPACE-complete in combined complexity, and NLOGSPACE-complete in data complexity. Thus, we can extend linear Datalog by allowing existentially quantified variables in rule heads, which essentially leads to IL, without affecting the complexity of query answering.

At this point, one maybe tempted to think that the same holds for piece-wise linear Datalog, i.e., we can extend it with existentially quantified variables in rule heads, which leads to PWL, without affecting the complexity of query answering, that is, PSPACE-complete in combined, and NLOGSPACE-complete in data complexity. However, if this is the case, then wardedness becomes redundant since the formalism that we are looking for is the class of piece-wise linear sets of TGDs, without the wardedness condition. It turned out that this is not the case. To our surprise, the following holds:

THEOREM 5.1. *CQAns(PWL) is undecidable in data complexity.*

To show the above result we exploit an undecidable tiling problem [9]. A *tiling system* is a tuple $\mathbb{T} = (T, L, R, H, V, a, b)$, where T is a finite set of tiles, $L, R \subseteq T$ are special sets of left and right border tiles, respectively, with $L \cap R = \emptyset$, $H, V \subseteq T^2$ are the horizontal and vertical constraints, and a, b are distinguished tiles of T called the start and the finish tile, respectively. A *tiling* for $\mathbb{T}$ is a function $f : [n] \times [m] \rightarrow T$, for some $n, m > 0$, such that $f(1,1) = a$, $f(1,m) = b$, $f(1,i) \in L$ and $f(n,i) \in R$, for every $i \in [m]$, and f respects the horizontal and vertical constraints. In other words, the first and the last rows of a tiling for $\mathbb{T}$ start with a and b, respectively, while the leftmost and rightmost columns contain only tiles from L and R, respectively. We reduce from the UnboundedTiling problem, that is, given a tiling system $\mathbb{T}$, decide whether there is a tiling for $\mathbb{T}$. Given a tiling system $\mathbb{T} = (T, L, R, H, V, a, b)$, the goal is to construct in polynomial time a database $D_{\mathbb{T}}$, a set of TGDs $\Sigma \in$ PWL, and a Boolean CQ q, such that $\mathbb{T}$ has a tiling iff $() \in \mathrm{cert}(q, D_{\mathbb{T}}, \Sigma)$; $()$ is the empty tuple. Note that Σ and q should not depend on $\mathbb{T}$.

The Database $D_{\mathbb{T}}$. It simply stores the tiling system $\mathbb{T}$:

$$\begin{aligned} & \{\mathrm{Tile}(t) \mid t \in T\} \cup \{\mathrm{Left}(t) \mid t \in L\} \cup \{\mathrm{Right}(t) \mid t \in R\} \\ \cup \quad & \{H(t,t') \mid (t,t') \in H\} \cup \{V(t,t') \mid (t,t') \in V\} \\ \cup \quad & \{\mathrm{Start}(a), \mathrm{Finish}(b)\}. \end{aligned}$$

The Set of TGDs Σ. It is responsible for generating all the candidate tilings for $\mathbb{T}$, i.e., tilings without the condition $f(1,m) = b$, of arbitrary width and depth. Whether there exists a candidate tiling for $\mathbb{T}$ that satisfies the condition $f(1,m) = b$ will be checked by the CQ q. The set Σ essentially implements the following idea: construct rows of size ℓ from rows of size $\ell - 1$, for $\ell > 1$, that respect the horizontal constraints, and then construct all the candidate tilings by combining compatible rows, i.e., rows that respect the vertical constraints. A row r is encoded as an atom $\mathrm{Row}(p, c, s, e)$, where p is the id of the row from which r has been obtained, i.e., the previous one, c is the id of r, i.e., the current one, s is the starting tile of r, and e is the ending tile of r. We write $\mathrm{Row}(c, c, s, s)$ for rows consisting of a single tile, which do not have a previous row (hence the id of the previous row coincides with the id of the current row), and the starting tile is the same as the ending tile. The following two TGDs construct all the rows that respect the horizontal constraints:

$$\begin{aligned} \mathrm{Tile}(x) &\rightarrow \exists z\, \mathrm{Row}(z, z, x, x), \\ \mathrm{Row}(\_, x, y, z), H(z, w) &\rightarrow \exists u\, \mathrm{Row}(x, u, y, w). \end{aligned}$$

Analogously to Prolog, we write "_" for a "don't-care" variable that occurs only once in the TGD. The next set of TGDs constructs all the pairs of compatible rows, i.e., pairs of rows (r_1, r_2) such that we can place r_2 below r_1 without violating the vertical constraints. This is done inductively as follows:

$$\begin{aligned} & \mathrm{Row}(x, x, y, y), \mathrm{Row}(x', x', y', y'), V(y, y') \rightarrow \mathrm{Comp}(x, x'), \\ & \mathrm{Row}(x, y, \_, z), \mathrm{Row}(x', y', \_, z'), \\ & \qquad\qquad \mathrm{Comp}(x, x'), V(z, z') \rightarrow \mathrm{Comp}(y, y'). \end{aligned}$$

We finally compute all the candidate tilings, together with their bottom-left tile, using the following two TGDs:

$$\begin{aligned} & \mathrm{Row}(\_, x, y, z), \mathrm{Start}(y), \mathrm{Right}(z) \rightarrow \mathrm{CTiling}(x, y), \\ & \mathrm{CTiling}(x, \_), \mathrm{Row}(\_, y, z, w), \mathrm{Comp}(x, y), \\ & \qquad\qquad \mathrm{Left}(z), \mathrm{Right}(w) \rightarrow \mathrm{CTiling}(y, z). \end{aligned}$$

This concludes the definition of Σ.

The Boolean CQ q. Recall that q is responsible for checking whether there exists a candidate tiling such that its bottom-left tile is b. This can be easily done via the query

$$Q \leftarrow \mathrm{CTiling}(x, y), \mathrm{Finish}(y).$$

By construction, $\Sigma \in$ PWL. Moreover, there is a tiling for $\mathbb{T}$ iff $() \in \mathrm{cert}(q, D_{\mathbb{T}}, \Sigma)$, and Theorem 5.1 follows.

6 EXPRESSIVE POWER

A class of TGDs naturally gives rise to a declarative database query language. More precisely, we consider queries of the form (Σ, q), where Σ is a set of TGDs, and q a CQ over $\mathrm{sch}(\Sigma)$. The *extensional (database) schema* of Σ, denoted $\mathrm{edb}(\Sigma)$, is the set of extensional predicates of $\mathrm{sch}(\Sigma)$, i.e., the predicates that do not occur in the head of a TGD of Σ. Given a query $Q = (\Sigma, q)$ and a database D over $\mathsf{edb}(\Sigma)$, the *evaluation* of Q over D, denoted $Q(D)$, is defined as $\mathsf{cert}(q, D, \Sigma)$. We write $(\mathsf{C}, \mathsf{CQ})$ for the query language consisting of all the queries (Σ, q), where $\Sigma \in \mathsf{C}$, and q is a CQ. The evaluation problem for such a query language, dubbed $\mathsf{Eval}(\mathsf{C}, \mathsf{CQ})$, is defined in the usual way. By definition, $\bar{c} \in Q(D)$ iff $\bar{c} \in \mathsf{cert}(q, D, \Sigma)$. Therefore, the complexity of $\mathsf{Eval}(\mathsf{C}, \mathsf{CQ})$ when $\mathsf{C} = \mathsf{WARD} \cap \mathsf{PWL}$ and $\mathsf{C} = \mathsf{WARD}$ is immediately inherited from Theorem 4.2 and Proposition 3.2, respectively:

THEOREM 6.1. *The following statements hold:*

(1) $\mathsf{Eval}(\mathsf{WARD} \cap \mathsf{PWL}, \mathsf{CQ})$ *is* PSPACE*-complete in combined, and* NLOGSPACE*-complete in data complexity.*
(2) $\mathsf{Eval}(\mathsf{WARD}, \mathsf{CQ})$ *is* EXPTIME*-complete in combined, and* PTIME*-complete in data complexity.*

The main goal of this section is to understand the relative expressive power of $(\mathsf{WARD} \cap \mathsf{PWL}, \mathsf{CQ})$ and $(\mathsf{WARD}, \mathsf{CQ})$. To this end, we are going to adopt two different notions of expressive power namely the classical one, which we call combined expressive power since it considers the set of TGDs and the CQ as one composite query, and the program expressive power, which aims at the decoupling of the set of TGDs from the actual CQ. We proceed with the details starting with the combined expressive power.

6.1 Combined Expressive Power

Consider a query $Q = (\Sigma, q)$, where Σ is a set of TGDs and $q(\bar{x})$ a CQ over $\mathsf{sch}(\Sigma)$. The *expressive power* of Q, denoted $\mathsf{ep}(Q)$, is the set of pairs $(D, \bar{c})$, where D is a database over $\mathsf{edb}(\Sigma)$, and $\bar{c} \in \mathsf{dom}(D)^{|\bar{x}|}$, such that $\bar{c} \in Q(D)$. The *combined expressive power* of a query language $(\mathsf{C}, \mathsf{CQ})$, where C is a class of TGDs, is defined as the set

$$\mathsf{cep}(\mathsf{C}, \mathsf{CQ}) = \{\mathsf{ep}(Q) \mid Q \in (\mathsf{C}, \mathsf{CQ})\}.$$

Given two query languages $\mathsf{Q}_1, \mathsf{Q}_2$, we say that Q_2 is *more expressive (w.r.t. the combined expressive power)* than Q_1, written $\mathsf{Q}_1 \leq_{\mathsf{cep}} \mathsf{Q}_2$, if $\mathsf{cep}(\mathsf{Q}_1) \subseteq \mathsf{cep}(\mathsf{Q}_2)$. We say that Q_1 and Q_2 are *equally expressive (w.r.t. the combined expressive power)*, written $\mathsf{Q}_1 =_{\mathsf{cep}} \mathsf{Q}_2$, if $\mathsf{Q}_1 \leq_{\mathsf{cep}} \mathsf{Q}_2$ and $\mathsf{Q}_2 \leq_{\mathsf{cep}} \mathsf{Q}_1$.

The next easy lemma states that $\mathsf{Q}_1 =_{\mathsf{cep}} \mathsf{Q}_2$ is equivalent to say that every query of Q_1 can be equivalently rewritten as a query of Q_2, and vice versa. Given two query languages Q_1 and Q_2, we write $\mathsf{Q}_1 \leq \mathsf{Q}_2$ if, for every $Q = (\Sigma, q) \in \mathsf{Q}_1$, there exists $Q' = (\Sigma', q') \in \mathsf{Q}_2$ such that, for every D over $\mathsf{edb}(\Sigma)$, $Q(D) = Q'(D)$.

LEMMA 6.2. *Consider two query languages* Q_1 *and* Q_2*. It holds that* $\mathsf{Q}_1 \leq_{\mathsf{cep}} \mathsf{Q}_2$ *iff* $\mathsf{Q}_1 \leq \mathsf{Q}_2$.

We are now ready to state the main result of this section, which reveals the expressiveness of $(\mathsf{WARD} \cap \mathsf{PWL}, \mathsf{CQ})$ and $(\mathsf{WARD}, \mathsf{CQ})$ relative to Datalog. Let us clarify that a Datalog query is essentially a pair (Σ, q), where Σ is a Datalog program, or a set of *full* TGDs, i.e., TGDs without existentially quantified variables, that have only one head atom, and q a CQ. We write FULL_1 for the above class of TGDs. In other words, piece-wise linear Datalog, denoted PWL-DATALOG, is the language $(\mathsf{FULL}_1 \cap \mathsf{PWL}, \mathsf{CQ})$, while Datalog, denoted DATALOG, is the language $(\mathsf{FULL}_1, \mathsf{CQ})$, and thus we can refer to their combined expressive power.

THEOREM 6.3. *The following statements hold:*

(1) PWL-DATALOG $=_{\mathsf{cep}}$ $(\mathsf{WARD} \cap \mathsf{PWL}, \mathsf{CQ})$.
(2) DATALOG $=_{\mathsf{cep}}$ $(\mathsf{WARD}, \mathsf{CQ})$.

Let us explain how (1) is shown; the proof for (2) is similar. We need to show that: (a) PWL-DATALOG $\leq_{\mathsf{cep}}$ $(\mathsf{WARD} \cap \mathsf{PWL}, \mathsf{CQ})$, and (b) $(\mathsf{WARD} \cap \mathsf{PWL}, \mathsf{CQ}) \leq_{\mathsf{cep}}$ PWL-DATALOG. By definition, $\mathsf{FULL}_1 \cap \mathsf{PWL} \subseteq \mathsf{WARD} \cap \mathsf{PWL}$. Thus, $(\mathsf{FULL}_1 \cap \mathsf{PWL}, \mathsf{CQ}) \leq (\mathsf{WARD} \cap \mathsf{PWL}, \mathsf{CQ})$, which, together with Lemma 6.2, implies (a). For showing (b), by Lemma 6.2, it suffices to show that:

LEMMA 6.4. $(\mathsf{WARD} \cap \mathsf{PWL}, \mathsf{CQ}) \leq$ PWL-DATALOG.

The key idea underlying the above lemma is to convert a linear proof tree $\mathcal{P}$ of a CQ $q(\bar{x})$ w.r.t. a set $\Sigma \in \mathsf{WARD} \cap \mathsf{PWL}$ of TGDs into a piece-wise linear Datalog query $Q = (\Sigma', q'(\bar{x}))$ such that, for every database D over $\mathsf{edb}(\Sigma)$, $\mathcal{P}(D) = Q(D)$. Roughly, each node of $\mathcal{P}$ together with its children, is converted into a full TGD that is added to Σ'. Assume that the node v has the children $u_1, \ldots, u_k$ in $\mathcal{P}$, where v is labeled by $p_0(\bar{x}_0)$ and, for $i \in [k]$, u_i is labeled by the CQ $p_i(\bar{x}_i)$ with $\bar{x}_0 \subseteq \bar{x}_i$. We then add to Σ'

$$C_{[p_1]}(\bar{x}_1), \ldots, C_{[p_k]}(\bar{x}_k) \rightarrow C_{[p_0]}(\bar{x}_0),$$

where $C_{[p_i]}$ is a predicate that corresponds to the CQ p_i, while $[p_i]$ refers to a *canonical renaming* of p_i. The intention underlying such a canonical renaming is the following: if p_i and p_j are the same up to variable renaming, then $[p_i] = [p_j]$. We also add to Σ' a full TGD

$$R(x_1, \ldots, x_n) \rightarrow C_{[p_R]}(x_1, \ldots, x_n)$$

for each n-ary predicate $R \in \mathsf{edb}(\Sigma)$, where $p_R(x_1, \ldots, x_n)$ is the atomic query consisting of the atom $R(x_1, \ldots, x_n)$. Since in $\mathcal{P}$ we may have several CQs that are the same up to variables renaming, the set Σ' is recursive, but due to the linearity of $\mathcal{P}$, the employed recursion is piece-wise linear, i.e., $\Sigma' \in \mathsf{FULL}_1 \cap \mathsf{PWL}$. The CQ $q'(\bar{x})$ is simply the atomic query $C_{[q]}(\bar{x})$. It should not be difficult to see that indeed $\mathcal{P}(D) = Q(D)$, for every database D over $\mathsf{edb}(D)$.

Having the above transformation of a linear proof tree into a piece-wise linear Datalog query in place, we can easily rewrite every query $Q = (\Sigma, q) \in (\mathsf{WARD} \cap \mathsf{PWL}, \mathsf{CQ})$ into an equivalent query that falls in PWL-DATALOG. We exhaustively convert each linear proof tree $\mathcal{P}$ of q w.r.t. Σ

such that $\mathsf{nwd}(\mathcal{P}) \leq f_{\mathsf{WARD}\cap\mathsf{PWL}}(q, \Sigma)$ into a piece-wise linear Datalog query $Q_{\mathcal{P}}$, and then we take the union of all those queries. Since we consider the canonical renaming of the CQs occurring in a proof tree, and since the size of those CQs is bounded by $f_{\mathsf{WARD}\cap\mathsf{PWL}}(q, \Sigma)$, we immediately conclude that we need to explore finitely many CQs. Thus, the above iterative procedure will eventually terminate and construct a finite piece-wise linear Datalog query that is equivalent to Q, as needed.

6.2 Program Expressive Power

The *expressive power* of a set Σ of TGDs, denoted $\mathsf{ep}(\Sigma)$, is the set of triples $(D, q(\bar{x}), \bar{c})$, where D is a database over $\mathsf{edb}(\Sigma)$, $q(\bar{x})$ is a CQ over $\mathsf{sch}(\Sigma)$, and $\bar{c} \in \mathsf{dom}(D)^{|\bar{x}|}$, such that $\bar{c} \in \mathsf{cert}(q, D, \Sigma)$. The *program expressive power* of a query language $(\mathsf{C}, \mathsf{CQ})$, where C is a class of TGDs, is defined as

$$\mathsf{pep}(\mathsf{C}, \mathsf{CQ}) = \{\mathsf{ep}(\Sigma) \mid \Sigma \in \mathsf{C}\}.$$

Given two query languages $\mathsf{Q}_1, \mathsf{Q}_2$, we say that Q_2 is *more expressive (w.r.t. program expressive power)* than Q_1, written $\mathsf{Q}_1 \leq_{\mathsf{pep}} \mathsf{Q}_2$, if $\mathsf{pep}(\mathsf{Q}_1) \subseteq \mathsf{pep}(\mathsf{Q}_2)$. Moreover, we say that Q_2 is *strictly more expressive (w.r.t. the program expressive power)* that Q_2, written $\mathsf{Q}_1 <_{\mathsf{pep}} \mathsf{Q}_2$, if $\mathsf{Q}_1 \leq_{\mathsf{pep}} \mathsf{Q}_2$ and $\mathsf{Q}_2 \not\leq_{\mathsf{pep}} \mathsf{Q}_1$.

Let us now establish a useful lemma, analogous to Lemma 6.2, which reveals the essence of the program expressive power. For brevity, given two classes of TGDs C_1 and C_2, we write $\mathsf{C}_1 \preceq \mathsf{C}_2$ if, for every $\Sigma \in \mathsf{C}_1$, there exists $\Sigma' \in \mathsf{C}_2$ such that, for every D over $\mathsf{edb}(\Sigma)$, and CQ q over $\mathsf{sch}(\Sigma)$, $Q(D) = Q'(D)$, where $Q = (\Sigma, q)$ and $Q' = (\Sigma', q)$.

LEMMA 6.5. *Consider two query languages* $\mathsf{Q}_1 = (\mathsf{C}_1, \mathsf{CQ})$ *and* $\mathsf{Q}_2 = (\mathsf{C}_2, \mathsf{CQ})$. *Then,* $\mathsf{Q}_1 \leq_{\mathsf{pep}} \mathsf{Q}_2$ *iff* $\mathsf{C}_1 \preceq \mathsf{C}_2$.

We are now ready to study the expressiveness (w.r.t. the program expressive power) of $(\mathsf{WARD} \cap \mathsf{PWL}, \mathsf{CQ})$ and $(\mathsf{WARD}, \mathsf{CQ})$ relative to Datalog. In particular, we show that:

THEOREM 6.6. *The following statements hold:*
(1) $\mathsf{PWL\text{-}DATALOG} <_{\mathsf{pep}} (\mathsf{WARD} \cap \mathsf{PWL}, \mathsf{CQ})$.
(2) $\mathsf{DATALOG} <_{\mathsf{pep}} (\mathsf{WARD}, \mathsf{CQ})$.

Let us explain how (1) is shown; the proof for (2) is similar. We need to show that: (a) $\mathsf{PWL\text{-}DATALOG} \leq_{\mathsf{pep}} (\mathsf{WARD} \cap \mathsf{PWL}, \mathsf{CQ})$, and (b) $(\mathsf{WARD} \cap \mathsf{PWL}, \mathsf{CQ}) \not\leq_{\mathsf{pep}} \mathsf{PWL\text{-}DATALOG}$. Since, by definition, $\mathsf{FULL}_1 \cap \mathsf{PWL} \subseteq \mathsf{WARD} \cap \mathsf{PWL}$, we immediately get that $\mathsf{FULL}_1 \cap \mathsf{PWL} \preceq \mathsf{WARD} \cap \mathsf{PWL}$, and thus, by Lemma 6.5, (a) follows. For showing (b), by Lemma 6.5, it suffices to show that:

LEMMA 6.7. $\mathsf{WARD} \cap \mathsf{PWL} \not\preceq \mathsf{FULL}_1 \cap \mathsf{PWL}$.

By contradiction, assume the opposite. We define the set of TGDs $\Sigma = \{P(x) \rightarrow \exists y\, R(x, y)\}$, the database $D = \{P(c)\}$, and the CQs $q_1 = Q \leftarrow R(x, y)$ and $q_2 = Q \leftarrow R(x, y), P(y)$. By hypothesis, there exists $\Sigma' \in \mathsf{FULL}_1 \cap \mathsf{PWL}$ such that $Q_1(D) = Q_1'(D)$ and $Q_2(D) = Q_2'(D)$, where $Q_i = (\Sigma, q_i)$ and $Q_i' = (\Sigma', q_i)$, for $i \in \{1, 2\}$. Clearly, $Q_1(D) \neq \emptyset$ and $Q_2(D) = \emptyset$, which implies that $Q_1'(D) \neq \emptyset$ and $Q_2'(D) = \emptyset$. However, it is easy to see that $Q_1'(D) \neq \emptyset$ implies $Q_2'(D) \neq \emptyset$, which is a contradiction, and the claim follows.

7 IMPLEMENTATION AND FUTURE WORK

The Vadalog system is currently optimized for piece-wise linear warded sets of TGDs in three ways: (i) the first one is related to the way that existential quantifiers interact with recursion; (ii) the second one is related to the optimizer, which detects and uses piece-wise linearity for the purpose of join ordering; (iii) the third way is related to the architecture of the system. Here are some directions for future research:

(1) As said in Section 1, NLogSpace is contained in the class NC_2 of highly parallelizable problems. This means that reasoning under piece-wise linear warded sets of TGDs is principally parallelizable, unlike warded sets of TGDs. We plan to exploit this for the parallel execution of reasoning tasks in multi-core settings and in the map-reduce model.
(2) Reasoning with piece-wise linear warded sets of TGDs is LogSpace-equivalent to reachability in directed graphs. Reachability in very large graphs has been well-studied and many algorithms and heuristics have been designed that work well in practice; see, e.g., [13, 18, 20]. We are confident that several of these algorithms can be adapted for our purposes.
(3) Reachability in directed graphs is known to be in the *dynamic* parallel complexity class Dyn-FO [14, 26]. This means that by maintaining suitable auxiliary data structures when updating a graph, reachability testing can actually be done in FO, and thus in SQL. We plan to analyze whether reasoning under piece-wise linear warded sets of TGDs, or relevant subclasses thereof, can be shown to be in Dyn-FO or some other dynamic complexity classes.

Acknowledgements. We thank the anonymous referees for their useful feedback. This work was supported by the EPSRC Programme Grant EP/M025268/ VADA, the EPSRC grant EP/S003800/1 EQUID, the WWTF grant VRG18-013, the EU Horizon 2020 grant 809965, the FWF grant W1255-N23, and a DOC fellowship of the Austrian Academy of Sciences.

REFERENCES

[1] Foto N. Afrati, Manolis Gergatsoulis, and Francesca Toni. 2003. Linearisability on datalog programs. *Theor. Comput. Sci.* 308, 1-3 (2003), 199–226.
[2] Marcelo Arenas, Georg Gottlob, and Andreas Pieris. 2014. Expressive languages for querying the semantic web. In *PODS*. 14–26.
[3] Marcelo Arenas, Georg Gottlob, and Andreas Pieris. 2018. Expressive Languages for Querying the Semantic Web. *ACM Trans. Database Syst.* 43, 3 (2018), 13:1–13:45.

[4] Patricia C. Arocena, Boris Glavic, Radu Ciucanu, and Renée J. Miller. 2015. The iBench Integration Metadata Generator. *PVLDB* 9, 3 (2015), 108–119.

[5] Catriel Beeri and Moshe Y. Vardi. 1981. The Implication Problem for Data Dependencies. In *ICALP*. 73–85.

[6] Luigi Bellomarini, Georg Gottlob, Andreas Pieris, and Emanuel Sallinger. 2017. Swift Logic for Big Data and Knowledge Graphs. In *IJCAI*. 2–10.

[7] Luigi Bellomarini, Emanuel Sallinger, and Georg Gottlob. 2018. The Vadalog System: Datalog-based Reasoning for Knowledge Graphs. *PVLDB* 11, 9 (2018), 975–987.

[8] Michael Benedikt, George Konstantinidis, Giansalvatore Mecca, Boris Motik, Paolo Papotti, Donatello Santoro, and Efthymia Tsamoura. 2017. Benchmarking the Chase. In *PODS*. 37–52.

[9] Peter Van Emde Boas. 1997. The Convenience of Tilings. In *Complexity, Logic, and Recursion Theory*. 331–363.

[10] Andrea Calì, Georg Gottlob, and Michael Kifer. 2013. Taming the Infinite Chase: Query Answering under Expressive Relational Constraints. *J. Artif. Intell. Res.* 48 (2013), 115–174.

[11] Andrea Calì, Georg Gottlob, Thomas Lukasiewicz, Bruno Marnette, and Andreas Pieris. 2010. Datalog+/-: A Family of Logical Knowledge Representation and Query Languages for New Applications. In *LICS*. 228–242.

[12] Andrea Calì, Georg Gottlob, and Andreas Pieris. 2012. Towards more expressive ontology languages: The query answering problem. *Artif. Intell.* 193 (2012), 87–128.

[13] Edith Cohen, Eran Halperin, Haim Kaplan, and Uri Zwick. 2003. Reachability and Distance Queries via 2-Hop Labels. *SIAM J. Comput.* 32, 5 (2003), 1338–1355.

[14] Samir Datta, Raghav Kulkarni, Anish Mukherjee, Thomas Schwentick, and Thomas Zeume. 2015. Reachability is in DynFO. In *ICALP*. 159–170.

[15] Ronald Fagin, Phokion G. Kolaitis, Renée J. Miller, and Lucian Popa. 2005. Data exchange: semantics and query answering. *Theor. Comput. Sci.* 336, 1 (2005), 89–124.

[16] Georg Gottlob, Giorgio Orsi, and Andreas Pieris. 2014. Query Rewriting and Optimization for Ontological Databases. *ACM Trans. Database Syst.* 39, 3 (2014), 25:1–25:46.

[17] Georg Gottlob and Andreas Pieris. 2015. Beyond SPARQL under OWL 2 QL Entailment Regime: Rules to the Rescue. In *IJCAI*. 2999–3007.

[18] Ruoming Jin, Yang Xiang, Ning Ruan, and Haixun Wang. 2008. Efficiently answering reachability queries on very large directed graphs. In *SIGMOD*. 595–608.

[19] David S. Johnson and Anthony C. Klug. 1984. Testing Containment of Conjunctive Queries under Functional and Inclusion Dependencies. *J. Comput. Syst. Sci.* 28, 1 (1984), 167–189.

[20] Valerie King. 1999. Fully Dynamic Algorithms for Maintaining All-Pairs Shortest Paths and Transitive Closure in Digraphs. In *FOCS*. 81–91.

[21] Mélanie König, Michel Leclère, Marie-Laure Mugnier, and Michaël Thomazo. 2015. Sound, complete and minimal UCQ-rewriting for existential rules. *Semantic Web* 6, 5 (2015), 451–475.

[22] Roman Kontchakov, Martin Rezk, Mariano Rodriguez-Muro, Guohui Xiao, and Michael Zakharyaschev. 2014. Answering SPARQL Queries over Databases under OWL 2 QL Entailment Regime. In *ISWC*. 552–567.

[23] David Maier, Alberto O. Mendelzon, and Yehoshua Sagiv. 1979. Testing Implications of Data Dependencies. *ACM Trans. Database Syst.* 4, 4 (1979), 455–469.

[24] Jeffrey F. Naughton. 1986. Data Independent Recursion in Deductive Databases. In *PODS*. 267–279.

[25] Jeffrey F. Naughton and Yehoshua Sagiv. 1987. A Decidable Class of Bounded Recursions. In *PODS*. 227–236.

[26] Sushant Patnaik and Neil Immerman. 1997. Dyn-FO: A Parallel, Dynamic Complexity Class. *J. Comput. Syst. Sci.* 55, 2 (1997), 199–209.

Decidable XPath Fragments in the Real World

David Baelde
Anthony Lick
Sylvain Schmitz
LSV, ENS Paris-Saclay & CNRS & Inria, Université Paris-Saclay
France

ABSTRACT

XPath is arguably the most popular query language for selecting elements in XML documents. Besides query evaluation, query satisfiability and containment are the main computational problems for XPath; they are useful, for instance, to detect dead code or validate query optimisations. These problems are undecidable in general, but several fragments have been identified over time for which satisfiability (or query containment) is decidable: CoreXPath 1.0 and 2.0 without so-called data joins, fragments with data joins but limited navigation, etc. However, these fragments are often given in a simplified syntax, and sometimes w.r.t. a simplified XPath semantics. Moreover, they have been studied mostly with theoretical motivations, with little consideration for the practically relevant features of XPath.

To investigate the practical impact of these theoretical fragments, we design a benchmark compiling thousands of real-world XPath queries extracted from open-source projects, and match them against syntactic fragments from the literature. We investigate how to extend these fragments with seldom-considered features such as free variables, data tests, data joins, and the `last()` and `id()` functions, for which we provide both undecidability and decidability results. We analyse the coverage of the original and extended fragments, and further provide a glimpse at which other practical features might be worth investigating in the future.

CCS CONCEPTS

• **Information systems** → **XPath**; XQuery; • **Theory of computation** → *Logic and verification.*

PODS'19, June 30-July 5, 2019, Amsterdam, Netherlands

ACM ISBN 978-1-4503-6227-6/19/06...$15.00
https://doi.org/10.1145/3294052.3319685

ACM Reference Format:
David Baelde, Anthony Lick, and Sylvain Schmitz. 2019. Decidable XPath Fragments in the Real World. In *38th ACM SIGMOD-SIGACT-SIGAI Symposium on Principles of Database Systems (PODS'19), June 30-July 5, 2019, Amsterdam, Netherlands.* ACM, New York, NY, USA, 18 pages. https://doi.org/10.1145/3294052.3319685

1 INTRODUCTION

The XPath language [47] is arguably the most popular querying language for selecting elements in XML documents. It is embedded in the XML processing languages XSLT [23] and XQuery [48], and widely used in general-purpose languages like Java or C# through third-party libraries. It combines the ability to navigate the XML tree—which finds its roots in modal logic [3]—with that of comparing data values found in several, distantly related attributes.

Alongside the *evaluation* of the set of elements selected in a document [e.g. 5, 13, 16, 35], the main computational problem associated with a query is the *satisfiability* problem: given an XPath query, and optionally a schema for the type of XML documents under consideration, does there exist at least one XML document on which this query would select some node? This abstract question actually allows to answer several questions on the reliability and performance of a query; to wit:

Usefulness: is the data query useful at all, i.e. will it select some parts of a well-formed document? The question is far from trivial in an environment where the data can be retrieved from external sources, prone to changes in their structure. This allows simple optimisations in batch processes, with significant savings [36].

Optimisation: can a query be replaced by another, simpler query? This is a classical question in query rewriting in database theory. This type of optimisation has for instance been applied to XPath queries without data joins by Genevès and Vion-Dury [33], with an appreciable impact on performance.

Unfortunately, the satisfiability problem is in general undecidable. Even CoreXPath 1.0, a simplified syntax based on the navigational fragment of XPath 1.0, is intractable, more exactly EXP-complete already when only using the `child` axis [3, 12, 45]. Thus with the exception of the work of Genevès et al. [32] on CoreXPath 1.0, most of the literature on the topic is of a theoretical nature [e.g. 2, 8, 15, 24–26, 29, 31, 39], and focuses on decidability and complexity questions in variants of CoreXPath 1.0 that allow limited forms of data joins.

While these results are technically impressive, it is not immediately clear how much is gained in practice by handling data joins. Indeed, data joins are not the sole source of difficulty in XPath: many real-life XPath queries perform calls to a standard library of functions [22]—including arithmetic and string-manipulating functions—that also lead to undecidable satisfiability.

Also, XPath 1.0 dates back to 1999; the more recent versions 2.0 and 3.0 feature path intersections, `for` loops, etc. [52]. As it evolves in pace with XQuery, XPath includes more and more general programming constructs, and is arguably not just a domain-specific language for path navigation—quite tellingly, in our benchmark, we found that only half of the queries use navigation.

In this paper, we evaluate the practical applicability of XPath fragments proposed in the theoretical literature from a basic, syntactic perspective: how many queries are captured by these fragments? The first step to this end is the compilation of a benchmark of 21,141 real-world XPath queries [6]. The queries are extracted from open-source projects that rely heavily on XSLT or XQuery. As described in Sec. 2, the benchmark offers for each XPath query an XML syntax tree representation in XQueryX [21]. The tools and the resulting benchmark are available from [6, 7] under open source licenses.

Our aim is then to check the queries in our benchmark against the syntax allowed in theoretical works on XPath satisfiability, namely by writing Relax NG specifications for PositiveXPath[31, 37], CoreXPath 1.0[34], CoreXPath 2.0[52], fragments of DataXPath [24, 25, 29], and fragments of XPath that can be interpreted in EMSO[2] [15] or using non-mixing MSO constraints [19] (see Sec. 4).

Naturally, the syntax defined in these works is simplified and was never meant to be used directly against concrete XPath inputs, while we need a concrete syntax for each one of these fragments in order to implement it in Relax NG. This leads to the interesting question of which XPath features can be 'reasonably' handled in these fragments without losing decidable satisfiability nor hampering its complexity (see Sec. 5.1). In turn, answering this type of question requires the definition of a palatable semantics for a substantial subset of XPath 3.0, which we provide in Sec. 3.

As could be expected, naively implementing the syntactic fragments from the literature does not lead to a good coverage (Sec. 4.2), and one should extend them whenever reasonable. In Sec. 5, we propose six extensions of the original fragments and evaluate their coverage on the benchmark. These extensions are root navigation, free variables, data tests against constants, positive data joins, and restricted calls to the functions `last()` and `id()`. Just as interestingly, we exhibit several cases where these extensions *cannot* be handled.

We analyse our experimental results in Sec. 6, notably concluding that higher coverage is obtained through basic extensions than by using complex academic fragments. We also identify increased function support as a promising direction for improved practical satisfiability checking, with an especially high potential for XPath queries from XSLT sources. We conclude in Sec. 7. Additional contents can be found in the full version of the paper available from https://hal.inria.fr/hal-01852475.

2 A REAL-WORLD BENCHMARK

We explain here the technical aspects of the construction of a benchmark of 21,141 queries [6]: the parser we developed to this end (Sec. 2.1), the sources we employed (App. A.2), and the way we processed the benchmark to check whether a given query belongs to a syntactic XPath fragment (Sec. 2.3). We finish the section by mentioning the limitations of the current benchmark.

2.1 Parser

We have slightly modified the W3C parser for XQuery 3.0 from https://www.w3.org/2013/01/qt-applets/, which is (almost) a superset of XPath 3.0, so that we can also use it for XPath queries extracted from XSLT documents. This parser uses a grammar automatically extracted from the language specification, so we are confident in its results. Our implementation [7]

(1) extracts XPath queries from XQuery files, by selecting 'maximal XPath subtrees' from the XQuery syntax tree, and
(2) outputs syntax trees in the XML format XQueryX [21]; this is what we process to determine to which XPath fragments each query belongs.

Duplicate queries within each source are removed. See App. B for an example XQuery document and the corresponding parser output.

2.2 Sources

Three XSLT and twenty-five XQuery sources have been chosen by searching through open source GitHub projects containing XSLT or XQuery files, selecting the most popular projects from which we could extract at least 50 queries. We also added one large project not hosted on GitHub, namely DocBook XSL.

Table 1: The benchmark's composition.

Sources	Queries	Coverage			
		XPath 1.0	XPath 2.0	XPath 3.0	XPath 3.0 std
XSLT	14,675	98.4%	100.0%	100.0%	91.3%
XQuery	6,466	76.1%	87.4%	99.8%	46.7%
Total	21,141	91.6%	96.1%	99.9%	77.7%

The XSLT projects aim to translate enriched text documents between different formats. The XQuery projects we include are most often libraries. The detailed composition is presented in App. A.2. We make no formal claim about the coverage of the benchmark, as it is certainly biased by the restriction to XSLT and XQuery sources. We rather see it as a first open-source release, which could be later enriched by adding XPath queries embedded in other programming languages (e.g., Python, Perl, ECMAScript).

2.3 Properties of the Benchmark

Standard Coverage. We exploit this benchmark by validating the syntax trees in XQueryX format against Relax NG [20] specifications. Table 1 presents the number of queries that fall within the scope of the three major revisions of the XPath standard (queries are unique as strings, per source). We can observe that the queries extracted from XSLT files are nearly all XPath 1.0 queries, which contrasts with queries extracted from XQuery sources, which rely more often on advanced XPath features from XPath 2.0 and XPath 3.0.[1]

Note that the coverage of XPath 1.0, 2.0, and 3.0 given in Tab. 1 does not restrict function calls to the standard library [22]. The last column 'XPath 3.0 std' shows the coverage of XPath 3.0 when restricted to standard functions. We see here an essential limitation of analysing XPath queries in isolation, without support for non-standard functions, and in particular for user-defined functions: more than half of the queries extracted from XQuery documents are beyond the scope of our analyses.

Functions. We show in Fig. 1 the number of occurrences for each of the 400 most frequently occurring functions (among 1,600) and the associated accumulated percentage of the total number of function calls. Darker dots correspond to standard XPath functions, and the darker line corresponds to the accumulated percentage achieved by these standard functions. Arithmetic operations do not figure here as they are classified syntactically as *operators* in XPath. They occur more than the tenth most frequent function.

[1]The output XQueryX representations of a handful of queries do not validate against XPath 3.0, due to out-of-bounds constant numerals; this is a very marginal effect.

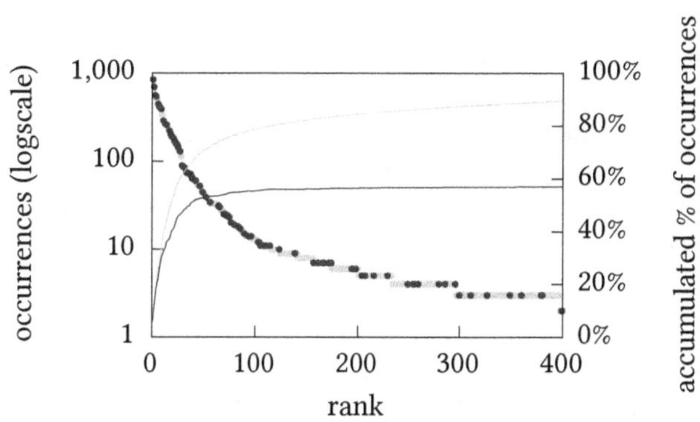

Figure 1: Occurrences of function calls.

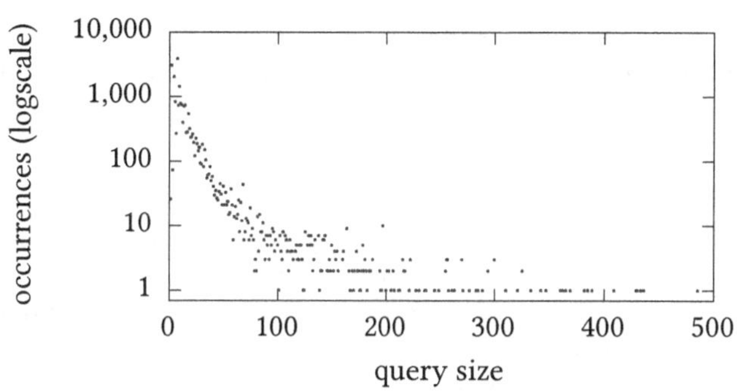

Figure 2: Distribution of query sizes.

The standard functions only represent 57.23% of the function calls in the benchmark. This is mostly due to queries from XQuery sources, which routinely use functions defined in the surrounding XQuery programs: when restricting to these sources, standard XPath functions represent 42.93% of the function calls. By contrast, when restricting to XSLT sources, we find only 210 functions and standard XPath functions represent 76.32% of the calls. Moreover, still within XSLT sources, the 16 functions with more than 100 occurrences each all belong to the XSLT or XPath standard, and account for 78.35% of the occurrences of function calls. In the XSLT sources, there are 4,650 queries (31.69%) performing at least one function call, roughly as many as the 4,556 queries (70.46%) found in the XQuery sources.

Size. Figure 2 shows the distribution of query sizes, defined as the number of nodes in their syntax trees. As might be expected, a majority of the queries have size at most 13, but there are nevertheless 256 queries of size 100 or more.

2.4 Limitations

The benchmark is made of uncurated data, thus no distinction is made between tiny XPath queries and more interesting ones. For instance, only 9,852 of the queries in the benchmark use at least one axis step. Also, as seen in Tab. 1, the numbers of queries from the various sources are not balanced, which means that results on the whole benchmark might not be very telling, and that one should distinguish the XSLT sources from the XQuery ones. Finally, the benchmark was compiled specifically for investigating the coverage of syntactic fragments of XPath. It is currently not really suitable for other ends:

XPath satisfiability: in both XSLT and XQuery files, no schema information on the XML to be processed is available. Furthermore, it seems likely that most queries are satisfiable—quite possibly all of them.

XPath evaluation: similarly, the benchmark does not provide examples of input XML documents on which the XSLT or XQuery should be evaluated.

The first limitation could be lifted by inspecting each source and manually adding the relevant schema when it can be identified.

2.5 Related Work

Regarding XPath and XQuery, the previous works [e.g. 4, 30, 49] on benchmarks focus on evaluating the performance of processors. These benchmarks are synthetic and of limited size, and accompanied with XML documents against which they should be evaluated. Compared to these works, we carry a large scale analysis of real-world queries, and analyse them with respect to the satisfiability problem rather than the evaluation problem; for the sake of completeness, we report on the coverage of our syntactic fragments on two such synthetic benchmarks in App. A.1.

Several large scale studies of real-world SPARQL queries harvest from semantic web search logs [17, 46]. Thanks to the availability of SPARQL logs, the latest one [17] includes over 50 million unique queries and carries out detailed analyses of query features that are relevant to their evaluation, including whether the queries belong to specific SPARQL fragments. While we did not focus on XPath fragments for which evaluation would be more efficient, our benchmark could certainly be exploited in this direction.

3 XPATH 3.0

The XPath 3.0 specification is arguably too complex to be reasoned about directly. We work instead with a well-defined sub-language, designed to capture accurately the constructions we witnessed in the benchmark. In order to be compatible with the semantics in the XPath literature, we provide a semantics on data trees, but in Sec. 3.6 we show how to capture the actual XPath semantics on XML documents.

3.1 Data Trees

Our models are an abstraction of XML DOM trees called *data trees*, which are finite trees where each node carries both a *label* from a finite alphabet Σ and a *datum* from an infinite countable domain $\mathbb{D}$ equipped with an order $<$.

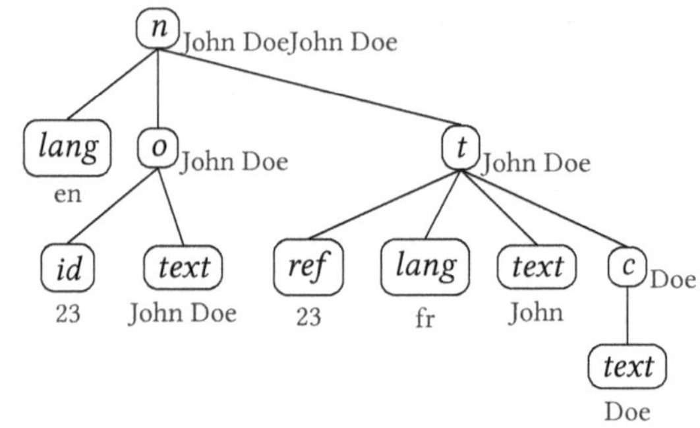

Figure 3: A data tree; labels from Σ are shown in the nodes, data from $\mathbb{D}$ in violet next to them.

$$[\![\texttt{self}]\!]_A \stackrel{\text{def}}{=} \{(p,p) \mid p \in N^2\}$$

$$[\![\texttt{child}]\!]_A \stackrel{\text{def}}{=} \downarrow \qquad [\![\texttt{parent}]\!]_A \stackrel{\text{def}}{=} \downarrow^{-1}$$

$$[\![\texttt{following-sibling}]\!]_A \stackrel{\text{def}}{=} \rightarrow^{+} \qquad [\![\texttt{ancestor}]\!]_A \stackrel{\text{def}}{=} (\downarrow^{-1})^{+}$$

$$[\![\texttt{preceding-sibling}]\!]_A \stackrel{\text{def}}{=} (\rightarrow^{-1})^{+} \qquad [\![\texttt{descendant}]\!]_A \stackrel{\text{def}}{=} \downarrow^{+}$$

Figure 4: The semantics of XPath axes.

Formally, a data tree is a finite rooted ordered unranked tree with labels in $\Sigma \times \mathbb{D}$: it is a pair $t = (\ell, \delta)$ of functions $\ell\colon N \to \Sigma$, $\delta\colon N \to \mathbb{D}$ with a common non-empty finite set of nodes $N \subseteq \mathbb{N}^*$ as domain; N must be prefix-closed (if $p \cdot i \in N$ for some $p \in \mathbb{N}^*$ and $i \in \mathbb{N}$, then $p \in N$) and predecessor-closed (if $p \cdot (i+1) \in N$ for some $p \in \mathbb{N}^*$ and $i \in \mathbb{N}$, then $p \cdot i \in N$); in particular it contains a root node ε. Nodes in N, being finite sequences of natural numbers, are totally ordered by the lexicographic ordering, which is known in this context as the *document order* and denoted by $\ll$. Figure 3 displays an example of a data tree. When working with first-order or monadic second-order logic, a data tree is seen as a finite relational structure $(N, \downarrow, \rightarrow, \sim, (P_a)_{a\in\Sigma}, (P_d)_{d\in\mathbb{D}})$ where

$$\rightarrow \stackrel{\text{def}}{=} \{(p \cdot i, p \cdot (i+1)) \in N^2 \mid p \in \mathbb{N}^*, i \in \mathbb{N}\}\,,$$

$$\downarrow \stackrel{\text{def}}{=} \{(p, p \cdot i) \in N^2 \mid p \in \mathbb{N}^*, i \in \mathbb{N}\}\,, \quad P_a \stackrel{\text{def}}{=} \{p \in N \mid \ell(p) = a\},$$

$$\sim \stackrel{\text{def}}{=} \{(p, p') \in N^2 \mid \delta(p) = \delta(p')\}\,, \quad P_d \stackrel{\text{def}}{=} \{p \in N \mid \delta(p) = d\}$$

denote the next-sibling relation, the child relation, the labelling predicates, data equivalence, and the data predicates.

3.2 Syntax

While our implementation works with concrete syntax, for the sake of readability we use an abstract syntax throughout the paper. It is nevertheless compatible with XPath 3.0: all the examples in this paper are written in actual XPath.

Let $\mathcal{X}$ be a countable infinite set of variables, and $\mathcal{F}$ be a ranked alphabet of function names; we denote by $\mathcal{F}_n$ its

$$
\begin{aligned}
\llbracket \alpha :: * \rrbracket^{\nu}_{\mathsf{P}} &\stackrel{\text{def}}{=} \llbracket \alpha \rrbracket_{\mathsf{A}} \\
\llbracket /\pi \rrbracket^{\nu}_{\mathsf{P}} &\stackrel{\text{def}}{=} N \times \llbracket \pi \rrbracket^{\nu}_{\mathsf{P}}(\varepsilon) \\
\llbracket \pi/\pi' \rrbracket^{\nu}_{\mathsf{P}} &\stackrel{\text{def}}{=} \llbracket \pi \rrbracket^{\nu}_{\mathsf{P}} \mathbin{⨾} \llbracket \pi' \rrbracket^{\nu}_{\mathsf{P}} \\
\llbracket \pi[\varphi] \rrbracket^{\nu}_{\mathsf{P}} &\stackrel{\text{def}}{=} \llbracket \pi \rrbracket^{\nu}_{\mathsf{P}} \cap (N \times \llbracket \varphi \rrbracket^{\nu}_{\mathsf{N}}) \\
\llbracket \pi \texttt{ union } \pi' \rrbracket^{\nu}_{\mathsf{P}} &\stackrel{\text{def}}{=} \llbracket \pi \rrbracket^{\nu}_{\mathsf{P}} \cup \llbracket \pi' \rrbracket^{\nu}_{\mathsf{P}} \\
\llbracket f(\pi_1, \ldots, \pi_n) \rrbracket^{\nu}_{\mathsf{P}} &\stackrel{\text{def}}{=} \{(p, \llbracket f \rrbracket_{\mathcal{F}}(\llbracket \pi_1 \rrbracket^{\nu}_{\mathsf{P}}(p), \ldots, \llbracket \pi_n \rrbracket^{\nu}_{\mathsf{P}}(p))) \mid p \in N\} \\
\llbracket \$\mathsf{x} \rrbracket^{\nu}_{\mathsf{P}} &\stackrel{\text{def}}{=} N \times \nu(\$\mathsf{x}) \\
\llbracket \texttt{let } \$\mathsf{x} := \pi \texttt{ return } \pi' \rrbracket^{\nu}_{\mathsf{P}} &\stackrel{\text{def}}{=} \{(p, \llbracket \pi' \rrbracket^{\nu[\$\mathsf{x} \mapsto \llbracket \pi \rrbracket^{\nu}_{\mathsf{P}}(p)]}_{\mathsf{P}}(p)) \mid p \in N\} \\
\llbracket \texttt{for } \$\mathsf{x} \texttt{ in } \pi \texttt{ return } \pi' \rrbracket^{\nu}_{\mathsf{P}} &\stackrel{\text{def}}{=} \{(p, p'') \in \llbracket \pi' \rrbracket^{\nu[\$\mathsf{x} \mapsto \{p'\}]}_{\mathsf{P}} \mid p' \in \llbracket \pi \rrbracket^{\nu}_{\mathsf{P}}(p)\}
\end{aligned}
$$

$$
\begin{aligned}
\llbracket \pi \rrbracket^{\nu}_{\mathsf{N}} &\stackrel{\text{def}}{=} \{p \in N \mid \exists p' \in \llbracket \pi \rrbracket^{\nu}_{\mathsf{P}}(p)\} \\
\llbracket a \rrbracket^{\nu}_{\mathsf{N}} &\stackrel{\text{def}}{=} P_a \\
\llbracket \texttt{false()} \rrbracket^{\nu}_{\mathsf{N}} &\stackrel{\text{def}}{=} \emptyset \\
\llbracket \texttt{not}(\varphi) \rrbracket^{\nu}_{\mathsf{N}} &\stackrel{\text{def}}{=} N \setminus \llbracket \varphi \rrbracket^{\nu}_{\mathsf{N}} \\
\llbracket \varphi \texttt{ or } \varphi' \rrbracket^{\nu}_{\mathsf{N}} &\stackrel{\text{def}}{=} \llbracket \varphi \rrbracket^{\nu}_{\mathsf{N}} \cup \llbracket \varphi' \rrbracket^{\nu}_{\mathsf{N}} \\
\llbracket \pi \texttt{ is } \pi' \rrbracket^{\nu}_{\mathsf{N}} &\stackrel{\text{def}}{=} \{p \in N \mid \exists p' . \{p'\} = \llbracket \pi \rrbracket^{\nu}_{\mathsf{P}}(p) = \llbracket \pi' \rrbracket^{\nu}_{\mathsf{P}}(p)\} \\
\llbracket \pi \vartriangle^{+} d \rrbracket^{\nu}_{\mathsf{N}} &\stackrel{\text{def}}{=} \{p \in N \mid \exists p' \in \llbracket \pi \rrbracket^{\nu}_{\mathsf{P}}(p) . \delta(p') \overset{\vartriangle^{+}}{\sim} d\} \\
\llbracket \pi \vartriangle \pi' \rrbracket^{\nu}_{\mathsf{N}} &\stackrel{\text{def}}{=} \{p \in N \mid \exists p', p'' . p' \in \llbracket \pi \rrbracket^{\nu}_{\mathsf{P}}(p) \\
&\qquad \wedge p'' \in \llbracket \pi' \rrbracket^{\nu}_{\mathsf{P}}(p) \wedge \delta(p') \overset{\vartriangle}{\sim} \delta(p'')\}
\end{aligned}
$$

Figure 5: The semantics of XPath path expressions and node expressions.

subset of symbols with arity n. As usual, our language has multiple sorts: *axes* denote directions in the data tree, with abstract syntax

$$\alpha ::= \texttt{self} \mid \texttt{child} \mid \texttt{descendant} \mid \texttt{following-sibling}$$
$$\mid \texttt{parent} \mid \texttt{ancestor} \mid \texttt{preceding-sibling}$$

path expressions describe binary relations between the nodes in a data tree, with abstract syntax

$$\pi ::= \alpha{::}* \mid /\pi \mid \pi/\pi \mid \pi[\varphi] \mid \pi \texttt{ union } \pi \mid f(\pi_1, \ldots, \pi_n)$$
$$\mid \$\mathsf{x} \mid \texttt{let } \$\mathsf{x} := \pi \texttt{ return } \pi \mid \texttt{for } \$\mathsf{x} \texttt{ in } \pi \texttt{ return } \pi$$

where $\$\mathsf{x}$ ranges over $\mathcal{X}$, n over $\mathbb{N}$, and f over $\mathcal{F}_n$, while *node expressions* describe sets of nodes, with abstract syntax

$$\varphi ::= \pi \mid a \mid \texttt{false()} \mid \texttt{not}(\varphi) \mid \varphi \texttt{ or } \varphi \mid \pi \texttt{ is } \pi \mid \pi \vartriangle \pi$$
$$\mid \pi \vartriangle^{+} d$$

where a ranges over Σ, d over $\mathbb{D}$, $\vartriangle$ over $\{\texttt{eq}, \texttt{ne}\}$ and $\vartriangle^{+}$ over $\{\texttt{eq}, \texttt{ne}, \texttt{le}, \texttt{lt}, \texttt{ge}, \texttt{gt}\}$. Note that only eq and ne are allowed when comparing paths, while the ordered structure of $\mathbb{D}$ is only available when comparing a path and a data constant: none of the fragments we consider is known to allow the richer path comparisons. We provide a detailed breakdown of how many queries from our benchmark use each one of these syntactic constructs in Sec. 3.7.

3.3 Data Tree Semantics

For a fixed data tree of domain N, we give in figures 4 and 5 the semantics of axes $\llbracket \alpha \rrbracket_{\mathsf{A}}$, path and node expressions $\llbracket \pi \rrbracket^{\nu}_{\mathsf{P}}$ and $\llbracket \varphi \rrbracket^{\nu}_{\mathsf{N}}$. The semantics is relative to a current variable valuation $\nu\colon \mathcal{X} \to 2^N$. The semantics of node expressions are sets of nodes of N, while those of axes and path expression are sets of pairs of nodes.

In order to interpret functions, each function symbol f from $\mathcal{F}_n$ comes with a semantics $\llbracket f \rrbracket_{\mathcal{F}}\colon (2^N)^n \to 2^N$. For instance, false() and not() are technically XPath functions, with semantics $\llbracket \texttt{false} \rrbracket_{\mathcal{F}} \stackrel{\text{def}}{=} \emptyset$ and $\llbracket \texttt{not} \rrbracket_{\mathcal{F}}(S) \stackrel{\text{def}}{=} N \setminus S$ for all $S \subseteq N$. Likewise, we interpret each comparison operator $\vartriangle^{+}$ as a data relation $\overset{\vartriangle^{+}}{\sim} \subseteq \mathbb{D} \times \mathbb{D}$: $\overset{\texttt{eq}}{\sim}$ is the equality $=$ over $\mathbb{D}$, and $\overset{\texttt{ne}}{\sim}$ the disequality $\neq$, $\overset{\texttt{lt}}{\sim}$ the strict order $<$, etc. For binary relations R, R', we employ relational compositions $R \mathbin{⨾} R' \stackrel{\text{def}}{=} \{(p, p'') \mid \exists p'.(p, p') \in R \wedge (p', p'') \in R'\}$, transitive closures R^+, converses $R^{-1} \stackrel{\text{def}}{=} \{(p', p) \mid (p, p') \in R\}$, and images $R(p) \stackrel{\text{def}}{=} \{p' \mid (p, p') \in R\}$.

Beware that the semantics of a path expression π changes when seen as a node expression. In particular, a variable $\$\mathsf{x}$ is a *path expression*, and when seen as a node formula, $\llbracket \$\mathsf{x} \rrbracket^{\nu}_{\mathsf{N}} = N$ unless $\nu(\$\mathsf{x}) = \emptyset$. XPath provides two quantifiers: for expressions bind singleton node sets, while let expressions bind node sets.

Example 3.1. Evaluating for \$x in child::*[o or t] return \$x[self::* eq \$x/child::*] at the root of the data tree in Fig. 3 binds \$x to each of the two children nodes labelled o or t in succession, and returns the o node. Evaluating let \$x := child::*[o or t] return \$x[self::* eq \$x/child::*] at the root binds \$x to the set containing both o and t, and returns both of them.

Our semantics is in line with the ones found in the literature. However, we note that it slightly differs from the actual XPath semantics. In particular, we only account for pure functions acting on paths, while functions from XPath's large standard library [22] may be polymorphic and have side-effects—two features that are anyway out of the reach of the current decidable fragments. Also, variables in XPath are bound to ordered collections of nodes and data values, while we only consider sets of nodes. This simpler semantics is not restrictive for our purposes, as discussed in Sec. 3.6.

3.4 The Satisfiability Problem

In this paper, we focus on the *satisfiability problem*: given a node expression φ, does there exist a data tree t such that $t \models \varphi$? As path expressions are also node expressions, this also captures the satisfiability of path expressions. In presence of a DTD, the data tree t should additionally belong to the DTD's language.

Remark 3.2. A related problem is *query containment*: for node expressions φ and φ', we say that φ is *contained* in φ' if, for all data trees and all variable valuations v, $[\![\varphi]\!]^v_N \subseteq [\![\varphi']\!]^v_N$. This is equivalent to asking the unsatisfiability of φ and not(φ'), so it reduces to the satisfiability problem when negation is allowed—which will not always be our case. The problem of *path containment* asks the same question for path expressions π and π', and is not captured by satisfiability. Furthermore, one might also consider variants where we ask whether for all data trees and variable valuations v and v', $[\![\varphi]\!]^v_N \subseteq [\![\varphi']\!]^{v'}_N$, which leads to rather different complexities [45].

3.5 Syntactic Sugar

3.5.1 XPath 1.0 Sugar. Beside standard definitions like true() $\stackrel{\text{def}}{=}$ not(false()) or φ and φ' $\stackrel{\text{def}}{=}$ not(not(φ) or not(φ')), we may use . $\stackrel{\text{def}}{=}$ self::* for referring to the current point of focus, .. $\stackrel{\text{def}}{=}$ parent::* for its parent, α::a $\stackrel{\text{def}}{=}$ α::*[a] for testing the label found after an axis step, and a single label a as a path formula for child::a.

The syntax also features more axes: descendant-or-self::* is defined as descendant::* union self::*; ancestor-or-self is defined similarly, while following::* is defined as the path ancestor-or-self::*/following-sibling::*/descendant-or-self::*. The preceding axis is defined similarly. The shorthand π//π' stands for π/descendant-or-self::*/π', and //π is defined similarly. Conditional node expressions, while only available in XPath 2.0 and later, are also easily handled: if (φ) then φ' else φ'' $\stackrel{\text{def}}{=}$ (φ and φ') or (not(φ) and φ'').

3.5.2 XPath 2.0 Sugar. As shown by ten Cate and Lutz [52], path intersection and complementation as introduced in XPath 2.0 can be expressed using for loops: π intersect π' is defined by

for \$x in π return for \$y in π' return \$x[\$x is \$y] (1)

and π except π' by

for \$x in π return .[not(π'[. is \$x])]/\$x (2)

Similarly, node quantification some \$x in π satisfies φ can be expressed using

for \$x in π return .[φ] (3)

and every \$x in π satisfies φ is defined dually. By first defining the non-standard *future*(φ)$\stackrel{\text{def}}{=}$(following::* union descendant::*)[φ] and *singleton*(π) $\stackrel{\text{def}}{=}$ π and not(π intersect π/*future*(true())), then we can also express standard *node comparisons* $\pi \ll \pi'$ with

singleton(π) and *singleton*(π')
and π' intersect (π/*future*(true())) (4)

In XPath, a path expression can select the last (according to the document order) node among those selected by a path π. This often appears as a predicate π[last()] or π[position() = last()] that calls the nullary last() function [22]. However, this syntax cannot be handled with our simplified semantics—and is a bit problematic—, thus we shall only consider the one-argument version of last() [22], with semantics $[\![\texttt{last}]\!]_{\mathcal{F}}(S) \stackrel{\text{def}}{=} \max_{\ll}(S)$ for any $S \subseteq N$. Then last(π) can be expressed in XPath 2.0 by

π except (π/ancestor::* union preceding::*) (5)

Example 3.3. In the data tree of Fig. 3, when evaluated at the c node, the path last(ancestor-or-self::*/child::*lang*) returns the *lang* node with data value 'fr.'

We will discuss the last() function further in Sec. 5.2.5.

3.6 XML Semantics

The XPath data model [54] specifies that nodes can fall into several categories, with multiple types and accessors. In data trees, there are only nodes, and two accessors ℓ and δ. Nevertheless, a large part of the XPath data model can be handled.

3.6.1 Data Tree of an XML Document. Elements, attributes, text nodes, and comments can all be encoded using distinguished labels: we let $\Sigma = E \uplus A \uplus \{text, comment\}$ where E is the set of element labels and A of attribute labels.

We see all the values as belonging to $\mathbb{D}$. The data in $\mathbb{D}$ associated with attribute nodes, text nodes, and comment nodes is their string value; for an element node, it is the concatenation of the string values of all its element and text children. The following XML document corresponds to the data tree of Fig. 3:

```
<n lang="en"><o id="23">John Doe</o><t
 ref="23" lang="fr">John <c>Doe</c></t></n>
```

3.6.2 XML-Specific Syntax. When considering XML documents rather than data trees as models, some additional features of XPath become meaningful. We enrich the syntax with the axis

α ::= ··· | attribute

and five *node tests*

τ ::= attribute() | comment() | element() | text()

φ ::= ··· | τ

π ::= ··· | α::node()

meant to select the appropriate node category, and new syntactic sugar: α::$\tau \stackrel{\text{def}}{=} \alpha$::node()[$\tau$] and @$a \stackrel{\text{def}}{=}$ attribute::*[a] for $a \in A$.

3.6.3 Interpretation into Data Trees. Given an XPath node expression φ with the XML semantics of [47], we interpret it as an XPath node expression $\ulcorner\varphi\urcorner$ and not(//.[*notxml*]) that uses the data tree semantics of Sec. 3.3.

The first conjunct $\ulcorner\varphi\urcorner$ is defined by induction on φ; the case of node tests τ is straightforward:

$$\ulcorner\texttt{attribute()}\urcorner \stackrel{\text{def}}{=} \texttt{or}_{a\in A}\, a \qquad \ulcorner\texttt{comment()}\urcorner \stackrel{\text{def}}{=} \mathit{comment}$$

$$\ulcorner\texttt{element()}\urcorner \stackrel{\text{def}}{=} \texttt{or}_{e\in E}\, e \qquad \ulcorner\texttt{text()}\urcorner \stackrel{\text{def}}{=} \mathit{text}$$

The semantics of atomic steps is modified to only visit element nodes, except when using the attribute axis or the node() test, and to forbid horizontal axes in attribute nodes: $\ulcorner\alpha$::node()$\urcorner \stackrel{\text{def}}{=} \alpha$::*, while $\ulcorner\alpha$::*$\urcorner$ is defined as child::*[or$_{a\in A}$ a] if α = attribute, as α::*[or$_{e\in E}$ e] if α = parent or α = ancestor, and as .[not(or$_{a\in A}$ a)]/α::*[or$_{e\in E}$ e] for all the other axes. The remaining cases of the induction are by identity homomorphism.

The second conjunct not(//.[*notxml*]) ensures that the data tree is indeed the encoding of an XML document, by forbidding the node expression *notxml* everywhere in the tree. We define it by first ensuring that attribute, comments, and text nodes are leaves:

$$(\mathit{comment}\ \texttt{or}\ \mathit{text}\ \texttt{or}\ \texttt{or}_{a\in A}\, a)\ \texttt{and}\ \texttt{child::*} \tag{6}$$

Note that this does not enforce the XML standard of having at most one a-labelled attribute for every element. This might actually be desirable, for instance for handling set-valued attributes, like the class ones in HTML 5. But it can be otherwise remedied with a disjunction with (7):

$$\cdots\ \texttt{or}\ \texttt{or}_{a\in A}(\texttt{for \$x in child::}a\ \texttt{return}$$
$$\texttt{for \$y in child::}a\ \texttt{return .[not(\$x is \$y)])} \tag{7}$$

In case we are working with a fragment without for and is, but with data joins, (8) ensures instead that all the a-labelled attributes share the same data

$$\cdots\ \texttt{or}\ \texttt{or}_{a\in A}(\texttt{child::}a\ \texttt{ne}\ \texttt{child::}a) \tag{8}$$

We might want to ensure that identifiers are unique. To simplify matters, let us assume that all the unique identifiers use the attribute name id $\in A$; then we add

$$\cdots\ \texttt{or}\ \big(\texttt{id and (. eq}\ \mathit{future}(\texttt{id}))\big) \tag{9}$$

Finally, we should also ensure that data values are consistent throughout the tree. Remember that the value of an element node should be the concatenation of the values of its element and text children. There is no way to do this without access to string-processing functions, so the XML semantics and data tree semantics do not quite coincide. Most of the literature

Table 2: Number of queries using each axis.

Axis	XSLT	XQuery	Total
ancestor(-or-self)	753 (5.1%)	27 (0.4%)	780 (3.6%)
attribute	3,048 (20.7%)	578 (8.8%)	3,626 (17.1%)
child	5,479 (37.3%)	1,122 (17.2%)	6,601 (31.1%)
descendant(-or-self)	488 (3.3%)	288 (4.4%)	776 (3.6%)
following	18 (0.1%)	2 (0.0%)	20 (0.0%)
following-sibling	223 (1.5%)	18 (0.2%)	241 (1.1%)
namespace	10 (0.0%)	0 (0.0%)	10 (0.0%)
parent	522 (3.5%)	56 (0.8%)	578 (2.7%)
preceding	49 (0.3%)	3 (0.0%)	52 (0.2%)
preceding-sibling	237 (1.6%)	13 (0.2%)	250 (1.1%)
self	557 (3.7%)	16 (0.2%)	573 (2.7%)
All axes	8,351 (56.8%)	1,501 (23.0%)	9,852 (46.5%)

Table 3: Number of queries using each construct.

Syntactic construct	XSLT	XQuery	Total
α::*	8,351 (56.8%)	1,501 (23.0%)	9,852 (46.5%)
$/\pi$	233 (1.5%)	39 (0.6%)	272 (1.2%)
π/π	3,355 (22.8%)	1,499 (23.0%)	4,854 (22.9%)
$\pi[\varphi]$	2,415 (16.4%)	1,070 (16.4%)	3,485 (16.4%)
π union π	1,155 (7.8%)	42 (0.6%)	1,197 (5.6%)
$f(\pi_1,\ldots,\pi_n)$	4,650 (31.6%)	4,555 (70.0%)	9,205 (43.4%)
\$x	6,896 (46.9%)	5,580 (85.8%)	12,476 (58.9%)
let \$x := π return π	0 (0.0%)	405 (6.2%)	405 (1.9%)
for \$x in π return π	5 (0.0%)	164 (2.5%)	169 (0.7%)
φ or φ, φ and φ	1,818 (12.3%)	234 (3.6%)	2,052 (9.6%)
π is π	1 (0.0%)	12 (0.1%)	13 (0.0%)
$\pi \vartriangle \pi$	545 (3.7%)	308 (4.7%)	853 (4.0%)
$\pi \vartriangle^{+} d$	4,029 (27.4%)	762 (11.7%)	4,791 (22.6%)

accordingly restricts data joins $\pi \vartriangle \pi'$ and data tests $\pi \vartriangle^{+} d$ to paths ending with an attribute step: only π/@$a \vartriangle \pi'$/@a' and π/@$a \vartriangle^{+} d$ are allowed in their syntax. We do not enforce this restriction in our concrete syntax specifications, but the effect is limited: there are only 381 occurrences in the benchmark of a data test $\pi \vartriangle^{+} d$ where π is neither a function call nor a variable and does not end with an attribute step.

3.7 Benchmark Occurrences

Table 2 shows the number of queries that use each specific axis, first for each type of source, and then globally; attribute and child are the most prominent axes.

Tables 3 and 4 show, for each syntactic construct, the number of queries that use it. Table 3 focuses on constructs from our restricted syntax, while Tab. 4 presents XPath constructs not supported by our abstract syntax. The difference between XSLT and XQuery sources is marked, with 'advanced' or unsupported constructs (let, for, map, etc.) used almost only in XQuery, and navigation and data tests against constants used significantly more in XSLT.

Table 4: Number of queries using unsupported syntactic constructs.

Unsupported construct	XSLT	XQuery	Total
simple map	0(0.0%)	44(0.6%)	44(0.2%)
dynamic function invocation	0(0.0%)	170(2.6%)	170(0.8%)
inline function	0(0.0%)	126(1.9%)	126(0.5%)
named function	0(0.0%)	31(0.4%)	31(0.1%)
range sequence	11(0.0%)	54(0.8%)	65(0.3%)
instance of	0(0.0%)	35(0.5%)	35(0.1%)
processing instruction	120(0.8%)	9(0.1%)	129(0.6%)
cast-related expressions	19(0.1%)	6(0.0%)	25(0.1%)

4 XPATH FRAGMENTS

We present here the fragments with decidable satisfiability and containment we have considered in our experiments. As there is such an abundant literature on the topic [e.g. 12, 13, 24–26, 29, 34, 39, 45, 50, 52], this is clearly an incomplete sample, but we think it is representative of the main lines of investigation.

The fragments we consider in our experiments and their inclusions are shown in Fig. 6, along with the complexity of satisfiability in each fragment. Regarding complexity, we use the DAG-size of the input expression, where isomorphic sub-expressions are shared. Note that Fig. 6 reports the complexity for the original logics, thus for EMSO^2 and non-mixing MSO constraints, the complexity of the XPath fragments we translate into the logics might be lower.

4.1 Decidable XPath Fragments

4.1.1 Positive XPath. Some of the earliest-studied fragments of XPath are based on tree patterns [37]. Geerts and Fan [31, Thm. 4] show that the following PositiveXPath fragment has an NP-complete satisfiability problem, even in presence of a DTD,

$$\pi ::= \alpha\texttt{::*} \mid \pi/\pi \mid \pi[\varphi] \mid \pi \texttt{ union } \pi \mid \pi \texttt{ intersect } \pi$$
$$\varphi ::= \pi \mid a \mid \texttt{false()} \mid \texttt{true()} \mid \varphi \texttt{ or } \varphi \mid \varphi \texttt{ and } \varphi \mid \pi \vartriangle \pi$$

where a ranges over Σ and $\vartriangle$ over {eq, ne}. This fragment has a semantics-preserving translation into the existential positive fragment of first-order logic over the relational signature $(\downarrow, \downarrow^*, \rightarrow, \rightarrow^*, (P_a)_{a\in\Sigma}, \sim, \nsim)$.

4.1.2 Core XPath 1.0. A landmark fragment is the language of Gottlob and Koch [34], known in the literature as 'CoreXPath'. This language is akin to propositional dynamic logic on trees [3], and is defined by the abstract syntax

$$\pi ::= \alpha\texttt{::*} \mid \pi/\pi \mid \pi[\varphi] \mid \pi \texttt{ union } \pi$$
$$\varphi ::= \pi \mid a \mid \texttt{false()} \mid \texttt{not}(\varphi) \mid \varphi \texttt{ or } \varphi$$

where a ranges over Σ. CoreXPath has an EXP-complete satisfiability problem, also in presence of a DTD. To the best

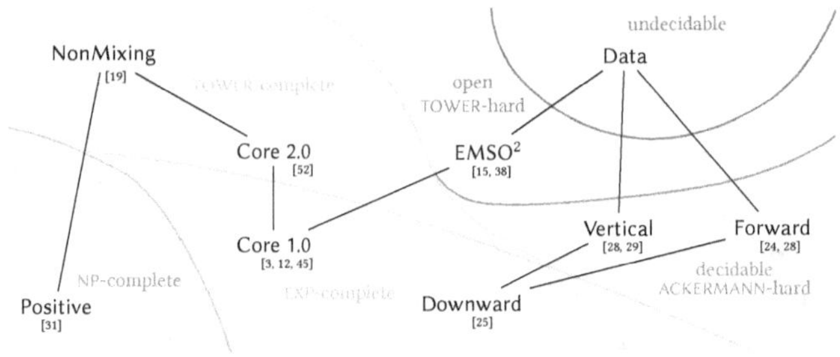

Figure 6: Inclusions and complexities of the fragments of Sec. 4.

of our knowledge, this is the only fragment in this section for which an implementation of a satisfiability procedure exists [32].

4.1.3 Core XPath 2.0. The main feature of XPath 2.0 was the introduction of `for` loops. Having `for` loops further enriches XPath with variable quantification, and provides a significant jump in expressiveness (see Sec. 3.5.2). Ten Cate and Lutz [52] study the extension of CoreXPath with

$$\pi ::= \cdots \mid \texttt{\$x} \mid \texttt{for \$x in } \pi \texttt{ return } \pi$$
$$\varphi ::= \cdots \mid \texttt{\$x is \$y} \mid \texttt{. is \$x}$$

where \$x and \$y range over $\mathcal{X}$; we call the resulting fragment CoreXPath 2.0. The syntax of node identity tests in [52] is slightly more restrictive than ours, but this can be fixed by defining π `is` π' as

$$\textit{singleton}(\pi) \texttt{ and } \textit{singleton}(\pi') \texttt{ and for \$x in } \pi \texttt{ return}$$
$$\texttt{for \$y in } \pi' \texttt{ return .[\$x is \$y]} \qquad (10)$$

A deeper difference lies in the semantics of variables: ten Cate and Lutz [52] assume that valuations map to single nodes. This does not make any difference regarding bound variables, since in CoreXPath 2.0 they must be bound by a `for` expression, but it does make one for free variables. This is not an issue, since the decision procedure for CoreXPath 2.0 can handle those.

Indeed, satisfiability in CoreXPath 2.0 is decidable in time bounded by a tower of exponentials, whose height depends on the size of the expression. This is seen by reducing the problem to satisfiability in $\text{MSO}(\downarrow, \rightarrow, (P_a)_{a\in\Sigma})$, using the usual *standard translation* of CoreXPath expressions into MSO formulæ [see, e.g., 3, 44]; the resulting TOWER complexity upper bound is tight [52, Thm. 31]. Thus our free XPath variables translate directly into free second-order variables in $\text{MSO}(\downarrow, \rightarrow, (P_a)_{a\in\Sigma})$.

4.1.4 Data XPath. A well-studied XPath fragment with the ability to test data equality and disequality is DataXPath [31]. It is obtained by adding *joins* to the syntax of CoreXPath as follows, where $\triangle$ ranges over {eq, ne}:

$$\varphi ::= \cdots \mid \pi \triangle \pi$$

Although DataXPath satisfiability is undecidable [31], restricting the navigational power restores decidability [27]. The first decidable fragment we consider is VerticalXPath, shown decidable by Figueira and Segoufin [29, Thm. 2.1], which restricts the syntax of DataXPath to only allow vertical navigation:

α ::= `self` | `child` | `descendant` | `parent` | `ancestor`

Another decidable fragment is ForwardXPath, shown decidable by Figueira [24, Thm. 6.4], where navigation is restricted to forward axes only:

α ::= `self` | `child` | `descendant` | `following-sibling`

We also consider DownwardXPath [25, Thm. 6.4], the intersection of VerticalXPath and ForwardXPath, where only downward navigation is allowed:

α ::= `self` | `child` | `descendant`

As seen in Fig. 6, the complexity of the satisfiability problem in these three fragments varies considerably: DownwardXPath is EXP-complete, but VerticalXPath and ForwardXPath are ACKERMANN-hard [28]. It is also notable that satisfiability of DownwardXPath also becomes ACKERMANN-hard in presence of DTDs [28].

4.1.5 Existential MSO². Bojańczyk, Muscholl, Schwentick, and Segoufin [15] investigate the satisfiability of formulæ of the form $\exists X_1 \cdots \exists X_n \,.\, \psi$, where $X_1, \ldots, X_n$ are monadic second-order variables and ψ is a first-order formula in the two-variable fragment

- over the signature $(\downarrow, \rightarrow, (P_a)_{a\in\Sigma}, \sim)$, which they denote by $\mathrm{EMSO}^2(\sim, +1)$, or
- over the signature $(\downarrow, \downarrow^+\!\rightarrow, \rightarrow^+, (P_a)_{a\in\Sigma}, \sim)$, which they denote by $\mathrm{EMSO}^2(\sim, <, +1)$.

In the first instance, they prove the decidability of satisfiability in 3-NEXP [15, Thm. 3.1], while the best known lower bound is NEXP-hardness, which holds already for first-order logic with two variables $\mathrm{FO}^2(\downarrow, (P_a)_{a\in\Sigma})$ [10, Thm. 5.1]. In the second instance, decidability is open, and equivalent to the reachability problem in an extension of branching vector addition systems [38], with a TOWER lower bound [41].

These results can be exploited for a fragment EMSO²-XPath of DataXPath: Bojańczyk et al. [15, Thm. 6.1] allow the following restricted joins in CoreXPath

$$\pi ::= \cdots \mid \pi \triangle /\pi \mid \texttt{.} \triangle \alpha\texttt{::*}[\varphi]$$

where $\triangle$ ranges over {eq, ne}. When the above π, π', and α are restricted to using the axes `self`, `child`, and `parent`, this can be translated into $\mathrm{EMSO}^2(\sim, +1)$, and the general form into $\mathrm{EMSO}^2(\sim, <, +1)$.[2] In spite of the unknown decidability status of $\mathrm{EMSO}^2(\sim, <, +1)$, we have run our benchmarks against the full logic.

4.1.6 Non-Mixing MSO Constraints. In [19], Czerwiński, David, Murlak, and Parys define *MSO constraints* as formulæ of the form $\psi(\bar{x}) \implies \eta_\sim(\bar{x}) \wedge \eta_\nsim(\bar{x})$, where ψ is an MSO formula over the signature $(\downarrow, \rightarrow, (P_a)_{a\in\Sigma})$ with the first-order variables $\bar{x}$ as its free variables, and $\eta_\sim$ and $\eta_\nsim$ are positive Boolean combinations of atoms, over the respective signatures $(\sim, (P_d)_{d\in\mathbb{D}})$ and $(\nsim, (\neg P_d)_{d\in\mathbb{D}})$. Hence data tests and data joins are permitted, as long as they are not *mixed.* Satisfiability is called 'consistency' in this context, and is decidable [19, Thm. 4]; better complexities are achievable when restricting ψ to conjunctive queries.

To quote Czerwiński et al. [19], their 'results imply decidability...of the containment problem in the presence of a schema for unions of XPath queries without negation, where each query uses either equality or inequality, but never both.' Here is indeed a NonMixingXPath fragment of XPath, which can be translated to MSO constraints:

$$\varphi_c ::= \varphi_{\mathsf{eq}} \mid \varphi_{\mathsf{ne}} \mid \varphi_c \texttt{ or } \varphi_c$$

where $\triangle$-*expressions*, for $\triangle$ in {eq, ne}, are defined by

$$\pi_\triangle ::= \alpha\texttt{::*} \mid \pi_\triangle/\pi_\triangle \mid \pi_\triangle[\varphi_\triangle] \mid \pi_\triangle \texttt{ union } \pi_\triangle$$
$$\varphi_\triangle ::= \texttt{true()} \mid \texttt{false()} \mid \pi_\triangle \mid \varphi \mid \varphi_\triangle \texttt{ or } \varphi_\triangle \mid \varphi_\triangle \texttt{ and } \varphi_\triangle \mid \pi_\triangle \triangle \pi_\triangle \mid \pi_\triangle \triangle d$$

where φ is any CoreXPath 2.0 node expression. As this fragment embeds CoreXPath 2.0, its satisfiability problem is TOWER-hard, which matches the upper bound for MSO constraints [19].

4.2 Baseline Benchmark Results

We have implemented the fragments of this section as Relax NG schemas. In each case we included obvious extensions, such as the syntactic sugars discussed in Sec. 3.5 (in particular, the `last()` function is included in CoreXPath 2.0 and NonMixingXPath).

The results of these fragments on the benchmark are presented in grey in figures 7 and 8 (p. 12). The fragments allowing free variables, namely CoreXPath 2.0, EMSO²XPath, and NonMixingXPath, have the best baseline coverage. We see here the practical interest of a fragment like NonMixingXPath with restricted negation but some support for variables, data tests $\pi \triangle d$, and data joins $\pi \triangle \pi$. The other fragments have an essentially negligible coverage in the XQuery benchmarks (Fig. 8). The support for unrestricted joins $\pi \triangle \pi'$ in the fragments of DataXPath from Sec. 4.1.4 has a very limited effect, and indeed we only found 65 relevant instances

[2] Bojańczyk et al. [15] actually also allow joins of the form $@a \triangle \alpha\texttt{::*}/@b$, but this is subject to a semantic condition.

Table 5: Occurrence counts of the syntactic extensions of Sec. 5 in the entire benchmark.

$/\pi$	\$x	$\pi \,\Delta^+\, d$	$\pi \,\Delta\, \pi$	last()	id()
272	12,476	4,791	853	1,203	31

in the entire benchmark, i.e. where neither π nor π' is a variable or a function call.

Of course, the fragments defined in the literature were not meant to be run against concrete XPath queries; we will see in the next section that several extensions can be made to these fragments.

5 EXTENSIONS

In this section, we introduce several extensions of the fragments from Sec. 4, while preserving the decidability and complexity of the corresponding satisfiability problems. As seen in Tab. 5, we consider first 'basic' extensions with considerable impact on the benchmark coverage in sections 5.2.1 to 5.2.3, and then 'advanced' ones with smaller impact in sections 5.2.4 to 5.2.6.

5.1 Handling an Extension in a Fragment

A first way to prove that an extension can be handled is, when given a node expression φ in the extended syntax, to compute an *equivalent* node expression φ' in the original fragment, i.e. such that for all data trees and valuations v, $[\![\varphi]\!]^v_{\mathsf{N}} = [\![\varphi']\!]^v_{\mathsf{N}}$— and similarly for path expressions. In such a case, we say that the extension can be *expressed* in the fragment, and *polynomially* so if φ' can be computed in polynomial time.

A second way is instead, when given a node expression φ in the extended syntax, to compute an *equisatisfiable* node expression φ' in the original fragment, i.e. such that there exists t with $t \models \varphi$ if and only if there exists t' with $t' \models \varphi'$. In such a case, we say that the extension can be *encoded* in the fragment, and that it can be *polynomially encoded* if φ' can be computed in polynomial time. Clearly, an extension that can be (polynomially) expressed can also be (polynomially) encoded, but the converse might not hold.

Last of all, the proof techniques employed to show the decidability of satisfiability in a fragment might allow to handle the extension at hand.

5.2 Extensions

5.2.1 $/\pi$: Root Navigation. In XPath, navigation to the root is possible through the $/\pi$ construct as well as using the nullary root() function [22], with semantics $[\![\mathsf{root}]\!]_{\mathcal{F}} \overset{\text{def}}{=} \{\varepsilon\}$.

We naturally allow these features in CoreXPath 1.0 and 2.0 as well as in the NonMixingXPath and EMSO^{2}XPath fragments, where navigation to the root is captured by

$$\texttt{ancestor-or-self::*[not(parent::*)]} \tag{11}$$

The same goes for VerticalXPath but not for the two other DataXPath fragments, where one cannot navigate upwards. It is clear that root navigation is not expressible in these fragments. In fact, it cannot even be encoded in ForwardXPath, since it becomes undecidable when extended with navigation to the root, as can be seen by adapting the proofs from [28].

Proposition 5.1. *Satisfiability in ForwardXPath extended with root navigation is undecidable.*

We leave open the question whether there is a (polynomial) encoding of root navigation in DownwardXPath.

Finally, regarding PositiveXPath, Hidders's original fragment [37] allowed root navigation, and his proof of a small model property (showing the satisfiability problem to be in NP) applies mutatis mutandis to the fragment with data joins defined in Sec. 4.1.1.

5.2.2 \$x: Free Variables. In most of our fragments, free variables are admissible. Indeed, any formula φ over Σ and $\mathbb{D}$ with a (necessarily finite) set of free variables $X \subseteq \mathcal{X}$ can be translated into an equisatisfiable formula φ^X over $\Sigma \times 2^X$ and $\mathbb{D}$ with no free variables. Let us write a_S for $(a, S) \in \Sigma \times 2^X$. The key translation steps are:

$$(\$x)^X \overset{\text{def}}{=} //.\Big[\mathop{\mathsf{or}}_{a\in\Sigma,\ \$x\in S\subseteq 2^X} a_S\Big] \quad (a)^X \overset{\text{def}}{=} \mathop{\mathsf{or}}_{a\in\Sigma,\ S\subseteq 2^X} a_S \tag{12}$$

Assuming without loss of generality that the variables bound by constructs such as `for` or `let` do not belong to X, they are not affected by this translation.

Proposition 5.2. *Free variables can be encoded in PositiveXPath, CoreXPath 1.0, CoreXPath 2.0, VerticalXPath, NonMixingXPath, and EMSO^{2}XPath.*

Note that although the encoding is exponential, the extension does not actually impact the complexity of satisfiability: in PositiveXPath and CoreXPath 1.0, a polynomial encoding can be obtained, leveraging a variant of the semantics where multiple propositions may hold at a node. In VerticalXPath, satisfiability is ACKERMANN-hard, so an exponential blow-up will not have an effect on the worst-case complexity. The decision procedures for the fragments CoreXPath 2.0, NonMixingXPath, and EMSO^{2}XPath are based on second-order logic, hence they actually allow XPath variables in their baseline version.

We finally observe that this translation is not available in DownwardXPath and ForwardXPath, because they cannot express the root path of (12). In fact, free variables cannot be encoded in ForwardXPath; this is similar to Prop. 5.1.

Proposition 5.3. *Satisfiability in ForwardXPath extended with one free variable is undecidable.*

5.2.3 $\pi \vartriangle^{+} d$: Data Tests against Constants. We now consider the extension with direct comparisons against constants from $\mathbb{D}$, assuming that $<$ is a dense total order:[3]

$$\varphi ::= \cdots \mid \pi \vartriangle^{+} d$$

where $\vartriangle^{+} \in \{\texttt{eq}, \texttt{ne}, \texttt{le}, \texttt{lt}, \texttt{ge}, \texttt{gt}\}$ and $d \in \mathbb{D}$.

PROPOSITION 5.4. *Data tests can be polynomially encoded in CoreXPath 1.0 and 2.0, Vertical, Downward, Forward and EMSO²XPath.*

We show that any formula over Σ and $\mathbb{D}$ featuring comparisons against constants in a finite subset $D \subseteq \mathbb{D}$ can be transformed into an equisatisfiable formula over an extended labelling set $\Sigma \times C_D$. This is similar to the treatment of free variables in Sec. 5.2.2, but requires to include data consistency constraints in the encoded formula when the fragment at hand supports data joins. Crucially, these consistency constraints are mixing, and thus not available in NonMixingXPath. Regarding PositiveXPath, the small model property [37, Lem. 1] still holds in the presence of data tests, hence satisfiability remains in NP for this extension.

Going slightly further, we allow comparisons against constant data *expressions* in our fragments, where constant expressions are built from constant values and the deterministic context-insensitive functions of the XPath specification [22]; e.g., @n eq 3 + 1 is allowed.

5.2.4 $\pi \vartriangle \pi$: Positive Data Joins. We observe that most of our fragments can be extended to allow restricted occurrences of data joins. Intuitively, we allow data joins in positions that guarantee that the join will be evaluated only once during satisfaction checking, which allows us to replace it by two tests against a specially chosen data constant. Hence, we extend any fragment with

$$\begin{aligned}\pi_+ &::= \pi \mid /\pi_+ \mid \pi_+/\pi_+ \mid \pi_+[\varphi_+] \mid \pi_+ \texttt{ union } \pi_+ \mid \pi_+ \texttt{ except } \pi \\ &\quad \mid \pi_+ \texttt{ intersect } \pi_+ \mid \texttt{some \$x in } \pi_+ \texttt{ satisfies } \varphi_+ \\ \varphi_+ &::= \varphi \mid \pi_+ \mid \varphi_+ \texttt{ or } \varphi_+ \mid \varphi_+ \texttt{ and } \varphi_+ \\ &\quad \mid \pi_+ \texttt{ is } \pi_+ \mid \pi_+ \vartriangle \pi_+ \mid \pi_+ \vartriangle d\end{aligned}$$

Productions for constructs such as navigation to the root, intersection, node comparison, etc. should only be considered in fragments where they are allowed. This works for all relevant fragments: NonMixingXPath does not support the mixing data tests required in our encoding, and PositiveXPath already supports positive data joins in its baseline version.

PROPOSITION 5.5. *Positive joins are expressible in CoreXPath 1.0, CoreXPath 2.0 and EMSO²XPath.*

[3] These assumptions are not met in the actual XPath model where comparisons are undefined between numeric and arbitrary string values, but this problem can be avoided e.g. when the type of attributes is known from a schema.

5.2.5 `last()`: Positional Predicates. The typical use of `last()` in XPath is through a *positional predicate* π[position() = last()] or π[last()] that only keeps the last node in the document order among all those selected by π. We can also check whether a node is the ith one for some $i > 0$ with $\pi[i]$, or not the last one with π[position() != last()] or not the ith one with π[position() != i]. As seen in Tab. 5, these constructions are quite frequent in the benchmark. Here we discuss the case of last() and its negation, but the other positional predicates can be handled in a similar fashion.

As explained in Sec. 3.5.2, this kind of predicates is not supported in our simplified semantics, thus we rather focus on the one-argument functions last(π) and *notlast*(π)—the latter is not a standard function—, with semantics $[\![\texttt{last}]\!]_{\mathcal{F}}(S) \stackrel{\text{def}}{=} \max_{\ll} S$ and $[\![\mathit{notlast}]\!]_{\mathcal{F}}(S) \stackrel{\text{def}}{=} S \setminus \{\max_{\ll} S\}$ for any $S \subseteq N$.

Recall from Sec. 3.5.2 that last() can be expressed natively in CoreXPath 2.0 and thus in NonMixingXPath. The question here is to which extent it can be handled in the other fragments. Our first result is that in some cases, the last() and *notlast*() functions cannot be expressed.

PROPOSITION 5.6. *The path* last(ancestor::a)[child::b] *is not expressible in VerticalXPath.*

This result, proved using bisimulation techniques, shows that last() cannot be expressed in VerticalXPath nor in DownwardXPath, even for simple one-step paths. Furthermore, we can show that it cannot be polynomially encoded in DownwardXPath by adapting the hardness proofs of [28].

PROPOSITION 5.7. *Satisfiability in DownwardXPath extended with both the path* last(descendant-or-self::*) *and the path* *notlast*(descendant-or-self::*) *is* ACKERMANN*-hard.*

However, we can still look for some uses of last() that can be reasonably allowed. In particular, the path expressions from the statement of Prop. 5.7 can be handled in ForwardXPath—or at least in its *regular* extension [51] with new axes and the Kleene plus and Kleene star operators on paths

$$\begin{aligned}\alpha &::= \cdots \mid \texttt{previous-sibling} \mid \texttt{next-sibling} \\ \pi &::= \cdots \mid \pi^{+} \mid \pi^{*}\end{aligned}$$

Their semantics are defined by $[\![\texttt{previous-sibling}]\!]_{\mathsf{A}} \stackrel{\text{def}}{=} \to^{-1}$, $[\![\texttt{next-sibling}]\!]_{\mathsf{A}} \stackrel{\text{def}}{=} \to$, $[\![\pi^{+}]\!]^{\nu}_{\mathsf{P}} \stackrel{\text{def}}{=} ([\![\pi]\!]^{\nu}_{\mathsf{P}})^{+}$, $[\![\pi^{*}]\!]^{\nu}_{\mathsf{P}} \stackrel{\text{def}}{=} ([\![\pi]\!]^{\nu}_{\mathsf{P}})^{*}$. As far as the computational complexity of satisfiability is concerned, this extension comes 'for free' in CoreXPath 1.0 [3, 44], ForwardXPath [24, Thm.6.4] (with next-sibling but without previous-sibling), VerticalXPath [29, Thm. 2.1], and DownwardXPath [25, Thm. 6.4] (without the new axes). We show in the full version that we can handle using this regular extension last(π) and *notlast*(π) on any *one-step* path argument of the form $\pi = \alpha$::*[φ].

Table 6: Number of new queries captured by the extensions of Sec. 5.2 in each fragment.

	basic	$\pi \triangle \pi$	last()	id()
Positive	7,653			
Core 1.0	7,895	+243	+54	
Core 2.0	4,309	+266		
Downward	1,993		+12	
Vertical	7,974		+25	+0
Forward	2,053		+26	
EMSO²	4,760	+241		+11
NonMixing	136			

5.2.6 id()*: Jumps.* Another interesting XPath feature in the XML document model is the id/idref mechanism [13, 43]. In full generality, this mechanism relies on attributes declared as identifiers in the XML schema, but we shall consider a simpler setting where the @id attribute plays this role. The function id() then takes a path as argument, and returns the nodes of the document (if any) that have an @id attribute matching the datum found at the end of the path given as argument.

$$[\![\mathtt{id}]\!]_{\mathcal{F}}(S) \stackrel{\text{def}}{=} \{p \mid \exists p' \in S \,.\, \delta(p') = \delta([\![@\mathtt{id}]\!]^{\mathcal{V}}_{\mathrm{P}}(p))\}$$

The function idref() is its inverse. For instance, in Fig. 3, evaluating id(@ref) at the t node returns the o node.

Adding id() jumps makes most of the fragments undecidable, as soon as we can also use (full) data joins or node tests π is π'. The proof reduces from Post's correspondence problem.

Proposition 5.8. *Satisfiability is undecidable in both DownwardXPath and CoreXPath 2.0 extended with* id()*.*

We show in the full paper that limited support for the id() function can be provided in VerticalXPath and EMSO²XPath.

5.3 Extended Benchmark Results

We have implemented the extensions of this section as Relax NG schemas. The results on the benchmark are presented in violet in figures 7 and 8. Generally, the differences observed before still hold but are significantly lessened. Strikingly, the extensions even bring CoreXPath 1.0 above NonMixingXPath: the latter only supports non-mixing data tests. It also differentiates VerticalXPath from the two other DataXPath fragments, due to its support for root paths, which in turn allows to support free variables.

Looking at the influence of each extension separately, Tab. 6 shows that the 'basic' extensions of sections 5.2.1 to 5.2.3 contribute most of the gains, while adding positive joins, positional predicates, or id() jumps to the basic extensions only brings small improvements. Regarding positional

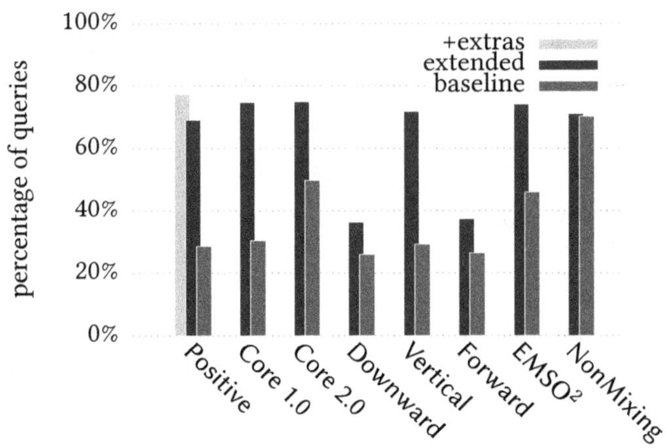

Figure 7: Coverage of the XSLT sources.

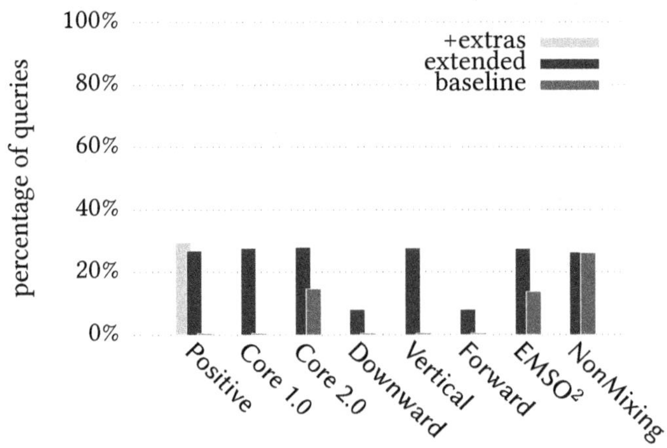

Figure 8: Coverage of the XQuery sources.

predicates, we found that many occurrences are of the form last($x), which is outside the scope of our treatment in Sec. 5.2.5. Regarding id(), Tab. 5 shows that there are *very* few occurrences of id() in the benchmark. A quick investigation of the usage of the id attribute in the benchmark shows that developers rather interact with it through variables and data tests.

6 DISCUSSION

Figures 7 and 8 show the coverage of the benchmark: in grey for the baseline fragments from Sec. 4 and in violet for their extensions described in Sec. 5; the yellow 'extras' are the topic of Sec. 6.2.2. The combined coverage of the extended fragments on the full benchmark is of 12,867 queries (60.86%).

Leaving DownwardXPath and ForwardXPath aside, the extended versions of the remaining six fragments have a somewhat similar coverage: for XSLT queries, between 69.16% for PositiveXPath and 75.03% for CoreXPath 2.0, and for XQuery ones, between 26.35% for NonMixingXPath and 28.08% for

CoreXPath 2.0. We look more closely at the differences between the fragments in Sec. 6.1.

Obviously, the coverage of XPath queries extracted from XQuery files is quite poor compared to that of XSLT files. Among the other factors, we see that the size of the query is (negatively) correlated (Tab. 7). Another correlation is the presence of at least one axis step, where the combined coverage is of 74.50%, but only 48.79% for queries without any axis step. The main factor we identify is however the presence of non-standard or unsupported function calls in the query, which we discuss in Sec. 6.2.

6.1 Comparisons Between Fragments

In the case of the extended fragments of Sec. 5, the inclusions of Fig. 6 are slightly changed: CoreXPath 2.0 now contains NonMixingXPath and PositiveXPath is included into CoreXPath 2.0 but disjoint from NonMixingXPath.

These theoretical inclusions are reflected in the difference matrix shown in Tab. 8 and the accompanying chord graph[4] of Fig. 9. There are three maximal incomparable fragments, namely CoreXPath 2.0, VerticalXPath, and EMSO^{2}XPath. Among the fragments of DataXPath, VerticalXPath benefits from the support of most extensions, while—as seen in Tab. 2—horizontal navigation is not used very frequently in the benchmark. The coverage of the extended CoreXPath 2.0 is almost as large as the combined coverage: only 30 queries from VerticalXPath are not captured by CoreXPath 2.0, and they all contain data joins under a negation; only 12 queries from EMSO^{2}XPath are not captured, which include 11 queries with `id()` plus one of the previous 30.

From a more practical perspective, we think that the extended versions of PositiveXPath and CoreXPath 1.0 are the most promising ones: satisfiability has a more manageable complexity (NP-complete and EXP-complete, resp.), and the coverage is not too far behind CoreXPath 2.0 (with 942 and 57 fewer queries, resp.). Note that PositiveXPath is nearly included into CoreXPath 1.0, with only four queries (featuring intersections) not captured by CoreXPath 1.0.

6.2 Supporting Functions

Due to the large number of calls to non-standard functions in the benchmark, the coverage of 'XPath 3.0 std' (cf. Tab. 1) is an upper bound on the achievable coverage. With respect to the number of queries captured by 'XPath 3.0 std', the combined coverage is 78.33%, and the precise coverage varies between 75.71% for PositiveXPath and 82.14% for CoreXPath 2.0 in XSLT sources and between 56.30% for NonMixingXPath

[4]A chord between fragments i and j has thickness proportional to entry (i, j) on its i end, and to entry (j, i) on its j end. The color of the chord is the one of the 'winning' value. An interactive version is available online at http://www.lsv.fr/~schmitz/xpparser/.

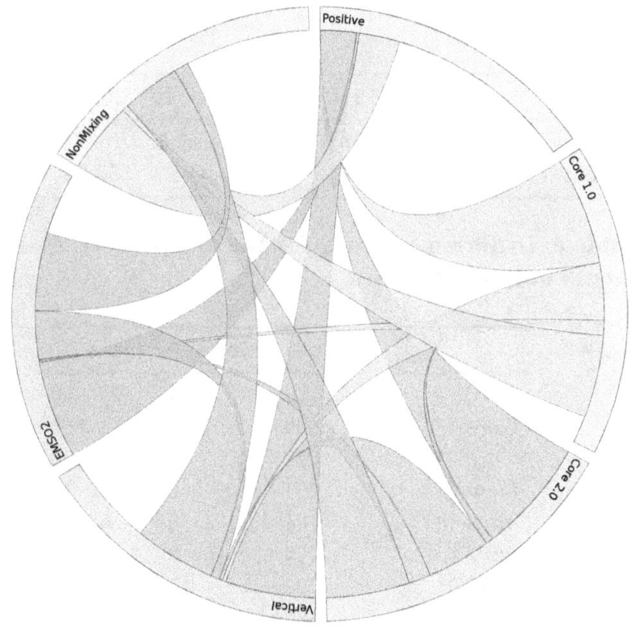

Figure 9: Chord graph of the difference matrix of Tab. 8, without Downward and ForwardXPath.

and 60.00% for CoreXPath 2.0 in XQuery sources: the latter sources are more complex even when leaving aside their higher reliance on non-standard functions.

A remaining issue is the support of standard functions. For instance, the four functions that occur the most frequently in the benchmark are in decreasing order `count()`, `concat()`, `local-name()`, and `contains()`, and they are all standard; `local-name()` is supported in our fragments, but the remaining three are not.

6.2.1 Aggregation. CoreXPath 1.0 extended with node expressions $\mathtt{count}(\pi) \mathbin{\Delta^{+}} i$ for an integer i can be translated into the two-variable fragment of first-order logic with counting on trees, which has an EXPSPACE decision procedure [9]. There are 314 occurrences of such expressions out of the 624 occurrences of `count()` in the benchmark, but unfortunately not a single query is gained by adding this feature to the extended CoreXPath 1.0 fragment. Capturing more occurrences of `count()` requires arithmetic operations, and leads to an undecidable fragment akin to AggXPath [13].

6.2.2 String Processing and Arithmetic. A promising direction for supporting more functions is the move to SMT solvers—even though it might also mean moving to semi-deciding satisfiability. Linear arithmetic is supported by all solvers, while theories comprising string concatenation, string length, and substring operations are also supported [e.g. 1, 40, 42, 53, 55]. SMT solvers have already been used in [11]

Table 7: Combined coverage of the extended fragments by query size.

sizes	1–4	5–8	9–12	13–16	17–20	21–24	25–28	29–32	33–36	37–40	41–44	45–48	≥ 49
queries	5,146	5,661	3,359	1,996	1,330	806	590	503	283	231	117	131	988
coverage	97.9%	58.7%	42.0%	44.2%	54.8%	44.9%	53.0%	42.7%	40.9%	47.6%	35.8%	46.5%	25.7%

Table 8: Difference matrix for the extended fragments. Cell (i, j) shows the number of queries covered by fragment i but not fragment j.

	Positive	Core 1.0	Core 2.0	Downward	Vertical	Forward	EMSO^2	NonMixing
Positive	0	4	0	6,283	300	6,159	23	331
Core 1.0	889	0	0	6,917	469	6,765	124	681
Core 2.0	942	57	0	6,974	526	6,822	181	689
Downward	251	0	0	0	0	0	12	83
Vertical	746	30	30	6,478	0	6,478	73	671
Forward	279	0	0	152	152	0	26	85
EMSO^2	796	12	12	6,817	400	6,679	0	639
NonMixing	584	49	0	6,368	478	6,218	119	0

to check XQuery inputs, using the classical interval encoding of trees, and the approach could be enriched to cover basic arithmetic and string support. Furthermore, a custom finite tree theory may be added to SMT solvers for more efficiency [e.g. 14, 18].

These considerations lead us to adding support in the extended PositiveXPath for linear arithmetic, the standard functions `concat()`, `contains()`, `string-length()`, and similar ones such as `ends-with()`. We view this fragment as a good candidate for practical satisfiability checking. At 62.75%, the coverage of this fragment, shown in yellow in figures 7 and 8, bests the combined coverage of our other fragments. This translates in particular to 84.77% of the subset of XSLT queries captured by 'XPath 3.0 std'.

This new fragment is incomparable with the others, with a new combined coverage of 67.40% (83.55% for XSLT sources). If we restrict our attention to the 14,732 queries (69.68%) that only use `not()` and the functions supported in this new fragment, the new combined coverage reaches 96.69% (98.10% for XSLT sources). Thus our fragments cover nearly all the queries that do not use unsupported or non-standard functions, from which we argue that improved function support is the most promising research avenue in order to gain over the extended fragments described in Sec. 5.

7 CONCLUDING REMARKS

We have designed a benchmarking infrastructure for testing the practical relevance of XPath fragments, based on the XQueryX format and Relax NG schemas. We have used this benchmark of over 20,000 queries, extracted from the XSLT and XQuery files of open-source projects, to evaluate the syntactic coverage of state-of-the-art XPath fragments for which decidability is known (or still open in the case of EMSO^{2}XPath). Concerning the benchmark itself, it would of course be interesting to incorporate new sources, to confirm our observations on a larger scale.

Our analysis shows that, in a hypothetical satisfiability checker for XPath, the differences between the fragments defined in the theoretical literature are not as important as the differences introduced by the *front-end* translating real XPath inputs to the restricted syntax on which the decision procedure operates. Among the features that such a front-end should support, the most impactful ones would be free variables, data tests against constants (and constant expressions), positive joins, and positional predicates.

According to our benchmark results, such a front-end combined with the decidable fragments from the literature would cover about 70%–75% of the XPath queries found in XSLT files. However, due to the high reliance on user-defined or ill-supported functions, this drops to less than 30% for XPath queries from XQuery files: full-blown program analysis techniques seem necessary for XQuery.

As the the support of XPath functions is a key factor, a promising approach might be to harness the power of modern SMT solvers to handle string-manipulating functions and linear arithmetic, which might cover 77.44% of the XPath queries from the XSLT sources.

ACKNOWLEDGMENTS

The authors thank the anonymous referees for their valuable comments and helpful suggestions. Work funded by ANR-14-CE28-0005 PRODAQ.

REFERENCES

[1] Parosh Aziz Abdulla, Mohamed Faouzi Atig, Yu-Fang Chen, Lukáš Holík, Ahmed Rezine, Philipp Rümmer, and Jari Stenman. 2015. Norn: An SMT solver for string constraints. In *CAV '15 (Lect. Notes in Comput. Sci.)*, Vol. 9206. Springer, 462–469. https://doi.org/10.1007/978-3-319-21690-4_29

[2] Sergio Abriola, Diego Figueira, and Santiago Figueira. 2017. Logics of repeating values on data trees and branching counter systems. In *FoSSaCS '17 (Lect. Notes in Comput. Sci.)*, Vol. 10203. Springer, 196–212. https://doi.org/10.1007/978-3-662-54458-7_12

[3] Loredana Afanasiev, Patrick Blackburn, Ioanna Dimitriou, Bertrand Gaiffe, Evan Goris, Maarten Marx, and Maarten de Rijke. 2005. PDL for ordered trees. *J. Appl. Non-Classical Log.* 15, 2 (2005), 115–135. https://doi.org/10.3166/jancl.15.115-135

[4] Loredana Afanasiev and Marteen Marx. 2008. An analysis of XQuery benchmarks. *Inform. Sys.* 33, 2 (2008), 155–181. https://doi.org/10.1016/j.is.2007.05.002

[5] Diego Arroyuelo, Francisco Claude, Sebastian Maneth, Veli Mäkinen, Gonzalo Navarro, Kim Nguyễn, Jouni Sirén, and Niko Välimäki. 2015. Fast in-memory XPath search using compressed indexes. *Softw. Pract. & Exp.* 45, 3 (2015), 399–434. https://doi.org/10.1002/spe.2227

[6] David Baelde, Anthony Lick, and Sylvain Schmitz. 2019. XPath benchmark, version 2.0. https://hal.inria.fr/hal-02079114

[7] David Baelde, Anthony Lick, and Sylvain Schmitz. 2019. XPath parser, version 1.0. https://hal.inria.fr/hal-02079276

[8] David Baelde, Simon Lunel, and Sylvain Schmitz. 2016. A sequent calculus for a modal logic on finite data trees. In *CSL 2016 (Leibniz Int. Proc. Inf.)*, Vol. 62. LZI, Article 32. https://doi.org/10.4230/LIPIcs.CSL.2016.32

[9] Bartosz Bednarczyk, Witold Charatonik, and Emanuel Kieronski. 2017. Extending two-variable logic on trees. In *CSL '17 (Leibniz Int. Proc. Inf.)*, Vol. 82. Schloss Dagstuhl–Leibniz-Zentrum fuer Informatik, Article 11. https://doi.org/10.4230/LIPIcs.CSL.2017.11

[10] Saguy Benaim, Michael Benedikt, Witold Charatonik, Emanuel Kieroński, Rastislav Lenhardt, Filip Mazowiecki, and James Worrell. 2016. Complexity of two-variable logic on finite trees. *ACM Trans. Comput. Logic* 17, 4, Article 32 (2016). https://doi.org/10.1145/2996796

[11] Michael Benedikt and James Cheney. 2010. Destabilizers and independence of XML updates. *Proc. VLDB* 3, 1 (2010), 906–917. https://doi.org/10.14778/1920841.1920956

[12] Michael Benedikt, Wenfei Fan, and Floris Geerts. 2008. XPath satisfiability in the presence of DTDs. *J. ACM* 55, 2, Article 8 (2008). https://doi.org/10.1145/1346330.1346333

[13] Michael Benedikt and Christoph Koch. 2009. XPath leashed. *ACM Comput. Surv.* 41, 1, Article 3 (2009). https://doi.org/10.1145/1456650.1456653

[14] Patrick Blackburn, Wilfried Meyer-Viol, and Maarten de Rijke. 1996. A proof system for finite trees. In *CSL '95 (Lect. Notes in Comput. Sci.)*, Vol. 1092. Springer, 86–105. https://doi.org/10.1007/3-540-61377-3_33

[15] Mikołaj Bojańczyk, Anca Muscholl, Thomas Schwentick, and Luc Segoufin. 2009. Two-variable logic on data trees and XML reasoning. *J. ACM* 56, 3, Article 13 (2009). https://doi.org/10.1145/1516512.1516515

[16] Mikołaj Bojańczyk and Paweł Parys. 2011. XPath evaluation in linear time. *J. ACM* 58, 4, Article 17 (2011). https://doi.org/10.1145/1989727.1989731

[17] Angela Bonifati, Wim Martens, and Thomas Timm. 2017. An analytical study of large SPARQL query logs. *Proc. VLDB* 11, 2 (2017), 149–161. https://doi.org/10.14778/3149193.3149196

[18] James Cheney. 2011. Satisfiability algorithms for conjunctive queries over trees. In *ICDT '11*. ACM, 150–161. https://doi.org/10.1145/1938551.1938572

[19] Wojciech Czerwiński, Claire David, Filip Murlak, and Paweł Parys. 2018. Reasoning about integrity constraints for tree-structured data. *Theor. Comput. Syst.* 62, 4 (2018), 941–976. https://doi.org/10.1007/s00224-017-9771-z

[20] James Clark (Ed.). 2002. *RELAX NG Compact Syntax*. OASIS Committee Specification. http://relaxng.org/compact.html

[21] Jim Melton (Ed.). 2014. *XQueryX 3.0*. W3C Recommendation. http://www.w3.org/TR/xqueryx-3/

[22] Michael Kay (Ed.). 2014. *XPath and XQuery Functions and Operators 3.0*. W3C Recommendation. https://www.w3.org/TR/xpath-functions-30/

[23] Michael Kay (Ed.). 2017. *XSL Transformations (XSLT) Version 3.0*. W3C Recommendation. http://www.w3.org/TR/xslt-30/

[24] Diego Figueira. 2012. Alternating register automata on finite words and trees. *Logic. Meth. in Comput. Sci.* 8, 1, Article 22 (2012). https://doi.org/10.2168/LMCS-8(1:22)2012

[25] Diego Figueira. 2012. Decidability of downward XPath. *ACM Trans. Comput. Logic* 13, 4, Article 34 (2012). https://doi.org/10.1145/2362355.2362362

[26] Diego Figueira. 2013. On XPath with transitive axes and data tests. In *PODS '13*. ACM, 249–260. https://doi.org/10.1145/2463664.2463675

[27] Diego Figueira. 2018. Automata column: Satisfiability of XPath on data trees. *SIGLOG News* 5, 2 (2018), 4–16. https://doi.org/10.1145/3212019.3212021

[28] Diego Figueira and Luc Segoufin. 2009. Future-looking logics on data words and trees. In *MFCS '09 (Lect. Notes in Comput. Sci.)*, Vol. 5734. Springer, 331–343. https://doi.org/10.1007/978-3-642-03816-7_29

[29] Diego Figueira and Luc Segoufin. 2017. Bottom-up automata on data trees and vertical XPath. *Logic. Meth. in Comput. Sci.* 13, 4, Article 5 (2017). https://doi.org/10.23638/LMCS-13(4:5)2017

[30] Massimo Franceschet. 2005. XPathMark – An XPath benchmark for XMark generated data. In *XSYM 2005 (Lect. Notes in Comput. Sci.)*, Vol. 3671. 129–143. https://doi.org/10.1007/11547273_10

[31] Floris Geerts and Wenfei Fan. 2005. Satisfiability of XPath queries with sibling axes. In *DBPL '05*. Springer, 122–137. https://doi.org/10.1007/11601524_8

[32] Pierre Genevès, Nabil Layaïda, Alan Schmitt, and Nils Gesbert. 2015. Efficiently deciding μ-calculus with converse over finite trees. *ACM Trans. Comput. Logic* 16, 2, Article 16 (2015). https://doi.org/10.1145/2724712

[33] Pierre Genevès and Jean-Yves Vion-Dury. 2004. Logic-based XPath optimization. In *DocEng '04*. ACM, 211–219. https://doi.org/10.1145/1030397.1030437

[34] Georg Gottlob and Christoph Koch. 2002. Monadic queries over tree-structured data. In *LICS '02*. IEEE, 189–202. https://doi.org/10.1109/LICS.2002.1029828

[35] Georg Gottlob, Christoph Koch, Reinhard Pichler, and Luc Segoufin. 2005. The complexity of XPath query evaluation and XML typing. *J. ACM* 52, 2 (2005), 284–335. https://doi.org/10.1145/1059513.1059520

[36] Jinghua Groppe and Sven Groppe. 2006. A prototype of a schema-based XPath satisfiability tester. In *DEXA '06 (Lect. Notes in Comput. Sci.)*, Vol. 4080. Springer, 93–103. https://doi.org/10.1007/11827405_10

[37] Jan Hidders. 2004. Satisfiability of XPath expressions. In *DBPL 2003 (Lect. Notes in Comput. Sci.)*, Georg Lausen and Dan Suciu (Eds.), Vol. 2921. Springer, 21–36. https://doi.org/10.1007/978-3-540-24607-7_3

[38] Florent Jacquemard, Luc Segoufin, and Jérémie Dimino. 2016. $FO^2(<, +1, \sim)$ on data trees, data tree automata and branching vector addition systems. *Logic. Meth. in Comput. Sci.* 12, 2, Article 3 (2016). https://doi.org/10.2168/LMCS-12(2:3)2016

[39] M. Jurdziński and R. Lazić. 2011. Alternating automata on data trees and XPath satisfiability. *ACM Trans. Comput. Logic* 12, 3, Article 19 (2011). https://doi.org/10.1145/1929954.1929956

[40] Adam Kiezun, Vijay Ganesh, Shay Artzi, Philip J. Guo, Pieter Hooimeijer, and Michael D. Ernst. 2013. HAMPI: A solver for word equations over strings, regular expressions, and context-free grammars. *ACM Trans. Softw. Eng. Methodol.* 21, 4, Article 25 (2013). https://doi.org/10.1145/2377656.2377662

[41] Ranko Lazić and Sylvain Schmitz. 2015. Non-elementary complexities for branching VASS, MELL, and extensions. *ACM Trans. Comput. Logic* 16, 3, Article 20 (2015). https://doi.org/10.1145/2733375

[42] Tianyi Liang, Andrew Reynolds, Nestan Tsiskaridze, Cesare Tinelli, Clark Barrett, and Morgan Deters. 2016. An efficient SMT solver for string constraints. *Form. Methods in Syst. Des.* 48, 3 (2016), 206–234. https://doi.org/10.1007/s10703-016-0247-6

[43] Maarten Marx. 2003. XPath and modal logics of finite DAG's. In *TABLEAUX '03 (Lect. Notes in Comput. Sci.)*, Vol. 2796. Springer, 150–164. https://doi.org/10.1007/978-3-540-45206-5_13

[44] Maarten Marx. 2005. Conditional XPath. *ACM Trans. Datab. Sys.* 30, 4 (2005), 929–959. https://doi.org/10.1145/1114244.1114247

[45] Frank Neven and Thomas Schwentick. 2006. On the complexity of XPath containment in the presence of disjunction, DTDs, and variables. *Logic. Meth. in Comput. Sci.* 2, 3, Article 1 (2006). https://doi.org/10.2168/LMCS-2(3:1)2006

[46] Francois Picalausa and Stijn Vansummeren. 2011. What Are Real SPARQL Queries Like?. In *SWIM '11*. ACM, Article 7, 6 pages. https://doi.org/10.1145/1999299.1999306

[47] Jonathan Robie, Don Chamberlin, Michael Dyck, and John Snelson (Eds.). 2014. *XML Path Language (XPath) 3.0.* W3C Recommendation. http://www.w3.org/TR/xpath-3/

[48] Jonathan Robie, Don Chamberlin, Michael Dyck, and John Snelson (Eds.). 2014. *XQuery 3.0: An XML Query Language.* W3C Recommendation. http://www.w3.org/TR/xquery-30/

[49] Albrecht Schmidt, Florian Waas, Martin Kersten, Michael J. Carey, Ioana Manolescu, and Ralph Busse. 2002. XMark: A benchmark for XML data management. In *VLDB '02*. VLDB Endowment, 974–985.

[50] Thomas Schwentick. 2004. XPath query containment. *SIGMOD Rec.* 33, 1 (2004), 101–109. https://doi.org/10.1145/974121.974140

[51] Balder ten Cate. 2006. The expressivity of XPath with transitive closure. In *PODS '06*. ACM, 328–337. https://doi.org/10.1145/1142351.1142398

[52] Balder ten Cate and Carsten Lutz. 2009. The complexity of query containment in expressive fragments of XPath 2.0. *J. ACM* 56, 6, Article 31 (2009). https://doi.org/10.1145/1568318.1568321

[53] Minh-Thai Trinh, Duc-Hiep Chu, and Joxan Jaffar. 2014. S3: A symbolic string solver for vulnerability detection in Web applications. In *CCS '14*. ACM, 1232–1243. https://doi.org/10.1145/2660267.2660372

[54] Norman Walsh, Anders Berglund, and John Snelson (Eds.). 2014. *XQuery and XPath Data Model 3.0.* W3C Recommendation. http://www.w3.org/TR/xpath-datamodel-30/

[55] Yunhui Zheng, Xiangyu Zhang, and Vijay Ganesh. 2013. Z3-str: A Z3-based string solver for web application analysis. In *ESEC/FSE '13*. ACM, 114–124. https://doi.org/10.1145/2491411.2491456

Table 9: The synthetic benchmarks' composition.

Sources	Queries	Coverage			
		XPath 1.0	XPath 2.0	XPath 3.0	XPath 3.0 std
XPathMark-FT	64	100.0%	100.0%	100.0%	100.0%
XPathMark-PT	38	100.0%	100.0%	100.0%	100.0%
XMark	66	92.4%	93.9%	100.0%	98.4%
Total	168	97.0%	97.6%	100.0%	99.4%

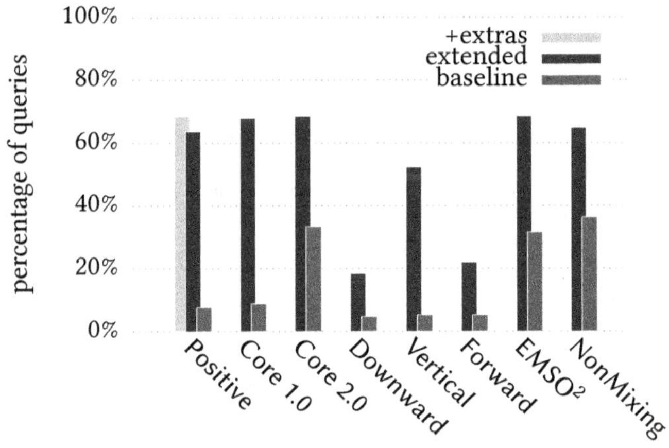

Figure 10: Coverage of the synthetic benchmarks.

A ADDITIONAL DATA

A.1 Synthetic Benchmarks

We did not include earlier synthetic benchmarks in our analysis, as we focus on real-world queries. We report here on two well-known synthetic benchmarks from the literature, XMark [49] and XPathMark [30]. The latter comprises two collections of queries: functional queries (XPathMark-FT) check the functional correctness of XPath processors, while performance queries (XPathMark-PT) allow to evaluate the performance of query evaluation in XPath processors.

A.1.1 Composition. Table 9 shows the composition of these benchmarks following the same format as in Tab. 1. The composition of these two synthetic benchmarks differs significantly from Tab. 1. The queries in these benchmarks are almost all from XPath 1.0, and although XMark is a benchmark of XQuery formulæ, it employs very few non-standard functions or complex constructs such as `map`.

A.1.2 Coverage. The coverage of the various syntactic fragments of XPath over these synthetic benchmarks is shown in Fig. 10, following the same format as figures 7 and 8.

As these sources total less than 200 queries, it is hard to draw any conclusions from this analysis. Nevertheless, we observe that the improvement brought by extensions is much more significant than for real-world queries, which might be explained by the fact that synthetic benchmarks aim for conciseness while attempting to achieve a complete coverage of XPath features. Similarly, the coverage of the extended VerticalXPath fragment is significantly lower, compared to other extended fragments, than for real-world queries, due to the higher proportion of horizontal navigation. Overall, the coverage of extended fragments is slightly lower than the one achieved for XSLT sources in the real-world benchmark.

A.2 Detailed Source Breakdown

The detailed composition of our benchmark [6] is given in Tab. 10, following the same structure as Tab. 1.

B EXAMPLE PARSER OUTPUT

Here is an XQuery snippet from the file `functx.xqy` of His-TEI:

```
module namespace functx = "http://www.functx.com" ;
declare function functx:id-from-element
  ( $element as element()? )  as xs:string? {
    data(($element/@*[id(.) is  ..])[1])
  } ;
```

The parser identifies 'data (($element/@*[id (.) **is** ..])[1])' as an XPath query inside this program, and returns the following information (note the normalisation of some of the syntactic sugar, like '@*' and ' .. '), including the syntax tree in XQueryX format [21] inside the <ast> element:

```
<?xml version="1.0"?>
<benchmark>
<xpath column="45" filename="benchmark/example-histei.xqy" line="4">
  <query>data(($element/ attribute:: *[( id (.) is parent::node ())])[1]) </query>
  <ast size="30">
    <xqx:functionCallExpr xmlns:xqx="http: //www.w3.org/2005/XQueryX">
      <xqx:functionName>data</xqx:functionName>
      <xqx:arguments>
        <xqx:pathExpr>
          <xqx:stepExpr>
            < xqx:filterExpr >
              <xqx:sequenceExpr>
                <xqx:pathExpr>
                  <xqx:stepExpr>
                    < xqx:filterExpr >
                      <xqx:varRef>
                        <xqx:name>element</xqx:name>
                      </xqx:varRef>
                    </ xqx:filterExpr >
                  </xqx:stepExpr>
                  <xqx:stepExpr>
                    <xqx:xpathAxis> attribute </xqx:xpathAxis>
                    <xqx:Wildcard/>
                    < xqx:predicates >
                      <xqx:isOp>
                        <xqx:firstOperand>
                          <xqx:functionCallExpr>
                            <xqx:functionName>id</xqx:functionName>
                            <xqx:arguments>
                              <xqx:contextItemExpr/>
                            </xqx:arguments>
                          </ xqx:functionCallExpr>
                        </ xqx:firstOperand >
                        <xqx:secondOperand>
                          <xqx:pathExpr>
                            <xqx:stepExpr>
                              <xqx:xpathAxis>parent</xqx:xpathAxis>
                              <xqx:anyKindTest/>
                            </xqx:stepExpr>
                          </xqx:pathExpr>
                        </xqx:secondOperand>
                      </xqx:isOp>
                    </ xqx:predicates >
                  </xqx:stepExpr>
                </xqx:pathExpr>
              </xqx:sequenceExpr>
            </ xqx:filterExpr >
            < xqx:predicates >
              <xqx:integerConstantExpr>
                <xqx:value>1</xqx:value>
              </xqx:integerConstantExpr>
            </ xqx:predicates >
          </xqx:stepExpr>
        </xqx:pathExpr>
      </xqx:arguments>
    </ xqx:functionCallExpr >
  </ ast >
</xpath>
</benchmark>
```

This syntax tree in XQueryX format can be validated against XML Schemas or Relax NG syntactic specifications in order to check whether it fits in some XPath fragments.

Table 10: The benchmark's list of sources.

Source	Queries	Coverage XPath 1.0	XPath 2.0	XPath 3.0	XPath 3.0 std	Core 2.0 extended
DocBook http://docbook.sourceforge.net/	7,620	100.0%	100.0%	100.0%	95.6%	79.3%
TEIXSL https://github.com/TEIC/Stylesheets	6,303	96.4%	100.0%	100.0%	86.1%	70.8%
HTMLBook https://github.com/oreillymedia/HTMLBook	752	100.0%	100.0%	100.0%	92.0%	66.4%
Total (XSLT)	14,675	98.4%	100.0%	100.0%	91.3%	75.0%
XQuery parser https://github.com/jpcs/xqueryparser.xq	1,659	83.1%	85.2%	99.9%	15.7%	12.6%
eXist-db https://github.com/eXist-db	1,151	76.7%	88.0%	100.0%	64.8%	33.1%
HisTEI https://github.com/odaata/HisTEI	483	74.7%	97.5%	100.0%	62.5%	30.2%
transform.xq https://github.com/jpcs/transform.xq	365	64.3%	70.4%	99.7%	45.7%	20.5%
ml-enrich https://github.com/freshie/ml-enrich	302	74.1%	96.3%	100.0%	55.2%	39.4%
xquerydoc https://github.com/xquery/xquerydoc	269	87.3%	98.8%	100.0%	52.7%	28.9%
openinfoman https://github.com/openhie/openinfoman	261	65.1%	96.1%	100.0%	47.8%	26.8%
Oxford Dict API https://github.com/AdamSteffanick/od-api-xquery	207	85.5%	97.5%	100.0%	57.4%	55.5%
MarkLogic Commons https://github.com/marklogic/commons	196	70.9%	93.8%	97.4%	45.4%	24.4%
datascience https://github.com/adamfowleruk/datascience	184	77.1%	91.8%	100.0%	40.7%	21.1%
Link Management BaseX https://github.com/dita-for-small-teams/dfst-linkmgmt-basex/	154	72.0%	96.7%	100.0%	73.3%	36.3%
Semantic Web https://github.com/HeardLibrary/semantic-web/	149	86.5%	93.9%	100.0%	81.2%	51.0%
eXist annotation store https://github.com/telic/exist-annotation-store/	133	80.4%	86.4%	100.0%	64.6%	48.8%
xqtest https://github.com/irinc/xqtest/	130	70.0%	99.2%	100.0%	46.9%	38.4%
data.xq https://github.com/jpcs/data.xq/	119	32.7%	33.6%	100.0%	34.4%	16.8%
graphxq https://github.com/apb2006/graphxq/	92	73.9%	78.2%	100.0%	76.0%	47.8%
ml-invoker https://github.com/fgeorges/ml-invoker/	92	89.1%	89.1%	100.0%	36.9%	32.6%
treedown https://github.com/biblicalhumanities/treedown/	92	94.5%	97.8%	100.0%	80.4%	59.7%
XQJSON https://github.com/joewiz/xqjson/	90	74.4%	100.0%	100.0%	67.7%	55.5%
fots BaseX https://github.com/LeoWoerteler/fots-basex/	73	65.7%	71.2%	100.0%	63.0%	28.7%
GPXQuery https://github.com/dret/GPXQuery/	57	73.6%	98.2%	100.0%	64.9%	29.8%
rbtree.qx https://github.com/jpcs/rbtree.xq/	57	22.8%	28.0%	100.0%	24.5%	0%
xquery-libs https://github.com/adamretter/xquery-libs/	53	79.2%	88.6%	100.0%	60.3%	49.0%
Guid-O-Matic https://github.com/baskaufs/guid-o-matic/	51	84.3%	96.0%	100.0%	56.8%	41.1%
functional.xq https://github.com/jpcs/functional.xq/	47	12.7%	14.8%	100.0%	21.2%	2.1%
Total (XQuery)	6,466	76.1%	87.4%	99.8%	46.7%	28.0%
Total	21,141	91.6%	96.1%	99.9%	77.7%	60.6%

Containment of Shape Expression Schemas for RDF

Sławek Staworko
CRIStAL, INRIA LINKS, CNRS
University of Lille
France
slawomir.staworko@inria.fr

Piotr Wieczorek
Institute of Computer Science
University of Wrocław
Poland
piotr.wieczorek@cs.uni.wroc.pl

ABSTRACT

We study the problem of containment of *shape expression schemas* (ShEx) for RDF graphs. We identify a subclass of ShEx that has a natural graphical representation in the form of *shape graphs* and whose semantics is captured with a tractable notion of *embedding* of an RDF graph in a shape graph. When applied to pairs of shape graphs, an embedding is a sufficient condition for containment, and for a practical subclass of *deterministic shape graphs*, it is also a necessary one, thus yielding a subclass with tractable containment. Containment for general shape graphs is EXP-complete. Finally, we show that containment for arbitrary ShEx is decidable.

CCS CONCEPTS

• **Information systems** → **Graph-based database models**; **Resource Description Framework (RDF)**; • **Theory of computation** → **Database theory**; Database interoperability.

KEYWORDS

RDF, Schema, ShEx, containment, counter-example

ACM Reference Format:

Sławek Staworko and Piotr Wieczorek. 2019. Containment of Shape Expression Schemas for RDF. In *38th ACM SIGMOD-SIGACT-SIGAI Symposium on Principles of Database Systems (PODS'19), June 30-July 5, 2019, Amsterdam, Netherlands.* ACM, New York, NY, USA, 17 pages. https://doi.org/10.1145/3294052.3319687

1 INTRODUCTION

Although RDF has been originally introduced schema-free, it has since become a standalone database format and the need for a schema language has been identified, with the emergence of new RDF applications previously reserved to relational and semi-structured databases [2, 37]. Recently introduced by W3C, and under continuous development, *shape expression schema* (ShEx) is a formalism for defining valid RDF graphs [21–23, 38]. ShEx allows to define a set of types, each type defined with a rule describing the admissible types of the outbound neighborhood of a node. Inspired by versatility of schema languages for XML [4, 19], the rules of ShEx are based on regular expressions.

An example of shape expression schema for RDF graphs storing bug reports is presented in Figure 1. The schema requires a bug report to have a description and a user who reported it. Optionally, a bug report may have an employee who successfully reproduced the bug. Also, a bug report can have a number of related bug reports. A user has a name and an optional email address while an employee has a name and a mandatory email address.

In this paper, we investigate the classical problem of *containment*: given two schemas S and S', is the set of instances satisfying S contained in the set of instances satisfying S'? This problem has applications to a vast number of problems that perform non-trivial reasoning tasks such as data exchange, query optimization, and inference [1, 3, 9, 10, 14, 16, 40]. The task at hand is difficult for a number of reasons.

Because the neighborhood of a node in an RDF graph is unordered, regular expressions define bag languages, also known as *commutative languages* [18], where the relative order among symbols is irrelevant. This lack of order gives raise to a significant degree of nondeterminism when working with *regular bag expressions* (RBE). For instance, membership for RBE i.e., deciding whether a bag of symbols belongs to the language defined by an RBE, is NP-complete [20]. Similarly, validation for ShEx i.e., deciding whether a RDF graph satisfies a ShEx, is NP-complete too [34]. The need for nondeterminism can be limited by disallowing disjunction and permitting the Kleene closure on atomic symbols only. This yields the class RBE_0 with tractable membership and tractable validation for the corresponding class of shape expression schemas ShEx_0. Similarly, single-occurrence regular bag expressions (SORBE) have tractable membership and give rise to *deterministic* shape expression schemas (DetShEx), where the same symbol can be used only once. Their validation is also tractable [34]. Both restrictions offer enough room to

PODS'19, June 30-July 5, 2019, Amsterdam, Netherlands

ACM ISBN 978-1-4503-6227-6/19/06...$15.00
https://doi.org/10.1145/3294052.3319687

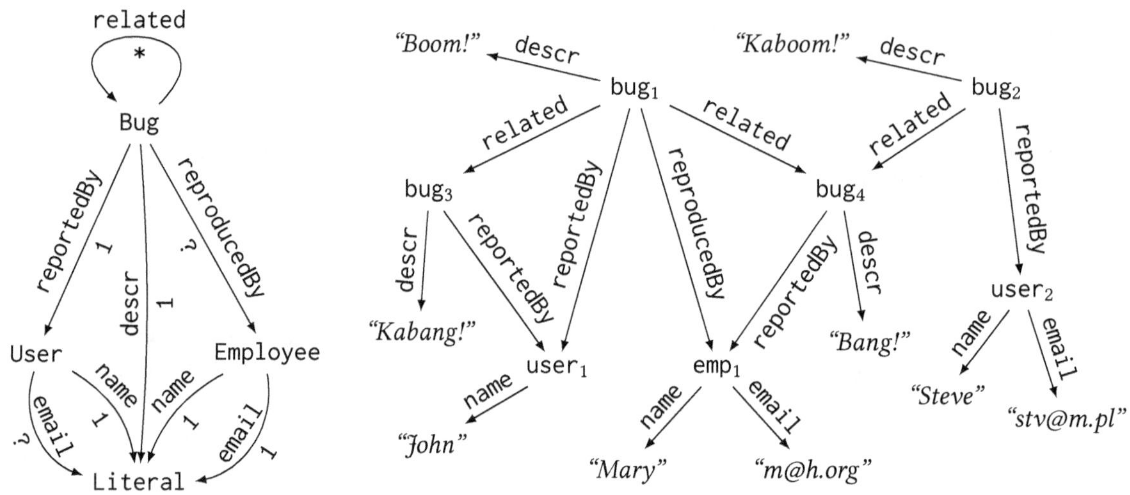

$\mathsf{Bug} \longrightarrow \mathtt{descr} :: \mathtt{Literal},\ \mathtt{reportedBy} :: \mathsf{User},\ \mathtt{reproducedBy} :: \mathsf{Employee}^?,\ \mathtt{related} :: \mathsf{Bug}^*$

$\mathsf{User} \longrightarrow \mathtt{name} :: \mathtt{Literal},\ \mathtt{email} :: \mathtt{Literal}^?$

$\mathsf{Employee} \longrightarrow \mathtt{name} :: \mathtt{Literal},\ \mathtt{email} :: \mathtt{Literal}$

Figure 1: An RDF graph with bug reports (top right) together with a shape expression schema (bottom) and the corresponding shape graph (top left).

accommodate practical uses, and in particular, the schema in Figure 1 belongs to them both.

Since ShEx is a schema language based on types, comparing two schemas requires the ability to compare types, and consequently, testing $S \subseteq S'$ revolves around questions whether a type t of S is *covered* by the union of types $s_1, \ldots, s_k$ of S'. Indeed, suppose that in the schema in Figure 1 we replace the type User with two types depending on whether or not the user has an email address:

$\mathsf{User}_1 \longrightarrow \mathtt{name} :: \mathtt{Literal}$
$\mathsf{User}_2 \longrightarrow \mathtt{name} :: \mathtt{Literal},\ \mathtt{email} :: \mathtt{Literal}$

and adapt the rest of the schema by replacing Bug with

$\mathsf{Bug}_1 \longrightarrow \mathtt{descr} :: \mathtt{Literal},\ \mathtt{reportedBy} :: \mathsf{User}_1,$
$\quad \mathtt{reproducedBy} :: \mathsf{Employee}^?,$
$\quad \mathtt{related} :: \mathsf{Bug}_1^*,\ \mathtt{related} :: \mathsf{Bug}_2^*$
$\mathsf{Bug}_2 \longrightarrow \mathtt{descr} :: \mathtt{Literal},\ \mathtt{reportedBy} :: \mathsf{User}_2,$
$\quad \mathtt{reproducedBy} :: \mathsf{Employee}^?,$
$\quad \mathtt{related} :: \mathsf{Bug}_1^*,\ \mathtt{related} :: \mathsf{Bug}_2^*$

Although no longer deterministic (the symbol related is used twice in the type definitions of Bug_1 and Bug_2), the modified schema is equivalent to the original one as the type Bug is covered by the union of the types Bug_1 and Bug_2, and the type User by the union of User_1 and User_2 (the latter also being equivalent to Employee).

Naturally, the fact that a type might be covered by a union of types is a source of complexity of the containment problem, and it is an interesting question if there is a class of schemas for which comparison on pairs of types alone would suffice. To answer this question, we use *shape graphs*, which are natural graphical representation of ShEx_0 (cf. Figure 1), and propose a graph-theoretic notion of an *embedding* between pairs of shape graphs. In essence, an embedding identifies in a simulation-like manner when a type is covered by another type, and therefore, is a sufficient condition for containment. We also identify a class $\mathsf{DetShEx}_0^-$ for which embedding is a necessary condition for containment. $\mathsf{DetShEx}_0^-$ is the class of deterministic shape expressions schema using RBE_0, which furthermore forbids the use of + and, intuitively, requires every ? to be referenced through $*$. In particular, the schema in Figure 1 belongs to $\mathsf{DetShEx}_0^-$ because the type User using $\mathtt{email} :: \mathtt{Literal}^?$ is (indirectly) referenced by $\mathtt{related} :: \mathsf{Bug}^*$ in type Bug.

Because embeddings are carefully crafted to be tractable, we obtain a class with tractable containment. The additional restrictions of $\mathsf{DetShEx}_0^-$ are necessary as we show the containment problem for full $\mathsf{DetShEx}_0$ to be intractable. Interestingly, for a schema S in $\mathsf{DetShEx}_0^-$ we construct a *characterizing* graph G such that G is satisfied by any schema S' in $\mathsf{DetShEx}_0^-$ if and only if $S \subseteq S'$.

Checking the containment $S \subseteq S'$ involves implicit negation: checking whether there is no *counter-example*, an instance that satisfies S and does not satisfy S'. The implicit negation allows to encode disjunction even in classes of schemas that explicitly forbid using disjunction in type definitions, such as ShEx_0. This renders ShEx_0 very powerful and allows for pairs of schemas for which the smallest counter-example is of exponential size. Not surprisingly, we observe a significant impact on complexity: testing containment for shape graphs is EXP-complete.

The picture of containment for arbitrary shape expression schemas is far from obvious. It is known that ∃MSO on graphs is alone insufficient to capture ShEx and needs to be enriched with Presburger arithmetic [34]. However, monadic extensions of Presburger arithmetic quickly become undecidable [13, 31]. The question whether containment for ShEx is decidable at all is non-trivial but we answer it positively and give an initial characterization of its complexity: coNEXP-hard and in $\text{co2NEXP}^{\text{NP}}$. The precise complexity of containment for ShEx remains an open question.

Our study has a number of outcomes:

- a thorough characterization of complexity of containment for classes of shape expression schemas;
- a set of bounds on the size of a minimal graph that satisfies one schema and violates another;
- a tractable notion of embeddings that is a sufficient condition for containment, and a necessary one of a subclass of deterministic shape expression schemas.

Related work. There is a large body of literature dealing with the containment problem for various database schema formalisms. The expressivity of ShEx has been studied in [34]. ShEx is not comparable to neither FO logic on graphs, nor to ∃MSO on graphs. In order to capture the cardinality contraints e.g., $(a \parallel b)^*$, expressible by RBE, ∃MSO has to be extended with Presburger Arithmetic (PA). Such extensions, as we have already mentioned, can easily get to be undecidable [13, 31]. It is, also, a classic result that MSO theory of $\mathbb{N}$ with addition is undecidable, it has been shown in [30] that even MSO theory of naturals with the double function, $\langle \mathbb{N}, +1, 2x, 0 \rangle$, is undecidable.

Schema languages for trees have been extensively studied in the context of XML. Most of the work, however, has been devoted to the case of ordered trees. Typically, schema languages for ordered trees (DTD, XML Schema) are captured by tree automata. A survey of basic decision problems for tree automata can be found in [36]. In particular, containment for nondeterministic tree automata is EXPTIME-complete [33] but becomes polynomial for deterministic tree automata. The containment of DTDs over the usual (ordered) nondeterministic regular expressions is PSPACE-complete and remains intractable even for very simple nondeterministic regular expressions [24] but drops to PTIME [25] if deterministic regular expressions are used as mandated by the XML standard [7]. We point out that in our case, however, determinism alone is not sufficient, in order to obtain tractability of the containment we need to enforce additional structural conditions on the shape graphs.

Various forms of DTDs with regular expressions interpreted under the commutative closure [28] have been studied. In the context of trees many formalisms have been introduced to express the numerical constrains on the occurrences of the different symbols among the children of some node, e.g., Presburger automata [31, 32], sheaves automata[12], TQL logic[8]. Unfortunately, the containment problem in all this settings is NP-hard [20].

The problem of containment of regular expressions with interleaving is EXPSPACE-complete [26]. A number of expressive formalisms with interleaving have been shown in [15] to have highly intractable inclusion.

Disjunctive multiplicity schemas (DMS) for unordered XML have been studied in [5]. A DMS is a formalism that defines for each label the language of allowed children labels using disjunctive multiplicity expressions (DIME) that are similar to RBE_0 but allow a limited form of disjunction. DMS assume similar form of determinism as DTDs since types of nodes are identified with their labels. Additionaly, DIMEs require each of the alphabet symbols from Σ to appear at most once. Nevertheless, the containment for DMS is in PTIME.

Organization. The paper is organized as follows. In Section 2 we present basic notions and introduce embeddings of shape graphs. In Section 3 we investigate decidability of containment for the full fragment of ShEx by bounding the size of a counter-example. In Section 4 we analyze the complexity of containment for shape graphs (ShEx_0) and show a tight exponential bound on the size of a counter-example. In Section 5 we identify a tractable subclass of deterministic shape expression schemas and investigate the complexity of constructing embeddings. We summarize our work and outline directions of further study in Section 6.

2 BASIC NOTIONS

Throughout this paper we employ elements of function notation to relations, and conversely, often view functions as relations. For instance, for a binary relation $R \subseteq A \times B$ we set $\mathsf{dom}(R) = \{a \in A \mid \exists b \in B.\, (a, b) \in R\}$, $\mathsf{ran}(B) = \{b \in B \mid \exists a \in A.\, (a, b) \in R\}$, $R(a) = \{b \in B \mid (a, b) \in R\}$ for $a \in A$, and $R^{-1}(b) = \{a \in A \mid (a, b) \in R\}$ for $b \in B$.

Intervals. We use pairs of numbers including the infinite constant ∞ to represent intervals: the pair $[n; m]$, with $n \leq m \leq \infty$, represents the set $\{i \mid n \leq i \leq m\}$. We assume that both n and m are stored in binary. We use a number of operators on intervals: every interval $I = [n; m]$ has its lower bound $\min(I) = n$ and its upper bound $\max(I) = m$. The point-wise addition of two intervals $A \oplus B = \{a + b \mid a \in A,\ b \in B\}$ has a natural interpretation: $[n_1; m_1] \oplus [n_2; m_2] = [n_1 + n_2; m_1 + m_2]$. Note that $[0; 0]$ is the neutral element of $\oplus$, and hence, for $k = 0$ the expression $I_1 \oplus \ldots \oplus I_k$ evaluates to $[0; 0]$. Also $[n_1; m_1] \subseteq [n_2; m_2]$ iff $n_2 \leq n_1 \leq m_1 \leq m_2$.

Four *basic intervals* are commonly employed in popular schema languages for semi-structured databases, listed here together with their shorthand notation: 1 stands for $[1; 1]$, ? for $[0; 1]$, + for $[1; \infty]$, and $*$ for $[0; \infty]$. We use I to denote the set of all intervals and M to denote the the set of basic intervals.

Bags. Let Δ be a finite set of symbols. Unordered words are represented with bags. Formally, a *bag* over Δ is a function $w : \Delta \to \mathbb{N}$ that maps a symbol to the number of its occurrences. The empty bag ε has 0 occurrences of every symbol i.e., $\varepsilon(a) = 0$ for every $a \in \Delta$. Bags are often presented using the notation $\{\!|a, \ldots|\!\}$ with elements possibly being repeated. For example, when $\Delta = \{a, b, c\}$, $w_0 = \{\!|a, a, a, c, c|\!\}$ represents the function $w_0(a) = 3$, $w_0(b) = 0$, and $w_0(c) = 2$. A *bag language* is a set of bags.

The equivalent of concatenation for unordered words is the *bag union* $w_1 \uplus w_2$ of two bags w_1 and w_2 is $[w_1 \uplus w_2](a) = w_1(a) + w_2(a)$ for all $a \in \Delta$. We also extend this operator to bag languages: $L_1 \uplus L_2 = \{w_1 \uplus w_2 \mid w_1 \in L_1, w_2 \in L_2\}$. Also, for a given bag language L, we define $L^0 = \{\varepsilon\}$ and $L^i = L \uplus L^{i-1}$ for $i > 0$.

Regular bag expressions. *Regular bag expressions* (RBE) are analogues of regular expressions for defining bag languages and use disjunction "|," unordered concatenation "||," and unordered repetition. Formally, they are defined with the following grammar:

$$E ::= \epsilon \mid a \mid (E|E) \mid (E \parallel E) \mid E^I,$$

where $a \in \Delta$ and I is an interval. Their semantics is defined as follows: $L(\epsilon) = \{\varepsilon\}$, $L(a) = \{\{\!|a|\!\}\}$, $L(E_1 \mid E_2) = L(E_1) \cup L(E_2)$, $L(E_1 \parallel E_2) = L(E_1) \uplus L(E_2)$, and $L(E^I) = \bigcup_{i \in I} L(E)^i$. By RBE_0 we denote the class of expressions of the form $a_1^{M_1} \parallel \ldots \parallel a_n^{M_n}$, where $a_i \in \Sigma$ and $M_i \in \mathsf{M}$ for $i \in \{1, \ldots, n\}$. We point out that occurrences of symbols need not be distinct e.g., $a \| a^+ \| b^*$ is RBE_0.

Graphs. We employ a general graph model that allows to capture RDF graphs as well as an important subclass of shape expression schemas (ShEx_0). Because shape expressions schemas do not constrain the predicates of the edges of an RDF graph, we assume a fixed set Σ of predicates names used to label edges of graphs. To represent (a subclass of) shape expression schemas as graphs, we additionally label each edge with an occurrence interval, which intuitively indicate the admissible number of edges of the given kind (cf. Definition 2.2). Also, the general graph model allows multiple edges connecting the same pair of nodes with the same predicate label, which is not allowed in standard RDF.

Definition 2.1. A *graph* is a tuple

$$G = (N_G, E_G, \mathsf{source}_G, \mathsf{target}_G, \mathsf{lab}_G, \mathsf{occur}_G),$$

where N_G is a finite set of *nodes*, E_G is a finite set of *edges*, the functions $\mathsf{source}_G : E_G \to N_G$ and $\mathsf{target}_G : E_G \to N_G$ identify resp. the origin node and end point node of an edge, $\mathsf{lab}_G : E_G \to \Sigma$ assigns a (predicate) label to an edge, and $\mathsf{occur}_G : E_G \to \mathsf{I}$ assigns an occurrence interval to an edge.

A graph is *simple* if it uses only the interval 1 and has no two edges with the same origin, the same end point, and the same label. By G_0 we denote the set of all simple graphs. A *shape graph* is a graph that uses only basic occurrence intervals (in M) and we denote the class of all shape graphs with ShEx_0. □

For the purposes of studying containment of shape expression schemas the class of simple graph captures adequately RDF graphs. Although RDF nodes are labeled with URIs, literal values, and blank identifiers, and shape expression schemas can constraint node labels, in general these constraints can, to some extent, be "simulated." For instance, if the schema imposes a type of admissible literal nodes (integer, date, etc.), literal nodes can be modified to include an outgoing edge labeled with the type name.

Shape expression schemas constrain the outbound neighborhood of a node, and for that purpose we identify the set of all outgoing edges of a node $n \in N_G$ with

$$\mathsf{out}_G(n) = \{e \in E_G \mid \mathsf{source}_G(e) = n\}.$$

Sometimes, if a node n has an outgoing edge leading to m, we shall call m a *child* of n (even if n and m are the same node). Also, we call an a-edge any edge labeled with $a \in \Sigma$, and analogously, an I-edge any edge with occurrence interval I.

Shape Expression Schemas. Again, we assume a fixed set of predicate labels Σ. Given a set of type names Γ, a *shape expression* over Γ is an RBE over $\Sigma \times \Gamma$ and in the sequel we write $(a, t) \in \Sigma \times \Gamma$ simply as $a :: t$. A *shape expression schema* (ShEx) is a pair $H = (\Gamma_H, \delta_H)$, where Γ_H is a finite set of types, and δ_H is a *type definition* function that maps elements of Γ_H to shape expressions over Γ_H. Typically, we present a ShEx H as a collection of rules of the form $t \to E$ to indicate that $\delta_H(t) = E$, where E is a shape expression. For a class of RBEs C, by $\mathsf{ShEx}(C)$ we denote the class of shape expression schemas using only shape expressions in C.

We recall the formal semantics of ShEx [34] and illustrate it on the example of a simple graph G_0 and a schema H_0 in Figure 2. A *typing* of a simple graph G w.r.t. H is a relation $T \subseteq N_G \times \Gamma_H$. For instance, a typing of G_0 w.r.t. H_0 is (for

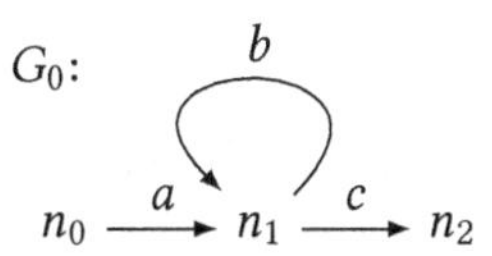

H_0: $t_0 \to a :: t_1$
$t_1 \to b :: t_2^* \parallel c :: t_3$
$t_2 \to b :: t_2^? \parallel c :: t_3$
$t_3 \to \epsilon$

Figure 2: A simple graph G_0 and a schema H_0.

clarity, we employ functional notation)

$$T_1(n_0) = \{t_0\},\ T_1(n_1) = \{t_1, t_2\},\ T_1(n_2) = \{t_3\}.$$

Note that a node may have a number of types. The *signature* of a node $n \in N_G$ w.r.t. T is an RBE expression

$$\mathsf{sign}_G^T(n) = \Vert_{e \in \mathsf{out}_G(n)} (|_{t \in T(\mathsf{target}_G(e))} \mathsf{lab}_G(e) :: t)$$

For instance, the signature of n_1 in G_0 w.r.t. T_1 is

$$\mathsf{sign}_{G_0}^{T_1}(n_1) = (b :: t_1 \mid b :: t_2) \parallel c :: t_3.$$

A node n *satisfies* a shape expression E w.r.t. a typing T iff $L(\mathsf{sign}_G^T(n)) \cap L(E) \neq \emptyset$. For instance, n_1 satisfies the type definition $\delta_{H_0}(t_2)$ of H_0 w.r.t. T_1. The typing T is *valid* iff every node satisfies the type definition of every type assigned to the node i.e., $L(\mathsf{sign}_G^T(n)) \cap L(\delta_H(t)) \neq \emptyset$ for every $(n, t) \in T$. Valid typings of G w.r.t. H form a semi-lattice, with the union as the meet operation [34]. Consequently, there exists a unique maximal typing, which we denote by $\mathsf{Typing}_{G:H}$, and in the sequel we say that a node n *has type* t if $(n, t) \in \mathsf{Typing}_{G:H}$. Now, G *satisfies* H if every node of G has at least one type i.e., $\mathsf{dom}(\mathsf{Typing}_{G:H}) = N_G$. By $L(H)$ we denote the set of all simple graphs that satisfy H.

Containment. In this paper, we investigate the containment problem for ShEx: given two shape expression schemas H and K we say that H is *contained* in K, in symbols $H \subseteq K$, if $L(H) \subseteq L(K)$. A *counter-example* for $H \subseteq K$ is any graph $G \in L(H) \setminus L(K)$.

Embeddings. We define a natural notion of embedding that allows to treat shape graphs as an alternative representation of ShEx(RBE$_0$).

Definition 2.2. Given two graphs G and H, a binary relation $R \subseteq N_G \times N_H$ is a *simulation* of G in H iff for any $(n, m) \in R$ there exists a *witness* of simulation of n by m w.r.t. R, i.e., a function $\lambda_{n,m} : \mathsf{out}_G(n) \to \mathsf{out}_H(m)$ such that for every $e \in \mathsf{out}_G(n)$

1. $\mathsf{lab}_G(e) = \mathsf{lab}_H(\lambda_{n,m}(e))$,
2. $(\mathsf{target}_G(e), \mathsf{target}_H(\lambda_{n,m}(e))) \in R$,

and for every $f \in \mathsf{out}_H(m)$

3. $\bigoplus\{\mathsf{occur}_G(e) \mid e \in E_G,\ \lambda_{n,m}(e) = f\} \subseteq \mathsf{occur}_H(f)$.

An *embedding* of G in H is a simulation R of G in H such that $\mathsf{dom}(R) = N_G$, and we write $G \preccurlyeq H$ if G there is an embedding of G in H. □

Figure 3 presents an example of an embedding between the simple graph G_0 and the shape graph corresponding to the shape expression schema H_0 in Figure 2.

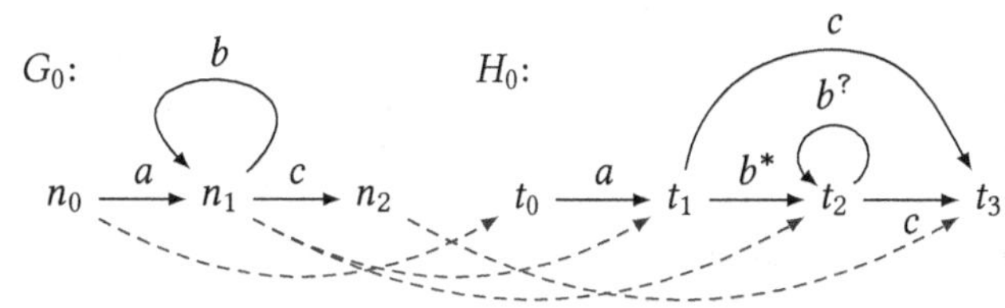

Figure 3: An embedding of G_0 in H_0.

The set of simulations of G in H is a semi-lattice (with the meet operation interpreted with the set union), and consequently, there exists exactly one *maximal simulation* of G in H. We use embeddings to treat graphs as schemas. The *language* of a graph H is the set of all simple graphs that can be embedded in H i.e., $L(H) = \{G \in \mathsf{G}_0 \mid G \preccurlyeq H\}$.

There is a natural correspondence between shape expression schemas using RBE$_0$ only and shape graphs, and we show that the existence of a witness of a simulation is equivalent to type satisfaction.

Proposition 2.3. *ShEx$_0$ captures precisely ShEx(RBE$_0$), i.e., for every ShEx(RBE$_0$) schema there is a shape graph in ShEx$_0$ defining the same language and for every shape graph in ShEx$_0$ there is a ShEx(RBE$_0$) schema defining the same language.*

Embeddings are closed under composition, which immediately gives the following.

Lemma 2.4. *For any G and H, $G \preccurlyeq H$ implies $G \subseteq H$.*

The converse does not hold as illustrated in Figure 4, where two equivalent graphs are given but embedding holds only in one direction. This example basically illustrates that a shape

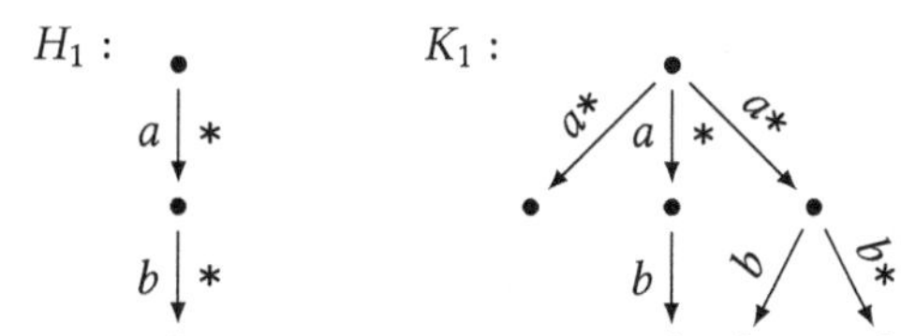

Figure 4: Containment does not imply an embedding: $H_1 \subseteq K_1$ but $H_1 \not\preccurlyeq K_1$.

expression $b :: t^*$ is equivalent to $\epsilon \mid b :: t \mid b :: t^+$, a (disjoint) union that enumerates cases of the original expression. In Section 5 we identify a practical subclass of shape graphs for which embedding is also a necessary condition for containment and then, we analyze the complexity of constructing an embedding.

3 SHAPE EXPRESSION SCHEMAS

In this section, we address the question of decidability of containment for ShEx, which is far from obvious as ShEx caries some expressive power of ∃MSO on graphs combined with Presburger arithmetic [34] and monadic extensions of Presburger arithmetic easily become undecidable [13]. We show a triple-exponential upper bound on the size of a counter-example, which can be compressed to double-exponential size. The compression does not change the complexity of validation, which permits us to give a preliminary upper bound on the complexity of testing containment for ShEx

3.1 Counter-example

To illustrate the analysis of the size of a counter-example we present in Figure 5 two shape expression schemas H_2 and K_2 and a counter-example G_2 for the containment $H_2 \subseteq K_2$. We

$$H_2: \quad t_0 \to a :: t_1^* \qquad t_1 \to b :: t_1^? \qquad\qquad K_2: \quad s_0 \to a :: s_1 \mid (a :: s_1 \parallel a :: s_2)^* \qquad s_1 \to b :: s_2^? \qquad s_2 \to \epsilon$$

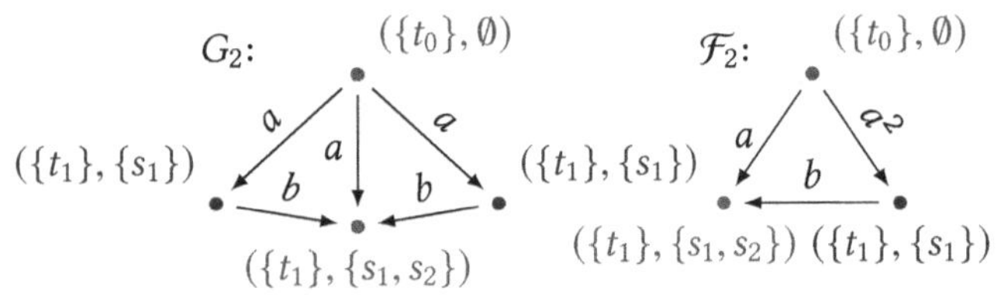

Figure 5: Two schemas $H_2 \not\subseteq K_2$ (top), a counter-example G_2 (bottom left), and its compression $\mathcal{F}_2$ (bottom right).

associate with every node of G_2 its *kind* (T, S), the set of all types T of H_2 and the set of all types S of K_2 that the node satisfies. Our goal is to construct a graph that has at most one node of any possible kind. We point out that in any counter-example there is at least one node that does not satisfy any type of K_2 (while it satisfies some types of H_2). In G_2 there is a single such node and its kind is $(\{t_0\}, \emptyset)$. This node has two a-children of the kind $(\{t_1\}, \{s_1\})$ and one a-child of the kind $(\{t_1\}, \{s_1, s_2\})$. Notice that none of the $(\{t_1\}, \{s_1\})$-nodes can be removed or the $(\{t_0\}, \emptyset)$-node would satisfy the type s_0 and the resulting graph would not longer be a counter-example. Instead, we *fuse* the $(\{t_1\}, \{s_1\})$-nodes into a single one, and use a singleton interval 2 to indicate two copies of the a-edge. Essentially, this allows to *compress* the counter-example into a graph with at most exponentially many nodes. We then use the existing results on solutions to Presburger arithmetic formulas to characterize bounds on the sizes of the intervals necessary in the compressed counter-examples.

Compression. Simple graphs do not allow multiple edges with the same label between the same pair of nodes. We propose a model that allows it by attaching to every edge a *cardinality* indicating the number of such edges. More precisely, a *singleton* interval is an interval of the form $[k; k]$ for any natural k, and a *compressed* graph is a graph that uses only singleton intervals on its edges and like simple graphs allows only one edge per label in Σ between a pair of nodes. Given a compressed graph $\mathcal{F}$, its *unpacking* is a simple graph obtained by making a sufficient number of copies of each node, each copy has the same outbound neighborhood but receiving at most one incoming edge.Since intervals are stored in binary, the unpacking of a compressed graph $\mathcal{F}$ is of size at most exponential in the size of $\mathcal{F}$.

Proposition 3.1. *The size of the unpacking of a compressed graph $\mathcal{F}$ is at most exponential in the size of $\mathcal{F}$.*

We adapt the definition of validation of ShEx to compressed graphs by extending the definition of node signature. Given a shape expression schema H and a compressed graph $\mathcal{F}$, the *signature* of a node $n \in N_{\mathcal{F}}$ w.r.t. a typing $T \subseteq N_{\mathcal{F}} \times \Gamma_H$ is

$$\mathsf{sign}_G^T(n) = \Vert_{e \in \mathsf{out}_{\mathcal{F}}(n)} \left(|_{t \in T(\mathsf{target}_{\mathcal{F}}(e))} \mathsf{lab}_{\mathcal{F}}(e) :: t \right)^{\mathsf{occur}_{\mathcal{F}}(e)}.$$

Again, the typing T is *valid* iff $L(\mathsf{sign}_G^T(n)) \cap L(\delta_H(t)) \neq \emptyset$ for every $(n, t) \in T$, there exists a unique maximal valid typing $\mathsf{Typing}_{\mathcal{F}:H}$ of $\mathcal{F}$ w.r.t. H, and also $\mathcal{F}$ satisfies H if $\mathsf{dom}(\mathsf{Typing}_{\mathcal{F}:H}) = N_{\mathcal{F}}$. Naturally, if $\mathcal{F}$ satisfies H, then its unpacking also satisfies H. Checking the satisfaction of ShEx for compressed graphs remains in NP and to prove it we employ known results on Presburger arithmetic that we present next.

Presburger Arithmetic. The *Presburger arithmetic* (PA) is the first-order logical theory of natural numbers with addition that has decidable satisfiability [29]. We point out that any natural number n can be easily defined with an existentially quantified formula of length linear in $\log(n)$. Since we use PA formulas to define bags, we use a convenient notation. When the set of symbols $\Delta = \{a_1, \ldots, a_k\}$ is known from the context, a bag w over Δ can be represented as a (Parikh) vector of k natural numbers $\langle w(a_1), \ldots, w(a_k) \rangle$ and if a vector of variables $\bar{x}$ is used to describe a bag over Δ, we use elements of Δ to index elements of $\bar{x}$: x_{a_i} designates $w(a_i)$, for $1 \leq i \leq k$. Also, we write $\varphi(w)$ to say that φ is valid for w.

We extend RBE with intersection $L(E_1 \cap E_2) = L(E_1) \cap L(E_2)$ because intersection is used to define satisfiability of a graph w.r.t. a schema and intersection is easily expressed in Presburger arithmetic. Now, for a regular bag expression E we recursively construct a formula $\psi_E(\bar{x}) = \psi(\bar{x}, 1)$ as follows.

$$\psi_\epsilon(\bar{x}, n) := \bigwedge_a x_a = 0$$
$$\psi_a(\bar{x}, n) := x_a = n \wedge \bigwedge_{b \neq a} x_b = 0$$
$$\psi_{E[k;\ell]}(\bar{x}, n) := (n = 0 \wedge \bigwedge_a x_a = 0) \vee (n > 0 \wedge \exists m.\, k \leq m \wedge m \leq \ell \wedge \psi_E(\bar{x}, m))$$
$$\psi_{E_1|E_2}(\bar{x}, n) := \exists \bar{x}_1, \bar{x}_2, n_1, n_2.\, n = n_1 + n_2 \wedge \bar{x} = \bar{x}_1 + \bar{x}_2 \wedge \psi_{E_1}(\bar{x}_1, n_1) \wedge \psi_{E_2}(\bar{x}_2, n_2)$$
$$\psi_{E_1 \| E_2}(\bar{x}, n) := \exists \bar{x}_1, \bar{x}_2.\, \bar{x} = \bar{x}_1 + \bar{x}_2 \wedge \psi_{E_1}(\bar{x}_1, n) \wedge \psi_{E_2}(\bar{x}_2, n)$$
$$\psi_{E_1 \cap E_2}(\bar{x}, n) := \psi_{E_1}(\bar{x}, n) \wedge \psi_{E_2}(\bar{x}, n)$$

The main claim, proven with a simple induction, is that $\psi_E(w, n)$ iff $w \in L(E)^n$ for any bag w over Δ and any $n \geq 0$. It follows that $L(E) \neq \emptyset$ iff $\exists \bar{x}.\psi_E(\bar{x})$ is valid. Validity of existentially quantified PA formulas is known to be in NP [17], and consequently, we obtain an upper bound on complexity of validation of compressed graphs.

PROPOSITION 3.2. *Validation of compressed graphs w.r.t.* ShEx *is in* NP.

The following result is instrumental in our analysis of upper bounds on the size of a counter-example for ShEx.

PROPOSITION 3.3 ([39]). *Let $\Phi = Q_1\bar{x}_1 \ldots Q_k\bar{x}_k.\varphi$ be a closed formula of Presburger arithmetic in prenex normal form with k quantifier alternations over the variables $\bar{x} = \bar{x}_1 \cup \ldots \cup \bar{x}_k$ (φ is quantifier-free). Then Φ is valid if and only if Φ is valid when restricting the first-order variables of Φ to be interpreted over elements of $\{0, \ldots, B\}$, where $\log(B) = O(|\varphi|^{3|\bar{x}|^k})$.*

Compressed counter-example. We take two schemas H and K such that $H \not\subseteq K$ and fix a counter-example $G \in L(H) \setminus L(K)$. We know that there is at least one node of G that satisfies at least one type of H but no type of K. In general, for a node n of G we identify a pair (T, S) consisting of a set T of types of H and a set of types S of K that n satisfies. We say that the node n is of the (T, S)-*kind* and we identify the set C of all kinds present in G.

$$kind(n) = (\mathsf{Typing}_{G:H}(n), \mathsf{Typing}_{G:K}(n)),$$
$$C = \{kind(n) \mid n \in N_G\}.$$

Shape expression schemas may only inspect the labels of the outgoing edges of a node and the types of the nodes at the end points of the edges. Consequently, if we replace a node by a node of the same kind, or more precisely we redirect all incoming edges of the node to the other node, then the types of the nodes in the graph do not change, in particular, it remains a counter-example. Furthermore, we can fuse the set of all nodes of the same kind into a single node that belongs to the same kind, and still obtain a graph that is a counter-example. When fusing several nodes we gather the incoming edges into a fused node but for the outgoing edges we use only the outgoing edges of one (arbitrarily chosen) of the fused nodes, while discarding the outgoing edges of the remaining nodes. We point out that the obtained graph needs not longer to be simple, fusing a set of nodes may lead to several incoming edges with the same label originating from the same node. Such multiple edges can, however, be easily compressed to a single one.

We describe the construction of the compressed counter-example $\mathcal{F}$ more precisely. First for every kind $\kappa \in C$ we pick an (arbitrarily chosen) representative node $n_\kappa \in G$ such that $kind(n_\kappa) = \kappa$. The set of nodes of $\mathcal{F}$ is the set of all kinds of G, $N_\mathcal{F} = C$. For every edge connecting two representative nodes $\mathcal{F}$ has a corresponding edge:

$$E_\mathcal{F} = \{\langle \kappa, a, \kappa' \rangle \mid \exists e \in E_G.\, \mathsf{source}_G(e) = n_\kappa, \mathsf{target}_G(e) = n_{\kappa'}, \mathsf{lab}_G(e) = a\}$$

and for $\langle \kappa, a, \kappa' \rangle \in E_\mathcal{F}$

$$\mathsf{source}_\mathcal{F}(\langle \kappa, a, \kappa' \rangle) = \kappa, \quad \mathsf{lab}_\mathcal{F}(\langle \kappa, a, \kappa' \rangle) = a,$$
$$\mathsf{target}_\mathcal{F}(\langle \kappa, a, \kappa' \rangle) = \kappa', \quad \mathsf{occur}_\mathcal{F}(\langle \kappa, a, \kappa' \rangle) = [k; k],$$

where

$$k = |\{e \in \mathsf{out}_G(n_\kappa) \mid \mathsf{lab}_G(e) = a,\ kind(\mathsf{target}_G(e)) = \kappa'\}|.$$

The main claim is that G and $\mathcal{F}$ satisfy precisely the same schemas. Furthermore, the number $|C|$ of possible kinds is at most exponential in the number of types in H and K, and from the above construction, $\mathcal{F}$ has at most one node per kind.

Bounding the node degree. The remaining question is how big the cardinalities of the edges of $\mathcal{F}$ must be. We answer this question with the help of Proposition 3.3 by describing the outbound neighborhood of a node of $\mathcal{F}$ with Presburger arithmetic formula.

For the kind $(T, S) \in C$ the formula $\Phi_{(T,S)}$ examines the existence of an outbound neighborhood of a node of that kind that satisfies all types in T and all types in S. This neighborhood is captured as a bag $\bar{x}$ over $\Delta_C = \{a :: (T', S') \mid a \in \Sigma,\ (T', S') \in C\}$, where an occurrence of the symbol $a :: (T', S')$ corresponds to one outgoing edge labeled with a and leading to a node of the kind (T', S').

$$\Phi_{(T,S)} := \exists \bar{x}.\ \bigwedge_{t \in T} \varphi_t(\bar{x}) \wedge \bigwedge_{t \in \Gamma_H \setminus T} \neg\varphi_t(\bar{x}) \wedge \bigwedge_{s \in S} \varphi_s(\bar{x}) \wedge \bigwedge_{s \in \Gamma_K \setminus S} \neg\varphi_s(\bar{x}).$$

The formulas $\varphi_t(\bar{x})$ and $\varphi_s(\bar{x})$ verify whether the types t of H and s of K are satisfied in this neighborhood. This is done in two phases and we present it only for $\varphi_t(\bar{x})$; the formula $\varphi_s(\bar{x})$ is defined analogously. The variable $x_{a::(T',S')}$ represents the number of outgoing edges with label a to nodes that satisfy all types in T' (and types in S'). In the context of satisfying definition of the type t each outgoing edge is used with exactly one type. Consequently, the next formula partitions the number of outgoing edges $x_{a::(T',S')}$ into all types in T'. Here, we use a vector $\bar{y}$ of variables over $\{a :: (T',S') \to a :: t' \mid a \in \Sigma,\ (T',S') \in C,\ t' \in T'\}$, where $y_{a::(T',S')\to a::t'}$ represents the part of $x_{a::(T',S')}$ edges that is to be used with the type t'.

$$\varphi_t(\bar{x}) := \exists \bar{y}.\ \bigwedge_{a::(T',S')\in\Delta_C} x_{a::(T',S')} = \sum_{t'\in T'} y_{a::(T',S')\to a::t'} \wedge \varphi'_t(\bar{y}).$$

Finally, the edges with the same label and type of the end point are aggregated in the vector $\bar{z}$ representing a bag over $\Delta_H = \Sigma \times \Gamma_H$, which is then is fed to the formula $\psi_{\delta_H(t)}$ that defines the type definition of t (cf. proof of Proposition 3.2).

$$\varphi'_t(\bar{y}) := \exists \bar{z}.\ \bigwedge_{a::t'\in\Delta_H} z_{a::t'} = \sum_{\substack{a::(T',S')\in\Delta_C \\ \text{s.t. } t' \in T'}} y_{a::(T',S')\to a::t'} \wedge \psi_{\delta_H(t)}(\bar{z}).$$

The formula $\Phi_{(T,S)}$ can be easily converted to prenex normal form, and then, it is of exponential length, uses an exponential number of quantified variables, and has only one alternation of quantifiers. Since $\Phi_{(T,S)}$ is valid for any $(T,S) \in C$, by Proposition 3.3 the satisfying values for the variables $\bar{x}$ are bound by a triple exponential, and consequently, have a binary representation whose size is bounded by double-exponential function in the size of H and K.

Theorem 3.4. *For any two* ShEx *H and K, if $H \not\subseteq K$, then there exists a compressed graph $\mathcal{F}$ that satisfies H, does not satisfy K, and whose size is at most double-exponential in the size of H and K.*

3.2 Complexity

Very recently containment for RBE has been shown to be coNEXP-complete [18], and immediately, we obtain this lower bound.

Proposition 3.5. *Containment for* ShEx *is* coNEXP*-hard.*

The upper bound follows from Theorem 3.4 and Proposition 3.2. A (universally) nondeterministic Turing machine for an input pair (H, K) guesses a compressed graph $\mathcal{F}$ and uses an NP oracle to verify that $\mathcal{F}$ satisfies the schema H and violates the schema K. The input pair is accepted if the test is passed on every computation path.

Corollary 3.6. *Containment for* ShEx *is in* $\text{co2NEXP}^{\text{NP}}$.

4 SHAPE GRAPHS

In this section we consider shape graphs ShEx_0, which correspond to the subclass $\text{ShEx}(\text{RBE}_0)$ of shape expression schemas that use only RBE_0 expression for type definitions (cf. Proposition 2.3). First, we show that the size of a counter-example is at most exponential and that the bound is tight. Then, we show that the complexity of the containment problem for ShEx_0 is EXP-complete.

4.1 Counter-example

In Section 3 we have presented an argument showing that a smallest counter-example has at most exponential number of nodes, and next we show that for ShEx_0 this bound is in fact tight.

Lemma 4.1. *For any n, there exist two shape graphs H and K such that $H \not\subseteq K$ and the smallest graph $G \in L(H) \setminus L(K)$ is of size exponential in n.*

Proof. In our construction the counter-example i.e., $G \in L(H) \setminus L(K)$, is essentially a binary tree of depth n modeled with the rules (for $i \in \{1, \dots, n\}$)

$$t^{(i)} \to L :: t^{(i+1)} \parallel R :: t^{(i+1)}$$

The leaves of this tree store each a subset of $A = \{a_1, \dots, a_n\}$, modeled with the two rules

$$t^{(n+1)} \to a_1 :: t_o^? \parallel \dots \parallel a_n :: t_o^? \quad t_o \to \epsilon$$

The schema H consists exactly of all the above rules while the schema K contains all but the rule defining type $t^{(1)}$. Clearly, at this point a counter-example of $H \not\subseteq K$ exists, one whose root node has type $t^{(1)}$ in H but no type in K, however, it may be small as it suffices to use a dag. To eliminate small counter-examples, by adding them to the language of K, we ensure that all leaves of the counter-example are labeled with distinct subsets of A. In essence, we require in the counter-example a node at level i to have all leaves of its left subtree labeled with subsets containing a_i and all leaves of its right subtree labeled with subsets missing a_i. For that purpose, we introduce types $s^{(j)}_{i,1,d}$ ($s^{(j)}_{i,0,d}$), which identify nodes at level j that are using (missing resp.) the symbol a_i; the additional parameter $d \in \{L, R\}$ is used to handle disjunction and essentially indicates the subtree from which the usage information comes from. The rules for leaves are (for $i \in \{1, \dots, n\}$, $M \in \{0, 1\}$, and $d \in \{L, R\}$)

$$s^{(n+1)}_{i,M,d} \to a_1 :: t_o^? \parallel \dots \parallel a_{i-1} :: t_o^? \parallel \\ a_i :: t_o^M \parallel a_{i+1} :: t_o^? \parallel \dots \parallel a_n :: t_o^?$$

The information of using a symbol a_i in a branch is propagated upward but only to the level $i + 1$ with the rules (for $i \in \{1, \dots, n\}, j \in \{i + 1, \dots, n\}$, and $M \in \{0, 1\}$)

$$s^{(j)}_{i,M,L} \to L :: s^{(j+1)?}_{i,M,L} \parallel L :: s^{(j+1)?}_{i,M,R} \parallel R :: t^{(j)}$$
$$s^{(j)}_{i,M,R} \to L :: t^{(j)} \parallel R :: s^{(j+1)?}_{i,M,L} \parallel R :: s^{(j+1)?}_{i,M,R}$$

Finally, a tree is invalid for our purposes if a node at depth i is missing the symbol a_i in a leaf of its left subtree or is using the symbol a_i in a leaf of its right subtree. This situation is identified and propagated to the root node with the rules (for $i \in \{1, \dots, n\}$ and $j \in \{1, \dots, i-1\}$)

$$p^{(i)}_{i,L} \to L :: s^{(i+1)?}_{i,0,L} \parallel L :: s^{(i+1)?}_{i,0,R} \parallel R :: t^{(i+1)}$$
$$p^{(i)}_{i,R} \to L :: t^{(i+1)} \parallel R :: s^{(i+1)?}_{i,1,L} \parallel R :: s^{(i+1)?}_{i,1,R}$$
$$p^{(j)}_{i,L} \to L :: p^{(j+1)?}_{i,L} \parallel L :: p^{(j+1)?}_{i,R} \parallel R :: t^{(j+1)}$$
$$p^{(j)}_{i,R} \to L :: t^{(j+1)} \parallel R :: p^{(j+1)?}_{i,L} \parallel R :: p^{(j+1)?}_{i,R}$$

Now, the claim, proven with a simple induction, is that for any $G \in L(H)$ unless G contains an exponential tree, any node that has the type $t^{(1)}$ of H also has a type $p^{(1)}_{i,d}$ of K for some $i \in \{1, \dots, n\}$, $M \in \{0, 1\}$, and $d \in \{L, R\}$. □

The lower bound on the size of a minimal counter-example for ShEx_0 is tight.

Theorem 4.2. *For any $H, K \in \mathsf{ShEx}_0$ such that $H \not\subseteq K$ there exists a graph $G \in L(H) \setminus L(K)$ whose size is at most exponential in the size of H and K.*

The proof consists of two parts. The first shows that there are at most exponentially many kinds of nodes, and we use the same argument in the proof of Theorem 3.4 in Section 3. The second part uses a pumping argument to show that the outbound degree of a minimal counter-example is polynomially bounded.

4.2 Complexity

The lower bound on the complexity of containment for ShEx_0 is obtained with a reduction from nondeterministic top-down tree automata known to be EXP-complete [11]. The reduction is non-trivial because RBE_0 does not allow directly the disjunction necessary to express nondeterminism, and the proof needs to account for graphs that might have cycles and do not represent trees.

Theorem 4.3. *Containment for ShEx_0 is EXP-hard.*

Since validation for ShEx_0 is polynomial [34], the bound on the size of a counter-example yields a coNEXP procedure for testing containment. We provide, however, a tight EXP bound with an exponential procedure for deciding containment of shape graphs. We outline the main ideas with the examples that follow. The first example gives a rough sketch of the framework, while the remaining examples present more challenging aspects of the problem at hand and how we address them.

Example 4.4. We consider the two shape graphs H_3 and K_3 in Figure 6, that represent the two shape expression schemas presented in Section 1. First, we introduce the notion of type covering, which essentially for every type t of H_3 identifies sets of types of K_3 that capture t. For instance, the type U is covered by $\{U_1, U_2\}$ and the type B is covered by the types $\{B_1, B_2\}$. Then, we prove an important property of *support* of type t being covered by a set of types S: the definition of the type t can be *unfolded* to a disjunction of type definitions of (a subset of) S. For instance, we take the type definition of U

$$\delta_{H_3}(U) = n :: L \parallel m :: L^?,$$

and decompose $m :: L^?$ into the following disjunction

$$(n :: L) \mid (n :: L \parallel m :: L)$$

which is equal to $\delta_{K_3}(U_1) \mid \delta_{K_3}(U_2)$. This indeed shows that U is covered by $\{U_1, U_2\}$. Here, the types L and E are the same in both schemas and for simplicity use the same name.

Because shape expression schemas are recursive, the notion of support needs to be defined in a (co)inductive fashion. For instance, for the type definition of B

$$\delta_{H_3}(B) = r :: B^* \parallel u :: U \parallel d :: L \parallel e :: E^?$$

since U is covered by $\{U_1, U_2\}$ we get

$$(r :: B^* \parallel u :: U_1 \parallel d :: L \parallel e :: E^?) \mid (r :: B^* \parallel u :: U_2 \parallel d :: L \parallel e :: E^?)$$

and since B is covered by $\{B_1, B_2\}$

$$(r :: B_1^* \parallel r :: B_2^* \parallel u :: U_1 \parallel d :: L \parallel e :: E^?) \mid$$
$$(r :: B_1^* \parallel r :: B_2^* \parallel u :: U_2 \parallel d :: L \parallel e :: E^?)$$

which is equal to $\delta_{K_3}(B_1) \mid \delta_{K_3}(B_2)$. This shows that B is covered by $\{B_1, B_2\}$ even though this very fact is assumed to hold when constructing the unfolding. □

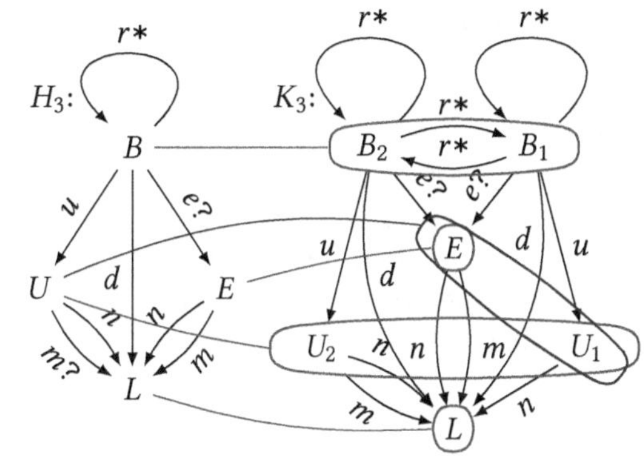

Figure 6: Covering between two shape graphs.

While unfolding atoms $a{::}t^1$ and $a{::}t^?$ is relatively straightforward, the next example shows that unfolding atoms $a :: t^*$ is more complicated than the previous example might suggest.

Example 4.5. Consider the following two schemas:

H_4: $t_0 \to a :: t^*$
$t \to a :: t_\varnothing \parallel a :: t_\varnothing^?$
$t_\varnothing \to \epsilon$

K_4: $s_0 \to a :: s_1^*$ $\quad s_0' \to a :: s_2^+ \parallel a :: s_1^*$
$s_1 \to a :: s_\varnothing$ $\quad s_2 \to a :: s_\varnothing \parallel a :: s_\varnothing$
$s_\varnothing \to \epsilon$

Clearly, $t_\varnothing$ is covered by $\{s_\varnothing\}$, and consequently, t is covered by $\{s_1, s_2\}$. We also point out that s_1 and s_2 are incomparable and so are s_0 and s_0'. Essentially, s_0 allows only outgoing edges that lead to nodes of type s_1, while s_0' requires at least one outgoing edge that leads to a node of type s_2 and an arbitrary number of edges that lead to nodes of type s_1. Naturally, t_0 is covered by $\{s_0, s_0'\}$. When constructing the unfolding of $\delta_{H_4}(t) = a :: t_0^*$ we observe that since t is covered by $\{s_1, s_2\}$ the type definition $a :: t^*$ can be unfolded to

$$a :: s_1^* \mid (a :: s_2 \parallel a :: t^*)$$

and then again to

$$a :: s_1^* \mid (a :: s_2 \parallel a :: s_1^* \parallel a :: s_2^*)$$

which after a simple normalization yields $\delta_{K_4}(s_0) \mid \delta_{K_4}(s_0')$. □

The next example illustrates why we trace the lineage of atoms in unfolding and why we additionally consider the problem of testing emptiness of intersection. In this example we use arbitrary intervals for brevity, and for instance, $a::t^{[1;2]}$ is short for $a :: t \parallel a :: t^?$.

Example 4.6. Consider the following two schemas:

$$\begin{aligned} H_5\colon\ & t_0 \to c :: t \\ & t \to a :: t_\varnothing^{[1;2]} \parallel b :: t_\varnothing^{[1;2]} \\ & t_\varnothing \to \epsilon \end{aligned}$$

$$\begin{array}{llll} K_5\colon & p_0 \to c :: p_1 \quad p_0' \to c :: p_2 & & s_0 \to c :: s_1 \\ & p_1 \to a :: t_\varnothing \parallel b :: t_\varnothing & & s_1 \to a :: t_\varnothing^2 \parallel b :: t_\varnothing^{[1;2]} \\ & p_2 \to a :: t_\varnothing^{[1;2]} \parallel b :: t_\varnothing^2 & & s_2 \to a :: t_\varnothing^3 \parallel b :: t_\varnothing^{[1;2]} \\ & p_3 \to a :: t_\varnothing^{[2;3]} \parallel b :: t_\varnothing & & t_\varnothing \to \epsilon \end{array}$$

It is easy to see that t is covered by $\{p_1, p_2, p_3\}$ and p_3 is covered by $\{s_1, s_2\}$. We shall prove that t_0 is covered by $\{p_0, p_0', s_0\}$ by constructing an unfolding of $\delta_{H_5}(t_0) = c :: t$. We first use the fact that t is covered by $\{p_1, p_2, p_3\}$ and obtain the following disjunction

$$c :: p_1 \mid c :: p_2 \mid c :: p_3 = \delta_{K_5}(p_0) \mid \delta_{K_5}(p_0') \mid c :: p_3$$

To further unfold the atom $c :: p_3$ one use the fact that p_3 is covered by $\{s_1, s_2\}$, which yields

$$\delta_{K_5}(p_0) \mid \delta_{K_5}(p_0') \mid \delta_{K_5}(s_0) \mid c :: s_2$$

The remaining atom $c :: s_2$ is in fact *void* and can be discarded. Indeed, if we inspect its lineage, we observe that the type t has been initially replaced by p_3 and then by s_2. However, the intersection of the types $t \cap p_3 \cap s_2$ is empty i.e., there is no graph with a node having the three types. □

4.2.1 Emptiness of intersection. To identify void atoms in derivations we present a method for identifying sets of types whose intersection is empty, a problem of independent interest. The method is based on techniques that are simpler versions of those central in proving Lemma 4.11, which are too complex to be presented in full detail.

We introduce the notion of *rooted graph*, which is a simple graph with one distinguished root node. We fix a shape graph H and for a shape expression E by $[\![E]\!]$ we denote the set of rooted graphs whose root nodes satisfy E. We extend this notion to sets of shape expressions $[\![\mathcal{E}]\!] = \bigcup\{[\![E]\!] \mid E \in \mathcal{E}\}$. Since shape expressions use RBE$_0$ and the unordered concatenation operator is commutative, we view shape expressions as unordered collections (bags) of atoms of the form $a :: t^M$ without repetitions of atoms using $*$. We also use the empty atom ϵ that is the neutral element of the unordered concatenation operator i.e., $E = E \parallel \epsilon$. W.l.o.g. we assume that the interval $+$ is not used: indeed $a :: t^+$ can be replaced by $a :: t \parallel a :: t^*$.

Our method is based on pumping and tagging shape expressions, which reduces the problem to (disjunctions) of single-occurrence expressions that use only the interval 1, denoted SORBE$_0$(1). Let $m = \max\{|\delta_H(t_1)|, \ldots, |\delta_H(t_k)|\}+1$, where $|E|$ is the number of atoms in E and $\Gamma_H = \{t_1, \ldots, t_k\}$. Pumping removes ? and $*$ by producing expressions with none or one occurrences of atoms using ? and up to m occurrences of atoms using $*$. For instance, for $m = 2$ pumping $a :: t^? \parallel b :: s \parallel c :: t^*$ yields

$$\begin{array}{ll} b :: s, & a :: t \parallel b :: s, \\ b :: s \parallel c :: t, & a :: t \parallel b :: s \parallel c :: t, \\ b :: s \parallel c :: t \parallel c :: t, & a :: t \parallel b :: s \parallel c :: t \parallel c :: t. \end{array}$$

Note that after pumping the obtained shape expression use only the interval 1. To obtain single-occurrence expressions we use tagging, which considers all permutations of atoms in an expression and numbers the symbols accordingly. For instance, the expression $a :: t \parallel a :: s \parallel b :: t$ has the following taggings

$$\begin{array}{ll} a_1 :: t \parallel a_2 :: s \parallel b_3 :: t, & a_1 :: t \parallel a_3 :: s \parallel b_2 :: t, \\ a_2 :: t \parallel a_1 :: s \parallel b_3 :: t, & a_2 :: t \parallel a_3 :: s \parallel b_1 :: t, \\ a_3 :: t \parallel a_1 :: s \parallel b_2 :: t, & a_3 :: t \parallel a_2 :: s \parallel b_1 :: t. \end{array}$$

Our procedure constructs the set $\mathcal{X}_H$ of all subsets of types of H whose intersection is nonempty

$$\mathcal{X}_H = \{\{t_1, \ldots, t_k\} \subseteq \Gamma_H \mid [\![\delta_H(t_1)]\!] \cap \ldots \cap [\![\delta_H(t_k)]\!] \neq \emptyset\}$$

Initially, we begin $\mathcal{X}_0 = \mathcal{P}(\Gamma_H)$ and we iteratively refine it as follows. Suppose, at an iteration we have a set $\mathcal{X} \subseteq \mathcal{P}(\Gamma_H)$. Let $E_1, \ldots, E_k$ be SORBE$_0$(1) expressions each having the same number n of atoms and using precisely the same labels $a_1, \ldots, a_n$ i.e., $E_i = a_1{::}t_{i,1}\|\ldots\|a_n{::}t_{i,n}$ for $i \in \{1, \ldots, k\}$. We say that $E_1, \ldots, E_k$ are *supported* by $\mathcal{X}$ if $\{t_{1,j}, \ldots, t_{k,j}\} \in \mathcal{X}$ for every $j \in \{1, \ldots, n\}$. Take any $\{t_1, \ldots, t_k\} \in \mathcal{X}$ and for $i \in \{1, \ldots, k\}$ let $\mathcal{E}_i$ be the set of SORBE$_0$(1) expressions obtained by pumping and tagging $\delta_H(t_i)$. We say that

$\{t_1, \ldots, t_k\}$ is *supported* by $\mathcal{X}$ if for every $i \in \{1, \ldots, k\}$ there is $E_i \in \mathcal{E}_i$ such that $E_1, \ldots, E_k$ are supported by $\mathcal{X}$. The one-step refinement function is

$$Refine(\mathcal{X}) = \{T \in \mathcal{X} \mid T \text{ is supported by } \mathcal{X}\}.$$

Naturally, the above function is monotone, and therefore, when iteratively applied to $\mathcal{X}_0 = \mathcal{P}(\Gamma_H)$ it has a fix-point $Refine^*(\mathcal{X}_0)$. We claim that this fix point is in fact $\mathcal{X}_H$. To prove that this procedure works in time exponential in the size of H it suffices to observe that each iteration of *Refine* removes from $\mathcal{X}$ at least one element, and therefore, the number of iteration is at most exponential in the number of types of H, and each iteration works in time exponential since the sets $\mathcal{E}_i$ have a number of expressions exponential in m and each expression is of size at most m^2.

Lemma 4.7. *Checking emptiness of intersection of a set of types of a shape graph is in* EXP.

4.2.2 *Type coverings.* We begin with a natural notion of coverage that captures the disjunction introduced by schemas. For technical reasons and in the interest of simplicity of presentation, the definitions in the reminder of this section are for a single shape graph $\mathcal{H}$ that is obtained by taking the disjoint union $H \uplus K$ of the two shape graphs H and K.

Definition 4.8. Given a shape expression schema $\mathcal{H}$, a type $t \in N_{\mathcal{H}}$ is *covered* by a set of types $S \subseteq N_{\mathcal{H}}$ iff in any simple graph G all nodes satisfying the type t also satisfy one of the types in S i.e.,

$$\forall G \in \mathsf{G}_0.\ \mathsf{Typing}_{G:\mathcal{H}}^{-1}(t) \subseteq \textstyle\bigcup_{s \in S} \mathsf{Typing}_{G:\mathcal{H}}^{-1}(s).$$

The *type covering* of $\mathcal{H}$ is the relation

$$\mathsf{Covering}_{\mathcal{H}} = \{(t, S) \in N_{\mathcal{H}} \times \mathcal{P}(N_{\mathcal{H}}) \mid t \text{ is covered by } S\}.$$

□

Type covering allows us to decide containment in a straightforward fashion.

Proposition 4.9. *$H \subseteq K$ if and only if for every $t \in N_H$ there is $S \subseteq N_K$ such that $(t, S) \in \mathsf{Covering}_{H \uplus K}$.*

We now fix a shape graph $\mathcal{H} = H \uplus K$ and propose an iterative algorithm for constructing the type covering of $\mathcal{H}$ using a local characterization of *support* for elements of type covering (Definition 4.10). The algorithm begins with the full relation $R = N_{\mathcal{H}} \times \mathcal{P}(N_{\mathcal{H}})$ and iteratively removes any (t, S) from R that is not supported by R. It returns the maximal self-supported relation R which is precisely the type covering (Lemma 4.11). We show that testing whether an element of R is supported can be done in exponential time (Lemma 4.12), and since R has an exponential number of elements and at most exponential number of iterations is performed, the algorithm works in exponential time (Theorem 4.13).

Unfolding. Again, we view shape expressions as unordered collections (bags) of atoms of the form $a :: t^M$, without repetitions of atoms using $*$, and we assume that the interval $+$ is not used. We propose a method that for a pair $(t, S) \in R$ uses R and basic properties of RBE_0 to unfold the type definition of t into a disjunction of shape expressions. If t can be unfolded into a disjunction contained in S, then (t, S) is supported by R and there is no reason to believe that t is not covered by S, and consequently, no reason to remove (t, S) from R (at this iteration).

The unfolding is defined with a set of unfolding operations on RBE_0 atoms that return a disjunction of RBE_0 expressions. This set captures: the disjunction from RBE_0

$$a{::}t^? \to \epsilon \mid a{::}t \qquad a{::}t^* \to \epsilon \mid (a{::}t \parallel a{::}t^*) \tag{1}$$

from every $(t, \{s_1, \ldots, s_m\}) \in R$ the straightforward disjunction

$$a{::}t^1 \to a{::}s_1^1 \mid \ldots \mid a{::}s_m^1 \tag{2a}$$

$$a{::}t^? \to a{::}s_1^? \mid \ldots \mid a{::}s_m^? \tag{2b}$$

as well as disjunction from $a :: t^*$ atoms (for $0 \leq k \leq m$)

$$a{::}t^* \to (a{::}s_1^* \parallel \ldots \parallel a{::}s_k^*) \mid (a{::}s_{k+1} \parallel a{::}t^*) \mid \ldots \mid (a{::}s_m \parallel a{::}t^*) \tag{2c}$$

and finally, the containment of RBE_0

$$\epsilon \to a{::}t^? \qquad a{::}t \to a{::}t^? \qquad a{::}t^? \to a{::}t^* \tag{3}$$

An *unfolding tree* w.r.t. R is a unranked tree whose nodes are labeled with RBE_0 expressions and if a non-leaf node is labeled with an expression $E \parallel e$, then there is an unfolding operation (w.r.t. R) $e \to e_1 \mid \ldots \mid e_m$ and the children of the node are labeled with the expressions $E \parallel e_1, \ldots, E \parallel e_m$. Furthermore, with a type t in a node we associate its *lineage*: the set of types $\{t, t_1, \ldots\}$ of its ancestors that have led to the type. A type used at a node is *void* if the intersection of its lineage is empty. A type t that is void at a node n of an unfolding tree is *pruned* as follows: if t is used in an atom $a :: t$, then the node and all its descendants are removed; if t is used in an atom $a :: t^?$ or $a :: t^*$, then the atom is removed from that the expression at that node and so is any derived atom in the descendants of the node. Now, an *unfolding* of an RBE_0 E w.r.t. R is a unfolding tree w.r.t. R whose root is labeled with all types pruned.

Support. We use unfolding to identify a defining property of the type covering.

Definition 4.10. Given a shape graph $\mathcal{H}$ and $R \subseteq N_{\mathcal{H}} \times \mathcal{P}(N_{\mathcal{H}})$, a pair $(t, S) \in N_{\mathcal{H}} \times \mathcal{P}(N_{\mathcal{H}})$ is *supported* by R if $\delta_{\mathcal{H}}(t)$ has an unfolding w.r.t. R contained in $\delta_{\mathcal{H}}(S) = \{\delta_{\mathcal{H}}(s) \mid s \in S\}$. $R \subseteq N_{\mathcal{H}} \times \mathcal{P}(N_{\mathcal{H}})$ is *self-supported* if every $(t, S) \in R$ is supported by R. □

Because the union of two self-supported relations is also self-supported, there exists precisely one maximal self-supported relation. The support property is an alternative definition of the type covering, which is the base of our algorithm for constructing the type covering.

Lemma 4.11. *For any* $\mathcal{H} \in$ ShEx$_0$, *the type covering of* $\mathcal{H}$ *is the maximal self-supported relation.*

Proof. The proof is non-trivial, technically complex, and we outline only the main key ideas. We show that type covering is self-supported i.e., if t is covered by S then $\delta_{\mathcal{H}}(t)$ has an unfolding (w.r.t. the type uncovering) contained in $\delta_{\mathcal{H}}(S)$, using a series of complex arguments. We generalize the notion of covering to shape expressions in the natural fashion.

First, we use a pumping and tagging technique, similar to the one in Section 4.2.1. We obtain the set of SORBE$_0(1)$ expression $\mathcal{E}$ from $\delta_{\mathcal{H}}(t)$ and the set $\mathcal{E}'$ from $\delta_{\mathcal{H}}(S)$, and we show that every $E \in \mathcal{E}$ is covered by $\mathcal{E}'$. We view a shape expression $E = a_1 :: t_1 \| \ldots \| a_n :: t_n$ as defining a n-cube Q that is covered by a set $\{Q_1, \ldots, Q_k\}$ of n-cubes corresponding to expressions from $\mathcal{E}'$. We then show that Q is covered by a single n-cube, which is captured with (3) operations or it can be decomposed into smaller n-cubes each covered by a proper subset of $\{Q_1, \ldots, Q_k\}$, which is captured with (2a) operations. This yields an unfolding of E into $\mathcal{E}'$ that we use as a skeleton for constructing an unfolding of $\delta_{\mathcal{H}}(t)$ into $\delta_{\mathcal{H}}(S)$. Furthermore, we observe that the height of the constructed unfolding is polynomially-bounded.

To show that the type covering is the maximal self-supported relation, we first prove the following claim.

Claim. *Let* $\mathcal{R}$ *be the maximal self-supported relation for* $\mathcal{H}$. *For any* $(t, S) \in \mathcal{R}$ *that is supported by* $\mathcal{R}$ *with an unfolding using the facts* $(t_1, S_1), \ldots, (t_k, S_k) \in \mathcal{R}$, *for any graph* G *and any node* $n \in N_G$ *of type* t, *if for every child* m *of* n *the fact that* m *has a type* t_i *also implies that* m *has a type in* S_i, *then* n *has a type in* S.

We use the above claim to show that for any $(t, S) \in \mathcal{R}$, in any graph G, any node of type t has also a type in S, and consequently, $(t, S) \in$ Covering$_{\mathcal{H}}$. □

Search graph. The polynomial bound on the depth of an unfolding allows to show that the number of relevant expressions derived from $\delta_{\mathcal{H}}(t)$ is bounded exponentially, even if we store the lineage information with every type. We construct an oriented hypergraph, whose nodes are all relevant expressions and oriented hyperedges represent one-step unfoldings with void atoms pruned with the help of Lemma 4.7. We reduce the problem of checking the existence of an unfolding to the reachability problem in alternating graphs, known to be P-complete. This gives us an exponential upper bound on testing the existence of a relevant unfolding.

Lemma 4.12. *For* $\mathcal{H} \in$ ShEx$_0$ *and* $R \subseteq N_{\mathcal{H}} \times \mathcal{P}(N_{\mathcal{H}})$, *checking that* $(t, S) \in R$ *is supported by* R *can be done in time exponential in the size of* $\mathcal{H}$.

Lemmas 4.11 and 4.12 together with Proposition 4.9 give.

Theorem 4.13. *Containment for* ShEx$_0$ *is in* EXP.

5 DETERMINISM

In this section we identify a tractable subclass of deterministic shape expression schemas that is arguably of practical use (recall that determinism forbids using the same edge label twice in type definition). We show that containment of deterministic shape expression schemas is intractable even if type definitions use RBE$_0$ only (Theorem 5.7). Interestingly, if the set of intervals is further restricted to 1 and $*$, containment is equivalent to the existence of embedding, which we show to be tractable (Theorem 5.4). Adding support for other basic intervals is tricky as unrestricted use of ? leads to intractability. Consequently, we employ the technique of *characterizing example* [27, 35] to find a relatively rich and tractable subclass of deterministic shape graphs that allows unrestricted use of 1 and $*$ and a restricted use of ?. We believe this subclass is of potential practical interest, and in particular it includes the schema in Figure 1. While our technique does allow to include +, the further restriction this addition causes render the class impractical, and consequently, we forbid + altogether (in practice using $*$ instead of + is often acceptable).

We first illustrate the method of characterizing example on the example in Figure 7, where we generate a characterizing example G_6 for the schema H_6 (which is a representation of the schema in Figure 1). The central property of G_6 is that any

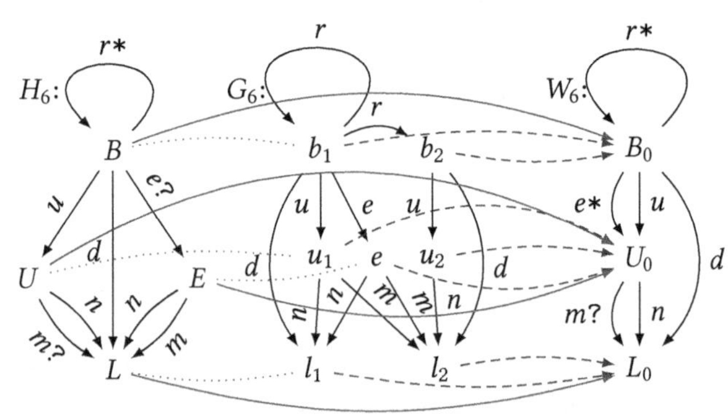

Figure 7: Constructing embedding of H_6 into W_6 from embedding of the characterizing example G_6 into W_6.

schema K (in DetShEx$_0^-$) that satisfies G_6 is satisfied by all graphs that satisfy H_6. In other words, H_6 can be embedded in any K such that $G_6 \in L(K)$ and hence for any $G' \in L(H_6)$ we have $G' \in L(K)$. The proof takes the embedding of G_6 in K and constructs an embedding of H_6 in K. Such a construction is feasible due to a key observation, which we illustrate on the schema W_6. Since the node b_1 has the type B_0, by determinism of W_6 the nodes b_1 and b_2 have the same type B_0. Transitively, the nodes u_1 and u_2 have the same type U_0 and similarly the nodes l_1 and l_2 have the same type L_0. The characterizing example G_6 is constructed in such a manner as to make sure that every type of H_6 is described by a set of nodes of G_6, all embedded into a corresponding type of W_6, which ensures embedding of the type of H_6 in the corresponding type of W_6. For instance, u_1 and u_2 are embedded into U_0 and since u_1 has an outgoing m-edge and u_2 does not, the definition of the corresponding type in W_6 must use $m :: L_0^?$ or $m :: L_0^*$.

We now define formally the subclass of shape expression schemas in question. Given a shape graph H and a type $t \in N_H$, a *reference* to t is any edge $e \in E_H$ that leads to t i.e. $\text{target}_H(e) = t$. A reference e is $*$*-closed* if $\text{occur}_H(e) = *$ or all references to $\text{source}_H(e)$ are $*$-closed.

Definition 5.1. A shape graph H is *deterministic* if for every node $n \in N_H$ and every label $a \in \Sigma$, n has at most one outgoing edge labeled with a. By DetShEx_0 we denote the class of all deterministic shape graphs. By DetShEx_0^- we denote the class of deterministic shape graphs that do not use + and any type using ? is referenced at least once and all references to it are $*$-closed. □

Intuitively, we require that any type using ? must be referenced and can only be referenced (directly or indirectly) through $*$. The schema in Figure 1 belongs to DetShEx_0^- since both uses of the ? operator are closed by the edge `related` with interval $*$.

5.1 Characterizing example

Interestingly, the class DetShEx_0^- allows construction of graphs that characterize any schema in DetShEx_0^- up to containment.

Lemma 5.2. *For any $H \in \text{DetShEx}_0^-$, there exists a simple graph $G \in L(H)$ of size polynomial in the size of H such that for any $K \in \text{DetShEx}_0^-$ we have that $G \preccurlyeq K$ implies $H \preccurlyeq K$.*

The precise construction of the graph G that characterizes H is in Appendix B. Here, we outline the main ideas and illustrate them on an example in Figure 8. In essence, for every type $t \in N_H$ the graph G needs to contain a number of nodes of type t that serve the purpose of characterizing t. If t has an outgoing $*$-edge e labeled with a that leads to the type s, then at least one node n of G that characterizes t needs to have at least two outgoing edges labeled with a that lead to nodes A that characterize the type s. When n is mapped to a

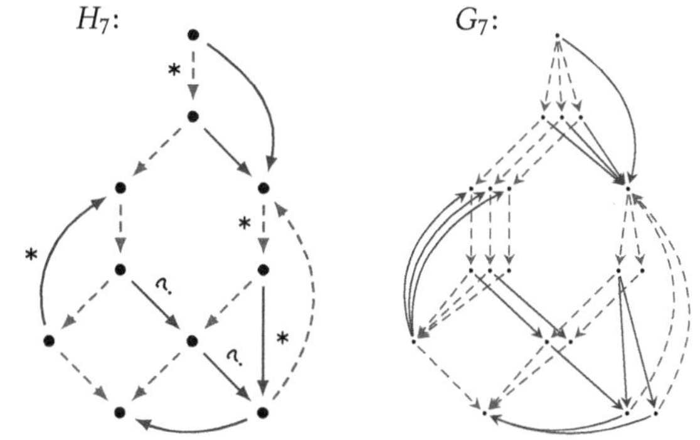

Figure 8: Characterizing example. Different colors denote different labels.

type t' of K that has an outgoing edge e' labeled with a and leading to s', all a-children A must to be mapped to s'. This shows that e' is an $*$-edge. Interestingly, this observation propagates to descendants of A. If the type s has an outgoing edge with label b that leads to the type u, then any b-child of a node in A must have the type u, and furthermore, they are all mapped to a type u' that is reachable from s' with an edge labeled with b, etc.

Now, for a type t with an outgoing ?-edge labeled with a we need two nodes in G that characterize t, which guarantee that the corresponding type in K uses the right occurrence interval: one node with one outgoing edge with label a and one node with no such outgoing edge. Naturally, we need to make sure that those two nodes are mapped to the same type in K and this is accomplished by making sure there is an ascending path from every ?-edge to every closest $*$-edge. In general, every type in H is characterized by a number of nodes that is at most 2 plus the number of ?-edges in H. Lemma 5.2 renders containment and embeddings equivalent.

Corollary 5.3. *For $H, K \in \text{DetShEx}_0^-$, $H \subseteq K$ iff $H \preccurlyeq K$.*

5.2 Complexity

To characterize the complexity of containment for DetShEx_0^- we study the complexity of testing embedding between two graphs. Interestingly, it turns out that constructing embeddings for shape graphs, which use only basic occurrence intervals, is tractable and becomes intractable if arbitrary intervals may be used. This rise in computational complexity does not come from binary encoding of intervals, in fact the results remain negative even if the arbitrary intervals are encoded in unary. We also point out that shape graphs using only basic intervals are as expressive as graphs using arbitrary intervals because RBE_0 with basic intervals and repetition are equivalent to RBE_0 with arbitrary intervals. The difference in complexity is not a contradiction but merely

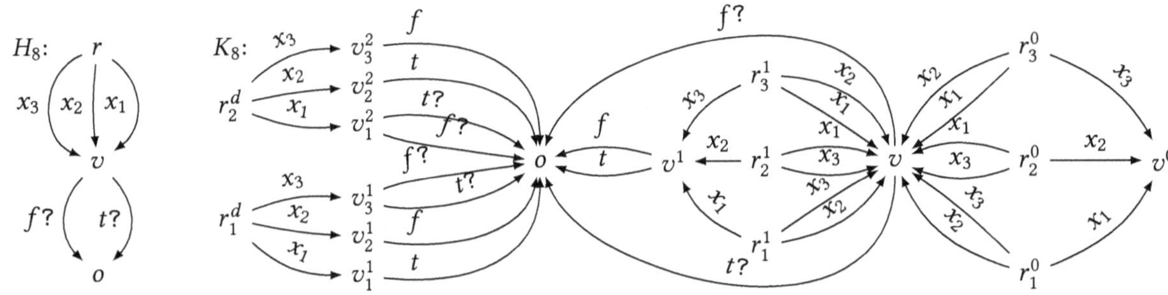

Figure 9: An example of reduction on $\varphi = (x_1 \land \neg x_2) \lor (x_2 \land \neg x_3)$.

reflects the fact that containment does not necessarily imply embedding.

THEOREM 5.4. *Testing the existence of embeddings between shape graphs is in* P.

The proof of the above theorem consisting of a polynomial algorithm constructing embeddings between two graphs can be found in Appendix A. As a result of Corollary 5.3 and Theorem 5.4, we obtain.

COROLLARY 5.5. *Containment for* $\mathsf{DetShEx}_0^-$ *is in* P.

Constructing an embedding becomes intractable if arbitrary intervals can be employed.

THEOREM 5.6. *Testing the existence of embeddings between graphs with arbitrary intervals is* NP*-complete.*

Finally, we observe that lifting the additional restrictions we impose on $\mathsf{DetShEx}_0^-$ leads to intractability.

THEOREM 5.7. *Containment for* $\mathsf{DetShEx}_0$ *is* coNP*-hard.*

PROOF (SKETCH). The proof is by reduction from tautology of DNF formulas, which we illustrate on the example of $\varphi = (x_1 \land \neg x_2) \lor (x_2 \land \neg x_3)$. We construct two deterministic schemas H_8 and K_8 presented in Figure 9. The schema H_8 is satisfied by all graphs defining a valuation of the variables of φ: a node with the root type r has outgoing edges labeled with the name of the variable leading to a node of type v that represents the value of the variable t or f. Because $\mathsf{DetShEx}_0$ does not allow disjunction, nodes of type v may also have both outgoing edges t and f, or neither of them. These cases are covered in K_8 by the types r_i^1's and r_i^0's respectively. The types r_j^d's capture precisely the valuations that satisfy the clauses of φ. Hence, K_8 is not satisfied by the graphs that correctly define a valuation that does not satisfy φ. Naturally, $H_8 \subseteq K_8$ iff φ is a tautology. ☐

6 CONCLUSIONS AND FUTURE WORK

This work was prompted by our recent work on data exchange for RDF [6] and ongoing work on schema inference for RDF, where not only do we ask the questions of type implication but are also interested in instances satisfying constraints expressed with the help of ShEx. In this paper, we have considered ShEx and its two practical subclasses ShEx_0 and $\mathsf{DetShEx}_0^-$. While the precise complexity of containment for ShEx remains open, the complexity results we have obtained, summarized in Figure 10, provide a good separation of the presented schema classes. Determinism shows

$\mathsf{DetShEx}_0^-$	ShEx_0	ShEx
P	EXP-complete	coNEXP-hard co2NEXP^{NP}

Figure 10: Summary of complexity results

promise in allowing reduction in complexity. For instance, containment for DetShEx is in co2NEXP since validation for DetShEx is in P. But its precise impact on complexity of containment needs to be studied further. It is an open question whether using arbitrary intervals in shape graphs has an impact on the complexity of testing containment; interestingly the answer to this question is negative for ShEx and positive for $\mathsf{DetShEx}_0^-$. The class of regular bag expression DIME that permits restricted use of disjunction yet allows for tractable containment for schemas for unordered XML [5] and it would also be interesting to see if there are any computational benefits that can be drawn for shape expression schemas using DIME.

ACKNOWLEDGMENT

We would like to thank the referees for many useful comments. This work has been supported by Polish National Science Center grant UMO-2014/15/D/ST6/00719. Part of this work has been done when one of authors was a fellow at the University of Edinburgh, funded by the EU DIACHRON project.

REFERENCES

[1] A. Abbas, P. Genevès, C. Roisin, and N. Layaïda. Optimising SPARQL query evaluation in the presence of shex constraints. In *BDA 2017*, pages 1–12, Nancy, France, November 2017.

[2] M. Arenas, C. Gutierrez, and J. Pérez. Foundations of RDF databases. In *Reasoning Web*, International Summer School on Semantic Technologies for Information Systems, pages 158–204, 2009. Invited Tutorial.

[3] M. Arenas, J. Pérez, Reutter J., C. Riveros, and J. Sequeda. Data exchange in the relational and RDF worlds. International Workshop on Semantic Web Information Management (SWIM), June 2011. Invited talk.

[4] G. J. Bex, F. Neven, and J. Van den Bussche. DTDs versus XML Schema: A practical study. In *WebDB*, pages 79–84, 2004.

[5] I. Boneva, R. Ciucanu, and S. Staworko. Schemas for unordered XML on a DIME. *Theoretical Computer Science (TCS)*, 57(2):337–376, 2015.

[6] I. Boneva, J. Lozano, and S. Staworko. Relational to RDF data exchange in presence of a shape expression schema. In *Alberto Mendelzon International Workshop on Foundations of Data Management*, May 2018.

[7] A. Brüggemann-Klein and D. Wood. One-unambiguous regular languages. *Information and Computation*, 142(2):182–206, 1998.

[8] L. Cardelli and G. Ghelli. TQL: a query language for semistructured data based on the ambient logic. *Mathematical Structures in Computer Science*, 14(3):285–327, 2004.

[9] Š. Čebirić, F. Goasdoué, P. Guzewicz, and I. Manolescu. Compact Summaries of Rich Heterogeneous Graphs. Research Report RR-8920, INRIA Saclay ; Université Rennes 1, July 2018.

[10] Š. Čebirić, F. Goasdoué, and I Manolescu. A Framework for Efficient Representative Summarization of RDF Graphs. In *International Semantic Web Conference (ISWC)*, Vienna, Austria, October 2017.

[11] H. Comon, M. Dauchet, R. Gilleron, C. Löding, F. Jacquemard, D. Lugiez, S. Tison, and M. Tommasi. Tree automata techniques and applications. 1997. Release 2007.

[12] S. Dal-Zilio and D. Lugiez. XML schema, tree logic and sheaves automata. In *Rewriting Techniques and Applications*, pages 246–263, 2003.

[13] C. C. Elgot and M. O. Rabin. Decidability and undecidability of extensions of second (first) order theory of (generalized) successor. *Journal of Symbolic Logic*, 31(2):169–181, 1966.

[14] M. F. Fernandez and D. Suciu. Optimizing regular path expressions using graph schemas. In *International Conference on Data Engineering (ICDE)*, pages 14–23, 1998.

[15] W. Gelade, W. Martens, and F. Neven. Optimizing schema languages for XML: Numerical constraints and interleaving. *SIAM Journal on Computing*, 38(5):2021–2043, 2009.

[16] F. Goasdoué, P. Guzewicz, and I. Manolescu. Incremental structural summarization of RDF graphs. In *International Conference on Extending Database Technology (EDBT)*, Lisbon, Portugal, March 2019.

[17] Erich Grädel. *The complexity of subclasses of logical theories.* PhD thesis, Universität Basel, 1987.

[18] C. Haase and P. Hofman. Tightening the complexity of equivalence problems for commutative grammars. In *Symposium on Theoretical Aspects of Computer Science (STACS)*, pages 41:1–41:14, 2016.

[19] A. Klarlund, T. Schwentick, and D. Suciu. XML: Model, schemas, types, logics and queries. In J. Chomicki, R. van der Meyden, and G. Saake, editors, *Logics for Emerging Applications of Databases.* Springer-Verlag, 2003.

[20] E. Kopczynski and A. To. Parikh images of grammars: Complexity and applications. In *Logic in Computer Science (LICS)*, pages 80–89, 2010.

[21] J. E. Labra Gayo, E. Prud'hommeaux, I. Boneva, and D. Kontokostas. Validating RDF data. *Synthesis Lectures on the Semantic Web: Theory and Technology*, 7(1):1–328, 2017.

[22] J. E. Labra Gayo, E. Prud'hommeaux, I. Boneva, S. Staworko, H. R. Solbrig, and S. Hym. Towards an RDF validation language based on regular expression derivatives. In *EDBT/ICDT Workshops (GraphQ & LWDM)*, pages 197–204, March 2015.

[23] J. E. Labra Gayo, E. Prud'hommeaux, H. Solbrig, and J. M. Alvarez Rodriguez. Validating and describing linked data portals using RDF Shape Expressions. In *Workshop on Linked Data Quality*, September 2015.

[24] W. Martens, F. Neven, and T. Schwentick. Complexity of decision problems for XML schemas and chain regular expressions. *SIAM Journal on Computing*, 39(4):1486–1530, 2009.

[25] W. Martens, F. Neven, T. Schwentick, and G. J. Bex. Expressiveness and complexity of XML schema. *ACM Transactions on Database Systems (TODS)*, 31(3):770–813, 2006.

[26] A. J. Mayer and L. J. Stockmeyer. The complexity of word problems - this time with interleaving. *Information and Computation*, 115(2):293–311, 1994.

[27] G. Miklau and D. Suciu. Containment and equivalence for a fragment of XPath. *Journal of the ACM*, 51(1):2–45, 2004.

[28] F. Neven and T. Schwentick. XML schemas without order. 1999.

[29] D. C. Oppen. A $2^{2^{2^{pn}}}$ upper bound on the complexity of Presburger arithmetic. *Journal of Computer and System Sciences*, 16(3):323–332, 1978.

[30] R. M. Robinson. Restricted set-theoretical definitions in arithmetic. In *Proceedings of the American Mathematical Society*, pages 238–242, 1958.

[31] H. Seidl, T. Schwentick, and A. Muscholl. Numerical document queries. In *ACM Symposium on Principles of Database Systems (PODS)*, pages 155–166, 2003.

[32] H. Seidl, T. Schwentick, and A. Muscholl. Counting in trees. In *Logic and Automata: History and Perspectives [in Honor of Wolfgang Thomas]*., pages 575–612, 2008.

[33] Helmut Seidl. Haskell overloading is dexptime-complete. *Information Processing Letters*, 52(2):57–60, October 1994.

[34] S. Staworko, I. Boneva, J. E. Labra Gayo, S. Hym, E. G. Prud'hommeaux, and H. Solbrig. Complexity and expressiveness of ShEx for RDF. In *International Conference on Database Theory (ICDT)*, pages 195–211, March 2015.

[35] S. Staworko and P. Wieczorek. Characterizing XML twig queries with examples. In *International Conference on Database Theory (ICDT)*, pages 144–160, March 2015.

[36] M. Veanes. On computational complexity of basic problems of finite tree automata. Technical Report 133, UPMAIL, January 1997.

[37] W3C. RDF validation workshop report: Practical assurances for quality RDF data. September 2013.

[38] W3C. Shape expressions language 2.0, 2017.

[39] V. Weispfenning. The complexity of almost linear diophantine problems. *Journal of Symbolic Computation*, 10(5):395–404, 1990.

[40] H. Zhang, Y. Duan, X. Yuan, and Y. Zhang. ASSG: adaptive structural summary for RDF graph data. In *International Semantic Web Conference (ISWC)*, pages 233–236, October 2014.

A CONSTRUCTING EMBEDDINGS

Theorem 5.4. Testing the existence of embeddings between shape graphs is in P.

PROOF. We fix shape graphs G and H and present a iterative procedure for constructing an embedding of G in H. The procedure begins with $R_0 = N_G \times N_H$ and iteratively refines it $R_i = \mathit{Refine}(R_{i-1})$ by removing any pair of nodes with no simulation witness

$$\mathit{Refine}(R) = \{(n, m) \in R \mid \text{there exists a witness } \lambda \text{ of simulation of } n \text{ by } m \text{ w.r.t. } R\}.$$

This process terminates at the earliest iteration k when a fix-point is reached $\mathit{Refine}^*(R_0) = R_k = \mathit{Refine}(R_k)$. The fix-point is in fact the maximal simulation of G in H and naturally, it is an embedding if its domain contains all nodes of G. The core difficulty is in testing the existence of a witness of simulation.

We fix a relation $R \subseteq N_G \times N_H$ and a pair of nodes $(n, m) \in R$. We abstract the problem of existence of a witness of simulation of n by m w.r.t. R as a *flow routing* problem, where we are given a set of sources $V = \mathsf{out}_G(n)$, a set of sinks $U = \mathsf{out}_H(m)$, and a source-to-sink connection table

$$E = \{(v, u) \in V \times U \mid \mathsf{lab}_G(v) = \mathsf{lab}_H(u) \land (\mathsf{target}_G(v), \mathsf{target}_H(u)) \in R\},$$

every source $v \in V$ outputs a volume of water between $v.min = \min(\mathsf{occur}_G(v))$ and $v.max = \max(\mathsf{occur}_G(v))$, and every sink $u \in U$ requires an input of at least $u.min = \min(\mathsf{occur}_H(u))$ but no more than $u.max = \max(\mathsf{occur}_H(u))$. The flow routing problem is to find a valid *routing* $\lambda : V \to U$ i.e., a routing such that $(v, f(v)) \in E$ for every source $v \in V$ and there are no deficits or overflows at any source. Formally, given a routing λ we estimate the inflow at a sink u with

$$\mathit{min\text{-}inflow}_\lambda(u) = \textstyle\sum_{\lambda(v)=u} v.min,$$
$$\mathit{max\text{-}inflow}_\lambda(u) = \textstyle\sum_{\lambda(v)=u} v.max.$$

A sink u is in *deficit* if $\mathit{min\text{-}inflow}_\lambda(u) < u.min$ and u is in *overflow* if $\mathit{max\text{-}inflow}_\lambda(u) > u.max$. Observe that the conditions 1 and 2 in Definition 2.2 are ensured by the definition of E while the condition 3 follows from lack of deficits and overflows. Also, w.l.o.g. we can assume that in E every source is paired with at least one sink.

In essence, the algorithm for constructing a valid routing (1) starts with an empty routing, (2) assigns it assigns a sink to every source while distributing any overflow by pushing it forth to other sinks, and (3) solves any deficit at a sink by pulling back the input from sources assigned to other sinks.

The main reason why this approach is successful is the use of basic occurrence intervals in shape graphs, which implies that the lower bounds are only 0 and 1 while the upper bounds are 1 and ∞. When constructing the routing λ we need to pay attention to *saturated* sinks that are unable to accept any additional inflow. However, saturated sinks are exactly those u's with $u.max = 1$ and $\mathit{max\text{-}inflow}_\lambda(u) = 1$. Furthermore, w.l.o.g. we can assume that $v.max \leq u.max$ for $(v, u) \in E$, and in particular a source with ∞ upper bound can only be routed to a sink with upper bound ∞. Consequently, any overflow created by the algorithm at a sink u is *singular* i.e., $\mathit{max\text{-}inflow}_\lambda(u) = 2$ and $u.max = 1$.

Given a (partial) routing λ and a source v with no assigned sink, the algorithm assigns to v any admissible sink u_0 i.e., such that $(v, u_0) \in E$. If an overflow is created at u_0, the algorithm attempts to find an acyclic path π from u_0 to fin in the *push-forth graph* $G_\lambda^{\rightarrow} = (N, A)$, where the nodes are $N = V \cup U \cup \{\mathit{fin}\}$ and the oriented edges A are (for $v \in V$ and $u \in U$):

- $u \to v$ if $\lambda(v) = u$ and u is saturated; an additional inflow of 1 at sink u must be redirected further and this can be done by redirecting the output of v to another sink.
- $v \to u$ if $(v, u) \in E$ but $\lambda(v) \neq u$; the source v can be routed to u and any additional inflow at u is at most 1.
- $u \to \mathit{fin}$ if u is not saturated; the sink can accept an additional inflow of 1.

Rerouting λ in accordance with a path from u to fin gives us a overflow-free routing.

When a total overflow-free routing λ is constructed, the algorithm identifies any sink u_0 with a deficit and tries to solve it by finding an acyclic path π from u_0 to fin in the *pull-back graph* $G_\lambda^{\leftarrow} = (N, A)$, where the nodes are $N = V \cup U \cup \{\mathit{fin}\}$, and oriented edges A are (for $v \in V$ and $u \in U$):

- $u \to v$ if $\lambda(v) \neq u$ and $v.min = 1$; rerouting v to u will solve a deficit of 1 at u and may create a overflow at u but only if $u = u_0$ and then the overflow is singular.
- $v \to u$ if $\lambda(v) = u$, $u.min = 1$, and v is the only source such that $\lambda(v) = u$ and $v.min = 1$; rerouting v away from u will create a deficit of 1 at u.
- $v \to \mathit{fin}$ if $\lambda(v).min \neq 1$, $v.min = 1$, and there is $v' \neq v$ such that $\lambda(v') = \lambda(v)$ and $v'.min = 1$; rerouting the source v from the sink $\lambda(v)$ will not create a deficit at $\lambda(v)$.

Rerouting λ in accordance with π renders λ deficit-free at u_0. If the rerouting creates a singular overflow at u_0, the algorithm uses the push-forth graph $G_\lambda^{\rightarrow}$ to find an acyclic path π' from u_0 to fin that is deficit-free i.e., with no edge $u \to v$ such that $u.min = v.min = 1$, which guarantees that further rerouting λ in accordance with π' yields a overflow-free routing with one sink node u_0 less in deficit.

Naturally, the algorithm is polynomial because the sizes of the push-forth and pull-back graphs are bounded by the size of E, and all constructed paths are acyclic. □

B CHARACTERIZING EXAMPLES FOR DETERMINISTIC SHAPE GRAPHS

Lemma 5.2. For any $H \in \mathsf{DetShEx}_0^-$, there exists a simple graph $G \in L(H)$ of size polynomial in the size of H such that for any $K \in \mathsf{DetShEx}_0^-$ we have that $G \preccurlyeq K$ implies $H \preccurlyeq K$.

Proof. Let $E_? = (e_1, \dots, e_m)$ be all edges in H with occurrence interval ?, in an arbitrary but fixed order. The graph G is constructed as follows. The graph has $m+2$ nodes per type of H: $N_G = N_H \times \{0, 1, \dots, m+1\}$, and for simplicity we shall write t^i for $(t, i) \in N_G$. The nodes are used to characterize the occurrence intervals used on the outgoing edges of the type. For an edge $e \in E_H$ such that $t = \mathsf{source}_H(e)$, $s = \mathsf{target}_H(e)$, and $a = \mathsf{lab}_H(e)$, we construct the following edges:

(1) if $\mathsf{occur}_H(e) = 1$, then t^i has one outgoing edge with label a that leads to s^i for $i \in \{0, \dots, m+1\}$;
(2) if $\mathsf{occur}_H(e) = ?$ and $e = e_\ell$ i.e., ℓ is the position of e on the list $\mathcal{E}_?$, then t^i has one outgoing edge with label a that leads to s^i for $i \in \{0, \dots, m+1\} \setminus \{\ell\}$ and t_ℓ has no outgoing edges with label a;
(3) if $\mathsf{occur}_H(e) = *$, then for $i \in \{0, \dots, m\}$ the node t^i has no outgoing edge with label a and the node t^{m+1} has an outgoing edge with label a that leads to t_j for every $j \in \{0, \dots, m+1\}$.

We now assume that $G \in L(K)$ and construct the following embedding of H in K:

$$
\begin{aligned}
R = {} & \{(t,u) \mid u \in \mathsf{Typing}_{G:K}(t^{m+1}),\ \mathsf{in}_H(t) = \emptyset\} \cup \\
& \{(t,u) \mid u \in \mathsf{Typing}_{G:K}(t^{m+1}),\ \exists e \in \mathsf{in}_H(t).\ \exists f \in \mathsf{in}_K(u). \\
& \quad \mathsf{lab}_H(e) = \mathsf{lab}_K(f) \wedge \mathsf{source}_H(e) = s \wedge \\
& \quad \mathsf{source}_K(f) \in \mathsf{Typing}_{G:K}(s^{m+1})\},
\end{aligned}
$$

where $\mathsf{in}_H(t) = \{e \in E_H \mid target_H(e) = t\}$. Essentially, R uses types of the nodes t^{m+1} but only essential ones: all types for root nodes (with no incoming edges) and for nodes with incoming edges only those types that are needed to ensure satisfaction of their predecessors. It is easy to see that $\mathsf{dom}(R) = N_H$. To prove that it is indeed an embedding we make several observations. First, we point out that for deterministic shape graphs the concept of witness is redundant since an edge with a given label can be mapped only to an edge with the same label. Consequently, we only need to make sure that R maps nodes in a manner consistent with the labels of the connecting edges and in quantities within the bounds of the occurrence interval.

Now we take any edge $e \in E_H$ and let $t = \mathsf{source}_H(e)$, $s = \mathsf{target}_H(e)$, and $a = \mathsf{lab}_H(e)$. We take any $u \in R(t)$, which implies that t^{m+1} of G has the type u. Since t^{m+1} has an edge labeled a and leading to s^{m+1}, there is an edge $f \in E_K$ with label a from u to some $v \in R(s)$. We can make the following observations about the occurrence interval on f:

- In general $\mathsf{occur}_G(f) \in \{1, ?, *\}$, which is adequate if $\mathsf{occur}_H(e) = 1$;
- If $\mathsf{occur}_H(e) = *$, then we observe that t^{m+1} has $m+2 \geq 2$ outgoing edges labeled with a, all of witch must be embedded in f, and therefore, $\mathsf{occur}_K(f) = *$.
- If $\mathsf{occur}_H(e) = ?$, then we diligently construct a path $e_k, \dots, e_1, e_0 = e$ such that $\mathsf{occur}_H(e_k) = *, \mathsf{occur}_H(e_j) \neq *$ for $j \in \{k-1, \dots, 1\}$, and $\mathsf{target}_H(e_i) = \mathsf{source}(e_{i-1})$ for $i \in \{k, \dots, 1\}$, together with two sequences of types $(t_{k+1}, \dots, t_1)$ and $(u_{k+1}, \dots, u_1)$ such that $t_i = \mathsf{source}_H(e_{i-1})$ for $i \in \{k+1, \dots, 1\}$, $(t_i, u_i) \in R$ for $i \in \{k+1, \dots, 1\}$ and there is an edge $f_i \in E_K$ from u_{i+1} to u_i for $i \in \{k+1, \dots, 1\}$. We let $t_1 = t$ and $u_1 = u$. Assume we have constructed the path up to e_i with type $t_i = \mathsf{source}_H(e_i)$ and the type u_i such that $(t_i, u_i) \in R$. If $\mathsf{occur}_H(e_i) = *$, we terminate the construction of the path. Otherwise, from construction of R there is a type of u' that is a parent of u_i with an edge with label a' as well as a type $t' \in N_H$ connected to t_i with an edge $e' \in E_H$ such that $(t', u') \in R$. We set $t_{i+1} = t$ and $u_{i+1} = u'$, and $e_{i+1} = e'$. This process terminates thanks to the definition of $\mathsf{DetShEx}_0^-$.
Now, let the edge e be the ℓ-th element in the ordering $E_?$. we take two corresponding paths in G:
$$t_{k+1}^{m+1}, t_k^{m+1} \dots, t_1^{m+1} \quad \text{and} \quad t_{k+1}^{m+1}, t_k^{\ell} \dots, t_1^{\ell};$$
both following the edges $e_k, \dots, e_1$. With a simple inductive proof we show that both t_1^ℓ and t_1^{m+1} have the same type u_1, and since t_1^ℓ does not have any outgoing edge labeled with a, the interval $\mathsf{occur}_K(f)$ must be either ? or $*$.

This concludes the proof. □

Complexity Bounds for Relational Algebra over Document Spanners

Liat Peterfreund
liatpf@cs.technion.ac.il
Technion
Haifa, Israel

Dominik D. Freydenberger
ddfy@ddfy.de
Loughborough University
Loughborough, United Kingdom

Benny Kimelfeld
bennyk@cs.technion.ac.il
Technion
Haifa, Israel

Markus Kröll
kroell@dbai.tuwien.ac.at
TU Wien
Vienna, Austria

ABSTRACT

We investigate the complexity of evaluating queries in Relational Algebra (RA) over the relations extracted by regex formulas (i.e., regular expressions with capture variables) over text documents. Such queries, also known as the regular document spanners, were shown to have an evaluation with polynomial delay for every positive RA expression (i.e., consisting of only natural joins, projections and unions); here, the RA expression is fixed and the input consists of both the regex formulas and the document. In this work, we explore the implication of two fundamental generalizations. The first is adopting the "schemaless" semantics for spanners, as proposed and studied by Maturana et al. The second is going beyond the positive RA to allowing the difference operator.

We show that each of the two generalizations introduces computational hardness: it is intractable to compute the natural join of two regex formulas under the schemaless semantics, and the difference between two regex formulas under both the ordinary and schemaless semantics. Nevertheless, we propose and analyze syntactic constraints, on the RA expression and the regex formulas at hand, such that the expressive power is fully preserved and, yet, evaluation can be done with polynomial delay. Unlike the previous work on RA over regex formulas, our technique is not (and provably cannot be) based on the static compilation of regex formulas, but rather on an ad-hoc compilation into an automaton that incorporates both the query and the document. This approach also allows us to include black-box extractors in the RA expression.

PODS'19, June 30-July 5, 2019, Amsterdam, Netherlands

ACM ISBN 978-1-4503-6227-6/19/06...$15.00
https://doi.org/10.1145/3294052.3319699

CCS CONCEPTS

• **Theory of computation** → *Models of computation*; *Formal languages and automata theory*; *Design and analysis of algorithms*; *Fixed parameter tractability*; *Database theory*; *Data modeling*; *Database query languages (principles)*; *Database query processing and optimization (theory)*; *Logic and databases*; • **Information systems** → *Information extraction*.

KEYWORDS

Information Extraction, Document Spanners, Regular Expressions, Relational Algebra, Polynomial Delay

ACM Reference Format:
Liat Peterfreund, Dominik D. Freydenberger, Benny Kimelfeld, and Markus Kröll. 2019. Complexity Bounds for Relational Algebra over Document Spanners. In *38th ACM SIGMOD-SIGACT-SIGAI Symposium on Principles of Database Systems (PODS'19), June 30-July 5, 2019, Amsterdam, Netherlands.* ACM, New York, NY, USA, 15 pages. https://doi.org/10.1145/3294052.3319699

1 INTRODUCTION

The abundance and availability of valuable textual resources position text analytics as a standard component in data-driven workflows. To facilitate the integration with textual content, a core operation is Information Extraction (IE)— the extraction of structured data from text. IE arises in a large variety of domains, including biology and biomedical analysis, social media analysis, cyber security,[1] system and network log analysis, and business intelligence, to name a

[1]See, e.g., the TA-COS workshop at http://www.ta-cos.org/.

few [4, 27]. *Rules* for IE are used in commercial systems and academic prototypes for text analytics, either as a standalone extraction language or within machine-learning models.

A common paradigm for rule programming is the one supported by IBM's SystemT [5, 18], which exposes a collection of *atomic* (sometimes called "primitive") extractors of relations from text (e.g., tokenizer, dictionary lookup, part-of-speech tagger and regular-expression matcher), together with a relational algebra for manipulating these relations.

In Xlog [29], user-defined functions provide the atomic extractors, and Datalog is used for relational manipulation. In DeepDive [26], rules are used for generating features that are translated into the factors of a statistical model with machine-learned parameters. Feature declaration combines atomic extractors alongside relational operators thereof.

Document spanners. In this work, we explore complexity aspects of IE within the framework of *document spanners* (or just *spanners* for short) [8]. In this framework, a *document* is a string over a fixed finite alphabet, and a *spanner* extracts from every input document a relation of intervals within the document. An interval, called *span*, is represented by its starting and ending indices in the document.

An example of a spanner is a *regex formula*, which is a regular expression with capture variables that correspond to the relational attributes. The most studied language for specifying spanners is that of the *regular* spanners: the closure of regex formulas under the classic relational algebra: projection, natural join, union, and difference [8]. Equally expressive formalisms include non-recursive Datalog over regex formulas [9] and the *variable-set automaton* (*vset-automaton* for short), which is a nondeterministic finite-state automaton (NFA) that can open and close variables while running.

Since the framing of the spanner framework, there has been a considerable effort to delineate the computational complexity of spanner evaluation, with a special focus on the regular representations (regex formulas and vset-automata) of the atomic extractors.

Florenzano et al. [10] studied the data complexity (where the spanner is fixed and the input consists of only the document), and so did Peterfreund et al. [25] who showed that the closure of regex formulas under Datalog characterizes the class of polynomial-time spanners. Freydenberger et al. [11–13] studied the *combined complexity* (where the input consists of both the query and the document) for conjunctive queries, and unions of conjunctive queries, over spanners. More recently, Amarilli et al. [1] presented an evaluation algorithm with tractability properties under both data and combined complexity; we further discuss this algorithm later on.

For complexity analysis, there are important advantages to yardsticks that take the atomic extractors (e.g., regex formulas or vset-automata) as input, rather than regarding them small or fixed. First, the size of these extractors can be quite large in practice. Taking examples from RegExLib.com, each of the regexes for recognizing the RFC 2822 mailbox format (regexp id 711) and date format (regexp id 969) uses more than 350 ASCII symbols, and a regex for identifying US addresses (regexp id 1564) uses more than 2,000 ASCII symbols. Furthermore, automata may be constructed by automatic (machine-learning) processes that achieve accuracy through the granularity of the automaton. The paradigm of Artificial Neural Networks (ANNs) in natural-language processing has motivated the conversion of ANN models such as *recurrent neural networks* and *convolutional neural networks* into automata [21, 22, 33], where the number of states may reach tens of thousands to match the expressiveness of the numeric parameters [33]. Another advantage of regarding the atomic extractors as input is more technical: polynomial-time combined complexity allows to incorporate vset-automata whose size may depend on the input document. This approach allows to establish tractability even if we join with schemaless spanners that cannot be represented as RA expressions over regular spanners, such as string equality [13].

Schema-based functionality vs schemaless sequentiality. As defined by Fagin et al. [8], the spanners are *schema-based* in the sense that every spanner is associated with a fixed and finite set X of variables, playing the roles of *attributes* in relational databases, so that every tuple they extract from a document assigns a value to each variable of X. The regex formulas conform to this property in the sense that every parse tree contains exactly one occurrence of each variable; such regex formulas are said to be *functional*. Freydenberger [11] applied the property of functionality to vset-automata: a vset-automaton is functional if every accepting path properly opens and closes every variable exactly once.

The functionality property can be tested in polynomial time for both regex formulas [8] and vset-automata [12]. Moreover, functional vset-automata generalize functional regex formulas in the sense that every instance of the former can be transformed in linear time into an instance of the latter (but not necessarily the other way around). Beyond that, functional vset-automata (and regex formulas) possess various desired tractability features [13]. First, they can be evaluated with polynomial delay under combined complexity. Second, the *natural join* of two functional vset-automata can be compiled in polynomial time into one functional vset-automaton, and so can the *union* of two vset-automata and the *projection* of a vset-automaton to a subset of its variables. Consequently, every combination of functional vset-automata can be evaluated with polynomial delay, as long as this combination is via the *positive* operators of the relational algebra.

More recently, Maturana et al. [19] introduced a *schemaless* version of spanners that allows for incomplete extraction from documents, in the spirit of the SPARQL model [23]. There, two extracted tuples may assign spans to different sets of variables. The analog of functionality is *sequentiality*: a regex formula is sequential is every parse tree includes *at most* one occurrence of every variable, and a vset-automaton is sequential if every accepting path properly opens and closes every variable *at most* once. Again, in polynomial time we can test for sequentiality and transform a sequential regex formula into a sequential vset-automaton; moreover, sequential vset-automata can be evaluated with polynomial delay under combined complexity [19]. In fact, the aforementioned algorithm of Amarilli et al. [1] enumerates with polynomial delay under combined complexity, and, under data complexity, with constant delay following a linear preprocessing of the document.[2] Since functional vset-automata are also sequential, this algorithm also applies to the schema-based spanners, and improves upon (and, in fact, generalizes the applicability of) the constant-delay algorithm of Florenzano et al. [10].

Contribution. The state of affairs leaves open two fundamental questions regarding the combined complexity of query evaluation.

- Does the tractability for the positive relational algebra generalize from the schema-based case to the schemaless case?
- Does the tractability extend beyond the positive operators (in either the schema-based or schemaless case)? In particular, can we enumerate with polynomial delay the *difference* between two functional vset-automata?

We prove that the answers to both questions are negative. More specifically, it is NP-complete to determine whether the natural join of two *sequential* regex formulas is nonempty (Theorem 3.1), and it is NP-complete to determine whether the difference between two given *functional* regex formulas is nonempty (Theorem 4.1).

We formulate various syntactic restrictions that allow to avoid hardness. In particular, we show that polynomial delay is retained if we bound the number of common variables between the two operands of the natural join and difference. For the natural join, we also present a normal form for schemaless regex formulas and vset-automata, namely *disjunctive functional*, that are more restricted than, yet as expressive as, their sequential counterparts; yet, the natural join of two disjunctive-functional vset-automata can be compiled into a disjunctive-functional vset-automaton in polynomial time (hence, evaluated with polynomial delay).

In contrast to the natural join, the tractability of the difference between vset-automata with a bounded number of common variables *cannot* be established via compilation into a single vset-automaton. This is due to the simple reason that, in the case of Boolean spanners, the problem is the same as the difference between two NFAs, where the compilation necessitates an exponential blowup [16]. Nevertheless, we establish the tractability by transforming the difference into a natural join with a special vset-automaton that is built ad-hoc for the input document.

In summary, our complexity upper bounds are established in two main approaches. The first is based on a document-independent compilation of the input vset-automata (or regex formulas) into a new vset-automaton. The second is based on a compilation of both the input vset-automata *and* the input document into a new, ad-hoc vset-automaton. We refer to the first approach as *static compilation* and to the second as *ad-hoc compilation*.

We compose our tractability results into more general queries by proposing a new complexity measure that is specialized to spanners. Recall that the evaluation problem has three components: the document, the atomic spanners (e.g., regex formulas), and the relational algebra that combines the atomic spanners, which we refer to as the *RA tree*. Under *combined complexity*, all three are given as input; under *data complexity*, the document is given as input and the rest are fixed; there is also the *expression complexity* [32] where the document is fixed and the rest are given as input. We propose the *extraction complexity*, where the RA tree is fixed, and the input consists of the document and the atomic spanners (mapped to their corresponding positions in the RA tree). We present and discuss conditions that cast the extraction complexity tractable (polynomial-delay evaluation) and intractable (NP-hard nonemptiness). Interestingly, since the tractability of an RA tree is based on ad-hoc compilation, we can incorporate there *any* polynomial-time spanner, as long as its dimension is bounded by a constant.

Organization. The rest of the paper is organized as follows. In Section 2, we present the basic terminology and concepts. We investigate the complexity of the natural-join operator in Section 3 and the difference operator in Section 4. We extend our development to the extraction complexity in Section 5, and conclude in Section 6. To meet space constraints, some of the proof are given in the full version of the paper [24].

2 PRELIMINARIES

We first introduce the main definitions and terminology, mainly from the literature on document spanners [8, 19].

2.1 Document Spanners

Documents and spans. We fix a finite alphabet Σ of symbols. By a *document* or *string* we refer to a finite sequence $\mathbf{d} = \sigma_1 \cdots \sigma_n$ over Σ (that is, each σ_i is in Σ), that is, a member

[2]This is the spanner analog of a recent line of work on the enumeration complexity of database and string queries [2, 3, 20, 28].

of Σ^*. The length n of the document $\mathbf{d} = \sigma_1 \cdots \sigma_n$ is denoted by $|\mathbf{d}|$. A *span* is a pair $[i, j\rangle$ of indices $1 \leq i \leq j \leq n+1$ that marks a substring of $\mathbf{d}$. The term $\mathbf{d}_{[i,j\rangle}$ denotes the substring $\sigma_i \cdots \sigma_{j-1}$.

Note that $\mathbf{d}_{[i,i\rangle}$ is the empty string, and that $\mathbf{d}_{[1,n+1\rangle}$ is $\mathbf{d}$. Note also that the spans $[i, i\rangle$ and $[j, j\rangle$, where $i \neq j$, are different objects, even though the substrings $\mathbf{d}_{[i,i\rangle}$ and $\mathbf{d}_{[j,j\rangle}$ are equal.

We denote by spans the set of all spans of all strings, that is, all expressions $[i, j\rangle$ where $1 \leq i \leq j$. By spans($\mathbf{d}$) we denote the set of all spans of $\mathbf{d}$.

Schemaless spanners. We assume a countably infinite set Vars of *variables*, and assume that Vars is disjoint from Σ and Σ^*. A *schemaless (document) spanner* is a function that maps each document into a finite collection of tuples (referred to as *mappings*) that assign spans to variables.

More formally, a *mapping* to $\mathbf{d}$ is a function μ from a finite set of variables, called the *domain* of μ and denoted dom(μ), into spans($\mathbf{d}$). A schemaless spanner is a function P that maps every document $\mathbf{d}$ into a finite set $P(\mathbf{d})$ of mappings.

For a schemaless spanner P and a document $\mathbf{d}$, different mappings in $P(\mathbf{d})$ may have different domains. This stands in contrast to the (schema based) spanners of Fagin et al. [8], where P is such that there exists a set V_P of variables where every document $\mathbf{d}$ and mapping $\mu \in P(\mathbf{d})$ satisfy dom(μ) = V_P; in this case, we may refer to P as a *schema-based spanner.*

Example 2.1. Let Γ be the alphabet consists of lowercase and uppercase English letters: a, ..., z, A, ..., Z; digits: 0, ⋯ , 9; and symbols: ␣ that stands for whitespace, '.' and '@'. Let $\Delta = \{\hookleftarrow\}$ where $\hookleftarrow$ stands for end of line. The input document $\mathbf{d}_{\mathsf{Students}}$ over $\Gamma \cup \Delta$ given in Figure 1 holds personal information on students. (Some of the positions are marked underneath for convenience.) Each line in the document describes information on a student in the following format: first name (if applicable), last name, phone number (if applicable) and email address. There are spaces in between these elements. The schemaless document spanner $P_{StudInfo}$ extracts from the input document $\mathbf{d}_{\mathsf{Students}}$ the following set of mappings, given in a table for convenience.

	x_{first}	x_{last}	x_{mail}	x_{phone}
μ_1 :	$[1,7\rangle$	$[8,19\rangle$	$[20,29\rangle$	
μ_2 :		$[30,37\rangle$	$[46,56\rangle$	$[38,45\rangle$
μ_3 :	$[57,62\rangle$	$[63,69\rangle$	$[78,89\rangle$	$[70,77\rangle$

Note that the empty cells in the table stand for undefined. That is, we have $x_{phone} \notin$ dom(μ_1) and $x_{first} \notin$ dom(μ_2). □

In the next sections, we discuss different representation languages for schemaless spanners. Whenever a schemaless spanner is represented by a description q, we denote by $\llbracket q \rrbracket$ the actual schemaless spanner that q represents. We are using the notation $\llbracket \cdot \rrbracket$ in order to clearly distinguish the schemaless semantics from the schema based semantics of Fagin et al. [8] who use $[\![\cdot]\!]$. This distinction is critical in the case of the *vset-automata* that we define later on.

2.2 Regex Formulas

One way of representing a schemaless spanner is by means of a *regex formula*, which is a regular expression with capture variables, as allowed by the grammar

$$\alpha := \emptyset \mid \epsilon \mid \sigma \mid (\alpha \vee \alpha) \mid (\alpha \cdot \alpha) \mid \alpha^* \mid x\{\alpha\}$$

where $\sigma \in \Sigma$ and $x \in$ Vars. For convenience, we sometimes put regex formulas in parentheses and also omit parentheses, as long as the meaning remains clear. For operator precedence, we assume that * comes before $\cdot$, which comes before $\vee$. We denote by Vars(α) the set of variables that appear in α. By RGX we denote the class of regex formulas.

Following Maturana et al. [19], we interpret regex formulas as schemaless spanners in the following manner. The following grammar defines the application of a regex formula α on a document $\mathbf{d} = \sigma_1 \cdots \sigma_n$, where the result is a pair (s, μ) where s is a span of $\mathbf{d}$ and μ is a mapping to $\mathbf{d}$.

- $[\emptyset](\mathbf{d}) := \emptyset$;
- $[\epsilon](\mathbf{d}) := \{([i, i\rangle, \emptyset) \mid i = 1, \ldots, n\}$;
- $[\sigma](\mathbf{d}) := \{([i, i+1\rangle, \emptyset) \mid \sigma_i = \sigma\}$;
- $[x\{\alpha\}](\mathbf{d}) := \{([i, j\rangle, \mu \cup \{x \mapsto [i, j\rangle\}) \mid ([i, j\rangle, \mu) \in [\alpha](\mathbf{d})$ and $x \notin$ dom(μ)$\}$;
- $[\alpha_1 \vee \alpha_2](\mathbf{d}) := [\alpha_1](\mathbf{d}) \cup [\alpha_2](\mathbf{d})$;
- $[\alpha_1 \cdot \alpha_2](\mathbf{d}) := \{([i, j\rangle, \mu_1 \cup \mu_2) \mid \exists i'$ s.t. $([i, i'\rangle, \mu_1) \in [\alpha_1](\mathbf{d}), ([i', j\rangle, \mu_2) \in [\alpha_2](\mathbf{d})$, and dom($\mu_1$)∩dom($\mu_2$) = $\emptyset\}$;
- $[\alpha^*](\mathbf{d}) := \bigcup_{i=0}^{\infty} [\alpha^i](\mathbf{d})$ where α^i stands for the concatenation of i copies of α.

The result of applying α to $\mathbf{d}$ is then defined as follows.

$$\llbracket \alpha \rrbracket(\mathbf{d}) = \{\mu \mid ([1, |\mathbf{d}|+1\rangle, \mu) \in [\alpha](\mathbf{d})\}$$

We denote by $\llbracket$RGX$\rrbracket$ the class of schemaless spanners that can be expressed using the regex formulas. Similarly, for every subclass R ⊆ RGX, we denote by $\llbracket$R$\rrbracket$ the class of spanners expressible by an expression in R.

Syntactic restrictions. Fagin et al. [8] introduced the class of regex formulas that are interpreted as schema-based spanners, namely the *functional* regex formulas. To define functional regex formulas, we first use the following inductive definition. A regex formula α is functional *for* a set $V \subseteq$ Vars of variables if:

- $\alpha \in \Sigma^*$ and $V = \emptyset$;
- $\alpha = \alpha_1 \vee \alpha_2$ and each α_i is functional for V;
- $\alpha = \alpha_1 \cdot \alpha_2$ and there exists $V_1 \subseteq V$ such that α_1 is functional for V_1 and α_2 is functional for $V \setminus V_1$;

`Rodion␣Raskolnikov␣rr@edu.ru` ↩ `Zosimov␣6222345␣mov@edu.ru` ↩ `Pyotr␣Luzhin␣6225545␣luzi@edu.uk` ↩ ···

1 8 20 30 38 46 57 63 70 78

Figure 1: The input document $\mathbf{d}_{\text{Students}}$

- $\alpha = \alpha_0^*$ and α_0 is functional for $\emptyset$;
- $\alpha = x\{\alpha_0\}$ and α_0 is functional for $V \setminus \{x\}$.

Finally, a regex formula α is *functional* if it is functional for the set $\mathsf{Vars}(\alpha)$ of its variables.

Maturana et al. [19] pointed at a wider fragment of regex formulas, namely the *sequential* regex formula, that has some desirable properties, as will be discussed later. A regex formula α is sequential if the following conditions hold:

- For every sub-formula $\alpha_1 \cdot \alpha_2$, we have $\mathsf{Vars}(\alpha_1) \cap \mathsf{Vars}(\alpha_2) = \emptyset$.
- For every sub-formula α^*, we have $\mathsf{Vars}(\alpha) = \emptyset$.
- For every sub-formula $x\{\alpha\}$, we have $x \notin \mathsf{Vars}(\alpha)$.[3]

We denote by funcRGX and seqRGX the classes of functional and sequential regex formulas, respectively.

As shown by Maturana et al. [19], it holds that funcRGX $\subsetneq$ seqRGX. That is, every functional regex formula is sequential, but some sequential regex formulas are *not* functional, as the next example illustrates.

Example 2.2. Let us define the following regex formulas over the alphabet $\Gamma \cup \Delta$ from Example 2.1:

$$\alpha_{\text{mail}} := x_{mail}\{\gamma @ \gamma . \gamma\}$$
$$\alpha_{\text{name}} := (x_{first}\{\delta\}␣x_{last}\{\delta\}) \lor (x_{last}\{\delta\})$$
$$\alpha_{\text{phone}} := x_{phone}\{\beta^*\}$$

where $\gamma := (\mathsf{a} \lor \cdots \lor \mathsf{z})^+$, $\delta := (\mathsf{A} \lor \cdots \lor \mathsf{Z}) \cdot (\mathsf{a} \lor \cdots \lor \mathsf{z})^*$, and $\beta := (0 \lor \cdots \lor 9)^+$.

Based on the previous regex formulas, we define the regex formula that represents the schemaless spanner $P_{StudInfo}$ from Example 2.1:

$$\alpha_{\text{info}} := \Gamma^* \cdot (\epsilon \lor \hookleftarrow) \cdot \alpha_{\text{name}} \cdot ␣ \cdot \Big((\alpha_{\text{phone}} \cdot ␣ \lor \epsilon) \cdot \alpha_{\text{mail}} \Big) \cdot \hookleftarrow \cdot \Gamma^*$$

Note that this is regex formula is sequential but not functional since the variables x_{first} and x_{phone} are optional. □

2.3 Vset-Automata

In addition to regex formulas, we use the *variable-set automata* (abbreviated *vset-automata*) for representing schemaless spanners, as defined by Maturana et al. [19] as a schemaless adaptation of the vset-automata of Fagin et al. [8].

A *vset-automaton*, VA for short, is a tuple (Q, q_0, F, δ), where Q is set of *states*, $q_0 \in Q$ is the *initial state*, $F \subseteq Q$ is the set of *accepting states*, [4] and δ is a transition relation consisting of *epsilon transitions* of the form (q, ϵ, p), *letter transitions* of the form (q, σ, p) and *variable transitions* of the form $(q, v{\vdash}, p)$ or $(q, {\dashv}v, p)$ where $q, p \in Q$, $\sigma \in \Sigma$, and $v \in \mathsf{Vars}$.

The symbols $v{\vdash}$ and ${\dashv}v$ are special symbols to denote the opening or closing of a variable v. We define the set $\mathsf{Vars}(A)$ as the set of all variables v that are mentioned in some transition of A. For every finite set $V \subseteq \mathsf{Vars}$ we define the set $\Gamma_V := \{v{\vdash}, {\dashv}v : v \in V\}$ of *variable operations*.

A *run* ρ over a document $\mathbf{d} := \sigma_1 \cdots \sigma_n$ is a sequence of the form

$$(q_0, i_0) \overset{o_1}{\to} \cdots (q_{m-1}, i_{m-1}) \overset{o_m}{\to} (q_m, i_m)$$

where:

- the i_j are indexes in $\{1, \ldots, n+1\}$ such that $i_0 = 1$ and $i_m = n + 1$;
- each o_j is in $\Sigma \cup \{\epsilon\} \cup \Gamma_{\mathsf{Vars}(A)}$;
- $i_{j+1} = i_j$ whenever $o_j \in \Gamma_{\mathsf{Vars}(A)}$, and $i_{j+1} = i_j + 1$ otherwise;
- for all $j > 0$ we have $(q_{j-1}, o_j, q_j) \in \delta$.

A run ρ is called *valid* if for every variable v the following hold:

- v is opened (or closed) at most once;
- if v is opened at some position i then it is closed at some position j with $i \leq j$;
- if v is closed at some position j then it is opened at some position i with $i \leq j$.

A run is called *accepting* if its last state is an accepting state, i.e., $q_m \in F$. For an accepting and valid run ρ, we define μ_ρ to be the mapping that maps the variable v to the span $[i_j, i_{j'}\rangle$ where $o_{i_j} = v{\vdash}$ and $o_{i_{j'}} = {\dashv}v$.

The result $[\![A]\!](\mathbf{d})$ of applying the schemaless spanner represented by A on a document $\mathbf{d}$ is defined as the set of all assignments μ_ρ for all valid and accepting runs ρ of A on $\mathbf{d}$.

We call a VA *sequential* if all of its accepting runs are valid, and it is called *functional* if each such run also include all of its variables $\mathsf{Vars}(A)$. Note that sequential VAs correspond to schemaless spanners, whereas functional correspond to complete.

In what follows, we assume that our VAs are *trimmed*, that is, for every state q we have that (1) q is reachable from the initial state, and (2) there is at least one accepting state that can be reached from q.

[3] We added this restriction to the original definition [19] since it was mistakenly omitted, as the authors confirmed.

[4] The original definition by Fagin et al. [8] used a single accepting state. We can extend this definition to multiple accepting states without changing the expressive power by simulating a multiple accepting states automaton by a single accepting state automaton with epsilon transitions.

Observe that given a VA we can construct an equivalent trimmed one in linear time.

EXAMPLE 2.3. Let A be the following sequential VA:

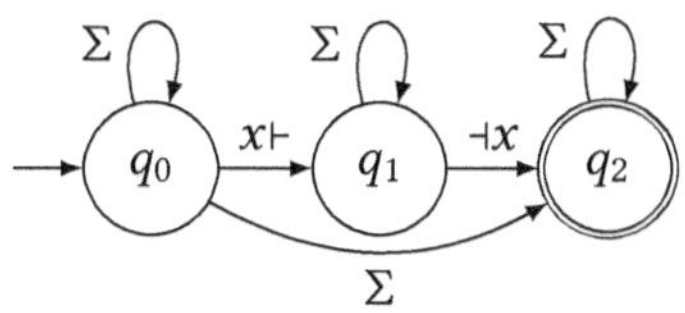

Omitting the transition from q_0 to q_2 results in a functional VA. The same schemaless spanner as that represented by A is given by the sequential regex formula $\alpha := (\Sigma^* x\{\Sigma^*\}\Sigma^*) \vee (\Sigma^+)$ where Σ^+ stands for $\Sigma \cdot \Sigma^*$. □

2.4 Algebraic Operators

Before we define the algebra over schemaless spanners, we present some basic definitions. Two mappings μ_1 and μ_2 are *compatible* if they agree on every common variable, that is, $\mu_1(x) = \mu_2(x)$ for all $x \in \mathsf{dom}(\mu_1) \cap \mathsf{dom}(\mu_2)$. In this case, we define $\mu := \mu_1 \cup \mu_2$ as the mapping with $\mathsf{dom}(\mu) = \mathsf{dom}(\mu_1) \cup \mathsf{dom}(\mu_2)$ such that $\mu(x) = \mu_1(x)$ for all $x \in \mathsf{dom}(\mu_1)$ and $\mu(x) = \mu_2(x)$ for $x \in \mathsf{dom}(\mu_2)$.

The correspondents of the relational-algebra operators are defined similarly to the SPARQL formalism [23]. In particular, the operators *union, projection, natural join,* and *difference* are defined as follows for all schemaless spanners P_1 and P_2 and documents $\mathbf{d}$.

- **Union:** The union $P := P_1 \cup P_2$ is defined by $P(\mathbf{d}) := P_1(\mathbf{d}) \cup P_2(\mathbf{d})$.
- **Projection:** The projection $P := \pi_Y P_1$ is defined by $P(\mathbf{d}) = \{\mu \upharpoonright Y \mid \mu \in P_1(\mathbf{d})\}$ where $\upharpoonright$ stands for the restriction of μ to the variables in $\mathsf{dom}(\mu) \cap Y$.
- **Natural join:** The *(natural) join* $P := P_1 \bowtie P_2$ is defined to be such that $P(\mathbf{d})$ consists of all mappings $\mu_1 \cup \mu_2$ such that $\mu_1 \in P_1(\mathbf{d})$, $\mu_2 \in P_2(\mathbf{d})$ and μ_1 and μ_2 are compatible.
- **Difference:** The difference $P := P_1 \setminus P_2$ is defined to be such that $P(\mathbf{d})$ consists of all mappings $\mu_1 \in P_1(\mathbf{d})$ such that no $\mu_2 \in P_2(\mathbf{d})$ is compatible with μ_1.

We allow the use of these operators for spanners represented by regex formulas or VAs and also for more complex spanner representations, e.g., $[\![A_1]\!] \bowtie [\![A_2]\!]$. In this case, we use the abbreviated notation $[\![A_1 \bowtie A_2]\!]$ instead of $[\![A_1]\!] \bowtie [\![A_2]\!]$. We make the clear note that when the above operators are applied on schema-based spanners, they are the same as those of Fagin et al. [8].

EXAMPLE 2.4. Let us consider our input document $\mathbf{d}_{\mathsf{Students}}$ from Figure 1. Assume one wants to filter out from the results obtained by applying the spanner $P_{StudInfo}$ from Example 2.2 on $\mathbf{d}_{\mathsf{Students}}$ the mappings that correspond with students from universities within the UK. It is given that students study in the UK if and only if their email addresses end with the letters 'uk'. We phrase the following regex formula that extracts such email addresses:

$$\alpha_{\mathsf{UKm}} := \left(\epsilon \vee (\Gamma^* \cdot \hookleftarrow)\right) \cdot \Gamma^* \cdot {\scriptstyle\sqcup} x_{mail}\{\gamma@\gamma.\mathsf{uk}\} \cdot \hookleftarrow \cdot \Gamma^*$$

where γ is as defined in Example 2.2. In this case, the desired output is given by $[\![\alpha_{\mathsf{info}} \setminus \alpha_{\mathsf{UKm}}]\!](\mathbf{d}_{\mathsf{Students}})$ which consists of the mappings μ_1 and μ_2 from Example 2.1. □

2.5 Complexity

Let $\mathcal{L}$ be a representation language for schemaless spanners (e.g., the class of regex formulas or the class of VAs). Given $q \in \mathcal{L}$ and a document $\mathbf{d}$, we are interested in the decision problem that checks whether $[\![q]\!](\mathbf{d})$ is not empty. In that case, we are also interested in evaluating $[\![q]\!](\mathbf{d})$. Note that we study the *combined complexity* of these problems, as both q and $\mathbf{d}$ are regarded as input.

Under the combined complexity, "polynomial time" is not a proper yardstick of efficiency for evaluating $[\![q]\!](\mathbf{d})$, since this set can contain exponentially many mappings. We thus use efficiency yardsticks of enumeration [17]. In particular, our evaluation algorithm takes q and $\mathbf{d}$ as input, and it outputs all the mappings of $[\![q]\!](\mathbf{d})$, one by one, without duplicates. The algorithm runs in *polynomial total time* if its execution time is polynomial in the combined size of q, $\mathbf{d}$ and $[\![q]\!](\mathbf{d})$. The *delay* of the evaluation algorithm refers to the maximal time that passes between every two consecutive mappings. A well-known observation is that polynomial total time implies polynomial delay (but not necessarily vice versa), and that NP-hardness of the nonemptiness problem implies that no evaluation algorithm runs in polynomial delay, or else P = NP.

While deciding whether $[\![q]\!](\mathbf{d}) \neq \emptyset$ is NP-hard whenever q is given as a VA [11], this is not the case for sequential (and hence functional) VA:

THEOREM 2.5. [1] *Given a sequential VA A and a document $\mathbf{d}$, one can enumerate $[\![A]\!](\mathbf{d})$ with polynomial delay.*

We call two schemaless spanner representations q_1 and q_2 *equivalent* if $[\![q_1]\!] \equiv [\![q_2]\!]$, that is, $[\![q_1]\!]$ and $[\![q_2]\!]$ are identical. Note that the translation of functional and sequential regex formulas to equivalent functional and sequential VAs, respectively, can be done in linear time [13, 19]. Hence, our lower bounds are usually shown for the nonemptiness of regex formulas and our upper bounds for the evaluation of VAs.

3 THE NATURAL-JOIN OPERATOR

To establish complexity upper bounds on the evaluation of schema-based spanners, Freydenberger et al. [13] used static compilation to compile the query (where the operands are regex formulas or VAs) into a single VA. In particular, they showed that two functional VAs can be compiled in polynomial time into a single equivalent VA that is also functional. Consequently, we can enumerate with polynomial delay the mappings of $[\![A_1 \bowtie A_2]\!](\mathbf{d})$, given functional VAs A_1 and A_2. The question is whether it generalizes to schemaless spanners: can we efficiently enumerate the mappings of $[\![A_1 \bowtie A_2]\!](\mathbf{d})$, given *sequential* (but not necessarily *functional*) A_1 and A_2? This is no longer the case, as the next theorem implies, even under the yardstick of *expression complexity* [32] in which the document is regarded as fixed. (Recall that a sequential regex formula can be translated in polynomial time into an equivalent VA [19].)

Theorem 3.1. *The following problem is* NP*-complete. Given two sequential regex formulas γ_1 and γ_2 and an input document* $\mathbf{d}$, *is $[\![\gamma_1 \bowtie \gamma_2]\!](\mathbf{d})$ nonempty? The problem remains* NP*-hard even if* $\mathbf{d}$ *is assumed to be of length one.*

Proof. Membership in NP is straightforward, so we focus on NP-hardness. We show a reduction from 3-CNF-satisfiability which is also known as 3SAT [15]. The input for 3SAT is a formula φ with the free variables $x_1, \dots, x_n$ such that φ has the form $C_1 \wedge \cdots \wedge C_m$, where each C_j is a clause. In turn, each clause is a disjunction of three literals, where a literal has the form x_i or $\neg x_i$ for $i = 1, \dots, n$. The goal is to determine whether there is an assignment $\tau : \{x_1, \dots, x_n\} \to \{\mathsf{t}, \mathsf{f}\}$ that satisfies φ. Given a 3CNF formula φ, we construct two sequential regex formulas γ_1 and γ_2 such that there is a satisfying assignment for φ if and only if $[\![\gamma_1 \bowtie \gamma_2]\!](\mathbf{d}) \neq \emptyset$, where $\mathbf{d}$ is the document that consists of a single letter a.

To construct γ_1 and γ_2, we associate every variable x_i with $2m$ corresponding capture variables $x_i^{j,\ell}$ for $1 \leq j \leq m$ and $\ell \in \{\mathsf{t}, \mathsf{f}\}$. We then define $\gamma_1 := \gamma_{x_1} \cdots \gamma_{x_n} \cdot \mathsf{a}$, where

$$\gamma_{x_i} := (x_i^{1,\mathsf{t}}\{\epsilon\} \cdots x_i^{m,\mathsf{t}}\{\epsilon\}) \vee (x_i^{1,\mathsf{f}}\{\epsilon\} \cdots x_i^{m,\mathsf{f}}\{\epsilon\}).$$

Intuitively, γ_{x_i} verifies that the assignment to x_i is consistent in all of the clauses. We then define

$$\gamma_2 := \mathsf{a} \cdot (\delta_1 \cdots \delta_m)$$

where δ_j is the disjunction of regex formulas β such that $\beta = x_i^{j,\mathsf{f}}\{\epsilon\}$ if $\neg x_i$ appears in C_j, and $\beta = x_i^{j,\mathsf{t}}\{\epsilon\}$ if x_i appears in C_j. Intuitively, γ_2 verifies that at least one disjunct in each clause is evaluated true.

Let us consider the following example where

$$\varphi := (x \vee y \vee z) \wedge (\neg x \vee y \vee \neg z).$$

In this case, we have

$$\delta_1 = x^{1,\mathsf{t}}\{\epsilon\} \vee y^{1,\mathsf{t}}\{\epsilon\} \vee z^{1,\mathsf{t}}\{\epsilon\}$$
$$\delta_2 = x^{2,\mathsf{f}}\{\epsilon\} \vee y^{2,\mathsf{t}}\{\epsilon\} \vee z^{2,\mathsf{f}}\{\epsilon\}$$

and, therefore,

$$\gamma_2 := \mathsf{a} \cdot (x^{1,\mathsf{t}}\{\epsilon\} \vee y^{1,\mathsf{t}}\{\epsilon\} \vee z^{1,\mathsf{t})}\{\epsilon\}) \cdot (x^{2,\mathsf{f}}\{\epsilon\} \vee y^{2,\mathsf{t}}\{\epsilon\} \vee z^{2,\mathsf{f}}\{\epsilon\}).$$

We also have

$$\gamma_1 := \left(x^{1,\mathsf{t}}\{\epsilon\}x^{2,\mathsf{t}}\{\epsilon\} \vee x^{1,\mathsf{f}}\{\epsilon\}x^{2,\mathsf{f}}\{\epsilon\}\right) \cdot \left(y^{1,\mathsf{t}}\{\epsilon\}y^{2,\mathsf{t}}\{\epsilon\} \vee y^{1,\mathsf{f}}\{\epsilon\}y^{2,\mathsf{f}}\{\epsilon\}\right) \cdot \left(z^{1,\mathsf{t}}\{\epsilon\}z^{2,\mathsf{t}}\{\epsilon\} \vee z^{1,\mathsf{f}}\{\epsilon\}z^{2,\mathsf{f}}\{\epsilon\}\right) \cdot \mathsf{a}.$$

It follows directly from the definition that both γ_1 and γ_2 are sequential. Moreover, $[\![\gamma_1 \bowtie \gamma_2]\!](\mathbf{d})$ is nonempty if and only if there are compatible mappings $\mu_1 \in [\![\gamma_1]\!](\mathbf{d})$ and $\mu_2 \in [\![\gamma_2]\!](\mathbf{d})$. Since γ_1 ends with the letter a whereas γ_2 starts with the letter a, it holds that $\mu_1 \in [\![\gamma_1]\!](\mathbf{d})$ and $\mu_2 \in [\![\gamma_2]\!](\mathbf{d})$ are compatible if and only if $\mathsf{dom}(\mu_1) \cap \mathsf{dom}(\mu_2) = \emptyset$. We will show that $[\![\gamma_1 \bowtie \gamma_2]\!](\mathbf{d})$ is nonempty if and only if there is a satisfying assignment to φ.

The "only if" direction. Suppose that $[\![\gamma_1 \bowtie \gamma_2]\!](\mathbf{d})$ is nonempty. In this case, a satisfying assignment τ to φ is encoded by the domain of γ_2 in the following way: if $x_i^{j,\ell} \in \mathsf{dom}(\mu_2)$ then $\tau(x_i) = \ell$. Observe that τ is well defined since $\mathsf{dom}(\mu_1) \cap \mathsf{dom}(\mu_2) = \emptyset$.

In our example, the mapping $\mu_1 \in [\![\gamma_1]\!](\mathsf{a})$ with

$$\mathsf{dom}(\mu_1) = \{x^{1,\mathsf{t}}, x^{2,\mathsf{t}}, y^{1,\mathsf{f}}, y^{2,\mathsf{f}}, z^{1,\mathsf{f}}, z^{2,\mathsf{f}}\}$$

and the mapping $\mu_2 \in [\![\gamma_2]\!](\mathsf{a})$ with

$$\mathsf{dom}(\mu_2) = \{x^{1,\mathsf{f}}, x^{2,\mathsf{f}}, y^{1,\mathsf{t}}, y^{2,\mathsf{t}}, z^{1,\mathsf{t}}, z^{2,\mathsf{t}}\}$$

are compatible, and the satisfying assignment τ is encoded by $\mathsf{dom}(\mu_2)$ and is given by $\tau(x) = \mathsf{f}$, $\tau(y) = \mathsf{t}$ and $\tau(z) = \mathsf{t}$.

The "if" direction. If there is a satisfying assignment τ to φ, then define the mappings $\mu_1 \in [\![\gamma_1]\!](\mathbf{d})$ and $\mu_2 \in [\![\gamma_2]\!](\mathbf{d})$ by $x_i^{j,\ell} \in \mathsf{dom}(\mu_2)$ whenever $j = \tau(x_i)$ and $x_i^{j,\ell} \in \mathsf{dom}(\mu_1)$ whenever $j \neq \tau(x_i)$. These mapping are compatible, since $\mathsf{dom}(\mu_1) \cap \mathsf{dom}(\mu_2) = \emptyset$. We conclude that $[\![\gamma_1 \bowtie \gamma_2]\!](\mathbf{d})$ is nonempty.

We conclude the NP-hardness of the problem of determining whether $[\![\gamma_1 \bowtie \gamma_2]\!](\mathbf{d})$ is nonempty, as claimed. □

In what follows, we suggest two different approaches to deal with this hardness.

3.1 Bounded Number of Shared Variables

We now consider the task of computing $[\![A_1 \bowtie A_2]\!](\mathbf{d})$, given sequential VAs A_1 and A_2 and a document $\mathbf{d}$. Next, we show that compiling the join into a new sequential VA is Fixed Parameter Tractable (FPT) when the parameter is the number of common variables.

Lemma 3.2. *The following problem is FPT when parametrized by* $|\mathsf{Vars}(A_1) \cap \mathsf{Vars}(A_2)|$. *Given two sequential VAs* A_1 *and* A_2, *construct a sequential VA that is equivalent to* $A_1 \bowtie A_2$.

Since we have a polynomial delay algorithm for the evaluation of sequential VAs (Theorem 2.5) and the size of the resulting VA is FPT in $|\mathsf{Vars}(A_1) \cap \mathsf{Vars}(A_2)|$, we have the following immediate conclusion.

Theorem 3.3. *Given two sequential VAs* A_1 *and* A_2 *and a document* $\mathbf{d}$, *one can evaluate* $[\![A_1 \bowtie A_2]\!](\mathbf{d})$ *with FPT delay parameterized by* $|\mathsf{Vars}(A_1) \cap \mathsf{Vars}(A_2)|$.

In the rest of this section, we discuss the proof of Lemma 3.2. As shown by Freydenberger et al. [13] if A is a functional VA then for every state q of A and every variable $v \in \mathsf{Vars}(A)$, all of the possible runs from the initial state q_0 to q include the same variable operations. Formally, for every state q there is a function c_q, namely *the variable configuration function*, that assigns a label from $\{\mathsf{o}, \mathsf{c}, \mathsf{w}\}$, standing for "open," "close," and "wait," to every variable in $\mathsf{Vars}(A)$, as follows. First, $c_q(x) = \mathsf{o}$ if every run from q_0 to q opens x but does not close it. Second, $c_q(x) = \mathsf{c}$ if every run from q_0 to q opens and closes x. Third, $c_q(x) = \mathsf{w}$ if no run from q_0 to q opens or closes variable x.

In sequential VAs, however, not all of the accepting runs open and close all of the variables and therefore it makes more sense to replace the label w with the label u that stands for "unseen". In addition, in sequential VAs as opposed to functional, there might be a state q for which there are two (different) runs from q_0 to q such that the first opens and closes the variable x whereas the second does not even open x. For this case, we add to the set of labels the label d that stands for "done" meaning that variable x cannot be seen after reaching state q. Hence, "done" can also be understood as "unseen or closed, depending on what happened before". We formalize these notions right after the next example.

Example 3.4. Let us examine the following two accepting runs of the sequential VA A from Example 2.3 on the input document $\mathbf{d} := \mathsf{a}$:

$$\rho_1 := (q_0, 1) \xrightarrow{x\vdash} (q_1, 1) \xrightarrow{\mathsf{a}} (q_1, 2) \xrightarrow{\dashv x} (q_2, 2)$$

$$\rho_2 := (q_0, 1) \xrightarrow{\mathsf{a}} (q_2, 2)$$

The run ρ_1 gets to state q_2 after opening and closing x while ρ_2 gets to q_2 without opening x. Thus, in state q_2 the variable configuration of x is d. □

This "nondeterministic" behavior of sequential VAs is reflected in an *extended variable configuration function* $\tilde{c}_q$ for every state q whose co-domain is the set $\{\mathsf{u}, \mathsf{o}, \mathsf{c}, \mathsf{d}\}$. Since all of the accepting runs of a sequential VA are valid, given a state q, exactly one of the following holds:

- all runs from q_0 to q open x; in this case $\tilde{c}_q(x) = \mathsf{o}$;
- all runs from q_0 to q (open and) close x; in this case $\tilde{c}_q(x) = \mathsf{c}$;
- all runs from q_0 to q do not open x; in this case $\tilde{c}_q(x) = \mathsf{u}$;
- at least one run from q_0 to q (opens and) closes x and at least one does not open x; in this case $\tilde{c}_q(x) = \mathsf{d}$.

A sequential VA A is *semi-functional for* x, if for every state q it holds that $\tilde{c}_q(x) \in \{\mathsf{u}, \mathsf{o}, \mathsf{c}\}$. We say that A is *semi-functional for* X if it is semi-functional for every $x \in X$.

Example 3.5. The sequential VA A from Example 2.3 is not semi-functional for x because $\tilde{c}_{q_2}(x) = \mathsf{d}$, as reflected from the runs ρ_1 and ρ_2 presented in the previous example. However, the following equivalent sequential VA A' is semi-functional for x:

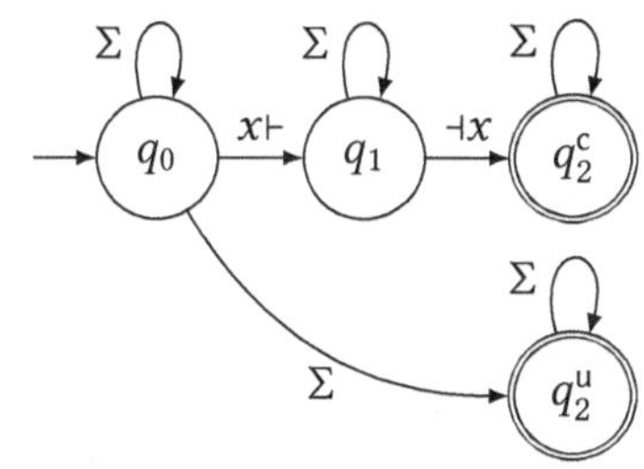

Observe that the ambiguity we had in state q_2 of A is resolved since it is replaced with two states, each corresponding to a unique configuration. □

We show that for every sequential VA A, every state q of A and every variable v, we can compute $\tilde{c}_q(v)$ efficiently, and based on that we can translate A into an equivalent sequential VA that is semi-functional for X. We show that the total runtime is FPT parameterized by $|X|$.

Lemma 3.6. *Given a sequential VA* A *and* $X \subseteq \mathsf{Vars}(A)$, *one can construct in* $O(2^{|X|}(n+m))$ *time a sequential VA* A' *that is equivalent to* A *and semi-functional for* X *where* n *is the number of states of* A *and* m *is the number of its transitions.*

Example 3.7. The sequential VA A' from Example 3.5 can be obtained from the automaton A from Example 2.3 by replacing q_2 with two states q_2^{u} and q_2^{c} such that q_2^{u} corresponds with the paths in from q_0 to q_2 in which variable x was unseen and q_2^{c} corresponds with the paths in from q_0 to q_2 in which variable x was closed, and by changing the transitions accordingly. The algorithm from the previous Lemma generalizes this idea. □

We refer the reader to Footnote 4 in the definition of a VA and note that, as in the previous example, there are cases where, to be semi-functional, a VA must have more than a single accepting state.

If two sequential VAs are semi-functional for their common variables, their join can be computed efficiently:

Lemma 3.8. *Given two sequential VAs A_1 and A_2 that are semi-functional for* $\mathsf{Vars}(A_1) \cap \mathsf{Vars}(A_2)$ *one can construct in polynomial time a sequential VA A that is semi-functional for* $\mathsf{Vars}(A_1) \cap \mathsf{Vars}(A_2)$ *and equivalent to* $A_1 \bowtie A_2$.

The proof of this Lemma uses the same product construction as that for functional VAs presented by Freydenberger et al. [13, Lemma 3.10]. What allow us to use the same construction is (a) the fact it ignores the non-common variables and (b) the fact we can treat both A_1 and A_2 as functional VAs over $\mathsf{Vars}(A_1) \cap \mathsf{Vars}(A_2)$.

We can now move to compose the proof of Lemma 3.2: Given two sequential VAs A_1 and A_2, we invoke the algorithm from Lemma 3.6 and obtain two equivalent sequential VAs $\tilde{A}_1$ and $\tilde{A}_2$, respectively, such that each $\tilde{A}_i$ is semi-functional for $\mathsf{Vars}(A_1) \cap \mathsf{Vars}(A_2)$. Then, we use Lemma 3.8 to join $\tilde{A}_1$ and $\tilde{A}_2$. Note that the runtime is indeed FPT parametrized by $\mathsf{Vars}(A_1) \cap \mathsf{Vars}(A_2)$.

3.2 Restricting to Disjunctive Functional

Another approach to obtain a tractable evaluation of the join is by restricting the syntax of the regex formulas while preserving expressiveness. A regex formula γ is said to be *disjunctive functional* if it is a finite disjunction of functional regex formula $\gamma_1, \ldots, \gamma_n$. We denote the class of disjunctive functional regex formulas as dfuncRGX.

Note that every disjunctive functional regex formula is also sequential. However, the regex formula $z\{\Sigma^*\} \cdot (x\{\Sigma^*\} \vee y\{\Sigma^*\})$ is sequential, yet it is not disjunctive functional. It also holds that every functional regex formula is disjunctive functional regex formula with a single disjunct. We can therefore conclude that we have the following:

$$\mathsf{funcRGX} \subsetneq \mathsf{dfuncRGX} \subsetneq \mathsf{seqRGX}$$

Note that here we treat the regex formulas as syntactic objects.

Equivalently, a *disjunctive functional* VA A is the sequential VA whose states are the disjoint union of the states of a finite number n of functional VAs $A_1, \ldots, A_n$ and whose transitions are those of $A_1, \ldots, A_n$, with the addition of a new initial state q_0 that is connected with epsilon transitions to each of the initial states of the A_i's.

We observe that being disjunctive functional is only a syntactic restriction and not semantic, based on the following proposition.

Proposition 3.9. *The following hold:*

1. *For every sequential regex formula there exists an equivalent disjunctive functional regex formula.*
2. *For every sequential VA there exists an equivalent disjunctive functional VA.*

Since funcRGX corresponds with schema-based spanners whereas seqRGX with schemaless and due to the previous proposition we can conclude the following:

$$[\![\mathsf{funcRGX}]\!] \subsetneq [\![\mathsf{dfuncRGX}]\!] = [\![\mathsf{seqRGX}]\!]$$

Note that here we refer to the schemaless spanners represented by the regex formulas.

Example 3.10. Consider the following sequential regex formula:

$$(x_1\{\Sigma^*\} \vee y_1\{\Sigma^*\}) \cdots (x_n\{\Sigma^*\} \vee y_n\{\Sigma^*\})$$

Note that if we want to translate it into an equivalent disjunctive functional regex formula then we need at least one disjunct for each possible combination $z_1\{\Sigma^*\} \cdots z_n\{\Sigma^*\}$ where $z_i \in \{x_i, y_i\}$. This implies a lower bound on the length of the shortest equivalent disjunctive functional regex formula. Similarly, let us consider the following sequential VA:

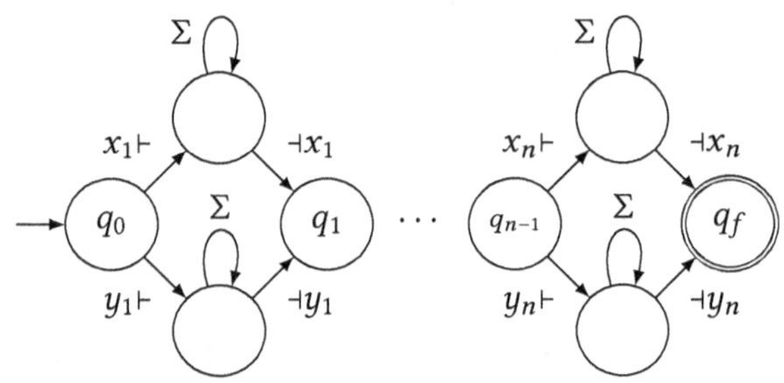

An equivalent disjunctive functional VA has at least 2^n accepting states since the states encode the variable configurations. □

We record this in the following observation.

Observation 3.11. *For every natural number n the following hold:*

1. *There exists a sequential regex formula γ that is the concatenation of n regex formulas of constant length such that each of its equivalent disjunctive functional regex formulas includes at least 2^n disjuncts.*
2. *There exists a sequential VA A with $3n + 1$ states such that each of its equivalent disjunctive functional VA has at least 2^n states.*

That is, the translation from sequential to disjunctive functional might necessitate an exponential blow-up. Although the translation cannot be done efficiently in the general case, the advantage of using disjunctive functional VAs lies in the fact that we can compile the join of two disjunctive functional VAs efficiently into a disjunctive functional VA.

Proposition 3.12. *Given two disjunctive functional VAs A_1 and A_2, one can construct in polynomial time a disjunctive functional VA A that is equivalent to $A_1 \bowtie A_2$.*

To prove this we can perform a pairwise join between the set of functional components of A_1 and those of A_2 and obtain a set of functional VAs for the join [13, Lemma 3.10].

Since disjunctive functional is a restricted type of sequential VA, we conclude the following.

Corollary 3.13. *Given two disjunctive functional VAs A_1 and A_2 and a input document* **d**, *one can enumerate the mappings of* $[\![A_1 \bowtie A_2]\!](\mathbf{d})$ *in polynomial delay.*

4 THE DIFFERENCE OPERATOR

When we consider the class of functional VAs, we know that we can compile all of the positive operators efficiently (i.e., in polynomial time) into a functional VA [13]. In the case of NFAs or regular expressions, compiling the complement into an NFA necessitates an exponential blowup in size [7, 16].

Since NFAs and regular expressions are the Boolean functional VA and Boolean regex formulas, respectively, we conclude that constructing a VA that is equivalent to the difference of two functional VAs, or two functional regex formulas, entails an exponential blowup. Therefore, the static compilation fails to yield tractability results for the difference.

In the case of NFAs and regular expressions, the membership of a string in the difference can be tested in polynomial time. In contrast, the following theorem states that, for functional regex formulas (and VAs), this is no longer true under the conventional complexity assumption P ≠ NP.

Theorem 4.1. *The following problem is* NP*-complete. Given two functional regex formulas γ_1 and γ_2 with* $\text{Vars}(\gamma_1) = \text{Vars}(\gamma_2)$ *and an input document* **d**, *is* $[\![\gamma_1 \setminus \gamma_2]\!](\mathbf{d})$ *nonempty?*

Proof. Membership in NP is straightforward: for functional regex formulas, membership can be decided in polynomial time [11]. Hence, we focus on NP-hardness.

We use a reduction from 3SAT as in the proof of Theorem 3.1. Here, however, we are restricted to functional regex formulas and therefore we cannot use the domains of the resulting mappings to encode the assignments. Recall that the input is a formula φ with the free variables $x_1, \dots, x_n$ such that φ has the form $C_1 \wedge \cdots \wedge C_m$, where each C_i is a clause. In turn, each clause is a disjunction of three literals, where a literal has the form x_i or $\neg x_i$.

Given a 3CNF formula, we construct two functional regex formulas γ_1 and γ_2, and an input document **d**, such that there is a satisfying assignment for φ if and only if $[\![\gamma_1 \setminus \gamma_2]\!](\mathbf{d}) \neq \emptyset$. We begin with the document **d**, which is defined by $\mathbf{d} := \mathsf{a}^n$.

The regex formulas γ_1 and γ_2 are constructed as follows. We associate every free variable x_i with a capture variable x_i. We start by defining the auxiliary regex formulas

$$\beta_i := ((x_i\{\epsilon\} \cdot \mathsf{a}) \vee x_i\{\mathsf{a}\})$$

for $1 \leq i \leq n$ and then define $\gamma_1 := \beta_1 \cdots \beta_n$. Intuitively, γ_1 encodes all of the legal assignments for φ in such a way that if x_i captures the substring 'a' then it corresponds with assigning t to the free variable x_i, and otherwise (in case it captures ϵ), it corresponds with assigning to it f. Before defining γ_2, for each $1 \leq i \leq m$ we denote the indices of the literals that appear in C_i by $i_1 < i_2 < i_3$ and define γ_2^i as follows:

$$\gamma_2^i := \beta_1 \cdots \beta_{i_1-1} \cdot \delta_{i_1} \cdot \beta_{i_1+1} \cdots \beta_{i_2-1} \cdot \delta_{i_2} \cdot \beta_{i_2+1} \cdots \beta_{i_3-1} \cdot \delta_{i_3} \cdot \beta_{i_3+1} \cdots \beta_n$$

where δ_ℓ is defined as $(x_\ell\{\epsilon\} \cdot \mathsf{a})$ if x_ℓ appears as a literal in C_i or as $(x_\ell\{\mathsf{a}\})$ if $\neg x_\ell$ appears as a literal in C_i.

Intuitively, γ_2^i encodes the assignments for which clause C_i is not satisfied. We then set

$$\gamma_2 := \bigvee_{1 \leq i \leq m} \gamma_2^i .$$

To emphasize the differences between this reduction and that in the proof of Theorem 4.1, we consider the same formula:

$$\varphi = (x \vee y \vee z) \wedge (\neg x \vee y \vee \neg z)$$

We have $\mathbf{d} := \mathsf{a}^3$ since we have three variables $\{x, y, z\}$ and

$$\gamma_1 = \Big((x\{\epsilon\} \cdot \mathsf{a}) \vee x\{\mathsf{a}\}\Big) \cdot \Big((y\{\epsilon\} \cdot \mathsf{a}) \vee y\{\mathsf{a}\}\Big) \cdot \Big((z\{\epsilon\} \cdot \mathsf{a}) \vee z\{\mathsf{a}\}\Big)$$

For the first clause we have

$$\gamma_2^1 := (x\{\epsilon\} \cdot \mathsf{a}) \cdot (y\{\epsilon\} \cdot \mathsf{a}) \cdot (z\{\epsilon\} \cdot \mathsf{a})$$

and for the second

$$\gamma_2^2 := (x\{\mathsf{a}\}) \cdot (y\{\epsilon\} \cdot \mathsf{a}) \cdot (z\{\mathsf{a}\})$$

It is left to show that $[\![\gamma_1 \setminus \gamma_2]\!](\mathbf{d}) \neq \emptyset$ if and only if φ has a satisfying assignment.

Note that for every assignment $\mu \in [\![\gamma_1]\!](\mathbf{d})$ and for every $1 \leq j \leq n$, it holds that $\mu(x_j)$ is either $[j, j\rangle$ or $[j, j+1\rangle$. Note also that the same is true also for $\mu \in [\![\gamma_2]\!](\mathbf{d})$.

Let us assume that there exists a satisfying assignment τ for φ. We define μ to be the mapping that is defined as follows: $\mu(x_i) := [i, i\rangle$ if $\tau(x_i) = \mathsf{f}$ and $\mu(x_i) := [i, i+1\rangle$, otherwise (if $\tau(x_i) = \mathsf{t}$). It then follows immediately from the definition of γ_2 that $\mu \in [\![\gamma_1 \setminus \gamma_2]\!](\mathbf{d})$.

On the other hand, assume that $\mu \in [\![\gamma_1 \setminus \gamma_2]\!](\mathbf{d})$. We can define an assignment τ is such a way that $\tau(x_i) = \mathsf{t}$ if $\mu(x_i) = [i, i+1\rangle$ and $\tau(x_i) = \mathsf{f}$ otherwise (if $\mu(x_i) = [i, i\rangle$). It follows directly from the way we defined γ_1 and γ_2 that τ is a satisfying assignment for φ.

In our example, the assignment τ defined by $\tau(x) = \tau(y) = \mathsf{t}$ and $\tau(z) = \mathsf{f}$ is a satisfying assignment. Indeed, the mapping μ corresponds to this assignment that is defined by $\mu(x) = [1, 2\rangle$, $\mu(y) = [2, 3\rangle$ and $\mu(z) = [3, 3\rangle$ is in $[\![\gamma_1]\!](\mathsf{a}^n)$ but is not in $[\![\gamma_2]\!](\mathsf{a}^n)$ since either (a) $\mu(x) = [1, 1\rangle$ and $\mu(y) = [2, 2\rangle$ or (b) $\mu(x) = [1, 2\rangle$ and $\mu(y) = [2, 2\rangle$.

Note also that the assignment μ defined by $\mu(x) = [1, 2\rangle$, $\mu(y) = [2, 3\rangle$ and $\mu(z) = [3, 4\rangle$ is in $[\![\gamma_1 \setminus \gamma_2]\!](\mathsf{a}^n)$ since it is in $[\![\gamma_1]\!](\mathsf{a}^n)$ and not in $[\![\gamma_2]\!](\mathsf{a}^n)$. Indeed, the assignment τ for which $\tau(x) = \tau(y) = \tau(z)$ is a satisfying assignment for φ. Hence, deciding nonemptiness of $[\![\gamma_1 \setminus \gamma_2]\!](\mathbf{d})$ is NP-hard. □

From Theorem 4.1 we conclude that, in contrast to the tractability of the natural join of disjunctive functional VAs (Corollary 3.13), here we are facing NP-hardness already for functional VAs. In the remainder of this section, we discuss syntactic conditions that allow to avoid this hardness.

4.1 Bounded Number of Common Variables

Theorem 4.1 implies that no matter what approach we choose to tackle the evaluation of the difference, without imposing any restrictions we hit NP-hardness. In this section, we investigate the restriction of an upper bound on the number of common variables shared between the operands. Recall that this restriction leads to an FPT static compilation for the natural join (Lemma 3.2).

Yet, in the case of difference, such static compilation necessitates an exponential blow-up, even if there are no variables at all (see the start of Section 4).

Therefore, instead of static compilation that is independent of the document, we apply an ad-hoc compilation that depends on the specific document at hand. In this case, we refer to the resulting automaton as an *ad-hoc VA* since it is valid only for that specific document.

Ad-hoc VAs were introduced (without a name) by Freydenberger et al. [13] as a tool for evaluating functional VAs with polynomial delay. The next lemma is based on this idea.

LEMMA 4.2. *Let k be a fixed natural number. Given two sequential VAs A_1 and A_2 where $|\mathsf{Vars}(A_1) \cap \mathsf{Vars}(A_2)| \leq k$ and a document $\mathbf{d}$, one can construct in polynomial time a sequential VA $A_{\mathbf{d}}$ with $[\![A_{\mathbf{d}}]\!](\mathbf{d}) = [\![A_1 \setminus A_2]\!](\mathbf{d})$.*

By Theorem 2.5, we can enumerate the results of a sequential VA in polynomial. We can conclude the following.

THEOREM 4.3. *Let k be a fixed natural number. Given two sequential VAs A_1 and A_2 where $|\mathsf{Vars}(A_1) \cap \mathsf{Vars}(A_2)| \leq k$ and a document $\mathbf{d}$, one can enumerate $[\![A_1 \setminus A_2]\!](\mathbf{d})$ with polynomial delay.*

PROOF SKETCH OF LEMMA 4.2. We construct two sequential VAs A and B (that share a bounded number of variables) such that evaluating the difference of A_1 and A_2 on $\mathbf{d}$ is the same as evaluating the natural join of A and B on $\mathbf{d}$. This natural join can be compiled into a sequential VA in polynomial time when the number of common variables is bounded by a constant (Theorem 3.3), and therefore, we establish the desired result.

Yet, unlike the schema-based model, difference in the schemaless case cannot be translated straightforwardly into a natural join (e.g., via complementation). For illustration, let us consider the case where there are $\mu_1 \in [\![A_1]\!](\mathbf{d})$ and $\mu_2 \in [\![A_2]\!](\mathbf{d})$ such that $\mathsf{dom}(\mu_1) \cap \mathsf{dom}(\mu_2) = \emptyset$. In this case, the assignment μ_1 is not in $[\![A_1 \setminus A_2]\!](\mathbf{d})$ since it is compatible with μ_2. Nevertheless, μ_1 will occur in the natural join of A_1 with every VA A_2', unless A_1 and A_2' share one or more common variables.

As a solution, we construct a VA that encodes information about the domains of the mappings μ, within the variables shared by A_1 and A_2, using new shared *dummy* variables. Specifically, we have a dummy variable $\hat{x}$ for every shared variable x. If $x \in \mathsf{dom}(\mu)$, then $\hat{x}$ is assigned the first empty span $[1, 1\rangle$, and if $x \notin \mathsf{dom}(\mu)$, then $\hat{x}$ is assigned the last empty span $[|\mathbf{d}| + 1, |\mathbf{d}| + 1\rangle$. (Here, we assume that $\mathbf{d}$ is nonempty; we deal separately with the case $\mathbf{d} = \epsilon$.)

We construct a VA A for the above extended mappings of A_1. In addition, we construct a VA B by iterating through all possible extended mappings over the shared variables, and for each such a mapping, if it is incompatible with all of the extended mappings of $[\![A_2]\!](\mathbf{d})$, then we include it in B. This construction can be done in polynomial time, since the number of common variables is bounded by a constant.

We conclude by showing that the extended mappings of $[\![A]\!](\mathbf{d})$ that have compatible mappings in $[\![B]\!](\mathbf{d})$ correspond to the mappings of $[\![A_1]\!](\mathbf{d})$ that have no compatible mappings in $[\![A_2]\!](\mathbf{d})$, and also that the extended mappings of $[\![A]\!](\mathbf{d})$ that have compatible mappings in $[\![B]\!](\mathbf{d})$ correspond to the mappings of $[\![A_1]\!](\mathbf{d})$ that do not have compatible mappings in $[\![A_2]\!](\mathbf{d})$. □*(Proof sketch)*

Theorem 4.3 shows that we can enumerate the difference with polynomial delay when we restrict the number of common variables. A natural question is whether the degree of this polynomial depends on this number; the next theorem answers this question positively, under the conventional assumptions of parameterized complexity.

THEOREM 4.4. *The following problem is* W[1]*-hard parametrized by $|\mathsf{Vars}(\gamma_1) \cap \mathsf{Vars}(\gamma_2)|$. Given two functional regex formulas γ_1 and γ_2 and an input document $\mathbf{d}$, is $[\![\gamma_1 \setminus \gamma_2]\!](\mathbf{d})$ nonempty?*

This result contrasts our FPT result for the natural join (Theorem 3.3). The proof uses a reduction from the problem of determining whether a 3-SAT formula has a satisfying assignment with at most p ones, where p is the parameter [6].

4.2 Restricting the Disjunctions

We now propose another restriction that guarantees a tractable evaluation, this time allowing the number of common variables to be unbounded. We begin with some definitions.

Let γ be a sequential regex formula and let $x \in \mathsf{Vars}$ be a variable. Then γ is *synchronized* for x if, for every subexpression of γ of the form $\gamma_1 \vee \gamma_2$, we have that x appears neither in γ_1 nor in γ_2. A regex formula γ is called *synchronized* for $X \subseteq \mathsf{Vars}$ if it is synchronized for every $x \in X$.

This notion generalizes to sequential VAs: A state q of a sequential VA A is called a *unique target state* for the variable operation $\omega \in \Gamma_{\mathsf{Vars}(A)}$, if for every state p of A we have that $(p, \omega, q) \in \delta$ implies $q = q_\omega$ where δ is the transition relation of A. In other words, q_ω is the only state that can be reached by processing ω. We say that A is *synchronized* for a variable $x \in \mathsf{Vars}$ if each of $x\vdash$ and $\dashv x$ has a unique target state and either all accepting runs of A open and close x, or no accepting run of A operates on x. Finally, A is *synchronized* for $X \subseteq \mathsf{Vars}$ if it is synchronized for every $x \in X$.

Example 4.5. Consider the regex formula $(x\{\Sigma^*\} \vee \epsilon) \cdot y\{\Sigma^*\}$ and this equivalent VA:

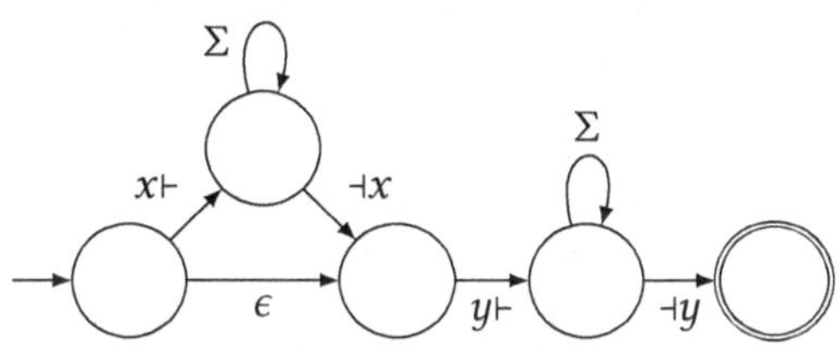

Both are synchronized for y and not for x: The regex formula has a subexpression of the form $(x\{\Sigma^*\} \vee \epsilon)$, whereas the variable y does not appear under any disjunction. In the VA, although each variable operation has a unique target state, not all of the accepting runs include the variable operations $x\vdash$ and $\dashv x$ (as opposed to $y\vdash$ and $\dashv y$, which are included in every accepting run). □

The following result states that conversions from regex formulas to VAs can preserve the property of being synchronized for X.

Lemma 4.6. *Let γ be a sequential regex formula that is synchronized for $X \subseteq \mathsf{Vars}$. One can convert γ in linear time into an equivalent sequential VA A that is synchronized for X.*

As one might expect, VAs that are synchronized (for some nonempty set X of variables) are less expressive than sequential or semi-functional VAs (that are defined in Section 3.1). In fact, even functional regex formulas can express spanners that are not expressible with VAs that are synchronized for all their variables:

Proposition 4.7. *There is no sequential VA that is synchronized for x and equivalent to $(\mathsf{a} \cdot x\{\epsilon\} \cdot \mathsf{a}) \vee (\mathsf{b} \cdot x\{\epsilon\} \cdot \mathsf{b})$.*

Hence, by using synchronized VAs, we sacrifice expressive power. But this restriction also allows us to state the following positive result on the difference of VAs:

Theorem 4.8. *Given an input document $\mathbf{d}$ and two sequential VAs A_1 and A_2 such that, for $X := \mathsf{Vars}(A_1) \cap \mathsf{Vars}(A_2)$, A_1 is semi-functional for X and A_2 is synchronized for X, one can construct a sequential VA $A_{\mathbf{d}}$ with $[\![A_{\mathbf{d}}]\!](\mathbf{d}) = [\![A_1 \setminus A_2]\!](\mathbf{d})$ in polynomial time.*

The full proof can be found in the full version of the paper [24]; we discuss some of its key ideas. The first key observation is that A_2 can be treated as a functional VA that uses only the common variables (similarly to the proof of Lemma 3.8). This allows us to work with the variable configurations of A_2, and construct the *match structure* $M(A_2, \mathbf{d})$ of A_2 on $\mathbf{d}$. This model was introduced (without a name) by Freydenberger et al. [13] to evaluate functional VAs with polynomial delay. As explained there, every element of $[\![A_2]\!](\mathbf{d})$ can be uniquely expressed as a sequence of $|\mathbf{d}| + 1$ variable configurations of A_2.

Every accepting run of A_2 on $\mathbf{d}$ can be mapped into such a sequence by taking the variable configurations of the states just before a symbol of $\mathbf{d}$ is read (and the configuration of the final state). The match structure $M(A_2, \mathbf{d})$ is an NFA that has the set of variable configurations of A_2 as its alphabet; and its language is exactly the set of sequences of variables configurations that correspond to elements of $[\![A_2]\!](\mathbf{d})$.

While determinizing match structures is still hard, the fact that A_2 is synchronizing on the common variables allows us to construct a deterministic match structure D_2 from $M(A, \mathbf{d})$. Using a variant of the proof of Lemma 3.8, we can then combine A_1 and A_2 into an ad-hoc VA $A_{\mathbf{d}}$ with $[\![A_{\mathbf{d}}]\!](\mathbf{d}) = [\![A_1 \setminus A_2]\!](\mathbf{d})$.

After creating $A_{\mathbf{d}}$ according to Theorem 4.8, we can use Theorem 2.5 to obtain the following tractability result:

Corollary 4.9. *Given an input document $\mathbf{d}$ and two sequential VAs A_1 and A_2 such that, for $X := \mathsf{Vars}(A_1) \cap \mathsf{Vars}(A_2)$, A_1 is semi-functional for X and A_2 is synchronized for X, one can enumerate the mappings in $[\![A_1 \setminus A_2]\!](\mathbf{d})$ in polynomial delay.*

We saw that disallowing disjunctions over the variables leads to tractability. Can we relax this restriction by allowing a fixed number of such disjunctions? Our next result is a step towards answering this question. A *disjunction-free* regex formula is a regex formula that does not contain any subexpression of the form $\gamma_1 \vee \gamma_2$.

Proposition 4.10. *The following decision problem is* NP-*complete. Given two sequential regex formulas γ_1 and γ_2 with $\mathsf{Vars}(\gamma_1) = \mathsf{Vars}(\gamma_2)$ and an input document $\mathbf{d}$ such that*

- *γ_1 is functional,*
- *γ_2 is a disjunction of regex formulas γ_2^i such that each is disjunction-free,*
- *for every variable $x \in \mathsf{Vars}(\gamma_2)$, it holds that x appears in at most 3 disjuncts γ_2^i of γ_2,*

is $[\![\gamma_1 \setminus \gamma_2]\!](\mathbf{d})$ nonempty?

Proof. This proof is an adaption of the proof of Theorem 4.1, using mostly the same notation. Instead of a general

3CNF formula, let $\varphi = C_1 \wedge \ldots \wedge C_m$ be a CNF formula, such that every clause C_i contains either 2 or 3 literals, and each of the variables appears in at most 3 clauses. Deciding satisfiability for such a formula is still NP-complete [31].

For γ_1 to not have any disjunctions, we first set set $\mathbf{d} = (\mathsf{bab})^n$ for some $\mathsf{a}, \mathsf{b} \in \Sigma$. We then define

$$\gamma_1 = (\mathsf{b}\, x_1\{\mathsf{a}^*\} \cdot \mathsf{a}^*\mathsf{b}) \cdots (\mathsf{b}\, x_n\{\mathsf{a}^*\} \cdot \mathsf{a}^*\mathsf{b}).$$

Intuitively γ_1 encodes all of the possible assignments. The regex formula γ_2 is defined analogously to γ_2 in the proof of Theorem 4.1 with an adaptation to the new input document and a slight simplification of the γ_2^is (since we do not need γ_2 to be functional any more). Formally, we set

$$\gamma_2^i = (\mathsf{bab})^{i_1-1}\delta_{i_1}(\mathsf{bab})^{i_2-i_1-1}\delta_{i_2}(\mathsf{bab})^{n-i_2}$$

if only variables x_{i_1}, x_{i_2} with $i_1 < i_2$ appear in clause C_i, and

$$\gamma_2^i = (\mathsf{bab})^{i_1-1}\delta_{i_1}(\mathsf{bab})^{i_2-i_1-1}\delta_{i_2}(\mathsf{bab})^{i_3-i_2-1}\delta_{i_3}(\mathsf{bab})^{n-i_3}$$

if variables $x_{i_1}, x_{i_2}, x_{i_3}$ with $i_1 < i_2 < i_3$ appear in clause C_i.

By the choice of the 3CNF formula φ, every variable x_j appears in at most three regex formulas of the form γ_2^i. Correctness of this reduction can be shown analogously to that of Theorem 4.1. □

We conclude that evaluating $\gamma_1 \setminus \gamma_2$ remains hard even if γ_1 is functional (and hence also semi-functional for the common variables) and γ_2 is a disjunction of disjunction-free regex formulas, and each of γ_2's variables appears in at most three such disjuncts.

It is open whether the problem becomes tractable if the variables are limited to at most one or two disjuncts.

5 EXTRACTION COMPLEXITY

In this section, we discuss queries that are defined as RA expressions over schemaless spanners given in a representation language $\mathcal{L}$ (e.g., regex formulas), which we refer to as the language of the *atomic* spanners. Formally, an *RA tree* is a directed and ordered tree whose inner nodes are labeled with RA operators, the out-degree of every inner node is the arity its RA operator, and each of the leaves is a placeholder for a schemaless spanner. For illustration, Figure 2 shows an RA tree τ, where the placeholders are the rectangular boxes with the question marks; the dashed arrows should be ignored for now. The RA tree corresponds to the relational concept of a *query tree* or a *logical query plan* [14, 30]. As in the rest of the paper, we restrict the discussion to the RA operators projection, union, natural join, and difference.

Let $\mathcal{L}$ be a representation language for atomic spanners, and let τ be an RA tree. An *instantiation* of τ assigns a schemaless spanner representation from $\mathcal{L}$ to every placeholder, and a set of variables to every projection. For example, Figure 2 shows an instantiation I for τ via the dashed arrows; here,

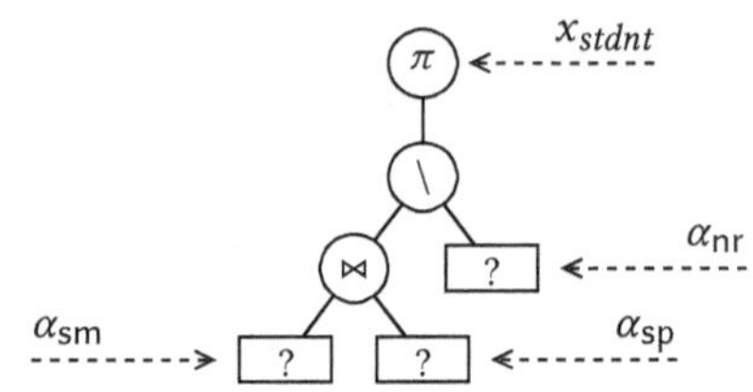

Figure 2: An RA tree τ with an instantiation I

we can think of $\mathcal{L}$ as the class of sequential regex formulas, and so, each α expression is a sequential regex formula.

An instantiation I of τ transforms τ into an actual schemaless spanner representation, where τ is the parse tree of its algebraic expression. We denote this representation by $I[\tau]$. As usual, by $[\![I[\tau]]\!]$ we denote the actual schemaless spanner that $I[\tau]$ represents.

Example 5.1. Assume that the input document $\mathbf{d}_{\mathsf{Students}}$ from the earlier examples is now extended and contains additional information about the students, including recommendations they got from their professors and previous hires. Let us assume that every line begins with a student's name and contains information about that student. Let us also assume that we have the following functional regex formulas:

- regex formula α_{sm} with capture variables x_{stdnt}, x_{ml} that extracts names with their corresponding email addresses;
- regex formula α_{sp} with variables x_{stdnt}, x_{phn} that extracts names with their corresponding phone numbers;
- regex formula α_{nr} with variables x_{stdnt}, x_{rcmnd} that extracts names with their corresponding recommendations.

Note that all of the regex formulas are functional, that is, they do not output partial mappings. The following query extracts the students that do not have recommendations.

$$\pi_{\{x_{stdnt}\}}\Big((\alpha_{\mathsf{sm}} \bowtie \alpha_{\mathsf{sp}}) \setminus (\alpha_{\mathsf{nr}})\Big)$$

This query is $I[\tau]$ for the RA tree τ and the instantiation I of Figure 2. This query defines the spanner $[\![I[\tau]]\!]$, and the set of extracted spans is $[\![I[\tau]]\!](\mathbf{d}_{\mathsf{Students}})$. □

We present a complexity measure that is unique to spanners, namely the *extraction complexity*, where the RA tree τ is fixed and the input consists of both the instantiation I and the input document $\mathbf{d}$. Specifically, the *evaluation problem* for an RA tree τ is that of evaluating $[\![I[\tau]]\!](\mathbf{d})$, given I and $\mathbf{d}$. Similarly, the *nonemptiness problem* for an RA tree τ is that of deciding whether $[\![I[\tau]]\!](\mathbf{d})$ is nonempty, given I and $\mathbf{d}$.

Clearly, some RA trees have an intractable nonemptiness and, consequently, an intractable evaluation. For example, if $\mathcal{L}$ is the class of sequential regex formulas and τ is the

RA tree that consists of a single natural-join node, then the nonemptiness problem for τ is NP-complete (Theorem 3.1). Also, if $\mathcal{L}$ is the class of functional regex formulas and τ is the RA tree that consists of a single difference node, then the nonemptiness problem for τ is NP-complete (Theorem 4.1). In contrast, by composing the positive results established in Sections 3 and 4, we obtain the following theorem, which is a consequence of Lemma 3.2 and Lemma 4.2.

Theorem 5.2. *Let $\mathcal{L}$ be the class of sequential VAs. Let k be a fixed natural number and τ an RA tree. The evaluation problem for τ is solvable with polynomial delay, assuming that for all join and difference nodes v of $I[\tau]$, the left and right subtrees under v share at most k variables.*

We restate that, while static compilation suffices for the positive operators, we need ad-hoc compilation to support the difference. Interestingly, the ad-hoc approach allows us to incorporate into the RA tree other representations of schemaless spanners, which can be treated as black-box schemaless spanners, as long as these spanners can be evaluated in polynomial time and are of a bounded degree. In turn, the *degree* of a schemaless spanner S is the maximal cardinality of a mapping produced over all possible documents, that is, $\max\{|\mathsf{dom}(\mu)| \mid \mathbf{d} \in \Sigma^*, \mu \in S(\mathbf{d})\}$.

Formalizing the above, we can conclude from Theorem 5.2 a generalization that allows for black-box schemaless spanners. To this end, we call a representation language $\mathcal{L}'$ for schemaless spanners *tractable* if $[\![\beta]\!](\mathbf{d})$ can be evaluated in polynomial time (for some fixed polynomial), given $\beta \in \mathcal{L}'$ and $\mathbf{d} \in \Sigma^*$, and we call $\mathcal{L}'$ *degree bounded* if there is a fixed natural number that bounds the degree of all the schemaless spanners represented by expressions in $\mathcal{L}'$.

Corollary 5.3. *Let $\mathcal{L}'$ be a tractable and degree-bounded representation system for schemaless spanners, and let $\mathcal{L}$ be the union of $\mathcal{L}'$ and the class of all sequential VAs. Let k be a fixed natural number and let τ be an RA tree. The evaluation problem of τ is solvable with polynomial delay, assuming that for all join and difference nodes v of $I[\tau]$, the left and right subtrees under v share at most k variables.*

Combining such black-box schemaless spanners in the instantiated RA tree increases the expressiveness, as it allows us to incorporate spanners that are not (and possibly cannot be) described as RA expressions over VAs, such as string equalities [8]. Other examples of such spanners are part of speech (POS) taggers, dependency parsers, sentiment analysis modules, and so on.

Example 5.4. Following Example 5.1, suppose that we now wish to extract the students that do not have any *positive* recommendations. Assume we have a black-box spanner for sentiment analysis, namely PosRec, with the variables x_{stdnt} and x_{posrec}, that extract names and their corresponding positive recommendation. Note that this spanner has the degree 2. We can replace α_{nr} in the instantiation I of Figure 2 with PosRec, and thereby obtain the desired result. If PosRec can be computed in polynomial time, then the resulting query can be evaluated in polynomial delay. □

6 CONCLUSIONS

We have studied the complexity of evaluating algebraic expressions over schemaless spanners that are represented as sequential regex formulas and sequential VAs. We have shown that we hit computational hardness already in the evaluation of the natural join and difference of two such spanners. In contrast, we have shown that we can compile the natural join of two sequential VAs (and regex formulas) into a single sequential VA, in polynomial time, if we assume a constant bound on the number of common variables of the joined spanners; hence, under this assumption, we can evaluate the natural join with polynomial delay. As an alternative to this assumption, we have proposed and investigated a new normal form for sequential spanners, namely disjunctive functional, that allows for such efficient compilation and evaluation.

Bounding the number of common variables between the involved spanners also allows to evaluate the difference with polynomial delay, even though this cannot be obtained by compiling into a VA—an exponential blowup in the number of states is necessary already for Boolean spanners. Evaluation with polynomial delay is then obtained via an ad-hoc compilation of both the spanners and the document into a VA. We have shown how the ad-hoc approach can be used for establishing upper bounds on general RA trees over regex formulas, VAs, and even black-box spanners of a bounded dimension. This has been done within the concept of *extraction complexity* that we have proposed as new lens to analyzing the complexity of spanners.

We believe that our analysis has merely touched the tip of the iceberg on the algorithms that can be devised under the guarantee of tractable extraction complexity. In particular, we have proposed sufficient conditions to avoid the inherent hardness of the natural join and difference, but it is quite conceivable that less restrictive conditions already suffice. Alternatively, are there conditions of extractors (possibly incomparable to ours) that are both common in practice and useful to bound the extraction complexity?

ACKNOWLEDGMENTS

The work of Liat Peterfreund was supported by the Technion Hiroshi Fujiwara Cyber Security Research Center and Israel Cyber Bureau. The work of Benny Kimelfeld and Liat Peterfreund was supported by the ISF Grant 1295/15. The work of Markus Kröll was supported by the FWF Grants P30930-N35 and W1255-N23.

REFERENCES

[1] Antoine Amarilli, Pierre Bourhis, Stefan Mengel, and Matthias Niewerth. Constant-delay enumeration for nondeterministic document spanners. *CoRR*, abs/1807.09320, 2018.

[2] Guillaume Bagan, Arnaud Durand, and Etienne Grandjean. On acyclic conjunctive queries and constant delay enumeration. In *CSL*, volume 4646 of *Lecture Notes in Computer Science*, pages 208–222. Springer, 2007.

[3] Nofar Carmeli and Markus Kröll. Enumeration complexity of conjunctive queries with functional dependencies. In *ICDT*, volume 98 of *LIPIcs*, pages 11:1–11:17. Schloss Dagstuhl - Leibniz-Zentrum fuer Informatik, 2018.

[4] Goutam Chakraborty, Murali Pagolu, and Satish Garla. *Text mining and analysis: practical methods, examples, and case studies using SAS.* SAS Institute, 2014.

[5] Laura Chiticariu, Marina Danilevsky, Yunyao Li, Frederick Reiss, and Huaiyu Zhu. Systemt: Declarative text understanding for enterprise. In *NAACL-HTL (3)*, pages 76–83. Association for Computational Linguistics, 2018.

[6] Rodney G Downey and Michael Ralph Fellows. *Parameterized complexity.* Springer Science & Business Media, 2012.

[7] Keith Ellul, Bryan Krawetz, Jeffrey Shallit, and Ming-wei Wang. Regular expressions: New results and open problems. *Journal of Automata, Languages and Combinatorics*, 10(4):407–437, 2005.

[8] Ronald Fagin, Benny Kimelfeld, Frederick Reiss, and Stijn Vansummeren. Document spanners: A formal approach to information extraction. *J. ACM*, 62(2):12, 2015.

[9] Ronald Fagin, Benny Kimelfeld, Frederick Reiss, and Stijn Vansummeren. Declarative cleaning of inconsistencies in information extraction. *ACM Trans. Database Syst.*, 41(1):6:1–6:44, 2016.

[10] Fernando Florenzano, Cristian Riveros, Martín Ugarte, Stijn Vansummeren, and Domagoj Vrgoc. Constant delay algorithms for regular document spanners. In *PODS*, pages 165–177, 2018.

[11] Dominik D. Freydenberger. A logic for document spanners. *Theory Comput. Syst.*, Sep 2018.

[12] Dominik D. Freydenberger and Mario Holldack. Document spanners: From expressive power to decision problems. *Theory Comput. Syst.*, 62(4):854–898, 2018.

[13] Dominik D. Freydenberger, Benny Kimelfeld, and Liat Peterfreund. Joining extractions of regular expressions. In *PODS*, pages 137–149, 2018.

[14] Hector Garcia-Molina, Jeffrey D. Ullman, and Jennifer Widom. *Database System Implementation.* Prentice-Hall, 2000.

[15] Michael R. Garey and David S. Johnson. *Computers and Intractability; A Guide to the Theory of NP-Completeness.* W. H. Freeman & Co., New York, NY, USA, 1990.

[16] Galina Jirásková. State complexity of some operations on binary regular languages. *Theor. Comput. Sci.*, 330(2):287–298, 2005.

[17] David S. Johnson, Christos H. Papadimitriou, and Mihalis Yannakakis. On generating all maximal independent sets. *Inf. Process. Lett.*, 27(3):119–123, 1988.

[18] Yunyao Li, Frederick Reiss, and Laura Chiticariu. SystemT: A declarative information extraction system. In *ACL*, pages 109–114. ACL, 2011.

[19] Francisco Maturana, Cristian Riveros, and Domagoj Vrgoc. Document spanners for extracting incomplete information: Expressiveness and complexity. In *PODS*, pages 125–136, 2018.

[20] Matthias Niewerth and Luc Segoufin. Enumeration of MSO queries on strings with constant delay and logarithmic updates. In *PODS*. ACM, 2018.

[21] Christian W. Omlin and C. Lee Giles. Extraction of rules from discrete-time recurrent neural networks. *Neural Networks*, 9(1):41–52, 1996.

[22] Hao Peng, Roy Schwartz, Sam Thomson, and Noah A. Smith. Rational recurrences. *CoRR*, abs/1808.09357, 2018.

[23] Jorge Pérez, Marcelo Arenas, and Claudio Gutiérrez. Semantics and complexity of SPARQL. *ACM Trans. Database Syst.*, 34(3):16:1–16:45, 2009.

[24] Liat Peterfreund, Dominik D. Freydenberger, Benny Kimelfeld, and Markus Kröll. Complexity bounds for relational algebra over document spanners. *CoRR*, abs/1901.04182, 2019.

[25] Liat Peterfreund, Balder ten Cate, Ronald Fagin, and Benny Kimelfeld. Recursive programs for document spanners. In *ICDT*, 2019.

[26] Christopher De Sa, Alexander Ratner, Christopher Ré, Jaeho Shin, Feiran Wang, Sen Wu, and Ce Zhang. Deepdive: Declarative knowledge base construction. *SIGMOD Record*, 45(1):60–67, 2016.

[27] Sunita Sarawagi. Information extraction. *Foundations and Trends in Databases*, 1(3):261–377, 2008.

[28] Luc Segoufin. Enumerating with constant delay the answers to a query. In *ICDT*, pages 10–20. ACM, 2013.

[29] Warren Shen, AnHai Doan, Jeffrey F. Naughton, and Raghu Ramakrishnan. Declarative information extraction using Datalog with embedded extraction predicates. In *VLDB*, pages 1033–1044, 2007.

[30] John Miles Smith and Philip Yen-Tang Chang. Optimizing the performance of a relational algebra database interface. *Commun. ACM*, 18(10):568–579, 1975.

[31] Craig A. Tovey. A simplified NP-complete satisfiability problem. *Discrete Applied Mathematics*, 8(1):85–89, 1984.

[32] Moshe Y. Vardi. The complexity of relational query languages (extended abstract). In *STOC*, pages 137–146. ACM, 1982.

[33] Gail Weiss, Yoav Goldberg, and Eran Yahav. Extracting automata from recurrent neural networks using queries and counterexamples. In *ICML*, volume 80 of *JMLR Workshop and Conference Proceedings*, pages 5244–5253. JMLR.org, 2018.

Reachability in Database-driven Systems with Numerical Attributes under Recency Bounding

Parosh Aziz Abdulla
Uppsala University
parosh@it.uu.se

C. Aiswarya
Chennai Mathematical Institute
aiswarya@cmi.ac.in

Mohamed Faouzi Atig
Uppsala University
mohamed_faouzi.atig@it.uu.se

Marco Montali
Free Univ. of Bozen/Bolzano
montali@inf.unibz.it

ABSTRACT

A prominent research direction of the database theory community is to develop techniques for verification of database-driven systems operating over relational and numerical data. Along this line, we lift the framework of database manipulating systems [3] which handle relational data to also accommodate numerical data and the natural order on them. We study an under-approximation called recency bounding under which the most basic verification problem –reachability, is decidable. Even under this under-approximation the reachability space is infinite in multiple dimensions – owing to the unbounded sizes of the active domain, the unbounded numerical domain it has access to, and the unbounded length of the executions. We show that, nevertheless, reachability is ExpTime complete. Going beyond reachability to LTL model checking renders verification undecidable.

KEYWORDS

database-driven systems; reachability; numerical constraints; recency

ACM Reference Format:
Parosh Aziz Abdulla, C. Aiswarya, Mohamed Faouzi Atig, and Marco Montali. 2019. Reachability in Database-driven Systems with Numerical Attributes under Recency Bounding. In *38th ACM SIGMOD-SIGACT-SIGAI Symposium on Principles of Database Systems (PODS'19), June 30-July 5, 2019, Amsterdam, Netherlands.* ACM, New York, NY, USA, 18 pages. https://doi.org/10.1145/3294052.3319705

PODS'19, June 30-July 5, 2019, Amsterdam, Netherlands

ACM ISBN 978-1-4503-6227-6/19/06...$15.00
https://doi.org/10.1145/3294052.3319705

1 INTRODUCTION

Verification of dynamic, database-driven systems operating over relational data, is a central task to support the integrated management of master data and business processes. Over the years, many researchers in the field of principles of data management have attacked this difficult problem, producing a flourishing plethora of formal, integrated models for processes and data, and corresponding technical results on identifying limits of decidability [12].

Within this broad literature, two main trends can be identified. A first line of research splits the data component of the database-driven system into two parts: a read-only part that is immutable and can only be queried by the process, and a "controlled" read-write part that can instead be updated while the process unfolds. Parameterized verification problems are then studied by checking whether the process satisfies a temporal property of interest irrespectively of the data contained in the read-only part (see, e.g., [10, 20, 26]). In this spectrum, verification has been studied also in the presence of numerical attributes and corresponding arithmetic constraints [17, 21]. In this challenging setting, decidability essentially requires to bound how the result of an arithmetic operation propagates to further arithmetic operations. In [17], this is ensured through the notion of *feedback freedom* (which prevents a variable to be updated based on the previous value stored in the same variable). In [21], instead, where the framework handles task hierarchies, this is achieved by controlling how parent tasks invoke their subtasks, in particular requiring that each subtask is called at most once between internal transitions of its parent task.

In a second, parallel line of research, the process can freely update the entire data component, and verification is studied by considering how the process evolves when starting from an initial, fixed database instance. Even without the parameterized flavor discussed above, verification turns out to be extremely challenging also in this setting, since it requires to analyze a transition system containing infinitely many different states, each one related to a different database instance. Towards decidability, two main strategies have been studied.

The first strategy is to focus on *state-bounded* systems, that is, systems where the size of each database instance cannot exceed a pre-defined, possibly unknown bound [5, 7]. Under this assumption, it is possible to construct a faithful, finite-state abstraction of the transition system that cannot be distinguished from the original one even by sophisticated temporal logics based on the first-order μ-calculus [13].

The second strategy is to consider *under-approximate verification*. Under-approximation has been proven very efficient for finding bugs in software verification [25]. Instead of checking a temporal property of interest over all the runs induced by the process, only a subset of the runs is considered. In [3], this notion has been applied for the first time ever to the verification of dynamic database-driven systems. In particular, processes operating over data are formalized there in a so-called *Database Manipulating Systems (DMS)*. A DMS consists of a relational database, and a set of actions that query and modify that database. Queries can be made using first order logic over the relational schema and they can be used as guards that enable/disable actions. Actions bring changes over the database that can result in 1) deleting facts from the relations, 2) adding new facts involving existing data elements to the relations, 3) adding new facts involving new data elements (that were not present in the current database instance) into the relations. The new data insertion is the key to model user-inputs or freshly generated data such as timestamps / UIDs. As in the other formal models for data-aware processes, this sophisticated modeling comes at the price of imminent undecidability of verification: even the most simple forms of verification, such as propositional reachability, enjoy decidability by putting severe restrictions on the modeling power of DMS [4].

In this setting, under-approximation is a good compromise between feasible verification and modeling power. In [3], the subset of runs carved out by under-approximation corresponds to the one where the answers to the queries posed over the data component are all returned from the most recent B elements introduced in the system. We call this *recency-bounded verification*. The set of database instances that we may encounter while abiding to recency-bounded runs is still infinite. Thus the coverage is far superior than any finite state abstraction. Furthermore, bounding recency is a natural choice for under-approximation – it appears naturally in processes where services are prioritized on a last-come-first-serve basis. In [3] we showed that not just reachability but also model checking against very powerful monadic second order logic that can reason about temporal properties of the database instances is decidable under the bounded recency assumption.

In spite of these encouraging results, little is known about verification of database-driven systems starting from an initial, fixed database instance, *when the system is equipped with numerical attributes*. The only existing result has been obtained for state-bounded systems [14]. The result essentially shows that, due to the state-bounded restriction, the implicit comparison predicate $\leq$ can be actually lifted into an explicit binary relation that suitably reconstructs comparison on all and only data objects present in the current active domain.

Unfortunately, this approach cannot be exploited under the recency-bounded restriction. For one reason the relations are total and hence appropriate update of the explicit relation would include adding facts involving *all* the unbounded elements in the current active domain, which would indeed violate the bound on recency. Even the case of a non-total relation such as "*smaller-but-closest* in the active domain" is problematic because the partner element may be very far away according to the recency and hence not accessible within the bound.

In some sense this has to be expected and permitted, because if we give the ability to build and maintain chains (eg. "successor" relations of two total orders), that could also easily lead to undecidability defeating our purpose.

This paper takes form at this juncture to precisely address this issue: *how to verify database-driven systems with numerical attributes under recency bounding*. First of all, we extend the framework of [3] so as to tackle processes operating over interpreted data and implicit relations over them, in particular numbers with implicit order $(\mathbb{Q}, \leq)$. Secondly, we study recency-bounded verification in this richer setting. Even without going to arithmetics, the extension to DMSs with numerical attributes makes this problem extremely difficult to attack: we cannot anymore resort to the technical machinery exploited in [3], but need to develop completely novel techniques.

Towards this we assume an uninterpreted data domain which is equipped with a numerical attribute. This is not an injective association, and hence there may be multiple elements with the same numerical value. Further we assume the numerical values to range from a dense domain such as rational numbers $(\mathbb{Q})$.

We lift the framework of DMS to handle dense orders on the numerical values as implicit relations. The action guards can check constraints on the numerical values. The constraints are Boolean combinations of inequality checks. Thus the guarding queries can be written as a union of conjunctive queries with possibly negated atoms over the extended vocabulary which consists of the schema as well as the implicit order relation.

Our main result states that recency-bounded reachability is decidable, in ExpTime, even with this rich feature. We also

show a matching lower-bound thus est
ity of our procedure. Further, we sho
reachability towards model checking ag
such as LTL-FO compromises decidabi

Our proof technique is to construct
(with finite states and stack alphabet) w
symbolic abstraction of the recency b
non-trivial because the pushdown sys
the numerical constraints faithfully th
to the relation instances. The numeri
jectively assigned to elements, and th
recency bounding or freshness, makin
merical values that are far outside th
also contribute to the constraints that n

The number of states and the size of
our symbolic pushdown system is exp
B, number of free variables in actions a
tions in a schema. We assume the arity
schema is fixed to have the reachabilit
the degree of the polynomial in the exp
to the maximum arity of the relations.

Outline. We will first give an overvie
the ExpTime procedure in Section 2.
model and the problem more formally
in Section 4, followed by an example (S
the modeling capabilities. Then we con
of the ExpTime procedure in Sections
lower bound and undecidability are m
for want of space. We discuss the relate
the paper with further research directions.

2 OVERVIEW

In this section, we give a high-level but detailed overv
the problem and our solution. First, we introduce *Da
Manipulating Systems (DMS)*, the recency semantics, a
reachability problem. Then, we describe a symbolic
sentation that allows to translate the reachability pr
under the recency semantics to the reachability probl
standard Push-Down Automata (PDA). More precise
show how the transitions of a PDA can simulate the a
of a DMS while preserving reachability properties.

2.1 Model

We consider *Database Manipulating Systems (DMS)* wh
elements from the data domain are equipped with nun
values. As usual, the database provides a set of *relation*
each with an *arity*. An *instance* I of the database consis
relation instance for each relation name R. A relation in
of R consists of a set of *facts* each of which is a vector
elements whose length is equal to the arity of R. The
domain ADOM (I) of I is the set of data elements that a

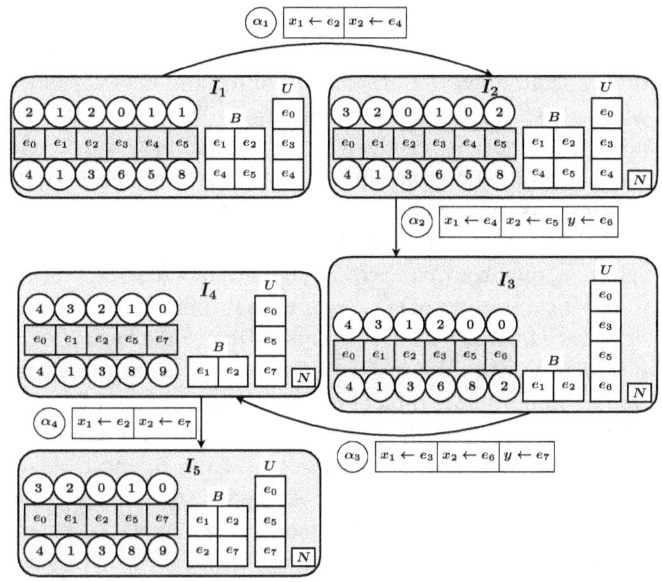

Figure 1: Database instances.

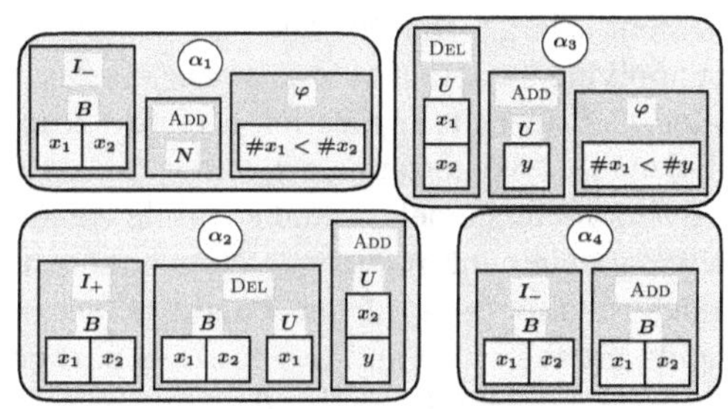

Figure 2: Actions.

of some fact in I. Fig. 1 depicts five instances $I_1, \ldots, I_5$. Let us consider I_1. The active domain contains six data elements, namely $e_0, \ldots, e_5$. The circle below each data element gives its numerical value which in general is a rational number. The numerical value of e_0 is given by $\#e_0 = 4$. For the time being, we will not explain the circles above the data elements (they will be used later when explaining the recency semantics.) The database has three relations names, namely B (for Binary) with arity 2, U (for Unary) with arity 1, and N (for Nullary) with arity 0. The instance I_1 contains the relation instances $\{\langle e_1, e_2\rangle, \langle e_4, e_5\rangle\}$ for B, and $\{\langle e_0\rangle, \langle e_3\rangle, \langle e_4\rangle\}$ for U. A nullary relation is treated as a proposition whose value is true if it occurs in the instance, and false otherwise. The value of N is false in I_1 and true in I_2.

The operational semantics of a DMS is defined as a transition relation on the set of instances. The relation is derived through a set of *actions*. Fig. 2 shows examples of four actions $\alpha_1, \ldots, \alpha_4$. Each action is defined using two sets of variables: the *old* variables that are instantiated to elements that are currently in the active domain, and the *new* variables that are instantiated to elements that will be added to the instance. In this section, we denote the sets of old and new variables using x resp. y (possibly with subscripts). The sets of old and new variables in α_2 are given by $\{x_1, x_2\}$ and $\{y\}$ respectively. The action may contain five parts (some of which may be missing), as follows. (i) The *positive database instance* I_+ requires that some facts should be present in the instance. The action α_2 requires that there should be a fact (corresponding to the instantiation of) $\langle x_1, x_2 \rangle$ in the instance of B. (ii) The *negative database instance* I_- requires that some facts should not be present in the instance. The action α_1 requires that there should not be a fact $\langle x_1, x_2 \rangle$ in the instance of B. (iii) The *delete part* DEL deletes some facts from the database. The action α_2 deletes the fact $\langle x_1, x_2 \rangle$ from B, and the fact $\langle x_1 \rangle$ from U. (iv) The *add part* ADD adds some facts to the database. The action α_3 adds a fact with a new data element to the unary relation U. (v) The *constraint* φ compares the numerical values of the data elements using the relations $\leq$ and $<$. The compared elements may be old or newly added. The action α_3 requires that the numerical value of the newly added element is larger that the one represented by x_1

Before applying an action to an instance, its variables are instantiated. Consider the application of α_2 to I_2 leading to I_3 as depicted in Fig. 1. We instantiate x_1 and x_2 to data elements in the active domain, namely e_4 and e_5, while we instantiate y to a new data element, namely e_6. Notice that the action will remove the fact $\langle e_4, e_5 \rangle$ from B and the fact $\langle e_4 \rangle$ from U, and adds the facts $\langle e_5 \rangle$ and $\langle e_6 \rangle$ to U. In particular, the element e_4 will not be in the active domain any more.

The *reachability problem* asks, given by a DMS, an instance I, and a proposition q, whether we can apply a sequence of actions to I to obtain an instance I' that contains q.

2.2 Recency Semantics

The recency semantics corresponds to an under-approximation where we only consider "recent" data elements when instantiating the variables when performing actions. To that end, we equip each data element in an instance with a *recency measure* that orders the elements according to the number of steps that have elapsed since they last participated in an action (i.e., since they were last used to instantiate a variable in action). More precisely, an element e_1 has a smaller recency measure than an element e_2 if the last time e_1 participated in an action was after the last time e_2 participated in an action. In particular, all the elements that participated in the latest action have recency measures that are equal to 0. The *band* of measure k is the set of elements with recency measures equal to k. The recency semantics is parameterized by a *recency bound* B. At any point of a run of the DMS, we identify the *current recency window* to be the set of elements whose recency measures do not exceed the bound B. When performing an action, we are only allowed to instantiate variables with elements in the current recency window. We reset the recency measures of all the elements that participate in the action to 0, while we increase the recency measures of all the other elements by 1. Notice that the recency measure of an element e may decrease after an action either because e participates in the action, or because the action removes all the elements in some band whose measure is smaller than the measure of e. In Fig. 1, we assume that the recency bound is $B = 2$. The recency measures of the elements are given in the circles above the element. In I_2, the band of measure 2 is given by the elements e_1 and e_5; and all the elements except e_0 are in the current recency window. When we perform an action, say α_2, we are only allowed to use elements with recency bounds up to 2 (e.g., e_4 and e_5 together with the new element e_6). However, we are not allowed to instantiate x_1 or x_2 by e_0 since its recency measure in I_2 is equal to 3. Since the recency measures may increase or decrease during a given run, some elements may repeatedly leave and enter the current recency window. The element e_1 is inside the window in I_1, I_2, and I_5, and outside the window in I_3 and I_4. An instance of the reachability problem under the recency semantics is defined in a similar manner to the original semantics. However, we are also given a recency bound B, and we are asked whether we can reach I' applying actions under the recency restriction.

Notice that, both under the standard and the recency semantics, we are solving the reachability problem for a transition system that is infinite in multiple dimensions. This is true since there is no bound on the number of objects that are generated during a given run. Furthermore, the objects have numerical values that are rational numbers, and they may participate in unbounded numbers of facts during the run.

In this paper, we solve the reachability problem by reducing it to the reachability problem for PDA. Given a DMS $\mathcal{D}$, we extract a PDA $\mathcal{B}$, called a *layered database*, such that $\mathcal{B}$ can faithfully simulate $\mathcal{D}$ wrt. reachability properties.

2.3 Layers

Simulating a DMS under the recency semantics using a PDA is not trivial. The reason is that in a PDA the symbols inside the stack are totally independent, while in the case of a database, there may exist dependencies between objects belonging to recency windows that are arbitrary far apart. One source of this dependency is that the objects may participate in common facts. Another source is that there may be constraints on their relative numerical values. A main challenge here is to store dependencies among arbitrary sets of objects

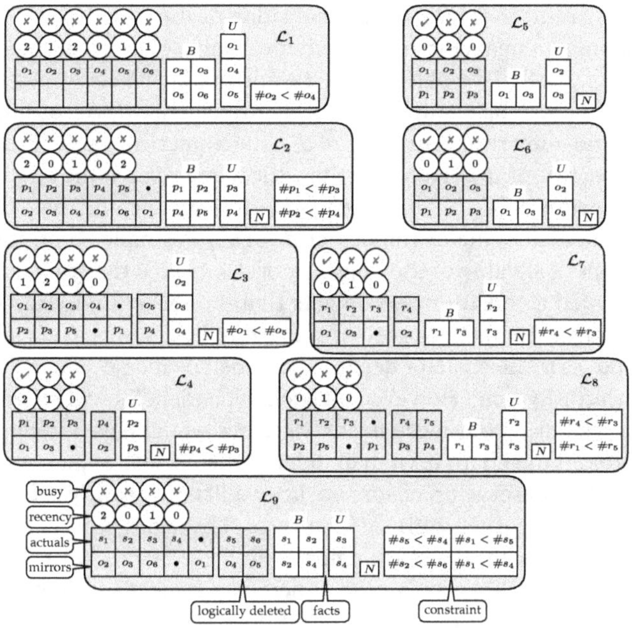

Figure 3: Layers.

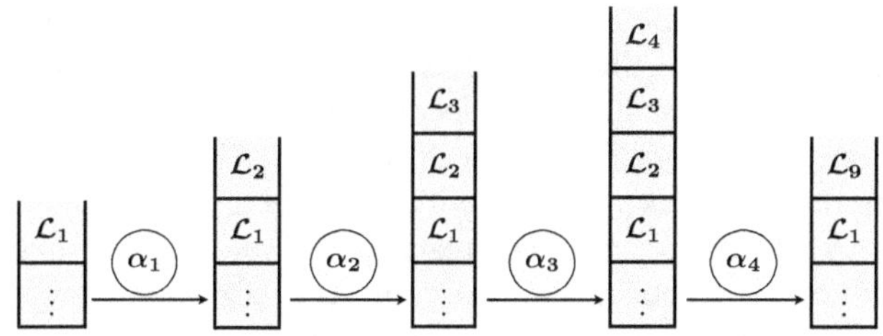

Figure 4: Actions of the layered database.

using only a finite stack alphabet. In order to solve this problem, we will capture the dependency between two objects that are in different places inside the stack by maintaining a "chain" of implicit dependencies between successive stack symbols leading from the first object to the second object. To that end, we will introduce an intricate encoding where each stack symbol, called a *layer*, represents one recency window. The layers correspond to recency measures that increase from the top to the bottom of the stack (see Fig. 3 and Fig. 4.) The top-most layer represents elements whose recency measures range from 0 to B. The next layer represents elements whose recency measures range from 1 to $B+1$, and so on. According to the recency semantics, we only need to consider the objects in the current recency window, and hence in our simulation we need only to consider the top-most layer when mimicking an action in the DMS (while we still need to maintain dependencies with other objects inside the stack, as explained above). A layer maintains different types of information about the objects (see layer $\mathcal{L}_9$ in Fig. 3.) These information types are introduced one by one below.

Actual Objects. First, the layer uses a set of *actual objects* representing elements of the data domain that lie in the current recency window, i.e., objects whose recency measures were up to the bound B when the layer was created. In Fig. 3, the layer $\mathcal{L}_1$ represents the recency window just before the action α_1 is performed in Fig. 1. Therefore, its objects correspond to the data elements in the recency window of I_1 in Fig. 1. The layer contains 6 actual objects $o_1, \ldots, o_6$ corresponding to the elements $e_0, \ldots, e_5$ respectively. Similarly, the layer $\mathcal{L}_2$ represents the recency window just after α_1 has been performed. The layer contains 5 actual objects $p_1, \ldots, p_5$ corresponding to the elements $e_1, \ldots, e_5$ respectively. The element e_0 is not represented in $\mathcal{L}_2$ since it is outside the recency window when $\mathcal{L}_2$ is created (its recency measure is 3 which exceeds the bound $B = 2$). Notice that the set of elements represented in two successive layers may overlap. For instance, the elements $e_1, \ldots, e_5$ are represented both in $\mathcal{L}_1$ and in $\mathcal{L}_2$. As we shall see later, the overlapping of elements between the successive layers will enable us to maintain the chain of dependencies among objects, thus avoiding the loss of precision. Consequently, the result of our simulation will be exact wrt. the recency semantics.

Mirrors. Since there is an overlap between the elements represented by successive layers, a layer also keeps a set of *mirror* objects that are copies of the actual objects from the next layer (the layer below the current layer in the stack). In Fig. 3, the layer $\mathcal{L}_2$ has six mirror objects $o_1, \ldots, o_6$ that are copies of the actual objects in the next layer in the stack, namely $\mathcal{L}_1$. In Fig. 3, we draw each mirror object below the object it mirrors. For instance, the object o_2 mirrors the object p_1 in $\mathcal{L}_2$ since they both represent the concrete data element e_1 in Fig. 1. The object o_1 does not mirror any object in $\mathcal{L}_2$ since it corresponds to the element e_0 in I_2 which is outside the recency window. In $\mathcal{L}_3$ (which corresponds to I_3), the object o_4 is not mirrored by any object. The reason is that o_4 corresponds to the element e_6 that is newly created (and hence not part of the previous layer $\mathcal{L}_2$). The fact that we keep mirror objects and also record which objects they mirror in the layer, allows to keep track of dependencies between objects (say o_1 and o_2) that lie in layers that are far apart in the stack (such objects belong to different recency windows.) This is possible since o_1 will be identified with its mirror, which in turn will be identified with its own mirror, and so on, until we reach a layer which contains both o_2 and a copy of o_1.

Actions. Fig. 4 depicts a run in the symbolic simulation that mimics the concrete run of Fig. 3. When performing an action, we check the top-most layer $\mathcal{L}$ in the stack, since

$\mathcal{L}$ represents the current recency window. We instantiate the variables of the actions using the actual objects of $\mathcal{L}$, and perform a sequence of operations on $\mathcal{L}$ to obtain a new layer $\mathcal{L}'$. In Figure 4, we perform α_1 on $\mathcal{L}_1$ by instantiating the variables x_1 and x_2 with the objects o_3 resp. o_5, and derive $\mathcal{L}_2$ as follows. We create new actual objects, make the actual objects in $\mathcal{L}_1$ mirror objects in $\mathcal{L}_2$, and define the correspondence between the actual and the mirror objects. Furthermore, we define the recency measures of the new actual objects. We add the proposition N as required by α_1, and add the numerical constraint in α_1 to the numerical constraint in $\mathcal{L}_1$, thus obtaining $\mathcal{L}_2$. We push $\mathcal{L}_2$ to the stack since it will now represent the current recency window and hence it should be the top stack symbol.

The transition from $\mathcal{L}_2$ to $\mathcal{L}_3$ through α_2 can be explained analogously. However, here we need three new aspects of our encoding namely *Busy flags*, *purification*, and *logical deletion.*

Busy Flags. The object p_1 in $\mathcal{L}_2$ is not copied as an actual object in $\mathcal{L}_3$. The reason is that p_1 corresponds to the object e_1 whose recency measure is 3 when $\mathcal{L}_3$ is created and hence it is outside the corresponding recency window. However, the object p_1 is involved in the fact $\langle p_1, p_2\rangle$ in $\mathcal{L}_2$ (which reflects the fact $\langle e_1, e_2\rangle$). Since p_1 is not an actual object in $\mathcal{L}_3$, the above fact will not be present in $\mathcal{L}_3$. This means that the object p_2 is not involved in any facts in $\mathcal{L}_3$. Therefore, we may mistakenly discard p_2 in the *purification* procedure that removes "useless" objects and that will be described below. To guard against accidental removal of objects which appear to be useless when only considering the current layer, we provide each actual object with a Boolean flag, called busy which tells whether the copies of the object are involved in facts further down the stack. In this case we set the flag of p_2 to true (in the figure we use the symbols ✓ and ✗ to represent the values true resp. false.)

Purification. In the transition from $\mathcal{L}_3$ to $\mathcal{L}_4$, the action α_2 deletes the facts $\langle o_2\rangle$ and $\langle o_4\rangle$ from U in $\mathcal{L}_3$. This means that o_2 and o_4 become *useless* in the since that (i) they do not participate in any facts in $\mathcal{L}_4$, and (ii) their busy-flags are false which means that they are not involved in facts further down the stack. In such a case, we *purify* the layer by removing the objects, i.e., not copying them as actual objects in $\mathcal{L}_4$.

Logical Deletion. In the previous paragraph, there is a difference between o_2 and o_4, since o_2 has a mirror p_3 in $\mathcal{L}_3$ while o_4 does not. In fact, o_2 is part of a chain of dependencies between objects in different layers as follows: (i) When applying α_3 to obtain $\mathcal{L}_4$ from $\mathcal{L}_3$, we instantiate the variables x_1 and y to the object o_2 in $\mathcal{L}_3$ and the new object p_3 in $\mathcal{L}_4$ (this corresponds to instantiating x_1 and y to e_3 and e_7 in the concrete run of Fig. 1.) To satisfy the numerical constraint in α_3, the numerical value of the object o_2 of $\mathcal{L}_3$ should be smaller than the numerical value of the new object p_3 of $\mathcal{L}_4$. (ii) The object p_3 of $\mathcal{L}_2$ mirrors the object o_2 of $\mathcal{L}_3$, and hence their numerical values are equal. (iii) According to the numerical constraint of $\mathcal{L}_2$, the numerical value of the object p_1 of $\mathcal{L}_2$ is smaller than the numerical value of the object p_3 of $\mathcal{L}_2$. From (i), (ii), and (iii) we conclude that the numerical value of the object p_1 of $\mathcal{L}_2$ is smaller than the numerical value of the object p_3 of $\mathcal{L}_4$. Notice that we have created a constraint on objects that do not lie in the same layer, and in fact not even in successive layers (the layers $\mathcal{L}_2$ and $\mathcal{L}_4$). The chain of dependencies between objects may be arbitrarily long. However, all such dependencies will be preserved using our mechanism. Here, we would have wrongly broken the chain if we had deleted the useless object o_2 of $\mathcal{L}_3$. To preserve precision, we keep a list of *logically deleted* objects together with their mirrors. These are objects that are useless but that have a mirror in the previous layer. The object p_4 will therefore be added as a logically deleted in $\mathcal{L}_4$ with mirror o_2, while o_4 that does not have a mirror in $\mathcal{L}_3$ will be completely deleted. The logically deleted objects will not be copied to the next layer. The fact that we remove useless objects and do not transfer logically deleted objects to the next layer are crucial for maintaining the finiteness of the stack alphabet.

Compactification. When we apply the action α_4 to $\mathcal{L}_4$ we get the layer $\mathcal{L}_5$ in which the band with measure 1 has disappeared. We *compactify* $\mathcal{L}_5$ by re-defining the recency measures of the higher bands (2 in this case) so that we are consistent with the definition of a recency measure (the object o_2 should have a recency measure 1 rather than 2.) This results in the layer $\mathcal{L}_6$.

Merging. Although $\mathcal{L}_6$ is compact in the sense described above, it does not represent the current recency window, since it missing the objects that currently have recency measure 2. Such objects may exist in layers that are currently in the stack. For instance the concrete element e_1 has a recency measure 2 after the application of α_4 (Fig. 1). However, this element is not represented in $\mathcal{L}_6$. In fact, its representative can be found first in layer $\mathcal{L}_2$ (object p_1). Therefore, we cannot push $\mathcal{L}_6$ to the stack (otherwise, we would violate the invariant that the top-most stack symbol represents the current recency window.) Therefore, we pop the current top-most stack symbol, which is the layer $\mathcal{L}_4$ and *merge* it with $\mathcal{L}_6$. The purpose of the merging operation is to search for objects that belong to the current recency window but are not part of $\mathcal{L}_6$. The operation "merges" the mirrors of $\mathcal{L}_6$ with the corresponding actual objects in $\mathcal{L}_4$, thus obtaining $\mathcal{L}_7$. For instance, the mirror object p_1 represents the same object as the actual object p_1 in $\mathcal{L}_4$. This means that the mirror of p_1 in $\mathcal{L}_4$, namely o_1 will be the mirror of the corresponding element in r_1 in $\mathcal{L}_7$. We update the recency measures, the busy-flags, and merge the facts and the numerical constraints in $\mathcal{L}_4$ and $\mathcal{L}_6$. In such a manner the layer $\mathcal{L}_7$ represents a *summary* of the layers $\mathcal{L}_4$ and $\mathcal{L}_6$. Notice that $\mathcal{L}_7$ is still missing one band. Therefore, we repeat the above operation now popping $\mathcal{L}_3$ and merging it with $\mathcal{L}_7$ to obtain $\mathcal{L}_8$. Finally, we pop $\mathcal{L}_2$ and merge it with $\mathcal{L}_8$ obtaining $\mathcal{L}_9$. Since $\mathcal{L}_9$ has all the bands, we push it to the stack.

Notice that the size of the stack may increase and decrease as layers are created and deleted, reflecting that the recency measures of the different objects change during a run.

3 PRELIMINARIES

Basic Notation. We use $\mathbb{B} = \{\text{true}, \text{false}\}$, $\mathbb{N}$, and $\mathbb{Q}$ to denote the sets of Booleans, natural numbers and rational numbers respectively. For a natural number $n \in \mathbb{N}$, we use $\widehat{n}$ to denote the set $\{0, 1, \ldots, n\}$.

For sets A and B, we write $f : A \to B$ to denote that f is a (possibly partial) function that maps elements from A to B. We write $f(a) = \bot$ to denote that f is undefined for a, and write $f : A \stackrel{\bullet}{\to} B$ to indicate that the function f is total. For a finite set A, we use $|A|$ to denote the size of A. For a relation $R \subseteq A \times B$, and a set $C \subseteq A$, we use $R\big|_C$ to denote the relation $R \cap (C \times B)$. In particular, for a function $f : A \to B$, we use $f\big|_C$ to denote the restriction of f to C.

For a set A, we use A^* to denote the set of words over A and use $w_1 \bullet w_2$ to denote the concatenation of the words w_1 and w_2.

Numerical Constraints. We will work with sets of objects each with a numerical value in $\mathbb{Q}$. As we shall see later, these objects can either be members of the data domains in (concrete) database instances, or be used in defining symbolic encodings of such instances. A *numerical constraint* φ over a set $O \subseteq \mathcal{O}$ of objects, is a set of inequalities each of the form $\#o_1 \sim \#o_2$ where $o_1, o_2 \in O$ and $\sim \in \{\leq, <\}$. We say that φ is *saturated* if whenever $(\#o_1 \sim_1 \#o_2) \in \varphi$ and $(\#o_2 \sim_2 \#o_3) \in \varphi$ then $(\#o_1 \sim_3 \#o_3) \in \varphi$ where $\sim_3$ is $\leq$ iff both $\sim_1$ and $\sim_2$ are $\leq$. We define saturate (φ) to be the smallest numerical constraint (wrt. set inclusion) φ' such that $\varphi \subseteq \varphi'$ and φ' is saturated. We say that φ is consistent if it does not contain two inequalities $\#o_1 \sim_1 \#o_2$ and $\#o_2 \sim_2 \#o_1$ such that either $\sim_1$ is $<$ or $\sim_2$ is $<$. For a numerical constraint φ and a set $O \subseteq \mathcal{O}$, we use $\varphi\big|_O$ to be the numerical constraint we get by removing all inequalities involving objects $o \notin O$.

4 MODEL

We consider databases where elements from the infinite data domain Δ are equipped with numerical values. The numerical value of each element in Δ is given by a function $\# : \Delta \to \mathbb{Q}$. The schema, as usual, contains a finite set of relation names with their arities: $\mathcal{R} = \{R_1/a_1, R_2/a_2, \ldots, R_{|\mathcal{R}|}/a_{|\mathcal{R}|}\}$. An *instance* of a relation R/a (or a relation instance) over the domain Δ is a set of a-tuples from Δ. A nullary relation is a proposition. In the rest of the paper, we fix the data domain Δ

A *database instance* over a schema $\mathcal{R}$ gives an instance of all the relations in the schema. Formally, a database instance I over a schema $\mathcal{R} = \{R_1/a_1, R_2/a_2, \ldots, R_{|\mathcal{R}|}/a_{|\mathcal{R}|}\}$ is given by $I = \left\langle R_1^I, R_2^I, \ldots, R_{|\mathcal{R}|}^I \right\rangle$ where $R_i^I \subseteq \Delta^{a_i}$ is an instance of the relation R_i/a_i in the schema. A *fact* in I is a vector that occurs in some relation instance in I, i.e., it is a vector $\langle e_1, \ldots, e_a \rangle \in R^I$ for some relation name R/a. The *active domain* of a database instance I, denoted $\text{ADOM}(I)$, is the set of elements from the domain present in the database instance. That is, $\text{ADOM}(I)$ is the set of data elements e such that there is some fact $\langle e_1, \ldots, e_a \rangle$ in I, and $e = e_i$ for some $i : 1 \leq i \leq a$. For a proposition $N/0$, we say N *occurs* in I if N^I is *true.*

DMS. A *Database Manipulating Systems (DMS)* $\mathcal{D}$ is given by a finite set ACTS of *actions.* An action $\alpha \in \text{ACTS}$ is a tuple $\langle \overline{x}, \overline{y}, I_+, I_-, \text{DEL}, \text{ADD}, \varphi \rangle$ where $\overline{x}$ and $\overline{y}$ are disjoint sets of variables, I_+, I_-, and DEL are database instances over $\overline{x}$, ADD is a database instance over $\overline{x} \cup \overline{y}$, and φ is a numerical constraint over $\overline{x} \cup \overline{y}$.

Semantics. The operational semantics of a DMS is defined to be an (infinite-state) transition system, where each configuration is a database instance over $\mathcal{R}$. Consider a database instance I and an action $\alpha = \langle \overline{x}, \overline{y}, I_+, I_-, \text{DEL}, \text{ADD}, \varphi \rangle$. A substitution $\nu : \overline{x} \cup \overline{y} \to \Delta$ is said to *instantiate* α at I if $\nu(x) \in \text{ADOM}(I)$ for all $x \in \overline{x}$, and $\nu(y) \notin \text{ADOM}(I)$ for all $y \in \overline{y}$. Let $\nu(I_+)$ be the database instance obtained by substituting every occurrence of a variable x in I_+ by $\nu(x)$, and similarly for $\nu(I_-)$, $\nu(\text{DEL})$, $\nu(\text{ADD})$, and $\nu(\varphi)$. For database instances I_1 and I_2, an action $\alpha = \langle \overline{x}, \overline{y}, I_+, I_-, \text{DEL}, \text{ADD}, \varphi \rangle$, and a substitution ν that instantiates α at I_1, we write $I_1 \xrightarrow{\alpha, \nu} I_2$ if $\nu(\varphi)$ holds and the following three conditions are satisfied for each relation name $R \in \mathcal{R}$: (i) $R^{\nu(I_+)} \subseteq R^{I_1}$. (ii) $R^{\nu(I_-)} \cap R^{I_1} = \emptyset$. (iii) $\langle e_1, \ldots, e_n \rangle \in R^{I_2}$ iff $\langle e_1, \ldots, e_n \rangle \in R^{I_1 - \nu(\text{DEL}) \cup \nu(\text{ADD})}$. We write $I_1 \xrightarrow{\alpha} I_2$ if $I_1 \xrightarrow{\alpha, \nu} I_2$ for some ν, and write $I_1 \to I_2$ if $I_1 \xrightarrow{\alpha} I_2$ for some α. We use $\xrightarrow{*}$ to denote the reflexive transitive closure of $\to$.

Reachability. The *reachability problem* asks, given a DMS $\mathcal{D}$, a database instance I, and a proposition $q \in \mathcal{R}$, whether there is a database instance I' such that $I \xrightarrow{*} I'$ and q occurs in I'.

The reachability problem is undecidable, even without numerical values and over very restrictive schema[3, 4]. We will hence resort to an under-approximate reachability problem, in which an instantiating substitution is limited to use only the recent elements.

Recency Semantics. Fix a *recency bound* $B \in \mathbb{N}$. An *augmented database instance* is a pair $J = \langle I, \mathsf{rcy} \rangle$ where I is a database instance and $\mathsf{rcy} : \textsc{Adom}(I) \to \mathbb{N}$ defines, for each element $e \in \textsc{Adom}(I)$, its *recency measure* $\mathsf{rcy}(e)$. We say that J is *compact* if for every $e \in \textsc{Adom}(I)$ and $j : 0 \leq j < \mathsf{rcy}(e)$, there is an $e' \in I$ where $\mathsf{rcy}(e') = j$. For $J = \langle I, \mathsf{rcy} \rangle$, we define $\mathsf{compactify}(J) := \langle I, \mathsf{rcy}' \rangle$ where $\mathsf{rcy}' : \textsc{Adom}(I) \to \mathbb{N}$ is the unique function such that $\langle I, \mathsf{rcy}' \rangle$ is compact and $\mathsf{rcy}'(e) \leq \mathsf{rcy}'(e')$ iff $\mathsf{rcy}(e) \leq \mathsf{rcy}(e')$ for all $e, e' \in \textsc{Adom}(I)$. A substitution $\nu : \overline{x} \cup \overline{y} \to \Delta$ is said to *instantiate* α at J if (i) ν instantiates α at I, and (ii) $\mathsf{rcy}(\nu(x)) \leq B$ for all $x \in \overline{x}$. For augmented instances $J_1 = \langle I_1, \mathsf{rcy}_1 \rangle$ and J_2, and a substitution ν that instantiates α at J_1, we write $J_1 \xrightarrow{\alpha,\nu}_B J_2$ to denote that there is a $J_3 = \left\langle I_3, \mathsf{rcy}_3 \right\rangle$ such that (i) $I_1 \xrightarrow{\alpha,\nu} I_3$. (ii) $\mathsf{rcy}_3(e) = 0$ if $e = \nu(x)$ for some $x \in \overline{x}$. (iii) $\mathsf{rcy}_3(e) = \mathsf{rcy}_1(e) + 1$ if $e \in \textsc{Adom}(I_1) - \nu(\overline{x})$. (v) $\mathsf{rcy}_3(e) = 0$ if $e = \nu(y)$ for some $y \in \overline{y}$. (v) $J_2 = \mathsf{compactify}(J_3)$. We define $\xrightarrow{\alpha}_B$, $\to_B$, and $\xrightarrow{*}_B$ in a similar manner to $\to$.

An instance of the reachability problem under the recency semantics is defined in a similar manner to above. However, we are also given a bound B and we are asked whether there is a database instance I' such that $I \xrightarrow{*}_B I'$ and q occurs in I'.

Our main theorem states that

Theorem 4.1. *Recency bounded reachability problem is* ExpTime*-complete.*

The lower bound is proved by a reduction from the intersection-non-emptiness problem of a pushdown automaton and n finite state automata. Our reduction does not need numerical constraints at all, showing that recency bounded reachability is ExpTime hard already for the DMS *à la* [3].

The upper bound is established by constructing an exponential sized pushdown automaton and translating the reachability problem to control state reachability problem in the constructed pushdown automaton. The construction is given in Sections 6 and 7.

We will also show that the decidability does not carry forward to the case of recency bounded model checking of LTL. We recall the definition of LTL-FO language and the recency bounded model checking problem in Appendix A.

Theorem 4.2. *Recency bounded model checking of DMS with numerical constraints against LTL-FO is undecidable.*

Proof is given in Appendix A. It is by a reduction from the control state reachability problem of Minsky machines.

5 EXAMPLE

To illustrate the main modelling features of our approach, we use a marketplace for recycling electronic devices. Users may bring broken devices to the marketplace, and such devices can then be fixed by reconditioning their broken/missing components using functioning components of other devices. Fully repaired devices can then be sold in the marketplace at a discounted price.

For simplicity, we consider only a single type of device, consisting of two components: a memory, and a cpu. Each device may differ, though, not only depending on which components are actually functioning, but also on the technical properties of such components, and on the ranges supported for such properties. For example, a device may come with a functioning memory of 1GB and no cpu, and with a working range of 32-64GB for its memory, and of 200-300MHz for its cpu.

Assuming that devices are identified using a code, the above data can be stored using the following schemas:

- Unary relation schemas to represent devices and their current status. In particular, $\mathsf{Device}(c)$ indicates that c is (the code of) a device, $\mathsf{Ok}(c)$ that c is fully operational, $\mathsf{NoMem}(c)$ (resp., $\mathsf{NoCpu}(c)$) that device c is missing the memory (resp., the cpu).
- Binary relation schemas to capture the properties of the working components. For simplicity, we focus on the simple properties of storage capacity and speed. Specifically, $\mathsf{Capacity}(c, v)$ indicates that device c has a functioning memory whose capacity is $\#v$ GB, while $\mathsf{Speed}(c, v)$ captures that device c has a functioning cpu whose speed is $\#v$ MGHz.
- Ternary relation schemas to capture the ranges for the memory capacity and the cpu speed that the device can support. Specifically, $\mathsf{SupCapacity}(c, \mathsf{min}, \mathsf{max})$ and $\mathsf{SupSpeed}(c, \mathsf{min}, \mathsf{max})$ respectively indicate that $\#\mathsf{min}$ and $\#\mathsf{max}$ are the minimum and maximum values that are compatible with device c in terms of memory capacity and cpu speed.

To introduce a new product into the marketplace, one has to indicate the device code, the device status, and the other properties related to the design. Since depending on the device status, certain properties are needed whereas others are not applicable, this input task is captured in the DMS as a set of actions, one per device status type. Below, we show the action for inserting into the marketplace a device with a missing cpu:

- $\varphi = \{\#y^c_{\mathsf{min}} \leq \#y^c_{\mathsf{max}}, \#y^m_{\mathsf{min}} \leq \#y^m, \#y^m \leq \#y^m_{\mathsf{max}}\}$
- $\textsc{Add} = \{ \mathsf{Device}(y), \mathsf{NoCpu}(y), \mathsf{Capacity}(y, y^m),$ $\mathsf{SupCapacity}(y, y^m_{\mathsf{min}}, y^m_{\mathsf{max}}), \mathsf{SupSpeed}(y, y^c_{\mathsf{min}}, y^c_{\mathsf{max}}) \}$
- $\textsc{Del} = \emptyset$

A similar action can be defined to insert a device with a missing memory.

As introduced above, devices can be combined so as to obtain a functioning device as a result. We define a *recondition* action capturing how a broken device can be made operational by incorporating the missing component from another device. In our simple representation of devices, we assume that it is easier to extract the memory component from a device rather than the cpu, and hence a broken device x_1 missing memory is reconditioned with the memory taken from another broken device x_2. As a result, x_1 becomes fully operational, whereas x_2 is removed from the marketplace since it does not have any other component that can be reused. This reconditioning can only be applied if the memory offered by x_2 is compatible with the memory range supported by x_1. Technically, the recondition action is then defined as follows:

- $I_+ = \{\mathsf{NoMem}(x_1), \mathsf{NoCpu}(x_2), \mathsf{Capacity}(x_2, x^2_{\mathsf{mem}}), \mathsf{SupCapacity}(x_1, x^{m1}_{\mathsf{min}}, x^{m1}_{\mathsf{max}})\}$
- $\varphi = \{\#x^{m1}_{\mathsf{min}} \leq \#x^2_{\mathsf{mem}}, \#x^2_{\mathsf{mem}} \leq \#x^{m1}_{\mathsf{max}}\}$
- $\textsc{Add} = \{\ \mathsf{Ok}(x_1), \mathsf{Capacity}(x_1, x^2_{\mathsf{mem}})\ \}$
- $\textsc{Del} = \{\ \mathsf{NoMem}(x_1), \mathsf{Device}(x_2), \mathsf{NoCpu}(x_2), \mathsf{Capacity}(x_1, x^2_{\mathsf{mem}}), \mathsf{SupCapacity}(x_2, x^{m2}_{\mathsf{min}}, x^{m2}_{\mathsf{max}}), \mathsf{SupSpeed}(x_2, x^{s2}_{\mathsf{min}}, x^{s2}_{\mathsf{max}})\ \}$

Finally, a fully operational device can be sold, which results in removing the device from the database. If we were following the recency bounded semantics, this deletion would enable less recent devices to pop up into the recency window.

Notice that, in this context, the bound of recency can be interpreted as a marketplace where recently introduced devices are put in a front-end showcase and can be used for reconditioning, whereas older devices are stored in a back-end warehouse. If the showcase gets free space (obtained by removing useless devices after a reconditioning action, or by selling functioning devices), then the most recent elements currently stored in the warehouse are moved into the showcase.

We consider two interesting safety properties to be checked on the marketplace recycling process.

The first property aims at ensuring that the device code is a key in all the relation schemas forming the marketplace database schema. This property can be turned into a propositional reachability property by introducing a proposition *key_viol* that is inserted in the database whenever one of the relations contains two distinct tuples that agree on the device code. This, in turn, is done by introducing one action per relation schema, whose query checks the violation of the key constraint on that relation, and whose effect is to raise the *key_viol* flag. For example, for relation Capacity we get:

- $I_+ = \{\mathsf{Capacity}(x, x^1_{\mathsf{mem}}), \mathsf{Capacity}(x, x^2_{\mathsf{mem}})\}$
- $\varphi = \{\#x^1_{\mathsf{mem}} \neq \#x^2_{\mathsf{mem}}\}$
- $\textsc{Add} = \{\ \mathit{key\_viol}\ \}, \textsc{Del} = \emptyset$

If the marketplace DMS reaches *key_viol*, then it violates the desired property.

The second property adopts a similar strategy used for the first one, this time to ascertain that no device in the marketplace contains components that are out of range. Towards this, we have actions that raise the `hit` flag whenever a faulty device (i.e., a device with memory and/or cpu plugged in but out of range) is spotted in the marketplace:

- $I_+ = \{\mathsf{Capacity}(x, x_{mem}), \mathsf{SupCapacity}(x, x^m_{\mathsf{min}}, x^m_{\mathsf{max}})\}$
- $\varphi = \{\#x_{\mathsf{mem}} \leq \#x^m_{\mathsf{min}}\}$
- $\textsc{Add} = \{\ \mathtt{hit}\ \}, \textsc{Del} = \emptyset$

We will have a similar action with different numerical constraint: $\varphi = \{\#x^m_{\mathsf{min}} \leq \#x_{\mathsf{mem}}\}$, and two more for the case of cpu.

If the marketplace DMS reaches `hit`, then it violates the property.

6 LAYERS

We give the definition and the different operations on layers.

6.1 Definition

We assume a finite set O of *objects*. In Appendix C we show that taking an O with $3m(B+2)$ elements will be sufficient for our encoding, where m is the maximum number of variables used in any action.

A *layer* $\mathcal{L}$ is a tuple $\langle A, D, \mathrm{rcy}, I, \mathrm{busy}, \varphi, M, g\rangle$ where $A \subseteq O$ is the set of *actual objects*, $D \subseteq O$ is a set of objects that have been *logically deleted* where $A \cap D = \emptyset$, $\mathrm{rcy} : A \to \widehat{B+1}$ defines the recency measures of the actual objects, I is a database instance over A, $\mathrm{busy} : A \to \mathbb{B}$ indicates whether a given actual object is involved in facts with objects whose recency measures are larger than B, φ is a numerical constraint over $A \cup D$, M is the set of *mirror objects* where $(A \cup D) \cap M = \emptyset$, and $g : A \cup D \to M$ is a function such that (i) for each $o \in M$ there is an o' with $g(o') = o$, and (ii) $g(o) \neq \bot$ if $o \in D$. The actual objects will have recency measures that are up to the bound B in the "stable" states of the symbolic simulation. However, during the simulation, the system may enter transient states in which the recency bounds of some actual objects become equal to $B + 1$. Objects whose recency measures remain equal to $B + 1$ will be "moved" to the next recency window. The injection g tells us which actual and mirror objects correspond to the same members of the data domain.

We say that $\mathcal{L}$ is *consistent* if φ is consistent. Given that the set O of objects is finite, there are only finitely many layers. In fact, the number of layers will be bounded by $2^{O(|\mathcal{R}|(mB)^{\mathrm{amax}})}$ where amax is the maximum arity of any relation in the schema. Details of this counting are given in Appendix C.

6.2 Compactification

For a database instance I over O, we write $o \in I$ if o occurs in some fact in I. An actual object $o \in A$ is said to be *useless* in $\mathcal{L}$ if $\mathsf{busy}(o) = \mathsf{false}$ and $o \notin I$. Intuitively, a useless object is not involved in any fact whether in the current or in the other recency windows. The logically deleted objects are useless but have a mirror in the layer. An object is said to be *useful* if it is not useless. We use $\mathcal{L}\cdot\mathsf{useless}$ and $\mathcal{L}\cdot\mathsf{useful}$ to denote the sets of useless and useful objects in $\mathcal{L}$ respectively. We say that $\mathcal{L}$ is *pure* if A does not contain any useless objects and all the objects in D have a mirror in $\mathcal{L}$. For a layer $\mathcal{L}_1 = \langle A_1, D_1, \mathsf{rcy}_1, I_1, \mathsf{busy}_1, \varphi_1, M_1, g_1\rangle$, we define $\mathsf{purify}(\mathcal{L}_1) := \langle A_2, D_2, \mathsf{rcy}_2, I_2, \mathsf{busy}_2, \varphi_2, M_2, g_2\rangle$ where

- $A_2 = \mathcal{L}_1\cdot\mathsf{useful}$. We keep only the useful objects in the set of actual objects.
- $D_2 = \{o \in \mathcal{L}_1\cdot\mathsf{useless} \mid g_1(o) \neq \bot\}$. The logically deleted objects are those that are useless but have a mirror.
- $\mathsf{rcy}_2 = \mathsf{rcy}_1\big|_{A_2}$. We restrict the recency function to the useful objects.
- $R^{I_2} = R^{I_1}\big|_{A_2}$ for each relation name R, where a is the arity of R. We do not include facts that contain useless objects.
- $\mathsf{busy}_2 = \mathsf{busy}_1\big|_{A_2}$, i.e., we restrict the busy function to the useful objects.
- $\varphi_2 = \varphi_1\big|_{A_2 \cup D_2}$. In the numerical constraint, we keep both the useful and logically deleted objects (but throw away constraints involving objects that are useless and that do not have mirrors in the layer). The reason for keeping the logically deleted objects is that they may impose numerical constraints on the objects that are in the next layer, but not in the current layer. This will be more clear in the definition of the merge operation below.
- $M_2 = M_1$. The mirror objects are not affected.
- $g_2 = g_1$. The injection to mirror objects is not changed (although some objects in the domain of g_2 may have moved to the logically deleted objects).

We define $\mathsf{present}(\mathcal{L}) := \{i \mid (1 \leq i \leq B+1) \wedge (\exists o \in A.\ \mathsf{rcy}(o) = i)\}$, i.e., it is the set of measures that are present among the actual objects of $\mathcal{L}$. We define $\mathsf{rcy}(\mathcal{L}) := \max\{\mathsf{rcy}(o) \mid o \in A\}$, i.e., it is the maximal recency measure that appears in $\mathcal{L}$.

A layer is said to be *compact* if $j \in \mathsf{present}(\mathcal{L})$ implies that $i \in \mathsf{present}(\mathcal{L})$ for every $i : 0 \leq i < j$. In other words, there is no gap below the recency measures of the actual objects in $\mathcal{L}$. For a layer $\mathcal{L}_1 = \langle A_1, D_1, \mathsf{rcy}_1, I_1, \mathsf{busy}_1, \varphi_1, M_1, g_1\rangle$, we define $\mathsf{compactify}(\mathcal{L}_1)$ to be the unique compact layer $\langle A_2, D_2, \mathsf{rcy}_2, I_2, \mathsf{busy}_2, \varphi_2, M_2, g_2\rangle$ such that $A_2 = A_1$, $D_2 = D_1$, $I_2 = I_1$, $M_2 = M_1$, and $\mathsf{rcy}_2(o) \leq \mathsf{rcy}_2(o')$ iff $\mathsf{rcy}_1(o) \leq \mathsf{rcy}_1(o')$ for all actual objects $o, o' \in A_1$. In other words, we get $\mathcal{L}_2$ from $\mathcal{L}_1$ by putting objects with successor recency measures next to each other.

Consider a compact layer $\mathcal{L} = \langle A, D, \mathsf{rcy}, I, \mathsf{busy}, \varphi, M, g\rangle$. We say that $\mathcal{L}$ is *under-loaded* if $\mathsf{rcy}(\mathcal{L}) < B$, i.e., there is no actual object $o \in A$ such that $\mathsf{rcy}(o) = B$. We say that $\mathcal{L}$ is *balanced* if $\mathsf{rcy}(\mathcal{L}) = B$, i.e., there is an actual object $o \in A$ such that $\mathsf{rcy}(o) = i$ but there there is no actual object $o \in A$ such that $\mathsf{rcy}(o) = B+1$. Finally, we say that $\mathcal{L}$ is *over-loaded* if $\mathsf{rcy}(\mathcal{L}) = B+1$, i.e., there is an actual object $o \in A$ such that $\mathsf{rcy}(o) = B+1$.

6.3 Running Actions

We describe how to apply an action to a layer $\mathcal{L}_1 = \langle A_1, D_1, \mathsf{rcy}_1, I_1, \mathsf{busy}_1, \varphi_1, M_1, g_1\rangle$. Consider an action $\alpha = \langle \overline{x}, \overline{y}, I_+, I_-, \textsc{Del}, \textsc{Add}, \varphi\rangle$, and a substitution $\nu : (\overline{x} \cup \overline{y}) \to O^{old} \cup O^{new}$ where $O^{old} \subseteq A_1$, $O^{new} \subseteq O$, $O^{new} \cap A_1 = \emptyset$, $\nu(x) \in O^{old}$ if $x \in \overline{x}$, and $\nu(y) \in O^{new}$ if $y \in \overline{y}$. Intuitively, the substitution maps the variables corresponding to old objects to members of A_1. This is consistent with the fact that we use A_1 to represent data belonging to the current recency window. Furthermore, the set O^{new} contains objects that correspond to the new data that will be created by the rule. We introduce a rule that explains the application of the action α to $\mathcal{L}$ under the substitution ν. The application will be captured by a transition relation $\xrightarrow{\alpha,\nu}$ on layers. The transition relation will be defined in several steps. First, we define an intermediate transition relation $\overset{\alpha,\nu}{\rightsquigarrow}$ that applies the action without purifying or compacting the resulting layer. Consider two layers $\mathcal{L}_1 = \langle A_1, D_1, \mathsf{rcy}_1, I_1, \mathsf{busy}_1, \varphi_1, M_1, g_1\rangle$ and $\mathcal{L}_2 = \langle A_2, D_2, \mathsf{rcy}_2, I_2, \mathsf{busy}_2, \varphi_2, M_2, g_2\rangle$. Define $A_1' = A_1 - O^{old}$. We write $\mathcal{L}_1 \overset{\alpha,\nu}{\rightsquigarrow} \mathcal{L}_2$ to denote that there is a bijection $h : A_2 \to A_1 \cup O^{new}$ such that the conditions below are satisfied. Notice that h means that the actual objects of $\mathcal{L}_2$ are renamings of the actual objects that are already in $\mathcal{L}_1$ and the new objects that are introduced by α.

- $A_2 \cap A_1 = \emptyset$.
- $D_2 = \emptyset$. We will identify the logically deleted objects when we purify $\mathcal{L}_2$ in the next step below.
- $\mathsf{rcy}_2(o) = 0$ if $h(o) \in O^{old} \cup O^{new}$, and $\mathsf{rcy}_2(o) = \mathsf{rcy}_1(o) + 1$ if $h(o) \in A_1'$, i.e, we reset the recency measures of the objects that are involved in the action α to zero, and increase the recency measures of the other objects by one.
- $R^{\nu(I_+)} \subseteq R^{I_1}$ and $R^{\nu(I_-)} \cap R^{I_1} = \emptyset$ for all relation names R. We check that all the facts in I_+ are present, and that all the facts in I_- are absent from $\mathcal{L}_1$.
- $\langle o_1, \ldots, o_n\rangle \in R^{I_2}$ iff $\langle h(o_1), \ldots, h(o_n)\rangle \in R^{I_1 - \nu(\textsc{Del}) \cup \nu(\textsc{Add})}$ for all relation names R. We remove the facts corresponding to $\textsc{Del}$ and add the facts corresponding to $\textsc{Add}$.
- $\mathsf{busy}_2(o) = \mathsf{false}$ if $h(o) \in O^{new}$ and $\mathsf{busy}_2(o) = \mathsf{busy}_1(h(o))$ if $h(o) \in A_1$. The busy-flags of the new objects are set to false since they are not involved in any

facts outside the current layer. The busy-flags of the other objects are maintained.

- $\varphi_2 = \{(o_1 \sim o_2) | (h(o_1) \sim h(o_2)) \in \mathsf{saturate}(\varphi \cup \nu(\psi))\}$. We add the new numerical query to the existing numerical constraint, and saturate the result. Notice that this may mean that the layer becomes inconsistent. As we will see later, we will block runs that reach inconsistent layers from the analysis.
- $M_2 = A_1$. The mirror objects in $\mathcal{L}_2$ are the actual objects in $\mathcal{L}_1$. Notice that $M_2 \cap A_2 = \emptyset$ since $A_2 \cap A_1 = \emptyset$.
- $g_2(o) = o'$ if $o' \in A_1$ and $h(o) = o'$. The actual objects in $\mathcal{L}_1$ will mirror the corresponding objects in $\mathcal{L}_2$.

The layer $\mathcal{L}_2$ may contain useless objects. Such objects are those involved in facts all of which are included in ν (DEL) and which are not involved in relations with objects outside the current recency window (i.e., their busy-flag is false). Therefore, we will purify $\mathcal{L}_2$. Assume that $\mathcal{L}_3 = \mathsf{purify}(\mathcal{L}_2)$ which means that the useless objects will be removed from the set of actual objects. Since, we have removed the useless objects, the layer $\mathcal{L}_3$ may not be compact, and hence we need to compactify $\mathcal{L}_3$. We define the transition relation $\rightarrow$ such that $\mathcal{L}_1 \xrightarrow{\alpha,\nu} \mathcal{L}_2$ if there is a layer $\mathcal{L}_3$ where $\mathcal{L}_1 \overset{\alpha,\nu}{\rightsquigarrow} \mathcal{L}_3$ and compactify (purify ($\mathcal{L}_3$)). The layer $\mathcal{L}_2$ is compact, but it may be under-loaded, balanced, or over-loaded. We will take these three cases into consideration when we later perform our simulation.

6.4 Merging and Truncation

As we saw above, applying $\overset{\alpha,\nu}{\rightsquigarrow}$ may result in a layer which can be under- or over-loaded. In both cases, we define operations that allow getting balanced layers. First, we consider the case of under-loading. An under-loaded-layer does not contain sufficient information about the current recency window since it does not contain all elements whose recency measures are up to B. In order to retrieve all these elements we *merge* the layer with the next layer. This will give access more objects without exceeding the bound B. Below, we define the merge operation.

Consider two layers $\mathcal{L}_1 = \langle A_1, D_1, \mathsf{rcy}_1, I_1, \mathsf{busy}_1, \varphi_1, M_1, g_1 \rangle$ and $\mathcal{L}_2 = \langle A_2, D_2, \mathsf{rcy}_2, I_2, \mathsf{busy}_2, \varphi_2, M_2, g_2 \rangle$ such that $\mathcal{L}_1$ is compact and under-loaded while $\mathcal{L}_2$ is compact and balanced. We define their merging $\mathcal{L}_1 \otimes \mathcal{L}_2$ in two steps. Define $A_2' := \{o \in A_2 | \, o \notin M_1\}$, i.e., it is the set of actual objects in $\mathcal{L}_2$ that do not mirror any objects in $\mathcal{L}_1$. Also, define $D_1' := \{o \in D_1 | \, g_2(g_1(o) \neq \bot)\}$, i.e., it is the set of logically deleted objects that have mirrors in $\mathcal{L}_2$ (notice that such objects have by construction mirrors in $\mathcal{L}_1$.) First we define $\mathcal{L}_1 \odot \mathcal{L}_2$ to be the set of layers including each layer $\mathcal{L}_3 = \langle A_3, D_3, \mathsf{rcy}_3, I_3, \mathsf{busy}_3, \varphi_3, M_3, g_3 \rangle$ such that there is an injection $h : A_3 \cup D_3 \overset{\bullet}{\rightarrow} A_1 \cup A_2' \cup D_1' \cup D_2$ satisfying the following conditions:

- $A_3 \cap D_3 = \emptyset$ and $(A_3 \cup D_3) \cap M_2 = \emptyset$. We need these conditions since they are required by the definition a layer. In particular, the second condition ensures that the set of actual objects A_3 will not intersect with the set of mirror objects M_3 (below, we will define M_3 to be the same as M_2).
- $h|_{A_3}$ is a bijection from A_3 to $A_1 \cup A_2'$. The actual objects in $\mathcal{L}_3$ correspond to the actual objects in $\mathcal{L}_1$ together with the actual objects in $\mathcal{L}_2$ whose recency measures are B.
- $h|_{D_3}$ is a bijection from D_3 to $D_1' \cup D_2$. The logically deleted objects in $\mathcal{L}_3$ correspond to the logically deleted objects in $\mathcal{L}_2$ together with logically deleted objects in $\mathcal{L}_1$ that have mirrors in $\mathcal{L}_2$.
- $\mathsf{rcy}_3(o) = \mathsf{rcy}_1(o)$ if $h(o) \in A_1$, and $\mathsf{rcy}_3(o) = \mathsf{rcy}_2(o) = B$ if $h(o) \in A_2'$. The objects in $\mathcal{L}_3$ take their recency measures from the corresponding objects in $\mathcal{L}_1$ and $\mathcal{L}_2$.
- For every relation name R, we have that $\langle o_1, \ldots, o_n \rangle \in R^{I_3}$ iff one of the following two conditions is satisfied:
  - There are objects $o_1', \ldots, o_n' \in A_1$ such that $\langle o_1', \ldots, o_n' \rangle \in R^{I_1}$ and $h(o_i) = o_i'$ for all $i : 1 \leq i \leq n$. In this case, the fact $\langle o_1', \ldots, o_n' \rangle$ involves objects that are all in the current recency window (defined by $\mathcal{L}_1$). Therefore, we copy the fact from $\mathcal{L}_1$ to $\mathcal{L}_3$ (while renaming according to h).
  - There are objects $o_1', \ldots, o_n' \in A_2$ such that the following three conditions are satisfied:
    - $\langle o_1', \ldots, o_n' \rangle \in R^{I_2}$,
    - $o_i' \in A_2'$ for some $i : 1 \leq i \leq n$.
    - For each $j : 1 \leq j \leq n$. either $o_i' \in M_1$ and $g(h(o_i)) = o_i'$, or $o_i \in A_2'$ and $h(o_i) = o_i'$.

    In this case, the fact $\langle o_1', \ldots, o_n' \rangle$ involves at least one element from A_2', and hence it cannot be found in $\mathcal{L}_1$. Therefore, we copy the fact from $\mathcal{L}_2$. Notice that (i) all the objects $o_1', \ldots, o_n'$ belong to A_2, (ii) each object o_i' either belongs to A_2' or mirrors some object in A_1, and (iii) an object in A_2 belongs either to M_1 or A_2'.
- $\mathsf{busy}_3(o)$ is defined as follows:
  - If $h(o) = o' \in A_1$ and $g_1(o') = \bot$ then $\mathsf{busy}_3(o) = \mathsf{false}$. The object o does not have a mirror object in the recency window defined by $\mathcal{L}_2$, and hence it cannot be part of facts that belong to $\mathcal{L}_2$ (or later layers).
  - If $h(o) \in A_1$ and $g_1(h(o)) = o'$ then $\mathsf{busy}_3(o) = \mathsf{busy}_2(o')$. The object o has a mirror in $\mathcal{L}_1$, and hence its busy-flag is defined by $\mathcal{L}_2$. Notice that the flag of the object may be true in $\mathcal{L}_1$ only because it is involved in a fact with objects whose recency measures are B in $\mathcal{L}_2$.
  - If $h(o) = o' \in A_2'$ then $\mathsf{busy}_3(o) = \mathsf{busy}_2(o')$. The object is part of $\mathcal{L}_2$ (but not $\mathcal{L}_1$) and hence its busy-flag is defined accordingly.

- $\varphi_3 = \{o_1 \sim o_2 \mid (h(o_1) \sim h(o_2)) \in \text{saturate}(\varphi_1 \cup \varphi_2)\} \cap (A_3 \cup D_3)$. In other words, we take the union of the numerical constraints, and saturate the result. Notice that it is important to include the objects that are logically deleted in $\mathcal{L}_1$ and that do not have mirrors in $\mathcal{L}_2$. when we saturate $\varphi_1 \cup \varphi_2$. The reason is that they may imply constraints among the other objects. However, after performing the saturation, these objects may be safely deleted. The definition of φ_3 ensures that the deletion will take place since we only include objects in $A_3 \cup D_3$.
- $M_3 = M_2$. The set of mirror objects are the same as in $\mathcal{L}_2$
- g_3 is defined as follows:
  - If $o \in A_3$, $h(o) \in A_1$, and $g_1(h(o)) = \perp$ then $g_3(o) = \perp$. If an object does not have a mirror in $\mathcal{L}_1$ then the corresponding object will not have a mirror in $\mathcal{L}_3$.
  - If $o \in A_3$, $h(o) \in A_1$, and $g_1(h(o)) \neq \perp$ then $g_3(o) = g_2(g_1(h(o)))$. If an object has a mirror in $\mathcal{L}_1$, and the mirror has in turn a mirror in $\mathcal{L}_2$, then the latter defines the mirror of o in the new layer $\mathcal{L}_3$.
  - If $o \in A_3$ and $h(o) \in A_2'$ then $g_3(o) = g_2(h(o))$. If an object is part of $\mathcal{L}_2$ then its mirror object is defined accordingly.
  - If $o \in D_3$ and $h(o) \in D_1'$ then $g_3(o) = g_2(g_1(h(o)))$. If an object is logically deleted in $\mathcal{L}_2$ but its mirror (in $\mathcal{L}_1$) has a mirror in $\mathcal{L}_2$, then the latter defines the mirror of o in $\mathcal{L}_3$.
  - If $o \in D_3$ and $h(o) \in D_2$ then $g_3(o) = g_2(h(o))$. If an object is logically deleted in $\mathcal{L}_2$ then the mirror of the corresponding object in $\mathcal{L}_3$ will be taken to be the same mirror.

Now we define the merging of $\mathcal{L}$ and $\mathcal{L}'$ by $\mathcal{L} \otimes \mathcal{L}' := \text{compactify}(\mathcal{L} \odot \mathcal{L}')$. Notice that $\mathcal{L} \otimes \mathcal{L}'$ can still be underloaded (but not over-loaded).

To handle the case where a layer is over-loaded we will use an operation that *truncates* the layer by removing the objects whose recency measures are equal to $B+1$. Consider a compact layer $\mathcal{L}_1 = \langle A_1, D_1, \text{rcy}_1, I_1, \text{busy}_1, \varphi_1, M_1, g_1\rangle$ such that $\text{rcy}(\mathcal{L}_1) = B+1$. We define $\mathit{truncate}(\mathcal{L}_1) := \langle A_2, D_2, \text{rcy}_2, I_2, \text{busy}_2, \varphi_2, M_2, g_2\rangle$, such the following conditions are satisfied:

- $A_2 = \{o \in A_1 \mid \text{rcy}(o) \leq B\}$. We include only the actual objects whose recency measures are up to the bound B.
- $D_2 = D_1$, i.e., we keep all the logically deleted objects.
- $\text{rcy}_2 = \text{rcy}_1\big|_{A_2}$. We restrict the recency function to the actual objects in $\mathcal{L}_2$.
- $R^{I_2} = R^{I_1}\big|_{A_1}$ for each relation name R. We only include facts that contain objects from the set A_2, and remove the rest of the facts.
- $\text{busy}_2(o) = \text{true}$ iff either $\text{busy}_1(o) = \text{true}$ or there is a relation name R and a fact $\langle o_1, \ldots, o_n\rangle \in R^{I_1}$ such that $o_i = o$ and $\text{rcy}_1(o_j) = B+1$ for some $i, j : 1 \leq i \neq j \leq n$. The busy-flag of an object is set to true if it is already true or if it is part of a fact that also involves an object whose recency measure is $B+1$. The reason for the latter case is that the second object will not be part of the current layer any more.
- $\varphi_2 = \varphi_1\big|_{A_2}$. We restrict the numerical constraint to the objects in A_2.
- $M_2 = \{o \in M_1 \mid \exists o' \in A_2.\ g_1(o) = o'\}$. We include only objects that mirror some object in the set A_2.
- $g_2 = g_1\big|_{A_2}$. We restrict the injection g_2 as expected.

7 LAYERED DATABASES

In this section, we present our symbolic simulation of DMS under the recency semantics. We will represent a database instance symbolically using a push-down automaton where the stack carries a word of layers. The layers in the stack encode recency windows with increasing recency measures, and in particular. the top-most layer represents the current recency window.

Push-Down Automata. We recall the classical model of Push-Down Automata (PDA). A PDA $\mathcal{P}$ is a tuple $\langle Q, q_{init}, \Gamma, T\rangle$ where Q is the set of *states*, $q_{init} \in Q$ is the *initial state*, Γ is the (finite) stack alphabet, and T is the set of *transitions*. A transition $t \in T$ is a triple $\langle q_1, op, q_2\rangle$ where $q_1, q_2 \in Q$ are states and op is an *operation* of one of three forms: (i) *nop* is an empty operation that does not change the content of the stack, (ii) *push* (a), where $a \in \Gamma$, adds a to the top of the stack, (iii) *pop* (a), where $a \in \Gamma$, removes the top-most stack symbol if this symbol is equal to a. A *configuration* β is a pair $\langle q, w\rangle$ where $q \in Q$ is the (local) state of the automaton, and $w \in \Gamma^*$ is the content of the stack. We define a transition relation $\rightsquigarrow_{\mathcal{P}}$ on the set of configurations as follows. For configurations $\beta_1 = \langle q_1, w_1\rangle$ and $\beta_2 = \langle q_2, w_2\rangle$, and a transition $t = \langle q_1, op, q_2\rangle$, we write $\beta_1 \overset{t}{\rightsquigarrow}_{\mathcal{P}} \beta_2$ to denote that one of the following three conditions is satisfied: (i) $op = nop$ and $w_1 = w_2$, (ii) $op = push(a)$ and $w_2 = a \bullet w_1$, or (ii) $op = pop(a)$ and $w_1 = a \bullet w_2$. We define $\rightsquigarrow_{\mathcal{P}} := \cup_{t \in T} \overset{t}{\rightsquigarrow}_{\mathcal{P}}$, and define $\overset{*}{\rightsquigarrow}_{\mathcal{P}}$ to be the reflexive transitive closure of $\rightsquigarrow_{\mathcal{P}}$. For a configuration β and a state q, we write $\beta \overset{*}{\rightsquigarrow}_{\mathcal{P}} q$ to denote that there is a word $w \in \Gamma^*$ such that $\beta \overset{*}{\rightsquigarrow}_{\mathcal{P}} \langle q, w\rangle$. An instance of the *reachability problem* consists of an (initial) configuration β_{init} and a (target) state q_F and we are asked whether $\beta \overset{*}{\rightsquigarrow}_{\mathcal{P}} q_F$.

Consider a DMS $\mathcal{D}$, a recency bound B, and a proposition p. The *layered database* $\mathcal{B}$ induced by $\mathcal{D}$ is a push-down automaton $\langle Q, q_{init}, \Gamma, T\rangle$ defined as follows.

Stack Alphabet. The stack alphabet Γ consists of the set of all compact layers, in addition to the *stack bottom* symbol BTM. By construction, the bottom symbol of the stack will be BTM, while all the other symbols will be compact layers. All the layers, except the one next to the bottom of the stack will be balanced. The layer next to the bottom of the stack may be under-loaded. This happens when all the objects represent data elements that are in the current recency window. No over-loaded layers will ever be pushed to the stack.

Initial Configuration. Let J be database instance over Δ, with $\text{ADOM}(J) = \{e_1, \ldots, e_n\}$. We will encode J as a layer $\text{encode}(J) = \langle A, D, \text{rcy}, I, \text{busy}, \varphi, M, g\rangle$ over the set objects O. For this, we may assume that $|\text{ADOM}(J)| < B$, as we can keep $\max\{|\text{ADOM}(J)|, B\}$ as the real B. [1] $A = \{o_1, \ldots, o_n\}$, $D = \emptyset$, $\text{rcy}(o) = 0$ for all actual objects $o \in A$, $\langle o_1, \ldots, o_n\rangle \in R^I$ iff $\langle e_1, \ldots, e_n\rangle \in R^J$ for every relation name R, $\text{busy}(o) = \text{false}$ for all actual objects $o \in A$, $(o_1 \sim o_2) \in \varphi$ iff $\#e_1 \sim \#e_2$, $M = \emptyset$, and $g(o) = \perp$ for all objects $o \in A \cup D$.

The initial configuration is defined by $\langle q_{init}, \text{encode}(J) \bullet \text{BTM}\rangle$

States. In addition to q_{init} and the target state q_F, the set Q contains the state ORIGIN which is the "stable state" from which we perform the actions of $\mathcal{D}$ on the top-most layer in the stack. Furthermore, the set Q contains a number of "transient states" that are used to mimic the actions. More precisely, for each compact layer $\mathcal{L}$, the set Q contains the following states:

- [FETCHED, $\mathcal{L}$]: we have fetched the layer $\mathcal{L}$ from the stack.
- [RESTORED, $\mathcal{L}$]: We have put back the layer $\mathcal{L}$ to the stack.
- [DERIVED, $\mathcal{L}$]: we have derived the layer $\mathcal{L}$ by applying an action to a layer that we have fetched from the stack.
- [MERGING, $\mathcal{L}_1, \mathcal{L}_2$]: we are about to merge the layers $\mathcal{L}_1$ and $\mathcal{L}_2$.

Transitions. The set T contains the following transitions.

- $\langle q_{init}, nop, \text{ORIGIN}\rangle$. We move from the initial state to the state ORIGIN from which we start the simulation.
- $\langle \text{ORIGIN}, pop(\mathcal{L}), [\text{FETCHED}, \mathcal{L}]\rangle$ for each compact layer $\mathcal{L}$. From the state ORIGIN, we can non-deterministically fetch a layer $\mathcal{L}$ from the stack.
- $\langle [\text{FETCHED}, \mathcal{L}], push(\mathcal{L}), [\text{RESTORED}, \mathcal{L}]\rangle$ for each compact and balanced layer $\mathcal{L}$. We restore the stack by immediately pushing pack the layer we have fetched in the previous step. The purpose of this transition (together with the previous transition) is to find out the top-most layer $\mathcal{L}$. Notice that $\mathcal{L}$ is stored in the definition of the state (each layer $\mathcal{L}$ has its own [FETCHED, $\mathcal{L}$]-state.) We also have a transition $\langle [\text{FETCHED}, \mathcal{L}], nop, [\text{RESTORED}, \mathcal{L}]\rangle$ if $\mathcal{L}$ is under-loaded.
- $\langle [\text{RESTORED}, \mathcal{L}_1], nop, [\text{DERIVED}, \mathcal{L}_2]\rangle$ for all compact layers $\mathcal{L}_1$ and $\mathcal{L}_2$ where $\mathcal{L}_1 \to \mathcal{L}_2$ and $\mathcal{L}_2$ is consistent. We consider the successors of $\mathcal{L}_1$ wrt. $\to$.
- $\langle [\text{DERIVED}, \mathcal{L}], push(\mathcal{L}), \text{ORIGIN}\rangle$ for each compact and balanced layer. If the layer is balanced we simply push it to the stack. An action has been performed, and we return back to the state ORIGIN from which we look for the next action.
- $\langle [\text{DERIVED}, \mathcal{L}_1], push(\mathcal{L}_2), \text{ORIGIN}\rangle$ for all compact layers $\mathcal{L}_1$ and $\mathcal{L}_2$ such that $\mathcal{L}_1$ is over-loaded and $\mathcal{L}_2 = truncate(\mathcal{L}_1)$. In case the derived layer is over-loaded, we truncate it first before we push it to the stack.
- $\langle [\text{DERIVED}, \mathcal{L}_1], pop(\mathcal{L}_2), [\text{MERGING}, \mathcal{L}_1, \mathcal{L}_2]\rangle$ where $\mathcal{L}_1$ is compact and under-loaded, and $\mathcal{L}_2$ is either a compact layer or equal to BTM. Since $\mathcal{L}_1$ is under-loaded it needs to be merged with another layer. Therefore, we fetch $\mathcal{L}_2$ from the stack.
- $\langle [\text{DERIVED}, \mathcal{L}], nop, q_F\rangle$ if the target proposition p occurs in $\mathcal{L}$.
- $\langle [\text{MERGING}, \mathcal{L}_1, \mathcal{L}_2], nop, [\text{DERIVED}, \mathcal{L}_3]\rangle$ for all compact layers $\mathcal{L}_1$ and $\mathcal{L}_2$ where $\mathcal{L}_3 \in \mathcal{L}_1 \otimes \mathcal{L}_2$. We have derived the layer $\mathcal{L}_3$ through the merging of the layers $\mathcal{L}_1$ and $\mathcal{L}_2$. We also have the transition $\langle [\text{MERGING}, \mathcal{L}, \text{BTM}], push(\mathcal{L}), \text{ORIGIN}\rangle$.

Correctness. Corresponding to any path $\pi_{\mathcal{D}}$ starting from the initial database instance J in the B-bounded configuration graph of $\mathcal{D}$, we have a path $\pi_{\mathcal{B}}$ in the configuration graph of our constructed PDA $\mathcal{B}$. Further, the length of $\pi_{\mathcal{D}}$ and the number of stable states in $\pi_{\mathcal{B}}$ are in bijection. Symmetrically, corresponding to any path $\pi_{\mathcal{D}}$ in the configuration graph of our constructed PDA which starts in the initial configuration and ends in a stable state, there exist at least one path $\pi_{\mathcal{D}}$ starting from J in the B-bounded configuration graph of the DMS. This can be proved by induction on the length of the paths. Further, in any database instance on a path $\pi_{\mathcal{D}}$, a proposition p occurs if, and only if, it also occurs in the corresponding stable state of $\mathcal{B}$ in the corresponding path $\pi_{\mathcal{B}}$. Thus, the target p is reachable in $\mathcal{D}$ if and only if the state q_F is reachable in $\mathcal{B}$.

Complexity: The PDA we construct is of size $n2^{O(|\mathcal{R}|(mB)^{\text{amax}})}$ where m is the maximum number of variables used in any action, n is the number of actions in the DMS and amax is the maximum arity of any relation in the schema. Control state reachability in pushdown systems is in linear time, and hence recency bounded propositional reachability can be done in $n2^{O(|\mathcal{R}|(mB)^{\text{amax}})}$. This is exponential time assuming amax is a constant. Detailed complexity analysis can be found in Appendix C.

This justifies the EXPTIME upper bound stated in Theorem 4.1. The lower bound is proved in Appendix B by a reduction from the language intersection non-emptiness problem of a pushdown automaton and n finite state automata.

[1] Note that since we are doing under-approximate verification, it will only increase coverage and not change the ExpTime upper bound we obtain.

8 RELATED WORK

Formal verification is very tempting due to its unmatched precision and the guarantee of correctness. Recent years have seen attempts to bring formal methods to the verification of business processes. This has resulted in a body of research papers throwing theoretical insight to a practical tool [23, 24] for data-centric work flow. Different formalisms to model database driven systems have been proposed in the literature.

The line of research followed in [10, 20, 26] assumes the system can start from an arbitrary initial database instance and evolve, as long as the instances agree to a constraint. This framework can now-a-days support rich features such as numerical data, task creation, hierarchical structure and limited concurrency. By introducing appropriate restrictions they get decidability for verification, which is ready to be put in practice [23].

In another line of research, in the works of [5, 6, 14, 18] the system starts from a fixed initial database and the actions result in bulk operations that add/delete an unbounded number of facts at a time. Two versions of bounded reachability has been studied in [5, 7] where the length of the run and size of the active domain are bounded respectively. These bounding strategies are an under-approximation, but they only admit a bounded number of distinct database instances modulo renaming.

The closest related work is indeed [3]. In [3] we showed that model checking of a weaker class of DMS which does not allow numerical values against a very expressive specification language (MSO-FO) is decidable. MSO-FO can relate data objects at different instances using global quantifiers. The proof idea was to encode the "data equality" using "same origin" in MSO, which crucially depended on the assumption on history-freshness – a newly inserted value must be different from any value ever used in the history of a run. Thus, it allowed to "interpret" the runs in nested words (analogous to tree-interpretation) on which MSO is decidable.

Our model, on the other hand, allows numerical values to be repeated freely, not restricted by freshness or recency. In fact we treat numerical values differently from the object of the data domain precisely to give it this freedom, which is crucial for most modelling applications. In the presence of non-fresh objects the proof from [3] fails, as the interpretation is not any more a nested word, but a data - nested word (analogous to "data-tree" [8]). This would make model checking against LTL undecidable (cf. Appendix A).

Hence we develop new proof techniques to handle this case by means of symbolic representation by layers and we capture the dynamics by a pushdown automaton. With this we could relax the restriction of history-freshness on data objects to local-freshness. Further the notion of recency is relaxed to recently *accessed* as opposed to recently *added.* Also, multiple elements are allowed to have the same recency. This increases the coverage of the under-approximation.

Pushdown systems with numerical values have been studied extensively in the literature [1, 2, 11, 16] but we have a much richer structure because we have to deal with unbounded database instances.

Formalisms for database-driven dynamic systems such as DMS are very similar, on the surface, to those used in planning and reasoning about actions (such as STRIPS and ADL). All such formalisms employ a first-order language (and fragments thereof) to capture the executability of actions and the updates they induce. In addition, the existence of a plan that brings the system from an initial to a target state can be formulated as a reachability problem. There is, however, a fundamental difference: planning and action languages are usually interpreted over a finite object domain, so that they simply provide a compact way for representing propositional action theories. To the best of our knowledge, the few approaches that attack planning problems over infinite object domains (such as [15, 22]) introduce conditions towards decidability that are different from those studied here, and that in fact make the resulting system *essentially finite state.*

9 CONCLUSIONS AND FUTURE WORK

We have lifted the framework of DMS [3] to handle elements from a dense domain with an implicit total order between them. We use an elegant symbolic encoding to show that the reachability problem under bounded recency restriction can be decided in ExpTime. We also give a matching lower-bound. We further show that going beyond reachability to model checking against liner-time properties is undecidable.

There are several directions for future research. An immediate step would be to see how the decidability/complexity varies if we allow full first-order guards in the actions.

It would be interesting to see which other interpreted data and relations can still give us decidable verification. In particular, whether it would be possible to extend the decidability results to the discrete domain. Another direction would be to use time as interpreted data and allow guards with timing constraints. Timing constraints are crucial for many database-driven transactions such as in banking domains or for security purposes. It is worth exploring the status of decidability and complexity in these settings. Another question is to see whether we could go beyond relations to interpreted functions such as arithmetic on numerical values.

Acknowledgments

C. Aiswarya has been partially supported by DST Inspire. Marco Montali has been partially supported by the UNIBZ projects REKAP and DACOMAN.

REFERENCES

[1] Parosh Aziz Abdulla, C. Aiswarya, and Mohamed Faouzi Atig. 2017. Data Multi-Pushdown Automata. In *CONCUR (LIPIcs)*, Vol. 85. Schloss Dagstuhl - Leibniz-Zentrum fuer Informatik, 38:1–38:17.

[2] P. A. Abdulla, M. F. Atig, G. Delzanno, and A. Podelski. 2013. Push-Down Automata with Gap-Order Constraints. In *FSEN (LNCS)*, Vol. 8161. Springer, 199–216.

[3] Parosh Aziz Abdulla, C. Aiswarya, Mohamed Faouzi Atig, Marco Montali, and Othmane Rezine. 2016. Recency-Bounded Verification of Dynamic Database-Driven Systems. In *PODS*. ACM, 195–210.

[4] Parosh Aziz Abdulla, C. Aiswarya, Mohamed Faouzi Atig, Marco Montali, and Othmane Rezine. 2018. Complexity of Reachability for Data-Aware Dynamic Systems. In *ACSD*. IEEE Computer Society, 11–20.

[5] Babak Bagheri Hariri, Diego Calvanese, Giuseppe De Giacomo, Alin Deutsch, and Marco Montali. 2013. Verification of Relational Data-Centric Dynamic Systems with External Services. In *PODS*. ACM Press.

[6] Francesco Belardinelli, Alessio Lomuscio, and Fabio Patrizi. 2012. Verification of GSM-Based Artifact-Centric Systems through Finite Abstraction. In *ICSOC (LNCS)*, Vol. 7636. Springer, 17–31.

[7] Francesco Belardinelli, Alessio Lomuscio, and Fabio Patrizi. 2014. Verification of Agent-Based Artifact Systems. *J. Artif. Intell. Res.* 51 (2014), 333–376.

[8] Mikolaj Boja'nczyk, Anca Muscholl, Thomas Schwentick, and Luc Segoufin. 2009. Two-variable logic on data trees and XML reasoning. *J. ACM* 56, 3 (2009), 13:1–13:48. https://doi.org/10.1145/1516512.1516515

[9] Mikolaj Bojanczyk, Anca Muscholl, Thomas Schwentick, Luc Segoufin, and Claire David. 2006. Two-Variable Logic on Words with Data. In *LICS*. 7–16.

[10] Mikolaj Bojanczyk, Luc Segoufin, and Szymon Torunczyk. 2013. Verification of Database-Driven Systems via Amalgamation. In *PODS*.

[11] B. Bollig, A. Cyriac, P. Gastin, and K. Narayan Kumar. 2012. Model Checking Languages of Data Words. In *FoSSaCS'12 (LNCS)*, Vol. 7213. Springer, 391–405.

[12] Diego Calvanese, Giuseppe De Giacomo, and Marco Montali. 2013. Foundations of Data-Aware Process Analysis: A Database Theory Perspective. In *PODS*. ACM Press.

[13] Diego Calvanese, Giuseppe De Giacomo, Marco Montali, and Fabio Patrizi. 2018. First-order μ-calculus over generic transition systems and applications to the situation calculus. *Inf. Comput.* 259, 3 (2018), 328–347.

[14] Diego Calvanese, Giorgio Delzanno, and Marco Montali. 2015. Verification of Relational Multiagent Systems with Data Types. In *AAAI*. AAAIP.

[15] Diego Calvanese, Marco Montali, Fabio Patrizi, and Michele Stawowy. 2016. Plan Synthesis for Knowledge and Action Bases. In *Proceedings of the Twenty-Fifth International Joint Conference on Artificial Intelligence, IJCAI 2016, New York, NY, USA, 9-15 July 2016*, Subbarao Kambhampati (Ed.). IJCAI/AAAI Press, 1022–1029. http://www.ijcai.org/Abstract/16/149

[16] Lorenzo Clemente and Slawomir Lasota. 2015. Reachability Analysis of First-order Definable Pushdown Systems. In *CSL 2015, (LIPIcs)*, Vol. 41. Schloss Dagstuhl - Leibniz-Zentrum fuer Informatik, 244–259.

[17] E. Damaggio, A. Deutsch, and V. Vianu. 2011. Artifact Systems with Data Dependencies and Arithmetic. In *ICDT*.

[18] Giuseppe De Giacomo, Riccardo De Masellis, and Riccardo Rosati. 2012. Verification of Conjunctive Artifact-Centric Services. *Int. J. Cooperative Inf. Syst.* 21, 2 (2012), 111–140. https://doi.org/10.1142/S0218843012500025

[19] Stéphane Demri and Ranko Lazić. 2009. LTL with the freeze quantifier and register automata. *ACM TOCL* 10, 3 (2009).

[20] Alin Deutsch, Richard Hull, Fabio Patrizi, and Victor Vianu. 2009. Automatic verification of data-centric business processes. In *ICDT*.

[21] A. Deutsch, Y. Li, and V. Vianu. 2016. Verification of Hierarchical Artifact Systems. In *Proc. of PODS*. ACM Press, 179–194.

[22] Jörg Hoffmann, Piergiorgio Bertoli, Malte Helmert, and Marco Pistore. 2009. Message-Based Web Service Composition, Integrity Constraints, and Planning under Uncertainty: A New Connection. *J. Artif. Intell. Res.* 35 (2009), 49–117. https://doi.org/10.1613/jair.2716

[23] Yuliang Li, Alin Deutsch, and Victor Vianu. 2017. VERIFAS: A Practical Verifier for Artifact Systems. *Proc. VLDB Endow.* 11, 3 (Nov. 2017), 283–296.

[24] Riccardo De Masellis, Chiara Di Francescomarino, Chiara Ghidini, Marco Montali, and Sergio Tessaris. 2017. Add Data into Business Process Verification: Bridging the Gap between Theory and Practice. In *AAAI*.

[25] Shaz Qadeer and Jakob Rehof. 2005. Context-Bounded Model Checking of Concurrent Software. In *TACAS*. Springer Berlin Heidelberg, 93–107.

[26] Victor Vianu. 2009. Automatic Verification of Database-Driven Systems: a New Frontier. In *Proc. of ICDT*. 1–13.

A LTL-FO MODEL CHECKING IS UNDECIDABLE

LTL-FO has been considered the apt temporal logic for evolving database driven systems. The reduction we present here will go through for a fragment of LTL-FO called LTL-UCQ where atomic formula can only check for the presence of a fact in the database instance.

The syntax of LTL-UCQ is given by:

$$\psi := \quad R(u_1, \dots u_a) \mid \#(u) \leq \#(v) \mid \psi \wedge \psi \mid \neg\psi \mid \mathsf{X}\psi \mid \mathsf{F}\psi \mid \mathsf{P}\psi \mid \psi \mathsf{U} \psi \mid \exists u \psi$$

where R/a is in the schema.

A formula ψ is evaluated on a sequence $\rho = I_0, I_1, I_2 \dots$ of database instances and an index $i \in \mathbb{N}$ together with a valuation $\nu : \mathsf{free}(\psi) \to \textsc{Adom}(\rho)$ of the free variables to the elements of the active domain of the database instance at i where $\textsc{Adom}(\rho) = \bigcup_i \textsc{Adom}(I_i)$. The semantics is given below:

$$\rho, i, \nu \models R(u_1, \dots u_a) \qquad \text{if } \langle \nu(u_1), \dots \nu(u_a) \rangle \in R^{I_i}$$

$$\rho, i, \nu \models \#(u) \leq \#(v) \qquad \text{if } \#(\nu(u)) \leq \#(\nu(v))$$

$$\rho, i, \nu \models \exists u \psi \qquad \text{if } \exists\, e \in \textsc{Adom}(I_i) \text{ such that } I_i, \nu' \models \psi$$

$$\text{where } \nu'(v) = \begin{cases} \nu(v) & \text{if } v \neq u \\ e & \text{if } v = u \end{cases}$$

The semantics of the standard temporal operators are as expected.

The recency bounded model checking problem asks, given a DMS S, and initial database instance I_0, a recency bound b and an LTL-UCQ sentence ψ, do we have $\rho, 0 \models \psi$ for all recency b - bounded runs $\rho = I_0, I_1, I_2, \dots$ of S ?

THEOREM A.1. *Recency bounded model checking problem of DMS against LTL-UCQ is undecidable.*

We will prove the undecidability of the model checking problem by demonstrating a reduction from the control state reachability problem in a two-counter machine (Minsky machines).

Two-counter machines. A two counter machine (2CM) is a tuple (States, init, Trans) where States is the finite set of states, init $\in$ States is the initial state, and Trans $\subseteq$ States $\times$ Ops $\times$ States is the set of transitions with $Ops = \{\mathtt{inc}_1, \mathtt{dec}_1, \mathtt{ifz}_1, \mathtt{inc}_2, \mathtt{dec}_2, \mathtt{ifz}_2\}$ denoting increment, decrement and zero-test on counter 1 and 2. We may assume, without loss of generality, that there are no transitions of the form (q, op, init).

The semantics is given by an infinite configuration graph whose set of nodes is States $\times \mathbb{N} \times \mathbb{N}$. A configuration (q, n_1, n_2) denotes that the machine is in state q, counter 1 has value n_1 and counter 2 has value n_2. We write $(q, n_1, n_2) \rightarrow (q', n_1', n_2')$ if one of the following conditions holds:

(1) $(q, \mathtt{inc}_1, q') \in Trans$, $n_1' = 1 + n_1$ and $n_2' = n_2$
(2) $(q, \mathtt{inc}_2, q') \in Trans$, $n_1' = n_1$ and $n_2' = 1 + n_2$
(3) $(q, \mathtt{dec}_1, q') \in Trans$, $n_1 > 0$, $n_1' = n_1 - 1$ and $n_2' = n_2$
(4) $(q, \mathtt{dec}_2, q') \in Trans$, $n_2 > 0$, $n_1' = n_1$ and $n_2' = n_2 - 1$
(5) $(q, \mathtt{ifz}_1, q') \in Trans$, $n_1' = n_1 = 0$ and $n_2' = n_2$
(6) $(q, \mathtt{ifz}_1, q') \in Trans$, $n_1' = n_1$ and $n_2' = n_2 = 0$

We denote the reflexive-transitive closure of $\rightarrow$ by $\rightarrow^*$.

The control-state reachability problem for two counter machines asks, given a 2CMand a target state $q_{\mathrm{target}} \in$ States, do we have $(\mathrm{init}, 0, 0) \rightarrow^* (q_{\mathrm{target}}, n_1, n_2)$ for some $n_1, n_2 \in \mathbb{N}$? The problem is well known to be undecidable.

Construction of the DMS. Our schema consists of a unary relations curr and propositions denoting state and the current operation. That is schema $\mathcal{R} = \{P_q/0 \mid q \in \mathrm{States}\} \cup \{P_{op}/0 \mid op \in \mathrm{Ops}\} \cup \{\mathtt{curr}/1\}$. A new element gets added in every action, and will be deleted in the subsequent one. Thus we maintain an invariant that there will be exactly one element in the active domain always (except for the very initial database instance). Corresponding to every transition $t = (q, op, q') \in$ Trans we have an action α_t with

- $I_+ = \{P_q, \mathtt{curr}(x)\}$
- DEL $= \{P_q, \mathtt{curr}(x), \{P_{op'}\}_{op' \in \mathrm{Ops}}\}$
- ADD $= \{P_{q'}, \mathtt{curr}(y), P_{op}\}$

We need an extra action α_{init} to handle the very first transition, as at that time the active domain is empty.

- $I_+ = \{P_{\mathrm{init}}\}$
- DEL $= \{P_{\mathrm{init}}, \{P_{op'}\}_{op' \in \mathrm{Ops}}\}$
- ADD $= \{P_{q'}, \mathtt{curr}(y), P_{op}\}$

Notice that the assumption of having no transitions with init as the target state is important to maintain the invariant of only one element in the active domain.

The DMS would run from the initial database instance (I_0) consisting of an empty active domain and a single proposition P_{init} being true. It also maintains an invariant that an any instance apart from I_0, exactly one proposition corresponding to the state, and one proposition corresponding to the type of the operation is true. The element added to the active domain keeps an identity of the operation which we will exploit using LTL for capturing faithful simulations.

LTL-UCQ formula characterising faithful simulation of 2CM. Notice that the DMS constructed could allow any sequence of actions as far the control states permit them. But these sequence of actions can take counters to negative values and zero-tests to be performed when the counter is not zero. We will rule out these spurious runs using the LTL-FO formulae. Our formula for faithful simulation (ψ_{faithful}) will be a conjunction of the following:

(1) $\neg(\mathsf{F}(\exists u\ (\mathsf{F}\ \exists v\ (\#u = \#v \wedge \mathsf{F}(\exists u\ \#u = \#v)))\ ))$
There must not be three elements with the same numerical value.
(2) $\mathsf{G}\ (\exists u\ \mathtt{dec}_1 \wedge \mathtt{curr}(u) \Rightarrow \mathsf{P}\ (\exists v\ \mathtt{inc}_1 \wedge \mathtt{curr}(v) \wedge \#u = \#v))$
Every decrement on counter 1 must have a corresponding increment on counter 1 before.
(3) $\mathsf{G}(\exists u\ \mathtt{dec}_2 \wedge \mathtt{curr}(u) \Rightarrow \mathsf{P}(\exists v\ \mathtt{inc}_2 \wedge \mathtt{curr}(v) \wedge \#u = \#v))$
Similarly for counter 2.
(4) $\mathsf{G}(\exists u\ \mathtt{inc}_1 \wedge \mathtt{curr}(u) \Rightarrow \neg\ \mathtt{ifz}_1 \mathsf{U}(\exists v\ \mathtt{dec}_1 \wedge \mathtt{curr}(v) \wedge \#u = \#v)$
Every increment on counter 1 must be decremented before a zero test on counter 1.
(5) $\mathsf{G}(\exists u\ \mathtt{inc}_2 \wedge \mathtt{curr}(u) \Rightarrow (\neg\ \mathtt{ifz}_1)\ \mathsf{U}\ (\exists v\ \mathtt{dec}_2 \wedge \mathtt{curr}(v) \wedge \#u = \#v)$
Similarly for counter 2.

Finally to check if a faithful run reaches the target state, we want to check if the formula $\psi_{\mathrm{faithful}} \wedge \mathsf{F} q_{\mathrm{target}}$ is satisfied by at least one run of the DMS. Since model checking asks whether all runs satisfy the given formula, we tweak the formula to $\psi_{\mathrm{faithful}} \implies \mathsf{G}\neg q_{\mathrm{target}}$. The model checking answers *no* if an only if the q_{target} is reachable by a faithful simulation (same as, q_{target} is reachable in 2CM). Thus the model-checking against LTL is undecidable.

Remark. Alternate proof: With recency bound 1, we can simulate a generic automaton generating all data words [9, 19]. The recency is applied only to objects, their values are completely free (to repeat or to be fresh). Using LTL-UCQ we can express Freeze-LTL [19] on datawords, for which it is undecidable to check satisfiability.

B LOWER BOUND

In this section we show that the recency bounded reachability problem for DMS is ExpTime-hard, already with a recency bound $B = 1$ starting from an initial database having a singleton active domain. Further our schema contains only unary relations, our actions employ only simple UCQN guards, and *do not* involve numerical constraints.

We will give a reduction from the intersection non-emptiness problem of the languages of a pushdown automaton and m finite state automata. The input is a pushdown automaton $\mathcal{A}_0$ and m finite state automata $\mathcal{A}_1, \ldots \mathcal{A}_m$, over the same finite alphabet Σ. The question is whether there exists a word $w \in \Sigma^*$ such that w is accepted by all $\mathcal{A}_i$.

Let the pushdown automaton $\mathcal{A}_0 = \langle \mathsf{States}_0, \Gamma, \mathsf{Trans}_0, \mathsf{init}_0, \mathsf{Acc}_0 \rangle$. We have $\mathsf{Trans}_0 \subseteq \mathsf{States}_0 \times \Sigma \times \Gamma \times \Gamma^* \times \mathsf{States}_0$, indicating the source state, the letter being read, the top of the stack symbol being popped, the sequence of symbols to be pushed onto the stack, and the target state. We define the set $\mathit{ToPush} \subseteq \Gamma^*$ to be the suffixes of the sequence of strings to be pushed to the stack in any transition of $\mathcal{A}_0$. That is, $\mathit{ToPush} = \{\alpha \mid \alpha \in \Gamma^* \text{ and } \exists (p, a, \gamma, \beta\alpha, p') \in \mathsf{Trans}_0$ for some $p, p' \in \mathsf{States}_0, a \in \Sigma$, and $\beta \in \Gamma^*\}$. Let the finite state automata be $\mathcal{A}_i = \langle \mathsf{States}_i, \mathsf{Trans}_i, \mathsf{init}_i, \mathsf{Acc}_i \rangle$ for $i : 1 \leq i \leq m$. Without loss of generality, we assume that the set of states States_i are disjoint for all $i : 0 \leq i \leq m$. We also assume that $|\mathsf{Acc}_i| = 1$, by letting the automata to be non-deterministic.

We will construct a DMS over a schema consisting of only unary relations and nullary relations (propositions). Our schema will contain:

- a unary relation U_γ for each stack symbol $\gamma \in \Gamma$,
- a proposition P_s for each state $s \in \bigcup_i \mathsf{States}_i$,
- a proposition P_a for each letter $a \in \Sigma$,
- a proposition $P_{\mathcal{A}_i}$ for each automaton $\mathcal{A}_i, i : 0 \leq i \leq m$
- a proposition P_α, for each $\alpha \in \mathit{ToPush}$ and
- two special values $P_\$$ and P_{Acc}.

That is, the schema $\mathcal{R} = \{U_\gamma/1 \mid \gamma \in \Gamma\} \cup \{P_s/0 \mid s \in \bigcup_i \mathsf{States}_i\} \cup \{P_a/0 \mid a \in \Sigma\} \cup \{P_{\mathcal{A}_i}/0 \mid 1 \leq i \leq m\} \cup \{P_\alpha/0 \mid \alpha \in \mathit{ToPush}\} \cup \{P_\$/0, P_{\mathsf{Acc}}/0\}$.

We will design the DMS to simulate a run of each of the automata on the same word, in synchronous rounds. In a round, every automaton will perform a transition and all of them will agree on the letter being read. A round is realized by a sequence of actions which simulate each automata in a round-robin fashion.

As an invariant we maintain that, there will always be exactly one proposition from $\{P_s/0 \mid s \in \mathsf{States}_i\}$ which is set to true, for each i. This will represent a global state, if we were doing a product construction of the automata.

Further, throughout a round exactly one and the same proposition from the set $\{P_a/0 \mid a \in \Sigma\}$ will be set to true. At the very beginning of a round, no proposition from the set $\{P_a/0 \mid a \in \Sigma\}$ is set to true. This enables us to simulate a synchronous transition in the product automata using a round.

Another invariant would be that every element present in the active domain will be present in exactly one unary relation from $\gamma \in \Gamma$. Thus the active domain along with the recency information represents a stack which is needed to simulate the run of the pushdown automaton $\mathcal{A}_0$.

At the beginning of a round the control will be given to the pushdown automaton $\mathcal{A}_0$, by setting $P_{\mathcal{A}_0}$ to true and every other $P_{\mathcal{A}_i}$ $(i \neq 0)$ would be false. The DMS would assert that no P_a is set to true, and simulate a transition of the pushdown automaton (it may take more than one action, we describe this below) and eventually give the control to the finite state automaton $\mathcal{A}_1$. The proposition P_a set to true by $\mathcal{A}_0$ would continue to remain true, and a consistent transition of $\mathcal{A}_1$ labelled by letter a would be simulated. Then the control will be given to $\mathcal{A}_2$ and so on. Finally once a transition of $\mathcal{A}_m$ is simulated the proposition P_a is set to false and DMS moves to a special stage intended to check for acceptance. This is marked by the special proposition $P_\$$. In this stage, an action will check if all automata are in Acc_i and if so, will set the target proposition P_{Acc} true, and else will set $P_{\mathcal{A}_0}$ to true in order to start the next round.

Formally, the DMS will have the following actions.

(1) $\alpha_{\text{Accept-yes}}$
   - $I_+ = \{P_\$, \{P_{\mathsf{Acc}_i}\}_i\}, I_- = \emptyset$
   - $\textsc{Add} = \{P_{\mathsf{Acc}}\}, \textsc{Del} = \emptyset$

   An accepting configuration sets the target proposition P_{Acc} true.

(2) $\alpha_{\text{Accept-no-i}}$
   - $I_+ = \{P_\$\}, I_- = \{P_{\mathsf{Acc}_i}\}$
   - $\textsc{Del} = \{P_\$\}, \ \textsc{Add} = \{P_{\mathcal{A}_0}\}$

   If not accepting as witnessed by Automaton $\mathcal{A}_i$, start the next round by giving the control to $\mathcal{A}_0$. We have one such transition for each i.

(3) α_t
   - $I_+ = \{P_{\mathcal{A}_0}, P_q, U_\gamma(x)\}, \quad I_- = \{\{P_a\}_{a \in \Sigma}\}$
   - $\textsc{Del} = \{P_q, U_\gamma(x)\}, \ \textsc{Add} = \{P_{q'}, P_a, P_\alpha\}$

   if $t = (q, a, \gamma, \alpha, q') \in \mathsf{Trans}_0$
   Checks if the transition is enabled, if yes sets the letter, updates the state, pops the top of the stack and remembers to push α to the stack by simulation. The control still is with $\mathcal{A}_0$ as $P_{\mathcal{A}_0}$ is still true.

(4) $\alpha_{\gamma\alpha}$
   - $I_+ = \{P_{\mathcal{A}_0}, P_{\gamma\alpha}\}, \quad I_- = \emptyset$
   - $\textsc{Del} = \{P_{\gamma\alpha}\}, \ \textsc{Add} = \{U_\gamma(y), P_\alpha\}$

   if $\gamma\alpha \in \mathit{ToPush}$

If $\gamma\alpha$ needs to be pushed to the stack, it first inserts an element to the unary relation U_γ and remembers that it has to still push α.

(5) α_ϵ
- $I_+ = \{P_{\mathcal{A}_0}, P_\epsilon\}, \quad I_- = \emptyset$
- $\textsc{Del} = \{P_\epsilon, P_{\mathcal{A}_0}\}, \ \textsc{Add} = \{P_{\mathcal{A}_1}\}$

If no more symbols needs to be pushed into the stack, then the control is given to $\mathcal{A}_1$.

(6) α_t
- $I_+ = \{P_{\mathcal{A}_i}, P_q, P_a\}, \quad I_- = \emptyset$
- $\textsc{Del} = \{P_{\mathcal{A}_i}, P_q\}, \ \textsc{Add} = \{P_{q'}, P_{\mathcal{A}_{i+1}}\}$

if $t = (q, a, q') \in \mathsf{Trans}_i$. We have one such transition for each $i : 1 \leq i \leq m - 1$.
Perform a transition labelled by the chosen letter and give control to the next automaton.

(7) α_t
- $I_+ = \{P_{\mathcal{A}_m}, P_q, P_a\}, \quad I_- = \emptyset$
- $\textsc{Del} = \{P_{\mathcal{A}_m}, P_q, P_a\}, \ \textsc{Add} = \{P_{q'}, P_{\mathcal{A}_\$}\}$

if $t = (q, a, q') \in \mathsf{Trans}_m$.
Once the round is finished, un-set the letter, and set the special proposition $P_\$$ (which will in turn check if the configuration is accepting, cf. Action in Item (1)).

Initially, the propositions P_{init_i} and the special proposition $P_\$$ are set to true, and all other propositions are set to false. Further all unary relations are empty except $U_\perp$ which contains one element, to mark the bottom of the stack. This defines I_0. The recency bound is 1. The target proposition is P_{Acc}.

Notice that I_0 ensures that all automata are in their respective initial states initially, and that the stack only contains the stack bottom symbol. A run of recency bound 1 will make sure that last-in-first-out policy of stacks is maintained on the elements of active domain along the run. Finally, if P_{Acc} is reachable then the automata have a non-empty intersection (the word whose length is the number of rounds in the run of the DMS, and the ith letter being the letter chosen at the ith round). Conversely, if the the automata have a non-empty intersection then there will be a run of the DMS which is recency bounded by 1.

Notice that the size of the schema is linear in the size of the input. The size of the DMS is polynomial in the size of the input. Thus we have a polynomial time reduction from the ExpTime complete problem to the bounded recency reachability problem thus establishing the ExpTime hardness of the latter.

C COMPLEXITY ANALYSIS

Complexity of our decision procedure will depend on the following parameters:

- m: the maximum number of variables used in any action
- amax: the maximum of the arities of the relations in the schema. That is, amax $= \max\{a \mid R/a \in \mathcal{R}\}$
- $|\mathcal{R}|$: number of relations in the schema
- B: the bound on recency and
- n: the number of actions in the DMS.

First we notice that the maximum number of elements that can be in a band (all having same value for rcy) is bounded by m. Next, we can observe that in a layer, the set A contains only the first $B+2$ bands. Hence the number of elements in A is bounded by $m\cdot(B+2)$. The sets D and M are also similar, in the worst case we need $3\cdot m\cdot(B+2)$ objects to be distributed across these. We can reuse the names for a different layer as long the conditions are satisfied. Hence we can establish a bound on the size of O. Let $N = |O| = 3\cdot m\cdot(B+2)$.

Now, keeping N as a loose upper bound, the number of different A, D, M possible are all 2^N. Number of different rcy is bounded by $(B+2)^N$. Number of different g is bounded by N^N. The number of different database instance over O is bounded by $2^{|\mathcal{R}|\cdot N^{\mathsf{amax}}}$. Hence the number of different layers possible is the product of these numbers, which is $2^{O(|\mathcal{R}|N^{\mathsf{amax}})}$ or equivalently $2^{O(|\mathcal{R}|(mB)^{\mathsf{amax}})}$.

Thus the number of states of the constructed PDA, as well as the stack alphabet be bounded by the same number. The number of transitions of the PDA is $O(n)$ where n is the number of actions in the DMS. Further the construction takes time $2^{O(|\mathcal{R}|(mB)^{\mathsf{amax}})}$.

Finally reachability in pushdown systems is in linear time, and hence recency bounded propositional reachability can be done in $2^{O(|\mathcal{R}|(mB)^{\mathsf{amax}})}$. Notice that this is exponential time assuming amax is a constant.

Remark. We will assume that the number of elements in the active domain of the initial database $|\textsc{Adom}(I_0)|$ is smaller than the recency bound. Otherwise, in the complexity analysis above we need to replace B by $\max\{|\textsc{Adom}(I_0)|, B\}$.

Compiling Existential-Positive Queries to Bounded-Variable Fragments

Christoph Berkholz*
Humboldt-Universität zu Berlin
Berlin, Germany
berkholz@informatik.hu-berlin.de

Hubie Chen†
Dept. of Computer Science and Information Systems
Birkbeck, University of London
London, United Kingdom
hubie@dcs.bbk.ac.uk

ABSTRACT

A crucial property of bounded-variable fragments of first-order logic is that they can be evaluated in polynomial time. It is therefore a useful preprocessing step to rewrite, if possible, a first-order query to a logically equivalent one with a minimum number of variables. However, it may occur that reducing the number of variables causes an increase in formula size. We investigate this trade-off for the existential-positive fragment of first-order queries, where variable minimisation is decidable in general. In particular, we study the blow-up in the formula size when compiling existential-positive queries to the bounded variable fragment of positive first-order logic. While the increase of the formula size is always at most exponential, we identify situations (based on the signature and the number of variables) where only a polynomial blow-up is needed. In all other cases, we show that an exponential lower bound on the formula size of the compiled formula that matches the general upper bound. This exponential lower bound is unconditional, and is the first unconditional lower bound for formula size with respect to the studied compilation; it is proved via establishing a novel interface with circuit complexity which may be of future interest.

*Funded by the Deutsche Forschungsgemeinschaft (DFG, German Research Foundation) – SCHW 837/5-1.

†Acknowledges the support of Spanish Project TIN2017-86727-C2-2-R.

PODS'19, June 30-July 5, 2019, Amsterdam, Netherlands

ACM ISBN 978-1-4503-6227-6/19/06...$15.00
https://doi.org/10.1145/3294052.3319693

CCS CONCEPTS

• **Theory of computation → Complexity classes; Finite Model Theory; Database query processing and optimization (theory).**

KEYWORDS

existential positive queries; bounded-variable logic; compilation; parameterized complexity

ACM Reference Format:
Christoph Berkholz and Hubie Chen. 2019. Compiling Existential-Positive Queries to Bounded-Variable Fragments. In *38th ACM SIGMOD-SIGACT-SIGAI Symposium on Principles of Database Systems (PODS'19), June 30-July 5, 2019, Amsterdam, Netherlands.* ACM, New York, NY, USA, 12 pages. https://doi.org/10.1145/3294052.3319693

1 INTRODUCTION

Overview. In this work we study the size blow-up that might occur when rewriting an existential-positive first-order query into a logically equivalent one that has a bounded number of variables. Existential-positive queries (EP) are those first-order queries that only use existential quantification (∃), conjunction (∧), and disjunction (∨)–so, those that disallow negation and universal quantification. This query language has been studied intensively in database theory and constraint satisfaction [6, 9, 10]. It can be alternatively described by the fragment of relational algebra that uses Select, Project, Join, and Union (SPJU), which is in turn semantically equivalent to the class of unions of conjunctive queries (UCQ).

Measures and their motivations. In addition to the *size* of a query, a fundamental complexity measure of first-order queries is the *number of variables*, by which is meant the total number of different variables that occur throughout a particular first-order query. The number of variables of query is essentially equivalent to the *width* of a query, which is defined to be the maximum number of free variables over all subformulas of the query. A query using k variables clearly has width at most k, and in the other direction, a query having width k can be rewritten, just by the syntactic renaming of variables, to a query using k variables. We thus freely interchange between these two measures in our discussions.

Every first-order query φ of width k can be evaluated on a database of size n in time $O(\|\varphi\| \cdot k \cdot n^k)$ by a straightforward bottom-up algorithm [20] that materialises for each subformula the result relation, which is of arity at most k. Therefore, it is a useful preprocessing step in query optimisation to rewrite, if possible, a first-order query into one having smaller, or even minimal, width. A classical example of a query where the width can be decreased via rewriting is the path query

$$\varphi(x,y) = \exists z_1 \cdots \exists z_k \big(E(x,z_1) \wedge E(z_1,z_2) \wedge \cdots \wedge E(z_{k-1},z_k) \wedge E(z_k,y)\big),$$

which can be equivalently formulated as the formula

$$\psi(x,y) = \exists z\Big(E(x,z) \wedge \exists x\big(E(z,x) \wedge \exists z(E(x,z) \wedge \cdots \wedge E(z,y))\big)\Big)$$

which uses 3 variables, and is obtained from $\varphi(x,y)$ by pushing in the quantifiers and renaming bounded variables. It is known that one can always compute, from an existential-positive query, an equivalent existential-positive query of minimal width [3, 4]. In fact, the existential-positive queries form a maximal fragment where this is computable: it is folklore that for full first-order logic width minimisation is undecidable, and the same holds true for positive first-order logic (PFO), which is the fragment of first-order logic where negation is disallowed [3].

From the viewpoint of parametrized complexity, width minimisation with a subsequent bottom-up evaluation is essentially *the only* way to achieve tractable query evaluation for existential-positive queries: model-checking for classes of existential-positive queries is fixed-parameter tractable[1] if and only every query in that class is equivalent to one of bounded width [6].

All together, this provides strong motivation for the study of rewriting existential-positive queries to logically equivalent ones of bounded width. Such a rewriting can always be done as follows [3, 18]: First transform the existential-positive formula into prenex normal form. Afterwards translate the quantifier-free part into a positive DNF (a disjunction of conjunctions of non-negated atoms) and push the existential quantifiers over the disjunction to obtain a disjunction of conjunctive queries, which is a UCQ. By minimising this UCQ using standard techniques, one can obtain an existential-positive formula of minimal width. This approach has one crucial drawback: due to the transformation into DNF form, the size of the query might increase exponentially! The main issue addressed in this paper is whether, and when, this exponential increase of the query size is necessary.

[1]Parameterized by the query size and assuming that the arity of each relation is bounded above by a constant.

1.1 Our contribution

Based on the signature[2] and the minimum width k of an equivalent query, we identify all cases where the exponential blow-up for width minimisation can be avoided. In these situations, it is always possible to compile an existential-positive formula into one that has minimum width and where the size is only polynomial in the size of the original query.

In all other cases, we show that there are families of existential-positive formulas φ_n of size n, which are equivalent to existential-positive k-variable formulas, but where any such k-variables formula have size $\Omega(2^{n^\varepsilon})$ for some absolute constant $\varepsilon > 0$. Our exponential lower bounds even hold when compiling formulas into equivalent positive formulas, which can also make use of universal quantification ($\forall$) and can have any finite number of variables. The upper and the matching lower bounds lead to a full characterisation of existential-positive queries where polynomial size compilation to negation-free bounded variable fragments is possible. We formalise the characterisation theorems in Section 4. The core of our lower bound argument builds on a rather special encoding of the clique problem in existential-positive logic. Our formula size lower bounds then follow from a translation from bounded-variable formulas to circuits, in conjunction with a novel use of the well-known lower bound for monotone Boolean circuits [16].

So, we show unconditional lower bounds on the size blow-up incurred by compilations from sentences to bounded-variable fragments, where a compilation is simply a mapping from sentences to sentences which preserves logical equivalence. We also complement these unconditional lower bounds with conditional lower bounds on the size blow-up incurred by compilations from sentences to arbitrary formats which then aid a polynomial-time decision procedure; these conditional lower bounds are proved alongside the unconditional lower bounds, and a summary and discussion thereof is provided in Section 6.

1.2 Related work

Closely related to our main goal of understanding the compilation to bounded variable fragments of existential-positive logic is the work of Bova and the second author of this paper [3], who investigated the computational complexity of deciding whether a given EP formula can be transformed into an equivalent one of width k. They showed that this decision problem is complete for the second level of the polynomial hierarchy. It follows that, unless PTIME = NP, there is no polynomial time algorithm that rewrites an EP query

[2]In this paper, a *signature* (sometimes called *schema*) will always be a (not necessarily finite) set of relation symbols. For completeness, we also allow nullary relation symbols, which are interpreted as Boolean variables.

into one of width k. Moreover, under the reasonable assumption that the polynomial hierarchy does not collapse, it is not possible to compile an EP query into a bounded-width query of size polynomial in the original query. Note that while this result implies a super-polynomial lower bound based on complexity theoretic assumptions, in this paper we are able to prove an explicit $\Omega(2^{n^{1/14}})$ lower bound on formula size that does not rely on any assumptions.

Also related to the main theme of our work is the notion of *succinctness* in finite model theory, which measures how much more succinctly properties can be expressed in one logic compared to another logic. Two logics $\mathcal{L}$ and $\mathcal{L}'$ are usually compared by their expressiveness: $\mathcal{L}$ is at least as expressive as $\mathcal{L}'$ if every property that can be expressed in $\mathcal{L}'$ can also be expressed in $\mathcal{L}$. Succinctness additionally takes the size of a formula into account: $\mathcal{L}$ is at least as succinct as $\mathcal{L}'$ if every property that can be expressed in $\mathcal{L}'$ can also be expressed in $\mathcal{L}$ by a sentence of roughly the same size. Moreover, $\mathcal{L}$ is exponentially more succinct as $\mathcal{L}'$ if in addition there is some $\varphi \in \mathcal{L}$ that expresses a property expressible in $\mathcal{L}'$, but for which the size of every $\psi \in \mathcal{L}'$ that is equivalent to φ is at least exponential in the size of φ.

Contrary to expressiveness and the well-studied complexity measures width, quantifier depth, and number of quantifier alternations, not that much is known about succinctness and the size of formulas. Wilke [22] showed that CTL^+ is exponentially more succinct that CTL and subsequent improvements of this succinctness gap have been obtained by Adler and Immerman [1] as well as Lange [15]. In particular, Adler and Immerman [1] developed a combinatorial method based on Ehrenfeucht-Fraïssé games for proving formula size lower bounds and applied it to prove an optimal succinctness gap between CTL^+ and CTL. Grohe and Schweikardt [14] used a related method to prove that first-order logic is exponentially more succinct than its 3-variable fragment FO^3 by showing that a linear order of length n can be defined by a 4-variable first-order formula of size $O(\log n)$, but requires FO^3 formulas of size $\Omega(\sqrt{n})$. Further succinctness results have been obtained for 2-variable logic on words [21] and for first-order and monadic second-order logic on structures of bounded tree-depth [12]. Here, we can also mention a qualitatively related succinctness result on navigational queries for graphs [19, Theorem 6.3].

Stated in terms of succinctness, our results imply that, for each $k \geq 1$, existential-positive first-order logic (EP) as well as positive first-order logic (PFO) are exponentially more succinct than their respective k-variable fragments EP^k and PFO^k. For $k \geq 4$ it is open, whether full first-order logic (FO) and is exponentially more succinct than its k-variable fragment FO^k.

The technical core of our compilation lower bound relies on a novel use of the well-known connection between descriptive complexity and Boolean circuit complexity. It is folklore that the circuit class DLOGTIME-uniform AC^0 corresponds to $\mathrm{FO}[\leq, +, \times]$, i. e., a property of relational structures can be computed by a uniform family of constant depth circuits, if and only if, it can be expressed in first-order logic with a linear order and the arithmetic predicates $+$ and $\times$ on the universe.

From this connection it follows that circuit lower bounds for AC^0 imply inexpressibility results for first-order logic, even in the presence of arithmetic predicates. Moreover, a fixed k-variable first-order formula can be translated to a family of AC^0 circuits of size $O(n^k)$ that decides the same problem. Hence, more fine-grained lower bounds for AC^0 provide inexpressibility results for the k-variable fragment. In his ground-breaking work [17], Rossman showed an $\omega(n^{k/4})$ AC^0 lower bound for k-clique and used the connection to descriptive complexity in order to show that FO^{k+1} has a strictly stronger expressiveness than FO^k on ordered graphs. Note that while from [14] it follows that FO^4 is exponentially more succinct than FO^3 on ordered structures, for $k \geq 4$ it is open whether there is a succinctness gap between FO^k and FO^{k-1} (even on the class of all structures).

We establish our succinctness results for EP and PFO through circuit lower bounds for *monotone* Boolean circuits and it is crucial for us that, contrary to the general case, there are lower bounds for monotone circuits of arbitrary depth [16]. While these size lower bounds for monotone circuits have been fruitfully applied in related ares, e. g., for query rewriting in ontology-based data access [13], we believe that its application to variable minimisation is a technical contribution might be of independent interest.

2 PRELIMINARIES

2.1 Logic and structures

We formalize our results using relational first-order logic, which we now review briefly.

A signature σ is a set of relation symbols, each of which has an associated arity; we permit each natural number $k \geq 0$ as an arity. We refer to a relation symbol of arity 0 as a *propositional symbol*, and a relation symbol of arity 1 as a *unary symbol*. We refer to a relation symbol that is of arity 2 or greater as an *at least binary symbol*.

A *structure* $\mathbf{B}$ over a signature σ consists of a non-empty set B called the *universe* of the structure, and, for each $R \in \sigma$, a relation $R^{\mathbf{B}}$ over B whose arity is that of R. We generally use the letters $\mathbf{A}, \mathbf{B}, \ldots$ to denote structures, and the corresponding letters $A, B, \ldots$ to denote their respective universes. When $\mathbf{A}$ and $\mathbf{B}$ are structures over the same signature σ, we define their union, denoted by $\mathbf{A} \cup \mathbf{B}$, as the structure with universe $A \cup B$ and where, for each relation symbol $R \in \sigma$, it holds that $R^{\mathbf{A} \cup \mathbf{B}} = R^{\mathbf{A}} \cup R^{\mathbf{B}}$.

An *atom* (over signature σ) is an equality of variables $u = v$ or a predicate application $R(v_1, \ldots, v_r)$ where $R \in \sigma$ is a relation symbol of arity r, and the v_i are variables. A predicate application $P()$ consisting of a relation symbol P of arity 0 is referred to as a *propositional atom*. A *formula* (over signature σ) is built from atoms (over σ), negation ($\neg$), conjunction ($\wedge$), disjunction ($\vee$), universal quantification ($\forall$), and existential quantification ($\exists$). We will sometimes use $\top$ and $\bot$ to denote the values true and false, respectively. We use free(φ) to denote the set of free variables of a formula φ; a *sentence* is a formula having no free variables.

When φ is a formula and the notation $\varphi(x_1, \ldots, x_k)$ is used, it is assumed that the free variables of φ are contained in $\{x_1, \ldots, x_k\}$. When $\varphi(x_1, \ldots, x_k)$ is a formula and $\mathbf{B}$ is a structure, we use the notation $\varphi(\mathbf{B})$ to denote the set of all tuples $(b_1, \ldots, b_k) \in B^k$ such that $\mathbf{B}, b_1, \ldots, b_k \models \varphi$.

2.2 Fragments and compilation between logics

We define a *primitive positive formula* to be a formula built from atoms, conjunction, and existential quantification. We define an *existential-positive formula* to be a formula built from atoms, conjunction, disjunction, and existential quantification. We define a *positive first-order formula* to be a formula that does not use negation. We refer to an existential-positive formula that is a sentence as an *existential-positive sentence*, and extend this convention to define primitive positive sentences, positive first-order sentences, etc. correspondingly.

We introduce the following notation, for each $k \geq 1$.

- Let PP^k denote the class containing each primitive positive sentence that uses at most k variables.
- Let $\approx\text{PP}^k$ denote the class containing each primitive positive sentence that is logically equivalent to a sentence in PP^k.
- Let EP^k denote the class containing each existential-positive sentence that uses at most k variables.
- Let $\approx\text{EP}^k$ denote the class containing each existential-positive sentence that is logically equivalent to a sentence in EP^k.
- Let PFO^k denote the class containing each positive first-order sentence that uses at most k variables.

By a sentence that *uses at most k variables*, we mean that when all variables occurring in the sentence are placed into a set, that set has size k or less. For each of these fragments, when σ is a signature, we add σ as a subscript to restrict to sentences over σ, so for example, EP^k_σ denotes the class of all sentences in EP^k that are over signature σ.

Proposition 2.1. *When σ is a signature that consists only of propositional symbols and unary symbols, it holds that every existential-positive sentence over σ is in $\approx\text{EP}^1_\sigma$.*

Proof. This follows directly from the argument in the first paragraph of [6, Proof of Theorem 4.3]. □

The *size* of a formula ψ, denoted by $\|\psi\|$, is defined inductively: $\|\alpha\| = 1$ when α is an atom; $\|\neg\varphi\| = \|\varphi\| + 1$; $\|\varphi \vee \psi\|$ and $\|\varphi \wedge \psi\|$ are defined as $\|\varphi\| + \|\psi\| + 1$; and $\|\exists v\varphi\|$ and $\|\forall v\varphi\|$ are defined as $\|\varphi\| + 1$. So, the size of a formula is essentially the number of atom occurrences plus the number of occurrences of connectives and quantifiers.

When $\mathcal{L}$ and $\mathcal{L}'$ are logics, a *compilation* from $\mathcal{L}$ to $\mathcal{L}'$ is a mapping $c : \mathcal{L} \to \mathcal{L}'$ such that for each $\varphi \in \mathcal{L}$, it holds that φ and $c(\varphi)$ are logically equivalent. The *size* of a compilation c is the function $f : \mathbb{N} \to \mathbb{N}$ defined by

$$f(n) = \max\{\|c(\varphi)\| \mid \varphi \in \mathcal{L}, \|\varphi\| = n\}.$$

2.3 Parameterized complexity and compilation

We present the framework that we will use for ruling out compilations to arbitrary polynomial-size formats. The framework given here comes from work [7, 8] of the second author.

Here, we use PTIME to denote the class of polynomial-time computable languages, and fPTIME to denote the class of polynomial-time computable functions.

By a *parameterization*, we refer to a polynomial-time computable map from Σ^* to Σ^*. Relative to a parameterization $\kappa : \Sigma^* \to \Sigma^*$, we say that $\kappa(x)$ is the *parameter* of the string x. It is typical in the literature to define a parameterization to be a map from Σ^* to $\mathbb{N}$; however, in the present article we want to apply compilation functions to parameters represented as strings and discuss the *length* of the results. In particular, we will study query evaluation, and the parameter of each instance will be the query to be evaluated.

A *parameterized problem* is a pair (Q, κ) consisting of a language Q and a parameterization κ. The parameterized problems that will be of focal study in this article are defined as follows.

Definition 2.2. When $\mathcal{L}$ is a logic, we define QueryEval($\mathcal{L}$) to be the parameterized problem (Q, κ) whose language Q is

$$\{(\varphi, \mathbf{B}) \mid \varphi \in \mathcal{L}, \mathbf{B} \models \varphi\}$$

and where $\kappa(\varphi, \mathbf{B}) = \varphi$.

A function $c : \Sigma^* \to \Sigma^*$ is said to be *polynomial length* if there exists a polynomial $\ell : \mathbb{N} \to \mathbb{N}$ such that for each $x \in \Sigma^*$, it holds that $|c(x)| \leq \ell(|x|)$. A function $g : \Sigma^* \to \Sigma^*$ is *poly-compilable* with respect to a parameterization κ if there exist $f \in$ fPTIME and a computable, polynomial length function $c : \Sigma^* \to \Sigma^*$ such that (for each $x \in \Sigma^*$) it holds that $g(x) = f(c(\kappa(x)), x)$.

We now present the parameterized complexity classes that will be used. Let us say that a parameterized problem (Q, κ) is *poly-compilable to* C if there exists a function $g : \Sigma^* \to \Sigma^*$ that is poly-compilable (with respect to κ) and a language $Q' \in C$ such that (for each $x \in \Sigma^*$) $x \in Q \Leftrightarrow g(x) \in Q'$. We define poly-comp-PTIME to be the class of parameterized problems that contains each parameterized problem that is poly-compilable to PTIME; and, we define poly-comp-NP to be the class of parameterized problems that contains each parameterized problem that is poly-compilable to NP. We define chopped-NP to be the class of parameterized problems that contains each parameterized problem (Q, κ) that is in poly-comp-NP via a poly-compilable function g for which there exists a polynomial $p : \mathbb{N} \to \mathbb{N}$ such that (for each $x \in \Sigma^*$) $|g(x)| \leq p(|\kappa(x)|)$.

We will use the following notion of reduction. We say that a parameterized problem (Q, κ) *poly-comp reduces* to another parameterized problem (Q', κ') if there exists a function $g : \Sigma^* \to \Sigma^*$ that is poly-compilable with respect to κ and a poly-length, computable function $s : \Sigma^* \to \wp_{\text{fin}}(\Sigma^*)$ such that (for each $x \in \Sigma^*$) it holds that $x \in Q \Leftrightarrow g(x) \in Q'$ and that $\kappa'(g(x)) \in s(\kappa(x))$. Here, when T is a set, we use $\wp_{\text{fin}}(T)$ to denote the power set of T restricted to finite sets, that is, the set $\{S \subseteq T \mid S \text{ is finite}\}$. We consider a parameterized problem to be chopped-NP-hard if every problem in chopped-NP poly-comp reduces to it.

Theorem 2.3. *[7, 8, Theorem 13] Poly-comp reducibility is transitive.*

We will establish chopped-NP-hardness results which provide evidence for non-containment in the parameterized class poly-comp-PTIME, as the following theorem shows.

Theorem 2.4. *(follows directly from [7, 8, Proposition 9 and Theorem 19]) A problem that is* chopped-NP-*hard is not contained in the class* poly-comp-PTIME, *unless the polynomial hierarchy collapses.*

In order to establish chopped-NP-hardness results, we will give reductions from the following problem. Let CLIQUE denote the clique problem, that is, the set of pairs (G, k) such that G is an undirected graph, $k \geq 1$, and G contains a clique of size k. Define ν-CLIQUE to be the parameterized problem (CLIQUE, ν) where ν is the parameterization such that $\nu(G, k)$ is equal to the number of vertices in G, expressed in unary; that is, $\nu(G, k) = 1^n$, where n is the number of vertices in G.

Theorem 2.5. *The parameterized problem* ν-CLIQUE *is* chopped-NP-*hard.*

Proof. By the argument in [8, Proof of Theorem 30], the parameterized problems ν-CLIQUE and (CLIQUE, len) are poly-comp interreducible; here, len denotes the parameterization that, given a string, returns the string's length in unary (that is, given x, returns $1^{|x|}$). The parameterized problem (CLIQUE, len) is chopped-NP-hard by [7, 8, Proposition 16]. □

3 UPPER BOUNDS

3.1 General upper bound

We establish the following general single-exponential upper bound on the length of compiling an existential-positive formula to the bounded-variable fragment.

Theorem 3.1. *(General upper bound) There exists a polynomial q such that for each $k \geq 1$, there is a compilation c from $\approx\mathrm{EP}^k$ to EP^k behaving as follows: when $\varphi \in \approx\mathrm{EP}^k$ is a sentence with $\|\varphi\| = n$, it holds that $\|c(\varphi)\| \leq 2^n q(n)$.*

To establish Theorem 3.1, we in fact prove the following theorem, which provides a more refined upper bound in the case of prenex sentences.

Theorem 3.2. *(General upper bound on prenex sentences) There exists a polynomial q such that for each $k \geq 1$, there is a compilation c from $\approx\mathrm{EP}^k$ to EP^k behaving as follows: when $\varphi \in \approx\mathrm{EP}^k$ is a sentence in prenex normal form with m occurrences of non-propositional atoms and $\|\varphi\| = n$, it holds that $\|c(\varphi)\| \leq 2^m q(n)$.*

Theorem 3.2 implies Theorem 3.1: any first-order formula can converted to prenex normal form via syntactic transformations that do not change its size; and, for any first-order formula, the number of occurrences of non-propositional atoms is bounded above by the formula's size.

Before proving Theorem 3.2, we establish a lemma. For any set of first-order formulas Φ, we let real(Φ) be the set of all $\Phi' \subseteq \Phi$ such that there is an interpretation I with $I \models \psi \iff \psi \in \Phi'$ for all $\psi \in \Phi$.

Lemma 3.3. *There exists a polynomial p such that, when φ is a formula that is a positive Boolean combination of propositional atoms and of positive formulas drawn from a finite set Φ, the formula φ is logically equivalent to a formula φ' such that*

$$\|\varphi'\| \leq |\operatorname{real}(\Phi)| \cdot p(\|\varphi\|),$$

and where φ' has the form

$$\bigvee_{\Phi' \in \operatorname{real}(\Phi)} (\varphi_{\Phi'} \wedge \bigwedge_{\psi \in \Phi'} \psi),$$

where each $\varphi_{\Phi'}$ is a positive Boolean combination of propositional atoms of size $O(\|\varphi\|)$.

Proof. For any $\Phi' \in \operatorname{real}(\Phi)$ let $\varphi_{\Phi'}$ be the formula obtained from φ by replacing every subformula in Φ' with $\top$ and every subformula in $\Phi \setminus \Phi'$ with $\bot$. We need to show that φ and φ' are equivalent. Let I be an interpretation that satisfies φ and let $\Phi' \subseteq \Phi$ be the set of formulas satisfied by

I. It follows from the definition that I satisfies $\varphi_{\Phi'} \wedge \bigwedge_{\psi \in \Phi'} \psi$ and hence φ'. For the other direction assume that I satisfies φ' and let $\Phi' \subseteq \Phi$ be such that I satisfies the disjunct $\varphi_{\Phi'} \wedge \bigwedge_{\psi \in \Phi'} \psi$. Since φ is a positive in the stated sense, it follows that $I \models \varphi_{\Phi''}$ where $\Phi'' \supseteq \Phi'$ contains exactly those formulas from Φ that are satisfied by I. By the definition of $\varphi_{\Phi''}$ it therefore holds that $I \models \varphi$. □

Let us remark that the just-given lemma is effective when the set Φ consists of primitive positive formulas, in the sense that φ' can be computed from φ. This is because entailment on primitive positive formulas is decidable, so the set real(Φ) can be computed from Φ.

Proof of Theorem 3.2. The compilation c is described as follows. Let $\varphi = \exists x_1 \dots \exists x_t \varphi^-$ be an $\approx$EP^k-sentence in prenex normal form and let Φ be the set whose elements are all non-propositional atoms that occur in φ^-. We have $|\Phi| \leq m$, so $|\operatorname{real}(\Phi)| \leq 2^m$. Apply Lemma 3.3 to the quantifier-free part φ^- of φ; one obtains a sentence of the form

$$\exists x_1 \dots \exists x_t (\bigvee_{i=1}^{r} \varphi^i)$$

and having size at most $2^m \cdot p(||\varphi||)$, where p is the polynomial from Lemma 3.3; this sentence is logically equivalent to $\bigvee_{i=1}^{r} \exists x_1 \dots \exists x_t \varphi^i$. Here, due to our choice of Φ and the statement of Lemma 3.3, each φ^i is a conjunction that contains (as a conjunct) up to one positive Boolean combination of propositional atoms, and otherwise contains non-propositional atoms. Each such φ^i can be rewritten, in a way that preserves logical equivalence, so that it contains no equalities; this is done by taking an equality $u = v$, replacing each instance of v with u, and then deleting the equality.

Now rewrite this last sentence so that it is *irredundant* in the sense that for no distinct i, j does it hold that $\exists x_1 \dots \exists x_t \varphi^i$ entails $\exists x_1 \dots \exists x_t \varphi^j$; this can be done simply by removing any disjunct $\exists x_1 \dots \exists x_t \varphi^i$ such that the entailment holds. Now, it is known from [3, Lemma 4] and from the assumption that $\varphi \in \approx$EP^k that each such disjunct of the irredundant sentence (neglecting the possible conjunct that is a positive Boolean of propositional atoms) is in $\approx$PP^k; each sentence in $\approx$PP^k can be converted to a sentence in PP^k without increasing its size [11]. This yields the theorem, for ever since the bound of $2^m \cdot p(||\varphi||)$ was computed, the transformations that have been applied were to duplicate the quantifier prefix, remove disjuncts, and perform the conversions from $\approx$PP^k to PP^k. □

3.2 The case of 1 variable

Theorem 3.2 gave a general exponential upper bound on the size of a compilation from $\approx$EP^k to EP^k. Now we turn to the 1-variable case. We provide two upper bounds: the first one in the case where the signature σ is finite and the second when σ consists of at most one non-propositional symbol, and any number of propositional symbols (even infinitely many).

Lemma 3.4. *Let σ be a finite signature. There exists a compilation c from $\approx$EP^1 to EP^1 with $\|c(\varphi)\| = O(2^{2^{\|\sigma\|}})$.*

Proof. We first make an observation. For any structure $\mathbf{B}$, define $\mathbf{B}^-$ to be the structure with the same universe as $\mathbf{B}$ and where

$$R^{\mathbf{B}^-} = R^{\mathbf{B}} \cap \{(b, \dots, b) \mid b \in B\}$$

for each relation symbol R. Then, when $\psi \in \approx$EP^1, it holds that $\mathbf{B} \models \psi$ if and only if $\mathbf{B}^- \models \psi$. It is sufficient to argue this for all $\psi \in$ EP^1; this holds because each atom $R(v_1, \dots, v_k)$ in such a ψ has $v_1 = \dots = v_k$.

We next turn to prove the theorem. Let $\varphi \in \approx$EP^1 be as described, and let us assume that φ is in prenex form. Define $\varphi^=$ to be the rewriting of φ where each atom $R(v_1, \dots, v_k)$ is replaced with

$$R(v_1, \dots, v_1) \wedge (v_1 = v_2) \wedge (v_2 = v_3) \wedge \dots \wedge (v_{k-1} = v_k).$$

We have, for any structure $\mathbf{B}$:

$$\mathbf{B} \models \varphi \Leftrightarrow \mathbf{B}^- \models \varphi \Leftrightarrow \mathbf{B}^- \models \varphi^= \Leftrightarrow \mathbf{B} \models \varphi^=.$$

Here, the first and last equivalences follow from the observation. We conclude that φ and $\varphi^=$ are logically equivalent.

Let $\exists x_1 \dots \exists x_t$ be the quantifier prefix of φ and $\varphi^=$, and let $R_1, \dots, R_s$ be the non-propositional symbols that appear in φ and $\varphi^=$. Observe that the quantifier-free part of $\varphi^=$ is a positive Boolean combination of propositional atoms, atomic formulas $R(x_i, \dots, x_i)$ and equalities $x_i = x_j$.

First, we transform this quantifier free part to DNF form. After doing so, the quantification $\exists x_1 \dots \exists x_t$ may be pushed in so that the result is a disjunction $\varphi^\vee$ of formulas each having the form $\exists x_1 \dots \exists x_t \bigwedge_{\psi \in \Phi'} \psi$; let us now refer here to such a formula as a disjunct.

Consider each disjunct $\exists x_1 \dots \exists x_t \bigwedge_{\psi \in \Phi} \psi$. One may eliminate each variable equality $x_i = x_j$ by replacing every instance of x_j with x_i. Then, by grouping together conjuncts that refer to the same variable, it can be seen that such a formula is logically equivalent to a conjunction of formulas each having the form $\theta_\tau = \exists x \bigwedge_{R \in \tau} R(x, \dots, x)$, where $\tau \subseteq \sigma$. Overall, we get a formula that is a disjunction of conjunctions of formulas θ_τ. It follows that the size of the formula is bounded by $2^{2^{O(\|\sigma\|)}}$. □

Lemma 3.5. *Let σ be a signature containing at most one non-propositional symbol. There exists a compilation c from $\approx$EP^1 to EP^1 with $\|c(\varphi)\| = \|\varphi\|$.*

Proof. The compilation is fairly simple: we just replace every variable in φ by x. It remains to prove that this is correct. If σ contains only propositional symbols, then the lemma is trivial. Otherwise, let R be the non-propositional symbol in σ and $\mathbf{B}$ an arbitrary σ-structure. We define the σ-structure $\mathbf{B}^-$ over the singleton universe $B^- = \{1\}$ by interpreting the propositional symbols as in $\mathbf{B}$ and defining $R^{\mathbf{B}^-} = \{(1,\ldots,1)\}$ if there is an $b \in B$ with $(b,\ldots,b) \in R^{\mathbf{B}}$ and $R^{\mathbf{B}^-} = \emptyset$ otherwise. It is not hard to verify that for every $\psi \in \mathrm{EP}^1$ it holds that $\mathbf{B} \models \psi \Leftrightarrow \mathbf{B}^- \models \psi$ and hence the same holds true for every $\psi \in {\approx}\mathrm{EP}^1$. Moreover, since $\mathbf{B}^-$ is a structure with singleton universe, it holds that $\mathbf{B}^- \models \varphi \Leftrightarrow \mathbf{B}^- \models c(\varphi)$. Thus, for any structure $\mathbf{B}$ we have

$$\mathbf{B} \models \varphi \Leftrightarrow \mathbf{B}^- \models \varphi \Leftrightarrow \mathbf{B}^- \models c(\varphi) \Leftrightarrow \mathbf{B} \models c(\varphi),$$

showing that φ and $c(\varphi)$ are logically equivalent. □

4 CLASSIFICATION THEOREMS

We state our classification theorems, and give proofs that make forward references to the next section, which contain the lower bounds; in particular, these proofs contain forward references to Theorems 5.3 and 5.5.

THEOREM 4.1. *Let σ be a signature.*

- *If σ is finite or contains at most one non-propositional symbol, then there exists a polynomial-size compilation from ${\approx}\mathrm{EP}^1_\sigma$ to EP^1_σ.*
- *Otherwise, for all $\ell \geq 1$, there exists $\varepsilon > 0$ such that any compilation from ${\approx}\mathrm{EP}^1_\sigma$ to PFO^ℓ_σ has size $\Omega(2^{n^\varepsilon})$.*

PROOF. The upper bound follows from Lemma 3.4 and Lemma 3.5. The lower bound follows from Theorem 5.3. □

THEOREM 4.2. *Let $k \geq 2$, and let σ be a signature.*

- *If σ contains only propositional and unary symbols and, in addition, is either finite or contains at most one unary symbol, then there exists a polynomial-size compilation from ${\approx}\mathrm{EP}^k_\sigma$ to EP^k_σ.*
- *Otherwise, for all $\ell \geq k$, there exists $\varepsilon > 0$ such that any compilation from ${\approx}\mathrm{EP}^k_\sigma$ to PFO^ℓ_σ has size $\Omega(2^{n^\varepsilon})$.*

PROOF. If the signature contains no symbols of arity strictly larger than one, then by Proposition 2.1 we have that ${\approx}\mathrm{EP}^k_\sigma$ and ${\approx}\mathrm{EP}^1_\sigma$ are equal. Hence, in this case the upper as well as the lower bounds immediately follow from Theorem 4.1. If σ contains one at least binary symbol, then the lower bound follows from Theorem 5.5. □

5 LOWER BOUNDS

On a high level, our unconditional lower bounds on compilations to bounded-variable positive logics will be based on previously established circuit lower bounds in conjunction with the fact (given soon as Lemma 5.1) that formulas can be translated to circuits that, in a way to be made precise, preserves formula semantics. As we establish these unconditional lower bounds, we also establish hardness results in the parameter compilation framework presented in Section 2.3; in particular, we establish chopped-NP-hardness results.

A monotone Boolean circuit C_N of size m is defined to be a directed acyclic graph over m vertices (the gates) with a designated output gate, N sources (the inputs), and where every non-source vertex is labelled with either $\wedge$ or $\vee$. The circuit naturally computes a monotone function $C_N\colon \{0,1\}^N \to \{0,1\}$. Assume σ to be a finite signature and $n \geq 1$; a monotone Boolean circuit C^σ_n that computes a function over all σ-structures $\mathbf{A}$ with universe $A = [n]$ is a monotone Boolean circuit C_N that contains, for every pair consisting of an r-ary relation symbol R and an r-tuple $(v_1,\ldots,v_r) \in [n]^r$, one input gate that indicates whether $(v_1,\ldots,v_r) \in R^{\mathbf{A}}$. We consider the *size* of a monotone Boolean circuit to be the number of gates that it contains.

In what follows, we use the term *k-ary signature* to refer to a signature wherein all relation symbols have arity k or less.

LEMMA 5.1. *(from formulas to circuits) For all $n, k \geq 1$, finite k-ary signatures σ and $\varphi \in \mathrm{PFO}^k_\sigma$ there exists a monotone circuit C^σ_n of size at most $(\|\varphi\| + \|\sigma\|)n^k$ that receives a σ-structure $\mathbf{A}$ with universe $A = [n]$ as input and decides whether $\mathbf{A} \models \varphi$.*

PROOF. The monotone circuit contains for every subformula $\psi(x_1,\ldots,x_k)$ of φ and every tuple $\mathbf{v} = (v_1,\ldots,v_k) \in [n]^k$ a gate $g^\psi_{\mathbf{v}}$ that computes whether $\mathbf{A}, \mathbf{v} \models \psi$. The construction of the circuit follows the inductive definition of φ:

- If $\psi = R(x'_1,\ldots,x'_r)$ is an atom, then $g_{\psi,\mathbf{v}}$ is defined to be the input gate for the pair consisting of R and the arity r subtuple $\mathbf{v}' \subseteq \mathbf{v}$ corresponding to $x'_1,\ldots,x'_r$.
- If $\psi = \psi_1 * \psi_2$ for $* \in \{\wedge,\vee\}$, then $g_{\psi,\mathbf{v}}$ is an $*$-gate with inputs $g_{\psi_1,\mathbf{v}}$ and $g_{\psi_2,\mathbf{v}}$.
- Finally, we let $\psi = \exists x_i \psi'$ ($\psi = \forall x_i \psi'$) and denote by $\mathbf{v}_w$ the k-tuple $(v_1,\ldots,v_{i-1},w,v_{i+1},\ldots,v_k)$. The gate $g_{\psi,\mathbf{v}}$ is an $\vee$-gate ($\wedge$-gate) with n inputs $g_{\psi',\mathbf{v}_w}$ for $w \in [n]$.

It is straightforward to verify that (for any $\mathbf{v}$) the gate $g_{\varphi,\mathbf{v}}$ decides whether $\mathbf{A} \models \varphi$. By construction, the circuit has $\sum_{R\in\sigma} n^{\mathrm{ar}(R)}$ input gates and at most $\|\varphi\|n^k$ non-input gates. □

We will make use of the following size lower bound for monotone circuits computing the clique function.

THEOREM 5.2 ([2]). *Let $\sigma = \{E\}$ be the signature of graphs and $k(n) = \lfloor \frac{1}{4}(n/\log n)^{2/3} \rfloor$. The size of monotone circuits C^σ_n that decide $k(n)$-clique on n-vertex graphs is lower bounded by $2^{\Omega((n/\log n)^{1/3})}$.*

5.1 Infinite signatures with two distinct non-propositional symbols

Theorem 5.3. *If σ is an infinite signature that contains two distinct non-propositional symbols, then for each $\ell \geq 1$, any compilation from* $\approx\mathrm{EP}^1_\sigma$ *to* PFO^ℓ_σ *has size* $\Omega(2^{N^{1/14}})$.

Proof. We prove this theorem under the assumption that σ contains infinitely many propositional symbols. This suffices, since when R is a non-propositional symbol of arity r, we may use the formula $\exists x R(x, \ldots, x)$ to simulate a propositional atom. We also make the assumption that σ contains two distinct unary symbols S_0 and S_1; this is justified, for if T_0 and T_1 are distinct non-propositional symbols, one may use $T_0(v, \ldots, v)$ and $T_1(v, \ldots, v)$ to simulate the atoms $S_0(v)$ and $S_1(v)$, respectively.

For $i, j \in \mathbb{N}$ we let P_{ij} be a propositional symbol in σ and use S_0 and S_1 to denote two distinct unary symbols in σ. Let

$$\sigma_n = \{P_{ij} \mid i, j \in [n]\} \cup \{S_0, S_1\}.$$

We have that $\sigma_n \subseteq \sigma$.

Suppose that $\mathbf{G}$ is a graph on $n = 2^d$ vertices $v_1, \ldots, v_n$ for some $d \in \mathbb{N}$. We let $\mathbf{A_G}$ be the σ-structure with universe $A_\mathbf{G} = \{0, 1\}$, $S_0^\mathbf{A} = \{0\}$, $S_1^\mathbf{A} = \{1\}$,

$$P_{ij}^\mathbf{A} = \begin{cases} \{\emptyset\}, \text{ if } (v_i, v_j) \in E^\mathbf{G} \\ \emptyset, \text{ else,} \end{cases} \tag{1}$$

for all $i, j \in [n]$, and $R^\mathbf{A} = \emptyset$ for all $R \in \sigma \setminus \sigma_n$.

Now we define an EP^k_σ sentence $\varphi_{n,k}$, which is satisfied by $\mathbf{A_G}$ if and only if $\mathbf{G}$ contains a k-clique. For every $i \in [n]$ we write $\langle i \rangle = (b_1, \ldots, b_d) \in \{0, 1\}^d$ to denote the d-bit binary encoding of the number $i - 1$. We define

$$\varphi_{n,k} = \exists x_1^1 \cdots \exists x_1^d \;\; \exists x_2^1 \cdots \exists x_2^d \;\; \cdots \;\; \exists x_k^d$$
$$\bigwedge_{\substack{i,j\in[n] \\ s,t\in[k] \\ s\neq t}} \Big(P_{ij} \vee \bigvee_{\substack{(b_1,\ldots,b_d) \\ \in\{0,1\}^d\setminus\{\langle i\rangle\}}} \bigwedge_{r\in[d]} S_{b_r}(x_s^r) \vee \bigvee_{\substack{(b_1,\ldots,b_d) \\ \in\{0,1\}^d\setminus\{\langle j\rangle\}}} \bigwedge_{r\in[d]} S_{b_r}(x_t^r)\Big).$$

The existential quantifiers guess the bit encoding of k vertices and the quantifier-free part ensures that they form a clique. In particular, the subformula

$$\bigvee_{\substack{(b_1,\ldots,b_d) \\ \in\{0,1\}^d\setminus\{\langle i\rangle\}}} \bigwedge_{r\in[d]} S_{b_r}(x_s^r)$$

is true if and only if the sth guessed vertex is not i; precisely, it is true if and only if the bits $x_s^1, \ldots, x_s^d$ are not equal to $\langle i \rangle$. Analogously, the subformula

$$\bigvee_{\substack{(b_1,\ldots,b_d) \\ \in\{0,1\}^d\setminus\{\langle j\rangle\}}} \bigwedge_{r\in[d]} S_{b_r}(x_t^r)$$

is true if and only if the tth guessed vertex is not j; precisely, it is true if and only if the bits $x_t^1, \ldots, x_t^d$ are not equal to $\langle j \rangle$. Hence, the quantifier-free part of $\varphi_{n,k}$ is true if and only if for all distinct $s, t \in [k]$, letting i' and j' denote the sth and tth guessed vertices, $P_{i'j'}$ holds; that is, if and only if the guessed vertices form a clique in $\mathbf{G}$.

We have that $\varphi_{n,k} \in \approx\mathrm{EP}^1_\sigma$ by Proposition 2.1. Let $\psi_{n,k}$ be an PFO^ℓ_σ sentence that is equivalent to $\varphi_{n,k}$. By Lemma 5.1 there exists a monotone Boolean circuit C_n^σ having size $O(\|\psi_{n,k}\| n^\ell)$ that evaluates $\psi_{n,k}$ on σ_n-structures over an n-element universe. By hard-coding all inputs that are different from F_{ij}, we obtain a monotone circuit $C_n^{\{E\}}$ that receives the adjacency matrix of an n-vertex graph $\mathbf{G}$ and decides whether $\mathbf{A_G}$ satisfies $\psi_{n,k}$. Since this is the case if and only if $\mathbf{G}$ contains a k-clique, we can choose $k = \lfloor \frac{1}{4}(n/\log n)^{2/3} \rfloor$ and obtain from Theorem 5.2 that C_n^σ has size $2^{\Omega((n/\log n)^{1/3})}$. It follows that $\|\psi_{n,k}\|$ is lower bounded by $2^{\Omega((n/\log n)^{1/3} - \ell \log n)}$. The Theorem follows from the observation that $N = \|\varphi\| = O(k^2 n^3 \log n) = O(n^{13/3})$. □

Theorem 5.4. *When σ is an infinite signature that contains two distinct non-propositional symbols, the parameterized problem*

$$\mathrm{QueryEval}(\approx\mathrm{EP}^1_\sigma)$$

is chopped-NP*-hard.*

Proof. We present a poly-comp reduction (g, s) from the problem v-CLIQUE; this suffices by Theorem 2.5 and Theorem 2.3. The mapping g, given an instance $(\mathbf{G}, k)$ of CLIQUE, outputs the pair $(\varphi_{n,k}, \mathbf{A_G})$ as defined in the proof of Theorem 5.3; here, n is the number of vertices in G. (We define g only on well-formed instances, in particular, instances with $k \leq n$; it is straightforwardly verified that this suffices.) This mapping is clearly polynomial-time computable; also, by the argumentation in the proof of Theorem 5.3, it holds that $(\mathbf{G}, k)$ is a yes instance of CLIQUE if and only if $\mathbf{A_G} \models \varphi_{n,k}$ if and only if $(\varphi_{n,k}, \mathbf{A_G})$ is a yes instance of $\mathrm{QueryEval}(\approx\mathrm{EP}^1_\sigma)$. The mapping s is defined by $s(n) = \{\varphi_{n,i} \mid i \leq n\}$. For all instances (G, k), we then have that $\varphi_{n,k} \in s(n)$. □

5.2 Signatures having an at least binary symbol

Theorem 5.5. *If a signature σ contains an at least binary symbol, then for each $\ell \geq 2$, there exists $\varepsilon > 0$ such that any compilation from* $\approx\mathrm{EP}^2_\sigma$ *to* PFO^ℓ_σ *has size* $\Omega(2^{n^\varepsilon})$.

We let E be a binary symbol, and prove the theorem in the case that $\sigma = \{E\}$; this suffices, since a higher arity symbol can simulate a binary symbol.

For each $n \geq 1$ and each $i \in [n]$, we define a structure $\mathbf{D}_{i,n}$ as follows. The universe $D_{i,n}$ is equal to

$$\{d\} \cup \{p_i^1, \ldots, p_i^i\} \cup \{q_i^{i-1}, q_i^i, \ldots, q_i^{n+1}\},$$

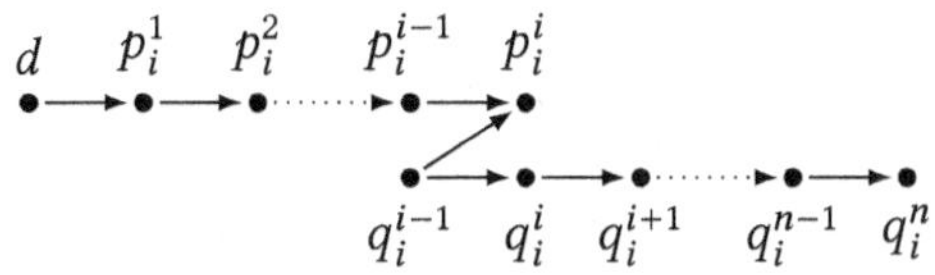

Figure 1: Structure $\mathbf{D}_{i,n}$

and $E^{\mathbf{D}_{i,n}}$ is defined as

$$\{(d, p_i^1)\} \cup \{(p_i^k, p_i^{k+1}) \mid k = 1, \ldots, i-1\} \cup$$
$$\{(q_i^{i-1}, p_i^i)\} \cup \{(q_i^k, q_i^{k+1}) \mid k = i-1, \ldots, n\}.$$

We refer the reader to the figure for a visualization of this structure.

Observe that for distinct values $i, i' \in [n]$, the only element in both of the universes $D_{i,n}$, $D_{i',n}$ is d, that is, we have $D_{i,n} \cap D_{i',n} = \{d\}$. For a non-empty subset $I \subseteq [n]$, let us use $\mathbf{D}_{I,n}$ to denote $\cup_{i \in I} \mathbf{D}_{i,n}$. In what follows, we will overload $\mathbb{N}$, and use it to denote the structure whose universe is the set $\mathbb{N}$ of natural numbers and where $E^{\mathbb{N}} = \{(k, k+1) \mid k \in \mathbb{N}\}$.

The following fact is straightforward to verify.

Proposition 5.6. *Let $n \geq 1$, and let $I \subseteq [n]$ be non-empty. For each $m \in \mathbb{N}$, there is a unique homomorphism h from $\mathbf{D}_{I,n}$ to $\mathbb{N}$ such that $h(d) = m$, namely, the homomorphism sending each element of the form p_i^k or q_i^k to $m + k$.*

We now establish a lemma showing that homomorphisms between certain structures of the described form must fix the element d.

Lemma 5.7. *Let $n \geq 1$, let $i \in [n]$, and let $J \subseteq [n]$ be non-empty. If there exists a homomorphism g from $\mathbf{D}_{i,n}$ to $\mathbf{D}_{J,n}$, then $g(d) = d$.*

Proof. Let h be the unique homomorphism (given by Proposition 5.6) from $\mathbf{D}_{J,n}$ to $\mathbb{N}$ such that $h(d) = 0$; observe that the image of h is $\{0, \ldots, n\}$, and that d is the only element sent to 0 by h. Assume for a contradiction that g is a homomorphism from $\mathbf{D}_{i,n}$ to $\mathbf{D}_{J,n}$ such that $g(d)$ is not equal to d. Set $m = h(g(d))$; it then holds that $m > 0$. But the composition $h(g)$ is a homomorphism from $\mathbf{D}_{i,n}$ to $\mathbb{N}$ sending d to m so by the description given by Proposition 5.6, the image of this homomorphism $h(g)$ contains $m + n$, which is strictly greater than n. This contradicts that the image of h is $\{0, \ldots, n\}$. □

Let $n \geq 1$. For each $i \in [n]$, we define the formula $\widetilde{\theta_{i,n}}(d)$ as $\exists p_i^1 \ldots \exists p_i^i \exists q_i^{i-1} \ldots \exists q_i^{n+1} \bigwedge_{(u,v) \in E^{\mathbf{D}_{i,n}}} E(u, v)$. We have that $\widetilde{\theta_{i,n}}(d)$ is logically equivalent to a two-variable sentence $\theta_{i,n}(d) \in \mathrm{PP}^2$ of the same size; indeed, since the formula $\widetilde{\theta_{i,n}}(d)$ is derived from the structure $\mathbf{D}_{i,n}$ which has a path-like shape, a rewriting similar to that performed in the introduction (Section 1) for the path query can be performed to obtain $\theta_{i,n}(d)$ from $\widetilde{\theta_{i,n}}(d)$.

For each non-empty $I \subseteq [n]$, we define $\theta_{I,n}(d)$ to be the conjunction $\bigwedge_{i \in I} \theta_{i,n}$. It is well-known and straightforward to verify that, for any structure $\mathbf{B}$, it holds that $b \in \theta_{i,n}(\mathbf{B})$ if and only if there exists a homomorphism h from $\mathbf{D}_{i,n}$ to $\mathbf{B}$ such that $h(d) = b$. Consequently, it holds that $b \in \theta_{I,n}(\mathbf{B})$ if and only if for every $i \in I$, there exists a homomorphism h from $\mathbf{D}_{i,n}$ to $\mathbf{B}$ such that $h(d) = b$.

The following lemma is thus directly implied by Lemma 5.7.

Lemma 5.8. *Let $n \geq 1$, and let $I, J \subseteq [n]$ be non-empty. It holds that $\theta_{I,n}(\mathbf{D}_{J,n})$ is equal to $\{d\}$ or $\emptyset$.*

Whereas the just-given lemma gives us information about the possible values of $\theta_{I,n}(\mathbf{D}_{J,n})$, the following lemma precisely characterizes this evaluation in terms of how I and J are related.

Lemma 5.9. *Let $n \geq 1$, and let $I, J \subseteq [n]$ be non-empty. It holds that $\theta_{I,n}(\mathbf{D}_{J,n})$ is equal to $\{d\}$ if $I \subseteq J$, and is equal to $\emptyset$ otherwise.*

Proof. It is sufficient to prove that $\theta_{i,n}(\mathbf{D}_{J,n})$ is equal to $\{d\}$ if $i \in J$, and to $\emptyset$ otherwise.

In the case that $i \in J$, the identity map is a homomorphism from $\mathbf{D}_{i,n}$ to $\mathbf{D}_{i,n}$, and is hence a homomorphism from $\mathbf{D}_{i,n}$ to $\mathbf{D}_{J,n}$, and so $d \in \theta_{i,n}(\mathbf{D}_{J,n})$; by Lemma 5.8, it follows that $\theta_{i,n}(\mathbf{D}_{J,n}) = \{d\}$.

In the case that $i \notin J$, we show that there is no homomorphism g from $\mathbf{D}_{i,n}$ to $\mathbf{D}_{J,n}$. We prove the contrapositive; suppose that there is such a homomorphism g. This homomorphism has $g(d) = d$ by Lemma 5.7. In $\mathbf{D}_{i,n}$, the element d has an outgoing edge to p_i^1; since d only has outgoing edges in $\mathbf{D}_{J,n}$ to elements of the form p_j^1, with $j \in J$, it holds that there exists $j \in J$ with $h(p_i^1) = p_j^1$. Since in $\mathbf{D}_{i,n}$, the element d has a directed path of edge length i coming out of it, this directed path must be mapped under h to a directed path of the same length. Observe that each vertex of the form p_ℓ^k only has outgoing edges to vertices of the same form; so, it holds that $h(p_i^2) = p_j^2, \ldots, h(p_i^i) = p_j^i$ and we have that $i \leq j$. But if q_i^{i-1} is mapped under h to p_j^{i-1}, then by the observation, q_i^i is mapped under h to p_j^i; since q_i^i has a directed path of edge length $n + 1 - i$ coming out of it, its image p_j^i must as well; but this is a contradiction, since by the definition of the $\mathbf{D}_{j,n}$ no point p_j^i has such a directed path (this would imply a directed path of edge length $n + 1$ coming out of d in $\mathbf{D}_{j,n}$). So q_i^{i-1} must be mapped under h to a point in $\mathbf{D}_{j,n}$ not equal to p_j^{i-1} but having an edge to $h(p_i^i) = p_j^i$; this point must be q_j^{j-1}, and so we conclude that $i = j$. □

The following theorem shows how one can simulate unary symbols with a binary symbol.

Theorem 5.10. *There exists a polynomial p such that, for any $m, s \geq 1$, there exist*

- *a set $B^+ \supseteq [s]$ of size less than or equal to $p(m, s)$,*
- *formulas $\psi_1(d), \ldots, \psi_m(d) \in \mathrm{EP}^2_{\{E\}}$, and*
- *a mapping t from the set*

$$\{E(v, w) \mid v, w \in B^+\}$$

to the set

$$\{U_i(j) \mid i \in [m], j \in [s]\} \cup \{\bot, \top\}$$

such that the following holds. Let $\mathbf{B}$ be any σ-structure with universe $[s]$ and $\sigma \supseteq \{U_i \mid i \in [m]\}$; when $\mathbf{B}'$ is defined as the $\{E\}$-structure with universe B^+ and where

$$\mathbf{B}' \models E(v, w) \text{ if and only if } \mathbf{B} \models t(E(v, w)),$$

it holds that (for each $i \in [m]$) $\psi_i(\mathbf{B}') = U_i^{\mathbf{B}}$.

Proof. We design the assignment t such that, for any structure $\mathbf{B}$ of the described form, the structure $\mathbf{B}'$ will be as follows. The universe B^+ of $\mathbf{B}'$ is $\cup_{i \in [m]} D_{i,m+1} \times [s]$. However, for each $j \in [s]$ we refer to the element (d, j) using the name j as well, so in this way we have $[s] \subseteq B^+$.

- For each $j \in [s]$, define I_j to be $\{i \in [m] \mid j \in U_i^{\mathbf{B}}\} \cup \{m + 1\}$, that is, I_j contains $m + 1$ and the subscripts of all unary symbols U_i such that $\mathbf{B} \models U_i(j)$.
- For $I \subseteq [m + 1]$ and $j \in [s]$, define $\mathbf{D}_{I,m+1} \times \{j\}$ as the structure obtained from $\mathbf{D}_{I,m+1}$ by renaming each element e as (e, j).
- Define $E^{\mathbf{B}'}$ as the union $\bigcup_{j \in [s]} E^{\mathbf{D}_{I_j,m+1} \times \{j\}}$.

From this description, it is evident that the desired assignment t exists: for $j \in [s]$, the edges in $E^{\mathbf{D}_{m+1,m+1} \times \{j\}}$ are always included in $E^{\mathbf{B}'}$; for $j \in [s]$ and $i \in [m]$, the edges in $E^{\mathbf{D}_{i,m+1} \times \{j\}}$ are included in $E^{\mathbf{B}'}$ depending on whether or not $\mathbf{B} \models U_i(j)$, and all other potential edges are never included in $E^{\mathbf{B}'}$.

For each $i \in [m]$, define $\psi_i(d) = \theta_{i,m+1}(d)$. To conclude the proof, we thus verify that $\psi_i(\mathbf{B}') = U_i^{\mathbf{B}}$. We have

$$\begin{aligned}
\psi_i(\mathbf{B}') &= \cup_{j \in [s]} \psi_i(\mathbf{D}_{I_j,m+1} \times \{j\}) && (2)\\
&= \cup_{j \in [s]} \{(d, j) \mid d \in \psi_i(\mathbf{D}_{I_j,m+1})\} && (3)\\
&= \cup_{j \in [s]} \{(d, j) \mid d \in \theta_{i,m+1}(\mathbf{D}_{I_j,m+1})\} && (4)\\
&= \cup_{j \in [s]} \{(d, j) \mid i \in I_j\} \text{ (by Lemma 5.9)} && (5)\\
&= \cup_{j \in [s]} \{j \mid i \in I_j\} = U_i^{\mathbf{B}}. && (6)
\end{aligned}$$

□

Now we are ready to prove the compilation lower bound for signatures that contain at least one at least binary symbol.

Proof of Theorem 5.5. Since an r-ary relation can be used to simulate a binary relation, it suffices to prove the theorem for the signature $\sigma = \{E\}$ that contains a single binary symbol E.

The proof follows closely and makes use of the proof of Theorem 5.3; in particular, we make use of the case of this theorem when the signature contains infinitely many unary symbols. We will use Theorem 5.10 to simulate unary relations by a single binary relation.

Consider the sentence $\varphi_{n,k}$ from the proof of Theorem 5.3 (adjusted accordingly so that all symbols are unary). By renaming the unary symbols we can assume that $\varphi_{n,k}$ is a sentence over the signature

$$\sigma_U^m = \{U_i \mid i \in [m]\}$$

where $m = n^2 + n$. By applying Theorem 5.10 for $m = n^2 + n$ and $s = n$, we obtain formulas

$$\psi_1(d), \ldots, \psi_m(d) \in \mathrm{EP}^2_\sigma$$

that can be used to simulate the unary symbol in σ_U^m. Let $\varphi_{n,k}^\sigma$ be the existential-positive σ-sentence obtained by replacing every occurrence of an atom $U_i(x)$ in $\varphi_{n,k}$ by $\psi_i(x)$ (from Theorem 5.10). Note that $\varphi_{n,k}^\sigma \in {\approx}\mathrm{EP}^2_\sigma$ because (by Proposition 2.1) there is a sentence $\psi_{n,k} \in \mathrm{EP}^1_{\sigma_U^m}$ that is logically equivalent to $\varphi_{n,k}$ and which can be transformed to an EP^2_σ-sentence that is logically equivalent to $\varphi_{n,k}^\sigma$ by the same replacement of atoms $U_i(x)$ by $\psi_i(x)$.

To prove the lower bound let $\psi \in \mathrm{PFO}^\ell_\sigma$ be a sentence that is logically equivalent to $\varphi_{n,k}^\sigma$ for $k = \lfloor \frac{1}{4}(n/\log n)^{2/3} \rfloor$. Let B^+ be the domain and t the mapping provided by Theorem 5.10. By Lemma 5.1 and the polynomial bound on $|B^+|$ there exists a monotone circuit $C_{|B^+|}^\sigma$ of size polynomial in n and $\|\psi\|$ that evaluates ψ on σ-structures over the universe B^+. Now we connect the inputs of this circuit to the inputs for σ_U^m-structures over the universe $[n]$ and $\bot, \top$ according to the mapping t. From Theorem 5.10 and the definition of $\varphi_{n,k}^\sigma$ it follows that the resulting circuit $C_n^{\sigma_U^m}$, which is of size polynomial in n and $\|\psi\|$, decides whether a σ_U^m-structure $\mathbf{B}$ with universe $[n]$ satisfies $\varphi_{n,k}$. As in the proof of Theorem 5.3, we can hard-code some inputs to obtain a circuit $C_n^{\{E\}}$ of the same size that decides the existence of a k-clique on n-vertex graphs. By applying Theorem 5.2 we obtain a lower bound of $2^{\Omega((n/\log n)^{1/3})}$ on the size of this circuit which is on the other hand bounded by a polynomial in $\|\varphi\|$ and n. Since $N = \|\varphi_{n,k}^\sigma\|$ is polynomial in n it follows that $\|\psi\| = \Omega(2^{N^\delta})$ for some $\delta > 0$ and the theorem is proven. □

Theorem 5.11. *When σ is an signature that contains an at least binary symbol, the parameterized problem*

$$\mathsf{QueryEval}({\approx}\mathrm{EP}^2_\sigma)$$

is chopped-NP*-hard.*

Proof. The proof is similar to the proof of Theorem 5.4. In that proof, we used the fact that $(\mathbf{G}, k)$ is a yes instance of CLIQUE if and only if $\mathbf{A_G} \models \varphi_{n,k}$; this in turn holds if and only if $\mathbf{A}'_\mathbf{G} \models \varphi_{n,k}^\sigma$, where $\mathbf{A}'_\mathbf{G}$ is obtained from $\mathbf{A_G}$ as described in the statement of Theorem 5.10. As in the proof of Theorem 5.4, it suffices to give a poly-comp reduction from v-CLIQUE to QueryEval($\approx$EP$^2_\sigma$). Define (g, s) as follows: g maps an instance $(\mathbf{G}, k)$ of CLIQUE to $(\varphi^\sigma_{n,k}, \mathbf{A}'_\mathbf{G})$, and $s(n) = \{\varphi^\sigma_{n,i} \mid i \leq n\}$. We have that g is polynomial-time computable, and (g, s) yields the desired poly-comp reduction. □

6 COMPILABILITY TO ARBITRARY FORMATS

In the classification theorems, for all fragments where we obtained an exponential lower bound on the size of compilation to PFO$^\ell$, we also can conditionally rule out compilations to arbitrary polynomial-size formats. The results can be formulated as follows.

THEOREM 6.1. *Assume that the polynomial hierarchy does not collapse; then, the following hold.*

- *When σ is an infinite signature that contains two distinct non-propositional symbols, it holds that the problem* QueryEval($\approx$EP$^1_\sigma$) *is not in* poly-comp-PTIME.
- *When σ is a signature that contains an at least binary symbol, it holds that the problem* QueryEval($\approx$EP$^2_\sigma$) *is not in* poly-comp-PTIME.

PROOF. The statements follow from Theorems 5.4 and 5.11, in conjunction with Theorem 2.4. □

Results of this form were previously shown by the second author [6, Theorem 4.3]. However, the present theorem, as indicated, is more comprehensive in that it provides a tight analysis: it provides a negative result for each value k and each signature σ such that $\approx$EP$^k_\sigma$ did not have a polynomial-size compilation according to our classification theorems. Also, the present article permits propositional symbols, whereas in the article [6], all symbols were assumed to be of arity 1 or greater.

Let us offer some discussion concerning the interpretation of Theorem 6.1. A parameterized problem (Q, κ) is in poly-comp-PTIME if there exists a computable, polynomial length function c such that when a string x is presented along with $c(\kappa(x))$, whether or not x is in Q can be decided in polynomial time.[3] In the case of one of our problems QueryEval($\mathcal{L}$), since the parameter of an instance $(\varphi, \mathbf{B})$ is the sentence φ, this means that one should consider the situation where each instance $(\varphi, \mathbf{B})$ is presented along with $c(\varphi)$. The theorem given above rules out (for the fragments presented) the possibility of a computable, polynomial length function c with the described properties. That is, it in essence rules out polynomial length compilations to an arbitrary format that consequently allow for polynomial-time decision.

[3] We remark that, for the poly-compilable function g in the definition of *poly-compilable to C*, it is straightforwardly verifiable that one can always take f to be the identity map; the described characterization follows from this remark.

This ruling out, however, is under the complexity-theoretic assumption that the polynomial hierarchy does not collapse. It can be contrasted with our unconditional results: for those, no complexity-theoretic assumption is invoked, but what is shown is that compiling to a *specific* format, namely that of bounded-variable positive first-order queries, requires exponential size.

7 CONCLUSION

Our main results, the characterisation theorems in Section 4, provide a thorough understanding of the increase in formula-size when compiling existential-positive queries to bounded variable fragments of existential-positive or positive first-order logic.

In general, our lower-bound results show that there exist existential-positive queries that can be rewritten as existential-positive queries of bounded width, but for which every such reformulation is exponentially larger than the original one. In terms of succinctness, these result implies that, for each $k \geq 1$, EP is exponentially more succinct than EP^k and that PFO is exponentially more succinct than PFO^k. While for EP this succinctness gap is tight, we do not have an exponential upper bound when rewriting PFO queries to equivalent queries of bounded width and it might be that unbounded quantifier alternation causes a non-elementary blow-up. We leave it as an open question whether there is a super-exponential succinctness gap between PFO and PFO^k.

Note that our lower bound results do not only provide exponential lower bounds when minimising the number of variables or compiling into a bounded variable fragment, but also when reducing the number of variables from k to k^δ for some $\delta > 0$. However, it would be worth to have a more fine-grained understanding of the blow-up when compiling an EP formula to one with fewer variables and whether reducing a finite number of variables by just one already implies an exponential blow-up: Does there exists a polynomial size compilation from EP$^{k+1} \cap \approx$EP^k to EP^k?

Our third open problem concerns the problem of compiling an existential-positive query into the bounded variable fragment of full first-order logic. By [5] we know that if an EP formula is equivalent to a formula in FO^k, then it is also equivalent to one in EP^k. Thus, width minimisation for existential-positive queries does not benefit from moving to full first-order logic. However, it might be that in FO^k the query can be expressed more succinct. Thus we ask: Is FO^k exponentially more succinct than EP^k? Note that a negative answer to this question would imply a compilation lower bound from $\approx$EP^k to FO^k.

Acknowledgements. The collaboration leading to this paper was partly carried out during the special semester program on Computational and Proof Complexity held in St.

Petersburg in 2016. The authors are grateful for having had the opportunity to attend, and thank the organizers Edward A. Hirsch and Sam Buss, as well as the rest of the program organization.

REFERENCES

[1] Micah Adler and Neil Immerman. 2003. An *n!* lower bound on formula size. *ACM Trans. Comput. Log.* 4, 3 (2003), 296–314. https://doi.org/10.1145/772062.772064

[2] Noga Alon and Ravi B. Boppana. 1987. The monotone circuit complexity of boolean functions. *Combinatorica* 7, 1 (01 Mar 1987), 1–22. https://doi.org/10.1007/BF02579196

[3] Simone Bova and Hubie Chen. 2014. The Complexity of Width Minimization for Existential Positive Queries. In *Proc. 17th International Conference on Database Theory (ICDT), Athens, Greece, March 24-28, 2014.* 235–244. https://doi.org/10.5441/002/icdt.2014.25

[4] Simone Bova and Hubie Chen. 2015. The complexity of equivalence, entailment, and minimization in existential positive logic. *J. Comput. Syst. Sci.* 81, 2 (2015), 443–457.

[5] Simone Bova and Hubie Chen. 2017. How Many Variables Are Needed to Express an Existential Positive Query?. In *20th International Conference on Database Theory, ICDT 2017, March 21-24, 2017, Venice, Italy.* 9:1–9:16. https://doi.org/10.4230/LIPIcs.ICDT.2017.9

[6] Hubie Chen. 2014. On the Complexity of Existential Positive Queries. *ACM Trans. Comput. Logic* 15, 1, Article 9 (March 2014), 20 pages.

[7] Hubie Chen. 2015. Parameter Compilation. In *10th International Symposium on Parameterized and Exact Computation, IPEC 2015, September 16-18, 2015, Patras, Greece.* 127–137. https://doi.org/10.4230/LIPIcs.IPEC.2015.127

[8] Hubie Chen. 2015. Parameter Compilation. *CoRR* abs/1503.00260 (2015). arXiv:1503.00260 http://arxiv.org/abs/1503.00260

[9] Hubie Chen and Stefan Mengel. 2016. Counting Answers to Existential Positive Queries: A Complexity Classification. In *Proceedings of the 35th ACM SIGMOD-SIGACT-SIGAI Symposium on Principles of Database Systems.* 315–326.

[10] Hubie Chen and Stefan Mengel. 2017. The logic of counting query answers. In *32nd Annual ACM/IEEE Symposium on Logic in Computer Science, LICS 2017, Reykjavik, Iceland, June 20-23, 2017.* 1–12.

[11] Víctor Dalmau, Phokion G. Kolaitis, and Moshe Y. Vardi. 2002. Constraint Satisfaction, Bounded Treewidth, and Finite-Variable Logics. In *Principles and Practice of Constraint Programming - CP 2002*, Pascal Van Hentenryck (Ed.). Springer Berlin Heidelberg, Berlin, Heidelberg, 310–326.

[12] Kord Eickmeyer, Michael Elberfeld, and Frederik Harwath. 2017. Succinctness of Order-Invariant Logics on Depth-Bounded Structures. *ACM Trans. Comput. Log.* 18, 4 (2017), 33:1–33:25. https://doi.org/10.1145/3152770

[13] Georg Gottlob, Stanislav Kikot, Roman Kontchakov, Vladimir V. Podolskii, Thomas Schwentick, and Michael Zakharyaschev. 2014. The price of query rewriting in ontology-based data access. *Artif. Intell.* 213 (2014), 42–59. https://doi.org/10.1016/j.artint.2014.04.004

[14] Martin Grohe and Nicole Schweikardt. 2005. The succinctness of first-order logic on linear orders. *Logical Methods in Computer Science* 1, 1 (2005). https://doi.org/10.2168/LMCS-1(1:6)2005

[15] Martin Lange. 2008. A purely model-theoretic proof of the exponential succinctness gap between CTL^+ and CTL. *Inf. Process. Lett.* 108, 5 (2008), 308–312. https://doi.org/10.1016/j.ipl.2008.06.003

[16] Alexander A. Razborov. 1985. Lower bounds on the monotone complexity of some Boolean functions. *Doklady Akademii Nauk SSSR* 285 (1985), 798–801.

[17] Benjamin Rossman. 2008. On the constant-depth complexity of k-clique. In *Proceedings of the 40th Annual ACM Symposium on Theory of Computing, Victoria, British Columbia, Canada, May 17-20, 2008.* 721–730. https://doi.org/10.1145/1374376.1374480

[18] Yehoshua Sagiv and Mihalis Yannakakis. 1980. Equivalences Among Relational Expressions with the Union and Difference Operators. *J. ACM* 27, 4 (1980), 633–655.

[19] Dimitri Surinx, George H. L. Fletcher, Dirk Leinders, Jan Van den Bussche, Marc Gyssens, Dirk Van Gucht, Stijn Vansummeren, and Yuqing Wu. 2015. Relative expressive power of navigational querying on graphs using transitive closure. *Logic Journal of the IGPL* 23, 5 (07 2015), 759–788.

[20] Moshe Y. Vardi. 1995. On the Complexity of Bounded-Variable Queries. In *Proceedings of the Fourteenth ACM SIGACT-SIGMOD-SIGART Symposium on Principles of Database Systems, May 22-25, 1995, San Jose, California, USA.* 266–276. https://doi.org/10.1145/212433.212474

[21] Philipp Weis. 2011. *Expressiveness and Succinctness of First-Order Logic on Finite Words.* Ph.D. Dissertation. University of Massachusetts Amherst. https://scholarworks.umass.edu/open_access_dissertations/407

[22] Thomas Wilke. 1999. CTL+ is Exponentially more Succinct than CTL. In *Foundations of Software Technology and Theoretical Computer Science, 19th Conference, Chennai, India, December 13-15, 1999, Proceedings.* 110–121. https://doi.org/10.1007/3-540-46691-6_9

Testability of Homomorphism Inadmissibility: Property Testing Meets Database Theory

Hubie Chen*
Dept. of Computer Science and Information Systems
Birkbeck, University of London
London, United Kingdom
hubie@dcs.bbk.ac.uk

Yuichi Yoshida†
National Institute of Informatics
Tokyo, Japan
yyoshida@nii.ac.jp

ABSTRACT

In this paper, we utilize the perspective of property testing to consider the testability of relational database queries. A primary motivation is the desire to avoid reading an entire database to decide a property thereof. We focus on conjunctive queries, which are the most basic and heavily studied database queries. Each conjunctive query can be represented as a relational structure **A** such that deciding if the conjunctive query is satisfied by a relational structure **B** is equivalent to deciding if there exists a homomorphism from **A** to **B**. We phrase our results in terms of homomorphisms.

Precisely, we study, for each relational structure **A**, the testability of homomorphism inadmissibility from **A**. We consider algorithms that have oracle access to an input relational structure **B** and that distinguish, with high probability, the case where there is no homomorphism from **A** to **B**, from the case where one needs to remove a constant fraction of tuples from **B** in order to suppress all such homomorphisms. We provide a complete characterization of the structures **A** from which one can test homomorphism inadmissibility with one-sided error by making a constant number of queries to **B**. Our characterization shows that homomorphism inadmissibility from **A** is constant-query testable with one-sided error if and only if the core of **A** is α-acyclic. We also show that the injective version of the problem is constant-query testable with one-sided error if **A** is α-acyclic; this result generalizes existing results for testing subgraph-freeness in the general graph model.

CCS CONCEPTS

• **Theory of computation → Streaming, sublinear and near linear time algorithms; Database query processing and optimization (theory).**

KEYWORDS

property testing; conjunctive queries; query evaluation; hypergraph acyclicity

ACM Reference Format:
Hubie Chen and Yuichi Yoshida. 2019. Testability of Homomorphism Inadmissibility: Property Testing Meets Database Theory. In *38th ACM SIGMOD-SIGACT-SIGAI Symposium on Principles of Database Systems (PODS'19), June 30-July 5, 2019, Amsterdam, Netherlands.* ACM, New York, NY, USA, 18 pages. https://doi.org/10.1145/3294052.3319679

1 INTRODUCTION

1.1 Background

Property testing. Traditional notions of algorithmic efficiency, such as that of polynomial time, permit each input to be read in its entirety. However, the modern necessity of performing computations on large bodies of data poses situations where inputs are so large that it is prohibitively expensive to fully read them. These situations motivate the study of algorithms that only read a part of each input. *Property testing* provides a framework wherein it is possible to present such algorithms.

In property testing, the input is typically read via random access queries, and an algorithm's desideratum is to distinguish between inputs that satisfy a property and inputs that are ϵ-*far* from satisfying the property. Intuitively speaking, an object is called ϵ-*far* from satisfying a property if one needs to modify more than an ϵ-fraction of the object in order for it satisfy the property; the exact definition depends on the context. The restriction on the allowed inputs leads

*Acknowledges the support of Spanish Project TIN2017-86727-C2-2-R.
†Supported by JSPS KAKENHI Grant Number JP17H04676.

PODS'19, June 30-July 5, 2019, Amsterdam, Netherlands

ACM ISBN 978-1-4503-6227-6/19/06...$15.00
https://doi.org/10.1145/3294052.3319679

to the possibility of algorithms that do not read the entire input.

A diversity of combinatorial objects have been studied in property testing, including functions [12, 45], graphs [30, 31], and constraint satisfaction problems (CSPs) [3, 51]; many properties have been shown to be testable with a constant number of queries, a most positive type of result. Moreover, general characterizations of constant-query testable properties have been achieved in several settings, including affine-invariant properties of functions over finite fields [49, 50], properties on dense graphs [4], and assignment testing of CSPs [11, 23]. See the surveys [43, 44] and the book [29].

Database theory, conjunctive queries, and relational homomorphisms. A central, fundamental computational task in the field of databases is the evaluation of a *query* on a *relational database*. In this article, we focus on *conjunctive queries*, the most basic and heavily studied class of database queries [46]. While there are numerous equivalent definitions, a *conjunctive query* may be defined as a first-order logical sentence built from predicate applications, conjunction, and existential quantification. (We focus here on *Boolean* conjunctive queries, which are conjunctive queries without so-called free variables and which evaluate to either true or false on a given database.) As is usual in database theory, we formalize a relational database as a *relational structure*, defined as an indexed set of relations, all over the same domain. As an example, consider the evaluation of the conjunctive query $\psi = \exists v_1 \exists v_2 \exists v_3 (E(v_1, v_2) \wedge E(v_2, v_3) \wedge E(v_3, v_1))$ on a simple undirected graph, whose edges are represented by a symmetric binary relation; this conjunctive query evaluates to true if and only if the graph contains a triangle.

A classical result in database theory [16] is that each conjunctive query ϕ can be naturally passed to a relational structure $\mathbf{A}[\phi]$, in a way such that, for any relational structure $\mathbf{B}$, the query ϕ evaluates to true on $\mathbf{B}$ if and only if there exists a *homomorphism* from $\mathbf{A}[\phi]$ to $\mathbf{B}$. Moreover, this passage can be naturally inverted. Hence, the problem of conjunctive query evaluation is equivalent to the *relational homomorphism problem* where, given a pair of relational structures, the goal is to decide if there exists a homomorphism from the first structure to the second.

Let us briefly present the relevant definitions and notions. Define a *relational structure* $\mathbf{A} = (A; R_1^{\mathbf{A}}, \dots, R_k^{\mathbf{A}})$ to consist of a finite set A, called the *domain*, and relations $R_i^{\mathbf{A}}$ $(i \in \{1, \dots, k\})$. Each relation symbol R_i has an associated arity $\mathrm{ar}(R_i)$, and each $R_i^{\mathbf{A}}$ is a relation of arity $\mathrm{ar}(R_i)$ over A, that is, a collection of tuples where each has length $\mathrm{ar}(R_i)$ and has entries drawn from A. When $\mathbf{A} = (A; R_1^{\mathbf{A}}, \dots, R_k^{\mathbf{A}})$ and $\mathbf{B} = (B; R_1^{\mathbf{B}}, \dots, R_k^{\mathbf{B}})$ are structures defined on the same symbols (that is, having the same *vocabulary*), a *homomorphism* from $\mathbf{A}$ to $\mathbf{B}$ is a mapping $h : A \to B$ such that for every $i \in \{1, \dots, k\}$ and every tuple $(a_1, \dots, a_{\mathrm{ar}(R_i)}) \in R_i^{\mathbf{A}}$, it holds that the tuple $(h(a_1), \dots, h(a_{\mathrm{ar}(R_i)}))$ belongs to $R_i^{\mathbf{B}}$. The relational structure $\mathbf{A}[\phi]$ corresponding to a conjunctive query ϕ (where all quantifiers are in front) has as domain the set of variables that occur, and, interprets each symbol R as the relation containing each tuple that R is applied to, in ϕ; for example, $\mathbf{A}[\psi]$ for $\psi = \exists v_1 \exists v_2 \exists v_3 (E(v_1, v_2) \wedge E(v_2, v_3) \wedge E(v_3, v_1))$ is equal to $(\{v_1, v_2, v_3\}; E^{\mathbf{A}[\psi]})$, where $E^{\mathbf{A}[\psi]} = \{(v_1, v_2), (v_2, v_3), (v_3, v_1)\}$.

The problem of conjunctive query evaluation and the relational homomorphism problem are, in fact, both considered formulations of the *constraint satisfaction problem* [26]. The complexity-theoretic aspects of these problems have been heavily studied over the years; see for example [1, 7, 20, 21, 33–35, 40, 41, 46] and the references therein.

1.2 Contributions

Despite the centrality of query evaluation as a computational problem in the field of databases, and the ability of the property testing framework to provide meaningful theoretical results for problems where examining the entire input is exceedingly costly, there has not been—to the best of our knowledge—any systematic study of database query evaluation from the viewpoint of property testing, on general relational databases. In this article, we initiate such a study: we present a natural oracle model under which relational structures can be accessed; and, we establish a dichotomy theorem that, in a certain precise sense, completely classifies the conjunctive queries that give rise to properties that are constant-query testable.

For cleanliness and ease of discussion, we work primarily with the homomorphism formulation of conjunctive query evaluation. When $\mathbf{A}$ and $\mathbf{B}$ are structures having the same vocabulary, let us say that $\mathbf{B}$ is $\mathbf{A}$*-free* if $\mathbf{B}$ does not admit a homomorphism from $\mathbf{A}$. We characterize precisely when, for a structure $\mathbf{A}$, one has constant-query testability of the property of $\mathbf{A}$-freeness; this property is here also referred to as the property of *homomorphism inadmissibility from* $\mathbf{A}$. Stated in the parlance of conjunctive queries, we characterize precisely when, for a conjunctive query ϕ, one has constant-query testability of the property of being false under ϕ; as each problem studied corresponds to a fixed conjunctive query ϕ and takes as input a structure $\mathbf{B}$ to be evaluated on ϕ, our study can be taken as a property testing characterization of the data complexity of each conjunctive query.

Model studied. Let $\mathbf{A}$ and $\mathbf{B}$ be relational structures over the same vocabulary, and let $\epsilon \in (0, 1)$; the structure $\mathbf{B}$ is called ϵ*-far* from $\mathbf{A}$-free if it is necessary to remove more than an ϵ-fraction of tuples from $\mathbf{B}$ in order to ensure that it does not admit a homomorphism from $\mathbf{A}$; it is called ϵ*-close* to A-free otherwise. In the problem of testing homomorphism inadmissibility from A, an algorithm is given an error parameter $\epsilon \in (0, 1)$ and is permitted query access to a relational structure **B** with the same vocabulary as **A**; its goal is to distinguish the case that **B** is **A**-free from the case that **B** is ϵ-far from **A**-free. An algorithm achieving this goal is called a *tester for* **A**-*freeness*. Such a tester is *constant-query* if the number of queries to **B** is a function only of ϵ; is said to *use* Q *queries*, where Q is a family of functions on the natural numbers, if for each ϵ there exists $q_\epsilon \in Q$ such that at most $q_\epsilon(|B|)$ queries are used when the presented error parameter is ϵ; and, is of *one-sided error* if it accepts every structure **B** that is **A**-free.

In our model, access to the structure **B** is via queries to what we term the *completion oracle*. Consider a relation $R^{\mathbf{B}}$ of arity r in **B** and a tuple $\mathbf{q} = (q_1, \dots, q_r) \in (B \cup \{*\})^r$, where B is the domain of **B** and $*$ is a special wildcard symbol. A tuple $\mathbf{t} = (t_1, \dots, t_r)$ is called a *completion* of $\mathbf{q}$ in $R^{\mathbf{B}}$ if (i) $t_i = q_i$ for every $i \in \{1, \dots, r\}$ with $q_i \in B$ and (ii) $\mathbf{t} \in R^{\mathbf{B}}$. The completion oracle allows two types of queries; for each, the oracle receives a relation symbol R and a tuple $\mathbf{q} = (q_1, \dots, q_r) \in (B \cup \{*\})^r$:

- To a *completion query*, the oracle returns a random completion of $\mathbf{q}$ in $R^{\mathbf{B}}$; if no such completion exists, it returns a special symbol $\perp$.
- To a *size query*, the oracle returns the number of completions of $\mathbf{q}$ in $R^{\mathbf{B}}$.

We discuss the relation between the completion oracle and the established *general graph* model later, in Section 1.3.

One may wonder why we do not test homomorphism admissibility instead of homomorphism inadmissibility. The reason is that, for any fixed structure **A**, we can add a constant number of tuples to a structure **B** to realize a homomorphism from **A** to **B**. Hence, we need to choose $\epsilon = O(1/\|\mathbf{B}\|)$ to make the testing problem meaningful, where $\|\mathbf{B}\|$ is the total number of tuples in **B**; otherwise, no ϵ-far instance exists and we can always answer that there is a homomorphism from **A** to **B**. However, when ϵ is so small, we can obtain the whole structure **B** with $O(1/\epsilon)$ queries, and can then exactly check whether there is no homomorphism from **A** to **B**. Hence, testing homomorphism admissibility is an uninteresting problem, under the employed lens of property testing.

We remark that the introduced model may permit the study of further properties, beyond **A**-freeness, that are *anti-monotone*; here, by an *anti-monotone* property, we mean a property on structures such that, when **B** is a structure that does not satisfy the property, adding tuples to **B** always results in a structure that also does not satisfy the property. We leave such a study as a potential avenue for future work.

Main results. The primary technical contribution of this work is a dichotomy theorem that completely characterizes the structures **A** for which the property of **A**-freeness is constant-query testable with one-sided error. In the following, n denotes the domain size $|B|$ of the structure **B** being tested.

Theorem 1.1. *Let* **A** *be any relational structure. The property of* **A**-*freeness is constant-query testable with one-sided error if and only if the core of* **A** *is* α*-acyclic. In particular, when the core of* **A** *is not* α*-acyclic, there exists a constant* $c \geq 1$ *such that testing* **A**-*freeness, with one-sided error, requires* $\Omega(n^{1/c})$ *queries.*

Here, α*-acyclicity* is an established notion of acyclicity for hypergraphs, and is applied to structures in a natural way; precise definitions are given in Section 2, where the definition of *core* is also given. Indeed, the notion of α*-acyclicity* is classical in database theory; it is known that there is a polynomial-time algorithm for the problem of deciding if an α-acyclic structure admits a homomorphism to another structure (see for example [1, Chapter 6.4]).

The just-presented dichotomy theorem may be restated in database parlance, as follows. By a *positive first-order query*, we here refer to a first-order logical sentence that does not contain negation; such a sentence evaluates to true or false when given a structure over the query's vocabulary. When ϕ is a positive first-order query, we say that a structure **B** is ϵ*-far* from ϕ-falsity if it is necessary to remove more than an ϵ-fraction of tuples from **B** to ensure that ϕ evaluates to false on **B**; we define the problem of testing ϕ-falsity analogously to how we defined the problem of testing **A**-freeness.

Theorem 1.2. *(Restatement of Theorem 1.1's dichotomy) Let* ϕ *be any conjunctive query; the property of* ϕ*-falsity is constant-query testable with one-sided error if and only if the core of* $\mathbf{A}[\phi]$ *is* α*-acyclic.*

In the area of databases, a heavily studied generalization of the class of conjunctive queries is the class of so-called *unions of conjunctive queries* [18, 25]. We formalize these logically as follows. A *union of conjunctive queries* is a disjunction of conjunctive queries; so, the class of structures on which it evaluates to true is equal to the union, over its constituent conjunctive queries θ, of the structures on which θ evaluates to true.

From Theorem 1.1, we may derive a more general dichotomy theorem, which describes the testability of each union of conjunctive queries. It is known that any union ϕ of conjunctive queries can be computably rewritten to a form, which we call the *normalization of* ϕ, wherein none of its disjuncts are redundant; see [13, Section 3].[1]

[1]In particular, a union of conjunctive queries as defined here is, in [13], referred to as an existential positive sentence in disjunctive form; by the

Corollary 1.3. *Let ϕ be any union of conjunctive queries, and let $\phi' = \phi_1 \vee \cdots \vee \phi_k$ be the normalization of ϕ. The property of ϕ-falsity is constant-query testable with one-sided error if and only if the following condition holds: for each $i \in [k]$, the core of $\mathbf{A}[\phi_i]$ is α-acyclic. When this condition does not hold, there exists a constant $c \geq 1$ such that testing ϕ-falsity, with one-sided error, requires $\Omega(n^{1/c})$ queries.*

In this article, we also consider the injective version of testing **A**-freeness [22]. We say that a relational structure **B** is *injectively* **A**-*free* if there is no injective homomorphism from **A** to **B**. Then, the testing problem is to distinguish the case that **B** is injectively **A**-free from the case that **B** is ϵ-far from being so. By building on and slightly modifying the positive result of Theorem 1.1, we show the positive testability result that, for any relational structure **A** that is α-acyclic, injective **A**-freeness is constant-query testable (Theorem 3.12).

Oracle implementation issues. In our view, the theory developed in this article evidences that our oracle model is mathematically robust and natural; again, we regard the presentation of this model as a contribution of this article. In Theorem 1.1 and the other dichotomy theorems presented above, however, oracle queries are treated as primitives; these theorems are agnostic about the particulars of how oracle queries are answered. While we hope that this article will engender further interaction between property testing and database theory, we here would like to point out that the oracle queries of our model can be resolved in polylogarithmic time in the case that the relations of the structure **B** being tested are represented as range trees [10], where we identify elements in B with values $1, \ldots, |B|$ through an arbitrary one-to-one correspondence. Precisely, consider the representation of each relation $R^{\mathbf{B}}$ of **B** by a range tree $T_{R^{\mathbf{B}}}$ of dimension ar(R). In each one-dimensional range tree T used in $T_{R^{\mathbf{B}}}$, a leaf node with value $b \in B$ is annotated with the number of tuples, in the relation represented by T, that begin with b; and each internal node v is annotated with the sum of the annotations over all leaf descendants of v. It is straightforward to verify that both completion queries and size queries concerning a relation $R^{\mathbf{B}}$ can be answered in time $O(\log^d |R^{\mathbf{B}}|)$, where $d = \text{ar}(R)$.

1.3 Relationship between our model and the general graph model

We may view each undirected graph as a relational structure $\mathbf{G} = (V; E^{\mathbf{G}})$ where $E^{\mathbf{G}}$ is a symmetric binary relation. Previous work [5, 39] studied the problem of testing, relative to a fixed graph **H**, whether a given graph **G** is injectively **H**-free or is ϵ-far from being injectively **H**-free.[2] Here, one often assumes that each graph $\mathbf{G} = (V; E^{\mathbf{G}})$ to be tested has $|E^{\mathbf{G}}| = \Omega(|V|)$, to avoid technical triviality. In the *general graph model* [5, 39], in addition to $|V|$ and $|E^{\mathbf{G}}|$, the graph **G** is provided through query access; the following four types of oracles are provided:

- Random edge oracle: It returns a random edge chosen uniformly at random from E.
- Random neighbor oracle: Given a vertex $u \in V$, it returns a random neighbor of v if a neighbor exists, and a special symbol $\perp$ otherwise.
- Adjacency oracle: Given a vertex pair $(u, v) \in V^2$, it returns yes if the edge $\{u, v\}$ exists in E, and no otherwise.
- Degree oracle: Given a vertex $v \in V$, it returns the degree of u.

Allowing these four types of oracles is equivalent to allowing queries to the completion oracle; this is seen as follows:

- A query to the random edge oracle corresponds to the completion query $(E, (*, *))$ to the completion oracle.
- The query $u \in V$ to the random neighbor oracle corresponds to the two completion queries $(E, (u, *))$ and $(E, (*, u))$ to the completion oracle. A response of v from the random neighbor oracle corresponds to the response of (u, v) or (v, u) from the completion oracle (respectively); a response of $\perp$ from the random neighbor oracle corresponds to the response of $\perp$ from the completion oracle.
- The query $(u, v) \in V^2$ to the adjacency oracle corresponds to the completion query $(E, (u, v))$ to the completion oracle. The response of *yes* from the adjacency oracle corresponds to the response of (u, v) from the completion oracle; the response of *no* from the adjacency oracle corresponds to the response of $\perp$ from the completion oracle.
- The query $u \in V$ to the degree oracle corresponds to the size queries $(E, (u, *))$ and $(E, (*, u))$ to the completion oracle.

We note that the answer to the size query $(E, (*, *))$ to the completion oracle is $|E^{\mathbf{G}}|$, and that the answer to the size query $(E, (u, v))$ to the completion oracle can be answered by asking the adjacency oracle whether u and v are adjacent: the answer is 1 if u and v are adjacent and 0 otherwise.

It was previously shown that the property of injective **H**-freeness is constant-query testable if **H** is a path of a constant

normalization of ϕ, we mean an existential positive sentence in disjunctive form that is *irredundant* in the sense of [13].

[2] Let us remark that, in the previous literature, *injective* **H**-*freeness* as defined in this article is sometimes referred to simply as **H**-*freeness*. In the present article, as the notion of homomorphism is of primary interest, we adhere to the terminology established in Section 1.2. Note that for a graph **G** to be injectively **H**-free is equivalent to **G** not containing **H** as a subgraph (up to isomorphism).

length [37], and requires $\omega(|V|^{1/2})$ queries when **H** is non-bipartite [5].

We can conceive of a generalization of the general graph model for k-uniform hypergraphs where, by specifying a set S of vertices of size at most k, an algorithm can obtain a random hyperedge containing S, as well as the number of such hyperedges. Our model encompasses testing injective **H**-freeness in such a model, though to the best of our knowledge, no prior work focused on this problem. Although testing properties of hypergraphs has been extensively studied [28, 38, 42], most works considered the *dense model*, in which we can ask whether there is a hyperedge spanning specific k vertices.

1.4 Proof Idea

We explain the proof idea of Theorem 1.1. We first note that, for a structure **A** and its core **C**, testing **A**-freeness and **C**-freeness are equivalent. Hence, we can assume that **A** itself is a core.

Algorithm. We here explain the idea of our algorithm, which only uses completion queries (that is, it does not use size queries). By the definition of α-acyclicity, we can order tuples in relations of **A** as $\mathbf{a}^1, \ldots, \mathbf{a}^m$ so that, for each $i > 1$, all the variables in $\mathbf{a}^i$ that appeared in $\mathbf{a}^1, \ldots, \mathbf{a}^{i-1}$ are contained in a single tuple $\mathbf{a}^j$ with $j < i$. Let $\{\mathbf{a}^k\}$ be the set of variables that appear in $\mathbf{a}^k$. Then, starting with an empty map $f^0 : \emptyset \to B$, we iteratively create a partial map $f^k : \bigcup_{\ell \in \{1,\ldots,k\}} \{\mathbf{a}^\ell\} \to B$ from f^{k-1} by assigning values to unassigned variables in $\mathbf{a}^k$ using completion queries. If a completion query returns $\perp$ along the way, then the algorithm accepts, claiming that there is no homomorphism from **A** to **B**. Otherwise, the algorithm rejects, claiming that **B** is ϵ-far from **A**-freeness.

If the algorithm successfully obtains a map f^m without ever getting $\perp$ from the completion oracle, this map always gives rise to a homomorphism from **A** to **B**. This means that the algorithm always accepts when **B** is **A**-free because there is no homomorphism from **A** to **B**.

The proof that the algorithm, with high probability, rejects any structure **B** that is ϵ-far from **A**-free consists of the following three steps. First, we take a large set of homomorphic images of **A** in **B** that are disjoint in a certain sense, and construct a substructure **B**$'$ of **B** consisting of tuples used in the homomorphic images. Then, we show that, if the probability that the algorithm rejects **B**$'$ is high, then the probability that the algorithm rejects **B** is also high. Finally, we show that the probability that the algorithm rejects **B**$'$ is high using the disjointness property, which establishes the correctness of the algorithm.

Lower bound. We now explain how we obtain a super-constant lower bound for testing **A**-freeness when it is not α-acyclic. We first show that there exists a structure **A**$'$ such that (i) a super-constant lower bound for testing **A**$'$-freeness implies a super-constant lower bound for testing **A**-freeness, (ii) **A**$'$ is symbol-distinct in the sense that each relation contains exactly one tuple, and (iii) the hypergraph constructed by regarding each tuple in **A**$'$ a hyperedge is (essentially) either a cycle or a *k-simplex*, which is, up to isomorphism, a $(k+1)$-vertex hypergraph with a hyperedge $\{1, \ldots, k+1\} \setminus \{i\}$ for each $i \in \{1, \ldots, k+1\}$. From (i), it suffices to show a super-constant lower bound for **A**$'$. We consider the cycle and simplex cases separately.

When the hypergraph is a cycle, we can show a super-constant lower bound by using the known lower bound for testing triangle-freeness in the general graph model [5] by a relatively simple reduction.

When the hypergraph is a simplex, we can show a super-constant lower bound by generalizing the argument used in [5]. Namely, we consider a distribution $\mathcal{D}$ over k-uniform hypergraphs generated as follows: We partition the vertex set into $k+1$ parts $V_1, \ldots, V_{k+1}$ of the same size, and for each set of k parts $\{V_{i_1}, \ldots, V_{i_k}\}$, we take random k-dimensional matchings spanning them. We can show that the created hypergraph G has many disjoint k-simplices and hence is $\Omega(1)$-far from k-simplex-freeness with high probability. Note that a one-sided error tester $\mathcal{A}$ can reject a hypergraph only when it finds a k-simplex as a subgraph. Considering when $\mathcal{A}$ finds the last hyperedge of a k-simplex, this means that $\mathcal{A}$ should query a tuple **q** with wildcard symbols and the returned completion **t** of **q** should consist only of vertices that already appeared in the process of $\mathcal{A}$. From the random construction of the hypergraph, however, we can show that the wildcard symbols in **q** are completed by vertices that have never appeared in the process as long as the number of queries is constant.

1.5 Related work

To the best of our knowledge, testing homomorphism inadmissibility, as formalized in this article, has not been systematically studied in the literature. The most relevant line of research is testing subgraph-freeness in the general graph model, as discussed above. There are several variations on the general graph model regarding the provided oracles. In [32, 39], a model with (a non-random version of) the random neighbor, adjacency, and degree oracles is considered. In [24], a model with essentially the random edge oracle is considered. In [37], a model with all of the random edge, random neighbor, adjacency, and degree oracles is considered. From the perspective of relational structures, it is natural to consider the model with all the oracles.

The computational problem of deciding, given a pair $(\mathbf{A}, \mathbf{B})$ of relational structures over the same vocabulary, if there exists a homomorphism from **A** to **B**, is a formulation of the constraint satisfaction problem, which is well-known to be NP-complete. There is an extensive literature that aims to identify restricted cases of this problem that are polynomial-time tractable. One main stream in this literature studies restricted cases where the target structure **B** is fixed, see for example [7, 15, 19, 52] and the references therein. Another stream, which is more closely aligned with the present study, considers cases that are based on limiting the permitted source structures **A**, see for example [18, 20, 21, 33–35] and the references therein.

In property testing, constraint satisfaction problems have been extensively studied; previous work can be classified into two categories:

- The first category is testing whether a given CSP instance, provided through a query access, is satisfiable. In the *dense model*, one restricts attention to CSP instances whose constraints have a fixed arity k, and an instance is considered ϵ-far from being satisfiable if one needs to remove more than ϵn^k constraints in order to make it satisfiable, where n is the number of variables. In this model, any CSP is known to be constant-query testable [3, 6, 47]. In the *bounded-degree model*, one restricts attention to CSP instances where each variable participates in a constant number, say, d, of constraints, and an instance is considered ϵ-far from being satisfiable if one needs to remove more than ϵdn constraints in order to make it satisfiable. In this model, a characterization is obtained via the LP integrality gap of the CSP [48].
- The second category is testing whether a given assignment to a CSP instance, through query access, is a satisfying assignment. This testing problem has been considered relative to fixed target structures **B**. Here, the CSP instance is explicitly provided to the algorithms. It was shown that 2-SAT is testable with $O(\sqrt{n})$ queries [27] and testing 3-SAT requires $\Omega(n)$ queries [9], where n is the number of variables. In [51], universal algebra is used to systematically study this problem. A characterization of constant-query testable Boolean CSPs was achieved in [11], and it was generalized to finite-domain CSPs in [23].

We also mention that, in the context of database theory, Ben-Moshe et al. [8, Section 6] studied the testability of a notion called *near-sortedness*. In their study, near-sortedness is a property of relations presented as an ordered list of tuples, whereas (as mentioned) in the present work, the oracle access to the structure being tested is not tied to a fixed representation of relations. In [2], the authors introduced a bounded-degree model for databases and showed that, if the databases have bounded tree-width, then every query definable in monadic second-order logic with modulo counting is testable with a constant number of oracle queries.

1.6 Organization

We introduce notions used throughout this paper in Section 2. We show that **A**-freeness is constant-query testable if the core of **A** is α-acyclic in Section 3; and, that it is not constant-query testable otherwise, in Section 4. We provide the proof of Corollary 1.3, our result on unions of conjunctive queries, in Section 5.

2 PRELIMINARIES

For each integer n, we use $[n]$ to denote the set $\{1, 2, \ldots, n\}$. We use bold symbols, such as $\mathbf{t}$, to denote tuples. For a tuple $\mathbf{t} = (t_1, \ldots, t_k)$, we use $\{\mathbf{t}\}$ to denote the set $\{t_1, \ldots, t_k\}$. For a function $f : A \to B$ and a tuple $\mathbf{a} = (a_1, \ldots, a_k)$ of elements of A, we define $f(\mathbf{a})$ to be the tuple $(f(a_1), \ldots, f(a_k))$. We use double brackets, as in $\{\{a, a, b, c\}\}$, to denote a multiset. When S is a multiset, we sometimes use $\#S$ to denote its size.

2.1 Relational structures and homomorphisms

A *vocabulary* is a set of relational symbols, where each relational symbol R has an associated *arity*, which is a positive integer and is denoted by $\mathrm{ar}(R)$. Throughout this paper, we assume that each vocabulary is finite. A *relational structure* (for short, *structure*) with vocabulary σ is a pair of the form $\mathbf{A} = (A, \{R^{\mathbf{A}}\}_{R \in \sigma})$, where A is a set, called the *domain* of $\mathbf{A}$, and each relation $R^{\mathbf{A}}$ is a subset of $A^{\mathrm{ar}(R)}$. We define a *multiset relational structure* (for short, *multiset structure*) similarly, with the difference that each relation $R^{\mathbf{A}}$ is a multiset whose elements are drawn from $A^{\mathrm{ar}(R)}$. In this article, each relational structure and each multiset relational structure under discussion is assumed to be *finite* in the sense that its domain is finite. We generally use the letters $\mathbf{A}, \mathbf{B}, \mathbf{C}, \ldots$ to denote structures and multiset structures, and the letters $A, B, C, \ldots$ to denote their respective domains. For a structure or multiset structure $\mathbf{A} = (A, \{R^{\mathbf{A}}\}_{R \in \sigma})$, we denote by $\|\mathbf{A}\|$ the total number of tuples in the relations of $\mathbf{A}$, that is, $\sum_{R \in \sigma} |R^{\mathbf{A}}|$.

For a structure $\mathbf{A} = (A, \{R^{\mathbf{A}}\}_{R \in \sigma})$ and a structure or multiset structure $\mathbf{B} = (B, \{R^{\mathbf{B}}\}_{R \in \sigma})$ having the same vocabulary σ, a *homomorphism* from $\mathbf{A}$ to $\mathbf{B}$ is a mapping $h : A \to B$ such that, for any $R \in \sigma$ and $\mathbf{t} = (a_1, \ldots, a_r) \in R^{\mathbf{A}}$, the image $h(\mathbf{t}) = (h(a_1), \ldots, h(a_r))$ belongs to $R^{\mathbf{B}}$.

An *endomorphism* of a structure $\mathbf{C} = (C, \{R^{\mathbf{C}}\}_{R \in \sigma})$ is a homomorphism from $\mathbf{C}$ to itself. A *core* is a structure such that each endomorphism thereof is a bijection. A *substructure* of a structure $\mathbf{A} = (A, \{R^{\mathbf{A}}\}_{R \in \sigma})$ is a structure $\mathbf{C} = (C, \{R^{\mathbf{C}}\}_{R \in \sigma})$

such that $C \subseteq A$ and $R^{\mathbf{C}} \subseteq R^{\mathbf{A}}$ for each $R \in \sigma$.[3] A *core of a structure* $\mathbf{A} = (A, \{R^{\mathbf{A}}\}_{R\in\sigma})$ is a substructure of $\mathbf{A}$ that is a core and that receives a homomorphism from $\mathbf{A}$. It is known that each structure has at least one core, and that all cores of a structure are isomorphic [36]; following a standard abuse, we thus speak of *the* core of a structure.

Example 2.1. Undirected graphs can be naturally represented as structures having a single binary relation that is symmetric. Under this representation, the following are well-known and straightforward to verify:

- any odd cycle is a core (that is, each endomorphism of an odd cycle is a bijection), and hence the core of any odd cycle is the odd cycle itself; and,
- the core of any even cycle is a single edge, that is, a two-vertex graph having a single edge between the two vertices. Indeed, the core of any bipartite graph (which contains at least one edge) is a single edge.

2.2 Hypergraphs and α-acyclicity

Let V be a set, and let $S, S_1, \ldots, S_k \subseteq V$. We say that S is an *ear* with respect to $S_1, \ldots, S_k$ when either $k = 0$ or there exists $j \in [k]$ such that $S \cap (\bigcup_{i\in[k]} S_i) \subseteq S_j$. A hypergraph $G = (V, \mathcal{E})$ with m hyperedges is called *α-acyclic* if there exists an ordering $S_1, \ldots, S_m$ of the hyperedges so that, for each $i \in [m]$, the hyperedge S_i is an ear with respect to the previous edges $S_1, \ldots, S_{i-1}$. For a relational structure $\mathbf{A} = (A, \{R^{\mathbf{A}}\}_{R\in\sigma})$, its associated hypergraph is defined as $G_{\mathbf{A}} = (A, \mathcal{E})$, where $\mathcal{E} = \{\{\mathbf{t}\} \mid R \in \sigma, \mathbf{t} \in R^{\mathbf{A}}\}$. We say that a relational structure $\mathbf{A}$ is *α-acyclic* if its associated hypergraph $G_{\mathbf{A}}$ is α-acyclic.

We say that a hypergraph $G = (V, \mathcal{E})$ on $k + 1$ vertices is *(k-)simplex* if, up to isomorphism, $V = [k + 1]$ and $\mathcal{E}$ consists of the $k + 1$ hyperedges of the form $[k + 1] \setminus \{i\}$, where $i \in [k + 1]$. We say that a hypergraph $(V, \mathcal{E})$ is a *cycle* if, up to isomorphism, it holds that $V = \{v_1, \ldots, v_m\}$ and $\mathcal{E} = \{(v_i, v_{i+1}) \mid i \in [m]\}$, where $v_{m+1} = v_1$.

Let $G = (V, \mathcal{E})$ be a hypergraph. For a subset $S \subseteq V$, the *hypergraph induced by* S, denoted by $G[S]$, is defined as $(S, \{e \cap S \mid e \in \mathcal{E}\} \setminus \{\emptyset\})$. The hypergraph $\mathcal{M}(G)$ is defined as $(V, \{e \in \mathcal{E} \mid \nexists f \in \mathcal{E}, e \subsetneq f\})$, that is, it is the hypergraph whose hyperedges are the inclusion maximal hyperedges of G. We will make use of the following known characterization; we recommend [14, Characterization 2.5] as a reference.

THEOREM 2.2. *A hypergraph $G = (V, \mathcal{E})$ is not α-acyclic if and only if there exists $S \subseteq V$ with $|S| \geq 3$ such that $\mathcal{M}(G[S])$ is either a simplex or a cycle.*

[3] Since a substructure $\mathbf{C}$ of a structure $\mathbf{A}$ is, by definition, a structure itself, it indeed holds that $R^{\mathbf{C}} \subseteq R^{\mathbf{A}} \cap C^{\mathrm{ar}(R)}$, for each symbol R.

2.3 Testing Homomorphism Inadmissibility

Throughout this paper, whenever we speak of testing $\mathbf{A}$*-freeness,* $\mathbf{A}$ *will be a structure, and the object* $\mathbf{B}$ *being tested will be a multiset structure.* The study of relational databases whose relations are multisets is established and natural in the database context; it is in line with so-called *multiset* or *bag* semantics [17].

For a structure $\mathbf{A}$, we say that a multiset structure $\mathbf{B}$ is *ϵ-far from* $\mathbf{A}$*-freeness* if we must remove more than $\epsilon\|\mathbf{B}\|$ tuples from relations in $\mathbf{B}$ in order to ensure that it does not receive a homomorphism from $\mathbf{A}$. Formally, a multiset structure $\mathbf{B}$ is *ϵ-far from* $\mathbf{A}$*-freeness* if, for any structure $\mathbf{B}'$ obtained from $\mathbf{B}$ by removing tuples from relations, $\|\mathbf{B}\| - \|\mathbf{B}'\| \leq \epsilon\|\mathbf{B}\|$ implies that $\mathbf{B}'$ admits a homomorphism from $\mathbf{A}$.

When testing a multiset structure $\mathbf{B}$, two types of queries are permitted. Each type of query receives a pair $(R, \mathbf{q})$ of a relation symbol R in the vocabulary of $\mathbf{B}$ and a tuple $\mathbf{q} \in (B \cup \{*\})^{\mathrm{ar}(R)}$, where $* \notin B$ is a special symbol. Let $S_{\mathbf{B}}(t) = B_1 \times \cdots \times B_{\mathrm{ar}(R)}$, where $B_i = B$ if $t_i = *$ and $B_i = \{t_i\}$ otherwise. We call each tuple in $S_{\mathbf{B}}(\mathbf{q})$ a *completion* of $\mathbf{q}$. The answer to a *completion query* is a random completion of $\mathbf{q}$ in $R^{\mathbf{B}}$, if a completion exists; formally, the result is a tuple chosen uniformly at random from the multiset $\{\{\mathbf{t} \in R^{\mathbf{B}} \mid \mathbf{t} \in S_{\mathbf{B}}(\mathbf{q})\}\}$ when this multiset is non-empty, and a special symbol $\perp$ otherwise. The answer to a *size query* is the size of the multiset $\{\{\mathbf{t} \in R^{\mathbf{B}} \mid \mathbf{t} \in S_{\mathbf{B}}(\mathbf{q})\}\}$. We use $\deg_{R,\mathbf{B}}(\mathbf{q})$ to denote $|\{\{\mathbf{t} \in R^{\mathbf{B}} \mid \mathbf{t} \in S_{\mathbf{B}}(\mathbf{q})\}\}|$, which is the number of completions of $\mathbf{q}$ in $R^{\mathbf{B}}$.

For a structure $\mathbf{A}$ with a finite vocabulary σ, we say that an algorithm is a *tester* for $\mathbf{A}$-freeness if, given a domain B, query access to a multiset structure $\mathbf{B}$ with the vocabulary σ, and an error parameter $\epsilon \in (0, 1)$, it accepts with probability at least $2/3$ if $\mathbf{B}$ is $\mathbf{A}$-free, and it rejects with probability at least $2/3$ if $\mathbf{B}$ is ϵ-far from $\mathbf{A}$-freeness. The notions of injective $\mathbf{A}$-freeness, of a tester for injective $\mathbf{A}$-freeness, etc. are defined analogously using injective homomorphisms.

3 CONSTANT-QUERY TESTERS FOR α-ACYCLIC RELATIONAL STRUCTURES

In this section, we present a constant-query tester for homomorphism inadmissibility from an α-acyclic relational structure. This positive result applies directly to any α-acyclic relational structure, even those that are not cores. We describe our algorithm in Section 3.1 and analyze it in Section 3.2. The modification needed to test injective homomorphism inadmissibility is given in Section 3.3. Throughout the section, we fix $\mathbf{A}$ to be an α-acyclic relational structure, and let $m = \|\mathbf{A}\|$.

Algorithm 1

procedure HI-TEST$_{\mathbf{A}}$(B, **B**)
  ▷ **B** is a multiset structure with domain B and having the same vocabulary as **A**.
  Let $(\mathbf{a}^1, R_1), \dots, (\mathbf{a}^m, R_m)$ be the ordering, as explained in the text.
  Let $f^0 : \emptyset \to B$ be the empty map.
  for $k = 1$ to m **do**
    Let $\mathbf{q}^k = (q_1^k, \dots, q_{\mathrm{ar}(R_k)}^k)$ be the tuple defined as

$$q_i^k = \begin{cases} f^{k-1}(a_i^k) & \text{if } a_i^k \in \bigcup_{\ell \in [k-1]}\{\mathbf{a}^\ell\} \\ * & \text{otherwise.} \end{cases}$$

    Pose the completion query $(R_i, \mathbf{q}^k)$ to **B**.
    if The answer is $\perp$ **then**
      Accept.
    else
      Let $\mathbf{b}^k = (b_1^k, \dots, b_{\mathrm{ar}(R_k)}^k)$ be the answer.
      Define $f^k : \bigcup_{\ell \in [k]}\{\mathbf{a}^\ell\} \to B$ by

$$f^k(a) = \begin{cases} f^{k-1}(a) & \text{if } a \in \bigcup_{\ell \in [k-1]}\{\mathbf{a}^\ell\} \\ b_i^k & \text{if } a \in \{\mathbf{a}^k\} \setminus \bigcup_{\ell \in [k-1]}\{\mathbf{a}^\ell\} \text{ and } a = q_i^k. \end{cases}$$

  Reject.

3.1 Algorithm

First, the algorithm preprocesses **A** before querying **B**. Consider the set $\mathcal{A} = \{(\mathbf{a}, R) \mid R \in \sigma, \mathbf{a} \in R^{\mathbf{A}}\}$. By the α-acyclicity of **A**, there is an ordering $(\mathbf{a}^1, R_1), \dots, (\mathbf{a}^m, R_m)$ of the elements in $\mathcal{A}$ such that, for each $k \in [m]$, the set $\{\mathbf{a}^k\}$ is an ear with respect to the sets $\{\mathbf{a}^1\}, \dots, \{\mathbf{a}^{k-1}\}$.

Our algorithm is a random process, called HI-TEST$_{\mathbf{A}}$ and detailed precisely in Algorithm 1. We give an overview here. The algorithm HI-TEST$_{\mathbf{A}}$ proceeds in m stages. Starting with an empty map $f^0 : \emptyset \to B$, the algorithm attempts to construct a partial map f^k: $\bigcup_{\ell \in [k]}\{\mathbf{a}^\ell\} \to B$ in the k-th stage. More specifically, in the k-th stage, the algorithm tries to extend the domain of f^{k-1} so that it is defined on all entries of the tuple $\mathbf{a}^k$, by making a completion query; if the answer to the query is $\perp$, then the algorithm gives up and claims that there is no homomorphism, by accepting. Let us say that the algorithm is *k-successful* if it did not fail in the first k-th stages and succeeded to define f^k. If the algorithm is m-successful, then the algorithm claims that there is a homomorphism, by rejecting.

It is clear that HI-TEST$_{\mathbf{A}}$ has a constant query complexity. Also, note that if we have succeeded to define the map f^k, then it is a homomorphism from **A** to **B** by construction. Hence, HI-TEST$_{\mathbf{A}}$ always accepts when **B** is **A**-free. In the next section, we show that HI-TEST$_{\mathbf{A}}$ rejects with a certain probability if **B** is ϵ-far from **A**-freeness.

3.2 Soundness analysis

The goal of this subsection is to establish the following.

LEMMA 3.1. *Suppose that* **B** *is ϵ-far from* **A**-*freeness for $\epsilon \in (0, 1)$. Then, there exists $\delta = \delta_{3.1}^{\mathbf{A}}(\epsilon) > 0$ such that* HI-TEST$_{\mathbf{A}}$(B, **B**) *rejects with probability at least δ. Here, we can choose $\delta_{3.1}^{\mathbf{A}}(\epsilon) = \Omega\left(\epsilon/(m2^{\bar{r}})\right)^m$, where $\bar{r} = \max_{R \in \sigma} \mathrm{ar}(R)$.*

In Section 3.2.1, we introduce the notion of a tuple-disjoint **A**-image, and show that we can restrict our attention to a relational structure constructed from tuple-disjoint **A**-images. Then, we analyze the rejection probability for it in Section 3.2.2.

3.2.1 Restriction to the tuple-disjoint case. Let **B** be a multiset structure that is ϵ-far from **A**-freeness. For a homomorphism $h : A \to B$ from **A** to **B**, we define $h(\mathbf{A})$ as the relational structure whose domain is B and $R^{h(\mathbf{A})} = \{h(\mathbf{a}) \mid \mathbf{a} \in R^{\mathbf{A}}\}$ for each $R \in \sigma$. We call $h(\mathbf{A})$ an **A**-*image* in **B**. We say that a multiset $\mathcal{I} = \{\{\mathbf{I}_1, \dots, \mathbf{I}_k\}\}$ of **A**-images are *tuple-disjoint* if, for each relation symbol $R \in \sigma$, the multiset union of $R^{\mathbf{I}_1}, \dots, R^{\mathbf{I}_k}$ is a subset of $R^{\mathbf{B}}$. For a set $\mathcal{I}$ of tuple-disjoint **A**-images in **B**, we define $\bigcup \mathcal{I}$ as the relational structure whose domain is B and $R^{\bigcup \mathcal{I}} = \bigcup_{\mathbf{I} \in \mathcal{I}} R^{\mathbf{I}}$ for each $R \in \sigma$; here, the union is taken as a multiset.

The following lemma states that we can analyze the rejection probability on **B** by analyzing the rejection probability on an instance induced by tuple-disjoint **A**-images.

LEMMA 3.2. *Suppose that* **B** *is a multiset structure, and $\mathcal{I}$ is a set of tuple-disjoint* **A**-*images in* **B** *where $|\mathcal{I}| \geq \alpha\|\mathbf{B}\|$ for a value $\alpha \in (0, 1)$. Then, there is a constant $\kappa = \kappa_{3.2}^{\mathbf{A}}(\alpha) > 0$ and a subset $\mathcal{I}' \subseteq \mathcal{I}$ with $|\mathcal{I}'| \geq |\mathcal{I}|/2$ such that, if the probability that* HI-TEST$_{\mathbf{A}}$($B, \bigcup \mathcal{I}'$) *rejects is p, then the probability that* HI-TEST$_{\mathbf{A}}$($B, \mathcal{B}$) *rejects is at least $\kappa^m p$. Here, we can choose $\kappa_{3.2}^{\mathbf{A}}(\alpha) = \alpha/2^{1+\max_{R \in \sigma} \mathrm{ar}(R)}$, where $\bar{r} = \max_{R \in \sigma} \mathrm{ar}(R)$.*

PROOF. Consider the sum $\sum_{R,\mathbf{t}} \deg_{R,\mathbf{B}}(\mathbf{t})$ over all pairs $(R, \mathbf{t})$ where $R \in \sigma$ and $\mathbf{t} \in (B \cup \{*\})^{\mathrm{ar}(R)}$. For any relation symbol R, a tuple $\mathbf{b} \in R^{\mathbf{B}}$ is a completion of $2^{\mathrm{ar}(R)}$ tuples $\mathbf{t}$. Thus, we have $\sum_{R,\mathbf{t}} \deg_{R,\mathbf{B}}(\mathbf{t}) \leq C\|\mathbf{B}\|$ for $C = 2^{\bar{r}}$.

Set $\kappa = \alpha/2C$ and initialize $\mathcal{I}'$ to be $\mathcal{I}$. Now, iterate the following process: if, for a pair $(R, \mathbf{t})$ of the described form, it holds that $\deg_{R,\bigcup \mathcal{I}'}(\mathbf{t}) < \kappa \cdot \deg_{R,\mathbf{B}}(\mathbf{t})$, remove each image $\mathbf{I}$ in $\mathcal{I}'$ such that $R^{\mathbf{I}}$ includes a completion of $\mathbf{t}$. As each pair $(R, \mathbf{t})$ is considered at most once in the process, at the end of the process, the total number of images removed is at most $\sum_{R,\mathbf{t}} \kappa \cdot \deg_{R,\mathbf{B}}(\mathbf{t}) \leq \kappa C\|\mathbf{B}\| = \alpha\|\mathbf{B}\|/2$. In particular, $\mathcal{I}'$ is non-empty. Moreover, we have $\deg_{R,\bigcup \mathcal{I}'}(\mathbf{t}) = 0$ or $\deg_{R,\bigcup \mathcal{I}'}(\mathbf{t}) \geq \kappa \cdot \deg_{R,\mathbf{B}}(\mathbf{t})$ for every pair $(R, \mathbf{t})$.

Now, we relate the probabilities that HI-TEST$_{\mathbf{A}}$(B, **B**) and HI-TEST$_{\mathbf{A}}$($B, \bigcup \mathcal{I}'$) reject. To this end, fix a sequence of tuples $\mathbf{b}^1 \in R_1^{\bigcup \mathcal{I}'}, \dots, \mathbf{b}^m \in R_m^{\bigcup \mathcal{I}'}$ that forms a homomorphism $g : \mathbf{A} \to \bigcup \mathcal{I}'$, that is, $g(\mathbf{a}^i) = \mathbf{b}^i$ for each $i \in [m]$. For $k \in [m]$, let $p_{\mathbf{B}}(\mathbf{b}^1,\ldots,\mathbf{b}^k)$ and $p_{\bigcup \mathcal{I}'}(\mathbf{b}^1,\ldots,\mathbf{b}^k)$ be probabilities that HI-TEST$_{\mathbf{A}}(B,\mathbf{B})$ and HI-TEST$_{\mathbf{A}}(B,\bigcup \mathcal{I}')$ obtain the sequence $\mathbf{b}^1,\ldots,\mathbf{b}^k$, respectively. Now, we show that $p_{\mathbf{B}}(\mathbf{b}^1,\ldots,\mathbf{b}^k)$ is at least κ^k times $p_{\bigcup \mathcal{I}'}(\mathbf{b}^1,\ldots,\mathbf{b}^k)$. Considering the case $k=m$ and summing up the inequalities over the sequence $\mathbf{b}^1,\ldots,\mathbf{b}^m$, we get the claim.

Suppose that we have obtained $\mathbf{b}^1,\ldots,\mathbf{b}^{k-1}$ through the oracle (both in HI-TEST$_{\mathbf{A}}(B,\mathbf{B})$ and HI-TEST$_{\mathbf{A}}(B,\bigcup \mathcal{I}')$). Then, the probability that HI-TEST$_{\mathbf{A}}(B,\mathbf{B})$ obtains $\mathbf{b}^k$ in the k-th stage is

$$\frac{1}{\deg_{R_k,\mathbf{B}}(\mathbf{q}^k)} = \frac{\kappa}{\kappa \deg_{R_k,\mathbf{B}}(\mathbf{q}^k)} \geq \frac{\kappa}{\deg_{R_k,\bigcup \mathcal{I}'}(\mathbf{q}^k)},$$

which is κ times the probability that HI-TEST$_{\mathbf{A}}(B,\bigcup \mathcal{I}')$ obtains $\mathbf{b}^k$. Note that $\deg_{R_k,\bigcup \mathcal{I}'}(\mathbf{q}^k)$ is not zero because of the existence of $\mathbf{b}^k \in R_k^{\bigcup \mathcal{I}'}$. By induction on k, it follows that $p_{\mathbf{B}}(\mathbf{b}^1,\ldots,\mathbf{b}^k) \geq \kappa^k \cdot p_{\bigcup \mathcal{I}'}(\mathbf{b}^1,\ldots,\mathbf{b}^k)$. □

In light of Lemma 3.2, it suffices to find a set of tuple-disjoint $\mathbf{A}$-images, and then analyze the rejection probability thereof.

3.2.2 Analysis on a relational structure constructed from tuple-disjoint $\mathbf{A}$*-images.* Now, we construct a large multiset of tuple-disjoint $\mathbf{A}$-images in $\mathbf{B}$. Let $\mathbf{B}$ be a multiset structure that is ϵ-far from $\mathbf{A}$-free, and let G be a maximal multiset of homomorphisms from $\mathbf{A}$ to $\mathbf{B}$ such that the multiset of the $\mathbf{A}$-images $\{\{g(\mathbf{A}) \mid g \in G\}\}$ are tuple-disjoint.

Let $G' \subseteq G$ be the subset with $|G'| \geq |G|/2$ given by applying Lemma 3.2 on G. Let $\mathbf{B}' = (B, \{R^{\mathbf{B}'}\}_{R\in\sigma})$ be the multiset structure obtained by taking the union of the images $\{\{g(\mathbf{A}) \mid g \in G'\}\}$, that is, the structure where $R^{\mathbf{B}'} = \bigcup_{g\in G'} R^{g(\mathbf{A})}$ for each $R \in \sigma$. For $k \in \{0,\ldots,m\}$, we say that the algorithm is *truly k-successful* if, for each $\ell \in [k]$, there exists $g \in G'$ such that $\mathbf{b}^\ell = g(\mathbf{a}^\ell)$, where $\mathbf{b}^\ell$ is the answer to the ℓ-th query. Let T_k denote the event of being truly k-successful.

LEMMA 3.3. *Suppose we run* HI-TEST$_{\mathbf{A}}(B,\mathbf{B}')$*. Then, it holds that* $\Pr[T_k \mid T_{k-1}] \geq \frac{1}{m}$ *for every* $k \in [m]$.

LEMMA 3.4. *We have* $|G| > \epsilon\|\mathbf{B}\|/m$.

PROOF. We could remove all $\mathbf{A}$-images in $\mathbf{B}$ by removing all tuples in $\{\{g(\mathbf{a}) \mid g \in G, R \in \sigma, \mathbf{a} \in R^{\mathbf{A}}\}\}$. This means that we can delete all homomorphisms from $\mathbf{A}$ to $\mathbf{B}$ by removing at most $m\cdot|G|$ tuples from $\mathbf{B}$. From the ϵ-farness of $\mathbf{B}$, we have $m\cdot|G| > \epsilon\|\mathbf{B}\|$, which yields the claim. □

LEMMA 3.5. *After the k-th stage of* HI-TEST$_{\mathbf{A}}(B,\mathbf{B}')$*, for any map* $h : \{\mathbf{a}^k\} \to B$*, we have*

$$\Pr\Big[f^k|_{\{\mathbf{a}^k\}} = h \mid T_k\Big] = \frac{\#\{\{g \in G' \mid g \text{ extends } h\}\}}{|G'|}.$$

PROOF. We prove this by induction. It is clear for $k=1$, since each of the tuples in $\{\{g(\mathbf{a}^1) \mid g \in G'\}\}$ is chosen with equal probability.

For $k > 1$, let $\ell < k$ denote an index such that $P_k := \{\mathbf{a}^k\} \cap \bigcup_{\ell'\in[k-1]}\{\mathbf{a}^{\ell'}\} \subseteq \{\mathbf{a}^\ell\}$; such an index ℓ exists due to $\mathbf{A}$ being α-acyclic. From the induction hypothesis on the ℓ-th stage, we have (by summing) that for any map $h : P_k \to B$,

$$\Pr\Big[f^\ell|_{P_k} = h \mid T_k\Big] = \Pr\Big[f^\ell|_{P_k} = h \mid T_\ell\Big] = \frac{\#\{\{g \in G' \mid g \text{ extends } h\}\}}{|G'|}.$$

We then have

$$\begin{aligned}
&\Pr\Big[f^k|_{\{\mathbf{a}^k\}} = h \mid T_k\Big]\\
&= \Pr\Big[f^\ell|_{P_k} = h|_{P_k} \mid T_k\Big]\\
&\quad\times \Pr\Big[f^k|_{\{\mathbf{a}^k\}\setminus P_k} = h|_{\{\mathbf{a}^k\}\setminus P_k} \mid T_k \wedge f^\ell|_{P_k} = h|_{P_k}\Big]\\
&= \Pr\Big[f^\ell|_{P_k} = h|_{P_k} \mid T_\ell\Big]\\
&\quad\times \Pr\Big[f^k|_{\{\mathbf{a}^k\}\setminus P_k} = h|_{\{\mathbf{a}^k\}\setminus P_k} \mid T_k \wedge f^\ell|_{P_k} = h|_{P_k}\Big].
\end{aligned}$$

The latter quantity is equal to the product of

$$\#\{\{g \in G' \mid g \text{ extends } h|_{P_k}\}\}/|G'|$$

and

$$\#\{\{g \in G' \mid g \text{ extends } h\}\}/\#\{\{g \in G' \mid g \text{ extends } h|_{P_k}\}\}$$

which yields the lemma. □

PROOF OF LEMMA 3.3. Let $P_k := \{\mathbf{a}^k\} \cap \bigcup_{\ell'\in[k-1]}\{\mathbf{a}^{\ell'}\}$ be the set of elements previously appeared.

Suppose that $P_k = \{\mathbf{a}^k\}$. Then, there exists $\ell \in [k-1]$ such that $\{\mathbf{a}^k\} \subseteq \{\mathbf{a}^\ell\}$. Then, as $\mathbf{q}^k = f^\ell(\mathbf{a}^\ell)|_{\{\mathbf{a}^k\}} = g(\mathbf{a}^\ell)|_{\{\mathbf{a}^k\}}$ for some homomorphism $g \in G'$, we have $\mathbf{q}^k = g(\mathbf{a}^k)$ and hence the process is truly k-successful.

Suppose that $P_k \subsetneq \{\mathbf{a}^k\}$. We define $Q \subseteq (B \cup \{*\})^{\mathrm{ar}(R_k)}$ as the set of tuples $\mathbf{q}$ such that (i) $\mathbf{q}(a) \neq *$ for $a \in P_k$, (ii) $\mathbf{q}(a) = *$ for $a \in \{\mathbf{a}^k\} \setminus P_k$, and (iii) $\mathbf{q}$ has a completion in $\{\{g(\mathbf{a}^k) \mid g \in G'\}\}$. For $\mathbf{q} \in Q$, we define $n_{\mathbf{q}}$ as the number of completions $\mathbf{b}$ of $\mathbf{q}$ such that $\mathbf{b} = g(\mathbf{a}^k)$ for some $g \in G'$. Note that $\sum_{\mathbf{q}\in Q} n_{\mathbf{q}} = |G'|$. For $\mathbf{q} \in Q$, we define $m_{\mathbf{q}}$ as the total number of completions $\mathbf{b} \in R_k^{\mathbf{B}'}$ of $\mathbf{q}$, that is, $\mathbf{b} = g(\mathbf{a}^\ell)$ for some $\ell \in [m]$ with $R_\ell = R_k$. Note that $\sum_{\mathbf{q}\in Q} m_{\mathbf{q}} \leq m\cdot\sum_{\mathbf{q}\in Q} n_{\mathbf{q}} = m|G'|$ because $\mathbf{A}$-images of homomorphisms in G' are tuple-disjoint. Also, $m_{\mathbf{q}} \geq n_{\mathbf{q}} > 0$ for any $\mathbf{q} \in Q$ from the definition of Q.

Let $\ell \in [k-1]$ be such that $P_k \subseteq \{\mathbf{a}^\ell\}$. For $\mathbf{q} \in Q$, define $h_{\mathbf{q}} : P_k \to B$ as $h(a) = \mathbf{q}(a)$ for every $a \in P_k$. By Lemma 3.5, we have

$$\Pr\Big[\mathbf{q}^k = \mathbf{q} \mid T_{k-1}\Big] = \Pr\Big[f^{k-1}|_{P_k} = h_{\mathbf{q}} \mid T_{k-1}\Big]$$

$$= \frac{\#\{\{g \in G' \mid g \text{ extends } h_{\mathrm{q}}\}\}}{|G'|} = \frac{n_{\mathrm{q}}}{|G'|}.$$

Hence, we have

$$\Pr\left[T_k \mid T_{k-1}\right] = \sum_{\mathrm{q} \in Q} \frac{n_{\mathrm{q}}}{|G'|} \frac{n_{\mathrm{q}}}{m_{\mathrm{q}}}. \tag{1}$$

Now we look at (1) as a function of $\boldsymbol{m} = \{m_{\mathrm{q}}\}_{\mathrm{q} \in Q}$ and write it as $p(\boldsymbol{m})$. Then, to get a lower bound on (1), we extend the domain of p from $\mathbb{N}^Q$ to $\mathbb{R}_+^Q$ and minimize it subject to $\sum_{\mathrm{q} \in Q} m_{\mathrm{q}} \leq m \cdot \sum_{\mathrm{q} \in Q} n_{\mathrm{q}}$. Notice that

$$(\nabla p)_{\mathrm{q}} = \begin{cases} -\frac{n_{\mathrm{q}}^2}{|G'| m_{\mathrm{q}}^2} & \text{if } m_{\mathrm{q}} > 0, \\ 0 & \text{otherwise.} \end{cases}$$

This in particular means that when $m_{\mathrm{q}} = 0$ for some $\mathrm{q} \in Q$, we can decrease the value of p by increasing m_{q} while decreasing another element. Hence, an optimizer $\boldsymbol{m}^* = \{m_{\mathrm{q}}^*\}_{\mathrm{q} \in Q}$ to (1) is not on the boundary of the domain $\mathbb{R}_+^Q$.

Then, we have for any $\mathrm{q}, \mathrm{q}' \in Q$ that

$$\nabla p(\boldsymbol{m}^*) \cdot (\boldsymbol{e}_{\mathrm{q}} - \boldsymbol{e}_{\mathrm{q}'}) = \frac{1}{|G'|} \left(\frac{n_{\mathrm{q}'}^2}{(m_{\mathrm{q}'}^*)^2} - \frac{n_{\mathrm{q}}^2}{(m_{\mathrm{q}}^*)^2} \right),$$

where $\boldsymbol{e}_{\mathrm{q}}$ is the characteristic vector with one in the q-th element and zeros elsewhere. As $\boldsymbol{m}^*$ satisfies $\nabla f(\boldsymbol{m}^*) \cdot (\boldsymbol{e}_{\mathrm{q}} - \boldsymbol{e}_{\mathrm{q}'}) = 0$ for all $\mathrm{q}, \mathrm{q}' \in B$, $n_{\mathrm{q}}/m_{\mathrm{q}}$ is constant regardless of the choice of q. It follows that

$$p(\boldsymbol{m}^*) \geq \sum_{\mathrm{q} \in Q} \frac{n_{\mathrm{q}}}{|G'|} \frac{n_{\mathrm{q}}}{m n_{\mathrm{q}}} = \frac{1}{m},$$

which implies the claim. □

Corollary 3.6. *The rejection probability of* HI-Test$_{\mathbf{A}}(B, \mathbf{B}')$ *is at least* $1/m^m$.

Proof. By Lemma 3.3, the probability that the algorithm is truly m-successful and hence finds a homomorphism from **A** to **B**$'$ is at least $1/m^m$. □

The proof of Lemma 3.1 is immediate from Lemma 3.2 and Corollary 3.6.

With Lemma 3.1, we can easily get a tester for **A**-freeness:

Theorem 3.7. *There exists a one-sided error tester for* **A**-*freeness with a constant number of queries. The query complexity is* $O(m2^{\bar{r}}/\epsilon)^m$, *where* $\bar{r} = \max_{R \in \sigma} \mathrm{ar}(R)$.

Proof. Our algorithm runs HI-Test$_{\mathbf{A}}(B, \mathbf{B})$ $\Theta(1/\delta)$ many times for $\delta = \delta_{3.1}^{\mathbf{A}}(\epsilon)$, and accepts if and only if all the runs accept.

If **B** is **A**-free, then HI-Test$_{\mathbf{A}}$ always accepts, and the algorithm also always accepts. If **B** is ϵ-far from **A**-freeness, then the rejection probability of the algorithm is at least $1 - (1 - \delta)^{\Theta(1/\delta)} \geq \frac{2}{3}$ by setting the hidden constant to be large enough. □

Algorithm 2

procedure IHI-Test$_{\mathbf{A}}(B, \mathbf{B})$ ▷ B is a domain, **B** is a multiset structure with the domain B and the same vocabulary as **A** provided through a query access.
  if HI-Test$_{\mathbf{A}}(B, \mathbf{B})$ accepts (by claiming that **B** is **A**-free) **then**
    Accept.
  else
    Let $g : A \to B$ be the obtained homomorphism.
    if g is not injective **then**
      Accept.
    else
      Reject.

Theorem 3.7 gives the "if" part of Theorem 1.1 because, if the core **A**$'$ of **A** is α-acyclic, then we can test **A**-freeness just by testing **A**$'$-freeness.

Suppose **A** represents an undirected graph H as in Section 1.3. Then, as $\bar{r} = 2$, the query complexity is $O(m/\epsilon)^m$, where m is the number of edges in H. This bound matches the previous result for testing k-path-freeness [37].

3.3 Injective homomorphism inadmissibility

In this section, we discuss how to test injective homomorphism inadmissibility. The modification to Algorithm 1 is simple: we check whether the obtained homomorphism is injective at the end of the algorithm. See Algorithm 2, called IHI-Test$_{\mathbf{A}}$ for details. It is clear that IHI-Test$_{\mathbf{A}}$ always accepts **B** that is injective **A**-free and that the query complexity is constant. Hence, we analyze its rejection probability when **B** is ϵ-far from injective **A**-freeness.

The analysis of IHI-Test$_{\mathbf{A}}$ is very similar to the one of HI-Test$_{\mathbf{A}}$. We use the reduction given by Lemma 3.2 and focus on a relational structure constructed from tuple-disjoint **A**-images. However, we carefully choose the images so that we get an injective homomorphism with high probability.

Now, we construct a large set of tuple-disjoint **A**-images. Let **B** be a multiset structure ϵ-far from injective **A**-freeness, and let G be a maximal set of injective homomorphisms from **A** to **B** such that the multiset of **A**-images $\{\{g(\mathbf{A}) \mid g \in G\}\}$ is tuple-disjoint.

Lemma 3.8. *We have* $|G| > \epsilon \|\mathbf{B}\|/m$.

Proof. We could remove all **A**-images in **B** by removing all tuples in $\{\{g(\mathrm{a}) \mid g \in G, R \in \sigma, \mathrm{a} \in R^{\mathbf{A}}\}\}$. This means that we can delete all injective homomorphisms from **A** to **B** by removing at most $m|G|$ tuples from **B**. From the ϵ-farness of **B**, we have $m|G| > \epsilon \|\mathbf{B}\|$, which yields the claim. □

Let $\phi : B \longrightarrow A$ be a map, which we call a *coloring* of B with $|A|$ colors. Then, we say that a homomorphism $g : A \longrightarrow B$ *admits the coloring* ϕ if $\phi(g(a)) = a$. We define G_ϕ as the multiset of injective homomorphisms in G that admit ϕ.

Lemma 3.9. *There exists a coloring* $\phi : B \longrightarrow A$ *such that* $|G_\phi| \geq |G|/|A|^{|A|}$.

Proof. Suppose that a coloring $\psi : B \longrightarrow A$ is randomly chosen, that is, $\Pr[\psi(b)] = 1/|A|$ for every $b \in B$ independently from others. Then, the probability that an injective homomorphism $g : A \longrightarrow B$ admits the coloring ψ is $1/|A|^{|A|}$. It follows that the expected number of homomorphisms in G that admit ψ is $|G|/|A|^{|A|}$. Hence, there exists a coloring $\phi : B \longrightarrow A$ with $|G_\phi| \geq |G|/|A|^{|A|}$. □

Fix a coloring $\phi : B \longrightarrow A$ with $|G_\phi| \geq |G|/|A|^{|A|}$, given by Lemma 3.9. Let $G'_\phi \subseteq G$ be the subset with $|G'_\phi| \geq |G_\phi|/2$ given by applying Lemma 3.2 on G_ϕ. Then, we define a multiset structure $\mathbf{B}'_\phi$ and the notion of being truly k-successful using G'_ϕ, as in Section 3.2.2.

The advantage of working with G'_ϕ is that, if the algorithm is truly m-successful with respect to G'_ϕ, then the obtained homomorphism is injective because any homomorphism g obtained when truly m-successful satisfies $\phi(g(a)) = a$ for every $a \in A$ and hence $g(a)$'s are distinct.

Modifying the proof of Corollary 3.6 by replacing $\mathbf{B}'$ with $\mathbf{B}'_\phi$, we obtain the following:

Corollary 3.10. HI-Test$_{\mathbf{A}}(B, \mathbf{B}'_\phi)$ *finds an injective homomorphism with probability at least* $1/m^m$.

Lemma 3.11. *Suppose that the multiset structure* $\mathbf{B}$ *is* ϵ*-far from injective* $\mathbf{A}$*-freeness for* $\epsilon \in (0, 1)$. *Then, there exists* $\delta = \delta^{\mathbf{A}}_{3.11}(\epsilon) > 0$ *such that* IHI-Test$_{\mathbf{A}}(B, \mathbf{B})$ *rejects with probability at least* δ.

Proof. It is immediate from Lemma 3.2 and Corollary 3.10 that there exists $\delta = \delta(\epsilon) > 0$ such that HI-Test$_{\mathbf{A}}(B, \mathbf{B})$ rejects and returns an injective homomorphism $g : A \longrightarrow B$ from A to $\mathbf{B}'_\phi$ with probability at least δ. As g is injective, IHI-Test$_{\mathbf{A}}(B, \mathbf{B})$ also rejects with probability at least δ. □

Theorem 3.12. *When* $\mathbf{A}$ *is* α*-acyclic, there exists a one-sided error tester for injective* $\mathbf{A}$*-freeness with a constant number of queries.*

Proof. Our algorithm run IHI-Test$_{\mathbf{A}}(B, \mathbf{B})$ $\Theta(1/\delta)$ many times for $\delta = \delta^{\mathbf{A}}_{3.11}(\epsilon)$, and accepts if and only if all the runs accept.

If there is no injective homomorphism from $\mathbf{A}$ to $\mathbf{B}$, then IHI-Test$_{\mathbf{A}}$ always accepts, and the algorithm also always accept. If $\mathbf{B}$ is ϵ-far from injective $\mathbf{A}$-freeness, then the rejection probability of the algorithm is at least $1 - (1 - \delta)^{\Theta(1/\delta)} \geq \frac{2}{3}$ by setting the hidden constant to be large enough. □

4 LOWER BOUND

In this section, we establish the following lower bound result.

Theorem 4.1. *Suppose that* $\mathbf{A}$ *is a relational structure whose core is not* α*-acyclic; then, testing* $\mathbf{A}$*-freeness is not constant-query testable with one-sided error.*

In order to establish this lower bound, we will make use of the following notion of reduction.

Definition 4.2. Let $\mathbf{A}_1, \mathbf{A}_2$ be structures. We say that testing $\mathbf{A}_1$-freeness *reduces* to testing $\mathbf{A}_2$-freeness if there exists a map f sending each multiset structure $\mathbf{B}_1$ to a multiset structure $\mathbf{B}_2 = f(\mathbf{B}_1)$ such that the following hold:

(i) For each structure $\mathbf{B}_1$, if $\mathbf{B}_1$ is $\mathbf{A}_1$-free, then $\mathbf{B}_2$ is $\mathbf{A}_2$-free.
(ii) For each $\epsilon_1 \in (0, 1)$, there exists $\epsilon_2 \in (0, 1)$ such that, for each structure $\mathbf{B}_1$, if $\mathbf{B}_1$ is ϵ_1-far from being $\mathbf{A}_1$-free, then $\mathbf{B}_2$ is ϵ_2-far from being $\mathbf{A}_2$-free.
(iii) There exists a constant $C \geq 1$ such that, for each structure $\mathbf{B}_1$, the answer to a query to the completion oracle for $\mathbf{B}_2$ can be computed from the answers to C many queries to the completion oracle for $\mathbf{B}_1$.
(iv) There exists a function $g(n) \in O(n)$ such that, for each structure $\mathbf{B}_1$, it holds that $|B_2| \leq g(|B_1|)$.

We will make tacit use of the following straightforwardly verified facts.

Proposition 4.3. *Suppose that* $\mathbf{A}_1, \mathbf{A}_2$ *are structures such that testing* $\mathbf{A}_1$*-freeness reduces to testing* $\mathbf{A}_2$*-freeness.*

- *If* $\mathbf{A}_2$*-freeness is constant-query testable with one-sided error, then so is* $\mathbf{A}_1$*-freeness.*
- *If* $k \geq 1$ *is a constant such that* $\mathbf{A}_2$*-freeness is testable in* $O(n^{1/k})$ *queries with one-sided error, then* $\mathbf{A}_1$*-freeness is also so testable.*

Towards proving Theorem 4.1, we next present two reductions. The first allows us to restrict attention to symbol-distinct structures, and the second allows us to pass to induced hypergraphs. Here, we say that a structure is *symbol-distinct* if each relation has exactly one tuple.

The full proofs of the following two theorems are included in the appendix.

Theorem 4.4. *For each structure* $\mathbf{A}$ *that is a core, there exists a symbol-distinct structure* $\mathbf{A}'$ *such that testing* $\mathbf{A}'$*-freeness reduces to testing* $\mathbf{A}$*-freeness, and such that* $\mathbf{A}$ *and* $\mathbf{A}'$ *share the same hypergraph, that is,* $G_{\mathbf{A}}$ *and* $G_{\mathbf{A}'}$ *are isomorphic.*

The idea behind the proof of Theorem 4.4 is as follows. The structure $\mathbf{A}'$ is defined on a vocabulary σ' having a relation symbol $R_{\mathbf{t}}$ interpreted as $\{\mathbf{t}\}$, for every relation symbol R of the vocabulary σ of $\mathbf{A}$ and for each $\mathbf{t} \in R^{\mathbf{A}}$. To reduce from testing $\mathbf{A}'$-freeness to testing $\mathbf{A}$-freeness, a structure $\mathbf{B}'$ with vocabulary σ' is translated to a structure **B** with vocabulary σ by marking the elements of $R_t^{\mathbf{B}'}$ with **t** and then placing them in $R^{\mathbf{B}}$. Establishing the correctness of the reduction uses the assumption that **A** is a core.

Theorem 4.5. *Let* **A** *be a symbol-distinct structure whose hypergraph is* $G_{\mathbf{A}}$*, and let* $S \subseteq A$*. There exists a symbol-distinct structure* **A**′ *whose hypergraph is* $G_{\mathbf{A}}[S]$ *such that testing* **A**′*-freeness reduces to testing* **A***-freeness.*

On a high level, Theorem 4.5 is established in the following way. For each relation symbol R in the signature σ of **A**, the structure **A**′ has a relation whenever the tuple $(a_1, \dots, a_r) \in R^{\mathbf{A}}$ contains an entry from S; that relation is interpreted as the relation having one tuple whose entries are the values among $a_1, \dots, a_r$ that are contained in S; the other coordinates are effectively removed. To reduce from testing **A**′-freeness to testing **A**-freeness, a structure **B**′ over signature σ' is translated to a structure **B** over signature σ essentially by filling out the coordinates that were removed, in each relation, with a value $+$ that is fresh in that it is not contained in B. In this way, any mapping $f : S \to B'$ can be naturally extended to a mapping $f' : A \to B$ where each element of $A \setminus S$ is sent to $+$; this correspondence has the property that f is a homomorphism from **A**′ to **B**′ if and only if f' is a homomorphism from **A** to **B**.

We now give a proof of Theorem 4.1 based on the following two theorems, whose proofs are deferred to Sections 4.1 and 4.2.

Theorem 4.6. *Let* **A** *be a symbol-distinct relational structure such that* $\mathcal{M}(G_{\mathbf{A}})$ *is a cycle. Then, testing* **A***-freeness requires* $\Omega(\sqrt{n})$ *queries, where n is the domain size of the input structure.*

Theorem 4.7. *Let* **A** *be a symbol-distinct relational structure such that* $\mathcal{M}(G_{\mathbf{A}})$ *is a k-simplex for* $k \geq 2$*. Then, testing* **A***-freeness with one-sided error requires* $\Omega(n^{1/k})$ *queries, where n is the domain size of the input structure.*

Proof of Theorem 4.1. Let **C** be the core of **A**. Since **A** and **C** are homomorphically equivalent (that is, there exist homomorphisms from each to the other), the properties of **A**-freeness and **C**-freeness are equivalent. Hence, it suffices to prove the lower bound for testing **C**-freeness. By Theorem 4.4, there exists a symbol-distinct structure **C**′ whose hypergraph G is not α-acyclic, and such that it suffices to prove the lower bound for testing **C**′-freeness. We now invoke Theorem 2.2; by this theorem, there exists a subset S of the domain of **C**′, with $|S| \geq 3$, such that $\mathcal{M}(G[S])$ is either a cycle or a simplex. By Theorem 4.5, there exists a symbol-distinct structure **C**″ whose hypergraph is $H = G[S]$ such that it suffices to prove the lower bound for testing **C**″-freeness. We have that $\mathcal{M}(H)$ is either a cycle or a simplex. The result follows from Theorems 4.6 and 4.7. □

4.1 Lower Bounds for Cycles

In this section, we prove Theorem 4.6. We use a reduction from testing triangle-freeness, which is hard as in the following theorem:

Theorem 4.8 ([5]). *Testing triangle-freeness in the general graph model requires* $\Omega(\sqrt{n})$ *queries, where n is the number of vertices in the input graph.*

The model studied in [5] did not consider queries of the form $(*, *)$. However, as the hardness is shown on a distribution over d-regular graphs for a fixed d, we can answer to the size query $(*, *)$ by returning $dn/2$ and to the completion query $(*, *)$ by sampling a vertex uniformly at random and returning a random edge incident to it using the random neighbor oracle.

Proof of Theorem 4.6. Let $A = \{a_1, \dots, a_k\}$, where $k \geq 3$. From the assumption, every relation in **A** is unary or binary, and any binary relation of **A** has a single tuple of the form (a_i, a_{i+1}) for $i \in [m]$, where $a_{k+1} = a_1$.

Now, we reduce testing triangle-freeness in the general graph model to testing **A**-freeness. Given a query access to a (regular) graph $G = (V, E)$, we construct a multiset structure **B** on the domain V as follows. For each unary relation $R^{\mathbf{A}}$, we define $R^{\mathbf{B}}$ as the set containing $2|E|/|V|$ many copies of (v) for each $v \in V$. Note that, as G is regular, $|V|$ always divides $2|E|$. For each binary relation of the form $R^{\mathbf{A}} = \{(a_i, a_{i+1})\}$ for $i \in [3]$, we define $R^{\mathbf{B}} = \{(u, v), (v, u) \mid \{u, v\} \in E\}$. For each binary relation of the form $R^{\mathbf{A}} = \{(a_i, a_{i+1})\}$ for $i \in \{4, \dots, k\}$, we define $R^{\mathbf{B}}$ as the set containing $2|E|/|V|$ many copies of (v, v) for each $v \in V$. Now, note that every relation contains exactly $2|E|$ tuples. Hence, $\|\mathbf{B}\| = 2\|\mathbf{A}\| \cdot |E|$.

Now, we check the reduction above satisfies the conditions of Definition 4.2. If G is triangle-free, then clearly **B** is **A**-free, which confirms (i). Suppose that G is ϵ-far from **A**-freeness whereas **B** is δ-close to **A**-freeness. Removing $\delta\|\mathbf{B}\|$ tuples from relations in **B** corresponds to removing at most $2\delta\|\mathbf{A}\| \cdot |E| = 2\delta\|\mathbf{A}\| \cdot |E|$ edges and at most $2\delta\|\mathbf{A}\| \cdot |E| \cdot |V|/2|E| = \delta\|\mathbf{A}\| \cdot |V|$ vertices from G. Recalling that G is regular, it results in removing at most $4\delta\|\mathbf{A}\| \cdot |E|$ edges. Hence, we must have $4\delta\|\mathbf{A}\| \geq \epsilon$, which confirms (ii). It is easy to see that we can answer to a query to the oracle for **B** using a constant number of queries to the oracle for G, which confirms (iii). Hence, testing **A**-freeness requires $\Omega(\sqrt{n})$ queries by Theorem 4.8. □

4.2 Lower Bounds for Simplices

In this section, we prove Theorem 4.7. The main ingredient of our proof is a hardness for testing simplex-freeness of hypergraphs. To state the hardness, we first introduce the general hypergraph model, which is an extension of the general graph model. In this model, an algorithm is given an integer n and a query access to a k-uniform hypergraph $G = (V, \mathcal{E})$ on n vertices. There are two types of queries, called *size queries* and *completion queries*. Each type of query receives a subset $Q \subseteq V$ of size at most k. A hyperedge $S \in \mathcal{E}$ is called a *completion* of Q in G if $S \cap Q = Q$. Then, the answer to the size query Q is the number of completions of Q in G, and the answer to the completion query Q is a random completion of Q in G if exists and a special symbol $\perp$ otherwise. In particular, if Q is empty, then it returns a random hyperedge (unless G is empty), and if Q is of size k, then it returns whether G has the hyperedge Q. A hypergraph $G = (V, \mathcal{E})$ is called *ϵ-far from simplex-freeness* if we must remove more than $\epsilon|E|$ hyperedges so that the resulting hypergraph has no simplex as its subgraph. A *tester* for simplex-freeness is an algorithm that, given an integer n, a query access to a graph $G = (V, \mathcal{E})$, and an error parameter $\epsilon \in (0, 1)$, accepts with probability at least 2/3 if G is simplex-free and rejects with probability at least 2/3 if G is ϵ-far from simplex-freeness. Then, we show the following lower bound for testing simplex-freeness.

THEOREM 4.9. *For any $k \geq 2$, testing k-simplex in a $(k+1)$-uniform hypergraph with one-sided error requires $\Omega(n^{1/k})$ queries, where n is the number of vertices in the input hypergraph.*

In Section 4.2.1, we provide a distribution of k-uniform hypergraphs that have many edge-disjoint k-simplices. In Section 4.2.2, we show that any one-sided error tester on a hypergraph sampled from the distribution requires $\Omega(n^{1/k})$ queries. We note that the proof of Lemma 4.9 follows the line of the proof of Theorem 4.8, but is more cumbersome. The proof of Theorem 4.7 is provided in Section 4.2.3. Missing proofs are given in Appendix C.

4.2.1 Lower-bound distribution. Let $\mathcal{D}_{n,k}$ be a distribution over k-uniform hypergraphs with n vertices and degree $d = \frac{k}{k+1} \cdot (\frac{n}{k+1})^{k-1-1/k}$ defined as follows. A hypergraph is generated by first partitioning the vertices into equal-size subsets of size $\bar{n} = n/(k+1)$, denoted $V_1, \ldots, V_{k+1}$. Next, for each subset $\{i_1, \ldots, i_k\} \subseteq [k+1]$ of size k, we select $\bar{d} = d/k = \bar{n}^{k-1-1/k}/(k+1)$ random perfect k-dimensional matchings among $V_{i_1}, \ldots, V_{i_k}$. In what follows, we assume that $\bar{n}$ is sufficiently large.

LEMMA 4.10. *For any n and k, a hypergraph sampled uniformly from $\mathcal{D}_{n,k}$ is $\Omega(1)$-far from simplex-freeness with probability at least $\delta_{4.10}(k) = \frac{1}{4(k+1)^k}$.*

4.2.2 Lower bound for one-sided error testers. The goal of this section is proving Theorem 4.9. Let $\mathcal{A}$ be any one-sided error tester for simplex-freeness. We can assume the probability that $\mathcal{A}$ errs is an arbitrarily small constant, say, $\delta_{4.10}(k)/2$ (Otherwise, we can run $\mathcal{A}$ many times to reduce the failure probability). If $\mathcal{A}$ views a simplex in the tested hypergraph, then clearly it can reject the hypergraph. However, since $\mathcal{A}$ is a one-sided error tester, if it terminates before viewing a simplex, then it must accept. Suppose that we run $\mathcal{A}$ on a hypergraph chosen according to $\mathcal{D}_{n,k}$ introduced in Section 4.2.1, with some (sufficiently small) constant ϵ. Since we have shown in Lemma 4.10 that, with probability at least $\delta_{4.10}(k)$, such a hypergraph is ϵ-far from being simplex free and the failure probability of $\mathcal{A}$ is at most $\delta_{4.10}(k)/2$, the probability that $\mathcal{A}$ terminates before viewing a simplex must be less than $1 - \delta_{4.10}(k)/2$. Hence, Theorem 4.9 follows from the following lemma:

LEMMA 4.11. *For any fixed k, any deterministic algorithm that detects a simplex in a hypergraph selected according to $\mathcal{D}_{n,k}$ with probability at least $\delta_{4.10}(k)/2$ (over the choice of the hypergraph and internal randomness) requires $\Omega(n^{1/k})$ queries.*

4.2.3 Proof of Theorem 4.7. We first show that testing **A**-freeness requires $\Omega(n^{1/k})$ queries. Suppose **A** is of the form

$$(A = \{a_1, \ldots, a_{k+1}\}, \{R^{\mathbf{A}}\}_{R \in \sigma}).$$

From the assumption, for every $i \in [k+1]$, there exists a k-ary relation $R^{\mathbf{A}} = \{(a_1, \ldots, a_{i-1}, a_{i+1}, \ldots, a_{k+1})\}$.

We reduce testing simplex-freeness on regular k-uniform hypergraphs to testing **A**-freeness. We only consider hypergraphs generated by the distribution given in Section 4.2.1. In particular, the input hypergraph $G = (V, \mathcal{E})$ is d-regular for $d = \Theta(n^{k-1-1/k})$ and the vertex set can be partitioned into $V_1, \ldots, V_{k+1}$ of the same size. For a set $I \subseteq [k+1]$ of size k, we define $\mathcal{E}_I$ as the set of hyperedges spanning V_i's for $i \in I$.

Now, we construct a multiset relational structure **B** on the domain V as follows. For a k-ary relation $R^{\mathbf{A}}$ of the form

$$\{(a_1, a_2, \ldots, a_{i-1}, a_{i+1}, \ldots, a_{k+1})\},$$

we define $R^{\mathbf{B}} = \mathcal{E}_{[k+1]\setminus\{i\}}$. Here, we identify a tuple

$$(v_1, \ldots, v_{i-1}, v_{i+1}, \ldots, v_{k+1})$$

and a hyperedge

$$\{v_1, \ldots, v_{i-1}, v_{i+1}, \ldots, v_{k+1}\}$$

with $v_1 \in V_1, \ldots, v_{i-1} \in V_{i-1}, v_{i+1} \in V_{i+1}, \ldots, v_{k+1} \in V_{k+1}$. For any other relation $R^{\mathbf{A}} = \{(a_{i_1}, \ldots, a_{i_\ell})\}$ of arity $\ell \leq k-1$, we define $R^{\mathbf{B}}$ as the set consisting of $|\mathcal{E}|/\bar{n}^\ell$ many copies of each tuple in $V_{i_1} \times \cdots \times V_{i_\ell}$, where $\bar{n} = n/(k+1)$. For simplicity, we assume that $\bar{n}^\ell$ divides $|\mathcal{E}|$ for every $\ell \leq k-1$, but we can easily extend the argument to the general case. Now, note that every relation in **B** has exactly $|\mathcal{E}|$ many tuples, which means that $\|\mathbf{B}\| \leq \|\mathbf{A}\| \cdot |\mathcal{E}|$

Now, we check the reduction above satisfies the conditions of Definition 4.2. If G is simplex-free, then **B** is **A**-free, which confirms (i). Suppose that G is ϵ-far from simplex-freeness, and $\mathbf{B}$ is δ-close to simplex-freeness. Then, removing at most $\delta||\mathbf{B}||$ tuples from $\mathbf{B}$ corresponds to removing $O(\delta||\mathbf{A}||||\mathbf{B}||) = O(\delta||\mathbf{A}||^2|\mathcal{E}|)$ hyperedges from G. Hence, we have $\delta = \Omega(\epsilon/||\mathbf{A}||^2)$, which confirms (ii). It is easy to see that we can answer to a query to the completion oracle for $\mathbf{B}$ with a constant number of queries to the completion oracle for G, which confirms (iii). Hence, testing $\mathbf{A}$-freeness requires $\Omega(n^{1/k})$ queries by Theorem 4.9. This concludes the proof of Theorem 4.7.

5 UNIONS OF CONJUNCTIVE QUERIES

In this section, we give a proof of Corollary 1.3.

By the results in [13, Section 3], ϕ may be computably rewritten to the form $\phi' = \phi_1 \vee \cdots \vee \phi_k$ that is normalized in the sense that for distinct $i, j \in [k]$, there does not exist a homomorphism from $\mathbf{A}[\phi_i]$ to $\mathbf{A}[\phi_j]$. Note that, given a structure $\mathbf{B}$, it holds that ϕ evaluates to true on $\mathbf{B}$ if and only if there exists $i \in [k]$ such that there is a homomorphism from $\mathbf{A}[\phi_i]$ to $\mathbf{B}$ (equivalently, $\mathbf{B}$ is not $\mathbf{A}[\phi_i]$-free).

For the positive result, assume that the condition in the statement of Corollary 1.3 holds. Given a structure $\mathbf{B}$, use the positive algorithmic result of Theorem 1.1 with an error parameter ϵ/k to test, for each $i \in [k]$, whether or not $\mathbf{B}$ is $\mathbf{A}[\phi_i]$-free. Reject to claim that ϕ is true if and only if one of the tests rejects (indicating that there is a homomorphism from some $\mathbf{A}[\phi_i]$ to $\mathbf{B}$). This algorithm rejects with probability at least $2/3$ when $\mathbf{B}$ is ϵ-far from ϕ-falsity because then $\mathbf{B}$ is ϵ/k-far from being $\mathbf{A}[\phi_i]$-free for some $i \in [k]$.

For the lower bound, assume that the condition in the statement of Corollary 1.3 does not hold; then, there exists $\ell \in [k]$ such that the core of $\mathbf{A}[\phi_\ell]$ is α-acyclic. By Theorem 1.1, it suffices to reduce from testing $\mathbf{A}[\phi_\ell]$-freeness to testing ϕ-falsity. We perform this by using the natural generalization of Definition 4.2. The reduction is to map a multiset structure $\mathbf{B}$ to the product $\mathbf{A}[\phi_\ell] \times \mathbf{B}$, by which we mean the structure with domain $A[\phi_\ell] \times B$ and where, for each relation symbol R, it holds that $R^{\mathbf{A}[\phi_\ell]\times\mathbf{B}} = \{\{((a_1, b_1), \ldots, (a_r, b_r)) \mid (a_1, \ldots, a_r) \in R^{\mathbf{A}[\phi_\ell]}, (b_1, \ldots, b_r) \in R^{\mathbf{B}}\}\}$; here, r denotes the arity of R. It is straightforward to verify that the first and second projections are homomorphisms from $\mathbf{A}[\phi_\ell] \times \mathbf{B}$ to $\mathbf{A}[\phi_\ell]$ and $\mathbf{B}$, respectively. Set $\mathbf{C} = \mathbf{A}[\phi_\ell] \times \mathbf{B}$.

Let us verify that this is indeed a reduction.

(i) We claim that if $\mathbf{B}$ is $\mathbf{A}[\phi_\ell]$-free, then $\mathbf{A}[\phi_\ell] \times \mathbf{B}$ causes ϕ to evaluate to false. Let us argue the contrapositive. Suppose that ϕ is true on the product. Then, there exists $i \in [k]$ such that $\mathbf{A}[\phi_i]$ has a homomorphism to the product $\mathbf{C} = \mathbf{A}[\phi_\ell] \times \mathbf{B}$; but since this product has a homomorphism to $\mathbf{A}[\phi_\ell]$, it follows that $\mathbf{A}[\phi_i]$ has a homomorphism to $\mathbf{A}[\phi_\ell]$, implying (by normalization) that $i = \ell$. Thus, $\mathbf{A}[\phi_\ell]$ has a homomorphism to this product, and hence to $\mathbf{B}$.

(ii) Let R be a relation symbol. By the definition of the product $\mathbf{A}[\phi_\ell] \times \mathbf{B}$, each tuple $(b_1, \ldots, b_r)$ in $R^{\mathbf{B}}$ gives rise to $|R^{\mathbf{A}[\phi_\ell]}|$ tuples in $R^{\mathbf{A}[\phi_\ell]\times\mathbf{B}}$; let us call these the *offshoots* of the tuple $(b_1, \ldots, b_r)$. It is evident that each tuple in $R^{\mathbf{A}[\phi_\ell]\times\mathbf{B}}$ is the offshoot of exactly one tuple in $R^{\mathbf{B}}$. Let K be the maximum, over relation symbols R, of $|R^{\mathbf{A}[\phi_\ell]}|$. We have $||\mathbf{C}|| \leq K||\mathbf{B}||$.

We claim that if a structure $\mathbf{B}$ is ϵ-far from being $\mathbf{A}[\phi_\ell]$-free, then $\mathbf{C}$ is ϵ/K-far from ϕ-falsity. Suppose that $\mathbf{C}'$ is obtained from $\mathbf{C}$ by removing $(\epsilon/K)||\mathbf{C}||$ tuples from relations. Let us say that a tuple $(b_1, \ldots, b_r)$ in a relation $R^{\mathbf{B}}$ of $\mathbf{B}$ is *partly removed in* $\mathbf{C}'$ if one of its offshoots was removed to obtain $\mathbf{C}'$ from $\mathbf{C}$. Then, the number of tuples of $\mathbf{B}$ that are partly removed in $\mathbf{C}'$ is bounded above by $(\epsilon/K)||\mathbf{C}|| \leq (\epsilon/K)K||\mathbf{B}|| = \epsilon||\mathbf{B}||$. Let $\mathbf{B}'$ be the structure obtained from $\mathbf{B}$ by removing each tuple that is partly removed in $\mathbf{C}'$. By assumption, there exists a homomorphism g from $\mathbf{A}[\phi_\ell]$ to $\mathbf{B}'$. It is straightforward to verify that the mapping h defined by $h(a) = (a, g(a))$ is a homomorphism from $\mathbf{A}[\phi_\ell]$ to $\mathbf{C}'$, and so ϕ is true on $\mathbf{C}'$.

(iii) Consider a query $(R, (c_1, \ldots, c_r))$ concerning the relation $R^{\mathbf{C}}$; here, $(c_1, \ldots, c_r) \in (C \cup \{*\})^r$ Define $(a_1, \ldots, a_r) \in (A[\phi_\ell] \cup \{*\})^r$ to be the tuple such that $a_i = *$ if $c_i = *$, and $a_i = d_i$ if c_i has the form (d_i, e_i). Analogously, define $(b_1, \ldots, b_r) \in (B \cup \{*\})^r$ to be the tuple such that $b_i = *$ if $c_i = *$, and $b_i = e_i$ if c_i has the form (d_i, e_i). If the query is a completion query, then to answer it, one can choose a random completion $\mathbf{a}'$ of $(a_1, \ldots, a_r)$, call the completion query for $\mathbf{B}$ to obtain a random completion $\mathbf{b}'$ of $(b_1, \ldots, b_r)$, and then return the product of $\mathbf{a}'$ and $\mathbf{b}'$. If the query is a size query, then to answer it, one can count the number M of completions of $(a_1, \ldots, a_r)$, call the size query for $\mathbf{B}$ to obtain the number N of completions of $(b_1, \ldots, b_r)$, and return $M \cdot N$.

(iv) We have $|C| = |A[\phi_\ell]| \cdot |B|$.

Acknowledgements. The first author thanks Amélie Gheerbrant and Cristina Sirangelo for a useful discussion.

REFERENCES

[1] S. Abiteboul, R. Hull, and V. Vianu. 1995. *Foundations of Databases.* Addison-Wesley.

[2] Isolde Adler and Frederik Harwath. 2018. Property Testing for Bounded Degree Databases. In *STACS.* 6:1–6:14.

[3] Noga Alon, W Fernandez de la Vega, Ravi Kannan, and Marek Karpinski. 2003. Random sampling and approximation of MAX-CSPs. *J. Comput. System Sci.* 67, 2 (2003), 212–243.

[4] Noga Alon, Eldar Fischer, Ilan Newman, and Asaf Shapira. 2009. A Combinatorial Characterization of the Testable Graph Properties: It's All About Regularity. *SIAM J. Comput.* 39, 1 (2009), 143–167.

[5] Noga Alon, Tali Kaufman, Michael Krivelevich, and Dana Ron. 2008. Testing Triangle-Freeness in General Graphs. *SIAM Journal on Discrete Mathematics* 22, 2 (2008), 786–819.

[6] Noga Alon and Asaf Shapira. 2002. Testing satisfiability. In *SODA*. 645–654.
[7] L. Barto and M. Kozik. 2009. Constraint Satisfaction Problems of Bounded Width. In *FOCS*. 595–603.
[8] Sagi Ben-Moshe, Yaron Kanza, Eldar Fischer, Arie Matsliah, Mani Fischer, and Carl Staelin. 2011. Detecting and exploiting near-sortedness for efficient relational query evaluation. In *ICDT*. 256–267.
[9] Eli Ben-Sasson, Prahladh Harsha, and Sofya Raskhodnikova. 2005. Some 3CNF Properties Are Hard to Test. *SIAM J. Comput.* 35, 1 (2005), 1–21.
[10] Jon Louis Bentley. 1979. Decomposable searching problems. *Inform. Process. Lett.* 8, 5 (1979), 244–251.
[11] Arnab Bhattacharyya and Yuichi Yoshida. 2013. An Algebraic Characterization of Testable Boolean CSPs. In *ICALP*. 123–134.
[12] Manuel Blum, Michael Luby, and Ronitt Rubinfeld. 1993. Self-testing/correcting with applications to numerical problems. *J. Comput. System Sci.* 47, 3 (1993), 549–595.
[13] Simone Bova and Hubie Chen. 2014. The Complexity of Width Minimization for Existential Positive Queries. In *ICDT*. 235–244.
[14] Johann Brault-Baron. 2016. Hypergraph Acyclicity Revisited. *Comput. Surveys* 49, 3 (2016), 54:1–54:26.
[15] Andrei A. Bulatov. 2017. A Dichotomy Theorem for Nonuniform CSPs. In *FOCS*. 319–330.
[16] Ashok K Chandra and Philip M Merlin. 1977. Optimal implementation of conjunctive queries in relational data bases. In *STOC*. 77–90.
[17] Surajit Chaudhuri and Moshe Y. Vardi. 1993. Optimization of *Real* Conjunctive Queries. In *PODS*. 59–70.
[18] Hubie Chen. 2014. On the complexity of existential positive queries. *ACM Trans. Comput. Log.* 15, 1 (2014).
[19] Hubie Chen and Benoit Larose. 2017. Asking the Metaquestions in Constraint Tractability. *TOCT* 9, 3 (2017), 11:1–11:27.
[20] Hubie Chen and Moritz Müller. 2015. The Fine Classification of Conjunctive Queries and Parameterized Logarithmic Space. *Transactions on Computation Theory* 7, 2 (2015), 7.
[21] Hubie Chen and Moritz Müller. 2017. One Hierarchy Spawns Another: Graph Deconstructions and the Complexity Classification of Conjunctive Queries. *ACM Trans. Comput. Log.* 18, 4 (2017), 29:1–29:37.
[22] Hubie Chen and Moritz Müller. 2017. The Parameterized Space Complexity of Embedding Along a Path. *Theory Comput. Syst.* 61, 3 (2017), 851–870.
[23] Hubie Chen, Matt Valeriote, and Yuichi Yoshida. 2016. Testing Assignments to Constraint Satisfaction Problems. In *FOCS*. 525–534.
[24] Anirban Dasgupta, Ravi Kumar, and Tamas Sarlos. 2014. On estimating the average degree. In *WWW*. 795–806.
[25] Ronald Fagin, Phokion G Kolaitis, Renée J Miller, and Lucian Popa. 2005. Data exchange: semantics and query answering. *Theoretical Computer Science* 336, 1 (2005), 89–124.
[26] T. Feder and M. Vardi. 1999. The computational structure of monotone monadic SNP and constraint satisfaction: A study through Datalog and group theory. *SIAM J. Comput.* 28 (1999), 57–104.
[27] Eldar Fischer, Eric Lehman, Ilan Newman, Sofya Raskhodnikova, Ronitt Rubinfeld, and Alex Samorodnitsky. 2002. Monotonicity testing over general poset domains. In *STOC*. 474–483.
[28] Jacob Fox, János Pach, and Andrew Suk. 2016. A Polynomial Regularity Lemma for Semialgebraic Hypergraphs and Its Applications in Geometry and Property Testing. *SIAM J. Comput.* 45, 6 (2016), 2199–2223.
[29] Oded Goldreich (Ed.). 2010. *Property Testing: Current Research and Surveys*. LNCS, Vol. 6390. Springer.
[30] Oded Goldreich, Shafi Goldwasser, and Dana Ron. 1998. Property testing and its connection to learning and approximation. *J. ACM* 45, 4 (1998), 653–750.
[31] Oded Goldreich and Dana Ron. 2002. Property Testing in Bounded Degree Graphs. *Algorithmica* 32, 2 (2002), 302–343.
[32] Oded Goldreich and Dana Ron. 2008. Approximating average parameters of graphs. *Random Structures & Algorithms* 32, 4 (2008), 473–493.
[33] Georg Gottlob, Nicola Leone, and Francesco Scarcello. 2001. The complexity of acyclic conjunctive queries. *J. ACM* 48, 3 (2001), 431–498.
[34] Georg Gottlob, Nicola Leone, and Francesco Scarcello. 2002. Hypertree decompositions and tractable queries. *J. Comput. System Sci.* 64, 3 (2002), 579–627.
[35] Martin Grohe. 2007. The complexity of homomorphism and constraint satisfaction problems seen from the other side. *J. ACM* 54, 1 (2007).
[36] P. Hell and J. Nesetril. 1992. The core of a graph. *Discrete Mathematics* 109 (1992), 117–126.
[37] Kazuo Iwama and Yuichi Yoshida. 2018. Parameterized Testability. *ACM Transactions on Computation Theory* 9, 4 (2018), 16–16.
[38] Felix Joos, Jaehoon Kim, Daniela Kühn, and Deryk Osthus. 2017. A characterization of testable hypergraph properties. In *FOCS*. 859–867.
[39] Tali Kaufman, Michael Krivelevich, and Dana Ron. 2004. Tight Bounds for Testing Bipartiteness in General Graphs. *SIAM J. Comput.* 33, 6 (2004), 1441–1483.
[40] Dániel Marx. 2010. Tractable hypergraph properties for constraint satisfaction and conjunctive queries. In *STOC*. 735–744.
[41] C. Papadimitriou and M. Yannakakis. 1999. On the Complexity of Database Queries. *J. Comput. System Sci.* 58, 3 (1999), 407–427.
[42] V Rödl and M Schacht. 2007. Property testing in hypergraphs and the removal lemma. In *STOC*. 488–495.
[43] Dana Ron. 2010. Algorithmic and Analysis Techniques in Property Testing. *Foundations and Trends in Theoretical Computer Science* 5 (2010), 73–205. Issue 2.
[44] Ronitt Rubinfeld and Asaf Shapira. 2011. Sublinear Time Algorithms. *Electronic Colloquium on Computational Complexity (ECCC)* 18 (2011). TR11-013.
[45] Ronitt Rubinfeld and Madhu Sudan. 1996. Robust Characterizations of Polynomials with Applications to Program Testing. *SIAM J. Comput.* 25, 2 (1996), 252–271.
[46] Nicole Schweikardt, Thomas Schwentick, and Luc Segoufin. 2009. Database Theory: Query Languages. In *Algorithms and Theory of Computation Handbook* (second ed.), Mikhail J. Atallah and Marina Blanton (Eds.). Vol. 2: Special Topics and Techniques. CRC Press, Chapter 19.
[47] Christian Sohler. 2012. Almost Optimal Canonical Property Testers for Satisfiability. In *FOCS*. 541–550.
[48] Yuichi Yoshida. 2011. Optimal constant-time approximation algorithms and (unconditional) inapproximability results for every bounded-degree CSP. In *STOC*. 665–674.
[49] Yuichi Yoshida. 2014. A Characterization of Locally Testable Affine-Invariant Properties via Decomposition Theorems. In *STOC*. 154–163.
[50] Yuichi Yoshida. 2014. Gowers Norm, Function Limits, and Parameter Estimation. In *SODA*. 1391–1406.
[51] Yuichi Yoshida. 2016. Testing list H-homomorphisms. *Computional Complexity* 25, 4 (2016), 737–773.
[52] Dmitriy Zhuk. 2017. A Proof of CSP Dichotomy Conjecture. In *FOCS*. 331–342.

A PROOF OF THEOREM 4.4

Proof. Let $\mathbf{A} = (A, \{R^{\mathbf{A}}\}_{R\in\sigma})$ be a core. We show how to construct a symbol-distinct structure $\mathbf{A}'$ such that testing $\mathbf{A}'$ reduces to testing $\mathbf{A}$.

Define σ' as the vocabulary $\{R_{\mathbf{t}} \mid R \in \sigma, \mathbf{t} \in R^{\mathbf{A}}\}$, where the arity of $R_{\mathbf{t}}$ is equal to that of $R \in \sigma$. Define $\mathbf{A}'$ to be the structure $(A, \{R_{\mathbf{t}}\}_{R_{\mathbf{t}} \in \sigma'})$ where $R_{\mathbf{t}}^{\mathbf{A}'} = \{\mathbf{t}\}$. For any structure $\mathbf{B}'$ with domain B' and vocabulary σ', we construct a structure $\mathbf{B}$ in the following way. The domain of $\mathbf{B}$ is $A \times B'$, and for each $R \in \sigma$, we define $R^{\mathbf{B}} = \{\{((a_1, b_1), \ldots, (a_r, b_r)) \mid (a_1, \ldots, a_r) \in R^{\mathbf{A}}, (b_1, \ldots, b_r) \in R^{\mathbf{B}'}_{(a_1,\ldots,a_r)}\}\}$. We have $\|\mathbf{B}\| = \|\mathbf{B}'\|$; moreover, there is clearly a natural bijection between the tuples of $\mathbf{B}'$ and the tuples of $\mathbf{B}$: namely, map the tuple $(b_1, \ldots, b_r) \in R^{\mathbf{B}'}_{(a_1,\ldots,a_r)}$ to the tuple $((a_1, b_1), \ldots, (a_r, b_r)) \in R^{\mathbf{B}}$.

Let $\mathbf{B}_-$ be a structure obtained from $\mathbf{B}$ by deleting tuples, and let $\mathbf{B}'_-$ be the corresponding structure obtained from $\mathbf{B}'$ by deleting the corresponding tuples under the bijection just given. We prove that $\mathbf{B}_-$ is $\mathbf{A}$-free if and only if $\mathbf{B}'_-$ is $\mathbf{A}'$-free, yielding properties (i) and (ii) in the definition of reduction. For any homomorphism h from $\mathbf{A}$ to $\mathbf{B}_-$, the composition $\pi_1(h)$ is readily seen to be an endomorphism of $\mathbf{A}$. (Here, π_1 denotes the first projection.) Since each endomorphism of $\mathbf{A}$ is a bijection (as $\mathbf{A}$ is a core), when h is a homomorphism from $\mathbf{A}$ to $\mathbf{B}_-$, by composing h with an appropriate power of $\pi_1(h)$, we obtain a homomorphism g from $\mathbf{A}$ to $\mathbf{B}_-$ such that $\pi_1(g)$ is the identity mapping. Hence, if there is any homomorphism from $\mathbf{A}$ to $\mathbf{B}_-$ at all, there is a homomorphism g such that $\pi_1(g)$ is the identity mapping; moreover, when such a homomorphism exists, the image $g(A)$ of g is straightforwardly verified to be the graph of a homomorphism from $\mathbf{A}'$ to $\mathbf{B}'_-$. In the other direction, if there is a homomorphism f from $\mathbf{A}'$ to $\mathbf{B}'_-$, then the mapping $a \mapsto (a, f(a))$ is readily verified to be a homomorphism from $\mathbf{A}$ to $\mathbf{B}_-$.

We verify property (iii) in the definition of reduction, as follows. Consider a query $(R, (q_1, \ldots, q_r))$ for $\mathbf{B}$.

- Let $(c_1, \ldots, c_r) \in (A \cup \{*\})^r$ be the tuple such that $q_i = *$ implies $c_i = *$ and $q_i \neq *$ implies $c_i = \pi_1(q_i)$.
- Let $(d_1, \ldots, d_r) \in (A \cup \{*\})^r$ be the tuple such that $q_i = *$ implies $d_i = *$ and $q_i \neq *$ implies $d_i = \pi_2(q_i)$.

Let $\mathbf{t}_1, \ldots, \mathbf{t}_k$ be the tuples in $R^{\mathbf{A}}$ that are completions of $(c_1, \ldots, c_r)$. We may use a size query $(R_{\mathbf{t}_i}, (d_1, \ldots, d_r))$ for $\mathbf{B}'$ to determine the number of completions m_i of $(d_1, \ldots, d_r)$ in $R^{\mathbf{B}'}_{\mathbf{t}_i}$. If the query $(R, (q_1, \ldots, q_r))$ was a size query, then the answer straightforwardly verified, from the definition of $\mathbf{B}$, to be $m_1 + \cdots + m_k$. If the query $(R, (q_1, \ldots, q_r))$ was a completion query, then it is answered in the following way. If $m_1 + \cdots + m_k = 0$, then return $\perp$. Otherwise, randomly pick an index $i \in [k]$, by selecting the index $i \in [k]$ with probability $m_i/(m_1 + \cdots + m_k)$; return the answer to a completion query $(R_{\mathbf{t}_i}, (d_1, \ldots, d_r))$ for $\mathbf{B}'$. Correctness is verified, again, from the definition of $\mathbf{B}$.

Property (iv) is clear: $|B| = |A| \cdot |B'|$. □

B PROOF OF THEOREM 4.5

Proof. Let σ' be the vocabulary and let $\mathbf{A}'$ be the symbol-distinct structure with domain S that are constructed as follows. For each $R \in \sigma$, if the unique tuple $(a_1, \ldots, a_r) \in R^{\mathbf{A}}$ contains at least one entry in S, then let $i_1 < \cdots < i_p$ be the indices from $[r]$ such that $a_{i_1}, \ldots, a_{i_p}$ are the entries among $a_1, \ldots, a_r$ that are contained in S; and, include a symbol R' in σ' whose arity is p, where $R'^{\mathbf{A}'} = \{(a_{i_1}, \ldots, a_{i_p})\}$. Let $\mathbf{B}'$ be any structure with domain B' over σ'. From $\mathbf{B}'$, we define a structure $\mathbf{B}$ as follows. The domain of $\mathbf{B}$ is $B = B' \cup \{+\}$. For each $R' \in \sigma'$, let $i_1 < \cdots < i_p$ be the indices defined above, and define $R^{\mathbf{B}}$ as the relation that contains, for each tuple $(b'_1, \ldots, b'_p) \in R^{\mathbf{B}'}$, the tuple $(b_1, \ldots, b_r)$ where $b_{i_1} = b'_1, \ldots, b_{i_p} = b'_p$, and where all other entries are equal to $+$. Clearly, there is a natural bijection between tuples in $R^{\mathbf{B}'}$ and $R^{\mathbf{B}}$. For each symbol $R \in \sigma$ that does not have a corresponding symbol $R' \in \sigma'$, define $R^{\mathbf{B}}$ as $\{\{(+, \ldots, +)\}\}$, where the multiplicity of $(+, \ldots, +)$ is $\|\mathbf{B}'\|$; let Z denote the number of such symbols $R \in \sigma$, and call each such symbol *trivialized*. We have $\|\mathbf{B}\| = (Z + 1)\|\mathbf{B}'\|$.

It is straightforward to establish that a mapping $f : S \to B'$ is a homomorphism from $\mathbf{A}'$ to $\mathbf{B}'$ if and only if the *canonical* extension $f' : A \to B$ of f that sends each element in $A \setminus S$ to $+$ is a homomorphism from $\mathbf{A}$ to $\mathbf{B}$. This establishes property (i) in the definition of reduction.

Let us establish property (ii) in the definition of reduction. We claim that if $\mathbf{B}'$ is ϵ'-far from being $\mathbf{A}'$-free, then $\mathbf{B}$ is $\epsilon'/(Z + 1)$-far from being $\mathbf{A}$-free. Consider the deletion of $(\epsilon'/(Z + 1))\|\mathbf{B}\| = \epsilon'\|\mathbf{B}'\|$ tuples from $\mathbf{B}$. Since each trivialized symbol R contains $\|\mathbf{B}'\|$ copies of $(+, \ldots, +)$, in effect, the deletion amounts to the deletion of at most $\epsilon'\|\mathbf{B}'\|$ tuples from the relations $R^{\mathbf{B}}$, over non-trivialized symbols R. Under the bijection given above, this is equivalent to the deletion of at most $\epsilon'\|\mathbf{B}'\|$ tuples from the relations of $\mathbf{B}'$. Since $\mathbf{B}'$ is assumed to be ϵ'-far from being $\mathbf{A}'$-free, this deletion of tuples from $\mathbf{B}'$ results in a structure that admits a homomorphism from $\mathbf{A}'$. By taking the canonical extension of this homomorphism, we obtain a homomorphism from $\mathbf{A}$ to $\mathbf{B}$ under the deletions, establishing our claim.

Let us establish property (iii) in the definition of reduction. A size query for $\mathbf{B}$ can clearly be resolved using size queries to $\mathbf{B}'$: for each trivialized symbol R, the size of $R^{\mathbf{B}}$ is $\|\mathbf{B}'\|$, and for each other symbol R, the size of $R^{\mathbf{B}}$ is equal to that of $R^{\mathbf{B}'}$. A completion query $(R, \mathbf{q})$ for $\mathbf{B}$ can be resolved in the following way. If the query concerns a trivialized symbol R, then the answer is $(+, \ldots, +)$ if this tuple is a completion of $\mathbf{q}$, and $\perp$ otherwise. Otherwise, an answer can be obtained from a completion query $(R, \mathbf{q}')$ for $\mathbf{B}'$.

Property (iv) is clear: $|B| = |B'| + 1$. □

C MISSING PROOFS FOR SECTION 4.2

Proof of Lemma 4.10. We shall show that with high probability over the choice of a hypergraph $G = (V, \mathcal{E})$ according to $\mathcal{D}_{n,k}$, there are at least $\gamma|\mathcal{E}|$ edge-disjoint simplices in the hypergraph, for some constant γ.

Let the vertices in each set V_b ($b \in [k+1]$) be denoted by $v_{b,1}, \ldots, v_{b,\bar{n}}$. For a tuple $\mathbf{b} = (b_1, \ldots, b_k) \in [k+1]^k$ of distinct indices and a tuple $\mathbf{i} = (i_1, \ldots, i_k) \in [\bar{n}]^k$, let $\alpha_{\mathbf{i}}^{\mathbf{b}}$ be an indicator of the event that there is a hyperedge spanning $v_{b_1,i_1}, \ldots, v_{b_k,i_k}$. Then, $\Pr[\alpha_{\mathbf{i}}^{\mathbf{b}} = 1] = 1 - \left(1 - \frac{1}{\bar{n}^{k-1}}\right)^{\bar{d}}$ and so $\Pr[\alpha_{\mathbf{i}}^{\mathbf{b}} = 1] \le \frac{\bar{d}}{\bar{n}^{k-1}}$, and

$$\Pr[\alpha_{\mathbf{i}}^{\mathbf{b}} = 1] \ge \frac{\bar{d}}{\bar{n}^{k-1}} - \binom{\bar{d}}{2}\frac{1}{\bar{n}^{2(k-1)}} \ge \frac{\bar{d}}{\bar{n}^{k-1}}\left(1 - \frac{1}{2(k+1)\bar{n}^{1/k}}\right)$$

Next, consider any choice of $\mathbf{i} = (i_1, \ldots, i_{k+1}) \in [\bar{n}]^{k+1}$. Let $X_{\mathbf{i}}$ denote the indicator of the event that there is a simplex spanning the vertices $v_{1,i_1}, \ldots, v_{k+1,i_{k+1}}$. Since the choices of the k-dimensional matchings on $V_{b_1}, \ldots, V_{b_k}$ for k-sized subsets $\{b_1, \ldots, b_k\}$ of $[k+1]$ are mutually independent, $\Pr[X_{\mathbf{i}} = 1] \le \left(\frac{\bar{d}}{\bar{n}^{k-1}}\right)^{k+1}$ holds, and

$$\Pr[X_{\mathbf{i}} = 1] \ge \left(\frac{\bar{d}}{\bar{n}^{k-1}}\right)^{k+1}\left(1 - \frac{1}{2(k+1)\bar{n}^{1/k}}\right)^{k+1}.$$

Let $\beta_{\mathbf{i}}$ denote the indicator of the event that there is a simplex different from $v_{1,i_1}, \ldots, v_{k+1,i_{k+1}}$ that includes one of the hyperedges. Since the probability of having a hyperedge $(v_{b_1,i'_1}, \ldots, v_{b_k,i'_k})$ conditioned on having the hyperedge $(v_{b_1,i_1}, \ldots, v_{b_k,i_k})$ for any choice of

$$|\{i'_1, \ldots, i'_k\} \cap \{i_1, \ldots, i_k\}| \ge 1$$

is at most $1 - (1 - \frac{1}{\bar{n}^{k-1}})^{\bar{d}-1} \le \frac{\bar{d}-1}{\bar{n}^{k-1}}$,

$$\begin{aligned}
&\Pr[X_{\mathbf{i}} = 1 \wedge \beta_{\mathbf{i}} = 1] = \Pr[X_{\mathbf{i}} = 1] \cdot \Pr[\beta_{\mathbf{i}} = 1 \mid X_{\mathbf{i}} = 1] \\
&\le \left(\frac{\bar{d}}{\bar{n}^{k-1}}\right)^{k+1} \cdot (k+1) \cdot (\bar{n}-1) \cdot \left(\frac{\bar{d}-1}{\bar{n}^{k-1}}\right)^k \\
&\le \left(\frac{\bar{d}}{\bar{n}^{k-1}}\right)^{k+1} \frac{(k+1)(\bar{d}-1)^k}{\bar{n}^{k^2-k-1}}
\end{aligned}$$

Let $\eta_{\mathbf{i}}$ be the indicator of the event that there is a simplex spanning the vertices $v_{1,i_1}, \ldots, v_{k+1,i_{k+1}}$ and there is no other simplex that shares any of its hyperedges. Then, we have

$$\begin{aligned}
&\Pr[\eta_{\mathbf{i}} = 1] = \Pr[X_{\mathbf{i}} = 1 \wedge \beta_{\mathbf{i}} = 0] \\
&= \Pr[X_{\mathbf{i}} = 1] - \Pr[X_{\mathbf{i}} = 1 \wedge \beta_{\mathbf{i}} = 0] \\
&\ge \left(\frac{\bar{d}}{\bar{n}^{k-1}}\right)^{k+1} \cdot \left(\left(1 - \frac{1}{2(k+1)\bar{n}^{1/k}}\right)^{k+1} - \frac{(k+1)(\bar{d}-1)^k}{\bar{n}^{k^2-k-1}}\right) \\
&\ge \frac{1}{2}\left(\frac{\bar{d}}{\bar{n}^{k-1}}\right)^{k+1}.
\end{aligned}$$

under our assumption that $\bar{n}$ is sufficiently large. Hence, the expected number of tuples $(v_{1,i_1}, \ldots, v_{k+1,i_{k+1}})$ that constitute a simplex that does not share a hyperedge with any other simplex is

$$\sum_{\mathbf{i}} \eta_{\mathbf{i}} \ge \bar{n}^{k+1} \cdot \frac{1}{2}\left(\frac{\bar{d}}{\bar{n}^{k-1}}\right)^{k+1} = \frac{\bar{d}\bar{n}}{2(k+1)^k} = \frac{dn}{2k(k+1)^{k+1}}.$$

Note that we have $\sum_{\mathbf{i}} \eta_{\mathbf{i}} \le dn/k(k+1)$ as we only have dn/k hyperedges and each simplex uses $k+1$ hyperedges. Let $\alpha = \frac{1}{4k(k+1)^{k+1}}$ and $p = \Pr[\sum_{\mathbf{i}} \eta_{\mathbf{i}} \le \alpha dn]$. Then, we have

$$\frac{dn}{2k(k+1)^{k+1}} \le \mathrm{E}\left[\sum_{\mathbf{i}} \eta_{\mathbf{i}}\right] \le p\alpha dn + (1-p)\frac{dn}{k(k+1)}$$

The last quantity is bounded above by $\alpha dn + (1-p)\frac{dn}{k(k+1)}$, implying $p \le 1 - \frac{1}{4(k+1)^k}$. □

We will also use the following, which states that, for every set of $k-1$ vertices belonging to different blocks, the number of hyperedges containing them is high.

Lemma C.1. *For any fixed k, a hypergraph sampled uniformly from $\mathcal{D}_{n,k}$ satisfies the following with probability $1 - O(1/n^{2k})$: For any set S of $k-1$ vertices belonging to different blocks and block V_b not containing any vertex in S, the number $m_{S,b}$ of hyperedges of the form $S \cup \{v\}$ for $v \in V_b$ is $\Omega(n^{1-1/k})$.*

Proof. Let $S = \{v_1, \ldots, v_{k-1}\}$ and let $V_{b_1}, \ldots, V_{b_{k-1}}$ be blocks to which $v_1, \ldots, v_{k-1}$ belong, respectively. For each $i \in [\bar{d}]$, the probability that the i-th k-dimensional matching spanning V_b and $V_{b_1}, \ldots, V_{b_{k-1}}$ has a hyperedge containing S is $p := 1/\bar{n}^{k-2}$. Hence, $\mu := \mathrm{E}[m_{S,b}] = p\bar{d} = \bar{n}^{1-1/k}/(k+1)$. By Chernoff's inequality, $\Pr\left[m_{S,b} < \frac{\mu}{2}\right] \le \exp\left(-\frac{\mu}{8}\right) \le \frac{1}{10n^{2k}}$. Here in the last inequality, we use the fact that n is sufficiently large. By union bound over the choice of S and b, we have $m_{S,b} \ge \bar{n}^{1-1/k}/(2k+2)$ for every S and b with probability at least $1 - O(1/n^{2k})$. □

Proof of Lemma 4.11. It will be convenient to view hypergraphs in the support of $\mathcal{D}_{n,k}$ as being represented by k-dimensional matchings over tables. Namely, there is a table $T_{b,B}$ for each $b \in [k+1]$ and a set $B \ni b$ of size k. Each table $T_{b,B}$ is of size $\bar{n} \times \bar{d}$ (recall that $\bar{n} = n/(k+1)$ and $\bar{d} = d/k$): there is a row for each vertex v in V_b, and each entry in v's row corresponds to one of the $\bar{d}$ hyperedges that are incident to v and to vertices in $V_{b'}$ with $b' \in B$. For $B = \{b_1, \ldots, b_k\}$, a hyperedge between $v_1 \in V_{b_1}, \ldots, v_k \in V_{b_k}$ is represented by $T_{b_1,B}[v_1, i_1], \ldots, T_{b_k,B}[v_k, i_k]$ for some $i_1, \ldots, i_k \in [\bar{d}]$. Hence, the $\bar{d}$ perfect k-dimensional matchings among $V_{b_1}, \ldots, V_{b_k}$ correspond to a single perfect k-dimensional matching among the entries of the tables $T_{b_1,B}$, $T_{b_2,B}, \ldots, T_{b_k,B}$, where $B = \{b_1, \ldots, b_k\}$.

Let $\mathcal{A}$ be a deterministic algorithm that performs $q(n) = o(n^{1/k})$ queries and whose goal is to detect a simplex with probability at least $\delta_{4.10}(k)$. The probability is taken over the choice of the hypergraph G in the support of $\mathcal{D}_{n,k}$ and internal randomness. Namely $\mathcal{A}$ is a (possibly probabilistic) mapping from query-answer histories $\langle(q_1, a_1), \ldots, (q_t, a_t)\rangle$, to q_{t+1} for every $t < q(n)$. We note that the mapping from query-answer histories to queries needs to be defined only on histories that are consistent with some hypergraph in the support of $\mathcal{D}_{n,k}$.

In what follows we define a process that answers the queries of the algorithm while generating a hypergraph according to $\mathcal{D}_{n,k}$. At any time t, the queries of the algorithm and the answers to them determine the knowledge hypergraph $G^t = (V^t, \mathcal{E}^t, \bar{\mathcal{E}}^t, D)$, where V^t are the vertices, $\mathcal{E}^t$ are the hyperedges, $\bar{\mathcal{E}}^t$ are the non-hyperedges, and D are degree informations. Namely, V^t consists of all vertices that appeared in queries of the algorithm or in answers to them. Similarly $\mathcal{E}^t$ consists of all hyperedges that were returned for completion queries, and $\bar{\mathcal{E}}^t$ consists of all sets that are found to be non-existent, that is, completions of completion queries whose answers were $\perp$ or completions of size queries whose answers were 0. Finally, D contains the information on the number of completions of sets of size at most k that were returned by size queries. For every hyperedge $S = \{v_1, \ldots, v_k\} \in \mathcal{E}^t$, the knowledge hypergraph will include the indices of the entries in the tables by which v_i's are connected (that is, $(i_1, \ldots, i_k)$ such that $T_{b_k,B}[v_i, i_1], \ldots, T_{b_k,B}[v_k, i_k]$ are matched, where $B = \{b_1, \ldots, b_k\}$ is a set with $v_i \in V_{b_i}$ for each $i \in [k]$).

We note that we cannot detect a simplex using size queries (as long as $q(n) = o(n)$). Hence, we upper bound the probability that we close a simplex using completion queries.

Completion queries of size k: Let $B = \{b_1, \ldots, b_k\}$; suppose a completion query $Q = \{v_1, \ldots, v_k\}$ with $v_i \in V_{b_1}$ for each $i \in [k]$ is given. Then, the process computes the probability, conditioned on the current knowledge hypergraph, that Q is a hyperedge. Namely, it considers all hypergraphs in the support of $\mathcal{D}_{n,k}$ that are consistent with G^t and answers positively, that is, Q, with probability that is proportional to the number of these hypergraphs that have the hyperedge Q. Let $U_{t,b_i,B}$ denote the number of unmatched entries in $T_{b_i,B}$ at time t (before the $(t+1)$-th query). Note that this number equals the number of unmatched entries in $T_{b_j,B}$ for every $j \in [k] \setminus \{i\}$ at the same time.

The probability that there is a hyperedge Q is bounded above by:

$$\frac{\bar{d} \cdot \bar{d}^{k-1}}{\prod_{i=2}^{k}(U_{t,b_i,B} - |\bar{\mathcal{E}}^t|\bar{d})} \tag{2}$$

To verify this consider an iterative process in which the (at most $\bar{d}$) unmatched entries in v_1's row in $T_{b_1,B}$ are matched one by one to unmatched entries in $T_{b_i,B}$'s for $i \in \{2, \ldots, k\}$. After τ steps, the probability of selecting any of the (at most $\bar{d}$) unmatched entries in v_i's row in $T_{b_i,B}$ for every $i \in \{2, \ldots, k\}$ is the number of combinations of unmatched entries in v_i's row in $T_{b_i,B}$ for $i \in \{2, \ldots, k\}$, divided by $\prod_{i=2}^{k}(U_{t,b_i,B} - |\bar{\mathcal{E}}^t|\bar{d})$. Here, the term $|\bar{\mathcal{E}}^t|\bar{d}$ is the maximum number of unmatched entries that cannot be matched to entries in v_1's row because they correspond to a hyperedge in $\bar{\mathcal{E}}^t$ containing v_1.

Note that $U_{t,b_i,B} \geq \bar{d}\bar{n} - t$ for every $i \in \{2, \ldots, k\}$. We also have $|\bar{\mathcal{E}}^t| \leq t$ with probability at least $1 - o(1)$ (over the choice of the hypergraph), as we get non-hyperedge only when the query is a set of size k from Lemma C.1. Recalling that $t = o(n)$, the probability (2) is $O(\bar{d}/\bar{n}^{k-1}) = O(n^{-1/k})$. It follows that the probability that the algorithm gets a positive answer, that is, Q, for any of the at most $o(n^{1/k})$ queries of size k is $o(1)$. But if the algorithm always gets $\perp$ or 0 for its completion queries of size k, it clearly cannot close a simplex with such a query.

Completion queries of size at most k − 1: Suppose that, for $B = \{b_1, \ldots, b_\ell\}$ with $\ell \leq k - 1$, a completion query $Q = \{v_1, \ldots, v_\ell\}$ with $v_i \in V_{b_i}$ for each $i \in [\ell]$ is given. By Lemma C.1, with probability at least $1 - o(1)$ (over the choice of the hypergraph), the process answers a completion $S = (v_1, \ldots, v_k)$ of Q according to the conditional probability that the entries $T_{b_1,B}[v_1, i_1], \ldots, T_{b_k,B}[v_k, i_k]$ are matched (where again, the conditioning is on the current knowledge hypergraph G^t). Here, we would like to upper bound the probability that any of the completed vertices, that is, vertices in $S \setminus Q$, already belongs to the knowledge hypergraph. Observe that the knowledge hypergraph G^t contains at most kt vertices and at most t hyperedges and non-hyperedges.

Suppose $Q = \emptyset$. Then, the probability that we hit a vertex in the knowledge hypergraph is upper bounded by

$$\prod_{i=1}^{k} \frac{kt}{\bar{n} - (kt + i - 1) - |\bar{\mathcal{E}}^t|} \leq \left(\frac{kt}{\bar{n} - k(t+1) - |\bar{\mathcal{E}}^t|}\right)^k = o(1)$$

as $t = o(n)$.

Suppose $Q \neq \emptyset$. Without loss of generality, we assume $q_1 \in V_{b_1}$ is a vertex and $q_2 = *$. Then, the conditional probability that $T_{b_1,B}[v_1, i_1]$ is matched to $T_{b_2,B}[v_2, i_2]$ for some $v_2 \in V^{t-1} \cap V_{b_2}$ and $i_2 \in [\bar{d}]$ at time t is upper bounded by

$$\frac{\bar{d}t}{\bar{d}\bar{n} - t - |\bar{\mathcal{E}}^t|\bar{d}} \leq \frac{\bar{d}t}{\bar{d}\bar{n} - t - t\bar{d}} = o\left(\frac{dn^{1/k}}{dn}\right) = o(n^{-1+1/k}).$$

as $t = o(n^{1/k})$.

To summarize, the probability that we hit a vertex in the knowledge hypergraph for any of the at most $o(n^{1/k})$ completion queries of size at msot $k - 1$ is $o(1)$. But if the algorithm always gets a new vertex for its completion queries of size at most $k - 1$, it clearly cannot close a simplex with such a query. □

The Selfish Models Property: Bounding the Complexity of Query Containment and Entailment Problems

Hubie Chen*
Dept. of Computer Science and Information Systems
Birkbeck, University of London
London, United Kingdom
hubie@dcs.bbk.ac.uk

ABSTRACT

Query containment is the fundamental problem of deciding, given two database queries, if the result of the first query is always contained in the result of the second query. For a number of established query classes, an instance of this problem can be decided by computing a set of models of the first query, and then evaluating the second query on each of the models. We formalize this phenomenon by introducing the *selfish models property*; this property gives an avenue for establishing both the decidability of and complexity upper bounds for containment problems. Using this property, we show how existing results can be uniformly derived, and we present two significant novel positive results for first-order query containment problems, exhibiting complexity upper bounds for containment problems that were not previously known to be decidable.

CCS CONCEPTS

• **Theory of computation → Complexity classes**; **Problems, reductions and completeness**; **Complexity theory and logic**; **Finite Model Theory**.

KEYWORDS

computational complexity; query containment; finite model theory

*Acknowledges the support of Spanish Project TIN2017-86727-C2-2-R.

PODS'19, June 30-July 5, 2019, Amsterdam, Netherlands

ACM ISBN 978-1-4503-6227-6/19/06...$15.00
https://doi.org/10.1145/3294052.3319682

ACM Reference Format:
Hubie Chen. 2019. The Selfish Models Property: Bounding the Complexity of Query Containment and Entailment Problems. In *38th ACM SIGMOD-SIGACT-SIGAI Symposium on Principles of Database Systems (PODS'19), June 30-July 5, 2019, Amsterdam, Netherlands.* ACM, New York, NY, USA, 16 pages. https://doi.org/10.1145/3294052.3319682

1 INTRODUCTION

1.1 Background

Query containment is the computational problem of deciding, given two database queries, if the result of the first query is always contained in the result of the second query; in logical formulation, it is the problem of deciding if a query *entails* a second one. This is a fundamental query reasoning problem that enjoys applications to and connections with many areas of database theory, including query optimization [1, 8, 28], view-based query answering [7, 25], and data integration [24]. While this problem has been studied over the years relative to many different types of database queries, we focus in this article on the fundamental class of *first-order queries*, queries formalizable in first-order logic. We also focus our discussion on *Boolean queries*, which are queries that, when evaluated on a structure, yield either true or false; in logical formulation, these correspond to *sentences*, that is, formulas not having free variables. This focus is not restrictive in that, by standard arguments, the results that we present can be extended to non-Boolean queries. It is well-known that, on general first-order queries, query containment is undecidable; in fact, this undecidability result holds even when one considers just query containment between positive first-order queries [13, Theorem 4.12].

There are important classes of queries where the problem of query containment is computably decidable, and where deciding if a query ϕ is contained in a query ψ can be reduced to checking that ψ holds on a finite set of models of ϕ. The most prominent and well-known example of a query class exhibiting this phenomenon is the class of *conjunctive queries*, which can be described logically as first-order queries built from conjunction and existential quantification. The classical work of Chandra and Merlin [8] showed that each conjunctive query ϕ can be efficiently mapped to a model $\mathbf{A}[\phi]$ of ϕ having the property that ϕ entails another conjunctive query ψ if and only if ψ evaluates to true on $\mathbf{A}[\phi]$; since query evaluation for conjunctive queries is in NP, this places query containment for such queries in NP as well. As another example, the class of *existential positive queries*—the extension of conjunctive queries where disjunction is also permitted—exhibits this phenomenon; here, it is known that each such query ϕ can be mapped to a finite set $\mathcal{A}^{\phi}$ of models of ϕ whereby another such query ψ contains ϕ if and only if ψ is true on each structure in $\mathcal{A}^{\phi}$ (this is due to Sagiv and Yannakakis [28], and there is a modern examination [4, 5] of the associated theory). Let us refer to the phenomenon of reducing query containment of ϕ in ψ to query evaluation of ψ on certain ϕ-models as the *selfish models phenomenon*; typically, the ϕ-models used—the *selfish models*—strongly reflect the structure of ϕ, and exhibit no dependence on ψ (as in the above two examples) or a minimal dependence on ψ. This phenomenon can be used in a number of situations to derive the decidability of and desirable complexity upper bounds on query containment problems.

Beyond the ability to derive positive results on the computability and complexity status of query containment problems, there is another reason for our interest in the selfish models phenomenon. There are now a number of dichotomy theorems that comprehensively describe, starting from a base class of queries (such as conjunctive queries), the subclasses (of the class) on which query evaluation is computationally tractable [9–12, 14–20, 22, 26]. To establish the hardness results for such dichotomy theorems, one typically exhibits a reduction from a known hard problem. In a number of cases, selfish models are used as a key component of these reductions; in particular, it is often gainful for a reduction to produce instances whose structure is some form of product of a selfish model with a structure based on an instance of a hard problem, as the evaluation of a query on a selfish model thereof often has a very restricted and reasonably analyzable form [9, 14, 18, 19, 22]. A relatively non-trivial example of such a use can be found in the hardness proof of a dichotomy theorem on so-called *block-sorted* quantified conjunctive queries [14].

Despite the prominence, importance, and relevance of the selfish models phenomenon, there has not been (to our knowledge) any theoretical framework for uniformly and tightly presenting positive results on query containment problems exhibiting this phenomenon. It is possible to reduce query containment to satisfiability; precisely, a query ϕ is not contained in a query ψ if and only if the query $\phi \wedge \neg\psi$ is satisfiable. In cases where the queries are drawn from classes exhibiting the selfish models phenomenon, one can restrict the satisfiability check to the selfish models; for example, for conjunctive queries, the given query $\phi \wedge \neg\psi$ is satisfiable if and only if it is satisfied by $\mathbf{A}[\phi]$, and for existential positive queries, the given query is satisfiable if and only if it is satisfied by a member of $\mathcal{A}^{\phi}$. In such cases, the class of queries $\phi \wedge \neg\psi$ has a strong form of the *finite model property*, namely, there is an algorithm that computes, given one of these queries, a bound on the size of structures that need to be considered to determine satisfiability (in that such a query is satisfiable if and only if it is satisfied by a finite structure whose size is within the bound). However, the canonical algorithmic technique corresponding to the finite model property is to guess a structure within the size bound and then evaluate the query on the structure. In general, this technique may be inefficient and may not tightly indicate the complexity of query containment in cases where the selfish models of a query ϕ can be computed directly from ϕ, or in cases where query evaluation on queries of the form $\phi \wedge \neg\psi$ exhibits higher complexity than query evaluation on the considered queries ψ; the latter occurs for conjunctive queries and existential positive queries. Let us indeed remark here that the classical query classes discussed here as examples (conjunctive queries and existential positive queries), as well as most of the query classes considered throughout the article, are *positive* in that negation is not present; thus, the reduction to satisfiability, which uses negation, results in queries that are outside of the classes into which the original queries fall.

1.2 Contributions

This article contains a few different forms of contributions, which we now turn to describe.

The selfish models property. We provide a theoretical framework for analyzing query containment problems demonstrating the selfish models phenomenon by defining the *selfish models property* (Section 3). In particular, we first give a basic definition (Definition 3.1) of what it means for a pair of query classes to have the selfish models property; when this holds, query containment of a query of the first class in a query of the second class is decidable. In addition, when the selfish models property holds, it is guaranteed that containment coincides with finite containment (that is, containment restricted to finite structures); this is essentially because the selfish models are by definition finite. Building on this first definition, we then define what it means for a pair of query classes to have the selfish models property via a pair of complexity classes (C, C'); this second definition (Definition 3.11) allows us to present complexity bounds on query containment problems. Roughly speaking, the first complexity class C bounds the complexity of generating the selfish models for queries in the first class, whereas the second complexity class C' bounds the complexity of evaluating queries in the second class on the generated selfish models.The first complexity class C is required to have a definition based on machines that permit oracle relativization; the particular formalization is in terms of what we call $\wedge$*-oracle machines*, which are oracle machines that accept an input if and only if, in the computation tree of the input, all oracle calls made return *accept*.

We believe that the selfish models property is worth formalizing because it permits the uniform derivation of a number of positive complexity results on query containment problems, and because it provides a conceptual framework for conveniently understanding and reasoning about query containment problems. Moreover, such a formalization opens up the possibility of proving that versions of the technique at hand do not apply to certain query containment problems, thus providing a more detailed, refined viewpoint on such problems and a scheme for organizing such problems.

Capture of existing results. We present a number of examples of query containment problems where the complexity can be bounded by establishing the selfish models property (throughout Section 3). All of the complexity results (in this section) are either known or are readily derivable from known techniques, and there is no claim whatsoever to any of these results being novel. Rather, there is a claim to the novelty of the viewpoint; the point of presenting these results is to evidence the utility of the selfish models property, by showing that this property permits an avenue for the clean, uniform derivation of these complexity results. Let us also point out that, as discussed throughout the section, all of the positive complexity results derived here are optimal in that when a query containment problem is shown to be in a complexity class C above P, it is the case that the problem is also C-complete.

Novel positive results for first-order query containment. Using the selfish models property, we present significant novel positive results for first-order query containment problems. The queries under study are formulated in multi-sorted first-order logic, in particular, in a specific such logic that we call *quantifier-sorted logic.* Quantifier-sorted logic has two sorts, denoted by u and e; universally quantified variables must have sort u, while existentially quantified variables must have sort e. In quantifier-sorted logic, we study two query containment problems.

- First, we study the problem of deciding if a *quantified conjunctive query* is contained in a positive query (Section 4.4). By *quantified conjunctive queries*, we refer to the extension of conjunctive queries where universal quantification is also permitted. We show that the selfish models property applies to this containment problem, and derive an NP upper bound for this problem. This is optimal, since this problem is NP-hard; it vastly generalizes the containment problem for conjunctive queries.
- Second, we study the problem of deciding of a positive query is contained in another positive query that is in prenex form and has a Π_2 quantifier prefix; so, we restrict the second query to allowing a single universal-existential quantifier alternation (Section 4.5). We show that the selfish models property applies to this containment problem, and use it to obtain a $\text{coNEXP}^{\text{NP}}$ complexity upper bound for this problem.

Let us emphasize that (to our knowledge) both of the containment problems studied were not known to be computably decidable, prior to this work.

Both of these positive results rely on a presentation of and study of selfish models for positive queries in quantifier-sorted logic (Section 4.3). It is readily seen that the selfish models presented here coincide with the known ones for conjunctive queries and for existential positive queries. The developed theory can thus be viewed as a vast and strong generalization of the classical theory of Chandra and Merlin [8] and of Sagiv and Yannakakis [28].

As discussed in the article (Remark 4.3), these positive results extend to generalizations of quantifier-sorted logic where multiple sorts are permitted, each sort is designated as having universal type or existential type, and the sort of each variable must have the type corresponding to the way in which it is quantified. We remark that the *block-sorted* queries studied in previous work [14] can be viewed as such a generalization.

Regarding the first positive result here, it was recently shown by Bova and Mogavero that containment of quantified conjunctive queries in one-sorted first-order logic is in NP [6]; this result followed a prior result showing decidability of this problem [13]. Our first result is incomparable to this recent result; the recent result studies containment of a quantified conjunctive query in another such query in one-sorted logic, whereas we study containment of a quantified conjunctive query in a positive query in quantifier-sorted logic. Moreover, in our view, our treatment reveals a more informative characterization of when containment holds (Theorem 4.15), since it explicitly presents selfish models and bounds the size of the selfish models that need to be considered.

2 PRELIMINARIES

When $f : A \longrightarrow B$ and $g : B \longrightarrow C$ are maps, we sometimes use $g(f)$ to denote their composition. When $f : A \longrightarrow B$ is a map and $S \subseteq A$, we use $f(S)$ to denote $\{f(a) \mid a \in S\}$; and, we use $f \upharpoonright S$ to denote the restriction of f to S. When A and B are sets, we sometimes use $[A \longrightarrow B]$ to denote the set of all maps from A to B.

2.1 Logic

In this article, we formulate our results logically, and we deal primarily with relational first-order logics and fragments thereof. We assume basic familiarity with the syntax and semantics of first-order logic. In particular, we work with usual one-sorted first-order logic in Section 3, and then work with a multi-sorted first-order logic in Section 4, which is introduced and defined in that section. Here, we recall and set some conventions and notation to be used.

In the context of one-sorted first-order logic, a *signature* is a finite set of relation symbols; each relation symbol has associated with it an *arity*, which is a natural number. We use the symbols $\mathbf{A}, \mathbf{B}, \ldots$ to denote structures, and the corresponding symbols $A, B, \ldots$ to denote their respective universes. A structure is *finite* if its universe is finite. In computational contexts, a natural representation of structures, which we will use, is the *explicit representation* whereby each relation is represented by an explicit list of the tuples that it contains.

When ϕ is a formula, we use free(ϕ) to denote the set of free variables of ϕ. In general, we say that a formula ϕ is a *sentence* when free(ϕ) $= \emptyset$. A formula ϕ is *prenex* or *in prenex form* if it has the form $Q_1 v_1 \ldots Q_n v_n \phi'$ where ϕ' is quantifier-free, that is, if all of the quantification occurs in the front of the formula; when ϕ is prenex, we refer to the quantifier-free part ϕ' as the *matrix* of ϕ, and denote it by matrix(ϕ). We generally assume that, in a prenex formula, no variable is quantified twice, and also that each variable that is quantified is an element of free(matrix(ϕ)). It is readily verified that a formula can be converted to a logically equivalent prenex formula in polynomial time, and we thus often assume formulas to be in prenex form. We use the term *atom* to refer to an atomic formula $R(v_1, \ldots, v_k)$ that is the application of a relation symbol to a tuple of variables.

We use the term *logic* to refer to a class of logical sentences. We assume that for each logic under discussion, the problem of deciding if a given string represents a sentence in the logic is polynomial-time decidable; we also assume that it is computable to decide, given a sentence ϕ in a logic and a finite structure $\mathbf{B}$, whether or not $\mathbf{B} \models \phi$.

We define the following logics. The logic of *conjunctive queries*, denoted by CQ, is the class of sentences built from atoms, conjunction, and existential quantification. The logic of *unions of conjunctive queries*, denoted by UCQ, is the class of sentences having the form $\phi_1 \vee \cdots \vee \phi_k$ where each ϕ_i is a conjunctive query. The logic of *existential positive queries*, denoted by EPQ, is the class of sentences built from atoms, conjunction, disjunction, and existential quantification. Clearly, we have CQ $\subseteq$ UCQ $\subseteq$ EPQ.

When ϕ and ψ are sentences, we say that ϕ *entails* ψ when for every structure $\mathbf{B}$, it holds that $\mathbf{B} \models \phi$ implies $\mathbf{B} \models \psi$; we say that ϕ *finitely entails* ψ when for every finite structure $\mathbf{B}$, it holds that $\mathbf{B} \models \phi$ implies $\mathbf{B} \models \psi$. For a pair of logics (Φ, Ψ), we say that *entailment and finite entailment coincide* when for all $\phi \in \Phi$ and $\psi \in \Psi$, it holds that ϕ entails ψ if and only if ϕ finitely entails ψ.

For the logic CQ of conjunctive queries, there is a neat and well-known characterization of entailment. For each prenex conjunctive query $\phi = \exists v_1 \ldots \exists v_n \text{matrix}(\phi)$, define $\mathbf{A}[\phi]$ to be the structure with universe $\{v_1, \ldots, v_n\}$ and where, for each relation symbol R, it holds that

$$R^{\mathbf{A}[\phi]} = \{(w_1, \ldots, w_k) \mid R(w_1, \ldots, w_k) \text{ occurs in matrix}(\phi)\}.$$

The following theorem is now classical.

THEOREM 2.1. *(Chandra-Merlin [8]) Let $\phi, \psi \in$ CQ, and assume ϕ to be prenex. The following are equivalent:*

- $\mathbf{A}[\phi] \models \psi$
- *ϕ entails ψ*
- *ϕ finitely entails ψ*

In particular, it holds that $\mathbf{A}[\phi] \models \phi$.

It follows immediately from this theorem that entailment and finite entailment coincide for (CQ, CQ).

2.2 Complexity

Let (Φ, Ψ) be a pair of logics. We define ENTAIL(Φ, Ψ) to be the computational problem of deciding, given a pair (ϕ, ψ) where $\phi \in \Phi$ and $\psi \in \Psi$, whether or not ϕ entails ψ. Analogously, we define FIN-ENTAIL(Φ, Ψ) to be the computational problem of deciding, given a pair (ϕ, ψ) where $\phi \in \Phi$ and $\psi \in \Psi$, whether or not ϕ finitely entails ψ. We tacitly assume that, in instances of these problems, each sentence is presented with an associated signature, and that attention is restricted to instances where the signatures of ϕ and ψ are equal.

We assume familiarity with typical complexity classes based on time and space bounds, as presented in standard references (such as the book by Papadimitriou [27]). Whenever we discuss completeness for a complexity class, it is with respect to many-one polynomial-time reducibility. By a *machine class*, we refer to a complexity class C defined as the class of languages of particular types of machines; we assume that the machines under consideration may permit access to an oracle via oracle calls. We always use established complexity classes and the standard machines used to define them. For example, P is a machine class; it is conventionally defined as the class of languages of polynomial-time deterministic Turing machines, and there is a well-established notion of oracle access for such machines. As another example, coNP is a machine class; it is typically defined as the class of languages of polynomial-time conondeterministic Turing machines, and again for such machines there is a well-established notion of oracle access. When C is a machine class, by a *C-machine*, we mean a machine of the type used to define C; by an *oracle C-machine*, we mean an oracle machine of the type used to define C. When M is an oracle machine and L' is a language, we use $M^{L'}$ to denote the combined machine where oracle calls made by M are resolved using the language L'. As usual, when C is a machine class and C' is a complexity classs, we use $C^{C'}$ to denote the class of languages that are decided by combined machines $M^{L'}$ where M is an oracle C-machine and L' is a language in C'.

We will make use of the following non-standard but natural notion. When C is a machine class and M is an oracle C-machine, we say that M is a *$\wedge$-oracle C-machine* if on any input, the machine M accepts if and only if, in the input's computation tree, each oracle call returned accept. Typically, when we use such machines, they are oracle C-machines for machine classes C that are defined in terms of deterministic or conondeterministic machines. Let C' be a complexity class. We use $C^{\wedge C'}$ to denote the class of languages that are decided by combined machines $M^{L'}$ where M is a $\wedge$-oracle C-machine, and L' is a language in C'. When C is a machine class and C' is a complexity class, it clearly holds that $C^{\wedge C'} \subseteq C^{C'}$.

To discuss a particular example, let us consider the case that C = P and C' = NP. It is straightforward to verify that $\mathsf{P}^{\wedge \mathsf{NP}} = \mathsf{NP}$. Notice, however, that in this case $\mathsf{P}^{\wedge \mathsf{NP}}$ is, a priori, not obviously equal to P^{NP}; it is known and is straightforward to verify that coNP $\subseteq \mathsf{P}^{\mathsf{NP}}$, whereas it is not known if coNP $\subseteq$ NP.

3 THE SELFISH MODELS PROPERTY

We begin by presenting our initial version of the *selfish models property*.

Definition 3.1. A pair (Φ, Ψ) of logics has the *selfish models property* if there exists a computable function $s : \Sigma^* \to \Sigma^*$ and a polynomial-time computable function $p : \Sigma^* \to \Sigma^*$ such that, for each $\phi \in \Phi$ and each $\psi \in \Psi$, $s(\phi, p(\psi))$ is equal to a finite set S of finite structures where:

- for each $\mathbf{B} \in S$, it holds that $\mathbf{B} \models \phi$, and
- if for each $\mathbf{B} \in S$ it holds that $\mathbf{B} \models \psi$, then ϕ entails ψ.

When the above conditions hold, we say that (Φ, Ψ) *has the selfish models property with respect to* (s, p).

Remark 3.2. Definition 3.1 can be intuitively explained in the following way. The first requirement holds that $s(\phi, p(\psi))$ is a set of finite models of ϕ. The second requirement holds that, in order to decide if ϕ entails ψ, it suffices to check that ψ is true on each structure in this set of models. The function p can be conceived of as an advice function that allows s to take into account some information from ψ. In most of the examples in this section, the function p will be constant and hence will play no real role; in later applications, this function, when used, will typically supply information about the size of ψ, in particular, information about the number of variables that ψ uses. □

Example 3.3. Let us argue that (CQ, CQ) has the selfish models property. Define p to be the constant function ϵ, and for each $\phi \in$ CQ, define $s(\phi, \epsilon) = \{\mathbf{A}[\phi]\}$. It is known that $\mathbf{A}[\phi] \models \phi$, and it is also known that for $\psi \in$ CQ that $\mathbf{A}[\phi] \models \psi$ if and only if ϕ entails ψ (Theorem 2.1). We therefore have that (CQ, CQ) has the selfish models property with respect to (s, p).

Example 3.4. Let us extend the previous example, and argue that (CQ, EPQ) has the selfish models property. Define p and s just as in the previous example (Example 3.3). We need to argue that, for any $\phi \in$ CQ and $\psi \in$ EPQ, if $\mathbf{A}[\phi] \models \psi$, then ϕ entails ψ. We use the known fact (discussed below in Example 3.10) that each sentence in EPQ is logically equivalent to a disjunction $\psi_1 \vee \cdots \vee \psi_k$ where it holds that each disjunct ψ_i is contained in CQ. If $\mathbf{A}[\phi] \models \psi$, then there exists $i \in \{1, \ldots, k\}$ such that $\mathbf{A}[\phi] \models \psi_i$; from this, it follows that ϕ entails ψ_i, and hence that ϕ entails ψ.

The following proposition identifies key consequences of the selfish models property. Namely, when the selfish models property holds on a pair of logics, entailment and finite entailment coincide, and are both decidable.

Proposition 3.5. *Suppose that (Φ, Ψ) is a pair of logics that has the selfish models property. Then, the following hold:*

- *For (Φ, Ψ), entailment and finite entailment coincide.*
- *The problem* ENTAIL(Φ, Ψ) *is decidable.*
- *The problem* FIN-ENTAIL(Φ, Ψ) *is decidable.*

Proof. Consider the following algorithm: given $\phi \in \Phi$ and $\psi \in \Psi$, compute $s(\phi, p(\psi))$; for each $\mathbf{B}$ in $s(\phi, p(\psi))$, check if $\mathbf{B} \models \psi$; accept if each check returns true, and reject otherwise. To establish the proposition, it suffices to show that the following are equivalent, for each instance (ϕ, ψ): (1) the algorithm accepts; (2) ϕ entails ψ; and, (3) ϕ finitely entails ψ. (1) implies (2) by the second requirement in Definition 3.1. (2) implies (3) is straightforwardly verified to be true in general. (3) implies (1), since each structure in $s(\phi, p(\psi))$ satisfies ϕ by the first requirement in Definition 3.1, so when ϕ finitely entails ψ, each such structure satisfies ψ. □

Example 3.6. We obtain directly from Example 3.4 and Proposition 3.5 that, for the pair of logics (CQ, EPQ), entailment and finite entailment coincide, and are both decidable. This was already known, but the selfish models property provides a general framework through which we will be able to uniformly present a number of pairs of logics that enjoy these positive properties.

REMARK 3.7. Suppose that (Φ, Ψ) is a pair of logics such that entailment and finite entailment coincide, and that the problems ENTAIL(Φ, Ψ) and FIN-ENTAIL(Φ, Ψ) are decidable. Then, when p is set to the identity function, so that $p(\psi) = \psi$ for each $\psi \in \Psi$, there exists a function s such that (Φ, Ψ) has the selfish models property with respect to (s, p). Namely, define $s(\phi, \psi)$ to be the output of the following algorithm: decide if ϕ entails ψ; if so, output the empty set $\emptyset$, otherwise exhaustively search for a finite model $\mathbf{B}$ of ϕ for which $\mathbf{B} \not\models \psi$, and output such a model when found. In the latter case, the exhaustive search must be successful, since if ϕ does not entail ψ, then ϕ does not finitely entail ψ, and so there exists a finite model of ϕ as described. There is thus a sense in which the converse to Proposition 3.5 holds. However, as indicated in Remark 3.2, the function p in this article will in general be constant or provide information about the size of the sentences ψ to which it is applied; thus, the use of the function p will generally veer away from the extreme of p simply acting as the identity function, as in the argument just given.

Intuitively speaking, one may view the case where p is constant as a pure form of the selfish models property, and conceive of p in general as a means of grading the proximity to this pure form. □

We now give a generic way of taking a pair (Φ, Ψ) of logics having the selfish models property, and extending this to another pair (Φ', Ψ) of logics having the selfish models property, where $\Phi' \supseteq \Phi$. For any logic Φ, define Disj(Φ) to be the class of disjunctions of sentences in Φ, that is, the class of sentences of the form $\phi_1 \vee \cdots \vee \phi_k$ where each ϕ_i is in Φ. We assume that the standard semantics are applied to such disjunctions.

PROPOSITION 3.8. *If a pair (Φ, Ψ) of logics has the selfish models property, then so does the pair* (Disj(Φ), Ψ).

PROOF. Suppose that the functions s, p witness that (Φ, Ψ) has the selfish models property. Define s' so that for all $\phi_1, \ldots, \phi_k \in \Phi$ and all strings $w \in \Sigma^*$, it holds that

$$s'(\phi_1 \vee \cdots \vee \phi_k, w) = s(\phi_1, w) \cup \cdots \cup s(\phi_k, w).$$

It is straightforward to verify that the functions s', p witness that (Disj(Φ), Ψ) has the selfish models property. □

Example 3.9. Observe that UCQ = Disj(CQ). Thus, we obtain directly from Example 3.4 and Proposition 3.8 that the pair of logics (UCQ, EPQ) has the selfish models property with respect to a pair (s', p) where p is the constant function ϵ.

Example 3.10. We now turn to show that the pair of logics (EPQ, EPQ) has the selfish models property. Our treatment is based on previous literature [5, 28].

It is known that each sentence in EPQ is logically equivalent to one in UCQ. This can be argued by showing that that, for any existential positive formula ϕ, we can define by induction a set of formulas $D(\phi)$ such that ϕ is logically equivalent to $\bigvee_{\phi' \in D(\phi)} \phi'$. This is performed as follows:

$$\begin{aligned} D(\alpha) &= \alpha \quad \text{whenever } \alpha \text{ is an atom} \\ D(\exists x\phi) &= \{\exists x\phi' \mid \phi' \in D(\phi)\} \\ D(\phi_1 \vee \phi_2) &= D(\phi_1) \cup D(\phi_2) \\ D(\phi_1 \wedge \phi_2) &= \{\phi_1' \wedge \phi_2' \mid \phi_1' \in D(\phi_1), \phi_2' \in D(\phi_2)\} \end{aligned}$$

Correctness of the equivalence is well-known and straightforwardly verified.

From the definition of $D(\cdot)$, it is evident that there in fact exists an algorithm that translates an input sentence in EPQ to a logically equivalent sentence in UCQ: given as input $\phi \in$ EPQ, output $\phi_d = \bigvee_{\phi' \in D(\phi)} \phi'$.

So, let (s', p) be the pair defined in Example 3.9; we have that p is the constant function ϵ. Define s'' to be a function such that $s''(\phi, \epsilon)$ is equal to $s'(\phi_d, \epsilon)$, where ϕ_d is the result of the described translation. It is then evident that (EPQ, EPQ) has the selfish models property with respect to (s'', p).

We next define a version of the selfish models property, according to which a pair of logics may have this property via a pair of complexity classes. The purpose of introducing this version of the selfish models property is to permit the derivation of upper bounds on the complexity of entailment and finite entailment.

Definition 3.11. Let (C, C') be a pair where C is a machine class, and C' is a complexity class. A pair (Φ, Ψ) of logics has the *selfish models property via* (C, C') if there exist:

- a computable function $s : \Sigma^* \to \Sigma^*$ and a polynomial-time computable function $p : \Sigma^* \to \Sigma^*$ such that (s, p) satisfy the criteria of Definition 3.1,
- an $\wedge$-oracle C-machine M, and
- a language L' in C'

such that, for all $\phi \in \Phi$ and $\psi \in \Psi$, the following hold:

- When M is run on (ϕ, ψ), the set of strings on which the oracle is called, in the computation tree, is equal to
$$\{(\mathbf{B}, \psi) \mid \mathbf{B} \in s(\phi, p(\psi))\}.$$
- When $\mathbf{B}$ is a structure in $s(\phi, p(\psi))$, it holds that $(\mathbf{B}, \psi) \in L'$ if and only if $\mathbf{B} \models \psi$.

In Definition 3.11, the condition on the behavior of M requires that the oracle calls made by the machine M correspond exactly to the structures in $s(\phi, p(\psi))$; in particular, the oracle calls must be equal to $(\mathbf{B}, \psi)$ over all such structures $\mathbf{B}$. The condition on the language L' requires that such a pair $(\mathbf{B}, \psi)$ is in L' if and only if $\mathbf{B} \models \psi$. Since by definition M is an $\wedge$-oracle machine, it accepts if and only if each oracle call returned accept, that is, if and only if $\mathbf{B} \models \psi$ for each $\mathbf{B} \in s(\phi, p(\psi))$. By Definition 3.1 and the proof of Proposition 3.5, we have that $M^{L'}$ decides both ENTAIL(Φ, Ψ) and FIN-ENTAIL(Φ, Ψ). We thus obtain the following proposition.

Proposition 3.12. *Suppose that a pair (Φ, Ψ) of logics has the selfish models property via (C, C'). Then, each of the two problems* ENTAIL(Φ, Ψ), FIN-ENTAIL(Φ, Ψ) *is in $C^{\wedge C'}$.*

Together, Definition 3.11 and Proposition 3.12 will allow us to give complexity upper bounds on the problems ENTAIL(Φ, Ψ) and FIN-ENTAIL(Φ, Ψ). In the rest of this section, we give a number of examples of such complexity upper bounds. We want to emphasize again the novelty in viewpoint that is presented here; the complexity upper bounds are not new, but they are derived in a uniform fashion via the selfish models property. We also want to point out that all of the upper bounds given in the rest of this section are tight in that whenever we show that an entailment problem is contained in a complexity class C, it is the case that the entailment problem is also C-complete; this is discussed in each situation.

Remark 3.13. In general, in using Definition 3.12, we do not commit to any particular representation of relational structures. Rather, when using this definition, any representation of structures, even a very implicit one, may be used to show that a pair of logics has the selfish models property. □

Example 3.14. We shall next consider the pair of logics (UCQ, EPQ). Define s and p as in Example 3.3; we then have $s(\phi, p(\psi)) = \{\mathbf{A}[\phi]\}$, for each $\phi \in$ CQ, $\psi \in$ EPQ, and that (CQ, EPQ) has the selfish models property with respect to (s, p). Next, define s' from (s, p) as in the proof of Proposition 3.8. By that proposition, as remarked in Example 3.9, we have that (UCQ, EPQ) has the selfish models property with respect to (s', p). For each disjunction $\phi = \phi_1 \vee \cdots \vee \phi_k$ of conjunctive queries, it holds that $s'(\phi, \epsilon) = \{\mathbf{A}[\phi_1], \ldots, \mathbf{A}[\phi_k]\}$.

Under the explicit representation of structures, this set of structures can clearly be computed from ϕ in polynomial time: simply loop over each disjunct ϕ_i and compute each structure $\mathbf{A}[\phi_i]$ in turn. There is thus an $\wedge$-oracle P-machine M that fulfills the condition on M in Definition 3.11: for each disjunct ϕ_i of ϕ, the machine computes each structure $\mathbf{A}[\phi_i]$ and makes an oracle call on $(\mathbf{A}[\phi_i], \psi)$; it accepts if and only if every oracle call accepted. Since query evaluation for EPQ on an explicitly represented structure is in NP, we thus have that (UCQ, EPQ) has the selfish models property via (P, NP). Since $\mathsf{P}^{\wedge \mathsf{NP}} = \mathsf{NP}$, we obtain by Proposition 3.12 that the problems ENTAIL(UCQ, EPQ) and FIN-ENTAIL(UCQ, EPQ) are in NP.

Let us remark that this complexity upper bound is optimal in that ENTAIL(UCQ, EPQ) is NP-complete. Indeed, even the more restricted problem ENTAIL(CQ, CQ) is NP-complete; this was shown in the article of Chandra and Merlin [8].

The next example examines the pair of logics (EPQ, EPQ). We derive a Π_2^p upper bound on entailment, and discuss its tightness; this forms an interesting contrast to the NP upper bound just derived for entailment for (UCQ, EPQ), since EPQ and UCQ have the same expressiveness (this was discussed in Example 3.10).

Example 3.15. Let us consider the pair of logics (EPQ, EPQ) again.

As discussed in Example 3.10, each $\phi \in$ EPQ is logically equivalent to $\bigvee_{\phi' \in D(\phi)} \phi'$, where the translation $D(\cdot)$ is given in that example. Let us define a recursive subroutine guess(θ) using conondeterminism that, when given an existential positive formula θ, guesses an element of $D(\theta)$. When θ is an atom, guess(θ) returns θ. When θ is of the form $\exists x \theta'$, guess(θ) returns $\exists x$ guess(θ). When θ is of the form $\theta_1 \vee \theta_2$, guess(θ) guesses an element $i \in \{1, 2\}$, and then returns guess(θ_i). When θ is of the form $\theta_1 \wedge \theta_2$, guess(θ) returns guess(θ_1) $\wedge$ guess(θ_2). From the definition of $D(\cdot)$, it is evident that the possible results of guess(θ) are precisely the elements of $D(\theta)$.

From this, it can be readily seen that there is a coNP-machine M satisfying the condition on M in Definition 3.11, such that the machine M, on an input (ϕ, ψ) with $\phi, \psi \in$ EPQ, makes an oracle call on $(\mathbf{A}[\phi'], \psi)$ for each $\phi' \in D(\phi)$. In particular, the machine M invokes guess(ϕ) to obtain a result ϕ'; it makes an oracle call on $(\mathbf{A}[\phi'], \psi)$; and, it accepts if and only if the oracle call did. Here, we also assume use of the explicit representation of structures.

We then have that (EPQ, EPQ) has the selfish models property via the classes (coNP, NP); recall that query evaluation for EPQ on an explicitly represented structure is in NP. Since $\mathsf{coNP}^{\wedge \mathsf{NP}} \subseteq \mathsf{coNP}^{\mathsf{NP}} = \Pi_2^p$, we obtain from Proposition 3.12 that each of the computational problems

ENTAIL(EPQ, EPQ), FIN-ENTAIL(EPQ, EPQ)

is in Π_2^p.

These complexity upper bounds are tight, as these problems are known to be Π_2^p-complete [5, 28].

In the next couple of examples, we will consider the class of *acyclic* conjunctive queries, denoted by ACQ. The key property that we will use is that query evaluation of an acyclic conjunctive query on an explicitly represented structure is in P. As the definition of *acyclic conjunctive query* is both well-known and not really needed in this extended abstract, we refer the reader to a reference [1] for the definition.

Example 3.16. Consider the pair of logics (UCQ, ACQ). Since ACQ $\subseteq$ EPQ, we have that (UCQ, ACQ) has the selfish models property with respect to the pair (s', p) discussed in Example 3.14. To analyze this pair of logics with respect to Definition 3.11, observe first that we may take M as in Example 3.14. Query evaluation of ACQ in this case, however, is in P, and thus it is possible to take $C' = \mathsf{P}$. By Proposition 3.12, we thus obtain that the problems ENTAIL(UCQ, ACQ) and FIN-ENTAIL(UCQ, ACQ) are in $\mathsf{P}^{\wedge\mathsf{P}} = \mathsf{P}$.

Example 3.17. Consider the pair of logics (EPQ, ACQ). Since ACQ $\subseteq$ EPQ, the machine M given in Example 3.10 satisfies the requirement on this machine in Definition 3.11. Since query evaluation of ACQ is in P, it is also possible to take $C' = \mathsf{P}$. From this, we thus obtain that the problems ENTAIL(EPQ, ACQ) and FIN-ENTAIL(EPQ, ACQ) are in $\mathsf{coNP}^{\wedge\mathsf{P}} = \mathsf{coNP}$.

This complexity upper bound of coNP is tight in that these problems are coNP-complete. Let us sketch a proof of coNP-hardness. First, we use the fact that query evaluation on the queries

$$\theta_k = \forall y_1 \ldots \forall y_k \exists x \bigwedge_{i=1}^{k} E_i(y_i, x)$$

is coNP-hard; this fact has been used in previous work, such as that of the author [10]. On a high level, this is proved by reducing from the complement of the *clique* problem; the universally quantified variables guess k vertices from the graph at hand, and the relations are configured in such a way that there exists a value for the variable x satisfying all of the atoms if and only if the k guessed vertices do not form a clique in the graph. Now, let us argue that this query evaluation problem reduces to ENTAIL(EPQ, ACQ). Given an instance $(\theta_k, \mathbf{B})$ of query evaluation, we create an instance (ϕ, ψ) of the entailment problem such that the sentences in $D(\phi)$ (where $D(\cdot)$ is the operator from Example 3.10) are precisely (up to logical equivalence) the sentences $\phi_{(b_1,\ldots,b_k)}$, over all $(b_1, \ldots, b_k) \in B^k$, where $\mathbf{A} = \mathbf{A}[\phi_{(b_1,\ldots,b_k)}]$ is equal to the expansion of $\mathbf{B}$ by the relations $U_1^{\mathbf{A}} = \{b_1\}, \ldots, U_k^{\mathbf{A}} = \{b_k\}$. This is achieved by setting ϕ to be the conjunction of sentence ϕ^- such that $\mathbf{A}[\phi^-] = \mathbf{B}$, with $\bigwedge_{i=1}^{k} \bigvee_{b \in B} U_i(b)$. Set ψ equal to be the following variant of θ_k:

$$\exists y_1 \ldots \exists y_k \exists x (\bigwedge_{i=1}^{k} E_i(y_i, x)) \wedge (\bigwedge_{i=1}^{k} U_i(y_i)).$$

It is then evident that $\mathbf{B} \models \theta_k$ if and only if ϕ entails ψ.

We next give an example that is qualitatively different from the previous examples. It does not fall strictly into our paradigm, but as discussed, it nearly does.

Example 3.18. This example concerns the theory of the dense linear order without endpoints; we supply a general reference [23, Section 5.3] for the notions used. In particular, we consider a pair of logics (Φ, Ψ) where the first contains just a single sentence. In particular, define ϕ to be an axiomatization of the named theory; the signature used throughout this example consists of a single binary relation symbol $<$. We overload the symbol $<$, and use it to denote an interpretation of the syntactic symbol when this is clear from context. Set $\Phi = \{\phi\}$.

It is known that the first-order sentences entailed by ϕ are exactly those true on the ordered rationals $(\mathbb{Q}, <)$. Let us take Ψ to be the set of all *existential* sentences over the signature at hand; by an *existential* sentence, we mean a prenex sentence using only existential quantification. For each $n \geq 1$, let $\mathbf{B}_n$ denote the induced substructure of $(\mathbb{Q}, <)$ on $\{1, \ldots, n\}$. Let $\psi = \exists v_1 \ldots \exists v_n \text{matrix}(\psi)$ be any existential sentence with n variables; it holds that

$$(\mathbb{Q}, <) \models \psi \text{ if and only if } \mathbf{B}_n \models \psi.$$

The backward direction is clear, from the fact that $\mathbf{B}_n$ is an induced substructure of $(\mathbb{Q}, <)$ and the assumption that ψ is existential; for the forward direction, suppose that $h : \{v_1, \ldots, v_n\} \to \mathbb{Q}$ is an assignment such that

$$(\mathbb{Q}, <), h \models \text{matrix}(\psi);$$

then, as $(\mathbb{Q}, <)$ is known to have a *set transitive* automorphism group, there exists an automorphism π thereof such that the image of $\pi(h)$ is contained in $\{1, \ldots, n\}$. We then have $(\mathbb{Q}, <), \pi(h) \models \text{matrix}(\psi)$, implying that $\mathbf{B}_n, \pi(h) \models \text{matrix}(\psi)$.

Take p to be the polynomial-time computable function where $p(\psi)$ is equal to the number of variables in ψ, for each $\psi \in \Psi$, and take $s(\phi, n)$ to be $\{\mathbf{B}_n\}$. (Here, we assume that the numbers at hand are represented in unary.) The pair (s, p) then satisfies the second condition in Definition 3.1, although it does not satisfy the first; indeed (as is well-known and relatively straightforward to verify), the sentence ϕ has no finite models! It is clear that (with the unary representation) given a pair (ϕ, ψ), it is possible to compute $s(\phi, p(\psi))$ in polynomial time. Since existential sentences may be evaluated on structures in NP, we obtain an NP bound on the ENTAIL(Φ, Ψ); given a pair (ϕ, ψ), compute $s(\phi, p(\psi))$, and then evaluate ψ on the single structure therein. This argument follows the schema of Definitions 3.1 and 3.11 and their respective propositions.

Note that ENTAIL(Φ, Ψ) is known to be NP-complete [2], and that this type of finitization technique has been previously studied [3], under the moniker of *sampling*.

We next present a relaxation of the selfish models property. As in the original definition, it is required that, based on a pair (ϕ, ψ), a finite set of structures can be computed, but two of the original requirements are dropped: first, the structures in the set are not required to be finite, and second, the structures are not required to be models of ϕ (this allows one to accommodate situations such as that discussed in Example 3.18).

Definition 3.19. A pair (Φ, Ψ) of logics has the *loosely selfish models property* if there exists a computable function $s : \Sigma^* \to \Sigma^*$ and a polynomial-time computable function $p : \Sigma^* \to \Sigma^*$ such that, for each $\phi \in \Phi$ and each $\psi \in \Psi$, $s(\phi, p(\psi))$ is equal to a finite set S of structures where:

- It holds that ϕ entails ψ if and only if for each $\mathbf{B} \in S$, it holds that $\mathbf{B} \models \psi$.

When the above conditions hold, we say that (Φ, Ψ) *has the loosely selfish models property with respect to* (s, p).

Here, we presume that, when one uses this definition, any representation of structures as strings may be used. We make the assumption that the following problem is decidable: given a sentence ψ in Ψ and a string representation of a structure, decide if ψ is true on the structure. Under this assumption, we have the following analog of Proposition 3.5.

Proposition 3.20. *Suppose that (Φ, Ψ) is a pair of logics that has the loosely selfish models property. Then, it holds that the problem* ENTAIL(Φ, Ψ) *is decidable.*

Proof. It is straightforward to verify that the algorithm given in the proof of Proposition 3.5 decides the stated problem. □

We now give an analog of Definition 3.11.

Definition 3.21. Let (C, C') be a pair where C is a machine class, and C' is a complexity class. A pair (Φ, Ψ) of logics has the *loosely selfish models property via* (C, C') if the conditions of Definition 3.11 hold, with the modification that (s, p) just need to satisfy the criteria of Definition 3.19.

We obtain the following analog of Proposition 3.12.

Proposition 3.22. *Suppose that a pair (Φ, Ψ) of logics has the loosely selfish models property via (C, C'). Then, the problem* ENTAIL(Φ, Ψ) *is in* $C^{\wedge C'}$.

Proposition 3.22 follows directly from the given definitions and the fact (discussed prior to Proposition 3.12) that Definition 3.21 provides an $\wedge$-oracle C-machine that accepts a pair (ϕ, ψ) if and only if $\mathbf{B} \models \psi$ for each $\mathbf{B} \in s(\phi, p(\psi))$.

4 QUANTIFIER-SORTED POSITIVE LOGIC

4.1 Multi-sorted logic

We here describe the formalization of multi-sorted relational first-order logic with which we will work.

A *signature* is a pair $(\sigma, \mathcal{S})$ where $\mathcal{S}$ is a set of *sorts* and σ is a finite set of relation symbols; each relation symbol $R \in \sigma$ has associated with it an element of $\mathcal{S}^*$ called the *arity* of R and denoted ar(R). Here, as usual, $\mathcal{S}^*$ denotes the set of all finite-length words built with $\mathcal{S}$ as the underlying alphabet.

A *structure* $\mathbf{B}$ on signature $(\sigma, \mathcal{S})$ consists of a family $B = \{B_s \mid s \in \mathcal{S}\}$ of sets called the *universe* of $\mathbf{B}$, and, for each symbol $R \in \sigma$, an interpretation $R^{\mathbf{B}} \subseteq B_{\text{ar}(R)}$. Here, for a word $w = s_1 \ldots s_k \in \mathcal{S}^*$, we use B_w to denote the product $B_{s_1} \times \cdots \times B_{s_k}$. In general, we use the symbols $\mathbf{A}, \mathbf{B}, \ldots$ to denote structures, and $A, B, \ldots$ to denote their respective universes. A structure $\mathbf{B}$ is *finite* if each member B_s of its universe is finite. We generally assume that for any sort-indexed family $B = \{B_s \mid s \in S\}$ of sets, the sets B_s are pairwise disjoint. When $A = \{A_s \mid s \in \mathcal{S}\}$, $B = \{B_s \mid s \in \mathcal{S}\}$ are two such families indexed by the same set of sorts, by a mapping $h : A \to B$, we mean a mapping that is defined on $\cup_{s \in \mathcal{S}} A_s$ and respects sorts in that $h(A_s) \subseteq B_s$, for each $s \in \mathcal{S}$.

Two structures $\mathbf{A}$ and $\mathbf{B}$ are *similar* if they are defined over the same signature $(\sigma, \mathcal{S})$; for two such structures, a *homomorphism* from $\mathbf{A}$ to $\mathbf{B}$ is a mapping $h : A \to B$ such that, for each relation symbol $R \in \sigma$ and each tuple $(a_1, \ldots, a_k) \in R^{\mathbf{A}}$, it holds that $(h(a_1), \ldots, h(a_k)) \in R^{\mathbf{B}}$. When $\mathbf{A}$ and $\mathbf{B}$ are similar structures over signature $(\sigma, \mathcal{S})$, $\mathbf{A}$ is a *substructure* of $\mathbf{B}$ if for each sort $s \in \mathcal{S}$ it holds that $A_s \subseteq B_s$, and for each relation symbol $R \in \sigma$ it holds that $R^{\mathbf{A}} \subseteq R^{\mathbf{B}}$.

In formulas over signature $(\sigma, \mathcal{S})$, each variable v has associated with it a sort $s(v)$ from $\mathcal{S}$. The permitted atomic formulas are those having the form $R(v_1, \ldots, v_k)$ where $R \in \sigma$ and $s(v_1) \ldots s(v_k) = \text{ar}(R)$; we refer to such an atomic formula as an *atom*.

4.2 Quantifier-sorted logic

We will focus on a particular multi-sorted first-order logic which we call *quantifier-sorted logic.* In quantifier-sorted logic, there are two sorts, denoted by u and e, which abbreviate *universal* and *existential.* In short, each universally quantified variable must have sort u, and each existentially quantified variable must have sort e. So formally, by a *quantifier-sorted formula*, we mean a formula over a signature of the form $(\sigma, \{u, e\})$, where in the formula, each instance $\forall y$ of universal quantification has $s(y) = u$, and each instance $\exists x$ of existential quantification has $s(x) = e$. We will focus on *positive quantifier-sorted formulas*, which are those quantifier-sorted formulas that can be built from atoms, conjunction, disjunction, universal quantification, and existential quantification (that is, formulas without negation). By a *quantifier-sorted structure*, we refer to a structure on a signature of the form $(\sigma, \{u, e\})$.

For the rest of this section, we generally assume that the formulas and structures under discussion are quantifier-sorted; nonetheless, we sometimes make this explicit for emphasis.

When ϕ is a prenex quantifier-sorted formula, we use X^ϕ to denote the set of variables having sort e that occur in ϕ, and we use Y^ϕ to denote the set of variables having sort u that occur in ϕ. When $x \in X^\phi$, we use $Y^\phi_{<x}$ to denote the set of variables in Y^ϕ that occur before x in the quantifier prefix of ϕ.

We will make use of the following well-known characterization of satisfaction. Let ϕ be a prenex sentence. A *Skolem family* for $(\phi, \mathbf{B})$ is a family of maps $\tau = (\tau_x : [Y^\phi_{<x} \to B_u] \to B_e)_{x \in X^\phi}$ such that for each $f : Y^\phi \to B_u$, the following holds: $\mathbf{B}, [f, \tau] \models \text{matrix}(\phi)$, where $[f, \tau] : (Y^\phi \cup X^\phi) \to B$ is the extension of f that sends each $x \in X^\phi$ to $\tau_x(f \upharpoonright Y^\phi_{<x})$.

Proposition 4.1. *Let ϕ be a prenex quantifier-sorted sentence. It holds that $\mathbf{B} \models \phi$ iff there exists a Skolem family for $(\phi, \mathbf{B})$.*

When $\mathbf{B}$ and $\mathbf{C}$ are similar quantifier-sorted structures, we define a $\forall$*-surjective homomorphism* from $\mathbf{B}$ to $\mathbf{C}$ to be a homomorphism h from $\mathbf{B}$ to $\mathbf{C}$ such that $h(B_u) = C_u$. The following theorem is a straightforwardly proved variant of the known fact that the models of any positive sentence in usual (one-sorted) first-order logic are closed under surjective homomorphism.

Theorem 4.2. *Let $\mathbf{B}$, $\mathbf{C}$ be similar quantifier-sorted structures. If there exists a $\forall$-surjective homomorphism from $\mathbf{B}$ to $\mathbf{C}$, then for each quantifier-sorted positive sentence ϕ such that $\mathbf{B} \models \phi$, it holds that $\mathbf{C} \models \phi$.*

Proof. Let h be a $\forall$-surjective homomorphism from $\mathbf{B}$ to $\mathbf{C}$. We prove that for any quantifier-sorted positive formula ψ and for any assignment f, it holds that $\mathbf{B}, f \models \psi$ implies $\mathbf{C}, h(f) \models \psi$. We prove this by induction on the structure of ψ.

When ψ is an atom, the claim follows immediately from the assumption that h is a homomorphism from $\mathbf{B}$ to $\mathbf{C}$. When ψ is a conjunction or disjunction, the claim follows immediately by induction.

Suppose that ψ has the form $\exists x \psi'$. We have that $\mathbf{B}, f \models \exists x \psi'$ implies that there exists $b \in B_e$ such that $\mathbf{B}, f[x \to b] \models \psi'$; by induction, this implies that $\mathbf{C}, h(f[x \to b]) \models \psi'$. Since $h(f[x \to b]) = (h(f))[x \to h(b)]$, we obtain that $\mathbf{C}, h(f) \models \psi$.

Suppose that ψ has the form $\forall y \psi'$. We have that $\mathbf{B}, f \models \forall y \psi'$ implies that for each $b \in B_u$, it holds that $\mathbf{B}, f[y \to b] \models \psi'$. We have $h(f[y \to b]) = (h(f))[y \to h(b)]$. By induction, we obtain that for each $b \in B_u$, it holds that $\mathbf{C}, (h(f))[y \to h(b)] \models \psi'$. Since h is $\forall$-surjective, we obtain that for each $c \in C_u$, it holds that $\mathbf{C}, (h(f))[y \to c] \models \psi'$. We thus conclude that $\mathbf{C}, h(f) \models \psi$. □

Remark 4.3. (On multiple sorts) A natural generalization of quantifier-sorted logic is a logic where, in place of two sorts, multiple sorts are permitted, each sort is designated as being of either universal or existential type, and each instance Qv of quantification has that $s(v)$ is of the type corresponding to Q. The theory and the positive complexity results obtained in this section can be straightforwardly extended to this more general logic; we prove them for quantifier-sorted logic primarily to reduce the intensity of required notation.

In fact, for the logics considered in Section 4.5, the generalization to the setting of multiple sorts can be obtained rather directly from the quantifier-sorted case, as follows. To check if ϕ entails ψ, in the case that these sentences come from the more general logic, perform the following. For each sort s of existential type, introduce a unary symbol V_s of arity e, and for each sort s of universal type, introduce a unary symbol W_s of arity u. Then, for each of the sentences ϕ and ψ, obtain new sentences ϕ' and ψ' as follows: replace each formula $\exists x \theta$ beginning with existential quantification with $\exists x (V_{s(x)} \wedge \theta)$, where x has sort e, and replace each formula $\forall y \theta$ beginning with universal quantification with $\forall y (W_{s(y)} \vee \theta)$. After replacement, existential quantification of a variable x is effectively performed over the interpretation of $V_{s(x)}$, and universal quantification of a variable y is effectively performed over the interpretation of $W_{s(y)}$. Thus, ϕ entails ψ if and only if ϕ' entails ψ'. □

4.3 Selfish models

Let us say that a quantifier-sorted sentence ϕ is *normal* if it is positive, prenex, and matrix(ϕ) has the form $\phi_1 \vee \cdots \vee \phi_d$ where each ϕ_i is a conjunction of atoms. Observe that each positive quantifier-sorted sentence is logically equivalent to a normal quantifier-sorted sentence; we focus on such normal sentences in this subsection.

Relative to a normal sentence ϕ, we now define sets of structures $\mathcal{A}^{\phi,Z}$ that will be shown to be models of ϕ. These structures will be used to exhibit the selfish models property.

Definition of $\mathcal{A}^{\phi,Z}$. Let ϕ be a normal quantifier-sorted sentence over signature $(\sigma, \{u, e\})$, and let Z be a non-empty set. We next define a set $\mathcal{A}^{\phi,Z}$ of structures. For each family $(M_f)_{f : Y^\phi \to Z}$ where each M_f is a value in $\{1, \ldots, d\}$, there is a structure $\mathbf{A}^{(M_f)}$ in $\mathcal{A}^{\phi,Z}$, defined as follows. The universe of this structure is defined by

$$A_u^{(M_f)} = Z, \; A_e^{(M_f)} = \{x^g \mid x \in X^\phi, g : Y^\phi_{<x} \to Z\}.$$

In order to define the relations of $\mathbf{A}^{(M_f)}$, we introduce the following general notation: for any map $g : Y^\phi \to S$, where

S is any set, we use $\hat{g}$ to denote the extension of g that maps each $x \in X^\phi$ to $x^{g \upharpoonright Y^\phi_{<x}}$. For each relation symbol $R \in \sigma$, define $R^{\mathbf{A}^{(M_f)}}$ as

$$\{(\hat{g}(v_1), \ldots, \hat{g}(v_k)) \mid g : Y^\phi \to Z, R(v_1, \ldots, v_k) \text{ is in } \phi_{M_g}\}.$$

For any fixed ϕ as above, when Z is finite, we have that the number of families $(M_f)_{f:Y^\phi \to Z}$ is finite, and also that for any particular family (M_f), both of the sets $A_u^{(M_f)}$ and $A_e^{(M_f)}$ are finite. We thus obtain the following.

Proposition 4.4. *When ϕ is a normal quantifier-sorted sentence, and Z is a non-empty finite set, the set $\mathcal{A}^{\phi,Z}$ of structures is finite, and each structure therein is finite.*

We now give examples concerning the contents of sets of the form $\mathcal{A}^{\phi,Z}$. We will consider normal sentences ϕ with $Y^\phi = \{y_1, y_2\}$ and the case where $Z = \{z_1, z_2\}$. For notational convenience, for $i, j \in \{1, 2\}$, we will use ij to denote the map $g : \{y_1, y_2\} \to \{z_1, z_2\}$ such that $g(y_1) = z_i$ and $g(y_2) = z_j$.

Example 4.5. Consider the normal sentence

$$\phi = \forall y_1 \forall y_2 \exists x (E(y_1, x) \wedge F(y_2, x)).$$

and $Z = \{z_1, z_2\}$. In this case, matrix(ϕ) does not contain any disjunction, so $d = 1$ and so the set $\mathcal{A}^{\phi,Z}$ contains a single structure; let us denote this structure by $\mathbf{A}$. We have $A_u = \{z_1, z_2\}$ and $A_e = \{x^{11}, x^{12}, x^{21}, x^{22}\}$. In this case, each of the relations $E^{\mathbf{A}}$, $F^{\mathbf{A}}$ contains a tuple for each map $g : \{y_1, y_2\} \to \{z_1, z_2\}$. In particular, it holds that

$$E^{\mathbf{A}} = \{(y_1, x^{11}), (y_1, x^{12}), (y_2, x^{21}), (y_2, x^{22})\},$$

and that

$$F^{\mathbf{A}} = \{(y_1, x^{11}), (y_2, x^{12}), (y_1, x^{21}), (y_2, x^{22})\}.$$

In the next example, disjunction is used.

Example 4.6. Consider next the normal sentence

$$\phi = \forall y_1 \forall y_2 \exists x (E(y_1, x) \vee F(y_2, x))$$

and $Z = \{z_1, z_2\}$. In this case, matrix(ϕ) has the form $\phi_1 \vee \phi_2$ where $\phi_1 = E(y_1, x)$ and $\phi_2 = F(y_2, x)$, and we have $d = 2$. In $\mathbf{A}^{\phi,Z}$, there is a structure $\mathbf{A}^{(M_f)}$ for each family $(M_f)_{f:Y^\phi \to Z}$. There are 4 maps $f : Y^\phi \to Z$, and thus $2^4 = 16$ many families. Let us consider the particular family given by $M_{11} = 1$, $M_{12} = 2$, $M_{21} = 2$, $M_{22} = 1$. To determine $E^{\mathbf{A}^{(M_f)}}$, observe that $E(y_1, x)$ is the only atom over E appearing in ϕ, and that it appears in ϕ_1. Since $M_g = 1$ when $g = 11$ or $g = 22$, we have $E^{\mathbf{A}^{(M_f)}} = \{(y_1, x^{11}), (y^2, x^{22})\}$. Similarly, towards determining $F^{\mathbf{A}^{(M_f)}}$, we have that $F(y_2, x)$ is the only atom over F appearing in ϕ, and that it appears in ϕ_2. We have $M_g = 2$ when $g = 12$ or $g = 21$, and so we have $F^{\mathbf{A}^{(M_f)}} = \{(y_2, x^{12}), (y_1, x^{21})\}$.

Properties of $\mathcal{A}^{\phi,Z}$. We now present the main properties of the sets $\mathcal{A}^{\phi,Z}$ of structures that make them suitable for establishing the selfish models property. *In the results that follow in the rest of this subsection, we assume throughout that ϕ is a normal quantifier-sorted sentence, and that Z is a non-empty set.*

We first verify that the structures in $\mathcal{A}^{\phi,Z}$ are all models of ϕ.

Theorem 4.7. *For each structure $\mathbf{A}^{(M_f)} \in \mathcal{A}^{\phi,Z}$, it holds that $\mathbf{A}^{(M_f)} \models \phi$.*

Proof. We define a Skolem family for $(\phi, \mathbf{A}^{(M_f)})$. For each $x \in X^\phi$, and each $h : Y^\phi_{<x} \to B_u$, define $\tau_x(h) = x^h$. For any map $g : Y^\phi \to Z$, we claim that $[g, \tau] = \hat{g}$. Clearly, these two maps agree on Y^ϕ. For each $x \in X^\phi$, we have $[g, \tau](x) = \tau_x(g \upharpoonright Y^\phi_{<x}) = x^{g \upharpoonright Y^\phi_{<x}} = \hat{g}(x)$. By definition of the relations of $\mathbf{A}^{(M_f)}$, it holds that $\mathbf{A}^{(M_f)}, \hat{g} \models \alpha$, for each atom α appearing in ϕ_{M_g}. It follows that $\mathbf{A}^{(M_f)}, \hat{g} \models \phi_{M_g}$, and hence that $\mathbf{A}^{(M_f)}, \hat{g} \models \text{matrix}(\phi)$. □

We next identify a connection between being a model of ϕ and receiving a homomorphism from a member of $\mathcal{A}^{\phi,Z}$.

Theorem 4.8. *Assume that $\mathbf{B}$ is a structure, and that $\mathbf{B} \models \phi$. For each map $h : Z \to B_u$, there exists a structure $\mathbf{A}^{(M_f)} \in \mathcal{A}^{\phi,Z}$ such that h can be extended to a homomorphism h^+ from $\mathbf{A}^{(M_f)}$ to $\mathbf{B}$.*

Proof. Let $(\tau_x)_{x \in X^\phi}$ be a Skolem family for $(\phi, \mathbf{B})$. For each $g : Y^\phi \to Z$, it holds that $\mathbf{B}, [h(g), \tau] \models \text{matrix}(\phi)$, and hence we obtain that there exists a value $i \in \{1, \ldots, d\}$ such that $\mathbf{B}, [h(g), \tau] \models \phi_i$; define M_g to be such a value i. We thus have that, for each $g : Y^\phi \to Z$, it holds that $\mathbf{B}, [h(g), \tau] \models \phi_{M_g}$.

Let us next define the extension h^+ of h. Let $x \in X^\phi$ and let $g : Y^\phi_{<x} \to Z$ be any map; define $h^+(x^g)$ to be τ_x applied to the map $h(g)$, that is, $h^+(x^g) = \tau_x(h(g))$.

We claim that h^+ is a homomorphism from $\mathbf{A}^{(M_g)}$ to $\mathbf{B}$. Let R be any relation symbol. Consider any tuple in $R^{\mathbf{A}^{(M_g)}}$; it has the form $(\hat{g}(v_1), \ldots, \hat{g}(v_k))$ where $g : Y^\phi \to Z$ is a map and where $R(v_1, \ldots, v_k)$ is in ϕ_{M_g}. We need to show that the tuple $(h^+(\hat{g}(v_1)), \ldots, h^+(\hat{g}(v_k)))$ is an element of $R^{\mathbf{B}}$. We argue that the map $h^+(g)$ is equal to $[h(g), \tau]$. In the case that v is a variable of sort u, we have $h^+(\hat{g}(v)) = h^+(g(v)) = h(g(v)) = [h(g), \tau](v)$; in the case that v is a variable of sort e, we have $h^+(\hat{g}(v)) = h^+(v^{g \upharpoonright Y_{<x}}) = \tau_v(h(g)) = [h(g), \tau](v)$. As we previously established that $\mathbf{B}, [h(g), \tau] \models \phi_{M_g}$, we have $\mathbf{B}, [h(g), \tau] \models R(v_1, \ldots, v_k)$ and thus we have that $\mathbf{B}, h^+(\hat{g}) \models R(v_1, \ldots, v_k)$; from this, we may infer that the tuple $(h^+(\hat{g}(v_1)), \ldots, h^+(\hat{g}(v_k)))$ is an element of $R^{\mathbf{B}}$. This establishes the claim. □

Corollary 4.9. *Assume that* $\mathbf{B}$ *is a structure, and that* $\mathbf{B} \models \phi$. *If there exists a surjective map from* Z *to* B_u, *then there exists a structure* $\mathbf{A} \in \mathcal{A}^{\phi,Z}$ *such that there is a* $\forall$*-surjective homomorphism from* $\mathbf{A}$ *to* $\mathbf{B}$.

Proof. Let $h : Z \rightarrow B_u$ be surjective. Then, apply Theorem 4.8 to h; the resulting structure $\mathbf{A}^{(M_f)}$ is the desired structure $\mathbf{A}$, and the resulting homomorphism h^+ is a $\forall$-surjective homomorphism from $\mathbf{A}$ to $\mathbf{B}$. □

By making use of the above results, we may now give a characterization of the models of a quantifier-sorted sentence ϕ.

Theorem 4.10. *Let* ϕ *be a normal quantifier-sorted sentence. For any quantifier-sorted structure* $\mathbf{B}$, *it holds that* $\mathbf{B} \models \phi$ *if and only if there exist a non-empty set* Z *and a structure* $\mathbf{A} \in \mathcal{A}^{\phi,Z}$ *such that there is a* $\forall$*-surjective homomorphism from* $\mathbf{A}$ *to* $\mathbf{B}$.

Proof. We first prove the forward direction. Set $Z = B_u$. Then, the identity map is a surjective map from Z to B_u; the result follows from Corollary 4.9.

We next prove the backward direction. Suppose that there exist a set Z and a structure $\mathbf{A}$ as described. Since $\mathbf{A} \in \mathcal{A}^{\phi,Z}$, by Theorem 4.7, we have $\mathbf{A} \models \phi$. By hypothesis, there is a $\forall$-surjective homomorphism from $\mathbf{A}$ to $\mathbf{B}$; by Theorem 4.2, we obtain $\mathbf{B} \models \phi$. □

This allows us to give a characterization of entailment for positive quantifier-sorted sentences.

Theorem 4.11. *Let* ϕ *be a normal quantifier-sorted sentence, and let* ψ *be a quantifier-sorted positive sentence. It holds that* ϕ *entails* ψ *if and only if, for every non-empty set* Z *and every structure* $\mathbf{B} \in \mathcal{A}^{\phi,Z}$, *it holds that* $\mathbf{B} \models \psi$.

Proof. The forward direction is immediate from Theorem 4.7. For the backward direction, suppose that $\mathbf{C} \models \phi$. It follows from Theorem 4.10 that there exists a set Z and a structure $\mathbf{B} \in \mathcal{A}^{\phi,Z}$ such that there is a $\forall$-surjective homomorphism from $\mathbf{B}$ to $\mathbf{C}$. By hypothesis, it holds that $\mathbf{B} \models \psi$. From this, it follows from Theorem 4.2 that $\mathbf{C} \models \psi$. □

4.4 Quantified conjunctive queries on the left

We say that a formula is *quantified conjunctive* if it is built from atoms, conjunction, universal quantification, and existential quantification; that is, if negation and disjunction are not used. We use $\mathrm{QCQ_{QS}}$ to denote the class of all quantifier-sorted quantified conjunctive sentences, and we use $\mathrm{PFO_{QS}}$ to denote the class of all positive quantifier-sorted sentences. In this subsection, we establish a characterization of entailment for $(\mathrm{QCQ_{QS}}, \mathrm{PFO_{QS}})$, and we use this characterization to show the selfish models property and an upper bound on the complexity of entailment.

Let ϕ be a normal quantified conjunctive sentence. Since disjunction is not used in ϕ, there is, for each set Z, only one family (M_f) of the form described at the beginning of Section 4.3; thus, there is a unique structure in $\mathcal{A}^{\phi,Z}$. Throughout this section, we denote this unique structure by $\mathbf{A}^{\phi,Z}$, and its universe by $A^{\phi,Z}$.

In the following proposition and throughout this subsection, we will use the following convention. Suppose that $\mathbf{A}$ is a structure of the form $\mathbf{A}^{\phi,Z}$. When x^g is an element of A_e and $h : Z \rightarrow Z'$ is a mapping defined on Z, we extend the action of h so that $h(x^g)$ is defined as $x^{h(g)}$.

The following proposition is immediate from the definitions.

Proposition 4.12. *Let* Z, Z' *be sets where* Z' *is non-empty. For any map* $h : Z \rightarrow Z'$, *it holds that* h *is a homomorphism from* $\mathbf{A}^{\phi,Z}$ *to* $\mathbf{A}^{\phi,Z'}$.

When W is a finite set of variables, we use $\sharp u(W)$ to denote the number of variables in W that have sort u, and respectively $\sharp e(W)$ to denote the number of variables in W that have sort e. When Z is a set and ϕ is a quantified conjunctive formula, we say that a positive quantifier-sorted formula ψ is *well-behaved* with respect to (Z, ϕ) if for every subformula ψ' of ψ, it holds that Z contains at least $\sharp u(\mathrm{free}(\psi')) + \sharp e(\mathrm{free}(\psi')) \cdot \sharp u(\mathrm{free}(\mathrm{matrix}(\phi)))$ many elements.

We next present a theorem that is a generalization of Proposition 4.12. It shows essentially that an assignment satisfying a well-behaved formula over $\mathbf{A}^{\phi,Z}$, when mapped under h, yields an assignment satisfying the same formula over $\mathbf{A}^{\phi,Z'}$.

Theorem 4.13. *Let* Z, Z' *be non-empty sets. Suppose that* ϕ *is a normal quantified conjunctive sentence, and that* ψ *is a positive quantifier-sorted formula that is well-behaved with respect to* (Z, ϕ). *For any assignment* f *defined on* $\mathrm{free}(\psi)$ *and any map* $h : Z \rightarrow Z'$, *if* $\mathbf{A}^{\phi,Z}, f \models \psi$, *then* $\mathbf{A}^{\phi,Z'}, h(f) \models \psi$.

Let us define a mapping appears defined on the universe $A^{\phi,Z}$ of $\mathbf{A}^{\phi,Z}$, as follows. Define $\mathrm{appears}(z) = \{z\}$ for each $z \in Z$, and $\mathrm{appears}(x^g) = \mathrm{image}(g)$. When f is a mapping from a set of variables V to the universe $A^{\phi,Z}$, let us define $\mathrm{appears}(f)$ as $\cup_{v \in V} \mathrm{appears}(f(v))$.

Proof. This is proved by induction on the structure of ψ. Suppose that $\mathbf{A}^{\phi,Z}, f \models \psi$. In the case that ψ is an atomic formula, the result is immediate from Proposition 4.12. In the case that ψ is a disjunction or conjunction, the result follows directly by induction.

In the case that ψ has the form $\exists v \psi'$, we argue as follows. There exists $a \in A_e^{\phi,Z}$ such that $\mathbf{A}^{\phi,Z}, f[v \rightarrow a] \models \psi'$, implying that $\mathbf{A}^{\phi,Z'}, h(f[v \rightarrow a]) \models \psi'$, from which we conclude that $\mathbf{A}^{\phi,Z'}, h(f) \models \psi$.

In the case that ψ has the form $\forall v \psi'$, we argue as follows. In the case that $v \notin \text{free}(\psi')$, the result follows directly by induction, since then ψ and ψ' are logically equivalent; so, let us assume that $v \in \text{free}(\psi')$. We further assume that the domain of f is free(ψ). Let us bound $|\text{appears}(f)|$; observe that each universal variable in free(ψ) contributes at most 1 to this value, and that each existential variable in free(ψ) contributes at most $\sharp u(\text{free}(\text{matrix}(\phi)))$ to this value. Since free(ψ') has a universal variable, namely v, that does not occur in free(ψ), we thus have $|\text{appears}(f)| < \sharp u(\text{free}(\psi')) + \sharp e(\text{free}(\psi')) \cdot \sharp u(\text{free}(\phi)) \leq |Z|$. By the bound $|\text{appears}(f)| < |Z|$, there exists a value $z \in Z$ such that $z \notin \text{appears}(f)$. Let $z \in Z'$ be arbitrary. Define h^- to be equal to $h[z \to z']$. It is then clear that $h^-(f[v \to z])$ maps v to z', and is elsewhere equal to $h(f)$. We have $\mathbf{A}^{\phi,Z}, f[v \to z] \models \psi'$; by induction, it follows that $\mathbf{A}^{\phi,Z'}, h^-(f[v \to z]) \models \psi'$ which is equivalent to $\mathbf{A}^{\phi,Z'}, (h(f))[v \to z'] \models \psi'$. Since z' was taken to be arbitrary, it follows that $\mathbf{A}^{\phi,Z'}, h(f) \models \forall v \psi'$. □

Let $f : \{v_1, \ldots, v_n\} \to A^{\phi,Z}$ be a mapping from a set of variables to a universe $A^{\phi,Z}$, and let $P = Q_1 v_1 \ldots Q_n v_n$ be a quantifier prefix on that set of variables. We say that f is a $\forall$-fresh assignment with respect to P when for each $i \in \{1, \ldots, n\}$, if v_i is a variable of sort u, then $v_i \notin \text{appears}(f \upharpoonright \{v_1, \ldots, v_{i-1}\})$. Roughly speaking, this means that if one inspects the value $f(v_1), f(v_2), \ldots$ one by one, whenever v_i is of the universal sort, its value $f(v_i)$ is fresh in the sense that it has not been seen before.

The following theorem shows that, relative to a selfish model $\mathbf{A}^{\phi,Z}$, the truth of a positive sentence ψ which begins with a sequence of quantification is implied by the existence of a $\forall$-fresh assignment that satisfies the portion of the sentence following the quantification.

Theorem 4.14. *Let ϕ be a normal quantified conjunctive sentence. Suppose that ψ is a positive quantifier-sorted sentence that the form*

$$Q_1 v_1 \ldots Q_n v_n \psi',$$

that is, ψ begins with the quantification of n variables; and, that Z is a set such that ψ is well-behaved with respect to (Z, ϕ). If $f : \{v_1, \ldots, v_n\} \to A^{\phi,Z}$ is a $\forall$-fresh assignment with respect to the prefix $Q_1 v_1 \ldots Q_n v_n$ such that $\mathbf{A}^{\phi,Z}, f \models \psi'$, then it holds that $\mathbf{A}^{\phi,Z} \models \psi$.

Proof. We prove this by induction on n. When $n = 0$, the theorem holds trivially, so suppose that $n > 0$. Set f^- equal to $f \upharpoonright \{v_1, \ldots, v_{n-1}\}$; observe that f^- is a $\forall$-fresh assignment with respect to $Q_1 v_1 \ldots Q_{n-1} v_{n-1}$.

If $Q_n = \exists$, then it holds that $\mathbf{A}^{\phi,Z}, f^- \models Q_n v_n \psi'$, so by induction, we obtain $\mathbf{A}^{\phi,Z} \models \psi$.

If $Q_n = \forall$, then we claim that for any $z \in Z$, it holds that $\mathbf{A}^{\phi,Z}, f[v_n \to z] \models \psi'$. Let $z \in Z$ be arbitrary. Let $h : Z \to Z$ the map that sends $f(v_n)$ to z, and fixes all other elements in Z. By Theorem 4.13, it holds that $\mathbf{A}^{\phi,Z}, h(f[v_n \to z]) \models \psi'$. Due to f being $\forall$-fresh, it holds that $h(f[v_n \to z]) = (h(f))[v_n \to z]$, and so we obtain $\mathbf{A}^{\phi,Z}, (h(f))[v_n \to z] \models \psi'$. Since $h(f^-) = f$, it follows that $\mathbf{A}^{\phi,Z}, f \models \forall v_n \psi'$. By induction, we obtain $\mathbf{A}^{\phi,Z} \models \psi$. □

We can now give a characterization of entailment for the logics under study.

Theorem 4.15. *Let ϕ be a normal quantified conjunctive sentence, and let*

$$\psi = Q_1 v_1 \ldots Q_n v_n \psi'$$

be a positive quantifier-sorted sentence in prenex form, where ψ' denotes the matrix of ψ. Let Z be a finite set of size at least

$$\sharp u(\text{free}(\psi')) + \sharp e(\text{free}(\psi')) \cdot \sharp u(\text{free}(\text{matrix}(\phi))).$$

The following are equivalent:

1. *ϕ entails ψ.*
2. *$\mathbf{A}^{\phi,Z} \models \psi$.*
3. *There exists a $\forall$-fresh assignment f with respect to the prefix $Q_1 v_1 \ldots Q_n v_n$ such that $\mathbf{A}^{\phi,Z}, f \models \text{matrix}(\psi)$.*

Proof. (1) implies (2) is immediate. (2) implies (3) follows directly from the semantics of ψ and the assumption on the size of Z. We argue that (3) implies (1) as follows.

By the choice of size of Z and the assumption that ψ is in prenex form, it follows that ψ is well-behaved with respect to (Z, ϕ). It follows by Theorem 4.14 that $\mathbf{A}^{\phi,Z} \models \psi$. Let Z' be any set. Then, Theorem 4.13 implies that $\mathbf{A}^{\phi,Z'} \models \psi$. Since Z' was arbitrary, we conclude by Theorem 4.11 that ϕ entails ψ. □

Using the previous characterization theorem, we can establish the selfish models property and present a complexity upper bound.

Theorem 4.16. *The pair of logics $(\text{QCQ}_{\text{QS}}, \text{PFO}_{\text{QS}})$ has the selfish models property via (P, NP), and each of the problems*

$$\text{ENTAIL}(\text{QCQ}_{\text{QS}}, \text{PFO}_{\text{QS}}), \text{FIN-ENTAIL}(\text{QCQ}_{\text{QS}}, \text{PFO}_{\text{QS}})$$

is NP-complete.

Proof. We first show that the pair of logics has the selfish models property. Let p be the polynomial-time computable function defined by $p(\psi) = |\text{free}(\text{matrix}(\psi))|$; here, we assume that ψ is prenex, and that the given quantity is represented in unary. When ϕ is a normal quantified conjunctive sentence, let $s(\phi, m)$ be defined as $\{\mathbf{A}^{\phi,Z_k}\}$ where Z_k is a finite set of size $m * \sharp u(\text{free}(\text{matrix}(\phi)))$. However, as the only structures that will ever be used to establish the selfish models property are of the form $\mathbf{A}^{\phi,Z_k}$ for various ϕ and various values of k, we represent such a structure succinctly, as a pair (ϕ, k). The pair of logics has the selfish model property with respect to (s, p), since $\mathbf{A}^{\phi, Z_k}$ is a model of ϕ (Theorem 4.7), and $\mathbf{A}^{\phi, Z_k} \models \psi$ implies that ϕ entails ψ.

We now argue that the pair of logics has the selfish models property via (P, NP). The machine M can be taken to be a P-machine which, when run on (ϕ, ψ), computes the structure $\mathbf{A}$ in $s(\phi, m)$ in the succinct representation, and then calls the oracle on $(\mathbf{A}, \psi)$. Checking whether or not $\mathbf{A} \models \psi$ can be performed in NP by using the characterization in Theorem 4.15 in terms of $\forall$-fresh assignments: an assignment can be guessed, and it can be checked that it is $\forall$-fresh and that it satisfies matrix(ψ). The complexity upper bounds claimed thus follow from Proposition 3.12; the lower bound of NP-hardness follows from the NP-hardness of ENTAIL(CQ, CQ) in the one-sorted setting. □

4.5 One alternation

We now study positive sentences with one alternation; in particular, let us use Π_2-PFO$_{QS}$ to denote the class of prenex sentences in PFO$_{QS}$ having a Π_2 quantifier prefix. We consider containment of positive sentences in sentences from Π_2-PFO$_{QS}$. We first establish the first version of the selfish models property, and then perform a complexity analysis.

Theorem 4.17. *Let ϕ be a normal quantifier-sorted sentence, let $\psi \in \Pi_2$-PFO$_{QS}$, and let n denote the number of universally quantified variables in ψ. Let Z_n be a set of size n; if for each $\mathbf{B} \in \mathcal{A}^{\phi, Z_n}$ it holds that $\mathbf{B} \models \psi$, then ϕ entails ψ.*

Proof. Let Z be an arbitrary set of size at least n, and let $\mathbf{A}^{(M_f)}$ be any element of $\mathcal{A}^{\phi, Z}$. By Theorem 4.11, it suffices to prove that $\mathbf{A}^{(M_f)} \models \psi$. Let $h : Y^{\psi} \to Z$ be any map. We want to show that h has an extension $h^+ : (Y^{\psi} \cup X^{\psi}) \to A^{(M_f)}$ such that $\mathbf{A}^{(M_f)}, h^+ \models \text{matrix}(\psi)$.

Let $Z' \subseteq Z$ be a set of size n such that $h(Y^{\psi}) \subseteq Z'$. Define $(M'_g)_{g : Y^{\phi} \to Z'}$ to be the natural subfamily of $(M_f)_{f : Y^{\phi} \to Z}$ such that for any $g : Y^{\phi} \to Z'$, it holds that $M'_g = M_f$, where $f : Y^{\phi} \to Z$ is the map that agrees with g at all points (that is, the map f such that, for all $y \in Y^{\phi}$, it holds that $f(y) = g(y)$).

Since Z' and Z_n have the same size, the structure $\mathbf{A}^{(M'_g)}$ is isomorphic to a structure in $\mathcal{A}^{\phi, Z_n}$; so by assumption, it holds that $\mathbf{A}^{(M'_g)} \models \psi$. Thus, h (viewed as a mapping from Y^{ϕ} to Z') has an extension $h^+ : (Y^{\psi} \cup X^{\psi}) \to A^{(M'_g)}$ such that $\mathbf{A}^{(M'_g)}, h^+ \models \text{matrix}(\psi)$. But, it is immediate from the definitions of the structures $\mathbf{A}^{(M_f)}$ and $\mathbf{A}^{(M'_g)}$ that $\mathbf{A}^{(M'_g)}$ is a substructure of $\mathbf{A}^{(M_f)}$. We thus conclude that $\mathbf{A}^{(M_f)}, h^+ \models$ matrix(ψ), as desired. □

Theorem 4.18. *Let p be the mapping where, for each $\psi \in \Pi_2$-PFO$_{QS}$, it holds that $p(\psi)$ is equal to the number of universally quantified variables in ψ. There exists a mapping s where, for each $\phi \in$ PFO$_{QS}$ and $n \geq 0$, it holds that $s(\phi, n) = \mathcal{A}^{\phi', Z_n}$, where Z_n is a set of size n, and ϕ' is a normal sentence which is logically equivalent to ϕ; and, where the pair (PFO$_{QS}$, Π_2-PFO$_{QS}$) has the selfish models property with respect to (s, p).*

Proof. From Theorem 4.17, we obtain that any s that both is defined as stated and is computable, along with the given p, satisfy Definition 3.1. It only needs to be argued that there exists such an s that is computable. Given $\phi \in$ PFO$_{QS}$, a normal sentence which is logically equivalent to ϕ can be obtained by converting ϕ to prenex form, and then processing the matrix so that disjunction is on the outside, by using the translation given in Example 3.10. □

Theorem 4.19. *The pair (PFO$_{QS}$, Π_2-PFO$_{QS}$) of logics has the selfish models property via (coNEXP, Π_2^p). We have that the problem ENTAIL(PFO$_{QS}$, Π_2-PFO$_{QS}$) as well as the problem FIN-ENTAIL(PFO$_{QS}$, Π_2-PFO$_{QS}$) are in coNEXP^{NP}.*

Proof. We argue that the conditions of Definition 3.11 are met by the functions (s, p) given in the statement and proof of Theorem 4.18. To give the machine M and to describe the language L', we use a succinct representation of the structures in $s(\phi, n)$. To specify such a structure, we need to provide ϕ and a family $(M_f)_{f : Y^{\phi} \to Z_n}$; the family is presented by giving, for each map $f : Y^{\phi} \to Z_n$, a disjunct in $D(\text{matrix}(\phi))$, where $D(\cdot)$ is the operator from Example 3.10. That is, we specify the disjuncts directly, as opposed to associating them with natural numbers. The machine M is an $\wedge$-oracle coNEXP-machine that conondeterministically guesses an element $\mathbf{B}$ of $s(\phi, n)$ by enumerating each map $f : Y^{\phi} \to Z_n$, guessing a disjunct in $D(\text{matrix}(\phi))$ using the procedure in Example 3.15, and writing down the map f along with the guessed disjunct; after $\mathbf{B}$ has been guessed, the oracle is called on $(\mathbf{B}, \psi)$, and the run accepts if and only if the oracle accepts. Each disjunct requires polynomial time to guess, and the number of maps can be bounded by 2^q for a polynomial q in the the input size $|(\phi, \psi)|$; thus, the guessing of $\mathbf{B}$ can be performed in conondeterministic exponential time, that is, by a coNEXP machine. We have coNEXP$^{\wedge \Pi_2^p} \subseteq$ coNEXP$^{\wedge \text{NP}} \subseteq$ coNEXP^{NP}, and thus obtain the complexity bounds on the two given problems from Proposition 3.12. □

Acknowledgements. The author thanks all of those with whom he has discussed the topics of this article, including André Hernich and Luc Segoufin. He also thanks Dániel Marx for prior collaboration [14].

REFERENCES

[1] S. Abiteboul, R. Hull, and V. Vianu. 1995. *Foundations of Databases.* Addison-Wesley.
[2] Manuel Bodirsky and Jan Kára. 2010. The complexity of temporal constraint satisfaction problems. *J. ACM* 57, 2 (2010).

[3] Manuel Bodirsky, H. Dugald Macpherson, and Johan Thapper. 2013. Constraint satisfaction tractability from semi-lattice operations on infinite sets. *ACM Trans. Comput. Log.* 14, 4 (2013), 30:1–30:19.
[4] Simone Bova and Hubie Chen. 2014. The Complexity of Width Minimization for Existential Positive Queries. In *ICDT*. 235–244.
[5] Simone Bova and Hubie Chen. 2015. The complexity of equivalence, entailment, and minimization in existential positive logic. *J. Comput. Syst. Sci.* 81, 2 (2015), 443–457.
[6] Simone Bova and Fabio Mogavero. 2017. Herbrand property, finite quasi-Herbrand models, and a Chandra-Merlin theorem for quantified conjunctive queries. In *32nd Annual ACM/IEEE Symposium on Logic in Computer Science, LICS 2017, Reykjavik, Iceland, June 20-23, 2017*. 1–12.
[7] Diego Calvanese, Giuseppe De Giacomo, Maurizio Lenzerini, and Moshe Y. Vardi. 2003. View-based query containment. In *Proceedings of the Twenty-Second ACM SIGACT-SIGMOD-SIGART Symposium on Principles of Database Systems, June 9-12, 2003, San Diego, CA, USA*. 56–67.
[8] Ashok K. Chandra and Philip M. Merlin. 1977. Optimal Implementation of Conjunctive Queries in Relational Data Bases. In *Proceddings of STOC'77*. 77–90.
[9] Hubie Chen. 2014. On the complexity of existential positive queries. *ACM Trans. Comput. Log.* 15, 1 (2014).
[10] Hubie Chen. 2017. The Tractability Frontier of Graph-Like First-Order Query Sets. *J. ACM* 64, 4 (2017), 26:1–26:29.
[11] Hubie Chen and Víctor Dalmau. 2016. Decomposing Quantified Conjunctive (or Disjunctive) Formulas. *SIAM J. Comput.* 45, 6 (2016), 2066–2086.
[12] Hubie Chen and Martin Grohe. 2010. Constraint Satisfaction with Succinctly Specified Relations. *J. Comput. System Sci.* 76, 8 (2010), 847–860.
[13] Hubie Chen, Florent R. Madelaine, and Barnaby Martin. 2015. Quantified Constraints and Containment Problems. *Logical Methods in Computer Science* 11, 3 (2015).
[14] Hubie Chen and Dániel Marx. 2013. Block-Sorted Quantified Conjunctive Queries. In *ICALP*.
[15] Hubie Chen and Stefan Mengel. 2015. A Trichotomy in the Complexity of Counting Answers to Conjunctive Queries. In *18th International Conference on Database Theory, ICDT 2015, March 23-27, 2015, Brussels, Belgium*. 110–126.
[16] Hubie Chen and Stefan Mengel. 2016. Counting Answers to Existential Positive Queries: A Complexity Classification. In *Proceedings of the 35th ACM SIGMOD-SIGACT-SIGAI Symposium on Principles of Database Systems*. 315–326.
[17] Hubie Chen and Stefan Mengel. 2017. The logic of counting query answers. In *32nd Annual ACM/IEEE Symposium on Logic in Computer Science, LICS 2017, Reykjavik, Iceland, June 20-23, 2017*. 1–12.
[18] Hubie Chen and Moritz Müller. 2015. The Fine Classification of Conjunctive Queries and Parameterized Logarithmic Space. *TOCT* 7, 2 (2015), 7.
[19] Hubie Chen and Moritz Müller. 2017. One Hierarchy Spawns Another: Graph Deconstructions and the Complexity Classification of Conjunctive Queries. *ACM Trans. Comput. Log.* 18, 4 (2017), 29:1–29:37.
[20] Hubie Chen and Moritz Müller. 2017. The Parameterized Space Complexity of Embedding Along a Path. *Theory Comput. Syst.* 61, 3 (2017), 851–870.
[21] J. Flum and M. Grohe. 2006. *Parameterized Complexity Theory*. Springer.
[22] Martin Grohe. 2007. The complexity of homomorphism and constraint satisfaction problems seen from the other side. *J. ACM* 54, 1 (2007).
[23] Shawn Hedman. 2004. *A First Course in Logic: An Introduction to Model Theory, Proof Theory, Computability, and Complexity (Oxford Texts in Logic)*. Oxford University Press, Inc., New York, NY, USA.
[24] Maurizio Lenzerini. 2002. Data Integration: A Theoretical Perspective. In *Proceedings of the Twenty-first ACM SIGACT-SIGMOD-SIGART Symposium on Principles of Database Systems, June 3-5, Madison, Wisconsin, USA*. 233–246.
[25] Alon Y. Levy, Alberto O. Mendelzon, Yehoshua Sagiv, and Divesh Srivastava. 1995. Answering Queries Using Views. In *Proceedings of the Fourteenth ACM SIGACT-SIGMOD-SIGART Symposium on Principles of Database Systems, May 22-25, 1995, San Jose, California, USA*. 95–104.
[26] Dániel Marx. 2013. Tractable Hypergraph Properties for Constraint Satisfaction and Conjunctive Queries. *J. ACM* 60, 6 (2013), 42.
[27] C.H. Papadimitriou. 1995. *Computational Complexity*. Addison-Wesley.
[28] Yehoshua Sagiv and Mihalis Yannakakis. 1980. Equivalences Among Relational Expressions with the Union and Difference Operators. *J. ACM* 27, 4 (1980), 633–655.

A PARAMETERIZED ENTAILMENT PROBLEMS

Here, we explore an implication that the selfish models property has in the setting of parameterized complexity theory. Here, we deal with the situation where the entailment problems are parameterized by the first sentence.

Let Σ be an alphabet over which strings and languages are formed. Define a *parameterization* to be a polynomial-time computable map $\kappa : \Sigma^* \to \Sigma^*$. Define a *parameterized problem* to be a pair (Q, κ) where Q is a language and κ is a parameterization. As we are about to deal with both classical complexity classes and parameterized complexity classes, which contain parameterized problems, let us define a *classical complexity class* as a class of computable languages. For each classical complexity class C, define para-C to be the parameterized complexity class that contains a parameterized problem (Q, κ) if there exists a computable map $c : \Sigma^* \to \Sigma^*$ and a language $Q' \in C$ of pairs such that, for each $x \in \Sigma^*$, it holds that $x \in Q$ if and only if $(c(\kappa(x)), x) \in Q'$. Essentially, this means that membership of a string x in Q can be decided in the class C when the string x is presented along with an advice string $c(\kappa(x))$ that depends only on its parameter $\kappa(x)$. It is known that para-P is equal to the parameterized compleixty class FPT [21, Chapter 1].

Let π_1 be the parameterization that, given a pair, returns the first entry, that is, such that $\pi_1(\phi, \psi) = \phi$.

- Define p-ENTAIL(Φ, Ψ) as the parameterized problem (ENTAIL$(\Phi, \Psi), \pi_1$).
- Define p-FIN-ENTAIL(Φ, Ψ) as the parameterized problem (FIN-ENTAIL$(\Phi, \Psi), \pi_1$).

We have the following.

Proposition A.1. *Suppose that (Φ, Ψ) is a pair of logics that has the selfish models property via (C, C') where the function p is the constant function ϵ. Then, each of the two problems* p-ENTAIL(Φ, Ψ), p-FIN-ENTAIL(Φ, Ψ) *is in* para-$(\mathsf{P}^{\wedge C'})$.

Proof. Let c be the computable function where $c(\phi) = s(\phi, \epsilon)$. Consider the language Q' that contains a pair (S, ψ)

when S is a set of structures such that, for each $\mathbf{B} \in S$, it holds that $\mathbf{B} \models \psi$. We have that $Q' \in \mathsf{P}^{\wedge C'}$, since in polynomial time it is possible, given a pair (S, ψ), to check membership in Q' by looping over each structure $\mathbf{B} \in S$ and check, using an L'-oracle, whether $\mathbf{B} \models \psi$. The language Q' witnesses that each of the given problems is in para-$\mathsf{P}^{\wedge C'}$, by the proof of Proposition 3.12. □

Example A.2. From Example 3.15 and Proposition A.1, we have that each of the two problems

$$\text{p-ENTAIL(EPQ, EPQ), p-FIN-ENTAIL(EPQ, EPQ)}$$

is in para-$\mathsf{P}^{\wedge \mathsf{NP}}$ = para-NP.

Example A.3. From Example 3.17 and Proposition A.1, we have that each of the two problems

$$\text{p-ENTAIL(EPQ, ACQ), p-FIN-ENTAIL(EPQ, ACQ)}$$

is in para-$\mathsf{P}^{\wedge \mathsf{P}}$ = para-P.

Attacking Diophantus: Solving a Special Case of Bag Containment

George Konstantinidis
g.konstantinidis@soton.ac.uk
University of Southampton

Fabio Mogavero
fabio.mogavero@unina.it
Università degli Studi di Napoli Federico II

ABSTRACT

Conjunctive-query containment is the problem of deciding whether the answers of a given conjunctive query on an arbitrary database instance are always contained in the answers of a second query on the same instance. This is a very relevant question in query optimization, data integration, and other data management and artificial intelligence areas. The problem has been deeply studied and understood for the, so-called, *set-semantics*, *i.e.*, when query answers and database instances are modelled as sets of tuples. In particular, it has been shown by Chandra and Merlin to be NPTIME-COMPLETE. On the contrary, when investigated under *bag-semantics*, *a.k.a. multiset semantics*, which allows for replicated tuples both in the underlying instance and in the query answers, it is not even clear whether the problem is decidable. Since this is exactly the standard interpretation for commercial relational database systems, the question turns out to be an important one. Multiple works on variations and restrictions of the *bag-containment problem* have been reported in the literature and, although the general problem is still open, we contribute with this article by solving a special case that has been identified as a major open problem on its own. More specifically, we study *projection-free queries*, *i.e.*, queries without existentially quantified variables, and show decidability for the bag-containment problem of a projection-free conjunctive query into a generic conjunctive query. We prove indeed that deciding containment in this setting is in Π_2^{P}. Our approach relies on the solution of a special case of the *Diophantine inequality problem* via a reduction to the *linear inequality problem* and clearly exposes inherent difficulties in the analysis of the general question.

PODS'19, June 30-July 5, 2019, Amsterdam, Netherlands

ACM ISBN 978-1-4503-6227-6/19/06...$15.00
https://doi.org/10.1145/3294052.3319689

KEYWORDS

Query Containment; Bag Semantics; Bag Containment; Multiset Semantics; Diophantine Inequalities

ACM Reference Format:
George Konstantinidis and Fabio Mogavero. 2019. Attacking Diophantus: Solving a Special Case of Bag Containment. In *38th ACM SIGMOD-SIGACT-SIGAI Symposium on Principles of Database Systems (PODS'19), June 30-July 5, 2019, Amsterdam, Netherlands.* ACM, New York, NY, USA, 15 pages. https://doi.org/10.1145/3294052.3319689

1 INTRODUCTION

The standard *query containment problem* can be defined as follows: given a *database schema* $\mathcal{S}$ and two *queries* q_1 and q_2 on $\mathcal{S}$, decide whether, for all *relational database instances* [12] $\mathcal{I}$ over $\mathcal{S}$, it is the case that $q_1^{\mathcal{I}} \subseteq q_2^{\mathcal{I}}$, in symbols $q_1 \sqsubseteq q_2$, with $q_i^{\mathcal{I}}$ being the set of answer tuples of query q_i on database $\mathcal{I}$. This is a problem of both great theoretical and practical significance, fundamental to databases [1] and knowledge representation systems [3], central to optimization and minimization of queries [5] and to data integration problems, such as view-based query answering [25, 27].

Conjunctive queries (CQs, for short) [5] are a restricted form of *first-order formulas* and correspond to the *select-project-join* fragment of relational algebra [12, 13], which is at the core of all major structured query languages, like SQL [1] and SPARQL [18]. Such types of queries have been extensively investigated by the database and artificial intelligence communities. In particular, in their breakthrough article [5], Chandra and Merlin solved the decidability of the containment problem for CQs, by proving that it is essentially the same problem as CQ evaluation, and it amounts to finding an *homomorphism* that syntactically maps one query into the other. This places the problem in NPTIME, and it is hard for the same class as well.

Although widely used as a language abstraction for SQL analysis, the classic *set-theoretic semantics* of CQs does not precisely capture the actual interpretation of SQL queries on relational databases. Under the standard semantics, indeed, both the answer to a CQ and all relations in the underlying database are modeled as sets of tuples. In practice, however, database systems allow for multiple replicas of a tuple in their tables. The answers to a query might also contain several occurrences of the same result. Motivated by this mismatch, Chaudhuri and Vardi [7] posed the question of deciding containment of CQs under *bag* or *multiset semantics*, where the answer and the database tables are collections of possibly replicated tuples, *i.e.*, *bags*. In their seminal work, they claimed that the relevant problem, referred to as *bag containment*, is Π_2^P-HARD, but its exact complexity, even worst its decidability, is unknown to date.

Several attacks on this problem (including two PhD theses) have failed [24]. However, there have been successful attempts, some of them reported in the following, to prove un-/decidability or complexity results for variations of the problem, usually focusing on extensions or restrictions of the CQ language. On one side, Ioannidis and Ramakrishnan [20] remarkably proved that the bag-containment problem for *unions of* CQs (UCQs, for short) is undecidable by applying a reduction from the *Diophantine inequality problem*, which is a variant of the well-known *Hilbert's 10th problem* [28] that, in turn, is about deciding whether a polynomial equation with integer coefficients has an all-integer solution. In more detail, they described a technique to derive, from two arbitrary polynomials $P_1(\overline{u})$ and $P_2(\overline{u})$, with natural coefficients, no constant terms, and same unknowns $\overline{u}$, two UCQs q_1 and q_2 such that q_1 is bag contained into q_2, in symbols $q_1 \sqsubseteq_b q_2$, *iff* $P_1(\overline{\xi}) \leq P_2(\overline{\xi})$, for all vectors of natural numbers $\overline{\xi} \in \mathbb{N}^{|\overline{u}|}$. By reducing from another variant of the same problem, Jayram *et al.* [21] showed that bag containment for CQ*s with inequalities* is also undecidable. On the other side, Kopparty and Rossman [26] proved the decidability of bag containment for a class of *Boolean* CQ*s* that enjoys certain graph-theoretic properties when syntactically interpreted as graphs. Their results exploit information-theory techniques based on entropy measures, but do not provide explicit complexity bounds. Finally, Afrati *et al.* [2] reported decidability and complexity results for five major subclasses of CQs that have important practical applications.

Apart form the original question, the major open problem out of those that Afrati *et al.* pointed out in their article is the bag containment of a *projection-free* CQ, *i.e.*, a conjunctive query with no existential variables, into a CQ that might have projections. In the present work, we solve this problem by providing a Π_2^P decidability procedure. Different from all other approaches aiming at a decidability result and inspired by the converse techniques of those exploited in the proofs of undecidability, we describe an exponential reduction to the solution of a Diophantine inequality system of a certain structure. The latter is then shown to be decidable in PTIME. In more detail, given a projection-free CQ q_1 and a generic CQ q_2, we first construct a family of monomial-polynomial pairs $\{(M_i(\overline{u}), P_i(\overline{u}))\}_{i=1}^k$, all with natural coefficients and no constant terms, such that $q_1 \sqsubseteq_b q_2$ *iff* $M_i(\overline{\xi}) \leq P_i(\overline{\xi})$, for all $\overline{\xi} \in \mathbb{N}^{|\overline{u}|}$ and $1 \leq i \leq k$. Both the number and the size of the polynomials $P_i(\overline{u})$ might be exponential in the size of the containing query q_2, but are polynomial in those of the containee query q_1. Then, we linearly reduce the solution of each converse *monomial-polynomial inequality* $M_i(\overline{u}) > P_i(\overline{u})$ to the search for a solution of a suitable *linear inequality system*. The latter problem is well-known to be computable in PTIME [29, 32]. Finally, we characterize the complexity of bag containment by relating it to the second level of the polynomial hierarchy, since it enjoys a witness whose correctness can be checked by a ∀∃-alternating Turing machine. As lower bound, we provide an NPTIME-hardness result.

We conclude by discussing possible generalizations of our approach to more expressive "containee" queries, pointing out difficulties for the general case. We hope this enables discussions for future research opportunities in the area.

2 PRELIMINARIES

A *bag* over a set I is a function $\mu \colon \mathrm{I} \to \mathbb{N}$ mapping every element $t \in \mathrm{I}$ to a non-negative integer value $\mu(t)$, called *multiplicity* of t *w.r.t.* μ in I, and it is *finite* if I is finite. We shall be writing a bag μ over a set I as the expression $\mathrm{I}^\mu = \{t^{\mu(t)} : t \in \mathrm{I}\}$. For two bags μ_1 and μ_2 over the sets I_1 and I_2, respectively, we say that μ_1 is a *subbag* of μ_2, in symbols $\mu_1 \subseteq \mu_2$, if $\mathrm{I}_1 \subseteq \mathrm{I}_2$ and $\mu_1(t) \leq \mu_2(t)$, for all $t \in \mathrm{I}_1$.

We use the standard mathematical logic notation of *relation*, *constant*, *variable*, and *term*, the latter denoting either a constant or a variable. An n-tuple $\overline{t}$ is an ordered list of n terms, with n its *arity* that can be also indicated by $|\overline{t}|$. Relations are also associated with a non-negative number called arity. A relation name R together with its arity n forms a *relation schema*. *Atoms* are syntactic expressions of the form $R(\overline{t})$, where R is a relation name having arity n and $\overline{t}$ is an n-tuple of terms. *Ground atoms*, *a.k.a. facts*, are atoms $R(\overline{c})$ where $\overline{c}$ is a tuple of constants only. Therefore, a relation (or relation instance) over relation schema R is essentially a set of facts $R(\overline{c})$. X and C denote the set of variables and constants, respectively. Sometimes it is convenient to interpret a variable (*resp.*, a tuple of variables) as constant (*resp.*, a tuple of constants). We call these *canonical constants* (disjoint from the set of constants in our language) and define a bisection between the canonical constant $\widehat{x}$ and the associated variable x (see [1]). Formally, $\mathrm{C} = \mathrm{C}_c \cup \mathrm{C}_l$, $\mathrm{C}_c \cap \mathrm{C}_l = \emptyset$, where C_c and C_l are the sets of canonical and language constants, respectively. Moreover, for a set of variables $\mathrm{V} \subseteq \mathrm{X}$, we have $\mathrm{can}(\mathrm{V}) \triangleq \{\widehat{x} : x \in \mathrm{V}\} \subseteq \mathrm{C}_c$. Note that $\mathrm{C}_c = \mathrm{can}(\mathrm{X})$.

A set of relation schemas is a *database schema* S. Accordingly, a *set database instance* (*set instance*, for short) I is a (possibly infinite) set of facts belonging in relation instances over relation schemas in S. The *active domain* adom(I) of a set database instance I is the set of all constants that occur in I. A bag over a set instance is a *bag instance.*

A *substitution* σ is a mapping of variables to constants. We write $\sigma = \{x_1 \mapsto c_1; \ldots; x_n \mapsto c_n\}$ to indicate that $\sigma(x_i) = c_i$, for $1 \leq i \leq n$. For α a term, a tuple of terms, an atom, or a set of atoms, $\sigma(\alpha)$ is obtained by replacing each occurrence of a variable x in α, that also occurs in the domain of σ, with $\sigma(x)$; variables outside the domain of σ remain unchanged. Given $\overline{x}$ an n-tuple of variables $x_1, \ldots, x_n$ and $\overline{t}$ an n-tuple of constants $t_1, \ldots, t_n$, we say that $\overline{x}$ and $\overline{t}$ *unify* with each other or are *unifiable*, if we can define the substitution σ in such a way that $\sigma(\overline{x}) = \overline{t}$. A substitution σ is a *homomorphism* of a set of atoms I_1 into a set of atoms I_2, if the domain of σ is the set of all variables occurring in I_1 and $\sigma(I_1) \subseteq I_2$.

A *conjunctive query* (CQ, for short) $q(\overline{x})$ with $\overline{x}$ the tuple of *free variables* (also denoted by q when we do not focus on its free variables) is a first-order formula of the form $\exists \overline{y} \bigwedge_i R_i(\overline{x}, \overline{y})$, where $\bigwedge_i R_i(\overline{x}, \overline{y})$ is a conjunction of atoms with variables from vector $\overline{xy}$. When $\overline{y}$ is empty, $q(\overline{x})$ is called a *projection-free* CQ. We usually use the datalog notation

$$q(\overline{x}) \leftarrow R_1(\overline{x}, \overline{y}), \ldots, R_n(\overline{x}, \overline{y})$$

in place of $q(\overline{x}) = \exists \overline{y} \bigwedge_{i=1}^{n} R_i(\overline{x}, \overline{y})$. As a syntactic object, the query $\exists \overline{y} \bigwedge_i R_i(\overline{x}, \overline{y})$ might contain repeated atoms, that is, there might be indexes i, j with $i \neq j$ such that $R_i(\overline{x}, \overline{y}) = R_j(\overline{x}, \overline{y})$. Traditionally, in set semantics, this repetition does not make any difference since it does not affect the result of a query. Under the bag perspective, however, we want to model these repetitions. The body of a CQ $q(\overline{x}) = \exists \overline{y} \bigwedge_i R_i(\overline{x}, \overline{y})$ is the set $\mathsf{body}(q(\overline{x}))$ that contains all distinct atoms in $\bigwedge_i R_i(\overline{x}, \overline{y})$. We can then define a bag $\mu_{q(\overline{x})}$ over $\mathsf{body}(q(\overline{x}))$, which given an atom in the body returns the number of occurrences of this atom in the expression $\bigwedge_i R_i(\overline{x}, \overline{y})$. Bag $\mu_{q(\overline{x})}$ is called the *body multiplicity* of $q(\overline{x})$. Any CQ can now be seen as the pair $\langle \overline{x}, \mu_{q(\overline{x})} \rangle$, which is called the *bag representation* of the corresponding CQ. Consider, for example, the query

$$q(x_1, x_2) \leftarrow R(x_1, y_1), R(x_1, y_1), R(x_1, y_2), P(y_2, y_3), P(y_2, y_3), P(x_2, y_4).$$

The bag representation of this CQ is $\langle x_1 x_2, \mu_q \rangle$, where μ_q is defined over the body

$$\mathsf{body}(q) = \{R(x_1, y_1), R(x_1, y_2), P(y_2, y_3), P(x_2, y_4)\},$$

with $\mu_q(R(x_1, y_1)) = \mu_q(R(y_2, y_3)) = 2$ and $\mu_q(R(x_1, y_2)) = \mu_q(R(x_2, y_4)) = 1$. To ease presentation, Table 1 reports a summary of our notations and examples of their usage.

We often write the bag representation of a conjunctive query by giving the datalog notation of the body with superscripts on the atoms in order to annotate them with their multiplicity. For instance, the bag representation of the previous example is

$$q(x_1, x_2) \leftarrow R^2(x_1, y_1), R^1(x_1, y_2), P^2(y_2, y_3), P^1(x_2, y_4).$$

Sometimes, we also omit the superscripts 1 as in

$$q(x_1, x_2) \leftarrow R^2(x_1, y_1), R(x_1, y_2), P^2(y_2, y_3), P(x_2, y_4).$$

For the sake of compactness, we might also write

$$\mathsf{body}(q) = \{R^2(x_1, y_1), R(x_1, y_2), P^2(y_2, y_3), P(x_2, y_4)\}.$$

The *active domain* $\mathsf{adom}(q)$ of a query q is the set of all constants that occur in it. The set of all variables in q is denoted $\mathsf{var}(q)$. The *canonical database instance* of q, denoted by I^q, is the set of facts obtained by replacing all variables x in $\mathsf{body}(q)$ with the associated canonical constant $\widehat{x}$ (see [1]).

For a given query q and substitution σ, the symbol $\sigma(q)$ denotes the query obtained by applying the substitution σ to each single atom in the body $\mathsf{body}(q)$. Informally, any repetition of atoms in q is carried over in $\sigma(q)$ and, in addition, the latter could result with more repeated atoms. Formally, $\sigma(q(\overline{x}))$ is a CQ with free variables $\sigma(\overline{x})$, body $\mathsf{body}(\sigma(q(\overline{x}))) = \sigma(\mathsf{body}(q(\overline{x})))$, and body multiplicity $\mu_{\sigma(q(\overline{x}))}$ defined as follows:

$$\mu_{\sigma(q(\overline{x}))}(\alpha) = \sum_{\beta \in \mathsf{body}(q(\overline{x}))}^{\sigma(\beta)=\alpha} \mu_{q(\overline{x})}(\beta). \tag{1}$$

For instance, consider the substitution $\sigma = \{y_1, y_2, y_3, y_4 \mapsto x_2\}$ and the query q of the above example. The bag representation of $\sigma(q)$ is

$$\sigma(q)(x_1, x_2) \leftarrow R^3(x_1, x_2), P^3(x_2, x_2).$$

When a tuple of free variables $\overline{x}$ is unifiable with a tuple of constants $\overline{t}$ via the substitution σ, the symbol $q(\overline{t})$ denotes the result of $\sigma(q(\overline{x}))$, *i.e.*, the Boolean query obtained by replacing $\overline{x}$ with $\overline{t}$ in q.

The *answer under set semantics* to a CQ $q(\overline{x})$ over an instance I, in symbols $q(\overline{x})^{I}$ or q^{I} when the tuple of free variables is not important, is the set of all tuples $\overline{c} \in \mathsf{adom}(I)^{|\overline{x}|}$ (tuples of constants from I) unifiable with $\overline{x}$, such that query $q(\overline{c})$ holds in I, *i.e.*, $\mathsf{body}(q(\overline{c})) \subseteq I$. For every answer tuple $\overline{c}$ of $q(\overline{x})$ over I, there is a homomorphism h of $\mathsf{body}(q(\overline{x}))$ into I such that $\mathsf{h}(\overline{x}) = \overline{c}$. We often say that such function h is a homomorphism of q into I and use $\mathrm{Hom}(q(\overline{x}), I)$ to denote the associated set of all these functions.

Let μ be a bag over a set instance I. The *answer under bag semantics* to a CQ $q(\overline{x}) = \exists \overline{y} \bigwedge_i R_i(\overline{x}, \overline{y})$ over μ, is the bag over $\mathsf{adom}(I)^{|\overline{x}|}$, denoted by $q^{\mu}(\overline{x})$, such that, for all tuples $\overline{c} \in \mathsf{adom}(I)^{|\overline{x}|}$ unifiable with $\overline{x}$, it holds that

$$q^{\mu}(\overline{c}) = \sum_{\mathsf{h} \in \mathrm{Hom}(q(\overline{x}), I)}^{\mathsf{h}(\overline{x})=\overline{c}} \prod_{\alpha \in \mathsf{body}(\mathsf{h}(q(\overline{x})))} \mu(\alpha)^{\mu_{\mathsf{h}(q(\overline{x}))}(\alpha)} \tag{2}$$

Note that, for all elements $\overline{c} \notin q(\overline{x})^{I}$, we have that $q^{\mu}(\overline{c}) = 0$, since the sum in Equation 2 ranges over an empty set of homomorphisms, *i.e.*, there are no homomorphisms h as

Table 1: Common notations.

Notation	Meaning	Example Usage
$\overline{t_i}$	a tuple of terms	$h(\overline{t_1}) = \overline{t_2}$
q or $q(\overline{x})$	a query (the semantic object)	$q_1 \sqsubseteq_s q_2$
$q(\overline{t})$	query obtained by replacing terms $\overline{x}$ in $q(\overline{x})$ with terms $\overline{t}$	$q(\overline{c})$ is Boolean if $\overline{c}$ is a tuple of constants, and in addition, it is ground if q is projection free
μ	a bag, i.e., a function $\mu\colon \mathrm{I} \to \mathbb{N}$ over a set I	a bag μ over a set instance I is a bag instance; for a tuple $\overline{t} \in \mathrm{I}$, $\mu(\overline{t}) > 0$
I^{μ}	convenience notation for μ, listing elements in I and multiplicities, i.e., $\mathrm{I}=\{t^{\mu(t)} : t \in \mathrm{I}\}$	if μ_1 and μ_2 both over I, and $\mu_1 \subseteq \mu_2$, then for all $\langle t^i, t^j\rangle \in I^{\mu_1} \times I^{\mu_2}$, $i \leq j$
$\exists \overline{y} \bigwedge_{i=1}^{n} R_i(\overline{x}, \overline{y})$	conj. queries in FOL	when $\overline{y} = \emptyset$, $\bigwedge_{i=1}^{n} R_i(\overline{x}, \overline{y})$ is projection free
$q(\overline{x}) \leftarrow R_1(\overline{x}, \overline{y}), \ldots, R_n(\overline{x}, \overline{y})$	conj. queries in datalog	$body(q) = \{R_1(\overline{x}, \overline{y}), \ldots, R_n(\overline{x}, \overline{y})\}$
q^{I}	the set answer of a query q over a set instance I	$q_1 \sqsubseteq_s q_2$ iff for all set instances J, $q_1^J \subseteq q_2^J$
I^q or $I^{q(\overline{x})}$	the canonical instance of q	$\overline{t}$ is an answer tuple of $q(\overline{x})$ over $\mathrm{I}^{q(\overline{t})}$
$\mu_{q(\overline{x})}$	body multiplicity of query $q(\overline{x})$, i.e., a bag over $body(q)$	if atom α appears twice in $q(\overline{x}) = \exists \overline{y} \bigwedge_{i=1}^{n} R_i(\overline{x}, \overline{y})$, then $\mu_{q(\overline{x})}(\alpha) = 2$
$\langle \overline{x}, \mu_{q(\overline{x})}\rangle$	bag representation of a query $q(\overline{x})$	$\langle \emptyset, \{R(\overline{x}) \to 2\}\rangle$ is the bag representation of Boolean query $\exists \overline{x} R(\overline{x}) R(\overline{x})$
q^{μ} or $q^{\mu}(\overline{x})$	a bag answer of $q(\overline{x})$ over μ	$(q^I)^{q^{\mu}} = \{\overline{t}^{q^{\mu}(\overline{t})} : \overline{t} \in q^{\mathrm{I}}\} \cup \{\overline{t}^0 : \overline{t} \notin q^{\mathrm{I}}, \overline{t} \in adom(I)^{\lvert\overline{x}\rvert}\}$

required. Thus, by restricting q^{μ} over $q(\overline{x})^{\mathrm{I}}$, we sometimes abuse the notation and represent the answer q^{μ} as

$$\left\{\overline{c}^{q^{\mu}(\overline{c})} : \overline{c} \in q(\overline{x})^{\mathrm{I}}\right\}.$$

To practice with the introduced notions consider the following example on the instance

$$\mathrm{I} = \{R(c_1, c_2), R(c_1, c_3), P(c_2, c_4), P(c_5, c_4)\}$$

and bag μ over it, such that

$$\mathrm{I}^{\mu} = \{R^2(c_1, c_2), R^1(c_1, c_3), P^1(c_2, c_4), P^3(c_5, c_4)\}.$$

Also, consider again the query from the previous example

$$q(x_1, x_2) \leftarrow R^2(x_1, y_1), R(x_1, y_2), P^2(y_2, y_3), P(x_2, y_4).$$

The answer under bag semantics to $q(x_1, x_2)$ over μ is

$$q^{\mu} = \{c_1c_2{}^{10}, c_1c_5{}^{30}\},$$

i.e., $q^{\mu}(c_1, c_2) = 10$ and $q^{\mu}(c_1, c_5) = 30$. To see why this is true, first notice that any homomorphism of $q(x_1, x_2)$ into I must map the two variables y_3 and y_4 to the constant c_4 and the variable y_2 to a constant which belongs to both a fact in R and one in P, and c_2 is the only value with this property. Hence, any such a homomorphism must be an extension of

$$\{x_1 \mapsto c_1; y_2 \mapsto c_2; y_3, y_4 \mapsto c_4\}.$$

For c_1c_2, i.e., when $x_2 \mapsto c_2$, we have two homomorphisms that give us this answer tuple:

$$\mathsf{h}_1 = \{x_1 \mapsto c_1; x_2, y_1, y_2 \mapsto c_2; y_3, y_4 \mapsto c_4\};$$
$$\mathsf{h}_2 = \{x_1 \mapsto c_1; x_2, y_2 \mapsto c_2; y_1 \mapsto c_3; y_3, y_4 \mapsto c_4\}.$$

Hence, according to Equation 2, we have

$$q^{\mu}(c_1, c_2) = \prod_{\alpha \in \mathsf{body}(\mathsf{h}_1(q(x_1,x_2)))} \mu(\alpha)^{\mu_{\mathsf{h}_1(q(x_1,x_2))}(\alpha)} + \prod_{\alpha \in \mathsf{body}(\mathsf{h}_2(q(x_1,x_2)))} \mu(\alpha)^{\mu_{\mathsf{h}_2(q(x_1,x_2))}(\alpha)}.$$

The bag representation of $\mathsf{h}_1(q(x_1, x_2))$ is

$$q(c_1, c_2) \leftarrow R^3(c_1, c_2), P^3(c_2, c_4),$$

while and the bag representation of $\mathsf{h}_2(q(x_1, x_2))$ is

$$q(c_1, c_2) \leftarrow R(c_1, c_2), R^2(c_1, c_3), P^3(c_2, c_4).$$

Hence, the above equation simplifies in

$$q^{\mu}(c_1, c_2) = 2^3 \times 1^3 + 2 \times 1^2 \times 1^3 = 10.$$

Similarly, for answer tuple c_1c_5, we have two homomorphisms from $q(x_1, x_2)$ to I:

$$\mathsf{h}_3 = \{x_1 \mapsto c_1; x_2 \mapsto c_5; y_1, y_2 \mapsto c_2; y_3, y_4 \mapsto c_4\};$$
$$\mathsf{h}_4 = \{x_1 \mapsto c_1; x_2 \mapsto c_5; y_1 \mapsto c_3; y_2 \mapsto c_2; y_3, y_4 \mapsto c_4\}.$$

The multiplicity of c_1c_5 is computed according to Equation 2 by means of the formula

$$q^{\mu}(c_1, c_5) = \prod_{\alpha \in \mathsf{body}(\mathsf{h}_3(q(x_1,x_2)))} \mu(\alpha)^{\mu_{\mathsf{h}_3(q(x_1,x_2))}(\alpha)} + \prod_{\alpha \in \mathsf{body}(\mathsf{h}_4(q(x_1,x_2)))} \mu(\alpha)^{\mu_{\mathsf{h}_4(q(x_1,x_2))}(\alpha)}.$$

For the bag representation of $\mathsf{h}_3(q(x_1, x_2))$, we have

$$q(c_1, c_5) \leftarrow R^3(c_1, c_2), P^2(c_2, c_4), P(c_5, c_4),$$

while $\mathsf{h}_4(q(x_1, x_2))$ has as bag representation

$$q(c_1, c_5) \leftarrow R(c_1, c_2), R^2(c_1, c_3), P^2(c_2, c_4), P(c_5, c_4).$$

Thus, the previous equation becomes

$$q^{\mu}(c_1, c_5) = 2^3 \times 1^2 \times 3 + 2 \times 1^2 \times 1^2 \times 3 = 30.$$

Given two CQs q_1 and q_2 we say that q_1 is set contained in q_2, in symbols $q_1 \sqsubseteq_s q_2$, if, for all instances I, the set of answer tuples under set semantics of q_1 on I is a subset of the answer tuples under set semantics of q_2 on I, that is $q_1^{\mathrm{I}} \subseteq q_2^{\mathrm{I}}$. Similarly, we say that q_1 is bag contained in q_2, in symbols $q_1 \sqsubseteq_b q_2$, if for all set instances I and bags μ over I, it holds that $q_1^{\mu} \subseteq q_2^{\mu}$. When discussing about a containment problem $q_1 \sqsubseteq_b q_2$, we shall refer to q_1 as the "*containee*" query and to q_2 as the "*containing*" one, even if the containment does not actually hold between two particular queries.

Chandra and Merlin [5] have proved that one can decide set query containment in NPTIME, by using the notion of *containment mappings*. Formally, a containment mapping from a CQ $q_2(\overline{x_2})$ to a CQ $q_1(\overline{x}_1)$ is a homomorphism $\mathsf{h} \in \mathrm{Hom}(\mathsf{body}(q_2(\overline{x}_2)), \mathsf{body}q_1(\overline{x}_1))$ from $q_2(\overline{x}_2)$ to $q_1(\overline{x}_1)$ such that $\mathsf{h}(\overline{x}_2) = \overline{x}_1$. Then, we have that $q_1 \sqsubseteq_s q_2$ *iff* there exists a containment mapping from $q_2(\overline{x_2})$ to $q_1(\overline{x}_1)$. Later in this work we make use of the set of all containment mappings from $q_2(\overline{x_2})$ to $q_1(\overline{x}_1)$ denoted by $\mathrm{CM}(q_2(\overline{x}_2), q_1(\overline{x}_1))$. Moreover, for a given tuple of terms $\overline{t}$, we make an abuse of notation by using $\mathrm{CM}(q_2(\overline{x}_2), q_1(\overline{t}))$ to represent the set of all compositions of a containment mapping $\mathsf{h} \in \mathrm{CM}(q_2(\overline{x}_2), q_1(\overline{x}_1))$ with a substitution σ such that $\sigma(\mathsf{h}(\overline{x}_2)) = \overline{t}$.

Observe that bag containment implies set containment, *i.e.*, for all pairs of queries $q_1(\overline{x_1})$ and $q_2(\overline{x}_2)$, if $q_1 \sqsubseteq_b q_2$ then $q_1 \sqsubseteq_s q_2$. This can be easily seen by unfolding the definitions. Indeed, if all tuples that appear in the answer of $q_1(\overline{x_1})$ with some multiplicity also appear in the answer of $q_2(\overline{x}_2)$ with at least the same multiplicity, then set containment holds by simply ignoring the multiplicities.

As an example of set and bag containment, consider the following three queries:

- $q_1(x_1, x_2) \leftarrow R^2(x_1, x_2), P^3(x_2, x_2)$;
- $q_2(x_1, x_2) \leftarrow R^3(x_1, x_2), P^3(x_2, x_2)$;
- $q_3(x_1, x_2) \leftarrow R^2(x_1, y_1), R(x_1, y_2), P^2(y_2, y_3), P(x_2, y_4)$.

It is not hard to see that:

(1) $q_1 \sqsubseteq_b q_2$ and $q_2 \sqsubseteq_s q_1$, but $q_2 \not\sqsubseteq_b q_1$;
(2) $q_1 \sqsubseteq_b q_3$ and $q_2 \sqsubseteq_b q_3$ (so, $q_1 \sqsubseteq_s q_3$ and $q_2 \sqsubseteq_s q_3$);
(3) $q_3 \not\sqsubseteq_s q_1$ and $q_3 \not\sqsubseteq_s q_2$ (so, $q_3 \not\sqsubseteq_b q_1$ and $q_3 \not\sqsubseteq_b q_2$).

Let us see why these statements hold.

(1) The identity substitution is the only containment mapping from $q_1(x_1, x_2)$ to $q_2(x_1, x_2)$ and *vice versa*. Moreover, every multiplicity of an atom, in an arbitrary instance, used as an image of $R(x_1, y_1)$, is raised to 2 in q_1 and 3 in q_2. So the bag containment of the first query into the second one trivially follows. To see why $q_2 \not\sqsubseteq_b q_1$, it is enough to observe that, on the bag instance $\mathrm{I}^{\mu} = \{R^2(c_1, c_2), P^1(c_2, c_2)\}$, we have $q_1^{\mu}(c_1, c_2) = 4$, but $q_2^{\mu}(c_1, c_2) = 8$.
(2) The substitution $\sigma = \{y_1, y_2, y_3, y_4 \mapsto x_2\}$ is the unique containment mapping of $q_3(x_1, x_2)$ to both $q_1(x_1, x_2)$ and $q_2(x_1, x_2)$. Since $\sigma(q_3(x_1, x_2)) = q_2(x_1, x_2)$, the statement follows from above.
(3) There are no containment mappings from $q_1(x_1, x_2)$ and $q_2(x_1, x_2)$ to $q_3(x_1, x_2)$.

3 A BAG-CONTAINMENT PROBLEM

In this section we start studying the bag-containment problem of a projection-free CQ into a generic CQ. In particular, we show that in order to verify that containment holds, it suffices to evaluate the two queries on a special class of infinitely many *canonical bags*. In other words, we use a particular class of canonical set instances and check the containment on all possible bags over all such instances. Note that this problem is trivial in the so-called bag-set semantics [2], since it is equivalent to set-containment, but requires non-trivial treatment in our case, as we show in the rest of the article.

The use of more than one canonical set databases, and in fact, exponentially many endomorphic versions of the canonical database of the containee query, has been already employed in query containment before, as in [23] for testing containment of CQs with arithmetic comparisons and in [34] for testing containment of CQs with negation. The set of instances that has been used in these approaches is obtained by taking the canonical instances of all queries that are "specializations" of the original containee query, *i.e.*, where some of its free variables have been equated to each other.

For our purposes, we exploit a variation of this idea and use all canonical instances where some of the free variables have been equated to each other or replaced with constants of the original query. In order to create such a set of instances, we shall ground the containee query $q(\overline{x})$, by substituting the free variables $\overline{x}$ with an appropriate *probe tuple* $\overline{t}$, whose terms are chosen from the canonical constants in $\mathsf{can}(\overline{x})$, as well as the preexisting constants in $\mathsf{adom}(q(\overline{x}))$. Obviously, $\overline{x}$ and $\overline{t}$ need to be unifiable, so that the query $q(\overline{t})$ derivable from the grounding is well-defined.

Definition 3.1. *Let $q(\overline{x})$ be a CQ defined over an n-tuple of free variables $\overline{x} \in \mathrm{X}^n$. An n-tuple of constants $\overline{t} \in \mathrm{C}^n$ is a* probe tuple *for $q(\overline{x})$ if (1) $\overline{t} \in \mathsf{adom}(\mathrm{I}^{q(\overline{x})})^n$ and (2) $\overline{t}$ is unifiable with $\overline{x}$.*

In the following, we use $\mathsf{prbtup}(q(\overline{x}))$ to denote the set of all probe tuples for a CQ $q(\overline{x})$.

As an example, consider the projection-free CQ

$$q(x_1, x_2) \leftarrow R(x_1, x_2), R(\mathrm{c}_1, x_2), R(x_1, \mathrm{c}_2).$$

It is not hard to see that there are sixteen probe tuples for $q(x_1, x_2)$, *i.e.*, all possible pairs over the elements $\{\widehat{x}_1, \widehat{x}_2, \mathrm{c}_1, \mathrm{c}_2\}$:

$$\left\{\begin{array}{c} \widehat{x}_1\widehat{x}_1, \widehat{x}_1\widehat{x}_2, \widehat{x}_2\widehat{x}_1, \widehat{x}_2\widehat{x}_2, \\ \widehat{x}_1\mathrm{c}_1, \widehat{x}_1\mathrm{c}_2, \widehat{x}_2\mathrm{c}_1, \widehat{x}_2\mathrm{c}_2, \mathrm{c}_1\widehat{x}_1, \mathrm{c}_1\widehat{x}_2, \mathrm{c}_2\widehat{x}_1, \mathrm{c}_2\widehat{x}_2, \\ \mathrm{c}_1\mathrm{c}_1, \mathrm{c}_1\mathrm{c}_2, \mathrm{c}_2\mathrm{c}_1, \mathrm{c}_2\mathrm{c}_2 \end{array}\right\}.$$

It is possible to prove that for our technique we do not need all probe tuples, but only those that are not isomorphic under a bijective function that preserves the language constants, but swaps the canonical constants. For the given example, we would only need the following ten tuples:

$$\left\{\begin{array}{c} \widehat{x}_1\widehat{x}_1, \widehat{x}_1\widehat{x}_2, \\ \widehat{x}_1\mathrm{c}_1, \widehat{x}_1\mathrm{c}_2, \mathrm{c}_1\widehat{x}_1, \mathrm{c}_2\widehat{x}_1, \\ \mathrm{c}_1\mathrm{c}_1, \mathrm{c}_1\mathrm{c}_2, \mathrm{c}_2\mathrm{c}_1, \mathrm{c}_2\mathrm{c}_2 \end{array}\right\}.$$

However, for the sake of simplicity in the presentation of the results we do not make use of the restricted set.

At this point, to characterize the bag-containment problem of interest, we make use of the specialized queries $q_1(\overline{t})$ and their canonical instances $\mathrm{I}^{q_1(\overline{t})}$, for each probe tuple $\overline{t}$ of the given projection-free containee query $q_1(\overline{x}_1)$. Next theorem states, indeed, that $q_1(\overline{x}_1)$ is bag contained into a generic CQ $q_2(\overline{x}_2)$ *iff*, for all possible bags μ over all such specialized canonical instances $\mathrm{I}^{q_1(\overline{t})}$, the multiplicity of $\overline{t}$ in the answer of $q_1(\overline{x}_1)$ over μ is less than or equal to that of $q_2(\overline{x}_2)$ over μ as well. In other words, if containment breaks for an arbitrary answer tuple over an arbitrary bag, there must be a probe tuple $\overline{t}$ and some bag μ over $\mathrm{I}^{q_1(\overline{t})}$ where containment breaks over this bag μ and for that particular tuple $\overline{t}$.

Theorem 3.1. *Given a projection-free* CQ $q_1(\overline{x}_1)$ *and a* CQ $q_2(\overline{x}_2)$, *it holds that* $q_1(\overline{x}_1) \sqsubseteq_b q_2(\overline{x}_2)$ iff, *for all probe tuples* $\overline{t} \in \mathsf{prbtup}(q_1(\overline{x}_1))$, *(1) $\overline{t}$ is unifiable with $\overline{x}_2$ and (2) $q_1^{\mu}(\overline{t}) \leq q_2^{\mu}(\overline{t})$, for all bags μ over the canonical instance $\mathrm{I}^{q_1(\overline{t})}$.*

Proof. **(Only if).** Assume $q_1(\overline{x}_1) \sqsubseteq_b q_2(\overline{x}_2)$. Then, $q_1^{\mu}(\overline{x}_1) \subseteq q_2^{\mu}(\overline{x}_2)$, for all instances I and bags μ over I. This means that, for all tuples $\overline{c} \in q_1^{\mathrm{I}}$, it holds that (i) $\overline{c}$ is unifiable with $\overline{x}_2$ and (ii) $q_1^{\mu}(\overline{c}) \leq q_2^{\mu}(\overline{c})$. Now, consider the canonical instance $\mathrm{I}^{q_1(\overline{t})}$ for $q_1(\overline{x}_1)$, a bag μ over it, and a probe tuple $\overline{t} \in \mathsf{prbtup}(q_1(\overline{x}_1)) \subseteq \mathsf{adom}(\mathrm{I}^{q_1(\overline{t})})^{|\overline{x}_1|}$. It is immediate to see that $q_1^{\mu}(\overline{t}) \leq q_2^{\mu}(\overline{t})$ holds. Hence, the thesis follows.

(If). Assume $q_1(\overline{x}_1) \not\sqsubseteq_b q_2(\overline{x}_2)$. This means that there exists an instance I and a bag μ over I such that $q_1^{\mu}(\overline{x}_1) \not\subseteq q_2^{\mu}(\overline{x}_2)$. Therefore, there has to exist a tuple $\overline{c} \in q_1^{\mathrm{I}}$ satisfying one of the following properties: (i) $\overline{c}$ is not unifiable with $\overline{x}_2$ or (ii) $\overline{c}$ is unifiable with $\overline{x}_2$, but $q_1^{\mu}(\overline{c}) > q_2^{\mu}(\overline{c})$. In the first case, the thesis is immediately, so, focus on the second one.

Since $q_1^{\mu}(\overline{c}) > q_2^{\mu}(\overline{c})$, we have that $q_1^{\mu}(\overline{c}) > 0$, which implies $\overline{c} \in q_1^{\mathrm{I}}(\overline{x}_1)$, *i.e.*, there exists an homomorphism h_1 from $q_1(\overline{x}_1)$ to I mapping $\overline{x}_1$ to $\overline{c}$, *i.e.*, $\mathsf{h}_1(\overline{x}_1) = \overline{c}$. Being projection-free, $q_1(\overline{x}_1)$ does not have existential variables, thus, h_1 is the only such homomorphism. Moreover, the image of the query under h_1, *i.e.*, $\mathsf{h}_1(q_1(\overline{x}_1))$, is exactly $q_1(\overline{c})$ and its body is equal to $\mathrm{I}^{q_1(\overline{c})} \subseteq \mathrm{I}$, since its atoms do not contain variables. Now, let μ' be the restriction of the bag μ to $\mathrm{I}^{q_1(\overline{c})}$. Obviously, it holds that $q_1^{\mu}(\overline{c}) = q_1^{\mu'}(\overline{c})$. In addition, $q_2^{\mu}(\overline{c}) \geq q_2^{\mu'}(\overline{c})$. The latter inequality is due to the following facts: (i) all the homomorphisms h_2 from $q_2(\overline{x}_2)$ to $\mathrm{I}^{q_1(\overline{c})}$, with $\mathsf{h}_2(\overline{x}_1) = \overline{c}$, are homomorphisms from $q_2(\overline{x}_2)$ to I as well, since $\mathrm{I}^{q_1(\overline{c})} \subseteq \mathrm{I}$; (ii) the contribution, through Equation 2, of each such homomorphism h_2 to the multiplicity $q_2^{\mu}(\overline{c})$ of $\overline{c}$ over the (bag μ over) I is exactly the same as the one over (the bag μ' over) $\mathrm{I}^{q_1(\overline{c})}$; observe that there might even exist homomorphisms from $q_2(\overline{c})$ to $\mathrm{I} \setminus \mathrm{I}^{q_1(\overline{c})}$. Thus, $q_1^{\mu'}(\overline{c}) > q_2^{\mu'}(\overline{c})$.

At this point, consider a function $\mathsf{f} : \mathrm{C} \rightarrow \mathsf{adom}(\mathrm{I}^{q_1(\overline{x}_1)})$ mapping constants to the active domain of the canonical database of the containee query $q_1(\overline{x}_1)$ such that (i) it is the identity on the active domain of $q_1(\overline{x}_1)$, *i.e.*, $\mathsf{f}(c) = c$, for all $c \in \mathsf{adom}(q_1(\overline{x}_1))$, and (ii) its restriction $\mathsf{f}\restriction\mathsf{adom}(q_1(\overline{c}))$ to the active domain of the ground query $q_1(\overline{c})$ is injective. Intuitively, f injectively replaces all constant in $\overline{c}$ that do not occur in the body of $q_1(\overline{x}_1)$ with some of the canonical constants of the free variables $\overline{x}_1$, leaving untouched the remaining ones. It is easy to see that (i) $\overline{t} \triangleq \mathsf{f}(\overline{c}) \in \mathsf{prbtup}(q_1(\overline{x}_1))$ and (ii) f is an isomorphism between the canonical instances $\mathrm{I}^{q_1(\overline{c})}$ and $\mathrm{I}^{q_1(\overline{t})}$. Now, let us define the bag $\mu^{\star}$ over $\mathrm{I}^{q_1(\overline{t})}$ as follows: $\mu^{\star}(\mathsf{f}(\alpha)) \triangleq \mu'(\alpha)$, for all atoms $\alpha \in \mathrm{I}^{q_1(\overline{c})}$. It is obvious that $q_1^{\mu^{\star}}(\overline{t}) = q_1^{\mu'}(\overline{c})$ and $q_2^{\mu^{\star}}(\overline{t}) = q_2^{\mu'}(\overline{c})$. Consequently, $q_1^{\mu^{\star}}(\overline{t}) > q_2^{\mu^{\star}}(\overline{t})$. Hence, the thesis follows. □

Note that, given a CQ bag-containment problem, in particular a projection-free CQ $q_1(\overline{x}_1)$, as in Theorem 3.1, the set of tuples in $\mathsf{prbtup}(q_1(\overline{x}_1))$ is finite, and so is the set of our specialized canonical instances $\mathrm{I}^{q_1(\overline{t})}$. To decide containment, however, we need to reason over all possible, infinitely many, bags μ over these instances. It is therefore natural to assume the exact values of μ as unknowns and try to verify whether we can prove the required properties for such all bags together.

From now on, we assume a countably infinite set U of symbols called *unknowns*, disjoint from the sets of variables and constants, and associate each possible atom with its "canonical" unknown in order to represent its unknown multiplicity. In more detail, we can assume a 1-to-1 correspondence between U and the countably infinite set of all possible atoms that can be constructed from relation names and having as arguments constants or variables. Through this correspondence, we associate each distinct atom α with its *canonical unknown* $u^\alpha \in \mathrm{U}$.

In the following, we shall use these unknowns in polynomial functions. In particular, we lift the above discussed association of atoms with unknowns to that of conjunctive queries with polynomial functions, so that the unknowns in the polynomials stand for the unknown values of a bag μ and the polynomial themselves stand for the multiplicity function of the answer tuples over μ.

First, we are going to associate a projection-free CQ $q(\overline{x})$ and a probe tuple $\overline{t} \in \mathrm{prbtup}(q(\overline{x}))$ with a monomial function $\mathsf{M}_{q(\overline{t})}(\overline{u})$. To do this, observe that there is only one homomorphism h, in fact an isomorphism, that maps $q(\overline{x})$ into the canonical instance $\mathrm{I}^{q(\overline{t})}$ such that $\mathsf{h}(\overline{x}) = \overline{t}$. This is precisely because $q(\overline{x})$ is projection-free. Thus, per Equation 2, the multiplicity of the tuple $\overline{t}$ in the answer of $q(\overline{x})$ over an arbitrary bag μ over the instance $\mathrm{I}^{q(\overline{t})}$ is:

$$q^\mu(\overline{t}) = \prod_{\alpha \in \mathsf{body}(\mathsf{h}(q(\overline{x})))} \mu(\alpha)^{\mu_{\mathsf{h}(q(\overline{x}))}(\alpha)} = \prod_{\alpha \in \mathsf{body}(q(\overline{t}))} \mu(\alpha)^{\mu_{q(\overline{t})}(\alpha)}.$$

Intuitively, if we interpret the values $\mu(\alpha)$ as unknowns, *i.e.*, we substitute $\mu(\alpha)$ with the canonical unknown u^α, we get the associated monomial for $q(\overline{x})$ and $\overline{t}$.

The *vector of unknowns* for a CQ $q(\overline{x})$ with $\mathsf{body}(q(\overline{x})) = \{\alpha_1, \alpha_2, \dots, \alpha_m\}$, denoted by $\overline{u}^{q(\overline{x})}$, is the vector of canonical unknowns $\overline{u}^{q(\overline{x})} = u^{\alpha_1} u^{\alpha_2} \cdots u^{\alpha_m}$. For convenience, in our definitions, we want to be able to deal with vectors of unknowns which are supersequences of the vector of unknowns for a given specific query. We introduce the notion of compatibility of a vector of unknowns $\overline{u} \in \mathrm{U}^k$, for some $k \in \mathbb{N}$, with a query $q(\overline{x})$: we say that $\overline{u}$ is *compatible* with $q(\overline{x})$ if, for all $\alpha \in \mathsf{body}(q(\overline{x}))$, it holds that u^α occurs in $\overline{u}$.

Definition 3.2. *For all projection-free* CQs $q(\overline{x})$ *for which* $\mathsf{body}(q(\overline{x})) = \{\alpha_1, \dots, \alpha_m\}$, *probe tuples* $\overline{t} \in \mathsf{prbtup}(q(\overline{x}))$ *unifiable with* $\overline{x}$, *and vectors of unknowns* $\overline{u} \in \mathrm{U}^k$ *compatible with* $q(\overline{x})$, *for some* $k \in \mathbb{N}$, *there is the associated* monomial

$$\mathsf{M}_{q(\overline{t})}(\overline{u}) \triangleq u_1^{e_1} \cdots u_k^{e_k},$$

where $e_i = \mu_{q(\overline{t})}(\alpha_i)$ *if* $u_i = u^{\alpha_i}$, *and* $e_i = 0$ *otherwise.*

As intuitively observed above, the monomial $\mathsf{M}_{q(\overline{t})}(\overline{u})$ allows us to compute the multiplicity of the answer $\overline{t}$ of the query $q(\overline{x})$ over any bag μ. Indeed, we just need to bind all unknowns u^{α_i} in $\overline{u}$ to the values given by μ for the corresponding atom $\alpha_i \in \mathsf{body}(q(\overline{x}))$, since the unknowns u_i that do not correspond to atoms in the body of query are cancelled out, as they are raised to 0.

To exemplify the above definition, consider the following bag variation of the projection-free CQ described in the example of the previous page:

$$q_1(x_1, x_2) \leftarrow R^2(x_1, x_2), R(\mathsf{c}_1, x_2), R^3(x_1, \mathsf{c}_2).$$

Moreover, consider probe tuple $\widehat{x}_1\widehat{x}_2 \in \mathsf{prbtup}(q_1(x_1, x_2))$. Then, it is easy to verify that

$$\mathsf{M}_{q_1(\widehat{x}_1, \widehat{x}_2)}(\overline{u}) = u_1^2 \cdot u_2 \cdot u_3^3, \quad \text{where}$$
$$u_1 = u^{R(\widehat{x}_1, \widehat{x}_2)}, u_2 = u^{R(\mathsf{c}_1, \widehat{x}_2)}, \text{ and } u_3 = u^{R(\widehat{x}_1, \mathsf{c}_2)},$$
$$\text{with } q_1(\widehat{x}_1, \widehat{x}_2) \leftarrow R^2(\widehat{x}_1, \widehat{x}_2), R(\mathsf{c}_1, \widehat{x}_2), R^3(\widehat{x}_1, \mathsf{c}_2).$$

At this point, once a projection-free CQ $q_1(\overline{x}_1)$, a probe tuple $\overline{t}$, and vector of unknowns $\overline{u}$ are fixed, as in Definition 3.2, we can associate any generic CQ $q_2(\overline{x}_2)$ with a polynomial $\mathsf{P}^{q_2(\overline{x}_2)}_{q_1(\overline{t})}(\overline{u})$. To do this, first let us observe that the multiplicity of $\overline{t}$ among the answers of $q_2(\overline{x}_2)$ for an arbitrary bag μ over the canonical instance $\mathrm{I}^{q_1(\overline{t})}$ is given by

$$\begin{aligned} q_2^\mu(\overline{t}) &= \sum_{\substack{\mathsf{h}(\overline{x}_2)=\overline{t} \\ \mathsf{h} \in \mathrm{Hom}(q_2(\overline{x}_2), \mathrm{I}^{q_1(\overline{t})})}} \prod_{\alpha \in \mathsf{body}(\mathsf{h}(q_2(\overline{x})))} \mu(\alpha)^{\mu_{\mathsf{h}(q_2(\overline{x}))}(\alpha)} \\ &= \sum_{\substack{\mathsf{h}(\overline{x}_1)=\overline{t} \\ \mathsf{h} \in \mathrm{CM}(q_2(\overline{x}_2), q_1(\overline{x}_1))}} \prod_{\alpha \in \mathsf{body}(\mathsf{h}(q_2(\overline{x})))} \mu(\alpha)^{\mu_{\mathsf{h}(q_2(\overline{x}))}(\alpha)} \\ &= \sum_{\mathsf{h} \in \mathrm{CM}(q_2(\overline{x}_2), q_1(\overline{t}))} \prod_{\alpha \in \mathsf{body}(\mathsf{h}(q_2(\overline{x})))} \mu(\alpha)^{\mu_{\mathsf{h}(q_2(\overline{x}))}(\alpha)}. \end{aligned}$$

The following definition becomes immediately clear, once one observes that, for any containment mapping $\mathsf{h} \in \mathrm{CM}(q_2(\overline{x}_2), q_1(\overline{t}))$, the monomial

$$\prod_{\alpha \in \mathsf{body}(\mathsf{h}(q_2(\overline{x})))} \mu(\alpha)^{\mu_{\mathsf{h}(q_2(\overline{x}))}(\alpha)}$$

has the same form of the multiplicity function for the Boolean, projection-free CQ $\mathsf{h}(q_2(\overline{x}))$.

Definition 3.3. *Let* $q_1(\overline{x}_1)$ *be a projection-free* CQ, $\overline{t} \in \mathsf{prbtup}(q_1(\overline{x}_1))$ *one of its probe tuples, and* $\overline{u} \in \mathrm{U}^k$ *a vector of unknowns compatible with* $q_1(\overline{x}_1)$, *for some* $k \in \mathbb{N}$. *Every* CQ $q_2(\overline{x}_2)$ *is associated with the polynomial*

$$\mathsf{P}^{q_2(\overline{x}_2)}_{q_1(\overline{t})}(\overline{u}) \triangleq \sum_{\mathsf{h} \in \mathrm{CM}(q_2(\overline{x}_2), q_1(\overline{t}))} \mathsf{M}_{\mathsf{h}(q_2(\overline{x}_2))}(\overline{u}),$$

w.r.t. $q_1(\overline{x}_1)$ *and* $\overline{t}$.

Notice that, for a given containment mapping from h from $q_2(\overline{x}_2)$ to $q_1(\overline{t})$, it holds that $\mathsf{h}(q_2(\overline{x}_2))$ is a subquery of $q_1(\overline{t})$, thus, the vector of unknowns $\overline{u}$ for $q_1(\overline{x}_1)$ is necessarily compatible with query $\mathsf{h}(q_2(\overline{x}_2))$. This ensures the monomial

$\mathsf{M}_{\mathsf{h}(q_2(\overline{x}_2))}(\overline{u})$ to be well-defined. Moreover, the multiplicity of $\overline{t}$ obtained just by such a homomorphism h on a bag μ over $\mathrm{I}^{q_1(\overline{t}_1)}$, *i.e.*, $(\mathsf{h}(q_2(\overline{x}_2)))^{\mu}(\overline{t})$, is obtained by taking the associated monomial for $\mathsf{h}(q_2(\overline{x}_2))$ and setting its unknowns to the corresponding values of μ for all the atoms in the query. Concluding, the associated polynomial for $q_2(\overline{x}_2)$ *w.r.t.* $q_1(\overline{x}_1)$ and $\overline{t}$, which sums all associated monomials derived from the mappings from $q_2(\overline{x}_2)$ to $q_1(\overline{t})$, gives us the multiplicity of $\overline{t}$ over a bag μ, by simply replacing each unknown u_i in $\overline{u}$ with the multiplicity $\mu(\alpha)$ for the atom α for which $u_i = u^{\alpha}$.

Before proceeding, consider again the projection-free CQ $q_1(x_1, x_2)$ of the previous example, together with its probe tuple $\widehat{x}_1\widehat{x}_2$, and the following additional CQ:

$$q_2(x_1, x_2) \leftarrow R^3(x_1, x_2), R^2(x_1, y_1), R^2(y_2, y_1).$$

Then, it is not hard to see that

$$\mathsf{P}^{q_2(x_1,x_2)}_{q_1(\widehat{x}_1,\widehat{x}_2)}(\overline{u}) = u_1^7 + u_1^5 \cdot u_2^2 + u_1^3 \cdot u_3^4.$$

Indeed, there are only the following three containment mappings from $q_2(x_1, x_2)$ to $q_1(\widehat{x}_1, \widehat{x}_2)$:

$$\mathsf{h}_1 = \{x_1, y_2 \mapsto \widehat{x}_1; x_2, y_1 \mapsto \widehat{x}_2\};$$
$$\mathsf{h}_2 = \{x_1 \mapsto \widehat{x}_1; x_2, y_1 \mapsto \widehat{x}_2; y_2 \mapsto c_1\};$$
$$\mathsf{h}_3 = \{x_1, y_2 \mapsto \widehat{x}_1; x_2 \mapsto \widehat{x}_2; y_1 \mapsto c_2\}.$$

Consequently, the queries $\mathsf{h}_i(q_2(x_1, x_2))$ obtainable from the homomorphisms h_i are:

$$\mathsf{body}(\mathsf{h}_1(q_2(x_1, x_2))) = \{R^7(\widehat{x}_1, \widehat{x}_2)\};$$
$$\mathsf{body}(\mathsf{h}_2(q_2(x_1, x_2))) = \{R^5(\widehat{x}_1, \widehat{x}_2), R^2(\mathsf{c}_1, \widehat{x}_2)\};$$
$$\mathsf{body}(\mathsf{h}_3(q_2(x_1, x_2))) = \{R^3(\widehat{x}_1, \widehat{x}_2), R^4(\widehat{x}_1, \mathsf{c}_2)\}.$$

Thus, the three monomials $\mathsf{M}_{\mathsf{h}_i(q_2(x_1,x_2))}(\overline{u})$ reported below can be derived, and the previous polynomial $\mathsf{P}^{q_2(x_1,x_2)}_{q_1(\widehat{x}_1,\widehat{x}_2)}(\overline{u})$ immediately follows:

$$\mathsf{M}_{\mathsf{h}_1(q_2(x_1,x_2))}(\overline{u}) = u_1^7;$$
$$\mathsf{M}_{\mathsf{h}_2(q_2(x_1,x_2))}(\overline{u}) = u_1^5 \cdot u_2^2;$$
$$\mathsf{M}_{\mathsf{h}_3(q_2(x_1,x_2))}(\overline{u}) = u_1^3 \cdot u_3^4.$$

We conclude this section by stating the following easy corollary of Theorem 3.1, which characterizes a given bag-containment problem of a projection-free CQ $q_1(\overline{x}_1)$ into a generic CQ $q_2(\overline{x}_2)$ in terms of a Diophantine inequality between the associated monomial $\mathsf{M}_{q_1(\overline{t})}(\overline{u})$ and polynomial $\mathsf{P}^{q_2(\overline{x}_2)}_{q_1(\overline{t})}(\overline{u})$. Note that, in the following, we use $\mathsf{P}(\overline{\xi}) \triangleq \mathsf{P}(\overline{u})|_{\overline{u}=\overline{\xi}}$ to denote the replacement of an unknown u_i in $\overline{u}$ with the value ξ_i in $\overline{\xi}$, for any polynomial P. Moreover, we say that an inequality $\mathsf{M}(\overline{u}) > \mathsf{P}(\overline{u})$ admits a Diophantine solution if there exists a natural vector $\overline{\xi} \in \mathbb{N}^{|\overline{u}|}$ such that $\mathsf{M}(\overline{\xi}) > \mathsf{P}(\overline{\xi})$.

Corollary 3.1. *Given a projection-free* CQ $q_1(\overline{x}_1)$ *and a* CQ $q_2(\overline{x}_2)$, *it holds that* $q_1(\overline{x}_1) \sqsubseteq_b q_2(\overline{x}_2)$ iff, *for all probe tuple* $\overline{t} \in \mathsf{prbtup}(q_1(\overline{x}_1))$, *(1)* $\overline{t}$ *is unifiable with* $\overline{x}_2$ *and (2) the inequality* $\mathsf{M}_{q_1(\overline{t})}(\overline{u}) > \mathsf{P}^{q_2(\overline{x}_2)}_{q_1(\overline{t})}(\overline{u})$ *does not admit any Diophantine solution.*

Note that in Theorem 5.3, we prove that in order to decide bag containment we actually need only one inequality between a monomial and a polynomial. Specifically, we shall just consider the *most-general* probe tuple which we define as the tuple of canonical constants that corresponds to the tuple of free variables of the containee query. However, to prove Theorem 5.3, we first need to use all probe tuples and Corollary 3.1 in order to develop the machinery for such a proof. Using a single probe tuple would obviously make a difference in an implementation of our decision method, but it does not change the asymptotic complexity of the problem.

4 DECIDING INEQUALITIES

We now investigate the problem of deciding whether a Diophantine inequality of a certain structure has an all-natural, *i.e.*, Diophantine, solution. Our inequalities, called *Monomial-Polynomial Inequalities* (MPIs, for short), compare a polynomial on n unknowns, with positive real coefficients, and natural exponents, to a monomial over the same unknowns with coefficient 1 and natural exponents. Although it might be quite evident from the previous sections how a decision procedure for MPIs can help us decide bag containment, the formal statement of the reduction between the two problems is deferred until Section 5. Here we focus on proving decidability for the aforementioned restriction of the generally undecidable *Diophantine inequality problem* [20]. We also discuss another variant of these inequalities, which we call *Generalized Monomial-Polynomial Inequalities* (GMPIs, for short), that differ from the MPIs in that they allow for real exponents.

Observe that, in the remaining part of this work, given two vectors $\overline{u}$ and $\overline{e}$ of the same dimension, we succinctly denote by $\overline{u}^{\overline{e}}$ the monomial $\prod_i {u_i}^{e_i}$. Moreover, recall that the degree of a polynomial is the maximal sum of the exponents over all its monomials.

Definition 4.1. *Given a n-dimensional unknown vector* $\overline{u} \in \mathrm{U}^n$, *m non-negative real values* $a_1, \ldots, a_m \in \mathbb{R}_{\geq 0}$, *and* $(m+1)$ *n-dimensional integer vectors* $\overline{e}, \overline{e}_1, \ldots, \overline{e}_m \in \mathbb{N}^n$, *with* $m, n \in \mathbb{N}_+$, *the* n-dimensional Monomial-Polynomial Inequality *(n-MPI, for short) with coefficients* $a_1, \ldots, a_m$ *and exponents* $\overline{e}, \overline{e}_1, \ldots \overline{e}_m$ *is the syntactic expression reported in the following:*

$$\mathsf{P}(\overline{u}) < \mathsf{M}(\overline{u}), \textit{ with } \mathsf{P}(\overline{u}) \triangleq \sum_{i=1}^{m} a_i \overline{u}^{\overline{e}_i} \textit{ and } \mathsf{M}(\overline{u}) \triangleq \overline{u}^{\overline{e}}. \quad (3)$$

A solution for 3 is a n-dimensional integer vector $\overline{\xi} \in \mathbb{N}^n$ *for which the numeric inequality* $\mathsf{P}(\overline{\xi}) < \mathsf{M}(\overline{\xi})$ *holds. Finally, a* n-dimensional Generalized Monomial-Polynomial Inequality *(*n*-GMPI, for short) is the expression 3, where the exponents* $\overline{e}, \overline{e}_1, \ldots, \overline{e}_m \in \mathbb{R}^n_{\geq 0}$ *are allowed to be positive real vectors.*

Our proof approach has two steps. First, we show that to decide whether a 1-GMPI admits a Diophantine solution, it is enough to compare the degrees between the two sides of the inequality. Then, we prove that for every solvable MPI over n unknowns, there exists a specific 1-GMPI admitting a solution as well. More specifically, we construct an inequality similar to a 1-GMPI, but containing unknowns in the exponents. To compare the degrees of this inequality we then need to solve a homogeneous linear inequality system and show how a Diophantine solution for such a system corresponds to a solution of our original MPI.

To begin, observe that 0 cannot be part of any solution of a n-GMPI $\mathsf{P}(\overline{u}) < \mathsf{M}(\overline{u})$, while 1 cannot be the only value of such a solution, for any $n \in \mathbb{N}_+$ of the unknown vector $\overline{u} \in \mathsf{U}^n$. As an example, consider the 3-MPI

$$u_1^7 + u_1^5 \cdot u_2^2 + u_1^3 \cdot u_3^4 < u_1^2 \cdot u_2 \cdot u_3^3$$

derived at the end of the previous section. Observe that there is no solution with $u_1 = 0$, independently of the value of the other two unknowns u_2 and u_3, since

$$(u_1^7 + u_1^5 \cdot u_2^2 + u_1^3 \cdot u_3^4)|_{u_1=0} = 0 \not< 0 = (u_1^2 \cdot u_2 \cdot u_3^3)|_{u_1=0}.$$

Obviously, the same holds for $u_2 = 0$ or $u_3 = 0$. For similar reasons, $u_1 = u_2 = u_3 = 1$ does not satisfy the 3-MPI under analysis, as

$$(u_1^7 + u_1^5 \cdot u_2^2 + u_1^3 \cdot u_3^4)|_{\substack{u_1=1\\u_2=1\\u_3=1}} = 3 \not< 1 = (u_1^2 \cdot u_2 \cdot u_3^3)|_{\substack{u_1=1\\u_2=1\\u_3=1}}.$$

On the contrary, $u_1 = 1, u_2 = 4$, and $u_3 = 3$

is one of infinitely many Diophantine solutions of the above 3-MPI, since

$$(u_1^7 + u_1^5 \cdot u_2^2 + u_1^3 \cdot u_3^4)|_{\substack{u_1=1\\u_2=4\\u_3=3}} = 98 < 108 = (u_1^2 \cdot u_2 \cdot u_3^3)|_{\substack{u_1=1\\u_2=4\\u_3=3}}.$$

Another solution is, for instance,

$$u_1 = 1, u_2 = 9, \text{ and } u_3 = 3.$$

The following proposition generalizes the previous observation to arbitrary GMPIs.

Proposition 4.1. *Let* $\overline{\xi} \in \mathbb{N}^n$ *be a Diophantine solution of an* n*-GMPI* $\mathsf{P}(\overline{u}) < \mathsf{M}(\overline{u})$, *with* $n \in \mathbb{N}_+$. *Then,* $\xi_j \geq 1$, *for all* $j \in [1, n]$, *and* $\xi_j > 1$, *for some* $j \in [1, n]$.

Proof. First notice that, if $\xi_j = 0$, for some $j \in [1, n]$, we would have $\mathsf{M}(\overline{\xi}) = 0$, thus, $0 \leq \mathsf{P}(\overline{\xi}) < 0 = \mathsf{M}(\overline{\xi})$, which is impossible. Now, suppose that $\xi_j = 1$, for all $j \in [1, n]$. Then, $\mathsf{M}(\overline{\xi}) = 1$, but $1 \leq \mathsf{P}(\overline{\xi})$, hence, $1 \leq \mathsf{P}(\overline{\xi}) < 1 = \mathsf{M}(\overline{\xi})$, which is impossible as well. □

As one might observe from the previous discussion, the relationship between the degree of the polynomial $\mathsf{P}(\overline{u})$ and the monomial $\mathsf{M}(\overline{u})$ in a n-GMPI does not constitute, in general, a criterion to decide whether this inequality admits a Diophantine solution. If $\mathsf{P}(u)$ has strictly lower degree than $\mathsf{M}(u)$, indeed, it can be shown that $\mathsf{P}(u) < \mathsf{M}(u)$ is necessarily solvable. However, a solution may even exist if the opposite holds, as exemplified by the above 3-MPI, where we have

$$\deg(u_1^7 + u_1^5 \cdot u_2^2 + u_1^3 \cdot u_3^4) = 7 > 6 = \deg(u_1^2 \cdot u_2 \cdot u_3^3).$$

In case of dimension 1, however, a 1-GMPI $\mathsf{P}(u) < \mathsf{M}(u)$ is solvable precisely when the degree of $\mathsf{P}(u)$ is strictly lower than the degree of $\mathsf{M}(u)$. For instance, $u^4 + u^2 < u^4$ is unsolvable, since $\deg(u^4 + u^2) = 4 \not< 4 = \deg(u^4)$. On the contrary, 3 is a solution for $2 \cdot u^4 + 1 < u^5$. Intuitively, a 1-GMPI is solvable whenever the monomial has an asymptotic grow that is greater than the one of the polynomial, so that there is necessarily a point after which $\mathsf{M}(\overline{u})$ assumes values greater than those assumed by $\mathsf{P}(\overline{u})$. The following lemma formalizes this concept.

Lemma 4.1. *A 1-GMPI* $\mathsf{P}(u) < \mathsf{M}(u)$ *admits a positive Diophantine solution* iff $\deg(\mathsf{P}(u)) < \deg(\mathsf{M}(u))$.

Proof. **(If).** Suppose that $\deg(\mathsf{P}(u)) < \deg(\mathsf{M}(u))$. Then, $e_i < e$, for all $i \in [1, m]$, where $e_i \in \mathbb{R}_+$ is the i-th exponent of the polynomial $\mathsf{P}(u) = \sum_{i=1}^m a_i u^{e_i}$ and $e \in \mathbb{R}_+$ is the exponent of the monomial $\mathsf{M}(u) = u^e$. Due to the well known special limit of rational functions, it holds that

$$\lim_{u \to +\infty} a_i u^{e_i} / u^e = 0,$$

where $a_i \in \mathbb{R}_+$ is the coefficient of the i-th monomial in the polynomial $\mathsf{P}(u)$. Therefore, by expanding the definition of limit, we have that there exists a positive real number $\ell_i \in \mathbb{R}_+$ such that

$$a_i u^{e_i} / u^e < 1/m,$$

for all $u \in \mathbb{R}_+$ with $u > \ell_i$. Now, assume

$$\xi^\star \triangleq 1 + \lceil \max_{i \in [1,m]} \ell_i \rceil \in \mathbb{N}_+.$$

By construction,

$$a_i \xi^{\star e_i} / \xi^{\star e} < 1/m, \text{ i.e., } a_i \xi^{\star e_i} < \xi^{\star e} / m,$$

for all $i \in [1, m]$. Consequently,

$$\mathsf{P}(\xi^\star) = \sum_{i=1}^m a_i \xi^{\star e_i} < \sum_{i=1}^m \xi^{\star e} / m = \xi^{\star e} = \mathsf{M}(\xi^\star).$$

So, $\xi^\star$ is a positive Diophantine solution for $\mathsf{P}(u) < \mathsf{M}(u)$.

(Only if). Suppose that $\deg(\mathsf{P}(u)) \geq \deg(\mathsf{M}(u))$. Then, there exists an index $i \in [1, m]$ such that $e_i \geq e$. Since $a_i \geq 1$, we have that

$$a_i u^{e_i}/u^e \geq u^{e_i}/u^e = u^{e_i - e}.$$

Moreover, $u^{e_i-e} \geq 1$, for all $u \in \mathbb{R}_+$ with $u \geq 1$, being $e_i - e$ non negative, which implies $a_i u^{e_i} \geq u^e$. Thus,

$$\mathsf{P}(u) = \sum_{i=1}^{m} a_i u^{e_i} \geq u^e = \mathsf{M}(u),$$

for all $u \in \mathbb{N}_+$. Consequently, $\mathsf{P}(u) < \mathsf{M}(u)$ cannot admit any positive Diophantine solution. □

In the multi-dimensional case, the reason why there is no similar simple dependence between the existence of a Diophantine solution for an GMPI $\mathsf{P}(\overline{u}) < \mathsf{M}(\overline{u})$ and the relationship between the degrees of its parts is that different unknowns may have different degrees in their contribution to the value of the polynomial $\mathsf{P}(\overline{u})$ and monomial $\mathsf{M}(\overline{u})$. For instance, in the search for a solution of the 3-MPI previously analyzed, it is counterproductive to have values for u_1 greater than 1, since this unknown appears in all monomials of

$$\mathsf{P}(\overline{u}) = u_1^7 + u_1^5 \cdot u_2^2 + u_1^3 \cdot u_3^4$$

with greater degree than the one in

$$\mathsf{M}(\overline{u}) = u_1^2 \cdot u_2 \cdot u_3^3$$

and thus it contributes more to value of the former than to that of the latter. On the contrary, u_2 and u_3 are completely decoupled in $\mathsf{P}(\overline{u})$ *w.r.t.* the operation of multiplication, since the first one only appears squared in the second monomial, while the second one just occurs in the third monomial as a fourth power. In other words, their combined contribution to $\mathsf{P}(\overline{u})$ is additive, while in $\mathsf{M}(\overline{u})$ is multiplicative. Consequently, by fixing $u_1 = 1$ and suitably choosing values for u_2 and u_3, we might be able to ensure that the sum

$$\mathsf{P}(\overline{u}) = 1 + u_2^2 + u_3^4$$

assumes smaller values than the product

$$\mathsf{M}(\overline{u}) = u_2 \cdot u_3^3,$$

if a certain linear relationship holds between the exponents as we show below (we already know that such values exist: $u_2 = 4$ and $u_3 = 3$). In order to find these values, we can express all unknowns as possibly different powers of a fresh unknown u transforming the 3-MPI

$$u_1^7 + u_1^5 \cdot u_2^2 + u_1^3 \cdot u_3^4 < u_1^2 \cdot u_2 \cdot u_3^3$$

into a parametric 1-MPI $\mathsf{P}^\star(u) < \mathsf{M}^\star(u)$, with

$$\begin{aligned}\mathsf{P}^\star(u) &\triangleq u^{7\epsilon_1} + u^{5\epsilon_1} \cdot u^{2\epsilon_2} + u^{3\epsilon_1} \cdot u^{4\epsilon_3}\\ &= u^{7\epsilon_1} + u^{5\epsilon_1+2\epsilon_2} + u^{3\epsilon_1+4\epsilon_3},\\ \mathsf{M}^\star(u) &\triangleq u^{2\epsilon_1} \cdot u^{\epsilon_2} \cdot u^{3\epsilon_3} = u^{2\epsilon_1+\epsilon_2+3\epsilon_3},\end{aligned}$$

such that the first inequality is solvable iff the second one is solvable as well, for some choice of the parameter vector $\overline{\epsilon} = (\epsilon_1, \epsilon_2, \epsilon_3)$. It is immediate to prove, indeed, that the scalar $\xi^\star \in \mathbb{N}_+$ is a solution for $\mathsf{P}^\star(u) < \mathsf{M}^\star(u)$ *iff* the vector $\overline{\xi} \in \mathbb{N}_+^3$ is a solution for $\mathsf{P}(\overline{u}) < \mathsf{M}(\overline{u})$, where $\epsilon_j \triangleq \log_{\xi^\star}(\xi_j)$ At this point, by exploiting the above lemma, we can verify the existence of a solution for $\mathsf{P}^\star(u) < \mathsf{M}^\star(u)$, by checking the existence of a real vector $\overline{\epsilon} \in \mathbb{R}^3$ for which

$$\begin{aligned}\deg(\mathsf{P}^\star(u)) &= \max(7\epsilon_1, 5\epsilon_1 + 2\epsilon_2, 3\epsilon_1 + 4\epsilon_3)\\ &< 2\epsilon_1 + \epsilon_2 + 3\epsilon_3\\ &= \deg(\mathsf{M}^\star(u))\end{aligned}$$

holds. The latter is then equivalent to the homogeneous linear inequality system

$$\begin{aligned}7\epsilon_1 &< 2\epsilon_1 + \epsilon_2 + 3\epsilon_3\\ 5\epsilon_1 + 2\epsilon_2 &< 2\epsilon_1 + \epsilon_2 + 3\epsilon_3\\ 3\epsilon_1 + 4\epsilon_3 &< 2\epsilon_1 + \epsilon_2 + 3\epsilon_3,\end{aligned}$$

which can be simplified into

$$\begin{aligned}-5\epsilon_1 + \epsilon_2 + 3\epsilon_3 &> 0\\ -3\epsilon_1 - \epsilon_2 + 3\epsilon_3 &> 0\\ -\epsilon_1 - \epsilon_2 + 3\epsilon_3 &> 0.\end{aligned}$$

A possible solution for this system is $\epsilon_1 = 0$, $\epsilon_2 = 2$, and $\epsilon_3 = 1$, from which we derive the 1-MPI

$$2 \cdot u^4 + 1 < u^5$$

having 3 as one of its infinite solutions. We finally compute the Diophantine solution $\xi_1 = 1, \xi_2 = 9, \xi_3 = 3$ for the 3-MPI under analysis by using the formula $\xi_j = \xi^{\star\epsilon_j}$. We can now state the general criterion. Observe that here we only present the result for MPIs, since this suffices for our purposes, and leave the more general version of the theorem as future work.

Theorem 4.1. *An n-MPI $\mathsf{P}(\overline{u}) < \mathsf{M}(\overline{u})$, with $n \in \mathbb{N}_+$, admits a positive Diophantine solution iff the system of n-dimensional homogeneous linear inequalities $\{(\overline{e} - \overline{e}_i)^\mathsf{T} \cdot \overline{\epsilon} > 0\}_{i=1}^m$ admits a Diophantine solution as well, where $\overline{e}, \overline{e}_1, \ldots \overline{e}_m \in \mathbb{N}^n$ are the exponents used in the n-MPI itself, with $m \in \mathbb{N}_+$.*

Proof. **(If).** Suppose that the system

$$\{(\overline{e} - \overline{e}_i)^\mathsf{T} \cdot \overline{\epsilon} > 0\}_{i=1}^m$$

admits a Diophantine solution $\overline{d} \in \mathbb{N}^n$ and consider the 1-MPI $\mathsf{P}^\star(u) < \mathsf{M}^\star(u)$ with

$$\mathsf{P}^\star(u) \triangleq \sum_{i=1}^{m} a_i u^{(\overline{e}_i{}^\mathsf{T} \cdot \overline{d})} \text{ and } \mathsf{M}^\star(u) \triangleq u^{(\overline{e}^\mathsf{T} \cdot \overline{d})},$$

where each $a_i \in \mathbb{R}_{\geq 1}$ is the i-th coefficient of the polynomial $\mathsf{P}(\overline{u})$. By construction, it holds that

$$\deg(\mathsf{P}^\star(u)) < \deg(\mathsf{M}^\star(u)),$$

since $(\overline{e}^{\mathsf{T}} \cdot \overline{d}) - (\overline{e}_i{}^{\mathsf{T}} \cdot \overline{d}) = (\overline{e} - \overline{e}_i)^{\mathsf{T}} \cdot \overline{d} > 0$, for all $i \in [1, m]$. Thus, by Lemma 4.1, we have $\mathsf{P}^{\star}(u) < \mathsf{M}^{\star}(u)$ admits a positive Diophantine solution $\xi^{\star} \in \mathbb{N}_{+}$. Now consider the n-dimensional natural vector $\overline{\xi} \in \mathbb{N}^n$ whose components are defined as $\xi_j \triangleq \xi^{\star d_j}$, for all $j \in [1, n]$. It is immediate to see that $\overline{\xi}$ is a Diophantine solution for the original n-MPI $\mathsf{P}(\overline{u}) < \mathsf{M}(\overline{u})$, since

$$\mathsf{P}(\overline{\xi}) = \mathsf{P}^{\star}(\xi^{\star}) < \mathsf{M}^{\star}(\xi^{\star}) = \mathsf{M}(\overline{\xi}).$$

Indeed,

$$\mathsf{M}(\overline{\xi}) = \overline{\xi}^{\overline{e}} = \prod_{j=1}^{n} \xi_j{}^{e_j} = \prod_{j=1}^{n} \xi^{\star d_j e_j} = \xi^{\star \sum_{j=1}^{n} e_j d_j} = \xi^{\star (\overline{e}^{\mathsf{T}} \cdot \overline{d})} = \mathsf{M}^{\star}(\xi^{\star}).$$

The same reasoning applies to each monomial of the polynomial $\mathsf{P}(\overline{u})$ and, so, to the polynomial itself.

(Only if). Suppose that $\mathsf{P}(\overline{u}) < \mathsf{M}(\overline{u})$ admits a Diophantine solution $\overline{\xi} \in \mathbb{N}^n$ and let $\xi^{\star} \triangleq \min_{j \in [1,n]}^{\xi_j > 1} \xi_j$. Observe that the existence of such a positive integer number $\xi^{\star}$ is ensured by Proposition 4.1. Now, let $\overline{r} \in \mathbb{R}^n_{\geq 0}$ be the n-dimensional real vector having components defined as $r_j \triangleq \log_{\xi^{\star}}(\xi_j)$, for all $j \in [1, n]$, whose existence is ensured again by Proposition 4.1, since $\xi_j \geq 1$. Obviously, $\xi_j = \xi^{\star r_j}$. Moreover, consider the 1-GMPI $\mathsf{P}^{\star}(u) < \mathsf{M}^{\star}(u)$ with

$$\mathsf{P}^{\star}(u) \triangleq \sum_{i=1}^{m} a_i u^{(\overline{e}_i{}^{\mathsf{T}} \cdot \overline{r})} \text{ and } \mathsf{M}^{\star}(u) \triangleq u^{(\overline{e}^{\mathsf{T}} \cdot \overline{r})},$$

where the coefficients a_i are the same as in the previous case. It is immediate to see that $\xi^{\star}$ is a positive Diophantine solution for $\mathsf{P}^{\star}(u) < \mathsf{M}^{\star}(u)$, since

$$\mathsf{P}^{\star}(\xi^{\star}) = \mathsf{P}(\overline{\xi}) < \mathsf{M}(\overline{\xi}) = \mathsf{M}^{\star}(\xi^{\star}).$$

Indeed,

$$\mathsf{M}(\overline{\xi}) = \overline{\xi}^{\overline{e}} = \prod_{j=1}^{n} \xi_j{}^{e_j} = \prod_{j=1}^{n} \xi^{\star r_j e_j} = \xi^{\star \sum_{j=1}^{n} e_j r_j} = \xi^{\star (\overline{e}^{\mathsf{T}} \cdot \overline{r})} = \mathsf{M}^{\star}(\xi^{\star}).$$

A similar reasoning applies to the polynomial $\mathsf{P}(\overline{u})$. At this point, by Lemma 4.1, we have that

$$\deg(\mathsf{P}^{\star}(u)) < \deg(\mathsf{M}^{\star}(u)),$$

which means that

$$\overline{e}_i{}^{\mathsf{T}} \cdot \overline{r} < \overline{e}^{\mathsf{T}} \cdot \overline{r}$$

and, so, $(\overline{e} - \overline{e}_i)^{\mathsf{T}} \cdot \overline{r} > 0$, for all $i \in [1, m]$. Hence, $\overline{r}$ is a solution in $\mathbb{R}^n_{\geq 0}$ for the linear system

$$\{(\overline{e} - \overline{e}_i)^{\mathsf{T}} \cdot \overline{\epsilon} > 0\}_{i=1}^{m}.$$

Now, due to the fact that the coefficients $\overline{e} - \overline{e}_i$ are all rational, there is necessarily an n-dimensional rational solution $\overline{q} \in \mathbb{Q}^n_{\geq 0}$ for $\{(\overline{e} - \overline{e}_i)^{\mathsf{T}} \cdot \overline{\epsilon} > 0\}_{i=1}^{m}$ [29]. Recall that, for every $j \in [1, n]$, there exist two natural numbers $a_i \in \mathbb{N}$ and $b_j \in \mathbb{N}_{+}$ with $\gcd(a_i, b_j) = 1$ such that we can write the jth component of $\overline{q}$ as $q_j = a_i / b_j$ and consider the n-dimensional natural vector $\overline{d} \in \mathbb{N}^n$ whose components are defined as follows: $d_j = b q_j$, for all $j \in [1, n]$, where $b \triangleq \mathsf{lcm}_{j=1}^{n}(b_j) \geq 1$. Then, it is evident that $\overline{d}$ is a Diophantine solution for the system as well, as $(\overline{e} - \overline{e}_i)^{\mathsf{T}} \cdot \overline{d} = b(\overline{e} - \overline{e}_i)^{\mathsf{T}} \cdot \overline{q} > 0$. □

At this point, it is not hard to prove that the Diophantine solution problem for a given n-MPI can be solved in PTIME by reducing it to the feasibility problem of the associated homogeneous linear inequality system.

THEOREM 4.2. *The Diophantine solution problem for an n-MPI $\mathsf{P}(\overline{u}) < \mathsf{M}(\overline{u})$, with $n \in \mathbb{N}_{+}$, is in PTIME.*

PROOF. Consider an n-MPI $\mathsf{P}(\overline{u}) < \mathsf{M}(\overline{u})$ defined over $(m+1)$ exponents $\overline{e}, \overline{e}_1, \ldots \overline{e}_m \in \mathbb{N}_n$, with $n, m \in \mathbb{N}_{+}$. By Theorem 4.1, it holds that $\mathsf{P}(\overline{u}) < \mathsf{M}(\overline{u})$ admits a Diophantine solution *iff* the system of n-dimensional homogeneous linear inequalities $\{(\overline{e} - \overline{e}_i)^{\mathsf{T}} \cdot \overline{\epsilon} > 0\}_{i=1}^{m}$ admits a Diophantine solution as well. As already observed in the proof of the above theorem, the latter question is equivalent to the classic rational feasibility problem of linear systems, which is solvable in polynomial time *w.r.t.* its size [29], *i.e.*, in the dimension n (unknowns in $\mathsf{M}(\overline{u})$), number of constraints (monomials in $\mathsf{P}(\overline{u})$), and value of the coefficients (exponents $\overline{e}, \overline{e}_1, \ldots \overline{e}_m$). Hence, the thesis immediately follows. □

5 COMPLEXITY RESULTS

By exploiting the decidability of the restricted version of the Diophantine inequality problem previously discussed, we are now able to decide the bag-containment problem of a projection-free CQ into a generic one [2].

A naive reduction from the problem we are interested in to the associated linear inequality problem, via Corollary 3.1 and Theorems 4.1 and 4.2, can be described as follows. First, the corollary allows to reduce a negative instance

$$q_1(\overline{x}_1) \not\subseteq_{\mathsf{b}} q_2(\overline{x}_2)$$

of the bag-containment problem to the solution of at least one among a set of MPI problems

$$\mathsf{P}^{q_2(\overline{x}_2)}_{q_1(\overline{t})}(\overline{u}) < \mathsf{M}_{q_1(\overline{t})}(\overline{u}),$$

each one for a different probe tuple $\overline{t} \in \mathsf{prbtup}(q_1(\overline{x}_1))$. Then, thanks to Theorem 4.1, the search of such a solution can be in its turn reduced to verify the existence of a solution for the associated inequality system

$$\{(\overline{e} - \overline{e}_{\mathsf{h}})^{\mathsf{T}} \cdot \overline{\epsilon} > 0\}_{\mathsf{h} \in \mathsf{CM}(q_2(\overline{x}_2), q_1(\overline{t}))},$$

where $\overline{e}$ and $\overline{e}_{\mathsf{h}}$ are the exponent vectors of the monomials $\mathsf{M}_{q_1(\overline{t})}(\overline{u})$ and $\mathsf{M}_{\mathsf{h}(q_2(\overline{x}_2))}(\overline{u})$, respectively, the latter being contained into the polynomial $\mathsf{P}^{q_2(\overline{x}_2)}_{q_1(\overline{t})}(\overline{u})$. Unfortunately, since there might be exponentially many containment mappings $h \in CM(q_2(\overline{x}_2), q_1(\overline{t}))$, this approach would let us obtain an ExpSpace decidability procedure only. Indeed, the size of the polynomial associated with the containee query, and so the number of inequalities in the linear system, is generally exponential in the size of the query itself. In order to avoid such exponential blow up in the required space, we put in practice a guess&check approach, which allows us to describe a procedure that decides containment, whose complexity is Π_2^P *w.r.t.* the size of the containing query and CoNPTime *w.r.t.* the size of the containee query. To do this, we make use of the following simple reformulation of a known result [32], which provides a polynomial bound on the size of a possible solution for an integer inequality system.

Lemma 5.1. *Let $\overline{e}_1, \ldots, \overline{e}_m \in \mathbb{Z}^n$ and $\overline{f} \in \mathbb{Z}^m$ be $(m+1)$ integer vectors, with $m, n \in \mathbb{N}_+$. An n-dimensional linear inequality system $\{\overline{e}_i^{\mathsf{T}} \cdot \overline{v} \leq f_i\}_{i=1}^m$ admits a positive solution* iff *it admits a natural one $\overline{\xi} \in \mathbb{N}^n$ with $\sum_{i=1}^n \xi_i \leq 6n^3\phi$, where $\phi \triangleq \max_{i=1}^m (f_i + \sum_{j=1}^n e_{i,j})$ is the maximum sum of the coefficients in an inequality of the system plus its constant term.*

The idea behind our guess&check approach is quite simple: suitably combine Corollary 3.1, Theorem 4.1, and Lemma 5.1 into a single criterion and then verify whether this holds by using a ∀∃-alternating Turing machine, *i.e.*, equivalently, a CoNPTime Turing machine with an NPTime oracle. In particular, in order to avoid the exponential blow-up in space complexity, we do not write down the entire system, but just guess which inequality might not be satisfied by a given proposed solution. In more detail, we first universally guess a probe tuple $\overline{t} \in \mathsf{prbtup}(q_1(\overline{x}_1))$ (one that would "break containment") and a hypothetical solution $\overline{d} \in \mathbb{N}^{|\overline{e}|}$ of the system $\{(\overline{e} - \overline{e}_h)^{\mathsf{T}} \cdot \overline{e} > 0\}_{h \in CM(q_2(\overline{x}_2), q_1(\overline{t}))}$ and then verify it by existentially guessing which inequality $(\overline{e} - \overline{e}_h)^{\mathsf{T}} \cdot \overline{e} > 0$ might be violated. Thanks to Lemma 5.1, the existence of a polynomial bound $\mathsf{sb}(q_1(\overline{t}), q_2(\overline{x}_2)) \triangleq \max_{h \in CM(q_2(\overline{x}_2), q_1(\overline{t}))} \sum_j (\overline{e} - \overline{e}_h)_j$ on a possible solution of the system ensures that the guessing has polynomial size. Note that in the inequalities of Theorem 4.1 there is no constant term (as f_i in Lemma 5.1). Next theorem formalizes the discussed criterion.

Theorem 5.1. *Let $q_1(\overline{x}_1)$ and $q_2(\overline{x}_2)$ be two CQs, the first of which is projection-free. Then, $q_1(\overline{x}_1) \sqsubseteq_b q_2(\overline{x}_2)$* iff, *for any probe tuple $\overline{t} \in \mathsf{prbtup}(q_1(\overline{x}_1))$, it holds that (i) $\overline{t}$ is unifiable with $\overline{x}_2$ and, (ii) assuming $n = |\mathsf{body}(q_1(\overline{t}))|$, for all natural vectors $\overline{d} \in \mathbb{N}^n$ with $\sum_j d_j \leq \mathsf{sb}(q_1(\overline{t}), q_2(\overline{x}_2))$, there exists a containment mapping $h \in CM(q_2(\overline{x}_2), q_1(\overline{t}))$ such that $(\overline{e} - \overline{e}_h)^{\mathsf{T}} \cdot \overline{d} \leq 0$, where $\overline{e}$ and $\overline{e}_h$ are the exponent vectors of the monomials $M_{q_1(\overline{t})}(\overline{u})$ and $M_{h(q_2(\overline{x}_2))}(\overline{u})$, respectively.*

Proof. By Corollary 3.1, we know that $q_1(\overline{x}_1) \sqsubseteq_b q_2(\overline{x}_2)$ *iff*, for all probe tuples $\overline{t} \in \mathsf{prbtup}(q_1(\overline{x}_1))$, it holds that (i) $\overline{t}$ is unifiable with $\overline{x}_2$ and (ii) the MPI

$$M_{q_1(\overline{t})}(\overline{u}) > \sum_{h \in CM(q_2(\overline{t}), q_1(\overline{t}))} M_{h(q_2(\overline{x}_2))}(\overline{u})$$

does not have a Diophantine solution. In addition, due to Theorem 4.1, we derive that the second item is equivalent to the fact that the inequality system

$$\{(\overline{e} - \overline{e}_h)^{\mathsf{T}} \cdot \overline{v} > 0\}_{h \in \mathrm{Hom}(q_2(\overline{t}), q_1(\overline{t}))}$$

does not have a Diophantine solution as well. This implies that, by Lemma 5.1, every natural vector $\overline{d} \in \mathbb{N}^n$ with $\sum_j d_j \leq \mathsf{sb}(q_1(\overline{t}), q_2(\overline{x}_2))$ cannot be a solution of the system *iff* this is unsolvable, which means that there exists at least one inequality $(\overline{e} - \overline{e}_h)^{\mathsf{T}} \cdot \overline{v} > 0$, and so one containment mapping $h \in CM(q_2(\overline{x}_2), q_1(\overline{t}))$, such that $(\overline{e} - \overline{e}_h)^{\mathsf{T}} \cdot \overline{d} \leq 0$ holds. The statement easily follows. □

At this point, we can prove our main result that concerns the upper-bound complexity of the bag-containment problem of a projection-free CQ into a generic one.

Theorem 5.2. *The bag-containment problem $q_1(\overline{x}_1) \sqsubseteq_b q_2(\overline{x}_2)$ of a projection-free* CQ *$q_1(\overline{x}_1)$ into a* CQ *$q_2(\overline{x}_2)$ is solvable in Π_2^P* w.r.t. *the size of containing query and in CoNPTime* w.r.t. *the size of containee query.*

Proof. To prove the required statement we describe a polynomial-size ∀∃-alternating procedure that, given the two queries $q_1(\overline{x}_1)$ and $q_2(\overline{x}_2)$ in input, exhibits an accepting computation *iff* $q_1(\overline{x}_1) \sqsubseteq_b q_2(\overline{x}_2)$ holds. We leave to the interesting reader the tedious but trivial translation of our procedure to an equivalent polynomial-size ∀∃-alternating Turing machine $\mathcal{M}$.

The procedure starts in a universal state s_0 by guessing a probe tuple $\overline{t} \in \mathsf{prbtup}(q_1(\overline{x}_1))$. If $\overline{t}$ is not unifiable with $\overline{x}_2$, the computation is rejected and the procedure terminates. Otherwise, a transit to a universal state $s_{\overline{t}}$ occurs, from which a natural vector $\overline{d} \in \mathbb{N}^n$ with $\sum_j d_j \leq \mathsf{sb}(q_1(\overline{t}), q_2(\overline{x}_2))$ and $n = |\mathsf{body}(q_1(\overline{t}))|$ is chosen. This step allows to reach an existential state $s_{\overline{t},\overline{d}}$. At this point, a containment mapping $h \in CM(q_2(\overline{x}_2), q_1(\overline{t}))$ is guessed as well and the procedure transits to the final state $s_{\overline{t},\overline{d},h}$, which is accepting *iff* the homogeneous linear inequality $(\overline{e} - \overline{e}_h)^{\mathsf{T}} \cdot \overline{d} \leq 0$ holds, where $\overline{e}$ and $\overline{e}_h$ are the exponent vectors of the monomials $M_{q_1(\overline{t})}(\overline{u})$ and $M_{h(q_2(\overline{x}_2))}(\overline{u})$, respectively. Now, one can make the following easy observations about the guessing points s_0, $s_{\overline{t}}$, $s_{\overline{t},\overline{d}}$ and the final state $s_{\overline{t},\overline{d},h}$:

(1) the probe tuple $\overline{t} \in \mathsf{prbtup}(q_1(\overline{x}_1))$ requires (in binary encoding) space $O(m \cdot \log(m + c))$, where m and c are the numbers of variables and constants in $\overline{x}_1$ and $q_1(\overline{x}_1)$, respectively;

(2) the natural vector $\overline{d} \in \mathbb{N}^n$ requires space $O(n \cdot \log(b))$, where the n atoms in $q_1(\overline{t})$ are not more than those in $q_1(\overline{x})$, and $b = \mathsf{sb}(q_1(\overline{t}), q_2(\overline{x}_2))$ is the maximum value an unknown can assume;
(3) the containment mapping $\mathsf{h} \in \mathsf{CM}(q_2(\overline{x}_2), q_1(\overline{t}))$ requires space $O(m \cdot \log(n))$, where n and m are the number of atoms in $q_1(\overline{t})$ and $q_2(\overline{x})$, respectively;
(4) the inequality $(\overline{e} - \overline{e}_{\mathsf{h}})^\mathsf{T} \cdot \overline{d} \leq 0$ contains n summands and we can verify it in PTime.

Evidently, thanks to the relationship between the alternation of quantification types among the guessing points and the levels of the polynomial hierarchy [4, 6], the procedure has complexity Π_2^P *w.r.t.* the size of containing query and in CoNPTime *w.r.t.* the size of containee query [33]. Finally, we can immediately observe that soundness and completeness of the described approach directly from Theorem 5.1. □

Before concluding with a hardness reduction, we provide a stronger result that simplifies our characterization via Diophantine inequalities, namely Corollary 3.1 and Theorem 5.1, without improving though the asymptotic complexity of the decision problem. Specifically, we show that we just need to evaluate the MPI associated with a bag-containment problem for the most-general probe tuple, similarly to what one would do for classic set-containment. The difference here is that, to do so, we cannot work only at the level of database instances and homomorphisms, but need to exploit the solution of an MPI via the corresponding linear system.

Theorem 5.3. *Given a projection-free* CQ $q_1(\overline{x}_1)$ *and a* CQ $q_2(\overline{x}_2)$, *it holds that* $q_1(\overline{x}_1) \sqsubseteq_b q_2(\overline{x}_2)$ iff *the inequality* $\mathsf{M}_{q_1(\overline{t}^\star)}(\overline{u}) > \mathsf{P}^{q_2(\overline{x}_2)}_{q_1(\overline{t}^\star)}(\overline{u})$ *does not admit a Diophantine solution, where* $\overline{t}^\star \in \mathsf{prbtup}(q_1(\overline{x}_1))$ *is the most-general probe tuple.*

Proof. Thanks to Theorem 5.1, we know that

$$q_1(\overline{x}_1) \not\sqsubseteq_b q_2(\overline{x}_2)$$

iff there exists a probe tuple $\overline{t} \in \mathsf{prbtup}(q_1(\overline{x}_1))$ and a natural vector $\overline{d} \in \mathbb{N}^n$, with $n = |\mathsf{body}(q_1(\overline{t}))|$, such that either (i) $\overline{t}$ is not unifiable with $\overline{x}_2$ or, (ii) for all containment mappings $\mathsf{h} \in \mathsf{CM}(q_2(\overline{x}_2), q_1(\overline{t}))$, it holds that

$$(\overline{e} - \overline{e}_\mathsf{h})^\mathsf{T} \cdot \overline{d} > 0,$$

where $\overline{e}$ and $\overline{e}_\mathsf{h}$ are the exponent vectors of the monomials $\mathsf{M}_{q_1(\overline{t})}(\overline{u})$ and $\mathsf{M}_{\mathsf{h}(q_2(\overline{x}_2))}(\overline{u})$, respectively. Consider the most-general probe tuple $\overline{t}^\star \in \mathsf{prbtup}(q_1(\overline{x}_1))$, the monomial $\mathsf{M}_{q_1(\overline{t}^\star)}(\overline{u})$, every monomial $\mathsf{M}_{\mathsf{h}^\star(q_2(\overline{x}_2))}(\overline{u})$ for some given containment mapping $\mathsf{h}^\star \in \mathsf{CM}(q_2(\overline{x}_2), q_1(\overline{t}^\star))$, and the corresponding exponent vectors $\overline{e}^\star$ and $\overline{e}^\star_{\mathsf{h}^\star}$, whose dimension is $n^\star = |\mathsf{body}(q_1(\overline{t}^\star))| = |\mathsf{body}(q_1(\overline{x}_1))|$. We now show that

$$q_1(\overline{x}_1) \not\sqsubseteq_b q_2(\overline{x}_2)$$

iff there exists a natural vector $\overline{d}^\star \in \mathbb{N}^{n^\star}$ such that

$$(\overline{e}^\star - \overline{e}^\star_{\mathsf{h}^\star})^\mathsf{T} \cdot \overline{d}^\star > 0,$$

for all containment mappings $\mathsf{h}^\star \in \mathsf{CM}(q_2(\overline{x}_2), q_1(\overline{t}^\star))$. First observe that every containment mapping $\mathsf{h}^\star \in \mathsf{CM}(q_2(\overline{x}_2), q_1(\overline{t}^\star))$ induces a containment mapping $\mathsf{h}^\star \circ \mathsf{f} \in \mathsf{CM}(q_2(\overline{x}_2), q_1(\overline{t}))$, where f is the unique surjective homomorphism from $q_1(\overline{t}^\star)$ to $q_1(\overline{t})$, *i.e.*, more precisely, from $\mathrm{I}^{q_1(\overline{t}^\star)}$ to $\mathrm{I}^{q_1(\overline{t})}$. Also, assume the bodies of the two queries $q_1(\overline{t}^\star)$ and $q_1(\overline{t})$ to be enumerated, *i.e.*,

$$\mathsf{body}(q_1(\overline{t}^\star)) = \{\alpha_1^\star, \ldots, \alpha_{n^\star}^\star\}, \mathsf{body}(q_1(\overline{t})) = \{\alpha_1, \ldots, \alpha_n\},$$

and let $\mathsf{g}\colon [1, n^\star] \to [1, n]$ be the unique surjective map between atom indexes induced by the homomorphism f as defined in the following: for all atoms $\alpha_i^\star \in \mathsf{body}(q_1(\overline{t}^\star))$, it holds that $\mathsf{f}(\alpha_i^\star) = \alpha_{\mathsf{g}(i)}$ is the $\mathsf{g}(i)$-th atom in $\mathsf{body}(q_1(\overline{t}))$. Obviously, the enumeration needs to associate every atom $\alpha_i^\star$ and α_j with the corresponding positions $i \in [1, n^\star]$ and $j \in [1, n]$ in all the vectors of the inequalities. At this point, we claim that the natural vector $\overline{d}^\star \in \mathbb{N}^{n^\star}$, with $d_i^\star \triangleq d_{\mathsf{g}(i)}$, for all $i \in [1, n^\star]$, satisfies all the required inequalities $(\overline{e}^\star - \overline{e}^\star_{\mathsf{h}^\star})^\mathsf{T} \cdot \overline{d}^\star > 0$, with $\mathsf{h}^\star \in \mathsf{CM}(q_2(\overline{x}_2), q_1(\overline{t}^\star))$. To do this, observe that

$$e_j = \sum_{\substack{i=1\\ \mathsf{g}(i)=j}}^{n^\star} e_i^\star \text{ and } e_{(\mathsf{h}^\star \circ \mathsf{f}), j} = \sum_{\substack{i=1\\ \mathsf{g}(i)=j}}^{n^\star} e^\star_{\mathsf{h}^\star, i}.$$

As a consequence, we have that

$$(\overline{e}^\star - \overline{e}^\star_{\mathsf{h}^\star})^\mathsf{T} \cdot \overline{d}^\star = (\overline{e} - \overline{e}_{(\mathsf{h}^\star \circ \mathsf{f})})^\mathsf{T} \cdot \overline{d} > 0.$$

Indeed, due to the above equalities and the choice of the vector $\overline{d}^\star$, it holds that

$$\overline{e}^{\star\mathsf{T}} \cdot \overline{d}^\star = \sum_{i=1}^{n^\star} e_i^\star d_i^\star = \sum_{j=1}^{n} \sum_{\substack{i=1\\ \mathsf{g}(i)=j}}^{n^\star} e_i^\star d_i^\star$$
$$= \sum_{j=1}^{n} d_j \sum_{\substack{i=1\\ \mathsf{g}(i)=j}}^{n^\star} e_i^\star = \sum_{j=1}^{n} e_j d_j = \overline{e}^\mathsf{T} \cdot \overline{d}.$$

Similarly,

$$\overline{e}^{\star\mathsf{T}}_{\mathsf{h}^\star} \cdot \overline{d}^\star = \overline{e}^\mathsf{T}_{(\mathsf{h}^\star \circ \mathsf{f})} \cdot \overline{d}.$$

Finally, the thesis follows by applying Theorem 4.1. □

We conclude by providing an NPTime hardness result.

Theorem 5.4. *The bag-containment problem* $q_1(\overline{x}_1) \sqsubseteq_\mathsf{b} q_2(\overline{x}_2)$ *of a projection-free* CQ $q_1(\overline{x}_1)$ *into a* CQ $q_2(\overline{x}_2)$ *is NPTime-hard* w.r.t. *the size of containing query.*

Proof. The proof generalizes the classic way to reduce the 3-colorability problem to the set-containment problem. Let $\mathcal{G}$ be a graph. It holds that $\mathcal{G}$ is 3-colorable *iff* there exists a homomorphism form $\mathcal{G}$ to a triangle graph $\mathcal{T}$. Now, consider the Boolean query $q_{\mathcal{G}}$ associated with $\mathcal{G}$ and the ground query $q_{\mathcal{T}} \leftarrow R(\mathsf{a},\mathsf{b}), R(\mathsf{b},\mathsf{c}), R(\mathsf{c},\mathsf{a})$ associated with $\mathcal{T}$. It holds that $\mathcal{G}$ is 3-colorable *iff* $q_{\mathcal{T}}$ is set-contained into $q_{\mathcal{G}}$. We now show that $\mathcal{G}$ is 3-colorable *iff* $q_{\mathcal{T}}$ is bag-contained into $q_{\mathcal{T}} \wedge q_{\mathcal{G}}$, as well.

(Only if). It is clear that the multiplicity of $q_{\mathcal{T}} \wedge q_{\mathcal{G}}$ is the product of the multiplicities of $q_{\mathcal{T}}$ and $q_{\mathcal{G}}$ in isolation, on any database instance, since $q_{\mathcal{T}}$ is ground. Now, suppose that $\mathcal{G}$ is 3-colorable. Then, there exists a containment mapping from $q_{\mathcal{G}}$ to $q_{\mathcal{T}}$ and, so, from $q_{\mathcal{T}} \wedge q_{\mathcal{G}}$ to $q_{\mathcal{T}}$. Therefore, it is immediate to see that $q_{\mathcal{T}}$ is bag-contained into $q_{\mathcal{T}} \wedge q_{\mathcal{G}}$, being the multiplicity of $q_{\mathcal{G}}$ greater than zero.

(If). If $q_{\mathcal{T}} \wedge q_{\mathcal{G}}$ bag-includes $q_{\mathcal{T}}$, it is obvious that $q_{\mathcal{G}}$ set-includes $q_{\mathcal{T}}$ too. Thus, $\mathcal{G}$ is 3-colorable. □

6 RELATED WORK

A very useful investigation for algebra operations on bags appeared in [17]. As discussed in the introduction, Chaudhuri and Vardi [7] posed the bag containment problem for CQs and stated, without giving a proof, that it is Π_2^{P}-HARD. Since then, and to the best of our knowledge, a proof for this claim has not been provided; our NPTime hardness obviously implies the same lower bound for the general case but this bound is loose and a tighter one remains to be investigated. Chaudhuri and Vardi [7] also formulated the problem of bag containment for UCQs, proved decidability of equivalence for UCQs, as well as introduced the problem of containment for bag-set semantics, *i.e.*, when the database is a set instance but the query answers could be bags. As mentioned, undecidability of the containment problem for UCQs was proved in [20]. In [2] containment for several restrictions of CQs is studied under bag and bag-set semantics, with the problem that we close in this paper, *i.e.*, bag containment of a projection-free CQ to a CQ, surfacing as the main open problem besides the general one.

Cohen [14] studied equivalence when *combining* set and bag-set semantics within the same query and in [15] expanded to queries that combine the three semantics altogether: set, bag-set, and bag. This combination is referred to as *combined semantics* and complete characterizations of equivalence were drawn for several classes of queries that include comparisons, disjunction and atomic negation. Further building on this work, Chirkova [8–10] investigated more query classes, where equivalence, as well as minimization, is decidable or tractable under combined semantics. Recently, [11] studied equivalence for SQL queries that use a mix of bag and bag-set semantics, taking into account also possible database dependencies. More recent work that looks into bag semantics of CQs in the face of dependencies, such as views, schema mappings, or ontologies, appeared in [16, 19, 30, 31].

7 DISCUSSION

We show that the problem of checking whether a projection-free CQ is contained into a CQ under bag semantics is decidable. In particular, it can be solved in Π_2^{P} and is at least NPTime-HARD. To the best of our knowledge, this has been a crucial open problem, right after the original one, which remains still open.

Our proof relies on the solution of a special case of the Diophantine inequality problem. Previous approaches that used Diophantine inequalities, notably [20] and [21], did so only for proving negative results: since the Diophantine inequality problem is undecidable, a reasonable approach is to reduce this problem to some version of bag containment in order to show undecidability of the latter. In contrast, here we focus on providing a positive result for a major class of conjunctive queries and in doing so we show decidability of an interesting restriction of the Diophantine problem. As far as we know, it is the first time that Diophantine inequalities are used as a positive tool and, in our opinion, this brings new hope for approaching the general problem. Indeed, if bag containment of CQs is eventually decidable, it must be the case that certain polynomial inequalities, and in particular those that would come out of an approach very similar to the one of Section 3, are decidable as well. Hence, a plan of attack for future works is to gradually generalize the language of the containee query and exploit the peculiarities of the structure of the associated polynomials in order to prove decidability. To do so, one can even try to reformulate the proposed technique inside the framework of functional aggregate queries [22].

Observe that the obtained mathematical results do not immediately apply to the general case, as we heavily exploit the fact that the inequalities corresponding to the studied bag containment problem compare polynomials against *monomials*. A starting point for generalization would be Lemma 4.1, which is about one variable GMPIs, and does not lift to the case of a polynomial in the right-hand side of the inequality, unless some further hypothesis is exploited that characterizes GMPIs on one unknown. In the future, we plan to further build on these results.

ACKNOWLEDGMENTS

The work by G. Konstantinidis was supported by the EU H2020 TheyBuyForYou project (780247). F. Mogavero acknowledges the support of the GNCS 2018 project "Metodi Formali per la Verica e la Sintesi di Sistemi Discreti e Ibridi".

REFERENCES

[1] S. Abiteboul, R. Hull, and V. Vianu. 1995. *Foundations of Databases.* Addison-Wesley.

[2] F.N. Afrati, M. Damigos, and M. Gergatsoulis. 2010. Query Containment under Bag and Bag-Set Semantics. *IPL* 110, 10 (2010), 360–369.

[3] R.J. Brachman and H.J. Levesque. 2004. *Knowledge Representation and Reasoning.* Morgan Kaufmann.

[4] A.K. Chandra, D. Kozen, and L.J. Stockmeyer. 1981. Alternation. *JACM* 28, 1 (1981), 114–133.

[5] A.K. Chandra and P.M. Merlin. 1977. Optimal Implementation of Conjunctive Queries in Relational Data Bases.. In *STOC'77.* ACM, 77–90.

[6] A.K. Chandra and L.J. Stockmeyer. 1976. Alternation.. In *FOCS'76.* IEEECS, 98–108.

[7] S. Chaudhuri and M.Y. Vardi. 1993. Optimization of Real Conjunctive Queries.. In *PODS'93.* ACM, 59–70.

[8] R. Chirkova. 2012. Equivalence and Minimization of Conjunctive Queries under Combined Semantics.. In *ICDT'12.* OpenProceedings.org, 262–273.

[9] R. Chirkova. 2014. Combined-Semantics Equivalence and Minimization of Conjunctive Queries. *TCJ* 57, 5 (2014), 775–795.

[10] R. Chirkova. 2016. Combined-Semantics Equivalence of Conjunctive Queries: Decidability and Tractability Results. *JCSS* 82, 3 (2016), 395–465.

[11] S. Chu, A. Cheung, and D. Suciu. 2018. *Axiomatic Foundations and Algorithms for Deciding Semantic Equivalences of SQL Queries.* Technical Report. arXiv.

[12] E.F. Codd. 1970. A Relational Model of Data for Large Shared Data Banks. *CACM* 13, 6 (1970), 377–387.

[13] E.F. Codd. 1972. Relational Completeness of Data Base Sublanguages. *DS* (1972), 65–98.

[14] S. Cohen. 2006. Equivalence of Queries Combining Set and Bag-Set Semantics.. In *PODS'06.* ACM, 70–79.

[15] S. Cohen. 2009. Equivalence of Queries that are Sensitive to Multiplicities. *PVLDB* 18, 3 (2009), 765–785.

[16] M. Console, P. Guagliardo, and L. Libkin. 2017. On Querying Incomplete Information in Databases Under Bag Semantics.. In *IJCAI'17.* 993–999.

[17] S. Grumbach and T. Milo. 1996. Towards Tractable Algebras for Bags. *JCSS* 52, 3 (1996), 570–588.

[18] S. Harris, A. Seaborne, and E. Prud´hommeaux. 2013. SPARQL 1.1 query language. W3C Recommendation.

[19] A. Hernich and P.G. Kolaitis. 2017. Foundations of Information Integration under Bag Semantics.. In *LICS'17.* ACM, 1–12.

[20] Y.E. Ioannidis and R. Ramakrishnan. 1995. Containment of Conjunctive Queries: Beyond Relations as Sets. *TODS* 20, 3 (1995), 288–324.

[21] T.S. Jayram, P.G. Kolaitis, and E. Vee. 2006. The Containment Problem for Real Conjunctive Queries with Inequalities.. In *PODS'06.* ACM, 80–89.

[22] M.A. Khamis, H.Q. Ngo, and A. Rudra. 2016. FAQ: Questions Asked Frequently.. In *PODS'16.* ACM, 13–28.

[23] A. Klug. 1988. On Conjunctive Queries Containing Inequalities. *JACM* 35, 1 (1988), 146–160.

[24] P.G. Kolaitis. 2013. The Query Containment Problem: Set Semantics vs. Bag Semantics.. In *AMW'13 (CEUR-WS 1949).*

[25] G. Konstantinidis and J.L. Ambite. 2011. Scalable Query Rewriting: A Graph-Based Approach.. In *SIGMOD'11.* ACM, 97–108.

[26] S. Kopparty and B. Rossman. 2011. The Homomorphism Domination Exponent. *EJC* 32, 7 (2011), 1097–1114.

[27] A.Y. Levy, A.O. Mendelzon, Y. Sagiv, and D. Srivastava. 1995. Answering Queries Using Views.. In *PODS'95.* ACM, 95–104.

[28] Y. Matiyasevich. 1993. *Hilbert's 10th Problem.* MIT Press.

[29] G.L. Nemhauser and L.A. Wolsey. 1988. *Integer and Combinatorial Optimization.* Wiley.

[30] C. Nikolaou, E.V. Kostylev, G. Konstantinidis, M. Kaminski, B.C. Grau, and I. Horrocks. 2017. The Bag Semantics of Ontology-Based Data Access.. In *IJCAI'17.* 1224–1230.

[31] C. Nikolaou, E.V. Kostylev, G. Konstantinidis, M. Kaminski, B.C. Grau, and I. Horrocks. 2019. Foundations of Ontology-based Data Access under Bag Semantics. *AI* 274 (2019), 91–132.

[32] A. Schrijver. 1986. *Theory of Linear and Integer Programming.* Wiley.

[33] L.J. Stockmeyer. 1976. The Polynomial-Time Hierarchy. *TCS* 3, 1 (1976), 1–22.

[34] J.D. Ullman. 2000. Information Integration Using Logical Views. *TCS* 239, 2 (2000), 189–210.

On Functional Aggregate Queries with Additive Inequalities

Mahmoud Abo Khamis
relationalAI

Ryan R. Curtin
relationalAI

Benjamin Moseley
Carnegie Mellon University

Hung Q. Ngo
relationalAI

XuanLong Nguyen
University of Michigan

Dan Olteanu
University of Oxford

Maximilian Schleich
University of Oxford

ABSTRACT

Motivated by fundamental applications in databases and relational machine learning, we formulate and study the problem of answering *functional aggregate queries* (FAQ) in which some of the input factors are defined by a collection of additive inequalities between variables. We refer to these queries as FAQ-AI for short.

To answer FAQ-AI in the Boolean semiring, we define *relaxed* tree decompositions and *relaxed* submodular and fractional hypertree width parameters. We show that an extension of the InsideOut algorithm using Chazelle's geometric data structure for solving the semigroup range search problem can answer Boolean FAQ-AI in time given by these new width parameters. This new algorithm achieves lower complexity than known solutions for FAQ-AI. It also recovers some known results in database query answering.

Our second contribution is a relaxation of the set of polymatroids that gives rise to the *counting* version of the submodular width, denoted by #subw. This new width is sandwiched between the submodular and the fractional hypertree widths. Any FAQ and FAQ-AI over one semiring can be answered in time proportional to #subw and respectively to the relaxed version of #subw.

We present three applications of our FAQ-AI framework to relational machine learning: k-means clustering, training linear support vector machines, and training models using non-polynomial loss. These optimization problems can be solved over a database asymptotically faster than computing the join of the database relations.

PODS'19, June 30-July 5, 2019, Amsterdam, Netherlands

ACM ISBN 978-1-4503-6227-6/19/06...$15.00
https://doi.org/10.1145/3294052.3319694

KEYWORDS

functional aggregate queries; inequality joins; in-database machine learning; non-polynomial loss

ACM Reference Format:
Mahmoud Abo Khamis, Ryan R. Curtin, Benjamin Moseley, Hung Q. Ngo, XuanLong Nguyen, Dan Olteanu, and Maximilian Schleich. 2019. On Functional Aggregate Queries with Additive Inequalities. In *38th ACM SIGMOD-SIGACT-SIGAI Symposium on Principles of Database Systems (PODS'19), June 30-July 5, 2019, Amsterdam, Netherlands.* ACM, New York, NY, USA, 18 pages. https://doi.org/10.1145/3294052.3319694

1 INTRODUCTION

We consider the problem of computing functional aggregate queries with inequality joins, or FAQ-AI queries for short. This is a fundamental computational problem that goes beyond databases: core computation for supervised and unsupervised machine learning can be formulated in FAQ-AI.

Inequalities occur naturally in scenarios involving temporal and spatial relationships between objects in databases. In a retail scenario (e.g., TPC-H), we would like to compute the revenue generated by a customer's orders whose dates closely precede the ship dates of their lineitems. In streaming scenarios, we would like to detect patterns of events whose time stamps follow a particular order [13]. In spatial data management scenarios, we would like to retrieve objects whose coordinates are within a multi-dimensional range or in close proximity of other objects [25]. The evaluation of Core XPath queries over XML documents amounts to the evaluation of conjunctive queries with inequalities expressing tree relationships in the pre/post plane [16].

1.1 Motivating examples

A key insight of this paper is that the efficient computation of inequality joins can reduce the computational complexity of supervised and unsupervised machine learning.

Example 1.1. The k-means algorithm divides the input dataset G into k clusters of similar data points [19]. Each cluster G_i has a mean $\boldsymbol{\mu}_i \in \mathbb{R}^n$, which is chosen according to the following optimization (similarity is defined here with respect to the ℓ_2 norm):

$$\min_{(G_1,\dots,G_k)} \sum_{i=1}^{k} \sum_{\boldsymbol{x}\in G_i} \|\boldsymbol{x} - \boldsymbol{\mu}_i\|_2^2 . \tag{1}$$

Let $\mu_{i,\ell}$ be the ℓ'th component of mean vector $\boldsymbol{\mu}_i$. For a data point $\boldsymbol{x} \in G$, the function c_{ij} computes the difference between the squares of the ℓ_2-distances from $\boldsymbol{x}$ to $\boldsymbol{\mu}_i$ and from $\boldsymbol{x}$ to $\boldsymbol{\mu}_j$:

$$c_{ij}(\boldsymbol{x}) = \sum_{\ell\in[n]} [\mu_{i,\ell}^2 - 2x_\ell(\mu_{i,\ell} - \mu_{j,\ell}) - \mu_{j,\ell}^2].$$

A data point $\boldsymbol{x} \in G$ is closest to mean $\boldsymbol{\mu}_i$ from the set of k means iff $\forall j \in [k] : c_{ij}(\boldsymbol{x}) \le 0$.

To compute the mean vector $\boldsymbol{\mu}_i$, we need to compute the sum of values for each dimension $\ell \in [n]$ over $G_i : \sum_{\boldsymbol{x}\in G_i} x_\ell$. If the dataset G is the join of database relations $(R_p)_{p\in[m]}$ over schemas $S_p \subseteq [n], \forall p \in [m]$, we can formulate this sum computation as a datalog-like query with aggregates [17]:

$$Q_1^{(i,\ell)}\left(\sum x_\ell\right) \leftarrow \left(\bigwedge_{p\in[m]} R_p(\boldsymbol{x}_{S_p})\right) \wedge \left(\bigwedge_{j\in[k]} c_{ij}(\boldsymbol{x}) \le 0\right).$$

The above notation means that the answer to query $Q_1^{(i,\ell)}$ is the sum of x_ℓ over all tuples $\boldsymbol{x}$ satisfying the conjunction on the right-hand side. Section 4 gives further queries necessary to compute the k-means. As we show in this paper, such queries with aggregates and inequalities can be computed asymptotically faster than the join defining G. □

Simple queries can already highlight the limitations of current evaluation techniques, as shown next.

Example 1.2. State-of-the-art techniques take time $O(N^2)$ to compute the following query over relations of size $\le N$:

$$Q_2() \leftarrow R(a,b) \wedge S(b,c) \wedge T(c,d) \wedge a \le d,$$

Examples 3.9 and 3.19 show how to compute Q_2 and its counting version in time $O(N^{1.5}\log N)$ using the techniques introduced in this paper. □

1.2 The FAQ-AI problem

One way to answer the above queries is to view them as *functional aggregate queries* (FAQ) [5] formulated in sum-product form over some semiring. We therefore briefly introduce FAQ over a single semiring.

First we establish notation. For any positive integer n, let $\mathcal{V} = [n]$. For $i \in \mathcal{V}$, let X_i denote a variable/attribute, and x_i denote a value in the discrete domain $\mathsf{Dom}(X_i)$ of X_i. For any $K \subseteq \mathcal{V}$, define $\boldsymbol{X}_K = (X_i)_{i\in K}$, $\boldsymbol{x}_K = (x_i)_{i\in K} \in \prod_{i\in K} \mathsf{Dom}(X_i)$. That is, $\boldsymbol{X}_K$ is a tuple of variables and $\boldsymbol{x}_K$ is a tuple of values for these variables.

Let a semiring $(\boldsymbol{D}, \oplus, \otimes, \boldsymbol{0}, \boldsymbol{1})$ and a **multi**-hypergraph $\mathcal{H} = (\mathcal{V} = [n], \mathcal{E})$. To each edge $K \in \mathcal{E}$ we associate a function $R_K : \prod_{v\in K} \mathsf{Dom}(X_i) \to \boldsymbol{D}$ called *factor*. An FAQ query over one semiring with free variables $F \subseteq \mathcal{V}$ has the form:

$$Q(\boldsymbol{x}_F) = \bigoplus_{\boldsymbol{x}_{\mathcal{V}\setminus F}\in\prod_{i\in\mathcal{V}\setminus F}\mathsf{Dom}(X_i)} \bigotimes_{K\in\mathcal{E}} R_K(\boldsymbol{x}_K). \tag{2}$$

Under the Boolean semiring $(\{\text{true}, \text{false}\}, \vee, \wedge, \text{false}, \text{true})$, the query (2) becomes a conjunctive query: The factors R_K represent input relations, where $R_K(\boldsymbol{x}_K) = \text{true}$ iff $\boldsymbol{x}_K \in R_K$, with some notational overloading. Under the sum-product semiring, the query (2) counts the number of tuples in the join result for each tuple $\boldsymbol{x}_F$, where the factors R_k are indicator functions $R_K(\boldsymbol{x}_K) = \boldsymbol{1}_{\boldsymbol{x}_K\in R_K}$. To aggregate over some input variable, say X_k, we can designate an identity factor $R_k(x_k) = x_k$.

Throughout the paper, we assume the query size to be a constant and state runtimes in data complexity. It is known [5] that over an arbitrary semiring, the query (2) can be answered in time $O(N^{\mathsf{fhtw}(Q)} \cdot \log N)$, where fhtw denotes the *fractional hypertree width* of the query and Q has no free variables [15]. If Q has free variables, fhtw-width becomes FAQ-width instead [5]. Here N is the size of the largest factor R_K. Over the Boolean semiring, the time can be lowered to $\tilde{O}(N^{\mathsf{subw}(Q)})$ [7], where subw is the *submodular width* [26] and $\tilde{O}$ hides a polylogarithmic factor in N.

Motivated by the examples in Section 1.1, we formulate a class of FAQ queries called FAQ-AI: the hyperedge multiset $\mathcal{E}$ is partitioned into two multisets $\mathcal{E} = \mathcal{E}_s \cup \mathcal{E}_\ell$, where s stands for "skeleton" and ℓ stands for "ligament". The input to our class of queries consists of the following: (1) to each hyperedge $K \in \mathcal{E}_s$, there corresponds a function $R_K : \prod_{i\in K} \mathsf{Dom}(X_i) \to \boldsymbol{D}$, as in the FAQ case; (2) to each hyperedge $S \in \mathcal{E}_\ell$, there corresponds $|S|$ functions $\theta_v^S : \mathsf{Dom}(X_v) \to \mathbb{R}$, one for every variable $v \in S$. The query we want to compute is the following:

$$Q(\boldsymbol{x}_F) = \bigoplus_{\boldsymbol{x}_{\mathcal{V}\setminus F}} \left(\bigotimes_{K\in\mathcal{E}_s} R_K(\boldsymbol{x}_K)\right) \otimes \left(\bigotimes_{S\in\mathcal{E}_\ell} \boldsymbol{1}_{\sum_{v\in S}\theta_v^S(x_v)\le 0}\right). \tag{3}$$

The summation $\bigoplus$ is over tuples $\boldsymbol{x}_{\mathcal{V}\setminus F} \in \prod_{i\in\mathcal{V}\setminus F} \mathsf{Dom}(X_i)$. The notation $\boldsymbol{1}_A$ denotes the indicator function of the event A in the semiring $(\boldsymbol{D}, \oplus, \otimes, \boldsymbol{0}, \boldsymbol{1})$: $\boldsymbol{1}_A = \boldsymbol{1}$ if A holds, and $\boldsymbol{0}$ otherwise. The (uni-variate) functions θ_v^S can be user-defined functions, e.g., $\theta_1^S(x_1) = x_1^2/2$, or binary predicates with one key in $\mathsf{Dom}(X_v)$ and a numeric value, e.g., a table `salary(employee_id, salary_value)` where `employee_id` is a key. The only requirement we impose is that, given x, the value $\theta^S_v(x)$ can be accessed/computed in $O(1)$-time.

If $\mathcal{E}_\ell = \emptyset$, then we get back the FAQ formulation (2).

Example 1.3. The queries in Section 1.1 are instances of (3):

$$Q_1^{(i,\ell)}() = \bigoplus_{\boldsymbol{x}_{[n]}} x_\ell \otimes \left(\bigotimes_{p\in[m]} R_p(\boldsymbol{x}_{S_p}) \right) \otimes \left(\bigotimes_{j\in[k]} \mathbf{1}_{c_{ij}(\boldsymbol{x})\leq 0} \right), \tag{4}$$

$$Q_2() = \bigoplus_{\boldsymbol{x}_{[4]}} R(x_1, x_2) \otimes S(x_2, x_3) \otimes T(x_3, x_4) \otimes \mathbf{1}_{x_1 - x_4 \leq 0}.$$

Q_1 is on the sum-product semiring. Q_2 can be on any semiring: Example 3.9 discusses the case of the Boolean semiring while Example 3.19 discusses the sum-product semiring. □

1.3 Our contributions

To answer FAQ queries of the form (2), currently there are two dominant width parameters: fractional hypertree width (fhtw [15]) and submodular width (subw [26]).[1] It is known that subw ≤ fhtw for any query, and in the Boolean semiring we can answer (2) in $\tilde{O}(N^{\text{subw}})$-time [7, 26]. For non-Boolean semirings, the best known algorithm, called InsideOut [5, 6], evaluates (2) in time $O(N^{\text{fhtw}} \log N)$. For queries with free variables, fhtw is replaced by the more general notion of FAQ-width (faqw) [5]; however, for brevity we discuss the non-free variable case here.

Following [6], both width parameters subw and fhtw can be defined via two constraint sets: the first is the set TD of all tree decompositions of the query hypergraph $\mathcal{H}$, and the second is the set of polymatroids Γ_n on n vertices of $\mathcal{H}$. The widths subw and fhtw are then defined as maximin or minimax optimization problems on the domain pair TD and Γ_n, subject to "edge domination" constraints for Γ_n. Section 2 presents these notions and other related preliminary concepts in detail.

Our contributions include the following:

Answering FAQ-AI *over Boolean semiring.* On the Boolean semiring, one way to answer query (3) is to apply the PANDA algorithm [26], using edge domination constraints on $\mathcal{E}_s$ and the set TD of *all* tree decompositions of $\mathcal{H} = (\mathcal{V}, \mathcal{E} = \mathcal{E}_s \cup \mathcal{E}_\ell)$. However, we can do better. In Section 3.2 we define a new notion of tree decomposition: *relaxed tree decomposition*, in which the hyperedges in $\mathcal{E}_\ell$ only have to be covered by adjacent TD bags. Then, we present a variant of the InsideOut algorithm running on these relaxed TDs, using Chazelle's classic geometric data structure [10] for solving the semigroup range search problem. We show that our InsideOut variant meets the "relaxed fhtw" runtime, which is the analog of fhtw on relaxed TD. The PANDA algorithm can use the InsideOut variant as a blackbox to meet the "relaxed subw" runtime. The relaxed widths are smaller than the non-relaxed counterparts, and are strictly smaller for some classes of queries, which means our algorithms yield asymptotic improvements over existing ones.

Answering FAQ *over an arbitrary semiring.* Next, to prepare the stage for answering FAQ-AI over an arbitrary semiring, in Section 3.3 we revisit FAQ over a non-Boolean semiring, where **no** known algorithm can achieve the subw-runtime. Here, we relax the set Γ_n of polymatroids to a superset Γ'_n of *relaxed polymatroids.* Then, by adapting the subw definition to relaxed polymatroids, we obtain a new width parameter called "sharp submodular width" (#subw). We show how a variant of PANDA, called #PANDA, can achieve a runtime of $\tilde{O}(N^{\#\text{subw}})$ for evaluating FAQ over an arbitrary semiring. We prove that subw ≤ #subw ≤ fhtw, and that there are classes of queries for which #subw is unboundedly smaller than fhtw.

Answering FAQ-AI *over an arbitrary semiring.* Getting back to FAQ-AI, we apply the #subw result under both relaxations: relaxed TD and relaxed polymatroids, to obtain a new width parameter called the relaxed #subw. We show that the new variants of PANDA and InsideOut can achieve the relaxed #subw runtime. We also show that there are queries for which relaxed #subw is essentially the best we can hope for, modulo k-sum-hardness.

Applications in relational Machine Learning. Equipped with the algorithms for answering FAQ-AI, in Section 4 we return to relational machine learning applications over datasets defined by feature extraction queries over relational databases. We show how one can train linear SVM, k-means, and ML models using Huber/hinge loss functions without completely materializing the output of the feature extraction queries. In particular, this shows that for these important classes of ML models, one can sometimes train models in time sub-linear in the training dataset size.

1.4 Related work

The full version of the paper [1] revisits two prior results on the evaluation of queries with inequalities through FAQ-AI lenses: Core XPath queries over XML documents and inequality joins over tuple-independent probabilistic databases [30]. Throughout the paper, we contrast our new width notions with fhtw and subw and our new algorithm #PANDA with the state-of-the-art algorithms PANDA and InsideOut for FAQ and FAQ-AI queries.

A seminal work considers the containment and minimization problem for queries with inequalities [22]. Efficient evaluation of such queries continues to receive good attention

[1]Section 2.1 overviews other notions of widths.

in the database community [21]. There is a bulk of work on queries with *dis*equalities (not-equal), e.g., [4, 23], which are at times referred to as inequalities. Queries with disequalities are a proper subclass of FAQ-AI (since $x \neq y$ can be represented as $x < y \vee x > y$). Prior works [4, 23] present several results for this proper subclass that are stronger than our general results for FAQ-AI in this work. In particular, for queries with disequalities it suffices to consider tree decompositions only for "skeleton" edges (ignoring "ligament" edges which -in this case- are the disequalities) [4, 23], whereas for the more general FAQ-AI we need to consider "relaxed" tree decompositions (see Def. 3.3).

Section 4 reviews relevant works on machine learning.

2 PRELIMINARIES

We assume without loss of generality in the paper that semiring operations $\oplus$ and $\otimes$ can be performed in $O(1)$-time. (When the assumption does not hold, for the set semiring for instance, we can multiply the claimed runtime with the real operation's runtime.) All missing proofs and details can be found in the full version of the paper [1].

2.1 Tree decompositions and polymatroids

We briefly define tree decompositions, fhtw and subw parameters. We refer the reader to the recent survey by Gottlob et al. [14] for more details and historical contexts. In what follows, the hypergraph $\mathcal{H}$ should be thought of as the hypergraph of the input query, although the notions of tree decomposition and width parameters are defined independently of queries.

A *tree decomposition* of a hypergraph $\mathcal{H} = (\mathcal{V}, \mathcal{E})$ is a pair (T, χ), where T is a tree and $\chi : V(T) \to 2^{\mathcal{V}}$ maps each node t of the tree to a subset $\chi(t)$ of vertices such that

(1) every hyperedge $S \in \mathcal{E}$ is a subset of some $\chi(t)$, $t \in V(T)$ (i.e. every edge is covered by some bag),
(2) for every vertex $v \in \mathcal{V}$, the set $\{t \mid v \in \chi(t)\}$ is a non-empty (connected) sub-tree of T. This is called the *running intersection property.*

The sets $\chi(t)$ are called the *bags* of the tree decomposition.

Let $\text{TD}(\mathcal{H})$ denote the set of all tree decompositions of $\mathcal{H}$. When $\mathcal{H}$ is clear from context, we use TD for brevity.

To define width parameters, we use the polymatroid characterization from Abo Khamis et al. [7]. A function $f : 2^{\mathcal{V}} \to \mathbb{R}_+$ is called a (non-negative) *set function* on $\mathcal{V}$. A set function f on $\mathcal{V}$ is *modular* if $f(S) = \sum_{v \in S} f(\{v\})$ for all $S \subseteq \mathcal{V}$, is *monotone* if $f(X) \leq f(Y)$ whenever $X \subseteq Y$, and is *submodular* if $f(X \cup Y) + f(X \cap Y) \leq f(X) + f(Y)$ for all $X, Y \subseteq \mathcal{V}$. A monotone, submodular set function $h : 2^{\mathcal{V}} \to \mathbb{R}_+$ with $h(\emptyset) = 0$ is called a *polymatroid.* Let Γ_n denote the set of all polymatroids on $\mathcal{V} = [n]$.

Given $\mathcal{H}$, define the set of *edge dominated* set functions:

$$\text{ED} := \{h \mid h : 2^{\mathcal{V}} \to \mathbb{R}_+, h(S) \leq 1, \forall S \in \mathcal{E}\}. \quad (5)$$

With this, we define the submodular width and fractional hypertree width of a given hypergraph $\mathcal{H}$:

$$\text{fhtw}(\mathcal{H}) := \min_{(T,\chi)\in\text{TD}} \max_{h\in\text{ED}\cap\Gamma_n} \max_{t\in V(T)} h(\chi(t)), \quad (6)$$

$$\text{subw}(\mathcal{H}) := \max_{h\in\text{ED}\cap\Gamma_n} \min_{(T,\chi)\in\text{TD}} \max_{t\in V(T)} h(\chi(t)). \quad (7)$$

It is known [26] that $\text{subw}(\mathcal{H}) \leq \text{fhtw}(\mathcal{H})$, and there are classes of hypergraphs with bounded subw and unbounded fhtw. Furthermore, fhtw is strictly less than other width notions such as (generalized) hypertree width and tree width.

Remark 2.1. Prior to Abo Khamis et al. [7], the commonly used definition of $\text{fhtw}(\mathcal{H})$ is

$$\text{fhtw}(\mathcal{H}) := \min_{(T,\chi)\in\text{TD}} \max_{t\in V(T)} \rho^*_{\mathcal{E}}(\chi(t)),$$

where $\rho^*_{\mathcal{E}}(B)$ is the fractional edge cover number of a vertex set B using the hyperedge set $\mathcal{E}$. It is straightforward to show, using linear programming duality [7], that

$$\max_{t\in V(T)} \max_{h\in\text{ED}\cap\Gamma_n} h(\chi(t)) = \max_{t\in V(T)} \rho^*_{\mathcal{E}}(\chi(t)), \quad (8)$$

proving the equivalence of the two definitions. However, the characterization (6) has two primary advantages: (i) it exposes the minimax / maximin duality between fhtw and subw, and more importantly (ii) it makes it completely straightforward to relax the definitions by replacing the $\text{ED} \cap \Gamma_n$ constraints by other applicable constraints, as shall be shown in later sections. □

Definition 2.2 (F-connex tree decomposition [8, 31]). Given a hypergraph $\mathcal{H} = (\mathcal{V}, \mathcal{E})$ and a set $F \subseteq \mathcal{V}$, a tree decomposition (T, χ) of $\mathcal{H}$ is *F-connex* if $F = \emptyset$ or the following holds: There is a nonempty subset $V' \subseteq V(T)$ that forms a connected subtree of T and satisfies $\bigcup_{t\in V'} \chi(t) = F$.

We use TD_F to denote the set of all F-connex tree decompositions of $\mathcal{H}$. (Note that when $F = \emptyset$, $\text{TD}_F = \text{TD}$.)

2.2 InsideOut and PANDA

To answer the FAQ query (2), we need a model for the representation of the input factors R_K. The support of the function R_K is the set of tuples $\boldsymbol{x}_K$ such that $R(\boldsymbol{x}_K) \neq \mathbf{0}$. We use $|R_K|$ to denote the size of its support. For example, if R_K represents an input relation, then $|R_K|$ is the number of tuples in R_K. In practice, there often are factors with infinite support, e.g., R_K represents a built-in function in a database, an arithmetic operator, or a comparison operator as in (3). To deal with this more general setting, the edge set $\mathcal{E}$ is partitioned into two sets $\mathcal{E} = \mathcal{E}_{\not\infty} \cup \mathcal{E}_\infty$, where $|R_K|$ is finite for all $K \in \mathcal{E}_{\not\infty}$ and $|R_K| = \infty$ for all $K \in \mathcal{E}_\infty$. For simplicity, we often state runtimes of algorithms in terms of the "input size" $N := \max_{K \in \mathcal{E}_{\not\infty}} |R_K|$. Moreover, we use $|Q|$ to denote the output size of Q. We always assume that $\bigcup_{S \in \mathcal{E}_{\not\infty}} S = \mathcal{V}$; otherwise the output size $|Q|$ could be infinite.

InsideOut *[5, 6]*. To answer (2), the InsideOut algorithm works by eliminating variables, along with an idea called the "indicator projection". Its runtime is described by the FAQ-*width* of the query, a slight generalization of fhtw. In the context of one semiring, we can define faqw(Q) by applying Definition (6) over a restricted set of tree decompositions and edge dominated polymatroids. In particular, let $F \subseteq \mathcal{V}$ denote the set of free variables in (2), and recall TD_F from Definition 2.2. Then,

$$\text{ED}_{\not\infty} := \{h \mid h : 2^{\mathcal{V}} \to \mathbb{R}_+, h(S) \le 1, \forall S \in \mathcal{E}_{\not\infty}\}, \quad (9)$$

$$\text{faqw}(Q) := \min_{(T,\chi) \in \text{TD}_F} \max_{h \in \text{ED}_{\not\infty} \cap \Gamma_n} \max_{t \in V(T)} h(\chi(t)) \quad (10)$$

$$(\text{remark 2.1}) = \min_{(T,\chi) \in \text{TD}_F} \max_{t \in V(T)} \rho^*_{\mathcal{E}_{\not\infty}}(\chi(t)) \quad (11)$$

Note that faqw(Q) = fhtw($\mathcal{H}$) when $F = \emptyset$ and $\mathcal{E}_\infty = \emptyset$ (i.e. $\mathcal{E} = \mathcal{E}_{\not\infty}$). A simple result from Abo Khamis et al. [5] is the following: (Recall that throughout the paper we assume the query size to be a constant and state runtimes in data complexity.)

Proposition 2.3. InsideOut *answers query* (2) *in time* $O(N^{\text{faqw}(Q)} \cdot \log N + |Q|)$.

To solve the FAQ-AI (3), we can apply Proposition 2.3 with $\mathcal{E}_\infty \supseteq \mathcal{E}_\ell$ (because all ligament factors are infinite). But this is suboptimal—later, we show a new InsideOut variant that is polynomially better.

PANDA *[7]*. In case of the Boolean semiring, i.e., when the FAQ query (2) is of the form

$$Q(\boldsymbol{x}_F) = \bigvee_{\boldsymbol{x}_{\mathcal{V} \setminus F} \in \prod_{i \in \mathcal{V} \setminus F} \text{Dom}(X_i)} \bigwedge_{K \in \mathcal{E}} R_K(\boldsymbol{x}_K), \quad (12)$$

we can do much better than Proposition 2.3. When $F = \emptyset$, Marx [26] showed that (12) can be answered in time $\tilde{O}(N^{O(\text{subw}(Q))})$. The PANDA algorithm [7] generalizes Marx's result to deal with general degree constraints, and to meet precisely the $\tilde{O}(N^{\text{subw}(Q)})$-runtime. In fact, PANDA works with queries such as (12) with free variables as well. In the context of this paper, we can define the following notion of *submodular* FAQ-*width* in a very natural way:

$$\text{smfw}(Q) := \max_{h \in \text{ED}_{\not\infty} \cap \Gamma_n} \min_{(T,\chi) \in \text{TD}_F} \max_{t \in V(T)} h(\chi(t)). \quad (13)$$

Then, the results from Abo Khamis et al. [7] imply:

Proposition 2.4. PANDA *answers query* (12) *in time* $\tilde{O}(N^{\text{smfw}(Q)} + |Q|)$.

These results only work for the Boolean semiring. Section 3 introduces a variant of PANDA, called #PANDA, that also works for non-Boolean semirings.

2.3 Semigroup range searching

Orthogonal range counting (and searching) is a classic and ubiquitous problem in computational geometry [12]: given a set S of N points in a d-dimensional space, build a data structure that, given any d-dimensional rectangle, can efficiently return the number of enclosed points. More generally, there is the semigroup range searching problem [10], where each point $\boldsymbol{p} \in S$ of the N input points also has a weight $w(\boldsymbol{p}) \in G$, where $(G, \oplus)$ is a *semigroup*.[2] The problem is: given a d-dimensional rectangle R, compute $\bigoplus_{\boldsymbol{p} \in S \cap R} w(\boldsymbol{p})$.

Classic results by Chazelle [10] show that there are data structures for semigroup range searching which can be constructed in time $O(N \log^{d-1} N)$, and answer rectangular queries in $O(\log^{d-1} N)$-time. Also, this is almost the best we can hope for [11]. There are more recent improvements to Chazelle's result (see, e.g., Chan et al. [9]), but they are minor (at most a log factor), as the original results were already very close to matching the lower bound.

Most of these range search/counting problems can be reduced to the dominance range searching problem (on semigroups), where the query is represented by a point $\boldsymbol{q}$, and the objective is to return $\bigoplus_{\boldsymbol{q} \le \boldsymbol{p}, \boldsymbol{p} \in S} w(\boldsymbol{p})$. Here, $\le$ denotes the "dominance" relation (coordinate-wise $\le$). We can think of $\boldsymbol{q}$ as the lower-corner of an infinite rectangle query.

3 RELAXED TREE DECOMPOSITIONS AND RELAXED POLYMATROIDS

3.1 Connection to a geometric data structure

We always assume that $\bigcup_{S \in \mathcal{E}_s} S = \mathcal{V}$; otherwise the output size $|Q|$ could be infinite. We start with a special case of (3) in which the skeleton part $\mathcal{E}_s$ contains only *two* hyperedges U and L. Consider the aggregate query of the form

$$Q(\boldsymbol{x}_F) = \bigoplus_{\boldsymbol{x}_{\mathcal{V} \setminus F}} \Phi_1(\boldsymbol{x}_U) \otimes \Phi_2(\boldsymbol{x}_L) \otimes \left(\bigotimes_{S \in \mathcal{E}_\ell} \mathbf{1}_{\sum_{v \in S} \theta^S_v(x_v) \le 0} \right), \quad (14)$$

where Φ_1 and Φ_2 are two input functions/relations over variable sets U and L, respectively. We prove the following very simple but important lemma:

Lemma 3.1. *Let* $N = \max\{|\Phi_1|, |\Phi_2|\}$, *and* $k = |\mathcal{E}_\ell|$, *then when* $F \subseteq U$, *query* (14) *can be answered in time* $O(N \cdot (\log N)^{\max(k-1,1)})$.

Proof. If there is a hyperedge $S \in \mathcal{E}_\ell$ for which $S \subseteq U$, then in a $O(N \log N)$-time pre-processing step we can "absorb" the factor $\mathbf{1}_{\sum_{v \in S} \theta^S_v(x_v) \le 0}$ into the factor Φ_1, by replacing $\Phi_1(\boldsymbol{x}_U)$ with $\Phi_1(\boldsymbol{x}_U) \otimes \mathbf{1}_{\sum_{v \in S} \theta^S_v(x_v) \le 0}$. A similar absorption

[2] In a semigroup we can add two elements using $\oplus$, but there is no additive inverse.

can be done with $S \subseteq L$. Hence, without loss of generality we can assume that $S \not\subseteq L$ and $S \not\subseteq U$ for all $S \in \mathcal{E}_\ell$. Furthermore, we only need to show that we can compute (14) for $F = U$, because after $Q(\boldsymbol{x}_U)$ is computed, we can marginalize away variables $\boldsymbol{x}_{U \setminus F}$ in $O(N \log N)$-time.

Abusing notation somewhat, for each $S \in \mathcal{E}_\ell$ and each $T \subseteq S$, define the function $\theta_T^S : \prod_{v \in T} \text{Dom}(X_v) \to \mathbb{R}$ by

$$\theta_T^S(\boldsymbol{x}_T) := \sum_{v \in T} \theta_v^S(x_v). \tag{15}$$

Fix a tuple $\boldsymbol{x}_U$ such that $\Phi_1(\boldsymbol{x}_U) \neq \boldsymbol{0}$. A tuple $\boldsymbol{x}_L$ is said to be $\boldsymbol{x}_U$*-adjacent* if $\pi_{U \cap L} \boldsymbol{x}_U = \pi_{U \cap L} \boldsymbol{x}_L$. We show how to compute the following sum in poly-logarithmic time:

$$\bigoplus_{\boldsymbol{x}_{L \setminus U}} \Phi_1(\boldsymbol{x}_U) \otimes \Phi_2(\boldsymbol{x}_L) \otimes \left(\bigotimes_{S \in \mathcal{E}_\ell} \boldsymbol{1}_{\sum_{v \in S} \theta_v^S(x_v) \leq 0} \right) = \tag{16}$$

$$\Phi_1(\boldsymbol{x}_U) \otimes \bigoplus_{\boldsymbol{x}_{L \setminus U}} \Phi_2(\boldsymbol{x}_L) \otimes \left(\bigotimes_{S \in \mathcal{E}_\ell} \boldsymbol{1}_{\theta_{S \cap U}^S(\boldsymbol{x}_{S \cap U}) \leq -\theta_{S \setminus U}^S(\boldsymbol{x}_{S \setminus U})} \right). \tag{17}$$

where the inner sum ranges over only tuples $\boldsymbol{x}_L$ which are $\boldsymbol{x}_U$-adjacent; non-adjacent tuples contribute $\boldsymbol{0}$.

Now, for the fixed $\boldsymbol{x}_U$ and for each $\boldsymbol{x}_L$ define the following k-dimensional points:

$$\boldsymbol{q}(\boldsymbol{x}_U) = (q_S(\boldsymbol{x}_U))_{S \in \mathcal{E}_\ell} \quad \text{where} \quad q_S(\boldsymbol{x}_U) := \theta_{S \cap U}^S(\boldsymbol{x}_{S \cap U}),$$

$$\boldsymbol{p}(\boldsymbol{x}_L) = (p_S(\boldsymbol{x}_L))_{S \in \mathcal{E}_\ell} \quad \text{where} \quad p_S(\boldsymbol{x}_L) := -\theta_{S \setminus U}^S(\boldsymbol{x}_{S \setminus U}).$$

We write $\boldsymbol{q}(\boldsymbol{x}_U) \leq \boldsymbol{p}(\boldsymbol{x}_L)$ to say that $\boldsymbol{q}(\boldsymbol{x}_U)$ is dominated by $\boldsymbol{p}(\boldsymbol{x}_L)$ *coordinate-wise*: $q_S(\boldsymbol{x}_U) \leq p_S(\boldsymbol{x}_L) \ \forall \ S \in \mathcal{E}_\ell$. Assign to each point $\boldsymbol{p}(\boldsymbol{x}_L)$ a "weight" of $\Phi_2(\boldsymbol{x}_L)$. Now, taking (17),

$$\bigoplus_{\boldsymbol{x}_{L \setminus U}} \Phi_2(\boldsymbol{x}_L) \otimes \left(\bigotimes_{S \in \mathcal{E}_\ell} \boldsymbol{1}_{\theta_{S \cap U}^S(\boldsymbol{x}_{S \cap U}) \leq -\theta_{S \setminus U}^S(\boldsymbol{x}_{S \setminus U})} \right)$$

$$= \bigoplus_{\boldsymbol{x}_{L \setminus U}} \left(\bigotimes_{S \in \mathcal{E}_\ell} \boldsymbol{1}_{q_S(\boldsymbol{x}_U) \leq p_S(\boldsymbol{x}_L)} \right) \otimes \Phi_2(\boldsymbol{x}_L) \tag{18}$$

$$= \bigoplus_{\boldsymbol{x}_{L \setminus U}} \boldsymbol{1}_{\boldsymbol{q}(\boldsymbol{x}_U) \leq \boldsymbol{p}(\boldsymbol{x}_L)} \otimes \Phi_2(\boldsymbol{x}_L). \tag{19}$$

The expression thus computes, for a given "query point" $\boldsymbol{q}(\boldsymbol{x}_U)$, the weighted sum over all points $\boldsymbol{p}(\boldsymbol{x}_L)$ that dominate the query point. This is precisely the dominance range counting problem, which—modulo a $O(N(\log N)^{\max(k-1,1)})$-preprocessing step—can be solved in time $O((\log N)^{\max(k-1,1)})$ [10], as reviewed in Section 2.3.

To conclude the proof, note that (14) can be written as (assuming $F \subseteq U$ as is the case in Lemma 3.1)

$$Q(\boldsymbol{x}_F) = \bigoplus_{\boldsymbol{x}_{U \setminus F}} \underbrace{\bigoplus_{\boldsymbol{x}_{L \setminus U}} \Phi_1(\boldsymbol{x}_U) \otimes \Phi_2(\boldsymbol{x}_L) \otimes \left(\bigotimes_{S \in \mathcal{E}_\ell} \boldsymbol{1}_{\sum_{v \in S} \theta_v^S(x_v) \leq 0} \right)}_{\text{same as (16)}},$$

where the outer sum ranges over N tuples $\boldsymbol{x}_U$ in Φ_1. □

Example 3.2. Let R be a binary relation. Suppose we want to count the number of tuples satisfying $R(a,b) \wedge R(b,c) \wedge a < c$, then by setting $F = \emptyset$, $U = \{a,b\}$, $L = \{b,c\}$, it is easy to see that the problem can be reduced to the form (14) with $k = 1$, $\mathcal{E}_\ell = \{\{a,c\}\}$. We can thus compute this count in time $O(N \log N)$. □

3.2 Relaxed tree decompositions

Equipped with this basic case, we can now proceed to solve the general setting of (3). To this end, we define a new width parameter.

Definition 3.3 (Relaxed tree decomposition). Let $\mathcal{H} = (\mathcal{V}, \mathcal{E} = \mathcal{E}_s \cup \mathcal{E}_\ell)$ denote a multi-hypergraph whose edge multiset is partitioned into $\mathcal{E}_s$ and $\mathcal{E}_\ell$. A *relaxed* tree decomposition of $\mathcal{H}$ (with respect to the partition $\mathcal{E}_s \cup \mathcal{E}_\ell$) is a pair (T, χ), where $T = (V(T), E(T))$ is a tree, and $\chi : V(T) \to 2^{\mathcal{V}}$ satisfies the following properties:

- The running intersection property holds: for each node $v \in \mathcal{V}$ the set $\{t \in V(T) \mid v \in \chi(t)\}$ is a connected subtree in T.
- Every "skeleton" edge $S \in \mathcal{E}_s$ is covered by some bag $\chi(t), t \in V(T)$.
- Every "ligament" edge $S \in \mathcal{E}_\ell$ is covered by the union of two *adjacent* bags: $S \subseteq \chi(s) \cup \chi(t)$, where $\{s,t\} \in E(T)$.

Let $\mathsf{TD}^\ell(\mathcal{H})$ denote the set of all relaxed tree decompositions of $\mathcal{H}$ (with respect to the skeleton-ligament partition). When $\mathcal{H}$ is clear from context we use TD^ℓ for the sake of brevity. Given $F \subseteq \mathcal{V}$, let TD_F^ℓ denote the set of all relaxed F-connex tree decompositions of $\mathcal{H}$.

3.2.1 FAQ-AI on a general semiring. We use relaxed TDs in conjunction with Lemma 3.1 to answer FAQ-AI with a relaxed notion of faqw. In particular, the *relaxed* width parameters of $\mathcal{H}$ are defined in exactly the same way as the usual width parameters defined in Section 2, except we allow the TDs to range over relaxed ones.

Definition 3.4 (Relaxed faqw). Let Q be an FAQ-AI query (3), and $\mathcal{H} = (\mathcal{V}, \mathcal{E} = \mathcal{E}_s \cup \mathcal{E}_\ell)$ be its hypergraph. Furthermore, let $\mathcal{E}_{\not\infty} \subseteq \mathcal{E}_s$ denote the set of hyperedges $K \in \mathcal{E}$ for which $|R_K| < \infty$. Then, the *relaxed* FAQ*-width* of Q is defined by

$$\mathsf{faqw}_\ell(Q) := \min_{(T,\chi) \in \mathsf{TD}_F^\ell} \max_{h \in \mathsf{ED}_{\not\infty} \cap \Gamma_n} \max_{t \in V(T)} h(\chi(t)) \tag{20}$$

When $F = \emptyset$, faqw_ℓ collapses to fhtw_ℓ, in which case we define the *relaxed* fhtw for FAQ-AI Q *without* free variables:

$$\mathsf{fhtw}_\ell(Q) := \min_{(T,\chi) \in \mathsf{TD}_\emptyset^\ell} \max_{h \in \mathsf{ED}_{\not\infty} \cap \Gamma_n} \max_{t \in V(T)} h(\chi(t)) \tag{21}$$

A relaxed tree decomposition (T, χ) of Q is *optimal* if its width is equal to faqw_ℓ, i.e.,

$$\text{faqw}_\ell(Q) = \max_{h \in \text{ED}_{\not\infty} \cap \Gamma_n} \max_{t \in V(T)} h(\chi(t)).$$

Theorem 3.5. *Any* FAQ-AI *query Q of the form* (3) *on any semiring can be answered in time* $O(N^{\text{faqw}_\ell(Q)} \cdot (\log N)^{\max(k-1,1)} + |Q|)$*, where k is the maximum number of additive inequalities covered by a pair of adjacent bags in an optimal relaxed tree decomposition.*[3]

Proof. We first consider the case of no free variables because this case captures the key idea. Fix an optimal relaxed TD (T, χ). We first compute, for each bag $t \in V(T)$ of the tree decomposition, a factor $\Phi_t : \prod_{i \in \chi(t)} \text{Dom}(X_i) \to \boldsymbol{D}$ such that

$$Q() = \bigoplus_{x_{\mathcal{V}}} \left(\bigotimes_{K \in \mathcal{E}_s} R_K(\boldsymbol{x}_K) \right) \otimes \left(\bigotimes_{S \in \mathcal{E}_\ell} \mathbf{1}_{\sum_{v \in S} \theta_v^S(x_v) \leq 0} \right) \quad (22)$$

$$= \bigoplus_{x_{\mathcal{V}}} \left(\bigotimes_{t \in V(T)} \Phi_t(\boldsymbol{x}_{\chi(t)}) \right) \otimes \left(\bigotimes_{S \in \mathcal{E}_\ell} \mathbf{1}_{\sum_{v \in S} \theta_v^S(x_v) \leq 0} \right). \quad (23)$$

To define the factors Φ_t, we need the notion of *indicator projection* [5, 6]. For a given $K \in \mathcal{E}_s$ and $t \in V(T)$ such that $J := K \cap \chi(t) \neq \emptyset$, the indicator projection of R_K onto the bag $\chi(t)$ is a function $\pi_{t,K} : \prod_{v \in J} \text{Dom}(X_v) \to \{\mathbf{0}, \mathbf{1}\}$ defined by

$$\pi_{t,K}(\boldsymbol{x}_J) := \begin{cases} \mathbf{1} & \exists \boldsymbol{x}_{K \setminus J} \text{ s.t. } R_K((\boldsymbol{x}_J, \boldsymbol{x}_{K \setminus J})) \neq \mathbf{0}, \\ \mathbf{0} & \text{otherwise.} \end{cases} \quad (24)$$

Recall from Definition 3.3 that every $K \in \mathcal{E}_s$ is covered by at least one bag $\chi(t)$ for $t \in V(T)$. Fix an arbitrary coverage assignment $\alpha : \mathcal{E}_s \to V(T)$, where K is covered by the bag $\chi(\alpha(K))$. Then, the factors Φ_t are defined by:

$$\Phi_t(\boldsymbol{x}_{\chi(t)}) := \bigotimes_{K \in \alpha^{-1}(t)} R_K(\boldsymbol{x}_K) \otimes \bigotimes_{\substack{K \in \mathcal{E}_s \\ K \cap \chi(t) \neq \emptyset}} \pi_{t,K}(\boldsymbol{x}_{K \cap \chi(t)}). \quad (25)$$

It is easy to verify that (23) holds. Using a worst-case optimal join algorithm [28, 29, 34] we can compute (25) in time

$$\tilde{O}(N^{\rho^*_{\mathcal{E}_{\not\infty}}(\chi(t))}) = O(N^{\max_{h \in \text{ED}_{\not\infty} \cap \Gamma_n} h(\chi(t))}). \quad (26)$$

Over all $t \in V(T)$, our runtime is bounded by $O(N^w)$, where

$$w = \max_{t \in V(T)} \max_{h \in \text{ED}_{\not\infty} \cap \Gamma_n} h(\chi(t)). \quad (27)$$

The support of each factor Φ_t has size bounded by N^w.

Next we compute (23) in time $\tilde{O}(N^w)$. We will make use of the fact that (T, χ) is a relaxed TD. Fix an arbitrary root of the tree decomposition (T, χ); following InsideOut, we compute (23) by eliminating variables from the leaves of (T, χ) up to the root. Without loss of generality, we assume that the tree decomposition is non-redundant, i.e., no bag is a subset of another in the tree decomposition (otherwise the contained bag factor can be "absorbed" into the containee bag factor). Let t_1 be any leaf of (T, χ), t_2 be its parent, where $L = \chi(t_1)$ and $U = \chi(t_2)$. Now write (23) as follows:

$$\bigoplus_{x_{\mathcal{V}}} \left(\bigotimes_{t \in V(T)} \Phi_t(\boldsymbol{x}_{\chi(t)}) \right) \otimes \left(\bigotimes_{S \in \mathcal{E}_\ell} \mathbf{1}_{\sum_{v \in S} \theta_v^S(x_v) \leq 0} \right)$$

$$= \bigoplus_{x_{\mathcal{V} \setminus (L \setminus U)}} \bigoplus_{x_{L \setminus U}} \left(\bigotimes_{t \in V(T)} \Phi_t(\boldsymbol{x}_{\chi(t)}) \right) \otimes \left(\bigotimes_{S \in \mathcal{E}_\ell} \mathbf{1}_{\sum_{v \in S} \theta_v^S(x_v) \leq 0} \right)$$

$$= \bigoplus_{x_{\mathcal{V} \setminus (L \setminus U)}} \left(\bigotimes_{t \in V(T) \setminus \{t_1, t_2\}} \Phi_t(\boldsymbol{x}_{\chi(t)}) \right) \otimes \left(\bigotimes_{\substack{S \in \mathcal{E}_\ell \\ S \cap (L \setminus U) = \emptyset}} \mathbf{1}_{\sum_{v \in S} \theta_v^S(x_v) \leq 0} \right)$$

$$\otimes \underbrace{\left[\bigoplus_{x_{L \setminus U}} \Phi_{t_1}(\boldsymbol{x}_L) \otimes \Phi_{t_2}(\boldsymbol{x}_U) \otimes \left(\bigotimes_{\substack{S \in \mathcal{E}_\ell \\ S \cap (L \setminus U) \neq \emptyset}} \mathbf{1}_{\sum_{v \in S} \theta_v^S(x_v) \leq 0} \right) \right]}_{\text{sub-query of the form (14)}}.$$

The third equality uses the semiring's distributive law. (Note that $S \cap (L \setminus U) \neq \emptyset$ implies that $S \subseteq (L \cup U)$ thanks to Definition 3.3 and the fact that t_2 is the only neighbor of t_1.) Lemma 3.1 implies that we can compute the sub-query in the allotted time. The above step eliminates all variables in $L \setminus U$. Repeatedly applying the above step yields the desired output $Q()$.

When the query has free variables, the algorithm proceeds similarly to the case of an FAQ with free variables [5]. □

Example 3.6. Given 3 binary relations R, S and T, consider a query Q about the number of tuples (a, b, c, d) that satisfy:

$$R(a, b) \wedge S(b, c) \wedge T(c, d) \wedge (a \leq c) \wedge (c \leq b) \wedge (d \leq b). \quad (28)$$

The query Q has $\mathcal{E}_s = \mathcal{E}_{\not\infty} = \{\{a, b\}, \{b, c\}, \{c, d\}\}$ and $\mathcal{E}_\ell = \mathcal{E}_\infty = \{\{a, c\}, \{b, c\}, \{b, d\}\}$. Let $N = \max\{|R|, |S|, |T|\}$. Note that $\text{faqw}(Q) = 2$. In fact, any of the previously known algorithms, e.g. [5, 6], would take time $O(N^2)$ to answer Q. However, this query has $\text{faqw}_\ell(Q) = 1$, and by Theorem 3.5, it can be answered in time $O(N \cdot \log N)$. (Note that here $2 = k < |\mathcal{E}_\ell| = 3$.) An optimal relaxed tree decomposition is shown in Figure 1. □

We next give a couple of simple lower and upper bounds for faqw_ℓ. The upper bound shows that, effectively faqw_ℓ is the best we can hope for, if the FAQ-AI query is arbitrary. The lower bound shows that, while the relaxed tree decomposition idea can improve the runtime by a polynomial factor, it cannot improve the runtime over straightforwardly applying InsideOut (over non-relaxed tree decompositions) by more than a polynomial factor.

[3]Note that k can be a lot smaller than $|\mathcal{E}_\ell|$.

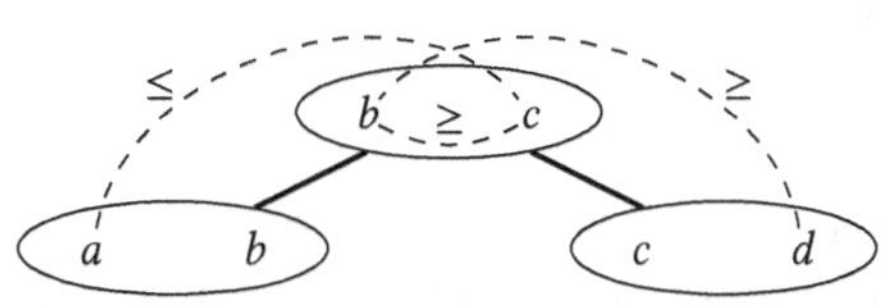

Figure 1: An optimal relaxed tree decomposition for the query in Example 3.6. *Ligament* edges are dashed. Each *skeleton* edge is held in one bag.

Proposition 3.7. *For any positive integer m, there exists an* FAQ-AI *query of the form* (3) *for which* $F = \emptyset$, $\mathsf{faqw}_\ell(Q) \geq m$ *and it cannot be answered in time* $o(N^{\mathsf{faqw}_\ell(Q)})$*, modulo* k-sum *hardness.*

Proposition 3.8. *For any* FAQ-AI *query* Q *of the form* (3)*, we have* $\mathsf{faqw}_\ell(Q) \geq \frac{1}{2}\mathsf{faqw}(Q)$*; in particular, when* Q *has no free variables* $\mathsf{fhtw}_\ell(Q) \geq \frac{1}{2}\mathsf{fhtw}(Q)$.

3.2.2 FAQ-AI *on the Boolean semiring.* Before explaining how we can adapt PANDA to solve an FAQ-AI query on the Boolean semiring, we give the intuition with an example.

Example 3.9. Consider the following FAQ-AI:

$$Q() \leftarrow R(a,b) \wedge S(b,c) \wedge T(c,d) \wedge a \leq d. \quad (29)$$

Here $\mathsf{faqw}_\ell(Q) = \mathsf{faqw}(Q) = 2$. Using fractional hypertree width measure and InsideOut (even with relaxed TDs and Theorem 3.5), the best runtime is $O(N^2)$, because no matter which (relaxed) TD we choose, the worst-case bag relation size is $\Theta(N^2)$. A key idea of the PANDA framework [7] is the use of a *disjunctive Datalog rule.* Consider the following disjunctive Datalog rule:

$$U(a,b,c) \vee W(b,c,d) \leftarrow R(a,b) \wedge S(b,c) \wedge T(c,d). \quad (30)$$

There are two relations in the head U and W, and they form a solution to the rule iff the following holds: if (a,b,c,d) satisfies the body, then either $(a,b,c) \in U$ or $(b,c,d) \in W$. Via information-theoretic inequalities [7], we are able to show that PANDA can compute a solution (U,W) to the above disjunctive Datalog rule in time $\tilde{O}(N^{1.5})$. In particular, both $|U|$ and $|W|$ are bounded by $N^{1.5}$.

Given the solution (U,W) to (30), it is straightforward to verify that the following also holds, using the distributivity of $\vee$ over $\wedge$:

$$(R(a,b) \wedge W(b,c,d)) \vee (U(a,b,c) \wedge T(c,d)) \leftarrow R(a,b) \wedge S(b,c) \wedge T(c,d). \quad (31)$$

By semijoin-reducing W against S, T, and semjoin-reducing U against R, S, we conclude that

$$(R(a,b) \wedge W(b,c,d)) \vee (U(a,b,c) \wedge T(c,d)) \equiv R(a,b) \wedge S(b,c) \wedge T(c,d).$$

Finally, we have a rewrite of the original body:

$$[R(a,b) \wedge W(b,c,d) \wedge a \leq d] \vee [U(a,b,c) \wedge T(c,d) \wedge a \leq d] \equiv R(a,b) \wedge S(b,c) \wedge T(c,d) \wedge a \leq d. \quad (32)$$

By defining intermediate rules, we can compute Q from them:

$$Q_1() \leftarrow R(a,b) \wedge W(b,c,d) \wedge a \leq d, \quad (33)$$

$$Q_2() \leftarrow U(a,b,c) \wedge T(c,d) \wedge a \leq d, \quad (34)$$

$$Q() \leftarrow Q_1() \vee Q_2(). \quad (35)$$

Q_1 and Q_2 are of the form (14), and thus they each can be answered in $\tilde{O}(N^{1.5})$-time (since $|U|, |W| \leq N^{1.5}$). This implies that Q can be answered in $\tilde{O}(N^{1.5})$-time overall. □

The strategy outlined in the above example uses PANDA to evaluate an FAQ-AI query over the Boolean semiring. The resulting algorithm achieves a natural generalization of the submodular FAQ-width defined in (13):

Definition 3.10. Given an FAQ-AI query Q (3) over the Boolean semiring. The *relaxed submodular* FAQ*-width* of Q is defined by

$$\mathsf{smfw}_\ell(Q) := \max_{h \in \mathsf{ED}_{\mathcal{P}} \cap \Gamma_n} \min_{(T,\chi) \in \mathsf{TD}_F^\ell} \max_{t \in V(T)} h(\chi(t)). \quad (36)$$

(Recall that the set of relaxed tree decompositions TD_F^ℓ was defined in Definition 3.3.)

Theorem 3.11. *Any* FAQ-AI *query* Q *of the form* (3) *on the Boolean semiring can be answered in time* $\tilde{O}(N^{\mathsf{smfw}_\ell(Q)} + |Q|)$.

The proof of Theorem 3.11 can be found in Appendix A.1.

3.3 Relaxed polymatroids

A key step in the proof of Theorem 3.11 is to find the Boolean tensor decomposition (72) of the product over R_K. In a non-Boolean semiring, this becomes a tensor decomposition on this semiring:

$$\bigotimes_{K \in \mathcal{E}_s} R_K = \bigoplus_{(T,\chi) \in \mathsf{TD}_F^\ell} \bigotimes_{t \in V(T)} S_{\chi(t)}^{(T,\chi)}. \quad (37)$$

In order to compute this tensor decomposition, we can still follow the script of the proof of Theorem 3.11, working on the parameter space of the input factors R_K; however, for the equality in (37) to hold (it is an identity over the value-space of the factors), we have to ensure the following property:

For any $\boldsymbol{x}_{\mathcal{V}}$ s.t. $\bigotimes_{K \in \mathcal{E}_s} R_K(\boldsymbol{x}_K) \neq \mathbf{0}$, there is *exactly one* tree decomposition $(T,\chi) \in \mathsf{TD}_F^\ell$ for which

$$\bigotimes_{t \in V(T)} S_{\chi(t)}^{(T,\chi)}(\boldsymbol{x}_{\chi(t)}) = \bigotimes_{K \in \mathcal{E}_s} R_K(\boldsymbol{x}_K), \quad (38)$$

while for the other TDs, the left-hand side above is $\mathbf{0}$.

Essentially, the property ensures that we do not have to perform inclusion-exclusion (IE) over the tree decompositions in TD^{ℓ}_F.[4] We do not know how to ensure this property in general. However, under a relaxed notion of polymatroids, the property above holds. Since this idea applies to FAQ queries in general, we start with our result on FAQ queries first, before specializing it to FAQ-AI.

3.3.1 FAQ *over an arbitrary semiring.* To explain how we can guarantee the property (38) for an FAQ query over an arbitrary semiring, consider the following example. Suppose that we would like to evaluate the (aggregate) query

$$Q() = \sum_{\boldsymbol{x}_{[4]}} R_{12}(x_1, x_2) R_{23}(x_2, x_3) R_{34}(x_3, x_4) R_{41}(x_4, x_1). \quad (39)$$

We write R_{ij} instead of $R_{ij}(x_i, x_j)$ for short. The factors R_{ij} are functions of two variables $R_{ij} : \mathsf{Dom}(X_i) \times \mathsf{Dom}(X_j) \to \mathbb{R}$, and they are represented by *ternary* relations in a database. Abusing notation we will also use R_{ij} to refer to its support, i.e., the binary relation over (X_i, X_j) such that $(x_i, x_j) \in R_{ij}$ iff $R_{ij}(x_i, x_j) \neq 0$.

There are only two non-trivial tree decompositions for the "4-cycle" query (39): one with bags $\{1, 2, 3\}$ and $\{3, 4, 1\}$, and the other with bags $\{1, 2, 4\}$ and $\{2, 3, 4\}$.[5] To evaluate the query, we first solve the relation equation (37), but only on the supports; i.e., we would like to find relations S_{123}, S_{341}, S_{234}, and S_{412} such that

$$\begin{aligned} R_{12} \wedge R_{23} \wedge R_{34} \wedge R_{41} \equiv (S_{123} \wedge S_{341}) \vee (S_{234} \wedge S_{412}) \equiv \quad (40) \\ (S_{123} \vee S_{234}) \wedge (S_{123} \vee S_{412}) \wedge (S_{341} \vee S_{234}) \wedge (S_{341} \vee S_{412}). \end{aligned}$$

The second $\equiv$ is due to the distributivity of $\vee$ over $\wedge$. Since the last formula is in CNF, we can solve each term separately by solving 4 different disjunctive Datalog rules:

$$(S_{123} \vee S_{234}) \leftarrow R_{12} \wedge R_{23} \wedge R_{34} \wedge R_{41}, \quad (41)$$

$$(S_{123} \vee S_{412}) \leftarrow R_{12} \wedge R_{23} \wedge R_{34} \wedge R_{41}, \quad (42)$$

$$(S_{341} \vee S_{234}) \leftarrow R_{12} \wedge R_{23} \wedge R_{34} \wedge R_{41}, \quad (43)$$

$$(S_{341} \vee S_{412}) \leftarrow R_{12} \wedge R_{23} \wedge R_{34} \wedge R_{41}. \quad (44)$$

Applying the proof-to-algorithm conversion idea from [7], the above disjunctive Datalog rules can be solved with the PANDA algorithm. It is beyond the scope of the main body of this paper to describe the PANDA algorithm in full details. However, we can describe a solution. Let $N = \max\{|R_{12}|, |R_{23}|, |R_{34}|, |R_{41}|\}$. For each input relation/factor, define their "light" parts as follows.

$$R^{\ell}_{ij} := \{(x_i, x_j) \in R_{ij} \ : \ |\sigma_{X_i = x_i} R_{ij}| \leq \sqrt{N}\}. \quad (45)$$

Also, for every R_{ij}, define $R^h_{ij} := R_{ij} \backslash R^{\ell}_{ij}$. Then, one can verify that the following is a solution to the relational equations (41)...(44) (and by semijoin-reducing each one of them with relations R_{ij}, they become a solution to (40) as well):

$$S_{ijk} = R_{ij} \ltimes R^l_{jk} \cup \pi_i R^h_{ij} \ltimes R_{jk}. \quad (46)$$

Furthermore, it is straightforward to verify that each S_{ijk} can be computed in $\tilde{O}(N^{1.5})$-time. Once we have obtained this solution to the relational equation, i.e., we have the relations S_{ijk}, we can extend them naturally into factors (so that they are represented by 4-ary relations) satisfying (38). In particular, as functions with range $\mathbb{R}$, they are defined by

$$S_{ijk}(x_i, x_j, x_k) := R_{ij}(x_i, x_j) \cdot R_{jk}(x_j, x_k). \quad (47)$$

The above sketch does not work for a generic FAQ query because we do not know how to guarantee that (38) is satisfied given the relational solution returned by PANDA. (If we were able to do so, then the notion of submodular width would apply also to #CSP and not just CSP.) However, we *are* able to prove that this strategy works (i.e., (38) can be ensured) under a relaxed notion of polymatroids and a corresponding "sharp submodular (FAQ) width".

Definition 3.12. Given a collection $\mathcal{E}$ of subsets of $\mathcal{V}$, a set function $h : 2^{\mathcal{V}} \to \mathbb{R}_+$ is said to be a *$\mathcal{E}$-polymatroid* if it satisfies the following: (i) $h(\emptyset) = 0$, (ii) $h(X) \leq h(Y)$ whenever $X \subseteq Y$, and (iii) $h(X \cup Y) + h(X \cap Y) \leq h(X) + h(Y)$ for every pair $X, Y \subseteq \mathcal{V}$ such that $X \cap Y \subseteq S$ for some $S \in \mathcal{E}$. In particular, a $2^{\mathcal{V}}$-polymatroid is a polymatroid as defined in Section 2.1. For $\mathcal{V} = [n]$, let $\Gamma_{n|\mathcal{E}}$ denote the set of all $\mathcal{E}$-polymatroids on $\mathcal{V}$.

The following definition is a straightforward generalization of smfw from (13), where we replace Γ_n by the relaxed polymatroids.

Definition 3.13. Given an FAQ query (2) whose hypergraph is $\mathcal{H} = (\mathcal{V}, \mathcal{E} = \mathcal{E}_{\not{\infty}} \cup \mathcal{E}_{\infty})$, its *#-submodular* FAQ*-width*, denoted by $\#\mathsf{smfw}(Q)$, is defined by

$$\#\mathsf{smfw}(Q) := \max_{h \in \mathsf{ED}_{\not{\infty}} \cap \Gamma_{n|\mathcal{E}_{\not{\infty}}}} \ \min_{(T,\chi) \in \mathsf{TD}_F} \ \max_{t \in V(T)} h(\chi(t)). \quad (48)$$

When there are no free variables, i.e., $F = \emptyset$, we define $\#\mathsf{subw}(Q) := \#\mathsf{smfw}(Q)$, to mirror the case when $\mathsf{faqw}(Q) = \mathsf{fhtw}(Q)$.

Under the above more restricted width parameter[6], our vision above with condition (38) can now be realized:

[4]IE is difficult for two reasons: (1) IE computation explodes the runtime, and (2) in a general semiring there may not be additive inverses and thus IE may not even apply.

[5]The trivial TD with one bag $\{1, 2, 3, 4\}$ can always be replaced by a non-trivial TD in the considered bounds/algorithms without making them any worse. Similarly, redundant TDs can be replaced by non-redundant ones.

[6]When we relax the polymatroids, the width goes *up*, and thus it is more restricted.

Theorem 3.14. *Any* FAQ *query Q of the form* (2) *on any semiring can be answered in time* $\tilde{O}(N^{\#\text{smfw}(Q)} + |Q|)$.

Appendix A.2 gives the proof of Theorem 3.14, which involves an appropriate adaptation of PANDA called #PANDA. Appendix A.3 shows that while #smfw(Q) can be larger than smfw(Q), it is not larger than faqw(Q) and can be unboundedly smaller for classes of queries.

Proposition 3.15 (Connecting #smfw to smfw and faqw).

(a) *For any* FAQ *query Q, the following holds:*

$$\text{smfw}(Q) \leq \#\text{smfw}(Q) \leq \text{faqw}(Q). \tag{49}$$

In particular, when Q has no free variables, we have

$$\text{subw}(Q) \leq \#\text{subw}(Q) \leq \text{fhtw}(Q). \tag{50}$$

(b) *Furthermore, there are classes of queries Q for which the gap between* #smfw(Q) *and* faqw(Q) *is unbounded, and so is the gap between* #subw(Q) *and* fhtw(Q).

Example 3.16. Consider again the count query Q in (39), which we showed earlier how to compute in time $\tilde{O}(N^{1.5})$. Since Q has no free variables, faqw(Q) = fhtw(Q) = 2 and #smfw(Q) = #subw(Q). In the proof of Proposition 3.15, we show that #subw(Q) ≤ 1.5. Therefore, the #PANDA algorithm from the proof of Theorem 3.14 can compute (39) in time $\tilde{O}(N^{1.5})$. In fact, the $\tilde{O}(N^{1.5})$ algorithm we described earlier for (39) is just a specialization of #PANDA. The proof of Proposition 3.15 offers a family of similar examples. □

3.3.2 FAQ-AI *over an arbitrary semiring.* Finally, we put everything together to solve the FAQ-AI problem. The only (very natural) change is to replace the tree decompositions by their relaxed version, and the technical details flow through.

Definition 3.17. Given an FAQ-AI query (3) whose hypergraph is $\mathcal{H} = (\mathcal{V}, \mathcal{E} = \mathcal{E}_s \cup \mathcal{E}_\ell = \mathcal{E}_{\not\infty} \cup \mathcal{E}_\infty)$, its *relaxed #-submodular* FAQ*-width*, denoted by #smfw$_\ell$(Q), is defined by

$$\#\text{smfw}_\ell(Q) := \max_{h \in \text{ED}_{\not\infty} \cap \Gamma_{n|\mathcal{E}_{\not\infty}}} \min_{(T,\chi) \in \text{TD}_F^\ell} \max_{t \in V(T)} h(\chi(t)). \tag{51}$$

When $F = \emptyset$, we define #subw$_\ell$(Q) := #smfw$_\ell$(Q).

Theorem 3.18. *Any* FAQ-AI *query Q of the form* (3) *on any semiring can be computed in time* $\tilde{O}(N^{\#\text{smfw}_\ell(Q)} + |Q|)$.

Example 3.19. Consider the following count query:

$$Q() = \sum_{a,b,c,d} R(a,b) \cdot S(b,c) \cdot T(c,d) \cdot \mathbf{1}_{a+b+c+d \leq 0}. \tag{52}$$

Let $N := \max\{|R|, |S|, |T|\}$. For the above query faqw(Q) = faqw$_\ell$(Q) = #smfw(Q) = 2. Any of the previously known algorithms, including the one from Theorem 3.5 *and* the one from Theorem 3.14, would need time $O(N^2)$ to compute Q. In Appendix A.4, we show that #smfw$_\ell$(Q) ≤ 1.5. As an example of Theorem 3.18, we also show how to compute the above query in $\tilde{O}(N^{1.5})$. (Using the same method, we can also solve the counting version of Q_3 from Example 1.2 in the same time.) □

4 APPLICATIONS TO RELATIONAL MACHINE LEARNING

Our FAQ-AI formalism and solution are directly applicable to learning a class of machine learning models, which includes supervised models (e.g., robust regression, SVM classification), and unsupervised models (e.g., clustering via k-means). In this section, we show that the core computation of these optimization problems can be formulated in FAQ-AI over the sum-product semiring.

4.1 Training ML models over databases

A typical machine learning model is learned over a training dataset G. We consider the common scenario where the input data is a relational database $\boldsymbol{I}$, and the training dataset G is the result of a feature extraction join query Q over $\boldsymbol{I}$ [2, 3, 18, 24]. Each tuple $(\boldsymbol{x}, y) \in G$ consists of a vector of features $\boldsymbol{x}$ and a label y. We consider that the feature extraction query Q has the hypergraph $\mathcal{H} = (\mathcal{V}, \mathcal{E}_s)$, where $\mathcal{E}_s$ is the set of its skeleton hyperedges.

A supervised machine learning model is a function $f_{\boldsymbol{\beta}}(\boldsymbol{x})$ with parameters $\boldsymbol{\beta}$ that is used to predict the label y for unlabeled data. The parameters are obtained by minimizing the objective function:

$$J(\boldsymbol{\beta}) = \sum_{(\boldsymbol{x},y) \in G} \mathcal{L}\left(y, f_{\boldsymbol{\beta}}(\boldsymbol{x})\right) + \lambda\Omega(\boldsymbol{\beta}), \tag{53}$$

where $\mathcal{L}(a, b)$ is a loss function, Ω is a regularizer, e.g., ℓ_1 or ℓ_2 norm, and the constant $\lambda \in (0, 1)$ controls the influence of regularization.

Previous work has shown that for polynomial loss functions, such as square loss $\mathcal{L}(a, b) = (a - b)^2$, the core computation for optimizing the objective $J(\boldsymbol{\beta})$ amounts to FAQ evaluation [3]. In many instances, however, the loss function is non-polynomial, either due to the structure of the loss, or the presence of non-polynomial components embedded within the model structure (e.g., ReLU activation function in neural nets) [27].

Examples of commonly used non-polynomial loss functions are: (1) hinge loss, used to learn classification models like linear support vector machines (SVM) [27], or generalized low rank models (glrm) with boolean principal component analysis (PCA) [33]; (2) Huber loss, used to learn regression models that are robust to outliers [27]; (3) scalene loss, used to learn quantile regression models [33]; (4) epsilon insensitive loss, used to learn SVM regression models [27]; and (5) ordinal hinge loss, used to learn ordinal regression models or ordinal PCA (another glrm) [33].

Any optimization problem with the above non-polynomial loss functions can benefit from our evaluation algorithm for FAQ-AI by reformulating computations in the optimization algorithm as FAQ-AI expressions over the feature extraction join query Q. We next exemplify this reformulation for two such problems: (1) learning a robust linear regression model using Huber loss, which can be solved with gradient-descent optimization, and (2) learning a linear support vector machine (SVM) for binary classification using hinge loss, which can be solved with subgradient-based optimization algorithms or with a cutting-plane algorithm for the primal formulation of linear SVM classification. The full version [1] details the cases of the scalene, epsilon insensitive, and ordinal hinge loss functions.

We also consider k-means unsupervised clustering and give an FAQ-AI reformulation of the computation done in an iteration of the algorithm over the dataset G.

The advantage of FAQ-AI reformulation is that the FAQ-AI expressions for the aforementioned optimization problems can be evaluated over relaxed tree decompositions of the feature extraction query Q and do not require the explicit materialization of its result G. The size of and time to compute G is $O(|I|^{\rho^*(Q)})$ [29]. The solution to these optimization problems can be computed in time sub-linear in the size of G, using InsideOut or #PANDA.

4.2 Robust linear regression with Huber loss

A linear regression model is a linear function $f_{\beta}(\mathbf{x}) = \boldsymbol{\beta}^{\top}\mathbf{x} = \sum_{i\in[n]} \beta_i x_i$ with features $\mathbf{x} = (x_1 = 1, x_2, \dots, x_n)$ and parameters $\boldsymbol{\beta} = (\beta_1, \dots, \beta_n)$. For a given feature vector $\mathbf{x}$, the model is used to estimate the (continuous) label $y \in \mathbb{R}$. We learn the model parameters by minimizing the objective $J(\boldsymbol{\beta})$ with the Huber loss function, which is defined as:

$$\mathcal{L}(a,b) = \begin{cases} \frac{1}{2}(a-b)^2 & \text{if } |a-b| \le 1, \\ \frac{1}{2}|a-b| - \frac{1}{2} & \text{otherwise.} \end{cases} \tag{54}$$

Huber loss is equivalent to the square loss when $|a - b| \le 1$ and to the absolute loss otherwise[7]. In contrast to the absolute loss, Huber loss is differentiable at all points. It is also more robust to outliers than the square loss.

To learn the parameters, we use batch gradient descent optimization, which repeatedly updates the parameters in the direction of the gradient $\nabla J(\boldsymbol{\beta})$ until convergence. We provide details on gradient-based optimization in [1]. In this section, we focus on the core computation of the algorithm, which is the repeated computation of the objective $J(\boldsymbol{\beta})$ and its gradient $\nabla J(\boldsymbol{\beta})$.

[7]Without loss of generality, we use a simplified Huber loss. The threshold between absolute and square loss is given by a constant δ and the absolute loss is $\frac{\delta}{2}|a-b| - \frac{\delta^2}{2}$.

The gradient $\nabla J(\boldsymbol{\beta})$ is the vector of partial derivatives with respect to parameters $(\beta_j)_{j\in[n]}$. The objective function $J(\boldsymbol{\beta})$ (with ℓ_2 regularization) and its partial derivative with respect to β_j are:

$$J(\boldsymbol{\beta}) = \frac{1}{2} \sum_{(\mathbf{x},y)\in G} \Big[(y - f_{\beta}(\mathbf{x}))^2 \cdot \mathbf{1}_{|y-f_{\beta}(\mathbf{x})|\le 1} + (|y - f_{\beta}(\mathbf{x})| - 1) \cdot \mathbf{1}_{|y-f_{\beta}(\mathbf{x})|>1}\Big] + \frac{\lambda}{2}\|\boldsymbol{\beta}\|_2^2, \tag{55}$$

$$\begin{aligned}\frac{\partial J(\boldsymbol{\beta})}{\partial \beta_j} &= \lambda\beta_j - \sum_{(\mathbf{x},y)\in G} \Big[(y - f_{\beta}(\mathbf{x})) \cdot x_j \cdot \mathbf{1}_{|y-f_{\beta}(\mathbf{x})|\le 1} \qquad (56)\\ &\quad + \frac{1}{2}(x_j \cdot \mathbf{1}_{y-f_{\beta}(\mathbf{x})>0} - x_j \cdot \mathbf{1}_{y-f_{\beta}(\mathbf{x})<0}) \cdot \mathbf{1}_{|y-f_{\beta}(\mathbf{x})|>1}\Big]\\ &= \lambda\beta_j - \sum_{(\mathbf{x},y)\in G} (y - f_{\beta}(\mathbf{x})) \cdot x_j \cdot \mathbf{1}_{|y-f_{\beta}(\mathbf{x})|\le 1}\\ &\quad - 1/2\sum_{(\mathbf{x},y)\in G} x_j \cdot \mathbf{1}_{y-f_{\beta}(\mathbf{x})>1} + 1/2\sum_{(\mathbf{x},y)\in G} x_j \cdot \mathbf{1}_{y-f_{\beta}(\mathbf{x})<-1}.\end{aligned}$$

Our observation is that we can compute $J(\boldsymbol{\beta})$ and $\frac{\partial J(\boldsymbol{\beta})}{\partial \beta_j}$ without materializing G, by reformulating their data dependent computation as a few FAQ-AI expressions. We exemplify the rewriting for $\frac{\partial J(\boldsymbol{\beta})}{\partial \beta_j}$; the rewriting for $J(\boldsymbol{\beta})$ is presented in [1]. We rewrite the first of the three summations in $\frac{\partial J(\boldsymbol{\beta})}{\partial \beta_j}$ as follows:

$$\begin{aligned}&\sum_{(\mathbf{x},y)\in G} (y - \sum_{i\in[n]} \beta_i x_i) \cdot x_j \cdot \mathbf{1}_{|y-f_{\beta}(\mathbf{x})|\le 1} \qquad (57)\\ &= \sum_{(\mathbf{x},y)\in G} y \cdot x_j \cdot \mathbf{1}_{|y-f_{\beta}(\mathbf{x})|\le 1} - \sum_{i\in[n]} \sum_{(\mathbf{x},y)\in G} \beta_i \cdot x_i \cdot x_j \cdot \mathbf{1}_{|y-f_{\beta}(\mathbf{x})|\le 1}\\ &= \sum_{(\mathbf{x},y)\in G} y \cdot x_j \cdot \mathbf{1}_{y-f_{\beta}(\mathbf{x})\le 1} \cdot \mathbf{1}_{y-f_{\beta}(\mathbf{x})>0}\\ &\quad + \sum_{(\mathbf{x},y)\in G} y \cdot x_j \cdot \mathbf{1}_{y-f_{\beta}(\mathbf{x})\ge -1} \cdot \mathbf{1}_{y-f_{\beta}(\mathbf{x})<0}\\ &\quad - \sum_{i\in[n]} \sum_{(\mathbf{x},y)\in G} \beta_i \cdot x_i \cdot x_j \cdot \mathbf{1}_{y-f_{\beta}(\mathbf{x})\le 1} \cdot \mathbf{1}_{y-f_{\beta}(\mathbf{x})>0}\\ &\quad - \sum_{i\in[n]} \sum_{(\mathbf{x},y)\in G} \beta_i \cdot x_i \cdot x_j \cdot \mathbf{1}_{y-f_{\beta}(\mathbf{x})\ge -1} \cdot \mathbf{1}_{y-f_{\beta}(\mathbf{x})<0}.\end{aligned}$$

The four terms can be expressed as $O(n)$ FAQ-AI expressions of the form (3). For instance, the first part of the expression is equivalent to the following FAQ-AI query:

$$Q() = \sum_{y,\mathbf{x}_{\mathcal{V}}} y \cdot x_j \cdot \underbrace{\mathbf{1}_{y-f_{\beta}(\mathbf{x})\le 1} \cdot \mathbf{1}_{y-f_{\beta}(\mathbf{x})>0}}_{\text{ligaments } \mathcal{E}_{\ell}} \cdot \left(\prod_{F\in\mathcal{E}_s} R_F(\mathbf{x}_F)\right).$$

The other two summations in $\frac{\partial J(\boldsymbol{\beta})}{\partial \beta_j}$ both aggregate over x_j and have one inequality that defines a ligament in $\mathcal{E}_{\ell}$. They can be expressed as FAQ-AI expressions. Overall, the gradient

$\nabla J(\boldsymbol{\beta})$ can be expressed as $O(n^2)$ FAQ-AI expressions. The full version [1] shows that the same holds for $J(\boldsymbol{\beta})$.

Theorem 4.1. *Let I be an input database where N is the largest relation in I, and Q be a feature extraction query. For any robust linear regression model $\boldsymbol{\beta}^\top \boldsymbol{x}$, the objective $J(\boldsymbol{\beta})$ and gradient $\nabla J(\boldsymbol{\beta})$ with Huber loss can be computed in time $\tilde{O}(N^{\#\mathsf{smfw}_\ell(Q)})$ with* #PANDA *and in time $O(N^{\mathsf{faqw}_\ell(Q)} \log N)$ with* InsideOut.

4.3 Linear support vector machines

A linear SVM classification model is used for binary classification problems where the label $y \in \{\pm 1\}$. For the features $\boldsymbol{x} = (x_1 = 1, x_2, \ldots, x_n)$, the model learns the parameters $\boldsymbol{\beta} = (\beta_1, \ldots, \beta_n)$ of a linear discriminant function $f_{\boldsymbol{\beta}}(\boldsymbol{x}) = \boldsymbol{\beta}^\top \boldsymbol{x}$ such that $f_{\boldsymbol{\beta}}(\boldsymbol{x})$ separates the data points in G into positive and negative classes with a maximum margin. The parameters can be learned by minimizing the objective function (53) with the hinge loss function:

$$\mathcal{L}(a, b) = \max\{0, 1 - a \cdot b\}. \tag{58}$$

Hinge loss is non-differentiable, and thus standard gradient descent optimization is not applicable. We next discuss two alternative approaches for solving this optimization.

The first approach is based on the observation that the loss function is convex, and the objective admits subgradient vectors, which generalize the standard notion of gradient. The optimization problem can be solved with subgradient based updates. Pegasos is a well-know algorithm for this approach [32].

The alternative approach is to solve the primal formulation of the problem, which avoids the non-differentiable objective by turning it into a constraint optimization problem with slack variables. Joachims proposed a cutting-plane algorithm which solves this optimization problem efficiently [20].

For both approaches, the number of iterations of the optimization algorithm is independent of the size $|G|$ of training dataset G [20, 32]. Thus, the time complexity for finding the solution is $O(|G|)$.

Despite the fact that the two approaches solve the same problem, they have been hugely influential in their own right. We therefore consider both approaches, and show that by reformulating their computation as FAQ-AI we can solve them asymptotically faster than materializing the training dataset G, i.e., sublinear in $|G|$.

4.3.1 Subgradient-based optimization for linear SVM classification. We first use subgradient-based optimization to compute the parameters of the SVM model; The full version [1] gives the details. The core of the optimization is the repeated computation of the objective and the partial derivatives in terms of $(\beta_j)_{j\in[n]}$. The objective $J(\boldsymbol{\beta})$ (with ℓ_2 regularization) and the partial derivative $\frac{\partial J(\boldsymbol{\beta})}{\partial \beta_j}$ are:

$$J(\boldsymbol{\beta}) = \sum_{(\boldsymbol{x},y)\in G} \max\{0, 1 - y(\boldsymbol{\beta}^\top \boldsymbol{x})\} + \frac{\lambda}{2} \|\boldsymbol{\beta}\|_2^2, \tag{59}$$

$$\frac{\partial J(\boldsymbol{\beta})}{\partial \beta_j} = -\sum_{(\boldsymbol{x},y)\in G} y \cdot x_j \cdot \mathbf{1}_{y(\boldsymbol{\beta}^\top \boldsymbol{x}) \le 1} + \lambda \beta_j. \tag{60}$$

Both $J(\boldsymbol{\beta})$ and $\frac{\partial J(\boldsymbol{\beta})}{\partial \beta_j}$ can be reformulated as FAQ-AI expressions and computed without materializing G. We first rewrite the objective (derivation steps shown in [1]):

$$\sum_{(\boldsymbol{x},y)\in G} \max\{0, 1 - y(\boldsymbol{\beta}^\top \boldsymbol{x})\} + \frac{\lambda}{2} \|\boldsymbol{\beta}\|_2^2 \tag{61}$$

$$= \frac{\lambda}{2} \|\boldsymbol{\beta}\|_2^2 + \underbrace{\sum_{(\boldsymbol{x},y)\in G} \mathbf{1}_{y=1} \mathbf{1}_{\boldsymbol{\beta}^\top \boldsymbol{x} \le 1}}_{\text{FAQ-AI of the form (3)}} - \underbrace{\sum_{i=1}^{n} \sum_{(\boldsymbol{x},y)\in G} \beta_i x_i \mathbf{1}_{y=1} \mathbf{1}_{\boldsymbol{\beta}^\top \boldsymbol{x} \le 1}}_{\text{FAQ-AI of the form (3)}}$$

$$+ \underbrace{\sum_{(\boldsymbol{x},y)\in G} \mathbf{1}_{y=-1} \mathbf{1}_{\boldsymbol{\beta}^\top \boldsymbol{x} \ge -1}}_{\text{FAQ-AI of the form (3)}} + \underbrace{\sum_{i=1}^{n} \sum_{(\boldsymbol{x},y)\in G} \beta_i x_i \mathbf{1}_{y=-1} \mathbf{1}_{\boldsymbol{\beta}^\top \boldsymbol{x} \ge -1}}_{\text{FAQ-AI of the form (3)}}.$$

$\frac{\partial J(\boldsymbol{\beta})}{\partial \beta_j}$ can also be rewritten into two FAQ-AI expressions:

$$-\sum_{(\boldsymbol{x},y)\in G} y \cdot x_j \cdot \mathbf{1}_{y(\boldsymbol{\beta}^\top \boldsymbol{x}) \le 1} + \lambda \beta_j \tag{62}$$

$$= \lambda \beta_j - \underbrace{\sum_{(\boldsymbol{x},y)\in G} x_j \cdot \mathbf{1}_{y=1} \mathbf{1}_{\boldsymbol{\beta}^\top \boldsymbol{x} \le 1}}_{\text{FAQ-AI of the form (3)}} + \underbrace{\sum_{(\boldsymbol{x},y)\in G} x_j \cdot \mathbf{1}_{y=-1} \mathbf{1}_{\boldsymbol{\beta}^\top \boldsymbol{x} \ge -1}}_{\text{FAQ-AI of the form (3)}}.$$

Theorem 4.2. *Let I be an input database where N is the largest relation in I, and Q be a feature extraction query. For any linear SVM classification model $\boldsymbol{\beta}^\top \boldsymbol{x}$, the objective $J(\boldsymbol{\beta})$ and gradient $\nabla J(\boldsymbol{\beta})$ with hinge loss can be computed in time $\tilde{O}(N^{\#\mathsf{smfw}_\ell(Q)})$ with* #PANDA *and in time $O(N^{\mathsf{faqw}_\ell(Q)} \log N)$ with* InsideOut.

4.3.2 Cutting-plane algorithm for linear SVM classification in primal space. An alternative to learning linear SVM via subgradient-based optimization is to pose the problem as a constraint optimization problem. The equivalent formulation for minimizing the objective (59) is the primal formulation of linear SVM [27]:

$$\min_{\boldsymbol{\beta}, \xi_{\boldsymbol{x},y} \ge 0} \quad \frac{1}{2} \|\boldsymbol{\beta}\|^2 + \frac{C}{|G|} \sum_{(\boldsymbol{x},y)\in G} \xi_{\boldsymbol{x},y} \tag{63}$$

$$\text{s.t.} \quad y f_{\boldsymbol{\beta}}(\boldsymbol{x}) \ge 1 - \xi_{\boldsymbol{x},y}, \qquad \forall (\boldsymbol{x}, y) \in G.$$

where $\xi_{\boldsymbol{x},y}$ are slack variables and C is the regularization parameter.

The optimization problem solves for the hyperplane $f_{\boldsymbol{\beta}}(\boldsymbol{x})$ that classifies the data points $(\boldsymbol{x}, y) \in G$ into two classes, so that the margin between the hyperplane and the nearest data

Algorithm 1: Training classification SVM via (64)

1 $\mathcal{W} \leftarrow \emptyset$; // Working set
2 $t \leftarrow 0$;
3 **repeat**
4 $\quad t \leftarrow t + 1$;
5 $\quad (\boldsymbol{\beta}^{(t)}, \xi^{(t)}) \leftarrow \arg\min_{\boldsymbol{\beta}, \xi \geq 0} \left\{ \frac{1}{2} \|\boldsymbol{\beta}\|_2^2 + C\xi \right.$;
6 $\quad\quad$ s.t. $\left. \frac{1}{|G|} \left\langle \boldsymbol{\beta}, \sum_{(\boldsymbol{x},y) \in T} y\boldsymbol{x} \right\rangle \geq \frac{|T|}{|G|} - \xi, \forall T \in \mathcal{W} \right\}$;
7 $\quad T^{(t)} := \{(\boldsymbol{x}, y) \in G \mid y \left\langle \boldsymbol{\beta}^{(t)}, \boldsymbol{x} \right\rangle < 1\}$;
8 $\quad \mathcal{W} \leftarrow \mathcal{W} \cup \{T^{(t)}\}$
9 **until** $\frac{|T^{(t)}|}{|G|} - \frac{1}{|G|} \left\langle \boldsymbol{\beta}^{(t)}, \sum_{(\boldsymbol{x},y) \in T^{(t)}} y\boldsymbol{x} \right\rangle \leq \xi^{(t)} + \epsilon$;

point for each class is maximized. For each $(\boldsymbol{x}, y) \in G$, the slack variable $\xi_{\boldsymbol{x},y}$ encodes how much the point violates the margin of the hyperplane.

Joachims' cutting-plane algorithm solves (63) in linear time over the training dataset [20]. The algorithm solves the following *structural classification* SVM formulation, which is equivalent to (63):

$$\min_{\boldsymbol{\beta}, \xi \geq 0} \quad \frac{1}{2} \|\boldsymbol{\beta}\|^2 + C\xi \tag{64}$$
$$\text{s.t.} \quad \frac{1}{|G|} \left\langle \boldsymbol{\beta}, \sum_{(\boldsymbol{x},y) \in T} y\boldsymbol{x} \right\rangle \geq \frac{1}{|G|} |T| - \xi, \quad \forall T \subseteq G.$$

This formulation has $2^{|G|}$ constraints, one for each possible subset $T \subseteq G$, and a single slack variable ξ that is shared by all constraints.

Algorithm 1 presents Joachims' cutting-plane algorithm for solving (64). It iteratively constructs a set of constraints $\mathcal{W}$, which is a subset of all constraints in (64). In each round t, it first computes the optimal value for $\boldsymbol{\beta}^{(t)}$ and $\xi^{(t)}$ over the current working set $\mathcal{W}$. Then, it identifies the constraint $T^{(t)}$ that is most violated for the current $\boldsymbol{\beta}^{(t)}$, and adds this constraint to $\mathcal{W}$. It continues until $T^{(t)}$ is violated by at most ϵ. Joachims showed that Algorithm 1 finds the ϵ-approximate solution to (64) in $O(1)$-many iterations [20]. Hence $|\mathcal{W}|$ and the number of constraints of the optimization problem are bounded by a number *independent* of $|G|$.

Next, we consider the inner optimization problem at line 5. Although $|\mathcal{W}|$ is small, the number n of variables can still be large. This prohibits solving with quadratic programming as it can take up to $O(n^3)$ [27]. Its Wolfe dual, on the other hand, is a quadratic program with only a constant number of variables that is independent of n and one constraint. Let $\boldsymbol{x}_T = \sum_{(\boldsymbol{x},y) \in T} y\boldsymbol{x}$. We next present the derived Wolfe dual (its derivation from (64) is in [1]):

$$\max_{\boldsymbol{\alpha} \geq 0} \quad -\frac{1}{2} \left\langle \sum_{T \in \mathcal{W}} \alpha_T \boldsymbol{x}_T, \sum_{T \in \mathcal{W}} \alpha_T \boldsymbol{x}_T \right\rangle + \sum_{T \in \mathcal{W}} |T| \alpha_T \tag{65}$$
$$\text{s.t.} \quad \sum_{T \in \mathcal{W}} \alpha_T \leq \frac{C}{|G|}$$

where $\boldsymbol{\alpha} = (\alpha_T)_{T \in \mathcal{W}}$ is the vector of constraints.

Theorem 4.3. *Let $\mathbf{I}$ be an input database where N is the largest relation in $\mathbf{I}$, and Q be a feature extraction query. A linear SVM classification model can be learned over the training dataset $Q(I)$ with Joachims' cutting-plane algorithm in time $\tilde{O}(N^{\#\text{smfw}_\ell(Q)})$ with* #PANDA *and in time $O(N^{\text{faqw}_\ell(Q)} \log N)$ with* InsideOut.

4.4 k-means clustering

We next consider k-means clustering, which is a popular example of an unsupervised machine learning algorithm.

An unsupervised machine learning model is computed over a dataset $G \subseteq \mathbb{R}^n$, for which each tuple $\boldsymbol{x} \in G$ is a vector of features without a label. A clustering task aims to divide G into k clusters of "similar" data points with respect to the ℓ_2 norm: $G = \cup_{i=1}^k G_i$, where k is a given fixed positive integer. Each cluster G_i is represented by a cluster mean $\boldsymbol{\mu}_i \in \mathbb{R}^n$. One of the most ubiquitous clustering methods, Lloyd's k-means clustering algorithm (also known as the k-means method), involves the optimization problem (1) with respect to the partition $(G_i)_{i \in [k]}$ and the k means $(\boldsymbol{\mu}_i)_{i \in [k]}$. Other norms or distance measures can be used, e.g., if we replace ℓ_2 with ℓ_1-norm, then we get the k-median problem. The subsequent development considers the ℓ_2-norm.

Lloyd's algorithm can be viewed as a special instantiation of the *Expectation-Maximization* (EM) algorithm. It iteratively computes two updating steps until convergence. First, it updates the cluster assignments for each $(G_i)_{i \in [k]}$:

$$G_i = \left\{ \boldsymbol{x} \in G \mid \|\boldsymbol{x} - \boldsymbol{\mu}_i\|^2 \leq \left\|\boldsymbol{x} - \boldsymbol{\mu}_j\right\|^2, \forall j \in [k] \setminus \{i\} \right\} \tag{66}$$

and then it updates the corresponding k-means $(\boldsymbol{\mu}_i)_{i \in [k]}$:

$$\boldsymbol{\mu}_i = \frac{1}{|G_i|} \sum_{\boldsymbol{x} \in G_i} \boldsymbol{x}. \tag{67}$$

Our observation is that we can reformulate the updating of the k-means as FAQ-AI expressions, without explicitly computing the partitioning $(G_i)_{i \in [k]}$. For a given set of k-means $(\boldsymbol{\mu}_j)_{j \in [k]}$, let $c_{ij}(\boldsymbol{x})$ be the following function:

$$c_{ij}(\boldsymbol{x}) = \sum_{\ell \in [n]} [(x_\ell - \mu_{i,\ell})^2 - (x_\ell - \mu_{j,\ell})^2]$$
$$= \sum_{\ell \in [n]} [\mu_{i,\ell}^2 - 2x_\ell(\mu_{i,\ell} + \mu_{j,\ell}) - \mu_{j,\ell}^2]. \tag{68}$$

where $\mu_{j,\ell}$ is the ℓ'th component of mean vector $\boldsymbol{\mu}_j$. A data point $\boldsymbol{x} \in G$ is closest to center $\boldsymbol{\mu}_i$ if and only if $c_{ij}(\boldsymbol{x}) \leq 0$ holds $\forall j \in [k]$.

We use this inequality to reformulate the mean vector $\boldsymbol{\mu}_i$ as $O(n)$ FAQ-AI expressions. First, we express $|G_i|$ as:

$$Q_i() = \sum_{\boldsymbol{x}} \left(\prod_{j \in [k]} \mathbf{1}_{c_{ij}(\boldsymbol{x}) \leq 0} \right) \left(\prod_{F \in \mathcal{E}_s} R_F(\boldsymbol{x}_F) \right). \tag{69}$$

Then, for each $\ell \in [n]$, the sum $\sum_{\boldsymbol{x} \in G_i} x_\ell$ can be reformulated in FAQ-AI as follows (similarly to (4)):

$$Q_{i\ell}() = \sum_{\boldsymbol{x}} x_\ell \left(\prod_{j \in [k]} \mathbf{1}_{c_{ij}(\boldsymbol{x}) \leq 0} \right) \left(\prod_{F \in \mathcal{E}_s} R_F(\boldsymbol{x}_F) \right). \tag{70}$$

Each component $(\mu_{i,\ell})_{\ell \in [n]}$ equals the division of $Q_{i\ell}$ by Q_i.

Overall, the mean vector $\boldsymbol{\mu}_i$ can be computed with $O(n)$ FAQ-AI expressions of the form (3).

Theorem 4.4. *Let $\boldsymbol{I}$ be an input database where N is the largest relation in $\boldsymbol{I}$, and Q be a feature extraction query where n is the number of its variables. Each iteration of Lloyd's k-means algorithm can be computed in time $\tilde{O}(N^{\#\mathsf{smfw}_\ell(Q)})$ with* #PANDA *and in time $O(N^{\mathsf{faqw}_\ell(Q)} \log^{k-1} N)$ with* InsideOut.

ACKNOWLEDGMENTS

This project has received funding from the European Union's Horizon 2020 research and innovation programme under grant agreement No 682588. LN gratefully acknowledges support from NSF grants CAREER DMS-1351362 and CNS-1409303, Adobe Research and Toyota Research, and a Margaret and Herman Sokol Faculty Award. BM's was supported in part by a Google Research Award, and NSF grants CCF-1830711, CCF-1824303, and CCF-1733873.

REFERENCES

[1] Mahmoud Abo Khamis, Ryan R. Curtin, Benjamin Moseley, Hung Q. Ngo, XuanLong Nguyen, Dan Olteanu, and Maximilian Schleich. 2018. On Functional Aggregate Queries with Additive Inequalities. *CoRR* abs/1812.09526 (2018).

[2] Mahmoud Abo Khamis, Hung Q. Ngo, XuanLong Nguyen, Dan Olteanu, and Maximilian Schleich. 2018. AC/DC: In-Database Learning Thunderstruck. In *2nd Workshop on Data Mgt for End-To-End ML (DEEM'18)*. 8:1–8:10.

[3] Mahmoud Abo Khamis, Hung Q. Ngo, XuanLong Nguyen, Dan Olteanu, and Maximilian Schleich. 2018. In-Database Learning with Sparse Tensors. In *PODS*. 325–340.

[4] Mahmoud Abo Khamis, Hung Q. Ngo, Dan Olteanu, and Dan Suciu. 2019. Boolean Tensor Decomposition for Conjunctive Queries with Negation. In *ICDT*. 21:1–21:19.

[5] Mahmoud Abo Khamis, Hung Q. Ngo, and Atri Rudra. 2016. FAQ: Questions Asked Frequently. In *PODS*. 13–28.

[6] Mahmoud Abo Khamis, Hung Q. Ngo, and Atri Rudra. 2017. Juggling Functions Inside a Database. *SIGMOD Rec.* 46, 1 (2017), 6–13.

[7] Mahmoud Abo Khamis, Hung Q. Ngo, and Dan Suciu. 2017. What Do Shannon-type Inequalities, Submodular Width, and Disjunctive Datalog Have to Do with One Another?. In *PODS*. 429–444.

[8] Guillaume Bagan, Arnaud Durand, and Etienne Grandjean. 2007. On Acyclic Conjunctive Queries and Constant Delay Enumeration. In *CSL*. 208–222.

[9] Timothy M. Chan, Kasper Green Larsen, and Mihai Pătraşcu. 2011. Orthogonal Range Searching on the RAM, Revisited. In *SoCG*. 1–10.

[10] Bernard Chazelle. 1988. A functional approach to data structures and its use in multidimensional searching. *SIAM J. Comput.* 17, 3 (1988), 427–462.

[11] Bernard Chazelle. 1990. Lower bounds for orthogonal range searching. II. The arithmetic model. *J. ACM* 37, 3 (1990), 439–463.

[12] Mark de Berg, Otfried Cheong, Marc van Kreveld, and Mark Overmars. 2008. *Computational geometry* (third ed.). Springer-Verlag, Berlin. xii+386 pages. Algorithms and applications.

[13] Lukasz Golab and M. Tamer Özsu. 2010. *Data Stream Management.* Morgan & Claypool Publishers.

[14] Georg Gottlob, Gianluigi Greco, Nicola Leone, and Francesco Scarcello. 2016. Hypertree Decompositions: Questions and Answers. In *PODS*. 57–74.

[15] Martin Grohe and Dániel Marx. 2014. Constraint Solving via Fractional Edge Covers. *ACM Trans. Alg.* 11, 1 (2014), 4.

[16] Torsten Grust. 2002. Accelerating XPath Location Steps. In *SIGMOD*. 109–120.

[17] Terry Halpin and Spencer Rugaber. 2015. *LogiQL: A Query Language for Smart Databases.* CRC Press.

[18] Joseph M. Hellerstein et al. 2012. The MADlib Analytics Library or MAD Skills, the SQL. *PVLDB* 5, 12 (2012), 1700–1711.

[19] Anil K. Jain. 2010. Data clustering: 50 years beyond K-means. *Pattern Recognition Letters* 31, 8 (2010), 651–666.

[20] Thorsten Joachims. 2006. Training Linear SVMs in Linear Time. In *SIGKDD*. 217–226.

[21] Zuhair Khayyat et al. 2015. Lightning Fast and Space Efficient Inequality Joins. *PVLDB* 8, 13 (2015), 2074–2085.

[22] Anthony C. Klug. 1988. On conjunctive queries containing inequalities. *J. ACM* 35, 1 (1988), 146–160.

[23] Paraschos Koutris, Tova Milo, Sudeepa Roy, and Dan Suciu. 2017. Answering Conjunctive Queries with Inequalities. *Theory of Computing Systems* 61, 1 (01 Jul 2017), 2–30.

[24] Arun Kumar, Jeffrey F. Naughton, and Jignesh M. Patel. 2015. Learning Generalized Linear Models Over Normalized Data. In *SIGMOD*. 1969–1984.

[25] Nikos Mamoulis. 2011. *Spatial Data Management.* Morgan & Claypool Publishers.

[26] Dániel Marx. 2013. Tractable hypergraph properties for constraint satisfaction and conjunctive queries. *J. ACM* 60, 6 (2013), Art. 42, 51.

[27] Kevin P. Murphy. 2013. *Machine learning : a probabilistic perspective.* MIT Press, Cambridge, Mass.

[28] Hung Q. Ngo. 2018. Worst-Case Optimal Join Algorithms: Techniques, Results, and Open Problems. In *PODS*. 111–124.

[29] Hung Q. Ngo, Ely Porat, Christopher Ré, and Atri Rudra. 2012. Worst-case optimal join algorithms: [extended abstract]. In *PODS*. 37–48.

[30] Dan Olteanu and Jiewen Huang. 2009. Secondary-storage confidence computation for conjunctive queries with inequalities. In *SIGMOD*. 389–402.

[31] Luc Segoufin. 2013. Enumerating with Constant Delay the Answers to a Query. In *ICDT*. 10–20.

[32] Shai Shalev-Shwartz, Yoram Singer, Nathan Srebro, and Andrew Cotter. 2011. Pegasos: primal estimated sub-gradient solver for SVM. *Mathematical Programming* 127, 1 (01 Mar 2011), 3–30.

[33] Madeleine Udell, Corinne Horn, Reza Zadeh, and Stephen Boyd. 2016. Generalized Low Rank Models. *Foundations and Trends in Machine Learning* 9, 1 (2016), 1–118.
[34] Todd L. Veldhuizen. 2014. Triejoin: A Simple, Worst-Case Optimal Join Algorithm. In *ICDT*. 96–106.

A MISSING DETAILS FROM SECTION 3

A.1 Proof of Theorem 3.11

Theorem 3.11. *Any* FAQ-AI *query Q of the form* (3) *on the Boolean semiring can be answered in time* $\tilde{O}(N^{\mathsf{smfw}_\ell(Q)} + |Q|)$.

Proof. As in the proof of Theorem 3.5, we first assume there are no free variables; the generalization to $F \neq \emptyset$ is trivial. When $F = \emptyset$, the query (3) is written in Datalog as:

$$Q() \leftarrow \bigwedge_{K \in \mathcal{E}_s} R_K \wedge \bigwedge_{S \in \mathcal{E}_\ell} \left[\sum_{v \in S} \theta_v^S \leq 0\right]. \tag{71}$$

We write R_K instead of $R_K(\boldsymbol{x}_K)$ and θ_v^S instead of $\theta_v^S(x_v)$ to avoid clutter. It will be implicit throughout this proof that the subscript of a factor/function indicates its arguments. To answer query (71), the first step is to find one relation $S_{\chi(t)}^{(T,\chi)}$ (over variables $\chi(t)$) for every bag $t \in V(T)$ of every relaxed tree decomposition $(T, \chi) \in \mathsf{TD}_\emptyset^\ell$ such that the relations $S_{\chi(t)}^{(T,\chi)}$ together form a solution to the following equation:

$$\bigwedge_{K \in \mathcal{E}_s} R_K \equiv \bigvee_{(T,\chi) \in \mathsf{TD}_\emptyset^\ell} \bigwedge_{t \in V(T)} S_{\chi(t)}^{(T,\chi)}. \tag{72}$$

Note that the right-hand side of (72) is a *Boolean tensor decomposition* of the left-hand side. The idea of using Boolean tensor decomposition to speed up query evaluation was used in [4] in the context of queries with *dis*equalities. Assuming that we can compute the intermediate relations $S_{\chi(t)}^{(T,\chi)}$ efficiently satisfying (72), then (71) can be answered by answering for each $(T, \chi) \in \mathsf{TD}_\emptyset^\ell$ an intermediate query:

$$Q^{(T,\chi)}() \leftarrow \bigwedge_{t \in V(T)} S_{\chi(t)}^{(T,\chi)} \wedge \bigwedge_{S \in \mathcal{E}_\ell} \left[\sum_{v \in S} \theta_v^S \leq 0\right]. \tag{73}$$

The final answer Q is obtained by the trivial Datalog rule:

$$Q() \leftarrow \bigvee_{(T,\chi) \in \mathsf{TD}_\emptyset^\ell} Q^{(T,\chi)}(). \tag{74}$$

The key point here is that each intermediate query (73) is an FAQ-AI query (3) with $\mathsf{faqw}_\ell = 1$, and thus from Theorem 3.5 each one of them can be answered in time $\tilde{O}(M)$ where

$$M = \max_{(T,\chi) \in \mathsf{TD}_\emptyset^\ell} \max_{t \in V(T)} |S_{\chi(t)}^{(T,\chi)}|. \tag{75}$$

It remains to show how to compute tables $S_{\chi(t)}^{(T,\chi)}$ that form a solution to (72); to do so, we apply distributivity of $\vee$ over $\wedge$ to rewrite the right-hand side of (72) as follows. Let $\mathcal{M}$ be the collection of *all* maps $\beta : \mathsf{TD}_\emptyset^\ell \to 2^{\mathcal{V}}$ such that $\beta(T, \chi) = \chi(t)$ for some $t \in V(T)$; in other words, β selects one bag $\chi(t)$ out of each tree decomposition (T, χ). Then, from the distributive law we have

$$\bigvee_{(T,\chi) \in \mathsf{TD}_\emptyset^\ell} \bigwedge_{t \in V(T)} S_{\chi(t)}^{(T,\chi)} \equiv \bigwedge_{\beta \in \mathcal{M}} \bigvee_{(T,\chi) \in \mathsf{TD}_\emptyset^\ell} S_{\beta(T,\chi)}^{(T,\chi)}, \tag{76}$$

which means to solve the relational equation (72) we can instead solve the equation

$$\bigwedge_{\beta \in \mathcal{M}} \bigvee_{(T,\chi) \in \mathsf{TD}_\emptyset^\ell} S_{\beta(T,\chi)}^{(T,\chi)} \equiv \bigwedge_{K \in \mathcal{E}_s} R_K. \tag{77}$$

To solve the above equation, for each $\beta \in \mathcal{M}$ we can find tables $S_{\beta(T,\chi)}^{(T,\chi)}$ that form a solution to the following equation

$$\bigvee_{(T,\chi) \in \mathsf{TD}_\emptyset^\ell} S_{\beta(T,\chi)}^{(T,\chi)} \equiv \bigwedge_{K \in \mathcal{E}_s} R_K. \tag{78}$$

To do that, for each $\beta \in \mathcal{M}$, we compute a solution to the following disjunctive Datalog rule:

$$\bigvee_{(T,\chi) \in \mathsf{TD}_\emptyset^\ell} W_{\beta(T,\chi)}^{(T,\chi)} \leftarrow \bigwedge_{K \in \mathcal{E}_s} R_K. \tag{79}$$

Once we obtain the relations $W_{\beta(T,\chi)}^{(T,\chi)}$, we can semijoin-reduce them against the input relations R_K, in order to obtain $S_{\beta(T,\chi)}^{(T,\chi)}$ that solve (77).

Finally, we evaluate each disjunctive Datalog rule (79) by running the PANDA algorithm, which computes the rule in time bounded by $\tilde{O}(N^{e(\beta)})$, where

$$e(\beta) = \max_{h \in \mathsf{ED}_{\not\to} \cap \Gamma_n} \min_{(T,\chi) \in \mathsf{TD}_\emptyset^\ell} h(\beta(T, \chi)). \tag{80}$$

Maximizing over $\beta \in \mathcal{M}$, the runtime is bounded by $\tilde{O}(N^w)$, where

$$\begin{aligned}
w &= \max_{\beta \in \mathcal{M}} e(\beta) && (81)\\
&= \max_{\beta \in \mathcal{M}} \max_{h \in \mathsf{ED}_{\not\to} \cap \Gamma_n} \min_{(T,\chi) \in \mathsf{TD}_\emptyset^\ell} h(\beta(T, \chi)) && (82)\\
&= \max_{h \in \mathsf{ED}_{\not\to} \cap \Gamma_n} \max_{\beta \in \mathcal{M}} \min_{(T,\chi) \in \mathsf{TD}_\emptyset^\ell} h(\beta(T, \chi)) && (83)\\
&= \max_{h \in \mathsf{ED}_{\not\to} \cap \Gamma_n} \min_{(T,\chi) \in \mathsf{TD}_\emptyset^\ell} \max_{t \in V(T)} h(\chi(t)) = \mathsf{smfw}_\ell(Q). && (84)
\end{aligned}$$

The first equality in (84) follows from the minimax lemma in [7]. Our reasoning above also shows that M from (75) is bounded by $N^{\mathsf{smfw}_\ell(Q)}$. □

A.2 Proof of Theorem 3.14

Theorem 3.14. *Any* FAQ *query Q of the form* (2) *on any semiring can be answered in time* $\tilde{O}(N^{\#\mathsf{smfw}(Q)} + |Q|)$.

Proof. The PANDA algorithm [7] takes as input a disjunctive Datalog query of the form

$$\bigvee_{B\in\mathcal{B}} G_B(\boldsymbol{x}_B) \leftarrow \bigwedge_{K\in\mathcal{E}} R_K(\boldsymbol{x}_K). \tag{85}$$

The above query has an input relation R_K for each hyperedge $K \in \mathcal{E}$ in the query's hypergraph $\mathcal{H} = (\mathcal{V}, \mathcal{E})$. The output to the above query is a collection of tables G_B, one for each "goal" (or "target") B in the collection of goals $\mathcal{B}$. The output tables $(G_B)_{B\in\mathcal{B}}$ must satisfy the logical implication in (85): In particular, for each tuple $\boldsymbol{x}_\mathcal{V}$ that satisfies the conjunction $\bigwedge_{K\in\mathcal{E}} R_K(\boldsymbol{x}_K)$, the disjunction $\bigvee_{B\in\mathcal{B}} G_B(\boldsymbol{x}_B)$ must hold. Query (30) is an example of (85). A disjunctive Datalog query (85) can have many valid outputs. The PANDA algorithm computes one such output in time $\tilde{O}(N^e)$, where

$$e = \max_{h\in\text{ED}_{\not\perp}\cap\Gamma_n} \min_{B\in\mathcal{B}} h(B). \tag{86}$$

(Recall notation from Section 2.2.)

In what follows, we describe a variant of PANDA, called #PANDA, that takes a disjunctive Datalog query (85), and computes the following:

- A collection of tables $(G_B)_{B\in\mathcal{B}}$ that form a valid output to query (85), i.e. that satisfy the logical implication in (85).
- Moreover, associated with each output table G_B, #PANDA additionally computes a collection of "filter" tables $\left(F_K^{(B)}\right)_{K\in\mathcal{E}}$, one table $F_K^{(B)}$ for each hyperedge $K \in \mathcal{E}$ in the input hypergraph $\mathcal{H}$. The output tables G_B along with the associated filters $\left(F_K^{(B)}\right)_{K\in\mathcal{E}}$ satisfy the following condition: For each tuple $\boldsymbol{x}_\mathcal{V}$ that satisfies the conjunction $\bigwedge_{K\in\mathcal{E}} R_K(\boldsymbol{x}_K)$, there is *exactly one* target $B \in \mathcal{B}$ where the conjunction $\bigwedge_{K\in\mathcal{E}} F_K^{(B)}(\boldsymbol{x}_K)$ holds, and for that target B, $G_B(\boldsymbol{x}_B)$ holds as well. In particular, the following equivalences hold:

$$\veebar_{B\in\mathcal{B}} \left[\bigwedge_{K\in\mathcal{E}} F_K^{(B)}(\boldsymbol{x}_K)\right] \equiv \bigwedge_{K\in\mathcal{E}} R_K(\boldsymbol{x}_K), \tag{87}$$

$$\left[\bigwedge_{K\in\mathcal{E}} F_K^{(B)}(\boldsymbol{x}_K)\right] \equiv \left[G_B(\boldsymbol{x}_B) \wedge \bigwedge_{K\in\mathcal{E}} F_K^{(B)}(\boldsymbol{x}_K)\right], \quad \forall B \in \mathcal{B}, \tag{88}$$

where $\veebar$ above denotes the exclusive OR.

#PANDA computes the above output tables $(G_B)_{B\in\mathcal{B}}$ and $\left(\left(F_K^{(B)}\right)_{K\in\mathcal{E}}\right)_{B\in\mathcal{B}}$ in time $\tilde{O}(N^{e'})$ where

$$e' = \max_{h\in\text{ED}_{\not\perp}\cap\Gamma_{n|\mathcal{E}_{\not\perp}}} \min_{B\in\mathcal{B}} h(B). \tag{89}$$

Now we briefly explain how to tweak the PANDA algorithm into #PANDA satisfying the above characteristics. We refer the reader to [7] for more details about PANDA. At a high level, the PANDA algorithm starts with proving an exact upperbound on e from (86) using a sequence of proof steps, called the *proof sequence.* Then PANDA interprets each step in the proof sequence as a relational operator, and then uses this sequence of relational operators as a query plan to actually compute the query in time $\tilde{O}(N^e)$. One of the proof steps used in PANDA is *the decomposition step* $h(Y) \to h(X) + h(Y|X)$ for some $X \subseteq Y \subseteq \mathcal{V}$. The relational operator corresponding to this decomposition step is the "partitioning" operator, in which we take an input (or intermediate) table R_Y and partition it into a small number $k = O(\log |R|)$ of tables $R_Y^{(1)}, \dots, R_Y^{(k)}$, based on the degrees of variables in Y with respect to variables in $X \subseteq Y$. In particular, define the degree of Y w.r.t. a tuple $\boldsymbol{t}_X \in \pi_X R_Y$ as

$$\deg_{R_Y}(Y|\boldsymbol{t}_X) := \left|\left\{\boldsymbol{t}'_Y \in R_Y \mid \boldsymbol{t}'_X = \boldsymbol{t}_X\right\}\right| \tag{90}$$

In the partitioning step, we partition tuples $\boldsymbol{t}_X \in \pi_X R_Y$ into k buckets based on $\deg_{R_Y}(Y|\boldsymbol{t}_X)$ and partition R_Y accordingly. After partitioning, PANDA creates k independent branches of the problem, where in the j-th branch, R_Y is replaced by $R_Y^{(j)}$, for each $j \in [k]$. PANDA continues on each branch independently and end up computing a target G_B for some $B \in \mathcal{B}$ that is potentially different for each branch.

From the proof sequence construction described in [7], we note the following: If the constructed proof sequence that is used to prove the bound on e in (86) contains a decomposition step $h(Y) \to h(X) + h(Y|X)$, then the proof of the bound on e must have relied on some submodularity constraint on h of the form $h(X) + h(Z \cup Y) \leq h(Y) + h(Z \cup X)$ for some $Z \subseteq \mathcal{V}$ where $Z \cap Y = \emptyset$. However, the new bound (89) used in #PANDA only relies on submodularities $h(X) + h(Z \cup Y) \leq h(Y) + h(Z \cup X)$ where $X \subseteq K$ for some $K \in \mathcal{E}$. (Recall $\Gamma_{n|\mathcal{E}_{\not\perp}}$ from Definition 3.12.) Therefore, in #PANDA, whenever we apply a partitioning step of R_Y into $R_Y^{(1)}, \dots, R_Y^{(k)}$ based on the degrees $\deg_{R_Y}(Y|\boldsymbol{t}_X)$ of $\boldsymbol{t}_X \in \pi_X R_Y$, we can add $\pi_X R_Y^{(j)}$ into the filter $F_K^{(B)}$ for some $K \in \mathcal{E}$, i.e. we can set $F_K^{(B)} \leftarrow F_K^{(B)} \ltimes \pi_X R_Y^{(j)}$ on the j-th branch. Semijoin-reducing $\pi_X R_Y^{(j)}$ into some $F_K^{(B)}$ is possible thanks to the fact that $X \subseteq K$ for some $K \in \mathcal{E}$. Moreover, this semijoin-reduction of filters $F_K^{(B)}$ maintains (87). (Initially, we start with filters $F_K^{(B)}$ that are identical to the input relations R_K, which trivially satisfies (87).)

Now that we have described the #PANDA algorithm satisfying the above properties, we explain how to use it as a blackbox to solve an FAQ query Q of the form (2) in time $\tilde{O}(N^{\#\text{smfw}(Q)} + |Q|)$. Following the same notation as in the proof of Theorem 3.11, let $\mathcal{M}$ be the collection of *all* maps $\beta : \text{TD}_F^\ell \to 2^\mathcal{V}$ such that $\beta(T, \chi) = \chi(t)$ for some $t \in V(T)$; in other words, β selects one bag $\chi(t)$ out of each tree decomposition (T, χ). For each $\beta \in \mathcal{M}$, we use #PANDA to solve the following rule:

$$\biguplus_{(T,\chi)\in\mathsf{TD}_F}\left[G_{\beta(T,\chi)}\wedge\bigwedge_{K\in\mathcal{E}}F_K^{(\beta(T,\chi))}\right]\equiv\bigwedge_{K\in\mathcal{E}}R_K. \quad (91)$$

The solutions collectively satisfy the following:

$$\bigwedge_{\beta\in\mathcal{M}}\biguplus_{(T,\chi)\in\mathsf{TD}_F}\left[G_{\beta(T,\chi)}\wedge\bigwedge_{K\in\mathcal{E}}F_K^{(\beta(T,\chi))}\right]\equiv\bigwedge_{K\in\mathcal{E}}R_K.$$

Now we distribute the outer conjunction $\bigwedge_{\beta\in\mathcal{M}}$ over the exclusive OR $\biguplus$, which results in an exclusive OR outside and a big conjunction inside. Using the same diagonalization argument from [7], we know that for this inner conjunction there must exist some tree decomposition $(\bar{T},\bar{\chi})\in\mathsf{TD}_F$ where the conjunction contains $G_{\bar{\chi}(t)}$ for all $t\in V(\bar{T})$. Thanks to (88), we can keep those terms $G_{\bar{\chi}(t)}$ in the conjunction and drop out all other terms $G_{\beta(T,\chi)}$ to get an equivalent conjunction. We interpret the resulting conjunction as an FAQ query: The input factors to this FAQ query are all filter $F_K^{(\beta(T,\chi))}$ in the conjunction along with $G_{\bar{\chi}(t)}$ for all $t\in V(\bar{T})$; all other $G_{\beta(T,\chi)}$ have been dropped. Now we solve this FAQ query by running InsideOut over the tree decomposition $(\bar{T},\bar{\chi})$. We repeat the above for every conjunction. Afterwards, because different conjunctions are joined together with an *exclusive* OR, we can simply add up individual query results.

From (89), the total runtime is $\tilde{O}(N^w+|Q|)$, where

$$\begin{aligned} w &= \max_{\beta\in\mathcal{M}}\max_{h\in\mathsf{ED}_{\not\!\!\:\!\!\:\!\!\:\!\!\:\mathcal{E}}\cap\Gamma_{n|\mathcal{E}_{\not\:\!\!\:\!\!\:\!\!\:\!\!\:}}}\min_{(T,\chi)\in\mathsf{TD}_F}h(\beta(T,\chi))\\ &= \max_{h\in\mathsf{ED}_{\not\!\!\:\!\!\:\!\!\:\!\!\:\mathcal{E}}\cap\Gamma_{n|\mathcal{E}_{\not\:\!\!\:\!\!\:\!\!\:\!\!\:}}}\max_{\beta\in\mathcal{M}}\min_{(T,\chi)\in\mathsf{TD}_F}h(\beta(T,\chi))\\ &= \max_{h\in\mathsf{ED}_{\not\!\!\:\!\!\:\!\!\:\!\!\:\mathcal{E}}\cap\Gamma_{n|\mathcal{E}_{\not\:\!\!\:\!\!\:\!\!\:\!\!\:}}}\min_{(T,\chi)\in\mathsf{TD}_F}\max_{t\in V(T)}h(\chi(t))=\#\mathsf{smfw}(Q). \end{aligned}$$

□

A.3 Proof of Proposition 3.15

Proposition 3.15.

(a) *For any* FAQ *query* Q*, the following holds:*

$$\mathsf{smfw}(Q)\le\#\mathsf{smfw}(Q)\le\mathsf{faqw}(Q). \quad (92)$$

In particular, when Q *has no free variables, we have*

$$\mathsf{subw}(Q)\le\#\mathsf{subw}(Q)\le\mathsf{fhtw}(Q). \quad (93)$$

(b) *Furthermore, there are classes of queries* Q *for which the gap between* #smfw(Q) *and* faqw(Q) *is unbounded, and so is the gap between* #subw(Q) *and* fhtw(Q).

Proof. First we prove part (a). The first inequality in (92) follows directly from the definitions of #smfw and smfw along with the fact that $\Gamma_n\subsetneq\Gamma_{n|\mathcal{E}_{\not\:\!\!\:\!\!\:\!\!\:\!\!\:}}$. To prove the second inequality in (92), we use the following variant of the *Modularization Lemma* from [7]:

Claim 1 (Variant of the Modularization Lemma [7]). *Given a hypergraph* $\mathcal{H}=(\mathcal{V}=[n],\mathcal{E})$ *and a set* $B\subseteq\mathcal{V}$*, we have*

$$\max_{h\in\mathsf{ED}\cap\Gamma_{n|\mathcal{E}}}h(B)=\max_{h\in\mathsf{ED}\cap\mathsf{M}_n}h(B), \quad (94)$$

where ED *is given by* (5) *and* M_n *denotes the set of all modular functions* $h:2^{\mathcal{V}}\to\mathbb{R}_+$*. (A function* $h:2^{\mathcal{V}}\to\mathbb{R}_+$ *is modular if* $h(X)=\sum_{i\in X}h(i),\forall X\subseteq\mathcal{V}$*.)*

Proof of Claim 1. Obviously, the LHS of (94) is lower-bounded by the RHS. Next, we prove LHS ≤ RHS. WLOG we assume $B=[k]$ for some $k\in[n]$. Let $h^*=\arg\max_{h\in\mathsf{ED}\cap\Gamma_{n|\mathcal{E}}}h(B)$. Define a function $\bar{h}:2^{\mathcal{V}}\to\mathbb{R}_+$ as follows:

$$\bar{h}(F)=\sum_{i\in F}(h^*([i])-h^*([i-1])).$$

Obviously $\bar{h}\in\mathsf{M}_n$ and $\bar{h}(B)=h^*(B)$. Next, we prove $\bar{h}\in\mathsf{ED}$ by proving that for every $F\subseteq[n]$ where $F\subseteq E$ for some $E\in\mathcal{E}$, the following holds: $\bar{h}(F)\le h^*(F)$.

The proof is by induction on $|F|$. The base case when $|F|=0$ is trivial. For the inductive step, consider some F where $F\subseteq E$ for some $E\in\mathcal{E}$. Let j be the maximum integer in F, then by noting that $|F\cap[j-1]|<|F|$, we have

$$\begin{aligned} \bar{h}(F) &= h^*([j])-h^*([j-1])+\sum_{i\in F-\{j\}}(h^*([i])-h^*([i-1]))\\ &= h^*([j])-h^*([j-1])+\bar{h}(F\cap[j-1])\\ &= h^*(F\cup[j-1])-h^*([j-1])+\bar{h}(F\cap[j-1])\\ &\le h^*(F\cup[j-1])-h^*([j-1])+h^*(F\cap[j-1])\le h^*(F). \end{aligned}$$

The first inequality above is by induction hypothesis, and the second inequality follows from the fact that h^* is a $\mathcal{E}$-polymatroid (recall Definition 3.12). Both steps rely on the fact that $F\cap[j-1]\subseteq E$ for some $E\in\mathcal{E}$. Consequently, $\bar{h}\in\mathsf{ED}\cap\mathsf{M}_n$. Since $\bar{h}(B)=h^*(B)$, this proves Claim 1. □

Now we prove the second inequality in (92):

$$\begin{aligned} \#\mathsf{smfw}(Q) &= \max_{h\in\mathsf{ED}_{\not\!\!\:\!\!\:\!\!\:\!\!\:\mathcal{E}}\cap\Gamma_{n|\mathcal{E}_{\not\:\!\!\:\!\!\:\!\!\:\!\!\:}}}\min_{(T,\chi)\in\mathsf{TD}_F}\max_{t\in V(T)}h(\chi(t))\\ &\le \min_{(T,\chi)\in\mathsf{TD}_F}\max_{h\in\mathsf{ED}_{\not\!\!\:\!\!\:\!\!\:\!\!\:\mathcal{E}}\cap\Gamma_{n|\mathcal{E}_{\not\:\!\!\:\!\!\:\!\!\:\!\!\:}}}\max_{t\in V(T)}h(\chi(t))\\ &= \min_{(T,\chi)\in\mathsf{TD}_F}\max_{t\in V(T)}\max_{h\in\mathsf{ED}_{\not\!\!\:\!\!\:\!\!\:\!\!\:\mathcal{E}}\cap\Gamma_{n|\mathcal{E}_{\not\:\!\!\:\!\!\:\!\!\:\!\!\:}}}h(\chi(t))\\ \text{(Claim 1)}\quad &= \min_{(T,\chi)\in\mathsf{TD}_F}\max_{t\in V(T)}\max_{h\in\mathsf{ED}_{\not\!\!\:\!\!\:\!\!\:\!\!\:\mathcal{E}}\cap\mathsf{M}_n}h(\chi(t))\\ \text{(Strong duality)}\quad &= \min_{(T,\chi)\in\mathsf{TD}_F}\max_{t\in V(T)}\rho^*_{\mathcal{E}_{\not\:\!\!\:\!\!\:\!\!\:\!\!\:}}(\chi(t))=\mathsf{faqw}(Q). \end{aligned}$$

The fact that $\max_{h\in\mathsf{ED}_{\not\:\!\!\:\!\!\:\!\!\:\!\!\:\mathcal{E}}\cap\mathsf{M}_n}h(\chi(t))=\rho^*_{\mathcal{E}_{\not\:\!\!\:\!\!\:\!\!\:\!\!\:}}(\chi(t))$ follows from the two sides being dual linear programs. (Recall the definition of ρ^* from Section 2.1.)

Now, we prove part (b) of Proposition A.3. In [7], we constructed a class of graphs/queries where the gap between fhtw and subw is unbounded. We will re-use the same construction here and prove that the upperbound on subw that we proved in [7] is also an upperbound on #subw. The upperbound proof is going to be different from [7] though since here we can only use $\mathcal{E}$-polymatroid properties to prove the bound (recall Definition 3.12).

Given integers m and k, consider a graph $\mathcal{H} = (\mathcal{V}, \mathcal{E})$ which is an "m-fold $2k$-cycle": The vertex set $\mathcal{V} := I_1 \cup \ldots \cup I_{2k}$ is a disjoint union of $2k$-sets of vertices. Each set I_j has m vertices in it, i.e., $I_j := \{I_j^1, I_j^2, \ldots, I_j^m\}$. There is no edge between any two vertices within the set I_j for every $j \in [2k]$, i.e., I_j is an independent set. The edge set $\mathcal{E}$ of the hypergraph is the union of $2k$ complete bipartite graphs $K_{m,m}$:

$$\mathcal{E} := (I_1 \times I_2) \cup (I_2 \times I_3) \cup \cdots \cup (I_{2k-1} \times I_{2k}) \cup (I_{2k} \times I_1).$$

Finally consider an FAQ query Q that has a finite-sized input factor R_K for every $K \in \mathcal{E}$, i.e., $\mathcal{E}_{\not\infty} = \mathcal{E}$ and $\mathcal{E}_\infty = \emptyset$ (recall notation from Section 2.2). Assuming Q has no free variables, then $\text{faqw}(Q) = \text{fhtw}(Q)$ and $\#\text{smfw}(Q) = \#\text{subw}(Q)$.

We proved in [7] that $\text{fhtw}(Q) \geq 2m$. Next we prove that $\#\text{subw}(Q) \leq m(2 - 1/k)$. Let h be any function in $\text{ED}_{\not\infty} \cap \Gamma_{n|\mathcal{E}_{\not\infty}}$. We recognize two cases:

- Case 1: $h(I_i) \leq \theta$ for some $i \in [2k]$. WLOG assume $h(I_1) \leq \theta$. Consider the TD

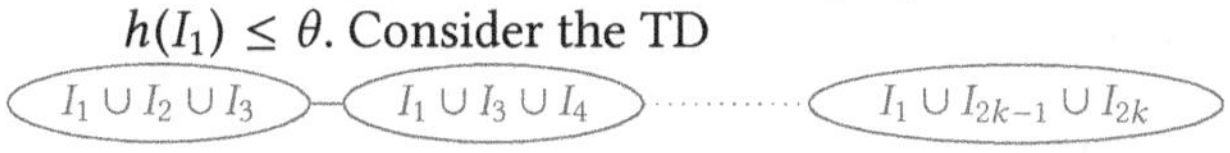

For bag $B = I_1 \cup I_i \cup I_{i+1}$, using $\mathcal{E}_{\not\infty}$-polymatroid properties (Definition 3.12), we have

$$\begin{aligned} h(B) &\leq h(I_1) + h(I_i \cup I_{i+1}) \\ &\leq h(I_1) + \sum_{j=1}^{m} h\left(\left\{I_i^j, I_{i+1}^j\right\}\right) \leq \theta + m. \end{aligned}$$

- Case 2: $h(I_i) > \theta$ for all $i \in [2k]$. Consider the TD

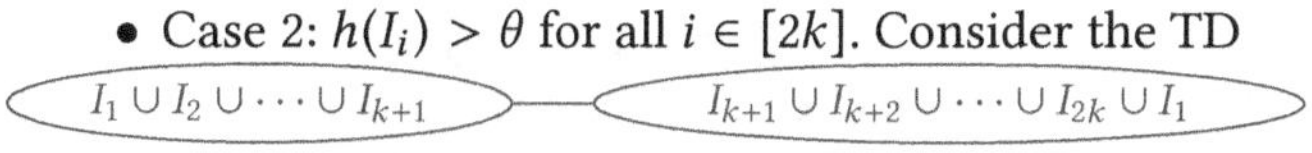

Bag B_1 Bag B_2

For convenience, given any vertex I_i^j, define the vertex set $\mathcal{V}_i^j$ as follows:

$$\mathcal{V}_i^j := I_1 \cup I_2 \cup \ldots \cup I_{i-1} \cup \left\{I_i^1, I_i^2, \ldots, I_i^{j-1}\right\}.$$

From $\mathcal{E}_{\not\infty}$-polymatroid properties, we have

$$\begin{aligned} h(B_1) &= h(I_1 \cup I_2) + \sum_{i=3}^{k+1} \sum_{j=1}^{m} h\left(\left\{I_i^j\right\} \cup \mathcal{V}_i^j \mid \mathcal{V}_i^j\right) \\ &\leq h(I_1 \cup I_2) + \sum_{i=3}^{k+1} \sum_{j=1}^{m} h\left(\left\{I_i^j, I_{i-1}^j\right\} \mid \left\{I_{i-1}^j\right\}\right) \\ &= h(I_1 \cup I_2) + \sum_{i=3}^{k+1} \sum_{j=1}^{m} h\left(\left\{I_i^j, I_{i-1}^j\right\}\right) - \sum_{i=3}^{k+1} \sum_{j=1}^{m} h\left(\left\{I_{i-1}^j\right\}\right) \\ &\leq h(I_1 \cup I_2) + \sum_{i=3}^{k+1} \sum_{j=1}^{m} h\left(\left\{I_i^j, I_{i-1}^j\right\}\right) - \sum_{i=3}^{k+1} h(I_{i-1}) \\ &\leq \sum_{i=2}^{k+1} \sum_{j=1}^{m} h\left(\left\{I_i^j, I_{i-1}^j\right\}\right) - \sum_{i=3}^{k+1} h(I_{i-1}) \leq km - (k-1)\theta. \end{aligned}$$

In a symmetric way, we can also show that $h(B_2) \leq km - (k-1)\theta$. By setting $\theta = (1 - 1/k)m$, we prove that $\#\text{subw}(Q) \leq m(2 - 1/k)$. Since $\text{fhtw}(Q) \geq 2m$, this proves part (b). □

A.4 More details on Example 3.19

Consider the count query from Example 3.19. First we prove that $\#\text{smfw}_\ell(Q) \leq 1.5$. Here $F = \emptyset$. We will use two *relaxed* tree decompositions in TD_F^ℓ: The first (T_1, χ_1) has two bags $\{a, b, c\}$ and $\{c, d\}$. The second (T_2, χ_2) has two bags $\{a, b\}$ and $\{b, c, d\}$. (Both are relaxed TDs because the ligament edge $\mathbf{1}_{a+b+c+d \leq 0}$ is not contained in any bag; recall Definition 3.3.) Following (51), for each $h \in \text{ED}_{\not\infty} \cap \Gamma_{n|\mathcal{E}_{\not\infty}}$, we will pick one TD or the other. In particular, given some $h \in \text{ED}_{\not\infty} \cap \Gamma_{n|\mathcal{E}_{\not\infty}}$:

- If $h(b) \geq 1/2$, then $h(bc|b) \leq 1/2$. We pick (T_1, χ_1). From $\mathcal{E}_{\not\infty}$-polymatroid properties (Def. 3.12), we have

$$\begin{aligned} h(abc) &= h(ab) + h(abc|ab) \leq h(ab) + h(bc|b) \leq 1.5, \\ h(cd) &\leq 1. \end{aligned}$$

- If $h(b) < 1/2$, we pick (T_2, χ_2).

$$\begin{aligned} h(ab) &\leq 1, \\ h(bcd) &= h(b) + h(bcd|b) \leq h(b) + h(cd) \leq 1.5. \end{aligned}$$

This proves that $\#\text{smfw}_\ell(Q) \leq 1.5$.

Finally, as a special case of #PANDA, we explain how to solve the above query in time $\tilde{O}(N^{1.5})$ (where recall $N := \max\{|R|, |S|, |T|\}$). Let

$$\begin{aligned} S^\ell &:= \left\{(b, c) \in S \mid |\{c' \mid (b, c') \in S\}| \leq \sqrt{N}\right\}, \\ S^h &:= S \setminus S^\ell. \end{aligned}$$

Now we can write

$$\begin{aligned} Q() &= \sum_{a,b,c,d} R(a, b) \left(S^\ell(b, c) + S^h(b, c)\right) T(c, d) \cdot \mathbf{1}_{a+b+c+d \leq 0} \\ &= Q^\ell() + Q^h(), \text{ where} \\ Q^\ell() &:= \sum_{a,b,c,d} \underbrace{R(a, b) \cdot S^\ell(b, c)}_{U(a,b,c)} \cdot T(c, d) \cdot \mathbf{1}_{a+b+c+d \leq 0}, \\ Q^h() &:= \sum_{a,b,c,d} R(a, b) \cdot \underbrace{S^h(b, c) \cdot T(c, d)}_{W(b,c,d)} \cdot \mathbf{1}_{a+b+c+d \leq 0}. \end{aligned}$$

Both U and W above have sizes $\leq N^{1.5}$. Using the algorithm from the proof of Theorem 3.5, Q^ℓ can be answered in time $O(N^{1.5} \log N)$ using the relaxed TD (T_1, χ_1), while Q^h can be answered in the same time using (T_2, χ_2).

Topology Dependent Bounds For FAQs

Michael Langberg
University at Buffalo

Shi Li
University at Buffalo

Sai Vikneshwar Mani Jayaraman
University at Buffalo

Atri Rudra
University at Buffalo

ABSTRACT

In this paper, we prove topology dependent bounds on the number of rounds needed to compute Functional Aggregate Queries (FAQs) studied by Abo Khamis et al. [PODS 2016] in a synchronous distributed network under the model considered by Chattopadhyay et al. [FOCS 2014, SODA 2017]. Unlike the recent work on computing database queries in the Massively Parallel Computation model, in the model of Chattopadhyay et al., nodes can communicate only via private point-to-point channels and we are interested in bounds that work over an *arbitrary* communication topology. This model, which is closer to the well-studied CONGEST model in distributed computing and generalizes Yao's two party communication complexity model, has so far only been studied for problems that are common in the two-party communication complexity literature.

This is the first work to consider more practically motivated problems in this distributed model. For the sake of exposition, we focus on two specific problems in this paper: Boolean Conjunctive Query (BCQ) and computing variable/factor marginals in Probabilistic Graphical Models (PGMs). We obtain tight bounds on the number of rounds needed to compute such queries as long as the underlying hypergraph of the query is $O(1)$-degenerate and has $O(1)$-arity. In particular, the $O(1)$-degeneracy condition covers most well-studied queries that are efficiently computable in the centralized computation model like queries with constant treewidth. These tight bounds depend on a new notion of 'width' (namely *internal-node-width*) for Generalized Hypertree Decompositions (GHDs) of acyclic hypergraphs, which minimizes the number of internal nodes in a sub-class of GHDs. To the best of our knowledge, this width has not been studied explicitly in the theoretical database literature. Finally, we consider the problem of computing the product of a vector with a chain of matrices and prove tight bounds on its round complexity (over a finite field of two elements) using a novel min-entropy based argument.

KEYWORDS

Topology Dependent Bounds, CONGEST model, Probabalistic Graphical Models, Boolean Conjunctive Query, Communication Complexity Lower Bounds.

ACM Reference Format:

Michael Langberg, Shi Li, Sai Vikneshwar Mani Jayaraman, and Atri Rudra. 2019. Topology Dependent Bounds For FAQs. In *38th ACM SIGMOD-SIGACT-SIGAI Symposium on Principles of Database Systems (PODS'19), June 30-July 5, 2019, Amsterdam, Netherlands.* ACM, New York, NY, USA, 18 pages. https://doi.org/10.1145/3294052.3319686

PODS'19, June 30-July 5, 2019, Amsterdam, Netherlands

ACM ISBN 978-1-4503-6227-6/19/06...$15.00
https://doi.org/10.1145/3294052.3319686

1 INTRODUCTION

In this paper, we prove topology dependent bounds on the number of rounds needed to compute Functional Aggregate Queries (FAQs) of [32] in a synchronous distributed network under the model considered by Chattopadhyay et al. [18, 19]. For ease of exposition, we consider the FAQ-SS problem [7, 32, 41] i.e., FAQ with a single semiring (also called *Marginalize a Product Function* in [3]), which is a special case of the general FAQ problem (defined in Section 5). In FAQ-SS, we are given a multi-hypergraph $\mathcal{H} = (\overline{\mathcal{V}}, \overline{\mathcal{E}})$ where for each hyperedge $e \in \overline{\mathcal{E}}$ we are given an input function $f_e : \prod_{v\in e} \text{Dom}(v) \to \mathbb{D}$. In addition we are given a set of *free variables*[1] $\mathcal{F} \subseteq \overline{\mathcal{V}}$ and our goal is to compute the function:

$$\phi_{\mathcal{F}}(\mathbf{x}) = \sum_{\mathbf{y}\in\prod_{v\in\overline{\mathcal{V}}}\text{Dom}(v):\mathbf{y}_{\mathcal{F}}=\mathbf{x}} \prod_{e\in\overline{\mathcal{E}}} f_e(\mathbf{y}_e) \quad (1.0)$$

for every $\mathbf{x} \in \prod_{v\in\mathcal{F}} \text{Dom}(v)$, where $\mathbf{y}_e$ and $\mathbf{y}_{\mathcal{F}}$ are $\mathbf{y}$ projected down to co-ordinates in $e \subseteq \overline{\mathcal{V}}$ for every $e \in \overline{\mathcal{E}}$ and $\mathcal{F} \subseteq \overline{\mathcal{V}}$ respectively. Further, all the operations are over the *commutative semiring*[2] $(\mathbb{D}, +, \cdot)$ with additive identity $\mathbf{0}$.

[1] We would like to mention here that our results hold only for specific choices of free variables.

[2] A triple $(\mathbb{D}, \oplus, \otimes)$ is a *commutative semiring* if $\oplus$ and $\otimes$ are commutative binary operators over $\mathbb{D}$ satisfying the following: (1) $(\mathbb{D}, \oplus)$ is a commutative monoid with an additive identity, denoted by $\mathbf{0}$. (2) $(\mathbb{D}, \otimes)$ is a commutative

As with database systems, we assume that the functions are given in *listing* representation i.e., the function f_e is represented as a list of its non-zero values: $R_e = \{(\mathbf{y}, f_e(\mathbf{y}))|\mathbf{y} \in \prod_{v \in e} Dom(v) : f_e(\mathbf{y}) \neq \mathbf{0}\}$.[3] We define $D = \max_{v \in \overline{\mathcal{V}}} |\text{Dom}(v)|$, $N = \max_{e \in \overline{\mathcal{E}}} |R_e|$, $k = |\overline{\mathcal{E}}|$ and r as the maximum arity among all functions.

Though our results are semiring agnostic, we mention two special problems that we consider in this paper. The first problem is when $\mathcal{F} = \emptyset$ and the semiring is the *Boolean semiring* $(\mathbb{D} = \{0, 1\}, \vee, \wedge)$. This corresponds to the *Boolean Conjunctive Query* (which we will call BCQ).[4] The other problem is when $\mathcal{F} = e$ for some $e \in \overline{\mathcal{E}}$ and the semiring is $(\mathbb{R}_{\geq 0}, +, \cdot)$, which corresponds to computing a *factor marginal* in *Probabilistic Graphical Models* (or PGMs) – here we think of f_e as a probability distribution. The FAQ setup (and even FAQ-SS) encompasses a large class of problems in varied domains. We refer the reader to the surveys [3, 33] for an overview of these applications.

Given a query $q = \left(\mathcal{H}, \{f_e\}_{e \in \overline{\mathcal{E}}}, \mathcal{F}\right)$, we will consider the number of rounds needed to compute q in a distributed environment. In particular, the underlying *communication topology*[5] $G = (V, E)$ is assumed to be a synchronous network and we would like to compute q on G with the following constraints [18, 19]. Initially, all functions $\{f_e\}_{e \in \overline{\mathcal{E}}}$ are assigned to specific nodes $K \subseteq V : 1 \leq |K| \leq k$ (called *players*). In each *round* of communication, $O(r \cdot \log_2(D))$ bits[6] can be simultaneously communicated on each edge in E (each such edge or *channel* is private to the nodes at its endpoints). At the end of the protocol, a pre-determined player in K knows the answer to q. Naturally, we would like to design protocols that minimize the total number of rounds of communication (rounds hereon) needed to compute q on G. More generally, we would like to obtain tight bounds depending on $\mathcal{H}$ and G for this problem for *every* query topology $\mathcal{H}$ and *every* network topology G. Note that we do not take into account the internal computation done by nodes in G and we assume that all nodes in V co-operatively compute the answer to q. Due to space constraints, many of the technical details are deferred to the version of this paper [38], which we refer to as full paper.

monoid with a multiplicative identity, denoted by $\mathbf{1}$. (In the usual semiring definition, we do not need the multiplicative monoid to be commutative.) (3) $\otimes$ distributes over $\oplus$. (4) For any element $d \in \mathbb{D}$, we have $d \otimes \mathbf{0} = \mathbf{0} \otimes d = \mathbf{0}$.

[3] We use function/relation interchangeably for f_e / R_e but both mean the same.

[4] $\mathcal{F} = \overline{\mathcal{V}}$ over the Boolean semiring is the natural join problem.

[5] Note that this is distinct from $\mathcal{H}$ and is just a simple graph: see Figure 1 for an example illustrating this difference.

[6] This is a natural choice since any tuple in any function can be communicated with at most $O(r \cdot \log_2(D))$ bits. Our bounds seamlessly generalize to the cases when each edge – (1) can transmit $B \neq r \cdot \log_2(D)$ bits and (2) has a different capacity, but for ease of exposition, we will not consider these generalizations in this paper.

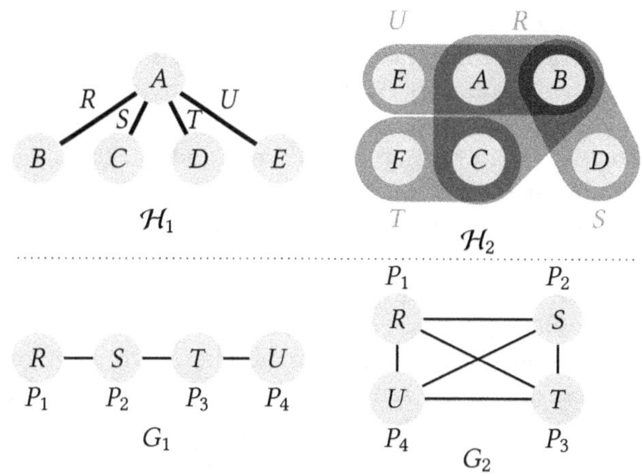

Figure 1: Two example queries $\mathcal{H}_1$ and $\mathcal{H}_2$ and two topologies – "line" G_1 and "clique" G_2. $\mathcal{H}_2$ has hyperedges $R(A, B, C)$, $S(B, D)$, $T(C, F)$ and $U(A, B, E)$.

1.1 Why this distributed model?

We believe that the strength of our model is its generality. Specifically, it captures query computation in three different paradigms, namely: (1) Computing the natural join query in the Massively Parallel Computation (MPC) model [2, 9, 10, 31, 36, 37], (2) Computing join and aggregation queries for sensor networks [13, 23, 40] and (3) Computation of FAQs on arbitrary topologies using *software defined networks* and optical reconfigurable networks like ProjecToR [24]. Before we discuss these in detail, we would like to mention that the CONGEST model in distributed computing has the same setup as ours [42] with one crucial difference. Unlike our case, where we can compute FAQs on *any* topology in the CONGEST model, the topologies for computing a fixed FAQ typically depend on the query itself.

The sequence of works in the MPC setting focus on computing the natural join q (which is a special case of FAQ-SS as mentioned earlier) on a topology G with p nodes, which is typically well-connected. Each round of communication has two phases – (1) internal computation among the nodes and (2) communication between the nodes bounded by a node capacity L. The goal in MPC is to minimize the number of rounds h needed for computing q. There are two different lines of work in this regime – one where p is fixed and the goal is to determine h, L [9, 10, 36, 37] and the other is when h, L are fixed and the goal is to determine p [2]. We compare both these classes of models with ours in Appendix A and present an executive summary here.

Roughly speaking, the MPC model defined in [9] is a special case of our model. We consider two different MPC models – one with no replication (which we call MPC(0) [9]) and one with replication (which we dub MPC(ϵ) [2, 36]). Both these models have some differences from ours and among themselves. For instance, both these models assume a specific network topology G' (as opposed to any topology G in our case), work on node capacities L (as opposed to edge capacities in our setting) and prove bounds for the natural join problem (in contrast, our bounds apply for the more general FAQ). The input functions are systematically assigned to players in MPC(0) and are uniformly distributed among players in MPC(ϵ). The instantation of these models for the setting where p is fixed and h, L is to be determined is the closest to our model. In particular, when $\mathcal{H}$ is a star, our protocols obtain the same guarantees as MPC(0) and are slightly worse in MPC(ϵ). Our model does not (yet) handle the scenario when L is fixed and the goal is to determine p. Sensor networks are typically tree-like topologies, where the goal is to efficiently and accurately report aggregate queries on data generated by the sensors. Since the sensors can store only little data, these queries are typically restrictive. We show in the full paper [38] that our results imply bounds for some of these queries. Recently, Internet of Things (IoT) devices [1] show the promise of expanding the data storage/class of queries that can be computed on sensor networks. We believe that our model/results will find more relevance in the IoT setting since the sensors used posess more computation power than those considered in [40]. Finally, our work initiates the study of computation on general topologies to be used in emerging technologies like ProjecToR [24], which has been proposed for use in data centers where topologies can be changed based on the workload.

1.2 Summary of Our Contributions

Table 1 lists our results and Section 2 contains a detailed overview of techniques used to obtain the results. We summarize our contributions here. For the sake of brevity, we focus on the BCQ problem. Our main result is the following. For (hyper)graphs $\mathcal{H}$ with constant degeneracy[7] (d) and constant arity (r), we prove tight bounds (up to constant factors) for computing *any* BCQ on *any* network topology G. Constant treewidth implies constant d and, as a result, queries having constant d encompass most well-studied queries that are efficiently computable in the centralized computation model.

Upper Bounds. Our upper bounds need protocols for solving the following two basic algorithmic tasks: (1) set intersection and (2) sending all inputs to a single node. For (1), our protocol is new in the FAQ literature and for (2), we use a standard protocol from flow networks. Interestingly, our results highlight a notion of width of *acyclic* queries– the number of internal nodes for a subclass of GHDs[8] (defined in Section 2.2.2), which to the best of our knowledge, has not been explicitly studied in the database literature.

Lower Bounds. Our lower bounds follow from known lower bounds on the well-studied TRIBES function in two-party communication complexity literature (defined in Section 2.2.2). At a high level, we start with an arbitrary TRIBES instance and show that it can be reduced to a suitable BCQ instance in our model. We then prove lower bounds on the BCQ instance using known lower bounds on TRIBES.

We note here that the simplicity of our techniques allows us to extend our results to the general FAQ problem. Further, we would like to mention that extending our bounds to d-degenerate graphs with non-constant d has a known bottleneck of solving BCQ of $\mathcal{H}$ on G when $\mathcal{H}$ is a clique and G is an edge. In particular, the gaps dependent on d in Table 1 cannot be resolved without addressing this bottleneck.

Finally, we consider the following FAQ-SS problem of Chain Matrix-Vector Multiplication (MCM): computing $\mathbf{A}_k \cdot \mathbf{A}_{k-1} \cdot \ldots \cdot \mathbf{A}_1 \cdot \mathbf{x}$, where each player gets $\mathbf{x}, \mathbf{A}_1, \ldots, \mathbf{A}_k$ in order and they would like to compute the product over the finite field $\mathbb{F}_2$.[9] Note that this problem is different from the well-known Online Matrix Vector Multiplication problem[10] and is related to k layer neural networks.[11] We prove a tight bound for this problem. The upper bound is simple but the lower bound argument (though conceptually simple) is technically the most involved part of the paper. We use an entropy-based argument using min-entropy instead of the standard Shannon's entropy. This requires more care since we can no longer use the chain rule.

2 OUR MODEL AND DETAILED OVERVIEW OF OUR RESULTS

In this section, our goal is to provide a walkthrough of our results and techniques used to prove them. We start with a formal definition of our model. Then, we illustrate with examples our results for the case when $\mathcal{H}$ has arity at most two and subsequently, our new notion of width for GHDs. We conclude this section with our results on Chain Matrix-Vector Multiplication (MCM).

2.1 Our Model

We first define our model.

[7] Degeneracy is defined as the smallest d such that every sub(hyper)graph in $\mathcal{H}$ has a vertex of degree at most d.

[8] An internal node is a non-leaf node in a GHD.

[9] $\mathbb{F}_2$ has two elements: the additive identity $\mathbf{0}$ and multiplicative identity $\mathbf{1}$. Addition and Multiplication are all modulo 2.

[10] We illustrate this difference in the full paper [38].

[11] In neural networks, a non-linear function is applied after each matrix-vector multiplication and the multiplication is over reals instead of $\mathbb{F}_2$. Our lower bounds hold for this setting as well.

Query	G	d, r	Gap	Ref
FAQ	L	$O(1), O(1)$	$\widetilde{O}(1)$	Thm 5.1
FAQ	A	$O(1), O(1)$	$\widetilde{O}(1)$	Thm 5.1
BCQ	A	$d, 2$	$\widetilde{O}(d)$	Thm 4.1
FAQ	A	d, r	$\widetilde{O}(d^2 r^2)$	Thm 5.2
MCM*	L	1, 2	$O(1)$	Sec 6

Table 1: The first and second columns denote the query that we compute and topology on which the query is computed. In the second column, L denotes a line and A denotes an arbitrary G. The third column denotes the degeneracy (Definition 3.3) and arity conditions (d, r). The fourth column denotes the gap between our upper and lower bounds ignoring polylogarithmic factors in N and G (denoted by $\widetilde{O}$). The final column denotes the relevant result in this paper. Note that all our results except MCM (denoted by a '*') assume worst-case assignment of input functions in the query to nodes in G.

Model 2.1. *We are given a query q, its underlying hypergraph $\mathcal{H} = (\overline{\mathcal{V}}, \overline{\mathcal{E}})$ with input functions f_e (having at most N non-zero values) for every $e \in \overline{\mathcal{E}}$ and a topology $G = (V, E)$. Further, each function is completely assigned to a unique node in V. It follows that there exists a subset $K : K \subseteq V$ that contains the players with functions and $|K| \leq k = |\overline{\mathcal{E}}|$. We assume $N \geq |V(G)|^2$ and consider worst-case inputs for the functions. We would like to compute* BCQ *(and more generally an* FAQ*) of $\mathcal{H}$ on G. To design a protocol for this computation, we assume that every node in G has the knowledge of $\mathcal{H}$ and G. In each round of the protocol, at most $O(r \cdot \log_2(D))$ bits can be communicated over every edge in E. In particular, this implies any subset of edges in G can communicate in the same round. Further, at the end of the protocol, a pre-determined player in K has the answer to q.*
Finally, given the above setup, our goal is to design protocols that minimize the total number of rounds needed to compute q assuming worst-case assignment of the functions to players in G. Note that we do not take into account the internal computation done by nodes in G and we assume that all nodes are always available in V (i.e., node failures do not happen) and they co-operatively compute the answer to q.

We prove both upper and lower bounds on the total number of rounds needed to compute q on G for every query hypergraph $\mathcal{H}$ and every topology G. While our upper bounds hold for any assignment of input functions to players in G, our lower bounds hold for a specific class of worst-case assignments of input functions to players in G. In Section 8, we further discuss the assumptions on $\mathcal{H}$ and G in the above model.
Before we move to our results for the case when $\mathcal{H}$ has arity at most two, we would like to point out that our bounds do not assume that the size of q is negligible compared to N, which is a standard assumption for computing database queries. Thus, our results are more general and in particular, for applications in PGMs, this is necessary since the size of q cannot be assumed as negligible w.r.t. N.

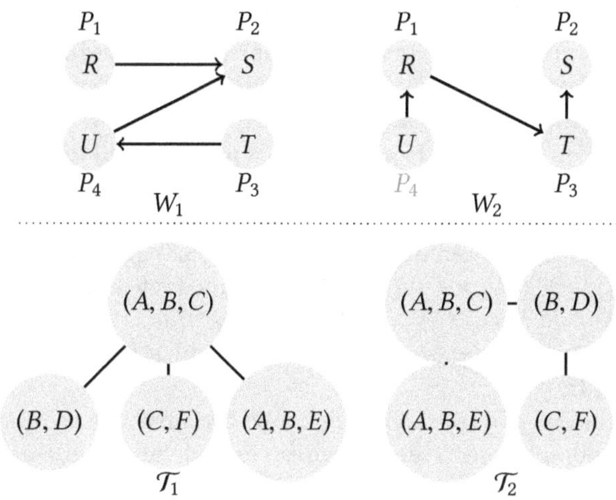

Figure 2: Two directed paths W_1 and W_2 for G_2 and two GHDs $\mathcal{T}_1$ (with 1 internal node) and $\mathcal{T}_2$ (with 2 internal nodes) both rooted at (A, B, C) for $\mathcal{H}_2$. G_2 and $\mathcal{H}_2$ are in Figure 1.

2.2 Arity Two $\mathcal{H}$

We consider the case when $\mathcal{H}$ has arity at most two and illustrate our upper and lower bound techniques through examples.

2.2.1 Upper Bounds. We start with a trivial protocol to compute any query $\mathcal{H}$ on any G. We then show how to improve upon it when $\mathcal{H}$ has a special structure. We use two extremal instances of G for an easy exposition of our results – a line (least connectivity) and a clique (full connectivity). We refer the reader to Figure 1 for all examples (except $\mathcal{H}_0$) considered in this section.

Trivial Protocol. There is always a *trivial protocol* to solve any query $\mathcal{H}$ on any G in which all players send their functions to one designated player who then computes the answer.
We consider the topologies G_1 and G_2 from Figure 1. We first start by computing a toy query $\mathcal{H}_0$ on G_1.

Example 2.1. Consider the query hypergraph $\mathcal{H}_0 = (\overline{\mathcal{V}} = \{A\}, \overline{\mathcal{E}} = \{R(A), S(A), T(A), U(A)\})$ i.e., all edges are self-loops on A and the line G_1. We would like to solve BCQ of $\mathcal{H}_0$ on G_1, which in Datalog format is $q_0() : -R(A), S(A), T(A), U(A)$. In G_1, player P_1 gets R, P_2 gets S, P_3 gets T and P_4 gets U. Then, solving BCQ of $\mathcal{H}_0$ on G_1 is equivalent to checking if

the set-intersection $R(A) \cap S(A) \cap T(A) \cap U(A)$ is empty. Let us assume that player P_4 needs to know the answer for this query.
We can solve this query in $N+2$ rounds as follows. In the first round, player P_1 sends a value $a \in \text{Dom}(A)$ such that there exists $R(a) = 1$ to player P_2 who then checks if $S(a) = 1$. More generally, in the i-th round, player P_j for $2 \leq j \leq 4$ receives an a from its left neighbor $(j-1)$ and checks if a is present in its table. If so, it passes a to its right neighbor $(j+1)$ (if $j \leq 3$) in the next $(i+1)$-th round. Otherwise, it does not pass anything. Notice that this protocol will terminate once all matching values of a are passed from P_1 to P_4 which takes $N+2$ rounds in the worst case. In other words, we are computing the semijoin (see Definition 3.5) query $((R(A) \ltimes S(A)) \ltimes T(A)) \ltimes U(A)$, which is equivalent to computing $R(A) \cap S(A) \cap T(A) \cap U(A)$. Note that this is much better than the *trivial protocol* for this case, which takes $3 \cdot N + 2$ rounds.
At the end of this protocol, P_4 knows the answer to the query. It is not too hard to see that we can extend the above protocol to the case when any other player say P_i for some $i \in [3]$ is designated to know the answer. In particular, we can orient G_1 in such a way that all paths are directed towards P_i and then run the protocol above simultaneously on all paths (there are at most two) towards P_i (recall that we assume knowledge of G for all nodes). Note that P_i would have the answer to the query and the new protocol takes $N+x$ rounds, where $x \leq 2$ depends on the choice of P_i.

It is not too hard to see that our protocol in the above example can be extended to the case when $\mathcal{H}$ is a star. We illustrate this in the following example.

Example 2.2. Consider the star $\mathcal{H}_1$ and the line G_1 in Figure 1. We would like to solve BCQ of $\mathcal{H}_1$ on G_1, which in Datalog format is $q_1() : -R(A,B), S(A,C), T(A,D), U(A,E)$. In G_1, player P_1 gets R, P_2 gets S, P_3 gets T and P_4 gets U. Then, BCQ of $\mathcal{H}_1$ is 1 iff $\pi_A(R) \cap \pi_A(S) \cap \pi_A(T) \cap \pi_A(U)$ is non-empty and 0 otherwise. Here, $\pi_A(\cdot)$ denotes the projection onto attribute A. We assume P_2 needs to know the answer for this query.
We can solve this query in $N+2$ rounds using the same protocol as in Example 2.1. In other words, we are computing the semjoin query[12] $((\pi_A(R) \ltimes \pi_A(S)) \ltimes \pi_A(T)) \ltimes \pi_A(U)$. Note that each node needs to compute $\pi_A(\cdot)$ internally but this doesn't need any communication between the nodes. At the end of this protocol, P_2 knows the answer to the query.

We now show how to do the same computation (i.e., BCQ of $\mathcal{H}_1$) on G_2.

[12]We would like to mention that casting the computation of BCQ on a star query as a semijoin is well-known [34].

Example 2.3. Consider the star $\mathcal{H}_1$ and the clique G_2 in Figure 1. We would like to compute BCQ of $\mathcal{H}_1$ on G_2, which in Datalog format is same as q_1 from Example 2.2. In G_2, player P_1 gets R, P_2 gets S, P_3 gets T and P_4 gets U. We assume that Dom(A) is split into two halves and P_2 needs to know the answer for this query.
We can solve this query in $\frac{N}{2} + 2$ rounds as follows. We consider the two edge-disjoint directed paths W_1 and W_2 (see Figure 2) on G_2 that end with P_2. Our protocol from Example 2.2 runs on both these paths simultaneously with one caveat – the values of a in the first half of Dom(A) are sent through W_1 and the ones in the second half of Dom(A) are sent through W_2. Since both these directed paths involve the same set of nodes, our protocol is valid and takes only $\frac{N}{2} + 2$ rounds as claimed above. Note that this is better than our bound in Example 2.2.

The protocols in Examples 2.2 and 2.3 can be generalized to solve any star $\mathcal{H}$ on any G. Given the protocol for a star, there is a natural extension to $\mathcal{H}$ being a tree (or more generally a forest): we handle all the stars of the tree in a bottom-up fashion (starting with the stars at the "end" of the tree) and recurse. In particular, we can apply our protocol for the star case as a black-box on each of these stars. To extend this result to general d-degenerate graphs $\mathcal{H}$, we first decompose $\mathcal{H}$ into a forest and a *core* that contains the roots of all trees in the forest and all remaining vertices not in the forest. We run the above protocol on the forest and use the *trivial protocol* on the core. For general G, note that we need to find optimal ways of applying these protocols – for the forest part, we extend the idea of packing edge-disjoint paths from Example 2.3 to a Steiner tree (Definition 3.8) packing and for the *trivial protocol*, we use standard ideas from network flows (Definition 3.12). We would like to mention here that our upper bounds hold even when more than one function is assigned to a player (i.e., $|K| < k$). We will crucially exploit this fact in our lower bounds. We present more details in Section 4.1.
We are now ready to talk about our lower bounds.

2.2.2 Lower Bounds. All our lower bounds follow from known lower bounds on the well-studied TRIBES function (see [18] and references therein) in two-party communication complexity literature. To this end, we first consider an arbitrary TRIBES instance of a specific size and show that it can be reduced to a suitable two-party BCQ instance. In particular, solving the two-party BCQ instance we constructed indeed solves the TRIBES instance we started with. Thus, known lower bounds on TRIBES imply lower bounds for BCQ. Finally, we generalize our results from the two-party setting to general G using ideas from [18, 19] and exploit the fact that our (upper and) lower bounds are for worst-case input

functions and worst-case assignments of input functions to players in G.
We start by defining the two-party communication complexity model as a special case of Model 2.1.

Model 2.2. *Consider two players Alice (a) and Bob (b) on a graph $\mathcal{G} = (V = \{a, b\}, E = \{(a, b)\})$ with strings $\bar{X} = (X_1, \ldots, X_m)$ and $\bar{Y} = (Y_1, \ldots, Y_m)$, where $X_i, Y_i \in \{0,1\}^N$. Further, Alice gets $\bar{X}$, Bob gets $\bar{Y}$ and both have knowledge of only their inputs. The goal for these two players is to compute the boolean function $f(\bar{X}, \bar{Y}) : \{0,1\}^{m \cdot N} \times \{0,1\}^{m \cdot N} \to \{0,1\}$. The randomized two-party communication complexity of computing f, denoted by $\mathcal{R}(f(\bar{X}, \bar{Y}), \mathcal{G}, \{a, b\})$, is defined as the minimum worst-case number of rounds*[13] *needed by a randomized protocol that deterministically computes $f(\bar{X}, \bar{Y})$ with error at most $\frac{1}{3}$.*

We would like to mention that considering the randomized two-party communication complexity over its deterministic counterpart makes our lower bounds only stronger. We define TRIBES and state the lower bound result that we will use in our arguments.

Theorem 2.3 (Jayram et. al [30]). *Let $\text{TRIBES}_{m,N}(\bar{X}, \bar{Y}) \equiv \bigwedge_{i=1}^{m} \text{DISJ}_N(X_i, Y_i)$, where $\text{DISJ}_N(X_i, Y_i)$ is 1 if $X_i \cap Y_i \neq \emptyset$ and 0 otherwise, $X_i, Y_i \in \{0,1\}^N$ for every $i \in [m]$ and $\bar{X} = (X_1, \ldots, X_m)$, $\bar{Y} = (Y_1, \ldots, Y_m)$. Note that in the two-party model, Alice gets $\bar{X}$ and Bob gets $\bar{Y}$. Given this setup, we have*

$$\mathcal{R}\left(\text{TRIBES}_{m,N}(\bar{X}, \bar{Y}), \mathcal{G}, \{a, b\}\right) \geq \Omega(m \cdot N).$$

We start with an arbitrary TRIBES instance $\text{TRIBES}_{m,N}(\bar{X}, \bar{Y})$ of a suitable size and show that it can be reduced to a suitable two-party BCQ instance $\text{BCQ}_{\mathcal{H},\bar{X},\bar{Y}}$, where m is a function of $\mathcal{H}$. In particular, such a reduction would imply

$$\mathcal{R}\left(\text{BCQ}_{\mathcal{H},\bar{X},\bar{Y}}, \mathcal{G}, \{a, b\}\right) \geq \mathcal{R}\left(\text{TRIBES}_{m,N}(\bar{X}, \bar{Y}), \mathcal{G}, \{a, b\}\right) \geq \Omega(m \cdot N),$$

where the final inequality follows from Theorem 2.3. The above inequality implies the following since we consider worst-case input functions for a fixed $\mathcal{H}$.

$$\mathcal{R}\left(\text{BCQ}_{\mathcal{H},N}, \mathcal{G}, \{a, b\}\right) \geq \mathcal{R}\left(\text{BCQ}_{\mathcal{H},\bar{X},\bar{Y}}, \mathcal{G}, \{a, b\}\right), \quad (1)$$

where $\text{BCQ}_{\mathcal{H},N}$ denote the class of problems where all functions in $\mathcal{H}$ have size at most N. We generalize the above result to any G using ideas from [18, 19]. We consider an appropriate cut $C = (A, B)$ of G that partitions V into two vertex-disjoint subsets A and B and a correponding assignment, where each function $e \in \overline{\mathcal{E}}(\mathcal{H})$ is assigned to a node in either A or B. Since this is a valid assignment of functions in $\mathcal{H}$ to players in G, the minimum number of rounds needed to compute an instance of $\text{BCQ}_{\mathcal{H},N}$ on G assuming worst-assignments of functions to players in K, denoted by $\mathcal{R}(\text{BCQ}_{\mathcal{H}}, G, K)$, is at least $\frac{\mathcal{R}(\text{BCQ}_{\mathcal{H},\bar{X},\bar{Y}}, \mathcal{G}, \{a,b\})}{\text{MinCut}(G,K)\lceil \log(\text{MinCut}(G,K)) \rceil}$. We reconsider $\mathcal{H}_1$ and G_1 from Example 2.2 here.

Example 2.4. Recall we proved an upper bound of $N + 2$ for computing BCQ of $\mathcal{H}_1$ on G_1. We start with an arbitrary $\text{TRIBES}_{m=1,N}(\bar{X} = (X_1), \bar{Y} = (Y_1))$ instance. With a slight abuse of notation, we treat X_1, Y_1 as subsets of $[N]$ (instead of elements in $\{0,1\}^N$). We now construct a corresponding $\text{BCQ}_{\mathcal{H}_1,\bar{X},\bar{Y}}$ instance from the TRIBES one as follows – we assign $R(A, B) = X_1 \times \{1\}$, $S(A, C) = T(A, D) = [N] \times \{1\}$ and $U(A, E) = Y_1 \times \{1\}$. It is not too hard to see that $\text{BCQ}_{\mathcal{H}_1,\bar{X},\bar{Y}}$ is 1 iff $\text{TRIBES}_{1,N}(\bar{X}, \bar{Y})$ is 1, implying that solving the BCQ instance would solve the TRIBES instance. Finally, to obtain a lower bound for computing $\text{BCQ}_{\mathcal{H}_1,\bar{X},\bar{Y}}$ on the line G_1, we only need a cut where R and U are on different sides. We consider the cut $C = (\{P_1, P_2\}, \{P_3, P_4\})$ of G_1 and the assignment where P_1 gets R, P_2 gets S, P_3 gets T and P_4 gets U. Then, we can us (1) and Theorem 2.3 to obtain the required lower bound of $\Omega(N)$ since $\text{MinCut}(G, K) = 1$. Note that the above lower bound holds for any star $\mathcal{H}$. The same TRIBES instance can be used for Examples 2.1 and 2.3 as well. While a similar assignment holds for Example 2.1, Example 2.3 requires a different assignment where $C = \{P_1\}, \{P_2, P_3, P_4\})$ and P_1 gets R and S, P_2 gets T and P_3 gets U. Note that more than one input function can be assigned to the same player in G.

For general d-degenerate graphs $\mathcal{H}$, we start by recalling that m (i.e., size of the TRIBES instance) is a function of $\mathcal{H}$. As mentioned in Section 2.2.1, we can decompose $\mathcal{H}$ into a forest and a *core*. We prove three different lower bounds on $\mathcal{H}$, where the size of the TRIBES instance m used in our reduction is the maximum of three different bounds, each one on a different part of $\mathcal{H}$. The first one is on $\mathcal{H}$'s forest part, the second and third ones are on $\mathcal{H}$'s *core* part – lower bounded by applying Moore's bound [5] and Turan's theorem [6] respectively. For each case, we show that we can reduce the TRIBES instance to a suitable two-party BCQ instance. Thus, known lower bounds on the TRIBES instance from Theorem 2.3 apply for the BCQ instance. Finally, to generalize our results from two-party BCQ to general G, we use ideas from [18, 19] to obtain an appropriate cut for G and use lower bounds from the induced two-party communication complexity problem across the cut. Note that the assignment of functions depends on the cut. We present the details in Section 4.2.
For constant d, our upper and lower bounds match. However, for non-constant d, we have a gap of $\widetilde{O}(d)$. We would like to note that there is a fundamental bottleneck in getting rid of this factor as the case of $\mathcal{H}$ being a clique is an outstanding

[13]In each round, we assume at most one bit is sent from a to b instead of $O(\log_2(r \cdot D))$ bits to be consistent with the two-party communication complexity literature.

open question[14] (even in Model 2.2) and seems beyond the reach of current communication complexity techniques [16].

2.3 Notion of Width

We start by defining the notion of *GHD*s and acyclic (hyper)graphs.

Definition 2.4 (GHD). *A GHD of $\mathcal{H} = (\mathcal{V}, \mathcal{E})$ is defined by a triple $\langle \mathcal{T}, \chi, \lambda \rangle$, where $\mathcal{T} = (V(\mathcal{T}), E(\mathcal{T}))$ is a tree, $\chi : V(\mathcal{T}) \to 2^{\mathcal{V}}$ is a function associating a set of vertices $\chi(v) \subseteq \mathcal{V}$ to each node v of $\mathcal{T}$, and $\lambda : V(\mathcal{T}) \to 2^{\mathcal{E}}$ is a function associating a set of hyperedges to each node v of $\mathcal{T}$ such that the following two properties hold. First, for each $e \in \mathcal{E}$, there is at least one node $v \in V(\mathcal{T})$ such that $e \subseteq \chi(v)$ and $e \in \lambda(v)$. Second, for every $V' \subseteq \mathcal{V}$, the set $\{v \in V(\mathcal{T}) | V' \subseteq \chi(v)\}$ is connected in $\mathcal{T}$, called the running intersection property (RIP hereon). We only consider rooted GHDs.*
A reduced-GHD *has the additional property that every hyperedge $e \in \overline{\mathcal{E}}$ has a unique node $v \in V(\mathcal{T})$ such that $\chi(v) = e$ (note that this is an equality).*

Definition 2.5 (Acyclicity). *A hypergraph $\mathcal{H} = (\overline{\mathcal{V}}, \overline{\mathcal{E}})$ is acyclic iff there exists a GHD $(\mathcal{T}, \chi, \lambda)$ in which for every node $v \in V(\mathcal{T})$, $\chi(v)$ is a hyperedge in $\overline{\mathcal{E}}$.*

We now define the sub-classes of reduced-GHDs that we consider in this paper. In particular, we construct reduced-GHDs using the GYO algorithm [28, 46, 51] (GYOA, also called GYO-Elimination order) and call them GYO-GHDs. We start by defining the *GYO-reduction* $\mathcal{H}'$ of a hypergraph $\mathcal{H}$.

Definition 2.6 (GYO-reduction and GYOA). *For any hypergraph $\mathcal{H}$, the GYO-reduction $\mathcal{H}'$ is defined as the leftover hypergraph after running GYOA on $\mathcal{H}$. We describe GYOA here. The input to GYOA is $\mathcal{H}$ and its output is a hypergraph $\mathcal{H}'$. It performs the following two steps iteratively on $\mathcal{H}'$ (starting with $\mathcal{H}' = \mathcal{H}$): (a) Eliminate a vertex that is present in only one hyperedge and (b) Delete a hyperedge that is contained in another hyperedge. GYOA terminates when it cannot perform any of the above two steps on $\mathcal{H}'$.*

We note here that running GYOA on an acyclic hypergraph $\mathcal{H}$ returns an empty $\mathcal{H}'$. For general hypergraphs $\mathcal{H}$, we start by running GYOA on $\mathcal{H}$, which returns a hypergraph $\mathcal{H}'$. Note that the hyperedges removed in this process form a forest of acyclic hypergraphs. For each hypertree in the forest of acyclic hypergraphs, we can construct a reduced-GHD and root it arbitrarily. We now define $\mathrm{C}(\mathcal{H})$ and $\mathrm{F}(\mathcal{H})$ based on the GYO-reduction $\mathcal{H}'$ and the reduced-GHDs constructed for the original hyperedges of $\mathcal{H}$ removed during GYOA.

Definition 2.7 ($\mathrm{C}(\mathcal{H}), \mathrm{F}(\mathcal{H})$). *$\mathrm{C}(\mathcal{H})$ is the union of $\mathcal{H}'$ and the root in each reduced-GHD we constructed. $\mathrm{F}(\mathcal{H}) = \mathcal{H} \setminus \mathcal{H}'$.*

[14] We state this problem formally in the full paper [38].

We are now ready to construct GYO-GHDs.

Construction 2.8. *Let $\mathcal{T}$ be the GYO-GHD be obtained from the following procedure. We define the root r' of $\mathcal{T}$ with $\chi(r') = V(\mathrm{C}(\mathcal{H}))$. For each edge $e \in \overline{\mathcal{E}}$ with $e \subset V(\mathrm{C}(\mathcal{H}))$, we create a new node v'_e in $\mathcal{T}$ with $\chi(v'_e) = e$ and add the edge (r', v'_e) to $\mathcal{T}$ in order to make it a reduced-GHD. For every reduced-GHD $\mathcal{T}'$ in $\mathrm{F}(\mathcal{H})$, we add the edge (r', r'') to $\mathcal{T}$, where r'' is the root of $\mathcal{T}'$. We add all the remaining nodes and edges in each reduced-GHD in $\mathrm{F}(\mathcal{H})$ to $\mathcal{T}$.*

We argue that the above procedure produces a reduced-GHD in the full paper [38]. Our new notion of width based on GYO-GHDs, which we call y (Internal Node Width), is defined as follows.

Definition 2.9.

$$y(\mathcal{H}) = \min_{\forall \mathcal{T} : \mathcal{T} \text{ is a GYO-GHD of } \mathcal{H}} y(\mathcal{T})$$

where $y(\mathcal{T})$ is the number of internal/non-leaf nodes in $\mathcal{T}$.

Unless specified otherwise, in the rest of the paper when we refer to GHDs, we are referring to GYO-GHDs. As an example in Figure 2, we consider two different GHDs $\mathcal{T}_1$ and $\mathcal{T}_2$ for the acyclic hypergraph $\mathcal{H}_2$ from Figure 1. Both are outcomes of Construction 2.8 and while $\mathcal{T}_2$ has two internal nodes, $\mathcal{T}_1$ has only one, implying $y(\mathcal{H}) = 1$. For $\mathcal{H}_1$ in Figure 1, it is easy to construct a GHD with one internal node (i.e., $y(\mathcal{H}) = 1$) by keeping (A, B) as the root and $(A, C), (A, D), (A, E)$ as leaves. We show how this can be achieved for simple graphs $\mathcal{H}$ in Section 4.

2.4 Chain Matrix-Vector Multiplication

Finally, in this work, we consider the problem of computing $\mathbf{A}_k \cdots \mathbf{A}_1 \mathbf{x}$ where the computation is over $\mathbb{F}_2$. The player P_i gets $\mathbf{A}_i$ for $i \in [k]$ and P_0 gets $\mathbf{x}$. Player P_{k+1} wants to know the answer (and does not have any input). The topology G is a line with P_i connected to P_{i+1} for $0 \le i \le k$. We show that when $k \le N$ the natural algorithm that computes the partial product $\mathbf{A}_i \cdots \mathbf{A}_1 \mathbf{x}$ at P_i taking $\Theta(kN)$ rounds is indeed optimal. By contrast, if the matrices are assigned randomly to the players then the optimal number of rounds is $\Theta(k^2 N)$ (this follows from a trivial protocol). On the other extreme, if all matrices are assigned to one player, then the problem is trivial. So we are proving a tight lower-bound for arguably the simplest assignment of matrices to players that is not trivial.

We note that the existing technique of [18] cannot prove a lower bound better than $\Omega(N)$ for this problem (see the full paper [38] for a more detailed description). To get a better lower bound of $\Omega(kN)$, we use an entropy based inductive argument to show that at end of the $\Omega(iN)$ rounds, in player P_i's view, $\mathbf{A}_{i-1} \cdots \mathbf{A}_1 \mathbf{x}$ has very high entropy. However, Shannon's entropy is too weak for this argument to go through and we use the stronger notion of min-entropy, which is omnipresent in pseudorandomness and cryptography [49]. Unfortunately, this means that we can no longer appeal to the chain rule and the arguments become a bit more delicate. Finally, in the process we prove the following natural result: if **A** and **x** have high enough min-entropy, then **Ax** has higher min-entropy than **x**. To the best of our knowledge this result is new, though it follows by combining known results in pseudorandomness.[15]

3 PRELIMINARIES AND NOTATION

In this section, we define some notions related to the query hypergraph $\mathcal{H}$ and network topology G. We conclude the section with some asymptotic notation.

Query (Hyper)graph $\mathcal{H}$.

DEFINITION 3.1 ($n_2(\mathcal{H})$). *Using Definition 2.7, we can decompose any $\mathcal{H}$ into a core $\mathrm{C}(\mathcal{H})$ and a forest $\mathrm{F}(\mathcal{H})$. We define $n_2(\mathcal{H}) = |V(\mathrm{C}(\mathcal{H}))|$.*

DEFINITION 3.2 (DEGREE). *The degree of a vertex $v \in \mathcal{H}$ is given by $\left|\{e \ni v : e \in \overline{\mathcal{E}}\}\right|$.*

DEFINITION 3.3 (d-DEGENERATE (HYPER)GRAPH [35]). *In a d-degenerate (hyper)graph, every sub(hyper)graph has a vertex of degree at most d.*

We now define *natural join* and *semijoin.*

DEFINITION 3.4 (NATURAL JOIN). *The* natural join *$J = \bowtie_{e\in\overline{\mathcal{E}}} R_e$ is a relation J with attribute set $V(\mathcal{H})$ satisfying the following condition (where $\bowtie$ denotes the* join *operator). A tuple $\mathbf{t} \in J$ iff for every $e \in E(\mathcal{H})$, the* projection *of $\mathbf{t}$ onto attributes in $v(e)$ - denoted by $\pi_{v(e)}(\mathbf{t})$ - belongs to R_e. Note that $J \subseteq \prod_{v\in V(\mathcal{H})} \mathrm{Dom}(v)$.*

DEFINITION 3.5 (SEMIJOIN). *A semijoin $J' = R_1 \ltimes R_2$ of relations R_1 and R_2 is defined as $J' = R_1 \bowtie \pi_{\mathrm{attr}(R_1)\cap\mathrm{attr}(R_2)}(R_2)$, where $\mathrm{attr}(\cdot)$ denotes the attribute set of the relations and $\ltimes$ is the semijoin operator.*

We show in the full paper [38] that *natural join* and *semijoin* are special cases of FAQ.

Network Topology G. We define some standard graph notions that will be used throughout the paper.

DEFINITION 3.6 ($\mathrm{MinCut}(G, K)$). *We denote the size of the minimum cut of G separating vertices in K by $\mathrm{MinCut}(G, K)$.*

DEFINITION 3.7 (STAR GRAPH). *A star is a tree on n vertices with one internal node and $n - 1$ leaves (e.g. $\mathcal{H}_1$ in Figure 1).*

[15] We thank David Zuckerman for showing us the high level proof idea of this result.

DEFINITION 3.8 (STEINER TREE). *Given a graph $G = (V, E)$ and a set of nodes $K \subseteq V$, we call a tree T a Steiner tree if it connects all vertices in K only using edges in E.*

In particular, we are interested in Steiner trees with diameter at most Δ (i.e., distance between any two nodes in K). Let $\mathcal{T}_{\Delta,K}$ denote the set of all such Steiner trees.

DEFINITION 3.9 ($\mathrm{ST}(G, K, \Delta)$). *$\mathrm{ST}(G, K, \Delta)$ denotes the maximum number of edge disjoint Steiner trees from $\mathcal{T}_{\Delta,K}$ that can be packed in G.*

We will need this result:

THEOREM 3.10 ([39]).

$$\mathrm{ST}(G, K, |V(G)|) = \Omega(\mathrm{MinCut}(G, K)).$$

Finally, we state a recent result under Model 2.1 on set-intersection queries over any topology G and any subset of players $K \subseteq V : |K| \le k$, which we will use frequently in our arguments.

THEOREM 3.11 ([18]). *Let $\mathbf{x}_u \in \{0, 1\}^N$ for every player $u \in K$. The number of rounds taken by a protocol that deterministically computes $\bigwedge_{u\in K} \mathbf{x}_u$ (where the $\wedge$ is bit-wise AND) is given by $\Theta\left(\min_{\Delta\in[|V|]}\left(\frac{N}{\mathrm{ST}(G,K,\Delta)} + \Delta\right)\right)$.*

We will use the following notation for a special case of a multi-commodity flow problem:

DEFINITION 3.12. *For every graph G, subset of players K and integer $N' \ge 0$, let $\tau_{\mathrm{MCF}}(G, K, N')$ be the minimum number of rounds needed to route at most $N' \log_2(N')$ bits from all players in K to any one player in K, assuming $\log_2(N')$ bits are sent in each round.* [16]

Let the minimum number of rounds taken by a protocol to determinstically compute BCQ of $\mathcal{H}$ on G be denoted by $\mathcal{D}(\mathrm{BCQ}_{\mathcal{H},N}, G, K)$, where each function in $\mathcal{H}$ has size at most N and is assigned to some player in $K \subseteq V, |K| \le k$. Recall that $\mathcal{R}(\mathrm{BCQ}_{\mathcal{H},N}, G, K)$ is themost minimum worst-case number of rounds needed to deterministically compute any instance in $\mathrm{BCQ}_{\mathcal{H},N}$ with error at most $\frac{1}{3}$. The *trivial protocol*, along with Definition 3.12, implies the following.

LEMMA 3.13.

$$\mathcal{D}(\mathrm{BCQ}_{\mathcal{H},N}, G, K) = O\left(\tau_{\mathrm{MCF}}(G, K, k \cdot r \cdot N)\right).$$

3.1 Asymptotic Notation

For notational clarity, we will ignore a factor of $\log_2(N) \cdot \log_2(\mathrm{MinCut}(G, K)) \cdot \log_2(n_2(\mathcal{H}))$ in our lower bounds. Further, we ignore these factors while arguing for the tightness of our bounds, which we denote by $\widetilde{\Omega}(\cdot), \widetilde{O}(\cdot)$ and $\widetilde{\Theta}(\cdot)$.

[16] Here, we will consider the worst-case over all possible ways the $N' \log_2(N')$ bits are distributed over K. While our upper bounds can be smaller than this, we use this worst-case measure to simplify our bounds.

4 $\mathcal{H}$ IS A SIMPLE GRAPH

In this section, we consider the class of queries $\text{BCQ}_{\mathcal{H},N}$ for a given d-degenerate graph $\mathcal{H}$ with arity r at most two and all functions have size at most N. We prove upper and lower bounds that are tight within a factor of $\widetilde{O}(d)$ for computing any query in $\text{BCQ}_{\mathcal{H},N}$. The following is our main result.

THEOREM 4.1. *For arbitrary topology G, subset of players K and d-degenerate simple graph $\mathcal{H}$, we have*

$$\mathcal{D}(\text{BCQ}_{\mathcal{H},N}, G, K) = O\left(y(\mathcal{H}) \cdot \min_{\Delta \in [|V|]}\left(\frac{N}{\text{ST}(G,K,\Delta)} + \Delta\right)\right) + O\left(\tau_{\text{MCF}}(G, K, n_2(\mathcal{H}) \cdot d \cdot N)\right). \quad (1.1)$$

Further, for all simple graphs $\mathcal{H}$, we have

$$\mathcal{R}(\text{BCQ}_{\mathcal{H},N}, G, K) \geq \widetilde{\Omega}\left(\frac{y(\mathcal{H}) \cdot N}{\text{MinCut}(G,K)}\right) + \widetilde{\Omega}\left(\frac{n_2(\mathcal{H}) \cdot N}{\text{MinCut}(G,K)}\right). \quad (1.2)$$

We would like to point out that our upper bound holds for every assignment of the functions f_e to players in K while our lower bound holds for some assignment of functions to players in K. We first prove the upper bound (1.1), followed by the lower bound (1.2). Finally, we argue how our bounds are tight up to a factor of $\widetilde{O}(d)$.

4.1 Upper Bound

We first consider the case when $\mathcal{H}$ is a star, which will be a basic building block for our algorithms for general $\mathcal{H}$.

4.1.1 $\mathcal{H}$ is a star. Let $P = (v_0, v_1, \ldots, v_k)$ be the vertices of the star with v_0 as it's center. In this case, $\mathcal{H}$ includes k relations of the form R_{v_0,v_i} for every $i \in [k]$. Note that computing the corresponding BCQ query q can be solved via a *set-intersection* problem where we compute $R'_P = \bigcap_{i=1}^{k} R'_{v_i}$, where $R'_{v_i} = \{a_0 | (a_0, a_i) \in R_{v_0,v_i}$ for some $a_i \in \text{Dom}(v_i)\}$. It is easy to see that the final output of q is 1 if $R'_P \neq \emptyset$ and 0 otherwise. We can solve the resulting set intersection problem using Theorem 3.11 to compute R'_P. The procedure to compute R'_P is described in Algorithm 1, which when combined with the fact that at most $O(\log_2(D))$ bits can be communicated in each round, implies the following result.

COROLLARY 4.2. *When $\mathcal{H}$ is a star, for arbitrary graphs G and subset of players K, we have*

$$\mathcal{D}(\text{BCQ}_{\mathcal{H},N}, G, K) = O\left(\min_{\Delta \in [|V|]}\left(\frac{N}{\text{ST}(G,K,\Delta)} + \Delta\right)\right).$$

For the case when G is a line with k vertices, note that $\text{ST}(G, K, \Delta) = 0$ for every $\Delta > k - 1$ and $\text{ST}(G, K, k-1) = 1$, which in turn implies the following.

COROLLARY 4.3. *Let $\mathcal{H}$ be a star and G be a line with k vertices. Then*

$$\mathcal{D}(\text{BCQ}_{\mathcal{H},N}, G, K) \leq N + k.$$

Note that the above result is a generalization of the upper bound in Example 2.2.

Algorithm 1 Algorithm for Star

1: **Input:** A star query with attributes $P = (v_0, \ldots, v_k)$ and relations $\{R_{(v_0,v_i)} : i \in [k]\}$. Note that v_0 is the center.
2: **Output:** R'_P
3: Each player containing a relation R_{v_0,v_i} computes $R'_{v_i} = \{a_0 | (a_0, a_i) \in R_{v_0,v_i} \exists a_i \in \text{Dom}(v_i)\}, \forall i \in [k]$ internally.
4: $R'_P = \bigcap_{i=1}^{k} R'_{v_i}$ is computed using Theorem 3.11.
5: **return** R'_P

4.1.2 $\mathcal{H}$ is a forest. We now use the above algorithm to obtain upper bounds for the case when $\mathcal{H}$ is a forest.

LEMMA 4.4. *For arbitrary G, subset of players K and $\mathcal{H}$ being a forest, we have*

$$\mathcal{D}(\text{BCQ}_{\mathcal{H},N}, G, K) = O\left(y(\mathcal{H}) \cdot \min_{\Delta \in [|V|]}\left(\frac{N}{\text{ST}(G,K,\Delta)} + \Delta\right)\right). \quad (2)$$

PROOF SKETCH. We keep removing stars from trees in $\mathcal{H}$ in a bottom-up fashion and solve the induced query on each removed star using Algorithm 1. Since the number of stars we remove in this process is $y(\mathcal{H})$, the stated bound follows. The details are in the full paper [38]. □

4.1.3 The general case: d-degenerate graphs. We now state our upper bound when $\mathcal{H}$ is a d-degenerate simple graph:

LEMMA 4.5. *For arbitrary G, subset of players K, and any d-degenerate simple graph $\mathcal{H}$, we have*

$$\mathcal{D}(\text{BCQ}_{\mathcal{H},N}, G, K) = O\left(y(\mathcal{H}) \cdot \min_{\Delta \in [|V|]}\left(\frac{N}{\text{ST}(G,K,\Delta)} + \Delta\right)\right) + O\left(\tau_{\text{MCF}}(G, K, n_2(\mathcal{H}) \cdot d \cdot N)\right). \quad (2.1)$$

PROOF SKETCH. We decompose $\mathcal{H}$ into two components using Definition 2.7 – forest ($\text{F}(\mathcal{H})$) and core ($\text{C}(\mathcal{H})$). We then use Lemma 4.4 to solve the induced query on $\text{F}(\mathcal{H})$. For the core, we use the *trivial protocol* of sending all the remaining relations to one player. The details are in the full paper [38]. □

4.2 Lower Bound

We start with an overview, followed by lower bounds for the case when $\mathcal{H}$ is a forest and conclude with lower bounds for all simple graphs $\mathcal{H}$.

4.2.1 Overview. As we showed in Section 2.2.2, we start by considering an arbitrary TRIBES instance of size m where m is a function of $\mathcal{H}$. We then show that it can be reduced to a suitable two-party BCQ instance, which is functionally equivalent to the TRIBES instance we started with. In particular, solving the BCQ instance we constructed indeed solves the TRIBES instance we started with. We denote this reduction succinctly by $\text{TRIBES}_{m,N} \leq \text{BCQ}_{\mathcal{H},N}$. Finally, we generalize our results from the two-party setting to general G using ideas from [18, 19]. We crucially exploit the fact that our lower bounds are for worst-case assignment of input functions to players in G and show a very specific class of assignments that achieves the required lower bound.

4.2.2 $\mathcal{H}$ is a forest. We prove the following lemma.

LEMMA 4.6. *When $\mathcal{H}$ is a forest, we have*

$$\text{TRIBES}_{\frac{y(\mathcal{H})}{2},N} \leq \text{BCQ}_{\mathcal{H},N}.$$

PROOF. For notational simplicity, define $y = y(\mathcal{H})$. Given $\mathcal{H}$ and a $\text{TRIBES}_{\frac{y}{2},N}$ instance we design a corresponding $\text{BCQ}_{\mathcal{H},N}$ instance. As $\mathcal{H}$ is bipartite, let (L, R) be the node partition of $\mathcal{H}$ and consider the set O_L (O_R resp.) consisting of all nodes of degree at least two included in L (R resp.). Let O equal the largest of O_L and O_R (i.e., O consists of nodes of odd or even distance from the roots of the forest). Note that $|O| \geq \frac{y}{2}$,[17] and assume w.l.o.g. that the size of O is exactly $\frac{y}{2}$ (otherwise we take a subset of O). We associate a pair of sets (S_o, T_o) from $\text{TRIBES}_{\frac{y}{2},N}$ with each node $o \in O$, such that

$$\text{TRIBES}_{\frac{y}{2},N}(\hat{S},\hat{T}) = \bigwedge_{o \in O} \text{DISJ}_N(S_o, T_o), \tag{3}$$

where $\text{DISJ}_N(S_o, T_o) = 1$ if $S_o \cap T_o \neq \emptyset$ and 0 otherwise.

We now construct a corresponding $\text{BCQ}_{\mathcal{H},N}$ instance in detail. We start by defining a pair of relations corresponding to each pair (S_o, T_o). Let $o \in O$. If o has a parent in $\mathcal{H}$, let o_p be its parent. Let o_c be a child of o. We consider the relations $R_{S_o} = S_o \times \{1\}$ and $R_{T_o} = T_o \times \{1\}$, where the attribute set of R_{S_o} is (o, o_c) and that of R_{T_o} is (o, o_p). Here we treat S_o and T_o as subsets of $[N]$ (instead of elements in $\{0,1\}^N$). In the case that o does not have a parent node, it is a root in $\mathcal{H}$ with at least two children, and thus we can set o_p to be a child of o that differs from o_c. Thus, $\text{TRIBES}_{\frac{y}{2},N}(\hat{S},\hat{T}) = 1$ iff for each $o \in O$, the join $R_{S_o} \bowtie R_{T_o}$ is not empty. To complete the description of the BCQ instance, for each $o \in O$, we associate all additional edges (o, v) adjacent to o in $\mathcal{H}$ with the relation $[N] \times \{1\}$ on attributes (o, v); and remaining edges (u, v) that are not adjacent to any $o \in O$ with the relation $\{1\} \times \{1\}$. Note that no two vertices $o_1, o_2 \in O$ are adjacent in $\mathcal{H}$. Let us denote the BCQ instance constructed above by $q_{\mathcal{H},\hat{S},\hat{T}}$.

To complete the proof, we show that $q_{\mathcal{H},\hat{S},\hat{T}} = 1$ iff $\text{TRIBES}_{\frac{y}{2},N}(\hat{S},\hat{T}) = 1$. If $q_{\mathcal{H},\hat{S},\hat{T}} = 1$ then there exists a tuple $\mathbf{t} \in \prod_{v \in V(\mathcal{H})} \text{Dom}(v)$ that satisfies all relations in $q_{\mathcal{H},\hat{S},\hat{T}}$, i.e. $\mathbf{t}_e \in R_e$ for every $e \in \overline{\mathcal{E}}$. Specifically, for each $o \in O$, $R_{S_o} \bowtie R_{T_o}$ is not empty which implies that $\text{TRIBES}_{\frac{y}{2},N}(\hat{S},\hat{T}) = 1$. Alternatively, if $\text{TRIBES}_{\frac{y}{2},N}(\hat{S},\hat{T}) = 1$, we can find a tuple $\mathbf{t} \in \prod_{v \in V(\mathcal{H})} \text{Dom}(v)$ that satisfies all relations in $q_{\mathcal{H},\hat{S},\hat{T}}$. For each $o \in O$ we set $\pi_o(\mathbf{t})$ to be any element in the intersection of S_o and T_o, and for all remaining nodes v we set $\pi_v(\mathbf{t}) = 1$. It holds that the relations corresponding to edges of the form (o, o_p), (o, o_c), (o, v), and (u, v) described above are all satisfied. This concludes our proof. □

Note that the above argument was independent of G. We now use the structure of G to obtain a lower bound on $\mathcal{R}(\text{BCQ}_{\mathcal{H},N}, G, K)$ using known results for $\text{TRIBES}_{\frac{y}{2},N}$.

Lower bounds dependent on G. We show the following lower bound for arbitrary G, assuming worst-case assignment of relations to players in K.

LEMMA 4.7. *For any topology G and $\mathcal{H}$ being a forest,*

$$\mathcal{R}(\text{BCQ}_{\mathcal{H},N}, G, K) \geq \widetilde{\Omega}\left(\frac{y(\mathcal{H}) \cdot N}{\text{MinCut}(G,K)}\right).$$

PROOF. We first consider a min-cut (A, B) of G that separates K, where A and B denote the set of vertices in each partition ($A \cup B = V$). Using the notation given in the proof of Lemma 4.6, let $q_{\mathcal{H},\hat{S},\hat{T}}$ be the query corresponding to a given instance $\text{TRIBES}_{\frac{y}{2},N}(\hat{S},\hat{T})$. We assign relations $\{R_{S_o}\}_{o \in O}$ to vertices in A and relations $\{R_{T_o}\}_{o \in O}$ to vertices in B. The other relations in $q_{\mathcal{H},\hat{S},\hat{T}}$ can be assigned arbitrarily. Note that any protocol to compute $q_{\mathcal{H},\hat{S},\hat{T}}$ on G gives a two-party protocol (Alice, Bob) for $\text{TRIBES}_{\frac{y}{2},N}$. In particular, Alice gets the sets $\{S_o\}_{o \in O}$ (corresponding to R_{S_o}) assigned to vertices in A and Bob gets the sets $\{T_o\}_{o \in O}$ (corresponding to R_{T_o}) assigned to vertices in B (ignoring the additional relations). It follows that if there exists a $\mathcal{R}(\text{BCQ}_{\mathcal{H},N}, G, K)$ round protocol on G, then we have a two-party protocol (i.e., on a graph $\mathcal{G} = (\{a, b\}, (a, b))$) with at most $\mathcal{R}(\text{BCQ}_{\mathcal{H},N}, G, K) \cdot \text{MinCut}(G, K) \cdot \lceil \log_2(\text{MinCut}(G, K)) \rceil$ rounds. Indeed, we can simulate the two-party protocol on G across the cut (A, B), where Alice is responsible for A and Bob for B. In particular, if Alice needs to send a message to Bob (or vice-versa), it will be sent across edges crossing the cut. Note that in each round, at most $\text{MinCut}(G, K)\lceil \log_2(\text{MinCut}(G, K)) \rceil$ bits will be exchanged between Alice and Bob. We need $\lceil \log_2(\text{MinCut}(G, K)) \rceil$ bits in order to know the edge on which the message was sent. We can now invoke (1) to obtain a lower bound of

$$\mathcal{R}(\text{BCQ}_{\mathcal{H},N}, G, K) \geq \widetilde{\Omega}\left(\frac{y(\mathcal{H}) \cdot N}{\text{MinCut}(G,K)}\right).$$

[17] Note that in the arity two case, it is easy to construct a GYO-GHD with y internal nodes using the structure of $\mathcal{H}$. Details in the full paper [38].

□

4.2.3 General $\mathcal{H}$. We are now ready to prove our general lower bound for all simple graphs $\mathcal{H}$.

THEOREM 4.8. *For arbitrary $G, K \subseteq V$, and graph $\mathcal{H}$, we have*

$$\mathcal{R}(\mathrm{BCQ}_{\mathcal{H},N}, G, K) \geq \widetilde{\Omega}\left(\frac{(y(\mathcal{H}) + n_2(\mathcal{H})) \cdot N}{\mathrm{MinCut}(G, K)}\right).$$

PROOF SKETCH. We present a proof sketch here. For notational convenience, define $y = y(\mathcal{H})$ and $n_2 = n_2(\mathcal{H})$. Let $m = \max\left(\frac{y}{2}, \frac{n_2}{2\log(n_2)}\right)$. In general, as in the proof of Lemma 4.6, given $\mathcal{H}$ and a TRIBES instance $\mathrm{TRIBES}_{m,N}(\hat{S}, \hat{T})$ we construct a BCQ instance $q_{\mathcal{H},\hat{S},\hat{T}}$ such that $q_{\mathcal{H},\hat{S},\hat{T}} = 1$ iff $\mathrm{TRIBES}_{m,N}(\hat{S}, \hat{T}) = 1$. To this end we need to "embed" the m pairs of sets (S_i, T_i) from $\mathrm{TRIBES}_{m,N}(\hat{S}, \hat{T})$ as relations in $q_{\mathcal{H},\hat{S},\hat{T}}$. For $m = \frac{y}{2}$, we embed the pairs (S_i, T_i) in the forest $\mathrm{F}(\mathcal{H})$ as done in Lemma 4.6. For $m = \frac{n_2}{2\cdot\log(n_2)}$, we consider $\mathrm{C}(\mathcal{H})$. We then show that it must be the case that $\mathrm{C}(\mathcal{H})$ either includes $\left(\frac{n_2}{2\log(n_2)}\right)$ vertex-disjoint cycles (or) it has an independent set of size $\Omega(n_2)$. In both cases, we show how one can embed $\frac{n_2}{2\log(n_2)}$ pairs (S_i, T_i) of $\mathrm{TRIBES}_{m,N}(\hat{S}, \hat{T})$ in $C(\mathcal{H})$. We defer the proof to the full paper [38].

Assuming the above embeddings, we conclude that $q_{\mathcal{H},\hat{S},\hat{T}} = 1$ iff $\mathrm{TRIBES}_{m,N}(\hat{S}, \hat{T}) = 1$, where $m = \max\left(\frac{y}{2}, \frac{n_2}{2\log(n_2)}\right)$. Since sum and max are within a factor 2 of each other, we can write $m \geq \frac{y}{4} + \frac{n_2}{4\log(n_2)}$. We can now apply ideas from the proof of Lemma 4.7 to obtain the required lower bound $\widetilde{\Omega}\left(\frac{(y+n_2)\cdot N}{\mathrm{MinCut}(G,K)}\right)$. □

Note that in Theorem 4.1, the upper bound follows from Lemma 4.5 and the lower bound from Theorem 4.8. We conclude this section by noting that when $N \geq |V|^2$, our upper and lower bounds differ by $\widetilde{O}(d)$ factor (for worst-case assignments of relations to players). In particular, Theorem 3.10 implies that the first two terms in the upper and lower bounds match up to an $\widetilde{O}(1)$ factor. In the full paper [38], we show that for worst-case assignment of relations, the second terms in the upper and lower bounds also differ by a $\widetilde{O}(d)$ factor, as desired.

5 HYPERGRAPHS $\mathcal{H}$ AND GENERAL FAQ

Our results generalize fairly seamlessly to hypergraphs $\mathcal{H}$. For constant d, r, our upper and lower bounds match. However, for non-constant d, we have a gap of $\widetilde{O}(d^2 \cdot r^2)$, which is worse than our gap of $\widetilde{O}(d)$ for the arity two case. Details are deferred to the full paper [38].

We extend our results from BCQ to the general FAQ problem. We define the general FAQ problem here, which is a generalization of FAQ-SS. We are given a multi-hypergraph $\mathcal{H} = (\overline{\mathcal{V}}, \overline{\mathcal{E}})$ where for each hyperedge $e \in \overline{\mathcal{E}}$, we also have an input function $f_e : \prod_{v\in e} \mathrm{Dom}(v) \to \mathbb{D}$. In addition, we are given a set of *free variables* $\mathcal{F} \subseteq \overline{\mathcal{V}} : |\mathcal{F}| = \ell$ and[18] we would like to compute the function:

$$\phi\left(\mathbf{x}_{[\ell]}\right) = \bigoplus^{(\ell+1)}_{x_{\ell+1}\in\mathrm{Dom}(x_{\ell+1})} \cdots \bigoplus^{(n)}_{x_n\in\mathrm{Dom}(x_n)} \bigotimes_{S\in\overline{\mathcal{E}}} f_S(\mathbf{x}_S), \quad (4)$$

where $\mathbf{x} = (x_u)_{u\in\overline{\mathcal{V}}}$ and $\mathbf{x}_S$ is $\mathbf{x}$ projected down to co-ordinates in $S \subseteq \overline{\mathcal{V}}$. The variables in $\overline{\mathcal{V}} \setminus \mathcal{F}$ are called *bound variables*. For every bound variable $i > \ell$, $\oplus^{(i)}$ is a binary (aggregate) operator on the domain $\mathbb{D}$. Different bound variables may have different aggregates. Finally, for each bound variable $i > \ell$ either $\oplus^{(i)} = \otimes$ (*product aggregate*) or $(\mathbb{D}, \oplus^{(i)}, \otimes)$ forms a commutative semiring (*semiring aggregate*) with the same additive identity $\mathbf{0}$ and multiplicative identity $\mathbf{1}$. As with FAQ-SS, we assume that the functions are input in the *listing* representation, i.e. the function f_e is represented as a list of its non-zero values: $R_e = \{(\mathbf{y}, f_e(\mathbf{y}))|\mathbf{y} \in \prod_{v\in e} Dom(v) : f_e(\mathbf{y}) \neq \mathbf{0}\}$. Note that when $\oplus^{(i)} = \oplus$ is the same semiring aggregate for every $\ell < i \leq n$, we have the FAQ-SS problem.

For any $\mathbb{D}$, let $\mathrm{FAQ}_{\mathbb{D},\mathcal{H},N,\mathcal{F}}$ denote the class of FAQ problems, where each function in $\mathcal{H}$ has at most N non-zero entries. (Note that we are not explicitly stating the operators for the bound variables $(\oplus^{(\ell+1)}, \ldots, \oplus^{(n)})$ since our upper and lower bounds hold for all such operators.) Let $\mathcal{R}(\mathrm{FAQ}_{\mathbb{D},\mathcal{H},N,\mathcal{F}}, G, K)$ denote the minimum worst-case number of rounds needed by a randomized protocol with error at most $\frac{1}{3}$ that computes any query in $\mathrm{FAQ}_{\mathbb{D},\mathcal{H},N,\mathcal{F}}$ on G with functions assigned to nodes in K. We prove the following results.

THEOREM 5.1. *For $O(1)$-degenerate hypergraphs $\mathcal{H}$ with $O(1)$-arity, we have*

$$\mathcal{R}(\mathrm{FAQ}_{\mathbb{D},\mathcal{H},N,\mathcal{F}}, G, K) = \widetilde{\Theta}\left(\frac{(y(\mathcal{H}) + n_2(\mathcal{H})) \cdot N}{\mathrm{MinCut}(G, K)}\right)$$

for any $\mathbb{D}$, specific choices of $\mathcal{F}$, arbitrary G and K. When G is a line (as in the first row in Table 1), $\mathrm{MinCut}(G, K) = 1$.

THEOREM 5.2. *For general degenerate hypergraphs $\mathcal{H}$ with arity at most r, we have*

$$\begin{aligned}&\mathcal{D}\left(\mathrm{FAQ}_{\mathbb{D},\mathcal{H},N,\mathcal{F}}, G, K\right)\\ &= O\left(y(\mathcal{H}) \cdot \min_{\Delta\in[|V|]}\left(\frac{N \cdot r}{\mathrm{ST}(G, K, \Delta)} + \Delta\right)\right)\\ &+ O\left(\tau_{\mathrm{MCF}}(G, K, n_2(\mathcal{H}) \cdot d \cdot r \cdot N)\right)\end{aligned}$$

and

$$\mathcal{R}\left(\mathrm{FAQ}_{\mathbb{D},\mathcal{H},N,\mathcal{F}}, G, K\right) \geq \widetilde{\Omega}\left(\frac{(d \cdot y(\mathcal{H}) + n_2(\mathcal{H})) \cdot N}{d \cdot r \cdot \mathrm{MinCut}(G, K)}\right).$$

[18]For a fixed $\mathcal{F}$, the vertices in $\overline{\mathcal{V}}$ can be renumbered so that $\mathcal{F} = [\ell]$ w.l.o.g.

The lower bound differs from the upper bound by a factor of $O(r^2d^2)$ in the worst case.

We would like to mention here once again that our upper bound is a deterministic protocol and the lower bound is for randomized protocols. Details are in the full paper [38].

6 MATRIX CHAIN MULTIPLICATION

We consider the following FAQ-SS problem. The network topology has $k+2$ players $P_0, \ldots, P_{k+1}$ such that (P_i, P_{i+1}) is an edge (i.e. G is a line) where P_0 receives $\mathbf{x} \in \mathbb{F}_2^N$ and P_i for $i \in [k]$ receives $\mathbf{A}_i \in \mathbb{F}_2^{N\times N}$. Player P_{k+1} wants to compute $\mathbf{A}_k \cdot \mathbf{A}_{k-1} \cdots \mathbf{A}_1 \cdot \mathbf{x}$. Alternatively, for every $i \in [k]$, define $\mathbf{y}_i = \mathbf{A}_i \cdot \mathbf{y}_{i-1}$, with $\mathbf{y}_0 = \mathbf{x}$. Note that we want to compute $\mathbf{y}_k$. Note that this is an FAQ-SS problem since we can re-write the above as

$$\phi(z_k) = \sum_{(z_i)_{i=0}^{k-1} \in [N]^k} \left(\prod_{j=1}^{k} A_j(z_j, z_{j-1}) \right) X(z_0), \tag{5}$$

where the functions satisfy $A_j(x, y) = \mathbf{A}_j[x, y]$ and $X(z) = \mathbf{x}[z]$ for every triple of indices $x, y, z \in [N]$. [19]

We note that this problem can be solved in $O(kN)$ rounds.[20]

Proposition 6.1. *The* FAQ-SS *problem from* (5) *can be computed in $O(kN)$ rounds.*

We prove this proposition in the full paper [38]. We remark that when k is large, a bottom-to-top fashion merge algorithm can achieve $O(N^2 \log k + k)$ rounds. (See the full paper [38] for details.) In the next section, we prove a tight lower bound of $\Omega(kN)$ for the case $k \le N$.

6.1 The Lower Bound

We will argue that the upper bound of $O(kN)$ rounds in Proposition 6.1 is tight if $k \le N$. Before we do that we collect some definitions and results related to the min-entropy of a random variable.

6.1.1 Background. The *min-entropy* of a random variable X is defined as $H_\infty(X) := -\log \max_{x \in \text{supp}(X)} \Pr[X = x]$. For a random variable X and an event $\mathcal{E}$ that is possibly correlated with X, define $H_\infty(X\mathcal{E}) = -\log \max_{x \in \text{supp}(X)} \Pr[X = x, \mathcal{E}]$. Notice that in the above definition, we do not "normalize" $\Pr[X = x, \mathcal{E}]$ by a factor of $\Pr[\mathcal{E}]$.

For random variables X and Y, the conditional smooth min-entropy $H_\infty^\epsilon(X|Y)$ is defined as

$$H_\infty^\epsilon(X|Y) = \sup_{\mathcal{E}} \min_{y \in \text{supp}(Y)} H_\infty(X\mathcal{E}|Y = y)$$
$$= \sup_{\mathcal{E}} \left(-\log \max_{(x,y) \in \text{supp}(X,Y)} \Pr[\mathcal{E}, X = x|Y = y] \right)$$

where the quantification over $\mathcal{E}$ is over all events $\mathcal{E}$ (which can be correlated with X and Y) with $\Pr(\mathcal{E}) \ge 1 - \epsilon$. When Y is a deterministic variable (in other words, we are not conditioning on any randomized variable), then we simply use $H_\infty^\epsilon(X)$:

$$H_\infty^\epsilon(X) = \sup_{\mathcal{E}} H_\infty(X\mathcal{E}), \tag{6}$$

where again the quantification over $\mathcal{E}$ is over all events $\mathcal{E}$ with $\Pr(\mathcal{E}) \ge 1 - \epsilon$.

The following lemma will be useful in our analysis:

Lemma 6.2 (Lemma 4 and Lemma 7 of [44]). *Let Y be a random variable with support size at most 2^ℓ. Then we have for any $\epsilon \ge 0, \epsilon' > 0$ and random variable X, that $H_\infty^{\epsilon+\epsilon'}(X|Y) \ge H_\infty^\epsilon(X) - \ell - \log(1/\epsilon')$.*

Finally, we will use the following result where $h(p) = -p\log_2 p - (1-p)\log_2(1-p)$:

Theorem 6.3. *Let the constant $\gamma > 0$ be small enough. Let $\mathbf{x} \in \mathbb{F}_2^N$, $\mathbf{A} \in \mathbb{F}_2^{N\times N}$ and $\mathbf{Y}$ be random variables such that for every $y \in \text{supp}(\mathbf{Y})$, $\mathbf{x}$ and $\mathbf{A}$ are independent conditioned on $\mathbf{Y} = y$. Moreover for some reals $\epsilon_1, \epsilon_2 \ge 0$, we have*

$$H_\infty^{\epsilon_1+\epsilon_2+2^{-\Omega(\gamma N)}}(\mathbf{Ax}|\mathbf{Y}) \ge \left(1 - \sqrt{2\gamma}\right) \cdot N,$$

where $\alpha \stackrel{def}{=} 3\gamma + \sqrt{2\gamma} + h(\sqrt{2\gamma})$. Then, we have

$$H_\infty^{\epsilon_1+\epsilon_2+2^{-\Omega(\gamma N)}}(\mathbf{Ax}|\mathbf{Y}) \ge \left(1 - \sqrt{2\gamma}\right) \cdot N.$$

The proof of Theorem 6.3 follows from known results in pseudorandomness [21, 52] and appears in the full paper [38].

6.1.2 Showing Proposition 6.1 is tight for $k \le N$. At a high level, we will prove by induction that for player P_i at time about $\gamma i N$, the min-entropy of $\mathbf{y}_{i-1}$ is at least $\alpha \cdot N$ (and the situation at P_{i+1} should be similar). Since by this time P_{i+1} would have received at most $O(\gamma i N) \le O(\gamma N^2)$ bits, this means $\mathbf{A}_i$ has min-entropy at least $(1-\gamma)N^2$. Thus, we can apply Theorem 6.3 to argue that at P_{i+1} the min-entropy of $\mathbf{y}_i = \mathbf{A}_i \cdot \mathbf{y}_{i-1}$ is large. To finish the inductive argument we have to wait for γN more steps but by Lemma 6.2, even then $\mathbf{y}_i$ will still have high enough min-entropy. It is natural to wonder if we can make the same argument using Shannon entropy instead of min-entropy. In the full paper [38], we show that this is not possible.

We define some useful notations before we prove the lower bound. At any given time t, let $\mathbf{m}^i(t)$ denote the transcript of messages exchanged on the link between P_{i-1} and P_i till time

[19]Note that N here is the dimension of the matrices as opposed to the number of non-zero entries used in the previous sections.

[20]Note that the trivial algorithm takes $\Omega(kN^2)$ rounds.

t. For $i \in [k+1]$, define $t_i = \frac{\gamma}{4} \cdot iN$, and $\widetilde{\mathbf{m}}^i = \mathbf{m}^i(t_i)$. For a random variable $\mathbf{m}$, we will use m to denote a specific value of the random variable $\mathbf{m}$. In addition, we use $\widetilde{\mathbf{m}}^{[i]}$ and $\widetilde{m}^{[i]}$ to denote the tuples $(\widetilde{\mathbf{m}}^1, \widetilde{\mathbf{m}}^2, \cdots, \widetilde{\mathbf{m}}^i)$ and $(\widetilde{m}^1, \widetilde{m}^2, \cdots, \widetilde{m}^i)$ respectively.

Let $\epsilon^* = 2^{-\Omega(\gamma N)}$ be at least thrice the maximum of $2^{-\gamma N/4}$ and the $2^{-\Omega(\gamma N)}$ term in Theorem 6.3. We will argue:

Lemma 6.4. *Let $\mathbf{A}_i$ for every $i \in [k]$ and $\mathbf{x}$ be all uniformly and independently distributed. Let $\gamma > 0$ be such that*[21]

$$4\gamma + \sqrt{2\gamma} + h(\sqrt{2\gamma}) \le 1, \tag{7}$$

and $\gamma N/4$ is an integer. Then we have the following for every $i \in [k+1]$:

$$H_\infty^{i\epsilon^*}\left(\mathbf{y}_{i-1}|\widetilde{\mathbf{m}}^{[i]}\right) \ge N(1-\gamma-\sqrt{2\gamma}). \tag{8}$$

Proof. We will prove the claim by induction. For the base case of $i = 1$, Lemma 6.2 implies that (recall that $\widetilde{\mathbf{m}}^1 = \mathbf{m}^1(t_1) = \mathbf{m}^1(\gamma N/4)$ and $\mathbf{y}_0 = \mathbf{x}$): $H_\infty^{\epsilon^*}\left(\mathbf{y}_0|\widetilde{\mathbf{m}}^1\right) \ge H_\infty(\mathbf{x}) - \gamma N/4 - \log(1/\epsilon^*) \ge N(1-\gamma/4-\gamma/2) \ge N(1-\gamma-\sqrt{2\gamma})$. Thus, (8) holds for $i = 1$.

We assume (8) holds for some $i \ge 1$; we prove that it also holds with i replaced by $i+1$. For any interval $[\ell, r]$ we use $\mathbf{A}_{[\ell:r]}$ to denote the tuple $(\mathbf{A}_\ell, \ldots, \mathbf{A}_r)$. Conditioned on $\widetilde{\mathbf{m}}^i = \widetilde{m}^i$, since all communication between $P_1, \ldots, P_{i-1}$ and $P_i, \ldots, P_{k+1}$ are independent, we have

(B1) $(\mathbf{x}, \mathbf{A}_{[1:i-1]})$ is independent of $\mathbf{A}_{[i,k]}$.
(B2) $\mathbf{y}_{i-1}$ and $\widetilde{\mathbf{m}}^{[i-1]}$ are determined by $(\mathbf{x}, \mathbf{A}_{[1:i-1]})$.
(B3) $\mathbf{m}^{i+1}(t_i)$ is determined by $\mathbf{A}_{[i:k]}$.

The above properties imply the following, which will be used many times in our analysis:

(C) Conditioned on $\widetilde{\mathbf{m}}^i = \widetilde{m}^i$, $(\mathbf{x}, \mathbf{A}_{[1:i-1]}, \mathbf{y}_{i-1}, \widetilde{\mathbf{m}}^{[i-1]})$ and $(\mathbf{A}_{[i,k]}, \mathbf{m}^{i+1}(t_i))$ are independent.

By (C), $\mathbf{y}_{i-1}\Big|\left(\widetilde{\mathbf{m}}^{[i]}, \mathbf{m}^{i+1}(t_i)\right) = \left(\widetilde{m}^{[i]}, m^{i+1}(t_i)\right)$ has the same distribution as $\mathbf{y}_{i-1}\Big|\widetilde{\mathbf{m}}^{[i]} = \widetilde{m}^{[i]}$. By the inductive hypothesis, we have

$$H_\infty^{i\epsilon^*}\left(\mathbf{y}_{i-1}\Big|\left(\widetilde{\mathbf{m}}^{[i]}, \mathbf{m}^{i+1}(t_i)\right)\right) = H_\infty^{i\epsilon^*}\left(\mathbf{y}_{i-1}\Big|\widetilde{\mathbf{m}}^{[i]}\right) \ge N(1-\gamma-\sqrt{2\gamma}). \tag{9}$$

We show in the full paper [38] that equality can be achieved in the above lemma. Further, Lemma 6.2 (with $\epsilon = 0$ and $\epsilon' = \epsilon^*/3$) implies that

$$H_\infty^{\epsilon^*/3}\left(\mathbf{A}_i\Big|\left(\widetilde{\mathbf{m}}^i, \mathbf{m}^{i+1}(t_i)\right)\right) \ge N^2 - 2i \cdot \frac{\gamma}{4} \cdot N - \log(\epsilon^*/3) \ge N^2(1-\gamma). \tag{10}$$

Again by (C), $\mathbf{A}_i\Big|\left(\widetilde{\mathbf{m}}^i, \mathbf{m}^{i+1}(t_i)\right) = \left(\widetilde{m}^i, m^{i+1}(t_i)\right)$ has the same distribution as $\mathbf{A}_i\Big|\left(\widetilde{\mathbf{m}}^{[i]}, \mathbf{m}^{i+1}(t_i)\right) = \left(\widetilde{m}^{[i]}, m^{i+1}(t_i)\right)$. Equality in (9) and (10) imply that

$$H_\infty^{\epsilon^*/3}\left(\mathbf{A}_i\Big|\left(\widetilde{\mathbf{m}}^{[i]}, \mathbf{m}^{i+1}(t_i)\right)\right) \ge N^2(1-\gamma). \tag{11}$$

By (9), (11), and (by (C)) the fact that $\mathbf{A}_i$ and $\mathbf{y}_{i-1}$ are independent conditioned on $(\widetilde{\mathbf{m}}^{[i]}, \mathbf{m}^{i+1}(t_i)) = (\widetilde{m}^{[i]}, m^{i+1}(t_i))$, we have the following via Theorem 6.3:

$$H_\infty^{(i+2/3)\epsilon^*}\left(\mathbf{y}_i = \mathbf{A}_i\mathbf{y}_{i-1}\Big|\left(\widetilde{\mathbf{m}}^{[i]}, \mathbf{m}^{i+1}(t_i)\right)\right) \ge N(1-\sqrt{2\gamma}),$$

as long as $1-\gamma-\sqrt{2\gamma} \ge 3\gamma + \sqrt{2\gamma} + h(\sqrt{2\gamma})$, which follows from (7). By applying Lemma 6.2 again (with $\epsilon = (i+2/3)\epsilon^*$ and $\epsilon' = \epsilon^*/3$), we get that[22]:

$$\begin{aligned} & H_\infty^{(i+1)\epsilon^*}\left(\mathbf{y}_i|\widetilde{\mathbf{m}}^{[i+1]}\right) \\ & \ge H_\infty^{(i+2/3)\epsilon^*}\left(\mathbf{y}_i\Big|\left(\widetilde{\mathbf{m}}^{[i]}, \mathbf{m}^{i+1}(t_i)\right)\right) - N\gamma/4 - \log(\epsilon^*/3) \\ & \ge N(1-\sqrt{2\gamma}-\frac{\gamma}{4}-\frac{\gamma}{2}) \ge N(1-\gamma-\sqrt{2\gamma}), \end{aligned}$$

as desired. □

The above immediately gives us our lower bound (the proof is deferred to the full paper [38]):

Theorem 6.5. *Any protocol that solves the* FAQ-SS *problem from (5) with $k \le N$ and large enough N, with success probability at least 1/2, takes $\Omega(kN)$ rounds.*

We will need the following result (the proof appears in the full paper [38]) in our proof.

Lemma 6.6. *Assume $H_\infty^\epsilon(X|Y) \ge L$. Then for every function $f : \mathrm{supp}(Y) \to \mathrm{supp}(X)$, we have $\Pr[f(Y) = X] \le \epsilon + 2^{-L}$.*

We are now ready to prove Theorem 6.5.

Proof of Theorem 6.5. Let Π be any protocol with at most $t_{k+1} = \gamma(k+1)N/4$ rounds. Lemma 6.4 implies that at the end of the protocol, we have

$$H_\infty^{(k+1)\epsilon^*}\left(\mathbf{y}_k|\widetilde{\mathbf{m}}^{[k+1]}\right) \ge N(1-\gamma-\sqrt{2\gamma}).$$

This implies that even if the player $k+1$ is given $\widetilde{\mathbf{m}}^{[k+1]}$ (instead of only $\widetilde{\mathbf{m}}^{k+1} = \mathbf{m}^{k+1}(t_{k+1})$), it can only output the correct answer with probability at most

$$(k+1)\epsilon^* + 2^{-N(1-\gamma-\sqrt{2\gamma})},$$

by Lemma 6.6 (here $f(Y)$ is the output at P_{k+1} for $Y = \widetilde{\mathbf{m}}^{[k+1]}$ and $X = \mathbf{y}_k$). For large enough N, the above quantity is less than 1/2. □

7 RELATED WORK

We now survey the most closely related work. Due to lack of space, a detailed discussion is deferred to the full paper [38].

[21] There exists a value $\gamma \ge 0.01$ (for large enough N) that satisfies the required conditions.

[22] Note that we are not conditioning on $\mathbf{m}^{i+1}(t_{i+1}) = \mathbf{m}^{i+1}(t_i + \gamma N/4)$ instead of the earlier $\mathbf{m}^{i+1}(t_i)$.

Parallel Database Query Computation. The MPC model has seen a lot of research activity in the last few years [2, 9, 10, 31, 36, 37]. We compared these models with ours in Section 1.1 and Appendix A.

Widths of GHDs. The Internal Node Width $y(\mathcal{H})$ of a GHD focuses on minimizing the number of internal (non-leaf) nodes in GHDs of acyclic hypergraphs. There is a related notion for Tree Decompositions called *Lean* Tree Decompositions (LTDs) [11, 22, 47]. The LTDs minimize the number of internal nodes in the following way – they try to retain only pairs of connected internal nodes whose intersection forms a bridge in the original graph $\mathcal{H}$. The other nodes are forced to become leaves of one of the internal nodes. While our construction procedure of GYO-GHDs tries to convert existing internal nodes to become leaves of some internal nodes, we do not (yet) see an exact one-to-one mapping from GYO-GHDs to LTDs. We would like to mention here that both the goals of GYO-GHDs and LTDs are the same i.e., to minimize the number of internal nodes. We would like to note here that $y(\mathcal{H})$ can potentially reduce the depth of the GHD as well. Reducing depth of GHDs (sometimes by increasing the treewidth) has been considered before [2, 4, 12].

For GHDs, the problem of computing GHDs that minimize certain cost functions of the HDs are studied in the framework of Weighted GHDs [29, 45]. For a given hypergraph $\mathcal{H}$, one way to map our notion of width to their setting is to consider a vertex aggregating function on every candidate HD $\mathcal{T}$ for $\mathcal{H}$. In particular, we can write

$$\Lambda_{H}^{f'}(\mathcal{T}) = \sum_{v' \in V(\mathcal{T})} f'_{\mathcal{H}}(v'), \tag{12}$$

where $f'_{\mathcal{H}} = 1$ if v' is a internal node and 0 otherwise. It follows that $f'_{\mathcal{H}}$ can be computed in linear time in size of $\mathcal{T}$. Given this setup, Theorem 3.4 in [29] proves that computing Minimal GHDs over HDs for arbitrary vertex aggregation functions is NP-Hard.

However, this does not hold in our case since there is always a GHD with one internal node (containing all the variables in $\mathcal{H}$). As a result, considering the minimization over all GHDs for our case is trivial and doesn't give use tight results. In particular, our setup is a bit different and we minimize over GYO-GHDs (Construction 2.8). For the tightness of our bounds for $\mathcal{H}$ with constant degeneracy and constant arity, we only need an $O(1)$-factor approximation of Internal-Node-Width, which we achieve (details in the full paper [38]).

We refer the reader to [27] for a recent survey on widths for GHD.

Distributed Computing and Communication Complexity. As stated earlier, our model is similar to (and different from) the CONGEST model in distributed computing [42]. Recently, there has been work on the same model as ours but instead of minimizing the number of rounds, they focus on minimizing the total communication of the protocols [14, 19, 20, 43, 48, 50]. Finally, [18] obtained results on minimizing the number of rounds of protocols in our setup for some well-studied functions in two-party communication complexity literature.

Entropy in Communication Complexity. Information complexity by now is a well-established sub-field of communication complexity that uses Shannon entropy to measure the amount of information exchanges in a two-party communication protocol. Information complexity was introduced in the work of Chakrabarti et al. [15] and later used in a systematic way to tackle multiple problems in [8]. To the best of our knowledge, min-entropy has only been used very recently in communication complexity [25, 26] though it has found numerous applications in pseudorandomness and cryptography for at least two decades [49]. Our work adds to the recently growing body of work that uses min-entropy to prove communication complexity results [17].

8 FUTURE WORK

We leave the following questions as future work: handling node failures, finding optimal assignments of functions to players in G, identifying the optimal topology for a given query and finally, closing the gap between our upper and lower bounds for d-degenerate graphs for super-constant d. We cannot (yet) handle the condition that N has to be larger than the size of G. We address the assumptions on the knowledge of q and G and the assumption that the input functions are completely assigned to players in G in the full paper [38].

ACKNOWLEDGMENTS

We thank the anonymous reviewers of PODS'19 for their helpful comments that greatly improved the presentation of the paper. We are greatly indebted to Arkadev Chattopadhyay and David Zuckerman for their insights that led to the results in Section 6. We thank Martin Grohe, Oliver Kennedy, Hung Ngo and Dan Suciu for helpful discussions at various stages of this work. This work was supported by NSF grant CCF-1717134.

REFERENCES

[1] Abu-Elkheir, M., Hayajneh, M., and Ali, N. A. Data management for the internet of things: Design primitives and solution. *Sensors 13*, 11 (2013), 15582–15612.

[2] Afrati, F. N., Joglekar, M. R., Ré, C., Salihoglu, S., and Ullman, J. D. GYM: A multiround distributed join algorithm. In *ICDT* (2017), pp. 4:1–4:18.

[3] Aji, S. M., and McEliece, R. J. The generalized distributive law. *IEEE Transactions on Information Theory 46*, 2 (Mar 2000), 325–343.

[4] Akatov, D. *Exploiting parallelism in decomposition methods for constraint satisfaction.* PhD thesis, University of Oxford, UK, 2010.

[5] Alon, N., Hoory, S., and Linial, N. The moore bound for irregular graphs. *Graphs and Combinatorics 18*, 1 (Mar 2002), 53–57.

[6] Alon, N., and Spencer, J. *The Probabilistic Method.* John Wiley, 1992.

[7] Bakibayev, N., Kociský, T., Olteanu, D., and Zavodny, J. Aggregation and ordering in factorised databases. *PVLDB 6*, 14 (2013), 1990–2001.

[8] Bar-Yossef, Z., Jayram, T. S., Kumar, R., and Sivakumar, D. An information statistics approach to data stream and communication complexity. *J. Comput. Syst. Sci. 68*, 4 (2004), 702–732.

[9] Beame, P., Koutris, P., and Suciu, D. Communication steps for parallel query processing. In *PODS* (2013), pp. 273–284.

[10] Beame, P., Koutris, P., and Suciu, D. Skew in parallel query processing. In *PODS* (2014), pp. 212–223.

[11] Bellenbaum, P., and Diestel, R. Two short proofs concerning tree-decompositions. *Combinatorics, Probability & Computing 11*, 6 (2002), 541–547.

[12] Bodlaender, H. L. Nc-algorithms for graphs with small treewidth. In *Graph-Theoretic Concepts in Computer Science, 14th International Workshop, WG '88, Amsterdam, The Netherlands, June 15-17, 1988, Proceedings* (1988), pp. 1–10.

[13] Bonnet, P., Gehrke, J., and Seshadri, P. Towards sensor database systems. In *Mobile Data Management, Second International Conference, MDM 2001, Hong Kong, China, January 8-10, 2001, Proceedings* (2001), pp. 3–14.

[14] Braverman, M., Ellen, F., Oshman, R., Pitassi, T., and Vaikuntanathan, V. A tight bound for set disjointness in the message-passing model. In *FOCS* (2013), pp. 668–677.

[15] Chakrabarti, A., Shi, Y., Wirth, A., and Yao, A. C. Informational complexity and the direct sum problem for simultaneous message complexity. In *FOCS* (2001), pp. 270–278.

[16] Chattopadhyay, A. Personal communication, 2018.

[17] Chattopadhyay, A., Koucký, M., Loff, B., and Mukhopadhyay, S. Simulation beats richness: New data-structure lower bounds. In *STOC* (2018).

[18] Chattopadhyay, A., Langberg, M., Li, S., and Rudra, A. Tight network topology dependent bounds on rounds of communication. In *SODA* (2017), pp. 2524–2539.

[19] Chattopadhyay, A., Radhakrishnan, J., and Rudra, A. Topology matters in communication. In *FOCS* (2014), pp. 631–640.

[20] Chattopadhyay, A., and Rudra, A. The range of topological effects on communication. In *ICALP* (2015), pp. 540–551.

[21] Dodis, Y., and Oliveira, R. On extracting private randomness over a public channel. In *RANDOM* (2003), pp. 252–263.

[22] Erde, J. A unified treatment of linked and lean tree-decompositions. *J. Comb. Theory, Ser. B 130* (2018), 114–143.

[23] Gehrke, J., and Madden, S. Query processing in sensor networks. *IEEE Pervasive Computing 3*, 1 (2004), 46–55.

[24] Ghobadi, M., Mahajan, R., Phanishayee, A., Devanur, N. R., Kulkarni, J., Ranade, G., Blanche, P., Rastegarfar, H., Glick, M., and Kilper, D. C. ProjecToR: Agile reconfigurable data center interconnect. In *SIGCOMM* (2016), pp. 216–229.

[25] Göös, M., Lovett, S., Meka, R., Watson, T., and Zuckerman, D. Rectangles are nonnegative juntas. In *STOC* (2015), pp. 257–266.

[26] Göös, M., Pitassi, T., and Watson, T. Query-to-communication lifting for BPP. In *FOCS* (2017), pp. 132–143.

[27] Gottlob, G., Greco, G., Leone, N., and Scarcello, F. Hypertree decompositions: Questions and answers. In *PODS* (2016), pp. 57–74.

[28] Graham, M. H. On the universal relation. In *Tech Report* (1979).

[29] Greco, G., Leone, N., and Scarcello, F. On weighted hypertree decompositions. In *Proceedings of the Twelfth Italian Symposium on Advanced Database Systems, SEBD 2004, S. Margherita di Pula, Cagliari, Italy, June 21-23, 2004* (2004), pp. 54–61.

[30] Jayram, T. S., Kumar, R., and Sivakumar, D. Two applications of information complexity. In *STOC* (2003), pp. 673–682.

[31] Joglekar, M., and Ré, C. It's all a matter of degree: Using degree information to optimize multiway joins. In *ICDT* (2016), pp. 11:1–11:17.

[32] Khamis, M. A., Ngo, H. Q., and Rudra, A. FAQ: questions asked frequently. In *PODS* (2016), pp. 13–28.

[33] Khamis, M. A., Ngo, H. Q., and Rudra, A. Juggling functions inside a database. *SIGMOD Record 46*, 1 (2017), 6–13.

[34] Kossmann, D. The state of the art in distributed query processing. *ACM Comput. Surv. 32*, 4 (2000), 422–469.

[35] Kostochka, A. V. On almost (k-1)-degenerate (k+1)-chromatic graphs and hypergraphs. *Discrete Mathematics 313*, 4 (2013), 366–374.

[36] Koutris, P., Beame, P., and Suciu, D. Worst-case optimal algorithms for parallel query processing. In *ICDT* (2016), pp. 8:1–8:18.

[37] Koutris, P., and Suciu, D. A guide to formal analysis of join processing in massively parallel systems. *SIGMOD Record 45*, 4 (2016), 18–27.

[38] Langberg, M., Li, S., Jayaraman, S. V. M., and Rudra, A. Topology Dependent Bounds For FAQs. UB-CSE Tech Report 2019-01, 2019. https://cse.buffalo.edu/tech-reports/2019-01.pdf.

[39] Lau, L. C. An approximate max-steiner-tree-packing min-steiner-cut theorem*. *Combinatorica 27*, 1 (2007), 71–90.

[40] Madden, S., Franklin, M. J., Hellerstein, J. M., and Hong, W. Tinydb: an acquisitional query processing system for sensor networks. *ACM Trans. Database Syst. 30*, 1 (2005), 122–173.

[41] Olteanu, D., and Závodný, J. Size bounds for factorised representations of query results. *ACM Trans. Database Syst. 40*, 1 (2015), 2:1–2:44.

[42] Peleg, D. *Distributed Computing: A Locality-Sensitive Approach.*

[43] Phillips, J. M., Verbin, E., and Zhang, Q. Lower bounds for number-in-hand multiparty communication complexity, made easy. In *SODA* (2012), pp. 486–501.

[44] Renner, R., and Wolf, S. Simple and tight bounds for information reconciliation and privacy amplification. In *ASIACRYPT* (Berlin, Heidelberg, 2005), Springer-Verlag, pp. 199–216.

[45] Scarcello, F., Greco, G., and Leone, N. Weighted hypertree decompositions and optimal query plans. In *PODS* (2004), pp. 210–221.

[46] Tarjan, R. E., and Yannakakis, M. Simple linear-time algorithms to test chordality of graphs, test acyclicity of hypergraphs, and selectively reduce acyclic hypergraphs. *SIAM J. Comput. 13*, 3 (1984), 566–579.

[47] Thomas, R. A menger-like property of tree-width: The finite case. *J. Comb. Theory, Ser. B 48*, 1 (1990), 67–76.

[48] Tiwari, P. Lower bounds on communication complexity in distributed computer networks. *J. ACM 34*, 4 (1987), 921–938.

[49] Vadhan, S. P. Pseudorandomness. *Foundations and Trends in Theoretical Computer Science 7*, 1-3 (2012), 1–336.

[50] Woodruff, D., and Zhang, Q. Tight bounds for distributed functional monitoring. In *STOC* (2012), pp. 941–960.

[51] Yu, C. T., and Ozsoyoglu, M. Z. An algorithm for tree-query membership of a distributed query. In *The IEEE Computer Society's Third International Computer Software and Applications Conference, COMPSAC 1979, 6-8 November, 1979, Chicago, Illinois, USA* (1979), pp. 306–312.

[52] Zuckerman, D. Simulating BPP using a general weak random source. *Algorithmica 16*, 4/5 (1996), 367–391.

A COMPARISON WITH RELEVANT MODELS

A.1 Basic MPC model

We formally define the MPC model used in [9] and the model adopted by [2] here, both in the language of our model

(Model 2.1). We consider the MPC with no replication, which is known as the basic MPC model in the literature.

Model A.1 (MPC(0)). *We are given a query q and its underlying hypergraph $\mathcal{H} = (\overline{\mathcal{V}}, \overline{\mathcal{E}})$ with input functions f_e having at most N non-zero values for every $e \in \overline{\mathcal{E}}$. We consider the network topology G' with $p+k$ nodes, defined as follows. There are k nodes, each assigned a function f_e for every $e \in \overline{\mathcal{E}}$. We call this set K. There are no edges between any pair of nodes in K. All nodes in K are directly connected by an edge to every node in a clique with p nodes that are disjoint from K (also a part of G'). Each vnode in K has capacity N and all the remaining nodes have capacity L. The capacity of a node bounds the number of bits it can receive in each round. Given this setup, we would like to compute* BCQ *(and more generally an* FAQ*) of $\mathcal{H}$ on G'.*

To design a protocol for this computation, we can assume that every node in G' has the knowledge of q and G'. At the end of the protocol, a pre-determined player in K knows the answer to q.

Finally, given the above setup, our goal is to design protocols that minimize the number of rounds to compute q on G. This model does not take into account the internal computation done by the $p+k$ nodes and assumes the nodes co-operatively compute the answer to q.

We now summarize the differences of this model from ours.

A.1.1 Differences from our Model.

- MPC(0) assumes a specific choice of a network topology G' as opposed to general topology G in our model.
- MPC(0) assumes a specific assignment of functions in $\overline{\mathcal{E}}$ to players in G'. Our upper bound techniques can handle any assignment but our lower bounds are for a specific class of assignments. We would like to mention here that this is true for the models in [2, 9] as well (i.e., upper bounds can handly any assignment whereas lower bounds are for a specific class of assignments) and we consider one such assignment in Model A.1.
- MPC(0) assumes node capacities whereas ours assumes edge capacities.
- The models in [2, 9] design protocols wherein the number of rounds is either constant or a function of k. The number of rounds in our model are a function of N.
- The models in [2, 9] generally prove results for computing natural join whereas we look at BCQ (and more generally FAQs). We note that the results of [2, 9] for natural join apply to BCQ as well. This is true for both upper and lower bounds in [9] and only for upper bounds in [2].

We consider two instantations of this model – one by [9] and the other by [2].

A.1.2 Fixing p and Determining L [9]. This model assumes N is larger than the size of G' and all the functions f_e are matchings (i.e., skew-free). In other words, for each variable $v \in e$, each of the values $x_v \in \text{Dom}(v)$ can occur in at most one tuple in f_e. Using Proposition 3.2 and Theorem 3.3 in [9], it can be shown that there exists an optimal one round protocol to solve BCQ of any star $\mathcal{H}$ on G' with $L = \Omega\left(\frac{k \cdot N}{p}\right)$. Further, when $\mathcal{H}$ is a forest, BCQ of $\mathcal{H}$ on G' takes $\Theta(\log(D'))$ rounds for the same L (where D' is the diameter of $\mathcal{H}$). We would like to mention here that a follow up work [10] handled input functions with specific types of skew and proved upper and lower bounds for the queries considered above. Since each node in the p-clique can have different capacities in this scenario, we do not discuss it further here.

A.1.3 Fixing L and Determining p [2]. This model assumes the size of G' is much larger than N. Assuming $L = (k \cdot N)^{\frac{1}{\delta}}$ for a fixed small constant $\delta > 1$, we can use the Main Results 1 and 2 from [2] and show that there exists a protocol to solve BCQ of any star $\mathcal{H}$ in: (1) $O(k)$ rounds with $p = (k \cdot N)^{2-\frac{2}{\delta}}$ and (2) $O(\log_2(k))$ rounds with $p = (k \cdot N)^{6-\frac{2}{\delta}}$.

Before we instantiate our model for a comparison with the above models, we would like to state that while our model can handle the constraint where the size of G' can be larger than N, our techniques cannot. Hence, we restrict our comparison to the model in Section A.1.2. We now instantiate our model (Model 2.1) with G' and assume that each edge in G' has capacity

$$L' = \frac{L}{k} = \frac{N}{p}. \tag{13}$$

Note that this is a weaker version of Model A.1 since node capacities don't necessarily translate to equal edge capacities when the goal is to compute q on G'. We take this route as it helps us make a fair comparison with Section A.1.2.

A.1.4 Our Results in Model A.1. We show how our upper bound techniques apply for solving BCQ of any star $\mathcal{H}$ on G'. We can instantiate Corollary 4.2 with capacity $\widetilde{\Theta}(1)$ to get $O\left(\min_{\Delta \in [|V(G')|]}\left(\frac{N}{\text{ST}(G',K,\Delta)} + \Delta\right)\right)$ rounds. We claim that $\min_{\Delta \in [|V(G')|]}\left(\frac{N}{\text{ST}(G',K,\Delta)} + \Delta\right) = O\left(\frac{N}{p}\right)$. To see this, we show such a Steiner tree packing containing p trees with diameter 2 – each node in the p-clique in G' along with all its k edges incident on K forms a Steiner tree. Since there are p such nodes, we can obtain such a packing. Recall that when each edge in G' has capacity L' (instead of the $O(\log_2(D))$ capacity in Model 2.1), our upper bound gets divided by L'. Thus, we have an upper bound of $O\left(\frac{N}{L' \cdot p}\right) = O(1)$ (using (13)) i.e., a constant number of rounds.

Note that a lower bound of one round on the number of rounds is trivial. Hence, we can obtain a tight bound of $\widetilde{\Theta}(1)$

for any star $\mathcal{H}$, resulting in an one round protocol matching results in Section A.1.2.

Given the tight results for the star case, there is a natural generalization for our protocol and bounds when $\mathcal{H}$ is a forest using ideas from the proof of Lemma 4.4. We start by noting that all stars at the same level in $\mathcal{H}$ can be computed simultaneously since each node in K is directly connected to each node in the (p)-clique. In particular, we can run the star protocol used above on all these stars simultaneously but we still need to be able to uniquely identify the stars computed. It's not too hard to see that this can be done with $O(\log(y(\mathcal{H})))$ additional information for each internal node v. This results in an upper bound of

$$O\left(D' \cdot \log(y(\mathcal{H})) \cdot \min_{\Delta \in [|V|]} \left(\frac{N}{\mathrm{ST}(G', K, \Delta)} + \Delta\right)\right) = O\left(\frac{D' \cdot \log(y(\mathcal{H})) \cdot N}{p}\right),$$

where $\mathrm{ST}(G', K, 2) = p$ and D' is the diameter of $\mathcal{H}$. If we divide our upper bound by L' and substitute its value from (13), we can use ideas similar to those used in the star case to obtain a protocol with $O(D')$ rounds. However, our lower bound techniques do not work for the assignment of functions to K in Model A.1. We would like to mention that the model in Section A.1.2 takes $\Theta(\log(D'))$ rounds for this case (though the upper bound only holds for the special case of matching databases).

Finally, for general simple graphs $\mathcal{H}$, we decompose $\mathcal{H}$ into a forest and a core by Definition 2.7. We use the *trivial protocol* on the core, which is basically sending all functions to one player in K and is independent of the induced query in the core. We would like to mention that this is worse than existing protocols [2, 9] for $\mathcal{H}$ with non-constant degeneracy d since we do not exploit any information about the query. Before we move to the next model, we would like to mention here that the results of Section A.1.2 and our results match up to a constant factor for the case when $\mathcal{H}$ is a star. The upper bounds match since the protocols in both cases split the input functions the same way – the model in Section A.1.2 uses hashes to achieve this and we use Steiner tree packings for the same. The results however start diverging even when $\mathcal{H}$ is a tree of small depth.

A.2 General MPC model

We now perform our second and final comparison. We formally define the model from [36], which is a followup of [9, 10] and performs a *worst-case analysis* of the communication cost for join queries. All the three models are described in [37]. We define it in the language of our model like we did for Model A.1.

Model A.2 (MPC(ϵ)). *Let ϵ be a fixed value s.t. $0 \le \epsilon < 1$. We are given a query q and its underlying hypergraph $\mathcal{H} = (\overline{\mathcal{V}}, \overline{\mathcal{E}})$ with input functions f_e having at most N non-zero values for every $e \in \overline{\mathcal{E}}$. We consider the network topology G'', which is a clique on p. The input of size $k \cdot N$ is uniformly partitioned across the p nodes. Let $K = V(G'')$. It follows that $|K| = p$. All nodes in G have capacity $L(\epsilon)$. The capacity of a vertex bounds the number of bits it can receive in each round. Given this setup, we would like to compute* BCQ *(and more generally an* FAQ*) of $\mathcal{H}$ on G''.*

To design a protocol for this computation, we can assume that every node in G'' has the knowledge of q and G''. At the end of the protocol, a pre-determined player in K knows the answer to q.

Finally, given the above setup, our goal is to design protocols that minimize the number of rounds to compute q on G''. This model does not take into account the internal computation done by the p nodes and assumes the nodes co-operatively compute the answer to q.

We now summarize the differences of this model from ours.

A.2.1 *Differences from our Model.*

- MPC(ϵ) assumes a specific choice of a network topology G'' as opposed to general topology in our model.
- MPC(ϵ) assumes a uniform distribution of the input across the p nodes instead of one function being completely assigned to a specific node in G'' in our model.
- MPC(ϵ) works with node capacities like Model A.1, whereas ours works on edge capacities.
- The model in [36] designs protocols wherein the number of rounds either constant or a function of k. The number of rounds in our model are a function of N.
- The model in [36] proves results for computing natural join whereas we look at BCQ (and more generally FAQs). Note that their upper results for natural join apply for BCQ as well (but lower bound results do not transfer).

We consider the instantiation of this model by [36]. We would like to mention here that the models studied in [2, 9, 10] can all be instantiated in this setting only for proving upper bounds.

A.2.2 Fixing p and Determining L [36]. This model assumes N is larger than the size of G' and there are no restrictions in the input functions. Using Theorems 3.1 and 3.3 of [36], it can be shown that there exists an optimal one round protocol to solve BCQ of any star $\mathcal{H}$ on G'' with $L\left(\epsilon = 1 - \frac{1}{k}\right) = \Omega\left(\frac{N}{p^{1-\epsilon}}\right) = \Omega\left(\frac{N}{p^{\frac{1}{k}}}\right)$. Further, when $\mathcal{H}$ is a forest, BCQ of

$\mathcal{H}$ on G'' takes $O(k)$ rounds[23] with $L\left(\epsilon = 1 - \frac{1}{\rho^*(\mathcal{H})}\right) = \Omega\left(\frac{N}{p^{1-\epsilon}}\right) = \Omega\left(\frac{N}{p^{\frac{1}{\rho^*(\mathcal{H})}}}\right)$ using ideas in Section 4 of [36]. Here, $\rho^*(\mathcal{H})$ denotes the edge cover number of $\mathcal{H}$ (i.e., size of the minimum edge cover of $\mathcal{H}$).
We now instantiate our model (Model 2.1) with G'' and assume that each edge in G'' has capacity

$$L'' = \frac{L(\epsilon)}{p}. \tag{14}$$

Further, we assume that the input functions are not distributed uniformly but rather based on some pre-determined hash functions. Note that this certainly makes our model (Model A.1) more restrictive since node capacities don't necessarily translate to equal edge capacities when the goal is to compute q on G'' and the hash-based split (see Appendix H in the full paper [38]) restricts the way in which input functions can be distributed across nodes in G''. We opt for this since it helps us make a fair comparison with Section A.2.2.

A.2.3 Our Results in Model A.2. We now show how our upper bound techniques apply in this model for solving BCQ of any star $\mathcal{H}$ on G'. We do not compare lower bounds here since (1) [36] lower bounds do not hold for BCQ (or at least it does not follow immediately from their lower bounds for the join quries) and (2) Our lower bounds for the case when the functions are uniformly distributed over the players are quantitatively very weak. For the upper bound, we can instantiate Corollary H.7 in the full paper [38] with capacity $\widetilde{\Theta}(1)$ to get $O\left(\min_{\Delta\in[p]}\left(\frac{N}{\mathrm{ST}(G'',K,\Delta)} + p\cdot\Delta\right)\right)$ rounds. We claim that $\min_{\Delta\in[p]}\left(\frac{N}{\mathrm{ST}(G'',K,\Delta)} + p\cdot\Delta\right) = O\left(\frac{N}{p} + p\right)$. To see this, we show a Steiner tree packing containing $\frac{p-1}{2}$ trees with diameter 1 – we can greedily keep picking and throwing out paths of length $p-1$ from G'' that contain all the p vertices. Each such path forms a Steiner tree. Since we can identify $\frac{p-1}{2}$ such paths, we can obtain such a packing. Recall that when each edge in G'' has capacity $L(\epsilon)$ instead of the standard $O(\log_2(N))$, our upper bound gets divided by L''. Thus, we have an upper bound of $O\left(\frac{\frac{N}{p}+p}{L''}\right)$. Using (14) and the fact $N \geq p^2$ (from Model 2.1), we get a $O\left(p^{\frac{1}{k}}\right)$ round protocol. Note that this is worse than the one round protocol by Section A.2.2.
For the case when $\mathcal{H}$ is a forest, we can instantiate Corollary H.7 in the full paper [38] with capacity $\widetilde{\Theta}(1)$ to get a bound of

$$O\left(y(\mathcal{H})\cdot \min_{\Delta\in[|V|]}\left(\frac{N\cdot r}{\mathrm{ST}(G'',K,\Delta)} + p\cdot\Delta\right)\right) = O\left(\frac{D'\cdot\log(y(\mathcal{H}))\cdot N}{p}\right),$$

where $\mathrm{ST}(G'',K,1) = p$ and D' is the diameter of $\mathcal{H}$. We can use ideas from Section A.1.4 and from those used in the star case to obtain a protocol with $O\left(D'\cdot p^{\frac{1}{\rho^*(\mathcal{H})}}\right)$ rounds. In particular, to get this bound, we divide our upper bound by L'' and substitute its value form (14). Note that this is worse than the $O(k)$ round protocol by Section A.2.2.
Finally, for general simple graphs $\mathcal{H}$, we decompose $\mathcal{H}$ into a forest and a core by Definition 2.7. We use the *trivial protocol* on the core, which is basically sending all functions to one player in K and is independent of the induced query in the core. As stated in Section A.1.4, this is worse than existing protocols [36] for $\mathcal{H}$ with non-constant degeneracy d since we do not exploit any information about the query.

A.3 Scope for Future Work

Many open questions arise out of this comparison. We summarize them here and leave them for future work.

- Can we modify our model to handle node failures like Models A.1 and A.2 do, using replication?
- Can we improve over our *trivial protocol* for cyclic queries using ideas from [2, 9, 10, 31, 36, 37]?
- Can our algorithmic ideas for set intersection be plugged into the Models A.1 and A.2?
- Can we extend our techniques to handle arbitrary distributions of input functions to nodes in the topology?

[23]For the case when we are interested in computing the join query of $\mathcal{H}$, then there is also a matching $\Omega(k)$ lower bound.

Instance and Output Optimal Parallel Algorithms for Acyclic Joins*

Xiao Hu
HKUST
xhuam@cse.ust.hk

Ke Yi
HKUST
yike@cse.ust.hk

ABSTRACT

Massively parallel join algorithms have received much attention in recent years, while most prior work has focused on worst-optimal algorithms. However, the worst-case optimality of these join algorithms relies on hard instances having very large output sizes, which rarely appear in practice. A stronger notion of optimality is *output-optimal*, which requires an algorithm to be optimal within the class of all instances sharing the same input and output size. An even stronger optimality is *instance-optimal*, i.e., the algorithm is optimal on every single instance, but this may not always be achievable.

In the traditional RAM model of computation, the classical Yannakakis algorithm is instance-optimal on any acyclic join. But in the massively parallel computation (MPC) model, the situation becomes much more complicated. We first show that for the class of r-hierarchical joins, instance-optimality can still be achieved in the MPC model. Then, we give a new MPC algorithm for an arbitrary acyclic join with load $O(\frac{\text{IN}}{p} + \frac{\sqrt{\text{IN}\cdot\text{OUT}}}{p})$, where IN, OUT are the input and output sizes of the join, and p is the number of servers in the MPC model. This improves the MPC version of the Yannakakis algorithm by an $O(\sqrt{\frac{\text{OUT}}{\text{IN}}})$ factor. Furthermore, we show that this is output-optimal when $\text{OUT} = O(p \cdot \text{IN})$, for every acyclic but non-r-hierarchical join. Finally, we give the first output-sensitive lower bound for the triangle join in the MPC model, showing that it is inherently more difficult than acyclic joins.

*This work was supported by Hong Kong RGC under grants 16200415, 16202317, and 16201318, and by grants from Microsoft and Alibaba.

PODS'19, June 30-July 5, 2019, Amsterdam, Netherlands

ACM ISBN 978-1-4503-6227-6/19/06...$15.00
https://doi.org/10.1145/3294052.3319698

CCS CONCEPTS

• **Theory of computation → Database query processing and optimization (theory).**

KEYWORDS

MPC algorithms; acyclic joins

ACM Reference Format:
Xiao Hu and Ke Yi. 2019. Instance and Output Optimal Parallel Algorithms for Acyclic Joins. In *38th ACM SIGMOD-SIGACT-SIGAI Symposium on Principles of Database Systems (PODS'19), June 30-July 5, 2019, Amsterdam, Netherlands.* ACM, New York, NY, USA, 14 pages. https://doi.org/10.1145/3294052.3319698

1 INTRODUCTION

A (natural) *join* is defined as a hypergraph $Q = (\mathcal{V}, \mathcal{E})$, where the vertices $\mathcal{V} = \{x_1, \ldots, x_n\}$ model the *attributes* and the hyperedges $\mathcal{E} = \{e_1, \ldots, e_m\} \subseteq 2^{\mathcal{V}}$ model the *relations*. Let $\text{dom}(x)$ be the *domain* of attribute $x \in \mathcal{V}$. An *instance* of Q is a set of relations $\mathcal{R} = \{R(e) : e \in \mathcal{E}\}$, where $R(e)$ is a set of *tuples*, where each tuple is an assignment that assigns a value from $\text{dom}(x)$ to x for every $x \in e$. We use $\text{IN} = \sum_{e \in \mathcal{E}} |R(e)|$ to denote the size of $\mathcal{R}$. The *join results* of Q on $\mathcal{R}$, denoted as $Q(\mathcal{R})$, consist of all combinations of tuples, one from each $R(e)$, such that they share common values on their common attributes. Let $\text{OUT} = |Q(\mathcal{R})|$ be the output size. We study the *data complexity* of join algorithms, i.e., we assume that the query size, namely n and m, are constants. In this paper, we focus on *acyclic joins*, i.e., when the hypergraph Q is acyclic (formal definition given later).

1.1 The model of computation

The problem gets much more interesting in the parallel setting. In this paper, we consider the *massively parallel computation* (MPC) model [1, 2, 6, 7, 21, 23, 25], which has become the standard model of computation for studying massively parallel algorithms, especially for join algorithms.

In the MPC model, data is initially distributed evenly over p servers with each server holding IN/p tuples. Computation proceeds in rounds. In each round, each server first sends messages to other servers, receives messages from other servers, and then does some local computation. The complexity of the algorithm is measured by the number of rounds and the *load*, denoted as L, which is the maximum message size received by any server in any round. A *linear load* $L = O(\frac{\text{IN}}{p})$ is the ideal case (since the initial load is already $\frac{\text{IN}}{p}$), while if $L = O(\text{IN})$, all problems can be solved trivially in one round by simply sending all data to one server. Initial efforts were mostly spent on what can be done in a single round of computation [2, 6, 7, 23, 25, 25], but recently, more interest has been given to multi-round (but still a constant) algorithms [1, 21, 23], since new main memory based systems, such as Spark and Flink, have much lower overhead per round than previous generations like Hadoop.

The MPC model can be considered as a simplified version of the BSP model [31], but it has enjoyed more popularity in recent years. This is mostly because the BSP model takes too many measures into consideration, such as communication costs, local computation time, memory consumption, etc. The MPC model unifies all these costs with one parameter L, which makes the model much simpler. Meanwhile, although L is defined as the maximum incoming message size of a server, it is also closely related with the local computation time and memory consumption, which are both increasing functions of L. Thus, L serves as a good surrogate of these other cost measures. This is also why the MPC model does not limit the outgoing message size of a server, which is less relevant to other costs.

All our algorithms work under the mild assumption $\text{IN} \geq p^{1+\epsilon}$ where $\epsilon > 0$ is any small constant. This assumption clearly holds on any reasonable values of IN and p in practice; theoretically, this is the minimum requirement for the model to be able to compute some almost trivial functions, like the "or" of IN bits, in $O(1)$ rounds. Our lower bounds hold under $\text{IN} \geq p^c$ for some constant c, which may depend on the particular lower bound construction.

We confine ourselves to *tuple-based* join algorithms, i.e., the tuples are atomic elements that must be processed and communicated in their entirety. The only way to create a tuple is by making a copy, from either the original tuple or one of its copies. We say that an MPC algorithm computes the join Q on instance $\mathcal{R}$ if the following is achieved: For any join result $(t_1, \dots, t_m) \in Q(\mathcal{R})$ where $t_i \in R(e_i)$, $i = 1, \dots, m$, these m tuples (or their copies) must all be present on the same server at some point. Then the server will call a zero-cost function $emit(t_1, \dots, t_m)$ to report the join result. Note that since we only consider constant-round algorithms, whether a server is allowed to keep the tuples it has received from previous rounds is irrelevant: if not, it can just keep sending all these tuples to itself over the rounds, increasing the load by a constant factor. All known join algorithms in the MPC model are tuple-based and obey these requirements. Our lower bounds are combinatorial in nature: we only count the number of tuples that must be communicated in order to emit all join results, while all other information can be communicated for free. The upper bounds include all messages, with a tuple and an integer of $O(\log \text{IN})$ bits both counted as 1 unit of communication.

1.2 Instance and output optimality

In worst-case analysis, the entire space of instances is divided into classes by the input size IN, and the running time is measured on the worst instance in each class. For many important computational problems, this is too coarse-grained and cannot accurately characterize the performance of the algorithm. For the join problem, no algorithm can do better than $O(\text{IN}^{1/\rho})$ time in the worst case, where ρ is the fractional edge cover number of the hypergraph Q [28, 32]. This bound drastically overestimates the running time on most typical instances.

A more refined approach is *parameterized analysis*, which further subdivides the instance space into smaller classes by introducing more parameters that supposedly better characterize the difficulty of each class. For the join problem, the output size OUT is a commonly used parameter, and each class of instances share the same input and output size. Let $\mathfrak{R}(\text{IN}, \text{OUT})$ be the class of instances with input size IN and output size OUT. Then the load of an MPC algorithm $\mathcal{A}$ is thus a function of both IN and OUT, defined as

$$L_{\mathcal{A}}(\text{IN}, \text{OUT}) = \max_{\mathcal{R} \in \mathfrak{R}(\text{IN}, \text{OUT})} L_{\mathcal{A}}(\mathcal{R}),$$

where $L_{\mathcal{A}}(\mathcal{R})$ denotes the load of $\mathcal{A}$ on $\mathcal{R}$. Algorithm $\mathcal{A}$ is *output-optimal* if

$$L_{\mathcal{A}}(\text{IN}, \text{OUT}) = O(L_{\mathcal{A}'}(\text{IN}, \text{OUT})),$$

for every algorithm $\mathcal{A}'$.

Further subdividing the instance space leads to more refined analyses. In extreme case when each class contains just one instance, we obtain instance-optimal algorithms. More precisely, an algorithm $\mathcal{A}$ is *instance-optimal* if

$$L_{\mathcal{A}}(\mathcal{R}) = O(L_{\mathcal{A}'}(\mathcal{R})),$$

for every instance $\mathcal{R}$ and every algorithm A'. Note that by definition, an instance-optimal algorithm must be output-optimal, and an output-optimal algorithm must be worst-case optimal, but the reserve direction may not be true.

In the traditional RAM model of computation, the classical Yannakakis algorithm [33] can compute any acyclic join in time $O(\text{IN} + \text{OUT})$, which is both output-optimal and instance-optimal, because on any instance $\mathcal{R}$, any algorithm has to spend at least $\Omega(\text{IN})$ time to read all the inputs[1] and $\Omega(\text{OUT})$ time to enumerate the outputs. Thus, the two

[1]To formally prove this claim, one will have to be more careful with the family of algorithms under consideration. In particular, if OUT = 0, then the algorithm may not have to do anything. One possible approach is to ask the algorithm to produce a *certificate* in addition to the join results [27]. We

notions of optimality coincide (but both are stronger than worst-case optimality). Fundamentally, this is because the difficulty of any instance $\mathcal{R}$ is precisely characterized by its input size and output size, and all instances in $\mathfrak{R}(\text{IN}, \text{OUT})$ have exactly the same complexity $O(\text{IN} + \text{OUT})$.

1.3 Join algorithms in the MPC model

The situation becomes much more interesting in the MPC model. First, it has been observed that the Yannakakis algorithm can be easily implemented in the MPC model with a load of $O(\frac{\text{IN}}{p} + \frac{\text{OUT}}{p})$ [1][2], but this is not optimal. In particular, it is known that the binary join $R_1(A, B) \bowtie R_2(B, C)$ can be computed with load $O(\frac{\text{IN}}{p} + \sqrt{\frac{\text{OUT}}{p}})$ [7, 16]. This is optimal by the following simple lower bound argument: Each server can only produce $O(L^2)$ join results in a constant number of rounds with the load limited to L, so all the p servers can produce at most $O(p \cdot L^2)$ join results. Thus, producing OUT join results needs at least a load of $L = \Omega(\sqrt{\frac{\text{OUT}}{p}})$. Meanwhile, since $L \geq \text{IN}/p$ by definition, the $O(\frac{\text{IN}}{p} + \sqrt{\frac{\text{OUT}}{p}})$ bound is optimal. Note that this argument can be applied on a per-instance basis, which means that the load complexity of any instance is still precisely captured by IN and OUT, and $O(\frac{\text{IN}}{p} + \sqrt{\frac{\text{OUT}}{p}})$ is both an instance-optimal and output-optimal bound.

However, when the join involves three relations, the situation becomes subtler, and we start to see a separation between the two notions of optimality, meaning that the load complexity of an instance may not depend only on IN and OUT. Let us start with the simplest 3-relation join $R_1(A) \bowtie R_2(B) \bowtie R_3(C)$, i.e., computing the Cartesian product of 3 sets of tuples. Consider a particular class $\mathfrak{R}(\text{IN}, \text{OUT})$ when $\text{OUT} = \text{IN}^2$. Suppose the 3 relations have sizes N_1, N_2, N_3, respectively. Then $\mathfrak{R}(\text{IN}, \text{OUT})$ consists of all instances with $N_1 + N_2 + N_3 = \text{IN}$ and $N_1 N_2 N_3 = \text{OUT} = \text{IN}^2$. Consider the following two instances: (1) $N_1 = N_2 = \Theta(\sqrt{\text{IN}})$, $N_3 = \Theta(\text{IN})$, applying the same argument above except that each server now can produce $O(L^3)$ join results, i.e., $p \cdot L^3 = \Omega(\text{OUT})$, we have $L = \Omega((\frac{\text{OUT}}{p})^{1/3})$; (2) if $N_1 = 1$, $N_2 = N_3 = \Theta(\text{IN})$, then the problem boils down to computing the Cartesian product of two sets, which has a lower bound of $L = \Omega((\frac{\text{OUT}}{p})^{1/2})$. The reason why instance (2) has a higher lower bound than instance (1) is that it has a higher skew, which causes more difficulty for the MPC model. Note that this phenomenon does not exist in the RAM model, in which both instances (in fact all instances in $\mathfrak{R}(\text{IN}, \text{OUT})$) have the same complexity of $O(\text{IN} + \text{OUT})$. Fundamentally, this is because the MPC model is all about *locality*: An MPC algorithm should strive to bring all related tuples to one server so as to produce as many join results as possible, while a higher skew reduces locality.

We can extend this argument to computing the Cartesian product of m sets of sizes $N_1, \ldots, N_m$. Any algorithm computing the full Cartesian product obviously must also compute the Cartesian product of any subset of the n sets, thus the load must be at least

$$L_{\text{Cartesian}}(p, \mathcal{R}) := \max_{S \subseteq \{1,\ldots,m\}} \left(\frac{\prod_{i \in S} N_i}{p} \right)^{\frac{1}{|S|}}. \quad (1)$$

It has been shown that the HyperCube algorithm [2] incurs a load of $L_{\text{Cartesian}}(p, \mathcal{R}) \cdot \log^{O(1)} p$ on any instance $\mathcal{R}$ [7]. Thus, it can be considered as an instance-optimal algorithm for computing Cartesian products, with an optimality ratio of $\log^{O(1)} p$.

The binary join and Cartesian products are the simplest joins. Then the obvious question is, do instance-optimal algorithms exist for larger classes of joins? If not, how about output-optimal algorithms? These are the main questions we wish to address in this paper.

1.4 Classification of acyclic joins

Before describing our results, we first define some sub-classes of acyclic joins.

Acyclic joins [8]. We use the common notion of acyclicity, which is also known as α-acyclicity. A join $Q = (\mathcal{V}, \mathcal{E})$ is *acyclic* if there exists an undirected tree $\mathcal{T}$ whose nodes are in one-to-one correspondence with the edges in $\mathcal{E}$ such that for any vertex $v \in \mathcal{V}$, all nodes containing v form a connected subtree. Such a tree $\mathcal{T}$ is called the *join tree* of Q. Note that the join tree may not be unique for a given Q.

Hierarchical joins [11]. A join $Q = (\mathcal{V}, \mathcal{E})$ is *hierarchical* if for every pair of vertices x, y, there is $\mathcal{E}_x \subseteq \mathcal{E}_y$, or $\mathcal{E}_y \subseteq \mathcal{E}_x$, or $\mathcal{E}_x \cap \mathcal{E}_y = \emptyset$, where $\mathcal{E}_x = \{e \in \mathcal{E} : x \in e\}$ is the set of hyperedges containing attribute x. Thus, all attributes can be organized into a forest, such that x is a descendant of y iff $\mathcal{E}_x \subseteq \mathcal{E}_y$. Hierarchical joins have been enjoyed nice properties in probabilistic databases [11, 12] and query answering under updates [9], but their role in the MPC model has not been studied so far.

r-hierarchical joins. We consider a slightly larger class of hierarchical joins. A *reduce* procedure on a hypergraph $(\mathcal{V}, \mathcal{E})$ is to remove an edge $e \in \mathcal{E}$ if there exists another edge $e' \in \mathcal{E}$ such that $e \subseteq e'$. We can repeatedly apply the reduce procedure until no more edge can be reduced, and the resulting hypergraph is said to be *reduced.* A join is *r-hierarchical*

will not digress to this direction since this paper is only concerned about MPC algorithms.

[2]The bound stated in [1] is actually $O(\frac{(\text{IN}+\text{OUT})^2}{p})$, because they used a sub-optimal binary join algorithm as the subroutine. Replacing it with the optimal binary join algorithm in [7, 16] yields the claimed bound, as observed in [24].

Joins	Instance-optimal		Output-optimal	
	one-round	multi-round	one-round	multi-round
tall-flat	$(\frac{\text{IN}}{p} + L_{\text{instance}}(p, \mathcal{R})) \log^{O(1)} p$ [7]	$\Theta\left(\frac{\text{IN}}{p} + L_{\text{instance}}(p, \mathcal{R})\right)$	-	
r-hierarchical w/o dangling tuples				
r-hierarchical w/ dangling tuples	$\omega\left(\frac{\text{IN}}{p} + L_{\text{instance}}(p, \mathcal{R})\right)$		$\omega\left(\frac{\text{IN}}{p} + \frac{\text{OUT}}{p}\right)$ [25]	-
acyclic	$\omega\left(\frac{\text{IN}}{p} + L_{\text{instance}}(p, \mathcal{R})\right)$			$\Theta\left(\frac{\text{IN}}{p} + \frac{\sqrt{\text{IN} \cdot \text{OUT}}}{p}\right)$ LB holds for $\text{OUT} \le O(p \cdot \text{IN})$
triangle				$\tilde{\Omega}\left(\min\left\{\frac{\text{IN}}{p} + \frac{\text{OUT}}{p}, \frac{\text{IN}}{p^{2/3}}\right\}\right)$

Table 1: Summary of results.

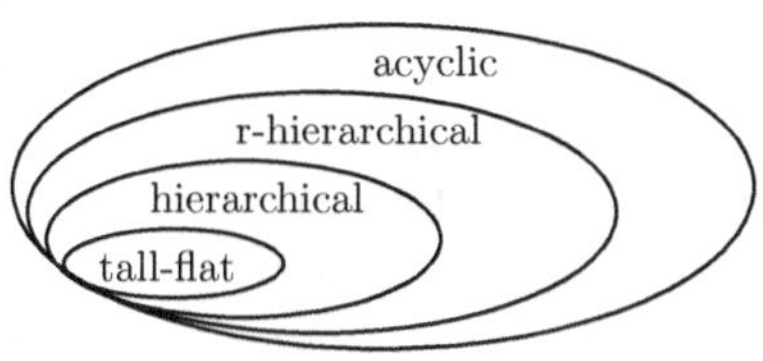

Figure 1: Relationships of joins.

if its reduced join hypergraph is hierarchical. A hierarchical join must be r-hierarchical, but not vice versa. For example, the join $R_1(A) \bowtie R_2(A, B) \bowtie R_3(B)$ is r-hierarchical but not hierarchical. On the other hand, an r-hierarchical join must be acyclic.

Tall-flat joins [25]. A join $Q = (\mathcal{V}, \mathcal{E})$ is *tall-flat* if one can order the attributes as $x_1, x_2, \cdots, x_h, y_1, y_2, \cdots, y_l$ such that (1) $\mathcal{E}_{x_1} \supseteq \mathcal{E}_{x_2} \supseteq \cdots \supseteq \mathcal{E}_{x_h}$; (2) $\mathcal{E}_{x_h} \supseteq \mathcal{E}_{y_j}$ for $j = 1, 2, \cdots, l$; and (3) $|\mathcal{E}_{y_j}| = 1$ for $j = 1, 2, \cdots, l$. Obviously, a tall-flat join must be hierarchical.

The relationships of these joins are illustrated in Figure 1.

1.5 Our results

This paper gives an almost complete characterization of acyclic joins with respect to instance-optimality and output-optimality in the MPC model. Our results are summarized in Table 1, and we explain them below in more detail.

Instance-optimality. First, we extend the Cartesian product lower bound (1) to a general join $Q = (\mathcal{V}, \mathcal{E})$. For any subset of relations $S \subseteq \mathcal{E}$, define

$$Q(\mathcal{R}, S) := (\bowtie_{e \in S} R(e)) \ltimes Q(\mathcal{R}),$$

i.e., the join results of relations in S that are part of a full join result. Clearly, any algorithm computing $Q(\mathcal{R})$ must implicitly also compute $Q(\mathcal{R}, S)$ for every S. Because each join result in $Q(\mathcal{R}, S)$ consists of $|S|$ tuples, one from each relation in S, a server can emit at most $O(L^{|S|})$ join results of $Q(\mathcal{R}, S)$, so we must have $p \cdot L^{|S|} = \Omega(|Q(\mathcal{R}, S|)$. Thus, we obtain the following per-instance lower bound on the load:

$$L_{\text{instance}}(p, \mathcal{R}) := \max_{S \subseteq \mathcal{E}} \left(\frac{|Q(\mathcal{R}, S)|}{p}\right)^{\frac{1}{|S|}}. \tag{2}$$

The BinHC algorithm [7] is a generalization of the HyperCube algorithm to general joins. The load of the BinHC algorithm is parameterized by the degrees of all subsets of attribute values (more detail given in Section 3). Beame et al. [7] show that BinHC is optimal (up to polylog factors) within the class of instances sharing the same degrees, among all one-round MPC algorithms. In this paper, we strengthen this result by giving a new analysis of the BinHC algorithm, showing that it is actually instance-optimal (up to polylog factors) for (1) all tall-flat joins, and (2) all r-hierarchical joins provided that the instance does not contain *dangling tuples* (a dangling tuple is one that does not appear in the join results). Furthermore, because the per-instance lower bound (2) also holds for multi-round algorithms, these instance-optimality results extend to multi-round algorithms as well. For r-hierarchical joins with dangling tuples, one-round algorithms cannot achieve $O(\frac{\text{IN}}{p} + L_{\text{instance}}(p, \mathcal{R}))$ load, but we can remove the dangling tuples in $O(1)$ rounds with $O(\frac{\text{IN}}{p})$ load [33], and then run then BinHC algorithm. This gives a multi-round, $(\frac{\text{IN}}{p} + L_{\text{instance}}(p, \mathcal{R})) \log^{O(1)} p$-load algorithm, where the $O(1)$ exponent depends on the query size, and is at least m, the number of relations. Then we give a new multi-round algorithm for r-hierarchical joins with load $O(\frac{\text{IN}}{p} + L_{\text{instance}}(p, \mathcal{R}))$, i.e., improving the instance-optimality ratio from $\log^{O(1)} p$ to $O(1)$.

The instance-optimal load $O(\frac{\text{IN}}{p} + L_{\text{instance}}(p, \mathcal{R}))$ is not achievable beyond r-hierarchical joins[3]. More precisely, we show that for every acyclic join that is not r-hierarchical, there is an instance $\mathcal{R}$ with $L_{\text{instance}}(p, \mathcal{R}) = O(\frac{\text{IN}}{p})$ but any

[3]But instance-optimal algorithms are still possible, if some higher per-instance lower bound can be derived.

multi-round algorithm must incur a load of[4] $\tilde{\Omega}(\frac{\text{IN}}{p^{1/2}})$ on $\mathcal{R}$. This is actually a corollary following our output-sensitive lower bound, which is described next.

Output-optimality. One-round algorithms have severe limitations with respect to OUT: As shown in [25], any non-tall-flat joins must incur load $\omega(\frac{\text{IN}}{p} + \frac{\text{OUT}}{p})$ if only one round is allowed. On the other hand, as mentioned, the classical Yannakakis algorithm is a multi-round MPC algorithm that works for all acyclic joins and has a load of $O(\frac{\text{IN}}{p} + \frac{\text{OUT}}{p})$ [1, 24]. Thus, our focus will be on multi-round algorithms and see if this result can be improved. An instance-optimal algorithm must also be output-optimal, so we have automatically obtained output-optimal algorithms for r-hierarchical joins. In fact, we show that $L_{\text{instance}}(p, \mathcal{R}) = O(\frac{\text{IN}}{p} + \sqrt{\frac{\text{OUT}}{p}})$ for all r-hierarchical joins, so this is already an asymptotic improvement over the Yannakakis algorithm. But the more important question is, how about acyclic joins that are not r-hierarchical?

Our main output-optimal result is a new MPC algorithm for acyclic joins achieving a load of $O(\frac{\text{IN}}{p} + \frac{\sqrt{\text{IN}\cdot\text{OUT}}}{p})$, which is an $O(\sqrt{\frac{\text{OUT}}{\text{IN}}})$-factor improvement from the Yannakakis algorithm. Interestingly enough, we observe that while the join order does not change the running time of the Yannakakis algorithm by more than a constant factor in the RAM model, it does have asymptotic consequences in the MPC model. However, there are instances on which no join order is good, in which case we recursively decompose the join into multiple parts, and choose a good join order for each part. The number of parts is exponential in the query size but constant in terms of data size. To achieve this result, we first give a simple algorithm on the line-3 join $R_1(A, B) \bowtie R_2(B, C) \bowtie R_3(C, D)$ (Section 4), and then extend it to arbitrary acyclic joins (Section 5).

We also give a matching lower bound (up to a log factor), thereby establishing the output-optimality of the algorithm. However, the lower bound only holds when $\text{OUT} = O(p \cdot \text{IN})$. This restriction on OUT is actually inherent, because the $O(\frac{\text{IN}}{p} + \frac{\sqrt{\text{IN}\cdot\text{OUT}}}{p})$ bound cannot be optimal for all values of OUT. When OUT is large enough, a worst-case optimal algorithm will take over. For example, on the line-3 join, the worst-case optimal algorithm, which has load $O(\frac{\text{IN}}{\sqrt{p}})$ [17, 23], becomes better when $\text{OUT} > p \cdot \text{IN}$. Our lower bound actually indicates that the $O(\frac{\text{IN}}{\sqrt{p}})$ bound is output-optimal (though it does not depend on OUT) for all $\text{OUT} > p \cdot \text{IN}$. Thus, we now have a complete understanding of the line-3 join with respect to output-optimality. For more complicated joins, their worst-case optimal algorithms have a higher load, and the output-optimality for OUT values in the middle is still unclear.

Next, we extend these results to *join-aggregate* (including *join-project*) queries that are *free-connex* (formal definition given in Section 6). More precisely, we give an MPC algorithm with linear load that removes all the non-output attributes of the query, converting it into an acyclic join. Then we apply our instance-optimal or output-optimal algorithm on the resulting acyclic join.

Finally in Section 7, we turn to the triangle join $R_1(B, C) \bowtie R_2(A, C) \bowtie R_3(A, B)$, which is the simplest cyclic join, and give the first output-sensitive lower bound $\tilde{\Omega}(\min\{\frac{\text{IN}}{p} + \frac{\text{OUT}}{p}, \frac{\text{IN}}{p^{2/3}}\})$ in the MPC model. Previously, only a worst-case bound of $\Omega(\frac{\text{IN}}{p^{2/3}})$ is known [23, 29] and that construction uses an instance with the maximum possible output size $\text{OUT} = \text{IN}^{3/2}$. Note that the second term in the lower bound is smaller as long as $\text{OUT} = \Omega(\text{IN} \cdot p^{1/3})$, which means that under this parameter range, the $\tilde{O}(\frac{\text{IN}}{p^{2/3}})$-load algorithm [23] is not only worst-case optimal but also output-optimal. For $\text{OUT} = o(\text{IN} \cdot p^{1/3})$, the lower bound becomes $\tilde{\Omega}(\frac{\text{IN}}{p} + \frac{\text{OUT}}{p})$ while we do not have a matching upper bound yet (some explanation on why this is difficult is given below). But at least, this shows a separation from acyclic joins, i.e., cyclic joins are harder than acyclic ones by at least a factor of $\tilde{\Omega}(\sqrt{\frac{\text{OUT}}{\text{IN}}})$.

1.6 Other related results

Most existing work on join algorithms in the MPC model has focused on the worst case. Here, the goal is to achieve a load of $O(\frac{\text{IN}}{p^{1/\rho}})$, where ρ is the fractional edge cover number of the hypergraph Q. So far, this bound has been achieved on Berge-acyclic joins[5] [17], joins where each relation has two attributes (i.e., Q is an ordinary graph) [21], and LW joins [23][6]. Whether this bound can be achieved for arbitrary joins, or even just α-acyclic joins, is still open. Assuming this is achievable, our output-sensitive algorithm is still better when $\text{OUT} = O(p^{2-2/\rho} \cdot \text{IN})$.

Joglekar et al. [19] described a multi-round MPC algorithm for arbitrary joins, whose load complexity depends on IN, OUT, as well as the degrees of the values. However, the load of their algorithm is at least $\Omega(\frac{\text{IN}}{p} + \frac{\text{OUT}}{p})$, i.e., no better than the Yannakakis algorithm on acyclic joins.

In the RAM model, output-sensitive join algorithms have been extensively studied. The running time of most algorithms is in form of $O(\text{IN}^w + \text{OUT})$, where w is certain notion of *width* of the hypergraph Q [13, 15, 22, 26]. However, it is not clear if this is optimal. Even for the triangle join,

[4]The $\tilde{O}$ and $\tilde{\Omega}$ notation suppresses polylog factors.

[5]A sub-class of α-acyclic joins.

[6]The LW join algorithm presented in [23] has a mistake, but it can be fixed, although non-trivially.

it is not known what the output-optimal bound is. For the triangle join, any notion of width has $w \geq 1.5$, thus these algorithms are no better than the worst-case optimal algorithm, which has running time $O(\text{IN}^{1.5})$. Recently, an improved triangle algorithm has been developed with a running time of $O(\text{IN}^{1.408} + \text{IN}^{1.222}\text{OUT}^{0.186})$ [10], which is better than the worst-case optimal algorithm when $\text{OUT} < \text{IN}^{1.495}$. On the lower bound side, it is known that when OUT ≥ IN, at least $\Omega(\text{IN}^{4/3-o(1)})$ time is needed, assuming the 3SUM conjecture [30]. Thus, output-optimal algorithms for cyclic joins still remain a wide open problem.

2 MPC PRIMITIVES

Assume $\text{IN} > p^{1+\epsilon}$ where $\epsilon > 0$ is any small constant. We first introduce the following primitives in the MPC model, all of which can be computed with linear load $O(\frac{\text{IN}}{p})$ in $O(1)$ rounds.

Multi-numbering [16]: Given IN (key, value) pairs, for each key, assigns consecutive numbers $1, 2, 3, \ldots$ to all the pairs with the same key.

Sum-by-key [16]: Given IN (key, value) pairs, compute the sum of values for each key, where the sum is defined by any associative operator.

Multi-search [16]: Given N_1 elements $x_1, x_2, \cdots, x_{N_1}$ as set X and N_2 elements $y_1, y_2, \cdots, y_{N_2}$ as set Y, where all elements are drawn from an ordered domain. Set $\text{IN} = N_1 + N_2$. For each x_i, find its predecessor in Y, i.e., the largest element in Y but smaller than x_i.

Semi-Join: Given two relations R_1 and R_2 with a common attribute x, the semijoin $R_1 \ltimes R_2$ returns all the tuples in R_1 whose value on x matches that of at least one tuple in R_2. This can be reduced to a multi-search problem: For each $t \in R_1$, if its predecessor on the x attribute in R_2 is the same as that of t , then it is in the semijoin.

Note that we can remove all dangling tuples in an acyclic-join [33] by a constant number of semi-joins, so it can be done in $O(1)$ rounds with linear load.

Parallel-packing: Given IN numbers $x_1, x_2, \cdots, x_{\text{IN}}$ where $0 < x_i \leq 1$ for $i = 1, 2, \cdots, \text{IN}$, group them into m sets $Y_1, Y_2, \cdots, Y_m$ such that $\sum_{i \in Y_j} x_i \leq 1$ for all j, and $\sum_{i \in Y_j} x_i \geq \frac{1}{2}$ for all but one j. Initially, the IN numbers are distributed arbitrarily across all servers, and the algorithm should produce all pairs (i, j) if $i \in Y_j$ when done. Note that $m \leq 1 + 2\sum_i x_i$.

We are not aware of an explicit reference on this primitive, but it can be solved quite easily, as shown in the full version of the paper [18].

Computing the output size OUT **of an acyclic join:** This primitive is a special case of our join-aggregate algorithm, which will be described in Section 6.

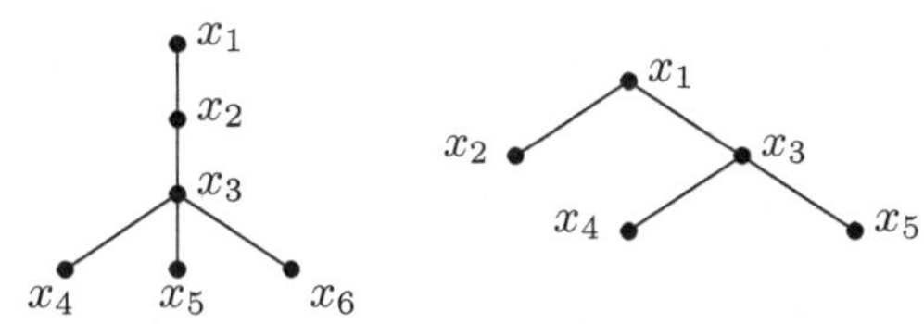

Figure 2: Examples of tall-flat and hierarchical join.

3 R-HIERARCHICAL JOINS

Recall that in a hierarchical join, all attributes can be organized into a forest, such that x is a descendant of y if and only if $\mathcal{E}_x \subseteq \mathcal{E}_y$. Each $e \in \mathcal{E}$ corresponds to a node x in the forest, such that e contains precisely x and all its ancestors. A subclass of hierarchical joins are tall-flat joins. For a tall-flat join, this attribute forest takes the form of a special tree, which consists of a single "stem" plus a number of leaves at the bottom. For example, $Q_1 = R_1(x_1) \bowtie R_2(x_1, x_2) \bowtie R_3(x_1, x_2, x_3) \bowtie R_4(x_1, x_2, x_3, x_4) \bowtie R_5(x_1, x_2, x_3, x_5) \bowtie R_6(x_1, x_2, x_3, x_6)$ is a tall-flat join; $Q_2 = R_1(x_1, x_2) \bowtie R_2(x_1, x_3, x_4) \bowtie R_3(x_1, x_3, x_5)$ is a hierarchical join (but not tall-flat). Their attribute forests (actually, trees for these two cases) are shown in Figure 2.

In this section, we study r-hierarchical joins. A join is r-hierarchical if its reduced join is hierarchical. For example, $Q_3 = Q_2 \bowtie R_4(x_3, x_5) \bowtie R_5(x_5)$ is an r-hierarchical join (but not hierarchical). After an r-hierarchical join is reduced, its hyperedges correspond to the leaves of the attribute forest.

3.1 BinHC algorithm revisited

We mentioned above that the HyperCube algorithm [2] is an instance-optimal algorithm for computing Cartesian products. The BinHC algorithm [7] is a generalization of the HyperCube algorithm to general joins. For a join Q, denote the residual query by removing attributes $\mathbf{x} \subseteq \mathcal{V}$ as $Q_{\mathbf{x}}$. Let $\mathbf{u}$ be any fractional edge packing of $Q_{\mathbf{x}}$ that saturates the attributes $\mathbf{x}$, i.e., $\sum_{e:x\in e} \mathbf{u}(e) \geq 1$ for every $x \in \mathbf{x}$, and $\sum_{e:x\in e} \mathbf{u}(e) \leq 1$ for every $x \in \mathcal{V} - \mathbf{x}$. Assuming knowing all degree information in advance, this algorithm computes Q on instance $\mathcal{R}$ in a single round with a load of $\widetilde{O}(\frac{\text{IN}}{p} + L_{\text{BinHC}}(p, \mathcal{R}))$, where

$$L_{\text{BinHC}}(p, \mathcal{R}) := \max_{\mathbf{x},\mathbf{u}} \left(\frac{\sum_{\mathbf{a}\in\text{dom}(\mathbf{x})} \prod_{e\in\mathcal{E}} |\sigma_{\mathbf{x}=\mathbf{a}} R(e)|^{\mathbf{u}(e)}}{p} \right)^{\frac{1}{\sum_{e\in\mathcal{E}} \mathbf{u}(e)}}$$

Here we define $0^0 = 0$. Note that for any $e \subseteq \mathbf{x}$, $|\sigma_{\mathbf{x}=\mathbf{a}} R(e)|$ is either 0 or 1, so we can just set $\mathbf{u}(e) = 0$ for each such e in the definition above.

We prove the following results and the proofs can be found in the full version of the paper [18].

THEOREM 3.1. *On any tall-flat join and any instance* $\mathcal{R}$, $L_{BinHC}(p, \mathcal{R}) = O(L_{instance}(p, \mathcal{R}))$.

THEOREM 3.2. *On any r-hierarchical join Q and instance $\mathcal{R}$ without dangling tuples, $L_{BinHC}(p, \mathcal{R}) = O(L_{instance}(p, \mathcal{R}))$.*

Note that since $L_{\text{instance}}(p, \mathcal{R})$ is a per-instance lower bound even for multi-round algorithms, this means that the BinHC algorithm is instance-optimal even among all multi-round algorithms, up to polylogarithmic factors. This result also incorporates the instance-optimality of the HyperCube algorithm on Cartesian products, which are special r-hierarchical joins without dangling tuples.

Remark. Koutris and Suciu [25] show that non-tall-flat joins cannot be done with load $\tilde{O}(\frac{\text{IN}}{p} + \frac{\text{OUT}}{p})$ by one-round algorithms. This does not contradict Theorem 3.2 since their lower bound construction uses dangling tuples. Our result implies that the key barrier for one-round algorithms is actually the dangling tuples. If they do not exist, one-round algorithms can go beyond tall-flat joins and solve r-hierarchical joins instance-optimally, up to polylog factors. On the other hand, once $O(1)$ rounds are allowed, dangling tuples become irrelevant, since they can be removed with linear load and $O(1)$ rounds.

3.2 An instance-optimal algorithm

We have shown that the BinHC algorithm is an instance-optimal algorithm for r-hierarchical joins, but it has an instance-optimality ratio of $\log^{O(1)} p$, where the $O(1)$ exponent depends on the query size, and is at least m, the number of relations. In this section, we improve the optimality ratio to $O(1)$, i.e., achieving a load of $O(\frac{\text{IN}}{p} + L_{\text{instance}}(p, \mathcal{R}))$. Our algorithm uses $O(1)$ rounds, but note that BinHC also needs $O(1)$ rounds to remove the dangling tuples if they exist. Furthermore, our algorithm is deterministic while BinHC is randomized.

As a preprocessing step, we remove all dangling tuples. Then we reduce the join hypergraph, since if $e \subseteq e'$, $R(e)$ will not affect the final join results after dangling tuples are removed[7]. Thus, we are left with a hierarchical join Q on an instance $\mathcal{R}$ with no dangling tuples.

Let $\mathcal{T}$ be the attribute forest of Q. Recall that after the join is reduced, each relation corresponds to a leaf of $\mathcal{T}$, whose attributes are precisely the leaf's ancestors in $\mathcal{T}$. Our algorithm is recursive. We will show that the load of this algorithm is $O(\frac{\text{IN}}{p} + L_{\text{instance}}(p, \mathcal{R}))$ for any hierarchical join Q on any instance $\mathcal{R}$. To simplify notation, we will not derive the exact constant in the big-Oh, which depends (exponentially) on the recursion depth. Since the recursion depth is proportional to (actually, twice) the height of $\mathcal{T}$, which is a constant, this is not a concern. Similarly, the number of servers employed by the algorithm will be $O(p)$, where the hidden constant may also depend on the recursion depth.

The base case is when Q has just one relation. In this case the algorithm just emits all tuples in the relation, achieving the bound $O(\frac{\text{IN}}{p} + L_{\text{instance}}(p, \mathcal{R}))$ trivially.

For a general hierarchical join Q and an instance $\mathcal{R}$, we proceed as follows. We first compute $L_{\text{instance}}(p, \mathcal{R})$: We use p servers to compute $|\bowtie_{e \in S} R(e)|$ for each $S \subseteq \mathcal{E}$ (recall that computing the output size of an acyclic join is an MPC primitive). This requires $O(p)$ servers with load $O(\frac{\text{IN}}{p})$. Note that $Q(\mathcal{R}, S) = \bowtie_{e \in S} R(e)$ when there is no dangling tuples in $\mathcal{R}$, so we can compute $L_{\text{instance}}(p, \mathcal{R})$ as defined in (2). Setting $L = \frac{\text{IN}}{p} + L_{\text{instance}}(p, \mathcal{R})$, we will show below how to compute the join with $O(p)$ servers and load $O(L)$.

Let k be the number of trees in $\mathcal{T}$. We handle the following two cases using different recursive strategies:

Case (1): $k = 1$. In this case, $\mathcal{T}$ is a tree. Suppose the root attribute of $\mathcal{T}$ is x, which is included in all the relations. Consider every $a \in \text{dom}(x)$, and let $\mathcal{R}_a = \{\sigma_{x=a} R(e) : e \in \mathcal{E}\}$. It suffices to compute the residual query Q_x on each $\mathcal{R}_a$, but all the $Q_x(\mathcal{R}_a)$'s have to be computed in parallel, using $O(p)$ servers in total. Thus, the key is to allocate servers to these residual queries appropriately so as to ensure a uniform load of $O(L)$. To do so, we first compute IN_a, the input size of $\mathcal{R}_a$, for all $a \in \text{dom}(x)$. Since $\text{IN}_a = \sum_{e \in \mathcal{E}} |\sigma_{x=a} R(e)|$, and each tuple belongs to exactly one $\mathcal{R}_a$, this is a sum-by-key problem, i.e., each tuple t with $\pi_x t = a$ has key a and weight 1. Note that $\text{IN} = \sum_a \text{IN}_a$.

An instance $\mathcal{R}_a$ is *heavy* if $\text{IN}_a > L$ and *light* otherwise. We handle heavy and light instances in different ways.

Case (1.1): Light instances. We use the parallel-packing primitive to put the light instances into $O(\frac{\text{IN}}{L}) = O(p)$ groups with each group having total input size $O(L)$. Then we simply use one server to solve the instances in each group. The load of each server is $O(L)$.

Case (1.2): Heavy instances. By definition, there are at most $\frac{\text{IN}}{L} = O(p)$ heavy instances. For each heavy instance $\mathcal{R}_a$, we allocate $p_a = \lceil p \cdot \frac{\text{IN}_a}{\text{IN}} \rceil$ servers to compute in parallel the join size $|Q_x(\mathcal{R}_a, S)|$ for all $a \in \text{dom}(x)$ and all $S \subseteq \mathcal{E}$. This uses $O(p)$ servers, and the load is $O(\max_a \frac{\text{IN}_a}{p_a}) = O(\frac{\text{IN}}{p})$. Next, for each heavy instance $\mathcal{R}_a$, we allocate

$$p_a = \max_{S \subseteq \mathcal{E}} \frac{|Q_x(\mathcal{R}_a, S)|}{L^{|S|}}$$

servers and compute $Q_x(\mathcal{R}_a)$ recursively in parallel. The number of servers used is

$$\sum_a p_a \leq \sum_a \sum_{S \subseteq \mathcal{E}} \frac{|Q_x(\mathcal{R}_a, S)|}{L^{|S|}} = \sum_{S \subseteq \mathcal{E}} \frac{|Q(\mathcal{R}, S)|}{L^{|S|}} = O(p).$$

[7]Strictly speaking, this violates the tuple-based requirement that when emitting a join result, all the participating tuples must be present. This can be easily fixed. Before removing $R(e)$, we attach each tuple $t \in R(e)$ to all tuples in $R(e')$ that join with t. This can be done by the multi-search primitive with linear load.

By the induction hypothesis, computing $Q_x(\mathcal{R}_a)$ with p_a servers has a load of (the big-Oh of)

$$\frac{\mathrm{IN}_a}{p_a} + L_{\mathrm{instance}}(p_a, \mathcal{R}_a) = \frac{\mathrm{IN}_a}{p_a} + \max_{S \subseteq \mathcal{E}} \left(\frac{|Q_x(\mathcal{R}_a, S)|}{p_a} \right)^{\frac{1}{|S|}}. \quad (3)$$

We bound each term of (3): For a heavy instance $\mathcal{R}_a$, there must exist at least one $e \in \mathcal{E}$ such that $|\sigma_{x=a}R(e)| \geq \frac{1}{|\mathcal{E}|} \cdot \mathrm{IN}_a$. Furthermore, since there are no dangling tuples, every tuple in $\sigma_{x=a}R(e)$ must be part of a join result of $Q_x(\mathcal{R}_a)$, so $|\sigma_{x=a}R(e)| = |Q_x(\mathcal{R}_a, \{e\})|$. Taking $S = \{e\}$, we have

$$p_a \geq \frac{1}{L} \cdot |Q_x(\mathcal{R}_a, \{e\})| = \frac{1}{L} \cdot |\sigma_{x=a}R(e)| \geq \frac{\mathrm{IN}_a}{|\mathcal{E}| \cdot L},$$

so $\frac{\mathrm{IN}_a}{p_a} = O(L)$. The second term of (3) is also bounded by L simply by the definition of p_a.

Case (2): $k > 1$. In this case, the join becomes a Cartesian product $Q_1(\mathcal{R}_1) \times \cdots \times Q_k(\mathcal{R}_k)$, where each $Q_i(\mathcal{R}_i)$ is a join under Case (1). One would attempt to first compute each $Q_i(\mathcal{R}_i)$ recursively, and then compute the Cartesian product, but this would not yield instance-optimality. Just consider an instance with $|Q_1(\mathcal{R}_1)| = 1$ and $|Q_2(\mathcal{R}_2)| = p \cdot \mathrm{IN}$, where $Q_2(\mathcal{R}_2) = R_1(A, B) \bowtie R_2(B, C)$ with $|\mathrm{dom}(B)| = 1, |R_1| = \mathrm{IN}, |R_2| = p$. On this instance, we have $L_{\mathrm{instance}}(p, \mathcal{R}) = \max(\frac{\mathrm{IN}}{p}, \sqrt{\mathrm{IN}})$, but if we took a two-step approach, merely storing the intermediate result $Q_2(\mathcal{R}_2)$ would incur a load of $\Omega(\mathrm{IN})$. This means that we have to interleave the two steps so as to avoid storing the intermediate results $Q_i(R_i)$ explicitly.

We arrange servers into a $p_1 \times p_2 \times \cdots \times p_k$ hypercube, where the dimensions $p_1, p_2, \cdots, p_k$ will be determined later. We identify each server with coordinates $(c_1, c_2, \cdots, c_k)$, where $c_i \in [p_i]$. For every combination $c_1, \ldots, c_{i-1}, c_{i+1}, \ldots, c_k$, the p_i servers with coordinates $(c_1, \cdots, c_{i-1}, *, c_{i+1}, \cdots, c_k)$ form a group to compute $Q_i(\mathcal{R}_i)$ (using the algorithm under Case (1)). Yes, each $Q_i(\mathcal{R}_i)$ is computed $p_1 \cdots p_{i-1} p_{i+1} \cdots p_k$ times, which seems to be a lot of redundancy. However, as we shall see, there will be no redundancy in terms of the final join results, and it is exactly due to this redundancy that we avoid the shuffling of the intermediate result and achieve an optimal load. Consider a particular server $(c_1, \ldots, c_k)$. It participates in k groups, one for each $Q_i(\mathcal{R}_i), i = 1, \ldots, k$. For each $Q_i(\mathcal{R}_i)$, it emits a subset of its join results, denoted $Q_i(\mathcal{R}_i, c_1 \ldots, c_k)$. Then the server emits the Cartesian product $Q_1(\mathcal{R}_1, c_1 \ldots, c_k) \times \cdots \times Q_k(\mathcal{R}_k, c_1 \ldots, c_k)$. Note that for each group of servers computing $Q_i(\mathcal{R}_i)$, the p_i servers in the group emit $Q_i(R_i)$ with no redundancy, so there is no redundancy in emitting the Cartesian product.

It remains to show how to set $p_1, \ldots, p_k$ so that $p_1 \cdots p_k = O(p)$ and each server has a load of $O(L)$. To do so, we first compute IN_i, the input size of $\mathcal{R}_i$, in the same way as in Case (1). An instance $\mathcal{R}_i$ is *heavy* if $\mathrm{IN}_i > L$ and *light* otherwise. For each heavy instance $\mathcal{R}_i$, we use p servers to compute $|\bowtie_{e \in S} \mathcal{R}_i(e)| = |Q_i(R_i, S)|$ for all $S \subseteq \mathcal{E}_i$, where $\mathcal{E}_i$ is the set of edges in Q_i. This requires $O(p)$ servers with load $O(\frac{\mathrm{IN}}{p})$. Then if $\mathcal{R}_i$ is light, we set $p_i = 1$; otherwise set

$$p_i = \max_{S \subseteq \mathcal{E}_i} \left\lceil \frac{|Q_i(\mathcal{R}_i, S)|}{L^{|S|}} \right\rceil.$$

Let $I = \{i \mid \mathcal{R}_i \text{ is heavy}\}$. The number of servers used is

$$\prod_{i \in I} p_i \leq \prod_{i \in I} \sum_{S \subseteq \mathcal{E}_i} \left(\frac{|Q_i(\mathcal{R}_i, S_i)|}{L^{|S|}} + 1 \right) \leq \sum_{S \subseteq \bigcup_{i \in I} \mathcal{E}_i} \frac{|Q(\mathcal{R}, S)|}{L^{|S|}},$$

which is bounded by $O(p)$.

Finally, consider the load of each server, which serves to compute each $Q_i(\mathcal{R}_i)$ with a group of p_i servers. For a light $\mathcal{R}_i$, $p_i = 1$ and it imposes a load of $O(L)$. For a heavy $\mathcal{R}_i$, by the induction hypothesis, the load is (the big-Oh of)

$$\frac{\mathrm{IN}_i}{p_i} + L_{\mathrm{instance}}(p_i, \mathcal{R}_i) = \frac{\mathrm{IN}_i}{p_i} + \max_{S \subseteq \mathcal{E}_i} \left(\frac{|Q_i(\mathcal{R}_i, S)|}{p_i} \right)^{\frac{1}{|S|}}.$$

This can be bounded by $O(L)$ using the same argument as Case (1.2). Summing over all $i = 1, \ldots, k$ increases the load by just a $k = O(1)$ factor.

The induction proof thus completes and we obtain the following result.

THEOREM 3.3. *On any r-hierarchical join query Q and any instance $\mathcal{R}$, there is an algorithm computing $Q(\mathcal{R})$ in $O(1)$ rounds with load $O(\frac{\mathrm{IN}}{p} + L_{instance}(p, \mathcal{R}))$.*

Since an instance-optimal algorithm is also output-optimal, we also obtain an output-optimal algorithm for r-hierarchical joins. In fact, we derive a closed-form formula of the output-optimal bound, described in Theorem 3.4. Moreover, we give a cleaner but not tight output-sensitive bound in Corollary 3.5. In particular, it will be used in the analysis of the output-sensitive algorithm for arbitrary acyclic joins in Section 5.1. Their proofs are shown in the full version of the paper [18].

THEOREM 3.4. *There is an algorithm that computes any r-hierarchical join with load $O\left(\frac{\mathrm{IN}}{p^{1/\max\{1, k^*-1\}}} + (\frac{\mathrm{OUT}}{p})^{\frac{1}{k^*}}\right)$ in $O(1)$ rounds, where $k^* = \lceil \log_{\mathrm{IN}} \mathrm{OUT} \rceil$. This bound is output-optimal.*

COROLLARY 3.5. *There is an algorithm that computes any r-hierarchical join in $O(1)$ rounds with load $O(\frac{\mathrm{IN}}{p} + \sqrt{\frac{\mathrm{OUT}}{p}})$.*

4 LINE-3 JOIN

The simplest acyclic but not r-hierarchical join is the line-3 join $R_1(A, B) \bowtie R_2(B, C) \bowtie R_3(C, D)$. In this section, we give an output-optimal MPC algorithm with load $O(\frac{\mathrm{IN}}{p} + \frac{\sqrt{\mathrm{IN} \cdot \mathrm{OUT}}}{p})$, together with a matching lower bound. In particular, the lower bound implies that instance-optimal algorithms are not possible for the line-3 join. In Section 5, we extend these results to arbitrary acyclic joins.

4.1 The Yannakakis algorithm revisited

The Yannakakis algorithm first removes all the dangling tuples, which is just a series of semi-joins and can be done with load $O(\frac{\text{IN}}{p})$. Then the algorithm performs pairwise joins in some arbitrary order. In the RAM model, the join order does not affect the asymptotic running time: After dangling tuples have been removed, any intermediate join result is part of a full join result, so the running time of the last join, which is $\Theta(\text{OUT})$, dominates that of any intermediate join. In fact, this argument applies on a per-instance basis, and the Yannakakis algorithm is instance-optimal on any instance with any join order.

Interestingly, the join order does matter in the MPC model. Consider the following instance of the line-3 join (see the top half of Figure 3). Attributes A, B, C, D have domain sizes $\frac{\text{OUT}}{N}, \frac{N^2}{\text{OUT}}, N, 1$, respectively. Set $R_1(A, B) = \text{dom}(A)\times\text{dom}(B)$, $R_2(B, C)$ is a one-to-many relation from $\text{dom}(B)$ to $\text{dom}(C)$, and $R_3(C, D) = \text{dom}(C) \times \text{dom}(D)$. Note that this instance has $\text{IN} = \Theta(N)$ and the output size is exactly OUT. Consider first the join plan $(R_1 \bowtie R_2) \bowtie R_3$, and note that $|R_1 \bowtie R_2| = |R_1 \bowtie R_2 \bowtie R_3| = \text{OUT}$. Using the $O(\frac{\text{IN}}{p} + \sqrt{\frac{\text{OUT}}{p}})$-load algorithm [7, 16] for binary joins, the load of computing $R_1 \bowtie R_2$ is $O(\frac{\text{IN}}{p} + \sqrt{\frac{\text{OUT}}{p}})$. However, since the output of the first join is the input of the second join, the input size for the second join is OUT, so the load of the second join is $O(\frac{\text{OUT}}{p} + \sqrt{\frac{\text{OUT}}{p}}) = O(\frac{\text{OUT}}{p})$. In general, the intermediate join result can be as large as $O(\text{OUT})$, which is why the Yannakakis algorithm incurs a load of $O(\frac{\text{OUT}}{p})$ (after dangling tuples are removed) on an acyclic join, as observed in [1, 24].

Now consider the alternative plan $R_1 \bowtie (R_2 \bowtie R_3)$. Note that $|R_2 \bowtie R_3| = O(\text{IN})$, so the load of computing $R_2 \bowtie R_3$ is $O(\frac{\text{IN}}{p})$, while the load of computing the second join is $O(\frac{\text{IN}}{p} + \sqrt{\frac{\text{OUT}}{p}})$. Crucially, the reason why the second plan is better is that it has a smaller intermediate join size. Note that a smaller intermediate join size does not matter in the RAM model, where the total cost is always dominated by the last join. But it does matter in the MPC model, because of the $O(\frac{\text{IN}}{p} + \sqrt{\frac{\text{OUT}}{p}})$ load complexity of a binary join, which has a linear dependency on the input size but sublinear in the output size. Fundamentally, this is because the MPC model is all about *locality*: algorithms strive to send all "related" tuples to the same server so as to maximize the number of join results that can be found by the server locally.

Now, the key question is if there is always a join plan with an intermediate join size asymptotically smaller than $O(\text{OUT})$. Unfortunately, the answer is no. A bad example can be easily constructed, by just putting two of the above instances together, but in opposite directions (see Figure 3).

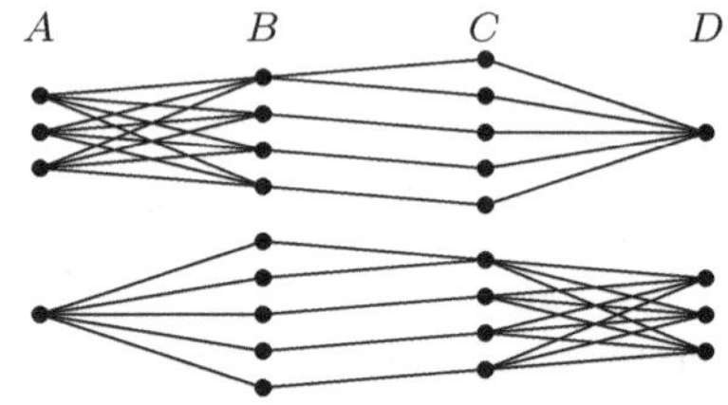

Figure 3: A hard instance for the Yannakakis algorithm.

Nevertheless, this bad example precisely points us to the right direction: Although a global best join order may not exist, but if we decompose the join into multiple pieces, it is possible to find a provably good join order for each. This is exactly the basic idea of our algorithm, presented next.

4.2 A new algorithm for the line-3 join

We first compute OUT (an MPC primitive). Then we proceed in two steps:

Step (1): Computing degrees. For a value in attribute B, it is *heavy* if its *degree* in relation R_1, i.e., $|\sigma_{B=b}R_1|$, is greater than τ (value to be determined later), otherwise *light*. We first use the sum-by-key primitive to compute the degrees of all b's for $b \in \text{dom}(B)$. After classifying the values in $\text{dom}(B)$ as heavy and light, we divide tuples in R_1 and R_2 also into heavy tuples and light tuples, depending on their B value. More precisely, a tuple in R_1 or R_2 is heavy if its B value is heavy, and light otherwise. This can be done by the multi-search primitive. We denote the heavy (resp. light) tuples in R_i as R_i^H (resp. R_i^L), for $i = 1, 2$.

Step (2): Decomposing the join. We decompose the join into the following two parts, and compute them using different join orders:

$$Q_1 = R_1^H \bowtie (R_2^H \bowtie R_3),$$
$$Q_2 = (R_1^L \bowtie R_2^L) \bowtie R_3.$$

Note that since R_1 and R_2 are both divided according to the B attribute, R_1^H do not join with R_2^L, R_1^L do not join with R_2^H.

Now we analyze the load. For Q_1, the intermediate join $R_{23} = R_2^H \bowtie R_3$ has size bounded by $\frac{\text{OUT}}{\tau}$, since each intermediate join result from R_{23} has a heavy B value, so it joins with at least τ tuples in R_1. Thus, the load of computing Q_1 is $O(\frac{\text{IN}}{p} + \frac{\text{OUT}}{p\tau} + \sqrt{\frac{\text{OUT}}{p}})$.

For Q_2, the intermediate join $R_{12} = R_1^L \bowtie R_2^L$ has size bounded by $\text{IN} \cdot \tau$, since each light tuple from R_2 can join with at most τ tuples from R_1. Thus, the load of computing Q_2 is $O(\frac{\text{IN}}{p} + \frac{\text{IN}\cdot\tau}{p} + \sqrt{\frac{\text{OUT}}{p}})$.

Setting $\tau = \sqrt{\frac{\text{OUT}}{\text{IN}}}$ balances the second term in both cases, and we obtain the claimed result (note that $\sqrt{\frac{\text{OUT}}{p}} \leq \frac{\sqrt{\text{IN}\cdot\text{OUT}}}{p}$ for $\text{IN} \geq p$):

Theorem 4.1. *There is an algorithm computing the line-3 join in $O(1)$ rounds with load $O\left(\frac{\text{IN}}{p} + \frac{\sqrt{\text{IN}\cdot\text{OUT}}}{p}\right)$.*

4.3 Lower bound

In the full version [18], we prove the following lower bound on any tuple-based algorithm for computing the line-3 join.

Theorem 4.2. *For any $\text{OUT} \geq \text{IN}$, there exists an instance $\mathcal{R}$ for the line-3 join with input size $\Theta(\text{IN})$ and output size $\Theta(\text{OUT})$, such that any tuple-based algorithm computing the join in $O(1)$ rounds must have a load of $\Omega\left(\min\left\{\frac{\sqrt{\text{IN}\cdot\text{OUT}}}{p\cdot\log\text{IN}}, \frac{\text{IN}}{\sqrt{p}}\right\}\right)$.*

Ignoring logarithmic factors, this lower bound completes our understanding of the line-3 join in terms of output-optimality: (1) When $\text{OUT} \leq \text{IN}$, the Yannakakis algorithm has linear load $O\left(\frac{\text{IN}}{p}\right)$. (2) When $\text{IN} < \text{OUT} \leq p \cdot \text{IN}$, the lower bound becomes $\tilde{\Omega}\left(\frac{\sqrt{\text{IN}\cdot\text{OUT}}}{p}\right)$, which is matched by our new algorithm. (3) When $\text{OUT} \geq p \cdot \text{IN}$, the lower bound is $\Omega\left(\frac{\text{IN}}{\sqrt{p}}\right)$, which is matched by the worst-case optimal algorithm in [17, 23]. In particular, this means that when OUT is large enough, the load complexity of the join is no longer output-sensitive. This also stands in contrast with the RAM model, where the complexity of any acyclic join always grows linearly with OUT.

An easy corollary (proof in the full version [18]) is the following result, which shows that instance-optimality is not achievable for the line-3 join.

Corollary 4.3. *For any $\text{IN} \geq p^{3/2}$, there is an instance $\mathcal{R}$ with input size $\Theta(\text{IN})$ for the line-3 join, such that any tuple-based algorithm computing the join in $O(1)$ rounds must have a load of $\Omega(\frac{\text{IN}}{p^{1/2}\log\text{IN}})$, while $L_{instance}(p, \mathcal{R}) = O(\frac{\text{IN}}{p})$.*

5 ACYCLIC JOINS

In this section, we first extend the results from the previous section to arbitrary acyclic joins. Specifically, the algorithm is a (nontrivial) generalization of the line-3 algorithm, but it is self-contained; the lower bound builds on top of the hard instance of the line-3 join.

5.1 Algorithm

As preprocessing, we remove all dangling tuples. Assume the output size OUT has been computed (an MPC primitive).

Recall that in an acyclic join $Q = (\mathcal{V}, \mathcal{E})$, the hyperedges $\mathcal{E}$ can be organized into a join tree $\mathcal{T}$, such that for each attribute $x \in \mathcal{V}$, the nodes corresponding to $\mathcal{E}_x$ are connected in $\mathcal{T}$. Given such a join tree $\mathcal{T}$, our algorithm recursively decomposes the join into multiple pieces, and apply a different join strategy for each.

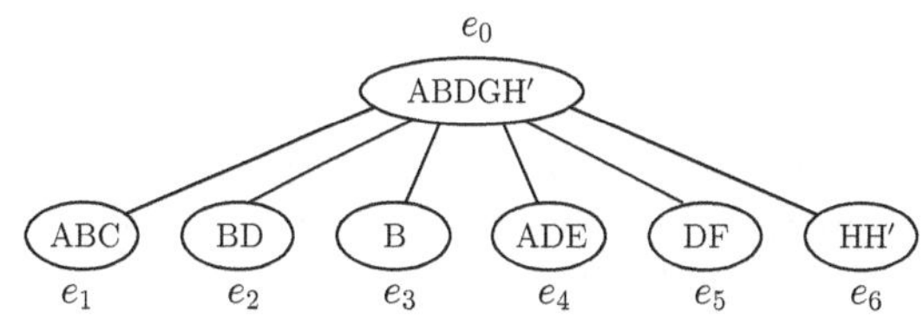

Figure 4: A node e_0 in the join tree $\mathcal{T}$ and its leaf children $e_1, e_2, e_3, e_4, e_5, e_6$.

We start from an internal node of $\mathcal{T}$ whose children are all leaves. Let this node be e_0, which has k leaf children $e_1, \cdots, e_k$ (see Figure 4 for an example). Let $s_i = e_0 \cap e_i$ be the set of join attributes between e_0 and e_i. We will assume $s_i \neq \emptyset$; otherwise we can add a dummy attribute to both e_0 and e_i and all tuples in $R(e_0)$ and $R(e_i)$ share the same value on this dummy attribute (e.g., we add a dummy attribute H' to both e_0 and e_6 in Figure 4). Note that the join tree ensures the property that if $x \in e_i \cap e_j$ for $i \neq j$, then $x \in e_0$.

Let $N_\alpha = \sum_{i=1}^{k} |R(e_i)|$ and $N_\beta = \text{IN} - N_\alpha$. We will actually prove a slightly tighter bound, that the load of our algorithm is bounded by $O(\frac{\text{IN}}{p} + \frac{\sqrt{N_\beta\cdot\text{OUT}}}{p} + \sqrt{\frac{\text{OUT}}{p}})$.

Set $\tau = \sqrt{\frac{\text{OUT}}{N_\beta}}$. Our algorithm proceeds in three steps.

Step (1): Computing data statistics. In each relation $R(e_i)$, $i = 1, \ldots, k$, let v be an assignment of values for attributes s_i. The set of *heavy* assignments in $R(e_i)$ is

$$H(s_i, e_i) = \{v \in \pi_{s_i} R(e_i) : |\sigma_{s_i = v} R(e_i)| \geq \tau\}.$$

Tuples in $R(e_i)$ can also be identified as *heavy* or *light*, depending on their projection on attributes s_i. More precisely, a tuple $t \in R(e_i)$ is heavy if $\pi_{s_i} t \in H(s_i, e_i)$. The set of heavy tuples and light tuples in $R(e_i)$ are denoted as $R_H(e_i)$ and $R_L(e_i)$, respectively. All the statistics can be computed in by the sum-by-key and multi-search primitives with linear load.

Let $\bar{\mathcal{E}} = \mathcal{E} - \{e_0, e_1, \cdots, e_k\}$. We decompose the join into the following sub-joins:

$$R(e_0) \bowtie R_?(e_1) \bowtie \cdots \bowtie R_?(e_k) \bowtie \left(\bowtie_{e\in\bar{\mathcal{E}}} R(e)\right),$$

where each ? can be either H or L. Note that there are 2^k, which is a constant, sub-joins, so we can afford to use p servers for each sub-join. If a sub-join involves at least one $R_H(e_i)$, we apply the procedure in step (2) to it. In step (3), we handle the case where all ? are L.

Step (2): Sub-joins with at least one $R_H(e_i)$. Without loss of generality, suppose $R_H(e_1)$ is in the sub-join, i.e., we need to compute the sub-join

$$R(e_0) \bowtie R_H(e_1) \bowtie R_?(e_2) \bowtie \cdots \bowtie R_?(e_k) \bowtie \left(\bowtie_{e\in\bar{\mathcal{E}}} R(e)\right),$$

where each ? can be either H or L. The algorithm consists of three steps:

(2.1) Compute $R'(e_0) = R(e_0) \ltimes R_H(e_1)$.
(2.2) Compute $R' = R'(e_0) \bowtie R_?(e_2) \bowtie \cdots \bowtie R_?(e_k) \bowtie (\bowtie_{e\in\bar{\mathcal{E}}} R(e))$ by any order.
(2.3) Compute $R_H(e_1) \bowtie R'$.

We analyze the load in each step: (2.1) is a primitive operation that incurs linear load. To bound the load of (2.2), observe that $|R'| \le \frac{\text{OUT}}{\tau}$, since each tuple in R' joins with at least τ tuples in $R_H(e_1)$, each producing one final join result. Thus, the load is bounded by $O(\frac{\text{IN}}{p} + \frac{\text{OUT}}{p\cdot\tau})$. The binary join in (2.3) has input size $\frac{\text{OUT}}{\tau} + \text{IN}$ and output size OUT, incurring a load of $O(\frac{\text{IN}}{p} + \frac{\text{OUT}}{p\cdot\tau} + \sqrt{\frac{\text{OUT}}{p}})$, which dominates the first two steps. Plugging in the value of τ, the total load is bounded by $O(\frac{\text{IN}}{p} + \frac{\sqrt{N_\beta\cdot\text{OUT}}}{p} + \sqrt{\frac{\text{OUT}}{p}})$, as desired.

Step (3): The sub-join with all $R_L(e_i)$. It remains to compute the following sub-join:

$$R(e_0) \bowtie R_L(e_1) \bowtie \cdots \bowtie R_L(e_k) \bowtie (\bowtie_{e\in\bar{\mathcal{E}}} R(e)).$$

We further divide $R(e_0)$ into heavy and light tuples, as follows. Let $s = s_1 \cup s_2 \cup \cdots \cup s_k$, and let v be an assignment over attributes s. The set of *heavy* assignments in $R(e_0)$ is define as

$$H(s, e_0) = \{v \in \pi_s R(e_0) : \prod_{i=1}^{k} |\sigma_{s_i=\pi_{s_i}v} R_L(e_i)| \ge \tau\}.$$

Tuples in $R(e_0)$ are classified as *heavy* or *light*, depending on their projection on attributes s, i.e., a tuple $t \in R(e_0)$ is heavy if $\pi_s t \in H(s, e_0)$, and light otherwise. Similarly, denote the heavy and light tuples in $R(e_0)$ as $R_H(e_0)$ and $R_L(e_0)$, respectively.

These statistics can also be computed using the primitives, but with some more care. For each relation $R_L(e_i)$, we first use sum-by-key to compute $|\sigma_{s_i=v_i} R_L(e_i)|$ for every $v_i \in \pi_{s_i} R_L(e_i)$. This gives us a list of $(v_i, |\sigma_{s_i=v_i} R_L(e_i)|)$ pairs. Then, we use multi-search to find, for each tuple $t \in R(e_0)$, the up to k pairs $(v_i, |\sigma_{s_i=v_i} R_L(e_i)|)$ such that $\sigma_{s_i} t = v_i$. After this step, each tuple $t \in R(e_0)$ is attached with k values, and we multiply them together to decide if t is heavy or light.

Step (3.1): The sub-join with $R_H(e_0)$. We first compute the following sub-join:

$$R_H(e_0) \bowtie R_L(e_1) \bowtie \cdots \bowtie R_L(e_k) \bowtie (\bowtie_{e\in\bar{\mathcal{E}}} R(e)).$$

The algorithm consists of three steps:

(3.1.1) Compute $R'(e_0) = R_H(e_0) \bowtie (\bowtie_{e\in\bar{\mathcal{E}}} R(e))$ by any order.
(3.1.2) Compute $R'(e_i) = R_H(e_0) \bowtie R_L(e_i)$ for each $i = 1, \cdots, k$.
(3.1.3) Compute $R'(e_0) \bowtie R'(e_1) \bowtie \cdots \bowtie R'(e_k)$. Note that each of these relations contains all attributes in e_0, so it is a hierarchical join (it is actually tall-flat), so we can use the instance-optimal algorithm in Section 3 to compute this join.

Now we analyze the load of each step: First, observe that $|R'(e_0)| \le \frac{\text{OUT}}{\tau}$. This is because the projection of each tuple in $R'(e_0)$ on s is a heavy assignment, so it will produce at least τ join results after joining with the $R_L(e_i)$'s. Therefore, the load of computing the join in (3.1.1) is $O(\frac{\text{IN}}{p} + \frac{\text{OUT}}{p\cdot\tau})$. Each binary join in (3.1.2) has a load of $O(\frac{\text{IN}}{p} + \sqrt{\frac{\text{OUT}}{p}})$. Note that each join result $R'(e_i)$ has size bounded by $N_\beta \cdot \tau$, since any tuple in $R(e_0)$ can join with at most τ tuples in $R_L(e_i)$. Thus, the hierarchical join in (3.1.3) has input size $O(N_\beta \cdot \tau + \frac{\text{OUT}}{\tau})$ and output size OUT, so the instance-optimal algorithm has load $O(\frac{N_\beta\cdot\tau}{p} + \frac{\text{OUT}}{p\cdot\tau} + \sqrt{\frac{\text{OUT}}{p}})$ according to Corollary 3.5. All the loads are bounded by $O(\frac{\text{IN}}{p} + \frac{\sqrt{N_\beta\cdot\text{OUT}}}{p} + \sqrt{\frac{\text{OUT}}{p}})$, as desired.

Step (3.2): The sub-join with $R_L(e_0)$. Finally, we are left with the sub-join

$$R_L(e_0) \bowtie R_L(e_1) \bowtie \cdots \bowtie R_L(e_k) \bowtie (\bowtie_{e\in\bar{\mathcal{E}}} R(e)).$$

This is actually the only case where we need recursion:

(3.2.1) Compute $R'_L(e_0) = R_L(e_0) \bowtie R_L(e_1) \bowtie \cdots \bowtie R_L(e_k)$ by any order.
(3.2.2) If $\bar{\mathcal{E}} \neq \emptyset$, compute $R'_L(e_0) \bowtie (\bowtie_{e\in\bar{\mathcal{E}}} R(e))$ recursively.

Now we analyze the load: First, we have $|R'_L(e_0)| \le N_\beta \cdot \tau$, since the projection of each tuple in $R_L(e_0)$ on s is a light assignment. Thus, the load of step (3.2.1) is $O(\frac{\text{IN}}{p} + \frac{N_\beta\cdot\tau}{p})$, which is also bounded by $O(\frac{\text{IN}}{p} + \frac{\sqrt{N_\beta\cdot\text{OUT}}}{p} + \sqrt{\frac{\text{OUT}}{p}})$. So far, we have completed the base case of the induction proof.

For the join to be computed recursively in step (3.2.2), its input size is at most $\text{IN} + N_\beta \cdot \tau$ and output size is at most OUT. More importantly, N_β can only become smaller, since e_0 becomes a leaf in the residual join and $|R(e_0)|$ is no longer included in N_β, no matter which node in the residual join is picked to be its new e_0. By the induction hypothesis, computing the residual join recursively incurs a load of $O(\frac{\text{IN}}{p} + \frac{N_\beta\cdot\tau}{p} + \frac{\sqrt{N_\beta\cdot\text{OUT}}}{p} + \sqrt{\frac{\text{OUT}}{p}})$, thus bounded by $O(\frac{\text{IN}}{p} + \frac{\sqrt{N_\beta\cdot\text{OUT}}}{p} + \sqrt{\frac{\text{OUT}}{p}})$.

Note that the recursion will increase the constant in the big-Oh, but as the recursion depth depends only on the query not the data size, it does not change the asymptotic result.

This completes the induction proof that the algorithm has a load of $O(\frac{\text{IN}}{p} + \frac{\sqrt{N_\beta\cdot\text{OUT}}}{p} + \sqrt{\frac{\text{OUT}}{p}})$. Observing that $N_\beta \le \text{IN}$ and $\sqrt{\frac{\text{OUT}}{p}} \le \frac{\sqrt{\text{IN}\cdot\text{OUT}}}{p}$, we obtain the following result.

THEOREM 5.1. *There is an algorithm that computes any acyclic join in $O(1)$ rounds with load $O(\frac{\text{IN}}{p} + \frac{\sqrt{\text{IN}\cdot\text{OUT}}}{p})$.*

5.2 Lower bound

In Section 4.2 we have constructed a hard instance for the line-3 join and have shown that any algorithm must incur a load of $\Omega(\min\{\frac{\sqrt{\text{IN}\cdot\text{OUT}}}{p\cdot\log \text{IN}}, \frac{\text{IN}}{\sqrt{p}}\})$ on this instance. In this section, we generalize this lower bound to an arbitrary acyclic join that is not r-hierarchical. Note that for r-hierarchical joins, we can achieve a smaller load $O(\frac{\text{IN}}{p} + \sqrt{\frac{\text{OUT}}{p}})$ (see the full version [18]), so this establishes a separation between r-hierarchical joins and acyclic joins.

The basic idea in the lower bound is that any acyclic join must "include" a line-3 join, such that any algorithm computing the acyclic join must also compute the line-3 join. This is more formally captured by the following structural lemma on acyclic and r-hierarchical joins. To state the lemma, we need some terminology. In a hypergraph $Q = (\mathcal{V}, \mathcal{E})$, a *path* between $x, y \in \mathcal{V}$, denoted $P(x, y)$, is a sequence of vertices starting with x and ending with y, such that each consecutive pair of vertices appear together in an edge. The length of a path is defined as the number of vertices in $P(x, y)$ minus 1. A path $P(x, y)$ is *minimal* if there is no other path $P'(x, y)$ that is a strict subsequence of $P(x, y)$. It is easy to see that $P(x_1, x_k) = (x_1, x_2, \cdots, x_k)$ is minimal if and only if there exists no edge $e \in \mathcal{E}$ containing x_i and x_j with $|j - i| > 1$. Note that a shortest path must be minimal, but not vice versa.

Lemma 5.2. *An acyclic join query is not r-hierarchical if and only if it has a minimal path of length* 3.

The proof is given in the full version [18]. With this lemma, we can extend the hard instance for the line-3 join to any acyclic but non-r-hierarchical join $Q = (\mathcal{V}, \mathcal{E})$.

Let (x_1, x_2, x_3, x_4) be a minimal path of length 3 in Q, and suppose $\{x_1, x_2\} \subseteq e_1, \{x_2, x_3\} \subseteq e_2, \{x_3, x_4\} \subseteq e_3$. Let $\mathcal{R} = \{R_1(x_1, x_2), R_2(x_2, x_3), R_3(x_3, x_4)\}$ be the hard instance for the line-3 join. We construct the hard instance $\mathcal{R}' = \{R'(e) : e \in \mathcal{E}\}$ for Q as follows. The domain of $x_i, i = 1, 2, 3, 4$ is the same as in $\mathcal{R}$. For any other attribute y, set $|\text{dom}(y)| = 1$.

Since the path is minimal, each $e \in \mathcal{E}$ must fall into one of the following three cases:

(1) For any e with $e \cap \{x_1, x_2, x_3, x_4\} = \emptyset$, $R'(e)$ contains only one tuple connecting the only value in the domains of attributes in e.
(2) If $e \cap \{x_1, x_2, x_3, x_4\} = \{x_i\}, i = 1, 2, 3, 4$, then $R'(e)$ contains $|\text{dom}(x_i)|$ tuples, each having a distinct value of $\text{dom}(x_i)$.
(3) If $e \cap \{x_1, x_2, x_3, x_4\} = \{x_i, x_{i+1}\}, i = 1, 2, 3$, then $R'(e)$ contains $|R_i(x_i, x_{i+1})|$ tuples such that $\pi_{x_i, x_{i+1}} R'(e) = R_i(x_i, x_{i+1})$.

It can be easily verified that $Q(\mathcal{R}')$ is exactly the join results of the line-3 join on $\mathcal{R}$, so the same lower bound applies.

However, since the output size of the line-3 join is at most IN^2, we do have a condition on OUT:

Theorem 5.3. *For an acyclic but non-r-hierarchical join and any* $\text{IN} \geq p^{3/2}, \text{OUT} \leq \text{IN}^2$, *there exists an instance* $\mathcal{R}$ *with input size* $\Theta(\text{IN})$ *and output size* $\Theta(\text{OUT})$ *such that any tuple-based algorithm computing it in* $O(1)$ *rounds must have a load of* $\Omega(\min\{\frac{\sqrt{\text{IN}\cdot\text{OUT}}}{p\cdot\log \text{IN}}, \frac{\text{IN}}{\sqrt{p}}\})$.

Similar to the line-3 join, this lower bound shows that our acyclic join algorithm is output-optimal (up to a logarithmic factor) when $\text{OUT} \leq p \cdot \text{IN}$.

Furthermore, the same argument for Corollary 4.3 can be used here to show that instance-optimal algorithms do not exist for any acyclic but non-r-hierarchical join.

Corollary 5.4. *For any* $\text{IN} \geq p^{3/2}$, *there is an instance* $\mathcal{R}$ *with input size* $\Theta(\text{IN})$ *for any acyclic but non-r-hierarchical join, such that any tuple-based algorithm that computes the join in* $O(1)$ *rounds must have a load of* $\Omega(\frac{\text{IN}}{p^{1/2}\log \text{IN}})$, *while* $L_{instance}(p, \mathcal{R}) = O(\frac{\text{IN}}{p})$.

6 JOIN-AGGREGATE QUERIES

We consider join-aggregate queries over *annotated relations* [14, 20]. Let $(\mathbb{R}, \oplus, \otimes)$ be a commutative semiring. Every tuple t is associated with an *annotation* $w(t) \in \mathbb{R}$. Let $Q = (\mathcal{V}, \mathcal{E})$ be a join hypergraph. The annotation of a join result $t \in Q(\mathcal{R})$ is $w(t) := \otimes_{t_e \in R(e), \pi_e t = t_e, e \in \mathcal{E}} w(t_e)$. Let $\mathbf{y} \subseteq \mathcal{V}$ be a set of *output attributes* and $\bar{\mathbf{y}} = \mathcal{V} - \mathbf{y}$ the non-output attributes. A *join-aggregate query* $Q_{\mathbf{y}}(\mathcal{R})$ asks us to compute $\oplus_{\bar{\mathbf{y}}} Q(\mathcal{R}) =$

$$\left\{(t_{\mathbf{y}}, w(t_{\mathbf{y}})) : t_{\mathbf{y}} \in \pi_{\mathbf{y}} Q(\mathcal{R}), w(t_{\mathbf{y}}) = \oplus_{t \in Q(\mathcal{R}): \pi_{\mathbf{y}} t = t_{\mathbf{y}}} w(t)\right\}.$$

In plain language, a join-aggregate query first computes the join $Q(\mathcal{R})$ and the annotation of each join result, which is the $\otimes$-aggregate of the tuples comprising the join result. Then it partitions $Q(\mathcal{R})$ into groups by their projection on $\mathbf{y}$. Finally, for each group, it computes the $\oplus$-aggregate of the annotations of the join results.

Many queries can be formulated as special join-aggregate queries. For example, if we take $\mathbb{R}$ to be the domain of integers, $\oplus$ to be addition, $\otimes$ to be multiplication, and set $w(t) = 1$ for all t, then it becomes the `COUNT(*) GROUP BY` $\mathbf{y}$ query; in particular, if $\mathbf{y} = \emptyset$, the query computes $|Q(\mathcal{R})|$.

The join-project query $\pi_{\mathbf{y}} Q(\mathcal{R})$, also known as a *conjunctive query*, is a special join-aggregate query, and we extend the terminology from [5] to join-aggregate queries. A *width-1 GHD* of a hypergraph $Q = (\mathcal{V}, \mathcal{E})$ is a tree $\mathcal{T}$, where each node $u \in \mathcal{T}$ is a subset of $\mathcal{V}$, such that

(1) (coherence) for each attribute $x \in \mathcal{V}$, the nodes containing x are connected in $\mathcal{T}$;
(2) (edge coverage) for each hyperedge $e \in \mathcal{E}$, there exists a node $u \in \mathcal{T}$ such that $e \subseteq u$; and

(3) (width-1) for each node $u \in \mathcal{T}$, there exists a hyperedge $e \in \mathcal{E}$ such that $u \subseteq e$.

Given a set of output attributes y (a.k.a. *free variables*), we say that $\mathcal{T}$ is *free-connex* if there is a subset of connected nodes of $\mathcal{T}$ including its root, denoted as $\mathcal{T}'$ (such a $\mathcal{T}'$ is said to be a *connex* subset), such that $\mathrm{y} = \bigcup_{u \in \mathcal{T}'} u$. A join-aggregate query Q_{y} is *free-connex* if it has a free-connex width-1 GHD.

As preprocessing, we remove the dangling tuples and apply the reduce procedure repeatedly to remove an $e \in \mathcal{E}$ if there is another $e' \in \mathcal{E}$ such that $e \subset e'$. Note that while dangling tuples can be just discarded, we cannot simply discard $R(e)$ in the reduce procedure. To ensure that the annotations will be computed correctly, we should replace $R(e')$ with $R(e) \bowtie R(e')$ and then discard $R(e)$. Note that by the earlier definition, the annotation of a join result is the $\otimes$-aggregate of the annotations of tuples comprising the join result, so the annotation in $R(e)$ are aggregated into those in $R(e')$.

We find a free-connex width-1 GHD $\mathcal{T}$ of Q [4, 5]. Note that the nodes of $\mathcal{T}$ also define a hypergraph, and can be regarded as another join-aggregate query, but with the property that it has a free-connex subset $\mathcal{T}'$ such that $\mathrm{y} = \bigcup_{u \in \mathcal{T}'} u$. We construct an instance $\mathcal{R}_{\mathcal{T}} = \{R(u) : u \in \mathcal{T}\}$ such that $Q_{\mathrm{y}}(\mathcal{R}) = \mathcal{T}(\mathcal{R}_{\mathcal{T}})$, where $\mathcal{T}(\mathcal{R}_{\mathcal{T}})$ denotes the result of running the query defined by $\pi_{\mathrm{y}}\mathcal{T}$ on $\mathcal{R}_{\mathcal{T}}$. Observe that on a reduced Q, the condition $e \subseteq u$ in property (2) of a width-1 GHD can be replaced by $e = u$, since if $e \subset u$ and $u \subseteq e'$ for some other $e' \in \mathcal{E}$ due to property (3), we would find $e \subset e'$. This implies that $\mathcal{T}$ has only two types of nodes: (1) all hyperedges in $\mathcal{E}$, and (2) nodes that are a proper subset of some $e \in \mathcal{E}$. Then we construct $\mathcal{R}_{\mathcal{T}}$ as follows. For each $u \in \mathcal{T}$ of type (1), we set $R(u) := R(e)$ where $e = u$; for each $u \in \mathcal{T}$ of type (2), we set $R(u) := R(e)$ for any $e \in \mathcal{E}, u \subset e$, but the annotations of all tuples in $R(u)$ are set to 1 (the $\otimes$-identity). Below, we will focus on computing $\mathcal{T}(\mathcal{R}_{\mathcal{T}})$.

Joglekar et al. [20] modified the Yannakakis algorithm into AggroYannakakis, and showed that it has load $O(\frac{\mathrm{IN}}{p} + \frac{\mathrm{OUT}}{p})$ on any free-connex join-aggregate query[8]. Since we want to avoid the sub-optimal $O(\frac{\mathrm{OUT}}{p})$ term, we modify their algorithm into LinearAggroYannakakis, which runs with linear load. It aggregates over all the non-output attributes, returning a modified query $\mathcal{T}'(\mathcal{R}_{\mathcal{T}'})$ that only has the output attributes. The details of LinearAggroYannakakis, as well as its guarantees stated in the following lemma, are given in the full version [18].

[8]The bound stated in [20] is actually $O(\frac{(\mathrm{IN}+\mathrm{OUT})^2}{p})$, because they used a sub-optimal binary join algorithm as the subroutine following [1]. Replacing it with the optimal binary join algorithm in [7, 16] yields the claimed bound. In addition, they only considered *simple* join-aggregate queries, which are a strict subclass of free-connex queries. But after our conversion from $Q_{\mathrm{y}}(\mathcal{R})$ to $\mathcal{T}(\mathcal{R}_{\mathcal{T}})$, their algorithm actually works for all free-connex queries.

Lemma 6.1. LinearAggroYannakakis *is a constant-round, linear-load algorithm that, given any free-connex width-1 GHD $\mathcal{T}$ and an instance $\mathcal{R}_{\mathcal{T}}$, returns an instance $\mathcal{R}_{\mathcal{T}'}$ such that $\mathcal{T}(\mathcal{R}_{\mathcal{T}}) = \mathcal{T}'(\mathcal{R}_{\mathcal{T}'})$, where $\mathcal{T}'$ is the free-connex subset of $\mathcal{T}$.*

Because $\mathcal{T}'$ is acyclic, we can run our output-optimal algorithm to compute $\mathcal{T}'(\mathcal{R}_{\mathcal{T}'})$. More precisely, when the algorithm emits a join result, we compute the $\otimes$-aggregate of the tuples comprising the join result. Note that in the following result, $\mathrm{OUT} = |Q_{\mathrm{y}}(\mathcal{R})|$, i.e., the size of the final output, which can be much smaller than $|Q(\mathcal{R})|$.

Theorem 6.2. *There is an algorithm that computes any free-connex join-aggregate query in $O(1)$ rounds with load $O(\frac{\mathrm{IN}}{p} + \frac{\sqrt{\mathrm{IN}\cdot\mathrm{OUT}}}{p})$.*

Observing that the join size of a (non-aggregate) join is a special join-aggregate query with $\mathrm{y} = \emptyset$, we obtain the following result, which has been used as a primitive. Note that there is no circular dependency here, because it only uses LinearAggroYannakakis.

Corollary 6.3. *For any acyclic join Q and any instance $\mathcal{R}$, $|Q(\mathcal{R})|$ can be computed in $O(1)$ rounds with load $O(\frac{\mathrm{IN}}{p})$.*

Furthermore, if $\mathcal{T}'$ is r-hierarchical, we run our instance-optimal algorithm to compute $\mathcal{T}'(\mathcal{R}_{\mathcal{T}'})$. In fact, we can precisely characterize the class of queries with an r-hierarchical $\mathcal{T}'$. A query is called *out-hierarchical* if it is free-connex and its residual query by removing all non-output attributes is r-hierarchical. We show the following result and its proof can be found in the full version [18].

Lemma 6.4. *A join-aggregate query Q_{y} is out-hierarchical if and only if it has a width-1 GHD $\mathcal{T}$ with a connex subset $\mathcal{T}'$ such that $\mathrm{y} = \bigcup_{u \in \mathcal{T}'} u$ and $\mathcal{T}'$ is r-hierarchical.*

Theorem 6.5. *For out-hierarchical query Q_{y} and any instance $\mathcal{R}$, there is an algorithm computing it in $O(1)$ rounds with load $O(\frac{\mathrm{IN}}{p} + L_{instance}(p, \mathcal{R}, \mathrm{y}))$.*

Note that the instance-optimal lower bound L_{instance} for a join-aggregate query is defined with respect to the output attributes only, i.e., $L_{\mathrm{instance}}(p, \mathcal{R}, \mathrm{y}) := \max_{S \subseteq \mathcal{E}} \left(\frac{|\pi_{\mathrm{y}} Q(\mathcal{R}, S)|}{p}\right)^{\frac{1}{|S|}}$, where $\pi_{\mathrm{y}} Q(\mathcal{R}, S) = \pi_{\mathrm{y}}((\bowtie_{e \in S} R(e)) \ltimes Q(\mathcal{R}))$.

7 A LOWER BOUND ON TRIANGLE JOIN

Finally, we look beyond acyclic joins. In particular, we give an output-sensitive lower bound on the triangle join $Q_{\triangle} = R_1(B, C) \bowtie R_2(A, C) \bowtie R_3(A, B)$. For $Q_{\triangle}$, a worst-case lower bound of $\Omega(\frac{\mathrm{IN}}{p^{2/3}})$ is known, by the following argument: A server loading L tuples can emit at most $O(L^{3/2})$ join results by the AGM bound [3], while the join size of $Q_{\triangle}$ can be as large as $\Omega(\mathrm{IN}^{3/2})$. Then setting $p \cdot L^{3/2} = \Omega(\mathrm{IN}^{3/2})$ yields this lower bound. However, if OUT is used as a parameter, this argument only leads to a lower bound of $\Omega((\frac{\text{OUT}}{p})^{2/3})$. Below, we improve this lower bound to the following:

THEOREM 7.1. *For any* $\text{IN}/\log^2 \text{IN} \geq 3p^3, \text{OUT}$, *there exists an instance* $\mathcal{R}$ *for* $Q_\triangle$ *with input size* $\Theta(\text{IN})$ *and output size* $\Theta(\text{OUT})$ *such that any tuple-based algorithm computing it in* $O(1)$ *rounds must have a load of* $\Omega(\min\{\frac{\text{IN}}{p} + \frac{\text{OUT}}{p \log N}, \frac{\text{IN}}{p^{2/3}}\})$.

The proof, given in the full version [18], is quite technical, but the intuition is simple: When $\text{OUT} = \Theta(\text{IN}^{3/2})$, the triangles are "dense" enough, so a server can achieve the maximum efficiency and emit $\Theta(L^{3/2})$ triangles. However, for small OUT, we can construct an instance in which the triangles are "sparse" so that a server cannot be as efficient. In fact, an instance constructed randomly (in a certain way) would have this property with high probability.

Our lower bound has the following consequences:

(1) When $\text{OUT} \geq \text{IN} \cdot p^{1/3}$, the lower bound becomes $\tilde{\Omega}(\frac{\text{IN}}{p^{2/3}})$, which means that the worst-case optimal algorithm of [23] is actually also output-optimal in this parameter range. Finding $\tilde{\Omega}(\text{IN} \cdot p^{1/3})$ triangles is as difficult as finding $\Theta(\text{IN}^{3/2})$ triangles.

(2) When $\text{IN} \leq \text{OUT} \leq \text{IN} \cdot p^{1/3}$, the lower bound becomes $\tilde{\Omega}(\frac{\text{OUT}}{p})$ while we do not have a matching upper bound yet. Nevertheless, this already exhibits a separation from acyclic joins, which can be done with load $O(\frac{\sqrt{\text{IN} \cdot \text{OUT}}}{p})$. The gap is at least $\tilde{\Omega}(\sqrt{\frac{\text{OUT}}{\text{IN}}})$.

REFERENCES

[1] F. Afrati, M. Joglekar, C. Ré, S. Salihoglu, and J. D. Ullman. GYM: A multiround join algorithm in MapReduce. In *Proc. International Conference on Database Theory*, 2017.

[2] F. N. Afrati and J. D. Ullman. Optimizing multiway joins in a map-reduce environment. *IEEE Transactions on Knowledge and Data Engineering*, 23(9):1282–1298, 2011.

[3] A. Atserias, M. Grohe, and D. Marx. Size bounds and query plans for relational joins. *SIAM Journal on Computing*, 42(4):1737–1767, 2013.

[4] G. Bagan. *Algorithmes et complexité des problèmes d'énumération pour l'évaluation de requêtes logiques.* PhD thesis, Université de Caen, 2009.

[5] G. Bagan, A. Durand, and E. Grandjean. On acyclic conjunctive queries and constant delay enumeration. In *International Workshop on Computer Science Logic*, pages 208–222. Springer, 2007.

[6] P. Beame, P. Koutris, and D. Suciu. Communication steps for parallel query processing. In *Proc. ACM Symposium on Principles of Database Systems*, 2013.

[7] P. Beame, P. Koutris, and D. Suciu. Skew in parallel query processing. In *Proc. ACM Symposium on Principles of Database Systems*, 2014.

[8] C. Beeri, R. Fagin, D. Maier, and M. Yannakakis. On the desirability of acyclic database schemes. *Journal of the ACM (JACM)*, 30(3):479–513, 1983.

[9] C. Berkholz, J. Keppeler, and N. Schweikardt. Answering conjunctive queries under updates. In *Proc. ACM Symposium on Principles of Database Systems*, 2017.

[10] A. Björklund, R. Pagh, V. V. Williams, and U. Zwick. Listing triangles. In *Proc. International Colloquium on Automata, Languages, and Programming*, 2014.

[11] N. Dalvi and D. Suciu. Efficient query evaluation on probabilistic databases. *The VLDB Journal*, 16(4):523–544, 2007.

[12] R. Fink and D. Olteanu. Dichotomies for queries with negation in probabilistic databases. *ACM Transactions on Database Systems*, 41(1), 2016.

[13] G. Gottlob, M. Grohe, N. Musliu, M. Samer, and F. Scarcello. Hypertree decompositions: structure, algorithms, and applications. In *Lecture Notes in Computer Science*, volume 3787, pages 1–15. Springer, 2005.

[14] T. J. Green, G. Karvounarakis, and V. Tannen. Provenance semirings. In *Proc. ACM Symposium on Principles of Database Systems*, 2007.

[15] M. Grohe and D. Marx. Constraint solving via fractional edge covers. *ACM Transactions on Algorithms*, 11(1):4, 2014.

[16] X. Hu, Y. Tao, and K. Yi. Output-optimal parallel algorithms for similarity joins. In *Proc. ACM Symposium on Principles of Database Systems*, 2017.

[17] X. Hu and K. Yi. Towards a worst-case I/O-optimal algorithm for acyclic joins. In *Proc. ACM Symposium on Principles of Database Systems*, 2016.

[18] X. Hu and K. Yi. Instance and Output Optimal Parallel Algorithms for Acyclic Joins. *arXiv e-prints*, page arXiv:1903.09717, Mar 2019.

[19] M. Joglekar and C. Ré. It's all a matter of degree: Using degree information to optimize multiway joins. In *Proc. International Conference on Database Theory*, 2016.

[20] M. R. Joglekar, R. Puttagunta, and C. Ré. AJAR: Aggregations and joins over annotated relations. In *Proc. ACM Symposium on Principles of Database Systems*, 2016.

[21] B. Ketsman and D. Suciu. A worst-case optimal multi-round algorithm for parallel computation of conjunctive queries. In *Proc. ACM Symposium on Principles of Database Systems*, 2017.

[22] M. A. Khamis, H. Q. Ngo, and D. Suciu. What do shannon-type inequalities, submodular width, and disjunctive datalog have to do with one another? In *Proc. ACM Symposium on Principles of Database Systems*, 2017.

[23] P. Koutris, P. Beame, and D. Suciu. Worst-case optimal algorithms for parallel query processing. In *Proc. International Conference on Database Theory*, 2016.

[24] P. Koutris, S. Salihoglu, and D. Suciu. *Algorithmic Aspects of Parallel Data Processing.* Now Publishers, 2018.

[25] P. Koutris and D. Suciu. Parallel evaluation of conjunctive queries. In *Proc. ACM Symposium on Principles of Database Systems*, 2011.

[26] D. Marx. Tractable hypergraph properties for constraint satisfaction and conjunctive queries. *Journal of the ACM*, 2013.

[27] H. Q. Ngo, D. T. Nguyen, C. Ré, and A. Rudra. Beyond worst-case analysis for joins with minesweeper. In *Proc. ACM Symposium on Principles of Database Systems*, 2014.

[28] H. Q. Ngo, E. Porat, C. Ré, and A. Rudra. Worst-case optimal join algorithms. In *Proc. ACM Symposium on Principles of Database Systems*, pages 37–48, 2012.

[29] R. Pagh and F. Silvestri. The input/output complexity of triangle enumeration. In *Proc. ACM Symposium on Principles of Database Systems*, 2014.

[30] M. Pătraşcu. Towards polynomial lower bounds for dynamic problems. In *Proc. ACM Symposium on Theory of Computing*, 2010.

[31] L. G. Valiant. A bridging model for parallel computation. *Communications of the ACM*, 33(8):103–111, 1990.

[32] T. Veldhuizen. Leapfrog triejoin: A simple, worst-case optimal join algorithm. In *Proc. International Conference on Database Theory*, 2014.

[33] M. Yannakakis. Algorithms for acyclic database schemes. In *Proc. International Conference on Very Large Data Bases*, pages 82–94, 1981.

HyperBench: A Benchmark and Tool for Hypergraphs and Empirical Findings

Wolfgang Fischl
TU Wien
wolfgang.fischl@tuwien.ac.at

Georg Gottlob
TU Wien & University of Oxford
georg.gottlob@cs.ox.ac.uk

Davide Mario Longo
TU Wien
davide.longo@tuwien.ac.at

Reinhard Pichler
TU Wien
reinhard.pichler@tuwien.ac.at

ABSTRACT

To cope with the intractability of answering Conjunctive Queries (CQs) and solving Constraint Satisfaction Problems (CSPs), several notions of hypergraph decompositions have been proposed – giving rise to different notions of width, noticeably, plain, generalized, and fractional hypertree width (hw, ghw, and fhw). Given the increasing interest in using such decomposition methods in practice, a publicly accessible repository of decomposition software, as well as a large set of benchmarks, and a web-accessible workbench for inserting, analysing, and retrieving hypergraphs are called for.

We address this need by providing (i) concrete implementations of hypergraph decompositions (including new practical algorithms), (ii) a new, comprehensive benchmark of hypergraphs stemming from disparate CQ and CSP collections, and (iii) HyperBench, our new web-interface for accessing the benchmark and the results of our analyses. In addition, we describe a number of actual experiments we carried out with this new infrastructure.

KEYWORDS

hypergraph decomposition methods, query answering, constraint satisfaction

ACM Reference Format:

Wolfgang Fischl, Georg Gottlob, Davide Mario Longo, and Reinhard Pichler. 2019. HyperBench: A Benchmark and Tool for Hypergraphs and Empirical Findings. In *38th ACM SIGMOD-SIGACT-SIGAI Symposium on Principles of Database Systems (PODS'19), June 30-July 5, 2019, Amsterdam, Netherlands.* ACM, New York, NY, USA, 17 pages. https://doi.org/10.1145/3294052.3319683

ACM ISBN 978-1-4503-6227-6/19/06...$15.00
https://doi.org/10.1145/3294052.3319683

1 INTRODUCTION

In this work we study computational problems on hypergraph decompositions which are designed to speed up the evaluation of Conjunctive Queries (CQs) and the solution of Constraint Satisfaction Problems (CSPs). Hypergraph decompositions have meanwhile found their way into commercial database systems such as LogicBlox [5, 8, 32, 33, 40] and advanced research prototypes such as EmptyHeaded [1, 2, 41, 48]. Hypergraph decompositions have also been successfully used in the CSP area [4, 29, 34]. In theory, the pros and cons of various notions of decompositions and widths are well understood (see [23] for a survey). However, from a practical point of view, many questions have remained open.

We want to analyse the hypertree width (hw) of hypergraphs from different application contexts. The investigation of millions of CQs [12, 42] posed at various SPARQL endpoints suggests that these real-world CQs with atoms of arity ≤ 3 have very low hw: the overwhelming majority is acyclic; almost all of the rest has $hw = 2$. It is, however, not clear if CQs with arbitrary arity and CSPs also have low hypertree width, say, $hw \leq 5$. Ghionna et al. [21] gave a positive answer to this question for a small set of TPC-H benchmark queries. We significantly extend their collection of CQs.

Answering CQs and solving CSPs are fundamental tasks in Computer Science. Formally, they are the same problem, since both correspond to the evaluation of first-order formulae over a finite structure, such that the formulae only use $\{\exists, \wedge\}$ as connectives but not $\{\forall, \vee, \neg\}$. Both problems, answering CQs and solving CSPs, are NP-complete [14]. Consequently, the search for tractable fragments of these problems has been an active research area in the database and artificial intelligence communities for several decades.

The most powerful methods known to date for defining tractable fragments are based on various decompositions of the hypergraph structure underlying a given CQ or CSP. The most important forms of decompositions are *hypertree decompositions (HDs)* [24], *generalized hypertree decompositions (GHDs)* [24], and *fractional hypertree decompositions (FHDs)* [27]. These decomposition methods give rise to three notions of width of a hypergraph H: the *hypertree width* $hw(H)$, *generalized hypertree width* $ghw(H)$, and *fractional hypertree width* $fhw(H)$, where, $fhw(H) \leq ghw(H) \leq hw(H)$ holds for every hypergraph H. For definitions, see Section 2.

Both, answering CQs and solving CSPs, become tractable if the underlying hypergraphs have bounded *hw*, *ghw*, or, *fhw* and an appropriate decomposition is given. This gives rise to the problem of recognizing if a given CQ or CSP has *hw*, *ghw*, or, *fhw* bounded by some constant k. Formally, for *decomposition* $\in$ {HD, GHD, FHD} and $k \geq 1$, we consider the following family of problems:

Check(*decomposition*, k)
input hypergraph $H = (V, E)$;
output *decomposition* of H of width $\leq k$ if it exists and answer 'no' otherwise.

Clearly, bounded *fhw* defines the largest tractable class while bounded *hw* defines the smallest one. On the other hand, the problem Check(HD, k) is feasible in polynomial time [24] while the Check(GHD, k) [25] and Check(FHD, k) [19] problems are NP-complete even for $k = 2$.

Systems to solve the Check(HD, k) problem exist [26, 44]. In contrast, for Check(GHD, k) and Check(FHD, k), apart from exhaustive search over possible decomposition trees (which only works for small hypergraphs), no implementations have been reported yet [1] – with one exception: very recently, an interesting approach is presented in [17], where SMT-solving is applied to the Check(FHD, k) problem. In [26], tests of the Check(HD, k) system are presented. However, a benchmark for systematically evaluating systems for the Check(*decomposition*, k) problem with *decomposition* $\in$ {HD, GHD, FHD} and $k \geq 1$ were missing so far. This motivates our first research goals.

Goal 1: Create a comprehensive, easily extensible benchmark of hypergraphs corresponding to CQs or CSPs for the analysis of hypergraph decomposition algorithms.

Goal 2: Use the benchmark from Goal 1 to find out if the hypertree width is, in general, small enough (say ≤ 5) to allow for efficient evaluation of CQs of arbitrary arity and of CSPs.

Recently, in [19], the authors have identified classes of CQs for which the Check(GHD, k) and Check(FHD, k) problems become tractable (from now on, we only speak about CQs; of course, all results apply equally to CSPs). To this end, the Bounded Intersection Property (BIP) and, more generally, the Bounded Multi-Intersection Property (BMIP) have been introduced. The maximum number i of attributes shared by two (resp. c) atoms is referred to as the intersection width (resp. c-multi-intersection width) of the CQ, which is similar to the notion of cutset width from the CSP literature [15]. We say that a class of CQs satisfies the BIP (resp. BMIP) if the number of attributes shared by two (resp. by a constant number c of) query atoms is bounded by some constant i.

A related property is that of bounded degree, i.e., each attribute only occurs in a constant number of query atoms. Clearly, the BMIP is an immediate consequence of bounded degree. It has been shown in [19] that Check(GHD, k) is solvable in polynomial time for CQs whose underlying hypergraphs satisfy the BMIP. For CQs, the BMIP and bounded degree seem natural restrictions. For CSPs, the situation is not so clear. This yields the following research goals.

Goal 3: Use the hypergraph benchmark from Goal 1 to analyse how realistic the restrictions to low (multi-)intersection width, or low degree of CQs and CSPs are.

Goal 4: Verify that for hypergraphs of low intersection width, the Check(GHD, k) problem indeed allows for efficient algorithms that work well in practice.

The tractability results for Check(FHD, k) [18, 19] are significantly weaker than for Check(GHD, k): they involve a factor which is at least double-exponential in some "constant" (namely k, the bound d on the degree and/or the bound i on the intersection-width). Hence, we want to investigate if (generalized) hypertree decompositions could be "fractionally improved" by taking the integral edge cover at each node in the HD or GHD and replacing it by a fractional edge cover. We will thus introduce the notion of *fractionally improved* HD which checks if there exists an HD of width $\leq k$, such that replacing each integral cover by a fractional cover yields an FHD of width $\leq k'$ for given bounds k, k' with $0 < k' < k$.

Goal 5: Explore the potential of fractionally improved HDs, i.e., investigate if the improvements achieved are significant.

In cases where Check(GHD, k) and Check(FHD, k) are intractable, we may have to settle for good approximations of *ghw* and *fhw*. For GHDs, we may thus use the inequality $ghw(H) \leq 3 \cdot hw(H) + 1$, which holds for every hypergraph H [3]. In contrast, for FHDs, the best known general, polynomial-time approximation is cubic. More precisely, in [38], a polynomial-time algorithm is presented which, given a hypergraph H with $fhw(H) = k$, computes an FHD of width $O(k^3)$. In [19], it is shown that a polynomial-time approximation up to a logarithmic factor is possible for any class of hypergraphs with bounded Vapnik–Chervonenkis dimension (VC-dimension; see Section 2 for a precise definition). The problem of efficiently approximating the *ghw* and/or *fhw* leads us to the following goals.

Goal 6: Use the benchmark from Goal 1 to analyse if, in practice, *hw* and *ghw* indeed differ by factor 3 or, if *hw* is typically much closer to *ghw* than this worst-case bound.

Goal 7: Use the benchmark from Goal 1 to analyse how realistic the restriction to small VC-dimension of CQs and CSPs is.

Results. Our main results are as follows:

• We provide *HyperBench*, a comprehensive hypergraph benchmark of initially over 3,000 hypergraphs (see Section 3). This benchmark is exposed by a web interface, which allows the user to retrieve the hypergraphs or groups of hypergraphs together with a broad spectrum of properties of these hypergraphs, such as lower/upper bounds on *hw* and *ghw*, (multi-)intersection width, degree, etc.

• We extend the software for HD computation from [26] to also solve the CHECK(GHD, k) problem. For a given hypergraph H, our system first computes the intersection width of H and then applies the *ghw*-algorithm from [19], which is parameterized by the intersection width. We implement several improvements and we further extend the system to compute also "fractionally improved" HDs.

• We carry out an empirical analysis of the hypergraphs in the HyperBench benchmark. This analysis demonstrates, especially for real-world instances, that the restrictions to BIP, BMIP, bounded degree, and bounded VC-dimension are astonishingly realistic. Moreover, on all hypergraphs in the HyperBench benchmark, we run our *hw*- and *ghw*-systems to identify (or at least bound) their *hw* and *ghw*. An interesting observation of our empirical study is that apart from the CQs also a significant portion of CSPs in our benchmark has small hypertree width (all non-random CQs have $hw \leq 3$ and over 60% of CSPs stemming from applications have $hw \leq 5$). Moreover, for $hw \leq 5$, in all of the cases where the *ghw*-computation terminates, *hw* and *ghw* have identical values.

• In our study of the *ghw* of the hypergraphs in the HyperBench benchmark, we observed that a straightforward implementation of the algorithm from [19] for hypergraphs of low intersection width is too slow in many cases. We therefore present a new approach (based on so-called "balanced separators") with promising experimental results. It is interesting to note that the new approach works particularly well in those situations which are particularly hard for the straightforward implementation, namely hypergraphs H where the test if $ghw \leq k$ for given k gives a "no"-answer. Hence, combining the different approaches is very effective.

Structure. This paper is structured as follows: In Section 2, we recall some basic notions. In Section 3, we present our system and test environment as well as our HyperBench benchmark. First results of our empirical study of the hypergraphs in this benchmark are presented in Section 4. In Section 5, we describe our algorithms for solving the CHECK(GHD, k) problem. A further extension of the system to allow for the computation of fractionally improved HDs is described in Section 6. Finally, in Section 7 we summarize related work and conclude in Section 8 by highlighting the most important lessons learned from our empirical study and by identifying some appealing directions for future work.

Due to lack of space, some of the statistics presented in the main body contain aggregated values (for instance, for different classes of CSPs). Figures and tables with more fine-grained results (for instance, distinguishing the 3 classes of CSPs to be presented in Section 4) will be provided in the full version of this paper.

2 PRELIMINARIES

Let ϕ be a CQ or CSP (i.e., an FO-formula with connectives $\{\exists, \wedge\}$). The *hypergraph corresponding to* ϕ is defined as $H = (V(H), E(H))$, where the set of vertices $V(H)$ is defined as the set of variables in ϕ and the set of edges $E(H)$ is defined as $E(H) = \{e \mid \phi$ contains an atom A, s.t. e equals the set of variables occurring in $A\}$.

Hypergraph decompositions and width measures. We consider here three notions of hypergraph decompositions with associated notions of width. To this end, we first need to introduce the notion of (fractional) edge covers:

Let $H = (V(H), E(H))$ be a hypergraph and consider a function $\gamma\colon E(H) \to [0, 1]$. Then, we define the set $B(\gamma)$ of all vertices covered by γ and the weight of γ as

$$B(\gamma) = \left\{ v \in V(H) \mid \sum_{e \in E(H), v \in e} \gamma(e) \geq 1 \right\},$$

$$weight(\gamma) = \sum_{e \in E(H)} \gamma(e).$$

The special case of a function with values restricted to $\{0, 1\}$, will be denoted by λ, i.e., $\lambda\colon E(H) \to \{0, 1\}$. Following [24], we can also treat λ as a set with $\lambda \subseteq E(H)$ (namely, the set of edges e with $\lambda(e) = 1$) and the weight as the cardinality of such a set of edges.

We now introduce three notions of decompositions.

Definition 2.1. A *generalized hypertree decomposition* (for short GHD) of a hypergraph $H = (V(H), E(H))$ is a tuple $\langle T, (B_u)_{u \in N(T)}, (\lambda_u)_{u \in N(T)} \rangle$, such that $T = \langle N(T), E(T) \rangle$ is a rooted tree and the following conditions hold:

(1) $\forall e \in E(H)$: there exists a node $u \in N(T)$ with $e \subseteq B_u$;

(2) $\forall v \in V(H)$: the set $\{u \in N(T) \mid v \in B_u\}$ is connected in T;

(3) $\forall u \in N(T)$: λ_u is defined as $\lambda_u\colon E(H) \to \{0, 1\}$ with $B_u \subseteq B(\lambda_u)$.

We use the following notational conventions throughout this paper. To avoid confusion, we will consequently refer to the elements in $V(H)$ as *vertices* of the hypergraph and to the elements in $N(T)$ as the *nodes* of the decomposition. For a node u in T, we write T_u to denote the subtree of T rooted at u. By slight abuse of notation, we will often write $u' \in T_u$ to denote that u' is a node in the subtree T_u of T. Finally, we define $V(T_u) := \bigcup_{u' \in T_u} B_{u'}$.

Definition 2.2. A *hypertree decomposition* (for short HD) of a hypergraph $H = (V(H), E(H))$ is a GHD, which in addition also satisfies the following condition:

(4) $\forall u \in N(T)$: $V(T_u) \cap B(\lambda_u) \subseteq B_u$

Definition 2.3. A *fractional hypertree decomposition* (for short FHD) [27] of a hypergraph $H = (V(H), E(H))$ is defined as a tuple $\langle T, (B_u)_{u \in N(T)}, (\gamma_u)_{u \in N(T)} \rangle$, where conditions (1) and (2) of Definition 2.1 plus the following condition (3') hold:

(3') $\forall u \in N(T)$: γ_u is defined as $\gamma_u \colon E(H) \to [0, 1]$ with $B_u \subseteq B(\gamma_u)$.

The width of a GHD, HD, or FHD is the maximum weight of the functions λ_u or γ_u, over all nodes u in T. The generalized hypertree width, hypertree width, and fractional hypertree width of H (denoted $ghw(H)$, $hw(H)$, $fhw(H)$) is the minimum width over all GHDs, HDs, and FHDs of H, respectively. Condition (2) is called the "connectedness condition", and condition (4) is referred to as "special condition" [24]. The set B_u is often referred to as the "bag" at node u. The functions λ_u and γ_u are referred to as the *λ-label* and *γ-label* of node u. Strictly speaking, only HDs require that the underlying tree T be rooted. We assume that also the tree underlying a GHD or an FHD is rooted where the root is *arbitrarily* chosen.

Favourable properties of hypergraphs. In [19], the following properties of hypergraphs were identified to allow for the definition of tractable classes of CHECK(GHD, k) and for an efficient approximation of CHECK(FHD, k), respectively.

Definition 2.4. The *intersection width* $iwidth(H)$ of a hypergraph H is the maximum cardinality of any intersection $e_1 \cap e_2$ of two edges $e_1 \neq e_2$ of H. We say that a hypergraph H has the *i-bounded intersection property (i-BIP)* if $iwidth(H) \leq i$. A class $\mathscr{C}$ of hypergraphs has the *bounded intersection property (BIP)* if there exists some constant i such that every hypergraph H in $\mathscr{C}$ has the i-BIP.

Definition 2.5. For positive integer c, the *c-multi-intersection width c-miwidth(H)* of a hypergraph H is the maximum cardinality of any intersection $e_1 \cap \cdots \cap e_c$ of c distinct edges $e_1, \ldots, e_c$ of H. We say that a hypergraph H has the *i-bounded c-multi-intersection property (ic-BMIP)* if c-*miwidth(H)* $\leq i$ holds. We say that a class $\mathscr{C}$ of hypergraphs has the *bounded multi-intersection property (BMIP)* if there exist constants c and i such that every hypergraph H in $\mathscr{C}$ has the ic-BMIP.

There are two more relevant properties of (classes of) hypergraphs: bounded degree and bounded Vapnik–Chervonenkis dimension (VC-dimension). It is easy to verify [19] that bounded degree implies the BMIP, which in turn implies bounded VC-dimension.

Definition 2.6. The *degree* deg(H) of a hypergraph H is defined as the maximum number d of hyperedges in which a vertex occurs, i.e., $d = \max_{v \in V(H)} |\{e \in E(H) \mid v \in E(H)\}|$. We say that a class $\mathscr{C}$ of hypergraphs has bounded degree, if there exists $d \geq 1$, such that every hypergraph $H \in \mathscr{C}$ has degree $\leq d$.

Definition 2.7 ([49]). Let $H = (V(H), E(H))$ be a hypergraph, and $X \subseteq V$ a set of vertices. Denote by $E(H)|_X = \{X \cap e \mid e \in E(H)\}$. X is called *shattered* if $E(H)|_X = 2^X$. The *Vapnik-Chervonenkis dimension (VC dimension)* of H is the maximum cardinality of a shattered subset of V. We say that a class $\mathscr{C}$ of hypergraphs has bounded VC-dimension, if there exists $v \geq 1$, such that every hypergraph $H \in \mathscr{C}$ has VC-dimension $\leq v$.

The above four properties help to solve or approximate the CHECK(GHD, k) and CHECK(FHD, k) problems as follows:

THEOREM 2.8 ([18, 19]). *Let $\mathscr{C}$ be a class of hypergraphs.*

- *If $\mathscr{C}$ has the BMIP, then the CHECK(GHD, k) problem is solvable in polynomial time for arbitrary $k \geq 1$. Consequently, this tractability holds if $\mathscr{C}$ has bounded degree or the BIP (which each imply the BMIP) [19].*
- *If $\mathscr{C}$ has bounded degree, then the CHECK(FHD, k) problem is solvable in polynomial time for arbitrary $k \geq 1$ [18].*
- *If $\mathscr{C}$ has bounded VC-dimension, then the fhw can be approximated in polynomial time up to a log-factor [19].*

3 HYPERBENCH BENCHMARK AND TOOL

In this section, we introduce our system, test environment, and HyperBench – our new benchmark and web tool.

System and Test Environment. In [26], an implementation (called `DetKDecomp`) of the hypertree decomposition algorithm from [24] was presented. We have extended this implementation and built our library (called `NewDetKDecomp`) upon it. This library includes the original hw-algorithm from [26], the tool `hg-stats` to determine properties described in Section 4 and the algorithms to be presented in Sections 5 and 6. The library is written in C++ and comprises around 8,500 lines of code. The code is available in GitHub at http://github.com/TUfischl/newdetkdecomp.

All the experiments reported in this paper were performed on a cluster of 10 workstations each running Ubuntu 16.04. Every workstation has the same specification and is equipped with two Intel Xeon E5-2650 (v4) processors each having 12 cores and 256-GB main memory. Since all algorithms are single-threaded, we were allowed to compute several instances in parallel. For all upcoming runs of our algorithms we set a timeout of 3600s.

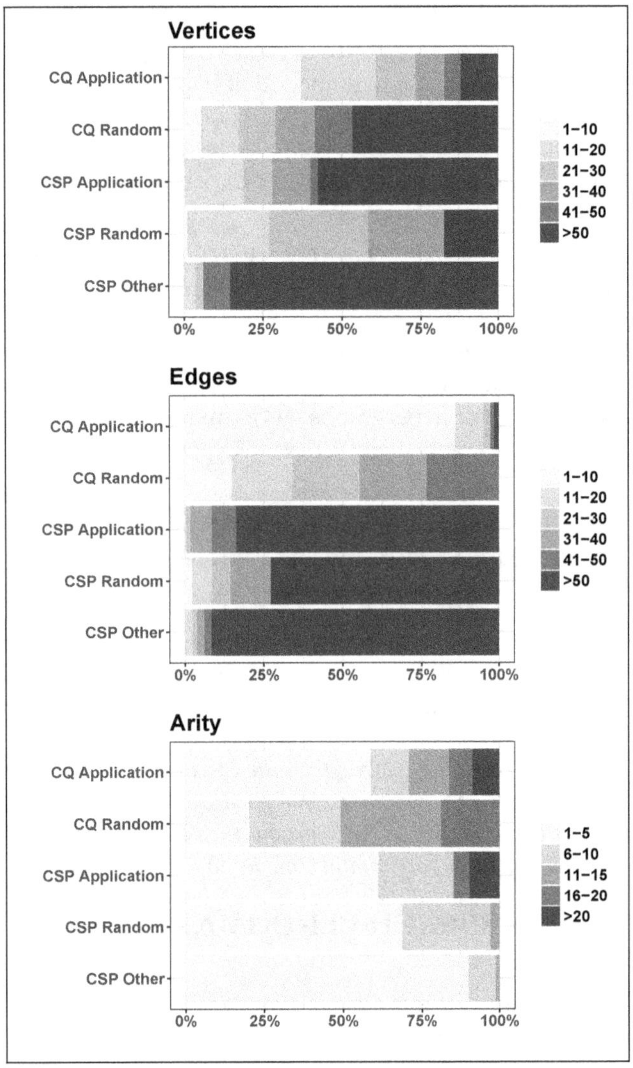

Figure 1: Hypergraph Sizes

Hypergraph benchmark. Our benchmark contains 3,070 hypergraphs, which have been converted from CQs and CSPs collected from various sources. Out of these 3,070 hypergraphs, 2,918 hypergraphs have never been used in a hypertree width analysis before. The hypertree width of 70 CQs and of 82 CSPs has been analysed in [26], [11], and/or [12]. An overview of all instances of CQs and CSPs is given in Table 1. They have been collected from various publicly available benchmarks and repositories of CQs and CSPs. In the first column, the names of each collection of CQs and CSPs are given together with references where they were first published. In the second column we display the number of hypergraphs extracted from each collection. The *hw* of the CQs and CSPs in our benchmark will be discussed in detail in Section 4. To get a first feeling of the *hw* of the various sources, we mention the number of cyclic hypergraphs (i.e., those with $hw \geq 2$) in the last column. When gathering the CQs, we proceeded as follows: of the huge benchmark reported in [12], we have only included CQs, which were detected as having $hw \geq 2$ in [12]. Of the big repository reported in [30], we have included those CQs, which are not trivially acyclic (i.e., they have at least 3 atoms). Of all the small collections of queries, we have included all.

Table 1: Overview of benchmark instances

	Benchmark	*No. instances*	$hw \geq 2$
CQs	SPARQL[12]	70 (out of 26,157,880)	70
	LUBM[10, 28]	14	2
	iBench[6, 10]	40	0
	Doctors[10, 20]	14	0
	Deep[10]	41	0
	JOB (IMDB) [36]	33	7
	TPC-H [9, 47]	33	1
	SQLShare [30]	290 (out of 15,170)	1
	Random [43]	500	464
CSPs	Application [7]	1,090	1,090
	Random [7]	863	863
	Other [11, 26]	82	82
	Total:	*3,070*	*2,580*

Below, we describe the different benchmarks in detail:

- *CQs*: Our benchmark contains 535 CQs from four main sources [9, 10, 12, 30] and a set of 500 randomly generated queries using the query generator of [43]. In the sequel, we shall refer to the former queries as *CQ Application*, and to the latter as *CQ Random*. The CQs analysed in [12] constitute by far the biggest repository of CQs – namely 26,157,880 CQs stemming from SPARQL queries. The queries come from real-users of SPARQL endpoints and their hypertree width was already determined in [12]. Almost all of these CQs were shown to be acyclic. Our analysis comprises 70 CQs from [12], which (apart from few exceptions) are essentially the ones in [12] with $hw \geq 2$. In particular, we have analysed all 8 CQs with highest *hw* among the CQs analysed in [12] (namely, $hw = 3$).

The LUBM [28], iBench [6], Doctors [20], and Deep scenarios have been recently used to evaluate the performance of chase-based systems [10]. Their queries were especially tailored towards the evaluation of query answering tasks of such systems. Note that the LUBM benchmark [28] is a widely used standard benchmark for the evaluation of Semantic Web repositories. Its queries are designed to measure the performance of those repositories over large datasets. Strictly speaking, the iBench is a tool for generating schemas, constraints, and mappings for data integration tasks. However, in [10], 40 queries were created for tests with the iBench. We therefore refer to these queries as iBench-CQs here. In summary, we have incorporated all queries that were either contained in the original benchmarks or created/adapted for the tests in [10].

The goal of the Join Order Benchmark (JOB) [36] was to evaluate the impact of a good join order on the performance of query evaluation in standard RDBMS. Those queries were formulated over the real-world dataset Internet Movie Database (IMDB). All of the queries have between 3 and 16 joins. Clearly, as the goal was to measure the impact of a good join order, those 33 queries are of higher complexity, hence 7 out of the 33 queries have $hw \geq 2$.

The 33 TPC-H queries in our benchmark are from the GitHub repository originally provided by Michael Benedikt and Efthymia Tsamoura [9] for the work on [10]. Out of the 33 CQs based on the TPC-H benchmark [47], 13 queries were handcrafted and 20 randomly generated. The TPC-H benchmark has been widely used to assess multiple aspects of the capabilities of RDBMS to process queries. They reflect common workloads in decision support systems and were chosen to have broad industry-wide relevance.

From SQLShare [30], a multi-year SQL-as-a-service experiment with a large set of real-world queries, we extracted 15,170 queries by considering all CQs (in particular, no nested SELECTs). After eliminating trivial queries (i.e., queries with ≤ 2 atoms, whose acyclicity is immediate) and duplicates, we ended up with 290 queries.

The random queries were generated with a tool that stems from the work on query answering using views in [43]. The query generator allows 3 options: chain/star/random queries. Since the former two types are trivially acyclic, we only used the third option. Here it is possible to supply several parameters for the size of the generated queries. In terms of the resulting hypergraphs, one can thus fix the number of vertices, number of edges and arity. We have generated 500 CQs with 5 – 100 vertices, 3 – 50 edges and arities from 3 to 20. These values correspond to the values observed for the *CQ Application* hypergraphs. However, even though these size values have been chosen similarly, the structural properties of the hypergraphs in the two groups *CQ Application* and *CQ Random* differ significantly, as will become clear from our analysis in Section 4.

- *CSPs*: In total, our benchmark currently contains 2,035 hypergraphs from CSP instances, out of which 1,953 instances were obtained from xcsp.org (see also [7]). We have selected all CSP instances from xcsp.org with less than 100 constraints such that all constraints are extensional. These instances are divided into CSPs from concrete applications, called *CSP Application* in the sequel (1,090 instances), and randomly generated CSPs, called *CSP Random* below (863 instances). In addition, we have included 82 CSP instances from previous hypertree width analyses provided at https://www.dbai.tuwien.ac.at/proj/hypertree/; all of these stem from industrial applications and/or further CSP benchmarks. We refer to these instances as *other CSPs*.

Our HyperBench benchmark consists of these instances converted to hypergraphs. In Figure 1, we show the number of vertices, the number of edges and the arity (i.e., the maximum size of the edges) as three important metrics of the size of each hypergraph. The smallest are those coming from *CQ Application* (at most 10 edges), while the hypergraphs coming from CSPs can be significantly larger (up to 2993 edges). Although some hypergraphs are very big, more than 50% of all hypergraphs have maximum arity less than 5. In Figure 1 we can easily compare the different types of hypergraphs, e.g. hypergraphs of arity greater than 20 only exist in the *CSP Application* class; the *other CSPs* class contains the highest portion of hypergraphs with a big number of vertices and edges, etc.

The hypergraphs and the results of our analysis can be accessed through our web tool, available at http://hyperbench.dbai.tuwien.ac.at.

4 FIRST EMPIRICAL ANALYSIS

In this section, we present first empirical results obtained with the HyperBench benchmark. On the one hand, we want to get an overview of the hypertree width of the various types of hypergraphs in our benchmark (cf. Goal 2 in Section 1). On the other hand, we want to find out how realistic the restriction to low values for certain hypergraph invariants is (cf. Goal 3 stated in Section 1).

Hypergraph Properties. In [18, 19], several invariants of hypergraphs were used to make the Check(GHD, k) and Check(FHD, k) problems tractable or, at least, easier to approximate. We thus investigate the following properties (cf. Definitions 2.4 – 2.7):

- *Deg*: the degree of the underlying hypergraph
- *BIP*: the intersection width
- *c-BMIP*: the c-multi-intersection width for $c \in \{3, 4\}$
- *VC-dim*: the VC-dimension

Table 2: Properties of all benchmark instances

CQ Application

i	Deg	BIP	3-BMIP	4-BMIP	VC-dim
0	0	0	118	173	10
1	2	421	348	302	393
2	176	85	59	50	132
3	137	7	5	5	0
4	87	5	5	5	0
5	35	17	0	0	0
6	98	0	0	0	0

CQ Random

i	Deg	BIP	3-BMIP	4-BMIP	VC-dim
0	0	1	16	49	0
1	1	17	77	125	20
2	15	53	90	120	133
3	38	62	103	74	240
4	31	63	62	42	106
5	33	71	47	28	1
6	382	233	105	62	0

CSP Application & Other

i	Deg	BIP	3-BMIP	4-BMIP	VC-dim
0	0	0	597	603	0
1	0	1037	495	525	0
2	597	95	57	23	1115
3	6	29	21	21	52
4	20	10	2	0	0
5	6	0	0	0	0
>5	543	1	0	0	0

CSP Random

i	Deg	BIP	3-BMIP	4-BMIP	VC-dim
0	0	0	0	0	0
1	0	200	200	238	0
2	0	224	312	407	220
3	0	76	147	95	515
4	12	181	161	97	57
5	8	99	14	1	71
>5	843	83	29	25	0

The results obtained from computing *Deg*, *BIP*, 3-*BMIP*, 4-*BMIP*, and *VC-dim* for the hypergraphs in the HyperBench benchmark are shown in Table 2.

Table 2 has to be read as follows: In the first column, we distinguish different values of the various hypergraph metrics. In the columns labelled "Deg", "BIP", etc., we indicate for how many instances each metric has a particular value. For instance, by the last row in the second column, only 98 non-random CQs have degree > 5. Actually, for most CQs, the degree is less than 10. Moreover, for the BMIP, already with intersections of 3 edges, we get 3-$miwidth(H) \leq 2$ for almost all non-random CQs. Also the VC-dimension is ≤ 2.

For CSPs, all properties may have higher values. However, we note a significant difference between randomly generated CSPs and the rest: For hypergraphs in the groups *CSP Application* and *CSP Other*, 543 (46%) hypergraphs have a high degree (>5), but nearly all instances have BIP or BMIP of less than 3. And most instances have a VC-dimension of at most 2. In contrast, nearly all random instances have a significantly higher degree (843 out of 863 instances with a degree >5). Nevertheless, many instances have small BIP and BMIP. For nearly all hypergraphs (838 out of 863) we have 4-$miwidth(H) \leq 4$. For 5 instances the computation of the VC-dimension timed out. For all others, the VC-dimension is ≤ 5 for random CSPs. Clearly, as seen in Table 2, the random CQs resemble the random CSPs a lot more than the CQ and CSP Application instances. For example, random CQs have similar to random CSPs high degree (382, corresponding to 76%, with degree > 5), higher BIP and BMIP. Nevertheless, similar to random CSPs, the values for BIP and BMIP are still small for many random CQ instances.

To conclude, for the proposed properties, in particular BIP/BMIP and VC-dimension, most of the hypergraphs in our benchmark indeed have low values.

Hypertree Width. We have systematically applied the *hw*-computation from [26] to all hypergraphs in the benchmark. The results are summarized in Figure 2. In our experiments, we proceeded as follows. We distinguish between *CQ Application*, *CQ Random*, and all three groups of CSPs taken together. For every hypergraph H, we first tried to solve the Check(HD, k) problem for $k = 1$. In case of *CQ Application*, we thus got 454 yes-answers and 81 no-answers. The number in each bar indicates the average runtime to find these yes- and no-instances, respectively. Here, the average runtime was "0" (i.e., less than 1 second). For *CQ Random* we got 36 yes- and 464 no-instances with an average runtime below 1 second. For all CSP-instances, we only got no-answers.

In the second round, we tried to solve the Check(HD, k) problem for $k = 2$ for all hypergraphs that yielded a no-answer for $k = 1$. Now the picture is a bit more diverse: 73 of the remaining 81 CQs from *CQ Application* yielded a yes-answer in less than 1 second. For the hypergraphs stemming from *CQ Random* (resp. CSPs), only 68 (resp. 95) instances yielded a yes-answer (in less than 1 second on average), while 396 (resp. 1932) instances yielded a no-answer in less than 7 seconds on average and 8 CSP instances led to a timeout (i.e., the program did not terminate within 3,600 seconds).

This procedure is iterated by incrementing k and running the *hw*-computation for all instances, that either yielded a

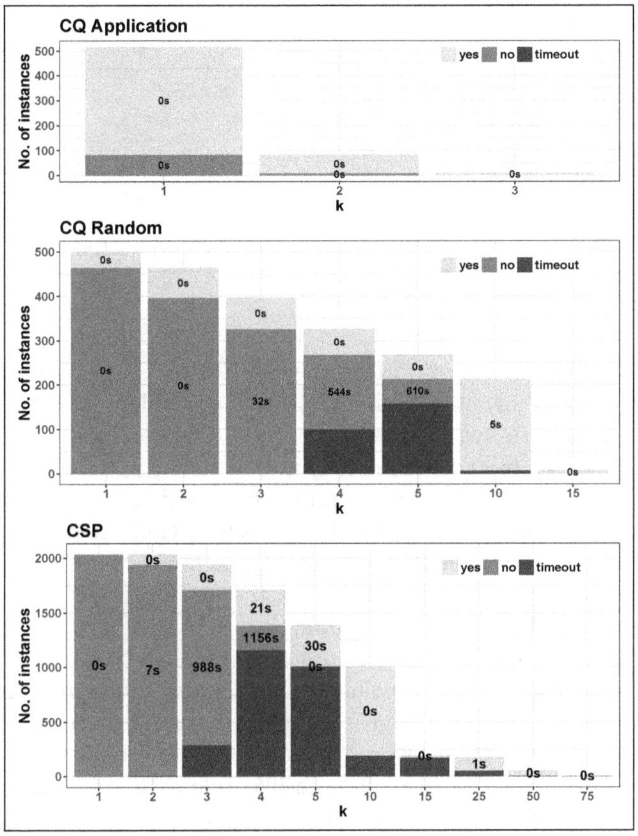

Figure 2: HW analysis (labels are avg. runtimes in s)

no-answer or a timeout in the previous round. For instance, for queries from *CQ Application*, one further round is needed after the second round. In other words, we confirm the observation of low *hw*, which was already made for CQs of arity ≤ 3 in [12, 42]. For the hypergraphs stemming from *CQ Random* (resp. CSPs), 396 (resp. 1940) instances are left in the third round, of which 70 (resp. 232) yield a yes-answer in less than 1 second on average, 326 (resp. 1415) instances yield a no-answer in 32 (resp. 988) seconds on average and no (resp. 293) instances yield a timeout. Note that, as we increase k, the average runtime and the percentage of timeouts first increase up to a certain point and then they decrease. This is due to the fact that, as we increase k, the number of combinations of edges to be considered in each λ-label (i.e., the function λ_u at each node u of the decomposition) increases. In principle, we have to test $O(n^k)$ combinations, where n is the number of edges. However, if k increases beyond a certain point, then it gets easier to "guess" a λ-label since an increasing portion of the $O(n^k)$ possible combinations leads to a solution (i.e., an HD of desired width).

To answer the question in *Goal 2*, it is indeed the case that for a big number of instances, the hypertree width is small enough to allow for efficient evaluation of CQs or CSPs: all instances of non-random CQs have $hw \leq 3$ no matter whether their arity is bounded by 3 (as in case of SPARQL queries) or not; and a large portion (at least 1027, i.e., ca. 50%) of all 2035 CSP instances have $hw \leq 5$. In total, including random CQs, 1,849 (60%) out of 3,070 instances have $hw \leq 5$, for which we could determine the exact hypertree width for 1,453 instances; the others may even have lower hw.

Correlation Analysis. Finally, we have analysed the pairwise correlation between all properties. Of course, the different intersection widths (BIP, 3-BMIP, 4-BMIP) are highly correlated. Other than that, we only observe quite a high correlation of the arity with the number of vertices and the hypertree width and of the number of vertices with the arity and the hypertree width. Clearly, the correlation between arity and hypertree width is mainly due to the CSP instances and the random CQs since, for non-random CQs, the *hw* never increases beyond 3, independently of the arity.

A graphical presentation of all pairwise correlations is given in Figure 3. Here, large, dark circles indicate a high correlation, while small, light circles stand for low correlation. Blue circles indicate a positive correlation while red circles stand for a negative correlation. In [19], we have argued that Deg, BIP, 3-BMIP, 4-BMIP and VC-dim are non-trivial restrictions to achieve tractability. It is interesting to note that, according to the correlations shown in Figure 3, these properties have almost no impact on the hypertree width of our hypergraphs. This underlines the usefulness of these restrictions in the sense that (a) they make the GHD computation and FHD approximation easier [19] but (b) low values of degree, (multi-)intersection-width, or VC-dimension do not pre-determine low values of the widths.

5 GHW COMPUTATION

In this section, we report on new algorithms and implementations to solve the Check(GHD, k) problem and on new empirical results.

Background. In [19], it is shown that the Check(GHD, k) problem becomes tractable for fixed $k \geq 1$, if we restrict ourselves to a class of hypergraphs enjoying the BIP. As our first empirical analysis with the HyperBench has shown (see Section 4), it is indeed realistic to assume that the intersection width of a given hypergraph is small. We have therefore extended the *hw*-computation from [26] by an implementation of the Check(GHD, k) algorithm from [19], referred to as the "*ghw*-algorithm" in the sequel. This algorithm is parameterized, so to speak, by two integers: k (the desired width of a GHD) and i (the intersection width of H).

The key idea of the *ghw*-algorithm is to add a polynomial-time computable set $f(H, k)$ of subedges of edges in $E(H)$ to the hypergraph H, such that $ghw(H) = k$ iff $hw(H') = k$

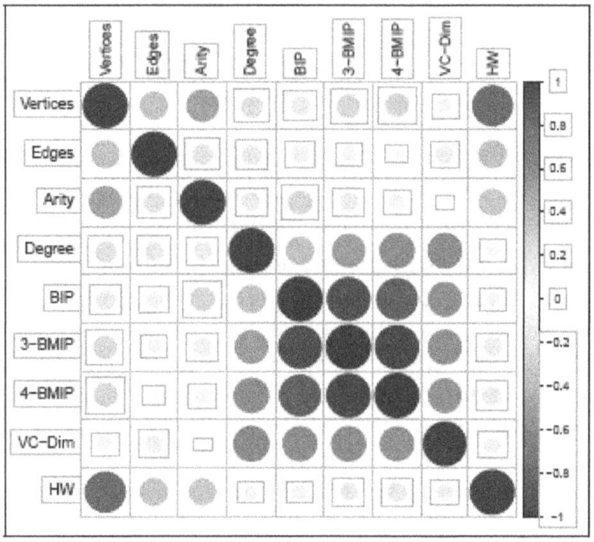

Figure 3: Correlation analysis.

with $H = (V(H), E(H))$ and $H' = (V(H), E(H) \cup f(H,k))$. Tractability of CHECK(GHD, k) follows immediately from the tractability of CHECK(HD, k). The set $f(H,k)$ is defined as

$$f(H,k) = \bigcup_{e \in E(H)} \Big(\bigcup_{e_1,\ldots,e_j \in (E(H) \setminus \{e\}),\, j \le k} 2^{(e \cap (e_1 \cup \cdots \cup e_j))} \Big),$$

i.e., $f(H,k)$ contains all subsets of intersections of edges $e \in E(H)$ with unions of $\le k$ edges of H different from e. By the BIP, the intersection $e \cap (e_1 \cup \cdots \cup e_j)$ has at most $i \cdot k$ elements. Hence, for fixed constants i and k, $|f(H,k)|$ is polynomially bounded.

"Global" implementation. In a straightforward implementation of this algorithm, we compute $f(H,k)$ and from this H' and call the hw-computation from [26] for the CHECK(HD, k) problem as a "black box". A coarse-grained overview of the results is given in Table 3 in the column labelled as 'GlobalBIP". We call this implementation of the ghw algorithm of [19] "global" to indicate that the set $f(H,k)$ is computed "globally", once and for all, for the *entire* hypergraph. We have run the program on each hypergraph from the HyperBench up to hypertree width 6, trying to get a smaller ghw than hw. We have thus run the ghw-algorithm with the following parameters: for all hypergraphs H with $hw(H) = k$ (or $hw \le k$ and, due to timeouts, we do not know if $hw \le k-1$ holds), where $k \in \{3,4,5,6\}$, try to solve the CHECK(GHD, $k-1$) problem. In other words, we just tried to improve the width by 1. Clearly, for $hw(H) \in \{1,2\}$, no improvement is possible since, in this case, $hw(H) = ghw(H)$ holds.

Table 3: GHW algorithms with avg. runtimes in s

$hw \rightarrow$		`GlobalBIP`		`LocalBIP`		`BalSep`
ghw	*total*	*yes*	*no*	*yes*	*no*	*no*
$3 \rightarrow 2$	310	-	128 (537)	-	195 (162)	307 (12)
$4 \rightarrow 3$	386	-	137 (2809)	-	54 (2606)	249 (54)
$5 \rightarrow 4$	427	-	-	-	-	148 (13)
$6 \rightarrow 5$	459	13 (162)	-	13 (60)	-	180 (288)

In Table 3, we report on the number of "successful" attempts to solve the CHECK(GHD, $k-1$) problem for hypergraphs with $hw = k$. Here "successful" means that the program terminated within 1 hour. For instance, for the 310 hypergraphs with $hw = 3$ in the HyperBench, the "global" computation terminated in 128 cases (i.e., 41%) when trying to solve CHECK(GHD, 2). The average runtime of these "successful" runs was 537 seconds. For the 386 hypergraphs with $hw = 4$, the "global" computation terminated in 137 cases (i.e., 35%) with average runtime 2809 when trying to solve the CHECK(GHD, 3) problem. For the 886 hypergraphs with $hw \in \{5,6\}$, the "global" computation only terminated in 13 cases (i.e., 1.4%). Overall, it turns out that the set $f(H,k)$ may be very big (even though it is polynomial if k and i are constants). Hence, H' can become considerably bigger than H. This explains the frequent timeouts in the GlobalBIP column in Table 3.

"Local" implementation. Looking for ways to improve the ghw-algorithm, we closely inspect the role played by the set $f(H,k)$ in the tractability proof in [19]. The definition of this set is motivated by the problem that, in the top down construction of a GHD, we may want to choose at some node u the bag B_u such that $x \notin B_u$ for some variable $x \in B(\lambda_u) \cap V(T_u)$. This violates condition (4) of Definition 2.2 (the "special condition") and is therefore forbidden in an HD. In particular, there exists an edge e with $x \in e$ and $\lambda_u(e) = 1$. The crux of the ghw-algorithm in [19] is that for every such "missing" variable x, the set $f(H,k)$ contains a subedge $e' \subseteq e$ with $x \notin e'$. Hence, replacing e by e' in λ_u (i.e., setting $\lambda_u(e) = 0$, $\lambda_u(e') = 1$ and leaving λ_u unchanged elsewhere) eliminates the special condition violation. By the connectedness condition, it suffices to consider the intersections of e with unions of edges that may possibly occur in bags of T_u rather than with arbitrary edges in $E(H)$. In other words, for each node u in the decomposition, we may restrict $f(H,k)$ to an appropriate subset $f_u(H,k) \subseteq f(H,k)$.

The results obtained with this enhanced version of the ghw-computation are shown in Table 3 in the column labelled "LocalBIP". We call this ghw-computation "local" because the set $f_u(H,k)$ of subedges of H to be added to the hypergraph is computed separately for each node u of the decomposition. Recall that in this table, the "successful" calls of the program are recorded. Interestingly, for the hypergraphs with $hw = 3$, the "local" computation performs significantly better (namely 63% solved with average runtime 162 seconds rather than 41% with average runtime 537 seconds). In contrast, for the hypergraphs with $hw = 4$, the "global" computation is significantly more successful. For $hw \in \{5, 6\}$, the "global" and "local" computations are equally bad. A possible explanation for the reverse behaviour of "global" and "local" computation in case of $hw = 3$ as opposed to $hw = 4$ is that the restriction of the "global" set $f(H, k)$ of subedges to the "local" set $f_u(H, k)$ at each node u seems to be quite effective for the hypergraphs with $hw = 3$. In contrast, the additional cost of having to compute $f_u(H, k)$ at each node u becomes counter-productive, when the set of subedges thus eliminated is not significant. It is interesting to note that the sets of solved instances of the global computation and the local computation are incomparable, i.e., in some cases one method is better, while in other cases the other method is better.

New alternative approach: "balanced separators". We now propose a completely new approach, based on so-called "balanced separators". The latter are a familiar concept in graph theory [16, 46] – denoting a set S of vertices of a graph G, such that the subgraph G' induced by $V(G) \setminus S$ has no connected component larger than some given size, e.g., $\alpha \cdot |V|$ for some given $\alpha \in (0, 1)$. In our setting, we may consider the label λ_u at some node u in a GHD as *separator* in the sense that we can consider connected components of the subhypergraph H' of H induced by $V(H) \setminus B_u$. Clearly, in a GHD, we may consider any node as the root. So suppose that u is the root of some GHD. Moreover, as is shown in [19] in the proof of tractability of Check(GHD, k) in case of the BIP, we may choose λ_u such that $B(\lambda_u) = B_u$ if the subedges in $f(H, k)$ have been added to the hypergraph.

By the HD-algorithm from [24], we know that an HD of H' (and, hence, a GHD of H) can be constructed in such a way that every subtree rooted at a child node u_i of u contains only one connected component C_i of the subhypergraph of H' induced by $V(H) \setminus B_u$. For our purposes, it is convenient to define the size of a component C_i as the number of edges that have to be covered at some node in the subtree rooted at u_i in the GHD. We thus call a separator λ_u "balanced", if the size of each component C_i is at most $|E(H')|/2$. The following observation is immediate:

Proposition 5.1. *In every GHD, there exists a node u (which we may choose as the root) such that λ_u is a balanced separator.*

This property allows us to design the algorithm sketched in Figure 4 to compute a GHD of H'. Actually, as will become clear below, we assume that the input to this recursive algorithm consists of a hypergraph plus a set Sp of "special edges" and we request that the GHD to be constructed contains "special nodes", which (a) have to be leaf nodes in the decomposition and (b) the λ-label of such a leaf node consists of a single special edge only. Each special edge contains the set of vertices B_u of some balanced separator λ_u further up in the hierarchy of recursive calls of the decomposition algorithm. The special edges are propagated to the recursive calls for subhypergraphs in order to determine how to assemble the overall GHD from the GHDs of the subhypergraphs. This will become clearer in the proof sketch of Theorem 5.2 which, for space reasons, is given in the appendix.

ALGORITHM Find_GHD_via_balancedSeparators
// high-level description

Input: hypergraph H', integer $k \geq 0$.
Output: a GHD $\langle T, B_u, \lambda_u \rangle$ of width $\leq k$ if exists, "Reject", otherwise.

Procedure Find_GHD (H: Hypergraph, Sp: Set of special edges)
begin
1. Base Case: if there are only two edges or special edges left then stop and return a GHD with one node for each edge or special edge, respectively.
2. Find a balanced separator: for all $\lambda\colon E(H') \longrightarrow \{0, 1\}$ check if λ_u is a balanced separator for H; if none is found then return Reject.
3. Split H into connected components $C_1, \ldots, C_\ell$ w.r.t. λ_u: $C_i \subseteq V(H) \setminus B(\lambda_u)$ for every i and C_i is connected in H and each C_i is maximal with this property.
4. Build the pair $\langle H_i, Sp_i \rangle$ (the subhypergraph based on C_i and the special edges in C_i) for each connected component C_i; add $B(\lambda_u)$ as one more special edge to each set Sp_i.
5. Call Find_GHD(H_i, Sp_i) for each pair $\langle H_i, Sp_i \rangle$; each successful call returns a GHD T_i for H_i if one call returns Reject then return Reject.
6. Create and return a new GHD for H having λ_u as root: each T_i has one leaf node labelled $B(\lambda_u)$; the new GHD is obtained by gluing together all subtrees T_i at the node with label $B(\lambda_u)$.

end

begin (* Main *)
  return Find_GHD (H', $\emptyset$);
end

Figure 4: GHD-algorithm via balanced separators

Theorem 5.2. *Let H be a hypergraph, let $k \geq 1$, and let H' be obtained from H by adding the subedges in $f(H, k)$ to $E(H)$. Then the algorithm Find_GHD_via_balancedSeparators*

Table 4: GHW of instances with average runtime in s

$hw \rightarrow ghw$	yes	no	timeout
$3 \rightarrow 2$	0	309 (10)	1
$4 \rightarrow 3$	0	262 (57)	124
$5 \rightarrow 4$	0	148 (13)	279
$6 \rightarrow 5$	18 (129)	180 (288)	261

given in Figure 4 outputs a GHD of width $\leq k$ if one exists and rejects otherwise.

If we look at the number of solved instances in Table 3, we see that the recursive algorithm via balanced separators (reported in the last column labelled BalSep) has the least number of timeouts due to the fast identification of negative instances (i.e., those with no-answer), where it often detects quite fast that a given hypergraph does not have a balanced separator of desired width. As k increases, the performance of the balanced separators approach deteriorates. This is due to k in the exponent of the running time of our algorithm, i.e. we need to check for each of the possible $O(n^{k+1})$ combinations of $\leq k$ edges if it constitutes a balanced separator. Note that the balanced separators approach only terminated in case of no-answers. We have therefore omitted the yes-column for this algorithm in Table 3.

Empirical results. We now look at Table 4, where we report for all hypergraphs with $hw \leq k$ and $k \in \{3, 4, 5, 6\}$, whether $ghw \leq k - 1$ could be verified. To this end, we run our three algorithms ("global", "local", and "balanced separators") in parallel and stop the computation, as soon as one terminates (with answer "yes" or "no"). The number in parentheses refers to the average runtime needed by the fastest of the three algorithms in each case. A timeout occurs if none of the three algorithms terminates within 3,600 seconds. It is interesting to note that in the vast majority of cases, no improvement of the width is possible when we switch from hw to ghw: in 98% of the solved cases and 57% of all instances with $hw \leq 6$, hw and ghw have identical values. Actually, we think that the high percentage of the *solved cases* gives a more realistic picture than the percentage of *all cases* for the following reason: our algorithms (in particular, the "global" and "local" computations) need particularly long time for negative instances. This is due to the fact that in a negative case, "all" possible choices of λ-labels for a node u in the GHD have to be tested before we can be sure that no GHD of H (or, equivalently, no HD of H') of desired width exists. Hence, it seems plausible that the timeouts are mainly due to negative instances. This also explains why our new GHD algorithm in Figure 4, which is particularly well suited for negative instances, has the least number of timeouts.

We conclude this section with a final observation: in Figure 2, we had many cases, for which only some upper bound k on the hw could be determined, namely those cases, where the attempt to solve CHECK(HD, k) yields a yes-answer and the attempt to solve CHECK(HD, $k - 1$) gives a timeout. In several such cases, we could get (with the balanced separator approach) a no-answer for the CHECK(GHD, $k - 1$) problem, which implicitly gives a no-answer for the problem CHECK(HD, $k-1$). In this way, our new ghw-algorithm is also profitable for the hw-computation: for 827 instances with $hw \leq 6$, we were not able to determine the exact hypertree width. Using our new ghw-algorithm, we closed this gap for 297 instances; for these instances $hw = ghw$ holds.

To sum up, we now have a total of 1,778 (58%) instances for which we determined the exact hw and a total of 1,406 instances (46%) for which we determined the exact ghw. Out of these, 1,390 instances had identical values for hw and ghw. In 16 cases, we found an improvement of the width by 1 when moving from hw to ghw, namely from $hw = 6$ to $ghw = 5$. In 2 further cases, we could show $hw \leq 6$ and $ghw \leq 5$, but the attempt to check $hw = 5$ or $ghw = 4$ led to a timeout. Hence, in response to *Goal 6*, hw is equal to ghw in 45% of the cases if we consider all instances and in 60% of the cases (1,390 of 2,308) with small width ($hw \leq 6$). However, if we consider the fully solved cases (i.e., where we have the precise value of hw and ghw), then hw and ghw coincide in 99% of the cases (1,390 of 1,406).

6 FRACTIONALLY IMPROVED DECOMPOSITIONS

The algorithms proposed in the literature for computing FHDs are very expensive. For instance, even the algorithm used for the tractability result in [18] for hypergraphs of low degree is problematical since it involves a double-exponential factor in the degree. Therefore, we investigate the potential of a simplified method to compute approximated FHDs. Below, we present two algorithms for such approximated FHD computations – with a trade-off between computational cost and quality of the approximation.

- The simplest way to obtain a fractionally improved (G)HD is to take either a GHD or HD as input and compute a fractionally improved (G)HD. To this end, an algorithm (which we refer to as SimpleImproveHD) visits each node u of a given GHD or HD and computes an optimal fractional edge cover γ_u for the set B_u of vertices. This algorithm is simple and computationally inexpensive, provided that we can start off with a GHD or HD that was computed before. In our case, we simply took the HD resulting from the hw-computation reported in Figure 2. Clearly, this approach is rather naive and the dependence on a concrete HD is unsatisfactory. We therefore move to a more sophisticated algorithm.

Table 5: Instances solved with `SimpleImproveHD`

hw	≥ 1	$[0.5, 1)$	$[0.1, 0.5)$	no	timeout
2	0	41	25	172	0
3	12	104	25	169	0
4	9	55	11	311	0
5	20	14	11	382	0
6	12	60	80	309	0

Table 6: Instances solved with `FracImproveHD`

hw	≥ 1	$[0.5, 1)$	$[0.1, 0.5)$	no	timeout
2	0	46	29	160	1
3	14	116	21	135	24
4	11	81	2	8	284
5	18	126	59	2	222
6	28	149	95	4	183

• The algorithm FracImproveHD has as input a hypergraph H and numbers $k, k' \geq 1$, where k is an upper bound on the hw and k' the desired fractionally improved hw. We search for an FHD $\mathcal{D}'$ with $\mathcal{D}' = SimpleImproveHD(\mathcal{D})$ for some HD $\mathcal{D}$ of H with $width(\mathcal{D}) \leq k$ and $width(\mathcal{D}') \leq k'$. In other words, this algorithm searches for the best fractionally improved HD over all HDs of width $\leq k$. Hence, the result is independent of any concrete HD.

The experimental results with these algorithms for computing fractionally improved HDs are summarized in Tables 5 and 6. We have applied these algorithms to all hypergraphs for which $hw \leq k$ with $k \in \{2, 3, 4, 5\}$ is known from Figure 2. The various columns of the Tables 5 and 6 are as follows: the first column (labelled hw) refers to the (upper bound on the) hw according to Figure 2. The next 3 columns, labelled ≥ 1, $[0.5, 1)$, and $[0.1, 0.5)$ tell us, by how much the width can be improved (if at all) if we compute an FHD by one of the two algorithms. We thus distinguish the 3 cases if, for a hypergraph of $hw \leq k$, we manage to construct an FHD of width $k-c$ for $c \geq 1$, $c \in [0.5, 1)$, or $c \in [0.1, 0.5)$. The column with label "no" refers to the cases where no improvement at all or at least no improvement by $c \geq 0.1$ was possible. The last column counts the number of timeouts.

For instance, in the first row of Table 5, we see that (with the SimpleImproveHD algorithm and starting from the HD obtained by the hw-computation of Figure 2) out of 238 hypergraphs with $hw = 2$, no improvement was possible in 172 cases. In the remaining 66 cases, an improvement to a width of at most $2 - 0.5$ was possible in 25 cases and an improvement to $k - c$ with $c \in [0.1, 0.5)$ was possible in 41 cases. For the hypergraphs with $hw = 3$ in Figure 2, almost half of the hypergraphs (141 out of 310) allowed at least some improvement, in particular, 104 by $c \in [0.5, 1)$ and 12 even by at least 1. The improvements achieved for the hypergraphs with $hw \leq 4$ and $hw \leq 5$ are less significant.

The results obtained with our FracImproveHD implementation are displayed in Table 6. We see that the number of hypergraphs which allow for a fractional improvement of the width by at least 0.5 or even by 1 is often bigger than with SimpleImproveHD – in particular in the cases where $k' \leq k$ with $k \in \{4, 5\}$ holds. In the other cases, the results obtained with the naive SimpleImproveHD algorithm are not much worse than with the more sophisticated FracImproveHD algorithm.

7 RELATED WORK

We distinguish several types of works that are highly relevant to ours. The works most closely related are the descriptions of HD, GHD and FHD algorithms in [19, 24] and the implementation of HD computation by the `DetKDecomp` program reported in [26]. We have extended these works in several ways. Above all, we have incorporated our analysis tool (reported in Sections 3 and 4) and the GHD and FHD computations (reported in Sections 5 and 6) into the `DetKDecomp` program – resulting in our `NewDetKDecomp` library, which is openly available on GitHub. For the GHD computation, we have added heuristics to speed up the basic algorithm from [19]. Moreover, we have proposed a novel approach via balanced separators, which allowed us to significantly extend the range of instances for which the GHD computation terminates in reasonable time. We have also introduced a new form of decomposition method: the fractionally improved decompositions (see Section 6), which allow for a practical, lightweight form of FHDs.

The second important input to our work comes from the various sources [6, 9–11, 20, 26, 30, 35, 47] which we took our CQs and CSPs from. Note that our main goal was not to add further CQs and/or CSPs to these benchmarks. Instead, we have aimed at taking and combining existing, openly accessible benchmarks of CQs and CSPs, convert them into hypergraphs, which are then thoroughly analysed. Finally, the hypergraphs and the analysis results are made openly accessible again.

The third kind of works highly relevant to ours are previous analyses of CQs and CSPs. To the best of our knowledge, Ghionna et al. [21] presented the first systematic study of HDs of benchmark CQs from TPC-H. However, Ghionna et al. pursued a research goal different from ours in that they primarily wanted to find out to what extent HDs can actually speed up query evaluation. They achieved very positive results in this respect, which have recently been confirmed by the work of Perelman et al. [41], Tu et al. [48] and Aberger et al. [1] on query evaluation using FHDs. As a side result, Ghionna et al. also detected that CQs tend to have low hypertree width (a finding which was later confirmed in [12, 42] and also in our study). In a pioneering effort, Bonifati, Martens, and Timm [12] have recently analysed an unprecedented, massive amount of queries: they investigated 180,653,910 queries from (not openly available) query logs of several popular SPARQL endpoints. After elimination of duplicate queries, there were still 56,164,661 queries left, out of which 26,157,880 queries were in fact CQs. The authors thus significantly extend previous work by Picalausa and Vansummeren [42], who analysed 3,130,177 SPARQL queries posed by humans and software robots at the DBPedia SPARQL endpoint. The focus in [42] is on structural properties of SPARQL queries such as keywords used and variable structure in optional patterns. There is one paragraph devoted to CQs, where it is noted that 99.99% of ca. 2 million CQs considered in [42] are acyclic.

Many of the CQs (over 15 million) analysed in [12] have arity 2 (here we consider the maximum arity of all atoms in a CQ as the arity of the query), which means that all triples in such a SPARQL query have a constant at the predicate-position. Bonifati et al. made several interesting observations concerning the shape of these graph-like queries. For instance, they detected that exactly one of these queries has $tw = 3$, while all others have $tw \leq 2$ (and hence $hw \leq 2$). As far as the CQs of arity 3 are concerned (for CQs expressed as SPARQL queries, this is the maximum arity achievable), among many characteristics, also the hypertree width was computed by using the original `DetKDecomp` program from [26]. Out of 6,959,510 CQs of arity 3, only 86 (i.e. 0.01‰) turned out to have $hw = 2$ and 8 queries had $hw = 3$, while all other CQs of arity 3 are acyclic. Our analysis confirms that, also for non-random CQs of arity > 3, the hypertree width indeed tends to be low, with the majority of queries being even acyclic.

For the analysis of CSPs, much less work has been done. Although it has been shown that exploiting (hyper-) tree decompositions may significantly improve the performance of CSP solving [4, 29, 31, 34], a systematic study on the (generalized) hypertree width of CSP instances has only been carried out by few works [26, 34, 45]. To the best of our knowledge, we are the first to analyse the *hw*, *ghw*, and *fhw* of ca. 2,000 CSP instances, where most of these instances have not been studied in this respect before.

It should be noted that the focus of our work is different from the above mentioned previous works: above all, we wanted to test the practical feasibility of various algorithms for HD, GHD, and FHD computation (including both, previously presented algorithms and new ones developed as part of this work). As far as our repository of hypergraphs (obtained from CQs and CSPs) is concerned, we emphasize open accessibility. Thus, users can analyse their CQs and CSPs (with our implementations of HD, GHD, and FHD algorithms) or they can analyse new decomposition algorithms (with our hypergraphs, which cover quite a broad range of characteristics). In fact, in the recent work on FHD computation via SMT solving [17], the Hyperbench benchmark has already been used for the experimental evaluation. In [17] a novel approach to *fhw* computation via an efficient encoding of the check-problem for FHDs to SMT (SAT modulo Theory) is presented. The tests were carried out with 2,191 hypergraphs from the initial version of the HyperBench. For all of these hypergraphs we have established at least some upper bound on the *fhw* either by our *hw*-computation or by one of our new algorithms presented in Sections 5 and 6. In contrast, the exact algorithm in [17] found FHDs only for 1.449 instances (66%). In 852 cases, both our algorithms and the algorithm in [17] found FHDs of the same width; in 560 cases, an FHD of lower width was found in [17]. By using the same benchmark for the tests, the results in [17] and ours are comparable and have thus provided valuable input for future improvements of the algorithms by combining the different strengths and weaknesses of the two approaches.

The use of the same benchmark has also allowed us to provide feedback to the authors of [17] for debugging their system: in 9 out of 2,191 cases, the "optimal" value for the *fhw* computed in [19] was apparently erroneous, since it was higher than the *hw* found out by our analysis; note that upper bounds on the width are, in general, more reliable than lower bounds since it is easy to verify if a given decomposition indeed has the desired properties, whereas ruling out the existence of a decomposition of a certain width is a complex and error-prone task.

8 CONCLUSION

In this work, we have presented HyperBench, a new and comprehensive benchmark of hypergraphs derived from CQs and CSPs from various areas, together with the results of extensive empirical analyses with this benchmark.

Lessons learned. The empirical study has brought many insights. Below, we summarize the most important lessons learned from our studies.

- The finding of [12, 42] that non-random CQs have low hypertree width has been confirmed by our analysis, even if (in contrast to SPARQL queries) the arity of the CQs is not bounded by 3. For random CQs and CSPs, we have detected a correlation between the arity and the hypertree width, although also in this case, the increase of the *hw* with increased arity is not dramatic.
- In [19], several hypergraph invariants were identified, which make the computation of GHDs and the approximation of FHDs tractable. We have seen that, at least for non-random instances, these invariants indeed have low values.

• The reduction of the *ghw*-computation problem to the *hw*-computation problem in case of low intersection width turned out to be more problematical than the theoretical tractability results from [19] had suggested. Even the improvement by "local" computation of the additional subedges did not help much. However, we were able to improve this significantly by presenting a new algorithm based on "balanced separators". In particular for negative instances (i.e., those with a no-answer), this approach proved very effective.

• An additional benefit of the new *ghw*-algorithm based on "balanced separators" is that it allowed us to also fill gaps in the *hw*-computation. Indeed, in several cases, we managed to verify $hw \leq k$ for some k but we could not show $hw \nleq k-1$, due to a timeout for Check(HD, $k-1$). By establishing $ghw \nleq k-1$ with our new GHD-algorithm, we have implicitly showed $hw \nleq k-1$. This allowed us to compute the exact *hw* of many further hypergraphs.

• Most surprisingly, the discrepancy between *hw* and *ghw* is much lower than expected. Theoretically, only the upper bound $hw \leq 3 \cdot ghw + 1$ is known. However, in practice, when considering hypergraphs of $hw \leq 6$, we could show that in 53% of all cases, *hw* and *ghw* are simply identical. Moreover, in *all* cases when one of our implementations of *ghw*-computation terminated on instances with $hw \leq 5$, we got identical values for *hw* and *ghw*.

Future work. Our empirical study has also given us many hints for future directions of research. We find the following tasks particularly urgent and/or rewarding.

• So far, we have only implemented the *ghw*-computation in case of low intersection width. In [19], tractability of the Check(GHD, k) problem was also proved for the more relaxed bounded multi-intersection width. Our empirical results in Table 2 show that, apart from the random CQs and random CSPs, the 3-multi-intersection is ≤ 2 in almost all cases. It seems therefore worthwhile to implement and test also the BMIP-algorithm from [19].

• The three approaches for *ghw*-computation presented here turned out to have complementary strengths and weaknesses. This was profitable when running all three algorithms in parallel and taking the result of the first one that terminates (see Table 4). In the future, we also want to implement a more sophisticated combination of the various approaches: for instance, one could try to apply our new "balanced separator" algorithm recursively only down to a certain recursion depth (say depth 2 or 3) to split a big given hypergraph into smaller subhypergraphs and then continue with the "global" or "local" computation from Section 5.

• Our new approach to *ghw*-computation via "balanced separators" proved quite effective in our experiments. However, further theoretical underpinning of this approach is missing. The empirical results obtained for our new GHD algorithm via balanced separators suggest that the number of balanced separators is often drastically smaller than the number of arbitrary separators. We want to determine a realistic upper bound on the number of balanced separators in terms of n (the number of edges) and k (an upper bound on the width). This will then allow us to compute also a realistic upper bound on the runtime of this new algorithm.

• Finally, we want to further extend the HyperBench benchmark and tool in several directions. We will thus incorporate further implementations of decomposition algorithms from the literature such as the GHD- and FHD computation in [39] or the polynomial-time FHD computation for hypergraphs of bounded degree in [18]. Moreover, we will continue to fill in hypergraphs from further sources of CSPs and CQs. For instance, in [1, 13, 21, 22] a collection of CQs for the experimental evaluations in those papers is mentioned. We will invite the authors to disclose these CQs and incorporate them into the HyperBench benchmark.

• Very recently, a new, huge, publicly available query log has been reported in [37]. It contains over 200 million SPARQL queries on Wikidata. In the paper, the anonymisation and publication of the query logs is mentioned as future work. However, on their web site, the authors have meanwhile made these queries available. At first glance, these queries seem to display a similar behaviour as the SPARQL queries collected by Bonifatti et al. [12]: there is a big number of single-atom queries and again, the vast majority of the queries is acyclic. A detailed analysis of the query log in the style of [12] constitutes an important goal for future research.

ACKNOWLEDGMENTS

This work was supported by the Austrian Science Fund (FWF) project P30930-N35. Davide Mario Longo's work was supported by the Austrian Science Fund (FWF) project W1255-N23. We would like to thank Angela Bonifati, Wim Martens, and Thomas Timm for sharing most of the hypergraphs with $hw \geq 2$ from their work [12] and for their effort in anonymising these hypergraphs, which was required by the license restrictions.

Appendix

Below, we give a proof a proof sketch of Theorem 5.2.

Proof Sketch. Steps 1–5 of the algorithm in Figure 4 essentially correspond to the computation of λ_u and B_u for the root node u in the HD-computation of [24]. The most significant modifications here are due to the handling of "special edges" in parameter Sp. A crucial property of the construction in [24] and also of our construction here is that each subtree below node u in the decomposition only contains vertices from a single connected component C_i w.r.t. $V(H) \setminus B_u$ (see Steps 3 and 4). Since the special edges come from such bags B_u, special edges can never be used as separators in recursive calls below. Hence, we can exclude special edges from the search for a balanced separator in Step 2. The base case (in Step 1) is reached for $|E(H) \cup Sp| \leq 2$.

The correctness of assembling a GHD (in Step 6) from the results of the recursive calls can be shown by structural induction on the tree structure of a GHD: suppose that the recursive calls in the algorithm for each hypergraph H_i with set Sp_i of special edges are correct, i.e., they yield for each hypergraph H_i a GHD $\mathcal{D}_i$ such that each special edge s in Sp_i is indeed covered by a leaf node in $\mathcal{D}_i$ whose λ-label consists of s only. In particular, since $s = B(\lambda_u)$ is a special edge contained in Sp_i for each i, there exists a leaf node t_i in $\mathcal{D}_i$ with $\lambda_{t_i} = \{s\}$. In a GHD, any node can be taken as the root. We thus choose t_i as the root node in each GHD $\mathcal{D}_i$. By construction, we have $B_u = B_{t_1} = \cdots = B_{t_\ell}$. Moreover, any two subhypergraphs H_i, H_j contain the vertices from two different connected components. Hence, apart from the vertices contained in the special edge s, any two GHDs $\mathcal{D}_i$, $\mathcal{D}_j$ with $i \neq j$ have no vertices in common. We can therefore construct a GHD $\mathcal{D}$ of H' by deleting the root node t_i from each GHD $\mathcal{D}_i$ and by appending the child nodes of each t_i directly as child nodes of u. Clearly, the connectedness condition is satisfied in the resulting decomposition. □

REFERENCES

[1] Christopher R. Aberger, Andrew Lamb, Susan Tu, Andres Nötzli, Kunle Olukotun, and Christopher Ré. 2017. EmptyHeaded: A Relational Engine for Graph Processing. *ACM Trans. Database Syst.* 42, 4 (2017), 20:1–20:44. https://doi.org/10.1145/3129246

[2] Christopher R. Aberger, Susan Tu, Kunle Olukotun, and Christopher Ré. 2016. Old Techniques for New Join Algorithms: A Case Study in RDF Processing. *CoRR* abs/1602.03557 (2016). arXiv:1602.03557 http://arxiv.org/abs/1602.03557

[3] Isolde Adler, Georg Gottlob, and Martin Grohe. 2007. Hypertree width and related hypergraph invariants. *Eur. J. Comb.* 28, 8 (2007), 2167–2181. https://doi.org/10.1016/j.ejc.2007.04.013

[4] Kamal Amroun, Zineb Habbas, and Wassila Aggoune-Mtalaa. 2016. A compressed Generalized Hypertree Decomposition-based solving technique for non-binary Constraint Satisfaction Problems. *AI Commun.* 29, 2 (2016), 371–392. https://doi.org/10.3233/AIC-150694

[5] Molham Aref, Balder ten Cate, Todd J. Green, Benny Kimelfeld, Dan Olteanu, Emir Pasalic, Todd L. Veldhuizen, and Geoffrey Washburn. 2015. Design and Implementation of the LogicBlox System. In *Proceedings of the 2015 ACM SIGMOD International Conference on Management of Data, Melbourne, Victoria, Australia, May 31 - June 4, 2015*, Timos K. Sellis, Susan B. Davidson, and Zachary G. Ives (Eds.). ACM, 1371–1382. https://doi.org/10.1145/2723372.2742796

[6] Patricia C. Arocena, Boris Glavic, Radu Ciucanu, and Renée J. Miller. 2015. The iBench Integration Metadata Generator. *PVLDB* 9, 3 (2015), 108–119. https://doi.org/10.14778/2850583.2850586

[7] Gilles Audemard, Frédéric Boussemart, Christophe Lecoutre, and Cédric Piette. 2016. XCSP3: an XML-based format designed to represent combinatorial constrained problems. http://www.xcsp.org/

[8] Nurzhan Bakibayev, Tomás Kociský, Dan Olteanu, and Jakub Zavodny. 2013. Aggregation and Ordering in Factorised Databases. *PVLDB* 6, 14 (2013), 1990–2001. https://doi.org/10.14778/2556549.2556579

[9] Michael Benedikt. 2017. CQ benchmarks. Personal Communication.

[10] Michael Benedikt, George Konstantinidis, Giansalvatore Mecca, Boris Motik, Paolo Papotti, Donatello Santoro, and Efthymia Tsamoura. 2017. Benchmarking the Chase. In *Proceedings of the 36th ACM SIGMOD-SIGACT-SIGAI Symposium on Principles of Database Systems, PODS 2017, Chicago, IL, USA, May 14-19, 2017*, Emanuel Sallinger, Jan Van den Bussche, and Floris Geerts (Eds.). ACM, 37–52. https://doi.org/10.1145/3034786.3034796

[11] Jeremias Berg, Neha Lodha, Matti Järvisalo, and Stefan Szeider. 2017. MaxSAT Benchmarks based on Determining Generalized Hypertree-width. *MaxSAT Evaluation 2017: Solver and Benchmark Descriptions* B-2017-2 (2017), 22.

[12] Angela Bonifati, Wim Martens, and Thomas Timm. 2017. An Analytical Study of Large SPARQL Query Logs. *PVLDB* 11, 2 (2017), 149–161. https://doi.org/10.14778/3149193.3149196

[13] Nofar Carmeli, Batya Kenig, and Benny Kimelfeld. 2017. Efficiently Enumerating Minimal Triangulations. In *Proceedings of the 36th ACM SIGMOD-SIGACT-SIGAI Symposium on Principles of Database Systems, PODS 2017, Chicago, IL, USA, May 14-19, 2017*, Emanuel Sallinger, Jan Van den Bussche, and Floris Geerts (Eds.). ACM, 273–287. https://doi.org/10.1145/3034786.3056109

[14] Ashok K. Chandra and Philip M. Merlin. 1977. Optimal Implementation of Conjunctive Queries in Relational Data Bases. In *Proceedings of the 9th Annual ACM Symposium on Theory of Computing, May 4-6, 1977, Boulder, Colorado, USA*, John E. Hopcroft, Emily P. Friedman, and Michael A. Harrison (Eds.). ACM, 77–90. https://doi.org/10.1145/800105.803397

[15] Rina Dechter. 2003. *Constraint Processing*. Elsevier. https://doi.org/10.1016/b978-1-55860-890-0.x5000-2

[16] Uriel Feige and Mohammad Mahdian. 2006. Finding small balanced separators. In *Proceedings of the 38th Annual ACM Symposium on Theory of Computing, Seattle, WA, USA, May 21-23, 2006*, Jon M. Kleinberg (Ed.). ACM, 375–384. https://doi.org/10.1145/1132516.1132573

[17] Johannes Klaus Fichte, Markus Hecher, Neha Lodha, and Stefan Szeider. 2018. An SMT Approach to Fractional Hypertree Width. In *Principles and Practice of Constraint Programming - 24th International Conference, CP 2018, Lille, France, August 27-31, 2018, Proceedings (Lecture Notes in Computer Science)*, John N. Hooker (Ed.), Vol. 11008. Springer, 109–127. https://doi.org/10.1007/978-3-319-98334-9_8

[18] Wolfgang Fischl, Georg Gottlob, and Reinhard Pichler. 2017. Tractable Cases for Recognizing Low Fractional Hypertree Width. *viXra.org e-prints* viXra:1708.0373 (2017). http://vixra.org/abs/1708.0373

[19] Wolfgang Fischl, Georg Gottlob, and Reinhard Pichler. 2018. General and Fractional Hypertree Decompositions: Hard and Easy Cases. In *Proceedings of the 37th ACM SIGMOD-SIGACT-SIGAI Symposium on Principles of Database Systems, Houston, TX, USA, June 10-15, 2018,*

Jan Van den Bussche and Marcelo Arenas (Eds.). ACM, 17–32. https://doi.org/10.1145/3196959.3196962

[20] Floris Geerts, Giansalvatore Mecca, Paolo Papotti, and Donatello Santoro. 2014. Mapping and cleaning. In *IEEE 30th International Conference on Data Engineering, Chicago, ICDE 2014, IL, USA, March 31 - April 4, 2014*, Isabel F. Cruz, Elena Ferrari, Yufei Tao, Elisa Bertino, and Goce Trajcevski (Eds.). IEEE Computer Society, 232–243. https://doi.org/10.1109/ICDE.2014.6816654

[21] Lucantonio Ghionna, Luigi Granata, Gianluigi Greco, and Francesco Scarcello. 2007. Hypertree Decompositions for Query Optimization. In *Proceedings of the 23rd International Conference on Data Engineering, ICDE 2007, The Marmara Hotel, Istanbul, Turkey, April 15-20, 2007*, Rada Chirkova, Asuman Dogac, M. Tamer Özsu, and Timos K. Sellis (Eds.). IEEE Computer Society, 36–45. https://doi.org/10.1109/ICDE.2007.367849

[22] Lucantonio Ghionna, Gianluigi Greco, and Francesco Scarcello. 2011. H-DB: a hybrid quantitative-structural sql optimizer. In *Proceedings of the 20th ACM Conference on Information and Knowledge Management, CIKM 2011, Glasgow, United Kingdom, October 24-28, 2011*, Craig Macdonald, Iadh Ounis, and Ian Ruthven (Eds.). ACM, 2573–2576. https://doi.org/10.1145/2063576.2064023

[23] Georg Gottlob, Gianluigi Greco, Nicola Leone, and Francesco Scarcello. 2016. Hypertree Decompositions: Questions and Answers. In *Proceedings of the 35th ACM SIGMOD-SIGACT-SIGAI Symposium on Principles of Database Systems, PODS 2016, San Francisco, CA, USA, June 26 - July 01, 2016*, Tova Milo and Wang-Chiew Tan (Eds.). ACM, 57–74. https://doi.org/10.1145/2902251.2902309

[24] Georg Gottlob, Nicola Leone, and Francesco Scarcello. 2002. Hypertree Decompositions and Tractable Queries. *J. Comput. Syst. Sci.* 64, 3 (2002), 579–627. https://doi.org/10.1006/jcss.2001.1809

[25] Georg Gottlob, Zoltán Miklós, and Thomas Schwentick. 2009. Generalized hypertree decompositions: NP-hardness and tractable variants. *J. ACM* 56, 6 (2009), 30:1–30:32. https://doi.org/10.1145/1568318.1568320

[26] Georg Gottlob and Marko Samer. 2008. A backtracking-based algorithm for hypertree decomposition. *ACM Journal of Experimental Algorithmics* 13 (2008), 1:1.1–1:1.19. https://doi.org/10.1145/1412228.1412229

[27] Martin Grohe and Dániel Marx. 2014. Constraint Solving via Fractional Edge Covers. *ACM Trans. Algorithms* 11, 1 (2014), 4:1–4:20. https://doi.org/10.1145/2636918

[28] Yuanbo Guo, Zhengxiang Pan, and Jeff Heflin. 2005. LUBM: A benchmark for OWL knowledge base systems. *J. Web Semant.* 3, 2-3 (2005), 158–182. https://doi.org/10.1016/j.websem.2005.06.005

[29] Zineb Habbas, Kamal Amroun, and Daniel Singer. 2015. A Forward-Checking algorithm based on a Generalised Hypertree Decomposition for solving non-binary constraint satisfaction problems. *J. Exp. Theor. Artif. Intell.* 27, 5 (2015), 649–671. https://doi.org/10.1080/0952813X.2014.993507

[30] Shrainik Jain, Dominik Moritz, Daniel Halperin, Bill Howe, and Ed Lazowska. 2016. SQLShare: Results from a Multi-Year SQL-as-a-Service Experiment. In *Proceedings of the 2016 International Conference on Management of Data, SIGMOD Conference 2016, San Francisco, CA, USA, June 26 - July 01, 2016*, Fatma Özcan, Georgia Koutrika, and Sam Madden (Eds.). ACM, 281–293. https://doi.org/10.1145/2882903.2882957

[31] Shant Karakashian, Robert J. Woodward, and Berthe Y. Choueiry. 2011. Reformulating R(*, m)C with Tree Decomposition. In *Proceedings of the Ninth Symposium on Abstraction, Reformulation, and Approximation, SARA 2011, Parador de Cardona, Cardona, Catalonia, Spain, July 17-18, 2011.*, Michael R. Genesereth and Peter Z. Revesz (Eds.). AAAI, 62–69. http://www.aaai.org/ocs/index.php/SARA/SARA11/paper/view/4234

[32] Mahmoud Abo Khamis, Hung Q. Ngo, Christopher Ré, and Atri Rudra. 2016. Joins via Geometric Resolutions: Worst Case and Beyond. *ACM Trans. Database Syst.* 41, 4 (2016), 22:1–22:45. https://doi.org/10.1145/2967101

[33] Mahmoud Abo Khamis, Hung Q. Ngo, and Atri Rudra. 2016. FAQ: Questions Asked Frequently. In *Proceedings of the 35th ACM SIGMOD-SIGACT-SIGAI Symposium on Principles of Database Systems, PODS 2016, San Francisco, CA, USA, June 26 - July 01, 2016*, Tova Milo and Wang-Chiew Tan (Eds.). ACM, 13–28. https://doi.org/10.1145/2902251.2902280

[34] Mohammed Lalou, Zineb Habbas, and Kamal Amroun. 2009. Solving Hypertree Structured CSP: Sequential and Parallel Approaches. In *Proceedings of the 16th RCRA workshop on Experimental Evaluation of Algorithms for Solving Problems with Combinatorial Explosion, RCRA@AI*IA 2009, Reggio Emilia, Italy, December 11-12, 2009 (CEUR Workshop Proceedings)*, Marco Gavanelli and Toni Mancini (Eds.), Vol. 589. CEUR-WS.org. http://ceur-ws.org/Vol-589/paper11.pdf

[35] Viktor Leis, Andrey Gubichev, Atanas Mirchev, Peter A. Boncz, Alfons Kemper, and Thomas Neumann. 2015. How Good Are Query Optimizers, Really? *PVLDB* 9, 3 (2015), 204–215. https://doi.org/10.14778/2850583.2850594

[36] Viktor Leis, Bernhard Radke, Andrey Gubichev, Atanas Mirchev, Peter A. Boncz, Alfons Kemper, and Thomas Neumann. 2018. Query optimization through the looking glass, and what we found running the Join Order Benchmark. *VLDB J.* 27, 5 (2018), 643–668. https://doi.org/10.1007/s00778-017-0480-7

[37] Stanislav Malyshev, Markus Krötzsch, Larry González, Julius Gonsior, and Adrian Bielefeldt. 2018. Getting the Most Out of Wikidata: Semantic Technology Usage in Wikipedia's Knowledge Graph. In *The Semantic Web - ISWC 2018 - 17th International Semantic Web Conference, Monterey, CA, USA, October 8-12, 2018, Proceedings, Part II (Lecture Notes in Computer Science)*, Denny Vrandecic, Kalina Bontcheva, Mari Carmen Suárez-Figueroa, Valentina Presutti, Irene Celino, Marta Sabou, Lucie-Aimée Kaffee, and Elena Simperl (Eds.), Vol. 11137. Springer, 376–394. https://doi.org/10.1007/978-3-030-00668-6_23

[38] Dániel Marx. 2010. Approximating fractional hypertree width. *ACM Trans. Algorithms* 6, 2 (2010), 29:1–29:17. https://doi.org/10.1145/1721837.1721845

[39] Lukas Moll, Siamak Tazari, and Marc Thurley. 2012. Computing hypergraph width measures exactly. *Inf. Process. Lett.* 112, 6 (2012), 238–242. https://doi.org/10.1016/j.ipl.2011.12.002

[40] Dan Olteanu and Jakub Závodný. 2015. Size Bounds for Factorised Representations of Query Results. *ACM Trans. Database Syst.* 40, 1 (2015), 2:1–2:44. https://doi.org/10.1145/2656335

[41] Adam Perelman and Christopher Ré. 2015. DunceCap: Compiling Worst-Case Optimal Query Plans. In *Proceedings of the 2015 ACM SIGMOD International Conference on Management of Data, Melbourne, Victoria, Australia, May 31 - June 4, 2015*, Timos K. Sellis, Susan B. Davidson, and Zachary G. Ives (Eds.). ACM, 2075–2076. https://doi.org/10.1145/2723372.2764945

[42] François Picalausa and Stijn Vansummeren. 2011. What are real SPARQL queries like?. In *Proceedings of the International Workshop on Semantic Web Information Management, SWIM 2011, Athens, Greece, June 12, 2011*, Roberto De Virgilio, Fausto Giunchiglia, and Letizia Tanca (Eds.). ACM, 7. https://doi.org/10.1145/1999299.1999306

[43] Rachel Pottinger and Alon Y. Halevy. 2001. MiniCon: A scalable algorithm for answering queries using views. *VLDB J.* 10, 2-3 (2001), 182–198. https://doi.org/10.1007/s007780100048

[44] Francesco Scarcello, Gianluigi Greco, and Nicola Leone. 2007. Weighted hypertree decompositions and optimal query plans. *J. Comput. Syst. Sci.* 73, 3 (2007), 475–506. https://doi.org/10.1016/j.jcss.2006.10.010

[45] Werner Schafhauser. 2006. *New heuristic methods for tree decompositions and generalized hypertree decompositions.* Master's thesis. Technische Universität Wien.

[46] Aaron Schild and Christian Sommer. 2015. On Balanced Separators in Road Networks. In *Experimental Algorithms - 14th International Symposium, SEA 2015, Paris, France, June 29 - July 1, 2015, Proceedings (Lecture Notes in Computer Science)*, Evripidis Bampis (Ed.), Vol. 9125. Springer, 286–297. https://doi.org/10.1007/978-3-319-20086-6_22

[47] Transaction Processing Performance Council (TPC). 2014. TPC-H decision support benchmark. http://www.tpc.org/tpch/default.asp

[48] Susan Tu and Christopher Ré. 2015. DunceCap: Query Plans Using Generalized Hypertree Decompositions. In *Proceedings of the 2015 ACM SIGMOD International Conference on Management of Data, Melbourne, Victoria, Australia, May 31 - June 4, 2015*, Timos K. Sellis, Susan B. Davidson, and Zachary G. Ives (Eds.). ACM, 2077–2078. https://doi.org/10.1145/2723372.2764946

[49] V. N. Vapnik and A. Ya. Chervonenkis. 1971. On the Uniform Convergence of Relative Frequencies of Events to Their Probabilities. *Theory of Probability & Its Applications* 16, 2 (jan 1971), 264–280. https://doi.org/10.1137/1116025

Algorithmic Fairness: Measures, Methods and Representations*

Suresh Venkatasubramanian
suresh@cs.utah.edu
University of Utah

ABSTRACT

What happens when we replace — or augment — human decision-making with algorithms? This is a simple question, but the answers now define a new field of study — a field that I call algorithmic fairness, and that spans issues of fairness, discrimination, accountability, transparency, interpretability and responsibility, and so much more. While some of the early work in the area came out of data mining and machine learning, the field is now truly transdisciplinary, with contributions from all across computer science, as well as from all disciplines that touch on aspects of society - whether it be economics, philosophy, sociology, political science, or communication.

In this tutorial, I'll try to do three things: I'll survey the main questions and some of the key insights we've developed over the years. I'll explain the web of connections between the technical and the social disciplines that make up this area, and I'll point to exciting directions that remain to be explored in both technical and social dimensions.

Along the way I hope to illustrate what I think are some interesting "collisions" between computer science and the social sciences, and call for a reimagining of core ideas in our field, including the very idea of how we think about data representation.

KEYWORDS

algorithmic fairness, interdisciplinary, decision-making

ACM Reference Format:

Suresh Venkatasubramanian. 2019. Algorithmic Fairness: Measures, Methods and Representations. In *38th ACM SIGMOD-SIGACT-SIGAI Symposium on Principles of Database Systems (PODS'19), June 30-July 5, 2019, Amsterdam, Netherlands.* ACM, New York, NY, USA, 1 page. https://doi.org/10.1145/3294052.3322192

*This work is partially supported by the National Science Foundation under grant IIS-1633724

PODS'19, June 30-July 5, 2019, Amsterdam, Netherlands

ACM ISBN 978-1-4503-6227-6/19/06.
https://doi.org/10.1145/3294052.3322192

Author Index

Abdulla, Parosh Aziz 335
Abo Khamis, Mahmoud 414
Aiswarya, C. 335
Amarilli, Antoine 89
Arenas, Marcelo 59
Assadi, Sepehr 236
Atig, Mohamed Faouzi 335
Baelde, David 285
Barceló, Pablo 2
Baumgartner, Alexander 2
Berger, Gerald 270
Berkholz, Christoph 353
Bertossi, Leopoldo 48
Borassi, Michele 254
Bourhis, Pierre 89
Calautti, Marco 104
Carmeli, Nofar 134
Chen, Hubie .... 353, , 383
Console, Marco 104
Croquevielle, Luis Alberto 59
Curtin, Ryan R. 414
Dalmau, Victor 2
Doleschal, Johannes 149
Dwork, Cynthia 1
Epasto, Alessandro 254
Fekete, Alan 269
Fischl, Wolfgang 464
Freydenberger, Dominik D. 320
Gottlob, Georg 270, 464
Grohe, Martin 17
Hu, Xiao 450
Indyk, Piotr 200
Jayaram, Rajesh 59, 218
Kallaugher, John 119
Karpov, Nikolai 236
Kimelfeld, Benny 2, 32, 74, 149, 320
Kolaitis, Phokion G. 32
Konstantinidis, George 399
Kröll, Markus 134, 320
Langberg, Michael 432
Lattanzi, Silvio 254
Li, Shi 432
Lick, Anthony 285
Lindner, Peter 17
Longo, Davide Mario 464
Mani Jayaraman,
Sai Vikneshwar 432
Martens, Wim 149
McGregor, Andrew 119
Medini, Dori 74
Mengel, Stefan 89
Mitzenmacher, Michael 164
Mogavero, Fabio 399
Montali, Marco 335
Morgan, Tom 164
Moseley, Benjamin 414
Nahshon, Yoav 149
Neven, Frank 149
Ngo, Hung Q. 414
Nguyen, XuanLong 414
Niewerth, Matthias 89
Olteanu, Dan 414
Patel, Sarvar 182
Persiano, Giuseppe 182
Peterfreund, Liat 320
Pichler, Reinhard 464
Pieris, Andreas 104, 270
Price, Eric 119
Ravid, Noam 74
Riveros, Cristian 59
Rudra, Atri 432
Sallinger, Emanuel 270
Schleich, Maximilian 414
Schmitz, Sylvain 285
Sharma, Gokarna 218
Staworko, Sławek 303
Su, Jianwen 47
Tibi, Muhammad 32
Tirthapura, Srikanta 218
Vakilian, Ali 200
Van Gucht, Dirk 47
Vassilvitskii, Sergei 254
Venkatasubramanian, Suresh 481
Vianu, Victor 47
Vorotnikova, Sofya 119
Wieczorek, Piotr 303
Woodruff, David P. 218
Yeo, Kevin 182
Yi, Ke 450
Yoshida, Yuichi 365
Zadimoghaddam, Morteza 254
Zhang, Qin 236

www.ingramcontent.com/pod-product-compliance
Lightning Source LLC
LaVergne TN
LVHW082026200926
848481LV00010B/2929